Lecture Notes in Computer Science 2363

Edited by G. Goos, J. Hartmanis, and J. van Leeuwen

Springer
Berlin
Heidelberg
New York
Barcelona
Hong Kong
London
Milan
Paris
Tokyo

Stefano A. Cerri   Guy Gouardères
Fábio Paraguaçu (Eds.)

Intelligent
Tutoring Systems

6th International Conference, ITS 2002
Biarritz, France and San Sebastian, Spain, June 2-7, 2002
Proceedings

Springer

Series Editors

Gerhard Goos, Karlsruhe University, Germany
Juris Hartmanis, Cornell University, NY, USA
Jan van Leeuwen, Utrecht University, The Netherlands

Volume Editors

Stefano A. Cerri
LIRMM, University of Montpellier II and CNRS
Montpellier, France
E-mail: cerri@lirmm.fr

Guy Gouardères
LIUPPA, IUT de Bayonne - University of Pau
Bayonne, France
E-mail: Guy.Gouarderes@iutbay.univ-pau.fr

Fábio Paraguaçu
Universidade Federal de Alagoas, Department of Information Technologies
Maceió, Brazil
on leave at
LIRMM, University of Montpellier II and CNRS
E-mail: paragua@lirmm.fr

Cataloging-in-Publication Data applied for

Die Deutsche Bibliothek - CIP-Einheitsaufnahme

Intelligent tutoring systems : 6th international conference ; proceedings /
ITS 2002, Biarritz, France and San Sebastian, Spain, June 2 - 7, 2002.
Stefano A. Cerri ... (ed.). - Berlin ; Heidelberg ; New York ; Barcelona ;
Hong Kong ; London ; Milan ; Paris ; Tokyo : Springer, 2002
    (Lecture notes in computer science ; Vol. 2363)
    ISBN 3-540-43750-9

CR Subject Classi cation (1998): K.3, I.2.6, H.5, J.1

ISSN 0302-9743
ISBN 3-540-43750-9 Springer-Verlag Berlin Heidelberg New York

Springer-Verlag Berlin Heidelberg New York
a member of BertelsmannSpringer Science+Business Media GmbH

http://www.springer.de

© Springer-Verlag Berlin Heidelberg 2002

Typesetting: Camera-ready by author, data conversion by PTP-Berlin, Stefan Sossna e.K.
Printed on acid-free paper   SPIN: 10870295   06/3142   5 4 3 2 1 0

Preface

After Montréal (in 1988, 1992, 1996, and 2000) and San Antonio, Texas (in 1998) it was Biarritz, France and San Sebastian, Spain that hosted the sixth International Conference on Intelligent Tutoring Systems in 2002.

Further to the logistic move to Europe, ITS 2002 also evolved in its scientific focus and in its quantitative impact.

We anticipated the shift in focus by extending the Program Committee to scientists not necessarily known in the specific area. We reinforced this choice by inviting presentations of scholars that have excellent records in complementary disciplines. The message was that any domain in Computing and the Human Sciences may contribute to the future of ITS, and conversely, ITS may add value to most traditionally separated domains, in Technologies and the Humanities. The message was also that these exchanges, in order to be fruitful, have to be rigorously placed at the top of current scientific research. We therefore enhanced the links to Programming Languages, Telematics, Knowledge Representation, Software Visualization, Natural Language understanding and generation, Logics.

At the strategic level, we wished to get out of the dangerous dichotomy "theory-application": instead of forcing industrial partners to listen to our successes or present their products to sell, we preferred to elicit the interests of people, projects, and institutions already seriously committed in technology transfer and large scale e-learning applications by inviting them to participate to special events. These colleagues include scientists, industrialists, as well as decision makers in public institutions. Panels have been reserved to discuss these issues.

We received 167 full papers, representing an increase of 150% in two years. This shows the vitality of the domain worldwide, a phenomenon that deserves attention and reflection. We will elaborate on this later in the preface.

The Program Committee (54 members) selected in a minimal time frame of 3 weeks, 93 of them for the main conference and the proceedings. The revision of papers and the selection of short, poster papers (18) required four more weeks. The files for the book were then presented to the publisher, Springer-Verlag. We were impressed by the competence and performance of the colleagues in the PC. Thank you.

In parallel, there were at least 13 proposed workshops, 6 tutorials, a Young Researcher's Track, and 6 panels, each managed by one or two specific chairs. There were twice as many complementary events as there were two years ago. We preferred to allow more time for the preparation of these events rather than force deadlines in order to meet the book's deadline. The rationale for the choice was to serve most of the collegues, with disparate awareness and interests, more than to serve our ambition to have an even richer single book. All events have been made public and all contributions acknowledged at some stage.

The Program Committee members carefully evaluated the competence and focus of each ITS paper. It was decided that the papers selected should be a testimony of research advancements in the intersection between Artificial Intelligence and Human Learning, neither of the two being ancillary to the other one, but instead in mutual synergy.

There is a consensus concerning human learning, even if some scholars priviledge cognitive and others social, contextual, organizational aspects; some focus on tutoring teacher's initiatives, others on learner's initiatives.

The role of "Intelligent Systems", i.e. Artificial Intelligence is more controversial, as may be expected. Traditional AI is currently challenged by an emerging attitude, perhaps stimulated by the Web, of considering the technological advancements that artificially facilitate "intelligence" in humans or groups as part of AI. The subjectivity of the borders between the two views is as evident as one's legitimate adoption of either of the two visions, provided the scientific mission is respected.

The program showed three emerging shifts in interests: the Web and Agents on it, Evaluations, and finally Dialogues, including studies on human motivation and emotions.

Most efforts focus on ITS on the Web. The challenge is not simple, as one is expected to demonstrate not just how the Web may be used for teaching, but how it should evolve in order to facilitate human learning.

Hardly any paper was accepted without requiring the proposed solutions to be seriously evaluated in concrete settings. Toy systems were criticized, real scale, well evaluated experiences were encouraged. Real size research on ITS favors real size research groups. As a result, many papers are signed by multiple authors. Geographically isolated scientists tend more and more to collaborate remotely via Web: many papers resulted from worldwide collaborations, which reinforces positively the vision of a virtual and dynamic scientific community, sometimes emerging even without local support. Statistics by first Author's Country of affiliation reflect less than before the distribution of competence: what may be more interesting to visualize are research networks across countries and institutions.

Dialogues, narrative, motivations, and emotions are central issues for the future of ITS. One sees a major leap in the maturity of the offered research results. Natural language, plan generation, and the pragmatics of interactions are no longer speculative hypotheses, but concrete modules in advanced ITSs in real size domains.

Finally, here are a few reflections on e-learning. The growth of ITS 2002 is probably a side effect of the e-learning fashion. The latter is probably a side effect of the e-commerce deception. Both e-learning and e-commerce deserve the attention due to important applications on the future Web, but at the same time they induce to a serious reflection on the difference between commercial keywords and real scientific and technical opportunities. At the time of writing, we know of at least five other conferences on e-learning announced for the next months worldwide. Many more exist on each of the subjects of our tracks and sessions.

We believe that our role is to keep a clear distinction between research and commercial implementations. Perhaps we should insist even more on this distinction by linking, coordinating, binding, and certifying scientific conferences in order to avoid the dispersion of interests of our younger colleagues. Certainly, the only way to achieve the mission with respect to future generations of scientists, is to reinforce both collaboration and competition in research. No science without both. No high level conference without rigorous selection and, at the same time, collaboration among peers. Probably, ITS has reached a size such that we may raise the selection level. France and Spain are among the most important wine producers in the world: we all know from history that high quality, highly selected wine requires a non profitable short term investment to ensure long term success and profit. We should probably implement the same rule to reinforce in the long run our recognition of excellence within the different research communities. Collaboration with neighboring disciplines, and newcomers from all over the world, should profitably be coupled with even more selection and competition.

ITS in Biarritz - San Sebastian further fertilized European research, at the same time, enhancing in quantity and quality the fundamental contributions of our colleagues from the USA and Canada. Perhaps it is also time to look even further, to Latin America or Asia for one of the next conferences, thus preparing ourselves to collaborate with new collegues, and also to compete in a common challenge: better human understanding and learning by means of advanced technologies.

Thanks are due to the other organizers Isabel Fernandez de Castro, General Organization Chair (San Sebastian), Esma Aimeur (Montreal) and Ken Koedinger (Pittsburgh) for the workshops, Gerhard Weber (Freiburg) for the panels, Cyrille Desmoulins (Grenoble) for the posters, Guy Boy (Toulouse) for the tutorials, Jon Elorriaga and Ana Arruarte (San Sebastian) for the Young Researcher's Track, and most especially, Peter King (Winnipeg), who was always present in the program construction process.

The conference was sponsored by the Association for Computing Machinery, the International Federation for Information Processing, the Artificial Intelligence in Education Society, the IEEE CS Learning Technology Task Force, the French Direction Générale de l'Armement, The Asociación Española para la Inteligencia Artificial. We are very grateful to both the sponsoring institutions and the corporate sponsors for their generous support.

A conference of this size cannot possibly succeed without the efforts and dedication of a large number of people; we are indebted to them all.

April 2002

Stefano A. Cerri
Guy Gouardères
Fábio Paraguaçu

Organization

Conference Chair

Guy Gouardères   IUT de Bayonne, Université de Pau, France

Program Committee Chair

Stefano A. Cerri   LIRMM, Université Montpellier II & CNRS, France

Program Committee

Esma Aimeur	Département d'Informatique et recherche opérationnelle, Université de Montréal, Canada
Gerardo Ayala	Center for Research in Information and Automation Technologies, Universidad de las Americas-Puebla, Mexico
Paul Bacsich	Telematics in Education Research Group, Sheffield Hallam University, UK
Guy Boy	EURISCO, European Institute of Cognitive Science and Engineering, France
Bert Bredeweg	Department of Social Science Informatics (SWI), University of Amsterdam, The Netherlands
Joost Breuker	Department of Computer Science & Law (LRI), University of Amsterdam, The Netherlands
Bernard Causse	IUT de Bayonne, Université de Pau, France
Stefano A. Cerri	LIRMM, Université Montpellier II & CNRS, France
Thierry Chanier	LIFC, Université de Franche-Comté, France
Looi Chee-kit	Institute of Systems Science, National University of Singapore, Singapore
Bill Clancey	Human-Centered Computing, NASA/Ames Research Center, USA
	Institute for Human and Machine Cognition, The University of West Florida, USA
Cristina Conati	Department of Computer Science, University of British Columbia, Canada
Ricardo Conejo	Department of Languages and Computational Sciences, Universidad de Malaga, Spain
Danail Dochev	Dept. of Artificial Intelligence - Knowledge Processing, Bulgarian Academy of Sciences, Bulgaria

John Domingue	Knowledge Media Institute, The Open University, UK
Ben DuBoulay	School of Cognitive and Computing Sciences, University of Sussex, UK
Isabel Fernández-Castro	Department of Computer Languages and Systems, University of the Basque Country, Spain
Claude Frasson	Département d'Informatique et recherche opérationnelle, Université de Montréal, Canada
Gilles Gauthier	Département d'Informatique, Université du Québec à Montréal, Canada
Guy Gouardères	IUT de Bayonne, Université de Pau, France
Art Graesser	Department of Psychology, The University of Memphis, USA
Monique Grandbastien	Institut National Agronomique, Paris-Grignon, France
	LORIA, Université Henri Poincaré, Nancy, France
Jim Greer	Department of Computer Science, University of Saskatchewan, Canada
Daniele Hérin	LIRMM, Université Montpellier II & CNRS, France
Ulrich Hoppe	Institute for Computer Science / Interactive Systems, University of Duisburg, Germany
W. Lewis Johnson	CARTE, Information Sciences Institute, University of Southern California, USA
Judith Kay	School of Information Technologies, University of Sydney, Australia
Peter R. King	Department of Computer Science, University of Manitoba, Canada
	LIRMM, Université Montpellier II & CNRS, France
Ken Koendinger	Human Computer Interaction Institute, Carnegie Mellon University, USA
Itoh Kojih	Department of Applied Electronics, Tokyo University of Science, Japan
Susanne Lajoie	Department of Educational and Counselling Psychology, McGill University, Canada
Vincenzo Loia	Dipartimento di Matematica e Informatica, Università di Salerno, Italy
James Lester	Department of Computer Science, North Carolina State University, USA
Gordon McCalla	Department of Computer Science, University of Saskatchewan, Canada
Alessandro Micarelli	Dipartimento di Informatica e Automazione, Università "Roma Tre", Italy
Riichiro Mizoguchi	Institute of Scientific and Industrial Research, Osaka University, Japan

External Reviewers Appointed by PC Members (Gratefully Acknowledged):

Ivon Arroyo	Department of Computer Science, University of Massachusetts, USA
Ana Arruarte Lasa	Department of Computer Languages and Systems, University of the Basque Country, Spain
Bora Arslan	Communication and Cognitive Technologies, ITC-IRST, Trento, Italy
Paolo Avesani	Communication and Cognitive Technologies, ITC-IRST, Trento, Italy
Marcel Barbulescu	Department of Computer Science, George Mason University, USA
Monique Baron	LIP6, Université de Paris 6, France
Canan Blake	Computers and Learning Group, IET, The Open University, UK
Cristina Boicu	Department of Computer Science, George Mason University, USA
Mihai Boicu	Department of Computer Science, George Mason University, USA
Denis Bouhineau	Laboratoire Leibnitz, Institut d'Informatique et de Mathématiques Appliqués de Grenoble, France
Anders Bouwer	Department of Social Science Informatics (SWI), University of Amsterdam, The Netherlands
Patrick Boylan	Dipartimento di Linguistica, Università "Roma Tre", Italy
Charles Callaway	Communication and Cognitive Technologies, ITC-IRST, Trento, Italy
Michel Chambreuil	LRL Département de Linguistique, Université de Clermont-Ferrand, France
Cleide Costa	Département Apprentissage et Evaluation, Université d'Aix-Marseille, France
	Departamento de letras, Universidade Federal de Alagoas, Brazil
Germana Da Nóbrega	LIRMM, Université Montpellier II & CNRS, France
Bertrand David	ICTT, Ecole Centrale de Lyon, France
Angel de Vicente	ICCS, Informatics, University of Edinburgh, UK
Arantza Diaz de Ilarraza	Department of Computer Languages and Systems, University of the Basque Country, Spain
Terry diPaolo	Computers and Learning Group, IET, The Open University, UK

Chris Eliot	Department of Computer Science, University of Massachusetts, USA
Jon Ander Elorriaga Arandia	Department of Computer Languages and Systems, University of the Basque Country, Spain
Jessica Faivre	GDAC Laboratory (Knowledge Management), University of Quebec at Montreal, Canada
Sophie Gouardères	LIUPPA, Université de Pau, France
Carlo Iacucci	ICCS, Informatics, University of Edinburgh, UK
Mitsuru Ikeda	Institute of Scientific and Industrial Research, Osaka University, Japan
Akiko Inaba	Institute of Scientific and Industrial Research, Osaka University, Japan
Mizue Kayama	Graduate School of Information Systems, The University of Electro-Communication, Japan
Bernard Lefebvre	Département d'Informatique, Université du Québec à Montréal, Canada
Jean Pierre Marciano	IUP MIAGE, Université d'Aix-Marseille, France
Dorin Marcu	Department of Computer Science, George Mason University, USA
Eva Millan	Department of Languages and Computational Sciences, Universidad de Malaga, Spain
Anton Minko	LIUPPA, Université de Pau, France
Erica Morris	Computers and Learning Group, IET, The Open University, UK
Paul Mulholland	Knowledge Media Institute, The Open University, UK
Antoinette Muntjewerff	Department of Computer Science & Law (LRI), University of Amsterdam, The Netherlands
Fábio Paraguaçu	LIRMM, Université Montpellier II & CNRS, France
	Department of Information Technologies, Universidade Federal de Alagoas, Maceió, Brazil
Josephine Pelleu	GDAC Laboratory (Knowledge Management), University of Quebec at Montreal, Canada
Tomas A. Perez	Department of Computer Languages and Systems, University of the Basque Country, Spain
Jose Luis Perez de la Cruz	Department of Languages and Computational Sciences, Universidad de Malaga, Spain
Emanuele Pianta	Communication and Cognitive Technologies, ITC-IRST, Trento, Italy
Christophe Reffay	LIFC, Université de Franche-Comté, France
Francesco Ricci	Communication and Cognitive Technologies, ITC-IRST, Trento, Italy
Michel Sala	LIRMM, Université Montpellier I, France

Jean Sallantin	LIRMM, Université Montpellier II & CNRS, France
Emmanuel Sander	Department of Psychology, Université de Paris 8, France
Bogdan Stanescu	Department of Computer Science, George Mason University, USA
Arthur Stutt	Knowledge Media Institute, The Open University, UK
Maite Urretavizcaya	Department of Computer Languages and Systems, University of the Basque Country, Spain

Organizing Committee Chair

Isabel Fernández-Castro	Department of Computer Languages and Systems, University of the Basque Country, Spain

Workshop's Chairs

Esma Aimeur	Département d'Informatique et recherche opérationnelle, Université de Montréal, Canada
Ken Koendinger	Human Computer Interaction Institute, Carnegie Mellon University, USA

Tutorial Chair

Guy Boy	EURISCO, European Institute of Cognitive Science and Engineering, France

Panel Chair

Gerhard Weber	Department of Psychology, Pädagogische Hochschule Freiburg, Germany

Poster Session Chair

Cyrille Desmoulins	Laboratoire CLIPS, Institut d'Informatique et de Mathématiques Appliquées de Grenoble, France

Young Researcher's Track Chairs

Ana Arruarte Lasa	Department of Computer Languages and Systems, University of the Basque Country, Spain
Jon Ander Elorriaga Arandia	Department of Computer Languages and Systems, University of the Basque Country, Spain

Publicity Chair

Michelle Rouet   Ecole Supérieure des Technologies Industrielles
                                 Avancées, CCI Bayonne, France

Local Arrangements

Bernard Causse   IUT de Bayonne, Université de Pau, France
Daniéle Hérin   LIRMM, Université Montpellier II & CNRS,
                                 France
Jean François Nicaud   Laboratoire Leibnitz, Institut d'Informatique
                                 et de Mathématiques Appliquées de Grenoble,
                                 France
Michelle Rouet   Ecole Supérieure des Technologies Industrielles
                                 Avancées, CCI Bayonne, France

Conference Treasurer & Registration Chair

Delphine Da Silva   IUT de Bayonne, Université de Pau, France

Local Organization Committee

Bernard Causse   IUT de Bayonne, Université de Pau, France
Jean-Roch Guiresse   Ecole Supérieure des Technologies Industrielles
                                 Avancées, CCI Bayonne, France
Philippe Aniorté   IUT de Bayonne, Université de Pau, France
Patrick Etcheverry   IUT de Bayonne, Université de Pau, France
Eric Gouardères   LIUPPA, Université de Pau, France
Sophie Gouardères   LIUPPA, Université de Pau, France
Nadine Couture   Ecole Supérieure des Technologies Industrielles
                                 Avancées, CCI Bayonne, France

ITS Steering Committee

Stefano A. Cerri	LIRMM, Université Montpellier II & CNRS, France
Claude Frasson	Département d'Informatique et recherche opérationnelle, Université de Montréal, Canada
Gilles Gauthier	Département d'Informatique, Université du Québec à Montréal, Canada
Guy Gouardères	IUT de Bayonne, Université de Pau, France
Marc Kaltenbach	Williams School of Business and Economics, Bishop's University, Canada
Judith Kay	School of Information Technologies, University of Sydney, Australia
Alan Lesgold	Learning Research and Development Center, University of Pittsburg, USA
Vimla Patel	Department of Psychology, McGill University, Canada
Elliot Soloway	Department of Electrical Engineering and Computer Science, University of Michigan, USA
Daniel Suthers	Department of Information and Computer Sciences, University of Hawaii at Manoa, USA
Beverly Woolf	Department of Computer Science, University of Massachusetts, USA

Table of Contents

Collaboration

Technologies

Architectures

Rules, Patterns, Hypermedia

Domain Oriented

Knowledge Acquisition, Reuse

Web

Dynamics

Ontologies

Training

Evaluation

Cognition

Authoring

Complex Domains

Instructional Design

Learning

Models

Simulation

Simulation 1

Simulation 2

Dialogue

Generic

Specific

Social

Learning

Architectures

Web

Meta-cognition

Evaluation

Technologies

Dynamics

Development

Narrative

Motivation and Emotions

Evaluation

Agents

Poster Papers

Living with Agents: From Human-Agent Teamwork to Cognitive Prostheses

Jeffrey M. Bradshaw

Institute for Human and Machine Cognition University of West Florida 40 South Alcaniz Pensacola, FL 32501 `jbradshaw@ai.uwf.edu`
http://www.coginst.uwf.edu/ jbradsha/

Abstract. Tomorrow's world will be filled with agents embedded everywhere in the places and things around us. Providing a pervasive web of sensors and effectors, teams of such agents will function as cognitive prostheses–computational systems that leverage and extend human intellectual, perceptual, and collaborative capacities, just as the steam shovel was a sort of muscular prosthesis or the eyeglass a sort of visual prosthesis. While these heterogeneous cooperating entities may operate at different levels of sophistication and with dynamically varying degrees of autonomy, they will require some common means of representing and appropriately participating in joint tasks. Just as important, developers of such systems will need tools and methodologies to assure that such systems will work together reliably, naturally, and effectively, even when they are designed independently. In this talk I will describe some of the principles and applications that are important to the design and implementation of effective human-agent systems.

References

1. Acquisti, A., Sierhuis, M., Clancey, W. J., & Bradshaw, J. M. (2002). Agent-based modeling of collaboration and work practices onboard the International Space Station. Proceedings of the Eleventh Conference on Computer Generated Forces and Behavior Representation, Orlando Florida, to appear.
2. Bradshaw, J. M., Beautement, P., and Raj, A. (2002). Toward a deliberative and reactive agent architecture for augmented cognition. DARPA Augmented Cognition Program White Paper, to appear.
3. Bradshaw, J.M., Acquisti, A., Gawdiak, Y., Jeffers, R., Suri, N. & Greaves, M. (2002). Brahms and KAoS agent framework support for human-robotic teamwork in practice.Support for Human-Robotic Teamwork in Practice, in Henry Hexmoor, Rino Falcone, and Cristiano Castelfranchi (Eds.), Agent Autonomy, Kluwer, to appear.
4. Bradshaw, J.M., Suri, N., Kahn, M., Sage, P., Weishar, D. and Jeffers, R. (2001) Terraforming Cyberspace: Toward a Policy-based Grid Infrastructure for Secure, Scalable, and Robust Execution of Java-based Multi-agent Systems. IEEE Computer, 49-56, July 2001.
5. Bradshaw, J. M., Boy, G., Durfee, E., Gruninger, M., Hexmoor, H., Suri, N. Tambe, M., Uschold, M., & Vitek, J. (2002). Human-Agent Interaction. In J. M. Bradshaw (Ed.) Software Agents for the Warfighter. ITAC Consortium Report. Cambridge, MA: AAAI/MIT Press, to appear.
6. Bradshaw, J.M. (Ed.) (1997). Software Agents. Cambridge, MA: AAAI Press/The MIT Press.

S.A. Cerri, G. Gouardères, and F. Paraguaçu (Eds.): ITS 2002, LNCS 2363, p. 1, 2002.

Computational Humor

Oliviero Stock

ITC-irst, Centro per la Ricerca Scientifica e Tecnologica
Povo (Trento), Italy
stock@itc.it

Humor is something we human beings cannot live without. It has been studied since the ancient times and in the Twentieth Century several theories have been introduced to explain it (see for instance [1]).

The challenge to come out with accurate modeling of the processes that underlie humor is very stimulating. Yet psychological, linguistic or philosophical theories in this area are not very detailed. Deep modeling of humor in all of its facets is not something for the near future. The phenomena are too complex; at the end humor is one of the most sophisticated forms of human intelligence. It is AI-complete: the problem of modeling it is as difficult to solve as the most difficult Artificial Intelligence problems. But some steps have been taken to achieve initial results. The treatment of verbal humor (computational interpretation and generation) is the area that has drawn most attention. And we can note that when something is realized humor has the methodological advantage (unlike, say, computer art) of leading to more directly falsifiable theories: the resulting humorous artifacts can be tested on human subjects in a rather straightforward manner.

Effort goes more naturally into the development of systems that automatically produce humorous output (rather than systems that appreciate humor). Basically, in order to be successfully humorous, a computational system should be able to: recognize situations appropriate for humor; choose a suitable kind of humor for the situation; generate an appropriately humorous output; and, if there is some form of interaction or control, evaluate the feedback.

I believe that some of the basic competences are within the state of the the the art of natural language processing. In one form or in another humor is most often based on some form of incongruity. In verbal humor this means that at some level different interpretations of material must be possible (and some not detected before the culmination of the humorous process) or various pieces of material must cause perception of specific forms of opposition [2]. Natural language processing research has often dealt with ambiguity in language. A common view is that ambiguity is an obstacle for deep comprehension. Most current text processing systems, for example, attempt to reduce the number of possible interpretations of the sentences, and a failure to do so is seen as a weakness of the system. The potential for ambiguity, however, can be seen as a positive feature of natural language. Metaphors, idioms, poetic language and humor use the multiple senses of texts to suggest connections between concepts that cannot, or should not, be stated explicitly. Fluent users of natural language are able to both use and interpret ambiguities inherent in the language and verbal humor is one of the most regular uses of linguistic ambiguity.

S.A. Cerri, G. Gouardères, and F. Paraguaçu (Eds.): ITS 2002, LNCS 2363, pp. 2–3, 2002.
© Springer-Verlag Berlin Heidelberg 2002

Looking at computational humor from an application-oriented point of view, one assumption is that in future human-machine interaction, humans will demand a naturalness and effectiveness that requires the incorporation of models of possibly all human cognitive capabilities, including the handling of humor [3]. There are many practical settings where computational humor will add value. Among them there are: business world applications (such as advertisement, e-commerce, etc...), general computer-mediated communication and human-computer interaction, increase in the friendliness of natural language interfaces, educational and edutainment systems. In particular in the educational field humor is an important resource for getting selective attention, help in memorizing names and situations etc. And we all know how important it is for children.

As for the scientific community, there have been a couple of workshops that have brought together most researchers in the field (see [4] and [5]).

I am also happy to report that the first European project devoted to computational humor, HAHAcronym [6], a Future Emerging Technologies (FET) EC project (contract number IST-2000-30039) in the context of the Information Society Technologies (IST) programme, has been successfully completed. I am confident it shows that time is ripe for taking the potential of computational humor seriously.

References

1. Freud, S.: Der Witz und seine Beziehung zum Unbewussten. Deutike, Leipzig and Vienna (1905)
2. Raskin, V.: Semantic Mechanisms of Humor. Reidel Pu. Co. Dordrecht/ Boston/ Lancaster (1985)
3. Stock, O.: Password Swordfish: Verbal humor in the interface. In Hulstijn, J. and Nijholt, A., editors, Proc. of International Workshop on Computational Humour (TWLT 12), University of Twente, Enschede (1996)
4. Hulstijn, J. and Nijholt, A., (eds.): Proceedings of International Workshop on Computational Humour (TWLT 12), University of Twente, Enschede (1996)
5. Stock, O., Strapparava, C. and Nijholt, A., (eds.): Proceedings of the Fools' Day Workshop on Computational Humour (TWLT 20), Trento (2002)
6. Stock, O. and Strapparava, C. HAHAcronym: humorous Agents for Humorous Acronyms. In Stock, O., Strapparava, C. and Nijholt, A., (eds.): Proceedings of the Fools' Day Workshop on Computational Humour (TWLT 20), Trento (2002)

Large-Scale Introduction of E-learning at Universities throughout Europe

Fred Mulder[1]

in collaboration with: Jos Rikers[1] and Piet Henderikx[2]

Open Universiteit Nederland, PO Box 2960, 6401 DL Heerlen, The Netherlands
{fred.mulder, jos.rikers}@ou.nl
European Association of Distance Teaching Universities (EADTU), PO Box 2960, 6401 DL
Heerlen, The Netherlands
secretariat@eadtu.nl

Abstract. In the last two years many initiatives to start so-called virtual universities have emerged in various countries throughout Europe. These mostly extensive projects are paving the way for really large-scale introduction of e-learning at the university level in Europe. Because of the substantial impact to be foreseen there is a need for a comparative state-of-the-art overview of the European landscape in this respect. We report the first results of such a study, in the future to be used as a base line for a monitoring instrument. This monitor will be established under the umbrella of the European Association of Distance Teaching Universities (EADTU), members of which are involved in many of the university level e-learning initiatives in Europe. The EADTU Monitor 'Universities in e-learning' aims to provide the needed continually updated information concerning Europe and relevant for educational professionals as well as policy makers.

1 Introduction

In spring 2001 EADTU held an exclusive Board Seminar in Rome dedicated to the development of e-learning at university level and more specifically the genesis of so-called virtual universities throughout Europe. The outcome was a very rich and impressive overview, however without being available to the public and presented in so many different forms that a systematic and comparative access is prohibited. In the meantime new initiatives have evolved and the existing ones are rapidly progressing with quite often changing focus and scope.

To enable the monitoring of all those large-scale e-learning initiatives at university level in Europe, it is preferred that the available information is collected and presented in a structured way. This enables the comparison of initiatives and the follow up in time. It should allow for a critical review on success and fail factors. And it offers references to various implementations in practice with lessons learned, in order to be helpful to all those who are considering similar large-scale projects.

The EADTU Monitor 'Universities in e-learning' is an instrument under development that should meet the above goals. It will be based on what we think are

S.A. Cerri, G. Gouardères, and F. Paraguaçu (Eds.): ITS 2002, LNCS 2363, pp. 4–5, 2002.

the most relevant parameters. But since we report a pilot version, the number of parameters and their definition is likely to change until we achieve a more stable monitor. We limit ourselves in this first version to EADTU member institutions, because of the easy availability of information within the EADTU, while at the same time the coverage of substantial e-learning initiatives in Europe is very large, simply because of the EADTU origin and characteristics. The EADTU Monitor will extend its range in the near future and will include non-member initiatives on invitation.

2   Parameters for the EADTU Monitor 'Universities in E-learning'

The parameters included in the initial version of the monitor are based on an analysis of available information on several initiatives known to the authors. The following parameters are introduced:
− Time scale
    Start date, end date and deliverables are reported. But also provisions for sustainability.
− Collaboration typology
    Here we will try to develop a typology of forms of collaboration. Examples we can mention already are e.g. consortia, with or without private partners, establishing a new institution or company by partners, etc.
− Functionalities
    The most interesting functionalities are e.g. inclusion or exclusion of commercial exploitation, the development and exchange of course material, and the provision of a support function through what one could call an Educational Service Provider (ESP).
− Public policy
    For the evaluation of every initiative it is important to know how it is related to the public (national and regional) policy on e-learning.
− Economic model
    The economic model describes the divide in funding between government, institutions and private partners. One could also address the 'business mechanism' underlying the initiative.
− Scale of impact
    This parameter refers to the absolute and relative number of students - potentially - involved.
− E-learning strategy
    How is the actual initiative related to the long term policy. What strategy is used to achieve the goals set.
− SWOT analysis
    A SWOT analysis provides a base line for evaluation of future developments.

3   Finally

The EADTU Monitor 'Universities in e-learning' is meant to be instrumental for critical review and further analysis of good practices and trends.

A Roadmap of Epistemic Logics for Learning Agents

Frédéric Koriche

LIRMM, UMR 5506, Université Montpellier II CNRS
161, rue Ada. 34392 Montpellier Cedex 5, France
koriche@lirmm.fr

1   Introduction

A student is facing a teacher, who is probing her knowledge of mathematics. The student is a new recruit and important questions must be answered: What are her strengths and weakness ? Which topics is she ready to study ? Should the student take a remedial course in some subject ? The teacher will ask a question and listen to the student's response. Other questions will then be asked. After a few questions, a picture of the student's state of knowledge will emerge, which will become increasingly sharper in the course of the examination.

However refined the questioning skills of the teacher may be, some important aspects of her task are not a priori beyond the capability of a learning agent (see e.g. [2]). Imagine a student sitting in front of a computer terminal. The agent selects a problem and displays it on the monitor. The student's response is recorded, and the knowledge base, which keeps track of the set of all feasible knowledge states consistent with the responses given so far, is updated. The next question is selected so as to refine the set of knowledge states. The goal is to converge on some knowledge state capable of explaining all the responses.

The broad purpose of this talk is to convey this perspective and to investigate the logical structure of knowledge states and their dynamics. To this end, we begin to propose a model of a learning agent which is based on the paradigm of *inductive reasoning*. Based on this model, we present a family of *epistemic logics* that capture cognitive actions underlying learning agents. Even so, we shall only scratch the surface, mostly ignoring such aspects as the computational representation and manipulation of knowledge states, the interplay between cognitive and physical actions, or multi-agent learning.

2   The Model

The first part of the talk sketches the concepts of our model in intuitive terms. The model is founded on the paradigm of inductive reasoning, first investigated by the philosopher C.S. Pierce [9], and recently studied by several authors in the artificial intelligence literature [4,5]. Inductive reasoning consists in a cycle of three steps: *hypothesis generation, prediction* and *evaluation.* The underlying model runs as follows. When confronted with a number of observed events she

S.A. Cerri, G. Gouardères, and F. Paraguaçu (Eds.): ITS 2002, LNCS 2363, pp. 6–7, 2002.
© Springer-Verlag Berlin Heidelberg 2002

seeks to explain, the learning agent comes up with a set of knowledge states which are consistent with the observations; then the agent investigates what are the consequences of the knowledge states; and finally, the agent evaluates the extent to which these predicted consequences agree with future events.

3 The Logics

The second part of this talk is devoted to the logical analysis of inductive reasoning. In the setting suggested by our approach, we present a family of epistemic logics that formalize the cognitive actions involved in inductive reasoning.

In order to describe the notion of knowledge state more precisely, we start with the concept of *basic epistemic logic*, first investigated by Hintikka in [7], and further studied in [3]. The key concept in this logic lies in possible-world semantics, which provide a good formal tool for capturing different properties of knowledge. Based on this logic, we progressively incorporate additional blocks that capture the essential features of inductive reasoning.

First, we stress the fact that learning agents need to introspect on both their knowledge and ignorance. In particular, we show that this notion is crucial for hypothesis prediction. To this aim, we examine the *logic of only knowing*, introduced by Levesque in [8], which includes an epistemic closure assumption. Secondly, we bring to the fore the notion "updating" knowledge which plays a central role in hypothesis generation. From this perspective, we present a *dynamic epistemic logic* inspired from investigations of Gerbrandy [6], and van Benthem [1]. Third and finally, we combine the two above components in a new system, called *dynamic only knowing*, which provides a formal and intuitive specification tool for learning agents.

References

1. J. van Benthem. *Exploring Logical Dynamics*. CSLI Publications, 1995.
2. J. P. Doignon and J. .C. Falmagne. *Knowledge Spaces*. Springer, 1999.
3. R. Fagin, J. Y. Halpern, Y. Moses, and M. Y. Vardi. *Reasoning About Knowledge*. MIT-Press, 1995.
4. P. A. Flach. *Conjectures : an inquiry concerning the logic of induction*. PhD thesis, Tilburg University, 1995.
5. P. A. Flach and A. C. Kakas (editors). *Abduction and Induction: Essays on their Relation and Integration*, volume 18 of *Applied Logic Series*. Kluwer Academic Publishers, 2000.
6. J. Gerbrandy. *Bisimulations on Planet Kripke*. PhD thesis, Institute for Logic, Language and Computation, 1999.
7. J. Hintikka. *Knowledge and Belief*. Cornell University Press, 1962.
8. H. J. Levesque. All I know: a study in autoepistemic logic. *Artificial Intelligence*, 42:263–309, 1990.
9. C.S. Peirce. *Collected papers of Charles Sanders Peirce*. Harvard University Press, 1958.

ITS, Agents, BDI, and Affection: Trying to Make a Plan Come Together

Rosa Maria Vicari

Federal University of Rio Grande do Sul, Brazil
Rosa@inf.ufrgs.br

In the IA group at UFRGS, Porto Alegre, Brazil, one of the main focus of work is on Intelligent Tutoring Systems. In this talk, I intend to present some of the aspects related to the construction of teaching and learning environments. Specifically, I will highlight the use of AI techniques and agents in the composition of these environments.

Most of the work that has been developed is concerned with the architecture of such systems. Our group has been using the concepts of agency and mental states as an abstraction to describe, design and build systems. As usual, architectures are too implementation-oriented. They provide schemas to build agents and systems but they are inadequate as analysis tool and, for the special case of pedagogical agents, there must be considered that sometimes it is not easy to respect the pedagogical theoretical foundations of such agents while building them. Formal models come into place, then, as we are interested both in describing and analyzing the autonomous behavior of (artificial and natural) agents in an Intelligent Tutoring System.

The purpose of having formal models of agents is to reduce the gap between specification and implementation. To achieve part of this goal, we have been using BDI (beliefs, desires and intentions) architectures with event calculus as a logical support for time and actions. Using this formal basis, we have been able to define static and dynamic aspects of the agents that composed the systems. Our current research includes looking for a formal model that can be used as a framework to specify and test (simulate, build, and execute) pedagogical agents.

The use of BDI architectures seems to be adequate to build teaching and learning agents because desires and intentions are pro-active mental states, i.e., they potentially lead agents to action. Another important characteristic is that desires may be contradictory (with other desires, and with the agent's beliefs) and beliefs allow the agents to constantly update its view of the world. These characteristics of mental states are very important to better represent the choreography that happens during a teaching/learning interaction.

Trying to go beyond the notion of behavior that mental states allows us to model, we have been updating these architectures to represent some affective aspects of learners, like effort, confidence and independence. The affective information improves the system, and allows it to provide a more adequate help for the student. In other words, we believe that the use of both mental states and affective aspects allows a more accurate selection of pedagogical strategies.

The long-term purpose of our research is to define an environment where there is no explicit tutor nor learner, but only a set of mental states and affective aspects that

S.A. Cerri, G. Gouardères, and F. Paraguaçu (Eds.): ITS 2002, LNCS 2363, pp. 8–9, 2002.
© Springer-Verlag Berlin Heidelberg 2002

generate learning and teaching attitudes that can be assumed by all agents that composed the environment.

References

1. Mora, M., Lopes, J. G., Coelho, H., Viccari, R. M.: Design Agents with Extended Logic Programming. Lecture Notes on Artificial Intelligence: ICSC-Symposium on Engineering of Intelligent Systems. E. Bogazici (Ed.). Berlin: Springer-Verlag. (1998).
2. Mora , M.C., Viccari ,R.M., Lopes, J. P., Coelho, H.: BDI models and systems: reducing the gap. ATAL'98 -Paris (1998).
3. Giraffa, L.M., Mora, M.C., Viccari, R.M.: Pedagogical Game Using ITS Architecture - IBERAMIA '98 - Workshop on Agents Application - Spain (1998)
4. Giraffa, L. M., Móra, M. C., Viccari, R.M.: Modelling an Interactive ITS Using a MAS Approach: from Design to Pedagogical Evaluation., R. M. ICCIMA'99 – 3rd International Conference on Computational Intelligence and Multimedia Applications. New Delhi, India (1999).
5. Viccari, R. M., Bercht, M.: Pedagogical Agents with Affective and Cognitive Dimensions. In: RIBIE 2000, V Congreso Iberoamericano de Informática Educativa, 2000, Vinã del Mar. RIBIE 2000, V Congreso Iberoamericano de Informática Educativa. 2000. v. CD-rom.
6. Viccari, R. M., Giraffa, L. M.: The Use of Multi Agent System to Build Intelligent Tutoring Systems. In: CASYS'01, 2001, Liege. CASYS'01 Abstract Book. Liege: CHAOS, 2001. v. 1, p. 13-13.
7. Bordini, R. H., Lesser, V., Viccari, R. M.; Bazzan, A. L., Janone, et ali.: Efficient Intention selection in BDI agents via Decision-Theoretic Task Scheduling. In: Autonomous Agents and Multiagents Systems, 2002, Bologna. Proceedings of the Autonomous and Multiagens Systems Conference. 2002.

An Intellectual Genealogy Graph Affording a Fine Prospect of Organizational Learning

Yusuke Hayashi, Hiroyuki Tsumoto, Mitsuru Ikeda, and Riichiro Mizoguchi

The Institute of Scientific and Industrial Research, Osaka University
8-1, Mihogaoka, Ibaraki, Osaka, 5670047, Japan
{hayashi, hiro_t, ikeda, miz}@ei.sanken.osaka-u.ac.jp

Abstract. The word of "learning", in a wide sense, is used as a part of the social system of education and it has been attracting researchers' interest in our research area of educational systems. The goal of this research is to support creation and inheritance of organizational intellect, that is, "learning" in an organization. In this paper, we will propose an "Intellectual Genealogy Graph," which is a model representing chronological correlation among persons, activities, and intellect in an organization. The intellectual genealogy graph is a basis of intelligent functions which is useful for surveying current learning conditions and clarifying the intellectual role of individuals, organizations, and documents in the organization.

1. Introduction

We continue to learn during our lifetimes. As researchers, for example, we learn basic knowledge through 'book learning', acquire up-to-date knowledge from the literature, develop original knowledge for ourselves, and then disseminate it to society. In this sense, we can share the idea that "life is a continuous process of learning." Usage of the word "learning" here has a rather wide sense; it is subtly different from the customary sense in which we use it to refer to the learning process established as a part of the social system of education.

"Learning" in a wide sense includes various forms of learning: for example, workplace learning, life-long learning, organizational learning, and so on. Viewing learning as an implicit, daily, long-term, practical activity is an important trend in many research areas related to the area of computers in education. As examples, the concepts of social constructionism in psychology [1], organizational learning [2] or knowledge creating companies [3] in management, and knowledge management systems in information technology [4][5] have been closely related to our research areas. In our area of intelligent educational systems, needless to say, "learning" in a wide sense has been attracting researchers' interest. Fisher's series of works on life-long learning [6] and integration of collaborative learning and knowledge management [7][8][9] are typical approaches in the same vein.

Along a similar line of thought, this research aims to develop a model of learning in a wide sense. Needless to say, we are all vaguely conscious of a similar model in our own minds which we apply to increase awareness of social relations among or-

S.A. Cerri, G. Gouardères, and F. Paraguaçu (Eds.): ITS 2002, LNCS 2363, pp. 10–20, 2002.

ganization members; however, that model is implicit and not systemic in most cases. We propose a model called a "dual loop model", which shows how intellect is formed in individual life in organizations and works as a fundamental component of a learning support platform. The dual loop model indicates an ideal relation between individual activity and organizational activity and clarifies roles of individuals, activities, and documents as a vehicle for intellectual communication in organizational learning.

In this research project, we have been developing an IT platform, Kfarm [10] [11], to develop users' pro-found social intellectual awareness in organization. Kfarm is a Web-browser-like workplace for users to carry out knowledge-oriented group activities, that is, searching, creating, organizing, and communicating information. All activities on Kfarm are recorded in organizational memory in the form of an "intellectual genealogy graph." This intellectual genealogy graph represents a trace of intellectual activities based on a dual loop model and shows how knowledge and the intellect are evolved in organization.

2. A Model of Organizational Learning

The terms 'knowledge,' 'intellect,' and so on are used with various meanings, so there appear to be no definite meanings for them [12]. Though it is difficult to define them strictly in a consistent manner, to show subjects of this study, we will take some exemplary definitions from the literature.

Brown and Duguid [13] argue convincingly that knowledge is more than just information because it
- usually entails a 'knower',
- appears harder to detach than information, and
- is something what we digest rather than merely hold.

Tobin draws distinctions between data, information, knowledge, and wisdom [14].
1. *Data*:
2. *Information*:   = *Data*+ relevance + purpose
3. *Knowledge*:   = *Information*+application
4. *Wisdom*:   = *Knowledge*+intuition + experience

In this research, the term 'intellect' is used to express our idea similar to Brown and Duguid's argument about 'knowledge' and Tobin's 'wisdom'. Having an intellect means not only merely knowing something, but also digesting it through creation or practical use. It also means that the intellect cannot be separated from a person because it includes skill and competency. Therefore, we aim to support creation and inheritance of organizational intellect by managing information concerned with intellect.

2.1. Organizational Learning

It is considered that there are two viewpoints to clarify the goal of creation and inheritance of organizational intellect. One is a practical view and the other is an educational one. The practical goal is to produce a novel and significant intellect for an organization. The educational goal is to properly transmit significant intellect from past to future members of an organization and import significant intellect from outside of it. For both viewpoint, it is necessary to clarify what intellect each organization member has and what kind of shared workplace (Nonaka et al. call this "*ba*"[15]) makes it easy to transmit each intellect.

We attempt to attain such goals through our usual communication. Typical activities are, for example, acquiring, creating, and distributing intellect through the organization. Linking the activities are vehicles, e.g. conversations, books, or documents. By interpreting the activities and the vehicles, we can gain an awareness of others' intellect; those members usually do various activities to achieve creation and inheritance of organizational intellect based on that awareness. Such individual activities run the organization. However, it is difficult for members to do that because of the implicit nature of an ideal process of creation and inheritance of organizational intellect and content of vehicles actually used in activities. Consequently, to be properly aware of intellect and decide activity to attain the goal, it is necessary to clarify a model representing relations among an organization, individuals, intellect, vehicles, and activities from the view of creation and inheritance of organizational intellect.

Landes et al. [16] proposed a model of organizational learning in which knowledge is augmented with experiences of its application and developed a support tool based on it. The augmentation process is represented by the dependency among the documented experiences. In the best applicable domain of their idea, general knowledge is treated on an abstract level and the essential details of how to apply that knowledge in very specific situations are absent. Basing improvement initiative on experiences has a number of advantages, particularly in such a domain. On the other hand, intellectual roles of a person and intellectual communication in an organization are relatively less focused in this model.

Nonaka and Takeuchi proposed the SECI model, representing a knowledge conversion process and "Middle up-down management", which is a form of an organization to activate process [3][15]. In Middle up-down management, a "Knowledge practitioner (K-practitioner)" plays the role of generating creative power previously mentioned, while a "Knowledge producer (K-producer)" plays the role of coordinating between the top's visions and the K-practitioners' practical activities. Typical activities of the K-producer are given below:

- Proper understanding of organizational conditions.
- Assimilating new intellect with the organizational intellect.
- Distributing organizational intellect based on their vision/strategy.

These activities give direction to K-practitioners' activities.

Several studies have been made on information systems to support creation and inheritance of organizational intellect. Klamma and Schlaphof [17] stated the importance of interrelation between the processes of knowledge creation and usage and normal business processes both on a conceptual and a systemic level; they proposed a model-based approach for solving that. Watanabe and Kojiri [8][18] arranged various kinds of educational support systems: CAI, CAL, ITS, and CSCL according to the SECI model and proposed a learning environment architecture in which learners are able to change their learning style freely. The former study addressed the practical viewpoint and the latter study addressed the educational viewpoint, but each study ignored the other viewpoint.

In the viewpoint of awareness of intellect, Ogata et al. defined awareness of one's own or another's knowledge as "Knowledge awareness" and developed Sherlock II which supports group formation for collaborative learning based on learners' initiatives with the knowledge awareness[19]. This study supports group formation by learners' own initiatives, but lacks the organizational perspective.

The purpose of this study is building an organizational learning environment from several perspectives: practical and educational; and organizational and individual.

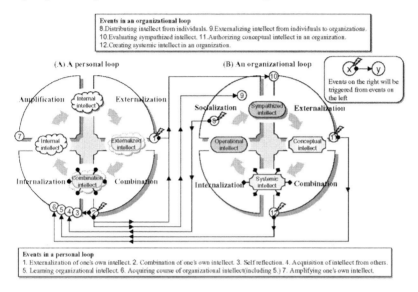

Fig. 1. Dual loop model (partly simplified)

2.2. Modeling an Organizational Intellect

We produced a model supporting creation and inheritance of organizational intellect from two separate models: a process model and a content model. The process model is a model representing creation and inheritance processes of intellect. The content model is a model of the domain of intellectual activities.

Process model. We modeled an ideal abstract process of creation and inheritance of organizational intellect as a "dual loop model". Figure 1 shows the most abstract level of the model, which describes constraint on the relation between activities and change of the property of intellect. For example, socialization prescribes that resultant intellect draws a certain amount of sympathy in the organization; then, externalization of the intellect should follow. These activities are structured as a multi-tiered abstraction hierarchy in which the bottom layer consists of observable activities, for example, reading a document or distributing one. The hierarchy does not prescribe content of intellect concerned with activity, but the property of intellect. The dual loop model explains these activities from both viewpoints of the 'individual' as the substantial actor in an organization (a personal loop: Figure 1(A)) and the 'organization' as the aggregation of individuals (an organizational loop: Figure 1(B)). This model as a whole represents an ideal interrelationship among an organization, its members, and vehicles of intellect for the goal of creation and inheritance of organizational intellect. Further details of the dual loop model are shown in [10].

Content model. Most document management systems manage a document with indexes. However, it is difficult to share it in the organization since the meaning of the indexes is implicit and does not ensure consistency. Even if the document is shared, that will often be done on an implicit premise. In order to share and inherit intellect properly in an organization, it is necessary to form a basis to clarify the meaning of intellect. Semantic web [20] is an attempt to build a global consensus to share resources on the WWW.

Ontology [21] has been brought to public attention as a foundation. Ontology is a set of definitions of concepts and relationships to be modeled. Concepts related to tasks and domains of an organization are defined as the ontology to describe document content. The description is called the "conceptual index". Thus, intellect content in an organization is modeled with an index described on the basis of an ontology.

3.   Intellectual Genealogy Graph

We compose a model of an organizational intellect as a combination of process and content, that is to say, the dual loop model and the ontology. The model is called an "intellectual genealogy graph". It represents chronological correlation among persons, activities, and intellect in an organization as an interpretation of activities of organization members based on these two models. Modeling an intellectual genealogy graph affords a good foundation for building intelligent support functions for the organizational activities given below.

- Clarifying a role for each member from a trail of his/her intellectual activities in organization. We call the role an "intellectual role", which characterizes a contribution of a person to the construction process of organizational intellect.
- Choosing a correct way to fill a gap between the current condition of organizational intellect and a desired one.

3.1.   Components of an Intellectual Genealogy Graph

Principal concepts appearing in an intellectual genealogy graph are as follows:
- *Person* is a career of intellect and a creator of it.
- *Intellect* is knowledge, skill, competency, and so on turned to practical use by a person. Categories of intellect are shown in Table 1.
- *Vehicle* is a representation of intellect and mediates intellect among people. As mentioned before, we assume that intellect can only exist in a person's mind and a vehicle of the intellect is not necessarily a complete representation of the intellect.
- *Activity* is activity related to the intellect or a vehicle. Categories of activities are shown partly in Table 2.

An intellectual genealogy graph is built by abstracting a causal structure of cognitive activities from concrete activities based on the dual loop model. The structure clarifies mutual relation among personal activities, social activities, and organizational activities.

Table 1. Types of intellect

Intellect type	Explanation
Personal intellect	An intellect, which a person has personally.
Organizational intellect	Types of intellect classified in view of relation to other's one and organizational one
Sympathized intellect	An intellect consented or sympathized by others
Conceptual intellect	An intellect acknowledged to be significant in an organization
Systemic intellect	A conceptual intellect combined with other conceptual ones.

Table 2. Types of activities (partial)

Activity type	Explanation
Concrete Activity	Observable activities in workplace.
Read	Reading, seeing a medium/vehicle.
Collect	Collecting a vehicle from other people.
Represent	Producing a vehicle.
Sort	Sorting a vehicle according to its meaning.
Distribute	Distributing a vehicle to other people.
Cognitive Activity	Activities affect on intellect
Personal Activity	Activities concerned with interpersonal activities
Create	Creating new intellect by oneself.
Acquire-1	Acquiring an intellect from others.
Organize	Assimilate a new intellect into his/her own structure of intellect.
Social Activity	An interaction activity as an aggregation of personal activities.
Pass	A person acquires an intellect imparted by another person.
Acquire-2	A person acquires an intellect from on his/her initiative.
Discuss	More than two persons communicate with each other.
Organizational Activity	Activities interpreted in an organizational perspective
Share	Members of the organization share a personal intellect.
Authorize	The organization authorizes a personal intellect.
Inherit	Members of the organization inherit an intellect.

3.2.   Modeling an Intellectual Genealogy Graph

An intellectual genealogy graph consists of a vehicle layer and an intellect layer. The vehicle layer comprises persons, vehicles, and concrete activities. On the other hand, the intellect layer is an interpretation of the vehicle layer and consists of persons, intellects, cognitive activities, and relations among intellects. These relations are classified into some types by characteristics of changes of intellect as shown in Table 3. In the intellect layer, these relations are built from activities.

Hard data for modeling an intellectual genealogy graph is a time-series of concrete activities observed in the workplace. Firstly, a vehicle layer of the graph is built from the data. Then, a series of cognitive activities are abstracted from the vehicle layer based on the dual loop model and an intellect layer of the graph is constructed. Figure

2 shows an example of interpretation from concrete activities into cognitive activity and relationships between intellects derived by the translation. In this way, the intellectual genealogy graph records the formation of an organizational memory from activities.

Table 3. Types of relations between intellects(partial)

Relation type	Explanation
created(?a)	A person originally creates an intellect *?a* with no reference to other intellects in the organization.
imported(?a)	A person acquires an intellect *?a* from the outside.
derived(?a, ?b)	A person acquires an intellect *?a* from another person's intellect *?b* in the same meaning.
inspired(?a, ?b)	A kind of *modified* relation, which represents the authorized significance of the conceptual leap from *?a* to *?b*.
authorized(?a, ?b)	A significance of an intellect *?b* is authorized as an organizational intellect *?a* by the organization

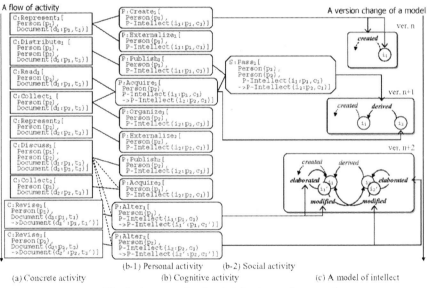

Fig. 2. An example of an intellect genealogy graph

4.   Kfarm: Affording Fine Prospect of Intellectual Activities

Kfarm is a system that we have been developing which embodies our conceptualization thus far. Kfarm is a distributed system consisting of a K-granary, at least one K-ranch house and some K-fields. The K-field and the K-ranch house are environments for a K-practitioner and a K-producer respectively. Those two play dual roles of sensors which watch a user's activities in a knowledge-oriented task and a display which shows information about the organizational intellect according to their roles. The K-granary is a server. It interprets K-producers' and K-practitioners' activities observed in the K-field and the K-ranch house and then aggregates and stores them as an organizational intellect.

4.1. K-Field

A K-field provides K-practitioners with information needed for their knowledge-intensive tasks. Typical K-field functions are given below. These are designed based on activities defined in the personal loop in the dual loop model.

Sorting documents by folders: A K-field provides a bookmark window as a tool to store documents in folders with indexes. The indexes are converted to conceptual indexes in the K-granary.

Communication with others: In a KW-window, a K-field indicates information about others and documents related to the document selected in the bookmark window. This information is based on intellectual roles of members and the document assigned on the intellectual genealogy graph.

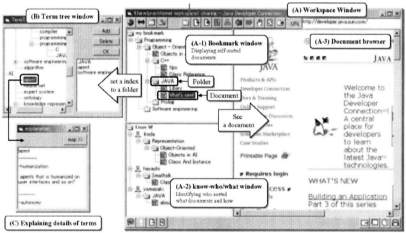

Fig. 3. K-field

4.2. K-Ranch House

A K-ranch house supports K-producers' activities, e.g., recognizing the organizational condition and coordinating communication, cooperative work, and collaborative learning between K-practitioners based on the organizational vision/strategy.

Figure 4 shows windows of the K-ranch house which is under development. A launcher window shown in Figure 4(A) informs K-producers about activities of K-practitioners in Kfarm. Figure 4(B) and (C) are monitor windows to provide a K-producer with detailed information of an organizational memory. In this case, an icon shown in Figure 4(A-1) indicates growth of an intellect supposed to be a sympathized intellect. If the K-producer clicks this icon, its details will be shown in the monitor window as shown in Figure 4(B) and (C). Figure 4(B) graphically indicates who sympathizes with the intellect through which document. Each node in Figure 4(C) indicates an intellect. Links between them indicate relations between intellects previously mentioned in Table 3.

Now, we will take a close look at the visualized intellectual genealogy graph. Figure 4(C) indicates a history of a generation of intellect in which the intellect (C-1) is the center of attraction. Broken arrows from intellect (C-2) to (C-1), for example, indicate an elaborated link. It is interpreted from the fact that *ikeda* makes a document referring to *hayashi*'s document concerned with intellect (C-2) and puts the same term index and additional ones on the document. This information help the K-producer to clarify intellectual roles of members and documents concerned with the intellect. To illustrate a case of this, for example, it is supposed that *hayashi* is a person who has made a seed of a new intellect (C-2) and documents concerned with intellects (C-3) can be used as background information.

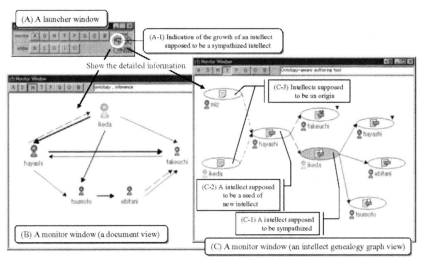

Fig. 4. K-ranch house (under development)

5. Conclusion

In order to support creation and inheritance of organizational intellect, that is, "learning" in a wide sense, it is important to abstract and interpret activities in the organization. In this paper, we have proposed the dual loop model and ontology as bases and introduced Kfarm as an embodiment of them. The intellectual genealogy graph is useful for individuals and organizations to survey current learning conditions and to clarify the intellectual role of individuals, organizations, and documents in the organization.

Future direction of this study will be to augment Kfarm in the following two ways.

• Support of arranging a collaborative learning space
• Model of the property of an organization

In the former, broadly speaking, it is considered that Kfarm itself is a space for less-regulated collaborative learning because it allows learner-directed communication. However, some processes of a dual loop model can be better achieved by rather regulated collaborative learning.

In the latter, generally, an organization has a hierarchical structure and a member belongs to some groups in the structure. Currently, we are introducing an organizational structure and developing a more flexible model of creation/inheritance of organizational intellect by considering that structure.

References

1. Doise W. and Mugny G.: The social development of the intellect, Oxford: Pergamon Press, 1984.
2. Senge P. M.: The Fifth Discipline: The Art and Practice of Learning Organization, Doubleday, 1990.
3. Nonaka I. and Takeuchi H.: The Knowledge-Creating Company: How Japanese Companies Create the Dynamics of Innovation, Oxford University Press, 1995.
4. Decker S. and Maurer F.: "Editorial: Organizational memory and knowledge management", Int. J. Human-Computer Studies, 51, pp. 511-516, 1999.
5. Fensel D.: Ontologies: A Silver Bullet for Knowledge Management and Electronic Commerce, Springer-Verlag Telos, 2001.
6. Fischer G.: "Lifelong Learning - More Than Training, Special Issue on Intelligent Systems/Tools in Training and Life-Long Learning". In Eds.: Mizoguchi R. and Piet A.M. Kommers, Journal of Interactive Learning Research, Vol. 11, No. 3/4, pp.265-294, 2000.
7. Eleuterio M. A., Bortolozzi F., and Kaestner C.A.: "The Roles of Ontologies in Collaborative Virtual Learning Environments", Proc. of ECAI2000 Workshop on Analysis and Modeling of Collaborative Learning Interactions, pp.31-35, 2000.
8. Watanabe, T.: "Knowledge Management architecture of Integrated Educational Support", Proc. of ICCE/SchoolNet 2001, pp.1138-1141, 2001.
9. Ayala G.: "Intelligent Agents Supporting the Social Construction of Knowledge in a Lifelong Learning Environment", Proc. of NTCL2000, pp.79-88, 2000.
10. Hayashi Y., Tsumoto H., Ikeda M., and Mizoguchi R.: "Toward an Ontology-aware Support for Learning-Oriented Knowledge Management", Proc. of ICCE/SchoolNet 2001, pp.1149-1152, 2001.
11. Hayashi Y., Tsumoto H., Ikeda M., and Mizoguchi R.: "Kfarm: A Knowledge Management Support System Based on Dual Loop Model", Proc. of PYIWIT'2002, pp.235-242, 2002.
12. Liebowitz J. (Eds.): Knowledge Management Hand Book, CRC Press, 1999.
13. Brown J. S. and Duguid P.: "The Social Life of Information", Harvard Business School Press, Boston, 2000.
14. Tobin D.: Transformational Learning: Renewing Your Company thought Knowledge and Skills, John Wiley and Sons, 1996.
15. Nonaka I., Toyama R., and Konno N.: "SECI, Ba, Leadership: a Unified Model of Dynamic Knowledge Creation", Long Range Planning, 33, pp. 5-34, 2000.

16. Landes D., Schneider K., and Houdek F.: "Organizational learning and experience documentation industrial software projects", Int. J. of Human-Computer Studies, 51, pp.643-661, 1999.
17. Klamma R. and Schlaphof A.: "Rapid Knowledge Deployment in an Organizational-Memory-Based Workflow Environment", Proc. of ECIS 2000, pp. 364-371, 2000.
18. Kojiri T., and Watanabe T.: "HARMONY: Web-based Adaptive Collaborative Learning Environment", Proc. of ICCE/SchoolNet 2001, pp.559-566, 2001.
19. Ogata H., Matsuura K., and Yano Y.: "Active Knowledge Awareness Map: Visualizing Learners Activities in a web Based CSCL Environment", Proc. of NTCL2000, pp.89-97, 2000.
20. W3C Semantic Web: http://www.w3.org/2001/sw/
21. Mizoguchi R. and Bourdeau J.: Using Ontological Engineering to Overcome AI-ED Problems, Int. J. of Artificial Intelligence in Education, Vol.11, No.2, pp.107-121, 2000

Group-Oriented Modelling Tools with Heterogeneous Semantics

Niels Pinkwart, H. Ulrich Hoppe, Lars Bollen, and Eva Fuhlrott

Institute for Computer Science and Interactive Systems
Faculty of Engineering, University of Duisburg
47048 Duisburg, Germany
Phone: (+49) 203 379-1403
pinkwart@collide.info

Abstract. This paper describes an approach of how to support collaborative modelling tasks. The presented system, Cool Modes, implements the approach using "plug-in" reference frames encapsulating the semantics of the used models. Details on the extensibility of the system and the definition and interpretation of these reference frames and models in the framework are shown and the co-operation support using the underlying MatchMaker communication server is explained. Furthermore, two examples from the domains "System Dynamics modelling" and "Jewish Ceremonies" are given.

1 Introduction

Currently, information technology or computer support for collaborative learning is mainly based on computer-mediated communication such as, e.g., on conferencing techniques and sharing of resources and materials as well as on digital archives. This implies that the information exchanged, voice, text or images, is "passed through" the system, but not semantically processed. On the other hand, originally motivated by the limitations of conventional individualised computer tutors, there was another tendency to have more interactivity in learning environments using rich and powerful "computational objects to think with". This lead to the development of interactive cognitive tools or "mind tools" [1], which were essentially based on the direct manipulation of visual objects by the user-learner but also based on the computational processing of related symbolic objects and representations. Typical examples are visual languages for argumentation and discussion as well as visual tools for simulation and scientific modelling. A first suggestion of how to support collaboration with modelling tools in "discovery learning" has been made by van Joolingen [2].
We see a new challenge in providing "computational objects to think with" in a collaborative, distributed computing framework. This is typically achieved through shared workspace environments which allows a group of learners to synchronously co-construct and elaborate external representations. Systems may differ considerably with respect to the degree of semantics or structure that is explicitly captured by the com-

S.A. Cerri, G. Gouardères, and F. Paraguaçu (Eds.): ITS 2002, LNCS 2363, pp. 21–30, 2002.

puterised representation: Whereas the internal structure of whiteboard (drawing) tools is based on strokes, colours, and geometrical shapes, concept mapping tools constitute "semantic" relations between certain objects or nodes. However, it is not clearly defined in how far the semantics of the representation is really interpreted by the machine. Internally, a concept mapping tool may just be based on an abstract graph structure, whereas more specific representations such as System dynamics models [3] or visual programming languages come with a clearly defined and rich internal operational semantics. They provide a complete semantic definition of all objects and thus allow for "running" the models. On the other hand, less specific systems like Belvedere [4] do not interpret the semantic content of the objects but the rhetorical or argumentative types and relations between objects (e.g. "hypothesis", "conclusion"). The system is aware of the developed argumentation structure and points out missing relations via a support agent. A recent example of a collaborative learning environment based on a domain-specific visual language is the COLER system [5] which supports the co-construction of entity-relationship (ER) models for database modelling.

The CardBoard environment [6] allows for creating "collaborative visual languages" by parameterising a general shared workspace environment. The particular language profile specifies the syntax of the respective language, i.e. the given set of relations, their argument slots, and the basic object types. To add semantics in terms of domain models or knowledge bases, an interface is provided that transfers actions from the visual language environment to the semantic plug-in component [7]. This architecture allows for flexibly defining semantically enriched tools, such as e.g. a co-operative editor and simulator for Petri Nets.

Our current work on the Cool Modes (*CO*llaborative *O*pen *L*earning and *MODE*lling *S*ystem) environment draws on the CardBoard experience, yet with an improved underlying communication mechanism (Java MatchMaker TNG) and the new orientation to provide multiple "language palettes" to choose from and the possibility of mixing different types of languages or representations, ranging form free-hand drawings over concept maps to semantically defined modelling languages (Petri Nets, System Dynamics), in one workspace.

In our vision of future applications (and already starting in our own practice), we see these multi-functional and multi-representational tools as digital, active extensions of chalkboard and paper & pencil as demonstrated in the NIMIS project [8]. The tools should ideally be used in networked ubiquitous and potentially mobile computing environments to support modelling, interactive presentation and group discussion in a variety of educational scenarios, including traditional lectures (presentation) as well as tutorials and collaborative work in small groups.

2   Cool Modes – An Extensible Platform

Cool Modes is a collaborative tool framework designed to support discussions and co-operative modelling processes in various domains. Like in some other environments [4,9], this is achieved through a shared workspace environment with synchronised visual representations. These representations together with their underlying semantics can be defined externally which offers the option to develop domain-dependent "plug-in" visual languages and interpretation patterns, encapsulated in so-called "palettes". The languages can differ considerably with respect to the underlying formal semantics (e.g. System dynamics simulation vs. handwriting annotation) but yet be mixed and used synchronously in the framework which from our point of view is a suitable approach for supporting open modelling tasks with potentially unknown means.

With the aim of having an extensible and useful platform suitable for the integrated use in multiple domain contexts, Cool Modes offers some generic representation elements and co-operation support. These are shortly described in 2.1, the extensibility of the system ("How can my favourite elements be integrated?") is shown in 2.2. and 2.3. These descriptions are mainly to outline the principles of realising semantically enriched extensions (e.g. simulations) in the framework, concrete examples are given in chapter 3.

2.1 Generic System Functions

Cool Modes allows the use of multiple workspaces represented in different windows which can be arranged freely. Each workspace consists of a number of transparent layers which can contain "solid" objects like e.g. handwriting strokes, images and other media types. Four predefined layers with different functionality exist by default - one for a background image, one for hand-written annotations and two for other objects - more can be dynamically added.

While the workspaces contain the results of the user's work and interaction with the system or other users, the elements for this interaction are available in "palettes". These can be dynamically added and removed and are the basic means of extending the system (cf. 2.2 and 2.3). Yet, some standard palettes useful for any domain are predefined: Cool Modes offers a "handwriting" palette allowing the user to directly annotate anything within a workspace. The second more general palette consists of different patterns for discussion support like "question" or "comment". The elements of this palette are designed to support the users in discussing their current work and structuring their argumentation.

As mentioned, the co-operation support integrated in Cool Modes basically relies on the provision of synchronously shareable representations. Technically, this is realised using the MatchMaker server [10,11] offering a replicated architecture, partial synchronisation features and dynamic synchronisation. According to the system structure with its workspaces and layers, the synchronisation of objects is flexibly possible, e.g. in the following different ways:

- By workspace, allowing the users to co-operate by the means of completely synchronised workspaces (and having private ones additionally).

- By layer, providing e.g. the option to have private hand-written annotations on synchronised workspaces as shown in figure 1.

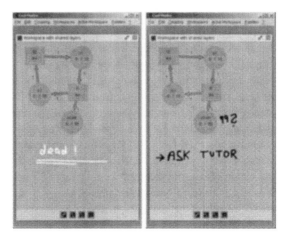

Fig. 1. Layer-wise synchronisation

- By Element. In this "low" level of synchronisation, the synchronised objects "to be discussed co-operatively" can be explicitly defined; any other objects will be private. It is imaginable to set up e.g. a modelling scenario in which only the model elements are shared, but the rest of the user's workspace content (like annotations, images, supporting notes and experimental results) is kept private.

MatchMaker supports this partial synchronisation by providing synchronisation trees. These trees normally reflect the structure of the coupled application, in the case of Cool Modes the subdivision workspace-layer-element. Applications can join different nodes in the tree and thus only receive and deliver synchronisation events concerning the selected shared parts of the representation.

2.2 Definition of Domain-Dependent Elements

The structures in Cool Modes containing the domain dependent semantics and thus offering the possibility for simulations, modelling and, more generally, integrating (potentially arbitrary) algorithms, are called reference frames. As outlined in [12] in more detail, these reference frames serve as structures which
- list the representation elements together with their semantic relations
- Cool Modes refers to in order to interpret the constructed results of user's work
- describe visual interfaces allowing the user to make use of the elements

The most important elements described in these reference frames are the visual elements it offers to the user, together with their semantics and, potentially, functions. The single available elements are called "nodes" and "edges", their relations are described in the reference frame itself whose visual interface is a "palette".

Palettes

A palette provides access to the reference frame for the users. Using the menu bar, it can at runtime be added and removed; the synchronous use of multiple palettes is possible. The two basic functions of palettes are:

- The provision of the nodes and edges defined in the reference frame. Nodes in a palette can be dragged into workspaces and connected via the edges
- The option of receiving and reacting to "global" events generated by the work-spaces, nodes or edges (cf. 2.3).

Nodes

A node is a standard Java object extending a predefined class `AbstractNode`. It is structurally divided in three parts:

- The node itself acting as controller, pointing to its reference frame and capable of receiving, sending and processing events - in both senses of "standard" Java events and internal, more semantically enriched, events within the Cool Modes system or even the reference frame (cf. 2.3).
- The node model, with information according to the definition in the reference frame. Due to the fact that the model is used by MatchMaker for coupling, it must implement `java.io.Serializable`.
- The view. Principally, any `javax.swing.JComponent` can be used as a view, yet Cool Modes offers some patterns like arbitrary-shaped views with auto-resizing text input fields.

Edges

Edges serve as connections between the nodes in the constructed graph structures and, similar to the nodes, consist of model, view and controller. Additionally, it is possible to define rule sets describing allowed and forbidden connections.

2.3   Interpretation of Domain-Dependent Semantics

While the principal way of *defining* custom semantically enriched components has been described in the previous chapter, the following part tries to give a rough idea about the general possibilities of *interpreting* the semantic relations within Cool Modes. Basically, the approach relies on four foundations:

1. The reference frame defines the semantic relations (expressed in data model types and associated algorithms) and is responsible for the objects of one domain "un-derstanding" each other.
2. General events generated through user actions contain node and edge model as parameter. These encapsulate the current state of the object, in terms of the asso-ciated domain.
3. There are "local" and "global" events and, accordingly, the option of having local and global listeners.
4. Specific, additional events can be freely defined in the reference frame.

Global Events and Control

A global event is fired upon a change in a workspace. Typically, the palettes and therefore, indirectly, the reference frames, listen and react to it:

```
void nodeAdded(NodeEvent e);
void nodeRemoved(NodeEvent e);
void nodeMoved(NodeEvent e);
void edgeAdded(EdgeEvent e);
void edgeRemoved(EdgeEvent e);
void edgeMoved(EdgeEvent e);
```

As the listening component has access to the workspace, it can check the workspace content upon reception of an event and can this way, e.g., check the following aspects:

Element presence / absence

As shown in chapter 3.2, the pure information about which nodes or edges are currently in a workspace might already be of interest. This type of "lightweight" model-checking is useful for some modelling tasks with a more or less predefined solution: the system can keep track if the required elements have already been added by the users and, if desired, give hints.

Spatial relations in the workspace

Making use of one more piece of available information allows the system to react upon the absolute or relative positioning of the nodes and edges in the workspace. An example for this is shown in chapter 3.2, where only the correct relative arrangement of four required images fulfils a task completely.

Abstract graph structure

In addition to the above point related to the visual positioning of workspace content, it is also possible to run arbitrary graph algorithms. This allows, e.g., connectivity checks in a Petri Net model or automatic testing of the correlation between topics of a discussion.

Node and Edge models

While the three ways of reaction to events listed above have been rather independent of a concrete domain, it is also possible for the global listener to interpret or change the semantics embedded in the node and edge models. An application for this is the global simulation of models through the use of control elements contained in the palette as shown in the System Dynamics example (chapter 3.1), although the "trigger" for this simulation is in this case not the change of the workspace content but a specific user action (pressing the "step"-button). Potentially, any domain-dependent algorithm that requires the whole graph structure as input, can be realised this way.

Local Events and Control

In addition to the global control and checking options and events pointed out above, some local events are available. Any node can be a listener for these and thus be kept up-to-date about changes within its direct neighbourhood in the graph. The events cover information about which other nodes have been attached by what type of edge, which nodes have been disconnected from the listener node and about model changes in the neighbour nodes and edges. Two typical applications that make use of these events are *local graph algorithms and model changes* (like e.g. the change of the activation status of transitions in a Petri net simulation whenever the model of a place or an edge has changed, or, more generally, searching or distance calculations in the graph) as well as the provision of *context-based feedback*. Even in an open task with no strict rules defined, it is possible to check the modified local structure against a known "ideal" solution or heuristic rule set and give hints.

3   Examples

3.1   System Dynamics: The DynaBoard

In this example we will show the basic functions of the „DynaBoard", one of the reference frames included in Cool Modes at the moment. The creation of the DynaBoard has been part of a master thesis [13] and provides basic support for modelling and

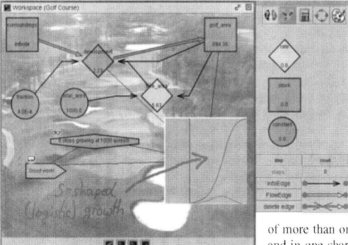

simulating System Dynamics models [3]. Figure 2 shows a group of learners trying to solve a problem about the growth of a golf course area with limited resources. Besides being an example for the use of more than one palette at a time and in one shared workspace, this figure shows the basic elements of the DynaBoard palette. You can see a stock (the „golf_area"), a

Fig. 2. Cool Modes: System Dynamics modelling

rate („development") and a constant („fraction"). By using different types of edges, you can distinguish between the flow of information (thin, black, cracked arrows) and the actual flow of values (thick, grey, straight arrows). The right part of figure 4 shows the user interface of the DynaBoard palette with buttons to control the simulation of the model.

3.2 Jewish Ceremonies

During an interdisciplinary project, students at the University of Duisburg developed the "Jewish Ceremonies" frame within Cool Modes. It addresses students at the age of 11-16 and, thought as addition to the curriculum of religious instruction, it gives the opportunity to test and to intensify knowledge about Jewish life and ceremonies. This task is inherently open like most things currently being supported by Cool Modes. Yet, there are some defined instructions and tasks together with their solution implicitly defined in the corresponding reference frame.

Available Palettes: "Ceremonial Objects" and "Hebrew"
The "Hebrew" palette can be used to write Hebrew words (from right to left) in special nodes. Consequently, the palette (see figure 3) contains this node and the available letters. Writing is done by clicking the buttons. To practise already known words and their pro-nunciation, the program gives feedback by presenting a loudspeaker icon if the word exists (in a local database) and is written correctly. Clicking the loudspeaker icon starts the matching sound file. Writing in this framework includes functions such as deleting a letter, inserting spacebars, changing letters automatically to "sofits" (if they appear at the end of a word) or the decision whether the text box shall be active and thus editable or not.

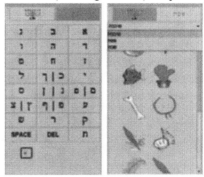

Fig. 3. "Jewish Ceremonies" palettes

The selection of one of the Jewish (religious) ceremonies takes place on top of the "Ceremonial Objects" palette (see figure 3) and returns a specific assortment of items on the palette. The names of the ceremonies are written in Hebrew. This palette shows pictures of items belonging to jewish rites, with Hebrew tool-tips. Not all of the items of one category are in correct context with the celebration. The user has to choose the right ones and to arrange them.

As usual in Cool Modes, these two palettes can be combined, showing the arranged items of both palettes at the same time in a workspace. An easy possible assignment could be to show an item and to ask the user to write its name.

Usage Scenario and Result Checking
Several assignment scenarios exist for the "Ceremonial Objects" palette. One assign-ment is to build a lulaw, a bunch of branches for the celebration of Sukkot. Four

branches of plants must be arranged correctly in a workspace to fulfil the task. As soon as the four items are in one workspace, a message box opens to report that they are complete and now have to be arranged (see figure 4). When the lulaw is built correctly, another message box comments that the task was completed successfully. Technically, this check is done using the events described in chapter 2.3. The listener here just has a list which contains the models of all needed items and compares it to all currently present items in the workspace. If this comparison succeeds, the internal

Fig. 4. Model-checking – constructing a lulaw

state "correct items" is entered and presented to the user via a message. If the internal state is already "correct items" and an item is moved, the second checking routine tests if the relative positions of the items are correct and, if so, delivers the final output that the task is fully completed.

4 Outlook

We see the Cool Modes environment with its example applications as a first step towards providing collaborative mind tools in a variety of realistic educational and training settings. The flexible coupling model provided by MatchMaker allows for flexibly supporting different co-operation modes with limited time and partial synchronisation. Ongoing work is focused on the following extensions:

- a standardised parameterisable protocolling mechanisms to support "undo" and several replay options on a general level, as well as the provision of action transcripts for analysis and reflection
- the development of "lightweight Cool Modes clients" to be used as mobile interactive frontends on wireless PDAs or tablets
- the enhancement of the included XML support towards using XML not only for data storage but also for synchronisation, e.g. by providing a SOAP interface.

References

1. Jonassen, D. H., Tessmer, M. & Hannum, W. H. (1999). Task Analysis Methods for Instructional Design. New York: Erlbaum.

2. Joolingen, W. R., van (2000). Designing for Collaborative Learning. In Gauthier, G., Frasson, C. & VanLehn, K. (Eds.): Intelligent Tutoring Systems (Proceedings of ITS 2000, Montreal, Canada, June 2000) (pp. 202-211). Berlin: Springer.
3. Forrester, J. W. (1968). Principles of Systems. Waltham, MA: Pegasus Communications.
4. Suthers, D. D., Weiner, A., Connelly, J., & Paolucci, M. (1995). Belevedere: Engaging students in critical discussion of science and public policy issues. In Proceedings of the World Conference on Artificial Intelligence in Education. Washington, DC: American Association for the Advancement of Computation in Education.
5. Constantino-González, M. & Suthers, D. D. (2000). A Coached Collaborative Learning Environment for Entity-Realationship Modeling. In G. Gauthier, C. Frasson & K. VanLehn (Eds.), Intelligent Tutoring Systems, 5th International Conference, Montréal, Canada. Berlin: Springer.
6. Hoppe, H.U., Gassner, K., Mühlenbrock, M. & Tewissen, F. (2000). Distributed visual language environments for cooperation and learning - applications and intelligent support. Group Decision and Negotiation (Kluwer), vol. 9, 205-220.
7. Mühlenbrock, M., Tewissen F. & Hoppe H. U. (1997). A Framework System for Intelligent Support in Open Distributed Learning Environments. In B. du Boulay & R. Mizoguchi (Eds.), Artificial Intelligence in Education: Knowledge and media in learning systems, Proceedings of the 8th International Conference on Artificial Intelligence in Education, AIED-97. Amsterdam: IOS Press.
8. Tewissen, F., Lingnau, A., H. Hoppe, H.U. (2000). "Today's Talking Typewriter" - Supporting early literacy in a classroom environment. In Gauthier, G.; Frasson, C.; VanLehn, K. (Eds.): Intelligent Tutoring Systems (Proceedings of ITS 2000, Montreal, Canada, June 2000) (pp. 252-261). Berlin: Springer.
9. Wang, W., Haake, J. & Rubart, J. (2001). The Cooperative Hypermedia Approach to Collaborative Engineering an Operation of Virtual Enterprises. . In Proceedings of CRIWG 2001 (Seventh International Workshop on Groupware, Darmstadt, Oktober 2001) (pp. 58-67). Los Alamitos: IEEE Press.
10. Tewissen, F., Baloian, N., Hoppe, H.U. & Reimberg, E. (2000). "MatchMaker" – Synchronising objects in replicated software architectures. In Proceedings of CRIWG 2000 (Sixth International Workshop on Groupware, Madeira, P, Oktober 2000) (pp. 60-67). Los Alamitos: IEEE Press.
11. Jansen, M., Pinkwart, N. & Tewissen, F. (2001). MatchMaker - Flexible Synchronisation von Java-Anwendungen. In R. Klinkenberg, S. Rüping, A. Fick, N. Henze, C. Herzog, R. Molitor & O. Schröder (eds.) LLWA 01 - Tagungsband der GI-Workshopwoche "Lernen-Lehren-Wissen-Adaptivität". Forschungsbericht 763, Oktober 2001. Universität Dortmund, Germany
12. Pinkwart, N., Hoppe, H.U., Gaßner, K. (2001). Integration of domain-specific elements into visual language based collaborative environments. In Proceedings of CRIWG 2001 (Seventh International Workshop on Groupware, Darmstadt, Oktober 2001) (pp. 142-47). Los Alamitos: IEEE Press.
13. Bollen, L. (2001). Integration einer visuellen Modellierungsprache in eine kooperative Diskussionsumgebung für den naturwissenschaftlichen Unterricht. Unpublished Master Thesis, University of Duisburg, Institute for Computer Science and Interactive Systems.

Social Network Analysis Used for Modelling Collaboration in Distance Learning Groups

Christophe Reffay and Thierry Chanier

Laboratoire d'Informatique de l'université de Franche-Comté
16 route de Gray, 25030 Besançon cedex, France
{Christophe.Reffay, Thierry.Chanier}@univ-fcomte.fr

Abstract. We describe a situation of distance learning based on collaborative production occurring within groups over a significant time span. For such a situation, we suggest giving priority to monitoring and not to guiding systems. We also argue that we need models which are easily computable in order to deal with the heterogeneous and the large scale amount of data related to interactions, i.e. models relying on theoretical assumptions which characterise the structures of groups and of interactions. Social Network Analysis is a good candidate we applied to our experiment in order to compute communication graphs and cohesion factors in groups. This application represents an essential part of a system which would enable tutors to detect a problem or a slowdown of group interaction.

1 Introduction

In computer science, as soon as several prototypes belonging to a sub-domain have been developed, we often try to establish a categorization among them, categorization often based on system functionalities. We then feel more secure, after having reduced the size of open-ended problems, introduced some ways of comparison and judgment among systems, and even indicated a direction for future research. This is what happened in CSCL –Computer Supported Collaborative Learning– with the often referred to Jerman & Al's paper [8], entitled "From mirroring to guiding: a review of the state of the art technology for supporting collaborative learning". Its authors classify CSCL environments according to their type of intervention defining three main categories: Mirroring Systems that reflect actions; Monitoring Systems that monitor the state of interaction; Guiding Systems that offer advice.

But this simplified presentation of CSCL work conceals several levels of problems which may be important issues in ITS. Among them: the nature and size of the data from which systems can make computations; the variety of learning situations; the relationship between tools/systems, models and theoretical perspectives.

Let us look at the data perspective first. At one end, Mirroring Systems seem to be reduced to basic computations of raw data –one if an email message has been sent, zero otherwise and, from there on, computation of the number of sent messages–, and, at the opposite end, Guiding Systems process various sorts of highly structured data. Experience from research in AI or from Student Modelling shows that, if we aim at developing systems that can make decisions and give advice to a learner on a specific

S.A. Cerri, G. Gouardères, and F. Paraguaçu (Eds.): ITS 2002, LNCS 2363, pp. 31–40, 2002.

learning task, it needs to heavily rely on domain-knowledge and on detailed task-descriptions. But domain-dependent approaches can hardly provide generic solutions. Systems developed to support collaboration during the learning process need to rely on the basic data, which often are textual data, coming from communication tools. CSCL literature presents interesting Monitoring Systems built on textual data, partially structured with a subpart made of sentence openers. Free input linguistic data are even accepted when the system includes NLP treatments. But what happens if the system has to deal with thousands of emails and conferences messages, thousands of speech-turns in synchronous dialogs –see, for example, the Simuligne figures? Then we are faced with a size and scale problem. In this case, it is worth reconsidering basic data: knowing whether one has opened/read a message –and not only whether a message has been sent– is a piece of information from which interesting inferences can be made, as we will see. Moreover, gathering and structuring communication data in large-scale environments is not straightforward.

The question of scale leads us to the second level of the problem, i.e. the non distinction often made among the variety of learning situations. As Fjuk & Al. [5] says:

"the problem area within most CSCL research in general, and in distributed collaborative learning in particular, is that their ecological validity could be considered low, since most studies are experiments or small-scale field trials. [Some] studies [...] are limited to experimental settings, or field trials where the time span of the learning activities is of short duration. [...]"

Besides time span, another characteristic of learning situations in CSCL is whether learning happens, on the one hand, in face-to-face or a mixture of face-to-face and distance situations or, on the other hand, in real distance learning situations. Confusing both and asserting that learning and teaching issues are the same is hardly convincing. Of course, we are not claiming that small-scale collaborative experiments, involving learners who have part of their syllabus in face-to-face courses are of no interest. We simply claim that the aim of supporting collaboration and interactions in real distance learning environments raises specific research priorities [7]. For example, because the role of the human tutor is critical in distance learning and her/his workload is more important than in face-to-face situations, it is worth having Distance Learning Management Systems –DLMS– that can automatically compute and show the structure of learning groups, as well as their cohesion and send warnings before the situation becomes irreversible.

Mentioning collaboration in distance learning groups brings us to the third concealed level of problems: the relationship between tools/systems, models and theoretical perspectives. Someone looking from outside how we, computer-scientists, sometimes deal with issues in CSCL may be surprised. On the one hand, from time to time, we may pretend developing generic tools unrelated to any theoretical concerns, and on the other hand, desperate for semantics, we may quote a citation of Vytgostky, coming from the thirties, as if it could exactly fit into our current concern! Even if the latter sentence is a caricature –for the sake of understanding–, it helps us introduce the fact that there can be a middle way. When involved in the improvement of existing DLMSs we are faced with new issues where interactions are not restricted to learner-system nor learner-learner pairs interactions but should be considered at a group level. There already exists models in sociology that see interaction at a structural level – "interactionisme structurel" in French or "Social Network Analysis" –SNA– in English. These models are computable and lead to tools which may be reused in our field. If we do think these tools are useful for the improvement of DLMSs –as Nurmela & Al [10] and Wortham [14] did when implementing specific SNA tools– we should also take into account the corresponding models and theoretical assumptions. Consequently, at a research level, it is worth considering spending time developing Monitoring Systems strongly linked to theoretical assumptions, before attempting to build Guiding Systems without knowing what exactly is at stake.

In the first section of this paper, we will give an overview of the Simuligne experiment. The learning situation will then be fixed and from there, the kind of DLMS we are concerned with. The second part will introduce the SNA approach and relate it to CSCL concerns. Researchers in SNA always had problems when collecting data. Within our electronic environments, data are accessible, provided that we decide which one to consider as relevant. This issue will be discussed in the third section. The following section will show how SNA-based-graphs algorithms can be applied to build our first learning group structures and measures of interactions on a subset of data collected in the Simuligne experiment.

2   The Simuligne Experimentation

Special thanks to which supports the ICOGAD project.

Simuligne was born in a trans-disciplinary research project named ICOGAD (Great-Britain), the Computer Science Laboratory of the Université de Franche-Comté (Besançon, France) and the Psychology Laboratory, Université de Nancy2. ICOGAD, sponsored by the French Minister of Research (MRT) and its cognitive science programme (Programme Cognitique 2000) whose partners are the Department of Language Learning at Open University, is the whole research project. It includes the conception, production and delivery of the online learning stage named Simuligne.

In Simuligne, we had 40 learners – English adults in professional training, registered at the Open University –, 10 natives – French teacher trainees from Université de Franche-Comté –, 4 tutors –teachers of French from the Open University– and one pedagogical coordinator. They can all be classified in one of the three classes of actors of this distance learning experiment: learners, experts –natives– and teachers –tutors and the coordinator. All actors were dispatched into four learning groups, namely Aquitania, Lugdunensis, Narbonensis and Gallia. In another group, the trainers' group, the coordinator, tutors and natives could share questions and answers while the simulation went on. French as a foreign language was the learning subject. Looking for a collaborative production-oriented project, we decided to adapt the method called "Simulation globale" for the first time to a distance situation. The global simulation method is based on role playing and is often used in intensive face-to-face language learning. Distance was the rule: everybody worked at a distance; no one had ever met before Simuligne, except the natives from Besançon. The only people working face-to-face were the technical team, some of the designers and the pedagogical coordinator in Besançon, where the DLMS server stands. Learners and tutors did not know the technical features of the DLMS beforehand. Consequently we had to train all the tutors, at a distance, before Simuligne really started. They were trained on the technical aspects of the platform as well as on the global simulation, a pedagogical method that most of them had never practised.

Other important factors of that experiment are sequence and duration. Simuligne spanned over 10 weeks, broken down into 4 parts:
- Stage 0: 2 weeks: self-introduction to the group and acquisition of technical skills,
- Stage 1: 3 weeks: designing the place of the simulation, –city, campus map, …
- Stage 2: 3 weeks: defining the various characters and putting them in various situations to solve some problems –explosion on campus, buses on strike...
- Stage 3: 2 weeks: discussing and voting for the favoured project.

Three groups out of four achieved the simulation, which is a high ratio in distance learning. When the Lugdunensis group broke up, its most active learners were transferred to another group. Posters produced by the three remaining groups presented rich and high quality language productions [3]. But what can be assessed afterwards by teachers on interaction and collaboration in the group need to be more carefully understood if we want to improve learning environments. The following section gives some representation of communications from which it is possible to have an overview of the interactions happening inside a distance learning group. These are the first steps if we want a system to be helpful to evaluate interaction.

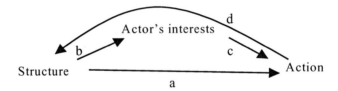

Fig. 1. Basic assumptions in structural theory.

3   Introduction to Structural Interactionism

Social Network Analysis [4,12] is a large research field in sociology and ethnology. Its major objective is to characterise the group's structure and, in particular, the influence of each of the members on that group, reasoning on the relationships that can be observed in that group. SNA has developed a theoretical approach thoroughly different from the traditional social analysis. In a traditional social quantitative analysis, the population is chosen for its variety, representative ness and is classified according to its individual characteristics such as age, sex, social class. Then, the study compares some extra attributes and uses statistic tools to give laws of dependency between some of these attributes. The main problem with this approach is that categories are defined before the analysis by describing the various attributes of individuals. On the contrary, SNA focuses on the relationships between individuals instead of the individuals themselves. In other words, in SNA, the basic item is the group where, as Block [2] says in holism theory: "*an individual acts according to the group he belongs to*".

In distance learning based on collaborative production, we start with individuals that have to socialise in order to form a group which shares goals and values. The existence of this group is a key issue if we want the group to produce collaboratively. Once this group exists, each visible action of each individual will alter the structure of the group. What holism says in the Structural Theory (Burt 1982 in [4]) – see figure 1 – is: the weight of this structure will influence a) the actions of the members and b) the members' interests so that if the member is a rational person, c) he will act according to his interests. The resulting new action will again d) modify the group's structure. The evolution of the structure, always modified by actions is well illustrated by Leydesdorff 1991 [4,p.15] who introduces time.

The structure of Burt (in figure 1) represents a basic collaborative learning group also called community. Woodruff [13] explains how cohesion is the key issue for collaborative learning and defines four cohesive factors he called "glue factors":

"1) function, 2) identity, 3) discursive participation, and 4) shared values. Briefly, function is the goal or purpose of the community; identity is the validation of 'self' through membership; discursive participation is the means by which the members' discourse helps to advance the function or goal of the community; and, shared values are the global beliefs held by members which unite them and help to promote an emerging discourse."

The third glue factor namely "discursive participation" is what we call interactions and is the most visible to the members, in so far as it gives a measure of group activity. For the researcher, this cohesive factor may be quantitatively valuable. More likely in a classical context, Homans in [4, p.95] pointed out the cohesion concept related to appreciation and interaction. He says that the cohesion of a given group enhances the appreciation of each of its members. The more people appreciate each other, the more they will interact. Interaction being a glue factor, it will reinforce cohesion. "Appreciation", in Homan's model, is probably very close to Woodruff's fourth cohesive factor, named "shared values". In fact, Woodruff says that the glue factors he identified are closely linked to one another: changes in one factor will inevitably have an effect on all the others.

These characterisations can be automatically computed by using matricial tools of the graph theory [1]. The difficulty in SNA in general, is to collect the large amount of data which define the relationships between individuals: collecting data is often a hand-made process. In our distance learning context, these data are stored in the DLMS. We have access to a large amount of data where it is sometimes very hard to find relevant information, as we will see in the next section.

4   Data for Communications and Interactions

The basic tools for communication in DLMS are e-mail, discussion forum –also named "conferencing system"– and chat. Communication is based on textual data and happens either asynchronously with the first two tools or synchronously for the latter one. Here are the figures coming from the Simuligne experiment:

- Discussion forum: 879 015 characters in 2686 messages, which represent: 45.11% of the communication flow measured in number of characters;
- E-mail: 834 753 characters in 4062 messages: 42.84%;
- Synchronous chat: 234 694 characters in 5680 speech turns: 12%.

Synchronous communications represent 12% of the whole set of data. Activities based on chat are interesting in language learning: it increases motivation, it develops abilities in conversations on the fly, provided that there is a limited number of participants who know which role to play and who have prepared it in advance. But activities using chat are difficult to integrate in the agenda and impedes the flexibility that characterises and make success of Distance Learning context.

Moreover e-mail and e-conference are generally considered as the core tools in distance learning, because they –not only– convey communications around the knowledge domain but also about the whole learning process [7,11].

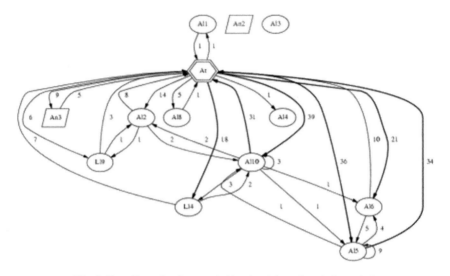

Fig. 2. E-mail graph of group A (Aquitania) on the whole period

Consequently, looking for structures that could automatically be built in order to reflect communications inside groups, we decided to apply SNA models to these asynchronous data, starting with e-mail. This supposes to retrieve detailed information on each of the messages. This information varies from one tool to another and is not straightforwardly accessible. Technically, the problem is to get the precise information among a very large and amount of basic data.

5   Building Graphs to Reflect Group Communications

In our model, we will try to ignore/mask all the messages that have not been opened by their recipient. Because such messages have been sent, we agree they have some influence on a *participation* index, but they may be ignored when dealing with an *interaction* index.

Using the resulting database, it becomes possible to compute, for each group, a graph of communications where we only select *messages that have been opened*.

From there, we can define a graph of group communications:

Let Go = (U, I) an oriented and valuated graph of order n where:

❑   U is the set of n vertices: the n group users: $X_1, X_2, ..., X_n$;

❑   I is a family of oriented and valuated relations representing interactions between the users of U. Each edge belongs to UxUxR represented by $(U_i, U_j,$

v) where source user U_i and destination user U_j are users of the set U and v defines the volume –number of messages– emitted by U_i and opened by U_j.

Having selected and restructured the kinds of data we need and defined our graph we are now able to design various representations.

The first step is to represent the volume and destination of all the communications sent by each user or the volume and source of all the communications received and opened by each user. Let us now illustrate this with e-mail messages.

The following example focuses on one of the four learning groups (Aquitania=A) during the whole period of the Simuligne experimentation (10 weeks). The communications represented are restricted to e-mail messages received and opened by their addressee(s). Extracting data from the databases mentioned previously, an e-mail matrix is built. Then, using the open source GraphViz package [6], we can automatically generate the visual representation of the e-mail graph (figure 2).

The edges of the graph are valued by the number of messages sent –by the user at the origin of the directed edge– and consulted –by the user at the end of the same edge. This picture immediately gives an idea of the central role of the Tutor –At– from/to whom the majority of the messages, sent and consulted, converge.

Let us now see what happens when we remove the tutor –At– and all the messages he is concerned with (see figure 3, top left corner for Aquitania). The notion of cohesive subgroup begins to be clear on that graph. It is not only the list of users interrelated by e-mail, but also who is in relation with the maximum number of other people and who is absolutely not connected –by e-mail– with others. In particular, we can see in this group that there is no e-mail communication with An2 and An3: the two natives of the group who where supposed to bring support as language experts if needed. Al2, Al5, Ll4, Ll9, Al6 and Al10 are the learners who successfully finished the Simuligne training by an actual production in the final group project result. Note that Ll4 and Ll9 are transferred students from the "dead" group Lugdunensis (L) to Aquitania (A).

The comparison given in figure 3 of the four groups on their consulted e-mail graph without tutor seems to be relevant for the way a group collaborated and produced.

Firstly, the data exposed in figure 3 are part of those needed by the global coordinator in charge of the inter-group regulation and of the tutor support. But these data are only partial data even for the communication part of the training.

Secondly, the main fact we are interested in, is to get a real value of a cohesion index for each group at each instant in order to give a comparative representation of the cohesion evolution of the four basic groups for each stage.

6   Cohesion in Communications

Starting from the list of all forum messages and for each of them, the list of the users who read it, let us describe the computing process of the cohesion index of the group for a given period –adapted from [4, p. 100].

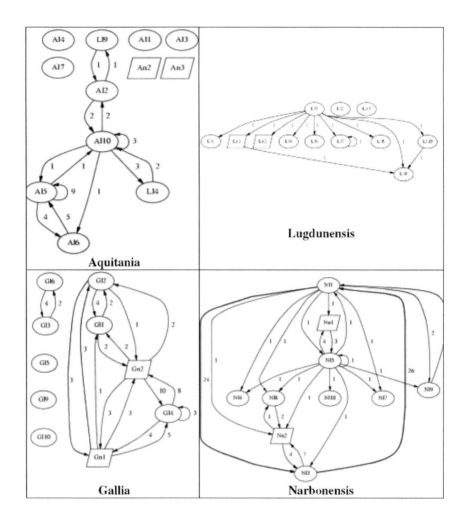

Fig. 3. Comparison of the consulted e-mail graph (without tutor's messages) of the four basic groups during the whole period of the Simuligne Experimentation.

Firstly, for each couple (L_i, L_j) of learners, we compute the number x_{ij} of forum messages posted by Li in the target period and read by L_j. We build the matrix A where $a_{ij}=1$ if $x_{ij}>0$. Then, the symmetric matrix S is given by $s_{ij}=\max(a_{ij}, a_{ji})$ for weak cohesion –a strong cohesion factor would be obtained replacing *max* by *min* function. S is the adjacency matrix representing the relations existing in the group. s_{ij} is 1 if L_i or L_j read at least one message posted by the other in the given period. Let n_i be the number of relations of L_i including himself. We have $n_i = \sum_k s_{ik}$, and if n_{ij} counts the relations shared by L_i and L_j, $n_{ij} = \sum_k \min(s_{ik}, s_{jk})$. It is then possible to compute d_{ij}:

the recovering degree of relations circles of L_i and L_j given by: $d_{ij} = \dfrac{n_{ij}}{n_i + n_j - n_{ij}}$. If

dij=1, it means that Li and Lj share all their relations and if dij=0, they don't have any common relation. The cohesion index of the group is then given by the means of dij values for all possible pairs Li and Lj of learners in the considered group for the target period.

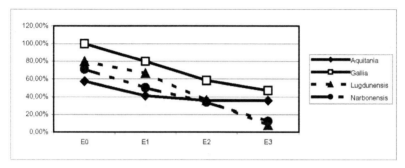

Fig. 4. Evolution of the cohesion factor in the four basic groups

By separating Simuligne in its four stages E0, E1, E2 and E3, we computed this cohesion factor for each group and for each stage. The resulted graph is shown in figure 4 where erosion – due to the abandon of some learners in normal proportion for distance learning – forces the evolution of the cohesion factor for each group to decrease. We can also notice that, during E0, the Gallia group obtained a maximum score for cohesion revealing that each member of Gallia had at least one interaction with all the others in the group.

It is also perceptible that in moving two active members from Lugdunensis to Aquitania, the Lugdunensis's cohesion factor fell while Aquitania's one remained the same during E2 and E3. Taking into account only the existence but not the number of interactions, this index much reduces the intensification of interactions between the remaining members of each group. The final means of d_{ij} is heavily thinned down by the entire lines and columns of zeros concerning the abandon, despite the fact that the values concerning the remaining learners are nearly all equal to one. The first method presented here to compute the cohesion index does not illustrate properly the growing cohesion of reduced and more and more active subgroups –empirically identified during the Simuligne experience. To avoid such a problem, we suggest we take into account the number of messages between each couple of members and we limit the computation of the cohesion index to the "interesting" subgroups.

7 Conclusion

We have described a situation of distance and online learning based on collaborative production. For such a complex situation we suggest we give priority to monitoring and not to guiding systems, even if other works in progress in our research group reconsider a whole DLMS as a multi-agent architecture in order to sustain interactions

[9]. We have to understand exactly what happened in the groups during such an experiment. We showed that Social Network Analysis gives an interesting theoretical background to compute various global indices such as communication graphs and the cohesion factor of a group. A complete access to communication data is needed in order to reorganise them in fruitful databases. We have started to show the interest of some sociometric measures using a large volume of data. This work is the first step in developing a software that would enable tutors or pedagogic coordinators to detect a problem or a slowing down of group interactions. In the near future, we need to refine the computation of the cohesion index and assess other SNA indices with respect to our Simuligne experience feedback.

References

1. Berge, C.: Graphs and Hypergraphs. Dunod, Paris (1973)
2. Block, N.: "Holism, Mental and Semantic". In The Routledge Encyclopedia of Philosophy (1998), http://www.nyu.edu/gsas/dept/philo/faculty/block/
3. Chanier, T.: Créer des communautés d'apprentissage à distance. Les dossiers de l'Ingénierie Educative, no 36 sur "Les communautés en ligne", CNDP, Montrouge (2001) 56-59, http://lifc.univ-fcomte.fr/RECHERCHE/P7/pub/cndpIE/cndpIE.htm
4. Degenne, A., Forsé, M. : Les réseaux sociaux. Armand Colin, Paris (1994)
5. Fjuk, A., Ludvigsen, S.: The Complexity of Distributed Collaborative Learning: Unit of Analysis. Proceedings of EURO-CSCL'2001 Conference, Maastricht (2001) http://www.mmi.unimaas.nl/euro-cscl/Papers/51.doc
6. GraphViz Home page (2000) http://www.graphviz.org
7. Henri, F., Lundgren-Cayrol, K.: Apprentissage collaboratif à distance. Presses de l'Université du Québec, Québec (2001)
8. Jermann, P., Soller, A., Muehlenbrock, M.: From mirroring to guiding: a review of state of art technology for supporting collaborative learning". Proceedings of EURO-CSCL'2001 Conference, Maastricht (2001) http://www.mmi.unimaas.nl/euro-cscl/Papers/197.pdf
9. Mbala, A., Reffay, C., Chanier, T.: Integration of automatic tools for displaying interaction data in computer environments for distance learning. This issue, Biarritz, France (2002)
10. Nurmela K.A., Lehtinen E., Palonen T.: Evaluating CSCL log files by Social Network Analysis. Proceedings CSCL'1999 Conference, Palo Alto, CA: Stanford University (1999) 434-444. http://kn.cilt.org/cscl99/A54/A54.HTM
11. Salmon, G.: E-moderating: The key to teaching and learning Online. Kogan, London (2000)
12. Scott, J.: Social Network Analysis. A handbook. SAGE Publication, London (1991)
13. Woodruff E.: Concerning the Cohesive Nature of CSCL Communities. Proceedings of CSCL'1999 Conference, Palo Alto, CA: Stanford University (1999) 677-680 http://kn.cilt.org/cscl99/A81/A81.HTM
14. Wortham D.W.: Nodal and matrix analyses of communication patterns in small groups. Proceedings CSCL'1999 Conference, Palo Alto, CA: Stanford University, (1999) 681-686 http://kn.cilt.org/cscl99/A82/A82.HTM

On the Social Rational Mirror: Learning E-commerce in a Web-Served Learning Environment

Germana M. da Nóbrega**, Stefano A. Cerri, and Jean Sallantin

LIRMM - Laboratoire d'Informatique, de Robotique et de Microélectronique de Montpellier.
161, Rue ADA - 34392 Montpellier Cedex 5 - France.
{nobrega,cerri,sallantin}@lirmm.fr

Abstract. Recent work in our teams focused on a methodology, called $Phi - calculus$, the aim of which is to study the process of interaction between a human - or a group - and a machine when the former is interested on using certain capabilities of the latter in order to improve the task of explicitating knowledge in a coherent and unambiguous fashion. Our more recent work consisted on examining how Phi-calculus might be instantiated in the context of Human Education. The result is a Web-served Learning Environment, called $PhiInEd$, to assist both the planning and the execution phases of a course. PhiInEd has been used by a class of D.E.A.[1] on Business Contracts.

1 Introduction

The methodology Phi-calculus [9,11] has appeared as an attempt to abstract a successful approach practiced since 1994 by the lawyers of the Company Fidal-KPMG grouping 1200 lawyers in France. Lawyer's daily activity consists of understanding, proving and comparing contracts. The issue for innovation for them is that laws, norms, and events change continuously, so contracts have to be conceived accordingly. The Company has identified classes of contracts, and for each class has decided to offer lawyers a *Reasoning Framework* (RF). A RF represents the knowledge that enables the artificial agent *fid@ct* to assist the lawyers in their activity. Whenever the Company identifies a class of contracts, it delegates the design of the corresponding RF to a team composed of a senior lawyer and two novice lawyers, who are supposed to interact with each other as well as with the fid@ct agent aiming to achieve a RF.

Fidal's methodology to design a RF may be summarized as follows (Figure 1): after having analysed a number of contracts previously written by experimented lawyers of the Company, the novice lawyers propose a RF, and then experiment

---

** Ph.D. student supported by CAPES, Brasília (Brazil). CAPES/COFECUB 291/99.

[1] *Diplome d'Études Avancés* - Advanced Studies Diplome. In certain countries this grade is acceptable as equivalent to the Master of Sciences.

S.A. Cerri, G. Gouardères, and F. Paraguaçu (Eds.): ITS 2002, LNCS 2363, pp. 41–50, 2002.
© Springer-Verlag Berlin Heidelberg 2002

and revise it under the supervision of the senior lawyer. The cycle is repeated until a RF is judged coherent by the senior. RFs thus constructed are used by fid@ct to assist about 400 lawyers of the Company, and it takes about 30 minutes instead of several hours, for a lawyer to write a contract assisted by the agent. The Company has patented both the methodology and the agent fid@ct.

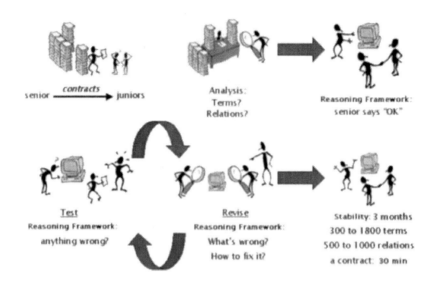

Fig. 1. Scenario of Fidal's methodology.

Recent relevant work on AIED focus on the *process* enabling Human Learning [1]. While a Reasoning Framework itself is the object of main interest for Fidal's lawyers, from the perspective of Human Learning, we are mainly interested in its *process of construction*. The main question we address is: do novice lawyers learn something due to the <u>interaction</u> both with the senior lawyer and the fid@ct agent during the process of construction of a RF? In a previous paper [10], we argue on a characterization of a Learning Environment (LE) [14] for Fidal's methodology. As a starting point, we adopt as a principle the view of Human Learning as a potential, indirect side effect of Dialogues, the agreement resulting from discussions by eminent scholars, as summarized in [7].

A popular property of LEs is that they often embody some "true" knowledge that is supposed to be "acquired" by the learner by interacting with the system. Socratic tutoring methods, on the contrary, attempt to emulate the autonomous discovery process for the causes of inconsistencies by the learner as a consequence of challenging him/her with dialectic arguments. In this direction, "the concept of discovery learning has appeared numerous times throughout history as a part of the educational philosophy of many great philosophers particularly Rousseau, Pestalozzi and Dewey, 'there is an intimate and necessary relation between the process of actual experience and education [12]'. It also enjoys the support of learning theorists/psychologists Piaget, Bruner, and Papert, 'Insofar as possible, a method of instruction should have the objective of leading the child to discover for himself' [6]" [5]. In spite of these pedagogical suggestions, few LEs are founded on these principles. Rather, most LEs developers wish "the truth in a domain" to be acquired by learners exposed to "the truth". In Fidal's methodology, in order to propose a RF, novice lawyers perform abstraction by themselves as they analyse achieved contracts in order to establish what terms should appear in a Reasoning Framework for the corresponding contract class. Also, they infer autonomously logical constraints stressing relations among those terms. Within fid@act, the prominent view that the "true" knowledge should be in the machine is changed, since it is provided only with the capability of handling propositional constraints among terms. Such a capability allows the agent to work like a *mirror*, reflecting thus to the novices inconsistencies in the knowledge that they have externalized during the process.

Discovery learning is also characterized as an iterative approach, in which errors work like a source of revision, as knowledge is supposed to be constructed by trial and error from experience. This issue is also present in the rationale of Fidal's lawyers: inconsistencies detected are exploited aiming to improve a RF. The convergence, often a problem with this kind of approach, is achieved thanks to the fact that knowledge explicitated in RFs reflect the way of thinking and working of a group, and according to the Law to which they are submitted. This meets the constructivist views of learning, from which knowledge and learning are dependent of context, person, and social situation [15].

Recent work [4] privilege methods and tools facilitating the acquisition of meta cognitive skills, the so called soft skills, with respect to domain independent "true" knowledge and skills. We see the development of cognitive skills as a potential consequence of discovery learning activities, since explanation and argumentation capabilities are crucial to perform tasks like build up a hypothesis or interpret experimental results such as needed to revise or confirm hypotheses. At the same time, soft skills are also a requirement whenever the control is transferred to the learner interacting with a system [2]. In Fidal's methodology these two (in principle controversing) perspectives co-exist and are even complementary since individuals are embedded in a *collaborative* environment. The relevance of collaborative learning has a classical consensus in the Educational community [8,13,3]. In addition, recent work on ITS [17] points out how discovery learning and collaborative learning may be put together to design effective learning environments.

The dialectic, autonomous, domain-independent, constructivist, and collaborative aspects of the Fidal's approach suggests us a positive answer to the question we are addressing (do novices lawyers learn anything...?). Expecting to confirm our assumption (that the answer is positive), we have decided to expose real learners to the methodology. In order to support the learner's work, we have implemented a Web-served LE, called *PhiInEd*. From a widespread perspective, the work on PhiInEd can be seen as an attempt to validate the methodology Phi-calculus when this latter meets the cause of Human Learning.

In §2 we briefly introduce the server PhiInEd through the phases of a course it supports. Then, in §3 we report the work carried out by a D.E.A. class supported by PhiInEd. Finally, we close the paper in §4.

2   Two Phases of a Course Supported by PhiInEd

Within the server PhiInEd, two phases of a course are currently taken into account, namely, *Planning* and *Running*, which are briefly introduced below.

2.1   Planning

Planning a course within PhiInEd consists of the elaboration of a *Plan* by the one who administrates the course, to which we will refer as the *Teacher*. A Plan consists of a sequence of *Lessons*, to be studied by the ones who follow the course, to whom we will refer as the *Learners*. The Teacher may provide each Lesson with a number of *Resources* and/or *Exercises*. Both Resources and Exercises are concretely provided within the server through Web pages. Resources may be seen as the course's content, while through Exercises the Teacher asks the Learners to react with respect to Resources. Indeed, we are particularly interested in reactions the memory of which would somehow be available for the Teacher. Such a memory corresponds to what we call a Reasoning Framework in §1.

Altogether - observation of Resources and construction of a Reasoning Framework - are expected to stimulate the development of certain capabilities of the Learner. The enumeration of these capabilities constitutes the list of the *Objectives* of the course. Then, the Lessons established should be those estimated by the Teacher as capable of leading a Learner to reach the Objectives of the course. When elaborating the Plan, one possibility for the Teacher could be to think firstly in terms of Global Objectives, and then decompose it into a list of Local Objectives from which the Lessons of the course would be elaborated.

2.2   Running

Running a course within PhiInEd consists of the execution of the course's Plan, causing the Learners to study its Lessons, guided by the Teacher. On the one hand, individual work is provided by PhiInEd such as to enable the Learners to elaborate a Reasoning Framework as a reaction to Resources observed. On the other hand, communication among participants is provided such as to allow (at least) both the Teacher to propose a Lesson to the Learners, and the Learners to present their RFs to the Teacher and/or to their peers.

The social level. The run of a course is organized as a *Sequence of Dialogues*. *Subjects* of Dialogues correspond to the title of the Lessons from the Plan. For instance, a course which Plan has three Lessons, will be executed within three Dialogues, one for each Lesson. A Dialogue is composed of a sequence of

Messages, and the Subject of a Message is, like for the Dialogue containing it, the title of a Lesson. The Teacher may declare a Lesson as *Studied* by a Learner, when the Dialogue about that Lesson has at least the two following Messages: (*i*) from the Teacher to the Learner, transporting the Lesson to be studied, and (*ii*) from the Learner to the Teacher, transporting the Reasoning Framework of the Learner with respect to the Lesson subject of the Dialogue. Besides these two Messages, additional ones may occur in a Dialogue, for instance, in the case that a Learner asks the Teacher some explanation while studying a Lesson.

3   Learning Business Contracts for E-commerce

A class of twenty-seven students of D.E.A., under the supervision of Prof. Dr. Didier Ferrier, have been using the server during seven sessions of three hours.

The subject of study. The chosen subject of study for the course was the so-called *General Conditions of Sale* (GCS). The definition of GCS requires the understanding of the process of formation of a contract. This latter is established whenever an offer meets an acceptance resulting in an agreement that constrains the behaviour that the two sides intend to adopt with respect to the other. In such a context, the GCS are defined as an offer of contracting addressed by a seller to any buyer interested on acquiring his products. This offer constitutes then the individual norm of the behaviour that the seller intends to impose to his potential buyers. The simple unconditional adhesion of the seller's conditions by a buyer should be enough to form the contract, and the individual norm composed of the seller's conditions becomes then the norm common to the two sides.

The scenario. The Teacher has initially fixed the GCS as the subject of study. A Reasoning Framework (RF) should then be constructed for this contract class. The goal was to obtain a single RF as a result of the work of the whole group. Firstly, students were distributed in seven working groups, each group working around a single machine. Each group should then prepare a RF by analyzing a GCS document from the Web. Secondly, a single RF should be generated as a fusion of RFs from the groups. Finally, this resulting RF should be revised under the supervision of the Teacher, up to be considered by the group as stable. We detail this scenario below through the Planning and then the Running phase.

3.1   Planning

Global Objectives. To be able to elaborate, criticize and improve particular contracts; to be able to apply general contractual techniques to specific contract classes.

The resulting Plan. The course was planned along six Lessons, each of which is introduced hereafter, through its local objectives, Resources/Exercises, and a report on how the students carried it out.

3.2   Running

Lesson 1: An overview of the server. The Local Objective is to apprehend the server through its components, their functionalities and information they handle. By means of an example - a very simplified RF of General Conditions of Buying - all the components are covered for the students to become familiarized with the work needed to construct a Reasoning Framework. A Resource is supplied with an explanative text, which is available in a Web page, while the students explore the server through the RF-example.

Students exhibited curious to discover PhiInEd, and some of them had preferred to work individually, instead of in groups. Also, they found it not evident to apprehend in a first moment "all the concepts" of the server.

Lesson 2: Let's start to work. The Local Objective is to stimulate the capacity of abstraction by analyzing examples. Concretely, to apprehend the notion of a good GCS from GCS documents. No Resource is foreseen for this Lesson. Part of a RF of General Conditions of Sale (GCS) is supplied, as a starting point for the work. Such part consists on a Hierarchy of Terms, voluntarily prepared to be incomplete. As an Exercise, the students are asked firstly to observe the Terms and how they are organized. Then to search on the Web, and then to retrieve, a page containing a GCS. They are instructed to analyze this page, and to improve the Hierarchy accordingly.

Faced with a real case to work out, students found positive the fact of working in small groups, since they could discuss with each other. In some cases, discussions were even too long: 20 minutes before they could agree on adding a single Term! They became more familiarized with the server, and even suggested improvements concerning the edition of the Terms Hierarchy. This necessity was due to the dynamism on updating the initial Terms Hierarchy, in part caused by discussions, in part caused by the progressive analysis of the Web page they have chosen to study.

Lesson 3: Entering a Document, and Constraints. One Local Objective is to be introduced to the activity of exemplification, i.e.: to instantiate a contract in a RF. Another Local Objective is to learn the link between clauses in a GCS, by constraining the use of Terms in clauses, through the identification of logical relations among Terms. The single Exercise asks students to describe the contents of their working GCS document, by using the Terms of their working Hierarchy. The Exercise asks them as well to identify relations among Terms and then to build up the corresponding Constraints. Figure 2 shows some of the Constraints from one group, who worked out a GCS document for spectacle tickets. An example of Constraint is "group fee *excludes* individual fee".

Students exhibited an initial difficulty to build up Constraints, although these were introduced in Lesson 1 through a simplified RF. Such a difficulty was quickly overcame, due both to the practice, and overall, to the understanding that Constraints were nothing but a formal way of stressing relations among Terms representing clauses, something to which they are, as lawyers, actually familiarized.

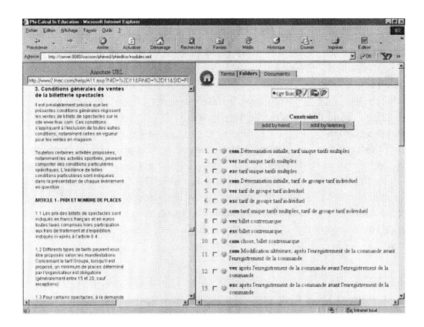

Fig. 2. Web page of GCS and some added Constraints.

Lesson 4: We present our results. A first Local Objective of this Lesson is to stimulate the capacity of comparison between an abstraction and an example. Concretely, since students have built a RF, they are supposed to have in mind the notion of a good GCS (at least their own!), and thus, they should be able to identify in GCS documents both positive and negative points with respect to their RF. Up to this point students work organized in seven groups. In this Lesson they are invited to work as a whole group. The single Exercise asks each group to present their RF to the larger group, to present their analysis about the RF they received, the Terms and Constraints they created, and yet to criticize the GCS they have chosen with respect to their own RF. Another Local Objective is to stimulate the capacity of argumentation and explanation, by means of debate: in case of different viewpoints (between groups) when students compare their RF with other's GCS documents, or even their RFs to each other. Before starting the expositions, the groups exchange their RFs by sending a message to each group.

The results presented were more complementary than conflicting to each other. An interesting case was the one of two groups that had chosen, as a coincidence, the same Web page to work out. They had, as expected, some common results, but also they had perceived different aspects in the document, over which they finally agreed as complementary.

Lesson 5: How about putting altogether? The Local Objective is to reinforce the capabilities stimulated in Lessons 2, 3, and 4: after knowing the others' work, students should formalize what they eventually apprehend from the debate with the larger group. Concretely, they should compose a reduced group responsible for generating a single RF, as a result of merging the RFs from the groups. The single Exercise asks students to consider the RF of their corresponding group, and to create a new RF resulting from all RFs together.

Voluntarily, a member of each group presented himself to compose the reduced group. They have adopted the strategy of performing partial fusions (two by two) due to the amount of information they obtained as a result of a single fusion. Finally, the complementarity observed in the previous session was not so confirmed, since they discussed yet a lot, before arriving to a final result. This lead us to think that even if they do not agree with other's work, students hesitate in criticizing. The fact of working together around a common and concrete objective seems to provide an actual collaborative environment, in such a way to make them naturally criticize without having the feeling of "hurting" their peers.

Lesson 6: Finally, did we work well? The Local Objective is to improve the notion of a good GCS that students have built up to this point. By proposing a number of GCS documents specially chosen to stimulate revision, the Teacher together with a group of several invited lawyers attempt to invalidate the Reasoning Framework representing the agreement among twenty-seven students.

By the time of preparation of this paper, this Lesson is yet to be run. By now, all that we have is the Teacher's certifying that the global objectives initially established were reached. Some specific points have hardly been identified by the invited lawyers in order to provoke the debate foreseen for this last Lesson.

4 Conclusion

In §1, we introduce an iterative and interactive method used by lawyers to explicitate the knowledge that enables an artificial agent to assist the tasks of contract analysis, verification, and construction. We also make the assumption that novice lawyers taking part in the process of knowledge explicitation learn something, thanks to the interaction both with humans and with the artificial agent. Such assumption is firstly supported by the identification of some features previously pointed out by researchers from the Educational Community, as important for learning events to occur in a Learning Environment. The results of the work carried out by real learners are for us an evidence (even if informal) that our initial assumption was right.

At this point, one might yet be attempting to find out where PhInEd's "intelligence" is. Despite of the fact that this is a notion yet waiting for a precise definition when applied to humans, the field of Artificial Intelligence (AI) is characterized by work on a number of sub-fields, e.g., machine learning, as well as work on older disciplines which purposes have been attracted AI researchers, e.g. logical reasoning. Although the agent giving support to the individual work within PhiInEd does have the capability of both learning[2] and performing logical reasoning, we cannot say that the main contribution of this work lies up there, since we have just been using these skills rather than developing. Our main focus is on the exam of how rationality emerges from - and simultaneously drives - the interactions between a human and an artificial agent both embedded in a process supposed to result in considerable intellectual gain for the human side. By replacing the notion of intelligence by that of rationality, we adopt the well-known view of Russell and Norvig of AI as the study and construction of rational agents [16]. By focusing on rationality of the overall system's behaviour instead of that from individual entities, we follow the purposes (even if not the means) of the reactive agents approach.

In cooperation with other researchers, future work include using PhiInEd to support courses in domains like Philosophy, Musical Theory, and Web page Design. Concerning improvement, one possibility is to provide communication as well in the Planning phase, such that a Plan could be the result of a negotiation between the Teacher and a Learner. Another possibility is to account also for the Analysis phase, such that the Teacher could get some assistance while analyzing Learner's works.

Acknowledgments. Part of the work presented was supported by the IST Projects MKBEEM[3] on e-commerce and LARFLAST[4], on e-Learning.

We would like to thank Mr. Daniele Maraschi, and Mr. Patrick Wittman for their attention and important contribution concerning both the design and the implementation of the server PhiInEd.

Our special thanks to Prof. Dr. Didier Ferrier and his D.E.A. class, without whom the experiment reported in the paper could not have been carried out. Also, many thanks to the lawyers Nicolas Eréséo and Christophe Granadas, who have elaborated part of the Resources used in the experiment, as well as the lawyer Cyrille Arlabosse, for his precious simulations always followed by constructive criticisms that allowed us to improve significantly the server.

References

1. F. N. Akhras and J. A. Self. Modelling learning as a process. In *8th World Conference on Artificial Intelligence on Education*, pages 418–425, Kobe, Japan, August, 18-22 1997. IOS Press.
2. V. Aleven and K. R. Koedinger. Limitations of student control: Do students know when they need help? In G. Gauthier, C. Frasson, and K. VanLehn, editors, *Intelligent Tutoring Systems 5th International Conference, ITS 2000 Montréal, Canada, June 2000*, Lecture Notes in Computer Science, pages 292–303. Springer, 2000.

---

[2] not exploited in this work.
[3] Multilingual Knowledge Based European Electronic Market place.
[4] LeARning Foreign LAnguage Scientific Terminology.

3. A. F. Andrade, P. A. Jaques, J. L. Jung, R. Bordini, and R. M. Vicari. A computational model of distance learning based on Vygotsky's social-cultural approach (MABLE-2001). In *10th International Conference on Artificial Intelligence on Education*, San Antonio, Texas, May, 19-23 2001.
4. M. Baker, E. de Vries, K. Lund, and M. Quignard. Interactions épistémiques médiatisées par ordinateur pour l'apprentissage des sciences: bilan de recherches. In C. Desmoulins, M. Grandbastien, and J.-M. Labat, editors, *Environnements Interactifs pour l'Apprentissage avec Ordinateur - EIAO*, La Villette, avril 2001.
5. J. Bartasis and D. Palumbo. Theory and technology: Design consideration for hypermedia/discovery learning environments. available on-line: http://129.7.160.115/INST5931/Discovery_Learning.html, 1995.
6. J. S. Bruner. *On Knowing: Essays for the Left Hand*. Harvard University Press, Cambridge, Mass, 1967.
7. S. A. Cerri. Models and systems for collaborative dialogues in distance learning. In M. F. Verdejo and S. A. Cerri, editors, *Collaborative Dialogue Technologies in Distance Learning*, volume 133 of *ASI Series F: Computers and Systems Sciences*, pages 119–125. Springer-Verlag, Berlin Heidelberg, 1994.
8. F. P. Duarte da Costa. *VYGOTSKY : Un Environnement d'Appentissage Social pour la programmation fondé sur la collaboration entre agents d'aide à la conception par cas*. PhD thesis, Université de Droit, d'Economie et des Sciences d'Aix-Marseille III, 1997.
9. G. M. da Nóbrega, E. Castro, P. Malbos, J. Sallantin, and S. Cerri. A framework for supervized conceptualizing. In V. R. Benjamins, A. Gómez Pérez, N. Guarino, and M. Uschold, editors, *Proceedings of the ECAI-00 Workshop on Applications of Ontologies and Problem-Solving Methods*, Berlin, Germany, 2000.
10. G. M. da Nóbrega, S. A. Cerri, and J. Sallantin. DIAL: serendipitous DIAlectic Learning. In T. Okamoto, R. Hartley, Kinshuk, and J. P. Klus, editors, *IEEE International Conference on Advanced Learning Technologies - ICALT'2001*, pages 109–110, Madison, Wisconsin (USA), August 6-8 2001. IEEE Computer Society.
11. G. M. da Nóbrega, P. Malbos, and J. Sallantin. Modelling through human-computer interactions and mathematical discourse. In L. Magnani and N. J. Nersessian, editors, *Logical and computational aspects of model-based reasoning*, Applied Logic Series. Kluwer Academic Press, Dordrecht, 2002. (forthcoming).
12. J. Dewey. *Experience and Education*. MacMillan, New York, 1938.
13. B. Goodman, A. Soller, F. Linton, and R. Gaimari. Encouraging student reflection and articulation using a learning companion. *International Journal of Artificial Intelligence in Education*, 9:237–255, 1998.
14. J. R. Hartley. Effective pedagogies for managing collaborative learning in on-line learning environments. *Educational Technology & Society*, 2(2):12–19, 1999.
15. D. H. Jonassen. Objectivism versus constructivism: Do we need a new philosophical paradigm? *Educational Technology Research & Development*, 39:5–14, 1991.
16. Stuart Russell and Peter Norvig. *Artificial Intelligence: A Modern Approach*. Pretice Hall Series in Artificial Intelligence. Prentice Hall, 1995.
17. W. R. van Joolingen. Designing for collaborative discovery learning. In G. Gauthier, C. Frasson, and K. VanLehn, editors, *Intelligent Tutoring Systems 5th International Conference, ITS 2000 Montréal, Canada, June 2000*, Lecture Notes in Computer Science, pages 202–211. Springer, 2000.

Including Malicious Agents into a Collaborative Learning Environment*

Natalia López, Manuel Núñez, Ismael Rodríguez, and Fernando Rubio

Dept. Sistemas Informáticos y Programación. Facultad de Informática.
Universidad Complutense de Madrid, E-28040 Madrid. Spain.
{natalia,mn,ir,fernando}@sip.ucm.es

Abstract. In this paper we introduce a collaborative environment for the development of medium-size programming projects. Our system provides the usual facilities for communication among members of the group as well as a friendly programming environment for the functional programming language Haskell. A relevant feature of our learning environment is that some of the *students* may be, in fact, *virtual* students. It is worth to point out that these agents will not always behave as *helpers*. On the contrary, it can happen that they produce, on purpose, wrong programs. By doing so, we pretend that students get the abilities to detect mistakes not only in their own code, but also in the code generated by other team-mates.

Keywords. Distributed learning environments, cooperative systems.

1   Introduction

The rapid development of network-based technologies has allowed distance partners to work collaboratively regardless of their location and time availability. In particular, there has been a great proliferation of systems providing collaborative learning environments (see e.g. [4,5,3,7]). We think that students should get used to work as part of a team already in their early stages of learning. In fact, team work encourages students to get some skills that are not covered by classroom lessons. In particular, we advocate that the last requirement of an introductory programming course should consist in the development of a medium-size programming project, where students are grouped into teams. Even though a teacher will evaluate the final result of the project, it is rather difficult to control all the activities of the group. That is why collaborative environments monitoring, among other tasks, the behavior of individual members of the group, may provide the appropriate feedback to the teacher.

In this paper we present a collaborative learning environment that can be used to develop such a medium-size project. We have chosen the programming language Haskell [12]. The reason for this is the same as the one for developing

---

* Research supported in part by the CICYT projects TIC2000-0701-C02-01 and TIC2000-0738, and the Spanish-British Acción Integrada HB 1999-0102.

S.A. Cerri, G. Gouardères, and F. Paraguaçu (Eds.): ITS 2002, LNCS 2363, pp. 51–60, 2002.

WHAT [8].[1] In contrast with other programming languages proposed to teach to first-year students, there are not friendly programming environments for Haskell. Therefore, in order to fairly compare the difficulties the students have to deal with their first programming language, a better interface is needed. Even though Haskell could be a good choice, the current environments are certainly not. However, the architecture of our system can be easily adapted to work under any other programming language.

Next, we briefly sketch the main capabilities of our system.

- It provides an environment to develop collaborative projects. In particular, it allows a *hierarchical* structure of the project. A group of students is partitioned into several teams. Each team has a distinguished member: The *team-leader*. Access privileges to different parts of the project will be given depending on the role of the corresponding student (the team where she[2] is located, considering if she is a team-leader, etc).
- It provides students with a friendly interface to write programs in Haskell. Let us remark that usual Haskell environments are quite verbose and far from friendly.
- It allows students to communicate among them. As pointed out in [10], these communications are specially relevant for the final development of the project, as they allow to monitor[3] the individual behavior of students inside a team. So, it will be possible to determine students attributes as activity/passivity, leadership capabilities, collaborative skills, etc.
- It allows students to test programs written by other team-mates. Students are not only supposed to write their assigned parts. On the contrary, they are responsible of the overall development of the project. So, they must control the programs produced by other team/group mates.

In addition to the previous characteristics, our system will incorporate intelligent agents[4] as part of the project. More precisely, we may include *virtual* agents as group members. They will have the same duties as a usual student. Thus, they are not supposed to (and they will not) be the *perfect student* who is solving all the problems appearing in the development of the project. Actually, they will also create (again, by simulating the behavior of usual students) problems: They may write wrong programs, they may be lazy, they may disobey its team-leader commands, etc. In conclusion, our agents are not really *malicious*. We use this term in order to clarify that their behavior do not correspond with the usual *angelic* conception of intelligent agents.

---

[1] WHAT (Web-based Haskell Adaptive Tutor) is a tool designed to help first year students having their first contact with the programming language Haskell.

[2] From now on, we assume that the gender of students and teachers is always female.

[3] In order to be able to monitor all the interactions, *physical* meetings among members of the project are restricted (as much as possible). In particular, *real* identities of project members are hidden.

[4] In terms of [14], our agents present as information attitude knowledge (versus belief) while as pro-attitudes we may remark commitment and choice (versus intention and obligation).

The main reason for including this kind of agents in our system is that we pretend to strengthen students collaborative skills. By adding a *distracting* colleague in the group, we pretend that students *learn by being disturbed* [2,1]. So, students will get used to pay attention not only to their assigned tasks but also to the ones developed by other team members. In this line, it is our intention that agents do not reveal their *true* identities. If students find out that some of their team-mates are (malicious) agents, they may be tempted to discard all the work performed by these *peers*. In order to *cover* agents we have the following *advantages*:

- Students are not identified by their real names.
- The number of students taking *Introduction to Programming* is around three hundred, distributed into six groups. These groups have different time-tables and they are located in different class-rooms.
- Students do not expect that some team-members are in fact artificial agents.

The rest of the paper is structured as follows. In Section 2 we briefly comment on the main capabilities of WHAT. Even though our collaborative learning environment is completely independent from WHAT, the teacher will use its *classes mechanism* to classify students in order to form groups/teams. In Section 3 we present our system. First, we describe the early stages of the project, where the teacher plays a fundamental role. Next, we show the system from the student point of view, that is, the possibilities that students have while interacting with our environment. Finally, we describe the behavior of our agents in the system. In Section 4 we present our conclusions and some lines for future work.

2   A Brief Introduction to WHAT

In this section we briefly review the main features of WHAT: A Web-based Haskell Adaptive Tutor [8]. The main duty of WHAT consists in providing exercises to students according to their current command on the language. In order to do that, the system does not only take into account the information gathered about the current student, but also all the information about previous *similar* students. Students are similar when they belong to the same classes. WHAT manages both *static* and *dynamic* classes. The former consider attributes as whether the student is taking the course for the first time, whether she already knows an imperative language, etc. Dynamic classes are used to handle information that is not known at the beginning of the course and that may vary along the academic year. For example, dynamic classes consider whether a student learns fast or whether she has good memory. In contrast with static classes, as dynamic attributes change (on the basis of interactions with the system) students can be automatically relocated into different dynamic classes.

WHAT handles three main categories of exercises: Typing functions, Evaluating expressions, and Programming assignments. For each problem, students are allowed to ask for hints. The proposed problems are chosen according to the student current knowledge of the language. At each moment, students are free to choose the category of exercises they want to practice. However, the system automatically points to the topic that better fits the current learning necessities of the student. In order to do that, WHAT provides a personalized following, by creating individualized profiles, that allows to offer better assistance to the student.

WHAT incorporates a complete help system for Haskell. Any concept covered during the academic year can be consulted by means of a friendly navigation interface.

Finally, our tutor provides the teacher with information about the skills the students are getting, how they are obtaining these skills, their typical mistakes, and their main difficulties. Thus, the teacher can improve her lessons in forthcoming years, explaining with more detail the parts of the course that seem to be harder.

3   The Collaborative Environment

In this section we introduce our collaborative environment. First, we present how the project is distributed among teams, how teams are formed, and the different roles played by students in the project. Next, we describe the system from the student point of view, explaining the different features. The view of the system will vary depending on the role of a student. For example, only team-leaders may communicate with other team-leaders. Finally, we present how we add agents into the collaborative environment. In particular, we define the theoretical models underlying the behavior of agents.

3.1   Distributing the Work

One of the main objectives of our system is that students learn good habits in programming (see e.g. [13]). A fundamental issue when developing real applications is the interaction with other programmers: Distributing the work, assuming/delegating responsibilities, putting pressure on other members of the team, etc. Thus, after a first course covering the basic concepts of programming, students confront a final project. In order to simulate a real software engineering application, this final assignment will be developed collaboratively by several students, organized in different groups. In this case, each project is assigned to a group of fifteen to twenty students. Besides, depending on the nature of the project, this group of students will be split into three to five teams. Given the fact that students still lack the necessary skills to develop on their own the whole project, the teacher plays a fundamental role in the specification of the different tasks. In particular, she will play both the roles of project owner and project manager.

In order to improve the coordination between teams, simple organizational design of projects structures are considered. There exists a project owner and a project manager. Each team has a *team-leader*. In addition to their duties as team-members, they have some additional responsibilities. First, they are in charge of the work assigned to the team. For example, they can (dynamically) decide to change the distribution of tasks in their teams, in the case that a member is too slow or is having problems with a particular task. They will also be responsible for putting pressure on their team-mates as well as on other teams. Actually, they are the *interface* of the team with the *outside world* (other teams and project manager/teacher).

As it is well known (see e.g. [6]), the learning efficiency of the individual students is strongly influenced by the relations among the members of the group. Thus, a critical teaching decision consists in the design of effective groups that guarantee educational benefits to the individual students. Fortunately, during the course, the learning of students was *controlled* by WHAT, so the teacher has been provided with relevant information about the characteristics of students. Hence, the composition of teams will be mainly determined by the attributes defined by WHAT (considering both static and dynamic classes of students). In particular, team-leaders will be appointed on the basis of their trajectory in the course.

The project manager (the teacher) is in charge of dividing the project into modules. Each module will be assigned to a different team of students. She will also perform the second refinement where each module is split into a set of tasks. Let us remark that this is not a typical software engineering strategy. In fact, it is a quite erroneous strategy in normal applications, as the project manager should abstract the distribution of the work inside each team. However, as we are dealing with first-year students, students are not yet prepared to perform these organizational tasks. Let us remark that even though tasks are initially distributed by the project manager, we allow students to *commerce* with their assigned tasks. Thus, each student can propose exchanging some tasks to other member of the team. Besides, she can also accept or reject such a proposal. In case students commerce adequately, a better distribution of tasks will be done, so that students specialize themselves on different topics, improving the overall performance of the project. As a byproduct we expect that students increase their *negotiation* skills, so that they can perform the tasks that are more attractive/easy for them. Let us remark that students are not allowed to commerce with members of other teams. This is a usual restriction and pretends to avoid tasks going out of the scope of the corresponding module.

3.2   The Student Point of View of the System

Students may access two different interfaces inside our collaborative environment: One devoted to *programming* and another one devoted to *communications*. The programming interface (left part of Figure 1) provides an area to write programs, another one to test programs already completed (by defining test cases), and several options to help the user (compile, run, load, save, etc.). In addition to that, students can always check the status of the functionalities of the project. They may consult the date/time of the last release of a given task, whether a finished task has been already tested, etc. Students can freely choose which of their pending tasks they want to work on. The state of this task is automatically updated in the programming environment. Finally, as our system is connected to

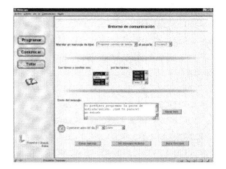

Fig. 1. Programming (left) and communication (right) environments

a Haskell compiler, both compilation errors and results from actual executions can be shown to the user.

The communication with the rest of users is done through a different interface (see right part of Figure 1). A student can either send messages to other peers, or read received messages (a list of her sent/received messages is always available). In order to be able to automatically monitor the communications among users, before a message is sent, students have to select the kind of message they want to transmit. By doing so, log files store all the relevant information about communications. These files are used to detect some characteristics (initiative, participation, leadership, etc.) of each student. The messages that can be sent are classified according to the following categories:

- Teams coordination.
- Tasks commerce.
- Project status.
- Other messages.

The first category of messages is enabled only for team-leaders, as they are responsible for coordinating the different modules of the project. They can put pressure on other teams to work on a specific functionality, to fulfill a deadline for performing a partial evaluation of the project, etc. Team-leaders will be also allowed to communicate with the project manager/teacher.

Regarding commerce of tasks, students may either accept or reject other users proposals. Moreover, students are also allowed to propose exchanges of a list of tasks with other users. Finally, team-leaders can also decide to redistribute the tasks of other member, just in case that a member is delaying the whole group.

Regarding the project status, a student can ask other members of her own team to work harder on a particular part of their tasks (because that part is critical for one of her pending tasks). The student has also the possibility to notify that she has already finished one of her assigned tasks. Finally, she can also detect that a functionality provided by other member is incorrect, and notify it. Let us remark that students do not have access to the source code being developed by other members of the group, but only to the interface of the modules. Thus, students must abstract implementation details and treat the programs of the other members as *black boxes*.

The last group of messages includes those communications associated with verbal conversations, so that, for instance, students can ask for help to other members of the team. Following the approach presented in [10], we allow students to send different kind of messages, like questions, answers, opinions, suggestions, encourages, acknowledgments, etc. As we have said, the monitoring of these communications allows us to detect the roles students are playing inside the teams, like discovering who is the real *leader* of the team.

3.3   Including Agents into the Collaborative Environment

In addition to students, intelligent agents will be added to the teams. Actually, students will not be informed about the fact that some of their team-mates could be *virtual* students. Thus, in order to hide their nature, they communicate using the same mechanisms as the rest of students, the only difference being that they do not need to use the web interface. Let us remark that, from the user point of view, both agents and real students are seen in the same way, as their user identities do not reveal the nature of them.

The characteristics of the agents will depend on the team members, so that they balance the *necessities* of the team. For instance, in case there are many brilliant students,[5] the behavior of the agent could be that of a not so brilliant student. Let us remark that there will be as many different *kinds* of agents as considered classes.[6] Thus, there will be different types of agents, depending on the skills learned in the course, depending on whether they learn fast or not, etc. Regarding the *malicious* adjective, as we already commented in the introduction, our agents are not always really *bad*: They mainly simulate the behavior of students. Let us remark that agents have access to the full code of two implementations of the project: the correct and complete one implemented by the teacher, and the incomplete one that the students are developing. That is, in order to provide programs solving their assigned tasks, they will (initially) use the right code (as provided by the teacher). However, they may introduce some errors. In order to write a wrong program, they will modify the right code according to the most commom mistakes of the (classes of) students that they are simulating. This information will be provided by WHAT (the tutor that students have been using along the course).

As pointed out in [6], the characteristics of the best learning group, for a particular user, are different at each moment. Thus, team components should ideally change dynamically. However, this solution is not feasible for students. Fortunately, our virtual students will dynamically adapt their attributes so that

---

[5] Let us remark that the student model is obtained by using WHAT.

[6] Formally, this number will be given by the cardinal of the set containing all the possible combinations of different (static and dynamic) classes (that is, a cartesian product of the corresponding sets).

they fit better the proper characteristics of the team. For instance, if a team temporarily lacks a person who press the rest of the members, an agent could adopt such behavior. Let us remind that the system dynamically detects the characteristics of each of the students, knowing whether they have initiative, participation, enthusiasm, etc. In addition, agents do not only balance groups/teams with behaviors that the components do not have. They can also strengthen some skills of students, as self-confidence and communication expertise. For instance, an agent could be lazy, so that it delays the whole group. The team should press the lazy member, and even decide to distribute its assigned tasks among the rest of members. We find this feature particularly useful for first-year students, as they are only used to solve problems individually.

In the following we present how agents react to the different interactions with real students. As we do not want students to know that some of their mates are virtual students, the way in which agents perform communications should be as similar as possible to the behavior of a real student. Obviously, it is not easy to perfectly simulate the communications performed by a student, as that is nearly equivalent to passing the Turing test. Logically, our aim is more modest: our agents will be able to ask simple questions, and also to answer them by using simple structures, as we show in the following paragraphs.

Regarding the commerce of tasks, the agent assigns a programming cost to each of the tasks. It suggests exchanging tasks when it can decrease its programming effort, and it accepts exchanges if they do not increase it. Actually, the underlying model is based on (a simplification of) PAMR [11]. This process algebra is very suitable for the specification of concurrent systems where *resources* can be exchanged between different components of the system. In our case, agents have a *utility function* relating all the tasks of the team, according to the programming costs. So, if a member of the group proposes an exchange, the agent will compute the corresponding utilities (before and after the exchange) and it will accept the offer if its utility does not decrease.

An important feature in the implementation of the agents consists in the definition of adequate response times. For example, if an agent is assigned to implement a difficult function, it could not be credible that the agent provides the code after a few seconds. It would be also erroneous to consider that the agent returns its programs after a fix amount of time, regardless the complexity of the corresponding program. In order to add realism to our agents, we have considered a model based on continuous time semi-Markov chains extended with probabilistic information (this theoretical framework is based on the work presented in [9]). Next, we briefly sketch how these models guide the temporal behavior of agents. For each of the tasks assigned to the agent, its response time will be defined by a discrete probability distribution function associated with the answer that the agent will provide. As we said before, agents may provide either a right answer (with probability p) or different (wrong) variations of the correct answer (the total probability of these answers is equal to $1 - p$). Besides, each probabilistic decision is associated with a random variable. These random variables decide the time that the agent will be delayed until the corresponding program is presented to the group. It is important to note that random variables will depend on the kind of answer that they are associated with. More precisely, the *wronger*[7] an answer is, the faster the agent will come out with a program. For the sake of simplicity, assume that all the random variables are exponentially distributed. Consider a *very wrong*, a *not so wrong*, and a *right* answers, having associated with them exponential distributions with parameters λ_1, λ_2, and λ_3, respectively.[8] We should have $\lambda_1 > \lambda_2, \lambda_3$ while $\lambda_2 \approx \lambda_3$. Let us remark that the probabilistic-stochastic model is not static. In other words, both probability distributions and random variables will vary not only according to the complexity of the given task but also according to the corresponding response time of other members of the group. For example, if the agent detects that it is faster than the rest of members, then forthcoming random variables will be *delayed*. In this line, agents consider a well-known property: Productivity (notably) increases as the deadline approaches. Finally, if the rest of the group urges the agent to finish a task, it may (probabilistically) decide to reduce the corresponding delays. However, if these delays are shortened, the probability distributions are also recomputed so that the probability associated with wrong answers increases.

Finally, an agent can also press other members of the project to work on a task, as the agent knows the tasks dependencies graph. In the same way, agents can also detect that a functionality provided by other user is wrong. Given the fact that to check equality of functions is undecidable, agents must use a *testing* procedure. Taking into account that agents have access to the right solution, provided by the teacher, they generate test cases covering the most problematic cases of the program. Then, they compare the results returned by the students implementation with the ones returned by the teacher implementation.

4   Conclusions and Future Work

In this paper we have described a collaborative environment for the development of medium-size programming projects. The system is designed to help first-year students to learn good programming habits. In order to obtain this objective, students need to collaborate to solve a common programming assignment. An important feature of our system is that not all the members of the group are real students (but students do not know this fact). Virtual students are added to the system in order to form effective groups that guarantee educational benefits to individual students. From the student point of view, our agents are not always helpers, as they can produce wrong programs, and they can even delay the work of the whole group. Nevertheless, agents are *real helpers*, as they help students to learn how to work inside heterogeneous groups.

As future work we plan to develop a similar tool for other programming languages, namely Pascal and Java. In fact, one of the main aims of our work

---

[7] The relative correctness is given by the type and number of errors that the agent is introducing.

[8] Let us remind that the mean of an exponential distribution with parameter λ is given by $\frac{1}{\lambda}$. So, the bigger λ is, the faster the delay is consumed.

is to compare the difficulties that first-year Mathematics students have learning different languages. By providing similar tools for the different languages that have been used in our department, we hope to help clarifying which language suits them better. As the environments will be analogous, we will be able to really compare the languages, without being disturbed by their environments. Besides, currently our system is now only in Spanish, as it is designed to be used by our students. However, it is trivial to translate it to any other language.

References

1. E. Aïmeur, H. Dufort, D. Leibu, and C. Frasson. Some justifications for the learning by disturbing strategy. In *AI-ED 97, World Conference on Artificial Intelligence and Education*, 1997.
2. E. Aïmeur and C. Frasson. Analyzing a new learning strategy according to different knowledge levels. *Computer and Education. An International Journal*, 27(2):115–127, 1996.
3. E. Aïmeur, C. Frasson, and H. Dufort. Co-operative learning strategies for intelligent tutoring systems. *Applied Artificial Intelligence. An International Journal*, 14(5):465–490, 2000.
4. G. Ayala and Y. Yano. GRACILE: A framework for collaborative intelligent learning environments. *Journal of the Japanese Society of Artificial Intelligence*, 10(6):156–170, 1995.
5. H.U. Hoppe. The use of multiple student modeling to parameterize group learning. In *7th Conference on Artifical Intelligence in Education*, pages 234–241, 1995.
6. A. Inaba, T. Supnithi, M. Ikeda, R. Mizoguchi, and J. Toyoda. How can we form effective collaborative learning groups? –Theoretical justification of "opportunistic group formation" with ontological engineering–. In *ITS 2000, LNCS 1839*, pages 282–291. Springer, 2000.
7. P. Jermann, A. Soller, and M. Muehlenbrock. From mirroring to guiding: A review of state of the art technology for supporting collaborative learning. In *1st European Conf. on Computer-Supported Collaborative Learning*, pages 324–331, 2001.
8. N. López, M. Núñez, I. Rodríguez, and F. Rubio. WHAT: A Web-based Haskell Adaptive Tutor. Submitted for publication, 2002.
9. N. López and M. Núñez. A testing theory for generally distributed stochastic processes. In *CONCUR'2001, LNCS 2154*, pages 321–335. Springer, 2001.
10. M. McManus and R. Aiken. Monitoring computer-based problem solving. *International Journal of Artificial Intelligence in Education*, 6(4):307–336, 1995.
11. M. Núñez and I. Rodríguez. PAMR: A process algebra for the management of resources in concurrent systems. In *FORTE 2001*, pages 169–185. Kluwer Academic Publishers, 2001.
12. S.L. Peyton Jones and J. Hughes. Report on the programming language Haskell 98, 1999. http://www.haskell.org.
13. A. Vizcaíno, J. Contreras, J. Favela, and M. Prieto. An adaptive, collaborative environment to develop good habits in programming. In *ITS 2000, LNCS 1839*, pages 262–271. Springer, 2000.
14. M. Wooldridge and N.R. Jennings. Intelligent agents: Theory and practice. *The Knowledge Engineering Review*, 10(2):115–152, 1995.

Learning with Virtual Agents: Competition and Cooperation in AMICO

Dorothée Rasseneur[1], Elisabeth Delozanne[1,2], Pierre Jacoboni[1], and Brigitte Grugeon[3,4]

[1]LIUM, Avenue Olivier Maessian, 72085 LE MANS Cedex 09, France
`{dorothee.rasseneur, elisabeth.delozanne,`
`pierre.jacoboni}@lium.univ-lemans.fr`
[2]IUFM de Créteil, Rue Jean Macé, 94861 BONNEUIL Cedex
[3]DIDIREM - Paris VII, 2, Place Jussieu, 75 251 PARIS Cedex 05, France
[4]IUFM d'Amiens 49, boulevard de Châteaudun 80044 AMIENS CEDEX,
`brigitte.grugeon@amiens.iufm.fr`

Abstract. This paper deals with the design and implementation of AMICO[1] , a prototype to enhance mathematics learning by interactions between a student (or a dyad) and virtual agents (several co-learner companions and a mathematician). This work is part of a multidisciplinary project, the project LINGOT that aims to give math teachers tools to improve their teaching. We first present the foundations of the project: the pedagogical assumptions, the design approach and the different kinds of virtual agents we propose. Then we present our virtual companions who allow students and teachers to use different learning and teaching strategies. They can play several characters: more or less trouble maker, more or less correct in their answers, more or less algebra speakers. In AMICO we propose two scenarios of interactions between students and virtual agents: competition and cooperation. We sketch the software architecture we propose in order to implement a simple authoring tool. Teachers specify problems, figures, the lists of common answers for students and companions. Then AMICO generates automatically and dynamically the dialogues between students and companions according to the companions' characters and students' answers. First user testing are encouraging and give perspectives.

1 Introduction

Learning with a virtual companion has been a focus of interest for ITS researchers for about ten years. Chan quoted that to bring up a future Chinese emperor an other boy was introduced to "learn with the prince" in order to improve the prince's learning. Chan proposed an ITS that allows students to learn with a virtual companion in the domain of indefinite integration. Since then, other Learning Companion Systems (LCS) have been created in different domains, although math is the most frequently

---

[1] AMICO sounds in French like an abbreviation for friendly companion and means Mathematical Learning by Interacting with Companions (in French: Apprentissage des Mathématiques par Interaction avec des COmpagnons)

S.A. Cerri, G. Gouardères, and F. Paraguaçu (Eds.): ITS 2002, LNCS 2363, pp. 61–70, 2002.
© Springer-Verlag Berlin Heidelberg 2002

chosen domain. Some systems support only one companion whereas others include both a virtual companion and a virtual tutor.

The aim of the multidisciplinary project Lingot is to provide mathematics teachers with software they can use in everyday classrooms in order to facilitate the teaching and learning of algebra. We agree with [10] that, from an educational perspective, the companions offer "a way to support the diversity of representations and perspectives inherent in human learning and teaching". Indeed in order to help student to make sense to algebraic expressions some teachers organize classrooms debates. Educational research in mathematics has shown that, on some types of problems and with a careful class management, this pedagogical strategy enhances comprehension of algebraic expressions [6]. We based our software on this work. Grugeon claims that according to level of rationality the students are engaged in (proof by numerical example, proof by argumentation, proof by school authority, proof by algebra) they use different types of justification (counter examples, correct rules, mal-rules, examples etc.). Those justifications are articulated in several representation modes: algebraic, graphical, numerical, "mathural" language. By "mathural", we mean a language created by students that mixes mathematics language and natural language: the formulations produced by the students in this language are not completely correct from a mathematical point of view but demonstrate a first level comprehension of mathematical notions [2]. To illustrate those table 1 shows an example of different justifications the students usually give and how those justifications are analysed in the educational research of Grugeon. Within this context, we assume that switching from one representation mode to another helps students to have a better understanding of algebraic expressions and to enter in a higher level of rationality.

Table 1. When stating that "$a^2 * a^3 = a^6$" isn't true for every a, examples of several students' proofs and their analysis in the model of algebra competencies that AMICO is based on

Level of rationality proof by …	Type of justification	Representation mode	Examples of students articulations
numerical example	To try with one or several numbers	numerical	"If I try with a = 1, 12 * 13 = 1 * 1 = 1 and 16 = 1"
argumentation	To give explanations	mathural language	"3*2 = 6 for exponents and not 2+3"
			"I have added the exponents"
school authority	To give rule relying on authority	mathural language	"We must never multiply exponents"
algebra	To take a counter-example	numerical	for a = 2, $2^2 * 2^3 = 4 * 8 = 32$ and 26 = 64
			"If we calculate for 2: $2^2 * 2^3 = 2*2 * 2*2*2 = 2^5$ and not 2^6"
	To give correct rule	algebraic	"for every a, we have $a^n * a^p = a^{n+p}$ and not a^{n*p}"
		mathural language	"To multiply powers of a same number, we add exponents"
			"When a number with an exponent is multiplied by this same number with an exponent, we add the exponents"

Our educational assumption is that an ITS based on interactions with virtual companions can improve the learning in inducing a socio-cognitive conflict. More precisely, we assume that to respond to the virtual peer's reactions, students may need to adapt their type of justification, and use several modes of representation. Our pedagogical goal is to find pedagogical scenarios to help the student in switching from one mode to another according to the situation, i.e. according to the problem or according to the interaction with the companion. In that context, our first objective is to test this idea by implementing AMICO.

For AMICO to be useful and usable by teachers in their classrooms, we have adopted methods of participative design based on the implementation of successive prototypes that are tested by students and teachers. This methodological choice led us to set a second objective: to define a flexible software architecture allowing fast modifications, flexible settings of parameters and automatic generation of the companions' interaction from data entered by teachers.

From those objectives come several research questions:

- As far as the pedagogical design is concerned:
    - Which interaction scenarios will induce socio-cognitive conflict and the use of several types of justification when a student (or a group of students) interacts with a companion?
    - What roles and features should the companions have in order to support different learning and teaching strategies? Is it necessary to introduce other virtual actors?
    - What types of relationships between human students and their virtual companions should be offered?
    - What learning situations can teachers set up when using AMICO in classrooms?
- As far as the software design is concerned:
    - Is the framework we propose powerful enough to allow teachers to adapt AMICO to the learning situations they want to set up?
    - What software architecture will be more effective to implement these situations and to generate instances of situations?

To begin to answer some of these questions, we introduce first the process that we adopted to find different types of companions and to design different interaction situations. Then we describe the "identity cards" of the companions we have designed in this prototype of AMICO and the different modes of interaction among the pedagogical actors. Next, we discuss the two scenarios proposed to elicit competition or cooperation between students and companions. Finally, we present the results of the tests we did and the teachers' opinions of our software.

2   The Design Process

As in our team's previous works [3] we based our work on a cognitive, epistemological and didactic analysis of a teaching problem. As mentioned above, we started from Grugeon's work [6] that has modeled the algebraic competence of students from (French) secondary schools. This model allows us both to analyse the set of exercises and to describe students' algebraic activity. Then we defined the context of use: AMICO is designed to be used in classrooms during individualised help sessions or when students work in dyads. The pedagogical objective is to have students confront several types of justifications and to use different representation modes. We selected from exercises used in schools, those that to trigger of a debate, especially those relying on proof. For each of them we collected about sixty students' answers for use in AMICO. Our pedagogical design decision was that the virtual companions should be students' peers and should express in a student's style, often in incomplete or erroneous ways. Therefore we did not try to correct the collected answers. We agree with many researchers that students need to construct their own explanations. In our opinion learning will be better if students can discuss and examine various types of justification, the correct answer being revealed later by a virtual agent, the mathematician.

Based on ITS research dealing with virtual companions, we defined four types of companions and two learning scenarios. A first mock-up was tested by team members. A second was tested by six students (between 14 and 16) in the lab. This early testing allowed us to validate our interaction design and improve interface usability. Then the prototype was implemented and a new learning scenario added. Finally, this prototype was tested by ten teachers and trainers for mathematics teachers.

3 Different Companions Characters

Educational agents and learning companions have been described in the literature. They have various objectives, and do not have necessarily educational or accurate domain expertise.

3.1 The Different Types of Educational Agents

Chan [4] described three types of learning activities with virtual companions. The first one is "computer as a co-learner". Here, the companion is at the same knowledge level as the learner. They solve the problem together, but they also may be in competition. The virtual teacher or tutor does not intervene in this case. The second form of learning activity is the "learning companion system". A virtual teacher is added to facilitate the human and virtual students' learning. Students and companions solve in parallel the problem set by the teacher and then compare and discuss their various solutions. The third form of learning activity is the "learning by teaching". In this scenario, companions have a weaker level of knowledge than students, and so students have to teach the companion by giving him examples or information.

For the educational researchers we work with, it is important to let the students make incomplete or erroneous articulations so that their misunderstanding can be confronted. If teacher's intervention occurs too early the student can be left with a false or partial conception. This is one of the reasons why, from our point of view, virtual companions should express themselves as students, and not in a formal way. Therefore we decided not to introduce a tutor or a teacher in AMICO.

However, the experienced mathematics teachers all agreed it is of primary importance to end classrooms debates with a moment when the correct answer is stated and identified as mathematical knowledge and not as an opinion ("institutionalisation phase"). To play this part, we introduced a virtual agent with the role of mathematician.

Educational researchers and teachers who share this conception on algebra learning and teaching agree with this design choice. It seems, although it remained to be confirmed, that teachers who have some more directive conceptions about teaching would wish to add a teacher agent who would explain and give several formulations to complete and correct the students' or companions' expressions.

3.2 Learning Companions in AMICO

[8] described research showing that not every student is satisfied by the same companion. Some prefer a very knowledgeable and self-confident companion; others prefer a less competent companion. We therefore decided to design different companions so that learners could choose according to their preferred learning strategies or teachers could select particular teaching strategies. [1] used some companions to disrupt learners deliberately by giving incorrect answers and by simply contradicting the learner. Such companions oblige students to confront theirs opinions with others and to justify their own ideas. In AMICO, we adopt this idea of disrupting companion. According to [11], better learning occurs when learners feel the need to teach something to their companion. Machine learning techniques could be used to implement the companion's learning. In AMICO, we did not explore this approach but we designed companions who make mistakes. We conjecture that students would want to explain their answers when they would think the companion was wrong.

Finally, to encourage understanding of algebraic expressions, our collaborating educational researchers recommended that students be incited to produce several types of justifications and to express these in several representation modes, in particular: algebraic language, natural language and numeric language. [7] estimated that the main difficulty for students when symbolizing word problems is that algebraic language is like a foreign language for the students. In their system, Ms Lindquist, they designed an artificial tutor who helps the students in developing this translation skill. In our project, it is a companion who incites the students to work in several representation modes. We designed a type of companion that almost always answers correctly but can use one of a number of representations. Choice of representation may be specified by the teacher. In AMICO two companions are of this type: the first almost always uses the algebraic language to justify his or her answers and the second uses the "mathural" language.

3.3 The Characters of the Pedagogical Agents in AMICO

In AMICO, we have chosen a range of features that can be parameterized by the teachers to define the characters of agents. The *mathematician* gives the correct mathematical answer to a question and a justification in an expression mode than can be specified by the teacher. For the companions, the first parameter is the degree of disrupting: it is the percentage of agreement or disagreement between the student's and companion's answers during a session. The second parameter is the frequency of use of different mathematical modes of representation (algebraic language, natural language, numeric language). The third concerns the companion's level of mathematical expertise which is represented by the percentage of correct answers the companion gives. The three others parameters (the companion's name, his or her picture and introductory message) are less relevant to the teaching strategy but are necessary for displaying the companion to students.

4   Interaction between the Software and the Students

The objective of AMICO is to encourage students to give explanations in different ways and develop connections between different modes of representations. We wanted to make it as easy as possible for the student to input answers whatever representation mode they choose. In addition, the interventions of the companions are not fixed but dynamically generated during the session according to the actions of the students and the character of the companion set by the teacher (or the student).

4.1   Students' Modes of Expression

In algebra, students answer in mathural language or with algebraic expressions. This led designers to choose between: providing students with an editor for algebraic expressions or providing students with a list of propositions to compose his or her answer. In AMICO we chose the second option. Its main advantage is of course that it is easy to implement and, for this reason, many systems use it, in standard software as in research software (for example, [7]). Moreover, students are often not clever with keyboard input and this solution facilitates their work. But numerous educational critiques have been made of this solution: if the only activities proposed to the students are choices in lists of predefined answers, students are not confronted with the task of producing and articulating their answer, which is an essential competence to be acquired. Our observations in the classrooms however showed that students' activity with software is not restricted to interaction with interface: some use a draft or a calculator, discuss with peers or with the teacher. In the scenario of use that we consider for AMICO, students are working partly with the software but also partly without it. The interaction with the software gives them the opportunity to synthesize the results of these various activities. In this context, forcing the students to choose a type of justification and its expression from a predefined list helps to generate a socio-cognitive conflict: the student is confronted by different arguments and must give his or her position with regard to propositions.

AMICO provides to students two types of input: choose a justification from a list or compose a sentence from predefined pieces. On the one hand a student giving an answer, sometimes has to justify it. In this case, AMICO offers the student a number of answers in several combo boxes, one corresponding to each representation mode. With respect to our educational objectives, this method is a compromise between easy self-expression and pedagogical constraint. The combo box lists offer students' answers that we collected earlier and that are not always correct. They are intended to approximate a student's articulation better than articulations of teachers or books. On the other hand, when one of the actors asks another actor for an explanation, the latter explains its reasoning process. As in [5;7], AMICO helps learners to write an explanation by providing sentence fragments. The list of fragments offered is made up dynamically according to students' previous choices. The companions' sentences are constructed from fragments in the same way because the companion's and students' role when interacting with AMICO are symmetric.

The effectiveness of this way of constructing explanations remains to be proved but first tests with students seem to raise no difficulties. However some teachers would prefer fewer choices. They ask for only one option chosen by us as prototype of students' answer for each type collected from our a priori educational analysis [9]. One teacher would prefer more academic formulations and opposes the design choice of displaying incomplete or wrong answers in the combo boxes. These reactions suggest to us that design choices can not be theoretically validated in isolation from teachers' conception of algebra education and their way of managing their classes.

4.2 Dynamic Evolution of Interactions with Companions

[13] proposed that educational agents must be autonomous i.e. they must be capable of pursuing goals in a complex environment and of adapting their behavior. The companions that we have designed in AMICO have very specific goal (disrupt the student or answer correctly or answer wrongly, or answer in algebraic language or in "mathural" language). In addition, each companion is able to adjust his or her goal. Companion's answers are not predefined but each interaction is calculated according to the step, the student's and companion's previous answers and the companion's goals. The companion will not answer the same way for two identical student answers. This is the reason we say that the interactions evolve dynamically.

5   Scenarios of Interaction

To create the scenarios of interaction, we began by finding types of exercises that allow discussion. We created two types of interaction: scenario of competition and cooperation. To test our ideas we looked for exercises in algebra that are suitable for discussion. In the prototype presented here, we choose three types of exercises:

- Deciding whether algebraic expressions are equivalent and justifying the answer
- Deciding whether a number is a solution of an equation and justifying the answer
- Comparing perimeters of polygons and justifying the answer

For each exercise, our a priori educational analysis identified a list of competencies involved in solving it. The educational analysis also identified a list of possible strategies.

Based on this educational work, we considered different scenarios. [12] proposed that the student can choose to solve the problem alone or in collaboration with the companion. For our part we invented two scenarios of interaction between the students (by dyad if possible) and the companion. The first scenario is founded on competition between the group of students and the companion, whereas the second is founded on their cooperation. In the competition scenario actors (students or companion) are required to justify their answers. For each exercise, AMICO asks the actors to answer "yes" or "no", and then to choose a justification in several combos boxes according to their expression mode. During the first user test we made in our lab, students said they were not feeling the companion's presence ("We haven't the feeling that the companion is here"). So we try to specify a more interactive scenario. In the cooperation scenario, the two actors can ask the other for an explanation. To improve the feeling of presence of the companion, we introduced the first names into the dialogue. When the two scenarios are available for the same exercise, we let the students choose the scenario. In all the cases, at the end of the exercise, the mathematician institutionalizes the knowledge.

The *competition scenario* is based on a three steps exchange: the companion and the group of learners take turns three times in all. The objective of this type of problem is, from a pedagogical point of view, to show the rules of formation of algebraic expressions the students have constructed, and the role they assign to + and * •signs, to parentheses and to exponents.

In the *scenario of cooperation*, the two actors (the group and the companion) cooperate to construct what they think is the best solution. This cooperation scenario only applies to problems that can be decomposed in two sub-problems. For example, an exercise presents two polygons including annotations carrying on the lengths of the sides and the question "Do the two polygons have the same perimeter?" The two sub-problems are in this case: "What is the perimeter of the first figure?" "What is the perimeter of the second figure?". The cooperative resolution of such a problem in AMICO has three steps. The first two steps require solving, after a discussion, the two sub-problems: find the perimeter of each figure. If the two actors agree on the solution (they agree on the two perimeters), they move to the third step (to say if the two perimeters are equal).

6   Testing AMICO with Students and Teachers

In the early tests we organized with the students we wondered if they would understand the trace of the dialogue generated by the system. We were concerned the dialogue was a little rigid and over-structured. These tests however did not raise difficulty in understanding the dialogue between the students and the companion. To the question "What do you think about companions", some answered "they are funny", "they are like us, sometimes they also make mistakes","he tried to disrupt us". To the question "Give strong points of the software", some answered "It is good because we aren't obliged to give the correct answers" "It is good because we can work with a companion and we aren't alone." Recall that in our design approach, these tests are not intended to establish a validation of the software in term of students' learning gains. This would require taking into account several other factors, for example the teachers' conceptions of the algebra education, their class management, the student's cognitive profiles and previous exposure to algebra teaching. The objective of these tests is to give design ideas, to test usability and to validate design choices.

Once the software was implemented, we tested it with five teachers. They were all interested in the idea of a virtual companion and in the fact that every companion has a different character. They thought that would please to students and motivate them. They appreciated that students and companions have several ways of expressing justifications and the diversity in the interaction, which, in their opinion would be beneficial for the students learning. They said that working on prototypic justifications and on various forms of expression would encourage students to question their conceptions. The teachers foresaw two types of uses in the classroom: a use with the whole class with a data show projector to initiate a discussion before a lesson about calculation with letters. This will allow the teacher to estimate the prior knowledge of the students in the class. The second is a use in individualised help sessions to elicit discussion in dyads and to challenge the students' misconceptions. According to the teachers, one of the strong points of AMICO is the scope for them to generate other exercises and to modify the answer lists used to construct students' and companions' explanations. One teacher wanted companions give only correct answers, more in conformity with the answers that a teacher would give. The four others mentioned the rigidity of the dialogue and suggested some improvements. They were not in complete agreement with the mathematician's answer when proving that the equality of two expressions is false: the mathematician gives a counter-example. Three on five considered that this answer is insufficient and that it would be necessary to supplement it with an explanation: either a commentary in natural language on the correct rule, or by its demonstration. Those comments enlighten that the institutionalization step includes two parts: the answer and a meta-mathematic indication explaining the answer

7 Conclusion

AMICO has been implemented in Java using a UML methodology to develop its architecture. It is based on educational research. This software offers two different scenarios of interaction with virtual companions: competition and cooperation. We implemented four characters for the companions. These various characteristic allow adaptation to different learning styles and teaching strategies. The main limitation of the prototype in the current state is the rigidity of the automatically generated dialogue. A possible solution would be to introduce an agent to lead the dialogue who could encourage a better fluidity of interaction. In the longer term, we could develop a model of richer dialogue by studying the dyads' dialogues while AMICO's use. In the current prototype exercises are defined in text files and a teacher interface would be necessary to allow teachers to input new exercises without the help of a designer.

In our opinion, the version of AMICO we described here presents a triple interest. At the computer science level, AMICO implement a generic model that allows interactions to be automatically generated from file text specifications. This approach allows to instrument participatory design: the early testing process informs the design choices but does not lead to a "spaghetti program" that is often criticized in rapid prototyping methods. At the educational level, this prototype supplies an environment to allow students to work on various types of justifications and various forms of expression. AMICO does not replace the teacher but can help as a catalyst in learning situations the teachers has set up. Finally, AMICO allows educational researchers to parameterize the companion and thus supplies them with a tool to study how students make sense with the different types of justifications.

Acknowledgements. We would like to thank Geoff Cumming who provided valuable insights and help us to improve the English version of this paper.

References

1. Aimeur, E., Dufort, H., Leibu, D., Frasson, C., Some justifications about the learning by disturbing strategy, AI-ED 97, Japan (1997) 119-126
2. Artigue, M., Aussadez, T., Grugeon, B., Lenfant, A., Teaching and learning algebra: Approaching complexity through complementary perspectives, 12th ICMI study, H. Chick, K. Stacey, J &J. Vincent, (Eds), Melbourne (Australia), vol 1(2001) 21-32
3. Bruillard, E., Delozanne, E., Leroux, P., Delannoy, P., Dubourg, X., Jacoboni , P., Lehuen, J., Luzzati, D., Teutsch, P., Quinze ans de recherche informatique sur les sciences et techniques éducatives au LIUM, Revue Sciences et Techniques Educatives, hommage à Martiel Vivet, Hermès, vol 7, n° 1, (2000) 87-145
4. Chan, T.-W., Some learning systems: an overview, Innovate adult learning with innovate technologies, North-Holland, Collis B. Davies G. (1995) 101-122
5. Craig, S. D., Gholson, B., Garzon, M. H., Hu, X., Marks, W., Weimer-Hastings, P., Lu, Z., Auto tutor and Otto Tudor, AI-ED' 99 Workshop on Animated and Personnified Pedagogical Agents, Le Mans (1999) 25-30
6. Grugeon, B., Etude des rapports institutionnels et des rapports personnels des élèves à l'algèbre élémentaire dans la transition entre deux cycles d'enseignement : BEP et Première, Thèse de doctorat, Université Paris VII (1995)
7. Heffernan, N. T., Koedinger, K. R., Intelligent tutoring systems are missing the tutor: building a more strategic dialog-based tutor, Workshop "Learning algebra with the computer", ITS 2000, Montréal (2000)
8. Hietala, P., Niemirepo, T., The competence of learning companion agents, International Journal of Artificial Intelligence in Education, vol 9, n° 3-4 (1998) 178-192
9. Jean, S., Delozanne, E., Jacoboni, P., Grugeon, B., A diagnostic based on a qualitative model of competence in elamantary algebra, in S. Lajoie, M. Vivet, AI&ED'99, IOS Press, Amsterdam, , Le Mans (1999) 491-498
10. Les, J., Cumming, G., Finch, S., Agents systems for diversity in human learning, in S. Lajoie, M. Vivet AI&ED'99, IOS Press, Amsterdam, Le Mans (1999) 13-20
11. Ramirez Uresti, J. A., Teaching a learning companion, The Tenth White house papers. Graduate research in the cognitive and computing sciences at Sussex, Brighton, Eds. J. Halloran & F. Retkowsky (1998)
12. Ramirez Uresti, J. A., LECORBA: A learning companion system for binary boolean algebra, AI-ED' 99 Workshop on Animated and Personnified Pedagogical Agents, Le Mans (1999) 56-61
13. Shaw, E., Ganeshan, R., Johnson W. L., Miller, D., Building a case agent-assisted learning as a catalyst for curriculum reform in medical education, AI-ED' 99 Workshop on Animated and Personnified Pedagogical Agents, Le Mans (1999) 70-79

Adaptive Tutoring Processes and Mental Plans

Alke Martens and Adelinde M. Uhrmacher

University of Rostock, Department of Computer Science,
18051 Rostock, Germany
{martens, lin}@informatik.uni-rostock.de

Abstract. Intelligent Tutoring Systems (ITS) and Adaptive Hypermedia Systems (AH) are state of the art in learning with computers. The
system PLAIT (Planning Agents in Intelligent Tutoring) is a web- and
case-based ITS. Typically, ITS adapt single pages to the learner's needs
and evaluate the learner's success according to his behavior at certain
checkpoints and interaction elements. In the case-based scenario it is of
particular interest to reason about the learner's skills according to the
question how to proceed in a concrete situation. To decide whether the
learner behaves logically coherent, the ITS requires some means to anticipate the learner's goals and intentions. For this purpose, the tutor
agent in PLAIT has access to a HTN (Hierarchical Task Network) plan.
The tutor agent evaluates the learner's behavior according to the plans.
It provides context dependent help and gives a summarizing feedback,
including information about the learner's problem solving skills.

1   Introduction

The history of Intelligent Tutoring Systems (ITS) can be traced back to the
early 1970s, when Carbonell [4] makes one of the first efforts in combining methods of Artificial Intelligence (AI) with Computer Aided Instruction (CAI). Since
then, a plethora of systems has been developed. Important developments have
taken place in the last years, pushed by the growing impact and the possibilities
of the WWW. According to the underlying pedagogical principle three types
of ITS can be distinguished, i.e. instructional, dialog-oriented, and case-based
ITS. Instructional ITS focus on modeling the complete instructional session, e.g.
[19], the underlying methodology is instructional planning. Focus of the dialog-
oriented system is to realize a dialog between the learner and the system, e.g.
[11]. Some early ITS, e.g. SCHOLAR [4] and GUIDON [6], used Socratic and
mixed initiative dialog, respectively. Case-based ITS follow the idea of "Case-
based Teaching", which aims at engaging the learner to train problem solving
and critical thinking in realistic situations. Case-based teaching has its origins
in law school in early 1800's [15] but is still state of the art in teaching decision-
making and procedural skills. Whereas in instructional and dialog-oriented ITS
the focus of tutoring changes according to the underlying system's philosophy
between tutor centered and learner centered approaches [5], the case-based training naturally lies in-between [18]. In the case-based scenario, the learner is the

S.A. Cerri, G. Gouardères, and F. Paraguaçu (Eds.): ITS 2002, LNCS 2363, pp. 71–80, 2002.

actor, his behavior steers the development of the case's storyline. In contrast to other approaches to learning theory, the learner should not be corrected immediately but should see the effects of his action in the stories development. The tutor can be reactive or (pro-)active, guiding and steering the learner's problem solving process, giving hints and advice, and preventing him from feeling lost. The tutor can engage the learner in a dialog, thus combining aspects of dialog and case-based ITS, as e.g. done in ADELE [10].

The approach presented in this paper is focused on strengthening the reasoning abilities of a virtual tutor. Based on learning goal hierarchies, a HTN planner is employed to reason about a learner's mental plans in a case-based ITS.

The system PLAIT (Planning Agents in Intelligent Tutoring) is an extension of the web- and case-based ITS "Docs 'n Drugs - The Virtual Hospital" [7], [9], [12], [13], which has been realized at the University of Ulm and constitutes an integral part of the medical curriculum. Based on the experiences made with "Docs 'n Drugs", PLAIT follows two main directions to enhance the possibilities of self-study. The first one, being partly realized in "Docs 'n Drugs", is a tutoring process that is flexible and adaptable to the learner's profile. This profile contains information about the learner's knowledge and skills in current and former training cases. The second one is aimed at mimicking human tutors' abilities to anticipate the learners intentions and to consider those in giving feedback. The hierarchical structure of learning goals allows to evaluate the success of students with respect to training case independent skills, e.g. knowledge about facts or knowledge about how to proceed. The gain of such an approach is to fine-tune reasoning about the learner's skills, broaden the feedback, and to enrich the learner profile. This information can be used to fine-tune the adaptable tutoring process.

2 PLAIT Planning Agents in Intelligent Tutoring

PLAIT is an extension of "Docs 'n Drugs". In Figure 1 the main elements of "Docs 'n Drugs" are depicted. The origin system "Docs 'n Drugs" has realized intelligent tutoring in a classical way. Certain checkpoints are part of the training case. They are used to reason about the learner's progress. Those checkpoints are interaction pages, where the learner must for example answer questions or mark a region in a picture. In the medical domain an exposed checkpoint is the differential diagnosis, which is used in "Docs 'n Drugs" as a reference point to check the learner's current intention. Reasoning about the learner's skills at these checkpoints is straightforward. However, no conclusions about process knowledge can be drawn, for example how to act and react appropriately in an emergency situation. If the learner starts to follow a wrong assumption, which he made not explicit by choosing a differential diagnosis, his choice of steps cannot be evaluated.

PLAIT is designed to enhance the possibilities of self-study by providing a more detailed feedback. The ideas are based on the experience made with the origin system. The main advantage of case-based training can be seen in the

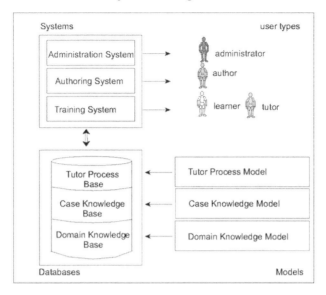

Fig. 1. Elements of "Docs 'n Drugs"

cognitive authenticity of the learning environment. Cognitive authenticity in a training case means, the learner should have an exploration space rather than a linear sequence of steps. As a consequence, the authors must embed not only correct but also wrong and alternative paths in the training case. Authoring thus becomes a very complex and time-consuming process.

As mentioned above, in "Docs 'n Drugs" one exposed point of control is the differential diagnosis. By forcing the learner to make every suspected diagnosis explicit, the intelligent tutor tries to reason about the learner's intentions and gives direct feedback and correction. However, the learners have claimed that this procedure is somewhat tiresome and far from real life situations. The question arises, how a virtual tutor can draw conclusions about the learner's procedural skills, how it can reason about a series of steps, each of which is wrong in the training cases overall context, but logically coherent. How can the reasoning abilities of the virtual tutor be enhanced without allowing the tutor to take over control? Some early approaches let the authors predesign libraries of possible bugs. Others tried to predefine each possible path and necessarily restrict the learner's exploration space.

Following the idea of perceiving "plans as complex mental attitudes", as described in [3], and [17] we use plans to draw conclusions about the learner's intention without forcing him to make his intention explicit. The usage of plans combines an expanded exploration space with intelligent feedback. At the same time it keeps the effort for the authors at bay.

Hierarchical plans provide the means to grasp the learner's learning skills. The underlying idea emerged from interviewing authors of training cases. When an author, being usually an expert in the application domain but not necessary an expert in pedagogy, develops a training case ad hoc, he faces a lot of difficulties, which can be avoided by a more systematic approach. An author can start to model a training case by identifying the skills the learner should acquire. Those skills are typically domain independent. For example, the author can define "a student should recognize essential facts within the text", afterwards "a student should interpret these facts in the given context", or "should choose an appropriate sequence of activities". This skeleton of a "partially ordered plan" is filled with domain dependent elements. For example in the domain of clinical medicine, the classical approach to acquire information is the anamnesis which often starts a training case, followed e.g. by body examination, diagnosis, and therapy. Based on this skeleton story line, the author models concrete elements. They will be reflected as actions and contents, i.e. pages, in the training case and form the tutoring process.

Hierarchical planning, however, cannot only be used to facilitate authoring. It is used to extend the tutor agent's abilities to reason about the learner's behavior, as the following sections will illustrate.

3   Agents and Tutoring Process in PLAIT

The story line of a case-based ITS and the web-based environment lend themselves for a multi-user scenario. To facilitate the support of multi-user interaction in the future, the learner and the intelligent tutor are implemented as agents. The learner model, which has grown in complexity, the learner's history in the current and past training cases, and his preferred learning styles are part of the learner agent. The learner agent steers and controls the tutoring process whereas the tutor agent reasons about the behavior of the learner, based on the hierarchical plans.

The tutoring process is a highly flexible and adaptable construct [13]. Each tutoring process consists of actions and contents. The contents can be coarsely divided into information and interaction elements, both equipped with information about the required learner level. Each page displayed to the learner consists of a set of elements and is composed by the learner agent according to the learner's level which depends on his performance in former and the current training case. Thus, the amount and type of questions and information showed to the learner vary. E.g. the display of additional information will help a weak learner in solving a task. Not only the contents are adapted, but also the amount and type of available actions. An action in a medical training case denotes what action the learner wants to perform next, e.g. "initial anamnesis", "body examination lower abdomen", etc.

4   Hierarchical Plans in PLAIT

Each training case is represented as an HTN plan [20]. The plan hierarchy consists of three levels. According to the terminology of HTN planners a plan distinguishes between tasks and actions. Each task can be reduced by a set of alternative task reduction schemata, each of which represents a sub-plan. The sub-plan again can comprise tasks and actions. Figure 2 shows the three layer hierarchy of PLAIT. At the topmost level A, the domain independent learning skills are located. They typically depend on the type of learning theory the author chose to adopt for the learning case. E.g. according to Bloom's "Taxonomy of Educational Objectives" [2] task 1 could be "Knowledge of Specific Facts", task2 could be "Knowledge of Convention", etc. The tasks can also be constructed according to Merrill's "Component Display Theory"[14], or according to the approach of Gagné [8].

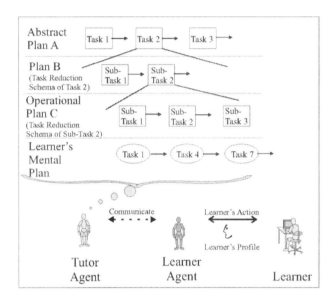

Fig. 2. The hierarchy of plans in PLAIT

Each of the tasks at plan level A is associated with at least one task reduction schema, the application of which will produce a sub-plan at level B. Level B plans consist of domain dependent tasks. In clinical medicine, those are e.g. "anamnesis", "body examination", etc. They denote phases of the case that are dedicated to teaching specific skills.

To reach level C each (sub-) task of level B is reduced. Typically, at level C, we find a partially ordered sequence of actions that do not necessitate a further reduction. It is important to clarify the relation between these actions and the steps a learner can choose in the tutoring process. With each single step in the tutoring process an action is associated. The actions at level C present a subset of the actions that are offered via steps to the learner in the tutoring process. The learner interacts with the tutoring process by choosing a step. Each of the steps that the learner chooses is compared with the plan at level C. If the steps are not covered by the plan at level C, the reasoner, i.e. the tutor agent, tries to relate the chosen steps to higher level tasks.

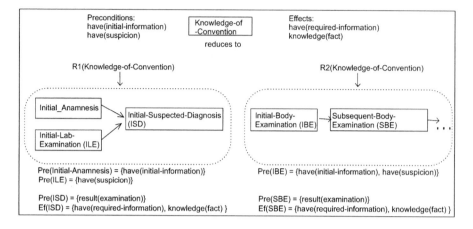

Fig. 3. Example of Task Reduction of Task "Knowledge of Convention"

In Figure 3 an example of two alternative task reduction schemata for level A tasks is shown. The reduction schemata R1 and R2 can be used to reduce the level A task "Knowledge of Convention" [2].

5   Sketching a Scene

For example, if the learner starts with the assumption, that a female patient with pain in the lower abdomen has appendicitis, he will likely make examinations that are testing appendicitis signs. If the patient suffers from extra uterine gravidity (EUG), these examinations are not correct. Taking into account that the learner starts with the assumption of appendicitis, his choice of examinations is correct. Moreover, a series of steps are required to falsify or confirm the suspicion. The tutor should not immediately guide the learner back to any correct path. But it should be able to give context sensitive feedback, which does not restrict the learner's exploration space, but helps him to follow and develop his own ideas. For example, the learner has checked one appendicitis sign and does not know how to proceed. The tutor could offer other appendicitis related examinations which will finally help to falsify the suspicion. The learner is not immediately told that he is following the wrong path instead he has the chance to reach the conclusion that he must exclude appendicitis.

The tutor will finally be able to give a summarizing feedback, e.g. the learner missed some facts in the anamnesis, or the learner seemingly has a lack of knowledge about how to proceed in examining appendicitis signs. Thus, with the help of the planning system the case on EUG has been (mis-)used by the student to learn something about the diagnosis and treatment of appendicitis. To decide whether the learner behaves in a coherent manner, and to make such a kind of final evaluation, the tutor has to anticipate the learner's goals and intentions.

6   Reasoning in PLAIT

If the learner starts a training case, a learner agent is created with the learner's history, his knowledge level and his profile information. The learner agent prepares the initial page by selecting the appropriate elements and the set of possible actions. The tutor agent constructs the plan hierarchy. It selects those elements from the database that are denoted to be the optimal plans, i.e. tasks, actions, and reduction schemata. The learner chooses the first step, leading him to the next page, which is again prepared by the learner agent: the learner has started his work with the training case. Reasoning about the learner's progress can take place at classical checkpoints, i.e. interaction elements. The learner agent records the learner's performance in its history and uses this information to continuously adapt the tutoring process, i.e. the content of the pages and the amount and type of possible next steps. The learner agent takes the past and the present into account to adapt the tutoring process. However, to anticipate the intentions of the learner and use those for adaptation and feedback planning is introduced in PLAIT. The tutor agent compares each of the learner's actions with the operational plan C (Figure 2) to reveal the learner's "mental plan". As the tutor agent can not directly access the tutoring process, it communicates its reasoning results to the learner agent (Figure 4).

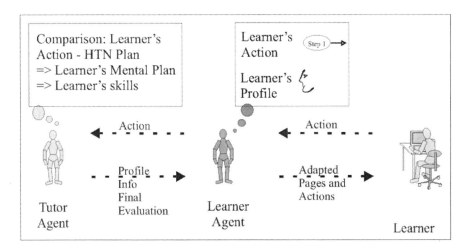

Fig. 4. The Agents Interaction

How does the tutor agent work? If the step the learner chooses does not correspond to the plan at level C, the tutor agent checks the plan library. If an alternative reduction schema for the level B task exists, that is consistent with the prior and current actions of the learner, the current plan is replaced. This is the typical procedure of plan recognition. If such a reduction schema does not exist, the tutor checks if re-planning is possible. If neither plan recognition nor re-planning works, the tutor agent can check whether the level B task can be replaced, i.e. it checks whether another suitable task reduction schema for the task at level A exists. If again plan recognition and re-planning fail, the tutor agent can offer help, e.g. by suggesting a "rollback"to the last correct step. If the learner does not want to use help, the tutor agent notes that the sub-plan at level C has failed and that the level B task will only be partially achieved. The tutor waits whether the learner succeeds in achieving the next task at level B.

In addition, each action is evaluated by either the tutor or the learner agent:

- The action is optimal, i.e. it is part of the optimal plan at level C.
- The action is unnecessary - it is not optimal but not wrong, i.e. it does not jeopardize the goal at level B. An alternative task reduction schema for the level B task exists, containing this action. However, in a time critical training case unnecessary actions will have cumulative negative effects. For example, if the patient shows signs for heart attack, and the learner selects several unnecessary anamneses (e.g. travel anamnesis, hobbies, job, family situation), the contents displayed are adapted. The patient will no longer answer the questions about his family situation, but his state of health deteriorates.
- The action is correct regarding the facts the learner has acquired so far. Even if the action itself is wrong in the case's overall context, it is logical coherent regarding the other actions chosen so far. Moreover, it can open an avenue to a series of actions, all of which are logical coherent and necessary. The later of course can only be deduced if alternative task reduction schemata exist.
- The action is entirely wrong, at least no suitable context is known to either of the two agents. The effects of such an action differ according to the action's importance. For example, in a medical training case a wrong anamnesis usually has fewer effects than ordering a wrong operation. Sometimes, as in the time critical training case, only cumulative effects might be critical.

Finally, the tutor agent evaluates the learner's performance based on the three levels of the plan hierarchy. For example, the learner has made some effort to check stomach flue and has seemingly continued with suspecting appendicitis. At some points in this process, he has failed to choose the correct examinations, at one point he has decided to check whether the patient is pregnant, which has finally lead him back to the optimal path, i.e. to the correct suspected diagnosis and the correct therapy. The tutor summarizes the following things: the learner had problems in taking all initial information into account, and he showed a lack of knowledge how to proceed in examinating appendicitis. Accordingly, the tutor will for example suggest to continue training with training cases that contain elaborated phases of knowledge extraction and some background information on appendicitis, it may also offer hints to additional information about appendicitis.

In the final evaluation the entire plan hierarchy is considered. Level C plans are used to reason about the learner's actions. The tasks at level B help to identify domain dependent lack of knowledge, for example how to proceed correctly in a clinical emergency scenario. The topmost level A allows assumptions about context independent learning skills, e.g. the learner is firm in re-producing fact but is uncertain how to apply his knowledge in a realistic scenario. Additional to the final feedback given to the learner, this information is stored in the learner's profile, and thus will influence the adaptation of the following training cases.

7 Conclusion and Ongoing Work

The system PLAIT (Planning Agents in Intelligent Tutoring) constitutes an extension of case- and web-based ITS, e.g. "Docs 'n Drugs". Two agents are embedded in the system, a learner agent, steering and controlling the tutoring process, and the tutor agent, reasoning about the learner's knowledge gain, his skills and behavior in the training case. Both provide help and explanation on demand in a context sensitive manner.

The main profit of case-based training can be seen in the cognitive authenticity of the problem to solve. The freedom to follow erroneous assumptions requires a feedback which takes the possible intentions of the learner into account. This is the responsibility of the tutor agent. The tutor agent employs an HTN planner to reason about the learner's assumed "mental plans", and finally to draw conclusions about the learner's skills. Unlike other approaches [19], [16], plans are not used to guide and steer the tutoring process but to reason about the learner's performance, which might affect the tutoring process indirectly.

Based on a medical training case and Bloom's "Taxonomy of Educational Objectives" [2] a first three layer plan hierarchy including learning skills, reduction schemata, and partially ordered action sequences has been developed. More are to follow to allow an evaluation of the presented approach.

References

1. Anderson, J.R., Corbett, A.T., Koedinger, K., Pelletier, W.: Cognitive Tutors: Lessons Learned. Journal of Learning Sciences, 4, (1995) 167–207
2. Bloom, B.S.: Taxonomy of Educational Objectives, Handbook I: Cognitive Domain. Davic McKay Company Inc, NY, 16th reprint (1971)
3. Bratman, M.E.: Intentions, Plans and Practical Reason. Harvard University Press,Cambridge (1987)
4. Carbonell, J.R.: AI in CAI: An Artificial Intelligence Approach to Computer Aided Instruction. IEEE Transactions on Man-Machine Systems,11, (1970) 190–202
5. Chi, M.T.H., Siler, S.A., Jeong, H., et.al.: Learning from Human Tutoring. Journal of Cognitive Science, 25 (2001) 471– 533
6. Clancey, W. J.: GUIDON. Journal of Computer Based Instruction, 10, 1/2, (1983) 1–15
7. "Docs 'n Drugs - The Virtual Hospital" - available at: http://www.docs-n-drugs.de

8. Gagné, R.M.: The Conditions of Learning and Theory of Instruction. Holt, Rinehart and Winston, NY, 4th edition (1985)

9. Illmann, T., Weber, M., Martens, A. and Seitz, A.: A Pattern-Oriented Design of a Web-Based and Case-Oriented Multimedia Training System in Medicine. 4th World Conference on Integrated Design and Process Technology, Dallas, US (2000)

10. Johnson, L., Shaw, E., Ganeshan, R.: Pedagogical Agents on the Web. Intelligent Tutoring Systems ITS98 (1998)

11. Freedman, R.: Using a Reactive Planner as the Basis for a Dialogue Agent. in Proceedings of the 13th Florida AI Research Symposium, Orlando, (2000)

12. Martens, A., Bernauer J., Illmann, T., and Seitz, A.: "Docs 'n Drugs - The Virtual Policlinic". to appear in Proc. of the American Medical Informatics Conference AMIA, Washington, US (2001)

13. Martens, A., Uhrmacher, A.M.: How to Execute a Tutoring Process. In: Proc. AI, Simulation, and Planning in High Autonomy Systems, Tucson, AZ (2000)

14. Merill,M.D.: The new Component Design Theory. Instructional Science, 16, (1987) 19–34

15. Merseth, K.: The early history of case-based instruction: Insights for teacher education today. Journal of Teacher Education, 42 (4), (1991) 243–249

16. Peachey, D., McCalla, G.: Using Planning Techniques in ITS. Journal of Man-Machine Studies (1987) 77–98

17. Pollack, M.: Plans As Complex Mental Attitudes. In: P.R. Cohen, J. Morgan, M.E. Pollack (eds.), Intentions in Communication, MIT Press (1990)

18. Teaching Models - available at: http://www.edtech.vt.edu/edtech/id/models/

19. Vassileva, J., Wasson, B.: Instructional Planning Approaches: from Tutoring towards Free Learning, EuroAIED (1996)

20. Yang, Q.: Intelligent Planning. Springer, Berlin, Heidelberg, NY (1997)

Architectural Patterns in Pedagogical Agents

Vladan Devedzic[1] and Andreas Harrer[2]

[1]Department of Information Systems, FON – School of Business Administration,
University of Belgrade, POB 52, 11000 Belgrade, Yugoslavia
`devedzic@galeb.etf.bg.ac.yu`
[2]Institut für Informatik, Technische Universität München, Orleansstr. 34, 81667 Munich,
Germany
`harrer@in.tum.de`

Abstract. One possible way to start from a firm and stable engineering backbone when developing the architecture of an Intelligent Tutoring System (ITS) is to use patterns for ITS architectures. Speaking architecturally, a pattern is a generalized solution of a typical problem within a typical context. Knowledge of patterns and using them definitely brings more engineering flavor to the field of ITS. It is also important to stress that it does not mean abandoning learning theories, teaching expertise, curriculum structuring, or instruction delivery as the cornerstones of any intelligent tutor. Using patterns is just taking more care about AIED systems themselves, especially about the way we develop them. This paper presents new results of our continuous efforts to analyze well-known ITS architectures from the patterns perspective.

1 Introduction

The big impact patterns had in the last years in the field of software engineering can be explained by the fact that patterns give general and reusable solutions for specific problems while developing software [2], [7]. Patterns emerge from successful solutions to recurring problems and with the knowledge of patterns it is not necessary to solve every software problem by oneself, but you can profit from the experience of other software engineers with similar problems. This is especially important because software systems tend to grow larger and larger and the need to keep the systems manageable and extendable is therefore getting bigger, too. Since intelligent tutoring systems are software systems with great complexity, it is advisable to transfer general knowledge and trends from the field of software design and architecture, such as that of software patterns, into the field of ITS. It would make possible to build ITS with reduced effort, or at least make them easier to maintain in the future.

This is not to say that one can talk of patterns in ITS only in the context of ITS architectures. On the contrary, there are many kinds of patterns in the way learners learn and in the way teachers teach, and all of them can be used as starting points when designing ITS. For example, patterns occur in speech acts of pedagogical interactions, in instructional design, in student modeling, and in teaching strategies [12], [14], [18]. However, in this paper we do not cover all possible subject areas of ITS where patterns do exist, just architectures. The nature of information we study is

S.A. Cerri, G. Gouardères, and F. Paraguaçu (Eds.): ITS 2002, LNCS 2363, pp. 81–90, 2002.
© Springer-Verlag Berlin Heidelberg 2002

the engineering one, hence we focus on *software* patterns in ITS design [7]. In the context of ITS architectures, we also don't cover all of them, but only selected ones. The focus is on pedagogical agents only; we do not cover other agents in ITS architectures in this paper. Note, however, that we have discovered a number of other patterns in ITS architectures (e.g., for student modeling and for collaborative learning). We could not present them here, though, due to space limitations.

There are several different kinds of general software patterns. The patterns described in this paper can be categorized as *analysis patterns* of agent-based ITS architectures. Analysis patterns are reusable models resulting from the process of software analysis applied to common business problems and application domains [5].

2   Pedagogical Agents and Software Patterns

Over the last several years there has been significant interest in the ITS research community for applying intelligent agents in design and deployment of ITS. The focus has been on *pedagogical agents*, i.e. autonomous agents that support human learning by interacting with students in the context of interactive learning environments [13]. Pedagogical agents monitor the dynamic state of the learning environment, watching for learning opportunities as they arise. They can support both collaborative and individualized learning, because multiple students and agents can interact in a shared environment. Pedagogical agents can provide numerous instructional interactions with students, promote student motivation and engagement, and effectively support students' cognitive processes. Some of them are represented by animated characters that give the learner an impression of being lifelike and believable, producing behavior that seems natural and appropriate for the role of a virtual instructor or guide. In distributed learning environments, multiple pedagogical agents can collaborate in different ways to help students in various learning activities.

We have analyzed a number of pedagogical agents described in the ITS literature, as well as some of them whose demos are available on the Web. The idea has been to see to what extent people designing pedagogical agents and multiagent systems use patterns (implicitly) in their design. The results shown here are related to the design of individual agents only. Note, however, that patterns exist also in different designs of multiagent educational systems.

We have found that numerous designers of pedagogical agents essentially follow the pattern shown in Figure 1, which we call *General Pedagogical Agent pattern*, or *GPA pattern*. The name comes from the fact that the pattern has been abstracted out of a number of agents playing different roles (such as learners, teachers, companions, and assistants) in different educational settings, yet having much in common. Boxes and data/knowledge flows represented by solid lines have been identified (under various names) in all the agents we have analyzed. Those represented by dashed lines have been found in a number of agents, but not in all of them.

The first mandatory participant in the GPA pattern is *Knowledge Base* that can include domain knowledge, pedagogical (instructional, tutoring) knowledge and/or strategies, and student model. Some of the examples include the Learning Tutor agent ([8], p. 446), Disciple agents [17], and pedagogical actors [6]. Only in the design of Disciple agents the *Knowledge Base Manager* is shown explicitly, although textual descriptions of most of other pedagogical agents also indicate its presence.

Knowledge Base Manager helps the other participants use and update all kinds of knowledge stored in *Knowledge Base*.

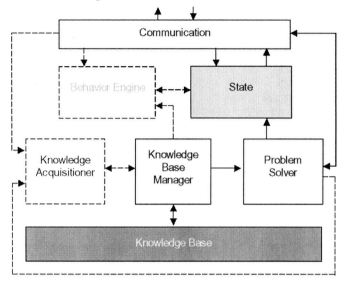

Fig. 1. The GPA pattern

Each pedagogical agent also has some kind of *Problem Solver* (i.e. *Logic*, or *Reasoning Engine*) that can include inferencing, case-based reasoning, student model evaluation, and other tasks normally associated with learning and teaching activities. For example, Learning Tutor agent has both a tutoring engine and an inference engine. The problem solver of pedagogical actors is essentially a control module and a decision maker that decides on whether the actor should take an action, how to do it, on what stimulus it should react, and the like [6]. Teachable Agent developed by Brophy et al. has explanation and simulation generators in the problem solving component ([14], p. 23).

The *Communication (Interface)* participant is responsible for perceiving the dynamic learning environment and acting upon it. Typically, perceptions include recognizing situations in which the pedagogical agent can intervene, such as specific student's actions, co-learner's progress, and availability of desired information. Examples of typical actions are "display a message", "show a hint", and "update progress indicator".

State is a general abstraction for many different kinds of states a pedagogical agent can be made "aware of", as well as both volatile and persistent factors that influence the states. It can refer to the agent's expression, expressiveness, emotions, and personality, as in the Classroom Agent Model ([8], p. 446). It can also represent the agent's different mental states and verbal behavior, as in the case of Vincent, the pedagogical agent for on-the-job training ([8], p. 588). Furthermore, *State* can contain current values of parameters of the agent's relationships with other agents - the relationships that the agent is able to create, reason about, and destroy, all according to its goals. This is the case of Social Autonomous Agents ([8], p. 567). Teachable Agent's state includes its disposition, or learning attitude, which may for example determine whether the agent will learn by picking a quick, reasonable solution, or will rather spend more time in order to come to a precise solution ([14], p. 24).

Occasional participants in the GPA pattern include *Knowledge Acquisitioner* and *Behavior Engine*. *Knowledge Acquisitioner* reflects the fact that apart from reactive, reasoning, and decision-making capabilities, cognitive pedagogical agents also possess a learning capability that makes possible for the agent to update and modify its knowledge over time, using some machine learning technique(s). For example, the Learning Tutor and Disciple agents include a machine learning and knowledge acquisition component explicitly ([8], p. 446, [17]). The cognitive layer of pedagogical actors provides them with self-improvement capabilities based on the analysis of the student's performance in different learning situations and machine learning techniques [6]. Essentially, it categorizes different learners using conceptual clustering techniques and builds a case base of situations. Self-improvement is done by using case-based reasoning to adapt the situation to a new case. In a similar way, cognitive agents can provide adaptivity and flexibility in learning in terms of autonomously establishing learning objectives, and creating, locating, tracking, and reviewing learning materials, such as diagnostic instruments, scenarios, learning modules, assessment instruments, mastery tests, etc. ([14], p.59).

If present in the design of a pedagogical agent, *Behavior Engine* (*Expression Engine*) is responsible for analysis of the agent's current internal state and possible modifications of (parts of) that state. In general, *Behavior Engine* depends on the current perception of the agent's environment supplied by the *Communication* module, the current *State*, and possibly on some heuristics specified in the *Knowledge Base*. Its output are changes in the current *State* that are then converted into appropriate actions by the action part of the agent's *Communication* module. Frequently used instances of *Behavior Engine* include Emotion generator and Behavior generator such as those included in the Classroom Agent Model ([8], p. 446), Emotive Behavior Sequencing Engine of lifelike pedagogical agents [13], physical behavior generator (i.e., layout handler, or the "Body") and dialog handler such as those of Vincent ([8], p. 588), and social behavior generator in pedagogical agents participating in multiagent systems ([8], p. 567). This last instance of *Behavior Engine* is always used for pedagogical agents participating in collaborative learning and collective decision-making processes.

As an illustration of how GPA is used in practical agent design, consider the Classroom Agent Model, shown in 2. Classroom Agents represent students in a classroom, each one having its own personalities and emotions (*Personality* and *Emotion* are, in fact, instances of *State*). *Learning* is the word that the Classroom Agents Model authors use to denote all kinds of problem solving activities associated with learning situations (an instance of *Problem Solver*). In these agents, *Behavior Engine* is split in two distinct parts, one to generate the agent's emotions (*Emotion Generator*), and another one (*Behavior Generator*) to formulate the agent's learning actions and pass them to the effector (the *Action* part of the *Communication* module). The idea is that for a learning agent perceiving an event that motivates it (e.g., an easy exercise) positive emotions will be generated and will promote its learning (and vice versa), which will certainly be reflected in *Behavior Generator* when formulating the agent's next actions.

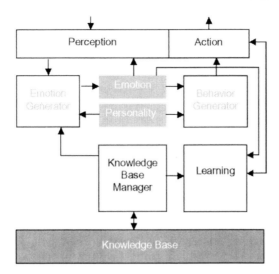

Fig. 2. An example of using the GPA pattern in the Classroom Agent Model (after [8], p. 488)

We have also identified several variants of the GPA pattern. For example, the pedagogical agent of the Adele system downloads its case task plan and an initial state, as well as student model, from the server, and only the reasoning engine and animated persona are on the client side [13]. Another variant can be seen in Vincent, where problem solving is done in the agent's Mind component ([8], p. 588). Vincent's Mind is a combination of a knowledge handler and a dialog handler - a kind of a mixture of functionalities of *Problem Solver* and *Behavior Engine*.

One last note about GPA: further abstraction of GPA-based agents can lead to the conclusion that they are essentially instances of *reflex agents with states*, *goal-based agents*, and *knowledge-based agents*, as higher-level abstractions of all intelligent agents [15]. Such a conclusion would be true - *State* corresponds to the agent's internal state in all these higher-level abstractions, *Problem Solver*, *Knowledge Acquisitioner*, and *Behavior Engine* reflect the agent's general ability to make inferences, decisions, and updates of its knowledge. However, going that far would take us completely out of the scope of ITS to much more general AI problems. That would, in turn, mean loosing the sense of context where the pattern applies - remember, a pattern is a generalized solution of a typical problem within a typical context.

3   Co-learner Pattern

Introducing an artificial learner (a program) acting as a peer in an ITS has proven to have a number of positive effects on the learner. It ensures the availability of a collaborator and encourages the student to learn collaboratively, to reflect on and articulate his past actions, and to discuss his future intentions and their consequences [9]. Artificial learners can take different roles, such as:

- *learning companion* [3], which learns to perform the same learning task as the student, at about the same level, and can exchange ideas with the student when presented the same learning material;
- *troublemaker* [6], which tries to disturb the student by proposing solutions that are at times correct, but are wrong at other times, thus challenging the student's self-confidence in learning;
- several *reciprocal tutoring* roles, as described in [4];
- roles that aim to stimulate collaboration and discussion within learning communities, such as *observer* ([1], p. 18), *diagnostician* or *mediator* [10].

In all these cases we can talk about a distinct learning paradigm that often goes under different names – *learning companion systems, co-learner systems,* and *simulated students*. We prefer the term co-learner.

It is important to note that *architecturally*, all ITS involving a co-learner have much in common regardless of the role the co-learner takes. In fact, we can talk about the *Co-Learner pattern*, represented in Figure 3. The classic 3-agents triad - *Tutor-Student-Co-Learner* - is shown in Figure 3a with more details than the literature on co-learners usually offers, due to the fact that all pattern diagrams have to show both the participants and their communication paths clearly. Hence that part of the figure stresses the "who communicates with whom" and "what knowledge and data are involved" issues. Moreover, since this is an architectural view, it is necessary to show details more-or-less irrelevant for instructional aspects of co-learner systems. For example, the *System* component acts as a supervisor and performs all the control and scheduling of activities of the three major agents. It is shown grayed, though, since it does not contribute essentially to the major knowledge and information flows.

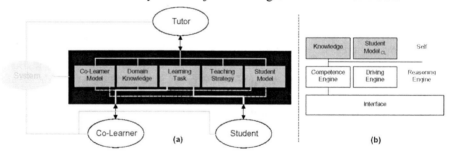

Fig. 3. Co-Learner pattern a) communication paths b) inside the Co-Learner

Furthermore, Figure 3a clearly indicates what kinds of knowledge and data each agent needs. Put this way, it turns out that the Co-Learner pattern belongs, in fact, to *blackboard architectures* [2]. All knowledge and data are on the blackboard, but usually only the *Tutor* agent accesses all of them. *Student* and *Co-Learner* normally have access only to the *Learning Task* part of the blackboard (thick data-flow lines). Variants are discussed in later paragraph (dashed data-flow lines).

If *T*, *S*, and *C* denote the *Tutor*, *Student*, and *Co-Learner* agents, then their communication in the Co-Learner pattern, Figure 3a, is as follows:

- T → S – present learning task and materials, explain the format of learning activities, generate problems, provide guidance, advice and hints, generate examples, evaluate solutions, generate final justifications of the solution and/or insightful retrospective comments, negotiate with the student [Chan & Baskin, 1988]. Most of this communication goes through the *Learning Task* part of the blackboard, while all the necessary domain knowledge is in the *Domain Knowledge* part. *Tutor* can use different *Teaching Strategies*, and during the course of the learning task it develops the *Student Model*.

- S → T – ask for clarifications & help, present solutions, request directions and references for future learning. Most of this communication goes through the *Learning Task* part of the blackboard.

- T → C – much like T → S for the learning companion role of the *Co-Learner* agent, but can vary a lot for other roles. For example, if *Co-Learner* is a troublemaker, it doesn't get much instruction or direction from the *Tutor*. On the contrary, troublemaker usually has access to *Domain Knowledge* as much as *Tutor*. Troublemaker has the level of competence superior to that of the student, in order to engage him. It is only disguised as a co-learner, while its role is pedagogically different. However, if *Co-Learner* is a true learning companion, it performs the learning task in much the same way as the student [3], and during the course of the learning task *Tutor* develops the *Co-Learner Model*.

- C → T – usually a highly restricted version of S → T, since the effects of co-learner's learning are of much less importance than those of student's learning. However, in some variants of reciprocal tutoring this communication can be much more important and much more elaborated [4].

- S → C – observe (watch) the co-learner working on the learning task individually, ask for assistance, give suggestions when asked, decide on problem-solving strategy, explain strategy, clarify problem, compare solutions, discover mistakes, correct mistakes [3], [9], [14] (p. 23). Also, in different variants of reciprocal tutoring, much of T → S and S → T [4]. An important consequence for system designers follows from that fact - all three major agents can be derived from the same, more general pedagogical agent, and should have similar functions (minor differences can be easily implemented using polymorphism).

- C → S – much like S → C for learning companions, but also much like T → C for other roles. For an excellent survey of co-learners' roles and activities in communication with human learners, see [9].

Figure 3b shows a fairly generalized version of the Co-Learner agent itself. Functionally, it is much like GCM (General Companion Modeling) architecture of Chou et al. ([14], p. 280). However, it stresses important details of Co-Learner's internal structure in terms of an analysis pattern. Note that, in general, Co-Learner can be a "mini-ITS". Depending on the role, it can have more or less of its own *Knowledge*, both domain and pedagogical. If Co-Learner has little knowledge, it is a novice learner; if its knowledge is comparable to *Tutor*'s, it is an expert. That knowledge can grow over time for teachable agents ([14], p. 23), and in all reciprocal-tutoring cases when Co-Learner switches the teaching and learning roles with another agent in the system [18]. For troublemakers, that knowledge can include details of the learning by disturbing strategy (although it is possible, in principle, to access it on the blackboard as well). Co-Learner constructs and maintains its own model of the human learner's knowledge and progress, *Student Model $_{CL}$*, which is generally different from the *Student Model* built by *Tutor*. Also, the agent's own internal state (attribute values, learning status, the level of independence, motivation, personality characteristics, the corresponding animated character (if any)) is stored in *Self*. Multiple co-learner systems can have Co-Learner agents with different *Self* characteristics.

Figure 3b is also an instance of the GPA pattern, Figure 1. Co-Learner's *Knowledge* corresponds to *Knowledge Base* in GPA, while *Student Model$_{CL}$* and *Self* are instances of GPA's *State*. Likewise, Co-Learner has a *Reasoning Engine* (an instance of *Problem Solver*), capable of simulating various activities in learning and teaching tasks, depending on the role Co-Learner plays (see C → S and C → T communication above). In fact, *Reasoning Engine* fully corresponds to the *Learning task simulation module* of GCM architecture, described in [14] (p. 23). *Driving Engine* (*Behavior Engine* of GPA pattern and *Behavior module* of GCM architecture) is responsible of generating specific behavior that drives the agent in playing a specific co-learning role (a learning companion, a peer tutor, and the like). *Competence Engine* (*Knowledge Acquisitioner* in GPA) is Co-Learner's mechanism to increase its competence by acquiring new knowledge, i.e. to learn and modify contents of its knowledge bases accordingly. For example, learning companions can employ machine-learning techniques or simulated knowledge acquisition (controlled externally, by the *System*, in order to adapt the companion's competence to the student's current knowledge level) [Chan and Baskin, 1998].

In practice, the Co-Learner pattern has many variants. Note, for example, that *Student* and *Co-Learner* can optionally access some parts of the blackboard other than *Learning Task* (the dashed lines in Figure 3a). Troublemakers have access to *Domain Knowledge* [6], and some authors have studied the benefits of letting the student access the *Student model* and the *Co-Learner Model* as well (e.g., [1], p. 130; [14], p. 271). Also, if Co-Learner is a troublemaker then the student explains his decisions to the troublemaker in a process controlled by the *Tutor* agent directly, and not by the *System* [1] (p. 123). *Tutor* can be even omitted from the system, as in teachable agents [14] (p. 23), in the similar "learning by teaching the learning companion" strategy [14] (p. 289), and in some other kinds of reciprocal tutoring [4]. Even group learning can be represented by the Co-Learner pattern (at least to an extent), by letting the system have multiple learning companions with different competences and different personas (peer group learning) [11]. Alternatively, the system can have multiple *Tutors* with different personas and the student can learn from them selectively, and *Co-Learner* can be the personal agent of another human learner on the network, as in distributed learning [Chan & Baskin, 1988].

4   Discussion

Patterns never exist in isolation - all knowledge and application domains are usually characterized by a number of patterns. When several related patterns in a given domain are discovered, named, described, and woven together in a collection, they form a pattern language for that domain [16]. The coverage of a domain by a corresponding pattern language can vary; yet each pattern language reflects a number of important issues in the domain (domain knowledge). Pattern languages are not formal languages, hence there are no language primitives, strict syntax, and things like that in such languages, just pattern names. The names provide specialists with vocabularies for talking about specific problems.

GPA and Co-Learner, along with other patterns we have discovered but didn't present in this paper, represent the initial collection of patterns in a pattern language that we are developing for ITS architectures. The patterns in that language condense parts of ITS-architectural design knowledge and sound practices of experienced designers and make it explicit and available to others.

There has been no actual application and practical evaluation of the language by now, because any pattern language has to be complete enough in order to become a useful design tool. Our language evolves and continues to accumulate new patterns, as they get discovered over time. But, pattern discovery takes time, hence all pattern languages grow slowly before they mature. We are perfectly aware of the fact that GPA and Co-Learner, presented the way we did it in the above sections, show just some parts and fragments of the language and its potential utility. However, once the number of patterns in the language grows sufficiently, developers of future ITS will have a good starting point in designing solutions to new problems without "reinventing the wheel".

5 Conclusions

Discovering patterns in ITS-related issues like ITS architectures is not a kind of search for *new* modeling and design solutions. It is more like *compiling* what we already know. Patterns enable us to see what kind of solutions ITS/AIED researchers and developers *typically* apply when faced with common problems. In the future, we expect discovery of many useful patterns other than those that we have discovered so far. The efforts in describing them in an appropriate way will follow, finally resulting in accumulation of the patterns in catalogues and repositories over time. This way the efforts will actually unveil common structures of frequently arising problems and will help describe and represent the knowledge of their contexts, solutions, driving forces and trade-offs in the form of explicit statements. Once we have explicitly represented such knowledge and experience, we can get a valuable feedback - we can use the patterns intentionally and systematically in other systems and applications, i.e. for further developments. In that sense, AIED/ITS patterns can be understood as many small tools for modeling and developing ITS, and AIED/ITS pattern languages, pattern catalogues, and repositories as the corresponding toolkits.

Many open issues about ITS/AIED patterns still remain and need to be further investigated. For example, do cognitive processes really work the way the discovered patterns (especially for GPA-agents) suggest? If so, to what extent? What kinds of interaction patterns exist among pedagogical agents in multiagent educational systems? Do they exist in the same way among human tutors, learners, peers, and assistants in different educational settings? In other words, further research on "cognitive justification" of patterns is necessary. However, we must not forget the fact that ITS are a kind of *software systems*, hence well-established practices of software analysis and design *do* matter.

References

1. Boulay, B. du, Mizoguchi, R. (eds.): Artificial Intelligence in Education. IOS Press, Amsterdam / OHM Ohmsha, Tokyo (1997)
2. Buschmann, F., Meunier, R., Rohnert, H., Sommerlad, P., Stal, M.,: A System of Patterns. John Wiley & Sons, Chichester (1996)
3. Chan, T.-W., Baskin, A.B.: Studying with the Prince – The Computer as a Learning Companion. Proc. First Int. Conf. ITS. Montreal, Canada (1988) 194-200
4. Chan, T.-W., Chou, C.-Y.: Exploring the Design of Computer Supports for Reciprocal Tutoring. Int. J. AIED 8 (1997) 1-29
5. Fowler, M.: Analysis Patterns: Reusable Object Models. Addison-Wesley, Reading, MA (1997)
6. Frasson, C., Mengelle, T., Aimeur, E.: Using Pedagogical Agents in a Multi-Strategic Intelligent Tutoring System. Proc. AIED'97 WS Pedag. Agents. Kobe, Japan (1997) 40-47
7. Gamma, E., Helm, R., Johnson, R., Vlissides, J.: Design Patterns: Elements of Reusable Object-Oriented Software. Addison-Wesley, Reading, MA (1995)
8. Goettl, B.R., Halff, H.M., Redfield, C.L., Shute, V.J.(eds.): Proc. Fourth Int. Conf. ITS. Lecture Notes in Computer Science, 1452. Springer-Verlag, Berlin Heidelberg New York (1998)
9. Goodman, B., Soller, A., Linton, F., Gaimari, R.: Encouraging Student Reflection and Articulation using a Learning Companion. Int. J. AIED 9 (1998) 237-255
10. Harrer, A.: Unterstützung von Lerngemeinschaften in verteilten intelligenten Lehrsystemen. Ph.D. Thesis, Technische Universität München, Institut für Informatik (2000), in German
11. Hietala, P., Niemirepo, T.: The Competence of Learning Companion Agents. Int. J. AIED 9 (1998) 178-192
12. Inaba, A., Ohkubo, R., Ikeda, M., Mizoguchi, R., Toyoda, J.: An Instructional Design Support Environment for CSCL - Fundamental Concepts and Design Patterns. In: Moore, J.D., Redfield, C.L., Johnson, W.L. (eds.), Artificial Intelligence in Education – AI-ED in the Wired and Wireless Future. IOS Press, Amsterdam (2001) 130-141
13. Johnson, W.L., Rickel, J., Lester, J.C.: Animated Pedagogical Agents: Face-to-Face Interaction in Interactive Learning Environments. Int. J. AIED 11 (2000) 47-78
14. Lajoie, S.P., Vivet, M. (eds.): Artificial Intelligece in Education. IOS Press, Amsterdam / OHM Ohmsha, Tokyo (1999)
15. Russell, S., Norvig, P.: AI – A Modern Approach. Prentice-Hall, Englewood Cliffs, NJ (1995)
16. Schmidt, D., Fayad, M., Johnson, R.E.: Software Patterns. Comm. ACM 39 (1996) 37-39
17. Tecuci, G., Keeling, H.: Developing Intelligent Educational Agents with Disciple. Int J. AIED 10 (1999) 221-237
18. Van Lehn, K., Ohlsson, S., Nason, R.: Applications of Simulated Students: An Exploration. J. AIED 5 (1994) 135-175

DÓRIS – Pedagogical Agent in Intelligent Tutoring Systems

Cássia Trojahn dos Santos[1], Rejane Frozza[2], Alessandra Dhamer[2],
and Luciano Paschoal Gaspary[2]

[1] Universidade de Santa Cruz do Sul, Av. Independência 2293, Santa Cruz do
Sul, RS – Brazil
cassia-ts@uol.com.br
[2] Universidade de Santa Cruz do Sul, Av. Independência 2293, Santa Cruz do
Sul, RS – Brazil
{frozza, adahmer, paschoal}@dinf.unisc.br

Abstract. Intelligent Tutoring Systems are characterised for incorporating
Artificial Intelligence techniques into their design and development, acting as
assistants in the teaching-learning process. Currently, Intelligent Agents
concepts have been applied to these systems as a way to improve them. DÓRIS
is a pedagogical follow-up agent for Intelligent Tutoring Systems developed to
perform tasks such as the following: follow students' interaction with the
intelligent tutor system, collect the information required for the modelling of
students' profile used to customise the environment assist and guide students
during the construction of their learning. This paper reports the characteristics
and functionality of this agent.

1 Introduction

There is a growing interest in the development of computer systems in the area of
education which has undergone changes with the emergence of alternative forms of
teaching, such as distance learning through the Internet and the use of Intelligent
Tutoring Systems (ITSs).

ITSs are a class of Artificial Intelligence (AI) systems that act as assistants in the
teaching-learning process. According to [1], the use of AI techniques in the design
and development of computerised teaching-learning environments has become the
object of greater investigation by researchers of Computer applied to Education due to
its potentialities.

These are systems that change their knowledge bases by interacting with students,
perceive students' interventions and can learn and adapt teaching strategies according
to students' performance. They are characterised mainly for building a Cognitive
Model of Students through the interaction formulation and proof of hypotheses about
students' knowledge. They have the ability of adapting teaching-learning strategies to
students and to the current situation [2].

S.A. Cerri, G. Gouardères, and F. Paraguaçu (Eds.): ITS 2002, LNCS 2363, pp. 91–104, 2002.

ITSs are designed to replicate in the computer a behaviour similar to that of a teacher. However, one of the greatest concerns of the researchers in this field is the interaction of the ITS with students, considering that a traditional ITS is based on a rigid interaction style, meaning that the system always has the control over it.

One of the ways to lessen this problem is the use of distributed artificial intelligence techniques which bring their contribution with the use of intelligent agents. The approach of agents in ITSs enables more natural interactions that are closer among students and the tutor system, where the initiative of the interaction is usually shared between the system and students. Such interactions are a precise contrast with the static documents that are usually found in materials of Internet-based courses.

In the context of educational activity, these intelligent agents are called pedagogical. According to [3], pedagogical agents are entities whose fundamental purpose is the communication with students in order to effectively perform the tutor role as part of the system's pedagogical mission.

Pedagogical agents act as monitors who observe the actions taken by students and who assist them during their learning process. Additionally, they exchange information with students in order to adapt the presentation with the content according to the student's ideal model, supervising the learning environment.

With the purpose of making research in the field of distance learning and teaching-learning environments the modelling and development of a pedagogical follow-up agent in an intelligent tutor system is presented in order to monitor and enrich students' learning in a distance learning program.

This paper is organised as follows: section 2 deals with the architecture of the environment, where the pedagogical agent is embedded. The aspects related to pedagogical agents are presented in section 3. The characteristics, architecture and functionality of the DÓRIS Agent are discussed in section 4. Finally, conclusions are presented.

2   Architecture of the Operation Environment of the Pedagogical Agent

The pedagogical agent is embedded in a distance learning environment that uses an ITS for the learning of a specific domain. Such environment is part of an institutional research project on distance learning at UNISC (Santa Cruz do Sul University). This project started in 1998, being designed to investigate mechanisms, tools and methods that could be used to provide a differentiated Web-based education, taking advantage of the web potentialities [4, 5, 6 and 7]. This project involved:
- the definition of knowledge representation in any given domain designed to manage the teaching material and the construction of a content editor;

- the development of a tool for the dynamic construction of pages designed to customise the presentation of the teaching material according to students' profiles;

- the application of the case-based reasoning module to help obtain the characteristics for students' profile diagnoses;

- the study of protocols for communication and agent transfer between the serving station and the customer's machine;

- the construction of a pedagogical follow-up agent.

The environment architecture is illustrated in Fig. 1.

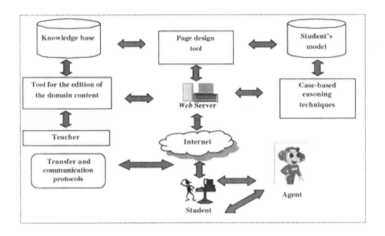

Fig. 1. DÓRIS agent's environment architecture

Students interact with the ITS through a Web interface. The pedagogical agent transfer and communication protocols operate in this interaction. The agent extracts information related to students' performance and action which is used by the case-based reasoning module. Every time students connect with the system the agent is sent to a student's machine to later return to the server with the collected information. Communication protocols are in charge of this task.

The teacher can use a tool to edit the content of the domain which is stored in the knowledge base of the ITS under a generic representation form, enabling the dynamic construction of the pages for the presentation of the teaching material based upon the student's profile, stored in a model base.

This paper discusses the characteristics and functionality of the pedagogical agent.

3 Pedagogical Agents

The agents are called pedagogical when they are embedded in an environment that makes up a teaching-learning system. This environment can be made up of a society of agents. The term pedagogical agent [8] was created because many systems developed for educational purposes adopt the paradigm of agents.

According to [9], incorporating agents into an educational software means to enhance the desirable pedagogical aspects in the environment. They provide advantages over conventional intelligent teaching environments because they enable more natural interactions that are closer between student and system.

Pedagogical agents have some essential properties of intelligent agents, such as autonomy, social capacity (interactions and communication) and adaptability to the environment. In addition to these properties, pedagogical agents are able to learn and in most cases they can be represented by a character. They are essentially cognitive[1]. However, they can have characteristics of reactive agents[2], reacting to changes in the environment where they are embedded.

These agents have a set of rules that determine the teaching methods and strategies to be used. The goal is to help students in the learning process.

They are responsible for following students' interaction with the educational system and, thus, they are able to guide students' actions so that students can learn efficiently.

The main goal of these agents is to help students learn effectively, enhancing quality from the pedagogical point of view for the environment where they are embedded. In order to do so, these agents can:

- guide students during their interaction with the system;
- monitor students' activities, providing assistant in critical situations;
- record information necessary to model students' profiles;
- select proper teaching strategies based on students' profiles;
- motivate students to learn;
- provide interactivity to the system, giving students the idea they have a tutor friend who will help them.

Next, the characteristics, behaviours and architecture of the *DÓRIS* pedagogical agent, developed and embedded in an ITS for distance learning are described. Several studies on pedagogical agents have been performed, including [10, 11, 12 and 13] to build *DÓRIS* Agent.

---

[1] Agents with knowledge, action planning and decision making capacity.
[2] Agents with behaviours such as response to stimuli from the environment.

4 DÓRIS – Pedagogical Agent

The main goal of pedagogical agents is to contribute to students' effective learning, enhancing quality, from the pedagogical point of view, for the environment where they are embedded.

This section describes the characteristics, behaviours and architecture of the Pedagogical Agent DÓRIS, whose main functions are the following:

- extract students' learning characteristics and make this information available to the system to be used for a latter modelling of students' profiles;

- guide and monitor students during their interaction with the teaching-learning environment, helping them in case of doubt and motivating them to learn.

4.1 Characteristics of the Pedagogical Agent DÓRIS

The pedagogical agent was designed to operate in an ITS with generic domain. Thus, the agent does not have specific knowledge on the domain that will be approached.

The DÓRIS agent has the following characteristics, coming from intelligent agents:

- *perception of the environment where it is embedded*: the agent extracts information from the students' learning environment which will be used to customise this environment;

- *autonomy*: the agent acts without human interference, being automatically evoked whenever students start the interaction with the system;

- *ability to operate in the environment*: the agent monitors and follows students in their learning process. This generates actions such as: change in attitudes by the agent and establishment of interaction between agents and students;

- *social ability*: the agent interacts with students in order to perform its follow-up and monitoring task;

- *adaptability*: the agent adapts to changes in the environment caused by the application of different teaching strategies;

- *mobility*: the agent can be taken to the students' machine when they download a given class module, returning to the central server in a predefined time;

- *it has knowledge*: the agent keeps an internal knowledge base where information extracted from students' interaction with the environment is stored;

- *representation through characters.*

4.2 Architecture of the Pedagogical Agent DÓRIS

Considering the pedagogical agent's characteristics, we can see that its architecture, illustrated in Fig. 2, reflects the following modules: *perceptive, cognitive* and *reactive*. Furthermore, the agent's architecture involves an internal knowledge base.

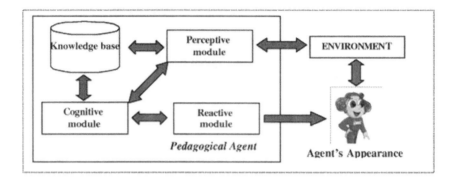

Fig. 2. Architecture of the pedagogical agent DÓRIS

Next is a description of each module of the agent's architecture.

4.2.1 Perceptive Module

The perceptive module is responsible for the extraction and storage of information related to students' interactions with the system. This module is used to monitor students' actions. This module checks:

- starting and finishing time of the interaction between students and the system; pages visited by students and how long they stayed in each of these pages;

- difficulties students had in the class; students' opinions about the elements used to prepare the class (whether they liked it or not);

- students' preferences in relation to the set of elements to be used in future classes;
- questions students had during the class.

4.2.2 Cognitive Module

The cognitive module is responsible for making inferences on the knowledge base, determining which actions should be taken by the agent based upon its perceptions. In this module the messages to be issued by the agent in its interaction with students are chosen and the audio-visual resources to be used are determined according to the agent's current emotional status.

The cognitive module comes into play in the following situations:

- choice of messages to be sent to students at intervals, such as tips, reminders and messages;

- choice of questions to check whether students are having difficulties or not;

- choice of questions to check whether they like the interaction and the elements used in the class or not;

- choice of agent's answers to students' questions;

- choice of messages to be sent to students when they no longer visit a page;

- choice of messages to be sent to students when the agent is activated or deactivated, such as welcome or farewell messages;

- choice of animation representing the agent to be shown with the corresponding messages. For example, if students say they are having difficulties, an animation that has to do with the answer should be chosen. In this case, an animation that conveys sadness.

4.2.3 Reactive Module

The reactive module is responsible for executing the actions indicated by the cognitive module. Additionally, it establishes the animated interface with students. It is through this module that agent's messages and animations are effectively presented to students.

4.2.4 Knowledge Base

The agent's internal knowledge base is made up of the following elements:

- *audio-visual resources base*: made up of the elements used to form the agent's appearance, such as images for the composition of its physical appearance. It is in this base that the animations activated according to the agent's emotional status are stored, together with the agent's audio resources;

- *class base*: contains information related to classes;

- *visited pages base*: contains information on pages checked by students;

- *content base*: contains information on class contents;

- *students' answers base*: contains answers to questions asked by students;

- *message base*: contains questions, tips and reminders used by the agent in its interaction with students;

- *students'questions base*: contains questions students had during the class. Answers to questions are edited by the teacher by an answer editor;

- *students' preferences base*: contains information on students' preferences in relation to the elements that can be used in the structure of a class, such as text, image, hypertext, exercise, animation, video or graphics.

4.3 Behaviours of the Pedagogical Agent

The agent DÓRIS is represented by a character with two types of behaviour: cognitive and reactive behaviour.

The cognitive behaviour is responsible for encouraging students to follow the class, sending them stimulus messages (tips, reminders, among others); selecting messages to be sent to students; and perceiving the interaction environment, storing information on students' actions in its internal knowledge base.

The reactive behaviour is responsible for the tasks that manipulate the agent's appearance, selecting an attitude according to the current situation.

The agent's representative character has different cartoons to convey the following emotional statuses: sadness, happiness and fellowship. Emotional statuses are defined according to the current status of the environment, being presented to students through animations, together with audio resources. Table 1 shows emotional statuses of the agent DÓRIS and the situations where they are presented to students.

Table 1. Emotional statuses of agent DÓRIS

Status	Situation
Sadness	Status achieved when students are having difficulties or do no like the interaction. This is perceived from the answers to questions asked at intervals by the agent.
Happiness	Status achieved when students have no difficulties and like the interaction. This is perceived from the answers to questions asked at intervals by the agent.
Fellowship	Agent's standard status shown during the agent's interaction with the environment.

Table 2 shows some of the cartoons used to build the animations corresponding to the agent's emotional status.

Table 2. Animations showing the emotional status of agent DÓRIS

Emotional statuses and cartoons		
Sadness	Happiness	Fellowship

As commented in section 3, the agent Doris' moldness was made based on the study of the others pedagogical agents. Soon, compare the agents that we have studied, with agent DÓRIS:

- *Vincent*[10]: responsible agent for deciding the educational action; autonomous, interactive, lively, perceptive, represented by sadness condition, happiness, friendship and impatience;

- Steve[15]: able to insert educational capacity in the system; autonomous, interactive, lively, perceptible; able to do head movements and gesture; communication possibility through the natural language;

- LANCA[12]: able to adapt strategies and teaching methods and represents teaching strategies through the characters; autonomous, perceptive, interactive and mobile;

- Multiple strategies[16]: able to adapt strategies and teaching methods and represents teaching strategies through the characters; autonomous, mobile, interactive and perceptible;

- Giant[13] responsible to interfere in the students' proposition; represents lively audiovisual attitudes, autonomous, mobile, interactive, lively, adaptable, represented by states of activities, lazyness, caution and curiosity;

- Dóris: able to extract students' learning characteristics, leading them and driving them during their interaction with the system; autonomous, perceptible, interactive, represented by a character ; represented by friendship, sadness and happiness condition.

4.4 Prototype of the Agent DÓRIS

For the construction of the prototype of the agent DÓRIS the agent's internal knowledge base was transferred to a set of tables in a physical database where every element that makes up the knowledge base corresponds to a table in the physical base, except for the audio-visual resources base which is inherent in the application.

Cartoons were used for the construction of the agent's animated representative character, manipulated in *Microsoft Agent Character Editor* [14]. The animations constructed through the *Microsoft Agent Character Editor* can be manipulated in programming environments that support *ActiveX* controls from the addition of the *Microsoft Agent* component [14]. An application was designed for the manipulation of agent DÓRIS' animations using the programming tool *Borland Delphi 4.0* and the *Microsoft Agent 2.0* component. The whole operation of agent DÓRIS is controlled by this application.

Then, it talks about a part of simulation of the applicative, as a way to give a general idea of its functioning, through the action of the agent DÓRIS.

When a student begins the navigation around a class, the communication module and the transfer does the agent inicialization. As soon as inicialized, the agent is presented in the screen, and a welcome message is sent to the student, as the example that can be checked in Fig. 3. The characteristic point at the representation through the characters as commented in section 4.1.

It's important to say that the message is customized through the addition of corresponding class title.

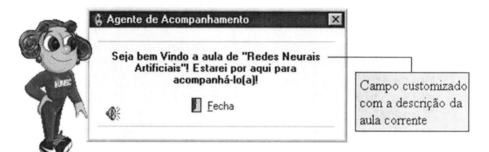

Fig. 3. Agent DÓRIS and welcome messages

Sometimes, tips and messages are sent. The Fig. 4 is an example.

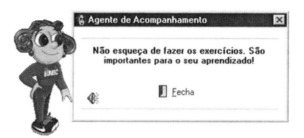

Fig. 4. Agent DÓRIS and message the make a remind.

Besides this, there are messages that ask the student about some difficulties that they have. The Fig. 5 shows this kind of message.

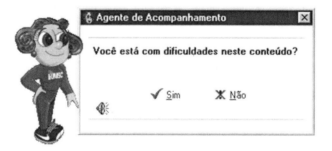

Fig. 5. Agent DÓRIS and message that relates the difficulty in question

In this example, if the student answered "yes" indicating that he has difficulty, a back message is sent and it gives the possibility that the student can inform his difficulty, as can be checked in Fig. 6.

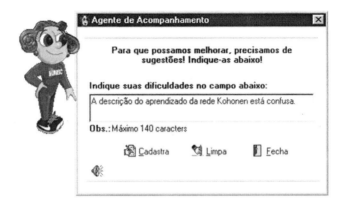

Fig. 6. Agent DÓRIS and back message.

If the student answered "no" indicating that he doesn't have difficulties, a back message is sent, as it is show in Fig. 7.

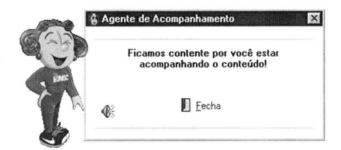

In this time, the DÓRIS agent' characteristics are pointed: environment perception and adaptation – because the back messages are sent as students answer.

Backing to the examples, if the student does have some question during the class, it can be filed. To do this, the student just have to double-click in the agent DÓRIS. The Fig. 8 shows this example. Besides that, through this screen, it can be accessed the screen that has the answered doubts, where it can be checked in Fig. 9.

Fig. 8. Agent DÓRIS and interface to file doubts

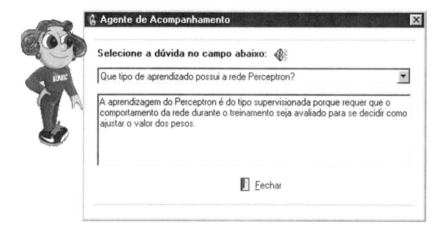

Fig. 9. Agent DÓRIS and interface to check the answers.

Besides theses presented messages, the others are sent to the student as in the following situations:

- when a student stays during a defined time in the same page, messages are sent and these messages ask the student about the interaction, as a way to check if the student are liking or not the page;
- when a student stays a long time in the same page, a message is sent asking the student about how is his learning between others questions;
- if the student doesn't visit any page during the navigation on the contents, a message is sent to the student, warning him about how important is to check all of the contents;
- when a student is on the last content of the class, a message is sent asking about part that the student would like to be used in the next classes (sounds, images, for example).

It's important to say that the agent DÓRIS is an application independent that can be called by other application. Then, the agent DÓRIS can run in whatever System Tutoring Intelligent.

5 Conclusion

Currently, research on ITSs are concerned with the construction of environments that enable a more efficient learning. In this context, the use of intelligent agents in these systems enables the development of different reasoning instances and the integration of several actions to achieve effective learning.

The use of the pedagogical agents technology can provide environments that are considerably efficient in relation to learning. This paper presented the complete modelling of a pedagogical follow-up agent in an ITS for distance learning, highlighting its architecture and behaviour, in addition to the presentation of the environment where it is embedded.

It can be proved that the use of ITSs has shown to be promising in distance learning environments due to the flexibility they provide in terms of adapting the material to students' profile, because they make use of different teaching strategies to promote more customised teaching. Thus, the use of pedagogical agents is designed to improve teaching in such environments, providing the desired educational quality.

The pedagogical follow-up agent developed enables a more pleasant interaction of students with learning systems, making the environment more attractive and, thus, motivating students to learn. Additionally, the agent performs the tasks of collecting relevant information on students, which is a big challenge in this field.

A prototype in the Artificial Neural Networks domain (Artificial Intelligence) has been developed in order to simulate the behaviours of agent DÓRIS. The next step scheduled in this project is, thus, the students'validation of the use of the pedagogical agent DÓRIS in a distance learning class.

References

[1]   GIRAFFA, L. M. M.. Seleção e Adoção de Estratégias de Ensino em Sistemas Tutores Inteligentes. Porto Alegre: UFRGS, 1997. (Exame de Qualificação).

[2]   VICCARI, R. Um Tutor Inteligente para a programação em Lógica –Idealização, Projeto e Desenvolvimento. Coimbra: Universidade de Coimbra, 1990. (Tese de Doutorado).

[3]   GIRAFFA, L. M. M.; VICCARI, Rosa M.. *ITS Built as Game like Fashion Using Pedagogical Agents*. Porto Alegre: UFRGS,1998. III Semana Acadêmica do PPGC.

[4]   DAHMER, A.; GASPARY, L. P.; FROZZA, R.; et al. Ambiente Integrado de Apoio ao Ensino a Distância: Gerenciamento de Aulas, Tutores Inteligentes e Avaliação Remota. Taller Internacional de Software Educativo. Santiago, Chile, 1999.

[5]   DAHMER, A.; GASPARY, L.P.; FROZZA, R.; et al. Um Ambiente para Desen-volvimento de Ensino a Distância. Workshop Internacional sobre Educação Virtual. Fortaleza,1999.

[6]   GASPARY, L. P.; FROZZA, R.; DAHMER, A.; et al. Uma Experiência de Ensino de Redes de Computadores via Internet. Workshop de Educação em Computação. Curitiba, 2000.

[7]   FROZZA, R; DAHMER, A.; GASPARY, L.P.. Uma Arquitetura para Acompanhamento Pedagógico. Workshop Internacional sobre Educação Virtual. Maceió, 2000.

[8]   GIRAFFA, L.M.M. Uma arquitetura de tutor utilizando estados mentais. Porto Alegre: UFRGS, 1999. (Tese de Doutorado).

[9]   PEREIRA, A. S. Um Estudo de Aplicações de Ensino na Internet Orientada a Agentes. Porto Alegre: UFRGS, 1997. (Trabalho Individual).

[10]   PAIVA, A.; MACHADO, I.. Vicent, an Autonomous Pedagogical Agent for on the Job Training. International Conference on Intelligent Tutoring System (ITS98), 4. Lecture Notes in Computer Science 1452. San Antônio, 1998.

[11]   RICKEL J., JOHSON, L. Animated Pedagogical Agents for Team Training. International Conference on Intelligent Tutoring System (ITS98), 4. Lecture Notes in Computer Science 1452. San Antônio, 1998.

[12]   FRASSON, C.; MARTIN, L.; GOUARDÉRES G.; AÏMEUR, E.. Lanca: A Distance Learning Architecture Based on Networked Cognitives Agents. International Conference on Intelligent Tutoring System (ITS98), 4. Lecture Notes in Computer Science 1452. San Antônio, 1998.

[13]   REICHEHHERZER, T; CANAS,A;.FORD, Kennneth.. The Giant: A Classrom Collaborator. International Conference on Intelligent Tutoring System (ITS98), 4. Lecture Notes in Computer Science 1452. San Antônio, 1998.

[14]   Disponível em : http://msdn.microsoft.cpm/workshop/c-frame.html#workshop/imedia/ agent/default.asp. (Acesso em Ago. 2000).

[15]   RICKEL J.; JOHSON, L. Animated Pedagogical Agents for Team Training. San Antonio: Texas, 1998. Intelligent Tutoring.

[16]   RASSON, C; MENGELLE, T; AIMEUR, E.. Using Pedagogical Agents in a Multi-Strategic Tutoring System. Kobe: Japan, 1997. Proceedings of Workshop V Pedagogical Agents.

Developing Distributed Intelligent Learning Environment with JADE – Java Agents for Distance Education Framework

Ricardo Azambuja Silveira[1] and Rosa Maria Vicari[2]

[1]Universidade Federal do Rio Grande do Sul – UFRGS
Universidade Luterana do Brasil - ULBRA
rsilv@inf.ufrgs.br
[2]Universidade Federal do Rio Grande do Sul – UFRGS
rosa@inf.ufrgs.br

Abstract. Over the last years, many organizations started to use Distance Teaching tools as instruments in employees' qualification programs, creating what we may call *E-learning* or *Virtual Training* in Human Resources Development Programs. However, usually these organizations tend to use technological resources already available, and do not shape their technological platform into a pedagogical project. Recent advances in the field of Intelligent Teaching Systems have proposed the use of Artificial Intelligence through architectures based on agents' societies. Teaching systems based on Multi-Agent architectures make possible to support the development of more interactive and adaptable systems. The objective of the paper is to discuss the feasibility of implementing Distributed Intelligent Learning Environment – DILE based on the Multi-Agents Architecture approach, aiming at the achievement of human resources qualification through Virtual Training. Besides, we present a proposal of an architecture named JADE - Java Agent Framework for Distance Learning Environments.

1 Introduction

Computer Science, together with Psychology and Education, has been trying to refine teaching computational tools towards personalized self-learning. Everyday, new approaches to the use of Computer and Education are bringing new perspectives to this area. The evolution of Computer and Education became computational teaching environments an excellent choice for Distance Learning, by bringing new vigor to this field of science. Computer Networks and Multimedia fields have provided tools for the development of Tutoring Systems based on client-server architectures. The popularity of Internet along with the extensive development and use of standard protocols and services make Internet very attractive for distance learning. There has been a big boom of tools and mechanisms available for implementation and support of Distance Learning.

Many business organizations have been using Distance Learning tools as an instrument to implement Human Resources development or qualification programs,

S.A. Cerri, G. Gouardères, and F. Paraguaçu (Eds.): ITS 2002, LNCS 2363, pp. 105–118, 2002.

by creating what we may name *Virtual Training*. However, these organizations usually use the legacy technological resources, and do not shape the technological platform with a pedagogical concern. The traditional Computer Assisted Instruction Systems approach (CAI) lacks to provide an adaptable learning process according to each individual student. The simple use of technological resources without an adequate pedagogical and organizational project results in inadequate virtual training programs, within learning environments excessively static and with quite directive teaching techniques. These issues claim for adequate implementation methodologies of virtual training programs and for suitable learning environment projects with adequate pedagogical proposal and proper use of technology.

According to Rosenberg [15], the use of modern technologies and delivering of good learning programs are essential but insufficient to guarantee the efficacy of these programs. The increase of human capital of an organization must be based on an E-learning strategy focused on factors that include building a learning culture marshaling true leadership support in consonance with the business model.

Projects of E-learning must take into consideration that there are different classes of students: the *non-cooperative*, those who act in a passive way or even try to frustrate the program's objective; the *cooperative,* who follow orientations, but do not necessarily know where to go; and the *pro-active* students, who know very well their objective, and search for aid to relief the task burden. The teaching methodology employed in each case is different and there must have a clear concern by the technological environment on the profile of the student that will use the system.

In order to reach this goal, cognitive student's modeling is required, and it must make a clear specification of the students' profiles. An intelligent teaching environment must build and update the student model according to what the student already knows, and this may vary from student to student. This difference must be considered when in the search for efficiency in the development of intelligent teaching environments. Student's performance in the domain, transparency of technical terminology, the student's objectives and expectations and his/her previous experience must be also taken into account. That is why the Intelligent Learning Environments, such as JADE, are a class of teaching instruments much more advanced from the pedagogical and organizational point of view, more adequate to the aims of Virtual Training in organizations.

The state of the art in Intelligent Tutoring Systems and Intelligent Learning Environments fields points to the use of Agent Society-Based Architectures. The fundamentals of the Multi-Agent systems have demonstrated to be very appropriate to design tutoring systems, since the teaching-learning problem could be handled in a cooperative approach [5] [7] [8] [10] [13]. Using Multi-Agents Systems approach to design Intelligent Tutoring Systems can result in more versatile, faster and at lower costs systems. The introduction of AI techniques and, specifically, the use of Multi-Agents architecture in these environments aim to provide student-modeling mechanisms [8]. We believe that these concepts can be used in modeling and implementation of Intelligent Distance Learning platforms aimed at qualification programs in organizations.

The objective of the paper is to discuss the feasibility of implementing Distributed Intelligent Learning Environment – DILE based on the Multi-Agents Architecture approach, aiming at the achievement of human resources qualification through Virtual Training. Besides, we present a proposal of an architecture named JADE - Java Agent Framework for Distance Learning Environments. This project was born in 1997

[16][17][18] as a thesis project. Different from the homonymous JADE (Java Agent DEvelopment Framework) [2], a FIPA [6] compliant software framework implemented in Java language which simplifies the implementation of multi-agent systems, the Java Agent Framework for Distance Learning Environments implements an agent framework with specific educational purposes.

2 Theoretical Issues

There is a new look upon Education developed in the last 20 years that has been highly influenced by Cognitive Science. The educational system has focused more and more on learning instead of on teaching. The development of learning theories has changed the nature of student's learning and perception. Knowledge is today considered something socially built throughout students' actions, communication and reflections. The classic approach of education on knowledge transmission has been changing into a model of practical experimentation and interaction that promotes changes in concepts and student's strategy, until he/she reaches proficiency. In this context, teachers perform the role of supporter instead of information provider.

As we pointed in previous papers [16] [17] [18], the idea of Distance Education, however not new, has showed a great capacity of integrating new technologies successfully. Lately there has been appearing a great deal of mechanisms and tools available for Distance Education support and implementation.

Classic definitions of distance teaching imply that the ideal situation for learning is the traditional one, with teacher and student face-to-face. From this viewpoint, Distance Education would be an "inferior" way of education, always trying to fill the lacks of the traditional model. This conception may be true in many cases, but a growing body of research, exploring other options, has been taking their place, in the light of new educational paradigms, changes in the social dynamics, and technological advance of means of communication and computational systems.

It is important to highlight that Distance Education cannot be seen as a replacement for traditional and presential education. They are two modalities of the same process. Distance Education does not compete with the conventional means, once this is not its objective. If Distance Education presents, as a basic characteristic, the physical and temporal separation between teaching and learning processes, this does not mean only a specific quality of this modality, but essentially a challenge to overcome, promoting the advance in the use of cooperative processes of teaching in a combined way.

Keegan [9] summarizes the central elements that characterize the concepts of Distance Education: Physical separation between student and teacher, different from Presential Teaching; Influence of the educational institution: planning, system-atization, and project, different from private learning; Use of technical means of communication to put teacher and student in contact and to send educational contents; Availability of a two-way communication, where the student benefits from the possibility of two-way dialogue initiatives; Possibility of occasional meetings.

We take a simpler and more encompassing definition, which explores new possibilities [19]: "Distance Education is a system that must provide educational opportunities anytime, anywhere for anyone".

According to Spodick [19], five basic points are essential in a successful Distance Education program: contact between teacher and student, active learning through student's answers, fast feedback to the teacher about the student's understanding level, fast feedback to the student about his/her own performance, the student has the opportunity to review and learn through his/her own mistakes.

2.1 Pedagogical Agents

One of the major problems of traditional computer based learning systems is how to provide adaptive teaching, suitable to each student. A Distance Education system must support as much as possible the problems caused by the physical distance among teacher, student, and classmates. This claims for more efficient mechanisms of adaptability and assistance in problem-solving processes. The system must perform the teacher's role as much as possible, building a robust student model for each user that would enable: Adapting the syllabus to each user; Helping him/her to navigate over the course activities; Giving support in the task accomplishment, and in exercises and problems to be solved; Providing help resources whenever is needed.

As the student's performance is rarely consistent, and it is impossible to preview the entire set of student's behavior, the ITS adaptability is limited and the classic ITS models are not robust enough to provide the minimum requirements necessary for an interactive learning environment. According to Mathoff [10], these requirements are: *Interactivity, Adaptable Instruction, Robustness, Direct Monitoring of the Learning Process, Empirical Evaluation* and *Parsimony*.

Most recent advances in the field of Intelligent Learning Environments have proposed the use of agent's society based architectures. The principles of Multi-Agent systems have showed a very adequate potential in the development of teaching systems, due to the fact that the nature of teaching-learning problems is more easily solved in a cooperative way. For that end, JADE , as well as other teaching environments [5], [7], [8], [12], [13], [20], uses this kind of architecture, implementing *Pedagogical Agents* as a specialized class of agents with the necessary abilities to deal with teaching strategies.

In this context an agent is described [3] as a software entity that works in a continuous and autonomous way in a particular environment, generally inhabited by other agents and able to interfere in that environment, in a flexible and intelligent way, not requiring human intervention or guiding. Ideally, an agent that works continuously for long periods of time must be able to learn through experience and, if it inhabits in an environment with other agents it must be able to communicate and cooperate with them, sharing a common world.

3 The JADE Project

The *Java Agent framework for Distance learning Environments* – JADE project [18] proposes an infrastructure of project, development and implementation of Distributed Intelligent Learning Environments – DILE, based on the approach of Multi-Agents architecture towards Distance Education, for multiple domains. In this project we implemented different versions of Eletrotutor prototype. Eletrotutor is a teaching environment for Electrodynamics teaching, and in each version we have been refining JADE architecture.

3.1 Architecture

JADE architecture encompasses a very short Multi-Agent family composed of just four types of agents: an agent responsible for the system's general control, one responsible for agents' communication, one in charge of student's environment, and a set of agents responsible for tasks related to teaching tactics (Pedagogical Agents), where each agent may have its tasks specified according to its goal.

The agent's architecture is designed as robust and standardized as possible and aims to enable reusing codes for different kinds of agents. The intelligence of the environment is strongly based on interaction among agents by message interchanging. The tasks performed in teaching are decomposed and performed individually or in groups of agents, and a set of messages is designed to be sent according to the knowledge base of each agent.

Communication between agents is performed through a KQML-based message set, implemented with communication resources of JAVA language objects named RMI (Remote Method Invocation), used in the project [1].

The system contains a special agent responsible for each teaching strategy (*Pedagogical Agents*), that is, for the domain knowledge retrieval over each point to be presented to the student, for the task of proposing exercises and evaluating proposals, examples and extra activities.

The Student's Model agent takes all actions of student's data accessing. When a Pedagogical agent is required to update the student's history, this agent sends to the Student Model agent the data to be updated, as well as any other change in the student's cognitive state.

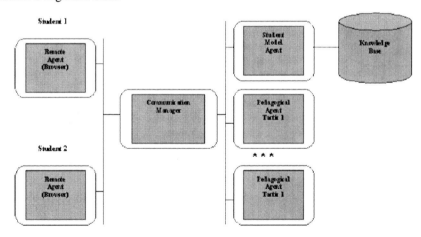

Fig. 1. System Architecture: The Architecture of JADE system is composed of a set of agents: (*Pedagogic Agent*) in charge of performing learning activities as examples, exercises, an others. One special agent (*Communication Agent*) performs communication management among the agents. There is an agent (*Student Model Agent*) responsible for student modeling and agents' coordination. The Browser component (*Remote Agent*) performs the student interface and the communication between the student and the system

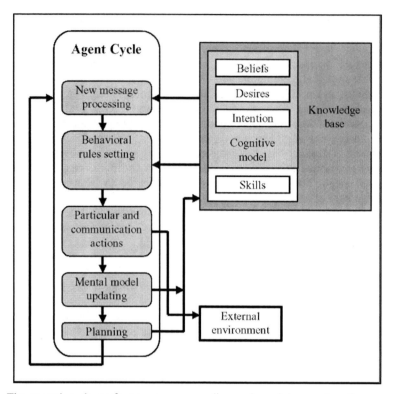

Fig. 2. The agents' cycle performs messages sending and receiving, and performs agents' specific task, according to the knowledge base. As the agent receives a new KQML message it processes the message according to its content, applying the adequate behavioral rule. According to these rules, the message-receiving event can trigger some message sending, mental model updating and some particular specific agent action

The cycle of agents' execution, showed in Figure 2, consists of the following steps:
- New messages processing: the task is decomposed;
- Determination of which rules are suitable in the current situation: analysis of task and if necessary delegation of other agent(s) task;
- Execution of actions specified for such rules: task execution;
- Mental state update according to those rules: management of knowledge about the world;
- Planning: module that must develop plans that reach goals specified by agents intentions.

JADE's Knowledge base implements BDI architecture [11] by using Java data structure and a relational data bank to represent beliefs, desires and intentions. The **Student Model agent** performs all actions related to knowledge base retrieval and updating. When a pedagogical agent needs to update the student's historic, for example, it will send data to the Student Model Agent. The major roles of the Student Model Agent are: To load the current student's state; to generate the overall student's historic; to generate the report of every student's steps; to generate the assessments results; to select the teaching strategies; to check the last access date and to verify tactics available for a certain lesson.

The **Pedagogical Agents** are generated from a tactics previously defined by the course specialist. Their tasks are defined according to the agent's needs. However, as the tutor is based on the content presentation (HTML pages presentation), some tasks are previously defined for all pedagogical agents:

- **Show current content**: when the pedagogical agent receives this request, it communicates with the Student Model manager agent to retrieve from the knowledge base the content that is being presented to the student and sends it to the student's browser.
- **Advance**: with that request, the pedagogical agent communicates with the Student Model Manager to retrieve from the knowledge base which content will be presented to the student.
- **Return**: the pedagogical agent retrieves, from the knowledge base and through the Student Model Manager, which is the content previous to the one the student sees at that moment.
- **Options**: if requested, the pedagogical agent can propose some tools or resources to the student, according to the teaching tactics s/he is performing
- **Update** historic: at every task implemented, the pedagogical agent must register at the Student Model the actions that were performed, as for example, date and hour the student left the current content, date and time of a new content input, etc.
- **Communication**: the agent implements a function that locates where the Communication Manager is in order to re-send information.
- **Evaluation**: the agent has evaluation mechanisms for the tactics the agent implements.

3.2   Teaching Methodology

The learning environments developed using the JADE framework can be used in two different ways: Tutorial and Autonomous modes. In the Autonomous mode, the student has total control over the study session, and can accomplish any lesson, follow any example or do any exercise, following the sequence she/he prefers. In this modality, the student can see the whole set of available activities and no student's data are recorded. In the Tutorial mode, the system undertakes the session control, defining the most adequate sequence of lessons, examples, and other activities. In this mode, the system uses information from its knowledge base to control actions developed with the student.

Teaching methodology used in the tutorial mode assumes a *Teaching Strategies* concept that is a set of *Teaching Tactics* sequence that will be proposed to the student. Evaluation is carried out while the student does the activities proposed, and the assessment of the student is continuously registered in the system's database. JADE knowledge base comprises the following aspects:

- **Student's Cognitive State**: the student model is based on the overlay method [8]: The system registers what the student has learned and compares against the course domain to propose the next topics. Through the guiding of every student's steps, the tutor could adapt the Teaching Strategy to the student and present some resources defined by specialists in order to reinforce his/her learning.

- **Teaching Strategies**: in the Teaching Strategies model, the specialist puts different strategies available by associating several tactics in different ways. According to the student's action within a teaching-learning tactics, the tutor can change the strategy of the next action, in order to better fit the student's abilities.
- **Assessment**: for each lesson presented to the student, the specialist must determine an evaluation method and define rules that will generate strategies to determine actions, according to the student's evaluation result in each lesson.

When the specialist designs the course, he/she can determine which resources or tools will be displayed to the student in each teaching strategy. The student will have at his/her disposal three kinds of resources:

1. Changing tactics: the specialist can create alternative tactics. When the tutor realizes the student is calling a new tactic, it activates another tactic related to this action and changes the way lesson's characteristics presentation.
2. Local tools: these tools are displayed on the screen and consist of: **Help** (explains to the student the interface's and tutor's function), **Hints** (hints on how to solve an exercise, learn a certain content, etc) and **Calculator** (used in exercises solving).
3. Online tools: the model proposed will put available several tools online in order to provide students with more resources to solve doubts, learn more about a topic, etc. These tools are chat, forum and search. The system is flexible and accepts the inclusion of other tools.

The course content can be developed using any kind of HTML authoring tools. Documents and multimedia resources created can be hosted at any web server. An **Administrative Tool** allows the specialist to build a course by designing lessons, strategies, tactics, and content associating all those resources from HTML pages. When designing the course, the Administrative Tool inserts in the database all the information the system needs to retrieve those pages and other documents developed by the authors.

3.3 Features

Some special features were implemented [14] aiming to expand JADE functions and to implement mechanisms that improve adaptability and dynamism to the system by creating a flexible structure that allows specialists to organize their web course content, as well as the strategies, tactics and help tools they want to provide when designing learning environments projects. Several **Learning Support Tools** are also available and can be included as additional features of the learning environments implemented with JADE. These tools were implemented as WEB oriented features to improve interaction among students and teachers as well as to provide on line help tools that avoid the student has to leave the teaching environment when using another tool. Nevertheless, with the number of resources available today on the Internet, it is normal that the student looks for other tools to complement his/her learning. The following tools are currently available:

- **On Line Calculator**: this tool is intended to help the student in problem solving tasks. The development of this tool used JavaScript in a HTML page, and it has functions of a scientific calculator that can be used by the student as a web page.

- **Chat**: this tool intends to allow students to chat within the tutor. Chat is automatically initiated with the student's login. In case the student leaves the tutor, the chat will automatically prevent this student to use it.
- **Forum**: This tool allows the students to discuss the course through topics. The student has always the possibility of sending a new message or reply an existent message just by clicking on the message and typing the text.
- **Search Tool**: This tool allows the student to research over any topic. This resource triggers the search in three search sites. After getting the answers, it collects the first three links of each site and builds a single page. The configuration of these sites was chosen at random (AltaVista, Yahoo and Google) but the implementation is flexible and any search site can be used.

Figure 3 shows a snapshot of the Eletrotutor prototype with the Learning Support Tools menu on the left side of the screen and the On Line Calculator window.

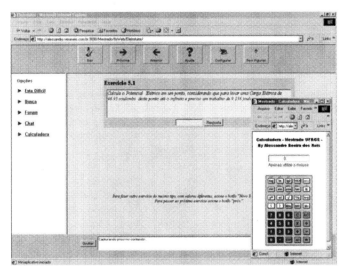

Fig. 3. Snapshot 1: This picture shows the features menu on the left side of the screen and the on line Calculator in the right side as an example. The features menu contain links to the **It is too hard** help feature (*Está Difícil*), **Search** tool feature (*Busca*), **Forum** tool *(Forum)*, **Chat** (*Chat*) and **Calculator** (*Calculadora*).

3.4   The ELETROTUTOR Prototype

The Eletrotutor prototype was implemented as a test bed to evaluate JADE platform. It is an Electrodynamics client-server intelligent learning environment designed according to JADE architecture (available in http://www.inf.ufrgs.br/~rsilv). Figures 4 and 5 show two snapshots of The Eletrotutor prototype.

As mentioned above, the environment may be used in two different ways: Tutorial, and Autonomous modes. In the Autonomous mode, the student has total control over the study session, and may perform any lesson, check any example or make any exercise in the sequence he/she chooses. In the Tutorial mode, the system undertakes

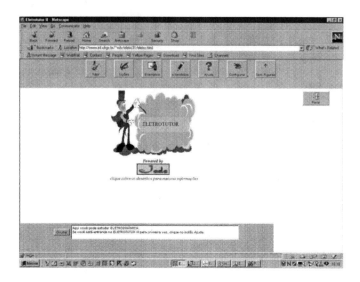

Fig. 4. Eletrotutor's snapshot 2 shows the main screen. The first button (*Tutor*) changes from the autonomous mode to the tutorial mode. The second (*Lições*) invokes the lessons menu. The third (*Exercícios*) invokes the exercises menu. The fourth (*Exemplos*) invokes the examples menu. The fifth (*Ajuda*) call the help system. The sixth (*Configurar*) seventh (*Sem* figures) and eighth (*parar*) change several interface configuration

the session control, defining the sequence of lessons, examples, and exercises. For that end, the tutor makes use of a student's cognitive diagnostic, taken through the record of every action the student takes. Thus, teaching strategies observe the student's historic before taking the next actions. Teaching strategies are the sequence of contents, examples and exercises that will be proposed to the student.

4 The System Evaluation

In order to have some partial evaluation of the teaching tactics used in this environment, we perform an experimental investigation comparing the performance of two groups of students in high school classes [16] [17]. The first group attended a special course using the Eletrotutor in non-tutorial mode. The second group attended a classic expositive class. The same test measured the knowledge acquired after the session class. Figure 6 shows the obtained results. The findings show that both groups have similar performance.

This evaluation shows that the experimental group has a performance similar to the control group. This shows the potential of the tools and teaching tactics implemented. Further work will evaluate the tutorial mode to verify how much the pedagogical agents can improve learning.

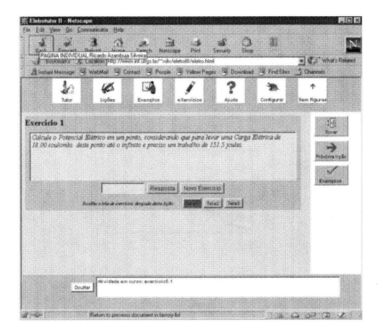

Fig. 5. Eletrotutor's snapshot 3 shows an exercise. The system presents as many exercises as the student want by clicking (*Novo Exercício*) button. This changes the instance of this kind of exercise. By clicking the buttons (*Tela1, Tela2, Tela3*) the student invokes different kinds of exercises for this lesson

5   Conclusions

Distance Education systems based on the Internet does not have any time or space constraint. Students can interact with the system anytime, anywhere. The available tools enable the communication between students and teachers very easily and allow quick feedback. Students and teachers can share information. Excellent teaching strategies may be taken through the available resources over the web, all over the world. Nowadays, it is possible to have access and display broad and advanced knowledge, not available until then. Students can decide what, how and when to learn, favoring teaching methodologies focused on the student and with an explorative and constructivist basis.

However, there are not only advantages in the www-based teaching. Some important aspects should be considered: Most of Distance Education systems based on the web are not intelligent or adaptable. Students usually get lost when they need to navigate choosing paths among the labyrinths of links displayed in HTML pages.

Web pages by themselves are not a teaching system. It is very hard for the student alone to get material that is of his/her interest, amid the great deal of material available.

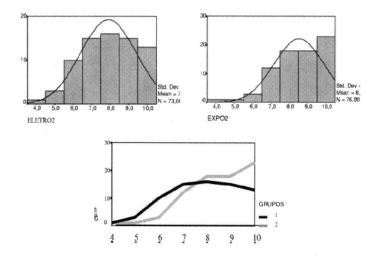

Fig. 6. The evaluation of Eletrotutor system compares the performance of an Experimental Group of students (*ELETRO2*) with a Control Group (*EXPO2*) in the same test. The Y-axis represents the number of students and the X-axis represents the score obtained in the test. The first group (dark *line*) had a little bit lower performance than the second group (*gray line*). But Parametric Statistic test shows that this difference is not significant. This experiment used Eletrotutor in the non-tutorial mode.

Research have turned towards three great directions: the use of adaptive www pages that use some method to verify the pages content and adapt them to the student's actions; the use of www systems based on ITS, which use the traditional architecture of Intelligent Tutors and use a www interface, including sometimes collaborative learning mechanisms; and architectures that use intelligent agents, as in the case of the architecture proposed in the present work.

However, all these issues have in common a strong dependence on a sharp and robust student modeling. Through the student model it is possible to provide customized teaching tactics, which reflect the knowledge level of each student, his/her learning abilities and objectives. The Student Model registers the student's mistakes in a way that the system can provide teaching strategies adequate for content review. Thus, the more precise this model is the better and higher is the system adaptability.

In this work we intend to bring some important contributions, refining the efficacy of learning environments, aggregating concepts of different areas to establish a methodology for the implementation of Distance Education projects, and stressing the use of cooperative problem solving paradigm using Multi-agent architecture.

Further work will integrate the JADE implementation of pedagogical agents with commercial or well-known academic learning environments or frameworks [4]. This integration takes advantage of the pedagogical and administrative resources of these environments and improves their adaptability using cognitive modeling and solving problem strategies of JADE framework. In addition we intend to consider the use of some FIPA-compliant communication framework. This will improve the message interchanging among the agents and provide more adaptability and flexibility to the system.

Acknowledgements. This project is granted by Brazilian research agencies: CAPES - PAPED program, CNPq – Protem-CC program and FAPERGS – ARD program. Thanks to Francine Bica, and Alessandro Boeira. Their master thesis are important part of this project.

References

1. BICA, Francine, *Eletrotutor III: Uma abordagem multiagente para o Ensino a distância.* Porto Alegre: CPGCC da UFRGS, 1999. Master Dissertation (Portuguese).
2. BELLIFEMINE, Fabio, POGGI, Agostino, RIMASSA, Giovanni. *JADE – A FIPA-compliant agent framework* CSELT internal technical report. Part of this report has been also published in: Proceedings of PAAM'99, London, April 1999, pagg.97-108.
3. BRADSHAW, J. M. An introduction to software agents In: BRADSHAW, J. M. Ed. *Software Agents.* Massachusetts: MIT Press, 1997.
4. Centre for Curriculum, Transfer & Technology. *Online educational delivery applications.* Disponível em: < http://www.c2t2.ca/landonline/>. Acesso em: 08 nov.2001.
5. CHEIKES, B. A. GIA: Agent Based Architecture for Intelligent Tutoring Systems. In: THE CIKM WORKSHOP ON INTELLIGENT INFORMATION AGENTS, 1995. *Proceedings... [S.l.: s.n],*1995
6. FIPA: The foundation for Intelligent Physical Agents. *Specifications.* Available by HTTP in http://www.fipa.org March 2002.
7. GIRAFFA L.M., VICCARI R. M.; SELF, J. *Multi-Agent based pedagogical games.* In: ITS, 4., 1998. *Proceedings...* [S.l.: s.n], 1998.
8. JOHNSON, W. Lewis; SHAW, Erin. Using agents to overcome deficiencies in web-based courseware. In: WORLD CONFERENCE ON ARTIFICIAL INTELLIGENCE IN EDUCATION, AI-ED, 8., 1997. *Proceedings... [S.l.: s.n]*, 1997. Disponível em: <http: //www.isi.edu/isd/johnson.html.>. Acesso em: 05 mar.2000.
9. KEEGAN, D. *Foundations of distance education.* 2nd ed. London: Routledge, 1991 apud NUNES, Ivônio Barros. *Noções de educação à distância.* Disponível por WWW em http: //www.Ibase.org.br/~ined/ivonio1.html (out. 1997).
10. MATHOFF, J.;VAN HOE, R. APEALL: A Multi-agent approach to interactive learning environments. In: EUROPEAN WORKSHOP ON MODELING AUTONO-MOUS AGENTS MAAMAW, 6., 1994. *Proceedings...* Berlin: Springer-Verlag, 1996.
11. MÓRA, Michael C. et al. BDI Models and Systems: Reducing the Gap.In: WORKSHOP ON AGENT THEORIES, ARCHITECTURES, AND LANGUAGES, 5., 1998. *Proceedings...* Berlin: Springer-Verlag, 1998.
12. NAKABAYASHI, Kiyoshi et al. Architecture of na intelligent tutoring system on the WWW. In: WORLD CONFERENCE OF THE AIED SOCIETY, 8., 1997, Kobe. *Proceedings...* [S.l.: s.n], 1997.
13. NORMAN, Timothy J.; JENNINGS, Nicholas R. Constructing a virtual training laboratory using intelligent agents. *International Journal of Continuos Engin-eering and Life-long Learning,* [S.l.], 2000.
14. REIS, Alessandro Boeira dos. *Um modelo do aluno adaptativo para sistemas na Web.* Porto Alegre: CPGCC da UFRGS, 2000. Master Dissertation (Portuguese).

15. ROSEMBERG, Marc J. *E-Learning: strategies for delivering knowledge in the digital age.* New York. McGrawHill, 2001
16. SILVEIRA, R. A.; VICCARI, R. M. Projeto Eletrotutor: Desenvolvimento e Avaliação de Ambientes Inteligentes de Ensino-Aprendizagem. In: CONFERENCIA LATINO-AMERICANA DE INFORMATICA, 23., 1997. *Proceedings...* Valparaíso: CLEI, 1997.
17. SILVEIRA, Ricardo et al. Desenvolvimento e avaliação de duas abordagens de ambientes de ensino inteligentes. In: SIMPÓSIO BRASILEIRO DE INFOR-MÁTICA NA EDUCAÇÃO, 8., 1997. *Anais...* São José dos Campos: [s.n.], 1997.
18. SILVEIRA, Ricardo Azambuja. Modelagem Orientada a Agentes Aplicada a Ambientes Inteligentes Distribuídos de Ensino – JADE - *Java Agent framework for Distance learning Environments* Porto Alegre: PPGC da UFRGS, 2000. Doctoral Thesis (Portuguese).
19. SPODICK, Edward F. *The evolution of distance learning.* Hong Kong: University of Science & Technology Library, 1995. Available in: <http: //sqzm14.ust.hk/distance.>. Acesso em: 08 ago. 1995.
20. WEBER, Gerhard; SPECHT, Marcus. User modeling and adaptative navigation support in WWW – based tutoring systems. In: USER MODELING INTER-NATIONAL CONFERENCE, 6., 1997. *Proceedings...* Viena: Springer-Verlag, 1997.

A Web-Based Intelligent Tutoring System Using Hybrid Rules as Its Representational Basis

Jim Prentzas, Ioannis Hatzilygeroudis, and John Garofalakis

University of Patras, School of Engineering
Dept of Computer Engin. & Informatics, 26500 Patras, Hellas (Greece)
prentzas@ceid.upatras.gr
&
Computer Technology Institute, P.O. Box 1122, 26110 Patras, Hellas (Greece)
(ihatz, garofala)@cti.gr

Abstract. In this paper, we present the architecture and describe the functionality of a Web-based Intelligent Tutoring System (ITS), which uses neurules for knowledge representation. Neurules are a type of hybrid rules integrating symbolic rules with neurocomputing. The use of neurules as the knowledge representation basis of the ITS results in a number of advantages. Part of the functionality of the ITS is controlled by a neurule-based inference engine. Apart from that, the system consists of four other components: the domain knowledge, containing the structure of the domain and the educational content, the user modeling component, which records information concerning the user, the pedagogical model, which encompasses knowledge regarding the various pedagogical decisions, and the supervisor unit that controls the functionality of the whole system. The system focuses on teaching Internet technologies.

1 Introduction

Intelligent Tutoring Systems (ITSs) form an advanced generation of Computer Aided Instruction (CAI) systems. Their key feature is their ability to provide a user-adapted presentation of the teaching material [1], [3], [13]. This is accomplished by using Artificial Intelligence methods to represent the pedagogical decisions and the information regarding each student. The emergence of the World Wide Web increased the usefulness of such systems [12].

Very significant for the development and operation of an ITS are the AI techniques it employs. The gradual advances in AI methods have been incorporated into ITSs resulting into more effective systems. During the past years, various AI formalisms have been developed for knowledge representation in knowledge-based systems such as symbolic rules, fuzzy logic, Bayesian networks, neural networks, case-based reasoning. Hybrid approaches (e.g. neuro-symbolic or neurofuzzy representations) integrating two or more formalisms have also been developed in an effort to create improved representations. A number of formalisms have been used for knowledge representation in ITSs [1], [7], [8], [9], [10]. Symbolic rules are perhaps the most prominent AI formalism used in ITSs. Till now, a few ITSs are based on hybrid

S.A. Cerri, G. Gouardères, and F. Paraguaçu (Eds.): ITS 2002, LNCS 2363, pp. 119–128, 2002.

formalisms (e.g. [7]). However, hybrid approaches can offer a number of benefits to ITSs not offered by single ones.

In this paper, we present the architecture and describe the functionality of a Web-based ITS, which uses a hybrid formalism for knowledge representation. The subject of the ITS is "Internet technologies". Course units covering the needs of users with different knowledge levels and characteristics are offered. The system models the students' knowledge state and skills and, based on this information, constructs lesson plans and selects the appropriate course units for teaching each individual user. The ITS uses neurules [4], a type of hybrid rules, to represent expert knowledge. Neurules offer a number of benefits to the ITS.

The paper is organized as follows. Section 2 presents an overview of the system's architecture. Section 3 presents the knowledge representation formalism and its advantages. Section 4 presents features of the domain knowledge. Section 5 describes the user modeling component. Section 6 presents the functionality of the pedagogical model. Finally, section 7 concludes.

2 System Architecture

Fig. 1 depicts the basic architecture of the ITS. It consists of the following components: (a) the *domain knowledge*, containing the structure of the domain and the educational content, (b) the *user modeling component*, which records information concerning the user, (c) the *pedagogical model*, which encompasses knowledge regarding the various pedagogical decisions and (d) the *supervisor unit*.

The ITS is based on an expert system aiming to control the teaching process. The expert system employs a hybrid knowledge representation formalism, called neurules [4]. According to their functionality, the neurules of the system are distributed into different neurule bases. More specifically, there are four neurule bases, one in the user modeling component and three in the pedagogical model (in the teaching method selection module, course units' selection module, evaluation module).

The supervisor unit supervises the function of the ITS. It interacts with the other components of the ITS calling the inference engine of the expert system whenever it is necessary. Furthermore, it plays a user interface role. The teaching subject (i.e. Internet technologies) of the ITS involves chapters such as the following: 'Basic aspects of computer networks', 'the Internet and its basic services', 'the World Wide Web', 'Email'.

The following sections elaborate on the system's key aspects.

3 Knowledge Representation

The expert system has an inference engine in order to make decisions based on known facts and the rule bases contained in the user modeling component and the pedagogical model.

Symbolic rules constitute a popular knowledge representation scheme used in the development of expert systems. Rules exhibit a number of attractive features such as naturalness, modularity and ease of explanation. One of their major drawbacks is the difficulty in acquiring rules through the interaction with experts. Methods based on decision trees construct rules from training examples and deal with this problem. Another drawback is the inability to draw conclusions when the value of one or more conditions is unknown.

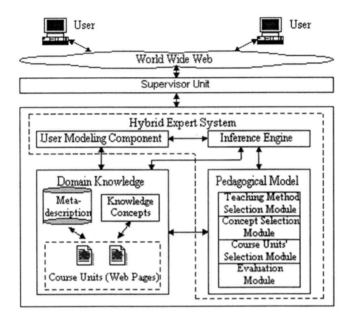

Fig. 1. The architecture of the ITS

During the last years, artificial neural networks are used quite often in the development of expert systems. Some of their advantages are the ability to obtain knowledge from training examples (with better generalization than the rules produced from decision trees), the high level of efficiency, the ability to reach conclusions based on partially known inputs and the ability to represent complex and imprecise knowledge. Their primary disadvantage is the fact that they lack the naturalness and modularity of symbolic rules. The knowledge encompassed in neural networks is in most cases incomprehensible.

The expert system's knowledge representation formalism is based on neurules, a type of hybrid rules integrating symbolic rules with neurocomputing. The attractive feature of neurules is that they improve the performance of symbolic rules [4] and simultaneously retain their naturalness and modularity [5] in contrast to other hybrid approaches.

3.1 Neurules

The form of a neurule is depicted in Fig. 2a. Each condition C_i is assigned a number sf_i, called its *significance factor*. Moreover, each rule itself is assigned a number sf_0, called its *bias factor*. Internally, each neurule is considered as an adaline unit (Fig. 2b). The *inputs* C_i ($i=1,...,n$) of the unit are the *conditions* of the rule. The weights of the unit are the significance factors of the neurule and its bias is the bias factor of the neurule. Each input takes a value from the following set of discrete values: [1 (true), -1 (false), 0 (unknown)]. The *output D*, which represents the *conclusion* (decision) of the rule, is calculated via the formulas:

$$D = f(a), \quad a = sf_0 + \sum_{i=1}^{n} sf_i C_i \tag{1}$$

where a is the *activation value* and f(a) the *activation function*, which is a threshold function returning '1' if a>=0 and '-1' otherwise. Hence, the output can take one of two values, '-1' and '1', representing failure and success of the rule respectively.

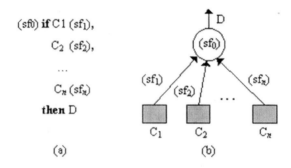

Fig. 2. (a) Form of a neurule (b) corresponding adaline unit

The general syntax of a condition C_i and the conclusion D:
<condition>::=<variable><l-predicate><value>
<conclusion>::=<variable><r-predicate><value>
where <variable> denotes a *variable,* that is a symbol representing a concept in the domain, e.g. 'teaching-method', 'examination-mark' etc. <l-predicate> denotes a symbolic or a numeric predicate. The *symbolic predicates* are {is, isnot}, whereas the *numeric predicates* are {<, >, =}. <r-predicate> can only be a symbolic predicate. <value> denotes a value. It can be a *symbol* or a *number*. The significance factor of a condition represents the significance (weight) of the condition in drawing the conclusion(s). So, the semantics of significance factors are quite different from that of certainty factors or probabilities.

Neurules are constructed offline either from empirical data (training patterns) or symbolic rules using the methods described in [4], [5]. With these methods significance and bias factors are calculated; the user does not need to explicitly specify them. In this way, the neurules contained in the neurule bases of the ITS are constructed. The inference mechanism is based on a hybrid rule-based inference engine [6]. Conclusions are reached based on the values of the condition variables and the weighted sums of the conditions.

3.2 Benefits of Neurules

The use of neurules as the representational basis of the ITS results in a number of benefits, which enhance the construction stage as well as the real-time operation stage of the ITS. More specifically:

- Neurules are time-efficient because they improve the performance of symbolic rules [4] and require fewer computations compared to other hybrid approaches in order to derive the inferences [6]. This is very important since an ITS is a highly interactive knowledge-based system requiring time-efficient responses to users' actions. The Web imposes additional time constraints.
- Neurules are space-efficient since it has been proven that when neurules are constructed from symbolic rules, the number of rules contained in the rule bases is decreased reducing their required amount of space [4].
- In contrast to symbolic rules, neurule-based reasoning can derive conclusions from partially known inputs. This is due to the fact that neurules integrate a connectionist component (adaline). This feature is useful, because, during a training session, certain parameters related to the user may be unknown.
- It is easy to update a neurule base because neurules retain the naturalness and modularity of symbolic rules enabling an incremental development of the neurule bases [4], [5]. One can easily add new neurules to or remove old neurules from a neurule base without making any changes to the knowledge base, since neurules are functionally independent units, given that they do not affect existing knowledge. This is difficult to do in other hybrid approaches. Ease of knowledge base updates is important, because there is always the possibility that the system's knowledge base should be changed.
- The explanation mechanism associated with neurules produces natural explanations justifying how conclusions were reached [6]. This feature can assist in the location of deficiencies in the neurule base when the prototype system is tested.
- Neurules can be constructed either from symbolic rules [4] or empirical data [5] enabling exploitation of alternative knowledge sources.

4   Domain Knowledge

Domain knowledge contains knowledge regarding the subject being taught as well as the actual teaching material. It consists of three parts: (a) *knowledge concepts*, (b) *concept (sub)groups* and (c) *course units*.

Knowledge concepts are elementary pieces of knowledge of the specific domain. Every concept has a number of general attributes such as name, level of difficulty, level of detail, lowest acceptable knowledge level. Furthermore, it can have links to other concepts. These links denote its prerequisite concepts. In this way, one or more *concept networks* are formed representing the pedagogical structure of the domain being taught.

Concepts are organized into *concept groups*. A concept group contains closely related concepts based on the knowledge they refer to. Therefore, the domain space is dissected into subdomains. Examples of subdomains in the 'Internet technologies' teaching subject are 'Computer Networks' and 'World Wide Web'. Concept groups may contain a number of subgroups.

A concept (sub)group is associated with a teaching method bias denoting preference to a specific teaching method (see Section 6) for teaching the concept (sub)group. Another important attribute is the detail level of a concept (sub)group which can be compared with the user's desired detail level of the presented educational content (see Section 5) in order to decide whether contents of the concept (sub)group will be presented or not. Furthermore, concept (sub)groups may be interconnected with precedence links used for the selection of the concept (sub)group to be taught. Some concept (sub)groups may be independent from the others meaning that their selection for teaching does not need to be preceded by the teaching of other (sub)groups.

The course units constitute the teaching material presented to the system users as Web pages. Each course unit is associated with a knowledge concept. The user is required to know this concept's prerequisite concepts in order to grasp the knowledge contained in the specific course unit. The course units present theory, examples or exercises.

The system keeps variants of the same page (course unit) with different presentations using the explanation variant method implemented by the page variant technique [2]. Domain knowledge includes a *meta-description* of the course units containing their general attributes such as the level of difficulty, the pedagogical type (theory, example, exercise), the multimedia type (e.g. text, images, animations, interactive simulations), the required Internet connection, the detail level. The meta-description of the course units is based on the ARIADNE recommendation.

5   User Modeling Component

The user modeling component is used to record information concerning the user which is vital for the system's user-adapted operation. It contains models of the system's users and mechanisms for creating these models.

The user model consists of four types of items: (i) *personal data,* (ii) *interaction parameters,* (iii) *knowledge of concepts* and (iv) *student characteristics.* The personal data concerns information necessary for the creation and management of the user's account (e.g. name, email). It is used for the identification of the user. The student characteristics and the knowledge of the concepts directly affect the teaching process whereas most of the interaction parameters indirectly.

The interaction parameters form the basis of the user model and constitute information recorded from the interaction with the system. They represent things like, the type and number of course units accessed, the concepts and concept groups for which the user has accessed some of their course units, the type and amount of help asked, the correct and wrong answers to exercises, the marks obtained from exercises, etc.

The student characteristics are mainly the following: (a) Multimedia type preferences (e.g. text, images, or animations) regarding the presented course units, (b) knowledge level (novice, beginner, intermediate, advanced) of the subdomains and the whole domain, (c) concentration level, (d) experience concerning the use of the

ITS, (e) available Internet connection, (f) desired detail level of the presented educational content.

Student characteristics are represented with the *stereotype model* that is, the user is assigned to predefined classes (stereotypes). Based on the way they acquire their values, the student characteristics are discerned into two groups: *directly obtainable* or *inferable*. The directly obtainable ones such as characteristics (a), (e), (f) obtain their values directly from the user whereas the values of the inferable ones such as characteristics (b)-(d) are inferred by the system based on the interaction parameters and knowledge of concepts. The user's knowledge of the domain is represented as a combination of a stereotype and an *overlay model* [2]. The stereotype denotes the (sub)domain knowledge level. The overlay model is based on the concepts associated with the course learning units.

A neurule base containing *classification neurules* is used to derive the values of the inferable characteristics. The variables of the classification neurules' conclusions correspond to inferable characteristics. The variables of the conditions correspond to the parameters the inferable characteristics are based on. More specifically, the knowledge level of the subdomains is inferred based on the user's knowledge of the concepts belonging in the subdomains. The knowledge level of the whole domain is deduced from the knowledge level of the subdomains. The concentration level depends on the marks obtained from the exercises, the type and amount of help asked and the percentage of wrong answers. Experience is deduced from the knowledge level of the whole domain and the percentage of accessed course units.

6   Pedagogical Model

The pedagogical model provides the knowledge infrastructure in order to tailor presentation of the teaching material according to the user model. The pedagogical model consists of four main components: (a) *teaching method selection module,* (b) *concept selection module,* (c) *course units' selection module* and (d) *evaluation module.* Each of these components but the concept selection module contains a neurule base.

In a specific learning session, the pedagogical model must perform the following tasks: (i) Select a concept (sub)group to teach, (ii) select-order the concepts to be taught, (iii) select a teaching method, (iv) select the course units to be presented, (v) evaluate the user's performance.

Selection of a concept (sub)group is based on the user's knowledge of the domain, links between concept (sub)groups, correspondence between concept (sub)groups' detail level and user's desired detail level of the presented educational content. Evaluation of the user's performance updates the inferable student characteristics and may create a feedback for tasks (iii) and (iv). In the following, the last four tasks are briefly described.

The task of the concept selection module is to construct a user-adapted lesson plan by selecting and ordering the appropriate concepts. This is based on the user's knowledge of the concepts, the user's (sub)domain knowledge level, the user's desired detail level, the concepts' detail level and the links connecting the concepts. More specifically, for the specific subdomain, the concepts for which the user's knowledge level is unsatisfactory are identified. These concepts are candidates for being selected in the construction of the lesson plan. Concepts whose detail level is incompatible with the user's desired detail level are eliminated from the candidate set. The lesson plan is formed based on the remaining set of concepts. Ordering of the selected concepts is performed based on the links connecting the concepts.

The teaching method selection module selects the appropriate teaching method using a neurule base. Selection is based on parameters concerning the user model and the specific concept (sub)group. User parameters considered include concentration level, knowledge level and percentage of accessed course units within the specific concept (sub)group. In addition, the concept group's teaching method bias is taken into account. These parameters appear in the conditions of the neurules used to select the teaching method. There are totally six teaching methods. For instance, according to one such method in order to teach the user a specific concept (sub)group, course units containing theory, examples and exercises should be presented. Another method states that only examples and exercises should be presented. Table 1 (left column) presents an example neurule for selecting the teaching method.

According to the plan constructed by the concept selection module, the course units' selection module selects and orders the course units that are suitable for presentation. For this purpose, the student characteristics of the user model, the selected teaching method as well as the meta-description of the course units are taken into account. Ordering of the course units is based firstly on their pedagogical type and secondly on their difficulty level. Ordering based on the pedagogical type is specified by the selected teaching method. A neurule base performs subsequent ordering based on the difficulty level. For instance, a specific ordering based on the difficulty level states that the presentation order of course units should start from course units with minor difficulty and proceed to more difficult ones. The variables of the neurules' conditions correspond to the inferable student characteristics and the teaching method.

Table 1. Example neurules for selecting the teaching method and assigning examination marks

TM-RULE	EVAL-RULE
(-2.4) **if** teach-meth-bias is examples-exercises (1.5)	(-11.2) **if** attempts-solution>2 (10.2),
concentration-level is low (1.2),	number-requested-examples=0 (9.9),
knowledge-level is low (1.0),	number-requested-examples=1 (6.4),
percent-accessed-cunits < 0.30 (0.9),	times-asked-assistance=1 (6.3),
teach-meth-bias is theory-examples-exercises (0.9)	times-asked-assistance=0 (3.3)
then teaching-method is theory-examples-exercises	**then** examination-mark is average

The evaluation module evaluates the user's performance based on the user's interaction with the system and updates accordingly the user model. More specifically, based on the interaction parameters, it assigns knowledge values to the concepts and updates the inferable student characteristics by using the classification neurules of the user modeling component. The evaluation module contains *evaluation neurules* for assigning marks to presented exercises. For each presented exercise, the user obtains a mark ranging from bad to excellent. The mark is given based on the number of times he/she asked for assistance, the number of related examples seen by the user and the number of answering attempts made by the user. Table 1 (right column) presents an example evaluation neurule.

Based on the acquired marks, the knowledge values of the concepts as well as the knowledge levels of the concept (sub)groups and the whole domain are derived. The user's knowledge level of each concept belonging in the initial lesson plan should be greater than or equal to its lowest acceptable knowledge level. If this is the case, another concept (sub)group will be selected and a new learning session will ensue. Otherwise, tasks (iii) and (iv) will be re-executed causing reselection of the teaching method and/or course units since different inputs will be given to the corresponding neurules.

7 Conclusions and Future Work

In this paper, we present the architecture and describe the functionality of a Web-based ITS, which uses a hybrid formalism for knowledge representation. The system's function is controlled by an expert system using neurules, a type of hybrid rules integrating symbolic rules with neurocomputing. The use of neurules instead of symbolic rules or other hybrid neuro-symbolic approaches offers a number of advantages. Neurules encompass the features desired by the knowledge representation formalism of an ITS. The use of hybrid approaches in ITSs is likely to gain interest in the following years. Hybrid approaches are more efficient than their component representations. In fact, hybrid intelligent systems have been proven effective in solving difficult problems.

Our future work is directed to the use of Distributed AI methods (such as the one in [11]) to achieve communication of the ITS with other intelligent educational systems teaching the same or related subjects.

References

1. Angelides, M., Garcia, I.: Towards an Intelligent Knowledge Based Tutoring System for Foreign Language Learning. Journal of Computing and Information Technology 1 (1993) 15-28.
2. Brusilovsky, P., Kobsa, A., Vassileva, J. (Eds.): Adaptive Hypertext and Hypermedia. Kluwer Academic Publishers, Dordrecht, Netherlands (1998).
3. Georgouli, K.: Modelling a Versatile Mathematical Curriculum for Low-attainers. Proceedings of the 8th Panhellenic Conference in Informatics (2001) 463-472.
4. Hatzilygeroudis, I., Prentzas, J.: Neurules: Improving the Performance of Symbolic Rules. International Journal on Artificial Intelligence Tools 9 (2000) 113-130.
5. Hatzilygeroudis, I., Prentzas, J.: Constructing Modular Hybrid Knowledge Bases for Expert Systems. International Journal on Artificial Intelligence Tools 10 (2001) 87-105.
6. Hatzilygeroudis, I., Prentzas, J.: An Efficient Hybrid Rule Based Inference Engine with Explanation Capability. Proceedings of the 14th International FLAIRS Conference. AAAI Press (2001) 227-231.
7. Magoulas, G.D., Papanikolaou, K.A., Grigoriadou, M.: Neuro-fuzzy Synergism for Planning the Content in a Web-based Course. Informatica 25 (2001) 39-48.
8. Martin, J., VanLehn, K.: Student assessment using Bayesian nets. International Journal of Human-Computer Studies 42 (1995) 575-591.
9. Nkambou, R.: Using Fuzzy Logic in ITS-Course Generation. Proceedings of the 9th IEEE International Conference on Tools With Artificial Intelligence. IEEE Computer Society Press (1997) 190-194.

10. Shiri, M. E., Aimeur, E., Frassen, C.: Student Modelling by Case-Based Reasoning. In Goettl, B.P., Halff, H.M., Redfield, C.L., Shute, V.J. (eds.): Fourth International Conference on Intelligent Tutoring Systems. Lecture Notes in Computer Science, Vol. 1452. Springer-Verlag, Berlin (1998) 394-404.

11. Solomos, K., Avouris, N.: Learning from Multiple Collaborating Intelligent Tutors: An Agent-Based Approach. Journal of Interactive Learning Research 10 (1999) 243-262.

12. Stern, M., Woolf, B.: Curriculum Sequencing in a Web-based Tutor. In: Goettl, B.P., Halff, H.M., Redfield, C.L., Shute, V.J. (eds.): Fourth International Conference on Intelligent Tutoring Systems. Lecture Notes in Computer Science, Vol. 1452. Springer-Verlag, Berlin (1998) 574-583.

13. Vassileva, J.: Dynamic Courseware Generation. Journal of Computing and Information Technology 5 (1997) 87-102.

Using Vector-Space Model in Adaptive Hypermedia for Learning

Jaakko Kurhila[1], Matti Lattu[2], and Anu Pietilä[2]

[1] Dept. of Computer Science, P.O. Box 26
FIN-00014 University of Helsinki, Finland
tel. +358 9 191 44664
`jaakko.kurhila@cs.helsinki.fi`
[2] Dept. of Teacher Education, University of Helsinki, Finland
`{mplattu,atpietil}@cc.helsinki.fi`

Abstract. Although many of the existing adaptive learning environments use other approaches, the vector-space model for information retrieval can be used in providing individualized learning with hypermedia. A system employing a modified version of the vector-space model is described. The approach taken is tested in a real-life setting to evaluate and train basic arithmetics skills of learners in elementary education. Although the impact on learning was not measured, the approach provides a useful evaluational help for the teacher to make observations about the learning processes of the learners.

1 Introduction

The common approach used in adaptive learning environments is to use methods of adaptive hypermedia [1,2]. Most of the existing solutions use overlay or stereotype models to provide the adaptation. AHMED is a system for individualized learning experiences: the learning material is organized as a vector space, where every piece of a learning material has a distinct position in the learning material space. There is still a difference between the vector-space model for information retrieval [7] and the learning space model for AHMED [5], discussed in the next section. The strength of the learning space model lies within the useful evaluational help the teacher or the experts assessing the learning processes can derive from the use of the system.

AHMED was originally developed to serve as a learning environment for disabled children [4] with deficits in *mental programming* [8], i.e. difficulties in composing a problem-solving strategy and organizing a task to meaningful sub-goals as well as difficulties in upholding motivation and attentiveness. However, the system can also be used in a regular education curriculum, especially in primary education due to the simple interface. Because of the obvious transfer, the evaluation presented in this paper is conducted in able-bodied education.

We briefly describe the system AHMED, and present the learning material collection called Matinaut used in the training and evaluation of addition skills in elementary education. The test results are shown and the possible uses of the visualized test results are discussed.

S.A. Cerri, G. Gouardères, and F. Paraguaçu (Eds.): ITS 2002, LNCS 2363, pp. 129–138, 2002.

2   The Description of Ahmed

The operation of AHMED. AHMED is a learning environment which consists of a collection of learning materials and an interface to the material. The learner is the person addressing the learning material so that he or she will have learning experiences in the learning environment.

AHMED relies on two principles: adaptation to individual learning processes and domain-independence of the learning materials. Adaptation is based on the actions a learner makes during a learning session in the learning environment. Domain-independence is assured by separating the adaptation mechanism completely from the domain knowledge, and allowing the learning material creation by a generic structured documentation language described based on XML.

The key issue in our learning environment is to lead the learner through the hypermedia learning material (which we call a *learning space*) so that the most suitable pieces of learning material (called *learning seeds*) are exposed to the learner (Fig. 1). To activate the learner, the material typically consists of various *tasks*, not just information items.

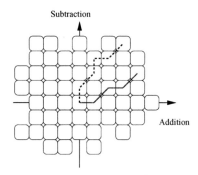

Fig. 1. A learning space with two dimensions and two individual paths through a set of seeds.

The difference between a learning space based on a vector-space model for information retrieval [7] and a standard hypermedia structure is that there are not necessarily links between the nodes (seeds). The seeds have their position in the space, defined by a vector containing a numerical parameter for every dimension. Formally, every seed s in learning space S is located by the corresponding n-dimensional ($n \in \mathbb{N}$) vector, called the *position* of s, denoted as

$$s = (s_1, s_2, ..., s_n),$$

where $s_i \in \mathbb{Z}$.

As a simple example, a learning space consisting of basic arithmetic might have two dimensions, namely "Addition" and "Subtraction". In such a case, the first exercise "1+1" might have a position of $(0,0)$ along these dimensions.

The learner is represented by a point in the learning space S at a given time t, $t = 1, 2, 3, \ldots$ In other words, the learner's location $s(t)$ at time t is indicated by a vector

$$s(t) = (s_1(t), s_2(t), \ldots, s_n(t)),$$

where $s_i(t) \in \mathbb{Z}$.

It should be noted that time t does not represent actual time; rather, time refers to discrete steps on a learner's path from one seed to another. To continue the previous example, a learner conducting the arithmetic exercises could be located in learning space S on a point $(0, 0)$, say, at time 1.

The seeds are thus positioned into the learning space similar to the way information retrieval entities (documents) are indexed in the vector space. However, in Salton's model [7], the key issue is to scatter entities in the space so that they can be retrieved efficiently, whereas AHMED's learning space model addresses guiding the learner to meaningful positions in the learning space. The guiding from one seed to another is conducted by assigning different *effects* for every action in a seed. An action refers to the choice a learner makes in a given seed s of space S. An action has an effect for the learner's position in the learning space. The effect can pertain 0 to n dimensions, and the strength of the effect can be arbitrary. Therefore, a negative effect is also possible. Thus, for every action a within a given seed s, the effect, or movement, is

$$\delta(s, a) = (\delta_1(s, a), \delta_2(s, a), \ldots, \delta_n(s, a)),$$

where $\delta_i(s, a) \in \mathbb{Z}$. For example, an action (in this example, the answer) "2" for assignment "1+1" could be parameterized to have an effect of $\delta((0, 0), 2) = (+1, +0)$ at the learner's position $(0, 0)$ in the learning space. This means that the effect depends not only on the action, but also on the position of the seed. In this particular case, the learner is considered to be ready to proceed one step along the "Addition" dimension but subtraction skills cannot be evaluated and therefore the effect for the "Subtraction" dimension is zero.

The action a learner takes within a seed s moves the learner to the seed that matches the learner's previous point in the space added with the effect from the last action a. Therefore, at a given time $t + 1$, the learner's location $s(t + 1)$ in the learning space is

$$s(t+1) = (s_i(t) + \delta_i(s(t), a))_{i=1,\ldots,n} = (s_1(t) + \delta_1(s(t), a), \ldots, s_n(t) + \delta_n(s(t), a)),$$

or, in practice, the seed closest to the new potential location $s(t + 1)$. Thus, if a learner in the learning space is located at point $(0, 0)$ and makes a choice with effect $(+1, +0)$, he or she is taken to point $(1, 0)$.

During a session, the learner's actions are recorded. Formally, for a given learner u, the learning process record $p(t, u)$ at a given time t is a sequence of actions

$$p(t, u) = (s(1, u), a(1, u), a(2, u), \ldots, a(t - 1, u), a(t, u)),$$

where $s(1, u)$ is the location of the first learning seed on learner u's learning path and $a(h, u)$ refers to the action learner u performed at time h. This record of a learner forms the individual path through the learning space. Therefore, the learner is not modeled as a mere point in the space but as a trail through the space, including the whole history of his or her learning process. This recorded trail is a *profile* of the learner, which can be represented visually and can be used for evaluational purposes.

In addition, every seed in the learning space can consist of an arbitrary amount of seeds within that seed, connected to each other with traditional hyperlinks. This possibility is added to the system because it adds simplicity when authoring the learning material, but also because it enables easy preparation of ready-made sub-problems to original problems that might be too challenging for the intended users. The possibility of using sub-problems is in harmony with supporting mental programming of learners.

3   Study Setting

Description of the test material. The functionality of AHMED was tested empirically by constructing a learning space for arithmetic addition. The learning space for the experiment is called Matinaut. The Matinaut material consisted of drilling material presenting addition exercises and general teaching material, "videos", for solving each type of exercise (Fig. 2). An exercise screen presents an exercise and two columns for multiple-choice answers. The learner is requested to select the answer from the first column if he or she has used the addition algorithm to solve the exercise. The second column is to be used if the answer was achieved by mental computation (as seen on the left in Fig. 2).

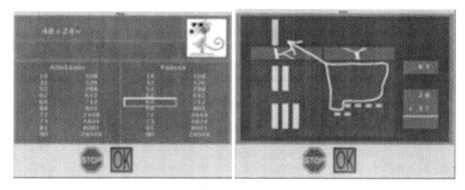

Fig. 2. The learner's view to the learning material. On the left, an exercise with multiple-choice answers is presented. On the right, a still of a "video" (general solving procedure to an exercise type) is presented

Authoring a learning space to AHMED is technically easy using the description language designed for the purpose, but there are conceptual difficulties caused by the freedom for the learning material author. There are at least four kinds of questions to be answered (discussed more thoroughly in [5]): What kind of dimensions to use, what the positions of the seeds in the learning space are, what the actions within the seeds are and what the effect of every action is.

The first issue to consider is to break the learning topic into meaningful dimensions. For addition exercises, several possibilities exist, but the Matinaut learning space was chosen to include three dimensions, namely "Number field", "Mental computation" and "Addition algorithm". "Number field" was divided into five discrete steps: numbers between 0 and 10, 10 and 20, 20 and 100, 100 and 1000, and 1000+. The corresponding dimension values were 0, 30, 70, 90, and 100. "Mental computation" was also divided into different categories, namely "Addition with no composing, bigger number first", "Addition with no composing, smaller number first", "Adding to 10/100/1000[1]", "Adding a ten or tens", "Addition with composing for ones", "Addition with composing for tens", "Addition with composing for hundreds or thousands", and "More than one addition with composing". The corresponding dimension values for "Mental computation" were 0, 10, 20, 30, 70, 80, 90 and 100. "Addition algorithm" was divided into seven categories: "No reason for addition algorithm", "no carry-over", "one carry-over", "more than one carry-over", "carry-over to the empty unit (such as 911+200)", "carry-over bigger than 1", and "more than one carry-over, zero to tens or hundreds slot". The corresponding dimension values for the dimension were -1, 10, 40, 50, 70, 90 and 100.

Examples of the position $(0, 0, 0)$ are 2+1 and 4+2. Examples from a position of $(70, 70, 40)$ are 29+32 and 48+24, because the Number field is from 20 to 100, there is a need for addition with composing for ones, and when using the addition algorithm, there is a need for one carry-over. Every possible position of the learning space had several exercises, and there were a total of 347 different exercises authored into the space.

It should be noted that the Matinaut space was not *complete*, i.e. the space had several "holes" since the dimensions chosen are not independent of each other. In other words, many locations in the space do not have seeds, since an exercise cannot fulfil the requirements for every dimension. For example, there cannot be a seed in a point $(0, 0, 40)$ since an exercise cannot have a number field between 0 and 10 and have carry-over. The space not being complete does not affect the functionality of AHMED, but it means that the movement from one point to another can be a "jump" even though the values for the learner's position would indicate only a small step. Figure 3 shows the actual positions of the seeds for the Matinaut learning space. Dark rectangles mark the positions where there are seeds and white rectangles mark the "holes" in the space. The three dimensions are shown pairwise.

The learning material author is also responsible for defining the actions a learner can make in a given seed as well as the effect of the action. Considering the Matinaut space, in the case of a correct answer by mental computation, the effect was $(+4, +2, +0)$ to dimensions Number field, Mental computation, and Addition algorithm. In the case of a correct answer by addition algorithm,

---

[1] The numbers to add give an answer of 10, 100 or 1000, such as 7+3, 40+60 etc.

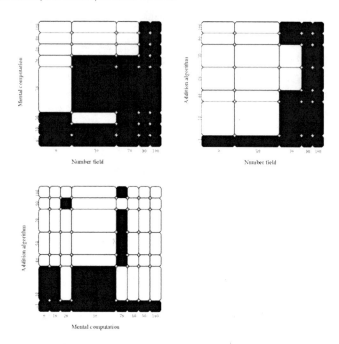

Fig. 3. The three-dimensional learning space for the Matinaut test is shown with two dimensions at a time.

the effect was $(+4, +0, +2)$. The learner progresses more rapidly on the Number field dimension to ensure that the learner does not have to stay with too easy problems too long.

All the erroneous answers for the multiple-choices were generated according to the known error types for both mental computation and addition algorithm. The errors for every exercise are straightforward to produce automatically. If the amount of generated errors based on the known error types was less than 20 (the amount of multiple choices was fixed to 20, see Fig. 2), the rest of the errors were produced by a random generator.

In the case of a wrong answer by mental computation with a choice that had an error-type generated error, the effect was $(+0, -1, +0)$ to dimensions Number field, Mental computation, and Addition algorithm. In the case of a wrong answer by mental computation with a choice that had a randomly generated error, the effect was $(-1, -1, +0)$.

In the case of a wrong answer by addition algorithm with a choice that had an error-type generated error, the effect was $(+0, +0, -1)$ to dimensions Number field, Mental computation, and Addition algorithm. In the case of a wrong answer by addition algorithm with a choice that had a randomly generated error, the effect was $(-1, +0, -1)$. The effect on the values for the dimensions for every answer is illustrated in Figure 4.

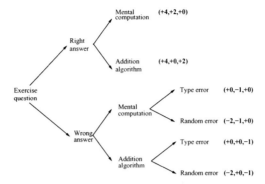

Fig. 4. The effects of possible actions for the values for every dimension.

A single point in the Matinaut learning space contained several different exercises of the same type. In addition, everyone of the seeds actually contained a chain of seeds. The rationale behind this was that it should be possible to try the same exercise after an error. After a second error, a video for general solving practice was to be presented. After the video, the same exercise can be tried once more. The effects on the values for the dimensions are the same as above for every time an exercise in the exercise chain is answered, except after the video the last trial of an exercise will not lower the values.

There are admittedly many possible ways to construct a learning space for addition. The approach taken in this experiment is partly based on the existing knowledge about the error-types and difficulty order of tasks included in mental computation and addition algorithm [3], and partly based on hands-on experiences of teaching elementary arithmetics.

The testees. Two classes of learners (n~35) at the age of 7 and 8 in an elementary school were chosen to be testees and were exposed to the system. Everyone in the class attended the tests. The testees were free to use the system during their spare time and during math classes. There were only three computers in each class so there was competition in who could have access to the system. The log files from the system were gathered after two weeks, during which time the learners started to learn the addition algorithm as a part of their curriculum.

4 Test Results

The evaluation was carried out without a control group and the testees and their test results were not reflected against the average. The focus of the evaluation was to see the individual trails left by the testees and find out if the trails alone can give any valuable information. In a way, the question is to evaluate the learning space schema by evaluating an instance of a learning space in a real-world setting.

The expected result was that the learners should progress rapidly to their skill level and after that the progress is slow unless the testees have some outside help (the teacher, the videos) to learn new things. In other words, the learners were assumed to achieve their zone of proximal development (ZPD) [9] and after that their progress is slowed but not stopped because they have the teacher teaching addition algorithm and the videos showing different methods of solving the exercises.

The data was gathered after two weeks of using the system. Some of the testees were still observed to be enthusiastic after two weeks, e.g. competing about who has the access to the system during the spare time on a lunch break.

Figure 5 shows a collection of trails of various learners. The trails are individual trails chosen to represent different categories of the progress expressed by the testees. It should be noted that the individual scores should not be compared against each other since the learners consumed different amounts of time working with the system.

The trails in Fig. 5 do not visualize the trails from a seed to another but the points gathered for each dimension. The points gathered are more informative for this purpose but an example of visualizing the trails between the actual seeds can be found in [6]. In Fig. 5, values for the x-axis indicate the exercises tried, and the values for the y-axis indicate the points gathered. In addition, the solid lines indicate progress in Number field, the dashed lines indicate progress in Mental computation, and the dotted lines indicate progress in Addition algorithm.

The testee presented in the first diagram in Fig. 5 (first row, first column) has reached her level on the mental computation dimension just before the 30th exercise. After not progressing for a while, the testee has moved from using mental computation to addition algorithm and ended up in her zone of proximal development. The testee presented in the second diagram in Fig. 5 (first row, second column) has not used mental computation at all. The progress has been slow but nearly constant. She has not reached her ZPD, but she has tried only less than forty exercises.

The testee presented in the third diagram in Fig. 5 (second row, first column) has apparently reached his ZPD even though he has used both the mental computation and the addition algorithm. The testee presented in the fourth diagram in Fig. 5 (second row, second column) has reached her ZPD with mental computation after 50 exercises, and switched to use addition algorithm at the very end. After the switch, her progress boosted.

The testee presented in the fifth diagram in Fig. 5 (third row, first column) has reached her ZPD with mental computation but has not started to use addition algorithm even though she has not progressed for the last 25 exercises. The testee presented in the last diagram in Fig. 5 (third row, second column) has used only addition algorithm and has progressed rapidly (virtually error-free and over 100 exercises completed).

The effect of videos. The seeds were organized in the Matinaut space so that after two wrong answers to an exercise, a video presenting the general solving method for that particular exercise was shown to the testee. An interesting issue

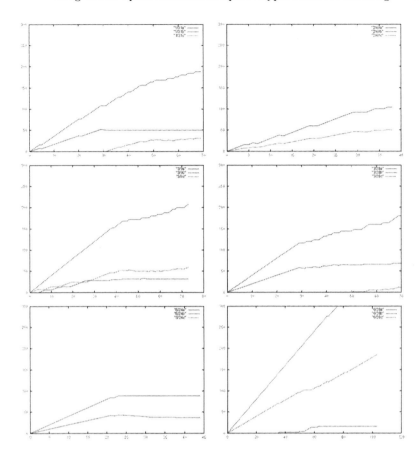

Fig. 5. The progress along three dimensions for six learners. Note the variable scale for x-axis.

to study is whether presenting the videos have any effect on the correctness of the answers. As anticipated, the effect of videos was not remarkable. The video was shown 357 times, and after watching the video, correct answer was given 95 times (27%). Although the videos were informative and included animations and speech for the solving of the exercise, they did not demand any interactivity and there was no direct reward for watching the video (since the video did not show an answer to that particular exercise). Also the observations in the classroom suggested only a small effect for videos, since in some cases when a video appeared after two wrong answers, the testee was not paying attention to the video.

However, interviews with the testees in the classroom indicated that some learners can indeed benefit from the videos if they possess metacognitive skills to understand the connection between the general solving strategy for the exercise and the actual exercise. When studying the effect of the videos individually, several testees showed much clearer effect than the average: 57% correct answers after a shown video (4/7), 50% (4/8), 40% (8/20), and 38% (5/13). In contrast, there were also several zero effects: 0/10, 0/10, 0/4 and 0/3, among others.

5   Conclusions

The presented learning space, Matinaut, is an example of using the learning space schema in elementary education. The constructed space is straightforward and simple, but the model is general enough to cater the needs of other types of learning material as well. Particularly suitable materials could be the ill-defined domains where there are no right and wrong answers, just different possibilities to cope with the situations.

Although the material to Matinaut learning space had to be authored beforehand, various generators and semi-automatic editors were used to speed up the authoring. The learning space schema enables adding seeds to an existing space directly. The teacher can add seeds without making any connections to seeds authored earlier: setting the position of a seed for each dimension is sufficient.

Another added value of the system and the learning space schema is that the teacher (the tutor or the evaluator) can instantly see by a glimpse at the visualizations which routes the learners have traversed and what kind of progress they have presented. It would be possible to make the information visible also for the learners for self-evaluation but in this version of the system it has not been implemented.

References

1. Brusilovsky, P.: Methods and Techniques of Adaptive Hypermedia. User Modeling and User-Adapted Interaction, 6(2-3), pp. 87–129 (1996).
2. Brusilovsky, P.: Adaptive Hypermedia. User Modeling and User-Adapted Interaction, 11(1-2), pp. 87–110 (2001).
3. Grinstein, L.S. and Lipsey, S.I.: Encyclopedia of mathematics education. New York: Routledge (2001).
4. Kurhila, J., Paasu, L., and Sutinen, E.: Adaptive support for brain deficits in special education. In Proceedings of ITS 2000, p. 658, Berlin: Springer (2000).
5. Kurhila, J., Sutinen, E. and Turull Torres, J.M.: How to Model a Platform for an Adaptive Learning Environment?. In Proceedings of Int'l Conference on Computers in Education (ICCE 2001), pp. 416–423, Seoul, Korea: Incheon National University of Education (2001).
6. Kurhila, J. and Varjola, H.: Using Adaptive Hypermedia to Evaluate Basic Arithmetic Skills in Special Education. To appear in Proceedings of Int'l Conference on Computers Helping People with Special Needs (ICCHP 2002), Linz, Austria (2002).
7. Salton, G., Wong, A., and Yang, C.S.: A Vector Space Model for Automatic Indexing. Communications of the ACM, 18(11), pp. 613–620 (1975).
8. Vilkki, J.: Neuropsychology of mental programming: an approach for the evaluation of frontal lobe dysfunction. Applied Neuropsychology 2, pp. 93–106 (1995).
9. Vygotsky, L.S.: Mind in Society: The development of higher psychological processes. Cambridge, MA: Harvard University Press (1978).

A System for the Specification and Development of an Environment for Distributed CSCL Scenarios

M.F. Verdejo, B. Barros, T. Read, and M. Rodriguez-Artacho

Departamento de Lenguajes y Sistemas Informáticos, U.N.E.D
Ciudad Universitaria s/n, 28040 Madrid, Spain
{felisa,bbarros,tread,martacho}@lsi.uned.es

Abstract. In this paper the 'Active Document system', grounded in the Activity Theory, is presented. This system serves both as a representational framework for the description of learning activities and a harness for the mechanisms necessary to support the creation and management of the corresponding computer-based scenarios. This system is made up of three components, firstly, a set of authoring tools for the creation and configuration of the different Active Documents required for specifying the learning activities. Secondly, a (distributed) repository of learning objects that consists of a variety of tools and resources for the described activities. Thirdly, an Active Document architecture that manages the Active Documents and generates the user environment necessary in order to carry out the described activities, together with the appropriate resources and tools. This proposal appears to offer a solution to the problems of producing reusable and customizible computer-based learning environments.

1 Introduction

A considerable amount of general-purpose (and domain specific) scientific software has proved to be highly suitable for learning scientific and technological principals; software such as visualizers, simulators and modelling tools. Furthermore, an increasing number of interactive and collaborative tools have become technically affordable for a wide spectrum of the educational community, opening up the possibility to support social constructivist learning approaches in computer-based environments. However, the production of a customized learning environment is still very time-consuming where even the complete coverage of a single subject area would require a very large amount of effort. The goal of the research presented in this paper is to provide a computational model and an underlying technological infrastructure that will permit the design and development of collaborative learning activities that involve a variety of resources. The approach adopted here is grounded in the Activity Theory (henceforth, AT) because it captures the social perspective of a learning community, and provides a unified view of how to specify a learning activity at a conceptual level: the different actors and their responsibilities, the context, the learning goals and the mediating tools. An authoring paradigm is presented that could meet the needs of various actors and which separates technical aspects of software creation from the design of collaborative learning activities. The focus of this work is

S.A. Cerri, G. Gouardères, and F. Paraguaçu (Eds.): ITS 2002, LNCS 2363, pp. 139–148, 2002.
© Springer-Verlag Berlin Heidelberg 2002

placed on learning experimental sciences where there is a pressing need for students to improve their learning processes with a better articulation of theory and practice throughout the academic year, especially in the context of distance learning. A way forward is to engage the students in a variety of activities, including the performance of experiments either in real or virtual settings, supported by a distributed collaborative computer environment. The premise here is to offer a persistent, structured, dynamic, active and personal work space to sustain their constructs in a long term learning process. For this purpose, the interoperability of tools and outcomes will be a central issue to be addressed.

2 Related Work

This work is related to three active research areas: (1) AT (2) sharing and interoperability issues, and (3) cognitive and communication tools to support active learning processes. What follows is a brief summary of ongoing initiatives that address these topics. AT views cognition as being a social activity. Individuals work and learn in groups and communities with organizational structure, interacting with others, using tools and resources, and following rules according to roles in order to perform purposeful actions. Socially oriented constructivism forms the basis of the Computer Supported Collaborative Learning paradigm (henceforth, CSCL). CSCL settings can take a great variety of forms. AT has proved to be a useful framework to describe and analyse collaborative settings [5][1]. However, very little work [2][10] has been undertaken which embodies AT in a computer model. The proposal presented here uses AT as the specification language for an authoring system that defines collaborative learning scenarios. The output of the complete authoring process is a set of XML data structures describing the learning activities, i.e., the community involved, the tasks and their interrelationship, the different roles participants can play with the tools to be used, as well as the objects of the activities. A system, implemented in Java, dynamically creates the learning environment specified by these data structures providing learners with an integrated workspace for the development of activities.

During the past seven years, a number of initiatives have been undertaken in order to define metadata schemas. Starting with Dublin Core (henceforth, DC), DC 1.0 in 1996, different communities have produced a large number of data and resource descriptions such as the educational metadata and content packaging specification proposed by the IMS project to describe learning resources, intended to be used for indexing and retrieval purposes in distributed repositories, to integrate multiple content on computer-based training courses. Extensible Markup Language (henceforth, XML), developed under the auspices of the WWW Consortium, offers amongst other things, the possibility of exchanging structured data between applications. Specifications such as DC and IMS can be expressed using XML. Developing standards for describing and reusing learning objects have crystallized in groups and committees such as the IEEE LTSC or the more recent initiative of CEN/ISSS. In parallel with the work being undertaken in this area, other research groups [7] have selected a software engineering framework that focuses on the definition of a component-based architecture, in order to support the building of interactive educational applications from software repositories. Their approach is to develop small components, typically developed in Java, which can be combined by powerful connections and sharing mechanisms (e.g., the ESCOT project, [3]). These objects are assembled in order to generate specific applications. The challenges here are to determine the right level of component granularity and connectivity for the application designer, in this case an educator, using an authoring-tool to assemble pieces in order to generate a domain oriented learning environment without the need to create or modify programs.

Other proposals such as [9], deal specifically with mechanisms supporting a tight integration of communication and task-oriented tools, to enhance the cognitive support in collaborative learning settings. Furthermore, the problem of how to combine diverse representational systems in a generic way by adding semantics without assuming a particular knowledge domain still exists. The benefit of multiple ways of viewing and manipulating objects using a variety of representations for learning purposes has been analysed by [8]. These alternative representational forms contribute to the idea of giving an active dimension to content objects, i.e., the meaning of the content would depend upon the domain context giving rise to a variety of perspectives but, most important, by being partially interoperable. Furthermore, the enrichment of not only the content behaviour but also the relations between objects has recently been explored in other tools [4] in a way that integrates highly specialized tools with a general-purpose cooperative visual language-based environment. The potential of visual language-based connective workspaces with intelligent plug-in components should be further pursued in order to reach more generic solutions.

The structure of the rest of the paper is as follows: in the next section the overall approach adopted in this work is described, what will be referred to as the Active Document (henceforth, AD) system. Subsequently, the potential of this system will be illustrated with examples taken from a learning scenario in the domain of chemistry, and finally, technical implementation issues about the underlying system architecture are discussed. We conclude with a summary and an outline of future work.

3   The Active Document System

The AD system provides both a representational framework for the description of learning activities together with a harness for the mechanisms necessary to support the creation and management of the corresponding computer-based scenarios. Using this approach, a set of learning activities can be formally described. The units of description are based on AT, explicitly considering all the concepts involved in an activity: the division of labour (tasks and subtasks), the mediating tools (learning objects), the norms (partially captured in terms of roles), the object as well as the community. The formalism for the description is inspired by the recent paradigm of Educative Modelling Languages, and by the experience of the development of an EML in this research group [6].

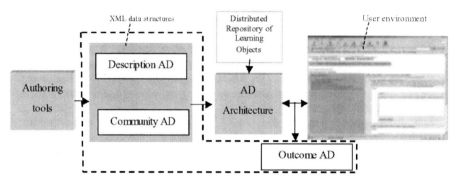

Fig. 1. The Active Document system

The AD system (figure 1) consists of a set of components necessary to create and process the ADs. The main components are: (1) Authoring tools for the creation and configuration of the different ADs required for specifying the learning activities. The authoring tools are currently XML editors which allow a lecturer to compose a set of ADs for specific learning applications. (2) A (distributed) repository of learning objects that consists of a variety of tools and resources for the described activities. It can include generic tools (such as editors) and specific tools like simulators or tele-operational devices, as well as domain-specific content repositories of semantically linked material. (3) An AD architecture that manages the ADs and generates the user environment necessary in order to carry out the described activities, together with the appropriate resources and tools.

4   The Specification of an Active Document

The concept of an AD includes three aspects of the learning process: a description of the activities, a description of the communities and the outcome of the work undertaken within the environment. The ADs are specified in XML and are defined by three pairs of document type definitions (or DTDs) and their corresponding XML document. The ADs are: (1) The description of the division of labour in the tasks and subtasks (referred to as the 'Description AD'). (2) The actors and roles involved in the collaborative tasks (referred to as the 'Community AD'). (3) The outcome of the activity (referred to as the 'Outcome AD'). As can be seen in figure 1, the Description AD, along with the specification of the actors that perform the collaborative activities (specified in the Community AD) are interpreted by the AD architecture that dynamically creates the appropriate user interface, according to the elements defined in the two XML structures. As the learning activity proceeds, the outcome produced by each student is represented in XML in the Outcome AD which stores the results of the learning process and the task structure described in the Description AD. These three ADs are described next. The 'Description AD' specifies a collection of activities, each of which reflect the components of an activity as described by AT, modelling the division of labour and the mediating tools associated with each task. Activities can be grouped within this AD, to provide (optional) sequencing and prerequisite dependences between *groups* of activities. The definition of an activity includes the following: (a) The description of the object of the activity. (b)The specification of the tasks and subtasks, and for each one (if applicable) the different roles that the participants involved in the task can play. (c) The tools and resources available for each role related to a task.

```
<activity id="Act_2" name="Activity Title>
   Description of the activity. Formatted text, graphics, external
   documents, etc., could be  also inserted here.
<taskbyrole id="Task_1" name="Task  1 Title" roles="student, teacher">
           Description of the task 1
         <mediating_tools>
             <resource_ref id="ref_tool 1" id_ref="Spectrum_Editor"
                 display="inside"  label="Spectrum Editor Tool">
             <parameter>
               <param name="text" value="Comment this result" />
               <param name="image" value="Act_1;Task_3" />
             </parameter>
             </resource_ref>
         </mediating_tools>
   </taskbyrole>
   <taskbyrole id="Task_2" name="Task  2 Title" roles="teacher">
           <mediating_tools ...>
                     <resource_ref ... />  <resource_ref ... />
         <mediating_tools .../>
   </taskbyrole>
</activity>
```

Fig. 2. An excerpt of an activity definition

Figure 2 shows an example of the components of the activity definition in the Description AD. The XML fragment would be interpreted by the AD architecture in order to produce a user interface for the learning environment where the activity called "Act_02" can be carried out, whose description can be seen to be divided into a set of tasks (Task_1 and Task_2), each of which to be performed by subjects in one or more roles (two roles are shown in the example: student and teacher). The description of this "task by role" (taskbyrole tag) consists of a description of the task to be carried out, followed by the declaration of the available tools, referred to as a type of resource. Each role involved in the activity will have its appropriate task by role definition. The definition of the Community AD will provide user assignment for the tasks. The resource_ref tag is a reference to a tool, also providing parameter values. The tool used in Task_1 is a collaborative graphical editor used here to annotate and interpret a chemical spectrum. Other possible resources include external document repositories or different types of tools. The objects generated as a result of an activity can be considered as input for another activity. For instance, Task_1 of Act_02 uses of the previously selected spectrum (the result of Task_3 in Act_01) as the input for the collaborative graphical editor. As well as the activities, the Description AD also can include:

- The definition of the overall structure of the learning scenario in which the activities are embedded. This structure is generic for a set of learning scenarios. In the case of a laboratory setting, this would include: the specification of an experiment with a fixed pattern to describe its aim, a theoretical component and safety guidelines, and one of more activities as described above.
- Content elements: A domain-specific repository that can be accessed to provide a semantically linked material.

These components are also expressed in XML in a similar way as an activity, but are not shown in the previous figure. **The Community AD** represents the activity organization in order to describe the assignment of roles for a specific task to the members of a given community. For each activity, a description of the community involved is provided. As has been previously stated, this description is processed by the AD architecture in combination with the Description AD in order to relate the appropriate tasks and tools to the corresponding members of the community. The use of a separate XML structure for the community gives rise to two interesting mechanisms: firstly, communities can change during the development of the activity, thus allowing dynamic role assignments to be made (amongst other possibilities); and secondly, different Community AD can be combined with the same Description AD, providing a flexible mechanism for the re-use of the same division of labour description for a set of different working groups. The **Outcome AD** specifies the way in which the results of the tasks performed in the environment are stored, thus providing an *active* component, a vision of the current work completed and in-progress. Thus, the Outcome AD is in fact the real *active* component of the AD organization, i.e., it is the result of the work generated by a specific actor involved in the activity described by the Description AD.This representation provides a definition, at the desired level of detail, of the work and the objects generated during the learning process. The Outcome AD, rather than a sequence of plain text can contain complex elements like graphics, tables, structured dialogs, maps, etc., in an XML format embedded into it, with links to non XML objects outside, e.g., a MS Word document. Furthermore, the AD architecture makes this structured collection of heterogeneous objects *persistent* during the life-cycle of the user within the environment, providing tools for their manipulation, storage and retrieval. This mechanism forms the basis for passing objects between tools in a transparent way for the user. Some interesting applications can be considered due to the nature of the Outcome AD representation. In the case of an experiment, it could for example, facilitate the creation of a report by the simple selection and copying of the relevant embedded objects once the experiment has terminated. The organization of the Outcome AD reproduces the structure of the Description AD in terms of the structure of activities and tasks, but differs from it in the sense of having an outcome tag for each of the performed tasks. Furthermore, there is an outcome AD XML structure for each actor involved in the activities described above.

5 Example

The definition of the AD presented above is sufficient to configure many different types of group activities. However, the aim here is to explore its capabilities for collaborative learning in experimental scenarios. What follows is an example of an activity, a part of an experiment, which has been developed to explore the current version of the AD system for a second year degree course in Organic Chemistry. An *experiment* usually involves several *activities* composed of *subtasks*. For each subtask, there are some indications about the particular constraints as well as the different possible resources and tools available to perform them. The experiment in question is the analysis and identification of the characteristics of a given chemical substance. Each group of students has to analyse a different substance, selecting the adequate subtasks and necessary steps. A *subtask* can be defined to be a basic (individual or group) action such as testing the material in the lab, annotating the results, deciding the next step to be done, reflecting on the results, elaborating a conclusion (considering the evidence), simulating the behaviour of a substance in the lab, etc. In the Description AD, one or more tools are associated with each subtask in order to carry out each action. These tools are invoked automatically and transparently in the environment when the students choose to undertake the corresponding subtask. What follows is a description of one of the activities of this experiment.

In this **activity** the student has to identify the compounds of the substance in question and from there infer what the substance actually is. This activity is composed of both individual and collaborative subtasks. It should be noted that each stage of the chemical analysis undertaken in this activity, which should eventually lead to the correct identification of the substance in question, is based upon the previous one. Therefore, depending on the result of a particular subtask, the students have to reflect upon the results obtained, describe the working situation, dismiss possibilities and decide upon the nature of next step to be taken in the analysis process Since these subtasks are essentially reflective in nature it is more appropriate to undertake them as a group. The structure of this activity can be seen in the environment on the left hand side of the figure 3. Students have to the select the most appropriate spectrum for this substance, based upon the data each student has gathered up until now. This subtask is undertaken collectively using the text-based collaborative discussion tool shown in the figure. As can be seen, from this tool the students can access a glossary of images of chemical spectra available for this choice. Once the decision has been made, the image selected from the glossary is automatically loaded into the collaborative visual markup tool to enable the students to perform the next task: the identification and characterization of the distinctive peaks within the spectrum. This is shown at the bottom right hand side of figure 3. Once the analysis of the spectrum of the substance has been undertaken, making use of the results of the previous activities, the students are finally in a position to decide upon the name of the substance. A visualization of the current state of the Outcome AD for this endeavor can be seen at the top right hand side of the figure 3. It should be noted that whilst some parts of this process have been collaborative in nature, the students have personal copies of the Outcome ADs that reflect their overall contributions.

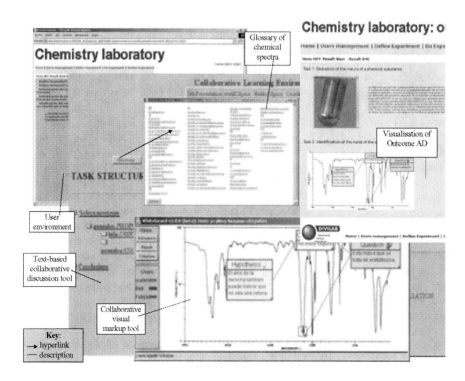

Fig. 3. Various snapshots of the user interface during the second activity

5.1   The Architecture

As can be seen in figure 4, the architecture is divided into various levels in order to accentuate operational flexibility and provide content reusability. This stratification has lead to the definition of the levels as follows: firstly, the presentation level completely separates aspects of the generation and management of the interface from other system functionality and also maintains persistent data during user sessions. Secondly, the configuration level undertakes the control of the data structures necessary both to manage the persistent user sessions and control the overall structure of the interface of the system. Thirdly, the application level manages the interchange of data between the external applications and the system during the experiments, which gives rise to the dynamic and active characteristics of the system. Fourthly and finally, the control level handles the low-level data interchange between the system and the underlying database. This architecture has been designed and developed using a combination of Java and XML technologies, where each functional level shown in the figure consists of several underlying components.

There have been three main goals in this design process. Firstly, the specification of each level enables parts of the system to be redefined without affecting overall functionality (for example, providing wider scenario scope by simply adding new presentation layer logic to permit Java-enabled hand-held devices or personal data assistants to connect to the system). Secondly, the declarative nature of the specification of the educational content in XML greatly simplifies its production and enhances its reusability. Thirdly, the production of a system that is portable between different computer hardware and operating systems with minimal configuration changes. The tools use established XML data standards to represent results in order to facilitate the reuse of the data. A couple of examples can be seen in the form of XHTML to represent formatted data such as paragraphs and tables and the use of Scalable Vector Graphics (henceforth, SVG) to represent the results of a graphical tools (such as a visual collaborative discussion tool), enabling the results to be viewed directly in any SVG-enabled tool (such as MS Internet Explorer) or automatically converted into other graphical formats, such as GIF or JPEG, for subsequent reuse in other applications (such as MS Word). As the user advances through an experiment the results of each tool used for a given task are incorporated into the outcome AD which 'grows' to reflect this progress. The control level serves as a transparent and persistent low-level data management device for the AD. The current version of the system can use any relational database that has a JDBC driver. The XML data that make up the various versions of the AD is collapsed into columns within the database. The standard limitation of this approach, that of not being able to search the XML data structures before extracting them from the database, is not a problem because additional columns in each table act as the search keys for data access.

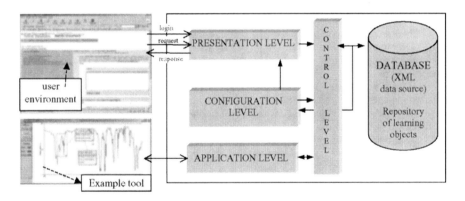

Fig. 4. The architecture of the AD system

6   Summary and Future Work

In this paper the 'Active Document system' has been presented for the design and development of resource-based collaborative learning activities. The two aspects most important in this work are: the computational specification of AT, which leads to an educational modelling language, which has been used to specify the ADs, and secondly the Outcome AD, which is the really active part of the system in the sense that it grows as the student progresses through the learning activities and represents the results of the work as objects that are reused by subsequent tools. Whilst its current domain of application has been that of an experimental science, namely chemistry laboratory sessions, it will also be applied to other non-science evaluation scenarios which should provide valuable insights into the ways in which it can be extended and improved. Finally, the presentation level of the AD architecture and the authoring tools that define the ADs can be identified as candidates for future work. The former needs to be extended to support non-desktop information devices computers, and the latter, needs to evolve from standard XML editors into a fully functional scenario authoring environment.

Acknowledgement. This work has been funded by Divilab IST-1999-12017 and EA_2C_2 CICYT TIC2001-007

References

1. B. Barros & M.F. Verdejo. 2000. "Analysing students interactions process for improving collaboration. The DEGREE approach". In *International Journal of Artificial Intelligence in Education*, vol 11, pp. 221-241.
2. G. Bourguin & A. Derycke. 2001. "Integrating the CSCL Activities into Virtual Campuses: Foundations of a new infrastructure for distributed collective activities". In P. Dillenbourg, A. Eurelings, K. Hakkarainen (eds.) *European Perspectives on Computer-supported Collaborative learning*, pp. 123-130.
3. C. DiGiano & J. Roschelle. 2000. "Rapid-assembly componentware for education". *Proceedings of the Int.Workshop on Advanced Learning Technologies*. IEEE Computer Society Press.
4. U. Hoppe, K. Gassner & N. Pinkwart. 2000. "Augmenting cooperative visual languages environments with object contexts and process semantics". In *Proceedings of New Technologies for Collaborative Learning NTLC 2000*, pp. 63-70.
5. K. Issroff & E. Scanlon. 2001. "Case studies revisited: what can activity theory offer?" In P. Dillenbourg, A. Eurelings, K. Hakkarainen (eds.) *European Perspectives on Computer-supported Collaborative learning*, pp. 316-323.
6. M. Rodríguez-Artacho & M. F. Verdejo. 1999. "Using a High Level Language to Describe and Create Web-based learning scenarios". In *Proceedings of the IEEE Frontiers in Education Conference*.
7. J. Roschelle, C. DiGiano, M.Koutlis, A. Repenning, J. Phillips, N. Jackiw & D. Suthers. 1999. "Developing Educational Software Components". *Computer*, September 99, pp 2-10.
8. D. Suthers. 1999. "Representational bias as guidance for learning interactions: a research agenda". In S.Lajoie & M.Vivet (eds.) *Artificial Intelligence in Education 99*, pp. 121-128. Editors. Amsterdam IOS Press. 1999
9. W. R. van Joolingen. 2000. "Designing for discovery collaborative learning". In *ITS 2000*, pp. 201-211. Springer-Verlag.
10. M.F. Verdejo, B. Barros, M. Rodriguez-Artacho. 2001. A proposal to support the design of experimental learning activities. In P. Dillenbourg, A. Eurelings, K. Hakkarainen (eds.) *Perspectives on Computer-supported Collaborative learning*, pp. 633-640.

Modelling of an Adaptive Hypermedia System Based on Active Rules

Hussein Raad and Bernard Causse

LIUPPA
Université de Pau
BP 576 64010 Pau cedex
Tel : 01.47.98.72.84
raadhussein@hotmail.com
Bernard.Causse@iutbay.univ-pau.fr

Abstract. This paper is a contribution to the modelling of adaptive hypermedia. The main feature of such a system is able to construct its adaptive behaviour easily. It is based on the concept of the active rule (Event-Condition-Action). The advantage of this concept resides in the integration of all existing adaptation techniques in the system. Furthermore, this system allows introducing new adaptation strategies easily. The system architecture consists of three main parts: first the traditional hypermedia subsystem that contains the navigational model, the interface model, and the multimedia resources; second the adaptive subsystem that contains the user model, the semantic network model, the events analyser, and the adaptive behaviour specification entity; third the tasks model which contain the strategic rules bases associated with the adaptive behaviour specification entity, the navigational rules bases associated with the navigational model, and the interface rules bases associated with the interface model.

1   Introduction

The emerging research domain Adaptive Hypermedia Systems (AHS) aims mainly to bridge the gap between traditional hypermedia systems and adaptive system. The goal of AHS is to help a wide range of users in a knowledge context largely diffused.
This study aims to model AHS based on the active rules (Event-Condition-Action). The paper reviews the literature of the adaptation methods, discusses the general aspects of the approach being adopted in the existing AHSs and proposes the general architecture of our AHS.

2   Adaptation Methods

We can distinguish between two adaptation methods: the first is based on the contents level (the so-called adaptive presentation); and the second is a link-based adaptation (the so-called adaptive navigation).

S.A. Cerri, G. Gouardères, and F. Paraguaçu (Eds.): ITS 2002, LNCS 2363, pp. 149–157, 2002.
© Springer-Verlag Berlin Heidelberg 2002

2.1   Adaptive Presentation

The idea is to adapt the content of a page accessed by a particular user to the current knowledge level, goals, and other characteristics of the user. Four techniques can be distinguished: additional, prerequisite, comparative and sorting explanations.

2.1.1   Additional Explanations
It is the addition of particular information to the basic content of a page. This information explains a concept that is related to a category of the users. The additional explanations can be presented or hidden according to the level of this category. This technique is used in the following systems: MetaDoc, KN-AHS, IPIAIM and Anatom-Tutor.

2.1.2   Prerequisite Explanations
This technique is based on the principle of the prerequisite links between the semantic concepts. Before presenting a concept explanation, the system inserts the explanations concerning the prerequisite concepts to facilitate the comprehension of this concept. The systems which apply this technique are Lisp-Critic and C-book.

2.1.3   Comparative Explanations
This technique is based on the principle of the similar links between the concepts. If there are two similar concepts, a comparative explanation can be offered to the user to show the similarities and the differences between these two concepts. The Comparative explanation is applied in the following systems: ITEM/PG, Lisp-Critic and C-book

2.1.4   Sorting Explanations
This technique consists in sorting information which will be explained to the user. This information which is related to a same semantic concept, takes into account the user formation and his knowledge. This technique is implemented in Hypadapter and EPIAIM

2.2   Adaptive Navigation

The idea of adaptive navigation techniques is to help the users to find their paths in hyperspace by adapting the style of link presentation to goals, knowledge and other characteristics of an individual user. The most popular techniques are: direct guidance, sorting links, hidden links and annotation links.

2.2.1   Direct Guidance
It is the simplest technique of adaptive navigation support. Direct guidance consists in selecting the next "best" node or page for the user to visit according to the user's goal and other parameters represented in the user model. Among the systems which use this technique are Web Watcher, ISIS-Tutor, SHIVA and HyperTutor.

2.2.2 Sorting Links

This technique consists in sorting all the links of a particular page according to the criteria indicated in the user model. This sorting is decreasing according to the links importance. This technique is applied in the following systems: Anatom-Tutor, Hypadapter, Adaptive HyperMan, HYPERFLEX and WebWatcher.

2.2.3 Hidden Links

The idea of hiding technique is to restrict the navigation space by hiding links to "not relevant" pages. This technique is easy to implement in the AHS. It avoids the user be lost in a large hyperspace. The systems which adopt this technique are: ISIS-Tutor, HyperTutor, SHIVA and WebWatcher.

2.2.4 Annotation Links

Annotation links technique consists in augmenting the links that can tell the user more about the current state of the nodes behind the annotated links. These annotations can be provided in textual form or in the form of visual cues using. This technique is applied in the systems: Excel Handbook, Elm-art, Item/pg, ISIS-Tutor, Hypadapter.

3   Structure of an Adaptive Hypermedia System

In this work, a novel tendency is adopted to build adaptive hypermedia systems. It consists in extending the traditional hypermedia systems towards the adaptive hypermedia systems using the adaptation techniques in the adaptive systems. We propose an adaptive hypermedia system which is based on active rules (Event-Condition-Action). More precisely, the specification of the components of this system, including the active rules, is based on the object concept. The advantage of active rules resides in the integration of all existing adaptation techniques in the system; it also allows easily introducing new adaptation strategies.

The architecture of this system consists of three main parts: an adaptive subsystem, a traditional hypermedia subsystem and a tasks model (fig.1).

3.1   Adaptive Subsystem

This part models the users' characteristics and the semantic concepts that must be acquired by these users. It also selects the corresponding adaptation behaviour and organizes the events coming from the user.

The adaptive subsystem contains the four following components: the user model, the semantic network model, the events analyser and the adaptive behaviour specification entity.

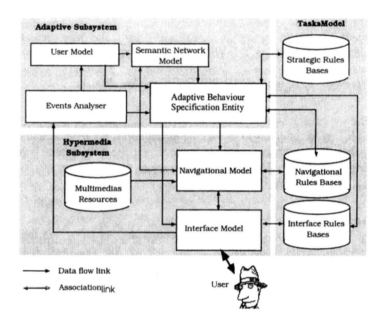

Fig. 1. Architecture of adaptive hypermedia system based on active rules

3.1.1 User Model

In the user model, we adopted stereotypic approach at the granularity level. This approach accounts for the concept of group that allows classifying the users into categories. This approach, however, does not exclude the individual aspect of the user. This model consists of three main parts:

- The individual part focuses on the user's personal information.
- The common part represents the groups' characteristics.
- The recovery part or the recovery model is devoted to represent the user's knowledge. This part is associated with the semantic concepts in the system.

3.1.2 Semantic Network Model

It constitutes an organization of concepts and the relationships between these concepts. Each concept may have a set of attributes to represent its semantic aspects. The relationships determine the nature of the links between the concepts. This model represents the user's knowledge and identifies the navigational entities.

3.1.3 Events Analyser

The events analyzer organizes the events coming from the user. This component feeds the user model by the events and sends the necessary events to the adaptive behaviour specification entity.

3.1.4   Adaptive Behaviour Specification Entity

This component determines the behaviour of the system by taking into account different users categories, the concepts. The adaptive behaviour specification entity selects and runs various rules bases: strategic bases, navigational bases and interface bases (to be explained later). This component respects the order in which the bases should be executed.

3.2   Hypermedia Subsystem

This part is responsible for modelling the navigational aspect of the system. The hypermedia subsystem contains three components: a navigational model, an interface model, and the multimedia resources.

3.2.1   Navigational Model

This model builds the navigational structures. It consists of two principal parts: the primitive elements like nodes and links; the navigational contexts which are based on the primitive elements.

3.2.2   Interface Model

This model specifies the visible entities which are presented to final user. Each node in the navigational model is associated with a corresponding interface node.

3.2.3   Multimedia Resources (Database Bases Multimedia)

This part contains all the multimedia resources that can be used in the system as text, image, audio, and video.

This component provides the navigational model by the necessary information while keeping the two parts clearly separated.

3.3   Tasks Model

The behavior of the system is obtained by integrating the rules with a specific form: Event-Condition-Action; also called active rules.

These rules are inspired from the production rules in the expert systems [Dayal *et al*, 88]. The active rules are applied in data bases domain to introduce an active aspect into these systems like HiPAC [Mccarthy & Dayal, 89] and ADACTIF [Tawbi, 96], but these rules are not largely used in the adaptive hypermedia domain.

The importance of the active rules resides in the facility of composition of the system behavior. The logic of the active rules takes the following form: with occurrence of an event E, if a condition C is satisfied then the system will run an action A.

A set of rules may compose a rules base. The base role is to run several elementary tasks which are coherent between them. In our system, we classified three categories of bases according to tasks type.

3.3.1   Strategic Rules Bases
This component represents a strategic view of the system. These bases determine the basic behavior of the system and select the navigational and interface bases.

3.3.2   Navigational Rules Bases
The navigational rules bases are devoted to specify the navigational behaviour. Each base selects the navigational context and suitable nodes and links.

3.3.3   Interface Rules Bases
This part is responsible to specify the interaction between the system and the user. Each interface node is associated with several interface rules bases.

3.4   Dynamic Model of Our System

The goal of the dynamic model is to study the principal states of the system during its life cycle. This dynamic model is based on a method notation OMT. The following figure explains the various states of the life cycle in the system.

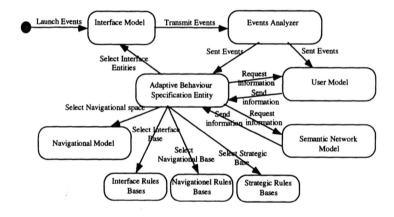

Fig. 2. Dynamic Model of adaptive hypermedia system

The first event comes from the user who requests a set of goals to be realized. The interface model will be active to provide screens corresponding to the user. This one gives information depending on its goals. The interface model transforms this information into intern events and transmits it towards the events analyzer. This last composes and transmits the events towards the adaptive behaviour specification entity and the user model.

The behavior specification entity will be active to select a strategic rules base by taking into account the user model and the semantic network model. According to the strategic base, the behavior specification entity selects navigational rules base, an interface entities and an interface rules base:

According to these steps, the system provides an adaptive behavior to the user's needs. The user, in turn, reacts to start another set of events.

4   Evaluation of the System

This system presents an excellent solution to extend an educational hypermedia system that conceived and implemented within project LINGUA. A simple example is given below to show how the rules bases specify the system behavior.

Initially, a strategic base will be activated by an event Held_Aims_List (Fig. 3). This base makes up two lists of bases: Navigational_Base_List and Interface_Base_List and filter it by choosing the bases corresponding to the user.

```
R1 :    When Held_Aims_List
        If Value(Group.Domain)= 'Education' et Value(Navigationnel_Base.Domain)='Education'
        Then Add(Base current, Navigational_Base_List)
R2 :    When Held_Aims_List
        If Value(Group.Domain)= 'Education' and Value(Interface_Base.Domain)='Education'
        Then Add(Base current, Interface_Base_Liste)
-- To select one or more navigational bases in the list " Navigational_Base_List "
R3 :    When Saturate(Navigational_Base_List)
        If Value(Group.Level)= 'Medium'
        Then Select_Base(Navigational_Base_List)
-- To select one or more interface bases in the list " Interface_Base_List "
R4 :    When Saturate(Interface_Base_List)
        If Value(Group.Level)= 'Medium'
        Then Select_Base (Interface_Base_List)
```

Fig. 3. Strategic base.

After the strategic base selects a navigational base this one chooses the nodes and the navigational links based on the concepts and the semantic links in the semantic network model (fig 4).

```
R1 :    When Aim_Identified
        If Belong(Aim, Concept_List)
        Then Activate_Final_Point (Aim, Concept)
R2 :    When Identified_Final_Point(But)
        If Value(True)
        Then Find(Concepts_Known_List, User) and Add(Concepts_Known_List, Path)
R3 :    When Added(Concepts_Known_List, Path)
        If Nb_Member(Concepts_Known_List) > 0
        Then Select_Links_Associated(Concepts_Known_List, Links_List) and Filter_List(Links_List,
        Educative_Links__List)
R4 :    When Filtered_Educative_Links__List
        If Nb_Member(Links_List) > 0
        Then Find(Concept_Associed_Link, Links_List) and Add(Concept_Associed_Link, Path)
```

Fig. 4. Navigational base.

The strategic base also selects an interface node and a corresponding interface base. This one specifies the interaction scenario between the user and the system (fig 5).

```
R1 :   When Activated(Educative_Navigational_Node)
       If Belong(User, Group)
       Then Activate(Points_Bar) and Activate(Field.explication) and Activate(Button.Vocabulary)
R2 :   When Button_Clicked(Button.Video)
       If Value(User.Score_Point) > 10
       Then Prevent(Annotation_Video)
R3 :   When Button_Clicked(Button.Video)
       If Value(User.Score_Point) < 10
       Then Activate(Annotation_Video))
```

Fig. 5. Interface base.

5   Conclusion

In this work, a novel AHS architecture model based fully on active rules (Event-Condition-Action) is presented. This model aims to facilitate the specification of the system adaptive behaviour. Based on the concept of active rules, this system applies all the adaptation techniques, which is not the case of the existing systems. For example, Anatom-Tutor and Adaptive HyperMan apply only two techniques "sorting links" and "hidden links", ISIS-Tutor applies three techniques "direct guidance", "hidden links" and "annotation links".

The separation between the behavioural part and the entities models makes it easy to add new adaptation techniques to our system. Moreover, the existence of three categories of rules bases supports the application of three adaptation types: adaptive presentation, adaptive navigation and strategic adaptation, whereas the existing systems don't. For example, EPIAIM and Lisp-Critic only offer adaptive presentation; HYPERFLEX and WebWatcher only offer adaptive navigation; Item/pg and Hypadapter jointly offer adaptive presentation and adaptive navigation.

On another side, according to the comparison between our system and those of intelligent tutor, it was observed that the model navigational in our system offers the intelligent navigational behavior, whereas the intelligent tutor systems do not have this characteristic. This one allows our system to be integrated in the Internet network.

References

[Dayal et al, 88]   DAYAL U., BLAUSTEIN B. et BUCHMANN A.: "The HiPAC Pro-ject: Combining Active Databases and Timing Constraints.", SIGMOD RECORD, vol 17, nº 1, pp 51-70, March 1988.

[Debevc et al., 94]   DEBEVC M., RAJKO S. & DONLAGIC D.: "Adaptive of Computing and Informatics," 18, pp 357-366, 1994.

[Kaplan et al., 93]   KAPLAN C., FENWICK J. & CHEN J.: "Adaptive hypertext navigation based on user goals and context", User Models and User Adapted Interaction 3(3), pp 193-220, 1993.

[Kaptelinin, 93]   KAPTELININ V.: "Item recognition in menu selection: The effect of practice", INTERCHI'93 Adjunct Proceedings, Amsterdam, pp183-184, 1993.

[Kay & Kummerfeld, 94]   KAY J. & KUMMERFELD R. J.: "An Individualised Course for the C Programming Language", Second Inter-national WWW Conference "Mosiac and the Web", Chicago,IL, http://www.ncsa.uiuc.edu/SDG/IT94/Proceedings/Educ/ kummerfeld/kummerfeld.html, 1994.

[Mccarthy & Dayal, 89]   MCCARTHY D.R. & DAYAL U.: "The Architecture of an Active Data Base Management System", Proceeding ACM-Sigmod Conference Portland, pp 215-224, may 1989.

[Tawbi, 96]   TAWBI C.: "ADACTIF : Extension d'un SGBD à l'Activité par une Approche Procédurale Basée sur les Rendez-vous", Thèse d'université, Toulouse, 1996.

[Widom & Finkelstein, 90] WIDOM J. & FINKELSTEIN S.: "A Syntax and Semantics for Set Oriented Production Rule in Relational Databases.", Proceedings of SIGMOD, Atlantic City NJ, June 1990.

The Architecture of Why2-Atlas: A Coach for Qualitative Physics Essay Writing

Kurt VanLehn, Pamela W. Jordan, Carolyn P. Rosé, Dumisizwe Bhembe,
Michael Böttner, Andy Gaydos, Maxim Makatchev, Umarani Pappuswamy,
Michael Ringenberg, Antonio Roque, Stephanie Siler, and Ramesh Srivastava

LRDC, University of Pittsburgh, Pittsburgh, PA 15260
vanlehn@cs.pitt.edu

Abstract. The Why2-Atlas system teaches qualitative physics by having students write paragraph-long explanations of simple mechanical phenomena. The tutor uses deep syntactic analysis and abductive theorem proving to convert the student's essay to a proof. The proof formalizes not only what was said, but the likely beliefs behind what was said. This allows the tutor to uncover misconceptions as well as to detect missing correct parts of the explanation. If the tutor finds such a flaw in the essay, it conducts a dialogue intended to remedy the missing or misconceived beliefs, then asks the student to correct the essay. It often takes several iterations of essay correction and dialogue to get the student to produce an acceptable explanation. Pilot subjects have been run, and an evaluation is in progress. After explaining the research questions that the system addresses, the bulk of the paper describes the system's architecture and operation.

1 Objectives

The Why2 project has three objectives. The first is to build and evaluate qualitative physics tutors where all student communication is via natural language text. In particular, we will compare their performance to text-based expository instruction and human tutoring. Text-based natural language (NL) technology has improved significantly but is still far from perfect. Are the inevitable disfluencies so confusing that they significantly retard learning, or are they no worse than the disfluencies of human-to-human text-based tutoring?

The second objective is to compare several different NL processing techniques. In particular, we are collaborating with the AutoTutor Research Group [1, 2] who are building a version of Why2 using latent semantic analysis, a statistical technique. Our version of Why2 is called Why2-Atlas; their version is called Why2-AutoTutor. Why2-Atlas is based on deep syntactic analysis and compositional semantics. It is more difficult to build but may yield better performance.

The third objective is to develop authoring tools that facilitate development of NL-based tutoring systems. Whereas a typical tutoring system's size is roughly determined by the amount of material it covers, an NL-based tutor's size is also a function of the diversity of the words and linguistic structures that students use.

S.A. Cerri, G. Gouardères, and F. Paraguaçu (Eds.): ITS 2002, LNCS 2363, pp. 158–167, 2002.
© Springer-Verlag Berlin Heidelberg 2002

Since this is a large effort, we chose a worthy pedagogical goal: qualitative physics understanding. It is well known that college physics students are often unable to construct acceptable qualitative explanations for simple physics questions, such as "what happens when two balls of different masses fall from the same height?" Sometimes they know what happens (the balls hit the ground at the same time) but they cannot explain *why* it occurs. Decades of experimental instruction have produced only limited progress toward universal qualitative understanding [3]. Even students with top grades in their classes get low scores on standardized measures of qualitative understanding, such as the Force Concepts Inventory [4].

The Why2-Atlas user interface is remarkably simple. There are three windows: the problem window, the essay window and the chat window. The problem window merely states a question, such as "Suppose you are running in a straight line at constant speed. You throw a pumpkin straight up. Where will it land? Explain." Students type their explanation into the essay window, then click on a submit button. The student and the tutor take turns typing in the chat window. For instance, one student's explanation was, "It would seem as though the ball would fall back into the man's hands at the end of T, but I do not think that this will happen…after the ball is thrown there is a lack of a force which results in the decrease of horizontal velocity." When this is entered in the essay window, Why2-Atlas analyzes it, which involves determining what "the ball" and "the man" refer to, among other things. The tutor determines that the student has a common misconception, which is that a moving object always slows down unless there is a force to propel it along. Switching to the chat window, the tutor engages the student in a dialogue, such as the one shown in Table 1. At its end, the tutor suggests that the student change the essay. If all goes well, the student will remove the misconception from the explanation, in which case the tutor can address any flaws that remain. If the student does not do so, then the tutor will either try a different dialogue.

Why2-Atlas is composed of several modules: A sentence-level understander (SLU), a discourse-level understander (DLU), a tutorial strategist and a dialogue engine. These four modules are controlled by a discourse manager. As the student enters an essay, the SLU parses it and produces a set of propositions expressed in a version of first-order logic. The discourse-level understander (DLU) assimilates them into a explanation. If a proposition is new, then the DLU augments the explanation with inferences that explain (prove abductively) the proposition. Next, the tutorial strategist analyzes the augmented explanation's completeness and correctness. If the explanation used rules that represent misconceptions (e.g., "If there is no force to propel an object along, it slows down."), then the tutorial strategist creates tutorial goals to remedy those misconceptions. If the explanation does not explicitly mention one of the points that the project physicists have indicated must be present in any acceptable essay, then the strategist creates a tutorial goal of eliciting that mandatory point. Next, the strategist uses heuristics to select the highest priority tutorial goal and attempts to achieve it by calling the dialogue engine to conduct a knowledge construction dialogue (KCD). If the student fails to remove the flaw after one or more KCDs, the system tells the student how to do so.

The remaining sections describe each of the modules in more detail and the relationship of this work to earlier work.

Table 1. A Knowledge Construction Dialogue (KCD)

• Tutor: OK, let's consider the relationship between force and acceleration in a different context. A hockey puck is resting on the rough ice surface of a skating rink (a hockey team has just finished practicing on it). You push with a force, F, during the time from t1 to t2. Assume that the only force acting horizontally on the puck is friction due to the ice surface (there is no air resistance). What will happen to the velocity of the puck after your push? • Student: it will get slower • Tutor: Good. A zamboni smoothes the ice so that the friction caused by the roughness of the ice surface is reduced. You push the same hockey puck with the same force as before (and for the same amount of time). How does the change in velocity of the hockey puck after this push compare to its change in velocity following the initial push? • Student: slows more slowly • Tutor: Correct. Now assume there exists a machine that can make the ice surface perfectly smooth, so that the friction caused by the ice surface is zero. Again assume the force of air resistance is zero. If you were to push a puck on this surface, what would happen to the velocity of the puck following the push? • Student: nothing • Tutor: Right. In general, according to Newton's first law, if there are no forces acting on a body, what happens to the body's velocity? • Student: not a darn thing • Tutor: Okay. In general, these and similar observations are summarized in Newton's first law, which states that if there are no forces acting on a body, its velocity will remain constant (or its acceleration will be zero)

2 The Sentence-Level Understander

The sentence-level understander (SLU) converts each sentence in the student's essay into a set of propositions. The propositions are expressed in a version of first-order logic. For instance, consider the following sentence: "Should the arrow have been drawn to point down?" Roughly speaking, this should be converted to:

$$\exists e \in events, \exists v \in vectors, \exists s \ draw(e, s, v) \& tense(e, past) \& mood(e, interrog) \& direction(v, down)$$

This is only an approximation of the real output. It illustrates the challenge of converting words into the appropriate domain-specific predicates. Notice how "arrow" has been converted to "vector." Another challenge is to interlink the predicate arguments correctly: Notice how the variable that denotes "the arrow" appears in both "draw" and "direction." Other aspects of the meaning of the utterance are not yet processed. For instance, "the arrow" probably refers to some specific vector mentioned earlier in the dialog, but the SLU makes no attempt to resolve that reference.

The SLU is composed of a lexical preprocessor, a parser, a repair module (which together comprise a package called CARMEL) and a statistical analyzer [5, 6]. As the student types in a sentence, the text is sent to the lexical preprocessing module, which looks up the words in a lexicon, doing spelling correction as necessary. It will also strip off prefixes and suffixes in order to uncover the root forms of the words. The resulting graph of root word forms is sent to the next module, the parser.

LCFlex [5, 7], is a flexible left-corner parser that does a deep syntactic analysis of each sentence. For instance, for the illustration sentence, the parser determines that "the vector" is both the deep object of "draw" and the deep subject of "point." As it builds a syntactic analysis, the parser builds the logical form as well. This allows it to check that the predicates are assigned arguments of the right type.

LCFlex copes with ungrammatical input by skipping words, inserting missing categories and relaxing grammatical constraints as necessary in order to parse the sentence. For instance, "Should the arrow has been drawn point down" would parse. When the parser produces too many analyses of the sentence, it uses statistical information on the frequency of word roots and grammatical analyses to determine the most probable parse.

If the parser cannot produce any complete analysis of the sentence, then its fragmentary analysis is passed to the repair module. The fragments can be viewed as domain-specific predicates that are looking for argument fillers, and domain-specific typed variables that are looking for arguments to fill. A genetic search is used to build a complete analysis from these fragments.

If the repair module fails, then the symbolic approach is abandoned, and the SLU's fourth module takes over. It uses text classification techniques. Given a statistical language model that indicates how strongly each word is associated with domain classifications (e.g., misconceptions), it computes the most likely classification of each sentence using either a naïve-Bayesian approach [8] or LSA.

Besides this statistical language model, the SLU requires three other large knowledge sources: a meaning-representation language definition, a grammar and a lexicon. The meaning-representation language definition specifies the domain predicates and types that can occur in the logical form output by the SLU. The definition of a predicate specifies type restrictions on its arguments. For instance, the definition of the "move" predicate specifies that its "agent" argument be an instance of the "concrete entity" type.

The grammar is a unification-augmented context-free grammar based on both Functional Grammar [9] and Lexical Functional Grammar [10]. Its main job is to assign deep syntactic roles to phrases in the sentence. For instance, in both the active sentence "I drew the vector" and the passive sentence "The vector was drawn," the noun phrase "the vector" is assigned to the same deep syntactic role (argument) of the verb "draw."

The lexicon defines word roots. For each one, it specifies their syntactic categorization, the possible semantic predicates or types, and the mapping from syntactic roles to semantic roles. For words like verbs that can have arguments, the lexical entry also specifies information about the syntactic and semantic argument restrictions. Words with multiple senses have multiple lexical entries. For instance, "draw" has 7 entries. The lexicon was built by adding semantic information and idioms to COMLEX [11].

Parts of the SLU (e.g., LCFlex) have been evaluated separately [5, 7], and some are being used by other projects [12, 13].

3 Discourse-Level Understanding

The discourse-level understander (DLU) receives logical forms and outputs a proof. Topologically, the proof is a forest of interwoven trees. The leaves are facts given in the problem statement or assumptions made while the proof is being constructed. The roots (conclusions) are student propositions. Other student propositions may occur in the middle of the forest. As an illustration, consider the following question and student essay:

Q: Suppose you are in a free-falling elevator and you hold your keys motionless in front of your face and then let go. What will happen to them? Explain.

A: The keys will fall parellel to the persons face because of the constant acceleration caused by gravity but later the keys may go over your head because the mass of the keys are less.

Although this essay has a misspelling, missing punctuation and grammatical errors, the SLU parses it and sends four propositions to the DLU. The first proposition corresponds to the student statement that the keys will fall parallel to the person's face. This conclusion is correct and becomes a root in the proof. The second proposition, that gravitational acceleration is constant, corresponds to an interior node in this proof. The third proposition, that the keys go over the person's head, is based on a common misconception, that heavier objects fall faster. It becomes a root in the proof. The last proposition, that the mass of the keys is less, corresponds to a node in the interior of the proof of the third proposition.

Proofs are constructed by Tacitus-lite+ [14], which is an extension of Tacitus [15]. Its knowledge base is a set of Horn clauses that represent both correct physics beliefs, such as "If a vector is vertical, its horizontal component is zero," and incorrect beliefs, such as "more massive objects have larger vertical accelerations." The goals in the body (the antecedents) of a rule each have a cost. Tacitus-lite+ can choose to assume the goal rather than prove it, in which case its cost is added to the overall cost of the proof. Tacitus-lite+ prefers proofs with the lowest costs. This mechanism, which is a form of abduction, is necessary to allow Tacitus-lite+ to "prove" false student statements.

When a goal that has unbound variables is proved, the variables often become bound to constants, terms or other variables. When Tacitus-lite+ assumes a goal, it can also bind unbound variables. To reduce the combinatorics when this occurs, all arguments in predicates and terms have types associated with them. The types constrain what existing constants, terms and variables may be bound to the unbound arguments of the goal that is being assumed. If a variable is used in several goals, it accumulates constraints from all of them.

Because variables accumulate constraints, the process of resolving referring expressions is interwoven with the construction of the proof. For instance, the student statement, "the mass of the keys is less," becomes a proposition similar to less(mass(keys1), X) where keys1 is a constant denoting the keys, mass(keys1) is a compound term denoting their mass, and X is a variable. That is, the student did not say what the mass was less than, so the DLU must resolve the implicit reference. Via accumulation of constraints and some discourse heuristics based on centering [16], the DLU ends up binding X to mass(person1). Sometimes objects must be created in order to refer to them. For instance, the temporal reference implicit in the student's statement, "later the keys may go over your head," requires dividing the fall of the keys into two time intervals, and stating that the keys are parallel to the person's face during the first interval but above the person's head during the second interval.

Creating time intervals in order to refer to them is just one of many complexities that must be handled when converting language to proofs. We have only tried to solve those that are necessary for our purposes. For instance, the modal "may" is ignored in "later the keys may go over your head."

4   The Tutorial Strategist

Once a proof has been constructed, the tutorial strategist analyzes it to find flaws. Each flaw is associated with patterns that match occurrences of the flaw in the proof. In the proof mentioned earlier, there are several flaws. The main one is that the misconception "heavier objects fall faster" has been used. In addition, several points that physicists consider mandatory for a sufficiently complete explanation have been implied but not stated. For instance, one is "the keys' acceleration and the person's acceleration are the same." Each detected flaw is queued as a tutorial goal to remedy the flaw.

Once tutorial goals have been queued, the strategist picks the highest priority goal from the queue. The priorities are: fix misconceptions before anything else, then fix self-contradictions, errors and incorrect assumptions, and lastly elicit missing mandatory points. Since most essays are missing several mandatory points, the choice of which one to tutor first is determined by a hand-authored list for each problem. This insures that the points will be elicited in a natural order.

5   The Dialogue Engine

The tutorial goals for remedying a misconception are associated with a specific *remediation* KCD, and those for eliciting a mandatory point are associated with a specific *elicitation* KCD. If one of these goals is chosen, then the dialogue manager, APE, is called with the name of the KCD.

KCDs are managed by finite state networks whose nodes are questions to the students. The links exiting a node correspond to expected responses to the question. The questions are written to invite short responses from the students so that simple techniques can be used to match the expected responses to the actual ones. For instance, Table 1 shows one KCD.

In order to determine which expected response is the best match to the student's answer, APE calls LCFlex with a simple semantic grammar. Each question has its own semantic grammar, although the grammar may share rules with other questions' grammars. The root categories in the grammar correspond to the expected responses. For instance, if the expected responses are "down" and "up," then the semantic grammar would have two rules such as "Ques32_down_resp => down_cat" and "Ques32_up_resp => up_cat" where down_cat and up_cat are categories used in several semantic grammars and are reduced by rules such as "down_cat => 'down'," "down_cat => 'downwards'," "down_cat => 'towards earth'," etc. Because LCFlex can skip words, it can find certain key words or phrases in the student's response even if they are surrounded by extra words, as in "Is it downwards?"

When the student has finished the KCD, the discourse manager inserts a segue, such as "Given what you've learned, please change your essay." The student should edit the essay, and resubmit it. When students fail to correct the essay, the same flaw will be detected and will probably be selected again for fixing. If the tutorial goal is important enough that multiple KCDs exist for remedying it, then a second KCD will be tried. If the discourse manager runs out of KCDs for fixing a flaw, then it gently suggests an explicit change to the essay. For example, if one of the required points is missing, the tutor says, "It could be that you have what I'm looking for in mind, but I'm just not able to understand what you're saying. Let me show you what I'd say was the point that should be covered in your essay: 'After their release, the only force acting on the keys is the downward force of earth's gravity.'"

6 Authoring Tools

The major knowledge sources in Why2-Atlas are the Tacitus-lite+ rules, the KCDs, the semantic grammars used in the KCDs, the syntactic grammar and the lexicon. We are working on tools for authoring all these knowledge sources. However, the only tools that are currently in routine use are the KCD editor and DAIENU, the semantic grammar authoring system.

The KCD editor is a graphically oriented editor designed for non-programmers [17, 18]. Typically the author starts by creating a main line of reasoning consisting of alternating questions and correct responses. Next the author enters expected incorrect answers for each question. The author then defines subsidiary KCDs, some of which may also be remediation KCDs, for the incorrect answers. It is typical to call the same KCDs from many different locations. As a result, KCDs can become so complicated that it would be difficult to navigate their links without the aid of the KCD editor.

The second tool, DAIENU, is used to create the semantic grammars required by the KCDs [19]. There are several hundred KCDs in the current version of Why2-Atlas, and each has several questions, so several hundred semantic grammars are needed. DAIENU begins by collecting all the expected student responses in the KCDs. Each is a string of expected student words, entered by the author, and a category standing for that particular expected response. The job of DAIENU is to create intermediate categories, similar to the down_cat and up_cat mentioned earlier, that will be used in the multiple semantic grammars. DAIENU suggests clusters of strings, based on shared words, to the author. The author can also add or subtract strings from the initial set. Together they come up with a set of strings that occurred in the KCD responses and have similar meaning, according to the author. DAIENU then finds commonalities between the sets such that it can construct a compact set of general grammar rules that will correctly classify the members of each set. When it has produced a candidate set of grammars, it generates novel strings labeled by the grammars, and presents them to the author. The author corrects their classifications, and the whole grammar induction process repeats.

7   Related Work

Development of Why2-Atlas is possible only because we borrowed many ideas from earlier efforts. This section highlights some of the similarities between Why2-Atlas and other NL-based tutoring systems.

Perhaps the first fully operational NL-based tutor was CIRCSIM-tutor [20]. It used information-extraction techniques and short-answer questions in order to conduct a dialogue about the student's qualitative analysis of a cardiophysiological feedback system. We also use short answer questions and word-based analysis of student responses in order to conduct a robust, fluent dialogue. In fact, the two tutors use nearly the same dialogue engine [21]. However, the CIRCSIM-tutor students express their cardiophysiological analysis by putting +/-/0 marks in a table, whereas our students enter an NL essay. Most of the current complexity in Why2-Atlas is devoted to analysis of this essay.

Another early NL-based tutor is AutoTutor [2]. It opens the dialogue by simply asking the student a question, such as "What happens when you boot up a computer?" It has a list of mandatory points that it wants the student to explicitly articulate, and will prompt the student more and more pointedly until the student says (types) them clearly. It also has a set of misconceptions that it anticipates the student will enter, and has remedial messages to deal with them. We use the same basic idea for analyzing the student essays: a set of mandatory points and a set of misconceptions. The main difference is that AutoTutor uses a statistical technique (LSA) to determine if a point has been mentioned, whereas Why2-Atlas uses symbolic analyses.

Whereas CIRCSIM-tutor and AutoTutor use shallow, word-based analyses of student text, Aleven, Popescu and Koedinger [12] are building a tutor that uses deep analyses of student explanations. Their tutor asks students simple geometry questions, such as whether two angles are the same. Students must provide both an answer and a NL explanation, such as "The sum of complementary angles is 180 degrees." Students typically do not provide such precise, complete explanations on their first attempt, so the tutor must prompt them more and more pointedly to add precision to their justification. Shallow, word-based analyses of these explanations would clearly not suffice, so the tutor uses the LCFlex parser [5, 7], a deep syntactic grammar, the Loom symbolic classifier, and a geometry ontology to analyze the students' explanations. For the same reasons, we also use the LCFlex parser and a deep syntactic grammar. However, our students' explanations often contain several clauses, compared to the single clause or phrase that typifies student justifications in the Geometry tutor. Consequently, we use an abductive theorem prover and a physics axiom set instead of a classifier and an ontology.

BEETLE [13] and PACO [22] are NL-based tutors for procedural tasks. The students need to do steps in a hierarchical, partial order which they may or may not know. A major challenge for these systems is allowing students to do steps when they can and offering hints when they can't. We have avoided (at least in this first version of the system) the problems of conducting a mixed initiative dialogue by giving the student all the initiative during the essay-entering phase, and having the tutor take the lead otherwise.

8 Conclusions

Our mission is to explore the cost-benefit space of NL-based tutoring. As an initial data point, we have constructed a baseline system and are evaluating it this spring. The evaluation compares Why2-Atlas to 3 other methods for teaching the same qualitative physics knowledge using the same 10 essay questions: (1) human tutors, (2) Why2-AutoTutor, a statistical NLP system described earlier, and (3) expository physics texts. Although Why2-Atlas is proving to be fast and robust enough, its knowledge sources are not nearly as well developed as we would like, so it often misunderstands the students. However, we anticipated this, and engineered its responses to yield reasonable dialogue despite its misunderstandings. We hypothesize that this baseline system should do about as well as Why2-AutoTutor. We expect both tutoring systems to be better than the expository texts, but not as good as the human tutors. Regardless of how this first evaluation turns out, we will use its log file data to improve our knowledge sources, then run the evaluation again. This will yield a second data point on the tradeoff between NLP sophistication and learning gains. Simultaneously, we are building tools that should lower the development effort for NL-based tutoring. Although the technology for NL-based tutoring is clearly still in its early stages, we hope to understand its benefits, its costs, and how to change both.

Acknowledgements. This research was supported by MURI grant N00014-00-1-0600 from ONR Cognitive Science, and by NSF grant 9720359. We're delighted to acknowledge the help of Art Graesser and his Tutoring Research Group, our partners in the Why2 project.

References

1. Graesser, A.C., et al., Using latent semantic analysis to evaluate the contributions of students in AutoTutor. *Interactive Learning Environments*, 2000.
2. Person, N.K., et al., Simulating human tutor dialog moves in AutoTutor. *International Journal of Artificial Intelligence in Education*, in press.
3. Hake, R.R., Interactive-engagement vs. traditional methods: A six-thousand student survey of mechanics test data for introductory physics students. *American Journal of Physics*, 1998. 66(4): p. 64-74.
4. Hestenes, D., M. Wells, and G. Swackhamer, Force concept inventory. *The Physics Teacher*, 1992. 30: p. 141-158.

5. Rose, C.P. A framework for robust semantic interpretation. In *The First Meeting of the North American Chapter of the Association for Computational Linguistics*. 2000.
6. Rose, C.P. A syntactic framework for semantic interpretation. In *The ESSLLI Workshop on Linguistic Theory and Grammar Implementation*. 2000.
7. Rose, C.P. and A. Lavie, Balancing robustness and efficiency in unification-augmented context-free parsers for large practical applications, in *Robustness in Language and Speech Technology*, J.C. Junqua and G.V. Noord, Editors. 2001, Kluwer Academic press.
8. McCallum, A.K., *Bow: A toolkit for statistical language modeling, text retrieval, classification and clustering*. 1996, CMU: Pittsburgh, PA.
9. Halliday, M.A.K., *An Introduction to Functional Grammar*. 1985: Adward Arnold: A division of Hodder and Stoughton.
10. Bresnan, J., *The Mental Representation of Grammatical Relations*. 1982, Cambridge, MA: MIT Press.
11. Grishman, R., C. Mcleod, and A. Meyers. COMLEX syntax: Building a computational lexicon. In *Proceedings of the 15th International Conference on Computational Linguistics (COLING-94)*. 1994.
12. Aleven, V., O. Popescu, and K.R. Koedinger. A tutorial dialogue system with knowledge-based understanding and classification of student explanations. In *Second IJCAI Workshop on Knowledge and Reasoning in Practical Dialogue Systems*. 2001. Seattle, WA.
13. Core, M.G., J.D. Moore, and C. Zinn. Supporting constructive learning with a feedback planner. In *AAAI Fall Symposium on Building Dialogue Systems for Tutorial Applications*. 2000. Cape Cod, MA.
14. Jordan, P.W., et al. Engineering the Tacitus-lite weighted abduction inference engine for use in the Why-Atlas qualitative physics tutoring system. submitted.
15. Hobbs, J., et al., Interpretation as abduction. *Artificial Intelligence*, 1993. 63(1-2): p. 69-142.
16. Strube, M. Never look back: An alternative to centering. In *Proceedings of the 17th International Conference on Computational Linguistics and the 36th Annual Meeting of the ACL*. 1998.
17. Jordan, P.W., C.P. Rose, and K. VanLehn, Tools for authoring tutorial dialogue knowledge, in *Artificial Intelligence in Education: AI-Ed in the Wired and Wireless future*, J.D. Moore, C. Redfield, and W.L. Johnson, Editors. 2001, IOS: Washington, DC. p. 222-233.
18. Graesser, A.C., et al., Intelligent tutoring systems with conversational dialogue. *AI Magazine*, 2001. 22(4).
19. Rose, C.P. Facilitating the rapid development of language understanding interfaces for tutoring systems. In *AAAI Fall Symposium on Building Tutorial Dialogue Systems*. 2000. Cape Cod, MA.
20. Evens, M.W., et al. Circsim-Tutor: An intelligent tutoring system using natural language dialogue. In *Twelfth Midwest AI and Cognitive Science Conference*. 2001. Oxford, OH.
21. Freedman, R., et al., ITS Tools for natural language dialogue: A domain-independent parser and planner, in *Intelligent Tutoring Systems: 5th International Conference, ITS 2000*, G. Gauthier, C. Frasson, and K. VanLehn, Editors. 2000, Springer: Berlin. p. 433-442.
22. Rickel, J., et al., Building a bridge between intelligent tutoring and collaborative dialogue systems, in *Artificial Intelligence in Education: AI-Ed in the Wired and Wireless Future*, J.D. Moore, C. Redfield, and W.L. Johnson, Editors. 2001, IOS: Washington, DC. p. 592-693.

Integrating Multimedia Technology, Knowledge Based System, and Speech Processing for the Diagnostic and Treatment of Developmental Dyslexia

L. Moreno, C. González*, V. Muñoz, J. Estévez, R. Aguilar, J. Sánchez, J. Sigut, and
J. Piñeiro

Centro Superior de Informática. University of La Laguna.
c/Delgado Barreto s/n 38200. Tenerife. Spain.

Abstract. SICOLE is a research effort to develop a software environment to help tutors of dyslexic children with the diagnostic and treatment tasks. This paper describes the architecture of the package already implemented where three important elements interact: a multimedia interface, an inference module and a database. This architecture provides the system with the flexibility to support a large variety of tasks, dynamic presentations, and complex teaching strategies. The application of speech recognition technology is also researched as an important part of the evaluation of the dyslexic children improvements. This package is being used at the present moment in several Spanish Schools as part of its validation process.

Keywords. Intelligent multimedia and hypermedia systems, case-based reasoning systems, developmental dyslexia.

1 Introduction

New technologies are a big support for helping people with learning difficulties, as research works about it recommend the using of adaptive software for training and teaching children with special needs (NEE) [1]. In this sense, this paper shows the design and implementation of a software package with the features of an intelligent system with two main objectives. Firstly, to establish which is the subtype of a student with developmental dyslexia by evaluating the linguistic and cognitive abilities and finding those ones where the student has deficits. Secondly, to propose and to apply the correct treatment based on exercises presented as attractive multimedia games to solve by the student. The name for this system is SICOLE.

It is very important to establish now the working conditions of SICOLE, because several decisions about the selected design are based on them. This system is a support tool for the professionals who work with dyslexic children. It has not been designed to work with the dyslexic child without the supervision of a human tutor. However, the

---

* Corresponding author: Carina González. E-mail: cjgonza@ull.es Phone: +34 922318287

S.A. Cerri, G. Gouardères, and F. Paraguaçu (Eds.): ITS 2002, LNCS 2363, pp. 168–177, 2002.

supervision level does not have to be high: the system should be robust enough to work in the conditions of a school room with one human tutor and several units of the SICOLE system.

SICOLE is based on the theoretical models selected by an expert team of psychologist specialized in dyslexia. These models are: double route of Colheart [2] where an explanation for the key characteristics of the developmental dyslexics is provided (difficulties in word recognition) and the cognitive theory of multimedia learning by Mayer and Moreno [3], where the cognitive processes that take place in an active multimedia learning are explained. In order to model and represent the expert knowledge structurally in the KBS we have used two methodologies: KADS [4] and IMMPS [5,6,7].

2   SICOLE: Functional Design and Implementation

2.1   Functional Design

The main functional subsystems are the database, the inference module and the interface. The database keeps crucial information about different aspects of the package. On one hand, it stores the available media components and the relation between these components and the concepts involved in the tasks. On the other hand, it stores the profile and history composing our student model.

This system has an inference module with the responsibility of selecting the next task to be proposed taking into consideration the information stored in the database. Furthermore, the media components to be used in the selected task are also chosen examining both the relation between all the components stored in the database, the specifications of the task and the profile and history of this user. The interface is a piece of software where the interaction with the user is controlled. The interface has to determine the basic parameters related to the media components to produce coherent responses to the user actions. To get this, once again the information stored in the database has to be analyzed.

2.2   Implementation Issues

Building a tool with the mentioned features requires the collaboration of a multidisciplinary team. In this sense, from the implementation point of view there are two important issues: the technical design (software engineering) and the artistic development of the media components.

This last point requires the collaboration of different groups. In our case, a multimedia specialist together with a professional artist under the supervision of the psychologists developed and produced most of the media included in SICOLE. The suitability of the artistic work was validated with a number of children asking them about the style and the contents of the drawings. An example of one of these drawings, showing the selected style for the SICOLE package is in figure 1. One of the key points that is very related to the motivation of the user is the variability of the scenarios and media components: at the moment there are about **200** original drawings produced and there are still another **600** to produce in the final system. There are also **2400** sounding elements (explanations, feedback, sounds related to the scenarios, ...) already produced and we are estimating that the final system will contain around **4000**. This high number of elements together with the capability of the system to dynamically compose coherent scenarios with continuous variations avoids the routine in each session, increasing the motivation and interest of the students. These numbers also explain the important role that the inference module plays in the coherent production of the multimedia presentation.

Fig. 1. Artistic style in the pictures of the SICOLE interface.

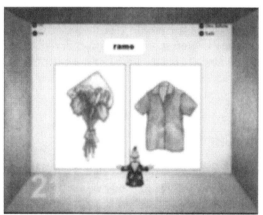

Fig. 2. Some examples of the presentations and demonstration tasks with the collaboration of an agent.

The other keystone of the package is the design of the software. SICOLE is based in a number of available tools to cover the different requirements of the system. At the present moment, the database is supported by the MySQL environment. This decision was made after evaluating other products from the point of view of robustness and fastness to maintain high amounts of data and to exchange pieces of information with other Windows applications that are also part of SICOLE. The core of the multimedia interface is based in commercial applications as Macromedia Authorware 6.0 and Flash 5.0. The media production was carried out with Macromedia Fireworks, Corel Draw and Corel Photo Paint. Finally, the inference module is based in the CLIPS environment and an interface between CLIPS and the database developed for this project with Microsoft Visual C++ 6.0. Additionally, an agent is used in the presentation to guide and motivate the student (figure 2): it is based on the Microsoft Agent Technology and programmed as an Active X object.

The software architecture is designed to allow the system for adapting each presentation to the individual characteristics of each student through a software module. This module generates activities dynamically and builds the presentation following the learning style of the student. In this framework the structure element is very important. The structure of a particular task is stored in the database. We can see this structure as a template that the inference module has to complete with data extracted from the database. The type of data included in a template is diverse: interaction types, definition of text containers, graphics, sounds and animation, input and output variables,...

The role of this structure elements in the whole system can be viewed in figure 3 where the interrelations between the basic software tools. As it is represented, the communication between the interface (Authorware presentation) and the inference module is always performed through the database. The CLIPS system is checking continuously a flag in a control data structure in the database. When the interface determines that a new inference is needed to change the state of the presentation, it changes this flag and waits until the CLIPS system produces all the required inferences. The result is to fill a number of required templates that are read by the Authorware module to change the media components and consequently the state of the presentation.

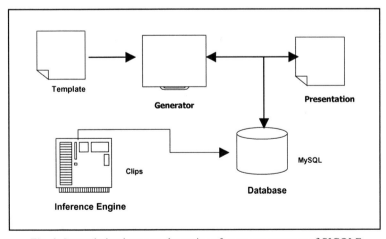

Fig. 3. Interrelation between the main software components of SICOLE.

3   SICOLE: An Approach for the Diagnostic and Treatment of the Dyslexia

The elements described above could be applied in general for any Intelligent Tutorial System with adaptive requirements. In this part of the paper, the particularities about the specific task of diagnosing and treating the dyslexia in children together with the solutions proposed and implemented in the SICOLE prototype are discussed.

3.1   Evaluation Modules

Evaluation process has two main phases: 1) classifies the student in one of the categories (phonologic, surface or mixture dyslexia) by a computer naming exercise, and 2) evaluates the specific reading deficits.

1) The distinction between the two subtypes of dyslexia is important because de deficits in the reading activity of the children in each category are of different nature. The phonologic dyslexic has a selective deficit reading pseudowords or unfamiliar words, while the surface dyslexic has a selective deficit reading irregular words despite the fact that he reads words and pseudowords correctly.

In the naming task, the student is asked to pronounce a sequence of words and pseudowords. The words are shown in the screen one after the other repeating the following operations: a blank screen is shown (200 ms.), a sound is emitted alerting the student about the immediate occurrence of the following word to read, the word is shown in the middle of the screen surrounded by a rectangle, and finally, the computer acquires and stores the word pronounced by the child, registering the reaction time (RT), i.e. the time from the moment the word is shown until the moment the child starts the reading activity. The time between the stimuli varies since the student must press a key to indicate that he has pronounced the word. That avoids a word would not be completely recorded as it will occur if recording time is fixed.

It must be remarked that once the sound is recorded, it is also analyzed using speech processing techniques for voiced and unvoiced segmentation. In order to identify an accurate RT, it is necessary to use signal processing techniques and calculate parameters as the Short Time Energy and Zero Crossing Rate values. Although the program determines other important features as the beginning and ending of each syllable, the most useful parameter in the actual implementation of SICOLE, is the reaction time (RT). Children with higher RT in pseudowords but under the upper limit of the confidence interval defined for normal readers reading familiar words, are identified by the SICOLE system as phonological dyslexic. On the other hand, those with higher RT reading familiar words but under the upper limit of the confidence interval defined for normal readers reading pseudowords are identified as surface dyslexic.

2) Once the system identifies the type of dyslexia affecting the student, SICOLE starts a functional evaluation to determine the processing deficits that are the cause of the low reading performance. This part of the diagnostic subsystem has three modules,

one for each processing level: lexical processing, perceptual processing and syntactic-semantic processing. Each one of these modules is also composed of different sub-modules where specific cognitive components affecting the different processing levels are evaluated.

The diagnostic modules and submodules to detect specific reading deficits are the follows: a) Sytactic (Gender, Number, Order, Functional Words, Assignation of Syntactic Roles, Punctuation), Auditory discrimination (Direct Syllabus, Double Syllabus, Rhyme, Auditory discrimination in words), Syllabic Conscience (Final Syllabic Omission, Final Trisyllabic Omission, Initial Bisyllabic Omission, Initial Trisyllabic Omission), Phonemic Conscience (Isolate, Omit, Synthesise), Knowledge of letters, Lexemes and Suffixes, Homophones Words.

The results of this intensive evaluation of the reading capabilities of the student are stored in the database and are used in the treatment modules. Taking into consideration the deficits discovered in each student, different treatments are applied.

3.2 Treatment Modules

Treatment modules are corresponding to deficits evaluation modules. A child will be treated only in problems founded in the evaluation. Each module has different submodules, complexity levels and types of task associated. Each child trajectory will be particular at his level progress.

As an example of a treatment module, an overview of the Syllabic Conscience Treatment Module (SCTM) is now given. This module has three submodules. There is a global set T of different tasks related to the SCTM. Each submodule is defined by a subset $Si < T$. Inside each submodule there are three different difficulty levels. A difficulty level is defined by the way in that a set of activities are combined in a presentation. For instance, a presentation of the most difficult level is a sequence of activities where all the possible deficits in the SCTM framework are combined, while a presentation in the easiest level has activities related to only one deficit. With this strategy, the training of the children with more problems is improved by focusing his attention in solving exercises with only a class of difficulties.

The first submodule is the most difficult one, and it is accessed by the student after the evaluation stage. It has three difficulty levels and the student will be passed to the adequate level depending on the results in the evaluation stage. The measure that determines which is the correct difficulty level for a student comes from the percentage of correctly performed activities in a presentation (sequence of activities). SICOLE considers that the SCTM is necessary for the children if his result in the Syllabic Conscience Evaluation Module (SCEM) was less than 70%.

Once the student has been placed in the level i of the first submodule a sequence of randomly generated multimedia activities is started. The activities are chosen in a random manner, but under the requirement that at least one activity belongs to each task in the set S1. In general the system drives the student through difficulty levels and submodules.

3.3   Automatic Speech Recognition and the Diagnosis and Treatment of Dyslexia

SICOLE is not only the development of a software package, but a research project also. In this sense, the SICOLE team is exploring how to take advantages of the current state of the art in the automatic speech recognition (ASR) technology. *The main motivation of including ASR in the SICOLE system is to extract the largest amount of information relevant to the diagnostic and treatment tasks from the waveform emitted by the child.* A part of this technology has been already included in the prototype as was described above (naming task). Obviously, the goal of automatically detecting each phoneme pronounced by the child and the time parameters related to them (starting time and end time of each phoneme) is more ambitious and it will require a deeper research and even an improvement of the state of the art in the ASR technology. However, we consider valuable all the research efforts to include the ASR technology in the SICOLE system for two main reasons:

– **Improvement of the evaluation stage.** Using the reaction time together with other parameters (for instance, time length of each phoneme, time separation between relevant phonemes in the word or the rhythm of the pronunciation) could be very valuable to get better results in classifying different types of children according to their reading capabilities.
– **Improvement of the training stage.** A better evaluation of the progress in the reading capabilities obtained by the system users would made the training stage more efficient. In this sense, the previously mentioned parameters are also useful.

It must be remarked that we are not trying to produce activities where all the interaction with the user is based in the ASR (for instance, pronouncing a word and automatically detecting the mistakes made by the user). According to our evaluation of different commercial and research ASR environments, the ASR technology under the established working conditions for SICOLE is not enough robust to make the system completely dependent on it. It must be considered the working conditions mentioned in the introduction of this paper, what makes necessary several features for the ASR:

– **Isolated word recognition.** Evaluation and training is most of the time based on reading correctly a sequence of isolated words and/or pseudowords. This implies that ASRs that make use of contextual information (sentence where the word is included) to reduce the mistakes are not valid for this application. The error rate of ASRs without contextual information is sensibly higher.
– **Recognition independent of the user.** Many ASR environments reduce the error rate through a previous supervised training with the utterances of the user. Taking into consideration again the working conditions and the fact that the users are not good readers, a supervised training stage could be inapplicable.
– **Phonemic level recognition.** The evaluation and training stages require information of the utterance at the phonemic level. This discards those ASRs that are specifically designed to recognize at the word level.

With these ideas in mind, a tool to study the applicability of the ASR to the evaluation of dyslexic children has been developed. The chosen ASR environment has been the CSLU toolkit [8]. Some of the benefits evaluated for this election have been:

- Fulfilment of the three previous requirements together with high accuracy and good technical support. Furthermore, this package is used by big organisations to develop their own ASR products.
- Open environment, not only from the application development point of view, but also for building new corpora. It also supports the Spanish language.
- Different levels of application development: visual environment for rapid application development (RAD), scripting language (TCL/TK) and finally C language.

The main objective is to present to the user a naming task. The words are read by the user and the utterances are analyzed by the prototype showing the most likely phonemes recognized, their time parameters and the confidence of the recognition. Each word in the naming list could have several related grammars. The grammar is a symbolic information that describes the expected utterance at the phonemic level. Grammars are flexible enough to consider many natural variations of the pronounced word. Using several grammars for the same word is a requirement because in our case (dyslexic readers) is not rare that the same word will be pronounced in many different ways. All the information about the users and the recognition results are stored in a database for further analysis.

Table 1. Grammar example and measurements carried out with the prototype for researching ASR applicability.

plastilina {$s1= {plas | ples | plis | plos | pas};	Phonem	Begin	End	Score
$s2={ta | te | ti | to | tu | tel};	<.pau>	0.0	10.0	-173.562
$s3= {ca | co};	<.pau>	10.0	20.0	-225.333
$s4={la | le | tili | lo | lu};	<.pau>	20.0	40.0	-373.909
$s5={na | ne | ni | no | nu};	$m_l8<m	40.0	80.0	-918.376
$sep = *sil%% [*any%%] *sil%%;	m>$m_r2	80.0	120.0	-122.279
$grammar = [$sep] <[$s1]> [$s2] [$s3] [$s4]	$a_l11<a	120.0	140.0	-424.705
[$s5] [$sep];}	<a>	140.0	270.0	-198.377
	a>$a_r6	270.0	320.0	-128.869
	$n_l0<n	320.0	370.0	-406.841
	n>$n_r0	370.0	440.0	-12.483
	<.pau>	440.0	470.0	-753.486
	Numerical results for an utterance.			
Example of a grammar defined for the word "plastilina"				

Table 1 shows an example grammar for the Spanish word "plastilina". Regular expressions are used to specify the utterance. Notice how the expected utterance can be obtained from basic building blocks, which can be combined allowing repetitions or omissions and including other "special sounds" as "garbage" or "silence". In the same table it is shown the output information: first column is the phonetic sound description, the following columns are the start and end times, and the confidence level.

4 Conclusions and State of the Project

This is a research about how a multimedia system can help in the diagnosis and treatment of the developmental dyslexia. We have developed the basic infrastructure to implement simple and complex pedagogical strategies. The software architecture designed is now supporting several modules that are able to establish an automatic diagnostic about the dyslexic subtypes and also to perform training routines to improve several reading deficits.

Regarding to the technical aspects it is a primary condition for any system of this type to be flexible enough to support a wide range of different solutions to the variety of individual dyslexic cases with different features. This has lead us to select the architecture described above to implement SICOLE.

One of the main benefits of this architecture is that it can incorporate new strategies and modifications to the implemented modules allowing the psychologist for experimenting different approaches for the expected problems.

The inference module based on a KBS has been found very useful to provide the system with the capability of composing dynamic presentations: tasks, media components, ... are chosen from the inference results that are based on both static and variable information stored in the database.

In this sense, the general strategy of using two dependent templates, one to be filled by the inference module and the other to be filled by the interface software has given flexibility in two different scales. The template filled by the KBS serves as the ground to complete the second template at the moment of generating the presentation.

The speech recognition technology has been also applied in several levels: basic parameters of the sound waveform (reaction time) are used to classify the dyslexic subtypes, while more ambitious applications as detecting mistakes at the phonemic level in the user utterance are still researched through an implemented prototype where the using of multiple grammars and interpretations has demonstrated to be a practical strategy.

Although the system has already been verified through the critic examination of a group of expert psychologists, at this moment the system is being used in some Schools with the purpose of validating and measuring the real benefits of SICOLE. We are using a reading level match design with pretest-postest control groups. The effect of SICOLE in the reading proficiency will be analyzed in a sample of students with learning difficulties in the reading activity divided as follows:

Experimental group composed of 30 retarded readers with ages between 8 and 9 years old coming from the second cycle of the Primary School. Control group for the chronological ages composed of 30 students with the same features as the ones in the experimental group. Control group for the reading level composed of 30 normal reader students with ages between 6 and 7 years old coming from the first year of the first cycle in the Primary School.

The experimental group is being trained with the SICOLE system, while the control groups are trained with other multimedia software in activities that are not related to the reading activity. The dependent variables are: reaction time in lexical decision tasks; latency time in word reading tasks; mistakes in the graph-phonemic decoding of the words; measurements of the reading level (i.e. lexical, syntactic and semantic processes).

Acknowledgements. This research has been founded by *Fondos Europeos para el Desarrollo Regional* (FEDER), 1FD97-1140, and the *Dirección General de Investigación Científica y Técnica* (DIGICYT), Spain. We are specially grateful to the group of expert psychologist of our research team: Juan E. Jiménez, Alicia Díaz Megolla, Eduardo García Miranda, Adelina Estévez Monzó, María del Rosario Ortiz González, Mercedes Rodrigo López, Remedios Guzmán   Rosquete and Isabel Hernández-Valle.

References

[1] González C.S. (2001), Sistema Tutorial Inteligente para niños con discapacidades intelectuales y cognitivas. Tesis doctoral. Universidad de La Laguna. Spain.

[2] Coltheart, M. (1978). Lexical access in simple reading tasks. En G. Underwood (ed.), Strategies of information processing. London: Academic Press.

[3] Mayer, R. E.Multimedia learning: Are we asking the right questions? *Educational Psychologist, 32,* 1-19. 1997.

[4] Schreiber G., Wielinga B., Breuker J., *KADS. A Principle Approach to Knowledge- Based System Development*, Ed. Academic Press Limited, 1993

[5] Bordegoni M., Faconti G., Rist T., Ruggieri S., Trahanias P., MD Wilson (1996), "Intelligent Multimedia Presentation Systems: A Proposal for a Reference Model Multimedia Modelling: Towards the Information SuperHighway p.3-20 JP Coutaz, M Diaz, P Senac (Eds), World Scientific Publishing Co., Singapore.

[6] Brusilovsky, P. (1999) Adaptive and Intelligent Technologies for Web-based Education. In C. Rollinger and C. Peylo (eds.), Special Issue on Intelligent Systems and Teleteaching, Künstliche Intelligenz, 4, 19-25.

[7] Karagiannidis C., Koumpis A., Stephanidis C. (1995), Media/Modalities Allocation in Intelligent Multimedia User Interfaces: Towards a Theory of Media and Modalities, in Proc First International Workshop on Intelligence and Multimodality in Multimedia Interfaces.

[8] The CSLU Toolkit is a product of the "Center for Spoken Language Understanding" at the OGI School of Science and Technology (Oregon Health and Science University). http://cslu.cse.ogi.edu.

The Aplusix-Editor: A New Kind of Software for the Learning of Algebra

Jean-François Nicaud, Denis Bouhineau, and Thomas Huguet

IMAG-Leibniz, Université de Grenoble
46, rue Félix Viallet, 38031 Grenoble cedex, France
{Jean-Francois.Nicaud,Denis.Bouhineau,Thomas.Huguet}@imag.fr
http://aplusix.imag.fr

Abstract. The first part of the paper presents our conception of a new kind of software for helping students to learn algebra. Such software has three main characteristics. First it includes an advanced editor that allows the student to build easily algebraic expressions. Second it reifies the student's reasoning as a tree. Third it verifies the student's calculations. In the second part, we present the Aplusix-Editor, a system of that kind that we have realised, and we describe the first tests of this system.

1 Introduction

Since 1980, there has been a lot of works devoted to formal algebra in AI-ED. Researchers built three main kinds of computer systems: humanlike solvers, microworlds and ITS. Humanlike solvers appeared first, e.g., PRESS [6] for simple equations, CAMELIA [20] for calculus, DISSOLVE [19] for equations. A few microworlds were realised later, e.g., ALGEBRALAND [10], and the McArthur's system [16]. Last, ITS were designed, e.g., ALGEBRA TUTOR [2] for simple equations, APLUSIX [17] for factorisations, MATHPERT [4] for algebra and calculus. More recently, appeared PAT [12] for word problems and simple equations, the Alpert's system [1] for simple equations on the Web, PÉPITE [11] for checking the student's competencies in algebra. A few systems became commercial products; this is the case for PAT and MATHPERT. Although controlled experiments proved that these systems are very useful to help students to learn algebra, the systems have currently a small penetration in education[1].

During the same period, the CAS (Computer Algebra System) community realised systems devoted to formal algebra, e.g., Maple [13], Mathematica [14], Derive [8]. These systems are commercial products that solve formal or numerical problems with powerful methods, with generally a presentation in one step, and that draw many kinds of graphs. They have been built for helping engineers and researchers to make calculations. Some of them have been implemented on calculators. Although they lack pedagogical features (they solve a strong problem in one step, they do not provide

---

[1] PAT, which is used in 600 schools in USA in December 2001, may be seen as an exception. However, this is not a general penetration.

S.A. Cerri, G. Gouardères, and F. Paraguaçu (Eds.): ITS 2002, LNCS 2363, pp. 178–187, 2002.

explanation), CAS are used in secondary education and there is a special group for CAS in the research community for mathematics education. This group has shown that the use of CAS in education has several problems and that a good understanding is essential to solve equations with a CAS [3]. Why is there a real penetration of CAS, and not of AI-ED systems, in education? We think that there are two main reasons for that. First, CAS are wildly available, even on calculators. Second, AI-ED systems are generally limited to a small sub-domain of algebra (PAT is limited to linear equations) or to a specific interaction mode (the use of MATHPERT consists of applying actions chosen in a menu, the student cannot input its own calculation steps).

Considering this situation, we thought that there was a place for a new kind of computer systems that will be ergonomic editors of algebraic expressions and reasoning, with a verification mechanism, systems allowing students to make their own calculations and verifying these calculations.

In this paper, we present our conception of such algebraic editor/verificator, we present the Aplusix-Editor, a system of that kind realised in our team, and we describe its first tests.

2 Our Conception of an Algebraic Editor/Verificator

An algebraic editor/verificator is a microworld with operators allowing to build algebraic expressions and steps of reasoning. However, the words "algebraic microworld" do not characterise such a system because there are other kinds of algebraic microworlds in which operators are transformation rules, e.g., l'Algebrista [7].

2.1 The Edition of Algebraic Expressions

An editor for algebra expressions must be 2D (two-dimensions), allowing to modify easily a given expression according to the student's wishes. First, an algebraic selection of any well-formed sub-expressions is required to allow making copy/cut/paste and drag&drop in an algebraic way. Second, several edition modes are necessary. We have defined in [5] three edition modes. The first one is the *structure* mode that takes into account the underlying tree. This mode allows to insert structured operators with one keystroke, e.g., two parentheses, a fraction, so that there is neither unbalanced parentheses nor fractions without a denominator. The second mode is the *text* mode where a part of an expression is seen as text. This is a non-algebraic mode, but a useful mode for actions like the insertion of digits, variables or unstructured operations like +. The *text* mode allows to insert unbalanced parentheses, which is sometime useful for modifying an expression. The third mode is the *equivalence* mode, a mode in which drag&drop makes calculations, i.e., respects the equivalence of the global expression.

With the *structure* mode as preferred mode, the editor teaches the structure of algebraic expressions. It allows, for example, to make algebraic substitutions with copy and paste, e.g., in order to substitute y–1 to x in 2x+3y=5, one first copies y–1 somewhere, then selects x, then pastes. As the paste is performed algebraically, the result is

$2(y-1)+3y=5$. With this mode, one may transform $8x=2+3x$ into $8x-3x=2$ by doing first a drag&drop of $3x$ to the left of "=", which produces $8x+3x=2$ (where $3x$ remains selected), second a hit of the "–" key that transforms $3x$ in $-3x$.

In the *equivalence* mode a drag&drop of $3x$ directly transforms $8x=2+3x$ in $8x-3x=2$.

Until recently, the editors of algebraic expressions were very poor. Most of the computer systems used a 1D editor (even if they used a 2D display). Progress has been made recently, some systems use a 2D editor (e.g., Mathematica [14], MathType [15]). However, their general behaviour is based on text and boxes, not on algebra. For example, with MathType 4, the selection is a text selection; for deleting the denominator of a fraction, one has to copy the numerator, then to select and delete the fraction, last to paste.

2.2   The Edition of Algebraic Reasoning

Solving a problem in formal algebra consists of searching a solution with the *replacement of equals* inference mode [9] that allows to replace any sub-expression by an equivalent one providing a global expression equivalent to the previous one. Reasoning by equivalence is a very important mechanism. It includes backtrack: in some situations, because of a difficult problem or a lack of knowledge, the student cannot be sure to solve the problem a direct way and needs to go back to a previous step in order to try another way. A good presentation and edition of a reasoning process by equivalence, including backtrack, is necessary.

CAS generally mix algebraic display and calculations with text processing. So they fulfil, in a sense, the above features but in a way asking the student to be in charge of the whole presentation of the reasoning. An editor of algebraic reasoning has to be in charge of the presentation.

2.3   The Verification of the Students' Calculations

Two algebraic expressions are equivalent if and only if they have the same semantics, called denotation [18]. For example, over the real numbers, the two expressions $(x-1)(x+1)-3$ and $(x-2)(x+2)$ are equivalent because the functions $x \rightarrow (x-1)(x+1)-3$ and $x \rightarrow (x-2)(x+2)$, from $\mathbf{R}$ to $\mathbf{R}$, are identical. This property allows to verify calculations without knowing what transformation has been done. So, it is possible to implement a verification mechanism in an editor of algebraic reasoning, which is very important for the student because it verifies his/her calculations.

As far as we know, there are no computer systems doing that, because all the systems for formal algebra (CAS or educational systems) are action driven, the action being performed by the computer, so the student do not input his/her own results. However, it is very important for the student to face situations where his/her errors are apparent. This favours learning by constructing more adequate knowledge.

3   Description of the Aplusix-Editor

The Aplusix-Editor we have designed and realised is an algebraic editor/verificator. It includes an advanced 2D editor, with the *text* and *structure* modes. The Editor uses the usual keyboard and a virtual keyboard (see Fig. 1). It includes a mechanism for selecting any well-formed sub-expression, including the situation where the sub-expression has several components. Fig. 2 shows a part of its behaviour.

Fig. 1. The virtual keyboard.

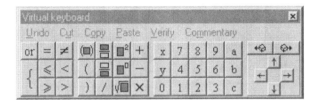

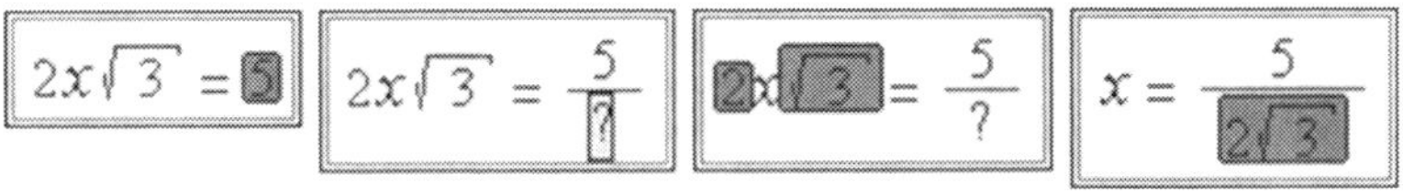

Fig. 2. A selection of 5, a click on the first fraction button of the virtual keyboard, a selection of 2 and $\sqrt{3}$, and a drag&drop to the denominator.

The drag&drop in the equivalence mode is not yet implemented. The Aplusix-Editor is able to work with complex expressions, see Fig. 3.

The edition of algebraic reasoning has been realised for reasoning by equivalence. The presentation is made of boxes that contain the expressions and links that indicate the transitions and the equivalence. An example with a backtrack is shown in Fig. 4.

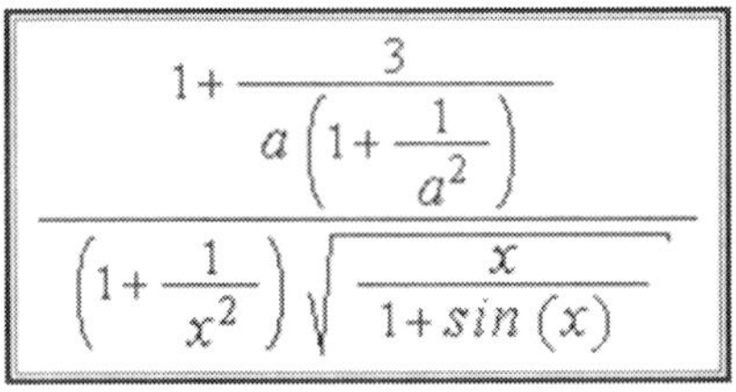

$$1+\cfrac{3}{a\left(1+\cfrac{1}{a^2}\right)}$$

$$\left(1+\frac{1}{x^2}\right)\sqrt{\frac{x}{1+sin\,(x)}}$$

Fig. 3. A complex expression

In order to verify the students' calculations, the Aplusix-Editor calculates the equivalence between the expressions. Currently, these calculations are implemented on the field of real numbers for polynomial expressions (n variables, degree p), for systems of linear equations (n variables, p equations), and for equations and inequa-lities (degree less or equal 3). At the present time, we use approximate calculations. They will be soon replaced by exact calculations for rational numbers. When the expressions are not equivalent, the system crosses the link between them (see Fig. 5).

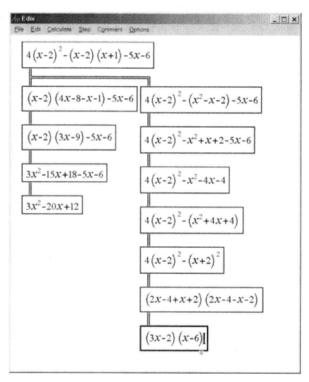

Fig. 4. The student tried a partial factoring of x-2 but did not get a common factor. Then (s)he expanded the expression but did not get an identity. At that moment, (s)he decided to backtrack to the first step in order to try a partial expansion.

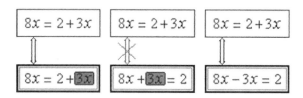

Fig. 5. (1) The equation is duplicated and 3x is selected. (2) A drag&drop of 3x: The equations are no more equivalent, the link is crossed in red. (3) A hit of "–": The equations are now equivalent, the equivalence link is restored.

4   First Tests of the Aplusix Editor

Our first tests took place in autumn 2001, inside a regular classroom, and in January 2002, as a controlled test. In both cases, we worked with beginners in algebra (14 - 15 years old).

4.1   Using the Aplusix-Editor in a Class

During the whole month of December 2001, the 18 students of a class used the system several times a week. The class was a special class with a lot of students having deep difficulties in mathematics. The students started learning expansions, simplifications and factorisations of simple expressions, and resolution of simple equations with the Aplusix-Editor. Some students worked alone with the computer, others worked in groups of two. Most of the students needed just a few minutes to become familiar with the software, even those who didn't have much familiarity with computers. Some of them acquired a great mastery of the drag&drop function, using it as well to copy some elements of an expression inside a new step, as to move parts of an expression to transform it, in particular to move a term from a side of an equation to the other.

For many students, what was usually opaque in algebra regained interest. Some of them, who generally didn't listen, all of a sudden began to ask questions. From passive, they became active. They all enjoyed the equivalence checking. This functionality moved the exchanges between the teacher and the students: "Is it right?" became "Why is it wrong?". This shifts to discuss on what really is a problem. All the students took pleasure in going to the computer lab and often asked to go there again. When working with the Aplusix-Editor, they solved more exercises than usually and more difficult exercises.

4.2   A Controlled Test

We conducted a controlled test of the Aplusix-Editor on the 9th and 16th of January 2002, with a group of 8 volunteers, coming from different classes. They worked apart from the normal classroom. Our objective was to check our first impressions by measuring the realised progresses and analysing the interactions. Fig. 6 shows the test plan.

Day	Phase	Duration
9 January	Knowledge pre-testing on paper	30 minutes
	Session with the Aplusix-Editor	1 h 30
16 January	Session with the Aplusix-Editor	1 h 30
	Knowledge post-testing on paper	30 minutes
	Questionnaire	15 minutes

Fig. 6. The test plan.

The first session dealt with the basic notions of equation solving (carry out the same operation – add, divide... – on both sides of the equal sign). The second one emphasized on the transformation rule that allows to move an additive term from a side of an equation to the other, changing its sign. Both sessions were driven by a teacher who began by briefly presenting the lesson. Then the students worked alone with the system, which was automatically supplied with exercises previously placed in a file. A large variety of exercises were proposed. In that context, the students were able to evolve according to their own speed. The teacher's role was to answer to the student's questions. He intervenes sometimes spontaneously. An observer was in charge of systematically taking notes on the exchanges between the teacher and the students.

Study of the pre-test and the post-test. From the pre-test to the post-test, the average of the group increased from 4.2 out of 10 to 7.9. Two good students progressed just a little; three students multiplied their note by three or four. Although these results have to be interpreted cautiously, because of the small effective and the imprecision of any assessment, we think that they testify of an important progression.

The students' learning didn't confine to the transformation rules. Some students, who often deconstructed their calculations, presented their calculations during the post-test as expected by the teacher. A few students who already had some mastery began to mentally apply some rules. See examples in Fig. 7.

	Pre-test	Post-test	Comment
S T U D E N T 1	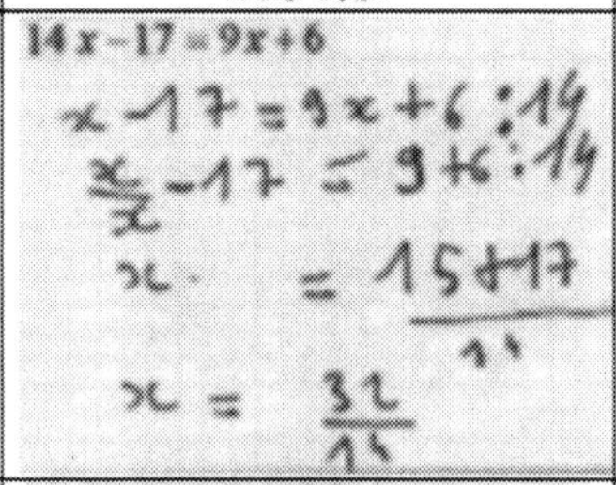 $14x-17=9x+6$ $x-17=9x+6:14$ $x-17=9x+6:14$ $x = 15+17$ $x = \frac{32}{15}$	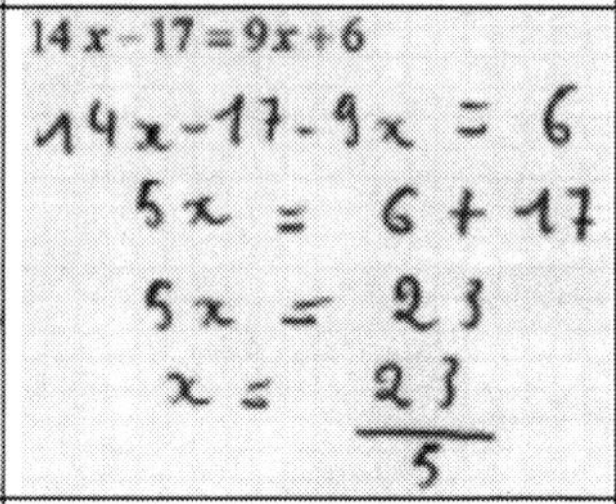 $14x-17=9x+6$ $14x-17-9x=6$ $5x = 6+17$ $5x = 23$ $x = \frac{23}{5}$	*The learning of transformation rules and the structuring of the calculation presentation.*
S T U D E N T 2	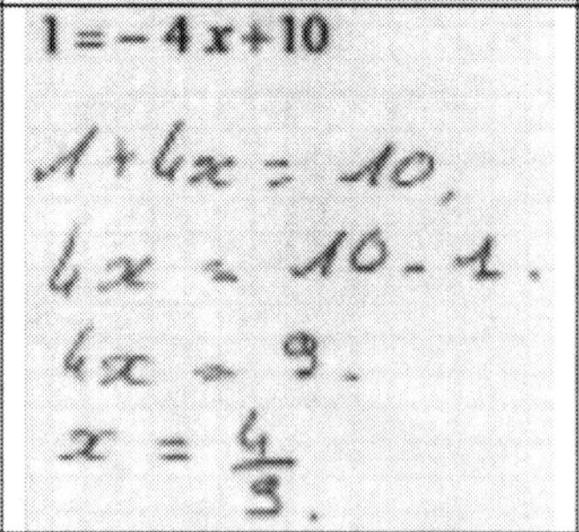 $1=-4x+10$ $1+4x=10$ $4x=10-1$ $4x=9$ $x=\frac{4}{3}$	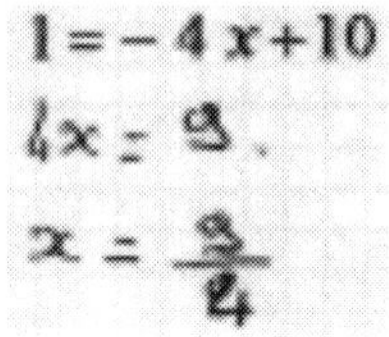 $1=-4x+10$ $4x=9$ $x=\frac{9}{4}$	*At the post-test, Student 2 appears to have done some intermediate calculations mentally.*

Fig. 7. Some improvements of students' behaviour between the two tests

Protocols analysis. The Aplusix-Editor saves the user's actions (keystrokes, drag&drop...). The protocols obtained in the two sessions are being analysed. We are currently extracting statistical information, replaying resolutions (the Aplusix-Editor allows to replay the interactions memorised in protocols like a video recorder) and reading the protocols. Fig. 8 indicates the minimal times (the fastest student), maximal time (the slowest student) and average time (group's average) taken by students to solve some exercises. We notice an increase of time when an exercise has something new (e.g., from 1a to 2a), a decrease of time after the software appropriation (e.g., from 4a to 10a) and a decrease of time between the first and the second session for similar exercises (e.g., from 3a to 2b).

	Exercise number	Equation	Time (in second)		
			Maximum	Average	Minimum
Session 1	1a	8x-7=13x+3	1094,2	371,1	129,6
	2a	7(2x+4)=-x-5	1743,5	607,9	182,9
	3a	-5x+7=2(-8x+9)	747,4	326,1	154,6
	4a	x+1=7x	955,8	297,3	77,1
	10a	10x+8+17x-13=6x+3	229,5	160,0	78,7
Session 2	1b	1+4x=x-3	359,2	265,0	162,1
	2b	3x+7=5(x+2)	248,8	172,0	108,7
	3b	2-2x=5x+3	376,7	136,2	76,7
	4b	2(x-1)=3(2+x)	388,5	160,8	79,3

Fig. 8. Times taken by students to solve some equations

With the protocols, it is possible to follow all the story of each resolution. We can see what the student tried, what worked and which algebraic points were problems.

Our analysis showed the important role of the equivalence checking functionality. Here is an example. A student made progress during the two sessions, beginning by adding the same expression to both sides of the equation/inequality, then moving an additive expression to the other side. He got confident in this procedure and applied it rather quickly. In the middle of the second session, he had to solve the inequality $4x-1-(2-3x) < 3x-5(2-x)+1$. He first expanded, typing $4x-1-2+3x < 3x-10+5x+1$. At the end of this input, the system indicated an equivalence. The student created then a new step and typed regularly $4x+3x+3x+5x < 1-10+2+1$. At the end of this input, the system indicated a non-equivalence. After 10 seconds without action, the student clicked before the second 3x, deleted the "+" and typed a "–". Again, the system indicated a non-equivalence. After 17 seconds without action, the student changed the sign of 5x and got the equivalence. It seams clear that the student had an idea of what could be wrong, because he went directly to the problem. What would have happened in a paper/pencil context? The student would just have continued the resolution with a wrong expression and would not have reinforced his learning of the correct procedure. On another exercise, later, the student began to combine several transformations, which requires several mental calculations. When he got a non-equivalence feedback, he deleted the entire expression and replaced it with another built with less mental calculations, and without error.

The observer's observations. During the second session, the observer noticed 28 exchanges between the teacher and the students: 13 came from a "Is it finished?" question and 15 dealt with algebraic difficulties, often beginning by a "Why is it not working?". The difficulties concerned calculations over fractions and negative integers. Reading the observer's notes, we became aware of the need of a feedback concerning the state of the problem. We did not implement such kind of feedback because the Aplusix-Editor is not aware of the problem type. This is possible because of the nature of algebra: the equivalence is defined by the denotation, which does not depend of a problem type. On the one hand, the student clearly needs information; on the other hand the editor is not a tutor and has not to know the problem type. We plan to solve this problem by installing components that will indicate a degree of the mains concepts that intervene in solved forms: degree of factoring, of expansion, of simplification, of being solved as an equation or an inequality.

Students' answers to the questionnaire. A part of the questionnaire was devoted to the interest of the system (compared to paper), its difficulty, and its usefulness. The results are:

Less interesting: 0	As interesting as: 1	More interesting: 7	
Very difficult: 0	Rather difficult: 3	Rather easy: 4	Very easy: 1
Entirely useless: 0	Rather useless: 0	Useful enough: 0	Very useful: 8

In their explanations, the students wrote that it is simpler to correct by typing on the keyboard and that it is very pleasant that the Aplusix-Editor verifies what they do.

One of the requests we found in the questionnaire was to use the Aplusix-Editor every week during the help-time (a moment in the week devoted to help students to solve their difficulties in French, History & Geography and Mathematics, driven by three teachers in a classical classroom).

5   Perspectives

The first couple of tests of the Aplusix-Editor is a real success and suggests that the system may fulfil a gap in educational software for algebra, as we thought. Of course, as we used beginners, we need to test now the system with novice and advanced students. We will do that soon. There are many perspectives for the Aplusix-Editor. First, we want to distribute it wildly. We will make a commercial product and, until we find a company for that, we will soon distribute a free version, limited in time, in several languages (http://aplusix.imag.fr). Second, we will build tools for analysing the protocols so that researchers in maths education and teachers may study the work of their students. Third, we will make it evolve towards an Ed-CAS (Educational Computer Algebra Systems), another new kind of system for algebra that we define as an algebraic editor/verificator with graph functionalities and commands like the ones we have in a CAS. Fourth, we will add a tutor over the system, for some problem types, and reuse, for that, our previous work on the Aplusix-Tutor.

References

1. Alpert, S.R., Singley, M.K., Fairweather, P.G. (1999). Deploying Intelligent Tutors on the Web: An Architecture and an Example, International Journal of Artificial Intelligence in Education, 10 (2), p. 183-197
2. Anderson J.R., Boyle C. F., Corbett A. T., Lewis M. W. (1990). Cognitive Modeling and Intelligent Tutoring. Artificial Intelligence, Vol 42, no 1.
3. Ball L. (2001). Solving equations: Will a more general approach be possible with CAS? Proceedings of the 12th ICMI Study Conference. The University of Melbourne.
4. Beeson, M. (1990). Mathpert, a computerized learning environment for Algebra, Trigonometry and Calculus, Journal of Artificial Intelligence in Education, p. 65-76.
5. Bouhineau D. Nicaud J.F., Pavard X., Sander E. (2001). A Microworld For Helping Students To Learn Algebra. Proceeding of ICTMT5, Austria.
6. Bundy A., Welham B. (1981). Using Meta-level Inference for Selective Application of Multiple Rewriting Rule Sets in Algebraic Manipulation. Artificial Intelligence, 16 (2).
7. Cerulli M., Mariotti, M.A. (2000). A symbolic manipulator to introduce pupils to algebra theory. Proceedings of Workshop W6 "Learning Algebra with the Computer, a Transdisciplinary Workshop". ITS'2000, Montreal.
8. Derive http://education.ti.com/product/software/derive/features/features.html
9. Dershowitz N, Jouannaud J.P. (1989). Rewrite Systems. In Handbook of Theoretical Computer Science, Vol B, Chap 15. North-Holland.
10. Foss C.L. (1987). Learning from errors in algebraland. IRL report No IRL87-0003.
11. Jean, S., Delozanne, E., Jacobini, P., Grugeon, B. (1999). A diagnosis based on a qualitative model of competence. Proc. of the Conference on AI in Education, IOS Press.
12. Koedinger, K.R., Anderson, J.R., Hadley, W.H., & Mark, M. A. (1997). Intelligent tutoring goes to school in the big city. Int. Journal of Artificial Intelligence in Education, 8.
13. Maple www.maplesoft.com
14. Mathematica www.wolfram.com
15. MathType www.mathtype.com/msee
16. McArthur D., Hotta Y. (1987). Learning problem-solving skills in algebra. Journal of education technology systems, 15.
17. Nicaud J.F., Aubertin C., Nguyen-Xuan A., Saïdi M., Wach P. (1990). APLUSIX: a learning environment for student acquisition of strategic knowledge in algebra. Proceedings of PRICAI'90. Nagoya.
18. Nicaud J.F., Bouhineau D. (2001). Syntax and semantics in algebra. Proceedings of the 12th ICMI Study Conference. The University of Melbourne.
19. Oliver J., Zukerman I. (1990). dissolve: An Algebra Expert for an Intelligent Tutoring System. Proceeding of ARCE, Tokyo.
20. Vivet M.(1984). Expertise mathématique et informatique: Camelia un logiciel pour raisonner et calculer. Thèse d'état, Université de Paris 6.

LKC: Learning by Knowledge Construction

Khalid Rouane, Claude Frasson, and Marc Kaltenbach*

Département d'Informatique et de Recherche Opérationnelle
Université de Montréal
C.P.6128, Succ. Centre-Ville
Montréal, Québec, Canada H3C 3J7
{rouane, frasson, kaltenba}@iro.umontreal.ca

Abstract. Domain knowledge is mainly communicated to learners via un-assessed content such as text. Lack of effective support in reading activity of this type of resources, induces students misconceptions while increasing their cognitive load, leading to their demotivation. In this paper, we present the Learning by knowledge Construction approach (LKC). This system provides full student support for knowledge acquisition in reading activity. Aspects such as document annotation, external representations and argumentation are all taken into account. We describe an ITS architecture that implements this approach and give details on the authoring and student learning environments.

1 Introduction

In 1988, William Johnson wrote [16], what can be considered as the supreme test for an ITS to be considered as effective: "If ITSs are to reach their promise, then the laboratory systems must operate and survive in the real world."

No need to answer the question 'How many ITSs have passed this test?'. Many reasons are behind this situation. The most important, in our opinion, are the drawbacks of the *expert system paradigm* that has deeply influenced the ITS's implementation [11][1], like the knowledge atomization [17], the loss of narration [13] and the complexity of implementation [11]. Moreover, knowledge modeled in systems using this paradigm, is aimed to support system inferences (or intelligence) and not to support the student in his knowledge acquisition, as this acquisition is still mainly achieved by reading resources such as text. Reading[1] stage can be considered as a *black box* for the system. Only student bad performance in exercises can indicate that something wrong (like misunderstanding and misconception) has happened inside this box and it's very difficult to find out where and when exactly this has happened.

Lack of student support at reading stage is the main cause of student's misconceptions. Knowing what is happening inside the reading *black box* can give the system the ability to track and correct misconceptions at their origin, which can be very efficient and maybe can prevent other misconceptions. The *Learning by knowledge Construction* approach (LKC) we are presenting in this paper, aims to

---

* Financial support from Bishop's University is gratefully acknowledged.
[1] Reading in a broad sense, dealing with text, figures, tables, images, …

S.A. Cerri, G. Gouardères, and F. Paraguaçu (Eds.): ITS 2002, LNCS 2363, pp. 188–198, 2002.
© Springer-Verlag Berlin Heidelberg 2002

provide a new paradigm for ITS construction with the objective to fully support students in every stage of reading activity, from document annotation to external representations and argumentation.

2 The Problem of the Un-assessed Content

The un-assessed content is any content that is presented to a learner without any evaluation of the level and the nature of knowledge acquisition it is expected to have triggered at the end of its presentation. A text document, an HTML page, a picture... are all kinds of un-assessed contents.

A rapid analysis of current ITSs' pedagogical activity shows the existence of a repetitive cycle of operations that can be summarized in three stages (Fig. 1, a):

- Presentation of un-assessed content: documents to read only.
- Presentation of assessed content: exercises and questions presented to evaluate knowledge acquisition.
- Pedagogical decision: decision about the next activity to select based on the result obtained in the previous stage.

It is important to note that most of pedagogical material presented to the student is un-assessed contents and that domain knowledge is mostly communicated to him via this kind of resources. But despite their huge importance as knowledge communicator, un-assessed contents are still presented to the student in a very passive way, without any effective support from the system. And that is, in our opinion, the origin of most misconceptions made by students, with a very large negative impact when committed at this stage and not corrected immediately.

Another drawback of misconceptions at the reading stage of un-assessed content is the waste of assessed contents such exercises, which become tools for misconception detection instead of being tools of assessment. Assessed content is very valuable, expensive to create, and can rarely be presented more than once. While an un-assessed content, is relatively cheaper to produce and can be presented indefinitely. The lack of effective student support at this stage is mainly due to the lack of adequate knowledge structuring.

To overcome this drawbacks and give students a real and effective support at reading stage, when the knowledge acquisition process is actually occurring, we propose a new approach and framework for an ITS that implies a radical shift in pedagogy cycle, content modeling, student modeling, and student-computer interaction.

3 The LKC System

Knowledge acquisition is still mainly achieved by reading activity. We consider *reading* in a broad sense that includes all kinds of un-assessed course content, ranging from raw text to video and animation.

The big issue at the reading stage is *understanding*. Understanding is different from competence (or performance) in a learning context. They are linked but not equal. Someone can perform well without understanding all aspects of a given problem, and the converse is true. Understanding is the outcome of higher-order learning while competence is the result of skill acquisition [15].

Reading activity as part of a knowledge acquisition in a learning process is not a passive task. Constructivist learning theory [4], states that learning is an active process in which learners construct new ideas based upon their current and past knowledge. The learner *selects* and *transforms information, constructs hypotheses,* and *makes decisions.* Passive learning will likely fail (and so passive reading), following Ben Ari [3]: because each student brings a different knowledge framework to the classroom, and will construct new knowledge in a different manner. Learning must be active (and so must be reading): the student must construct knowledge *assisted by guidance* from the teacher and *feedback from other students.*

Much ITS research work has been done in the skill acquisition area, dealing with problem solving, exercises, task performance and so on, but little has been done to enhance knowledge acquisition and better understanding at the reading stage. The LKC system presented here is our attempt to solve this problem. It aims to give students an effective support in their reading activity by *assisting* and *guiding* them in the process of knowledge construction. Students will successively use the system, as indicated in Fig. 1,b:

- first in *reading* documents, which results in the selection and transformation of information,
- then in *representing*, to make external representations of their ideas, and construct argumentations,
- and in receiving instant *feedback* from the system.

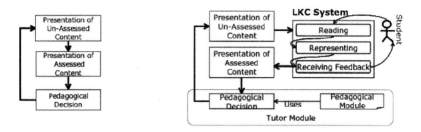

(a) The Classical ITS Pedagogical Cycle   (b) The New Pedagogical Cycle

Fig. 1. Pedagogical Cycle

The main objective is to use very efficiently the bulk of un-assessed content used to transmit the domain knowledge and to avoid the pitfalls of early misconceptions and cognitive overload demotivation, while promoting and facilitating understanding and knowledge acquisition.

This introduces a change in the traditional pedagogical cycle, which requires a new approach in knowledge modeling and structuring.

3.1 Three Steps in Knowledge Structuring

Knowledge construction in the reading process, especially in a higher education context on which we focus, involves three steps of knowledge structuring to be undertaken by the student: *microstructures construction, macrostructures construction* and *external representations construction*.

Microstructures Construction. A. van Dijk and W. Kintsch, state in their theory about *discourse comprehension* [7] that understanding in the reading process is assumed to be an essentially 'bottom-up' process, starting with microstructures construction where the learner gathers successive fragments of read text to make basic building blocks, called *microstructures*. Sentences for instance could be considered as microstructures. The basic understanding that can be carried by a given micro-structure is called microproposition or cognitive unit. The external manifestation that could be linked to micro-structuring is annotation activity, especially by underlining and marking [14].

Macrostructures Construction. Through the action of various rules of combination and reduction, microstructures are successively reduced in an iterative fashion to produce higher order macrostructures, which convey macropropositions. A. van Dijk and W. Kintsch [7] give three macrorules for this transformation:

- *Deletion*: propositions that are not direct or indirect condition of interpretation of an other proposition can be deleted.
- *Generalization*: a sequence of propositions may be substituted by one proposition if this proposition is entailed by each of the members of this sequence.
- *Construction*: a sequence of propositions may be substituted by one proposition if this proposition is entailed by this joint set of propositions.

The application of these macrorules to produce macrostructures is a transformation process that simplifies the read document and gives it an additional organizational structure. Macrostructures are not the structure of the document (the discourse) but are the structure assigned by the reader to this document. Failing to make a valid macrostructure organization can lead to misconceptions.

External Representations Construction. To focus the attention on the relationships among the different ideas in the text (expressed now in macrostructures), the reader uses various types of graphical representations to link these ideas [14]. *External representations* (ERs) is a general term used to define this kind of graphical representations [6]. Concept maps are a well-known example of ERs [2], but all figures in this paper are kinds of ERs. The importance of ERs in education comes from their weak expressiveness (limited number of possible interpretation) that makes inference and reasoning more tractable for the student [6][18].

Many systems were made to deal with ERs in education, such as MindManager [12] and Inspiration [10]. But as they don't integrate any conceptual knowledge about what is represented; they provide no automated support to the student and can only be used as tools of communication between students.

3.2 LKC Knowledge Models

Taking into account the knowledge structuring process accompanying learners reading activity, we propose in the LKC system that the designer creates a *reference model* of this knowledge to give learners an effective support at each stage of this structuring process (Fig. 2).

The reference model contains the following knowledge model:

- **Microstructure Model (Mi).** This model deals with the organization of the text at the level of microproposition (words and sentences). It will be used to help students, at the step of microstructure construction, to annotate a document easily and efficiently. Three types of microstructures can be created:
  - *Atomic microstructure (Mi-Atomic)*: can be seen as a clause in natural language like a group of words or sentences.
  - *Composed microstructure (Mi-Composed)*: is a set of atomic microstructures, which are all at the same level.
  - *Complex microstructure (Mi-Complex)*: is a set of microstructures with at least one microstructure that is not atomic (i.e. is composed or complex).

$$Mi = Mi\text{-}Atomic \cup Mi\text{-}Composed \cup Mi\text{-}Complex$$

$$Mi\text{-}Atomic = \{ \text{ Text fragments from source document } \}$$

$$Mi\text{-}Composed = \{ (a_1, a_2, a_3, \ldots a_n) \mid a_i \in Mi\text{-}Atomic \}$$

$$Mi\text{-}Complex = \{ (c_1, c_2, c_3, \ldots c_n) \mid c_i \in Mi\text{-}Atomic \cup Mi\text{-}Composed \}$$

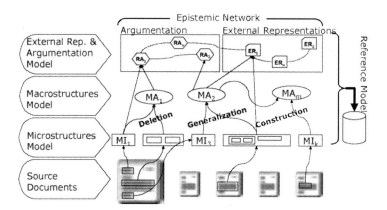

Fig. 2. Knowledge Structuring Models

- **Macrostructure Model (Ma).** To help students in constructing a valid organization at the level of macropropositions and to give them critics and hints about construction the LKC system will use a *Macrostructure Model*. Macrostructures are obtained by applying *Deletion*, *Generalization* and *Construction* operations on sets of microstructures and/or macrostructures.

$$Ma = \{ f(m_1, m_2, m_3, \ldots m_n) \} \text{ where } m_i \in Mi \cup Ma \text{ and}$$
$$f \in \{ \text{ Deletion, Generalization, Construction } \}$$

- **External Representations (ER).** To give learners an automated support in ERs construction, the designer will create a set of ERs as part of the reference model of the content. As the definition of each ER's element is based on macrostructures and microstructures elements, the system can explain the presence of this element, at different levels of details, by following the path from to top-level macrostructures linked to this element, to the root text in source document. In this first implementation of LKC system, we will limit ERs definition to graph forms only, as they are very general (like concept maps) and can be easily represented and formulated:

$$Er = \{N, A\} \text{ where}$$
$$N = \{ e_1, e_2, e_3, \ldots e_n \mid e_i \in Mi \cup Ma \cup Er \cup Ar \}$$
$$A = \{ (e_a, e_b) \mid e_a \in N \text{ and } e_b \in N\}$$

- *Argumentation Model (Ar).* One special form of external representations are *argumentation diagrams*. They are special in that they deal with argumentation and have some kind of formalism. Belvedere is an example of system using argumentation diagrams [19]. In LKC, we use a simple but powerful definition of argumentation based on the Toulmin view of Argumentation [20]. The set of argumentation diagrams made by the designer will constitute the Argumentation Model.

$$Ar = \{ (d, w, b, q, r, c) \mid d, w, b, q, r \text{ and } c \in Mi \cup Ma \cup Er \cup Ar \}$$

d = datum is the evidence supporting the claim.
w = warrant is the principle, provision or chain of reasoning that connects the datum to the claim.
b = backing is justifications and reasons to back up the warrant.
q = quantifier is specification of limits to claim, warrant and backing.
r = refutable is exceptions to the claim; description and rebuttal of counter-examples and counter-arguments.
c = claim is the position or claim being argued for; the conclusion of the argument.

- *Epistemic Network Model (En).* External representation elements from Er model and argumentation elements from Ar model are merged in one big network, the epistemic network, noted En, using links such as *Similar*, *Uses* and *Special-case-of*. This model is constructed by the course designer as part of the reference model of the document and has a important role in pedagogical planning.

$$En = \{ r(m, n) \mid m \text{ and } n \in Er \cup Ar \} where$$
$$r \in \{ Uses, \text{ } Help\text{-}in, \text{ } Similar, \text{ } More\text{-}difficult, \text{ } Special\text{-}case\text{-}of \}$$

4   Authoring Environment

The first version of the LKC prototype has been implemented in MS Visual C++ and uses MS Access as database. The type of resources is limited in this version to html document and interactions with the document are managed by using dynamic html. The LKC prototype consists of an *authoring environment* and a *learning environment*.

The authoring environment is a set of graphical editors used by the course designer to create and update the *reference model* of a raw document (Fig. 3): *microstructures editor, macrostructures editor, external representations editor, argumentation editor and epistemic network editor*. All these editors are specialized graph editors, dealing with nodes and links, except for the *microstructures editor* as it deals directly with the source document. The design work starts by the creation of atomic microstructures in the microstructures editor. Special html tags are inserted in html source document to delimit an atomic microstructure:

```
<span   id="at789">here is the text of an atomic
...</span>
```

An Id is generated for this microstructure (id="at789") and stored in the database as a *unique* reference to it. This Id is used for generating interaction with this element, like for event triggering (mouse click for instance) and attribute controlling (highlight this element by the instruction *at789.style.background="yellow"*).

The outcome of authoring process is the creation of an augmented document, which is the combination of a raw document and its reference model. This reference model is not to be considered as an absolute model (of truth) but merely as the designer's vision of the subject matter and will only be used as a starting point of learning that can be eventually criticized and enhanced.

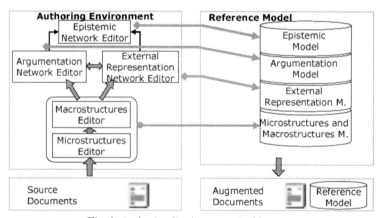

Fig. 3. Authoring Environment Architecture

5   The Student Learning Environment

The student learning environment is implemented with the objective to facilitate the learners knowledge construction. They can use the LKC system in two modes: in a controlled or supervised mode and in free or unsupervised mode (Fig. 4).

5.1 Controlled Reading Activity

The objective of the controlled reading activity is to ensure that student understanding of read material is near or similar to the understanding of the designer. The student is invited to read the document while performing some epistemic tasks. We define an epistemic task as the construction by the student of an external representation or an argumentation present in the reference model of the document and previously created by the designer. The reason behind asking the student to reconstruct these representations instead of showing them as part of the content is that self-constructed ERs have been shown to be more effective than prefabricated ones [9] and have similar pedagogical effect as self-explanations [5].

The system uses all its knowledge of an epistemic task to support the student. As each external representation or argumentation of an epistemic task is linked to source text in the document, via macrostructure and microstructure elements, the system can provide a very sophisticated annotation mechanism (with the *intelligent annotation module*) and help effectively the student in the construction of this external representations and argumentations.

Many components work together to provide this help. The ET[1] *Planner and Selector*, uses knowledge from *epistemic network* to plan and order the ET that the student must perform. The *Strategy Selector* is in charge of selecting the most appropriate strategy depending on the learner and the current ET. The simplest strategy, but the most difficult for the student, is to give him a blank screen and ask him to execute the ET based only on its definition. Another strategy would be to give him graph with empty slots that he must fill with appropriate elements.

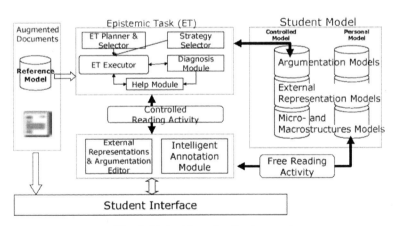

Fig. 4. Student Learning Environment

The *Diagnosis Module* is in charge of analyzing the work of the student and finds out what are the differences in respect to the reference model. Based on this diagnostic and on the selected strategy, the *Helper Module* can give help to the student in different forms. It can be text highlight of a single part in the source

---

[1] ET : Epistemic Task

document to guide the attention of the student (use of microstructures). It can be the highlight of many parts of the text linked to a particular idea (use of macrostructures). Or it can be the recall of similar ETs that was successfully performed by this student in the past (use of epistemic network and student model).

The *ET Executor* is a control component in charge of managing all other components and of starting and ending all ETs.

To performing epistemic tasks, student can uses two tools: an *intelligent annotation module,* and an *external representations and argumentation editor.* The intelligent annotation module gives the student means to select and highlight text fragment to construct microstructures and organize them in macrostructures. This module takes into account the current epistemic task to perform, to intelligently guide the student's attention to the right area of a text document to read or re-read. This enhances the reading experience. The external representations and argumentation editor, like one used by the designer, gives the student means to construct graphical representation of text ideas requested by the current epistemic task.

The result of the student's modeling work is stored in the *controlled student model.* This is an open learner model [8] as it is build by the student. It plays the function of student cognitive profile and has a great importance in pedagogical planning performed by the planner and selector module.

5.2 Free Reading Activity

In free reading activity, the student uses the same editing tools as in controlled reading activity (the *intelligent annotation module* and *external representations and argumentation editor*), but he is free to construct his own vision of the read document if he feels that the reference model is not sufficient or he can do better. The result of this modeling activity is stored in another part of the student model, the *personal student model* (Fig. 4).

However, even if this is a free activity, the system can still give valuable help and feedback to the student. To achieve this goal, the *system supervision component* of the LKC system uses his knowledge of the *collective model* (a compilation of all free works done by students) and the current context, to find matches between the student construction and similar constructions of other students in the same context (Fig. 5). The student can reuse other's work or can even argument if he disagrees with them (using standard argumentation template as those of *Ar* model). This argumentation and critics from the student, and maybe counter argumentation from the creators, become part of the collective model and will automatically be used by the system in the future to provide feedbacks and critics about students' work.

Periodic analysis of the collective model can be a valuable source of course enhancement. Students' knowledge representations can sometime be more understandable for peer students than the designer's work. *Course enhancement module* is in charge to analyze the collective model and suggest to the designer interesting students' knowledge representations (external representations and argumentation) it finds. Designer can then integrate these new findings in the reference model to enhance the course quality in an incremental way.

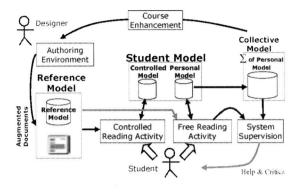

Fig. 5. Course Enhancement Cycle

6   Conclusion

This paper has presented the LKC system architecture oriented to support knowledge construction in the reading process and facilitate students understanding. The potential value of this approach is that it valorizes the use of un-assessed content such as text in ITS context. Far from been seen as simple resources, they are considered in the LKC approach as the main vehicle of knowledge transmission. The LKC system support to readers aims to overcome the problem of misconceptions at the reading stage by their early detection and correction.

To achieve this goal, the framework provides a way to augment a raw document by several knowledge models to support the student at every stage in the reading process, from document annotation to ideas representation and argumentation. The Knowledge representation required by the LKC system is entirely based on the narrative in the source document. The permanent link between modeled knowledge and narrative keep clear and visible the context in which this knowledge is elicited and used. Testing is under way to determine how this approach facilitates understanding and recall. A first prototype version of the LKC system is being implemented and experimented in an industrial application.

References

[1]   Anderson, J. (1988). *The expert module.* In M.C. Polson and J.J. Richardson (eds.), Foundations of Intelligent Tutoring Systems. Hillsdale, New Jersey, LEA.

[2]   Anderson-Inman, L. and Zeitz, L. (1999). Computer-Based Concept Mapping: A Tool for Negotiating Meaning. *The Computing Teacher*, 26(08).

[3]   Ben-Ari, M. (1998). Constructivism in computer science education. Proceedings of the twenty-ninth SIGCSE technical symposium on Computer science education, pages 257–261.

[4]   Bruner, J. (1973). *Going Beyond the Information Given.* New York: Norton.

[5]   Chi, M., Bassok, M., Lewis, M., Reimann, P., and Glaser, R. (1989). *Self-explanation: How students study and use examples in learing to solve problems*, volume 13. Cognitives Science. Pages 145-182.

[6]   Cox, R. and Brna, P. (1995). Supporting the use of external representations in problem solving: the need for flexible learning environments. *Journal of Artificial Intelligence in Education*, 6(2), pages 239–302.

[7]   Dijk, T. A. V. and Kintsch, W. (1983). *Strategies of discourse comprehension.* Academic Press, New York.

[8]   Dimitrova, V., Self, J., and Brna, P. (1999). The interactive maintenance of open learner models. *Proceedings of the 9th International Conference on Artificial Intelligence in Education*, pages 405–412.

[9]   Grossen, G. and Carnine, D. (1990). *Diagramming a logic strategy: Effect on difficult problem types and transfer*, volume 13, pages 168–182. Learning Disability Quarterly.

[10]   Inspiration, I. (2002). Inspiration Software. http://www.inspiration.com.

[11]   Luger, G. and Stubblefield, W. (1998). *Artificial Intelligence, Structure And Strategies For Complex Problem Solving.* Addison-Wesley, Massachusetts, 3 edition.

[12]   Mindjet   (2002).   MindManager   Business   and   Standard   Edition. http://www.mindjet.com/.

[13]   Murray, T. (1998). Authoring Knowledge Based Tutors: Tools for Content, Instructional Strategy, Student Model, and Interface Design. *Journal of the Learning Sciences*, 7(1), pages 5–64.

[14]   O'Hara, K. (1996). *Towards a Typology of Reading Goals.* Technical Report EPC-1996-107, Xerox Palo Alto Research Center.

[15]   Ohlsson, S. (1996). *Learning to do and learning to understand. in Reimann*, P. and Spada, H. (Eds.), Learning in humans and machines, Pergamon, oxford edition.

[16]   Polson, M. and Richardson, J. (1988). *Foundations of Intelligent Tutoring Systems.* LEA, Hillsdale, New Jersey.

[17]   Rodenburg, D. (2001). Learning System Design: More than Atomic Science. Learning Technology, *IEEE Computer Society (LTTF)*, 3(1).

[18]   Stenning, K. and Oberlander, J. (1995). *A cognitive theory of graphical and linguistic reasoning: Logic and implementation*, volume 19. Cognitive Science. Pages 97-140.

[19]   Suthers, D., Weiner, A., Connelly, J., and Paolucci, M. (1995). Belvedere: Engaging students in critical discussion of science and public policy issues. *7th World Conference on Artificial Intelligence in Education (AI-ED 95).* Washington, DC.

[20]   Toulmin, S. (1958). *The uses of argument.* Cambridge, MA: Cambridge University Press.

Generating Intelligent Tutoring Systems from Reusable Components and Knowledge-Based Systems

Eman El-Sheikh[1] and Jon Sticklen[2]

[1] Department of Computer Science, University of West Florida, 11000 University Parkway,
Pensacola, FL 32514 USA
eelsheikh@uwf.edu
[2] Intelligent Systems Laboratory, Computer Science and Engineering Department,
Michigan State University, East Lansing, MI 48824 USA
sticklen@cse.msu.edu

Abstract. This research addresses the need for easier, more cost-effective means of developing intelligent tutoring systems (ITSs). A novel and advantageous solution to this problem is the development of a task-specific ITS shell that can *generate* tutoring systems for different domains within a given class of tasks. Task-specific authoring shells offer an appropriate knowledge representation method to build knowledgeable tutors as well as flexibility for generating ITSs for different domains. In this paper, we describe the development of an architecture that can generate intelligent tutoring systems for different domains by interfacing with existing generic task-based expert systems, and reusing the other tutoring components. The architecture was used to generate an ITS for the domain of composite materials fabrication using an existing expert system.

1 Introduction

There is a growing need for effective tutoring and training in both academic and industrial settings, especially in technical fields that demand the learning of complex tasks and the use of large knowledge stores. In the last two decades, intelligent tutoring systems (ITSs) have been proven to be highly effective as learning aides, and numerous ITS research and development efforts were initiated. However, few tutoring systems have seen widespread use, mainly because the development of ITSs is difficult, time-consuming, and costly. There is a need for easier, more cost-effective means of developing tutoring systems.

This paper reports a novel ITS authoring methodology from which tutoring systems for different domains may be generated. We describe the development of an architecture that interacts with any generic task-based (GT) expert system and generates an ITS for the domain knowledge represented in that expert system.

Intelligent tutoring systems are characterized by the principle that individualized learning offers the most effective and efficient learning for most students [3, 5, 12]. In recent studies, Shute evaluated several ITSs to judge how they live up to the two main promises of ITSs: (1) to provide more effective and efficient learning in relation to traditional instructional techniques, and (2) to reduce the range of learning outcome measures where a majority of individuals are elevated to high performance levels

S.A. Cerri, G. Gouardères, and F. Paraguaçu (Eds.): ITS 2002, LNCS 2363, pp. 199–207, 2002.

[17]. Results of such studies show that tutoring systems do accelerate learning with no degradation in final outcome [1, 13].

Although ITSs are becoming more common and proving to be increasingly effective, each application is usually developed independently, from scratch, and is very time-consuming and difficult to build [15]. Another problem is that there is very little reuse of tutoring components between applications or across domains. The dilemma that Clancey and Joerger noted at the First International Conference on Intelligent Tutoring Systems that "...the endeavor is one that only experienced programmers (or experts trained to be programmers) can accomplish..." still faces us today [9]. In addition, there often exists a gap between the tutoring content and the underlying knowledge organization. There is a need for ITS authoring tools that can bridge this gap by making the knowledge organization used for tutoring more explicit.

Commercial authoring systems for traditional CAI and multimedia-based training give instructional designers and domain experts tools to produce visually appealing and interactive screens, but do not provide a means of developing a rich and deep representation of the domain knowledge and pedagogy. Indeed, most commercial systems allow only a shallow representation of content.

The motivation for our work comes from the need for reusable intelligent tutoring systems and from the leverage that the generic task (GT) development methodology offers in solving this problem. The assumption of the GT approach is that there are basic "tasks" or problem solving strategies and corresponding knowledge representation templates from which complex problem solving may be decomposed [7]. GT systems utilize a deep domain knowledge representation and an explicit inferencing strategy. Our approach involves developing an ITS architecture that can interact with different GT knowledge-based systems, to produce tutoring systems covering the domain knowledge represented in those systems. The ITS shell is domain-free, and this allows it to be reused for different domains. The architecture makes the underlying knowledge organization of the expert systems explicit, and reuses both the problem solving and domain knowledge for tutoring [10, 11].

2   ITS Generation Using a Task-Specific Approach

Task-specific authoring environments focus on the development of ITSs for a specific class of tasks. They incorporate pre-defined notions of teaching strategies, system-learner interactions, and interface components that are intended to support a specific class of tasks rather than a single domain. Task-specific authoring systems offer considerable flexibility, while maintaining rich semantics to build knowledgeable tutors. They can support rapid prototyping and reusability since they can be used to develop tutoring systems for a wide range of domains, within a class of tasks.

Related research efforts on task-specific authoring tools include IDLE-Tool, the Investigate and Decide Learning Environments Tool [2]. IDLE-Tool supports the design and implementation of educational software for investigate and decide tasks, which the author defines as a type of goal-based scenario in which the learner's task involves performing some investigations and then making a decision based on the supporting knowledge acquired from those investigations. Another example task-specific authoring environment is TRAINER [16], a shell for developing training systems for tasks such as medical diagnosis.

3   Generic Tasks: A Task-Specific Approach for Knowledge-Based Systems Development

Generic tasks are task-specific building blocks, implemented as reusable shells, for knowledge-based systems analysis and implementation. Each GT is defined by an input and output form, a knowledge structure, and an inferencing strategy [8]. To develop a system following this approach, a knowledge engineer first performs a task decomposition of the problem, which proceeds until a sub-task matches an individual generic task, or another method (e.g., a numerical simulator) is identified to perform the sub-task. The knowledge engineer then implements the identified GT instances using off-the-shelf GT shells by obtaining the appropriate domain knowledge to fill in the identified GT knowledge structure. Having a pre-enumerated set of generic tasks and corresponding knowledge engineering shells from which to choose guides the knowledge engineer during the analysis phase of system development. Several atomic generic tasks, such as structured or hypothesis matching, hierarchical classification and routine design, have been identified and implemented.

The architecture developed focuses on hierarchical classification (HC), a knowledge representation and inferencing technique for selecting among a number of hierarchically organized options [6]. Knowledge is organized in the form of a hierarchy of pre-specified categories. The higher level categories represent the more general hypotheses, while the lower level categories represent more specific hypotheses. Inferencing uses an algorithm called *establish-refine*; each category attempts to establish itself by matching patterns of observed data against pre-defined matching patterns. Once a category is established, it is refined by having its sub-categories attempt to establish themselves. Pruning the hierarchy at high levels of generality eliminates some of the computational complexity inherent in the classification problem. While automobile engine diagnosis and medical diagnosis are very different in terms of the knowledge involved, they both can utilize the same type of classification problem solving. Analysis of one of the two problems thereby contributes to analysis of the other.

4   An Architecture for ITS Generation from GT Expert Systems

The ITS architecture extends the GT framework with an ITS shell that can interact with any HC-based expert system to produce a tutoring system for the domain addressed by the system. The learner interacts with both the ITS shell (to receive instruction, feedback, and guidance), and the expert system (to solve problems and look at examples), in an integrated environment as shown in figure 1.

The architecture, which is shown in figure 2, consists of three main components: a GT expert system, an extended domain knowledge component, and the ITS shell. The expert system is used by the tutoring shell and the learner to derive problem solving knowledge and solve examples, and is developed as an instance of a hierarchical classification-based GT expert system. The extended domain knowledge component stores knowledge about the domain that is necessary for tutoring, but not available from the expert system. The ITS shell has four main components: the expert model, student model, instructional manager, and user interface, which are described next.

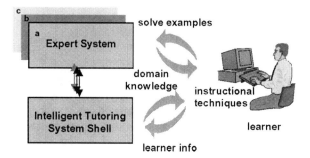

Fig. 1. The learner's interaction with the ITS architecture

The expert model component of the ITS shell models a GT expert system. Rather than re-implement the expert model for each domain, the ITS shell interfaces with a GT expert system to extract domain knowledge. This facilitates the reuse of the instructional manager, student model, and user interface components for different domains. The quality of the tutoring knowledge is thus affected by the expert system's knowledge representation. A GT's deep knowledge representation and structured inferencing strategy allows the extraction of well-defined tutoring knowledge. The expert model extracts three types of knowledge:

- Decision-making knowledge
- Knowledge of the elements in the domain data base
- Knowledge of the problem solving strategy and control behavior

Generic task expert systems have well defined knowledge structures and reasoning processes that can be reused for tutoring support. A typical GT system is composed of agents, each of which has a specific goal, purpose, and plan of action. The expert system solves problems using a case-by-case approach. Individual cases can be extracted from the expert system, to present as either examples or problems for the learner to solve. The expert model uses this knowledge, along with an encoding of the expert system's structure, to formulate domain knowledge as required by the ITS.

The student model component uses the expert system as a model of how to solve problems in the domain. The student model compares the performance of the student during problem solving to the expert system's solution to make inferences about how the learner is progressing. An overlay model is used to assign performance scores to the problems that the learner solves. Each question that the learner answers is assigned a score based on how many hints and/or attempts the learner needed, and on whether or not the learner was able to determine the correct answer. Each topic has an overall score that is computed as the average score of all the questions covered on that topic. The instructional manager uses this information to direct the instruction. For example, if the learner's overall topic score is low, the tutor presents more examples. If the score is high, the tutor can ask the learner to solve more questions, or move on to the next topic.

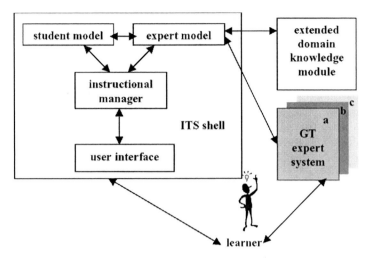

Fig. 2. Architecture for generating ITSs from GT-based expert systems

Using a runnable and deep model of expertise allows fine-grained student diagnosis and modeling. As a result, the tutor can give learners very specific feedback and hints that explain the problem solving process when their behavior diverges from that of the expert system's. Moreover, if the learner is having difficulties, he or she can ask the tutor to perform the next step or even to solve the problem completely.

The ITS architecture's pedagogical approach incorporates two main instructional strategies, learning by doing and example-based teaching. These teaching strategies are a good match for this framework, since the learner can interact with both the expert system to solve problems and the tutoring system. Learning by doing is implemented within the architecture by having the learner solve real problems using the expert system, with the tutor watching over as a guide. In the other learning mode, the tutor makes use of the predefined cases in the expert system's knowledge base. The instructional manager presents prototypical cases as examples, which serve as a basis for learning from new situations. It can also present new examples, posed as questions, and ask the learner to solve them. The goal is to help the user develop knowledge of how to solve problems in the domain by looking at and solving examples.

The instructional manager uses an instructional plan that incorporates a cognitive apprenticeship approach; learners move from looking at examples to solving problems as their competence level of the domain increases. The curriculum includes:

- Presentation of an overview on the domain topic.
- Presentation of problem solving examples on each topic of the domain.
- Asking the learner to solve problems covering the domain topics.

The architecture gives the author flexibility in determining the content of the examples and questions presented to the user. The author selects these from the set of cases defined in the expert system. The author can also determine the number of questions to ask the user for each topic. The pedagogical strategy also includes techniques for giving the learner feedback and hints. During a tutoring session, the tutor gives the learner appropriate feedback according to whether the learner solved problems correctly or not. If the learner's answer is incorrect, the tutor gives the learner a hint specific to the mistake committed, and then re-asks the question. The pedagogical strategy supports giving the learner up to three levels of hints and attempts to solve a problem, after which the tutor presents the correct answer if the learner still did not answer the question correctly.

Overall, the instructional approach utilized by the architecture attempts to reflect important findings about effective learning. Namely, for learners to become competent in a domain, they need to not only have a deep knowledge base of information related to that domain, but they must also be able to understand that knowledge within the context of a conceptual framework, and be able to organize that knowledge in a manner that facilitates its use [4]. Research studies have also indicated that effective learning environments should aim to bring real-world problems to the learning environment, provide "scaffolding" support to learners during the learning process, and also increase opportunities for learners to receive feedback and guidance.

The architecture employs a simple user interface that has been designed for tutoring using a problem solving approach. Since the tutoring content is mainly generated from the expert system, the user interface is tailored to allow the learner to interact with both the ITS shell and expert system in a transparent manner.

The ITS architecture requires additional pedagogical knowledge, which is obtained from the extended knowledge component and used by the ITS shell in presenting information to the user. This knowledge includes a high-level description of the domain, and the list of examples and questions used in the curriculum.

5 Implementation and Use of the Architecture

The architecture described above was implemented as a system named Tahuti[1], which consists of three main components: the ITS shell, the GT expert system, and the extended knowledge module. The architecture runs as a CD-based stand-alone environment, and was developed in VisualWorks Smalltalk. Any hierarchical classification-based GT expert system developed using the Intelligent Systems Laboratory's Integrated Generic Task Toolset developed can be plugged into the architecture to generate tutors for different domains. The extended knowledge module is implemented as a structured text file. It includes a problem overview and the curriculum topics. To generate an ITS using the Tahuti architecture, an author perform three main steps:

1. Identify an existing GT-based expert system for that domain or develop one using the Integrated Generic Task Toolset developed and used at the Intelligent Systems Laboratory, Michigan State University.
2. Construct the extended knowledge module by filling in the template provided as a structured text file. The ITS author fills in the template with a description of the domain, and a list of the examples and questions to be used in the curriculum.
3. Generate the ITS. The author links the expert system and extended knowledge module to the ITS shell, after which, the ITS is generated automatically.

The architecture was used to generate several ITSs including one for teaching the fabrication process of composite materials systems, which is described here. The

---

[1] The architecture is named after Tahuti, the ancient Egyptian god of knowledge, wisdom, learning, and magic. ITS development and use, in a way, involves a bit of all these aspects.

Composite Materials (CM) Tutor was generated from an existing expert system named COFATE2 [14], developed using the ISL's Integrated Generic Task Toolset. Figure 3 shows the CM Tutor's main interface.

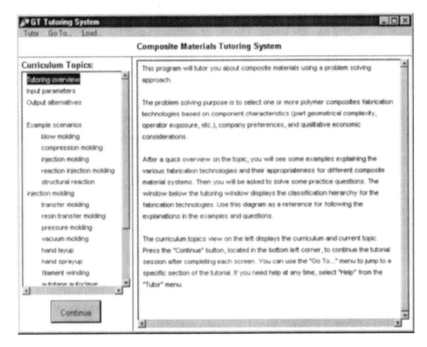

Fig. 3. Composite Materials Tutor – main user interface

The tutoring session begins with a topic overview. The tutor then presents examples for each topic defined in the curriculum, and asks the learner to solve practice questions. For each question, the tutor presents a scenario and asks the learner to select the appropriate fabrication technology. The tutor gives feedback according to the current instructional objective and learner's performance. If the learner selects an incorrect answer, the tutor gives the learner one or more hints, and asks again. Finally, the tutor presents explanations of the correct answers. The hints and explanations provided by the tutor are based on the hierarchical classification of fabrication technologies illustrated in figure 4. This classification structure is an integral part of the architecture. It is used by the expert system during problem solving, by the tutor in generating the hints and explanations, and also by the learners as a conceptual framework to map their knowledge onto as they learn. When the learner has achieved competency on the curriculum topics, the tutoring session ends, and the tutor displays a summary report.

6   Conclusions

The focus of this research work is the need for easier and more cost-effective means of developing intelligent tutoring systems. In this paper, we suggest that a task-

Fig. 4. Hierarchy of fabrication technologies shown to the learner by the CM Tutor

specific authoring approach can provide a useful solution to this problem. Specifically, we describe the development of a task-specific ITS shell that can generate tutoring systems for different domains within a class of tasks. Task-specific authoring shells offer flexibility in generating ITSs for different domains, while still being powerful enough to build knowledgeable tutors.

Our approach leverages the knowledge representation and reasoning capabilities of Generic Task knowledge-based systems, and reuses them for tutoring. More specifically, we have developed an architecture for generating ITSs for different domains by interfacing with Hierarchical Classification-based expert systems and reusing the other tutoring components. The architecture employs a runnable deep model of domain expertise, facilitates fine grained student diagnosis, offers an easy method for generating ITSs from expert systems, and allows the core ITS shell components to be reused with different knowledge bases, among other features. The effort involved in ITS development problem is reduced to identifying or developing an appropriate expert system, and the focus becomes tailoring problem solving domains to classification-based expert systems.

Future research paths include generating more ITSs using the architecture, and evaluating the tutors generated within instructional settings, for example, as aides to classroom learning. In addition, by incorporating different instructional strategies or new content formats, the architecture developed could serve as a component of a virtual laboratory for experimentation with new learning approaches and technologies. We also hope to extend the framework to support expert systems developed as integrated generic tasks.

References

1. Anderson, J. R. (1990). Analysis of Student Performance with the LISP Tutor. Diagnostic Monitoring of Skill and Knowledge Acquisition. N. Frederiksen, R. Glaser, A. M. Lesgold and M. Shafto. Hillsdale, NJ, Lawrence Erlbaum Associates.
2. Bell, B. (1999). Supporting educational software design with knowledge-rich tools. International Journal of Artificial Intelligence in Education 10: 46-74.
3. Bloom, B.S. (1984). The 2-Sigma Problem: The Search for Methods of Group Instruction as Effective as One-to-one Tutoring. Educational Researcher 13: 4-16.
4. Bransford, J.D., A.L.Brown. (2000). How People Learn. Washington, DC, National Academy Press.
5. Burton, R. R. and J. S. Brown (1982). An Investigation of Computer Coaching for Informal Learning Activities. Intelligent Tutoring Systems. Sleeman and Brown. London, UK, Academic Press.
6. Bylander, T. and S. Mittal (1986). CSRL: A Language for Classificatory Problem Solving. AI Magazine 7(2): 66-77.
7. Chandrasekaran, B. 1986. Generic tasks in knowledge-based reasoning: high-level building blocks for expert system design. IEEE Expert 1(3):23-30.
8. Chandrasekaran, B. and J.R.J.R. Josephson (1997). The Ontology of Tasks and Methods. Symposium on Ontological Engineering, Stanford, CA, AAAI.
9. Clancey, W. and K. Joerger (1988). A Practical Authoring Shell for Apprenticeship Learning. Proceedings of ITS'88: First Intl. Conf. on Intelligent Tutoring Systems, Montreal, Canada.
10. El-Sheikh, E. (1999). Development of a Methodology and Software Shell for the Automatic Generation of ITSs from Existing Generic Task-based Expert Systems. AAAI-99: Sixteenth National Conf. on Artificial Intelligence, Orlando, Florida, AAAI Press.
11. El-Sheikh, E. and J. Sticklen (1998). A Framework for Developing Intelligent Tutoring Systems Incorporating Reusability. IEA-98-AIE: 11th International Conference on Industrial and Engineering Applications of Artificial Intelligence and Expert Systems, Benicassim, Spain, Springer-Verlag (Lecture Notes in Artificial Intelligence, vol. 1415).
12. Juel, C. (1996). Learning to Learn From Effective Tutors. Innovations in Learning: New Environments for Education. L. Schauble and R. Glaser. Mahwah, NJ, Lawrence Erlbaum.
13. Lesgold, A., S. Lajoie, et al. (1990). A Coached Practice Environment for an Electronics Troubleshooting Job. Computer Assisted Instruction and ITSs Establishing Communication and Collaboration. C. Larkin. Hillsdale, NJ, Lawrence Erlbaum.
14. Moy, B., J. McDowell, et al. (1994). Expansion of an Intelligent Decision Support System for Process Selection and Process Design in Polymer Composites. 26th International SAMPE Technical Conference, Atlanta, Georgia.
15. Murray, T. 1998. Authoring Knowledge-Based Tutors. The Journal of the Learning Sciences 7(1):5-64.
16. Reinhardt, B. and S. Schewe (1995). A Shell for Intelligent Tutoring Systems. AI-ED 95 7th World Conference on Artificial Intelligence in Education, Washington, DC.
17. Shute, V., and Psotka, J. 1996. Intelligent Tutoring Systems: Past, Present, and Future. Handbook of Research for Educational Communications and Technology. D. Jonassen, ed. New York, NY: Macmillan.

Evaluating and Revising Courses from Web Resources Educational

Daniéle Hérin, Michel Sala, and Pierre Pompidor

LIRMM - Université Montpellier II / CNRS
161, rue Ada 34 392 - Montpellier cedex 5
Phone : (33) 4 67 41 85 85 Fax : 33 4 67 41 85 00
{dh, sala, pompidor}@lirmm.fr

Abstract. The World Wide Web offers a great availability of heterogeneous educational resources. This suggests the idea that such materials can be re-used in compose courses. In this paper we address this issue by proposing an architecture for composing teaching courses using "the best parts" of heterogeneous educational materials available on the Web. Course composition relies on a simple but effective evaluation methodology which reproduces real techniques used by teachers in composing and improving classroom courses. The final goal of this article is to help the teacher to construct his course until the obtension of a steady course.We present our initial work and discuss about future developments.

1 Introduction

Nowadays, the WWW (World Wide Web) constitutes the biggest source of educational courses of the globe. Following different approaches, many efforts have been done towards providing learners with courses able to teach without the help of a real teacher. From the simplest courses which appear as a sequence of web-pages displaying educational contents, to the more sophisticated ones, provided by educational applications which try to support the learner during the learning process in a more or less intelligent way, respectively ITSs (Intelligent Tutoring Systems) or CAL (Computer Assisted Learning). Among all courses teaching the same subject and developed according to different computer based learning educational paradigms, there are not any absolutely better than others: each of them is able to teach better than the others certain parts of the course. This can be due to the characteristics of the particular approach used or simply because the course is better designed or because it presents higher quality contents.

So far, most of teaching courses built according to each different educational paradigm have been composed using didactic material expressly designed or adapted for them. To the first category belong courses available as a sequence of web-pages and most of CAL applications or ITS [1]; in other cases, teaching materials are produced by modifying existing ones [3]. Other applications allow building instructional courses from already existent educational materials [2,4], but re-used materials for composing

S.A. Cerri, G. Gouardères, and F. Paraguaçu (Eds.): ITS 2002, LNCS 2363, pp. 208–218, 2002.

the course are of the same type, i.e. homogeneous (e.g. all HTML-files, all CAL materials). Using homogeneous didactic materials for composing courses guarantees semantic coherence between the different parts composing the course itself. Moreover, when didactic material is designed explicitly for a given course the quality of the teaching material is not put in discussion.

We focus our attention on the problem of re-using existent on-line educational materials developed according to different instructional paradigms and of composing the best parts of them in order to obtain high-level teaching courses which combine all best characteristics of different approaches. We propose a methodology and an architecture which constitute a support for teachers in building educational courses using "the best parts" of heterogeneous educational materials available on the WWW. Teacher is helped in detecting which parts of existing educational materials are the best to use for composing teaching courses and in checking that among different parts composing the built course holds semantic coherence even if they come from heterogeneous sources. This is done by proposing each composed course to students and by evaluating its effectiveness on the basis of comprehension the students have of contents of the course. Starting from such evaluation, learning is made on the quality of the course and feedback is provided for revising and improving it. In particular, the evaluation of students' reaction to the proposed course gives advice on both the quality of single parts composing it and on effectiveness of the whole course, i.e. it reveals if the order of the parts of the course (curriculum) is a good one and if semantic coherence holds among them. Learning, in our approach, relies on a pragmatic methodology of evaluation and revision of built courses, which reproduces the real way according to which teachers compose and improve traditional classroom courses.

In this paper we describe our initial efforts in designing an architecture responding to the characteristics described above. We also propose a first version of the evaluation methodology that constitutes the main part of our work. We present successively the proposed approach, the conceptual structures and the evaluation methodology. There were already works on the domain from P. Brusilovsky [5,6] on the Web-Based Education (WBE).

2   The Approach

2.1   Classical Course Construction

The approach we consider relies on observations coming from real-life teaching experiences where teachers build progressively teaching courses by iteration on different steps: composition of the course, teaching session, evaluation of different parts of the course by testing students.

The overall process is characterised by the following steps:

1. Consensual contents of the course: contents of a teaching course generally constitute a consensus for what concerns the main concepts to teach in the course. For ex-

ample, a teaching course on programming languages is accepted to be composed of two main parts: data structures and algorithmic structures. In many cases, a concept constitutes a prerequisite for another concept: in this case, we say that the two concepts are *related*.

2. Use of different textbooks: when a teacher builds a course, he consults different books or articles treating the subject of the course. In general, a teaching course is built by composing pieces of knowledge selected from different textbooks.

3. Content planning: each teacher has his own teaching method according to which he decides about relevant concepts to teach in the course and their teaching order. We call *curriculum* of a teaching course the ordered sequence of concepts taught in a course. Each teacher sequences his own curriculum.

4. Composition of the course: once a curriculum has been sequenced, associating each concept in it with pieces of knowledge selected from different textbooks substantiates it.

5. Teaching session: the composed course is presented to students.

6. Course evaluation by testing students: teacher evaluates effectiveness of his course by examining how students perform on quizzes and tests on all concepts composing the teaching course. In particular, the teacher detects which are typical errors made by students on the different parts of the course.

2.2 Analogy with Classical Course Construction

We propose an architecture (figure 1) and an evaluation methodology based on an analogy with observations listed above:

1. Global Ontology (GO) describes consensual contents of the course: we dispose of a consensual conceptual structure, GO, which represents the consensual knowledge about a given teaching course. It contains all concepts composing the course as well as prerequisites holding among them. Concepts in GO are called *Educational Units (EUs)*. Prerequisites among EUs are represented by *precedence constraints.*

2. *Local Ontologies* (LO) describe different *didactic tools*: on-line educational materials, called didactic tools replace traditional textbooks. The teacher disposes of a great deal of didactic tools available on the Web treating the same subject of a given teaching course. A didactic tool teaches a set of EUs. Each didactic tool is described by a conceptual structure called LO containing all EUs taught by the didactic tool.

3. *Curriculum Planner* to help teacher in sequencing the curriculum: the teacher sequences his own curriculum and the Curriculum Planner checks its consistency with respect to GO. A consistent curriculum is a sequence of EUs present in GO respecting all precedence constraints.

4. *Course Composer* to compose the course: the Course Composer composes the course by associating curriculum EUs with the parts of didactic tools able to teach them. This is done by instantiating each EU in the curriculum with one of the corresponding EUs contained in LO.

5. *Teaching Session*: during the Teaching Session the course is taught to students.

6. Evaluation methodology: the teacher makes the evaluation of the effectiveness of a teaching course by testing students on all EUs composing the curriculum. For each tested EU he gives a *teaching coefficient* indicating how well the EU has been "learned" by students and detects *errors* made on it. The evaluated course is stored in the *Curricula Database*.

In the setting of this paper, we won't take in account the problems of homogeneity of the different sources. On the other hand this homogenization is necessary to construct a curriculum. We consider solely that the GO is defined by the teacher and that the LO of every source is gotten while using a parser [7].

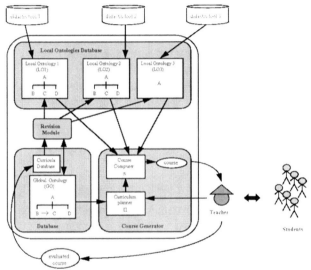

Fig. 1. General architecture

3   Conceptual Structures

3.1   Global Ontology

Global Ontology is represented by a hierarchy of aggregation in which nodes are EUs and the root is the subject (or teaching goal) taught by the course. A EU can be either composed or elementary. We call "elementary" a EU that cannot be decomposed in smaller EUs, i.e. that have to be taught as a whole. Because of aggregation relationship holding among EUs in GO, a composed EU is taught when all its component EUs have been taught. It follows that all knowledge to teach is contained in the leaves of the hierarchy. Prerequisites required by each EU are represented by precedence constraints. If a EU B is prerequisite for another EU C, the precedence constraint holding between B and C is denoted as $B \rightarrow C$ and indicates that C can be taught if and only if

B has already been taught. To each EU can also be associated some errors (cf. §5.2) that represent concepts taught in the EU.

An example of Global Ontology GO1 of a course teaching the subject A is denoted as follows:

GO1 = {*A*(*B*[er1],*C*,*D*[er2,er3]), {*B* →*C*}}

where GO1 identifies a particular Global Ontology; *A* is a composed EU; *A*(*B*,*C*,*D*) means that *A* is composed of *B*, *C*, and *D*; *B*, *C* and *D* are elementary EUs; er1, er2 and er3 are errors and *B*[er1] means that error er1 is relative to *B*; {*B*→*C*} is the set of prerequisites holding among EUs composing GO1 and *B* → *C* means that between *B* and *C* holds a precedence constraint.

We can think at GO as a textbook teaching the subject *A* where *A* is the whole book, *B* and *C* are chapters; the precedence constraint that holds among *B* and *C* means that chapter *B* teaches concepts which are necessary for understanding contents of chapter *C*.

The GO of a teaching course is built consensually by many teachers. We consider it as given. It is used as a scheme of reference to generate curricula of the course.

3.2 Didactic Tool and Local Ontology

Didactic tool is the name given to denote heterogeneous educational materials available on the Web. Each didactic tool is an entity that has been developed autonomously according to different instructional paradigms and for different purposes. It can be, for example, a text, a picture, CAL materials or an educational software application. A didactic tool teaches a set of EUs on a given domain. EUs taught by a didactic tool correspond to the smaller unit that can be identified by an http-address into which the tool can be decomposed. For example, while sections teaching different concepts can be recognized and isolated in a text, it could not be possible to decompose in sub-parts a software application presenting a course on, for example, "Programming Languages". In this case we can only say that the software application teaches the EU "Programming Languages". We use EUs coming from different didactic tools for composing teaching courses. Because of the heterogeneity of such materials we need to define a common representation for describing contents taught by different didactic tools. Contents of a didactic tool are described by a LO.

Local Ontology of a didactic tool is represented as a hierarchy of aggregation whose nodes represents EUs taught by the tool. Given the GO of a teaching course, LO of a didactic tool is built using GO as scheme of reference. For each EU appearing in GO, the same EU is searched in the didactic tool; found EUs are then organized respecting the hierarchy indicated in GO. The resulting LO constitutes a subset of the GO of reference.To each EU composing LO is associated the following additional information:

Errors

Each EU composing the LO is associated with errors made by students in learning the EU. *B*[er*j*] indicates that error er*j* with $j \in$ N is associated to EU *B*. For each detected error is also indicated the percentage of students that have made it. In the notation $B[erj_p]$ the parameter p represents the percentage of students that have made erj associated to the EU B. The percentage p is calculated by the following

$$p = (e/s)*100 \qquad\qquad (1)$$

where s is the number of students that have learned B and e is the number of students that have made error erj.

Teaching Coefficients

For each EU in Local Ontology a teaching coefficient indicates how well the didactic tool teaches the EU. In the notation B_x x represents the teaching coefficient of EU B; it is calculated according to the following equation:
notation B_x x represents the teaching coefficient of EU B; it is calculated according to the following equation:

$$x = (n/s) \quad \text{where } n = \Sigma_{i=1..s} n_i \qquad\qquad (2)$$

where s is the number of students that have been taught with B and n_i is a score indicating how well B has been learned by student i. The score is given with respect to a parameter of reference r and depends on the teacher t who has given the evaluation. An example of score indicating how well a student has learned a given EU could be 5/10 where $n_i = 5$ and $r = 10$.

The following example of Local Ontology
$$LO1 = \{A_9(B_8[er1_{60\%}],C_9,D_8[er2_{80\%},er3_{50\%}])\}$$
describes the Local Ontology LO1 of the didactic tool 1 which teach the EUs A, B, C, D where B_8 indicates that the EU B has teaching coefficient $x = 8$ (for $r=10$); $B[er1]$ means that error $er1$ is relative to B and $er1_{60\%}$ is the percentage $p = 60\%$ of students that have made error $er1$.

Considering the above GO1, the following examples of Local Ontologies are relative to didactic tools 1, 2 and 3 respectively
$$LO1 = \{A_9(B_8[er1_{60\%}],C_9,D_8[er2_{80\%},er3_{50\%}])\}$$
$$LO2 = \{A_{8.5}(B_{7.5}[er1_{80\%}],C_{9.5},D_{8.5}[er3_{50\%}])\}$$
$$LO3 = \{A_7\} \qquad\qquad\qquad ......$$

The construction of LO can be made semi-automatically by a parser (it is not the objective of this paper) which tries to individuate in the didactic tool the block of information concerning a particular EU. Such block of information is identified by a http-address. To each EU composing a LO is associated the http-address that corresponds to the physical location on the Web where educational material teaching that EU is located.

4 Course Generator

The Course Generator is the component that helps the teacher in sequencing the curriculum of the course and that creates the course by substantiating the concepts in the curriculum with educational materials able to teach them. Each of these tasks is carried out by one of the following components:

4.1 The Curriculum Planner

The first step in building a teaching course is sequencing the curriculum, i.e. deciding which EUs are to teach in the course and their teaching order. Making reference to the Global Ontology which describes the teaching course, the teacher t sequences his own curriculum by choosing and ordering EUs he wants to teach in the course. He also indicates which are errors associated to EUs in GO that he wants to minimize (for example, making reference to GO, the teacher can choose that he wants to build a course that minimizes er3 on D). Then is invoked the Curriculum Planner that checks if teacher's curriculum has been built respecting all constraints imposed by GO. A curriculum is considered correct if:

- EUs composing the curriculum are a subset of EUs appearing in GO;
- all precedence constraints among concepts indicated in GO are respected.

The Curriculum Planner guides the teacher in composing a correct curriculum by pointing out inconsistencies of the proposed curriculum and suggesting possible solutions. The result of interaction between the teacher and Course Planner is the generation of a correct curriculum that is a sequence of EUs present in Global Ontology and respecting all precedence constraints. We call such a curriculum the "non-instantiated" curriculum of the course.

Making reference to the above Global Ontology GO1, an example of correct curriculum could be:

$$\Pi 1_{(GO1)} = <B,C,D>. \tag{3}$$

$\Pi 1_{(GO1)}$ identifies is the non-instantiated curriculum of a course teaching the subject described by the Global Ontology GO1; $<B,C,D>$ are the EUs that have to be taught during the course. (3) is a correct curriculum in the sense that it satisfies both the conditions listed above, i.e. EUs B, C, D that compose it constitute a subset of EUs composing GO1 and the precedence constraint among concepts B and C is respected.

4.2 The Course Composer

Given the non-instantiated curriculum of the course, the Course Composer generates the teaching course by substantiating each EU of the non-instantiated curriculum with one of the corresponding EUs contained in LO. The choice of the EU to associate to a concept in the curriculum is made according to one of the following strategies:

- choosing the EU with the higher teaching coefficient (cf. §5.1). If there are many EUs with the same teaching coefficient, it is chosen the one which minimizes errors associated to the corresponding EU in GO;
- choosing the EU that minimizes errors indicated by the teacher in the phase of course planning.

In this sense, the obtained "instantiated" curriculum is composed of "the best parts" of available didactic tools.

An instantiated version of curriculum $\Pi 1_{(GO1)}$ with respect to Local Ontologies LO1, LO2, LO3 is the following

$$\pi_{(\Pi1,GO1)}=<B_{(LO1,8)},C_{(LO2,9.5)},D_{(LO1,8)}> \qquad (4)$$

where $B_{(LO1)}$ indicates that EU B is taken from Local Ontology LO1. B has been chosen from the Local Ontology with the higher teaching coefficient for it:

$$B_{(LO1,8)}=\max_{\text{teaching coefficient}}\{B_{(LO1,8)},B_{(LO2,7.5)}\};$$

D has been chosen in order to minimize er3, as indicated by the teacher in the previous section:

$$D_{(LO1,8)}=\min_{\text{percentage er3}}\{D_{(LO1,8)}[er3_{50\%}],D_{(LO2,8.5)}[er3_{80\%}]\}.$$

5   Evaluation Methodology

We present the initial version of the evaluation methodology on which our system is based. We will describe how teaching courses are evaluated on the basis of students' mastering of course contents and how evaluations are used to improve the quality of courses built in the future.

The instantiated curriculum representing the teaching course is proposed to students and a teaching session takes place. At the end of the teaching session the course is evaluated on the basis of knowledge acquired by students on the subject taught. The teacher who tests students on all EUs composing the curriculum makes course evaluation. For each tested EU, the teacher detects which are errors made on that EU. These errors determine how well the EU has been learned. On the basis of made errors, the teacher also indicates a teaching coefficient that is a numeric value representing the level of mastering gained by students on the EU.

Errors

Each EU appearing in the curriculum of a course is associated with errors made by students in learning that EU. The notation $B[erj]$ indicates that error erj with $j \in$ N has been made by students in learning the EU B. Errors detected on EUs can be of different types:

– errors caused by the didactic tool that is not good at teaching the EU: each error represents a misconception of the student on the part of the EU that is not taught well. For example, $B[er1]$ indicates that students have not well learned the part of B corresponding to er1.

– errors given by wrong sequencing of the curriculum: the EU has not well understood because it requires a prerequisite EU that have not been put in the curriculum. In this case, prerequisites among EUs in the curriculum are not respected.

– errors propagated between related EUs: if a EU is prerequisite for another EU making an error on the first EU causes bad understanding of its related EU.

Errors detected on EUs are indicated in the evaluated curriculum of the course.

For each detected error is also indicated the percentage of students that have made it. In the notation $B[erj_p]$ the parameter p represents the percentage of students that have made erj associated to the EU B. If s is the number of students that have learned B and e is the number of students that have made error erj, the percentage p is calculated using equation (1).

Teaching Coefficients

Teaching coefficients are associated to each tested EU: they indicate how well a EU is learned by students. In the notation B_x x represents the teaching coefficient of EU B. Let s be the number of students that have been quizzed on B and n_i with $i=1..s$ be a score indicating how well B is learned by student i, which depends on a reference r and on a teacher t; the teaching coefficient x relative to the EU B is calculated using equation (2).

Results of evaluation of a course are stored in the instantiated curriculum of the course. Let's consider (4); its evaluation given by a teacher t on a class k of students is the following

$$\pi_{(\Pi1,GO1)}=<B_{(LO1,8.5)}[er1_{55\%}],C_{(LO2,8)}[er4_{80\%}],D_{(LO1,8.5)}[er2_{65\%},er3_{45\%}]> \qquad (5)$$

where $B[er1]$ means that error $er1$ is made on the EU B; $er1_{55\%}$ indicates the percentage $p=55\%$ of students that have made error $er1$ which is calculated using equation (1); in $B_{(LO1,8.5)}$, $x = 8.5$ is the teaching coefficient representing students' comprehension of B which is calculated using equation (2). The evaluated instantiated curriculum of the course is stored in Curricula Database.

According to the new evaluations of EUs in the course, Local Ontologies are updated: teaching coefficients and percentages of errors given for EUs in the curriculum are used for re-calculating teaching coefficients and error percentages of the corresponding EUs in Local Ontologies. Let $y=(m/k)$ with $m=\sum_{i=1..k} m_i$ be the teaching coefficient representing the evaluation given by the teacher for a EU and let $x=(n/s)$ with $n=\sum_{i=1..s} n_i$ be the teaching coefficient of the in Local Ontology to which it refers. The new teaching coefficient z on this Local Ontology is obtained using the following equation: $z=(n+m)/(s+k)$.

On the contrary, let $p=(d/k)*100$ be the percentage of students that make a particular error on a EU in the course and let $q=(e/s)*100$ be the percentage of the same error on the corresponding EU in Local Ontology. The new percentage w on Local Ontology is calculated using the following equation: $w=[(e+d)/(s+k)]*100$.

Next time curriculum $\Pi1_{(GO1)}$ is instantiated, the association of EUs in the curriculum with EUs in Local Ontologies LO1, LO2 and LO3 will be made according to the modified teaching coefficients and error percentages.

6   Conclusions and Future Work

In this paper we proposed an approach which is pragmatic and involves strongly the teacher. It reposes on the fact that course evaluation and, indirectly, the evaluation of the quality of used educational materials is completely left to the free will of the teacher (even if we check coherence among evaluations given on the same course by different teachers). We only point out if students have "well passed or not" the course. In this sense we help "mass teaching", like that of collective teaching made in class-rooms, instead of individualized teaching. Our goal is not that of determining emotional or psychological implications that can cause bad understanding of certain parts of the course; we leave these problems to specialists in the domain of education.

We have also described how the domain knowledge of the course, i.e. the GO, is modified on the basis of successive teaching experiences by adding relevant information about the teaching. We are interested in studying more deeply how GO can be widen in order to complete the knowledge it expresses. In order to do that, we would reject the hypothesis made in this paper that LO and curriculum of the course are composed by a subset of EUs composing GO: in fact, we have supposed the only knowledge to which make reference is the consensual one. In the reality, on the contrary, didactic tools are able to teach more EUs other than that ones contained in GO. If we accept this hypothesis, we can learn how to complete GO by learning about EUs taught by didactic tools and present in curricula sequenced by the teacher.

Future work will consist in revising the teaching course which relies on the analysis of errors made by students who have been taught with that course. Error analysis makes it possible to recognize the type of errors made and, as a consequence, to determine the cause that generates them. It allows deciding about actions to take in order to improve course effectiveness. The Revision Module on the basis of evaluated courses stored in the Curricula Database makes error analysis. It recognizes the types of the errors associated to the different EUs composing the course and modifies LO and GO in order to improve the future Course Planner and Course Composer work. Another goal with consist in developing a prototype for validating our evaluation and revision methodology. We also intend to investigate how machine learning techniques can be applied for improving their effectiveness and how they can be used in order to provide more intelligent support to the teacher in planning his curriculum.

References

1. P. Brusilovsky, E. Schwarz and G. Weber, ELM-ART: An Intelligent Tutoring System on World Wide Web, *Intelligent Tutoring System*, (1996) pp. 261-269.
2. K. Nakabayashi et al., An Intelligent Tutoring System on World-Wide Web: Towards an Integrated Learning Environment on a Distributed Hypermedia, *ED-MEDIA '95: World conference on educational multimedia and hypermedia*, AACE, (1995) pp. 488-493.
3. M. Stern, B. Park Woolf, J. F. Kurose, Intelligence on the Web ? *AI-ED'97: Artificial Intelligence in Education* (1997) pp. 4 90-497.

4. J. Vassileva, Dynamic Courseware Generation : at the Cross Point of CAL, ITS and Authoring, *ICCE'95: Int. Conf. of Computer and Education, Singapore,* AACE, Charlottesville (1995) pp. 290-297.
5. P. Brusilovsky: adaptative Web-based Educational Systems ITS'2000 Tut. T2
6. P. De Bra, P. Brusilovsky, and C-J. Houben, ACM Computing Surveys, Vol 31, Number 4es, December 1999.
7. M-S Segret, P Pompidor, D Herin, M Sala: Use of ontologies to integrate some information semi-structured exits of pages web, INFORSID'2000, Lyon pp 37-55

Adaptive Postviewer for Constructive Learning in Hyperspace

Akihiro Kashihara, Kunitaka Kumei, Shinobu Hasegawa, and Junichi Toyoda

The Institute of Scientific and Industrial Research, Osaka University
8-1, Mihogaoka, Ibaraki, Osaka 567-0047, JAPAN
kasihara@ai.sanken.osaka-u.ac.jp
http://www.ai.sanken.osaka-u.ac.jp/thome2/kasihara/index-e.html

Abstract. Self-directed learning in hyperspace requires learners to monitor their navigation process involving knowledge construction, which they have carried out so far, since what and how they have learned becomes hazy as the navigation progresses. Although the reflective monitoring is an important activity in the self-directed learning, it is hard for them to keep it during navigating pages. The main issue addressed here is how to support the reflective monitoring. Our approach to this issue is to provide learners with the postviews of their knowledge construction adapted to their navigation process. Following the idea of adaptive postviewing, we have proposed an adaptive postviewer for self-directed learning with existing web-based resources. It generates page postviews and knowledge map, which display information suitable for their reflective monitoring to promote the constructive learning in hyperspace.

1 Introduction

Hypermedia/hypertext-based learning resources for education/learning generally provide learners with hyperspace, which consists of pages and links among the pages. In hyperspace, they can navigate the pages in a self-directed way to learn the domain concepts/knowledge [8]. The self-directed navigation often involves constructing knowledge, in which they would make semantic relationships among the contents learned in the navigated pages [2,6]. Knowledge constructed is shaped according to the navigation process. Such knowledge construction would enhance learning [2].

On the other hand, learners often fail in constructing knowledge during navigation in hyperspace since what and how they have navigated so far becomes hazy as the navigation progresses [5,8]. The self-directed learning in hyperspace accordingly requires them to monitor the navigation process with knowledge construction, which has been carried out so far [2,5]. We call such monitoring reflective monitoring, which can be viewed as meta-cognitive activity in the self-directed learning. However, it is not so easy for learners to keep the reflective monitoring during navigating pages since they would focus on comprehending the contents of the pages [5].

The important point towards resolving the problem is how to provide learners with information about the navigation process that they have carried out and information about the knowledge construction such as the contents they have learned in the pages navigated and the semantic relationships they have made among the pages learned.

S.A. Cerri, G. Gouardères, and F. Paraguaçu (Eds.): ITS 2002, LNCS 2363, pp. 219–228, 2002.

Current work on educational hypermedia/hypertext has provided a number of aids such as navigation history and concept/spatial maps, which represent information of navigation process in hyperspace [1]. These aids allow learners to recall the pages they have navigated. However, they provide insufficient information of why the learners have navigated the pages and how they have constructed knowledge in a self-directed way. The reasons why learners have navigated, which are called navigation goals, have a great influence on how to construct knowledge [2,6]. It is accordingly necessary for them to be aware of the navigation goals in the reflective monitoring.

In order to give learners an awareness of navigation goals, we have developed an interactive history, which allows them to annotate their navigation history with navigation goals arising from navigating pages in hyperspace provided by existing web-based learning resources [7]. The annotated navigation history enables them to monitor their self-directed navigation process.

In this paper, we propose an adaptive postviewer for reflective monitoring in the self-directed learning with web-based resources, which displays information related to the knowledge construction process with the interactive history. It generates the page postviews, which include the contents learners have learned at the web pages, and a visual representation called knowledge map, which shows the semantic relationships among the pages. The information of the web pages to be postviewed depends on the topic, on which the learners have focused in visiting the pages. The adaptive postviewer accordingly identifies the focal topic from their navigation process, and generates the page postviews according to the focal topic. Such adaptive postviewing enables learners to keep reflective monitoring, and facilitates their self-directed learning in hyperspace.

2   Reflective Monitoring Support

Before discussing the reflective monitoring support, let us first reconsider self-directed learning in hyperspace, and then demonstrate the interactive history that enables learners to monitor their navigation process in a proper way.

2.1 Self-Directed Learning in Hyperspace

The self-directed learning generally involves navigating hyperspace from one page to others by following the links among the pages. It also involves constructing knowledge from the contents navigated. Knowledge constructed depends on the navigation process even if the learning goal is the same.

In hyperspace, learners generally start navigating with a learning goal. The movement between the various pages is often driven by a local goal called navigation goal to search for the page that fulfills it. Such navigation goal is also regarded as a sub goal of the learning goal. We refer to the process of fulfilling a navigation goal as primary navigation process [6,7]. This is represented as a link from the starting page where the navigation goal arises to the terminal page where it is fulfilled.

Table 1. Navigation Goals and Visual Representation.

Navigation Goals	Visual Representation	
Supplement	Inclusion	
Elaborate	Set	
Compare	Bidirection arrow	
Justify	Vertical arrow	
Rethink	Superposition	
Apply	Arrow	

○ Starting page ● Terminal page

A navigation goal may have several terminal pages with one starting page. Navigation goal, represented as verb, signifies how to develop or improve the domain concepts and knowledge learned at the starting page. We currently classify navigation goals as shown in Table 1. A navigation goal arising from visiting a page is not always fulfilled in the immediately following page. In such case, learners need to retain the goal until they find the appropriate terminal page/s. While searching for the fulfillment of the retained goal, it is possible for other navigation goals to arise.

The navigation process can be modeled as a number of primary navigation processes. In constructing knowledge during navigation, learners would make a semantic relationship among the domain concepts/knowledge in the starting and terminal pages of each primary navigation process, and then combine each semantic relationship to integrate a number of primary navigation processes. In educational hypermedia/hypertext systems with concept maps representing domain concepts to be learned, learners can derive such semantic relationship from the maps [1]. Most existing web-based learning resources, on the other hand, do not specify the semantic relationship [7]. The learners accordingly need to identify it by themselves.

The semantic relationship would be shaped according to the navigation goal. For instance, a learner may search for the meaning of an unknown term to supplement what he/she has learned at the current page or look for elaboration of the description given at the current page. Each navigation goal provides its own way to make relationship between the starting and terminal pages.

The self-directed learning also requires learners to reflect on their navigation process since the primary navigation processes, which have been carried out so far, become hazy as the navigation progresses. The reflection involves monitoring the navigation process, which would also involve reconstructing knowledge with the monitored information [2]. It can be viewed as meta-cognitive activity of the navigation process. Such meta-cognitive activity is indispensable in the self-directed learning [5]. The reflective monitoring particularly holds a key to success in the knowledge construction. However, it is difficult for learners to keep the reflective monitoring since they would focus on comprehending the contents of the pages navigated, and since they have a limit of memorizing primary navigation processes [5]. Supporting the reflective monitoring is accordingly necessary for facilitating the reflection and learning in hyperspace.

2.2 Interactive History

In order to help learners reflect on their navigation process in hyperspace, we have implemented the interactive history system, which provides them with a navigation history annotated with navigation goals [7]. The system first enables learners to annotate a navigation history, which includes web pages sequenced in order of time they have visited, with primary navigation processes. In order to help learners note down the navigation goals, the system provides them with a list of navigation goals, and requires them to select one from the list when a navigation goal arises. The learners are also asked when they find the terminal page/s. The interactive history system annotates the navigation history with the information noted down. The annotated navigation history enables the learners to retain the primary navigation processes. The learners are also enabled to directly manipulate the annotated navigation history to modify/delete the primary navigation processes and to add new primary navigation processes.

Fig. 1 shows the user interface of the interactive history system. Learners can explore web pages with one learning goal in the Web browser. When they want to set up a navigation goal in visiting a page, they are required to mouse-click the corresponding page in the *Annotated Navigation History* window. The *Navigation Goal Input* window then appears as shown in Fig. 1. The learners can select one corresponding to the goal from the navigation goal list in the window. The page visited currently is also recorded as the starting page of the navigation goal. After inputting the navigation goal, the window disappears.

When the learners find a terminal page of the navigation goal, they are required to mouse-click the navigation goal in the *Annotated Navigation History* window. The *Navigation Goal Input* window then appears. They can input the terminal page by dragging the title of the terminal page and pasting into the terminal page section in the window.

Using the information inputted from the learners, the system generates the annotated navigation history as shown in Fig. 1 so that the primary navigation processes can be viewed clearly. In the annotated history, each page has its page title. The starting page of each goal is linked with the corresponding terminal page/s. There may be some primary navigation processes without terminal pages since they have not been found yet. The learners can look at the annotated navigation history on their demand during navigation.

Learners can also directly manipulate the annotated navigation history. Each manipulation is done by means of mouse-clicking/dragging parts of the primary navigation processes. There are three basic manipulations: deleting and changing navigation goals/links between starting and terminal pages, and adding new primary navigation process.

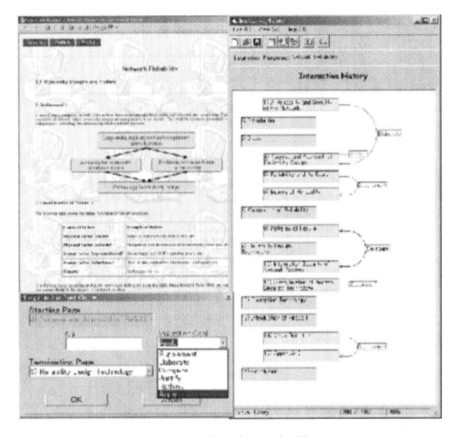

Fig. 1. User Interface of Interactive History.

Learners are not always required to input the above information whenever they visit pages. Nevertheless, inputting the information during navigation may be troublesome for learners. However, it enables the learners to promote the goal awareness to make their navigation more constructive [2,7]. From the results of the case study, which we had with the interactive history, we have ascertained that the interactive history can promote the goal-awareness in navigation and facilitate reflection on primary navigation processes [7].

2.3 Framework

Let us now discuss how the adaptive postviewer supports the reflective monitoring. The information necessary for the reflective monitoring can be broadly divided into:
    (1) Information about the navigation process, and
    (2) Information related to the knowledge construction process.
Learners can obtain information about their navigation process by using the interactive history. The adaptive postviewer provides them with information related to

the knowledge construction process, which information is identified from the navigation process.

The adaptive postviewer first identifies the contents learners have learned at the starting and terminal pages included in the primary navigation processes. The identified contents are regarded as the page postview. Web page generally includes several topics. Not every topic needs to be postviewed since it is not always learned. Which topic should be postviewed depends on the topic learners have focused on in the page. We call it focal topic. In navigating web pages, learners select an anchor of link in one page to move to the next page. In both the page including the anchor and the page the anchor points to, they seem to have an interest in the topic implied by the anchor. We accordingly consider the anchor indicates the focal topic. The adaptive postviewer identifies the focal topic of learners with the contextual information of the navigation process, and then identifies the contents to be postviewed.

The adaptive postviewer next generates a knowledge map according to their navigation process, which visually represents the semantic relationships among the primary navigation processes. Mouse-clicking any node in the knowledge map, which corresponds to the web page, learners can take a look at the page postview generated by the adaptive postviewer. The knowledge map accordingly enables learners to reflect on the relationships not only among the pages but also among the contents learned at the pages. It would be substantially fruitful for the learners to monitor the knowledge construction process they have carried out.

3   Adaptive Postviewer

3.1   Page Postview

The adaptive postviewer generates postviews of starting and terminal pages included in primary navigation processes since learners would primarily learn the contents included in these pages during navigation. The page postview generation consists of two processes:

(a) To identify the focal topic of learners, and
(b) To identify the contents of web pages to be postviewed.

The adaptive postviewer first identifies the focal topic with keywords included in the anchor of link that learners have selected in visiting web page. Following the hierarchy of heading tags such as *Title*, *H1*, *H2*, etc., in the HTML document file of the page, the adaptive postviewer next divides the document into sections, which are indicated by the tags. The heading tags describe the topics of the sections. Among these sections, the adaptive postviewer then identifies the section to be postviewed according to the focal topic. The page postview generated are shown to the learners on the knowledge map.

How to generate postview of the starting page of a primary navigation process are different from the one of the terminal page. As for the starting page, the adaptive postviewer identifies the focal topic from the anchor, which learners have selected in the starting page. Using the HTML document file of the starting page, it then identifies a section including the anchor as the section to be postviewed.

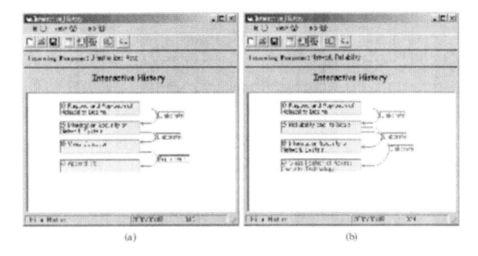

(a)   (b)

Fig. 2. Annotated Navigation Histories Generated by Interactive History.

As for the terminal page, the adaptive postviewer uses the HTML document file of the terminal page, and then identifies a section whose heading tag indicates the focal topic as the section to be postviewed. If no heading tag indicates the focal topic, it finds in which section keywords representing the focal topic appear most frequently.

Let us demonstrate the adaptive page postviewing with a simple example. In this example, we consider a learner who navigates as shown in Fig. 2(a) with the learning goal of exploring factors reducing the reliability of computer networks. In the web page *Purpose and Approach of Reliability Design* as shown in Fig. 1, he/she selects the anchor *Unauthorized Acts* to elaborate *Human factor*, which is one of the causes of computer network failure, and then visits the web page *Information Security of Network System*. In generating page postviews of the starting and terminal pages, the adaptive postviewer identifies his/her focal topic with *Unauthorized Acts*. It then extracts the section including the selected anchor from the HTML document file of the starting page as the page postview, which is shown in Fig. 3(a). It also extracts the section whose heading tag indicates *Unauthorized Acts* from the HTML document file of the terminal page, which is shown in Fig. 3(b). This page also turns into the starting page of the second primary navigation process in Fig. 2(a). In the page, he/she selects the anchor *virus detection* to elaborate *Unauthorized Acts*. Since the anchor is included in the same section that the heading tag *Unauthorized Acts* indicates, the postview of the starting page is accordingly the same as shown in Fig. 3(b).

Let us next consider the second example with another learner who navigates as shown in Fig. 2(b). In learning the page *Information Security of Network System*, he/she moves from the page *Reliability and its Scale* by selecting the anchor *About Concept of Security*. In this case, the adaptive postviewer extracts the section whose heading tag indicates *About Concept of Security* from the HTML document file of the terminal page, which is shown in Fig. 3(c). Although Fig. 3(b) and 3(c) are extracted from the same web page, these have different contents. In this way, the contents to be postviewed depends on the focal topic learners have interest in navigating pages.

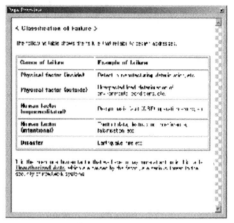

(a) Postview of Starting Page.

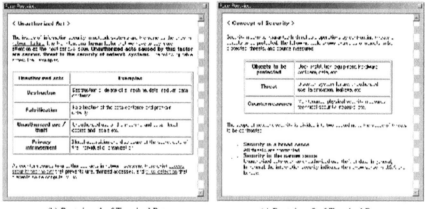

(b) Postview-1 of Terminal Page.   (c) Postview-2 of Terminal Page.

Fig. 3. Examples of Page Postviews.

3.2   Knowledge Map

In the knowledge map generation, the adaptive postviewer first transforms each primary navigation process into a visual representation by means of the visualization scheme shown in Table 1 [7]. This table shows the correspondence of a navigation goal to a visual representation of the relationship between the starting and terminal pages. For example, a navigation goal to *Elaborate* is transformed into a set that visualizes the starting page as a total set and the terminal page as the subset. The adaptive postviewer next generates a knowledge map by combining visual representation of each primary navigation process. The knowledge map generation is executed on learners' demand.

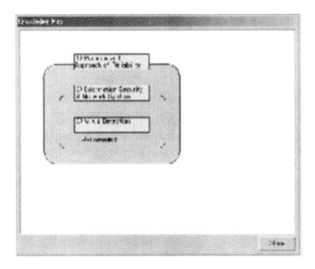

Fig. 4. A Knowledge Map.

When any node in the knowledge map is mouse-clicked, the postview of the corresponding page appears. Concurrently looking at several page postviews, learners can view the relationships among the contents learned at the pages.

Fig. 4 shows the knowledge map that is generated from Fig. 2(a). Viewing the map, for example, the learner can recall that he/she elaborated the contents learned at *Purpose and Approach of Reliability* by visiting *Information Security of Network System*. He/she can also mouse-click these corresponding nodes to concurrently view the page postviews shown in Fig. 3(a) and 3(b).

4   Related Work

Let us next compare with related work to consider the usefulness of the adaptive postviewer. As representative reflective monitoring support, there are currently concept maps. Learners can look at concept maps to reflect on what they have learned and the relationships among the concepts learned. They are helpful for learners who have lower capability of constructive learning in hyperspace since the direction of knowledge construction is visible to them [2]. In the context of self-directed learning, however, learners would often identify semantic relationships among the domain concepts learned, which are different from those defined in the concept maps [3]. In other words, they do not always construct the same knowledge structure as the structure of the domain concepts predefined. In addition, most existing web-based learning resources have no concept maps.

The adaptive postviewer, on the other hand, provides learners with more proper information of the knowledge construction process they have carried out in a self-directed way. Even in learning with existing web-based resources whose concept maps are not prepared, it can provide postviews of the pages navigated and the knowledge construction process according to their navigation process obtained from the interactive history. Such adaptive postviewing is an important aid for reflective monitoring of constructive learning particularly on the Web.

5 Conclusions

This paper has claimed that self-directed learning in hyperspace requires learners to monitor their navigation process involving knowledge construction, which they have carried out. It has also stated that keeping the reflective monitoring during navigation holds a key to success in the self-directed learning. However, the reflective monitoring is not so easy for the learners.

This paper has accordingly proposed an adaptive postviewer for supporting self-directed learning with web-based learning resources. The adaptive postviewer generates the page postviews and knowledge map according to their navigation process, which show information necessary for their reflective monitoring to promote the constructive learning in an adaptive way.

In future, we need to evaluate the effectiveness of the adaptive postviewer. We would also like to improve it according to the results.

References

1. Brusilovsky, P. Methods and Techniques of Adaptive Hypermedia, Journal of User Modeling and User-Adapted Interaction, 6, pp.87-129 (1996).
2. Cunninghan, D.J., Duffy, T.M., and Knuth, R.A. The Textbook of the Future, in McKnight, C., Dillon, A., and Richardson, J. (eds): HYPERTEXT A Psychological Perspective, Ellis Horwood Limited, pp.19-49 (1993).
3. Dillon, A., McKnight, C, and Richardson, J. Space-the Final Chapter or Why Physical Representations are not Semantic Intentions, in McKnight, C., Dillon, A., and Richardson, J. (eds): HYPERTEXT A Psychological Perspective, Ellis Horwood Limited, pp.169-191 (1993).
4. Gaines, B.R. and Shaw M.L. G. WebMap: Concept Mapping on the Web, in Proc. of Second International WWW Conference, http://www.w3.org/Conferences/ WWW4/Papers/134 (1995).
5. Hammond, N. Learning with Hypertext: Problems, Principles and Prospects, in McKnight, C., Dillon, A., and Richardson, J. (eds): HYPERTEXT A Psychological Perspective, Ellis HorwoodLimited, pp.51-69 (1993).
6. Kashihara, A., Ujii, H., and Toyoda, J. Reflection Support for Learning in Hyperspace, Educational Technology, 39, 5, pp.19-22 (1999).
7. Kashihara, A., Hasegawa, S., and Toyoda, J. An Interactive History as Reflection Support in Hyperspace, Proc. of ED-MEDIA 2000, pp.467-472 (2000).
8. Thuering, M., Hannemann, J., and Haake, J.M. Hypermedia and Cognition: Designing for Comprehension. Communication of the ACM, 38, 8, ACM Press, pp.57-66 (1995).

Adaptive Visualization Component of a Distributed Web-Based Adaptive Educational System

Peter Brusilovsky and Hoah-Der Su

School of Information Sciences
University of Pittsburgh
Pittsburgh PA 15260
peterb@mail.sis.pitt.edu

Abstract. Adaptive visualization is a technology that can enhance the power of program visualization. The idea of adaptive visualization is to adapt the level of details in a visualization to the level of student knowledge about these constructs. This paper presents an adaptive visualization system, WADEIn, that was developed to explore visualization of expression execution during program execution - a under-explored area in visualization research. WADEIn has been designed as a component of our distributed Web-based adaptive educational system KnowledgeTree, however it also can be used as a standalone educational tool. The system has been pilot-tested in the context of a real university course with 40 students and is available on the Web for public use.

1 Introduction

Program visualization is one of the most powerful educational tools in computer science education. It can provide a clear visual metaphor for understanding complicated concepts and uncover the dynamics of important processes that are usually hidden from the student's eye. Many papers and projects have been devoted to visualization of program execution. Visualization has been explored in the context of machine level languages [9], various high level languages [12; 13; 18], and algorithms and data structures [1]. While several studies show the positive value of visualization, some other studies have demonstrated that visualization is not a silver bullet [10; 17]: often in the presence of a well-developed visualization the students still fail to understand what is happening inside a program or an algorithm. In our past research, we have explored several ways to improve the efficiency of visualization [3; 7]. One of the directions we have explored was adaptive visualization.

Adaptive visualization is based on an assumption that a student may have different level of knowledge of different *elements* of a program or an algorithm that is being visualized. For the case of a program, the student may know some high-level language constructs or machine level language commands better than others. For the case of algorithm animation the student may understand some steps of an algorithm better than others. In this context, regular visualization that animates all constructs or steps for each user with the same level of details may not be the best approach. For a troublesome construct the level of detail may not be deep enough to for the student to understand its behavior. At the same time, by showing a visualization of a well-

S.A. Cerri, G. Gouardères, and F. Paraguaçu (Eds.): ITS 2002, LNCS 2363, pp. 229–238, 2002.

understood construct with unnecessary details, the visualization system distracts the student and make it harder to focus on and thus comprehend the behavior of the constructs that are still poorly understood by the student.

Adaptive visualization matches the level of details in visualization of each construct or step to the level of student knowledge about it. The less the level of understanding of a construct, the greater the level of details in visualization. Naturally, with a demonstrated increase in student knowledge about specific constructs, the level of visualization of those constructs should decrease. This approach allows a student to focus attention on the least understood components while still being able to understand the whole visualization. Our experimental evaluation of several kinds of enhanced visualization in the context of program debugging has confirmed our hypothesis that adaptive visualization can increase the power of visualization [2].

Our current work continues our research on adaptive visualization in the slightly different context of visualization of expression evaluation in C programming language. For the students of our programming and data structure course based on C language, the expression evaluation is one of the most difficult to understand parts. They have problems with both understanding the order of operator execution in a C expression and understanding the semantics of operators. To help the students, we have developed a Web-based Adaptive Expression Interpreter (WADEIn, pronounced as wade-in). WADEIn has been designed as a component of our distributed Web-based adaptive educational system KnowledgeTree; however it also can be used as a standalone educational tool. The system has been pilot-tested in the context of a real university course with 40 students and is available on the Web for public use. WADEIn and the technology of adaptive visualization used in it are the central topics of this paper. The following sections present, in order: the user interface, the architecture of WADEIn, and its use in two contexts: as a component of KnowledgeTree and as a standalone tool. At the end we discuss our research contribution and the plans of future work.

2 WADEIn: The User's View

The front-end of WADEIn is an expression interpreter that can work in either exploration or evaluation mode. In *exploration mode* the user can observe the process of evaluating a C expression step-by-step. An expression can be typed in or one can be selected from a menu of suggested expressions. At the beginning of evaluation, the system indicates the order in which various operations in the expression will be performed (Fig. 1). After that, the system starts visualizing the execution of each operation. The goal here is to show the results and the process of executing an operator. To show the results, the system visualizes a "shrinking" copy of the original expression and the values of all involved variables.

The execution of every operation is split in several sub-steps. At first, the system highlights the operations to be executed and its operands on the "shrinking" copy of the expression and re-writes it to the *evaluation area* field (gray rectangle in the center of the window). Next, it shows the *value* of the expression (2 on Fig. 1). In case of assignment and increment/decrement operations, WADEIn also shows the new value of the variable involved (Fig. 1). On the next sub-step, it replaces the whole highlighted operation in the "shrinking" copy with the calculated value. If a variable has changed its value as a side effect of evaluation, it also changes the value of the variable (Fig. 2). On this sub-step the system may use animation by "flying" the numbers from the working field to their destinations in an expression or in the variable area. Finally, the system removes all highlighting, "shrinks" the simplified expression, and prepares for the next step.

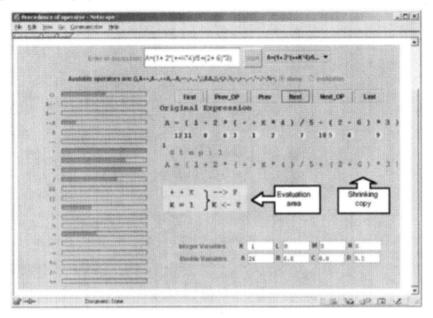

Fig. 1. The user starts working with an expression. Numbers in circles show the order of calculation. The applet starts visualizing the execution of the first operation ++K (the current value of variable K shown below is 1).

The level of detail in executing an operation depends on the user's current level of knowledge about it. For the minimal level of knowledge (1.0), the system will perform all sub-steps and will show the animation in a slow motion. As the user learns an operation increasingly better and his or her knowledge level improves from 1 to 5, the system degrades gracefully the level of detail in the visualization by increasing the speed of animation and removing some sub-steps. For the maximal level of knowledge (5.0) there will be no sub-steps and no animation - the operation will be executed in one step.

To control the process of expression interpretation, the user has six buttons. *First* and *Last* let the user move to the beginning or the end of expression execution; *Next_OP* and *Prev_OP* let the user move in one step to the beginning of interpretation of the next or previous operation; *Next* and *Prev* move the user one adaptive step forward and backwards. Normally, the user would use only *Next* button (or simply hit Return key). Other buttons can be used to watch the same operations and sub-steps again and again forwards and backwards or to skip sub-steps or operations.

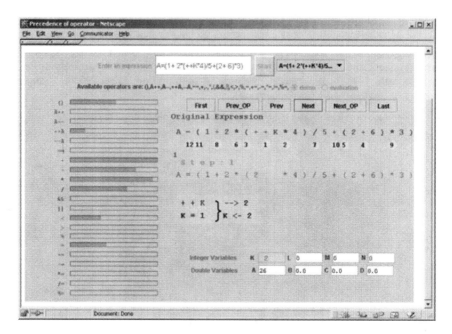

Fig. 2. The results of calculating an operation are "flying in" to replace the original operation and operands in a working expression and the old value of the variable involved.

To show to the user the system's opinion about his or her knowledge, we use progress indicator bars also known as a *skillometer*. This convenient interface feature that makes the user model viewable for a student was introduced in Carnegie Mellon cognitive tutors [16] and has been used since that in some other ITS [19]. One of our assumptions is that even passive watching of the visual execution of various operators contributes to student's knowledge about these operators. After visual execution of every expression, the progress indicators are updated. A more reliable way to check student knowledge and to update the student model is the *evaluation mode*. The student's work with an expression in evaluation mode starts with a request to indicate the order of execution of the operations in the expression (Fig. 3). After that, the system shows the correct of execution, and starts evaluating an expression (Fig. 4). The process of evaluation is quite similar to the evaluation in an exploration mode (the execution of every operation is adaptively visualized), but two aspects are different. First, the students have no freedom in navigation through the solution. Only two actions are possible - quit an exercise and move to the next operator (Fig. 4). Second, if the student knowledge of the current operation is low, the system will not calculate the result of the operation, but instead requests it from the user (Fig. 4). If the user makes an error, the correct result is provided, so the calculation of the expression will always be correct.

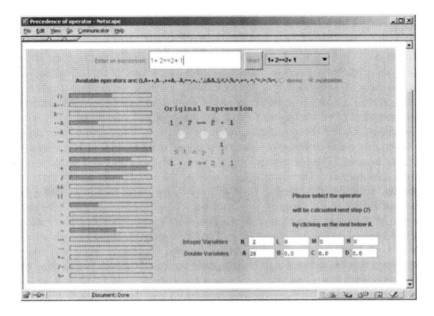

Fig. 3. At the beginning of executing an expression in the evaluation mode, the system requests the user to mark the order in which the operators will be executed.

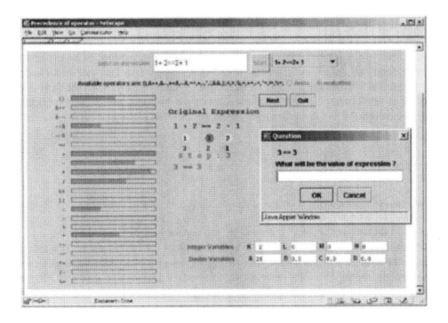

Fig. 4. In evaluation mode, the system requests the result of each operation from the user if his or her level of knowledge about this operation is low.

3 The Implementation

Architecturally, WADEIn is a distributed client-server application written in Java. It consists of a client-side applet and a servlet-based server side. The server side maintains authentication and provides a top-level interface for the user. It also accepts the information about the student progress from the applet, provides information about the student to all components and hosts the student model updating interface.

The client and the server side maintain two-way communication, however, each way is implemented differently. Server to client communication is maintained by parameter passing. The interpreter applet is very flexible and can be controlled by multiple parameters. The parameters define the mode of work (exploration, evaluation, or both), the starting level of user knowledge, the order and subset of operations visible on the progress indicator bar, the expressions that will be shown in the menu of expressions to choose, and a few other things. This flexibility allows the applet to be used in several contexts. In WADEIn systems the set of parameters are generated by a presentation server. More exactly, the server generates the whole HTML page that embeds the applet, including necessary parameters in the <applet> tag. In particular, it uses parameters to pass the current level of student knowledge about each operator. However, the requirement to use the interpreter applet with a server seriously reduces the applicability of this applet in a real classroom. The mechanism of parameters lets teachers who are interested to use the interpreter to create a static embedding page to host the applet. The values of parameters on this static page can be set to tune the applet to the needs of the class. In this context the applet will be able to function without the server component (though the student model will not be stored from session to session).

Client to server communication is essentially reporting the results of the student's work back to the server. After the student completes the work with an expression, the applet sends all information in the form of raw events to the user modeling server (next section explains it in more details). The communication with the user modeling server is implemented using a simple http-based protocol that is very similar to the one we have used in our earlier distributed system PAT-InterBook [6].

4 The Student Modeling

The student modeling component of WADEIn was developed following our *centralized user modeling* approach [4; 5]. One of the main ideas of this approach is that an educational system is composed of several adaptive components that all use the same central student model. The central student model assembles the information about the student from multiple sources. The student model is formed on the basis of the domain model that is a network of elementary knowledge elements. It stores an evidence of student knowledge for each of these knowledge elements separately. In our case, every C operator is an independent knowledge element. At the same time, the central student model is not a classic overlay that "cooks" all evidences about student knowledge of an element into a single number. In our central model the information is stored in a relatively "raw" form that avoids information loss and distinguishes different sources and events. This is important since the student model is used by different adaptive components that have different needs. Processing a flow of events into a classic vector overlay is usually done for the needs of one of the components and may lose an information important for other components.

WADEIn uses two different sources that can produce four kinds of events for the central student model. The main source is the interpreter applet that produces three types of events. The first type is "the student has seen a visual execution of an operator". The parameter for the event is the level of visualization. The second event is "the student has performed an operation". The third is "the student has identified the order of execution for an operator". The parameter for the latter two events is correctness. These events are sent to the user modeling server after the completion of every expression.

The second source of information is the student himself. The student model server maintains an open student model [8] and provides an interface where the students can self-evaluate their knowledge of every operator. All these events are stored independently and can be retrieved by any client of the central student model.

As mentioned above, the interpreter applet itself uses a regular overlay model for its own needs - the level of knowledge of each operator is modeled and visualized by progress indicators as a real number from 1 to 5. This overlay model is obtained as a *projection* of the central student model by applying a polynomial formula (1).

$$K = a_1 N_{user} + a_2 N_{seen} + a_3 N_{eval} \qquad (1)$$

Here N_{user} is the user own evaluation, N_{seen} is the number of times the user have seen an evaluation and N_{eval} is the number of times the user has done a correct evaluation. For experimental purposes, weights a_{1-3} can be provided as applet parameters.

5 WADEIn as a Component of KnowledgeTree

WADEIn was designed to serve as one of the *activity servers* for our KnowledgeTree learning portal. The KnowledgeTree portal allows a teacher to create a course support Web site that can use course materials distributed among different servers. With KnowledgeTree, a teacher is able to specify the objectives for every lecture and to request relevant learning activities of different kinds from different activity servers. At runtime the portal will retrieve relevant activities from different activity servers according to the objectives of the lecture and student knowledge (Fig. 5). The kinds of learning activities currently provided by WADEIn are a sets of expressions to be evaluated in either exploration or evaluation mode. Each set is developed to practice one or more operations.

Currently, KnowledgeTree/WADEIn does not support full-featured adaptive sequencing, but it does support mastery learning [11]: the student can work with the expressions until the target level of knowledge for the operations to be learned is achieved. In the future we are planning to add full adaptive sequencing of expressions to the WADEIn system - i.e., an ability to generate a small set of most appropriate examples at any point of a student's work with the system. This will let us use the system not only in conjunction with a course but also for self-guided Web-based education.

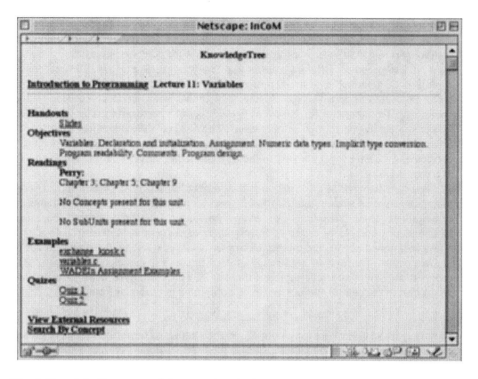

Fig. 5. KnowledgeTree, a portal for accessing distributed Web-based course support material. The window shows a view of a lecture with associated learning material. Different items are usually served by different activity servers.

6 Conclusion

This paper presents WADEIn system that lets the students explore the process of calculating the value of expressions in C language and evaluates the student knowledge of various C operators. WADEIn uses adaptive visualization to let students focus their attention on less understood C operators. The system is designed to be a component of a large adaptive educational system based on centralized student modeling. Currently we use WADEIn as a component of a learning portal KnowledgeTree, however, the interpreter applet that is a core of the system could also be used without any portal or server. The system was pilot-tested in a practical C course and got very positive student feedback. Many students considered WADEIn as the most useful tool among all tools that are currently connected to the KnowledgeTree portal. Currently we are running a larger and more formal evaluation of the system in an introductory programming class. Our plans are to provide WADEIn as a free tool that could be used for teaching programming in many places.

In addition to the practical need, the work on WADEIn was stimulated by two research goals. Our first goal is to develop an open architecture for adaptive distributed educational systems. To achieve a progress in this direction, we need set of diverse adaptive components that can be used to explore various aspects of the architecture and evaluate different student modeling approaches. In this context, an adaptive visualization system serves as one of the components.

Our second goal is to explore adaptive visualization as a way to increase the educational value of program visualization. It has been shown in several experiments [10; 17] that the educational effect of observing visualization is unexpectedly low. Different approaches to make visualization work have been suggested [3; 14; 15]. Adaptive visualization is one of these approaches. Our earlier experiments show promising results [3] and we want to continue this direction of work. Along this direction we plan a series of experiments with WADEIn to evaluate different aspects of adaptive visualization.

References

1. Brown, M. H. and Najork, M. A.: Collaborative Active Textbooks: A Web-Based Algorithm Animation System for an Electronic Classroom. In: Proc. of IEEE Symposium on Visual Languages (VL'96), Boulder, CO (1996) 266-275, available online at http://www.research.digital.com/SRC/JCAT/vl96
2. Brusilovsky, P.: Program visualization as a debugging tool for novices. In: Proc. of INTERCHI'93 (Adjunct proceedings), Amsterdam (1993) 29-30
3. Brusilovsky, P.: Explanatory visualization in an educational programming environment: connecting examples with general knowledge. In: Blumenthal, B., Gornostaev, J. and Unger, C. (eds.) Human-Computer Interaction. Lecture Notes in Computer Science, Vol. 876. Springer-Verlag, Berlin (1994) 202-212
4. Brusilovsky, P.: Student model centered architecture for intelligent learning environment. In: Proc. of Fourth International Conference on User Modeling, Hyannis, MA, MITRE (1994) 31-36
5. Brusilovsky, P.: Intelligent learning environments for programming: The case for integration and adaptation. In: Greer, J. (ed.) Proc. of AI-ED'95, 7th World Conference on Artificial Intelligence in Education, Washington, DC, AACE (1995) 1-8, available online at http://www.contrib.andrew.cmu.edu/~plb/papers/AIED-95.html
6. Brusilovsky, P., Ritter, S., and Schwarz, E.: Distributed intelligent tutoring on the Web. In: du Boulay, B. and Mizoguchi, R. (eds.) Artificial Intelligence in Education: Knowledge and Media in Learning Systems. IOS, Amsterdam (1997) 482-489
7. Brusilovsky, P. L.: Adaptive visualization in an intelligent programming environment. In: Gornostaev, J. (ed.) Proc. of East-West International Conference on Human-Computer Interaction, Moscow, ICSTI (1992) 46-50
8. Bull, S., Brna, P., and Pain, H.: Extending the scope of the student model. User Modeling and User-Adapted Interaction 6, 1 (1995) 45-65
9. Butler, J. E. and Brockman, J. B.: A Web-based learning tool that simulates a simple computer architecture. SIGCSE Bulletin - inroads 33, 2 (2001) 47-50
10. Byrne, M. D., Catarambone, R., and Stasko, J. T.: Evaluating animations as student aids in learning computer algorithms. Computers & Education 33, 5 (1999) 253-278
11. Corbett, A. T. and Anderson, J. R.: Student modeling and mastery learning in a computer-based programming tutor. In: Frasson, C., Gauthier, G. and McCalla, G. I. (eds.) Intelligent Tutoring Systems. Springer-Verlag, Berlin (1992) 413-420
12. Domingue, J. and Mulholland, P.: An Effective Web Based Software Visualization Learning Environment. Journal of Visual Languages and Computing 9, 5 (1998) 485-508

13. Haajanen, J., Pesonius, M., Sutinen, E., Tarhio, J., Teräsvirta, T., and Vanninen, P.: Animation of user algorithms on the Web. In: Proc. of VL '97, IEEE Symposium on Visual Languages, IEEE (1997) 360-367, available online at http://www.cs.helsinki.fi/research/aaps/Jeliot/vl.ps.gz

14. Hansen, S. R., Narayanan, N. H., and Schrimpsher, D.: Helping learners visualize and comprehend algorithms. Interactive Multimedia: Electronic Journal of Computer-Enhanced Learning 2, 1 (2000)

15. Hundhausen, C. D. and Douglas, S. A.: Using Visualizations to Learn Algorithms: Should Students Construct Their Own, or View an Expert's? In: Proc. of IEEE Symposium on Visual Languages, Los Alamitos, CA, IEEE Computer Society Press (2000) 21-28, available online at http://lilt.ics.hawaii.edu/~hundhaus/writings/VL2000-Experiment.pdf

16. Koedinger, K. R., Anderson, J. R., Hadley, W. H., and Mark, M. A.: Intelligent tutoring goes to school in the big city. In: Greer, J. (ed.) Proc. of AI-ED'95, 7th World Conference on Artificial Intelligence in Education, Washington, DC, AACE (1995) 421-428

17. Stasko, J., Badre, A., and Lewis, C.: Do Algorithm Animations Assist Learning? An Empirical Study and Analysis. In: Proc. of INTERCHI'93, New York, ACM (1993) 61-66

18. Tung, S.-H. S.: Visualizing Evaluation in Scheme. Lisp and Symbolic Computation 10, 3 (1998) 201-222, available online at ftp://140.125.81.71/pub/tungsh/lasc.ps.Z

19. Weber, G. and Brusilovsky, P.: ELM-ART: An adaptive versatile system for Web-based instruction. International Journal of Artificial Intelligence in Education 12, 4 (2001) To appear

Dynamic Profiling in a Real-Time Collaborative Learning Environment

Jaakko Kurhila[1], Miikka Miettinen[2], Petri Nokelainen[2], and Henry Tirri[2]

[1] Dept. of Computer Science
P.O. Box 26
FIN-00014 University of Helsinki
Finland
tel. +358 9 191 44664
`Jaakko.Kurhila@cs.helsinki.fi`
[2] Complex Systems Computation Group
Helsinki Institute for Information Technology
Finland
{`Miikka.Miettinen, Petri.Nokelainen, Henry.Tirri`}`@hiit.fi`

Abstract. EDUCO is system for collaborative web-based learning. Collaboration is enabled by real-time social navigation and support for social interaction via synchronous and asynchronous discussions. However, the system and the use of the system in collaborative learning could benefit from dynamic profiling as well as active recommendations for the students working in the learning environment. The paper describes the system and discusses the generation of profiles and recommendations.

1 Introduction

EDUCO is a system for on-line collaborative learning. EDUCO employs a form of *social navigation* [10] by visualizing the actions of other participants currently present in the learning environment. Since the actions of the users are visible to the other users in real-time, the social navigation is *direct* [1].

Many of the contemporary systems incorporating social navigation use *collaborative filtering*. It means that these "systems provide the user with recommendations of their likely interest in data items on the basis of 'interest matches' derived from ratings from the set of users" [2].

The approach to social navigation taken in EDUCO brings the *feel* of live companions into web-based learning [8]. The feel can promote pedagogically meaningful communication and collaboration. To amplify the social aspects of learning and to make the system adaptive for different needs, effective profiling of the students and active recommendations are appropriate features.

One approach to profiling of the users is to use data gathered with questionnaires. Kurhila et al. [7] introduced an adaptive questionnaire designed both for the construction of profiles and adaptive questioning. However, the scope of this paper is to examine the possibility of constructing dynamic profiles based on the users' behavioral patterns without any prior data. The profiles can be utilized

S.A. Cerri, G. Gouardères, and F. Paraguaçu (Eds.): ITS 2002, LNCS 2363, pp. 239–248, 2002.

in EDUCO to support collaborative learning and to enable adaptive recommendation of potential documents to different users.

2 Description of EDUCO

From the users' point-of-view, EDUCO consists of six different views for various activities, a document area and a discussion area (Fig. 1). The views are map, chat, search, alarm, preferences and help. They are presented in a tool resembling a handheld computer (upper-left corner in Fig. 1, now in "map" view). The largest area on the right-hand side is the document viewing area for documents gathered into an Web-course in EDUCO. The space below the EDUCO (bottom-left corner in Fig. 1) is reserved for the asynchronous discussions.

Fig. 1. The user interface of EDUCO. Map view presents documents gathered in EDUCO.

"Map view" presents documents ordered into clusters of in EDUCO. Documents are presented as paper-icons and the users are presented as dots. The colour of a dot indicates a group membership. The dot is located next to the document the user is currently viewing. When a user places the mouse pointer on top of a document or a dot representing a user, a tool tip text appears showing the name of the person or the title of the document. In Fig. 2, the pointer is on a document called "Where did all the people go?". Double clicking a document opens the document into the right-hand side of the browser window and moves the dot representing the user to a corresponding location on the map view of every user in EDUCO.

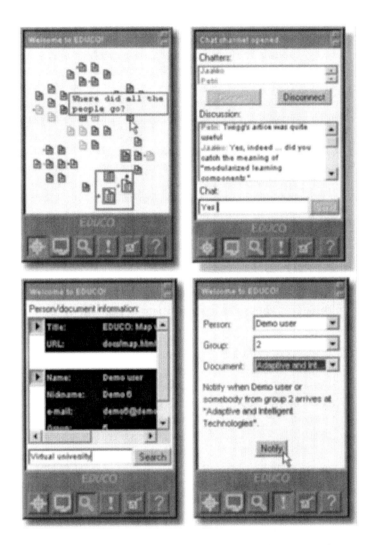

Fig. 2. The "map" (top-left), "chat" (top-right), "search" (bottom-left) and "alarm" (bottom-right) views of EDUCO.

The documents change their colour on the map depending on how much the users have viewed the document relative to the other documents. The colours range from bright to dimmed, indicating heavily viewed and nearly ignored documents, respectively. This way the user can get the historical navigation information at a glance and does not have to be on-line all the time to know where the other users have navigated and where they have stayed for long periods of time. The change in the colour of an individual document is determined by the distance of its moving average for the last 24 hours from the same average for all the documents.

Other functions of EDUCO include a chat and a bulletin-board for asynchronous discussions. Any user can easily initiate a chat discussion with other users simply by clicking the corresponding user symbols and then clicking the "Connect" button in the chat view (Fig. 2). Asynchronous discussions are document-specific. Users of EDUCO can write a comment when viewing a document. The comment is visible to users navigating to that document. Other users can comment on the comment, thus continuing the chain of comments as illustarted in Fig. 1.

The third view is "Search". Users can search other users and documents in an instance of EDUCO. When a user searches a user or a document, the results are shown textually in search view (Fig. 2) and graphically in map view by highlighting the corresponding user or document.

"Alarm view" gives users the possibility to set up an alarm that is triggered if the requested condition occurs. For example, if a user seeks another user also interested in a certain document, he or she can tell the system to give a notifying message when someone else arrives to the document (Fig. 2).

The last two views are "Preferences" and "Help". While viewing "Preferences", the user is allowed to change personal settings in the system. Help view provides information about the system usage in general.

3   Educo Architecture

From a technological point of view, EDUCO consists of a server, a Java applet for every user and a number of CGI-scripts. The most important task of the server is to keep track of the state of the distributed system and inform the clients as changes occur. An example of typical change in the system is a navigation step: If one of the users moves to another page, the new location has to be sent to everyone currently present in EDUCO. This type of implementation of communication without delays requires that the clients maintain an open socket connection to the server throughout the session.

To avoid copyright issues and to make the use of EDUCO simpler for the EDUCO-administrator (i.e., the course teacher), we have taken the approach that the documents (HTML-files) for a particular instance of EDUCO do not need to be copied to the EDUCO server. Instead, they can be located anywhere on the Web. To operate properly, the server still needs to know which document the user is reading to be able to send that information to all the other users in the environment. This has to work even when the users navigate along the hyperlinks in the documents and are not using the map view by double-clicking the document symbols. We have solved this problem by using the EDUCO server as a proxy. The documents are routed through the server instead of being sent to the client directly from their actual location. Two additional operations are required: clients are informed about the new location of the user and all of the links in the document are changed so that they point to their destination indirectly through the proxy. If the user then navigates to another document along one of the links, the same procedure is repeated.

4 Dynamic Profiling and Document Recommendations

4.1 Data Set

The data set used for evaluating the profiling and recommendation possibilities in EDUCO was collected in the Fall 2001 during a course entitled "Web-based learning" given at the University of Helsinki, Finland. The course was a web-based course, and the use of EDUCO was mandatory. The course was an advanced course in Computer Science. Twenty-four students participated in the course, some of them adult learners with varying backgrounds and degrees but most of them were Computer Science majors.

The type of the course was a "seminar" which means that the students have to pick a topic, prepare a 10-page paper on a topic and present it to the teacher and other students in the course. However, there were also small weekly assignments to complete. These assignments required navigation in EDUCO, and interaction with the other participants in the course. The weekly assignments introduced the students to the concepts and issues essential to the course.

The course material was organized to six different document clusters in EDUCO. The clusters were: 1) Implications of Web-based education on the society, 2) History of Web-based education, 3) Web-based education research, 4) Pedagogical issues, 5) Adaptive educational systems and 6) Learning environments (i.e. course delivery systems). The document cluster sizes varied from six to nine, giving a total of 43 documents.

The course included only two face-to-face meetings. The first was an initial meeting where the structure and requirements for the course were explained and the EDUCO system was introduced. The second face-to-face meeting was the final meeting where the students presented their papers. Everything else between the initial and final meeting was conducted on-line using EDUCO.

Because of the small student population participating the course, it was possible that there will not be enough students at the same time using EDUCO. We wanted to make sure that students will see other live users in the environment, so we fixed a primary time slot for the students to visit EDUCO. However, the time slot was not restrictive in any way. In practice, the majority of the students visited EDUCO right after the weekly assignment was published on Mondays, and that was also the primary time slot.

4.2 Profiling the Users

A significant amount of useful information about the students' interactions with the system was accumulated during the course. Exact data about the times students viewed the documents and word histograms of chat discussions as well as the use of "search" and "alarm" was logged. Besides being of value to researchers studying the social aspects of group formation and collaboration [8], the data can be used for adaptation.

It could be possible to profile the users based on the data gathered by observing the social behaviour (chatting, comments, searching people and setting alarms) of the users. Besides social activity, dynamic profiling of the users can be based on other sources of information. The approach taken in this paper is to study the use of navigation and viewing times of documents, i.e. *navigational patterns*, as a basis for effective profiling.

The idea of dynamically profiling the users based on their navigational patterns defines some requirements for the technical implementation. We would like to form, update and discard clusters dynamically based on the data available at a particular point in time. However, there is no need to reconsider the whole clustering every time one of the students moves to another page. It is sufficient to update the profiles on a daily or weekly basis. The data set used in our preliminary analysis made weekly updating a natural choice. Most of the activity took place on Mondays, when the students were given small assignments due on the same day. For the reason, the experimental clustering was conducted with 8 different data sets, each consisting of the data accumulated by the end of the particular session.

The amount of the consolidated data was small from a statistical point of view, since there were only 24 students attending the course. This will likely to be the case with other courses of the same kind, so an important requirement for the clustering method is its ability to give useful results even with small data sets. In other applications it is often appropriate to balance the complexity of the model with the amount of data, but placing all the students to one cluster would not be helpful for our present purposes. On the other hand, algorithms that determine the number of clusters automatically would in principle be preferable.

As discussed above, the original idea was to profile the students on the basis of the amount of time they had spent viewing particular topics (i.e. groups of documents). However, some of the visits to the documents appearing in the logged data lasted for several hours. It is obvious that the user had left the browser window open rather than studied the document actively for the whole time. To prevent this type of data from distorting the profiles, we ignored additional time after a certain limit. The limit was set to 10 minutes, affecting about 9% of the data. It is certainly possible that more time was spent on active studying, but a relatively low limit is appropriate for evaluating the distribution of the viewing time over topics rather than individual documents.

Ideally, the clustering algorithm should learn incrementally from a small set of training examples, adjusting the number of clusters as needed. A method called COBWEB [3] attempts to address these issues. The clusters are represented as probability distributions calculated from the instances assigned to each cluster. The clustering process is guided by a heuristic evaluation function known as *category utility* [5] that attempts to maximize both the similarities within clusters and differences between clusters. When encountering a new instance, COBWEB calculates the category utility for various alternative modifications of the previous clustering. New clusters are formed and old ones are splitted and merged as needed. Incremental learning, in addition to automatic determination of the number of clusters and applicability to small data sets, made COBWEB an attractive solution for the problem at hand. However, the method did not perform adequately on our data set. Almost every student was assigned to a different cluster, which made the results useless for the purpose. The problem, known as overfitting, is an issue in almost all forms of machine learning. Fortunately, better performance can be achieved with other methods.

One practical solution is the k-means algorithm [6]. The data vectors are first assigned randomly to k clusters, and the center of each cluster is determined by calculating the mean of the data vectors assigned to it. The centers and the clustering are then redefined repeatedly until a stable configuration is found. More specifically, each data vector is moved to the cluster that maximizes its probability, after which the cluster means are re-calculated. When none of the assignments changes any more, the algorithm has converged to a local optimum. Alternative solutions can be created by restarting from a new randomly generated clustering.

When using the k-means algorithm, the number of clusters has to be fixed beforehand. This is not a major problem, however, since the suitable range is rather narrow. In order to constitute student profiles of practical value, the clusters should not be too big, and our focus on the social aspects of learning implies that we do not prefer clusters of one or two people either. Considering the available data set of 24 users, the optimal cluster size iis in our opinion 5 to 6, suggesting that there should be 4 clusters. Trials with 3 and 5 clusters also produced satisfactory results.

After the clusters have been constructed on the basis of topic level viewing times, it is useful to examine differences within the clusters more carefully. In particular, it seems possible to implement a small scale recommendation system if the viewing statistics and the clustering algorithm are indeed successful in capturing useful information about the interests of the students. Some students in a cluster may have spent a reasonable amount of time viewing a particular document, and assuming that viewing time indicates interest, the document could be recommended to others in the same cluster who have not looked at it yet. The viability of the idea can be tested by looking if such differences exist, and if they have predictive power in the sense that sooner or later everyone in the cluster ends up viewing the interesting document. We currently base the recommendations on the following heuristic rule: if more than one third of the people in the cluster have viewed a certain document 5 minutes or one fourth of the people 10 minutes, the document is recommended to the others.

4.3 Empirical Results

The clustering was conducted for 8 different data sets, each successive set including the additional data of one more week. The viewing times of the documents were transformed into a discrete 3 point scale. Based on some experimentation, the ranges were set to 0–10 minutes, 10–20 minutes and more than 20 minutes. The k-means algorithm was executed with the amount of clusters fixed to 4.

About the clusters. Because of the small data sets (only 24 cases and 6 variables), it was straightforward to see that the results of the clustering appeared to be "good" in the sense that items within clusters were remarkably similar to each other and clusters were reasonably different from each other. From the eight periods, the only confusing exception was period 3. For some reason, all of the items were in one cluster, and the others were empty. In period 4, which contained the same data and one more week, the results looked good again. The third period was left out from the other analyses, since it seemed to be an odd exception among otherwise consistent results.

Figure 3 shows as an example of the clusters identified in period 1. The bars indicate the average amount of time spent viewing each of the topics of the course. As can be seen from the figure, there are clear differences between the clusters regarding both the total amount of time spent in the system and its distribution over the topics.

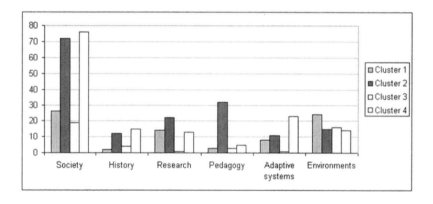

Fig. 3. Average viewing times of the topics in the first period.

The students in clusters 2 and 4 had been online much more than the ones in clusters 1 and 3. In all clusters the most popular topic was the "Implications of Web-based education on the society". The documents discussing those issues accounted for 34 to 52% of the total viewing time. "Learning environments" appeared to be another focus of interest in clusters 1 and 3. Their main difference is that the topic having the third longest viewing time is "Web-based education research" in cluster 1 and "Adaptive educational systems" in cluster 3. The students in cluster 2 seemed to be more interested in education than technology as documents related to society, pedagogy and research comprised 77% of the total viewing time. In cluster 4 the most popular topics were "Implications of Web-based education on the society" and "Adaptive educational systems".

Stability of the clusters. In order to evaluate the stability of the clusters, we calculated the proportion of the students who stayed in the same cluster for two successive periods. Each cluster of the first period was paired with one of the clusters of the second period in such a way that the overall degree of similarity, defined in terms of the overlap between the two clusterings, was maximized. On average, the similarity was 78%. The similarities of individual pairs of clusterings varied between 46% and 96%, largely reflecting the rate of the accumulation of data. The more additional data was received during the period, the more the clusters tended to change. Only 5 people of the 24 stayed in the same (gradually evolving) cluster for the whole time. It seemed that there were no major variations between individuals regarding the difficulty of profiling them, since nobody was moved to another cluster more than 3 times.

Recommending the documents. The idea of recommending documents within clusters was also tested in a simulation. Since each clustering generates a set of recommendations independently, there is no straightforward way of comparing the results of different periods. For this reason, we did our analysis on one data set chosen from the middle of the course (period 4). Significant differences in the viewing times of individual documents were first identified using the criteria discussed above. The system would have given 42 recommendations in total. Only 3 of these were found in the smallest cluster, which contained only 2 students. It is obvious that the variation among 2 people cannot be sufficient for the purpose. The other clusters received 12-15 recommendations each. For individual students the number ranged from 0 to 6, with an average of 1.8. People who had spent the least time in the system were generally in the upper end and the most active readers in the lower end.

The recommendations generated at the middle of the course were also compared to the final data set, which included the actual viewing times of each document. In particular, it was interesting to see if the students eventually found their way to the potentially meaningful material without guidance. The proportion of recommended documents, in which the particular students spent more than 5 minutes during the latter part of the course, was 18%. Since 31% of all viewing times were above 5 minutes, the students were actually less likely to indicate interest in the recommended documents than all documents in general. However, in 67% of the cases the recommended document was not visited at all. Therefore, it seems possible that the recommendation facility would be helpful in finding relevant material.

5   Conclusions

EDUCO is a learning environment with built-in support for real-time on-line social collaboration. The underlying principles of EDUCO could benefit from dynamical user profiling and active recommendations of potentially interesting documents to users. The paper presented a method to provide the profiling and recommendations using a data set gathered from an actual web-course where EDUCO was used. Analyzing the data suggests that merely the navigation and viewing of documents are enough to provide sufficient data for meaningful and efficient profiling of the learners, and the adaptive recommendations are possible from the same data.

Examining the navigational patterns of the users of EDUCO elaborates the idea that human thinking can be viewed to occur at least partly outside the mind [4]. In the case of EDUCO, *insight* (new learning method or view into the course material) can come from *outside* (new tools for direct social navigation) the mind. In a way, McCalla et al.[9] address the same issue when they state that intelligent tutoring systems of the future do not have a learner model as a single distinct entity. Instead, they will have a virtual infinity of models, computed as needed during the learning process.

References

1. Dieberger, A.: Social Navigation in Populated Information Spaces. In A. Munro, K. Höök and D. Benyon (Eds.), Social Navigation of Information Space, pages 35–54. London: Springer (1999).
2. Dourish, P.: Where the Footprints Lead: Tracking Down Other Roles for Social Navigation. In A. Munro, K. Höök and D. Benyon (Eds.), Social Navigation of Information Space, pages 15–34. London: Springer (1999).
3. Fisher, D.H.: Knowledge Acquisition via Incremental Conceptual Clustering. Machine Learning 2, 139–172 (1987).
4. Gigerenzer, G.: Adaptive Thinking. New York: Oxford University Press (2000).
5. Gluck, M.A. and Corter, J.E.: Information, uncertainty, and the utility of categories. Proceedings of The 7th Annual Conference of the Cognitive Science Society, pages 283–287 (2001).
6. Jain, A.K., Murty, M.N. and Flynn, P.J.: Data Clustering: A review. ACM Computing Surveys 31, 264–323. (1999).
7. Kurhila, J., Miettinen, M., Niemivirta, M., Nokelainen, P., Silander, T. and Tirri, H.: Bayesian Modeling in an Adaptive On-Line Questionnaire for Education and Educational Research. Proceedings of The 10th International PEG2001 Conference, pages 194–201 (2001).
8. Kurhila, J., Miettinen, M., Nokelainen, P. and Tirri, H.: EDUCO - A Collaborative Learning Environment using Social Navigation. To appear in Proceedings of Adaptive Hypermedia and Adaptive Web-based Systems (AH2002)(2002).
9. McCalla, G., Vassileva, J., Greer, J. and Bull, S.: Active Learner Modelling. Proceedings of the Intelligent Tutoring Systems (ITS2000), pages 53–62. Berlin: Springer (2000).
10. Munro, A., Höök, K. and Benyon, D.: Footprints in the Snow. In A. Munro, K. Höök and D. Benyon (Eds.), Social Navigation of Information Space, pages 1–14. London: Springer (1999).

Dynamic Generation of an Interface for the Capture of Educational Metadata

Issam Rebaï[1] and Brigitte de La Passardière [2]

[1] Université René Descartes – Paris 5
CRIP5
12 rue de l'école de médecine –75270 Paris cedex 06
Issam.Rebai@math-info.univ-paris5.fr
[2] Université Pierre et Marie Curie – Paris 6
LIP6 – case 169
4 place Jussieu –75252 Paris cedex 05
Brigitte.de-la-Passardiere@lip6.fr

Abstract. Faced with a multiplicity of educational applications on the web, various initiatives can be found defining sets of metadata to be used to describe them. It is indeed of critical importance that everyone (teacher, trainer, learner) can find these materials when needed. This is why the IEEE proposes a Learning Object Metadata (LOM) standard. Given, however, the habits of communities or institutions and the practices of groups, we will wish to characterise their learning resources according to their own point of view. In order to take this diversity into consideration we have developed a tool to dynamically generate an interface which permits a group of users to work on its own metadata set, while at the same time, granting it the possibility to be in conformity with the standards which are coming into existence.

1 Introduction

What web surfer has not submitted a query on a search engine and either seen "no result" or, on the contrary, hundreds of references which have no relation to the subject. The case is not rare and cannot be considered as an exception. Where the search for learning resources is concerned, the phenomenon is much greater. The web is crawling with sites to help students revise for the "baccalauréat" (final year examination in French secondary schools) but requests submitted through the usual search engines return little or even nothing within the area specified. It is therefore urgent that a way is found in which to characterize these applications so that everybody can benefit from these online resources. To achieve this, researchers and users are working on defining metadata sets. What then remains is to offer tools to those involved in producing these materials to help them capture these descriptions. The work that we are presenting here takes this into consideration. In effect, the customs of a community, the habits of an institution and the practices of a group will define the ways in which each one will wish to characterize its learning resources according to its own point of view. This is the reason why we are proposing a tool to dynamically generate an interface which will permit a group of users to work on its

S.A. Cerri, G. Gouardères, and F. Paraguaçu (Eds.): ITS 2002, LNCS 2363, pp. 249–258, 2002.

own metadata set, while, at the same time, granting it the possibility to be in conformity with the standards which are coming into existence.

2 Metadata for Educational Applications

Educational applications demand more specific metadata [1] than those used to describe an electronic document[1]. In addition to the technical characteristics of the resource, it is necessary to specify the uses, environment and other information which may help the user in his choices [2], [6]. In fact, several propositions are being developed currently by the major organisations or national communities.

The IMS global Learning Consortium which is specialized in promoting open specifications for facilitating online distributed learning activities such as locating and using educational content has proposed an IMS Learning Resource Metadata Specification[2]. It's an XML-compliant schema for indexing learning objects. This schema has a growing popularity among e-learning projects such as SCORM[3] (Sharable Content Object Reference Model), MERLOT[4] (Multimedia Educational Resource for Learning and Online Teaching) and others. This work is also at the origin of national proposals. Thus, CanCore[5] is a subset of this Metadata Specification, tailored slightly for the Canadian context. The CanCore element and vocabulary set was developed in early 2001 by educators and metadata specialists representing several national research initiatives. The Australians have also integrated these proposals in the framework of their work in the MetaWeb project. In this project they have selected 6 of the 15 Dublin Core metadata tags, in order to create skeleton records for pre-determined sites. In actual fact approximately 10 major institutions support the Dublin Core metadata, notably EDNA (Education Network Australia)[6]. This education community online, funded by all the Australian government departments proposes a metadata which consists of all the 15 DC elements and 9 specific EdNA.

Besides the national initiatives, other projects have also flourished, notably European projects such as ARIADNE(Alliance of Remote Instructional Authoring and Distribution Network for Europe)[7] Beginning in 1995 this project focused on the development of tools and methods to produce, manage and reuse learning resources. These are regrouped in a "knowledge pool", a repository in which the entire educational materials are available. In fact, the project began, at an early stage, to be preoccupied by the development of tools for indexing to enable their retrieval in the knowledge pool.

Thus IMS and ARIADNE co-operated within the Learning Technology Standards Committee (LTSC), Learning Objects Metadata working group of the IEEE with a

---

[1] http://dublincore.org/

[2] http://www.imsglobal.org/metadata/ (version 1.2.2 – 2001)

[3] http://xml.coverpages.org/scorm.html

[4] http://www.merlot.org/Home.po

[5] http://www.cancore.ca/

[6] http://standards.edna.edu.au/metadata/

[7] http://www.ariadne-eu.org/

view to defining a common metadata set [4] in order to establish a standard for the description of the "Learning Object Metada" (LOM)[8].

Other major institutions can also be seen to be preoccupied with this domain of application. The Dublin Core Metadata Initiative thus created the DC Education Working Group[9] in April 1999, a working group dealing with this question. Its objectives are to continue discussion and development of proposals for the use of Dublin Core metadata in the description of learning resources. It works in the development of qualifiers and domain-specific elements, element qualifiers and value qualifiers to describe educational materials for the purpose of enhancing resource discovery.

But it should also be noted that, in December 2000, cooperation was officially announced between the LTSC-Learning Objects Metadata working group of the IEEE and the Dublin Core Metadata. The work of this group is carried out in conformity with LOM elements, such as interactivityType, interactivityLevel, TypicalLearningTime…

In sum, it can only be noted that the description of electronic educational material is a necessity felt by many communities and that ARIADNE implements metadata which are compatible with LOM in the same manner as other platforms such as « Campus virtuel » [7].

3   Habits in Communities

Today, the tendency is moving towards the creation of a certain stability and even a standard around the IEEE propositions.

Nevertheless, in the institutions or the communities, the reality is quite different. Depending on the discipline, the public and the usage, specific work habits, references, ways and customs can be found. As a matter of fact they would like to be able to have their own metadata implemented as DTD [3]. We would like to offer these groups the possibility of working according to their own needs, while allowing them to conform with the standard. It is essential to have generic tools which allow to make up for this instability of metadata and their tedious capture. That's why the system we are presenting in this paper offers a tool to enable dynamic interface generation, which, for teachers, will be easier to use than those usually available.

Starting with users' needs and their own metadata set, we propose, in this work, to provide them with an interface based on their needs and automatically generated.

4   Dynamic Generation of the Interface

The dynamic generation of the interface consists in creating an interface to capture data and generate an XML document in conformity with the DTD from which it is created [5]. Our system also offers help to users by filling some fields automatically, defining lists of values, using default values or evaluating value from other input data.

---

[8] http://ltsc.ieee.org/doc/
[9] http://dublincore.org/groups/education/

To achieve these goals, four operations are required: the analysis of the source DTD, the configuration of the interface, its construction, and finally the generation of the XML document. Consequently, the system architecture is organized around four main components, and deals with each one of these operations (Fig. 1).

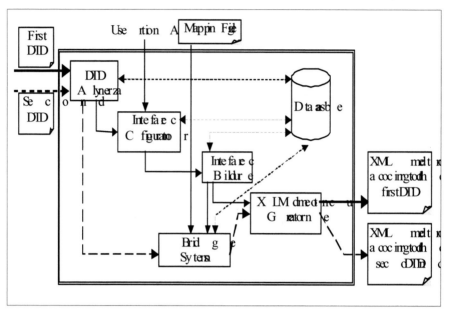

Fig. 1. System architecture

The system offers two operating modes. The first one is a « normal mode », which permits the building of an interface based on a default configuration with just a few clicks, and the production of XML document. The second one is an « advanced mode » which permits the configuration of the interface and the supply of help to the user when he captures data.

Hereunder we present this last mode which is more difficult to bring into operation, but allows a researcher's or practitioner's community to appropriate themselves the tool and to work in their usual way.

4.1 DTD Analyser

The analyser is aimed at checking the validity of the DTD and extracting the useful data for the interface construction and storing this information in a data structure usable for the interface configurator. For this, the analyser executes six operations.

```
<!ELEMENT exercise_geneval (head_gii, body_gii)>
<!ELEMENT head_gii (name, author, meta_informations)>
<!ELEMENT meta_informations (date, language, difficulty?)>
<!ELEMENT body_gii (autoevaluation_criterions, question*)>
<!ELEMENT question (name, nota?, method*)>
<!ELEMENT method (name, help+, short_answer*)>
```

Fig. 2. An example of DTD source[10]

- The first one consists in proceeding to the analysis of the DTD source (Fig. 2) by a "validating parser". This makes sure that there is neither syntactic, nor structural errors.
- The second one imports information from external files. If the DTD includes external references, the analyser replaces these references by the referenced text.
- The third one analyses and extracts elements and attributes. For this operation, the DTD will be gone through several times. It's necessary to locate parameter entities (« < !ENTITY % ») and replace them by the entity content. Then it must extract the elements (« < !ENTITY % ») to create a list of couples (element name, element content). And finally, the last traversal permits the extraction of attributes (« < !ATTLIST ») and, for each found instance found, the analysis of the data included between delimiters. Then, for each element of the DTD, a list with all the attributes and their characteristics is created.
- The fourth one has to determine which element is the root of the DTD. So the analyser defines all the elements as potential roots. For each element, it checks if it has a parent. If this is the case, it is not considered as a root anymore. At the end of the process, the number of roots is counted. If there are more than one, the user has to choose which one he wants to keep as a candidate.
- The fifth one carries out the construction on the hierarchical tree of the DTD. To do this, it first proceeds with a pretreatment to delete parenthesis and replace them by face values. The aim of this is to be able to associate, in the place of the text between parenthesis, a graphic container according to its type (optional, mandatory, multiple) and implement the operation (insert or delete) for its handling. Then all elements must be located and replaced. Finally, starting with the root, the analyst constructs a binary tree corresponding to the hierarchical structure of the DTD. For each node, it determines its indicator of occurrences, its type, its parent, child and first sibling nodes, and for the latter, if they are ordered (separated by coma) or not (separated by |).
- The sixth operation consists in storing the tree in a data structure usable by the interface constructor. For this, information on the elements and on the attributes (name, predefined value) is stored. The storage of the result of the previous analysis in a database is a time saver, since later on, it will not be necessary to analyze the DTD again in order to generate the interface.

---

[10] Unmentionned element have a PCDATA type. Extract from the GENEVAL DTD (Ariadne project).

4.2   Interface Configurator

This component is, as already indicated, only usable in the advanced mode. It provides the interface builder with information related to the display and the management of the DTD. Some of the information is valid for all interfaces, while other parts of it are specific to a DTD. Like for the tree resulting from the analysis, this information is stored in the database. This component is particularly dedicated to specifying the ways in which to present the different types of element, to associating help and comments to each element of the DTD, to creating lists of values and attaching them to elements, to establishing a hierarchy in these lists of values, to defining default values for elements and attributes, to attaching events to some elements, to managing users' and institutions' profiles and, at another level, to managing the different DTD.

For the user, the interface configurator looks like a graphic application, which allows him to manage a series of DTD known by the system. It's able not only to define the set of interface graphic parameters, such as police font, background color, alignment, border, and so on, but also the vocabularies used in the different languages available. Furthermore, the interface configurator permits the management of events in order to render an interface capable of reacting to user' s actions.

An event is characterized by a source element, an event type and its parameter, and a target element. An event is triggered when the user acts with the source element. Event type specifies if it is a query, a graphic change, an action or a program, which is to be executed. Target element defines the element to which the event has to be applied. This can be the source element itself or any other of elements used in the interface.

For example, in the case of metadata with which we are concerned here, the user, in order to characterize learning resources, chooses a discipline, and the system responding to this event, will execute a query to search for the sub-discipline which corresponds. It then affects the result to the ad hoc element.

This component also fulfills another major function. It permits the definition and management of user and group profiles. In reality, there is nothing more tedious for an author, e.g. a teacher, to complete a series of metadata which can be automatically filled in by the system. Those profiles are only used for this purpose. For example, if you are producing a series of learning resources related to a topic, plenty of metadata can be found from the different profiles, one for the users, one for the institutions, or one for the series.

4.3   Interface Builder

This component constitutes the core of the system. Its role consists in associating a graphic panel to each tree node. For this, we have defined three types of panel:
1. A *DATA panel* permitting the graphic representation of a leaf of the tree (element type PCDATA or EMPTY). If the element doesn't have an associated list, it is a text field, or, if it does, it is a pull-down list.
2. An *AND panel* permitting the graphic representation of a tree node with mandatory and ordered descendants.

3. An *OR panel* permitting the graphic representation of a tree node with optional descendants. By using radio buttons one can thus select, display and activate only one descendant at a time.

For multiple elements, panels include a button or a command bar that allows the display of a pop-up menu through which it is possible to introduce new instances and to delete them. One can note that the generating of a new tree node also means that a new series of all its descendants is created.

To generate the interface, the builder begins with a first traversal of the tree. It associates a panel to each node, configures it according to the data from the database and integrates the events (dynamic function). Then it continues with a second traversal to assemble the components embedding them according to the hierarchical structure of the DTD. The interface builder then proceeds to a third traversal in order to build windows to capture attributes of elements, if needed, and to attach them to the corresponding graphic panel. At the end of this assembly only one panel is obtained which corresponds to the root element of the DTD. This one will be integrated in a window and displayed on the screen.

4.4 XML Documents' Generator

This component permits the generation of an XML document from the interface whilst at the same time respecting the structures of the DTD source and the input data. To achieve this the generator first of all prepares a prologue composed of the declaration of the XML document, the declaration of the type of document, an optional commentary, and the URL of the style sheet. For this, the user has, at his disposal, a window where he can introduce the two last pieces of information.

To generate the XML document body, the generator requests the panel which corresponds to the root to extract its contents. The operation of extraction differs depending on the panel type.

For the *DATA panels* representing leaves of the tree, the extraction is limited to the creation of an open tag with the name of the element. As many open tags are created as there are occurrences in the panel. For the *AND panels* representing the node of the tree, the extraction operation creates an open tag with the name of the element and its attributes and then retrieves relative information. For the *OR panels* representing nodes with optional children, the extraction operation checks which one has been chosen and creates an open tag with the name of the element and its attributes, inserts the result of the extraction of its panel content and adds the chosen tag. This takes place on each occurrence in the panel.

The optional elements without data are not taken into account during the XML document generation. At the end of its recursive treatment a text corresponding to the body of the XML document is obtained. This is in accordance with the structure of the source DTD and contains all data provided through the interface. This text is linked with the prologue and stored in a file.

4.5 Data Storage

In order to store information needed for interface management and DTDs, the system supports a data modeling which can be divided into four parts (Fig. 3).

• *Information on DTD*

Regarding the DTD, the system stores general data on the source file (i.e. URL address and date of modification). These two attributes allow the system to check if the file has been modified. If that is the case, the user will be notified as to whether he wants to consequently update the database. It also stores the results of the analysis.

• *Information on users*

This part of the data storage includes information related to user profiles and user groups together with information as to their identities.

• *Information on the interface configuration*

This corresponds to design data, labels, tips that can be displayed for each element, and, moreover, to complementary help that can be displayed in the status bar or in a special help window, and this, in the various languages available. This part also includes a series of lists of elements of the DTD, which can be organized in a hierarchical order.

• *Information on events*

This allows the storage of a 4-uplet already defined through the interface configurator.

With this database all information needed for the application is stored. It thus allows saving time in both building the interface and using it for capturing data. Then, as in every database, coherency, integrity and information sharing are ensured by DBMS.

5   A Bridge from One DTD to Another

To achieve our final objective one other major element must be present in this process. Up to now, we have been presenting what is required to generate an appropriate interface so as to reach this objective. We now have to present the tool for generating a document which transforms it to meet the standards which are coming into existence regarding metadata for educational materials and, more specifically, the LOM.

In other words, we need a bridge mechanism to map from one DTD to another. This can be considered as a binding between two DTD. For this we must not only establish correspondence between vocabularies in the two DTD but also, and, above all, between their structures.

This brings with it several difficulties, such as missing elements in one or other of the DTDs, correspondence between elements which don't have the same number of occurrences (this problem appears more specifically when an element is optional or multiple in one, and mandatory or single in the other), and correspondence between one element in one and several elements in the other. In this case we have to deal with a problem of linguistic analysis.

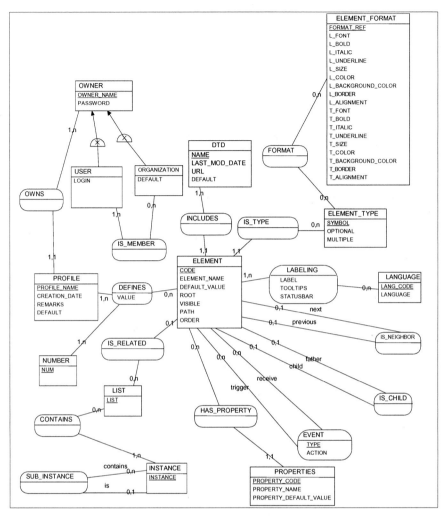

Fig. 3. Data model

For simple cases, i.e. without any of the above-mentioned difficulties, it is possible to build a bridge if we have the two tree structures and a corresponding table between elements. The principle consists in transferring the information carried by the leaves of the first tree to the second data tree and executing the XML document generator on the newly obtained tree.

6 Conclusion

UTES[11] (Using Educational Technologies in Sciences) is an autodidactical center where our university students may go to study on computers. This center provides

---

[11] Usages des Technologies Educatives en Sciences – Université Paris VI.

more than the equivalent to 600 hours of learning materials. There, it is exactly as we describe it: a metadata set has been defined in order to fit in better with the characteristics of its learning resources which are mainly dedicated to scientific domains. Actually, this set is not definitively fixed. Under these conditions, the tool we have developed permits authors to have an interface automatically generated and to obtain XML documents in conformity with their own TD and standards such as LOM or ARIADNE. Those documents can be opened by any browser recognizing XML syntax and used in index to search out resources.

To conceive of metadata remains a problem. But, having a tool at one's disposal which can adapt itself to the specific needs of both sides, i.e. institutions and international standards, is a major trump. Further evolution will be at a lower cost. The generic character of our tool permits, on the one hand, to be totally independent from the standards and the specific metadata set, and, on the other, to fit in with other XML applications. For example, it could be used to capture content, if the DTD modeling the pedagogical activity is available.

Presently, we are working with this tool in order to describe the entire educational materials available in the UTES center.

References

1. Berners L.: Metadata Architecture (1997)
   http://www.w3.org/DesignIssues/Metadata.html
2. Bourda Y., Hélier M.: Métadonnées et XML: Applications aux «objets pédagogiques», In: TICE 2000 - Technologies of Information and Communication in Education for engineering and industry, Troyes (France), (2000), 135-141
3. Crampes M., Bayart L., Gelly A,. Uny P.: Spécification et proposition d'une DTD pour la qualification des matériaux pédagogiques adaptatifs. In: Revue Science et Techniques EducativesEditions Hermès, Vol 6, n°2 (1999) 343-374
4. McMurray E.: Des normes pour les technologies de la formation,
   http://sic.epfl.ch/SA/publications/FI00/fi-4-00/4-00-page3.html
5. Michard A.: XML Langage et application, Eyrolles, ISBN :2-212-09052-8 (1999)
6. de La Passardière B., Giroire H.: XML au service des applications pédagogiques, In: Revue Science et Techniques Educatives, Editions Hermès, vol 8, n°1-2 (2001))99-112
7. Viéville C.: Learning Activities in a Virtual Campus, In: The Digital University - Building a Learning Community, Reza Hazemi and Stephen Hailes (Eds), Springer, serie Computer Supported Cooperative Work (2001) 215-226

Ontology-Centered Personalized Presentation of Knowledge Extracted from the Web

Stefan Trausan-Matu[1], Daniele Maraschi[2], and Stefano Cerri[2]

[1]Computer Science Department, "Politehnica" University of Bucharest
Romanian Academy Research Centre for Machine Learning, Computational Linguistics, and
Conceptual Modeling, Calea 13 Septembrie nr. 13, Bucharest
ROMANIA
trausan@cs.pub.ro, http://www.racai.ro/~trausan
[2]LIRMM, rue Ada, Montpellier, FRANCE
cerri@lirmm.fr, maraschi@lirmm.fr

Abstract. The paper presents an approach for the dynamic generation of a complex structure of personalized web pages for learning purposes, reflecting the ontology of the considered domain. The need of assuring a holistic character for the body of knowledge induced in the learner's mind is emphasized. This is very important in the learning processes, especially nowadays, in the context of the huge amount of information available on the web and of its permanent evolution. The approach permits the adaptation of the content of the generated web pages to the incoming information from the web. New information is extracted, annotated and coherently integrated in the body of knowledge in order to keep the holistic character of the body of knowledge. Personalization is achieved by filtering the semantic network according to the learner model, which keeps the list of concepts known or unknown by the learner. The approach was used in an EU INCO Copernicus project for computer aided language learning.

1 Introduction

One of the main goals of any human learning process consists in the progressively construction of a body of declarative knowledge for the considered domain (a "model" of the domain) in the mind of the learner. This must also be, of course, one of the main goals of any Intelligent Tutoring System ("ITS") or learning environment.

What we consider very important, especially nowadays, in the context of the huge amount of information available on the web and of its permanent evolution, is the need of assuring a holistic character of the constructed body of knowledge. The learning process must induce the sense of the whole in the learner's mind. This simplifies the understanding of complex sets of concepts, being in consonance with the cognitive ergonomic rule of reducing the cognitive load [11].

A second way to facilitate learning is the usage of metaphors. Every professor, even in the most abstract domains, uses metaphors (consider, for example, the "trees" in mathematics and programming). Metaphors may appear every day and they are needed for a correct understanding of a concept. An important problem is that metaphors are not easy to tackle by a foreign speaker of a language [16] (e.g. "to

S.A. Cerri, G. Gouardères, and F. Paraguaçu (Eds.): ITS 2002, LNCS 2363, pp. 259–269, 2002.

sustain a loss" [16]). This problem of metaphors becomes more important in the context of the explosion of documents (and potential new metaphors).

Another important idea of the paper, related with the above ones, rose especially after the success of the web. It is a reality that everyday some new relevant information might appear on the web and must be included in the learning process. This new information must be coherently integrated in the learned body of knowledge in order to keep the its holistic character.

The skeleton of the above-mentioned knowledge body may be considered as a semantic network of the main concepts involved in that domain. These concepts are usually taxonomically organised, have several attributes and relations connecting them with other concepts. From a knowledge-based perspective, we might say that the learner must articulate in his mind the so-called ontology of the domain.

The word "ontology" is used in philosophy to denote the theory about what is considered to exist. Any system in philosophy starts from an ontology, that means from the identification of the concepts and relations considered as fundamental. In artificial intelligence, the same word is now often used as "a specification of a conceptualization.... an ontology is a description (like a formal specification of a program) of the concepts and relationships that can exist for an agent or a community of agents" [7].

The approach presented in this paper follows the previous ideas, combining agents that search for information, text mining (for metaphors) techniques, learner modeling, and personalized web page generation. The visible result is the fact that the semantic network of the concepts from the domain ontology is mapped on a network of personalised web pages automatically generated. Personalization is achieved by filtering the semantic network according to the learner model, which keeps the list of concepts known or unknown by the learner. The generated web pages contain relevant excerpts from documents continuously retrieved from the web.

The idea of assuring the inclusion in the learning process of the latest information available on the web is provided by searching relevant documents, extracting necessary knowledge and including it in the generated web pages. The domain ontology has a determinant role in all these three activities this central role providing also the needed holistic character.

The novelty of the approach presented in the paper resides on the dynamic generation of a complex structure of personalized web pages that reflects the domain ontology (having a holistic character). Another novel feature is the possibility of continuously updating the content of the generated web pages, considering the incoming information from the web. Other approaches [2], [10] provide adaptability starting from local policies ("adaptive navigation support" – [2]), driven by learner's model and goals. They do not follow any holistic principles. They also do not process (by selection and annotation, as in our approach) new information and do not include it in a complex structure. They rather provide support for relevant web pages in a given context [3], [8]. Eventually, the usage of metaphors for enhancing understandability is also new.

Our approach was used for the development of an ITS distributed on the web (with three servers, in France, Romania, and Bulgaria) under the INCO Copernicus project LarFLaST ("Learning Foreign Language Scientific Terminology" – see http://www-it.fmi.uni-sofia.bg/larflast/). This project had as main objectives to provide a set of tools available on the World Wide Web for supporting Romanian, Bulgarian and Ukrainian people to learn foreign (English) terminology in finance.

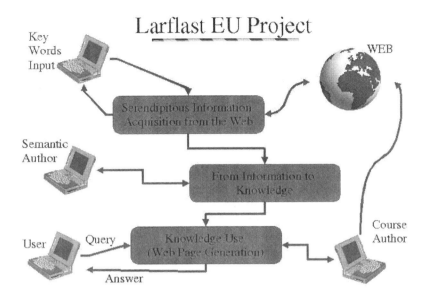

Fig. 1. Information acquisition, annotation and usage in Larflast

The next section presents our approach for extracting new, relevant information from the web. Gathered information is further edited for semantic (knowledge) annotation. Eventually, annotated documents are used to extract excerpts to be included in the generated web pages. The third section exemplifies the usage of this framework in the LarFLaST project. The fourth section presents the dynamic generation of ontology-centred, personalized web pages that include information obtained with the framework discussed in the previous two sections.

2 Intelligent Search, Annotation, and Usage of Information from the Web

The World Wide Web (WWW or the "web") is a huge hypermedia on Internet, browsable with very simple, direct manipulation interfaces. Its explosive growth in only several years is the best prove of its usefulness. Two of the causes of this phenomenon are, probably, the ease of "publishing", of communicating something through text and/or images on the web. From the other direction of the communication process, it is very easy for everybody to explore the network of web pages. As a consequence, we notice the extremely dynamic character of information nowadays, the availability of the Web today having definitely changed the information scenario. What happens is that the time between the appearance of new information in some domain and the use of this information by people has extremely shortened comparatively with some years ago. Therefore, information may become obsolete very quickly or be replaced by some other Information. A good tutoring system should consider this scenario, and consequently be able to update its Information continuously.

The process of extracting and using the most relevant information from the web involves three phases: information acquisition performed by searching the web, knowledge identification by semantic editing and the usage of this knowledge, as in the below figure.

The domain ontology plays important roles in each of the three mentioned phases. The keywords used by a web spidering agent [4] for the search of relevant documents are obtained from the domain ontology. The process controlled by this agent searches on the web by means of activating a number of search engines. During this phase, data mining techniques may be applied in order to better select automatically the fit between the requested information and the retrieved one.

The set of raw Web pages is stored in a DBMS of XML (XHTML) pages (generated by transforming HTML pages with JTIDY) in order to facilitate the crucial activity of knowledge construction by the "semantic author" [18]. This semantic author is either a human agent (e.g. the professor) that edits the documents by means of a special, "semantic editor" or a natural language processing program that transforms the XML documents.

We have built two "semantic editors". The first one may be used remotely (accessed through a Web browser). The second semantic editor (which will be presented in the next section) was built for a specific purpose (metaphor identification and annotation) and is used only offline.

The authored XML documents are stored in a XML database, to be subsequently used by the web page generator or by the "course author" for composing the Course. By applying XSL files to XML authored files, the "semantic author" may visualise the appearance of each knowledge unit in order to check the interface with the learner.

The XML web-based editor is generic with respect to any chosen XML mark-up choice. For these reasons, the same editor may be used both by the "semantic author" and the "course author" (described hereafter).

Once the knowledge units have been made available on the XML DBMS, the course author (by using the same XML Web editor) may compose the course at his-her choice. At the end, the course will be published and delivered on the Web. Another possibility, described in the next section, is the dynamic generation of web pages.

3   Metaphor Identification, Annotation, and Usage as Aid for Learning Financial Terminology

An instance of the process discussed in the previous section is used for the identification, annotation, and usage of metaphors for aiding learning foreign finance terminology [14]. This approach was implemented in the LarFLaST project.

Metaphors are often used to give insight in what a concept means, like in the following example: "Stocks are very sensitive creatures" (NYSE, New York Stock

Exchange web page, http://www.nyse.com/). Such insight cannot be obtained in knowledge-based approaches centred on taxonomic ontologies. For example, these systems will explain the concept "stock" in terms of its super-concepts like "securities", "capital", "asset" or "possession". Its attributes and relations with other concepts may provide more details.

Metaphor processing was used for aiding language learning in the LarFLaST project and it involved the three phases discussed in the previous section:

- gathering relevant texts from the web,
- identification (acquisition) of metaphors in the selected texts and their XML mark-up of the identified metaphors,
- personalised usage of the metaphors.

The following picture illustrates the whole process:

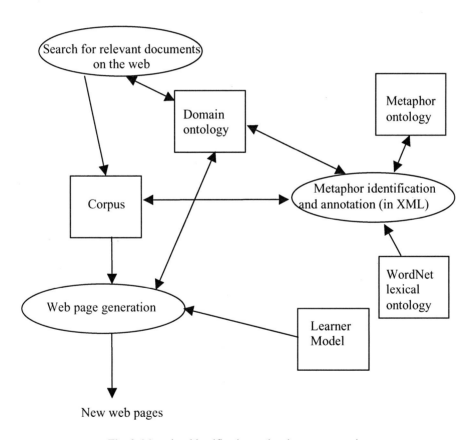

Fig. 2. Metaphor identification and web page generation

The DBMS (corpus) of relevant texts is the raw material for the second phase, metaphor identification and annotation. This phase may be considered similar to a knowledge acquisition process, in which XML semantic annotations are added in the texts. A specialized acquisition tool, written in Java, supports this semantic editing (the second type of semantic editor mentioned in the previous section). The interface for this tool is presented in the next figure.

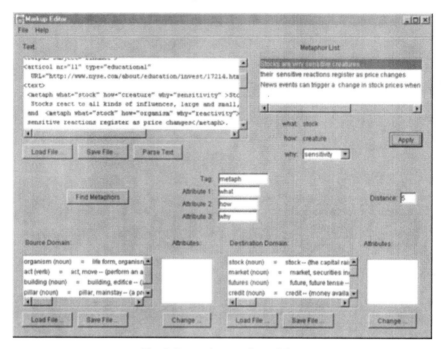

Fig. 3. Semantic metaphor editing

Metaphor identification in the corpus is performed by searching for occurrences of pairs of concepts from source (metaphor) and destination (domain) ontologies. These concepts are loaded from XML files and are displayed in the two bottom text areas in the figure. The lexical ontology WordNet (http://www.cogsci.princeton.edu/~wn) is used for extending the search to related (synonyms, hyperonyms, hyponyms, meronyms) concepts. Identified metaphors are listed in the top right text area. If the user approves, the selected proposed metaphor is annotated in the corpus.

The metaphor-annotated corpus may be further used for several purposes. In LarFLaST, the corpus is used in the dynamically generated Web pages for metaphor examples and explanations tailored to a learner model, in a given context (see next section). For this purpose, XSL descriptions are used for the personalized web pages.

A concept ontology editor is used for editing concept ontologies, and for controlling the process of metaphor search by stating which relations from WordNet are considered. This editor allows the user to add, remove or modify a concept. For a specific concept you can set its part of speech, its WordNet sense number, its attributes and the related concepts, which will be considered for metaphor identification. The ontologies may be saved in XML files, to be used as source and domain ontologies for finding new metaphors (see the above figure).

The next figure illustrates the concept ontology editor:

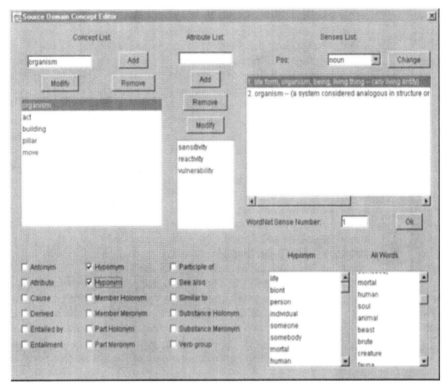

Fig. 4. Concept editor

4   Ontology-Centered Presentation on the Web

An intelligent tutoring system is a knowledge-based, interactive computer program that can be used by a learner as a personal, tireless teacher, which adapts to the learner's cognitive particularities and his/her individual progress. A major emphasis is paid in ITS to the choice of domain and learner models.

The domain model (the knowledge base or ontology) is one of the most important parts in such applications. In most ITS, the domain model is build once for all, at define time, before the conversations with the learners will occur. Usually, the learner model is developed in correspondence with the domain model. By consequence, the structure of the learner model is as well decided once for all, at define time.

In our approach we challenge this view, and attempt to transform the construction and the delivery of knowledge into dynamic processes, continuously updated by incoming Information, on the domain (from the Web) and on the learner. The central issue remains to be able to tune the generation of domain knowledge according to what can be derived from the learner's model as well as to update permanently this model as a result of learner testing.

In LarFLaST, the learner model ("LM") includes correct, erroneous and incomplete learner's beliefs (about which he is or not aware), misunderstandings and misconceptions about concepts [5]. From a knowledge-based perspective, LM includes what knowledge has the learner, what knowledge misses or has been wrongly acquired: LM may be inferred starting from the analysis of the results at tests or from other data, as the path followed by the learner during browsing [5].

WWW is a perfect place for learning. The synergetic integration of ITS with the Web might provide a learning environment able to change totally the way we learn. This idea is supported by the fact that hypertext was introduced by Douglas Engelbart, in the early sixties, as a "Conceptual Framework for Augmenting Human Intellect" [6]. Moreover, Theodor Nelson, who coined the term "hypertext", defined it as the hyperspace of concepts from a given text (Nelson 1995) or "a system for massively parallel creative work and study ... to the betterment of human understanding" [9].

A natural consequence of the above idea is the usage of the web "hyperspace of concepts" for facilitating the conceptualisation and understanding in learning processes. For assuring a best conceptualisation, the conceptual map of the considered domain (the ontology) should be filtered according to the learner model. After the filtering, the concepts considered as relevant and the relations among them are mapped in a network of web pages. Each concept is mapped to a Web page and each relation to a link, according to explicit (e.g. "is-a", "part-of", "agent", "instrument" etc.) or implicit (e.g. "similar") relations [12]. The result is that the ontology, the network of generated web pages, and the conceptual map to be induced in the mind of the learner have the same (semantic network like) structure. As mentioned in the introduction, this mapping assures the holistic character of the knowledge body in the mind of the learner.

This idea was used in the GenWeb system, for the dynamic generation of highly structured web pages for learning functional programming [12] and in the INCO Copernicus project LarFLaST. The web page generator is written in the Lisp-based knowledge-based framework XRL [1]. Personalization is obtained by dynamically tailoring the content of the Web pages according to each learner's model [12], [13]. That means, for example, that explanations refer only to known concepts, while the structure of the generated collection of Web pages is centred on unknown concepts.

Information about metaphors (the third phase, the "usage" of metaphors from the above section) is added in the generated pages. This information is personalized through the selection only of the relevant metaphors accordingly to the learner model. The attributes of the XML metaphor annotation are used for this purpose.

Three examples of dynamically generated Web pages are given in the fig.5. They are personalized accordingly to the learner model [5], from which a fragment is shown below:

```
know(john,money_market,[[b_def,2025,80],[b_def,20,80]],u_1_d_1,1,none
,4).
not_know(john,investment,[[b_def,2006,80]],u_1_d_1,1,none,5).
not_know(john,investment,[[b_def,2006,80]],u_1_d_1,2,none,6).
know_wrongly(john,secondary_market,[[b_def,2004,80]],u_1_d_1,3,none,7
).
know_wrongly(john,financial_market,[[b_def,2001,80]],u_1_d_1,2,none,1
4).
not_know(john,open_market,[[b_def,2016,80]],u_1_d_1,1,none,15).
not_know(john,open_market,[[b_def,2016,80]],u_1_d_1,2,none,16).
```

Fig. 5. A screenshot with dynamically generated, personalized web pages

The left (biggest) window in the figure contains some metaphorical phrases extracted with the framework presented in the second section. This window contains, in the bottom, the structure (the taxonomy) of domain concepts. Links are generated only to the concepts unknown or wrongly known by the learner (listed in the upper right window). A web page from the taxonomy is illustrated in the third, bottom-right window.

5   Conclusions

The approach presented in this paper is centred on the domain ontology. This ontology is used as a start point in the serendipitous search. The same ontology is used for the XML semantic annotation of the retrieved documents. The ontology is used for the retrieval of relevant metaphors from the XML annotated documents. The structure of the dynamically generated web pages reflects the domain ontology. In addition, the ontology is driving the construction of the learner's model and the filtering of the amount of concepts and facts presented. This omnipresence of the ontology induces the holistic character discussed in the introduction, assuring the coherence of the presentation, which has direct effects on the learning process.

The good effects of the structuring of the generated web pages according to the ontology were emphasized in a study performed with students in the end of the

LarFLaST project. They remarked (not being asked explicitly about it) that the taxonomic organisation is very helpful.

Other systems for learning on the web usually have a static domain model from which they construct (not dynamically) web pages. Even if they have some dynamic characteristics, like adaptive hypermedia [3], [17] or planning the content of the presented material [10], [15], they miss a holistic character. Adaptive hypermedia is obtained, for example, by local policies ("adaptive navigation support" – [3]) like flexible link sorting, hiding or disabling or by conditionally showing text fragments etc. [3]. Planning the content of the generated web pages is also not concerned with a global, holistic approach, but more with local decisions based on the learner model.

The permanent inclusion of new information gathered and annotated from the web is another novel feature, not included in other systems. Existing approaches only provide intelligent recommend interesting web pages, according to the user profile [3], [8]. They do not permit the inclusion of relevant facts in the structure of ontology-centred structure.

Eventually, the usage of metaphors is a novel approach. It has a lot of implications discussed in detail in [14]

References

1. Barbuceanu, M. and Trausan-Matu, S. (1987) Integrating Declarative Knowledge Programming Styles and Tools in a Structured Object Environment, in J. Mc.Dermott (ed.) Proceedings of 10-th International Joint Conference on Artificial Intelligence IJCAI'87, Italia, Morgan Kaufmann Publishers, Inc.
2. deBra, P., Brusilovsky, Houser, G.J., Adaptive Hypermedia: From Systems to Framework, ACM Computing Surveys, 31(4), 1999.
3. Breese, J.,Heckerman, D., Kadie, C., Empirical Analysis of Predictive Algorithms for Collaborative Filtering, Procs. Of 14th Conf. On Uncertainty in AI, Morgan Kaufmann, 1998
4. Cerri, S.A., Loia, V., Maffioletti, S., Fontanesi, P., and Bettinelli, A. (1999) Serendipitous acquisition of Web knowledge by Agents in the context of Human Learning. In: Proceedings of THAI-ETIS: European Symposium on Telematics, Hypermedia and Artificial Intelligence, Varese, Italy.
5. Dimitrova, V., Self, J., Brna, P., 'Maintaining a Joinly Constrcted Student Model', in S.A.Cerri (ed.), Artificial Intelligence, Methodology, Systems, Applications 2000, Springer-Verlag, ISBN 3-540-41044-9, pp.221-231.
6. Engelbart, D.C. (1995) Toward Augmenting the Human Intellect and Boosting our Collective IQ, Communications of the ACM, vol.38, no. 8, pp. 30-33.
7. Gruber, T., What is an Ontology, http://www-ksl.stanford.edu/kst/what-is-an-ontology.html
8. Lieberman, H., Letizia: An Agent That Assists Web Browsing, International Joint Conference on Artificial Intelligence, Montreal, August 1995.
9. Nelson, T.H. (1995), 'The Heart of Connection: Hypermedia Unified by Transclusion', Communications of the ACM, vol.38, no. 8, pp. 31-33.
10. Siekmann, J., Benzmuller, C, and all, Adaptive Course Generation and Presentation, Proceedings of the International Workshop on Adaptive and Intelligent Web-based Educational Systems, Montreal, 2000
11. Thuering, M., Hannemann, J., Haake, J.M., Hypermedia and Cognition: Designing for Comprehension, Communications of the ACM, vol.38, no. 8, pp. 57-66, aug. 1995.

12. Trausan-Matu, St. (1997) 'Knowledge-Based, Automatic Generation of Educational Web Pages', in Proceedings of Internet as a Vehicle for Teaching Workshop, Ilieni, June 1997, pp.141-148, See also http://rilw.emp.paed.uni-muenchen.de/99/papers/Trausan.html

13. Trausan-Matu, St. (1999) 'Web Page Generation Facilitating Conceptualization and Immersion for Learning Finance Terminology', in Proceedings of RILW99. See also http://rilw.emp.paed.uni-muenchen.de/99/papers/Trausan.html

14. Trausan-Matu, St. (2000) 'Metaphor Processing for Learning Terminology on the Web', in S.A.Cerri (ed.), Artificial Intelligence, Methodology, Systems, Applications 2000, Springer-Verlag, ISBN 3-540-41044-9, pp.232-241.

15. Vassilieva, J., http://julita.usask.ca/homepage/AIED'97.ps 16.   Vitanova,   I.   (1999) English for Finance. Understanding Money and Markets, Research report, Larflast project, http://www-it.fmi.uni-sofia.bg/larflast/

17. Weber, G., Specht, M., User Modeling and Adaptive Navigation Support, in WWW-based Tutoring Systems, http://www.psychologie.uni-trier.de:8000/projects/ELM/Papers/UM97-WEBER.html

18. Wittman, P., Evolution de l'activite editoriale face a un nouvel ordinateur: le Web, Eng. These, Univ. Montpellier, France, 2002

Ontological Support for Web Courseware Authoring

Lora Aroyo[1], Darina Dicheva[2], and Alexandra Cristea[1]

[1] Technische Universiteit Eindhoven, The Netherlands
{l.m.aroyo, a.i.cristea}@tue.nl
[2] Winston-Salem State University, United States of America
dichevad@wssu.edu

Abstract. In this paper we present an *ontology-oriented authoring support* system for Web-based courseware. This is an elaboration of our approach to knowledge classification and indexing in the previously developed system AIMS (Agent-based Information Management System) aimed at supporting students while completing learning tasks in a Web-based learning/training environment. By introducing *ontology-based layers* in the courseware authoring architecture we aim at using *subject domain ontology* as a basis for formal semantics and reasoning support in performing generic authoring tasks. We also focus on *cooperative authoring*, which allows re-usage and sets the basis for *authoring collaboration*. To exemplify our method we define a set of generic tasks related to *concept-based courseware authoring* and present their ontological support by the newly added operational and assistant layers in the AIMS architecture.

1 Introduction

Courseware and its authoring acquire a new meaning in the context of Web-based education. Courseware, a term initially coined to name computer-supported presentation and use of teaching material aimed at improving the student's course work by instruction individualization, traditionally consists of *teaching material*, divided into learning units (or frames), and a *courseware delivery engine*. The goal of courseware authoring was to support authors in creating and linking frames. The second generation was the *multimedia courseware* [4,10], based on the same principles but allowing multi-modality in material presentation thus significantly improving content presentation. The third generation was the *hypermedia courseware* [6,9]. The novelty was to remove the constraints of predefined paths in the learning material. In adaptive *educational hypermedia* [7,11] a student could browse and explore e-book links and pages by following an adaptable knowledge path. However, frames were still locally stored documents.

Nowadays, with the revolution that the Web has brought to information access worldwide, the meaning of courseware is changing again. Web-based courseware can be viewed as a *gateway* to a variety of Web educational materials related to specific

S.A. Cerri, G. Gouardères, and F. Paraguaçu (Eds.): ITS 2002, LNCS 2363, pp. 270–280, 2002.

topics or educational goals, developed by the course author (instructor) and stored locally, or represented by Web addresses and descriptions. This dramatic change obviously affects the courseware authoring process, too [1,18, 19].

To efficiently organize and maintain Web-based resources we employ a powerful approach for *knowledge classification and indexing* in on-line learning environments, based on conceptualisation of the course subject domain. A significant aspect of the proposed approach is building a *subject domain ontology* [2], in line with recent Semantic Web research (e.g., layered architecture [5]) and ontologies [12].

In this paper we present our view on ontological support of Web-based courseware authoring, which is an elaboration of our approach to knowledge classification and indexing, aimed at supporting students in retrieving, evaluating, and comprehending information when performing learning tasks in a Web-based learning/training environment. We start by shortly presenting authoring Web-based courseware with AIMS. Next we propose a layered approach to support courseware authoring. Then, we define a set of generic tasks related to concept-based courseware authoring and their possible support. Finally, we present some conclusions and future perspectives.

2   AIMS – An Example of Courseware Authoring

From an enterprise point of view, the main actors in the proposed solution for information handling in a Web-based educational system (e.g., AIMS), are *student*, *courseware author* and *administrator* (with their set of responsibilities and tasks). The student is responsible for interpreting and processing information. Authoring includes information maintenance, i.e. creating, editing, structuring. The administrator is responsible, among others, for system information-access policies. In this paper we focus only on authoring roles related to domain and course authoring. By supporting these activities we aim at increasing the efficiency of information reuse and of collaboration between course authors. The AIMS authoring environment consists of three main modules: Domain Editor, Library Editor, and Course Editor [3]. These three modules correspond to the three layers in the system's information base: library metadata, domain ontology, and course information (Fig. 1). The last two are represented as concept maps (CM) of domain concepts and links among them.

The *Domain Editor* enables the author to construct a domain concept mapping structure. It provides facilities to add, delete and update domain terms and links between them. For each new term the author specifies a name and definition along with its classification in a simple hierarchy within the concept map (including category, sub-category, topic and sub-topic). The editor also allows authors to create new types of links and links between a domain term and existing documents in the AIMS library.

The *Course Editor* enables the author to define a structure of a course within a specific domain by using domain terms as basic framework of the structure definition. It allows the author to define course topics and course tasks and relate them to domain terms by assigning a list of keywords to each task. Each topic and task is given a definition and a reference (link to a main document in the library). One course can consist of several topics and each topic can have several tasks. A topic usually corresponds to the course weekly session and the tasks to the course weekly assignments. As the tasks are directly related to domain terms and the domain terms to library documents, this provides a link between the course structure and the appropriate course material.

The *Library Editor* provides means for maintaining a collection of information related to different courses and domains. It provides simple options typical for most of the library systems. Each document is described both task- and use-oriented. For example, each document description includes its instructional and presentation formats, indicating the way this document could be used for instructional purposes and whether it is in an appropriate presentation format. Each document description includes also a list of keywords (not necessarily belonging to the domain ontology).

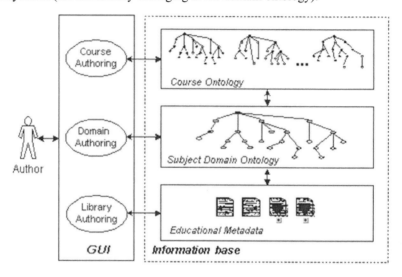

Fig. 1. AIMS authoring architecture

Since the authoring of concept-based Web courseware is three-fold, including domain-, course-, and library authoring, this process is more complicated and labor intensive than the process of 'standard' courseware authoring. Such authoring is extremely difficult and time-consuming and needs specialized, modern authoring support and re-usage [2,17], cooperation and collaboration among authors. The further needs of support in concept-based courseware authoring are the following:

- automatic or semi-automatic performance of some authoring activities,
- intelligent assistance to the author in the form of hints, recommendations, etc.,
- supporting the activities of different instructors for collaborative building and/or cooperative reuse of domain and course ontologies.

Collaborative authoring [19] occurs in project-like settings, where authoring sub-tasks are delegated to a group of authors. This kind of authoring needs synchronization, dialogue support and coordination of the whole project. In contrast, *cooperative authoring* [8] mainly involves asynchronous re-usage of authoring products, such as course materials, libraries, ontologies, etc. In our current work we focus on the latter, more precisely, on supporting primitive interaction activities in cooperative authoring.

The key idea of our approach is that to provide enhanced support for authoring concept-based Web courseware we use the system's domain concept map, i.e. the ontology, which captures the semantics of the subject domain terminology used by students when searching for relevant information necessary to perform course tasks. The same ontology can be used by courseware authors to ask authoring-related questions or by the system to perform (semi-)automatically some authoring activities. Thus we introduce additional *ontology-based layers* to the courseware authoring architecture, which allow *intelligent assistance* of courseware authors. The idea is to use the existing domain and course ontologies for all generic authoring tasks related to concept-based Web courseware authoring, as a basis for formal semantics and reasoning support. In our work the ontologies are represented as concept maps [3,8]. Consequently, authoring involves manipulating concept maps, i.e., creating and modifying CMs. The proposed semantic layers for intelligent authoring assistance include reasoning, consistency check, and introduce additional operations on CMs (such as comparing CMs, mapping and merging CMs, extracting subsets of CM, analyzing CMs). Next we describe the suggested layered approach to support Web courseware authoring.

3 Ontology-Based Layered Support to Courseware Authoring

To support cooperative concept-based courseware authoring, we aim at creating a re-usage based cooperative environment [19]. The primitive interaction activities among participants in this environment during both cooperative and collaborative authoring are: planning/creation, data/idea sharing, coordination/control/initiative/supervision, observation/suggesting and dialogue (with interaction). The support system should provide all appropriate tools for these activities. Furthermore, refined cognitive tools (e.g., concept mapping tools [1,8]) are required to facilitate group collaborative authoring [19], corresponding to the activities enumerated above. We propose a 2D-layer approach (Fig. 2) for concept-based courseware authoring support. This approach allows re-usage, in the sense of authoring cooperation, and sets the basis for authoring collaboration. The *Y-axis* represents the main information objects in the information base of the courseware system (library objects, domains, courses). The *X-axis* targets system's support for information objects authoring (*GUI, Assisting -, Operation -, Information layer*) and is represented by a layered architecture implementing system functionality. The *GUI layer* supports user-system communication. The *Information layer* contains the layered description and structuring of the information objects in the courseware system (*educational metadata, subject domain ontology, course ontology*). The educational metadata layer contains the description of the data sources. The two new layers in the extended architecture are the *Assisting* and the *Operation layer*.

The *Operation layer* handles the operations related to data in each information layer thus providing means for modeling data into ontology and creating alternative goal-oriented structures of courses. The Operation layer is also responsible for facilitating information manipulation, consistency and co-operation. It consists of three processing engines: (a) *course engine*, (b) *domain engine* and (c) *library engine*. All of them include two types of support operations: (a) *consistency check*, and (b) *co-operation support*. The consistency modules perform their activities over each sub-layer within the information layer. They provide functions to facilitate the process of authoring the domain ontology, course ontology and educational metadata in a semi-automatic way. These modules also guarantee the consistency of the educational sources [17]. They should deal with tasks such as: handling notions of *semantic equivalence* [21] and conflict, conflict resolution rules, equivalence comparison rules, enhancing the resulting ontology and defining additional constraints if necessary.

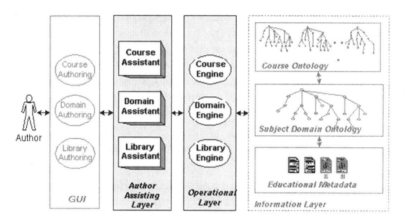

Fig. 2. 2D-layer approach towards courseware authoring support

The co-operation support modules offer on one hand a set of operations to check the consistency in alternative (simultaneous) course structure building by different authors and on another - predefined functions (patterns and templates) to facilitate effective reusability of the available course structures developed by different authors.

Concerning the reusability support, we pay special attention to the issues associated with merging ontologies [16], such as: extracting portions of an ontology to be merged with another [21], identifying which frames are to be extracted from the source ontology, determining if the extracted information has semantic overlaps or conflicts with the target ontology, assisting in merging ontologies, recording the sources of inserted sub-ontologies for later reference and update, selecting patterns, templates in an educational ontology for presenting them as predefined objects to other authors.

Among the issues of importance when merging two ontologies are those related to the following types of semantic overlaps and conflicts: semantically equivalent concepts but with different names [21], semantically different concepts but with the same name, semantically equivalent concepts with the same name but different definitions, semantically equivalent concepts linked to different /conflicting concepts, etc.

While the Operation layer actually implements the authoring operations, the Assisting layer, which is based on the ontological mapping of the domain, is responsible for helping the author in the process of courseware authoring. For example, it gives hints to the author of how to create a course structure, or how to link a document to the ontology, or how to link a course item to the ontology, etc.

According to the computational semantics of an ontology [15], the ontologies we consider here can be situated at *level 1* (term collection, as shown previously (Fig. 1,2) and *level 3* (executable task ontologies). We still lack the connection given by *level 2* (formal definitions, constrains and axioms).

4 Generic Authoring Tasks Support

In this section we discuss generic authoring tasks supported by the operation sets [15] of the Operation layer and the presentation options provided by the Assisting layer.

Table 1. Atomic operation definitions

Atomic operation	Range	Description
'Add'	performed over sets of objects $\{T_o, T_a, C_o, L_l, D_{oc}\}$, where: $T_o \in \{course\ topics\}$, $T_a \in \{course\ tasks\}$, $C_o \in \{domain\ concepts\}$, $L_l \in \{domain\ links\}$, $D_{oc} \in \{library\ documents\}$.	adds each object to either course structure, domain ontology or metadata library.
'Del',	as above	deletes an object from the corresponding structure
'Edit'	as above	edits the object settings
'U'	set $\{CM, CS, EML\}$, where: CM=Concept Map, CS=Course structure, EML=Educational Metadata Library.	ensures current state update of the corresponding information structure of set
'L'	sets $\{DirLC, RelC, RelC_o, RelT_a, RelD_{oc}\}$, where: $DirLC_o$ = Directly linked concepts, $RelC$ = Related courses, $RelC_o$= Related concepts, $RelT_a$ = Related tasks, $RelD_{oc}$= Related documents.	lists the objects of the set(s)
'V'	set $\{Graph, Text\}$, where '$Graph$' is a graphical and '$Text$' gives a textual results view.	gives alternative views of the *engine* results to the author
'Chk'	set $\{T_a, T_o, C_o, L_l, D_{oc}, RelC_o, RelT_a, RelD_{oc}, DirLC\}$	checks the existence of objects within the set(s)

We are defining a complete set of generic authoring tasks at all three information layers (course, subject domain and library) that are supported by the course, domain and library engines. In this paper however we present only an excerpt from the course engine supported authoring tasks (Table 2). We further illustrate the interaction between the course engine and the course assistant in supporting the author by presenting an activity diagram of the support for the atomic authoring task 'add topic' (Fig. 3). Table 1 above presents abbreviations and definitions of atomic operations used in this section. There are number of composite actions such as 'delete all topics of a course', 'delete all concepts of a topic', 'delete all tasks of a topic', 'delete all concepts of a task' or 'give value 'a' to all the concept weights of a task', which can be implemented with a repetitive call to the atomic operations called 'delete topic' and 'list all topics' and the corresponding operations for tasks and concepts. In Table 2 we present an excerpt of the course authoring ontology with a selection of basic atomic tasks and the interaction between course engine and assistant.

Table 2. Course engine supported authoring tasks

Task	Course Assistant	Course Engine	Result

Add $(T_o,$ CS)	▪ suggest options for the author:
	▪ add or delete *course engine* results
	▪ give alternative presentation:
	  – V (Text, RelC, Relevance %)
	  – V (Graph, Course Trees, Matched Concepts) –highlighted
	  – V (Graph, Domain Ontology, Matched concepts) – 'you are here'
	▪ notify other authors of adding T_o to CS
		▪ perform a keyword search on T_o expression within:
		  - DO (domain &
		  - CO (course ontology)
		▪ store results for reuse
		▪ U (T_o)
		▪ U (CS)
			▪ L (RelC, keyword percentage)
			▪ L $(RelC_o,$ depth within DO)

Add (T_a ,T_o)	▪ if a new connection to the domain concept is discovered, options are:
	  – Del (connection)
	  – Add (C_o, T_o)
	  – Add (C_o, T_a)
	  – V $(RelT_a)$
	  – Copy $(RelT_a)$
	▪ notify other authors of adding T_a to T_a
		▪ Chk $(T_a, ∃)$ = true
		▪ Chk $(T_o, C_o,$ compatibility) = true
		▪ deduce *assistant* activity
		▪ Chk $(RelT_a,$ other courses) = true
		▪ U (T_o)
		U (CS)
			▪ L $(RelT_a,$ other courses) – ordered by their weight-related relevance
			▪ L $(RelT_a,$ same course)

Add (C_o ,T_a)	▪ if Chk $(C_o, T_a, ∃)$ = true:
	  – Notify the user
	  – Change the weight of the C_o
	▪ if Chk $(C_o, T_a, ∃)$ = false γV (C_o, T_a)
	▪ notify other authors of adding C_o to T_a
		▪ Chk $(C_o, T_a, ∃)$ = true
		▪ U (T_a, C_o)
		▪ U (T_o)
		▪ U (CS)
			▪ L $(T_a, ∋ C_o)$
			▪ L $(T_a,$ other courses)
			▪ L $(RelC_o)$
			▪ L (all $C_o, T_a)$

Add (C_o ,T_o)	▪ if Chk $(C_o, T_o, ∃)$ = true ▪ notify the user ▪ if Chk $(C_o, T_o, ∃)$ = false ▪ V (C_o, T_o) ▪ notify other authors of adding C_o to T_o	▪ Chk $(C_o, T_o, ∃)$ = true ▪ U (T_o, C_o) ▪ U (CS)	▪ L $(T_o, ∋ C_o)$ ▪ L $(T_o,$ other courses) ▪ L $(RelC_o)$ ▪ L (all $C_o, T_o)$ ▪ L $(T_a, ∋ C_o)$ ▪ L $(T_a,$ other courses)

E (C_o, T_a)	▪ V (options to choose):
	  – change $(C_o,$ weight)
	  – Del (C_o, T_a)
	  – Del $(C_o, RelT_o)$
	▪ Notify other authors of editing T_a in C_o
		▪ U (C_o, W)
		▪ U (C_o)
		▪ U (C_o, T_a) within different system modules
			L (C_o, T_a)

Del (C_o ,T_o)	▪ if Chk $(C_o, T_a, ∃)$ = true
	▪ notify the user
	▪ V (options to choose):
	  – Del (Co, all Ta)
	  – Del (Co, some Ta)
	  – Del (Co, To)
	  – Cancel Del option
	▪ notify others of deleting T_a in C_o
		▪ Chk $(C_o, T_a, ∃)$ = true
		▪ Chk $(C_o, T_o, ∃)$ = true
		▪ U (T_o) within different system modules
		▪ U (CS)
			L $(RelC_o, T_o)$ - updated

Due to space restrictions we are not presenting the full ontology for the domain and educational metadata authoring. Other possible course authoring tasks not mentioned here relate to document library and education metadata: 'link a document to a topic', 'link a document to a task', 'delete a document from a task' and 'delete a document from a topic'.

Domain. The interaction stream between *domain assistant* and *engine* is triggered by common authoring tasks, e.g., 'create/edit/copy-domain','merge-domains'. These tasks involve basic concept-maintenance such as 'add/delete/edit concept', 'create/delete/edit link/type' between concepts. At a higher level, authoring tasks include:'remove-all-direct-links-to-concept','remove-all-segments-of-a-path-between-two-concepts', 'edit/create-the-domain-map' (ontological domain structure) or 'make-links-between-domain-structure-and-library'. These tasks trigger operations performed by the domain engine over the ontological domain structure.

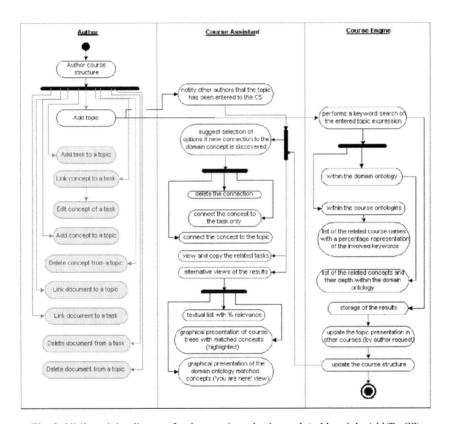

Fig. 3. UML activity diagram for the atomic authoring task 'add topic': *Add(T_o, CS)*

The operations ensure data consistency by performing domain specific checks for conflicts. For instance, when the authoring task *Add(C_o, CM)* is performed by the author (Fig. 3, Table 2 task 1) the domain engine performs *Chk(C_o, CM, exist)*, i.e. checks whether the concept Co is already in the map, updates the CM with *U(C_o, CM)*, performs *Add(C_o, weight)* and finally provides the results to the domain assistant for analysis and presentation to the author. Depending on whether the concept has been found in the CM, the domain engine returns: (a) $L(C_o, synonyms)$ (b) $L(DirLC_o)$ and (c) notification that the new concept C_0 has been added to the CM. These results are input to the domain assistant, which is responsible for the customization and presenting them in an appropriate format to the author so as to support his/her task most efficiently. In this case the domain assistant performs the alternative operations allowing the author to choose from $V(Text, DirLC_o)$, $V(Graph, DirLC_o)$ and another set of alternative views for the synonyms $V(Text, C_o, synonyms)$, $V(Graph, C_o, synonyms)$. There are a number of composite actions such as 'delete all direct links of a given concept' or 'delete all segments of a path between two concepts', which can be implemented with a repetitive call to the atomic operation called 'remove a link in the CM'.

Library. The interaction stream between the library assistant and library engine is triggered by a set of common authoring tasks, such as 'create/edit existing library', 'add/delete document', 'link/unlink a document to domain concepts', 'add/delete keywords to a document', 'edit the weights of the keywords', 'link/unlink a document to course topics and tasks'. Due to lack of space the details of all possible library-authoring tasks are skipped.

5   Conclusions

In this paper we have introduced a 2D-layer approach to support Web-based courseware authoring. The main idea is to use *system's domain ontology*, capturing the semantics of the subject domain terminology, in order to provide enhanced authoring support for concept-based courseware. We propose introducing additional ontology-based layers to the courseware authoring architecture, which allow intelligent authoring assistance. We elaborate on the various types of support that these layers should provide for the authoring actions within a courseware-authoring environment (for example AIMS, but not restricted to it). We consider also issues of re-usage and cooperative information sharing, towards collaborative authoring, in the sense of simultaneous performance of authoring activities. This is motivated by the increase in need for authors' cooperation and collaboration, especially in Web-authoring, where information is plentiful and has only to be molded into the different shapes adequate for learning.

The processing presented in the paper is self-contained. However, many more aspects can be analysed, and further research direction pursued. A direction already pointed to in section 2 is towards collaborative authoring environments. This would mean a merge between re-usage based cooperative environments, such as the one presented here, and collaborative means of working extracted from previous researches on collaborative learning environments. Furthermore, such environments can benefit from the creation of a user model of the author. Another important direction is towards merging of ontologies. Here we will rely heavily on the developments and research in this field [21].

This paper represents a contribution towards collaborative and cooperative course-ware authoring by both structuring, and adding semantics to the courseware in the sense of the standardization efforts of the semantic Web community.

References

1. Aroyo (2001). Task-oriented approach to information handling support within Web-based education. PhD Thesis, University of Twente, The Netherlands
2. Aroyo L., Dicheva D. (2001). AIMS: Learning and Teaching Support for WWW-based Education. Int. J. for Continuing Eng. Education and Life-long Learning, 11(1/2), 152-164.
3. Aroyo L., Dicheva D., Velev I. (2001). A Concept-Based Approach to Support Learning in a Web-based Course Environment. J. Moore et al. (Eds.) AI in Education, Amsterdam: IOS Press, Frontiers of AI and Applications, 68, 1-10.
4. Benyon, D., Stone, D., & Woodroffe, M. (1997). Experience with developing multimedia courseware for the World Wide Web: the need for better tools and clear pedagogy, Int. J. Human–Computer Studies, 47, 197–218
5. Berners-Lee, T. (1998). Semantic Web road map. Internal note, World Wide Web Consortium. http://www.w3.org/DesignIssues/Semantic.html.
6. Bolter, J.D., Joyce, M., Smith, J.B. (1990) Storyspace: Hypertext Writing Environment for the Macintosh. Computer Software. Cambridge, MA: Eastgate Systems.
7. Brusilovsky, P. (2001). Adaptive Educational Hypermedia. In: Proceedings of Tenth International PEG conference, Finland, pp. 8-12.
8. Cristea, A. and Okamoto, T., (2001). Object-oriented Collaborative Course Authoring Environment supported by Concept Mapping in MyEnglishTeacher, Educational Technology and Society, 4 (2), April, http://ifets.ieee.org/periodical/vol_2_2001/v_2_2001.html
9. De Bra, P. & Calvi, L. (1998). AHA! An open Adaptive Hypermedia Architecture, The New Review of Hypermedia and Multimedia, 4, 115-139.
10. De Vries, E. (1996). Educational multimedia for learning and problem solving, EuroAIED: European conference on artificial Intelligence in Education, Lisbon, 157-163.
11. Kay, J. & Kummerfeld,B (1994). Adaptive Hypertext for Individualised Instruction, Workshop on Adaptive Hypertext and Hypermedia, User Modelling '94, Cape Cod.
12. Gruninger, M. & Lee, J. (2002) Ontology: Applications and Design. Communications of the ACM, 45(2), 39-41
13. Hubscher. R., Puntambekar, S. (2001). Navigation Support for Learners in Hypertext Systems: Is More Indeed Better? J. Moore et al. (Eds.) AI in Education, Amsterdam: IOS Press, Frontiers in AI and Applications, 68, 13-20.
14. Lambiotte, J.G., Dansereau, D.F., Cross, D.R. and Reynolds, S.B. (1989). Multirelational semantic maps. Educational Psychology Review 1(4), 331-367.
15. Mizoguchi, R., Bourdeau, J. (2000). Using Ontological Engineering to Overcome Common AI-ED Problems, International Journal of AI in Education, 11 (2), 107-121.
16. McGuinness, D.L. et al. (2000). An Environment for Merging and Testing Large Ontologies, KR00, Breckenridge, Colorado. April 12-15.
17. Murray, T. (1999). Authoring Intelligent Tutoring Systems: An analysis of the state of the art. International Journal of AI in Education, 10, 98-129.
18. Murray, T., Shen, T., Piemonte, J., Condit, C., Thibedeau, J. (2000). Adaptivity in the MetaLinks Hyper-Book Authoring Framework, Workshop Proceedings of Adaptive and Intelligent Web-Based Education Systems workshop at ITS 2000, Montreal, June 2000.

19. Okamoto, T., Cristea, A. (2001). A Distance Ecological Model for Individual and Collaborative-learning support, Educational Technology and Society, 4(2) April.
20. Okamoto, T., Kayama, M. and Cristea, A. (2001) Considerations for building a Common Platform of Collaborative Learning Environment, ICCE'01, Ed.: C.-H. Lee, 2, 800-807.
21. Sowa, J. F. (2001). Building, Sharing, and Merging Ontologies, http://www.jfsowa.com/ontology/ontoshar.htm

Hypermedia Environment for Learning Concepts Based on Inter-domain Analogies as an Educational Strategy

Cécile Meyer

ICTT research laboratory
Ecole Centrale de Lyon,
36 avenue Guy de Collongue
69134 Ecully Cedex, FRANCE
Tél. +33 4 72 18 65 80
Cecile.Meyer@ictt.ec-lyon.fr

Abstract. Analogies are recognized as one possible teaching strategy for facilitating acquisition of concepts. We consider in our work analogy between semantically separate domains (inter-domain analogy), and we also consider analogy as a metacognitive tool: learning activities are based on analogies and they are explained. This use of analogy is rarely found in computer based learning environments. We propose an innovative environment which is based on analogy as an educational strategy, and also on two other elements which support learning activities : concept maps and hypermedia. A first application in the field of computer networks was designed and evaluated with students, and one of the results is the importance of creation of analogies by students.

1   Introduction

Analogy can be seen as one teaching strategy which can facilitate acquisition of concepts and problem solving (Mayer 1993, Duit 1991). The process of analogical reasoning has been widely studied in cognitive psychology, especially for problem solving tasks, producing various theories on how operate this cognitive process (Gentner 1983, Holyoak 1984, Indurkhya 1987).

In our work we consider analogy as similitude between elements from semantically separate knowledge domains: it is *inter-domain analogy*, like the classical analogy between electrical circuits and water circuits.

Intelligent tutoring systems take into account analogy : this strategy can be found, as well as other strategies (like providing examples) in multiples strategy authoring systems (Major 1997, Abou-Jaoude & Frasson 1998). But it seems that inter-domain analogy is quite rarely implemented in ITS. This can probably be explained by the fact that it is already very complex to model the knowledge for a problem-solving task. Modeling analogies implies an other level of complexity and this constitutes an important limitation as Wenger noted (1987, p. 334).

The orientation we took in our work focus on concepts learning rather than on problem solving. We defined an innovative generic learning environment founded on inter-domain analogy as a teaching strategy and on hypermedia and concept mapping. This environment has been tested with an early prototype. However complete

S.A. Cerri, G. Gouardères, and F. Paraguaçu (Eds.): ITS 2002, LNCS 2363, pp. 281–290, 2002.
© Springer-Verlag Berlin Heidelberg 2002

specifications exist (Meyer 2001) and they will be implemented soon in a full prototype.

In this paper, we mainly describe the principles and the structure of this environment from a conceptual view and we focus more on analogy as a teaching strategy.

2   Inter-domain Analogies as a Teaching Strategy

The principle of inter-domain analogy as a teaching strategy is to base the knowledge to be acquired in a domain (target domain) on prior knowledge in an other known domain (source domain).

We consider that one target domain may have analogies in several source domains (Fig. 1). So one concept of the target domain is possibly related to several analog concepts from several source domains.

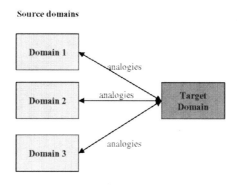

Fig. 1. Inter-domain analogies

2.1   Classification of Uses of Analogies

Sticht (1993) has defined several uses of analogies in education (Fig. 2). As a communication tool, analogies are used as a linguistic tool which helps to bring back information into active memory of the learner, as theorized by (Ortony 1975). In this case the learner doesn't realize any learning activity based on analogies, this situation is like the very common use of analogies in a classroom when a teacher gives a lecture. On the contrary, analogies as a reflection tool implies that the learner realizes activities based on analogies.

Two cases are distinguished: in the case of analogies as intuitive tool, analogies are underlying learning activities but are not explained. In the case of analogy as a metacognitive tool, case that we consider in our work, analogies are explained : the relations between the knowledge domains are analyzed by learners (the adequacy as well as the limits) with adequate activities. According to Sticht, this use stimulates creation of knowledge and not only retention, and also extend the capabilities of analytical thought.

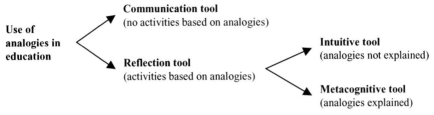

Fig. 2. Use of analogies in education

2.2 Learning Environments Based on Analogies as a Metacognitive Tool

As far as we know, there are very few systems based on inter-domain analogies as a metacognitive tool. The only one we know is the prototype AMPS, Analogical Model based Physical System (Brna & Duncan 1996). This system is based on a simulation of each domain of the analogy, for example, a simulation of electrical circuits and water circuits. The learner can construct a circuit in each domain and define the properties of its components with editors. Then he/she can simulate each circuit and compare the two simulations.

3 Principles and Components of the Environment

Compared to AMPS, which is founded on learning activities relying on simulation, our approach is different. We wanted the learner to have a more direct access to his/her representation of the domain to be learned, and to be able to act on his/her representation. This is provided in our environment by learning activities based on concepts maps (Novak & Gowin 1984, Jonassen 1997). Concept maps are used as cognitive tool by the learner : he/she constructs his own map, which reflect his/her comprehension of the domain.

We wanted also the system to handle a lot of analogies : that several source domains can exist for one target domain, and that each concept of the target domain can have multiple analogies, taken from different source domains. This feature is provided by hypermedia, which is, with analogies and concept maps, the third element of our environment (Fig. 3). The aim of hypermedia in this environment is to link the knowledge domains containing analogies: each domain, the target domain and the source domains, is described by hypermedia documents and analog concepts in those documents are linked together with hypertext semantic links.

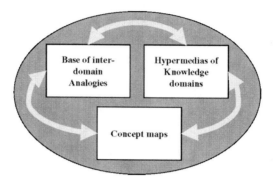

Fig. 3. Components of the environment: analogies, hypermedia and concept maps are closely inter-related : analogies are embedded in hypermedia, and concept maps contain reference to both analogies and hypermedia documents

4 Structure of the Environment

Giving those principles, we have defined a generic structure, independent from a knowledge domain, containing various components organized in four level (Fig. 4). In this structure, components on the left hand side are specific to the presence of analogies, while components on the right hand side are not specific to analogies. Components at each level of the environment are associated to other components with semantic hypertext links. This allows the learner to navigate from one component to another through the links, as to navigate between a source domain and the target domain.

4.1 Hypermedia Level

This level contains several hypermedia modules (a module is a set of documents). Each module describes a domain - source or target - with text, pictures, sounds, etc. Analog elements of a source and a target domain are linked together by semantic analogy hypertext links.

As each source domain may contain several analogies, and as the target domain may have several source domains, we can see that an important number of analogy links can exist between the domains.

For each analogy, the analog concepts are represented by items which can be words, but also pictures (drawing, photo, video, etc.) or sounds.

It has also to be noted that the source domain is described according to the target domain, which means that only the concepts of the source domain having an analog in the target domain are described.

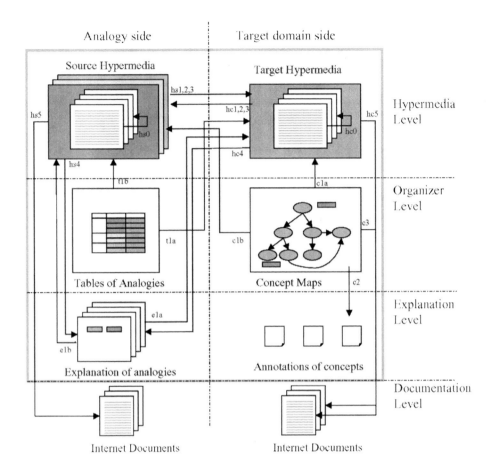

Fig. 4. Generic structure of the environment: various components are organized in four levels and linked together with different kind of hypertext links (identified by labels). The learner can navigate from one component to another, like to navigate between a source domain and the target domain through analogy hypertext links

4.2 Organizer Level

This level contains tools for organizing knowledge of the source and target domains. Concepts maps are a kind of graphical organizer used by learner, and tables of analogies are a semi-textual organizer listing analogous concepts in each domain. Each organizer can have various forms, depending on the type of learning activity which is performed.

Concerning concept maps built by students, two representations at least are possible in order to indicate analogies : a concept map of the target domain indicating source concepts on it (Fig. 5 is an example of such a map) or the opposite, a concept map of a source domain indicating target concepts on it.

4.3   Explanation Level

This level contains textual explanation of analogies and annotations of concepts map or hypermedia documents. An explanation is a text describing which elements of source and target domain are analog, what is the adequacy of the analogy (why this analogy works well) and what are the limits of the analogy. An explanation can contain hypertext links to target and source domains.

4.4   Documentation Level

This level is external, it contains reference to documents related either to source or target domain (like Web documents on the Internet). This level is important in order to link the learning environment to "real" information, for example web sites of companies describing technical products.

4.5   Learning Activities and Scenarios

A lot of different activities can be done by the learner within this environment:

- Hypermedia navigation: reading a document of a domain (source or target), browsing between source and target domain through semantic analogy links, browsing in a source domain, browsing in the target domain, annotating a document.
- Concept mapping: creating a map of a domain (target or source), annotating the map, indicating analogies on the map, linking the map with documents.
- Analogy creation: creating correspondence between concepts of source and target domain, either in the concept map, or in the table of analogies. Creating a document describing the source concepts (possibly creating a new source domain), creating analogy links between this document and the document of the target concepts.
- Collaborative activities: showing a map to other students, annotating the map of an other student, constructing a map with other students, constructing analogies with other students.

These activities can be organized into scenarios, which depend partly on the strategies adopted in using analogies as a metacognitive tool. For example one strategy is to use analogies as a starting point to go from the source domain towards the target domain. This implies to favor navigation from a source domain to a target domain, that is to activate hypertext links in this direction and to inhibit links in the other direction.

4.6   Functionalities of the System and Implementation

The functionalities of the system correspond to the various activities of the actors of the system (teacher, designer, students), in particular to the learning activities of students. One important functionality comes from the need to manage the browsing complexity:

- One target concept can have multiple corresponding source concepts. This implies that hypertext links can have multiple destinations. We see two solutions for this problem. In the first one, all destinations are proposed to the user and he/she has to choose at each time which source domain he/she wants. In the second solution, the user chooses once a source domain among all the possible source domains, then this domain becomes the current context and the links are activated according to this context.
- The various possible scenarios implies also different ways of browsing through the hypermedia, like navigating from a source to the target or from the target to a source.

Consequently, the system has to adapt both to the choices of the user and to the current pedagogic scenario. This can be obtained by the techniques of adaptive hypermedia (Brussilovsky 1996). We have defined an architecture based on a adaptive hypermedia mechanisms, on an object model of analogies and documents, and on several databases. As we said in introduction, this environment is not implemented yet in a full prototype (we plan to reuse an existing hypermedia generator).

5   An Application for Learning Computer Networks

We have a simple hypermedia application in order to test the approach on a real training ground and in a specific technical domain: computer networks. This domain seems to be especially rich for analogies, the "information highway metaphor" being the most famous one. Historically this application was designed before we created the generic structure, and it was also designed for test purposes, which explains it offers only a subset of the generic structure.

5.1   Design of the Application

We choose a specific topic, routing in computer networks, which concerns how information is routed from one point to another in a computer network. This topic was chosen because it is, according to teachers, complex and difficult to teach. We realized an application which is rather simple from a technical point of view, but which required an important effort regarding the design of analogies. We followed several stages, as advised by several authors in human-computer interaction field (Caroll & al. 1988; Madsen 1994)

- *Generating potential analogies.* We collected analogies in several source domains by different means: from teachers, from students, from books and by searching on web sites. The result was more than 60 analogies from 12 source domains. For example, a router can be seen as analogous to a sorting post office, where packets are sent to various destinations.

- *Evaluating and choosing analogies.* We choose three source domain that we estimated familiar to the targeted audience: road networks, postal systems and railway networks. Then we studied several analogies in each domain: the concepts involved, the adequacy and the limits. We found this stage time consuming because a detailed study of analogies brings about fundamental questions on the knowledge domain.
- *Developing analogies in the design task.* This stage involved searching meaningful illustrations for source domains (in our case we choose photographic pictures), writing textual explanation of analogies, and linking source and target domains.

The application has three hypermedia source module (postal, road, railway) and one target module (routing in computer networks). Compared to the generic structure, the differences are the following : the target module is not a full hypermedia module but is composed of slide documents previously used in a lecture; each source module has only one document and explanations of analogies are stored in this document; hypertext links are one way from source to target; table of analogies are not proposed.

This application will be, in a next stage, extended in order to fully implement the possibilities of the generic structure. This design experience was also fruitful because we draw from it a first draft of a generic method (independent from a knowledge field) for designing learning environments based on analogies and concept maps.

5.2   Evaluation

This application was tested in a real education ground with seven students in continuing education: a master degree in management of computer networks. In a first stage, students had a lecture on routing, without analogies. In a second stage, students had to construct a concept map on this topic. In a third stage, students could browse the application and they had to work again their map and to indicate analog concepts of their choice on it. For each student and each session were collected a concept map and a questionnaire. An example of map created by a student in the third stage is shown in (Fig. 5): the target domain is routing in computer networks, and we can see that the source domain chosen by the student is the postal system. Here are some results of this evaluation:

- *Feature of application*: need for a non-graphical tool to associate analog concepts, for a more detailed formalism to indicate analogies in concept maps, for more guidance for creating concept maps and analogies.
- *Base of analogies*: the most quoted source domain was the road network (5 students), which is not surprising given the popularity of the information highway metaphor, but the postal system was also chosen by 2 students.
- *Comprehension and motivation*: all students were motivated by using analogies. Moreover, we found that the understanding of 3 students was really enhanced by this approach.

Another very interesting result was that all students, not only indicate analogies on their concepts maps, but also indicate new analogies, that is, analogies which were not present in the test application: they wanted to create their own analogies.

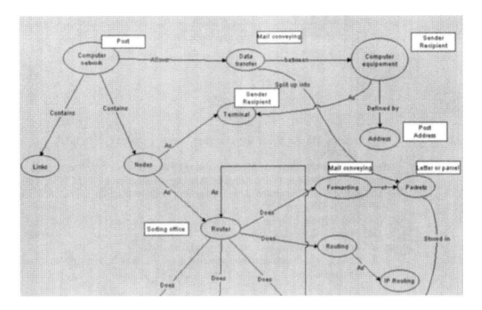

Fig. 5. Part of a concept map of the target domain elaborated by a student. The concepts of target domain are in oval shapes while the concepts of source domain are in rectangular shapes. A source concept set close to a target concept indicates an analogy

6 Conclusion

This first evaluation of a test application with real students raises questions about the principles and the design of the system: indeed, we designed a system able to handle a lot of analogies, but the students want to create their own analogies. Does the system need to contain a lot of different analogies that the student can choose from or do we have to consider an initially "analogy empty" system that is filled by students ? This raises also questions about the role of analogy: should it be considered more as a teaching strategy or more as a learning strategy ?

Maybe the answer is somewhere in between: the system should contain some analogies in order to provide students with models of what are analogies, but tools should exist to help them creating their own analogies, either derived from existing analogies, or completely new analogies in existing source domains or in brand new source domains.

But if the students become very creative, there is an even greater necessity of guidance to help them and to prevent them from drawing incorrect analogies. An orientation is to introduce intelligent tools, that is tools being able to diagnose the "correctness" of analogies, but this is probably a very complex issue because it requires a detailed model of analogies and it needs to take into account a lot of domains. Another orientation, which seems more pragmatic, is to have this help provided by a human tutor who guides the students through the creation of analogies.

Acknowledgements. I would like to thank René Chalon, Bertrand David, Christian Bessière of Ecole Centrale de Lyon and Gérard Beuchot of INSA de Lyon.

References

Abou-Jaoude, S.C., Frasson, C.: An agent for selecting learning strategy. NTCIF'98. Rouen, Novembre (1998). 353-358.

Brna, P., Duncan, D.: The Analogical Model-based Physics System: A Workbench to Investigate Issues in How to Support Learning by Analogy in Physics. CALISCE'96, Third International Conference on Computer Aided Learning and Instruction in Science and Engineering. (1996) 331-339.

Brusilovsky, P.: Adaptive Hypermedia: an Attempt to Analyze and Generalize. In: Multimedia, Hypermedia, and Virtual Reality, P., Brusilovsky, P., Kommers and N., Streitz (eds.). Lecture Notes in Computer Science, Vol. 1077, (1996). 288-304.

Caroll, J., Mack, R., Kellog, W.: Interface metaphors and user interface design. In: Handbook of Human-Computer Interaction. Edited by Helander, M.G., Elsevier Science Publishers North-Holland (1988). 67-85.

Duit, R.: On the Role of Analogies and Metaphors in Learning Science. Science Education, Vol. 75 N.6. (1991) 649-672.

Gentner, D.: Structure-mapping: a theoretical framework for analogy. Cognitive Science, 7(2), (1983). 155-170.

Holyoack, K.J.: Analogical thinking and human intelligence. In: R.J. Sternberg (ed.), Advances in the psychology of human intelligence (vol. 2), Hillsdale, New Jersey, Lawrence Erlbaum, (1984).

Indurkhya, B.: Approximate semantic transference: A computational theory of metaphors and analogies. Cognitive Science, Vol. 11, (1987). 445-480.

Jonassen, D.H., Reeves, T., Hong, N., Harvey, D., Peters, K.: Concept Mapping as cognitive learning and assessment tools. Journal of Interactive Learning Research, Vol. 8 N. 3/4. (1997) 289-308.

Madsen, K.H.: A guide to metaphorical design. Communications of the ACM Vol. 37 N. 12 (1994). 57-62.

Major, N.: REDEEM: Exploiting symbiosis between psychology and authoring environment. International Journal of Artificial Intelligence in Education, Vol 8. (1997). 317-340.

Mayer, R.E.: The instructive metaphor: Metaphoric aids to student's understanding of science. In: Metaphor and thought. Edited by Ortony A., Cambridge, UK : University Press, (1993) (2nd ed.). 562-578.

Meyer, C.: A learning environment based on metaphors and analogies. Young researchers tracks of AI-ED'99, International Conference on Artificial Intelligence in Education. Le Mans, France, July (1999). 51-52.

Meyer, C.: Un environnement d'apprentissage fondé sur les métaphores, les hypermédias et les cartes de concepts. Application aux réseaux informatiques. PhD thesis in computer science of Ecole Centrale de Lyon, France (2001).

Novak, J.D., Gowin, D.B.: Learning How to Learn. New York : Cambridge University Press (1984).

Ortony, A.: Why metaphors are necessary and not just nice. Educational theory, 25, (1975).

Sticht, T.S. Educational uses of metaphor. In Metaphor and thought. Edited by Ortony A. Cambridge, UK: University Press, (1993) (2nd ed.). 621-632.

Wenger, E.: Artificial Intelligence and tutoring systems. Los Altos, Californie: Morgan Kauffman, (1987).

Towards a Specification of Distributed and Intelligent Web Based Training Systems

Claus Moebus, Bernd Albers, Stefan Hartmann, Heinz-Juergen Thole, and
Jochen Zurborg

Innovative Learning and Teaching Systems,
Department of Computing Systems,
University of Oldenburg

Abstract. Modern e-Learning Systems are expected to be innovative
not only concerning comprehensive representation of content enriched
by multimedia, but also in the integration of learning situations in contexts suitable for students. Suitable, motivating contexts can be "fun"
as found in strategic games or business simulations or of a more "serious" variety in the form of virtual data labs. In the new BMBF Project
EMILeAstat[1] (e-stat) 13 partners from different organisations are cooperating to construct such an innovative intelligent web based training
(I-WBT) system for applied statistics.

This paper describes the formal specification, the architecture, and the
implementation of e-stat from a knowledge and content engineering
point of view, applying pedagogical and psychological criteria where
necessary. Towards the end of the paper we compare our approach with
an emerging e-Learning engineering approach which is based on EML a
special XML-dialect.

Keywords. Architectures, Authoring Systems, Cognitive Approaches,
Distributed Learning Environments, Intelligent Distance Learning, Internet Environments, Learning Environments, Content-Engineering, Intelligent Web Based Training (I-WBT), Specification of e-Learning Systems, Unified Modeling Language (UML), Extensible Markup Language
(XML), Educational Modeling Language (EML).

1 The I-WBT-System "E-stat"

E-stat is an attempt to go beyond the scope of existing WBT systems by using
a strong integration concept in combining well-structured content with a high
diversity of methodical and didactical approaches. Special emphasis is placed on
reuse and sharing of contents, clean separation of factual contents and its didactical motivated presentation, as well as the avoidance of proprietary solutions.
This ambitious approach creates the need for new research and evaluation. For
example, a method for the presentation of coherent and user-adaptive content

---

[1] The German Federal Ministry of Education and Research finances e-stat by means of
the NMB funding program "Neue Medien in der Bildung" (New Media in Education).

S.A. Cerri, G. Gouardères, and F. Paraguaçu (Eds.): ITS 2002, LNCS 2363, pp. 291–300, 2002.

(learning objects) supplied by a variety of sources has to be found. E-stat is motivated by pedagogical plurality. So it integrates different learning-methods, scenarios, and a consulting component into a knowledge landscape. The question is whether existing methods of specification [1] [2] [3] have to be modified accordingly, to ensure a systematic method for production of content. In the course of the project we decided to use the standard approach of software engineering modified by special educational and cognitive needs. For development and analysis purposes we make use of concept and notations supplied by object orientated analysis (OOA) and object orientated design (OOD) [4]. For the implementation we develop a special XML-dialect to give structure to the learning objects and the learning environment.

1.1   Specifications

What is the purpose of specifications? We borrow some general requirements [5], which were published for the slight different purpose of an Educational Modeling Language (EML). A specification or an EML should meet the general requirements: (1) formalization, (2) pedagogical flexibility, (3) explicitly typed learning objects, (4) completeness, (5) reproducibility, (6) personalization, (7) medium neutrality, (8) interoperability and sustainability, (9) compatibility, (10) reusability, and (11) life cycle. We will take these criteria as a frame of reference.

Specification of IPSEs. In our group we started our ITS research with the development of Intelligent Problem Solving Environments [6] (IPSEs) a special type of ITS. They are instances of intelligent problem based learning systems [7]. To us they seem to be the most effective intelligent systems for enabling problem solving learning. Though they contain a comprehensive expert system or an oracle that is able to check the correctness of students' solution proposals, they lack other expensive components like teaching or student models. The curricular component in form of a teaching model is abandoned in favor of a simple sequence of task relevant problems. In place of student models individualization is achieved by the ability of the system to respond intelligently to student hypotheses. In IPSEs an expert system and the current student hypothesis are sufficient to generate adaptive help. The development is based on a cognitive meta-learning theory, which we called ISP-DL-Theory, an acronym for "Impasse-Success-Problem-Solving-Driven-Learning" [8]. This theory is influenced by the cognitive theories of Anderson [9] [10], Newell [11], and Van Lehn[12] as well as by the motivational "Rubikon" theory of Heckhausen [13] and Gollwitzer [14].

To guide the work of our group we developed an abstract specification of the IPSE philosophy. We define formally the concept of a hypothesis in a knowledge revision framework. We show that hypothesis testing can be integrated into theory revision [15] and knowledge acquisition processes of an abstract problem solver. Stating and testing of hypotheses is the most important concept in the development of IPSEs. Though most have an intuitive idea what a hypothesis is we have to give a formal definition. We try to be as abstract as possible so that hypothesis testing in various IPSEs can be extended as special cases. The main points are summarized in Figure 1.

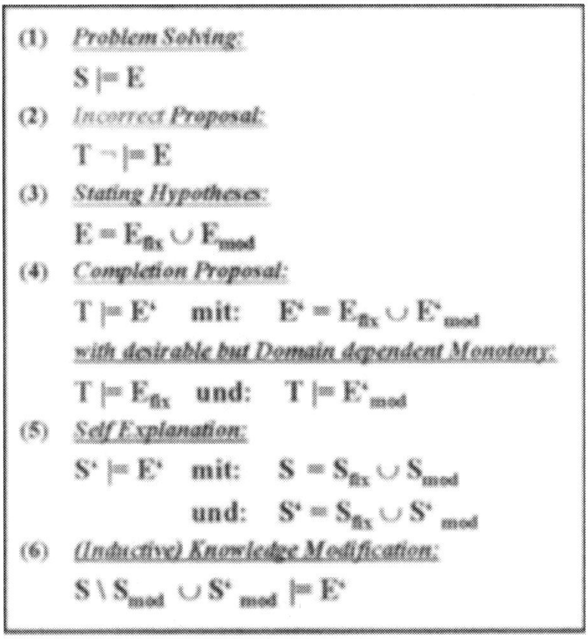

(1) *Problem Solving:*

$$S \models E$$

(2) *Incorrect Proposal:*

$$T \neg \models E$$

(3) *Stating Hypotheses:*

$$E = E_{fix} \cup E_{mod}$$

(4) *Completion Proposal:*

$$T \models E' \quad \text{mit:} \quad E' = E_{fix} \cup E'_{mod}$$

with desirable but Domain dependent Monotony:

$$T \models E_{fix} \quad \text{und:} \quad T \models E'_{mod}$$

(5) *Self Explanation:*

$$S' \models E' \quad \text{mit:} \quad S = S_{fix} \cup S_{mod}$$
$$\text{und:} \quad S' = S_{fix} \cup S'_{mod}$$

(6) *(Inductive) Knowledge Modification:*

$$S \setminus S_{mod} \cup S'_{mod} \models E'$$

Fig. 1. Problem Solving, Hypotheses Testing, Self Explanation and Inductive Knowledge Modification in IPSEs

According to ISP-DL theory there are several steps when acquiring knowledge with IPSEs. (1) Using his subjective theory S the problem solver generates evidence or an artifact E, which may be a solution proposal to a task. From the viewpoint of an ideal expert this proposal may be wrong. (2) This proposal E is submitted to the system. If the proposal is in error it cannot be explained by the system's domain theory T contained in the expert system. The learner gets an according feedback. (3) Thus the system offers the problem solver to generate a hypothesis and he may partition his proposal E into two parts E_{fix} and E_{mod}. The student has the hypothesis that E_{fix} can be embedded into a correct solution. (4) Now, the system generates with its theory T a system response to the hypothesis. E' is a system generated solution proposal, which contains E_{fix}. E'_{mod} is help information for the student which in our IPSEs is shown to the student stepwise on demand. (5) After these events (hopefully) we have some knowledge acquisition events on the learner side. According to ISPDL-theory we expect some self-explanation: the student tries to explain E' with its parts E_{fix} and E'_{mod} to himself. As a result, the learner generates new knowledge S'_{mod}. As indicated in (6), this new knowledge gives him the opportunity to understand E'. According to (6) this is an inductive inference, because S'_{mod} can be inferred inductively from $S \setminus S_{mod} \cup \{E'\}$. The comparison of (1) with (5) results in a revised theory S'.

Though this specification was a good guide for the development of various IPSEs in our group, it was not useful for the development of I-WBT systems in a multiparty consortium with several content-providers. The specification is too abstract, even if it had been translated to UML with abstract classes T, E and an entailment relation between some classes. For instance the oracle within the IPSE was not specified in detail. In some domains you need grammars and in other domains model checkers to check the correctness of student proposals. Which of the 11 requirements are not met by the IPSE-specifications: (2), (4), (9), (10), and (11). So we had to look for other specification approaches which are suitable for a distributed development.

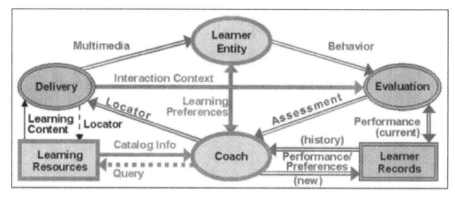

- Primary design issues: learner/tutor choose direction, acquires knowledge during use of tutoring tool, learning resources may be implicit (not explicitly defined) in tutor
- Secondary design issues: tutor does evaluation, tools and delivery support experimentation

Fig. 2. LTSA mapped to intelligent tutoring tool

Specification of the LTSA. Following their authors the LTSA [16] (Learning Technology Systems Architecture) specification covers a wide range of systems, commonly known as e-learning technology. The LTSA specification is pedagogically neutral, content-neutral, culturally neutral, and platform-neutral. The LTSA is neither prescriptive nor exclusive. Many systems may satisfy the requirements of the LTSA specification although they don't provide all the components, have differing organizations, or have differing designs.

The specification (Fig. 2) mentions stores (rectangles), processes (ovals), and flows (arrows) in a kind of YOURDON-notation. Figure 2 demonstrates the view a developer should have when developing an ITS according to the LTSA-standard.

As can be seen from the Figures 1 and 2 it is possible to map the IPSE-specification to the LTSA-specification. The former is more specific than the latter. The IPSE-specification would extend the LTSA-specification if we would translate both to UML. Which of the 11 requirements are not met by the LTSA-specifications: (1), (3), (4), (6), (8), (10), and (11). The lesson learned for e-stat was, that LTSA is too vague for a distributed development in a multi-party consortium.

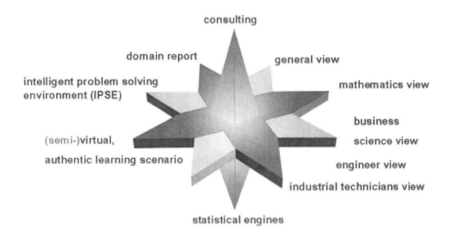

Fig. 3. The Wind Rose as a metaphor for pedagogical plurality

Specification of e-stat. In the beginning of the project the wind rose [17] (Fig. 3) was used as a metaphor for the e-stat idea. It was meant to express e-stats ambition to supply applicable solutions with changing didactical demands [18] [19] (e.g. instructional, cognitive, and constructive): courses of differing levels of complexity for mathematicians, managers, psychologists and engineers but also for people with a special need of practical experience like industrial technicians.

e-stat furthermore contains methods to integrate existing statistical engines, (semi-) virtual learning scenarios, an automated glossary, and the case based consulting component for the "hasty user". Next the wind rose was transferred into use-cases of the semiformal UML-Notation [20] (Fig. 4). A use-case is a typical application of e-stat. Due to the open nature of the e-stat system, the process of defining new use-cases has not been finalized.

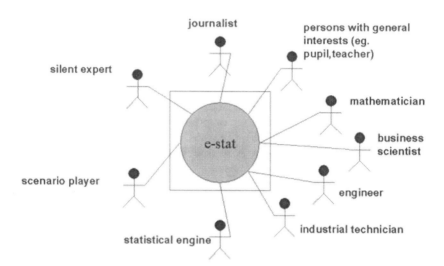

Fig. 4. Use-Cases of e-stat

The next step in the OOA constitutes the construction of the static system structure using a class diagram. A class defines structure (attribute), behaviour (operations), and relations (associations and inheritance structures) for a collection of certain objects [21].

As can be seen in our class diagram, e-stat is a composite aggregate of views (Fig. 5). Views are shared aggregates of scenarios, courses, course units and concepts. Concepts have recursive structure. They can be built up by text blocks (text leafs) module frames, and/or concepts. This architecture ensures the representation of hierarchically organized lessons. Module frames are again composite aggregates of modules, which are the smallest building blocks or knowledge-units of e-stat.

Types (e.g. moduleType) were provided to us by the statistical content providers, which are members of the department of mathematics at our university. Inside module frames, modules are interlinked to define a partial order (e.g. "X depends on Y").
The ontological links will be specified reflexively by the association "up" inside the class "moduleframe" (Fig. 5). A conceptual map of the e-stat content can be created automatically using this pointer structure. On the right hand side of Figure 6 a cut-out of the ontology is illustrated which will be used in the consulting component of e-stat to deepen explanations on demand.

This consulting component is based on methods of case-based reasoning. The cases consist of Question-Answer-Pairs (QAPs). In the beginning the QAPs will be extracted from consulting sessions with experts to initialize the component.

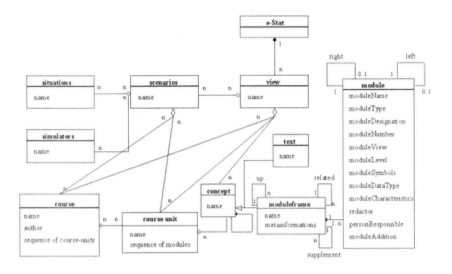

Fig. 5. Class Diagram of the Content Aspect

With the use of formal [22] and relational concept analysis [23] we will build up both question and answer concept lattices. The root nodes of the concept lattices are the most general question or answer node. The leaf nodes represent more specific questions respective answers.

If the hasty user asks a question, the consulting component will indicate the most similar question using the similarities given by the question concept lattice. To response the consulting component makes a search in the answer concept lattice for the appropriate answer, which is next to the question. This response is displayed to the user. If he needs detailed explanations or relevant hints for the reinforcement of his learning the ontologically structured content of e-stat serves to meet his needs.

Only if the response is not helpful for the user, the unanswered question will be transferred via asynchronous communication to human consultants. After the answer of the human expert satisfied the user, both the question and the answer are integrated into the respective concept lattice. So we have some learning mechanism in the system [24].

Due to this learning capability, the quality of the automatic consulting component will be steadily increased. After a period of time, we expect that only really difficult and interesting questions will be delivered to the consultants.

Which of the 11 requirements are not met by the momentary e-Stat-specifications: (4) and (9). The main deficits are the lack of completeness and the lack of integrating (educational) standards. The former point is not serious because the project just started 6 months ago. The latter deficit is really not a deficit, because the existing standards are not convincing.

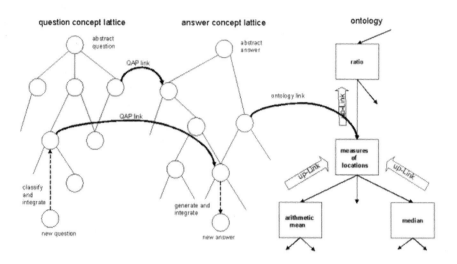

Fig. 6. The consulting component of e-stat

1.2   Implementing E-stat Using a 4-Tier Architecture

Most classes of the class diagram are implemented using the standardised XML language. XML allows to create semantic tags additional to syntactic tags (HTML). Authors receive the respective document type definitions (DTDs) to generate valid class objects. DTDs for modules and module frames have been developed. Modules are specified by following attributes taken form the class-diagram (Fig. 5): moduleName, moduleType, moduleDesignation, moduleNumber, moduleView, moduleLevel, modulSymbols, moduleDataType, moduleCharacteristics, redactor, personResponsible, and moduleAddition. This module structure is the result of an interactive process between domain experts, content providers, and knowledge engineers. Depending on the separation of content and layout the authors will also get a XSL-file, which is responsible for the layout. While developing content, authors have preview permanently.

E-stat is implemented using a 4-tier architecture. The presentation tier supplies content providers and students with suitable graphical user interfaces (GUIs). The view-author GUI will be powerful enough to enable authors to construct a course for his particular target group from the certified e-stat modules by means of a system similar to "shopping cart" systems used by many e-shops. It should only be necessary to construct new modules in very special cases.

Authors can use current XML-editors instead of a special e-stat content authoring GUI. In the logic-tier we use an Apache server, which is installed in Oldenburg. On this server our e-stat-control-system is implemented. Interactions with our database and other statistical-engines will be managed in this tier, as well as the handling of the user-administration. The native XML-database

TAMINO is represented in the data-tier. Statistical engines (Xplore, SPSS, qs-stat) and scenario engines for simulation (e.g. handling business planning, production or stock exchange) are part of the application tier.

2   Related Work

During the work in our project we came across the EML initiative [25] [26].The pedagogical meta-model consists of four (conceptually) packages: (1) Theories of learning and instructions, (2) Learning Model, (3) Unit of Study Model, (4) Domain Model. These partially overlap with our approach. The parts (1) and (4) are identical to our ideas. Part (2) is a generalization of the ISP-DL-Theory. ISPDL-Theory allows more specific empirical hypotheses and more constraints for the development process of learning systems. The Unit-of-Study Model overlaps partially with the e-stat-Class-Diagram. The e-stat-Classes are at the present time partly not so semantically rich. Especially the left upper triangle concerned with scenarios has to be worked out further. Otherwise is the right lower triangle of the e-stat-Class-Diagram more semantically elaborated in comparison to the knowledge object structure of EML. What could be said at the moment is, that we could not meet the requirements of our mathematical partners using an unmodified EML. At the present moment we try to use an unmodified EML in a less demanding nonmathematical domain.

3   Contact

Prof. Dr. Claus Moebus, Innovative Learning and Teaching Systems, Department of Computing Systems, University of Oldenburg, D-26111 Oldenburg, Germany mailto:moebus@informatik.uni-oldenburg.de

References

1. Aviation Industry CBT Committee (AICC)
2. Learning Technology Standards Committee (LTSC) mit den Work Groups IEEE P1484.1 Architecture and Reference Model WG: Learning Technology Systems Architecture (LTSA) und IEEE P1484.12 Learning Object Metadata WG: LOM Standards
3. Alliance of Remote Instructional Authoring and Distribution Networks for Europe (ARIADNE)
4. BALZERT, H., Lehrbuch der Objektmodellierung, Heidelberg: Spektrum Akademischer Verlag, 1999
5. KOPER, R., Modelling Units of Study from a Pedagogical Perspective: The Pedagogical Meta-Model behind EML, Educational Technology Expertise Centre, Open University of the Netherlands, First Draft, Version 2, 2001
6. MOEBUS, C., Towards an Epistemology of Intelligent Problem Solving Environments: The Hypothesis Testing Approach, in J. Greer (ed), Artificial Intelligence in Education, Proceedings of AI-ED 95, Charlottesville: AACE, 1995

7. BARROWS, H.S. & TAMBLYN, R.M. Problem-based learning: an approach to medical education, New York: Springer, 1980
8. MOEBUS, C., SCHROEDER, O. & THOLE, H.J., Diagnosing and Evaluating the Acquisition Process of Programming Schemata, in J.E. Greer, G. McCalla (eds), Student Modelling: The Key to Individualized Knowledge-Based Instruction, Berlin: Springer (NATO ASI Series F: Computer and Systems Sciences, Vol. 125), 1994
9. ANDERSON, J.R., Knowledge Compilation: The General Learning Mechanism. In: R.S. Michalski et. al., Machine Learning II. Kaufman, 1986
10. ANDERSON, J.R., A Theory of the Origins of Human Knowledge, Artificial Intelligence, 1989
11. NEWELL, A., Unified Theories of Cognition, Cambridge, Mass.: Harvard University Press, 1990
12. VANLEHN, K., Toward a Theory of Impasse-Driven Learning, in H. Mandl et. al.(eds), Learning Issues for Intelligent Tutoring Systems, Berlin: Springer, 1988
13. HECKHAUSEN, H., Motivation und Handeln, Heidelberg: Springer, 1989
14. GOLLWITZER, P.M., Action Phases and Mind-Sets, in: E.T. Higgins & R.M. Sorrentino (eds), Handbook of Motivation and Cognition, Vol. 2, 1990
15. DE RAEDT, L., Interactive Theory Revision, San Diego: Academic Press, 1992
16. LTSA Draft 9, LTSA Home page, http://edutool.com/ltsa/, 2001
17. Foerderantrag an das BMBF, Foerderkennzeichen 08NM058A, 2000
18. JANK, W & MEYER, H., Didaktische Modelle, Frankfurt a. M.: Cornelsen Scriptor, 1994,
19. BRUNS, B. & GAJEWSKI, P., Multimediales Lernen im Netz: Leitfaden für Entscheider und Planer, Berlin: Springer Verlag, 1999,
20. BOOCH, G. & RUMBAUGH, J. & JACOBSON, I., The unified Modeling Language User Guide, Addison-Wesley, 1999,
21. BALZERT, H., UML kompakt, Heidelberg: Spektrum Akademischer Verlag, 2001,
22. GANTER, B. & WILLE, R., Formal Concept Analysis: mathematical foundations, Springer Verlag, 1999,
23. PRISS, U., Relational Concept Analysis: Semantic Structures in Dictionaries and Lexical Databases, Dissertation, TH-Darmstadt
24. HEINRICH, E. & MAURER, H., Active Documents: Concept, Implementation and Applications, Journal of Universal Computer Sciences 6, 2000
25. KOPER, R., Modeling Units of Study from a Pedagogical Perspective: The Pedagogical Meta-Model behind EML, Educational Technology Expertise Centre, Open University of the Netherlands, First Draft, Version 2, 2001
26. KOPER, R., From Change to Renewal: Educational Technology Foundations of Electronic Learning Environments, 2000, http://eml.ou.nl/introduction/articles.htm/

A Virtual Assistant for Web-Based Training in Engineering Education

Frédéric Geoffroy[(1)], Esma Aimeur[(2)], and Denis Gillet[(1)]

[(1)] Swiss Federal Institute of Technology in Lausanne (EPFL)
LA-I2S-STI, CH – 1015 Lausanne, Switzerland
Phone: +41 21 693-5168, FAX: + 41 21 693-2574,
frederic.geoffroy@epfl.ch, denis.gillet@epfl.ch
[(2)] Université de Montréal,
Département IRO
C.P. 6128, Succursale Centre-Ville, Montréal (Québec), H3C 3J7 Canada
aimeur@IRO.UMontreal.CA

Abstract. Experimentation has always been an essential ingredient to sustain the learning activities in engineering education. During traditional laboratory sessions, a huge amount of work is carried out by the assistant who is in charge of supporting and evaluating the students. In a Web-based experimentation setting students ask for more feedback while they work on simulation or remote manipulation. We present in this paper a virtual assistant for Web-based training. The training and the evaluation process are shared between real and virtual assistants in order to deliver a tutoring scheme adapted to Web-based experimentation.

1 Introduction

The Swiss Federal Institute of Technology in Lausanne (EPFL) currently supports various new learning technologies projects for promoting active and flexible learning in engineering education. The *eMersion* project [8] is an initiative integrated in this framework with the main objective of sustaining hands-on practice and active learning through Web-based experimentation. The Web-based experimentation environment implemented at the EPFL features Web-based simulation and remote manipulation facilities.

Web-based education is getting an increasing popularity due to its clear benefits: Classroom and platform independence. We know only four Web-based educational systems that have influenced a number of more recent systems, among which ELM-ART [4] and InterBook [3].

If we consider simulation, several Web-based systems exist such as Cardiac Tutor [6], Belvedere [10], and Simquest [9]. The purpose of these systems and the methods used are numerous and varied. For example, [11] use induction to generate feedback in simulation-based discovery learning.

S.A. Cerri, G. Gouardères, and F. Paraguaçu (Eds.): ITS 2002, LNCS 2363, pp. 301–310, 2002.
© Springer-Verlag Berlin Heidelberg 2002

We propose a scheme to expand the level of support provided at EPFL [7] to students involved in Web-based experimentation activities by providing a Virtual Assistant. This solution is introduced to compensate for the students' remoteness as well as to sustain learning by providing feedback [5] or by proposing challenges to test the confidence of the student [1], [2].

During laboratory activities, a huge amount of work is traditionally performed by the assistants in charge of supporting and evaluating the students. In a Web-based experimentation framework there is a need for new cooperative learning and teaching strategies. The teaching and the evaluation process could be shared between real and virtual assistants in order to deliver an adapted teaching[1].

We propose an Intelligent Tutoring System that integrates three agents: the Real Instructor, the Real Assistant (RA) and the Virtual Assistant (VA). The aim of the VA is to provide feedback during the evaluation process to reinforce learning. Since the VA is never tired, the students can interact with it at any time.

In this paper, we first describe the Cockpit-like environment the students used at EPFL to carry out Web-based experimentation. Then, we introduce a Virtual Assistant in the context of flexible learning, including some elements of justification for the VA. We also present a complete description of the goal and the functioning of the VA before going through a practical case study. We end with concluding remarks.

2   The Cockpit-Like Web-Based Experimentation Environment

2.1 The Cockpit Functionalities

The Web-based experimentation environment provided to students has a Cockpit-like graphical user interface. This so-called *Cockpit* environment (Figure 1) contains all the components necessary to successfully complete laboratory assignments. In particular, the Cockpit includes two main parts: the *experimentation console* and the *Laboratory Journal*. The Cockpit also includes a *navigation bar* from which the students can launch useful functionalities in other browser windows, such as an experimental protocol, which describes the procedures necessary to perform the laboratory assignment.

The experimentation console can be regarded as the interactive part of the environment. It enables the actual realization of experiments. The interactions that can be sustained are mainly in the form of changes that the students can make to parameters or algorithms that effect actuations on the physical or virtual piece of equipment.

The laboratory journal is the collaborative part of the environment. It permits documenting and reporting the observations and results, and it facilitates the key activities of *knowledge integration and knowledge sharing*. The laboratory journal has been designed as an extended electronic version of the traditional notebook used by students to document their laboratory work.

The laboratory journal belongs to a group (restricted access to the group members), but at any time the group can decide to make the journal visible for the teaching staff

---

[1] The term teaching here is being used to describe either the explanations given by tutors or feedback provided during the evaluation process.

in order to get feedbacks. For this purpose, the assistant can annotate the different paragraphs of the journal. There is a journal edited for each Web-based experimentation module. A module typically corresponds to a non-consecutive 2 hours hands-on learning session.

2.2 Initial Validation of the Environment

Since October 2001, EPFL students have used a prototype of the Cockpit environment, including a basic laboratory journal, for their practical work in mechatronics. The first validation was conduced with a group of 28 volunteer students (working in pairs). They had to realize three experimental modules in mechatronics for the modeling and digital control of an electrical drive (Figure 1).

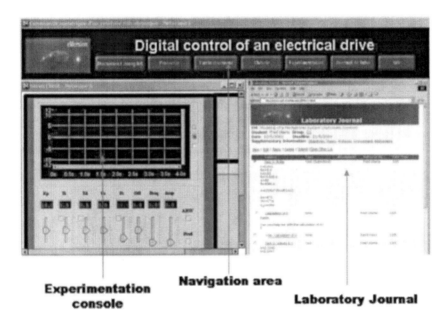

Fig. 1. Example of a Cockpit environment for Web-based experimentation in automatic control.

The progress of the experiment occurred as follow: (i) Students where asked to answer some preliminary questions listed in the protocol window (Figure 2). They answered it by editing paragraphs or attaching documents (example: script file) in their laboratory journal. When this work was finished, the students marked it visible to the assigned assistant. (ii) These questions were corrected and annotated by the assistants in the laboratory journal. (iii) Then they were authorized to perform the practical part of the experiment module using the experimentation console of the Cockpit. Then they were authorized to perform the practical part of the experiment module using the experimental console of the Cockpit.

1. Write a Matlab™ script that realizes the identification of A and τ coefficients according to the least square method.
2. Give the numerical values of A and τ coefficients obtained using your script and corresponding to the provided sample data.
3. Draw the measures and the theoretical values obtained with the coefficients determined under number 2.
4. Determine using an analytic method the "a priori" command to be imposed if the reference speed Ω_c is 60 [rad/s].

Fig. 2. Example of preliminary questions of the protocol

The volunteers have been observed and interviewed by pedagogues to measure their reaction while they were working with such an environment. Most of them have asked for more feedback during the experimental activities and the journal editing. In the implemented flexible setting, providing the students with synchronous feedback would require for this task an assistant dedicated 24 hours a day. Thus the only way to give such feedback is to implement some automatic response features. This is done by the introduction of the VA as described in the next section. The evaluation of a laboratory journal is a very complex task strongly related to the semantic, which has nothing to do with the automatic evaluation of a quiz for example. The main consequence is that the VA can't send all the necessary feedback, but only part of it. So the VA actions are combined with the *Real Assistant* and *Real Instructor* actions.

3   The Virtual Assistant

3.1   Functionalities

In this section we introduce a *Virtual Assistant* (VA) using parts of an *Intelligent Tutoring System* (ITS). This VA is designed to give regular feedback on the structure of the laboratory journal produced by students and also on the semantics of the results and analysis. The typical role assignation is the following: (i) Structural feedback and partial semantic feedback are provided by the VA; (ii) Detailed semantic feedback is under the responsibility of the RA; (iii) Final evaluation and appreciation are handled by the Instructor.

Each laboratory journal, corresponding to an experiment, produced by a group of students goes through a life cycle, which includes interventions of the VA, the RA and the Instructor at determined steps (Figure 3). The document produced evolves from a version 1 to a version N, until it becomes stable with respect to the evaluation and feedback given by the VA, RA and the Instructor.

3.2   Initialization

When the group connects to the system for the first time, it is asked to fill a questionnaire to determine the profile of the group. Each group is assigned to a student model, which is used by the VA to customize its action. The student model is made up of two parts: (i) The cognitive part: an overlay of the capabilities of the group compared to the capabilities in the curriculum (expert knowledge); (ii) The affective part: concerning several parameters such as attention, rapidity, motivation, and confidence.

The initialization of the student model is mainly concerned by the following criteria: (i) *Personal information*: names, ages, addresses; (ii) *Initial background*: self confidence about the subject matter to be taught; (iii) *Affective state*: interaction, preferences for graphics, sound, video or texts, motivation, rapidity, need of support; (iv) *Other parameters* are not initialized until the end of the learning session, where the Instructor, the RA and the VA can provide the information.

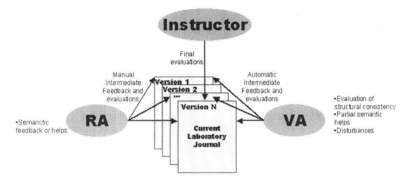

Fig. 3. The different type of feedback in the editing process of the laboratory journal.

3.3   Structural Consistency

The laboratory journal produced by the group has to be valid with respect to a predefined structure. The aim of this structure is to ensure that students will produce organized and structured documents. It is not too restrictive for students to produce such documents because they have several degrees of freedom in editing the laboratory journal. They just have to respect some rules. To reach this goal we use XML technology, which allows high document structuring. We define a DTD (Document Type Definition) that defines the document class "laboratory journal" (Figure 4).

According to the DTD each laboratory journal is composed of a mandatory introduction, and can have 1 to N recursive sections. Finally a conclusion is required. Each section is composed of a mandatory title and a list of paragraphs. The paragraphs contain any type of elements: text, images formulas, links, and attached files. The student assigns a predefined type relevant to the content. The different paragraph types are: theory, configuration, measurement, observation, and analysis.

The structural consistency is checked with two criteria analysis: (i) the consistency of the document (in XML) with the DTD of the laboratory journal. (ii) The consistency with a list of constraints.

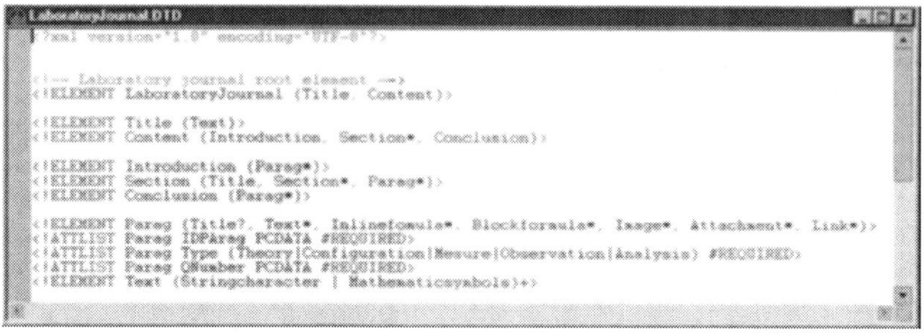

Fig. 4. DTD fragment (document Type Definition) of the laboratory journal.

We can sum up the different constraints as follow:
1. Several following paragraphs of the same type are possible,
2. A "configuration" type paragraph is followed by a paragraph of the same type or a "measurement" type,
3. A "measurement" type paragraph is followed by a paragraph of the same type or a "observation" type, or a "analysis" type,
4. A "observation" type paragraph is followed by a paragraph of the same type or a "analysis" type,
5. In a laboratory journal there is at least one instance of "configuration", "measurement" and "analysis" types.

We can see bellow (Figure 5) three sample structures of documents, answering the first two questions of the protocol given in Figure 2. They represent the same content, but the last one doesn't respect the DTD and the constraints. It has no conclusion and it doesn't respect the fourth constraint.

Experiment 1	The electrical drive in opened loop	The electrical drive in opened loop
1. Introduction		
2. Theory reminders	1. Introduction	1. Introduction
3. Experimental results	2. Identification of parameters A and T.	2. Experimental results 2.1 Response in speed
3.1 Response in speed	2.1 Calculation of numerical value	2.2 Static gain
3.2 Static gain	2.2 Theory graphs	3. Configuration and analysis
4. Observations and analysis	3. Step response in speed	3.1 Configuration on the measurements of the response in speed
4.1 Response in speed	3.1 Measurements 3.2 Analysis	3.2 Analysis of the response in speed
4.2 Time constant	4. Static gain 4.1 Measurements 4.2 Analysis	3.3 Analysis of the static gain
5. Conclusion	5. Conclusions	
Well-structured document	Well-structured document	Ill structured document

Fig. 5. Example of well-structured and ill-structured documents.

The group submits the laboratory journal to the VA who is in charge of checking the structural consistency. By enabling structural consistency check by the VA, we ensure that the students strengthen their scientific approach and make it more rigorous.

3.4 Semantic Consistency

There are two ways to ensure semantic consistency: an automatic one provided by the VA and a manual one by the RA (see section 4). In this section we focus on the semantic feedback given by the VA. It is called *partial semantic feedback*, in contrast with the feedback given by the RA, which is a more detailed semantic feedback.

There are three kinds of feedback elements given by the VA: evaluation, disturbances and hints. Disturbances are questions that are intended to test the confidence of the students about their work. Hints are documents (text, graphs, formulas, etc.) related to a particular question of the experimental protocol that help students find by themselves possible errors or problems. Disturbances and hints have been predefined and stored in a disturbance and hints databases respectively by the authors (professor, assistants). The authors may associate one or more disturbances to some learning concepts. When the VA is considering these concepts it chooses from the database the most suitable one. However, the group can ask anytime to receive a disturbance. Doing so, he can challenge or test his self-confidence with regard to the subject. When a hint is sent it is stored in a hint box that the group is free to consult or not.

Each time a group creates a new paragraph in the laboratory journal, this paragraph is identified by the paragraph type (theory, measurement, etc.) and with the question of the experimental protocol (defined by the authors in the Cockpit) it is connected with. So the VA can find which disturbance or hint in the databases correspond to it.

3.5 Profile Update

During the work session the profile is updated with 3 different processes:
- During the working process the VA checks different actions and updates the profile with the collected information. The parameters set this way in the profile are different from the ones set by the questionnaire.
- When the work on a laboratory journal is finished there is a final evaluation by the Instructor, which is taken into account to update the profile.
- The group can update its profile at any time. Especially when it estimates it has changed its working organization, its learning strategy. Of course it cannot access the elements updated by the VA, the RA and by the Instructor.

4 Implementation

4.1 Architecture of the System

The three different actors (VA, RA, Instructor) perform different actions such as initialization of the profile, feedback on the structure and on the semantic of the laboratory journal, profile update, and final evaluation. This tutoring scheme is represented in Figure 6 to illustrate the actors, their tasks and interactions and described with the following pseudo algorithm.

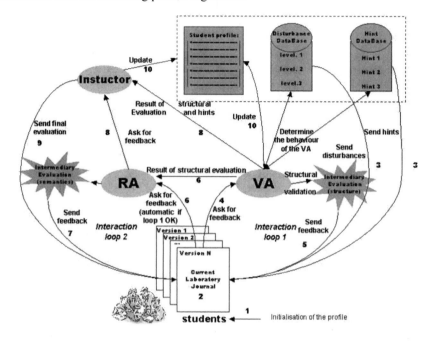

Fig. 6. Intervention of the VA, RA and Instructor in the life cycle of a laboratory journal.

1. When the group log on for the first time it has to fill a questionnaire to initialize the profile. With the result of this questionnaire the VA assign the group to a "student model".
2. Edition of the current version of the laboratory journal.
3. The VA sends some hints (partial semantic feedback) and/or disturbances (taken in the databases), for the selected paragraph, according to the student model. The consultation of the hints is optional (the hints are stored in a hint box that the group is free to consult or not). The consultation of the disturbance is required (they are automatically displayed in a pop up window). *Remark*: At any time the group can also ask the VA for feedback on the current paragraph.
4. The group asks the VA for a feedback on its current version of the report.
5. The VA checks the structural consistency and can also send some new hints and disturbances to the group. If the structure is correct go to step 6, else go back to step 2 for a new version of the journal.
6. (i) The laboratory journal is automatically sent to the RA. (ii) The VA sends the results of the structural evaluation (number of errors before a correct version, number of times where the same error is detected, number of versions, etc.) and the use of hints (number of hints used or asked), but also some other available information. *Remark*: The group has also the freedom to send its report and ask for feedback from the RA when it wants during steps 2 to 5.

7. The RA sends a semantic feedback (detailed semantic feedback) to the group. It also sends a general appreciation on the quality of the report. If the appreciation is correct go to step 8 else go back to step 2.
8. The VA sends to the Instructor the final version of the report plus a summary of the evaluation.
9. The Instructor sends to the group the final evaluation (mark).
10. Information collected by the VA and the result of the final evaluation are used to update the profile.

4.2 Example of Deployment

Let us consider as an example the completion of the prelab assignment. In an early stage, the group of students may have just answered questions 1 and 2 (Figure 2). Thus, there is still not enough material to perform a structural consistency check. However, the students are already looking for feedback at that point to make sure they have taken the right direction. Moreover, the results of question 2 are necessary to succeed to question 3. The fact that they have been requested to write code to perform calculation on a sample data set is helpful in order to enable the virtual assistant to provide semantic consistency feedback. The virtual assistant can run the proposed code and first check whether it is free of bugs. If not, error messages can be returned with an explanatory hint. If the code is running smoothly, the concordance of the computed numerical values can by checked against the expected answers.

By having the virtual assistant handling the semantic consistency evaluation in an automatic way, it is now possible to produce different sample data set customized for each group of students. This enables to have a more personalized and efficient learning. It also helps in detecting early mistakes that may have induced further misinterpretation or motivation decrease if not detected soon enough by the students.

5 Concluding Remarks

The main goal of our Web-based training environment is to strengthen the knowledge acquisition. A first step has already been experimented by reintroducing hands-on experimentation in the curriculum of engineering students by means of a Web-based environment.

Students also need to benefit from a tutoring system, which is able to provide the necessary feedback while they are carrying out their experiments. A Virtual Assistant (VA) provides this feedback automatically or on request in case of:

- hints, they allow the group to realize what were its errors. In that way we support knowledge acquisition with an auto-evaluation process.
- disturbances, they allow the group to strengthen its knowledge and its self-confidence with regard to the domain.
- evaluations of the journal structure, they force the group to think of the best way to present its results and personal analysis.

As we can see the VA combines different types of feedback and help that have different impact in the knowledge acquisition process improving the "learning by doing approach".

The benefit of the Virtual assistant is to give more freedom and less constraints to the students seeking for feedback. In addition, the presence of a Virtual Assistant sustains the development of autonomy by being more independent of the tight protocols usually needed in a distance-learning framework.

References

1. Aïmeur, E., Frasson, C., *Analysing a New Learning Strategy According to Different Knowledge Levels*, Computer and Education, An International Journal , vol 27, no 2, pp. 115-127, 1996.
2. Aïmeur E., Frasson C., Dufort H., *Co-operative Learning Strategies for Intelligent Tutoring Systems*, Applied Artificial Intelligence. An International Journal, Vol 14(5), pp. 465-490, 2000.
3. Brusilovsky P., Eklund J., Schwartz E., *Web-based education for all: A tool for developing adaptive courseware*. Computer Networks and ISDN Systems. 30, 1-7, pp. 291-300, 1998.
4. Brusilovsky P., Schwartz E., Weber G., *ELM-ART: An Intelligent tutoring system on World Wide Web*. ITS'96 Conference, Third International Conference on Intelligent Tutoring Systems. Lecture Notes in Computer Sciences, no 1086, Frasson C., Gauthier G., Lesgold A. Editors, Springer Verlag, Montréal, pp. 261-269, 1996.
5. Callear D., *Intelligent tutoring environment as teacher substitutes: Use and feasibility*, Educational technology journal, September - October 1999, pp.6-8, 1999
6. Eliot C.R., Woolf B., *Reasoning about the user within a simulation-based-real time training system*, Fourth International Conference on User Modeling, Hyannis Cape Cod, Mass, pp. 15-19 August, 1994.
7. Gillet D., Salzmann C., Latchman H.A., and Crisalle O.D., *Advances in Remote Experimentation*, 19th American Control Conference, Chicago, Illinois, USA, pp. 2955-2956, 2000
8. Gillet D., Fakas G., *eMersion: A new paradigm for Web-based training in engineering education*, International Conference on Engineering Education, pp. 8B4-10 - 8B4-14, Oslo, 2001.
9. Jong T., Joolingen W.T., King S., *The authoring Environment SimQuest and the need for author support. Supporting authors in the design of simulation-based- discovery environment*. Servive project deliverable D 8.1. Enschede, University of Twente, 1997.
10. Suthers D., and Jones D., *An architecture for Intelligent Collaborative Educational Systems, AI-Ed 97,* World Conference on Artificial Intelligence and Education, Japan, pp. 55-62, 1997.
11. Veermans K., and Van Joolingen W.R., *Using Induction to generate Feedback in Simulation Based Discovery Learning Environment*, ITS-98, Fourth International Conference on Intelligent Tutoring Systems, Lecture Notes in Computer Sciences, no. 1452, Goettl B.P., Halff H.M., Redfield C.L., Shute V.J. Editors, Springer Verlag, San Antonio, Texas, pp. 196-205, 1998.

Web-Based ITS for Training System Managers on the Computer Intrusion

Chong-woo Woo[1], Jin-woo Choi[1], and Martha Evens[2]

[1] School of Computer Science, Kookmin University, Seoul, Korea
[2] Department of Computer Science, Illinois Institute of Technology, Chicago, IL
cwwoo@kookmin.ac.kr, evens@iit.edu

Abstract. Recently, unauthorized computer access has become becomes a big social problem. Of course, there are many commercial solutions for protecting systems against the intruder. But mostly we tend to rely on the system manager's field experience for maintaining the system. Therefore, the manager needs to keep up with the existing knowledge, along with any new threats. In the research described here, we have designed and implemented a simulated training environment to combat computer intrusions. The system begins with a menu outlining a curriculum focused on UNIX security, which is generated from the knowledge base dynamically. The selected topic (a goal) from the curriculum is then expanded into several missions (subgoals). The student can complete each mission by entering a sequence of UNIX commands that together provide an appropriate solution to the problem at hand. Since the system keeps track of the solution paths, the student's problem solving steps can easily be monitored and interrupted with appropriate hints, as needed. The tutor is designed as a client/server system, so the student needs only a web browser to access the system. Moreover, the student can manipulate the tasks in this virtual OS environment, according to the learning scenario.

1 Introduction

The rapid development of computer communication networks has brought many benefits to our society, but this new technology has brought with it some serious side effects, especially the tremendous increase in malicious computer intrusions. The Intrusion Detection System (IDS) serves a useful purpose in this environment [6][9], and being further studied with various issues, such as an intelligent agent [2]. The recent IDS detect the intrusion only. So that when the IDS signals an intrusion alert, the system manager of the attacked system needs to take care of all the operations including the recovery or re-installation of the damaged parts of the system. We tend to rely mostly on the system manager's field experience in this recovery process, but recovery from attack is not easy to perform since this is not an everyday situation. So the manager needs to keep up with the existing knowledge, along with any new threats

S.A. Cerri, G. Gouardères, and F. Paraguaçu (Eds.): ITS 2002, LNCS 2363, pp. 311–319, 2002.

that arise. Therefore, there is a strong need to emphasize education about security mechanisms and to provide a simulation program to train system managers.

Recent research on security education for system managers includes the ID-Tutor [8]. This system creates an audit file using a planning methodology, and the student can simulate the system, and get tutored on weaknesses based on the tutoring rules. The system provides a good framework for security education, since the simulation can give more comprehensive insights for understanding the underlying mechanisms [7][10]. But the ID-tutor has some limitations. For example, the student cannot enter the answer directly since the system runs in a menu environment. In real world, the UNIX environment needs to type in commands, which is another practice. Second, the system simulates intrusion according to the generated audit data, so that the student can practice diverse intrusion case. But this case study cannot cover the entire UNIX security issues. So, we need to have a solid curriculum to train the student. Third, since the system is designed by the case study, it does not analyze the student's entire performance, or it does not diagnose the student's weakness on some specific issue. Rather it focuses on providing hints based only the student's individual actions.

In this paper, we describe a security simulation system designed to train system managers to combat computer intrusions. We have selected UNIX security problems as the test domain. Since UNIX security topics are too diverse to implement with a single tutoring system, we have limited the curriculum scope to 'vulnerability' issue. We selected this issue since vulnerability is one of the most important areas that system managers need to check every day; they also need to learn the step-by-step procedures carefully [4]. The main focus is the creation of a virtual learning environment and intelligent tutoring based on the student's performance. We are aiming to build a web-based Intelligent Tutoring System (ITS)[1][3], so we have adapted a standard ITS architecture. And since this architecture is based on the client/server model, the student needs only a web browser to access and carry out the tasks following the learning scenario.

2 System Overview

The system managers need to be trained with various security topics. In this system, we have designed a simulated tutoring system to teach the system managers on the 'vulnerability' issue of the UNIX system. The system is not based on the real intrusion data rather we have focused on building a tutoring system with a regular curriculum. Therefore, the system begins by suggesting a curriculum, which is generated from the knowledge base dynamically. The student can select any one of these topics freely, since the order is not so important. If the student selects a topic, then this is further expanded into several missions. And then each mission can be carried out by the student by entering a sequence of the UNIX commands. When the student finishes one topic, then the student can proceed to the next by selecting one from the curriculum. Since the system maintains the solution paths, the student's problem solving steps are monitored, and are interrupted with appropriate hint messages when the student misses some steps or asks for a hint. The architecture of the system is based on a standard ITS structure, including the expert module, the student module, and the tutoring module as shown in Figure 1. We will first describe basic components of the system, and then explain how to generate learning material for the student dynamically

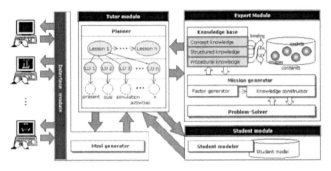

Fig. 1. The Overall Architecture of the System

2.1 ITS Structure

The Expert. The expert module consists of a domain knowledge base, a problem solver, and a mission generator. The domain knowledge base is designed using an object-oriented structure, and includes the concept knowledge required in explanations requested by the student, procedural knowledge to check the student's progress and give hints when necessary, and some other objects, such as image objects and applet objects to combine with the text knowledge. The mission generator collects the necessary objects, such as the applets and some related knowledge, and combines them together to generate a simulation exercise. The problem solver provides appropriate feedback after analyzing the student's performance during the simulation.

The Tutor. The tutor is basically in charge of planning the entire lesson contents. In this system, the tutor provides a curriculum first, and then based on the student's selection, the tutor generates a lesson plan, alternating concept explanation, step-by-step practice, and simulation. The concepts include basic security definitions, usage of UNIX commands, etc. The tutor also provides a simple problem as a quiz, and finally asks the student to solve a simulation exercise. The system control is basically mixed-initiative: at the beginning of the lesson, the student can select the scenario on the given menu, or the student can ask the system to suggest a topic. In both cases, the tutor plans a lesson on the selected topic dynamically.

The Student Model. For the current version of our system, we have implemented the student model in the minimal, which records the student's performance on the given quiz. This model will be expanded by including the 'number of hint or help asked by the student', 'result of solving quiz', and 'time spent for completing the simulation' for the next version of the system. This model is designed in overlay method, and it needs to be studied further, including the issues on the adaptive presentation.

2.2 The Learning Environment

For the simulation, we have built a virtual learning environment in the form of a Java applet. Within this virtual OS, the student can practice the security exercise. Unlike the ID-tutor, which runs on the menu only, we have made the system interactive. This approach has several advantages:

– First, the student can actually simulate the given exercise by typing a sequence of UNIX commands into the applet, and the command is actually executed in the simulation. The student can perform UNIX commands, such as **ls** or **cd**, and observe the results in our telnet-like environment. For example, if the student's command is **mkdir temp**, then directory **temp** is created, by extending the simulation knowledge base. This feature is designed by using 'S-expressions', similar to the fundamental structures used in LISP. The S-expressions can be extended or manipulated easily using this knowledge structure. This is important since we do not actually create the physical directory in the system, rather we get the same effect by just extending the knowledge structure. So we have provided an S-expression interpreter, which is similar to a LISP interpreter. In order to allow this expression, we prepare LISP-like templates, and provide the same environment to the student. In Figure 2, the directory permission belongs to the 'root'; it is fixed in the beginning. The $username is bound to the user login ID.

– Second, when the simulation applet is sent to the student, the other necessary information (or knowledge) will be sent also. For example, for the 'password checker' mission, the 'password cracker' explanation will also be sent together with the applet.

– Third, the knowledge base is designed in terms of S-expressions, which allows easy manipulation for the simulation process. In other words, the virtual OS is expressed as a string. Since this is a string, it does not need to be executed on the Server side. Therefore, the simulation does not affect the actual file system, so that the system memory is not physically occupied. Actually, the real 'telnet' application uses the network resource and the memory space. Also, the student's commands do not execute the actual system processes, which help avoid overloading the system.

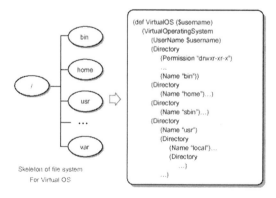

Fig. 2. The Structure of the Virtual OS

3 Mission-Based Simulation

The security exercise described in this paper is the 'vulnerability' issue. The 'vulner-ability' will be further classified into several categories, and each of them will be accomplished by performing a few tasks. In Figure 3, a selected single topic (a lesson goal) is further expanded into a few detailed sub-tasks (sub-goals). This procedure can be explained as follows. First, the system proposes a curriculum in which each item is a kind of vulnerability, such as 'password vulnerability' or 'student environment vul-nerability'. We consider each topic on this curriculum as a lesson goal or a scenario. If the student selects one item in the curriculum, then the selected one will be expanded into several sub-tasks. For example, the 'password vulnerability' topic will be accom-plished by performing the 'password checker, system booting checker, and password file checker' in sequence. We treat this sequence of sub-tasks as a lesson plan, and consider each sub-task as a subgoal or a mission. Each mission can be carried out, by performing some pre-defined UNIX commands. When the student finishes all the missions, then the selected topic is completed, and the student can proceed with an-other topic.

Fig. 3. Virtual Scenario for the system 'vulnerability' System

3.1 Mission Generator

The Mission Generator collects necessary knowledge from the knowledge base for the selected mission. It consists of three parts: the Initializer, the Fact Generator, and the Knowledge Constructor as shown in Figure 4.

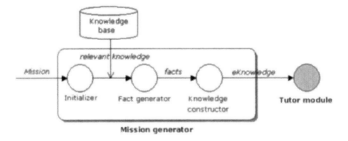

Fig. 4. Mission Generator.

In Figure 4, the ***Initializer*** initializes java objects for the selected mission, and collects necessary knowledge from the knowledge base. The ***Fact Generator*** creates some 'facts' according to the given mission. For example, if the given mission is the 'password checker', then the 'facts' to be created are the '(student ID, Password)'. Different versions of this pair will be provided to different users. The ***Knowledge Constructor*** organizes the 'facts' acquired from the 'fact generator', and sends the package to the planner in the form of an S-expression to be used in the simulation. Figure 5 shows this process in detail. The numbered process can be explained as follows.

1   Selected mission, "password checker" is received by the mission generator
2   Mission generator initializes/collects mission knowledge from knowledge base
3   Interprets the knowledge
4   Requests the result of the interpretation in sequence from the Fact Generator
5   Fact Generator loads the requested objects and returns the result
6   Repeat steps 4 and 5 for each user.
7   Collects the procedural knowledge
8   Sends the extended knowledge to the Knowledge Constructor
9   Knowledge Constructor builds an S-expression structure

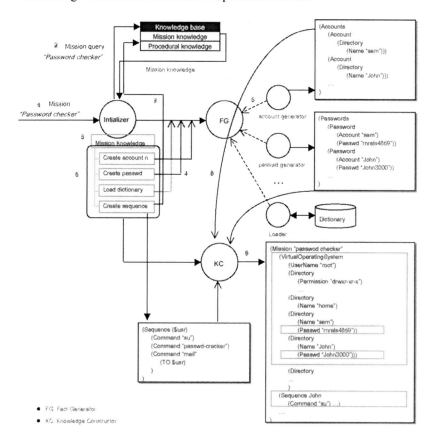

Fig. 5. Internal Processing in the Mission Generator

3.2 Evaluation of the Simulation

When the mission is selected, the system generates the correct answer as a sequence of UNIX commands, such as, 'su, passwd-cracker, and mail' as shown in Figure 6. Then the student's response is received and re-organized by retracing only the UNIX commands. The student modeler compares the revised student's answer with the system generated one. Then, the tutor receives the final result from the modeler, and replies to the student with appropriate acknowledgements. Also, the generated correct sequence by the system can be used as a basis for providing help when the student gets in trouble during the problem solving.

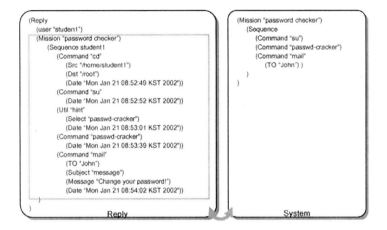

Fig. 6. Mission *"Password checker"*

3.3 User Interface

The user can interact with the system through the web-browser. On the top, the system shows a menu consists of 'directory, mission, view, window, and help'. The 'Directory' menu shows the virtual OS as a tree structure. The result appears in the upper left window, and the current user's location inside of the directory is indicated in a different color. This feature could help the user understand where am I. For example, in Figure 7, the 'John' in the directory is colored, which means that the user is in that location. The 'Mission' menu shows brief explanations about the mission to perform. This action shows in the middle window. And the student can enter UNIX commands directly in this window, and get an immediate response. The output is designed to look like UNIX 'telnet' output in order to make the simulation environment seem real to the user. When the lesson has been completed, the student can push the 'done' button. The 'View' menu displays information about the currently open windows. The 'Window' menu organizes the opened windows in vertical or horizontal locations. Finally, the 'Help' menu gives help messages about the simulation procedure.

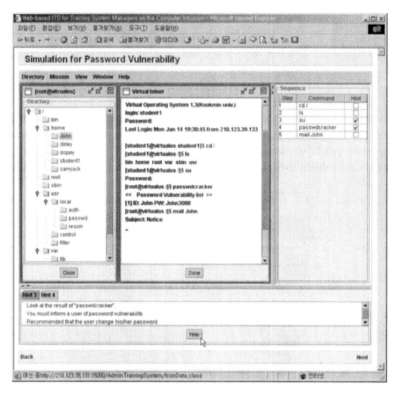

Fig. 7. The Simulation Provided given by System (mission "password checker")

3.4   Hint Generation

During the problem solving process the student should have a chance to ask for a hint or help, occasionally. The hints may take various forms [5]. In our system, the hint comes in two different forms. First, the upper right window of Figure 7 records the student's performance, and the student can ask for hints at each step by clicking on the 'check-box' next to the command lists. Then the generated hint message appears in the bottom window. When the student asks for a hint, which is related to the commands in the 'check-box', the hint request get assigned a number. And the 'hint number' also appears in the bottom Hint window, and the student can toggle between the multiple hint messages. A second source of hints is the 'help' button in this same window. For example, in Hint 4 the message says 'inform the user about password security'. But the student does not know whom to inform, and so asks for help. In that case, the system indicates that the user is 'John' by blinking the directory folder.

4   Conclusion

We have designed and implemented a security simulation system intended to train system managers to combat computer intrusion. The system begins by providing a curriculum for UNIX security issues that is generated from the knowledge base dynamically, and the student learns about these issues by solving security problems in a realistic simulated environment.

This system embodies several significant advances. First, the student can actually interact with the system by typing in UNIX commands; this is a step beyond the IDtutor where the student just can select one of the commands from the menu. Second, since the computer security consists of diverse topics, our system is designed by providing the student a global lesson contents as a curriculum. Third, the system keeps track of all solution paths, which are used to monitor the student's problem solving steps and to provide hints when they are needed. Fourth, the system is designed using a client/server model, so the student needs only a web browser to access the system, and it is built as an applet, so the student can manipulate the tasks in this virtual OS following the learning scenario.

We have not done any evaluation on this version of the system yet, since the system is still under development, and we are starting to expand the system to cover the rest of the issues. Also we are planning to enhance the student model including more detailed student's learning performance, and to include more adaptive tutoring strategy.

References

1. Alpert, S., Singley, K., and Fairweather, P.: Porting a Standalone Intelligent Tutoring System on the Web. Proceedings of ITS'2000 workshop (2000) 1-11.
2. Balasubramaniyan, S., Garcia-Fernandez, O., Isacoff, D., Spafford, E., and Zamboni, D.: An Architecture for Intrusion Detection using Autonomous Agents. Technical Report 98-05, COAST Laboratory, Purdue University, West Lafayette, In 47907-1398 (1998).
3. Brusilovsky, P., Eklund, J., and Schwarz, E.: Web-based education for all: A tool for developing adaptive courseware. The Proceedings of the 7th WWW conference (1998) 291-300.
4. Farmer, D., and Spafford, E. H.: The COPS Security Checker System. In Proceedings of the Summer USENIX Conference (1990) 165-170.
5. Hume, G., Michael, J., Rovick, A., and Evens, M.: Hinting as a tactic in one-on-one tutoring. The Journal of Learning Sciences, 5(1) (1996) 23-47.
6. Kumar, S.: Classification and Detection of Computer Intrusions. PhD thesis, Purdue University (1995)
7. Reddy, Y., Fox, M., Hussain, N., and McRoberts, M.: The Knowledge-based Simulation System. IEEE Software, Vol 3. No.2 (1986) 26-37.
8. Rowe, N. C. and Schiavo, S.: An Intelligent Tutor for Intrusion Detection on Computer Systems. Computers and Education (1998) 395-404.
9. Sebring, M., Shellhouse, E., Hanna, M. and Whitehurst, R.: Expert Systems in Intrusion Detection: A Case Study. Proceedings of the 11th National Computer Security Conference (1988) 74-81.
10. Shannon, R. E.: Introduction to Simulation. Proceedings of the 1992 Winter Simulation Conference (1992) 65-73.

A La Recherche du Temps Perdu, or As Time Goes By: Where Does the Time Go in a Reading Tutor That Listens?

Jack Mostow, Greg Aist[1], Joseph Beck, Raghuvee Chalasani, Andrew Cuneo, Peng Jia, and Krishna Kadaru

Project LISTEN[2], Carnegie Mellon University
RI-NSH 4213, 5000 Forbes Avenue, Pittsburgh, PA 15213-3890
mostow@cs.cmu.edu
http://www.cs.cmu.edu/~listen

Abstract. Analyzing the time allocation of students' activities in a school-deployed mixed initiative tutor can be illuminating but surprisingly tricky. We discuss some complementary methods that we have used to understand how tutoring time is spent, such as analyzing sample videotaped sessions by hand, and querying a database generated from session logs. We identify issues, methods, and lessons that may be relevant to other tutors. One theme is that iterative design of "non-tutoring" components can enhance a tutor's effectiveness, not by improved teaching, but by reducing the time wasted on non-learning activities. Another is that it is possible to relate student's time allocation to improvements in various outcome measures.

1 Introduction

The title of Marcel Proust's magnum opus (English translation: "In Pursuit of Lost Time") aptly expresses what this paper is about: Where does time really go when students use intelligent tutors? And how can we tell? We address both questions based on our experience with successive versions of Project LISTEN's automated Reading Tutor, which listens to children read aloud, and helps them learn to read [1].

The question of where time goes is obviously important because the effectiveness of tutorial interaction depends on how time is allocated. For example, a study of one-on-one literacy tutoring [2] compared more versus less successful tutor-student dyads, and found significant differences in their time allocation among different activities.

---

[1] Now at RIACS, NASA Ames Research Center, Moffett Field, California.

[2] This work was supported in part by the National Science Foundation under Grant No. REC-9979894. Any opinions, findings, conclusions, or recommendations expressed in this publication are those of the authors and do not necessarily reflect the views of the National Science Foundation or the official policies, either expressed or implied, of the sponsors or of the United States Government. We thank other members of Project LISTEN who contributed to this work, especially Al Corbett and Susan Eitelman for discussion of their video analysis; mySQL's developers; and the students and educators at the schools where the Reading Tutor records data.

S.A. Cerri, G. Gouardères, and F. Paraguaçu (Eds.): ITS 2002, LNCS 2363, pp. 320–329, 2002.

Within the intelligent tutoring community, analysis of time allocation showed that Stat Lady spent much longer than necessary on remediation [5]. Followup work [6] estimated the potential reduction in tutoring time from various modifications.

In human tutoring, the tutor can control where time is spent. But when a student uses educational software, the student controls time to a greater extent – not necessarily with educational goals as the top priority. Children have their own agenda when using software, which may or may not match the desired educational outcome. As Hanna et al. [7] said, "When analyzing usage by children, we look at the goals of the product and the goals of children. The goal of the product may be to teach the alphabet, but children will probably not play with the product because they want to learn the alphabet. A child's goal may be to explore and find out what happens or to win a game" For example, children spend much of the time in "edutainment" software playing with on-screen animations [8], clicking on them a considerable amount [9]. The Reading Tutor's goal is to help students learn to read. A student's goal may be reading a particular story, writing a story, exploring the story menus, or something else.

Ideally a session on any intelligent tutor would be devoted almost entirely to educational useful activities, with a minimum of wasted time. But in reality, considerable time may be spent non-productively, whether from confusion or on purpose. What actually happens? More precisely, we want to know:

1. *What typically happened?* On average, where did time go? This question is important in identifying bottlenecks.

2. *How did students differ?* For example, did a few of the students waste most of their time? That is, where are the loopholes or escape routes that let students spend time on the tutor without useful learning?

3. *How did differences affect outcomes?* Where did high- and low-gain students differ? That is, how do different allocations of time influence – or at least reflect – what is learned by students?

4. *Did students fall into a few types?* What were the principal components of variation? Were there clusters? That is, what types of students are there? How can we identify them? To what extent do their differing profiles explain or predict what and how they learn?

This paper looks at #1 and #2, and begins to address #3, in the context of Project LISTEN's Reading Tutor.

2 Project LISTEN's Reading Tutor

Project LISTEN's Reading Tutor is shown in and described in detail elsewhere [1]. Here we summarize the aspects relevant to this paper.

Children have used the Reading Tutor at schools since 1996. A session on the Reading Tutor operates as follows. The Reading Tutor runs on dedicated PCs configured to automatically reboot themselves and launch the Reading Tutor every morning. Launching takes a minute or two, so the Reading Tutor is normally left running. First the student logs in to the Reading Tutor by clicking a *Hello* icon, selecting her name from a menu, selecting her birth month from another menu, and reading her name aloud to make sure the Reading Tutor can hear spoken input.

A new student receives an automated tutorial on how to operate the Reading Tutor. Next it's time to pick an activity, such as a story to read or write. The 2001 Reading Tutor takes turns with the student picking activities. It picks (or encourages the student to pick) stories at a recommended reading level, which it adjusts based on the student's performance. talking menu (see 1-click picker in Fig. 1c lists stories to pick and provides access to more stories at the same level, and to other story levels.

The student then performs the activity with the assistance of the Reading Tutor. The Reading Tutor may insert a preview before the activity and/or a review after the activity. The activity lasts until the student completes it, clicks *Back* through each sentence or step of the activity to return to story-picking, clicks *Goodbye* to stop using the Reading Tutor, or remains inactive long enough to trigger a timeout.

Controlled comparisons of successive versions of the Reading Tutor have shown significantly higher gains than baseline instruction or independent reading practice in word comprehension [10], reading comprehension [11], and other reading skills. Although these results are encouraging, we believe that the Reading Tutor has the potential to be even more effective. To tap that potential, we first need to analyze where the time goes when children use the Reading Tutor.

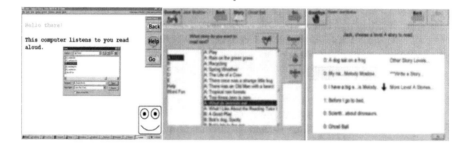

Fig. 1. a. Adult-assisted picker, 1996*; b.* 2-click picker, 1998; **c.** 1-click picker, 1999

3   Analyzing Time Allocation

Determining how students spend time on a tutor is difficult for several reasons:
- Multimodal dialogue is rich, and students' speech data are especially messy.
- Student behavior varies among students, and may be affected by observation.
- The tutor itself may change, both in how it appears to students and how it logs their interactions.
- Logs introduced for other purposes, such as debugging, may not be conducive to analysis.
- Anomalies, rare events, software crashes, and missing data can distort results of automated analysis methods that lack common sense.

To answer questions about time allocation in the Reading Tutor, we have therefore combined various complementary analysis methods, including live observation, anecdotal reports, video analysis, manual inspection of sample data captured by the tutor, and automated analysis of tutor-recorded event logs.

Our automated methods started with special-purpose perl scripts to parse this data to answer specific questions. More recently, we have parsed logged data from 2000-2001 into a database on which we can run SQL queries to answer a broader class of questions. It takes considerable time to parse and import into our database an entire year's worth of data down to the millisecond level, so we are working with a subset of the data for students who used the Reading Tutor for the entire year.

Automated methods permit comprehensive analysis of the copious data from months of daily use by hundreds of children. However, the mappings from actual tutoring to recorded logs to analysis results are too complex to trust on their own. There is no substitute for picking several cases randomly (to ensure a representative sample) and analyzing them by hand (to include common sense).

Because the logs are too detailed to see the forest for the trees, we have also found it important to generate more understandable views at different levels of detail. At first we extended the Reading Tutor to generate such views itself, such as class rosters and student portfolios. Now we use a database to dynamically generate human-readable views in the form of HTML tables at different levels.

We now analyze several aspects of time allocation in various versions of the Reading Tutor, including overhead, delay, mixed initiative, and distribution of time among different functions and interaction types.

4 Session Overhead: Logging In

The Reading Tutor uses login mechanisms to identify and authenticate students so that it can distinguish among them, keep their records straight, and adapt its behavior to the individual student. We have not previously quantified how long login takes. However, we observed in early versions of the Reading Tutor, in a summer lab used by over 60 children, that finding one's name on a long list is a hard task for a small child. More recent versions of the Reading Tutor display only the students who use that particular machine, and read the list aloud. Analysis of data from 2000-2001 shows that login averaged 15 seconds on a machine with 4 readers enrolled.

To reduce the risk of one child reading under another's login, the Reading Tutor times out after 15 seconds of inactivity in case the current reader has gotten up and left, so as to ensure that the next reader logs in as him- or herself. If the same reader is still there, she must log back in, which takes up additional time. How often does this occur? Analysis [11] of 541 sessions in a controlled classroom evaluation of the Spring 1998 Reading Tutor found a total of 1028 "mini-sessions" ("time from login to *Goodbye* or timeout") each lasting an average of 6.2 minutes. The difference between the total session time and the total mini-session time averaged 1.6 minutes. Apparently the average 13.5 minute session in Spring 1998 included a nearly 2-minute hiatus, followed by logging back in. Analysis of the database from 2000-2001 showed that total session length averaged 21 minutes. 38% of sessions included one or more hiatuses, whose duration averaged 1 minute and 21 seconds.

5   Response Time: Waiting for the Reading Tutor

Another source of waste is the time the student spends after processing a stimulus, waiting for the computer to respond. Response delay can eat up an embarrassingly large portion of time on tutor. Delayed response has adverse indirect consequences as well, by causing the student's attention to wander off-task, wasting additional precious seconds before coming back on-task after the tutor responds.

Previous analysis [10] of a sample of 25 sessions videotaped out of 3,833 sessions from the 1999-2000 Reading Tutor revealed that in the course of an average 20-minute session, the student spent over 8 minutes waiting for the Reading Tutor to respond – almost as long as the 9 minutes actually spent reading!

Part of this delay involved several seconds of preparatory computation (especially database accesses) prior to displaying the next sentence to the student. This component of delay was reduced by rewriting code to make it more efficient. Another source of delay involved deliberately waiting for 2 seconds of silence before responding, to ensure that the student was done speaking. This delay was reduced by modifying the Reading Tutor to respond more promptly when it heard the last two words of the sentence (at the cost of barging in prematurely a bit more often).

However, the sample was not large enough to characterize how time spent waiting *varied* among students. Worse, this sample was vulnerable to observer effects due to the presence of the video camera operator, so it was not even guaranteed to be representative of typical sessions. Finally, we wanted to determine whether wait time was still a problem now that we had sped up Reading Tutor response time.

To calculate wait time for the 2000-2001 school year, we used the database generated from log data. Communication between the Reading Tutor and the student is mixed-initiative, so it is difficult to define precisely when a turn ends. If the student finishes reading a sentence, waits for a second, becomes frustrated, rereads the sentence, and waits for a few more seconds, how much of that time should be counted as waiting for the Reading Tutor? The manual analysis used human coders' listening and judgment to distinguish between "processing the stimulus" (that is, reading the displayed sentence) versus "waiting" (such as rereading the sentence when the Reading Tutor didn't respond quickly enough). We decided to estimate wait time as starting when the Reading Tutor accepted the last word of the sentence, and ending when the Reading Tutor displayed the next sentence, or reached the end of the passage. The resulting estimate should provide an upper bound in that it overestimates delay time compared to the videotape analysis.

This estimate indicated that students averaged less than 16% of total session time waiting in stories, and less than 4% waiting in previews and reviews. According to this analysis, wait time per 20-minute session averaged less than half the 8-minute average seen in the 1999-2000 Reading Tutor, according to hand-coded videos. Apparently the changes to reduce wait time had succeeded.

6   Task Choice Overhead: Picking a Story to Read

What about the time it takes to choose a story? Previous work [12] compared the time to pick stories in 3 versions of the Reading Tutor, shown in Fig. 1 To include time spent "browsing," the comparison measured the time to settle on a story as the time from the last sentence of one story to the first sentence of the next story that the student stayed in long enough to proceed to the second sentence.

To estimate story selection time in the 1996 through 1999 versions, 10 transitions were chosen at random and analyzed by hand [3]. This procedure exposed behaviors (e.g. reading the same story twice in a row) and anomalies (e.g. timing out) that a more automated analysis might not have found.

In the 1996 version, children used the Reading Tutor under the individual supervision of a school aide who helped them pick stories using a generic Windows file picker. This process averaged about 3 minutes – a considerable time cost for each story choice, especially given that sessions averaged only 14 minutes in duration [13].

In the 1998 version, children used the Reading Tutor in their regular classrooms. The student clicked on a story title to make the Reading Tutor speak it, and clicked on an *OK* button to pick that story. Including time spent rating the just-completed story as "easy, hard, or just right" and "fun, boring, scary, or silly," this process took about 2 minutes – about as long as it took to actually read the story, according to analysis of log data for the 1931 story readings in all 541 sessions in a spring 1998 study [11]. 1931/541 comes to an average of 3.6 stories per session. So roughly half the average session duration of 13.5 minutes was spent choosing stories!

In the 1999 version, the Reading Tutor recited the menu, and a single click sufficed to pick the story. Moreover, the Reading Tutor took turns picking stories. Videotape analysis showed the time to choose each story averaged only about 30 seconds – significantly shorter (p = .02).

To confirm the reduction in story selection time, we queried the database of logs from the 2000-2001 Reading Tutor, using the same criterion as before, but averaging per student. Student story choice averaged 33 seconds, ranging from 16 seconds for the fastest student to 50 seconds for the slowest. Reading Tutor choice averaged 5 seconds, ranging from 4 seconds for the fastest student to 11 seconds for the slowest.

To summarize, in 1996, story choice took about 3 minutes using a generic file picker. In 1998 it required about 2 minutes using a select-and-confirm picker. In 1999 it required about 30 seconds using a one-click picker. In 2000 it averaged only 19 seconds, based on automated analysis of hundreds of sessions.

7 Time Battles: Equal Time vs. Equal Turns

Did turn taking work as designed? That is, did the Reading Tutor manage to equalize the number of stories chosen by student and tutor? One source of evidence is an "opinion poll" story review activity in the 2000-2001 Reading Tutor that asked the reader to rate the quality, difficulty, and length of the story. Analysis of the poll data showed that of the 4,560 completed story readings represented in the poll, 2,296 were chosen by the student, and 2,264 by the Reading Tutor. Thus the turn taking mechanism successfully achieved 50-50 division in terms of *finishing* stories.

As for time allocation, querying our database showed that students spent 70% of their story time on stories selected by the Reading Tutor and only 30% of their time on stories that they picked. The reason is that students generally picked stories less challenging than the Reading Tutor's selections, and students were likelier to back out of a story the Reading Tutor picked (which did not affect whose turn it was to pick).

8   Where Time Went in the 2000-2001 Reading Tutor

Table 1 summarizes where time went for 34 students whose 2000-2001 data we have parsed so far into the database. To avoid skewing the results toward students who used the Reading Tutor more, we first computed per-student averages, and then averaged across students. "Story" refers to time spent reading stories, writing, listening to the tutor read, and waiting for the tutor to respond. "Pre/Review" is time spent on activities that precede and/or follow a story, such as introducing or practicing new words. "Tutorial" is time spent on three tutorials that train students how to operate the Reading Tutor. "Task choice" is time selecting stories. "Out of tutor" is time spent logging in to the Reading Tutor, and time spent outside of a session because the student logged out, the Reading Tutor timed out due to student inactivity, or the computer crashed.

Table 1. Per-student breakdown of time spent on Reading Tutor

	Mean	Min	Max
Stories	67%	43%	80%
Pre/Review	13%	6%	46%
Tutorial	2%	0%	9%
Task choice	5%	1%	13%
Out of tutor	7%	2%	14%

But what did student and tutor actually do during these educational activities? Anecdotal field reports brought to our attention one student who managed to spend almost all his time on the Reading Tutor "writing" junk stories. How did he defeat the intent of the turn taking mechanism? Quite simply: When it was the Reading Tutor's turn to pick a story, he read the story. The Reading Tutor was picking stories that he read in a couple of minutes – not quite fast enough to get promoted to higher levels. But when it was his turn, he picked a writing activity and then often spent the rest of the session in the story editor. With this student, we were winning the story choice battle, but losing the time on task war. Changing his behavior took a visit by his mother to the lab, after which he followed her orders to read instead of "write."

The Reading Tutor's stories, previews, and reviews are all expressed as sequences of a few types of steps. The most common types are assisted reading and writing, both of which may range from single words to sentences to entire stories. Other types of steps include narrating student-written text, listening to the Reading Tutor read aloud, choosing from a talking menu, and oral spelling. Fig. 2 shows how time spent on stories and pre/reviews was split among these types of steps.

In general, few students spent a significant portion of their time writing. In our database of 34 students, the minimum was 2%, the average was 10%, and the maximum was 43%. Moreover, this analysis includes all writing – not just writing stories, but exercises such as typing in a "trouble word" to review it.

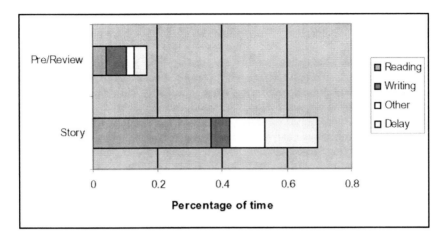

Fig. 2. Where the time went (averaged per student)

9   How Did Time Allocation Relate to Student Gains?

To compute how students' reading abilities improved over the course of a year, we pre- and post-tested specific reading skills using 4 subtests of the Woodcock Reading Mastery Test (WRMT) [14], an individually administered reading test. To control for pretest scores, we computed the gains (i.e. the posttest – pretest score for each student).

We used partial correlations in SPSS to relate students' gains on these tests to the percentages of time they spent reading, writing, in Pre/Review activities, picking stories, or in hiatus between parts of a session. To avoid confounds with initial differences among students, we controlled for student grade and (grade-normed) pretest score. Percentage of time spent on Pre/Review activities correlated positively with gains in word identification (R=.40, p=0.03) and word comprehension (R=.51, p=.004). Percentage of time spent writing correlated negatively with gains in word attack (R=-.36, p=0.05) and word identification (R=-.38, p=0.03).

These results suggest that the Pre/Review activities succeeded in helping students learn new words, since the percentage of time spent on those activities accounted for variance that grade and pretest did not. Time spent "writing" at the expense of reading may have hurt students who needed to improve their word decoding skills. Also, time spent outside of tutoring activities apparently did little harm, since the percentage of time spent picking stories or outside of the Reading Tutor did not correlate negatively with gains. However, we have not proved that time allocation actually *caused* gains; perhaps it only *reflected* gains, or individual differences (such as motivation) that our analysis did not control for.

10   Conclusions

This paper addressed the question of where tutoring time goes, and how to find out. More specifically, how much tutoring time goes to educational activities, as opposed to overhead? How is time spent during those activities? How much time is wasted waiting for the tutor to respond? How is time allocation related to student gains? We addressed each of these questions in the context of the Reading Tutor, in some cases quantifying improvements between successive versions. We identified several methods for answering these questions, each with its own strengths and weaknesses.

Analyzing videotaped sessions is informative but too labor-intensive for more than a few sessions. Videotaping provides a detailed record, but may distort student behavior. Manual analysis allows human judgment, but hence is harder to replicate.

Automated analysis of tutor logs is more comprehensive but less trustworthy. It can compute large-sample statistics, but lacks common sense. Logs of multimodal tutorial dialogue designed for other purposes, such as debugging and performance speedup, are messy and bug-prone to parse and analyze. Log formats tend to evolve along with the tutor, limiting parsing and analysis code to specific versions of the tutor. Instantaneous events may be easy to log on a "fire and forget" basis, but events that span time intervals are trickier to log correctly because their interim state must be stored, and the tutor must remember to log their completion in every possible case. The log format is designed before the logs are generated, and therefore may not anticipate needs that do not become clear until data analysis is underway.

Organizing log data into a database incurs a considerable up-front cost to design the database. Also, populating the database with parsed logs takes time – too much to redo every time a bug is found. That said, SQL queries have been a much quicker way of answering research questions than writing specialized analysis scripts in perl to operate directly on logs as in [1]. We also consider the queries somewhat trustworthier because they are shorter and subject to fewer kinds of programming errors than general-purpose procedural code. However, writing SQL queries to answer research questions is a difficult art to master, and is no guarantee of correctness. One simple but useful lesson when computing averages is also to compute minimum and maximum, as a quick way to spotlight anomalous cases. For example, a supposed 12-minute-long wait exposed a missing case in our analysis.

Analyzing randomly chosen examples by hand applies to many more research problems than time allocation in tutors, but it is very helpful in getting a sense of typical student-tutor interaction, and in spotting bugs. At first such analysis consisted of consulting the detailed log, or the speech recognizer output for individual utterances. The detail made it hard to see the forest for the trees. Then we augmented the Reading Tutor to output student portfolios listing each session's activities [10]. Now we have a log viewer that uses the database to dynamically generate human-readable views at different grain sizes. Such views are invaluable in exposing previously hidden bugs, cases, and patterns.

Like Proust, we have focused on the "pursuit of lost time." How can analyzing where time goes improve tutors? Identifying bottlenecks can help reduce time waste. Relating time allocation to student gains indicates which activities seem to help which skills. We hope that the issues, methods, and lessons identified in this paper help researchers make time allocation more efficient in other automated tutors.

References

1. Mostow, J. and G. Aist. Evaluating tutors that listen: An overview of Project LISTEN. In *Smart Machines in Education*, K. Forbus and P. Feltovich, Editors. 2001, MIT/AAAI Press.
2. Juel, C. What makes literacy tutoring effective? *Reading Research Quarterly*, 1996. *31*(3): p. 268-289.
3. Aist, G. and J. Mostow. Faster, better task choice in a reading tutor that listens. In *Speech Technology for Language Learning*, P. DeCloque and M. Holland, Editors. in press, Swets & Zeitlinger Publishers: The Netherlands.
4. Aist, G. Challenges for a mixed initiative spoken dialog system for oral reading tutoring. *Proc. Computational Models for Mixed Initiative Interaction: Working Notes of the AAAI 1997 Spring Symposium*. 1997.
5. Shute, V. SMART Evaluation: Cognitive Diagnosis, Mastery Learning and Remediation. *Proc. 7th World Conference on Artificial Intelligence in Education*. 1995. Washington, DC: Springer-Verlag.
6. Gluck, K.A., V.J. Shute, J.R. Anderson, and M.C. Lovett. Deconstructing a Computer-Based Tutor: Striving for Better Learning Efficiency in Stat Lady. *Proc. 4th International Conference on Intelligent Tutoring Systems*. 1998. San Antonio, Texas: Springer-Verlag.
7. Hanna, L., K. Risden, M. Czerwinski, and K.J. Alexander. The role of usability research in designing children's computer products. In *The Design of Children's Technology*, A. Druin, Editor. 1999, Morgan Kaufmann: San Fransisco. p. 3-26.
8. Snow, C.E., M.S. Burns, and P. Griffin. Preventing Reading Difficulties in Young Children. 1998, National Academy Press: Washington D.C.
9. Underwood, G. and J.D.M. Underwood. Children's interactions and learning outcomes with interactive talking books. *Computers in Education*, 1998. *30*(1/2): p. 95-102.
10. Mostow, J., G. Aist, P. Burkhead, A. Corbett, A. Cuneo, S. Eitelman, C. Huang, B. Junker, C. Platz, M.B. Sklar, and B. Tobin. A controlled evaluation of computer- versus human-assisted oral reading. In *Artificial Intelligence in Education: AI-ED in the Wired and Wireless Future*, J.D. Moore, C.L. Redfield, and W.L. Johnson, Editors. 2001, Amsterdam: IOS Press: San Antonio, Texas. p. 586-588.
11. Mostow, J., G. Aist, C. Huang, B. Junker, R. Kennedy, H. Lan, D.L. IV, R. O'Connor, R. Tassone, B. Tobin, and A. Wierman. 4-Month Evaluation of a Learner-controlled Reading Tutor that Listens. In *Speech Technology for Language Learning*, P. DeCloque and M. Holland, Editors. in press, Swets & Zeitlinger Publishers: The Netherlands.
12. Aist, G. and J. Mostow. Improving story choice in a reading tutor that listens. *Proc. Fifth International Conference on Intelligent Tutoring Systems (ITS'2000)*. 2000. Montreal, Canada.
13. Aist, G. and J. Mostow. When Speech Input is Not an Afterthought: A Reading Tutor that Listens. *Proc. Workshop on Perceptual User Interfaces*. 1997. Banff, Canada.
14. Woodcock, R.W. *Woodcock Reading Mastery Tests - Revised (WRMT-R/NU)*. 1998, Circle Pines, Minnesota: American Guidance Service.

An Empirical Assessment of Comprehension Fostering Features in an Intelligent Tutoring System

Santosh A. Mathan and Kenneth R. Koedinger

Center for Innovation in Learning / Human-Computer Interaction Institute
Carnegie Mellon University
Pittsburgh, PA 15213, USA
mathan@andrew.cmu.edu, koedinger@cmu.edu

Abstract. This paper describes the design and evaluation of two features in an Intelligent Tutoring System designed to facilitate a deeper conceptual understanding of domain principles in conjunction with the development of procedural skills. The first feature described here relates to the timing of feedback. Some researchers have argued that immediate corrective feedback, as embodied in many cognitive tutors, can block the exercise of activities that may enable students to gain a deeper conceptual understanding of a domain. These include self-monitoring, error detection, and error correction skills. We compare an immediate feedback tutor with a tutor that allows students to reflect on problem solving outcomes, and engage in error detection and correction activities. The other feature reported here is a component of declarative instruction. We assess the use of Ex-ample Walkthroughs as a comprehension-fostering tool. Prior to procedural practice, Example Walkthroughs step students through the study of example problems and guide them to reflect on the reasoning involved in going from a problem statement to a solution. An evaluation has shown that the best learning outcomes were associated with a combination of immediate feedback and Example Walkthroughs. There are indications that a combination of lower cognitive load during procedural practice and a robust and accurate encoding of declarative concepts contributed to the observed outcomes.

1 Introduction

The research reported in this paper seeks to facilitate the joint development of procedural and conceptual knowledge. We focus on features of declarative instruction and problem solving feedback in an Intelligent Tutoring System designed toward this end. We begin with a description of the theoretical motivations underlying our design decisions. Later in the paper we describe how these ideas were implemented in the context of a tutor for Microsoft Excel and present results from an empirical evaluation of their efficacy.

1.1 Feedback: When?

Some of the most widely used intelligent tutoring systems provide immediate feedback on errors [6]. Empirical findings suggest that skill acquisition is most efficient with immediate feedback. For instance, Corbett and Anderson [5] compared the pedagogical benefits of immediate and delayed feedback in the context of their LISP tutor.

S.A. Cerri, G. Gouardères, and F. Paraguaçu (Eds.): ITS 2002, LNCS 2363, pp. 330–343, 2002.

While their comparison did not reveal statistically significant differences in terms of posttest performance, they did see reliable differences in the learning rate. Students in the immediate feedback condition completed training significantly faster. Immediate feedback served to minimize floundering and keep the learning process efficient.

Despite the fact that tutors based on such an approach have been very successful in classroom contexts [6], the principle of immediate feedback has been criticized on at least two grounds. First, critics point out that immediate feedback offered by cognitive tutors is qualitatively different from that offered by human tutors. For instance, Merrill et al. [10] found that human tutors do not intervene immediately on errors that may provide learning opportunities. Instead, they often guide learners through error detection and correction activities. Second, immediate feedback has been criticized on the basis of empirical studies that highlight benefits of delayed feedback. For instance, in a study involving a genetics tutor [9], students either received feedback as soon as an error was detected or at the end of a problem. As in Corbett and Anderson [5], students who received immediate feedback completed training problems significantly faster during training and performed equally well on near transfer tasks. However, students who received delayed feedback performed significantly better on a far transfer task. Similar comparisons in other domains (LISP [17]; Motor Learning [16]) show that while performance differences may not be apparent during or immediately following training, students trained in delayed feedback conditions may show better retention of skills over time.

The Guidance Hypothesis
The guidance hypothesis proposed by Schmidt et al. [15] provides an account of the suggested trade-off between the benefits offered by immediate feedback and those offered by delayed feedback. According to the guidance hypothesis, feedback serves to precisely direct learner actions following each presentation. This has the effect of boosting performance during and immediately following training. However, feedback can negatively impact learning in two ways. First, feedback could obscure important task cues – that is, learners may come to depend on feedback instead of cues inherent in the natural task environment. Second, feedback may prevent important skill components of a task from being exercised. In many academic tasks, these skills could include error detection & correction, and metacognitive skills.

The guidance hypothesis suggests that immediate feedback may promote the development of *generative skills* – that is, skills involved in selection and implementation of operators in specific task contexts. However, *evaluative skills* – skills called for in evaluating the effect of applying these operators, implementing steps to remedy errors, and monitoring one's own cognitive process may go unpracticed. These evaluative functions are instead delegated to feedback. As a consequence, performance may be compromised in transfer and retention tasks where the likelihood of errors is high and both generative and evaluative skills must be jointly exercised. Additionally, the exercise of evaluative skills may provide an opportunity for a deeper conceptual understanding. As Merrill et al. [10] have suggested, errors provide an opportunity to develop a better model of the behavior of operators in a domain.

The Designers Dilemma

The research on feedback just summarized presents the designer with a dilemma. Immediate feedback speeds up the learning process. Furthermore, some of the most effective and efficient cognitive tutors are based on this scheme [6]. However, a designer may also wish to realize benefits such as the development of debugging and metacognitive skills offered by delayed feedback. Unfortunately, the research reviewed here offers little guidance as to what an appropriate level of delay might be. At best, an inappropriate level of delay can reduce the efficiency of the learning process. At worst, delayed feedback can recede to a no-feedback condition. Unproductive floundering and frustration may characterize the learning process in such circumstances.

An Integrative Perspective

The mutually exclusive choice just described stems partly from the fact that much of the debate concerning when to provide feedback is cast in terms of feedback latency. We suggest that a more appropriate focus is on the underlying model of desired performance that serves as the basis for providing feedback to students.

Expert Model

Currently feedback in cognitive tutors is based on what is broadly referred to as an *Expert Model*. Such a model characterizes the end-goal of the instructional process as error-free task execution. Feedback is structured so as to lead students towards such performance. An Expert Model based tutor focuses on the generative components of a skill. Figure 1 (L) illustrates the student interaction with an Expert Model tutor.

Intelligent Novice Model

An alternative model that could serve as the basis for feedback in cognitive tutors is that of an *Intelligent Novice*. The assumption underlying such a model is that an intelligent novice, while progressively getting skillful, is likely to make errors. Recognizing this possibility, the Intelligent Novice model incorporates both self-monitoring, error detection and error correction activities as part of the task. Feedback based on such a model would support the student in both the generative and evaluative aspects of a skill while preventing unproductive floundering. Immediate feedback with respect to such a model would resemble delayed feedback with respect to an Expert Model. Figure 1 (R) outlines student interaction with a tutor based on an Intelligent Novice model.

Later in this paper we will detail the design of two versions of an Excel Tutor – one based on an Expert model the other on an Intelligent Novice model. We will also present results of a study evaluating learning outcomes associated with each. However, before we do so, we describe the theoretical motivations underlying the design of declarative instruction that precedes procedural practice with the two models.

1.2 Declarative Instruction

Declarative knowledge plays a crucial role in early skill acquisition. Under the ACT-R theory of skill acquisition [1], declarative knowledge serves to structure initial problem solving attempts. Over the course of practice, knowledge compilation processes transform declarative encodings into efficient, context specific production rules. Besides playing a guiding role in the initial stages of skills acquisition, declarative knowledge of principles underlying a domain can provide the basis for transfer of skills to novel task domains [18].

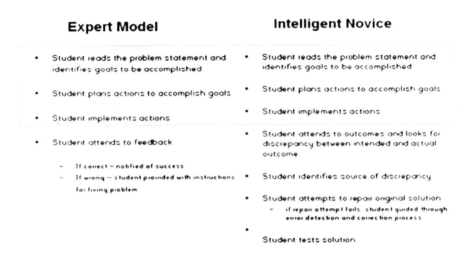

Fig. 1. Interaction with an Expert Model Tutor (L) and Intelligent Novice Model (R)

The study of examples has been used as a tool for fostering the development of conceptual understanding [3]. Examples serve to introduce learners to the range of operators relevant to the solution of a class of problems, the specific conditions under which these operators apply, the transformations that result from the application of operators in specific problem contexts, and the overall sequence in which these operators are applicable. Recent research by Renkl, Atkinson, and Maier indicates that the effectiveness of examples can be enhanced by integrating elements of problem solving into the study of examples [14]. That is, students who study fully worked out examples, then complete intermediate steps in partially incomplete examples before problem solving, outperform students who transition directly to problem solving from the study of fully worked out examples. As Renkl et al. have suggested, elements of such an approach – that is, the progression from modeling of solutions with examples, to fading of scaffolds to independent problem solving – can be found in a variety of successful instructional techniques. These include: Reciprocal Teaching [12], and Cognitive Apprenticeship [4]. Jones and Fleishman [8] have theorized – on the basis of a CASCADE model of fading examples – that partially worked out examples focus attention on crucial parts of a problem, thus providing an opportunity for self-explanation. Furthermore, as a consequence of making problem-solving decisions at these points, students acquire search control knowledge (knowledge of the sub-goal structure for solving the task).

Declarative Instruction in the tutor described here incorporates what we call *Example Walkthroughs* to guide students in the study of examples. Students read textual expositions of concepts and watch video illustrations of the application of these concepts in the context of examples. Subsequently, instead of progressing directly into problem solving, students solve the examples demonstrated in the video with the help of Example Walkthroughs. These walkthroughs step students through the reasoning necessary to solve the example problems. At each step of the solution process, students are prompted with questions that serve to help them make the inferences necessary to perform the task correctly. Incorrect inferences, which may result from an inaccurate or partial encoding of relevant declarative knowledge, are remedied with brief messages that clarify the knowledge necessary to make the appropriate inference.

Example Walkthroughs differ from conventional approaches to declarative instruction in several ways. First, declarative information is typically presented in a passive form (usually in the form of text, lecture, or video expositions). In contrast, walkthroughs actively engage students in elaborating on information presented. Secondly, walkthroughs provide an opportunity to check and correct knowledge encoding in the context of representative tasks. Thirdly, walkthroughs allow conceptual gaps to be remedied immediately following the exposition of a concept, instead of being deferred to problem solving contexts where cognitive load may be high.

We now describe implementation of feedback and declarative instruction based on the analysis just presented. We do so in the context an Excel Tutor.

2   Excel Tutor

Spreadsheets have been widely regarded as exemplary end-user programming environments [11]. They allow non-programmers to perform sophisticated computations without having to master a programming language. However, despite decades of evolution in spreadsheet design, there are aspects of spreadsheet use that are sources of difficulty for novice and expert spreadsheet users (e.g. [7]). A commonly reported usability problem concerns the appropriate use of absolute and relative references – these are schemes that allow users to perform iterative computations. These difficulties exist despite an abundance of manufacturer and third-party training materials. The tutor reported in this paper was designed to enable students to master cell referencing concepts. We elaborate on the tutorial domain below and go on to detail features of the tutor based on the theoretical analysis presented earlier.

2.1   Overview of Tutorial Domain

A spreadsheet is essentially a collection of cells on a two dimensional grid. Individual cells may be addressed by their column and row indices. Column indices (also called column references) are denoted by number, whereas row indices (often called row references) are denoted by letter. Cells may contain alphanumeric data and formulas. Formulas can refer to values in specific cells by referring to their addresses. So, a user could specify a formula in cell C3 (in column C and row 3) that adds the contents of cell A3 and B3 by entering: '=A3+B3'.

Formulas may be reused to perform iterative operations. This is accomplished through a scheme called relative referencing. Consider the spreadsheet depicted in Figure 2. One could enter a formula in cell B5 that adds the contents of cells B2, B3, and B4. The corresponding operation can be performed in cells C5 and D5 simply by copying the formula entered in cell B5 and pasting it into these new locations. When pasted, Excel modifies the formula to refer to cells that lie at the same relative location as the original formula. For example the formula in Cell B5 referred to the 3 cells above it. When the formula is copied and pasted into cells C5 and D5 the formulas are modified to refer to the three cells above these new locations.

In order to determine the appropriate relative references at new locations, Excel updates formulas based on where the formula is moved. When a formula is moved into a cell in a different column, Excel updates column references in the formula by the number of columns moved (see Figure 2, =B2+B3+B4 becomes =D2+D3+D2 when moved across columns from B5 to D5). Similarly, when a formula is copied and pasted into a cell in a different row, all row references in the formula get updated by the number of rows moved (see Figure 2, =B2+C2+D2 becomes =B4+C4+D4 when moved across rows from E2 to E4).

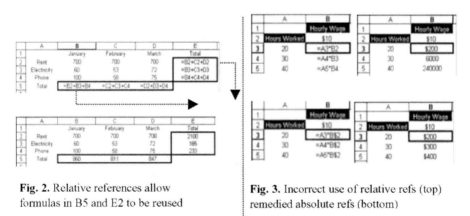

Fig. 2. Relative references allow formulas in B5 and E2 to be reused

Fig. 3. Incorrect use of relative refs (top) remedied absolute refs (bottom)

While relative referencing works in many task contexts, it is sometimes necessary to hold a row or column reference fixed regardless of where a formula is moved. Consider the example in Figure 3. The value in cell B2 (Hourly Wage) has to be multiplied with the values in cells A3, A4, and A5 (Hours Worked). If the formula, =A3*B2 is entered into B3 and pasted into cells B4 and B5, all row references will change in order to refer to cells that lie at the same relative location as those referred to by the formula in B3. This would produce =A4*B3 in B4 and =A5*B4 in B5 (instead of =A4*B2 and =A5*B2 respectively). In order for the formula to continue to refer to cell B2, the row reference 2 has to be held fixed as an absolute reference. This can be done by placing a '$' ahead of '2'. Thus, in order for the formula in B3 to work appropriately when copied and pasted, it would be modified to read =A3*B$2.

2.2   Expert Model Tutor Description

As mentioned earlier the Expert Model emphasizes generative skills. Details of the design of declarative instruction and feedback design based on such a model are presented below.

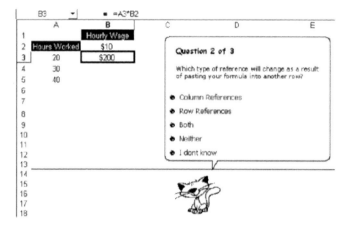

Fig. 4. Screenshot from Example Walkthrough for Expert Model Tutor Example Walkthrough

Example Walkthroughs corresponding to the Expert Model tutor focus on generative skills. Students are provided with a 3-step procedure, described below, in order to generate solutions to cell-referencing problems. As mentioned earlier, in order to determine where an absolute reference may be needed, users have to be able to identify the references in a formula that will change as a result of copying and pasting. Depending on where a formula will be pasted, row and/or column references will change. Each reference that will change must be inspected. Of these, references changes that are to be prevented must be preceded by a '$' symbol – an absolute reference. The Expert Model Walkthrough guides students through these inferences by posing a series of questions (Figure 4): [Which way will you be pasting your formula? (into another column/row/both?) , Which type of reference will change when moved? (column/row/both?) Of the references that will change, which ones should you prevent?]. Students respond to these questions by picking from multiple-choice options. The system provides succinct explanations in response to errors.

Problem Solving Feedback

During problem solving, students working with an Expert Model based tutor receive feedback as soon as an error is detected. The error notification message presents students with the choice of correcting the error on their own or getting help from the system in generating a correct answer. If help is sought, the student is guided through the process of identifying where, if any, absolute references are required in a particular problem context. Students are interactively guided by question prompts to solve the problem deductively (see Figure 4).

2.3   Intelligent Novice Tutor Description

In addition to generative skills emphasized by Expert Model based tutors, the Intelligent Novice Model provides practice in evaluative skills.

Example Walkthrough

In addition to helping students solve example problems, the Intelligent Novice Example Walkthrough guides students through the reasoning associated with the exercise of evaluative skills. First, students are prompted to indicate the values and formulas they should see in each cell if the formula works correctly. Subsequently, students copy and paste a formula without any absolute references into each cell of the example. Students, then note the values and formulas produced as a result of copying the original formula. They are prompted to examine discrepancies between the actual and intended formulas. Prompts then guide learners to use the identified discrepancies to determine where an absolute reference may be necessary. Figure 5 illustrates a portion of the Intelligent Novice Example Walkthrough.

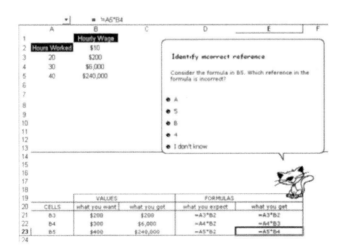

Fig. 5.   Screenshots   from   Example   Walkthrough   for Intelligent Novice Model Tutor

Problem Solving Feedback

In contrast to the Expert Model based tutor, the Intelligent Novice Model allows students to enter an incorrect formula and copy and paste it to observe the consequences of the error. The student is given an opportunity to detect the source of the error and correct the formula. Hints requested by students can guide them through the error detection and correction process. An error in the formula correction step will result in immediate corrective feedback to minimize floundering and frustration. If a student fails to detect an error and tries to start a new problem, feedback directs the student to check for errors and request hints if needed. The error notification message at the formula correction step presents students with the choice of correcting the error on their own or doing so with help from the system.

If help is sought, the student is asked to specify formulas and values that should result if the original formula were referenced appropriately. This is noted in a table on the spreadsheet. Subsequently, the student is asked to enter a formula without any absolute references and copy and paste it. The student then prompted to note the values and formulas produced. The student is prompted to use the discrepancy between actual and intended formulas to determine where absolute references, if any, may be appropriate (see Figure 5).

3 Method

An evaluation of the features described here was conducted with a group of 40 participants recruited from a local temporary employment agency. All subjects had general computer experience, including proficiency with word processing, email, and web applications – however, they were all spreadsheet novices. We randomly assigned students to one of four conditions associated with the manipulation of two factors: Model – Expert or Intelligent Novice (EX, IN), Declarative Instruction – With or Without Example Walkthrough (WT, noWT).

The evaluation was conducted over the course of three days. On *Day-1*, students came in for a 90-minute instructional session. Declarative instruction provided all students with an exposition of basic spreadsheet concepts: everything from data entry, copying and pasting to formula creation and cell referencing. Cell referencing lessons for all students included video examples of cell referencing problems being solved. Students in the Walkthrough conditions stepped through Example Walkthroughs immediately following the videos, prior to problem solving. Students in the No Walkthrough conditions went directly to problem solving. Declarative instruction took approximately 60 minutes for students whose instruction included walkthroughs, and 50 minutes for those whose instruction did not. The remainder of the session was spent on procedural practice. Students solved a variety of problems that called for the exercise of cell referencing skills. The session was preceded by a pre-test and was followed by a post-test. On *Day-2*, students came in the next day for 50 minutes of procedural practice with the tutor. A post-test was administered following the instructional session. On *Day-3*, eight days after Day-2, students came in for a third instructional session. Students attempted a pre-test and transfer task to measure retention prior to the instructional session. The third session consisted of 30 minutes of proce-dural practice and was followed by a post test

The pre and post-tests had two components: a test of problem solving and a test of conceptual understanding. The problem-solving test consisted of problems isomorphic to training tasks. The conceptual test consisted of two parts: the first part required students to exercise predictive skills. Students had to identify an outcome (from a selection of screenshots) that could have resulted from copying and pasting a given formula. The second called for students to exercise error attribution skills. Students had to examine a given spreadsheet table and identify which of several formula alter-natives could have produced the observed outcome. The transfer task called for the exercise of cell referencing skills in the context of a structurally complex spreadsheet. Students also were also asked to complete a computer experience questionnaire. The questionnaire asked them to indicate the frequency with which they use various com-puter applications and rate their proficiency at each.

4 Results

An analysis of pre-test scores showed student performance in all conditions to be close to zero. However, we suspected that computer proficiency might influence learning outcomes. The computer experience questionnaire provided the basis to assign a com-puter experience score to each participant. Analysis has shown the computer experi-ence score to be a significant predictor of student performance ($F=8.57$, $p < 0.007$). The results reported in this paper control for computer experience as a covariate.

As shown in Figure 6A, a repeated measure ANCOVA, over all the tests, did not show a significant main effect for Model or Walkthrough. However, the analysis did reveal a significant Model-Walkthrough interaction ($F= 5.10$, $p < 0.03$). Overall, students in the Expert-Walkthrough condition outperformed students in all other con-ditions (Figure 6A). Though not shown in Figure 6, a similar pattern of scores was observed in the conceptual ($F=7.12$, $p < 0.02$) and problem-solving tests ($F= 7.4$, $p < 0.01$).

As shown in Figure 6B, students in the Expert-Walkthrough condition demon-strated the greatest immediate learning as measured by the Day-1 and Day-2 post-tests, and the most robust retention of material. A similar pattern was observed when the problem solving and conceptual understanding scores were examined separately. A Model-Walkthrough interaction on the transfer task suggests that students in the Ex-pert-Walkthrough condition also demonstrated the highest performance on the transfer test ($F=4.49$, $p<0.05$) (Figure 6C). There is also some indication of an aptitude treat-ment interaction (Figure 6D). While High computer experience students performed at about the same level on the transfer task regardless of condition, low computer experi-ence students got a performance boost in the Expert-Walkthrough condition ($F = 3.56$, $p < 0.07$).

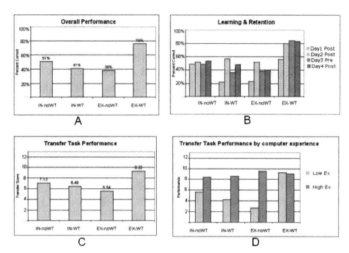

Fig. 6. Evaluation Results

We observed qualitative differences in the way students in each condition dealt with errors. Students in the Expert-Walkthrough condition were able to understand the error messages, repair their solutions, and get back on track efficiently. In contrast, several students in the Expert-noWalkthrough condition were unable to fully comprehend terms and concepts used in the error correction dialogs – several students had forgotten or expressed confusion about concepts described during declarative training. They tended to get to the solution by trial and error attempts at placing absolute references. Students in the Intelligent Novice conditions experienced the greatest frustration. The error analysis and fixing process appeared to become a fairly lengthy and involved problem-solving episode in itself – this frustration was particularly pronounced among low computer experience students.

5   Discussion

Contrary to our expectations, our evaluation did not reveal a main effect for Model or Example Walkthrough. Instead, a conjunction of features associated with Expert Model based feedback and Example Walkthroughs had the greatest impact on learning, retention and transfer outcomes. We examine features of declarative and procedural instruction associated with the Expert-Walkthrough condition below:

Explicit Procedure to Guide Problem Solving
Students in the Expert-Walkthrough condition had the benefit of a three-step procedure (expressed in the form of the three questions) to guide their problem solving efforts. Students were introduced to this procedure during Example Walkthroughs. Furthermore Expert Model based feedback during procedural practice kept students focused on applying these rules to solve problems. Prior research suggests that a pro-

cedure for interpreting declarative concepts in problem solving contexts contributes to better learning outcomes [13]. The Intelligent Novice Walkthrough on the other hand focused on imparting an understanding of the mechanism underlying cell referencing. Students had to generate a procedure based on their understanding of underlying concepts.

Cognitive Load under Intelligent Novice Model
Procedural practice with the Intelligent Novice model was more taxing on working memory than with the Expert Model tutor for at least two reasons [cf. 2]. First, error diagnosis and recovery steps under the Intelligent Novice condition often became extended problem-solving episodes in their own right. These episodes are likely to have interfered with the acquisition of solution generation schemas. Second, artifacts of the interface may have imposed additional cognitive load on learners. The error recovery steps required students to split attention between 3 areas: the problem, the table used to track expected and actual values and formulas, and messages from the office assistant (see Figure 5). These two features were also inherent in the Intelligent Novice Example Walkthroughs, potentially compromising their efficacy.

Accuracy and Robustness of Declarative Encodings
Expert-Walkthrough condition students are likely to have benefited from comprehension checks and the opportunity to elaborate on video examples during declarative instruction. There are indications that Expert Model students whose declarative instruction included walkthroughs had a more robust and accurate encoding to guide them during procedural practice. Students in the Expert-Walkthrough condition made half as many errors as those in the Expert-noWalkthrough condition on the first six problems – these problems represented the first presentation of the six types of problems included in the tutor (1.01 errors per problem vs. 2.79, F=3.09, p < 0.09).

6   Conclusion

Empirical results suggest that the best learning outcomes were associated with the combined use of Expert Model based feedback and Example Walkthroughs. Overall, students in the Expert-Walkthrough condition exhibited the strongest performance in transfer tests, tests of conceptual understanding, and on problem solving tasks isomorphic to those encountered during training. Furthermore, students in the Expert-Walkthrough condition exhibited robust retention of learning over the course of an eight-day retention interval. We have suggested that a combination of relatively low cognitive load during practice, the provision of an explicit procedure for applying declarative knowledge, and a robust and accurate declarative encoding contributed to observed outcomes.

The research reported here has implications for the design of cognitive tutors. First, Example Walkthroughs show the potential for boosting learning outcomes associated with cognitive tutors. Walkthroughs provide an opportunity for students to elaborate on video and textual expositions of examples. Furthermore they provide a way to check and remedy student comprehension of concepts prior to procedural practice. Expert-Walkthrough students are likely to have benefited from an explicit procedure (in the form of 3 questions) for applying declarative knowledge in problem contexts. Additionally, students were guided through the process of applying the procedure in the context of examples. Second, the exercise of evaluative skill, as afforded by the Intelligent Novice tutor, comes at a cost – if these activities become extended problem solving episodes, they have the potential for disrupting the acquisition of schemas [cf. 2] associated with generative skills.

References

1. Anderson, J. R. (1993). Rules of the mind. Hillsdale, N.J: LEA
2. Chandler, P. & Sweller, J. (1991). Cognitive load theory and the format of instruction. Cognition and Instruction, 8, 293-332.
3. Chi, M. T. H., Bassok, M., Lewis, M. W., Reimann, P., & Glaser, R. (1989). Self-explanations: How students study and use examples in learning to solve problems. Cognitive Science, 13, 145-182
4. Collins, A., Brown, J. S., & Newman, S. E. (1989). Cognitive apprenticeship: Teaching the crafts of reading, writing, and mathematics. In L. B. Resnick (Ed.), Knowing, learning, and instruction (453-494). Hillsdale, NJ: LEA
5. Corbett, A. T., Anderson, J. R. (2001) Locus of feedback control in computer-based tutoring: impact on learning rate, achievement and attitudes. Proceedings of CHI 2001, ACM, 2001 245-252
6. Corbett, A. T., Koedinger, K. R., & Hadley, W. (2001). Cognitive Tutors: From the research classroom to all classrooms. In Goodman, P. (Ed) Technology Enhanced Learning (235-263). Mahwah, NJ: LEA
7. Hendry, D. G. and Green, T. R. G. (1994) Creating, comprehending, and explaining spreadsheets: a cognitive interpretation of what discretionary users think of the spreadsheet model. Int. J. Human-Computer Studies, 40(6), 1033-1065
8. Jones, R. M., Fleischman, E. S. (2001). Cascade Explains and Informs the Utility of Fading Examples to Problems. Proceedings of the 23rd Conf. of the Cognitive Sc. Society (pp. 459-464). Mahwah, NJ: LEA
9. Lee, A.Y. (1992) Using tutoring systems to study learning. Behavior Research Methods, Instruments, & Computers, 24(2, 205-212)
10. Merrill, D.C., Reiser, B.J., Merrill, S.K., and Landes, S. "Tutoring: Guided Learning by Doing". Cognition and Instruction, 1995, 13(3). 315-372.
11. Nardi, B. (1993). A Small Matter of Programming. Cambridge: MIT Press
12. Palincsar, A.S., & Brown, A.L. (1984). Reciprocal teaching of comprehension-fostering and comprehension-monitoring activities. Cognition and Instruction, 1, 117-175
13. Reif, F. & Allen, S. (1992). Cognition for interpreting scientific concepts: A study of acceleration. Cognition and Instruction, 9, 1-44
14. Renkl, A., Atkinson, R. K., & Maier, U. H. (2000). From studying examples to solving problems: Fading worked-out solution steps helps learning. In L. R. Gleitman & A. K. Joshi (Eds.), Proceedings of the Twenty-Second Annual Conference of the Cognitive Science Society, 393-398. Mahwah, NJ: LEA.

15. Schmidt, R.A., Young, D.E., Swinnen, S., & Shapiro, D.C. (1989). Summary knowledge of results for skill acquisition: Support for the guidance hypothesis. *J. of Experimental Psychology: Learning, Memory, and Cognition, 15*, 352-359
16. Schmidt, R.A., Bjork, R.A. (1992). new conceptualizations of practice: common principles in three paradigms suggest new concepts for training. Psychological Science, 3 (4), 207-217
17. Schooler, L. J. & Anderson, J. R. (1990). The disruptive potential of immediate feedback. Proceedings of the Twelfth Annual Conference of the Cognitive Science Society, 702-708, Cambridge, MA
18. Singley, M. K. & Anderson, J. R. (1989). Transfer of Cognitive Skill. Cambridge, MA: Harvard

Pilot-Testing a Tutorial Dialogue System That Supports Self-Explanation

Vincent Aleven, Octav Popescu, and Kenneth Koedinger

Human Computer Interaction Institute
Carnegie Mellon University
{aleven, koedinger}@cs.cmu.edu, octav@cmu.edu

Abstract. Previous studies have shown that self-explanation is an effective metacognitive strategy and can be supported effectively by intelligent tutoring systems. It is plausible however that students may learn even more effectively when stating explanations in their own words and when receiving tutoring focused on their explanations. We are developing the Geometry Explanation Tutor in order to test this hypothesis. This system helps students, through a restricted form of dialogue, to construct general explanations of problem-solving steps in their own words. We conducted a pilot study in which the tutor was used for two class periods in a junior high school. The data from this study suggest that the techniques that we chose to implement the dialogue system, namely a knowledge-based approach to natural language understanding and classification of student explanations, are up to the task. There are a number of ways in which the system could be improved within the current architecture.

1 Introduction

Recently, many researchers have embraced the notion that tutorial dialogue systems will make a dramatically more effective "3rd generation" of computer-based instructional systems (Graesser, et al., 2001; Evens, et al., 2001; Rosé & Freedman, 2000; Aleven, 2001). But what pedagogical approaches should underlie the dialogues conducted by these systems? A number of cognitive science studies have shown that self-explanation is an effective metacognitive strategy (Bielaczyc, Pirolli, & Brown, 1995; Chi, 2000; Renkl, et al., 1998). That is, when students study textbooks or worked-out examples, they learn with greater understanding to the extent that they explain the materials to themselves. However, not all students self-explain spontaneously and even when prompted to self-explain, it is difficult for students to arrive at good explanations (Renkl, et al., 1998).

This has led a number of researchers to investigate how self-explanation can be supported effectively by intelligent tutoring systems (Aleven & Koedinger, in press; Conati & VanLehn, 2000) or other instructional software (Renkl, in press). In previous work, we showed that even simple means of supporting self-explanation within an intelligent tutoring system, such as menus, can help students learn with greater understanding, as compared to tutored problem solving without self explanation (Aleven & Koedinger, in press). It is plausible that students learn even better when they explain

S.A. Cerri, G. Gouardères, and F. Paraguaçu (Eds.): ITS 2002, LNCS 2363, pp. 344–354, 2002.

in their own words. However, the potential advantages of "free-form" explanation do not seem to materialize when the system merely prompts students to explain but does not provide feedback on students' explanations (Aleven, et al., 2000).

Our long-term goal is to find out whether a tutorial dialogue system can effectively tutor students as they produce self-explanations and whether it thereby can help them learn with greater understanding. We are developing a tutorial dialogue system that supports self-explanation in the domain of geometry, the Geometry Explanation Tutor (Aleven, Popescu, & Koedinger, 2001). This system helps students, through a restricted form of dialogue, to produce explanations that not only get at the right mathematical idea but also state the idea with sufficient precision. The system evaluates whether students' explanations are correct and sufficiently precise and is able to detect common omissions and errors in explanations. We have opted for a knowledge-based approach to natural language understanding, with a logic-based representation of semantics, similar in spirit to those discussed in Allen (1995). We have presented our arguments for our choice elsewhere (Popescu & Koedinger, 2000). Further, we have opted to keep dialogue management as simple as possible, adopting a "submit and critique" approach described below.

In this paper we present the results of a short pilot study in a school and discuss how far along we are towards having a robust and effective tutorial dialogue system that is ready for the classroom. Further, we discuss whether the techniques we have chosen to implement our tutorial dialogue system are adequate and were a good choice.

2 The Geometry Explanation Tutor

The Geometry Explanation Tutor was built on top of an existing Cognitive Tutor (Anderson, et al., 1995) for geometry problem solving, the Geometry Cognitive Tutor™. This tutor was developed by our research group in tandem with a full-year high school geometry curriculum. The combination of these two components has been shown to be better than traditional geometry classroom instruction (Koedinger, et al, 2000). The tutor and the curriculum are being marketed commercially and are in use in about 100 schools in the United States (see http://www.carnegielearning.com).

The Geometry Explanation Tutor provides for guided problem-solving practice. In addition, it requires that students provide general explanations of their problem-solving steps in their own words (Aleven, et al., 2001). It helps students, through a restricted form of dialogue, to improve their explanations and arrive at explanations that are mathematically precise (see Figure 1, which shows a dialogue with the system collected during the pilot study described below). So far, the dialogues deal with the topics covered in one of the six units that make up the tutor curriculum, the Angles unit, which deals with the geometric properties of angles.

The system's architecture has been described elsewhere (Aleven, et al, 2001) so here we provide only a short outline. An important knowledge source is the system's hierarchy of 149 explanation categories, which represent the most common ways in which students express or attempt to express geometry rules in their own words. For each relevant geometry rule, the hierarchy contains one or more categories representing correct and complete ways of stating the rule. For example, category COMPLEMENTARY-ANGLES-SUM-90 represents all correct and complete statements of the definition of complementary angles, including "the sum of the measures of complementary angles is 90 degrees". For each relevant geometry rule the explanation hierarchy also contains numerous categories that represent commonly-occurring incomplete or incorrect ways of stating the rule. For example, category COMPLEMENTARY-ANGLES-90 represents sentences meaning "complementary angles are 90 degrees," which falls just short of being a complete and correct explanation.

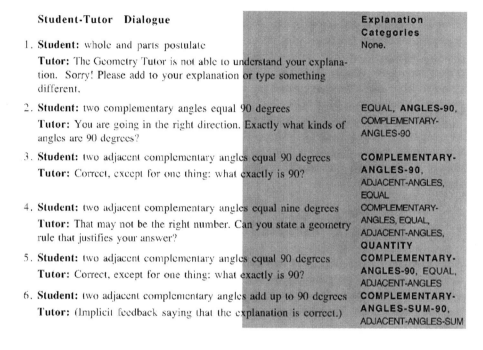

Student-Tutor Dialogue	Explanation Categories
1. **Student:** whole and parts postulate **Tutor:** The Geometry Tutor is not able to understand your explanation. Sorry! Please add to your explanation or type something different.	None.
2. **Student:** two complementary angles equal 90 degrees **Tutor:** You are going in the right direction. Exactly what kinds of angles are 90 degrees?	EQUAL, ANGLES-90, COMPLEMENTARY-ANGLES-90
3. **Student:** two adjacent complementary angles equal 90 degrees **Tutor:** Correct, except for one thing: what exactly is 90?	COMPLEMENTARY-ANGLES-90, ADJACENT-ANGLES, EQUAL
4. **Student:** two adjacent complementary angles equal nine degrees **Tutor:** That may not be the right number. Can you state a geometry rule that justifies your answer?	COMPLEMENTARY-ANGLES, EQUAL, ADJACENT-ANGLES, QUANTITY
5. **Student:** two adjacent complementary angles equal 90 degrees **Tutor:** Correct, except for one thing: what exactly is 90?	COMPLEMENTARY-ANGLES-90, EQUAL, ADJACENT-ANGLES
6. **Student:** two adjacent complementary angles add up to 90 degrees **Tutor:** (Implicit feedback saying that the explanation is correct.)	COMPLEMENTARY-ANGLES-SUM-90, ADJACENT-ANGLES-SUM

Fig. 1. Example dialogue with the Geometry Explanation Tutor

The system has a natural language understanding (NLU) component, primarily knowledge-based, whose task is to construct a logic-based representation of the semantic content of student input and classify that representation with respect to the explanation categories. In this regard our system is different from many other tutorial dialogue systems, which rely on statistical approaches (Graesser, et al., 2001), keyword spotting (Evens et al., 2001), or bypass language understanding altogether (Heffernan & Koedinger, 2000) and from systems that use hybrid approaches combining deep and shallow methods (e.g., Wahlster, 2001).The NLU component uses a left-corner chart parser with a unification-based grammar formalism to parse the input (Rosé & Lavie, 1999). It uses the Loom description logic system (MacGregor, 1991) to construct a semantic representation of student input. Once the semantic representation has been constructed, it is classified with respect to the explanation hierarchy. This may result in a set of explanation categories, as is illustrated in Figure 1, rightmost column.

If the student's explanation was classified as a complete and correct statement of an applicable geometry theorem, the tutor accepts the explanation, as illustrated in step 6 of the dialogue shown in Figure 1. Otherwise, if the explanation was classified under one or more categories that represent incomplete or incorrect statements of an applicable geometry theorem, the tutor selects one of these categories randomly and displays the feedback message associated with the selected category. In Figure 1, the explanation category on which the tutor feedback was based is shown in bold face in the rightmost column. The system also appropriately handles explanations that are merely references to geometry rules (student gave the name of a geometry rule) and explanations that focus on the wrong rule. Since the pilot study described in this paper, a number of improvements have been made to the system, as described below. Nonetheless, it is fair to say that the techniques for dialogue management used by the Geometry Explanation Tutor are fairly straightforward compared to those used in other systems (Graesser, et al., 2001; Evens, et al., 2001; Wahlster, 2001).

3   A Pilot Study

At the end of the 2000-2001 school year, we conducted a pilot study in order to get a sense of how well the system was working. During this study, the Geometry Explanation Tutor was used briefly in a suburban junior high school in the Pittsburgh area, as part of a 9th-grade Integrated Mathematics II course. This course covered a number of topics in geometry and algebra. Approximately 30 students of ages 14 and 15 participated in the pilot study. The students were "honors students," which means that within their school they were among the best of their grade level in terms of academic ability and diligence. During two 40-minute class periods, the students worked in pairs on the Geometry Explanation Tutor, running the tutor on the school's wireless PC laptops. Earlier during the semester, they had learned about angles and their interrelationships (the topics covered in the tutor's Angles unit, on which we focused in the study) but they did not have any computer tutoring related to these topics.

4   Effectiveness of Student-Tutor Dialogues

The logs of the student-tutor interactions were analyzed in order to evaluate how effective the student-system dialogues were. The logs contained information about 185 dialogues comprising 791 explanation attempts to explain a geometry theorem or definition, or 12.3 ± 4.6 dialogues per pair of students. Students arrived at a complete explanation in 75% of the 185 dialogues. About half of the incomplete dialogues occurred simply because the bell rang at the end of the period. For the other half, the logs indicate that the students' work on the problem ended abnormally. Such abnormal

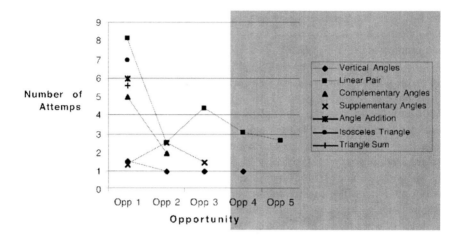

Fig. 2. Number of attempts to explain a given geometry rule, by opportunity

endings were especially likely to occur with geometry theorems that require longer statements (angle addition and angle bisection) and seem to have been caused by long system response times.

First, we looked at the number of attempts that it took students to complete their explanations. This variable provides a measure of how difficult it is to explain problem-solving steps, assisted by the system's feedback. In advance, we did not have a clear expectation of what the value of this variable should be. However, if practice with the system helps students learn to explain, one should see a decline in the number of attempts needed to explain any given theorem as students gain experience.

Overall, it took students 3.6 ± 4.5 attempts to get an explanation right. This average breaks down as follows: On the first opportunity to explain any given theorem, students needed 4.7 ± 5.6 attempts, whereas on later opportunities, they needed 2.5 ± 2.5 attempts. This decrease over time in the number of attempts was observed for most of the theorems, as is illustrated in Figure 3, which provides a more detailed break-down of the data. This figure shows also that some theorems are considerably more difficult to explain than others. Overall, the number of attempts that were needed to arrive at complete explanations seems reasonable. Further, our expectation that this number would go down as students gained experience was clearly borne out. Thus, students learned to explain the various geometry rules as they worked with the tutor.

A different way of measuring the effectiveness of the student-system dialogues is to see how often students were able to improve their explanation from one attempt to the next, assisted by the system's feedback. *A priori,* it is not clear on what percentage of attempts one would expect to see such progress. If students would rarely make progress, this would obviously not be a good sign. On the other hand, if they would make progress on every attempt, this might indicate that the tutor feedback makes the task too easy for students. As a very rough rule of thumb, then, let us say that a minimum criterion is that students make progress more often than not.

We define progress as follows: an attempt at explaining a geometry rule constitutes progress over a previous attempt if

(a) it is a correct and complete statement of an applicable geometry rule, or

(b) if it is closer to a complete statement than the previous attempt, meaning that it classifies under a more specific category in the explanation hierarchy, or

(c) if the attempt focuses on an applicable geometry rule whereas the previous attempt focused on a geometry rule that does not apply to the current step.

For example, in the dialogue shown in Figure 1, attempts 2, 5, and 6 constitute progress according to this criterion. The actual criterion is slightly more complicated due to the fact that some explanations are references to geometry rules and also because explanations can fall under multiple categories.

We define regression as the opposite of progress, see for example step 4 in Figure 1. Some explanations constitute neither progress nor regression. These may be explanations that classify under the same set of categories as the previous attempt or explanations that are classified under a different set of categories but constitute "lateral movement". This means either that the explanation is better than the previous attempt in one respect but worse in another, or that the explanation is different from the previous attempt but no closer to the correct explanation. An example of the latter type is shown in Figure 1, step 3: although not wrong, it was not necessary to add the term "adjacent".

In assessing this kind of local progress, we obviously need not be concerned with the first attempt at explaining any given step (185 attempts). Further, we disregard steps where the student's input was identical to the previous attempt. Such repetitions occurred rather frequently (namely, 218 times), but we suspect that they are mostly unintentional, due to imperfections in the system's user interface that have been fixed meanwhile. Therefore, we focus on the remaining 388 explanation attempts. For each, we computed whether or not it constitutes progress based on the explanation categories assigned by a human rater, namely, the first author. We found that of the 388 attempts, 44% constituted progress over previous attempts, 26% were classified under the same set of categories as the previous attempt (even though the explanation was different), 17% represented lateral movement, and 14% constituted regression. Thus, the percentage of attempts in which students made progress was close to the 50% threshold presented above, although ideally, it would be somewhat higher than it was.

Some changes have been made within the current dialogue management framework that are likely to improve the progress rate. First, due to its policy of selecting randomly when a student explanation classifies under multiple explanation categories, the tutor did not always base its feedback on the most appropriate category. For example, in step 2 in Figure 1, it would have been better if the tutor had selected category COMPLEMENTARY-ANGLES-90. We have meanwhile changed the tutor's selection criterion so that the tutor selects the explanation category that is closest to a complete and correct explanation. Second, the tutor feedback can likely be improved by associating multiple levels of (increasingly specific) feedback messages with each explanation category. This enables the system to provide more specific feedback when the student's explanation classifies under the same explanation categories as the previous attempt and may help reduce the amount of stagnation in the dialogues. This technique has since been implemented. Third, some parts of the explanation hierarchy are not yet fine-grained enough to detect certain improvements to explanations. We have added 18 categories already (for a total of 167), based on the analysis of the current data set and will likely add more. Finally, it is likely to be useful if the tutor pointed out to the student whether an explanation attempt implies progress or not. The criterion for progress used here will be a good stating point. While these improvements are very likely to raise the progress rate, we cannot rule out that for some of the more difficult-to-state geometry theorems, such as angle addition, we will need to model more elaborate dialogue strategies that do not easily fit within the current framework.

5   Evaluation of the System's NLU Performance

We also evaluated the system's NLU component, to get an idea of how well it works and because the question of how well knowledge-based natural language understanding works in analyzing mathematical explanations by novices is an interesting research question in its own right. We focused on the accuracy with which the system's NLU component is able to classify student explanations with respect to its set of explanation categories. There is inherent ambiguity in this classification task: for some explanations, it is difficult even for human raters to determine what the correct category or categories are. Therefore, rather than compare the labels assigned by the system against a "correct" set of labels, we ask to what extent the agreement between system and human raters approaches that between human raters. This design was used also in earlier studies, for example a study to evaluate an automated method for essay grading (Foltz, Laham, & Landauer, 1999).

From the set of explanations collected during the pilot study, we removed those explanations that are identical to the previous attempt. As mentioned, we strongly suspect that these repetitions were unintentional, caused by small flaws in the user interface, which meanwhile have been fixed. Therefore, these repetitions should not influence the evaluation of NLU performance. Three human raters (two authors and a research assistant) labeled the remaining set of 573 examples, assigning one or more labels to each explanation. Each rater went through the data twice, in an attempt to achieve maximum accuracy. After the first round, we selected 24 "difficult" examples, explanations that all raters had labeled differently. The raters discussed these examples extensively, in order to calibrate their labeling approaches. We then removed the 24 examples from the data and all raters made a second pass through the data, independently revising their labels. The sets of labels assigned by the human raters and by the system were then processed automatically, in an attempt further to reduce labeling errors, inconsistencies, and irrelevant differences between label sets. These changes preserved the intention of the raters and would not have affected the system's responses. Out of the 167 labels that could be assigned (the categories in the explanation hierarchy plus some extras for explanations that were references to geometry rules), 91 were actually used, combined in 218 different sets of labels.

Table 1. Average pair-wise inter-rater agreement between human raters and average pair-wise agreement between the system and each human rater.

	κ	Actual Agreement	Chance Agreement
Set equality			
Avg Human-Human	0.77	0.77	0.033
Avg System-Human	0.60	0.61	0.030
Overlap			
Avg Human-Human	0.81	0.81	0.043
Avg System-Human	0.65	0.66	0.039
Weighted overlap			
Avg Human-Human	0.88	0.91	0.26
Avg System-Human	0.75	0.81	0.25

To compute the inter-rater agreement, we use the κ statistic (Cohen, 1960), as is customary in the field of computational linguistics and other fields (Carletta, 1996). The κ statistic provides a measure of how much agreement there is between raters beyond the agreement expected to occur by chance alone. We computed κ in three different ways: First we computed κ based on "set equality" – two raters were considered to agree only if they assigned the exact same set of labels to an explanation. However, this measure seems unduly harsh when there are small differences between label sets. Therefore, we also computed two versions of "weighted κ" (Cohen, 1968), a version of the κ statistic that takes into account the degree of difference between labels (or in our case, label sets). So, second, we computed a weighted κ based on "overlap" – meaning that the degree of disagreement was computed as the ratio of the number of unshared labels versus the total number of labels. Third, we computed a weighted κ based on "weighted overlap" – to take into account a (somewhat rough) measure of semantic similarity between the individual labels, measured as the distance in the explanation hierarchy between the labels. In the discussion that follows, we interpret the set equality measure as a lower bound on the agreement and focus mostly on the other two measures.

For each of the three agreement measures, we computed the average of the κ for each pair of human raters, as well as the average of the κ between the system and each human rater. As can be seen in Table 1, the average human-human κ was good. The set equality gives a lower bound of .77. According to the (more appropriate) overlap and weighted overlap measures, the human-human agreement is .81 and .88, respectively. The system-human κs were reasonable but somewhat lower than the corresponding human-human κs. The system-human κ according to the overlap measure is .65, according to the weighted overlap measure, it was .75. Thus, while the comparison of human-human κ and human-system κ indicates that the system's classification accuracy was quite good, there seems to be some room for improvement.

In an attempt to find ways to improve the NLU component, we examined cases where there was high agreement among the human raters (i.e., at least 2 out of the 3 human raters were in full agreement, according to the set equality measure), but where the system's classification did not agree with the majority of human raters. There were 170 such cases. A detailed examination of those cases revealed about 32 different causes for the system's failure, ranging from difficult to very minor. The most difficult problems deal with insufficient flexibility in the face of ungrammatical language and cases where the system's semantics model was not developed enough to deal with the complexity of the meaning of the student's explanations. The system needs better repair capabilities to deal with ungrammatical sentences such as "the measures of the two angles in the linear pair are add up to 180 degree." Also, the system needs a better semantic representation of coordinated structures, to handle for example the sentence "adjacent supplementary angles form a straight line and are a linear pair."Further, a number of problems of medium difficulty need to be addressed, dealing with quantifiers, relative clauses, multi-clause sentences, and the semantics of certain predicate constructs (e.g., "isosceles triangles have two sides equal"). Finally, there are a number of small flaws with various components of the system that can easily be fixed. A number of problems have been fixed already. While it will take a considerable amount of time to address all problems, overall the evaluation results suggest that knowledge-based NLU with logic-based semantics is able to perform the detailed analysis of student explanations necessary to provide helpful feedback.

6 Discussion and Conclusion

We are developing the Geometry Explanation Tutor in order to evaluate the hypothesis that natural language self-explanation can be tutored effectively by an intelligent tutoring system and leads to improved learning, as compared to alternative ways of supporting self-explanation. We conducted a pilot study to get an idea of the effectiveness of the current system and of the techniques chosen to implement it. This pilot study constituted the first time that the system was used in a school by a group of students from the target population and thus represents a realistic test for the Geometry Explanation Tutor. It does not yet represent a full test, given the limited time and scope; it covered about half the geometry theorems and definitions of the relevant curriculum unit. Also, the students probably were somewhat better prepared and of somewhat higher ability than the students in the target population.

We found evidence that the student-system dialogues are beginning to work well. The logs of student-system dialogues showed evidence that students were learning to explain geometry theorems. On the other hand, the data also revealed some room for improvement. We would like to see a higher completion rate for the dialogues. Also, the number of attempts within dialogues on which students made progress was decent but could be higher. We have described a number of measures that we took in order to improve the system's feedback, which we expect will lead to better progress rates.

Further, there was evidence that the system's knowledge-based NLU component is reaching a reasonably good level of performance in classifying student explanations. We found that the system's classification of student explanations was quite reasonable: it was not too far behind the agreement between human raters, no mean feat given that we are classifying with respect to a fine-grained set of categories. All in all, the results are encouraging but also indicate room for improvement.

What does the evaluation say about the particular techniques we have chosen for dialogue management and natural language understanding? For some geometry theorems, such as vertical angles, linear pair, and supplementary angles, it seems quite clear that the current dialogue management framework is adequate. It is still an open question however, whether this kind of architecture is going to help students to explain such difficult-to-state theorems as angle addition. At this point, we need to leave open the possibility that we will need more elaborate dialog strategies. Knowledge-based natural language understanding with logic-based semantics seems to be able to deal with challenging input such as students' mathematical explanations.

The broader goal of our project is to get students to learn with greater understanding, as compared to other (simpler) forms of tutored self-explanation. We are currently involved in a larger evaluation study, involving two schools, three teachers, and four classes, in which we compare the current system to a version where students explained their steps by making reference to a rule in a glossary.

References

Aleven, V. (Ed.). (2001). Papers of the AIED-2001 Workshop on Tutorial Dialogue Systems (pp. 59-70). Available via http://www.hcrc.ed.ac.uk/aied2001/workshops.html.

Aleven, V. & Koedinger, K. R. (in press). An effective metacognitive strategy: Learning by doing and explaining with a computer-based Cognitive Tutor. *Cognitive Science, 26*(2).

Aleven V., Popescu, O., & Koedinger, K. R. (2001). Towards Tutorial Dialog to Support Self-Explanation: Adding Natural Language Understanding to a Cognitive Tutor. In J. D. Moore, C. L. Redfield, & W. L. Johnson (Eds.), *Artificial Intelligence in Education: AI-ED in the Wired and Wireless Future* (pp. 246-255). Amsterdam, IOS Press.

Aleven, V. & Koedinger, K. R. (2000). The Need for Tutorial Dialog to Support Self-Explanation. In C. P. Rose & R. Freedman (Eds.), *Building Dialogue Systems for Tutorial Applications, Papers of the 2000 AAAI Fall Symposium* (pp. 65-73). Technical Report FS-00-01. Menlo Park, CA: AAAI Press.

Allen, J. (1995). *Natural Language Understanding* (2nd Ed.). Redwood City, CA: Cummings.

Anderson, J. R., Corbett, A. T., Koedinger, K. R., & Pelletier, R. (1995). Cognitive Tutors: Lessons Learned. *The Journal of the Learning Sciences, 4,* 167-207.

Bielaczyc, K., Pirolli, P. L., & Brown, A. L. (1995). Training in Self-Explanation and Self-Regulation Strategies: Investigating the Effects of Knowledge Acquisition Activities on Problem Solving. *Cognition and Instruction, 13,* 221-252.

Carletta, J. (1996). Assessing Agreement on Classification Tasks: The Kappa Statistic. *Computational Linguistics, 22*(2):249-254.

Chi, M. T. H. (2000). Self-Explaining Expository Texts: The Dual Processes of Generating Inferences and Repairing Mental Models. In R. Glaser (Ed.), *Advances in Instructional Psychology,* (pp. 161-237). Mahwah, NJ: Erlbaum.

Cohen, J. (1960). A coefficient of agreement for nominal scales. *Educational and Psychological Measurement, 20,* 37-46.

Cohen, J. (1968). Weighted kappa: Nominal scale agreement with provision for scaled disagreement or partial credit. *Psychological Bulletin, 70,* 213-220.

Conati C. & VanLehn K. (2000). Toward Computer-Based Support of Meta-Cognitive Skills: a Computational Framework to Coach Self-Explanation. *International Journal of Artificial Intelligence in Education*, 11, 398-415.

Evens, M. W., Brandle, S., Chang, R.C., Freedman, R., Glass, M., Lee, Y. H., Shim L.S., Woo, C. W., Zhang, Y., Zhou, Y., Michael, J.A. & Rovick, A. A. (2001). CIRCSIM-Tutor: An Intelligent Tutoring System Using Natural Language Dialogue. In *Twelfth Midwest AI and Cognitive Science Conference, MAICS 2001* (pp. 16-23).

Foltz, P. W., Laham, D. & Landauer, T. K. (1999). Automated Essay Scoring: Applications to Educational Technology. In *Proceedings of EdMedia '99*.

Graesser, A. C., VanLehn, K., Rosé, C. P., Jordan, P. W., & Harter, D. (2001). Intelligent Tutoring Systems with Conversational Dialogue. *AI Magazine*, 22(4), 39-51.

Heffernan, N. T. & Koedinger, K. R. (2000). Intelligent Tutoring Systems are Missing the Tutor: Building a More Strategic Dialog-Based Tutor. In C. P. Rose & R. Freedman (Eds.), *Building Dialogue Systems for Tutorial Applications, Papers of the 2000 AAAI Fall Symposium* (pp. 14-19). Menlo Park, CA: AAAI Press.

Koedinger, K. R., Corbett, A. T., Ritter, S., & Shapiro, L. (2000). *Carnegie Learning's Cognitive Tutor ™: Summary Research Results*. White paper. Available from Carnegie Learning Inc., 1200 Penn Avenue, Suite 150, Pittsburgh, PA 15222, E-mail: info@carnegielearning.com, Web: http://www.carnegielearning.com.

MacGregor, R, (1991). The Evolving Technology of Classification-Based Knowledge Representation Systems. In J. Sowa (ed.), *Principles of Semantic Networks: Explorations in the Representation of Knowledge*. San Mateo, CA: Morgan Kaufmann.

Popescu, O., & Koedinger, K. R. (2000). Towards Understanding Geometry Explanations In *Proceedings of the AAAI 2000 Fall Symposium, Building Dialog Systems for Tutorial Applications* (pp.80-86). Menlo Park, CA: AAAI Press.

Renkl, A., Stark, R., Gruber, H., & Mandl, H. (1998). Learning from Worked-Out Examples: the Effects of Example Variability and Elicited Self-Explanations. *Contemporary Educational Psychology, 23*, 90-108.

Renkl, A. (in press). Learning from Worked-Out Examples: Instructional Explanations Supplement Self-Explanations. *Learning and Instruction*.

Rosé, C. P. & R. Freedman, (Eds.). (2000). *Building Dialogue Systems for Tutorial Applications. Papers from the 2000 AAAI Fall Symposium*. Menlo Park, CA: AAAI Press.

Rosé, C. P. & Lavie, A. (1999). LCFlex: An Efficient Robust Left-Corner Parser. User's Guide, Carnegie Mellon University.

Wahlster, W. (2001). Robust Translation of Spontaneous Speech: A Multi-Engine Approach. Invited Paper, *IJCAI-01, Proceedings of the Seventeenth International Joint Conference on Artificial Intelligence* (pp. 1484-1493). San Francisco: Morgan Kaufmann.

When and Why Does Mastery Learning Work: Instructional Experiments with ACT-R "SimStudents"

Benjamin MacLaren and Kenneth Koedinger

Carnegie Mellon University, Pittsburgh PA
(ben@cs.cmu.edu), (koedinger@cmu.edu)

Abstract. Research in machine learning is making it possible for instructional developers to perform formative evaluations of different curricula using simulated students (VanLehn, Ohlsson & Nason, 1993). Experiments using simulated students can help clarify issues of instructional design, such as when a complex skill can be better learned by being broken into components. This paper describes two formative evaluations using simulated students that shed light on the potential benefits and limitations of mastery learning. Using an ACT-R based cognitive model (Anderson & Lebiere, 1998) we show that while mastery learning can contribute to success in some cases (Corbett & Anderson, 1995), it may actually impede learning in others. Mastery learning was crucial to learning success in an experiment comparing a traditional early algebra curriculum to a novel one presenting verbal problems first. However, in a second experiment, an instructional manipulation that contradicts mastery learning led to greater success than one consistent with it. In that experiment learning was better when more difficult problems were inserted earlier in the instructional sequence. Such problems are more difficult not because they have more components but because they cannot be successfully solved using shallow procedures that work on easier problems.

1 Introduction

This paper describes some early experiments with a "pedagogical domain theory" we have developed for "early algebra" problem solving (Koedinger & MacLaren, 2002). This theory posits knowledge-specific generalizations about quantitative reasoning and yields explanations of and predictions about student problem-solving and learning behavior during the transition from arithmetic to algebraic competence. We describe our first efforts at using the EAPS (Early Algebra Problem Solving) theory to experiment with alternative teaching strategies.

First we will briefly review developmental data from early algebra learners, followed by an ACT-R model of this data that provides an explanation of how students acquire knowledge. Then we will describe two "SimStudent" (simulated student) experiments, teaching the model according to a standard and a novel curriculum. These experiments test some of the conditions under which Mastery learning does and does not work. And because these experiments are based on a symbolic model, we can provide a detailed explanation for when and why mastery learning works or does not. Finally, we discuss some of the limitations of the current work and how future research might address some of these concerns.

S.A. Cerri, G. Gouardères, and F. Paraguaçu (Eds.): ITS 2002, LNCS 2363, pp. 355–366, 2002.
© Springer-Verlag Berlin Heidelberg 2002

1.1 Mastery Learning

Mastery learning theory (e.g., Bloom, 1987) presumes that complex skills can be broken down into components, and claims that "mastering" the components first will yield better performance in the long run. Mastery learning is based on the idea that the "failure to learn prerequisites skills is likely to interfere with students' learning of later skills" (Slavin, 1987).

Many researchers have supported the ideas behind mastery learning (Corbett & Anderson, 1995; Kulik, Kulik & Bangert-Drowns, 1990) but there are still some who remain unconvinced (e.g., Slavin, 1987). The main concern raised by Slavin is that remedial efforts made to benefit most of the students in a classroom will harm the learning of the better students. While this concern is well addressed by the use of individualized instruction using computer tutors, there are still unresolved issues in designing mastery learning curricula. For example, what exactly does it mean to break down a problem into "easier" problems, or prerequisites?

A more detailed explanation of when and why mastery learning works would help shed light on the debate about the value of mastery learning. We provide such an explanation based on the EAPS theory of quantitative knowledge and the utility learning mechanism of the ACT-R theory (Anderson & Lebiere, 1998).

1.2 An Integrated Model of Story and Equation Problem Solving

EAPS is designed to model student knowledge behind two kinds of quantitative reasoning tasks, story problem solving and equation solving, that have been addressed separately in prior research. The theory is informed by this prior research, by the constraints of ACT-R, and by difficulty factor assessments (DFAs) comparing student performance on story problems and matched equations (Koedinger & Nathan, 2002).

	Result-Unknown Problems	**Start-Unknown Problems**
Story Problems	After buying donuts at Wholey Donuts, Laura takes the $1.10 she paid and subtracts the 10 cents charge for the box they came in. Then she divides the resulting amount by the donut price of 25 cents to find the number of donuts bought. How many donuts did she buy?	After buying donuts at Wholey Donuts, Laura multiplies the number of donuts she bought by their price of 25 cents per donut. Then she adds the 10 cents charge for the box they came in and gets $1.10. How many donuts did she buy?
Word Equations	Starting with 1.10, if I subtract 0.10 and then divide by 0.25, I get a number. What is it?	Starting with some number, if I multiply by 0.25 and then add 0.10, I get 1.10. What number did I start with?
Equations	$(1.10 - 0.10) / 0.25 = X$	$X * 0.25 + 0.10 = 1.10$

Fig. 1. Example problems from DFA study with different combinations of difficulty factors for the problem representation and directionality

Two factors from these DFAs are illustrated in Figure 1, unknown position and presentation type. The pair of problems in each row of Figure 1 differs in where the problem unknown is positioned. The problems in column 1 are called Result-Unknowns because the unknown is the result of the process described. The problems in column 2 are called Start-Unknown because the unknown is at the start. Variations within the columns illustrate a second factor. They require the same underlying arithmetic, but differ in the representation in which they are presented. The "Story Problems" in the first row are presented verbally and include reference to a real world situation (e.g., wages). The "Word Equations" in the second row are also presented verbally but do not include a situation. Finally, "Equations" are presented symbolically and have no situational information.

In contrast with common expectations (Nathan & Koedinger, 2000), students performed better, not worse, on story problems than matched equations. The results are summarized in Figure 2. Students were 65% correct on verbal problems (like those in the top two rows of Figure 1) but only 42% correct on equations (the bottom row).

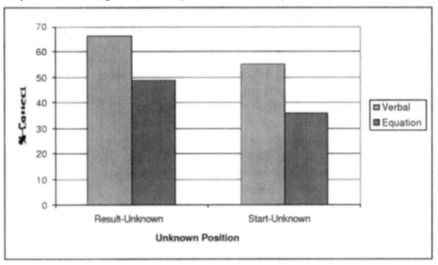

Fig. 2. Results from DFA study showing main effect of problem representation

2 A Cognitive Model of the Empirical Data

We have developed a series of cognitive models to explain these and other observations in the DFA data, called EAPS (Koedinger & MacLaren, 2002). In EAPS the general flow of control is 1) comprehend the problem presentation (whether story, word, or equation) to extract relevant arithmetic operators and their arguments, 2) manipulate the operators as necessary (e.g., invert them), and 3) solve any arithmetic subgoals that are produced. EAPS models two general classes of errors: arithmetic and conceptual. Conceptual errors include things like forgetting to change the sign when removing an operator in the verbal representation or confusing the order of operations in the symbolic representation. For arithmetic errors, we model bugs (miss-alignment of decimal places in doing arithmetic) and slips (e.g., 2*3=5).

EAPS explains the DFA results by hypothesizing differences in verbal versus equation comprehension processes. First, consistent with students' extended English language experience and limited symbolic algebra language experience, the production rules that comprehend verbal representations are more likely to fire than those that comprehend equations. Second, the equation comprehension productions include certain buggy productions that result from shallow processing of past instructional experiences (e.g., not respecting order of operations).

EAPS is implemented in the ACT-R production system (Anderson & Lebiere, 1998). Components of knowledge include declarative chunks to represent quantities and quantitative relations and if-then production rules to represent procedures for quantitative reasoning.

2.1 ACT-R's Utility Learning Mechanism

One central issue in production-based cognitive architectures like ACT-R is how to choose which production to fire when several match. If the condition side of several productions applies, there is a conflict that needs to be resolved. To model these situations, ACT-R includes a "rational" component for conflict resolution based on decision theory. To determine which production to fire if there is a conflict, the expected gain of each production is computed. The expected gain or utility of a production is defined to be equal to PG–C, where G is the estimated value of the current goal, P is the estimated likelihood that executing the production will eventually satisfy the current goal and C is the estimated cost of executing the production.[1]

The P term is determined by another equation: $R_{alpha} / (R_{alpha}+R_{beta})$, where R_{alpha} and R_{beta} refer to the number of eventual successes and failures that occurred when a given production fired respectively (Lovett, 1998). These successes and failures include those before a simulation (estimated from empirical data) and those during a simulation. As a model runs and gets feedback, it updates the R_{alpha} and R_{beta} values for each production that fires in a problem, thus changing their estimated R values.

In ACT-R's conflict resolution mechanism, the production with the highest utility is not always chosen. Rather, there is a stochastic process implemented as a Gaussian noise parameter that will sometimes cause a production with a lower utility to be selected. The probability of selecting a given production with expected gain g_i from n possibilities is determined by the Likelihood Ratio equation (Anderson & Lebiere 1998, p. 65):

Probability of production i firing =

$$p(\mathit{firing}(\Pr odi)) = \frac{e^{g_i/t}}{\sum e^{g_n/t}}$$

where g is equal to PG-C, t is:

$$\sqrt{6}\sigma/\pi$$

where g is equal to PG-C, t is sqrt(6)* σ/π, with σ being the standard deviation of the noise, and the summation is across the n productions in the conflict set. Produc-

---

[1] ACT-R does not propose that people explicitly analyze their problem-solving choices using decision theory, but rather that their choices conform with this analysis.

tion rule utilities, combined with the Gaussian noise parameter, provide a useful approach to modeling student choice behavior.

Using ACT-R's utility mechanism just described, we tuned our EAPS cognitive model to behave in accordance with a detailed coding of students' strategies and errors (Koedinger & MacLaren, 2002). For setting initial values for R_{alpha} and R_{beta} we used an estimate of what the value of P should be and also the number of relevant problems the student is likely to have seen in prior experience (i.e., R_{alpha} plus R_{beta}).

A key subset of the 11 parameters used to fit EAPS can be seen in Table 1. The first two (VC, SC) deal with comprehension of a verbal versus a symbolic representation. OA, Operate-on-Adjacent-Numbers, is an over-general production that ignores operator precedence in an equation and, thus, sometimes produces incorrect results. CRH is for comprehending relations with hi-priority operators (e.g., "*" and "/"). The next three (AR, SL, BG) capture behavior on arithmetic.

Table 1. Subset of Parameters for the Math Model

VC	(92%)	– Comprehend-Verbal-Relation
SC, CN, CO	(78%)	– Comprehend-Symbolic-Relation,Comp-Number,Comp-Operator
OA	(4%)	– Operate-on-Adjacent-Numbers
CRH	(69%)	– Comprehend-Relation-Hi (relation with high-precedence operator)
AP	(97%)	– Arithmetic-Procedure
SL	(3%)	– Arithmetic-Slip
BG	(0%)	– Arithmetic-Bug

The math model equation representing the probability of a correct solution on a result-unknown story problem is shown in Table 2a. EAPS needs to comprehend two verbal relations and perform two arithmetic operations. Using the likelihood that these productions will fire for the average student, shown in parentheses in Table 1, we get $VC_1(.92) * AP(.97) * VC_1(.92) * AP(.97) = 80\%$ correct story result unknowns.

The model of a correct solution to a result-unknown equation like "25 * 4 + 10 = X" is a bit more complex as we explicitly represent the comprehension of the elements in the equation.[2] As can be seen in Table 2b, EAPS must comprehend two numbers (CN) and two operators (CO) before it can comprehend the symbolic relations (SC) and perform the arithmetic. A path resulting in an Order-of-Operations error is shown in Table 2b. After comprehending "800 – 30" (CN * CO * CN), EAPS decides to operate on these adjacent numbers and subtract them (OA * AP) instead of continuing to comprehend the rest of the equation. This results in an Order-of-Operations error, 100 ((80 - 30) * 2) instead 20 (80 - (30 * 2)). For more details on how the cognitive model was used to guide the creation of the math model equations and how we tuned the resulting math model see Koedinger & MacLaren (2002).

---

[2] We chose not to model verbal comprehension in contrast to equation comprehension because beginning algebra students had little difficulty comprehending the word problems used.

Table 2. Subset of Math Model Equations for Paths through Model

a. Paths leading to a correct answer for Result-unknown problems (with integer arithmetic):
   Story Problem: VC * AP * VC * AP
   Equation: CN * CO * CN * CO * CN * SC * AP * SC * AP
b. A path for an Order-of-Operations error on problems like"80–30*2=X"
   Equations: CN * CO * CN * OA * AP * CO * CN * SC * AP

3 Developmental Models for Early Algebra Problem Solving

EAPS did a good job of capturing the main effects of the student error and strategy selection behavior for the "average" student, but in order to begin to simulate instruction using EAPS, we needed models of students at different performance levels. We needed versions of EAPS that model weaker students, that could be "taught" to become more like the better performers in our empirical data. We separated students into six developmental "zones," shown in Table 3, and then fit a version of EAPS to model each one of these zones.

Table 3. Performance Groups of Students Based on Categories of Problems Correctly Solved
   Zone 0 – None
   Zone 1 – Verbal arithmetic problems (top 2 on the left in Figure 1)
   Zone 2 – Verbal problems (verbal algebra as well as verbal arithmetic) (top 4 problems)
   Zone 3 – Arithmetic problems (symbolic as well as verbal arithmetic) (3 problems on left)
   Zone 4 – All problems but symbolic algebra (all but the problem on bottom right)
   Zone 5 – All problems.

Most traditional textbooks (Nathan, Long & Alibali, 2002) present arithmetic symbol problems first, followed by arithmetic word problems, symbolic algebra problems, and finally algebra word problems. This "Textbook curriculum" is shown in Table 4a. However, students in Koedinger and Nathan (2000) got 67% of the arithmetic word problems correct, but only 49% of symbolic arithmetic problems correct. Given this data, it was natural to ask why the more difficult problems should be given earlier in the curriculum? Students might learn better following a different curriculum, which we call Verbal Precedence, shown in Table 4b, where informal verbal reasoning skills precede the equivalent reasoning skills in the symbolic representation.

Table 4. Curricula for SimStudent Experiment 1
a. Control Condition: Textbook curriculum:
   1. Arithmetic equations   49% correct in DFA data
   2. Arithmetic word problems   67% "
   3. Algebra equations   36% "
   4. Algebra word problems   56% "
b. Experimental Condition: Verbal Precedence curriculum:
   1. Arithmetic word problems   67% correct in DFA data
   2. Arithmetic equations   49% "
   3. Algebra word problems   56% "
   4. Algebra equations   36% "

4   SimStudent Experiment 1: Textbook vs. Verbal Precedence

The EAPS theory and simulation provide a means to evaluate whether the Verbal Precedence curriculum can lead to more effective learning than the Textbook curriculum and to provide an explanation for why it might.

We used eight hundred SimStudents in the experiment, one hundred in each of the eight conditions resulting from crossing the three dimensions shown in Table 5.

Table 5. Variables for the Eight Instructional Conditions in SimStudent Experiment 1

1. **Ordering** – Half of each of these groups followed the Verbal Precedence Curriculum where word problems were practiced before symbolic problems. The other half followed the Textbook Curriculum where symbolic problems were given first.
2. **Mastery** – Half the SimStudents solved 1-operator problems before 2-operator problems, while SimStudents in the non-mastery control condition only solved 2-operator problems.
3. **Initial competence** – Half of each group was made up of SimStudents parameterized to be in the lowest performance group (Zone 0), while the other half started with an ability to solve Verbal-Arithmetic problems (Zone 1). We used these two performance groups simply because they represent students most in need of instruction.

Procedure. Each SimStudent was presented with ten problems at each level in the chosen curriculum. If the simulated student solved eight of the ten problems successfully, it was moved on to the next problem in the curriculum sequence. If it failed to reach this level of success, it was given the same problem type again. If it failed to get eight out of ten problems correct after four attempts at any level, the SimStudent failed. SimStudents are given feedback after each problem and are performing utility learning during the presentation of each of these problems, so its performance can improve with practice. This enables EAPS to strengthen the productions that transfer from simpler problems to the harder ones that follow.

The feedback given is only whether the problem is correct or incorrect, not what the exact error was. If EAPS makes it all the way through all the problem sets in the curriculum sequence, it is considered to have passed the curriculum. If the student gives up before actually writing anything down on a problem, the productions fired up to that point were not penalized. This is because if EAPS gives up, it does not know that the productions used to that point are wrong.

The results of this experiment can be seen in Table 6. 59% of Zone 1 SimStudents make it through all levels of the Verbal Mastery curriculum, and 44% make it through all levels of the Textbook Mastery. By breaking down the problems presented into parts, the probability of getting a problem correct increases. Initial performance on a problem like "X*2=10", for example, is much greater than performance on a problem like "X*4+2=10". This performance difference dramatically improves the learning process as positive feedback is much more likely and thus good productions do not get penalized along with bad ones.

Table 6. Results from SimStudent Experiment 1

	Zone 0	Zone 1
Verbal Mastery	28%	59%
Textbook Mastery	24%	44%
Verbal Control	14%	32%
Textbook Control	6%	26%

Two conclusions can be drawn. First, the Verbal Precedence curriculum was consistently more effective than the traditional Textbook curriculum. Second, Mastery Learning proved to be a much more effective pedagogical strategy than the control. For the two curricula compared, the Mastery condition made it more likely that a SimStudent would successfully complete the curriculum. When the SimStudent did fail on a problem, feedback was more likely to be focused on those skills responsible, making blame assignment more effective.

5   Experiment 2: Discouraging Shallow Knowledge

Another set of predictions from our model that we wanted to explore followed from EAPS' representation of bugs as overly general knowledge.[3] Like other learning mechanisms, ACT-R's utility learning mechanism yields learning outcomes that are sensitive to the order in which problems are presented. In particular, some presentation orders can lead to a greater likelihood of over-general productions than others can. In poorly designed instruction, the sequences of examples and practice problems may be such that students can initially learn and be successful with an overly general production. In this case, continued practice on such problems would yield increasing utility estimates for the overly general productions. It would be then necessary to distinguish the overly general production from the correct one. This potential confusion suggests that curricula should have problems early on that will cause overly general rules to fail. In such cases, more specific correct productions increase in utility and further practice will replace the over-general production.

An example problem that will cause the over-general Operate-on-Adjacent-Numbers production to fail is "800 – 40 x 4". This production can apply to the first part of this expression and incorrectly subtract 40 from 800. It could also apply to the second relation, "40x4", and produce a correct answer. It seems a plausible instructional hypothesis that problems like "800–40x4" should be introduced early in a curriculum so that overly general productions can receive negative feedback before they have a chance to accumulate a significant utility value.

The first step we took was to modify the most successful curriculum in SimStudent Experiment 1 (using parameter setting three and Zone 1) by replacing the fourth problem with a 2-operator symbolic problem "10 + 4 * 25 = X" to the curriculum. The first four problems of the resulting curriculum are shown in Table 7.

---

[3] In ACT-R new productions are created by analogy from example problem solving traces. ACT-R hypothesizes that bugs are introduced from incorrect generalizations during analogy.

Table 7. Control Curriculum1 for SimStudent Experiment 2

1. 1-operator Story Arithmetic problems (equivalent to "4 * 25 = X")
2. 2- operator Story Arithmetic problems (equivalent to "4 * 25 + 10 = X")
3. 1- operator Symbolic Arithmetic – indifferent to Order-of-Operations: 10 * 4 = X
4. 2- operator Symbolic Arithmetic – discouraging Order-of-Operations: 10 + 4 * 25 = X
5.

As before, we then ran one hundred SimStudents on this curriculum. The SimStudents did not succeed at all with this curriculum. This failure was due to the over-general Operate-on-Adjacent-Numbers, which succeeded on single operator problems (problem category 3 in Table 7) and had its utility dramatically increased. Then, once the model started attempting two operator problems like "10 + 4 * 25" (problem category 4 in Table 7) it would usually fail because Operate-on-Adjacent-Numbers had such high utility. Thus, not only would Operate-on-Adjacent-Numbers be penalized but many other good productions that fired with it would as well.

As a potential solution to the problem of prematurely strengthening Operate-on-Adjacent-Numbers, we decided to introduce problems earlier in the curriculum where Operate-on-Adjacent-Numbers would fail, like "10 + 4 * 25". We also *raised* the R_{alpha} and R_{beta} values of the lower level symbolic comprehension productions to make them more resistant to change, and *lowered* R_{alpha} and R_{beta} values of Operate-on-Adjacent-Numbers production, to make it more sensitive to change. Using two versions of two operator result-unknown equations as the third and fourth problems in the sequence, we created two new curricula, shown in Table 8:

Table 8. Curricula for SimStudent Experiment 2

a. Control Curriculum2:
1. 1- operator Story Arithmetic problems (equivalent to "4 * 25 = X")
2. 2- operator story arithmetic problems (equivalent to "4 * 25 + 10 = X")
3. 2- operator Symbolic Arithmetic – indifferent to Order-of-Operations: 10 * 4 * 25 = X
4. 2- operator Symbolic Arithmetic – discouraging Order-of-Operations: 10 + 4 * 25 = X

b. Experimental Curriculum to challenge shallow (overly-general) knowledge:
1. 1- operator Story Arithmetic (equivalent to "4 * 25 = X")
2. 2- operator Story Arithmetic (equivalent to "4 * 25 + 10 = X")
3. 2- operator Symbolic Arithmetic – discouraging Order-of-Operations: 10 + 4 * 25 = X
4. 2- operator Symbolic Arithmetic – indifferent to Order-of-Operations: 10 * 4 * 25 = X

On the third problem category in Control Curriculum2, Operate-on-Adjacent-Numbers produces a correct answer. Operate-on-Adjacent-Numbers is then strengthened, so that when the fourth problem category in the Control Curriculum is reached, Operate-on-Adjacent-Numbers will be more likely to operate on "10+4." However, it is incorrect in this case, and all the other correct productions that fired to reach the resulting incorrect answer will also be penalized.

On the third problem in the Experimental Curriculum the situation is different. When Operate-on-Adjacent-Numbers fires on "10+4" it results in an incorrect solution. The resulting errors make it more likely that Operate-on-Adjacent-Numbers will be penalized and weakened before it has become strengthened too much.

The results of SimStudent Experiment 2 are shown in Table 9. Thirty-six percent of students made it through the experimental curriculum, compared to six percent for the control. In the control, Operate-on-Adjacent-Numbers was strengthened as it produced correct answers on the problem "10*4*25" in problem set 3. When EAPS then attempted problem set 4, "10+4*25" it often failed (because Operate-on-Adjacent-Numbers would not yield a correct answer when it applied to "10+4"), driving not only its R value down, but more importantly weakening the non-buggy productions that fired along with it to produce an answer (as can be seen in Table 2b) and reducing the likelihood of success.

Table 9. Results from SimStudent Experiment 2

	Zone 1
Challenge Shallow Knowledge	36%
Control Condition	6%

In the experimental condition where Operate-on-Adjacent-Numbers was discouraged early, its R-value was lowered by the problems in set 3, "10+4*25", before it had a chance to get strengthened. By the time EAPS got to problem set 4 Operate-on-Adjacent-Numbers was no longer firing – it had been successfully weeded out.

It was not obvious that our hypothesis about how to weed out shallow knowledge was correct. It is in conflict with the mastery learning prescription to have students master easier problems before moving to more difficult ones. Experiment 2 was designed to test this hypothesis, namely to see whether early introduction of more difficult problems that challenge over-general knowledge hurts or helps learning.

6   Discussion and Future Work

Our SimStudent experiments targeted two instructional principles that appear to be in conflict with each other. The "Mastery Learning" principle suggests that presentation and mastery of simpler component problems should precede presentation of more complex problems. A second "Challenge Shallow Knowledge" principle suggests that certain harder problems should be introduced earlier in a curriculum to prevent students from over-practicing shallow strategies that only work on simpler problems. Together these principles result in an instructional dilemma. The Mastery Learning principle encourages the use of simple problems early in the curriculum while the Challenge Shallow Knowledge principle encourages the use of harder problems early in the curriculum.

The acquisition of shallow, over-general productions appears more likely for certain classes of problems than others. For those problem categories where shallow knowledge acquisition is less likely, the Mastery Learning principle should be heeded, that is, curricula should start with simpler problems. For problem categories where shallow production acquisition is likely, we suspect the Challenge Shallow Knowledge principle is more important and harder problems should be introduced early. Results of experiment 2 are consistent with this claim, but we need to do further experiments and sensitivity analysis.

A broader issue is how faithfully our simulated student experiments have captured the notion of learning. For example, we do not model the knowledge-level learning process (i.e., the acquisition of productions via ACT-R's analogy mechanism). We could add this functionality, but analogy produces a number of productions at different levels of generality, which then need to be pruned by experience. We feel this pruning process is more central than the knowledge level learning, and hypothesize the results presented here would not be affected if we enabled EAPS to acquire productions via analogy.

There are also three main issues that need to be considered with respect to Mastery Learning. The first issue that needs to be considered is the nature of the feedback students receive. In our experiments the SimStudents were simply told they were right or wrong. Clearly giving the model more directed feedback, or giving the model the ability to provide some of this corrective feedback, would be a more accurate model of a good instructional environment. This kind of more directed feedback is not possible with hidden skills, so it is possible to imagine a combination of directed and blanket feedback being used in future work with simulated students.

A second issue that needs to be addressed is the corrective instruction students receive if they have not mastered the lesson they are currently working on. According to Bloom (1987) if students are having trouble with a given lesson the teacher should provide corrective instruction using a different approach. However, we are currently only modeling learning as an increase in the utility estimate of the knowledge, and the student just applies the same approach again, so different ways of assisting EAPS needs to be looked into.

We have considered some ways in which the credit and blame attribution might be improved in our SimStudents learning processes including: 1) a better blame attribution algorithm, which assigns blame in proportion to current strength of productions involved, and 2) more deliberate reasoning in blame attribution whereby the student reasons about which subgoal is at fault. Beyond the challenge of implementing such improvements, it is an interesting question whether human learner behavior is consistent with such improvements or is more like ACT-R's current model of blame attribution.

It is interesting to note in retrospect that the two curricula in SimStudent1 did not contain problems that frequently resulted in an error when the Operate-on-Adjacent-Numbers production fired, which means that the SimStudents that pass those curricula may still make Order-of-Operations errors. However it is also probably the case that curricula being used in schools today do the same thing, leaving large amounts of shallow knowledge present in *real* students!

References

Anderson, J. R., & Lebiere, C. (1998). The Atomic Components of Thought. Laurence Erlbaum.

Bloom, B. (1987). A Response to Slavin's Mastery Learning Reconsidered, 57, 507-508.

Corbett, A.T. and Anderson, J. R. (1995). Knowledge decomposition and subgoal reification in the ACT programming tutor. Artificial Intelligence and Education, 1995: The Proceedings of AI-ED 95. Charlottesville, VA: AACE.

Koedinger, K.R., & MacLaren, B. A. (2002). Developing a Pedagogical Domain Theory of Early Algebra Problem Solving. CMU-HCII Tech Report 02-100. Accessible via http://reports-archive.adm.cs.cmu.edu/hcii.html

Koedinger, K. R. & Nathan, M. J. (Under review). The real story behind story problems: Effects of representations on quantitative reasoning.

Kulik, C. C., Kulik, J. A., & Bangert-Drowns, R. L. (1990). Effectiveness of mastery learning programs: A meta-analysis. Review of Education Research, 60, 265-299.

Lovett, M. (1998). Choice. In The Atomic Components of Thought. Anderson J.R. & Lebiere, C. (pp255-296) Laurence Erlbaum Associates .

Nathan, M. J. , Long, S. D. & Alibali, M. W. (in press). An analysis of the presentation of arithmetic and algebraic topics in common mathematics textbooks. In preparation.

Slavin, R. (1987). Mastery learning reconsidered. Review of educational research, 57, 175-213.

VanLehn, K., Ohlsson, S., & Nason, R. (1994). Applications of simulated students: An exploration. Journal of Artificial Intelligence and Education, 5(2), 135-175.

Minimally Invasive Tutoring of Complex Physics Problem Solving

Kurt VanLehn[1], Collin Lynch[1], Linwood Taylor[1], Anders Weinstein[1],
Robert Shelby[2], Kay Schulze[2], Don Treacy[2], and Mary Wintersgill[2]

[1] LRDC, University of Pittsburgh, Pittsburgh, PA USA 15260
VanLehn@cs.pitt.edu, lht@lzri.com, {collinL,andersw}@pitt.edu
http://www.pitt.edu/~vanlehn/andes.html
[2] US Naval Academy, Annapolis, MD, USA
{Shelby, Schulze, Treacy, MWinter}@usna.edu

Abstract. Solving complex physics problems requires some kind of knowledge for selecting appropriate applications of physics principles. This knowledge is tacit, in that it is not explicitly taught in textbooks, existing tutoring systems or anywhere else. Experts seem to have acquired it via implicit learning and may not be aware of it. Andes is a coach for physics problem solving that has had good evaluations, but still does not teach complex problem solving as well as we would like. The conventional ITS approach to increasing its effectiveness requires teaching the tacit knowledge explicitly, and yet this would cause Andes to be more invasive. In particular, the textbooks and instructors would have to make space in an already packed curriculum for teaching the tacit knowledge. This paper discusses our attempts to teach the tacit knowledge without making Andes more invasive.

1 Objectives

The Andes project [1-3] began with three objectives [4]. The first was to improve the learning of university physics students. This goal has been accomplished. In large-scale field evaluations at the US Naval Academy over the last three years, students who did their homework with Andes learned significantly more than students who did similar homework on paper. These results are discussed below.

The second objective was to see if Andes could be minimally invasive. In particular, could students adopt Andes for doing their homework while virtually nothing else in the physics course changed? The professors would give the same lectures, use the same textbooks, assign the same homework problems and conduct the same labs and recitations. We think that Andes will have a much wider impact if it can be used with many kinds of teaching, both conventional and reformed. This goal has been difficult to achieve, and our progress is discussed below.

The third objective was to test three help systems. The Conceptual Helper is called when Andes decides that the student is unfamiliar with a specific principle of physics or has a misconception. The Conceptual Helper uses "minilessons" that are adapted to the context of the student's problem solving. Students using Andes with the Con-

S.A. Cerri, G. Gouardères, and F. Paraguaçu (Eds.): ITS 2002, LNCS 2363, pp. 367–376, 2002.

ceptual Helper learned more than students using a version of Andes with ordinary hint sequences [5, 6]. Recent work has replaced the expository minilessons of the Conceptual Helper with natural language dialogs run by Atlas, and has shown that this results in an improvement in student understanding [7].

The Self-Explanation Coach coaches students as they study a solved physics problem (i.e., an example). In order to determine if the student has self-explained an example adequately, it monitors the location and latency of the student's visual attention. If it appears that the student fails to self-explain specific key aspects of the example, the coach guides the student in doing so. Some students who used the SE Coach learned more than students who studied the same examples without the coach [8, 9].

The Procedural Helper answers help requests while students are solving problems [10]. In particular, if the student gets stuck and asks, "What do I do next?" the Procedural Helper will suggest a goal or action. If Andes marks a student entry wrong and the student asks, "What's wrong with that?" the Procedural Helper gives advice based on determining whether the error is the result of either an incorrect inference or a correct inference that does not lead to the goal. The Procedural Helper has been evaluated repeatedly, as described below. Although it is improving, it is still not as effective as we would like.

In short, although we have achieved many of our objectives, two remain: reducing the invasiveness of Andes and increasing the effectiveness of the Procedural Helper. This paper reviews our progress towards achieving those goals.

2 The Andes1 User Interface

This paper only discusses the part of Andes that coaches students as they solve problems. A typical physics problem and its solution on the Andes screen are shown in Figure 1. Students read the problem (top of the upper left window), draw vectors and coordinate axes (bottom of the upper left window), define variables (upper right window) and enter equations (lower right window). These are exactly the actions that they should do when solving physics problems with pencil and paper. The main difference between Andes and paper are:

1. Andes gives immediate feedback by turning correct entries green and incorrect entries red. If a red entry is the result of a low-level error (e.g., illegal algebraic syntax), an error message pops up saying so.
2. Andes answers "what should I do next?" and "what's wrong with that?" help requests. Most help requests are answered by canned-text and menu dialogues in the tutor window (lower left). If Andes determines that the student has flawed physics knowledge, it invokes either the Conceptual Helper, which conducts a hypertext-based minilesson, or Atlas, which conducts a natural language dialogue in the tutor window.
3. Andes will solve algebraically the equations that the student has entered, provided that student has entered enough correct ones.
4. Variables must be defined before they are used in equations, and the only way to define certain variables is to draw vectors and/or coordinate axes.

With the exception of the fourth point, which will be discussed later, Andes acts simply as an unobtrusive but helpful piece of paper.   This should facilitate transfer to unsupported, paper-based problem solving.

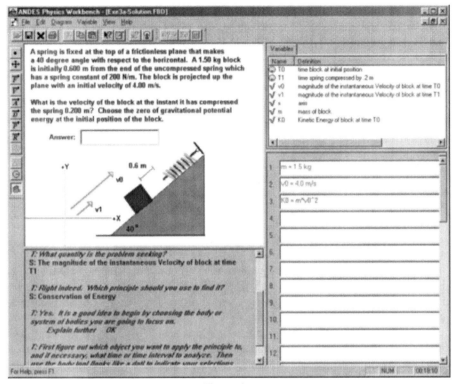

Fig. 1. The Andes screen.

3   The Andes1 Procedural Help System

Two major versions of Andes have been developed. From the student's view, they differed only in the kind of help they gave when asked "What's next?" or "What's wrong?" That is, they had the same user interface but completely different Procedural Help systems. This section briefly describes the first version of Andes, called Andes1. Subsequent sections discuss its evaluation, then Andes2 and its evaluation.

When the student was stuck and asked Andes1 "What should I do next?", it would first select a target step then give a sequence of hints intended to suggest that action to the student. The hint sequences were similar to those used by many intelligent tutoring systems, but the method of selecting a target step was unique. Andes1 precomputed all possible solutions to the problem and stored them as a Bayesian network called the *solution graph* [11, 12]. The nodes in the solution graph represented goals, facts and other propositions, as well as the inferences (rule applications) that connected the propositions. Andes1 searched the solution graph for a target step as follows [10]. Starting from the student's most recent correct action, it found a goal in the network that was likely to be the one dominating that action. It then searched for another action dominated by that goal that had not yet been entered and was probably one that the student didn't know how to do. This was selected as the target step.

If the student made an incorrect entry and asked Andes1 "What's wrong with that?", it again selected a target step and gave a hint sequence. The target step was selected by comparing the incorrect entry to all possible entries of that type and selecting the closest matching one [13]. The position of the target step in the solution graph was not used.

4   Evaluations of Andes1

The first full-scale evaluation of Andes1 occurred during the fall of 1999 as part of the regular US Naval Academy physics course. For about 6 weeks, 173 students used Andes1 to do their homework, and 162 students did their homework using pencil and paper. The Andes1 students scored significantly higher (t=2.2, p=.036) on a midterm exam given at the end of the intervention period, and the effect size was a modest 0.21 standard deviations [14].

More detailed evaluations were undertaken to find ways to improve Andes1. Students at the University of Pittsburgh who had recently taken physics were asked to solve problems on Andes while giving a verbal protocol. They were often totally lost and seldom found Andes' help useful.

In order to get a more formal evaluation at this level of detail, we extracted from the log files 40 episodes where a student had asked Andes1 "what's wrong?" with an equation. We printed screen snapshots just before Andes1 gave its advice. Working independently, the three USNA physicists wrote on the snapshots the advice that they would give to the student. Often the advice was somewhat different, but on 21 snapshots their advice was the same. However, Andes' advice was the same as the physicists' advice on only 3 of the 21 snapshots.

Two patterns stood out in the physicists' advice. One was that they often insisted that students do any steps that they had skipped in the procedure for applying a principle. For instance, many students had trouble writing a correct equation for Newton's second law, and they had skipped drawing the force and acceleration vectors. Instead of helping the students correct their equation, the physicists would usually ask the students to draw the missing vectors.

The second pattern was that when the student was lost, the physicists would not just select a target step and hint it as Andes would. Instead, they would help the students infer a target step themselves via a dialogue such as the following:

Tutor: What quantity is the problem seeking?
Student: The acceleration of the car.
Tutor: What principle should you use to find it?
Student: Newton's second law.

If the student had not yet applied Newton's second law, then the physicists would coach the hypothetical student through the steps in its procedure. If the student had already applied Newton's second law, the physicists would say, "I see you've applied it already as equation 4. What quantities in the equation are unknown?" When the student answers, "the frictional force on the car," the process repeats and the physicists ask for a principle to find that quantity, etc.

Lastly, we discovered that Andes would frequently give outlandish advice when asked "What's wrong?" with an incorrect equation. Often it would suggest replacing a piece of the equation with a specific number or expression, creating an equation that none of the physicists could recognize. This turned out to be due to its basic algorithm for selecting a target step for "What's wrong" help. Even if the student was just beginning to solve the problem, it would consider target equations from the very end of the solution. Moreover, it would consider all possible algebraic combinations of correct equations even if that combination didn't participate in the solution. Consequently, it would hint writing an equation that the student wasn't intending to write and should never write. Unfortunately, when students took Andes' advice and entered the suggested equation, it would turn green (correct). Students probably found this terribly confusing.

The second full-scale evaluation occurred during fall of 2000 at the US Naval Academy. The major goal was to increase the amount of physics covered, so the intervention lasted longer (10 weeks), covered more problems (60) and covered more topics. We also made some limited changes to cure the problems found in the analyses of the 1999 log files: (1) Students were required to draw vectors rather than define vector variables without drawing them. (2) The plan inference method described in [10] was replaced with a simpler technique. These changes left Andes1 giving essentially the same feedback and help as the 1999 version. Nonetheless, the Andes1 students scored significantly higher on a midterm exam just after the intervention ($t=7.74$, $p<.00001$), and this time the effect size was a satisfying 0.92 standard deviations [14]. However, Andes' advice still differed substantially from the advice given by the physicists, so it seemed that there was still room for improvement.

5   The Objectives of Andes2

The physicists clearly had a goal hierarchy in mind when they gave advice to the students. The lower levels of the goal hierarchy corresponded to well-known methods for applying principles, which are printed in textbooks. For instance, the method for applying Newton's second law to an object is to draw all the forces acting on the object, draw its acceleration, draw coordinate axes and write an equation. The upper levels of the goal hierarchy seemed to correspond to a search that starts at the sought quantity, applies a principle containing the sought, and then recurses to find values for any unknowns in the principle's equation. This corresponds to a backwards search strategy used by many expert physics problem solving systems [e.g., 15]. Although empirical studies have not precisely identified the strategies used by human experts, it appears that they use this backwards search some of the time, but more often hold principle applications in memory until they have planned out a complete solution, then they write equations as they solve them [16]. Our physicists' advice was consistent with just one strategy, backwards search, so we decided to teach that, along with the well-known procedures for applying principles.

Our first task was to invent a display that reified the goal hierarchies. When we implemented such a display (two of them, in fact), the physicists carefully considered them but ultimately rejected them as too invasive. For students to use these displays, they would have to be explicitly taught the backwards search algorithm, a vocabulary for specifying goals and some tools for navigating and editing the goal hierarchies. This seemed to the physicists to require too much class time. Even if they changed their curriculum, they doubted that any of their colleagues would be willing to. In short, the goal of minimal invasiveness was incompatible with the standard technique of reifying goals and explicitly teaching a problem solving strategy.

Thus, we decided to have Andes teach the problem solving strategy in the same way that the physicists seemed to teach it: as part of their advice when asked for help. That is, when a student asks "What should I do next?" Andes should engage the student in the same question-answer dialogue that the physicists did.

6   The Implementation of Andes2

Many changes were required in order to implement Andes2. First, we had to restructure the physics knowledge base. Instead of a flat set of several hundred inference rules as used in Andes1, the new knowledge base was organized as about 100 principles, each with its textbook method for applying it.

The solution graph was restructured as a *bubble graph* and a set of *method graphs*. The bubble graph is composed of two kinds of nodes: nodes representing quantities and nodes representing principle applications. A node representing a principle application is linked to the nodes representing the quantities that appear in the principle application's equation. Associated with each principle application node is a graph of propositions similar to the ones used in Andes1. This graph, called the method graph, represents how to actually accomplish the application of the principle.

When the student asks "What should I do next?", Andes2 conducts a dialogue based on the solution graph. It always starts by asking the student, "What quantity does the problem seek?" It offers the student a hierarchical menu of all physics quantities. The student gets negative feedback and another chance if the student fails to pick a quantity that is actually sought by the problem. Otherwise, the tutor asks, "What principle should be used to find it?" and offers a hierarchical menu of all principle applications. To evaluate the student's selection, it starts at the sought quantity's node in the bubble graph and sees if the student's selected principle application is indeed on a solution path for this problem. If not, Andes2 says so and asks the student to try again. If the selected principle application is appropriate and not yet finished, then Andes2 enters the method graph for that principle. It locates the first unaccomplished step, and composes a hint sequence for that step. These hints drive the rest of the dialogue. On the other hand, if the principle has already been applied, Andes2 says so and asks the student which unknowns in the equation should be determined next. The student selects a quantity, and Andes2 uses the bubble graph to check that it is indeed an unknown in the principle application. From this point on, the process recurses. Eventually the tutor and the student end up at an unfinished principle application, traverse its method graph, select a target step and accomplish it.

Since Andes2 locates a target step by asking a sequence of questions of the student, it has no need to guess a target step based on probabilistic reasoning. Thus, Andes2 does not use a Bayesian network. We would revive it if Andes needed estimates of the student's mastery of principles in order to decide which problem to assign next and whether to go on to the next chapter. However, having different students do different homework was believed to be too invasive for the US Naval Academy. For instance, students who were assigned more physics problems could justifiably complain that Andes hurt their grades in their other courses.

We also revised the help that Andes gives when students ask, "What's wrong with that?" Instead of finding a closest matching target step then hinting the difference between it and the student's step, Andes2 has a set of error handlers. Each can recognize a specific type of error. For instance, there is an error handler for using the wrong time specifier on a given quantity, which is usually due to a misreading of the problem statement. There is an error handler for failing to include a minus sign on a vector component when the vector is parallel to the axis; this is usually due to a misunderstanding of vector algebra. Each error handler has hints and/or minilessons designed to remedy the error and any misconceptions that might underlie it. If none of the error handlers recognizes the student's incorrect entry, then the student is advised to ask, "What should I do next?"

Joel Shapiro, a physicist who visited our group for a year, implemented a fundamental change in the way Andes recognizes equations [17]. Andes1 precomputed a table of all algebraic combinations of principle applications. This allowed it to recognize $T\_y-mg=m*a\_y$ even though it is composed of several principle applications: $T\_y+W\_y=m*a\_y$ and $W\_y = -W = -m*g$. This precomputation became intractable as Andes1 began to handle more complex problems. Andes2 recognized which primitive equations have been combined to form the student's equation by taking the gradient of the student's equation at a particular point, then seeing whether there is a set of principle applications such that the gradients of their equations sum to the gradient of the student's equation. This made it possible to handle problems with several hundred principle applications.

7   Evaluations of Andes2

Andes2 was evaluated in fall 2001 at the US Naval Academy. The intervention lasted around 12 weeks. Once again, the Andes students learned significantly more than the control students ($t=3.14$, $p=.0012$). The 0.52 effect size was respectable but less than Andes1 achieved in Fall 2000.

It was quite clear, both from log file analysis and from the comments of the students to the instructors, that Andes2 was simply young software. Although we had succeeded in removing bugs that would crash the system or cause obvious malfunctions, many pedagogical bugs remained. For instance, since all the hint sequences were new, many of the hints were phrased in confusing ways. The error handlers sometimes misrecognized errors. There were hundreds of these little "pedagogical bugs." Pilot testing would have uncovered them, but we could only run a few pilot subjects before the Naval Academy semester began. In contrast, Andes1 was tuned using log files from several hundred subjects by the time it reached the Fall 2000 evaluation, so it was much more mature software.

The instructors were happy to report that Andes2 did not suggest outlandish equations when students asked what was wrong with one of their equations. Moreover, student acceptance of the tutor appears not to have been hurt, and may even have gone up slightly. When asked at the end of the intervention if they would chose to continue using Andes if they could, 33% of the Fall 2001 students reported that they would versus 28% of the Fall 2000 students. Although this is good news, there is still room for improvement.

8 Conclusions and Future Work

We are finally beginning to understand the problem faced by Andes. Physics knowledge can be divided into (1) principles and the multi-step methods used to applying them, and (2) some kind of problem solving strategy, such as backwards search, that is used to *select* a principle application. All the stakeholders agree that physics students should learn principles and the methods for applying them. Indeed, recent textbooks print the application method for Newton's law, the application method for translational kinematics, and the application methods for many other major principles. However, there is no consensus on whether to explicitly teach a strategy for *selecting* principle applications. On the one hand, many successful tutoring systems have been built around the common wisdom that one should first find out what tacit knowledge is required for successful problem solving, then design a tutoring system that teaches that knowledge explicitly [e.g., 18]. On the other hand, today's experts probably acquired their principle selection strategy via implicit learning. There are even computational models of how such implicit learning could occur [19, 20]. Perhaps it would be best if students were not explicitly taught a principle selection strategy, but instead learned it implicitly. Moreover, explicit teaching of a principle selection strategy would be more invasive than implicit teaching. It would require augmentation of the textbooks, changes to the lectures, mastery of a notation for goals and reallocation of precious student time from learning principles to learning strategies.

Since we do not know whether implicit or explicit learning is better for principle selection knowledge, we designed Andes2 as a compromise between them. It offers explicit teaching of the backwards search strategy for selecting principles, but only when asked.

Clearly, the next major goal for the Andes project is an experiment that measures the effectiveness of different amounts of explicit teaching of principle selection knowledge. The current plan is to use 3 versions of Andes2. One has help turned off, so that students must learn principle selection knowledge implicitly. The second is the current version, which teaches some but not all the necessary principle selection knowledge. The third is a new version, which explicitly teaches principle selection knowledge. It will reify goals and be accompanied by printed materials with copious examples. A modified curriculum will be developed that inserts explicit teaching of principle selection knowledge at key points (e.g., when students are able to solve single-principle problems easily, but have not yet begun to solve multiple-principle problems). All three versions of Andes2, along with the printed instructional material, should be thoroughly pilot tested in order to remove pesky pedagogical bugs like the ones that plagued the Fall 2001 version.

Depending on the results of this experiment, we may move to the next obvious study, which is seeing which versions of the tutor are acceptable to instructors and students. That is, how much better do the more explicit tutors have to be in order to justify their invasiveness?

At issue here is perhaps one of the oldest pieces of advice in the ITS literature: explicate tacit knowledge, then teach it. We hope to discover whether that advice is correct for physics.

Acknowledgements. This research was supported by grant N00014-96-1-0260 from ONR Cognitive Sciences.

References

1. Gertner, A.S. and K. VanLehn, Andes: A coached problem solving environment for physics, in *Intelligent Tutoring Systems: 5th international Conference, ITS 2000*, G. Gautheier, C. Frasson, and K. VanLehn, Editors. 2000, Springer: New York. p. 133-142.
2. Schulze, K.G., et al., Andes: An intelligent tutor for classical physics. *The Journal of Electronic Publishing*, 2000. 6(1).
3. Schulze, K.G., et al., Andes: An active learning intelligent tutoring system for Newtonian physics, in *THEMES in Education*. 2000, Leader Books: Athens, Greece. p. 115-136.
4. VanLehn, K., Conceptual and meta learning during coached problem solving, in *ITS96: Proceeding of the Third International conference on Intelligent Tutoring Systems.*, C. Frasson, G. Gauthier, and A. Lesgold, Editors. 1996, Springer-Verlag: New York.
5. Albacete, P.L. and K. VanLehn, The Conceptual Helper: An intelligent tutoring system for teaching fundamental physics concepts, in *Intelligent Tutoring Systems: 5th International Conference, ITS 2000*, G. Gauthier, C. Frasson, and K. VanLehn, Editors. 2000, Springer: Berlin. p. 564-573.
6. Albacete, P.L. and K. VanLehn, Evaluation the effectiveness of a cognitive tutor for fundamental physics concepts, in *Proceedings of the Twenty-Second Annual Conference of the Cognitive Science Society*, L.R. Gleitman and A.K. Joshi, Editors. 2000, Erlbaum: Mahwah, NJ. p. 25-30.
7. Rose, C.P., et al., Interactive conceptual tutoring in Atlas-Andes, in *Artificial Intelligence in Education: AI-Ed in the Wired and Wireless future*, J.D. Moore, C. Redfield, and W.L. Johnson, Editors. 2001, IOS: Washington, DC. p. 256-266.
8. Conati, C. and K. VanLehn, Further results from the evaluation of an intelligent computer tutor to coach self-explanation, in *Intelligent Tutoring Systems: 5th International Confer-

ence, ITS 2000, G. Gauthier, C. Frasson, and K. VanLehn, Editors. 2000, Springer: Berlin. p. 304-313.

9. Conati, C. and K. VanLehn, Toward computer-based support of meta-cognitive skills: A computational framework to coach self-explanation. *International Journal of Artificial Intelligence in Education*, 2000. 11: p. 398-415.

10. Gertner, A., C. Conati, and K. VanLehn, Procedural help in Andes: Generating hints using a Bayesian network student model., in *Proceedings of the 15th national Conference on Artificial Intelligence*. 1998.

11. Conati, C., A. Gertner, and K. Vanlehn, Using Bayesian networks to manage uncertainty in student modeling. *User Modeling and User-Adapted Interactions*, in press.

12. Conati, C., et al., On-line student modeling for coached problem solving using Bayesian networks, in *User Modeling: Proceedings of the Sixth International conference, UM97*, A. Jameson, C. Paris, and C. Tasso, Editors. 1997, Spring Wien: New York.

13. Gertner, A.S., Providing feedback to equation entries in an intelligent tutoring system for Physics, in *Intelligent Tutoring Systems: 4th International Conference*, B.P. Goettl, et al., Editors. 1998, Springer: New York. p. 254-263.

14. Shelby, R.N., et al. The Andes Intelligent Tutor: an Evaluation. In *Physics Education Research Conference*. 2001. Rochester, NY.

15. Bundy, A., et al., Solving mechanics problems using meta-level inference, in *Proceedings of the Sixth International Joint Conference on AI*. 1979, Morgan Kaufmann: San Mateo, CA. p. 1017-1027.

16. Priest, A.G. and R.O. Lindsay, New light on novice-expert differences in physics problem solving. *British Journal of Psychology*, 1992. 83: p. 389-405.

17. Shapiro, J.A., Algebra subsystem for an intelligent tutoring system. *International Journal of Artificial Intelligence in Education*, submitted.

18. Anderson, J.R., et al., Cognitive Tutors: Lessons Learned. *The Journal of the Learning Sciences*, 1995. 4(2): p. 167-207.

19. VanLehn, K., R.M. Jones, and M.T.H. Chi, A model of the self-explanation effect. *The Journal of the Learning Sciences*, 1992. 2(1): p. 1-59.

20. Elio, R. and P.B. Scharf, Modeling novice-to-expert shifts in problem-solving strategy and knowledge organization. *Cognitive Science*, 1990. 14: p. 579-639.

KERMIT: A Constraint-Based Tutor for Database Modeling

Pramuditha Suraweera and Antonija Mitrovic

Intelligent Computer Tutoring Group
Computer Science Department, University of Canterbury
Private Bag 4800, Christchurch, New Zealand
pramu16@hotmail.com, tanja@cosc.canterbury.ac.nz

Abstract. KERMIT is an intelligent tutoring system that teaches conceptual database design using the Entity-Relationship data model. Database design is an open-ended task: although there is an outcome defined in abstract terms, there is no procedure to use to find that outcome. So far, constraint based modelling has been used in a tutor that teaches a database language (SQL-Tutor) and a system that teaches punctuation and capitalisation rules (CAPIT). Both systems have proved to be extremely effective in evaluations performed in real classrooms. In this paper, we present experiences in using CBM in an open-ended domain. We describe system's architecture and functionality. KERMIT has also been evaluated in the context of genuine teaching activities. We present the results of an evaluation study with students taking a database course, which show that KERMIT is an effective system. The students enjoyed the system's adaptability and found it a valuable asset to their learning.

1. Introduction

In previous work, we have shown that Constraint-Based Modeling (CBM) [14] is extremely effective. We have implemented SQL-Tutor [11], an Intelligent Tutoring System (ITS) for the SQL database language, and CAPIT [10], a punctuation and capitalization tutor. This paper presents our experiences in implementing another constraint-based tutor, this time in the area of database design. This domain is different from the ones we have previously worked in, as it is an open-ended domain. Although the final database design is described in abstract terms (i.e. the features of a good quality design are known generally), there is no procedure to use to arrive at the final solution. We therefore wanted to test CBM in such a domain.

The Entity-Relationship (ER) data model, proposed by Chen [3], is the most widely used model for conceptual database design. Although the ER model is relatively simple, students have many problems developing ER diagrams. The text of the problem is often ambiguous and incomplete. ER modelling is not a well-defined process. There is no single best solution for a problem, and often there are several possible schemas for the same requirements. Although the traditional method of

S.A. Cerri, G. Gouardères, and F. Paraguaçu (Eds.): ITS 2002, LNCS 2363, pp. 377–387, 2002.

learning ER modelling in a classroom environment may be sufficient as an introduction to the concepts of database design, students cannot gain expertise in the domain by attending lectures only. In tutorials, a single tutor must cater for the needs of the entire group of students, and it is inevitable that they obtain only limited personal assistance. Therefore, the existence of a computerized tutor, which would support students in acquiring database design skills, would be highly important.

We start by reviewing related work. Section 3 describes the overall architecture of the system. Section 4 presents the evaluation study that showed the effectiveness of the system. The conclusions are given in the last section.

2. Related Work

There have been only two attempts at developing ITSs for DB modelling. ERM-VLE [9] is a text-based virtual learning environment for ER modelling, in which students design databases by navigating the virtual world and manipulating objects. The virtual world consists of different rooms, such as entity creation rooms and relationship creation rooms. The authors claim that the organisation of the environment reflects the task structure. The student issues commands such as *pick up*, *drop*, *name*, *evaluate*, *create* and *destroy* to manipulate objects. The effect of a command is determined by the location in which it was issued. For example, a student creates an entity whilst in the entity creation room.

The interface of ERM-VLE contains the definition of the problem, and a graphical representation of the solution, but the student does not directly interact with the graphical representation. The student interacts with the virtual world solely by issuing textual commands. The problem's ideal solution is embedded in the virtual world. The learner is only allowed to create objects that correspond to the ones in the ideal solution. When the system was evaluated, the experienced designers felt that the structure of the virtual world had restricted them [8]. On the other hand, novices felt that they had increased their understanding of ER modelling. However, these comments cannot be treated as a proof of the system's effectiveness since the system has not been evaluated properly.

ERM-VLE restricts the learner since he/she is forced to follow the identical solution path to the ideal one. This method has a high tendency to encourage shallow learning as users are prevented from making errors and they are not given explanation about their mistakes. Moreover, a text-based virtual reality environment is not a natural environment in which to construct ER models. Students who learn to construct ER models using ERM-VLE would struggle to become accustomed to modelling databases outside the virtual environment.

The other tutor for database modelling is COLER [5,6], a web-based collaborative learning environment for ER modelling. Students initially solve problems individually and then join a group to develop a group solution. The designers argue that this process helps to ensure that students participate in discussions and that they have the necessary raw material for negotiating differences with other members of the group. The student's individual solution is constructed in the private workspace, whereas the collaborative solution is created in the shared workspace. Students are provided with a chat window through which they can communicate with each other.

The private workspace also allows the student to experiment with different solutions. Once a group of students agree to be involved in collaboratively solving a problem, the shared workspace is activated. Only a single member can edit the shared workspace at any time. After each change in the shared workspace, the students are required to express their opinions by voting, with either *agree*, *disagree* or *not sure*. The personal coach resident in the interface gives advice in the chat area based on the group dynamics: student participation and the group's ER model construction.

COLER encourages and supervises collaboration, and we believe it has the potential in helping students to acquire collaboration skills. However, it does not evaluate the ER schemas produced, and cannot provide feedback regarding their correctness. In this regard, even though the system is effective as a collaboration tool, the system would not be an effective teaching system for a group of novices with the same level of expertise. From the authors' experience, it is very common for a group of students to agree on the same flawed argument. Accordingly, it is very likely that groups of students unsupervised by an expert may learn flawed concepts of the domain. In order for COLER to be an effective teaching system, an expert should be present during the collaboration stage.

3. KERMIT: A Knowledge-Based ER Modelling Tutor

KERMIT [12] is a problem-solving environment, in which students construct ER schemas that satisfy a given set of requirements. The system provides feedback tailored towards each student's knowledge. The system supports the ER model as defined in [7]. The architecture of the system is given in Figure 1. The main components of KERMIT are its user interface, pedagogical module and student modeller, discussed in this section. KERMIT contains a number of predefined database problems and ideal solutions, specified by a human expert. Each problem describes the requirements of a database that the student is to design. The problem text is represented internally with embedded tags that specify the mapping to the objects in the ideal solution. The tags are not visible to the student since they are extracted before the problem is displayed.

Users interact with KERMIT's interface to construct ER schemas for the problems presented to them by the system. The pedagogical module drives the whole system by selecting the instructional messages and problems that best suit the particular student.

The student modeller evaluates the student's solution. In contrast to typical ITSs, KERMIT does not have a problem solver, as developing a problem solver for ER modelling is extremely difficult. One of the major obstacles that would have to be overcome is natural language processing (NLP), as the problems in the domain are presented using natural language text. NLP would

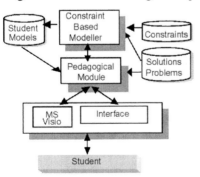

Fig. 1. Architecture of KERMIT

have to be used to extract the requirements of the database from the problem text. However, the NLP problem is far from being solved. Other complexities arise from the nature of the task. There are assumptions that need to be made during the composition of an ER schema. These assumptions are outside the problem description and are dependent on the semantics of the problem itself. Although this obstacle can be avoided by explicitly specifying these assumptions within the problem description, ascertaining these assumptions is an essential part of the process of constructing a solution and would over simplify the problems.

Although there is no problem solver, KERMIT is able to diagnose students' solutions by using its domain knowledge represented as a set of constraints. The system contains an ideal solution for each of its problems, which is compared against the student's solution according to the system's knowledge base. The knowledge base consists of constraints used for testing the student's solution for syntax errors and comparing it against the system's ideal solution. KERMIT's knowledge base enables the system to identify student solutions that are identical to the system's ideal solution. More importantly, this knowledge also enables the system to identify alternative correct solutions, i.e. solutions that are correct but not identical to the system's solution.

KERMIT's knowledge base consists of 92 constraints. Each constraint consists of a relevance condition, a satisfaction condition and feedback messages. The feedback messages are used to compose hints that are presented to students when the constraint is violated. The constraints can be roughly divided into syntactic and semantic ones. The syntactic constraints describe the syntactically valid ER schemas and are used to identify syntax errors in students' solutions. These constraints only deal with the student's solution. They vary from simple constraints such as "an entity name should be in upper case", to more complex constraints such as "the participation of a weak entity in the identifying relationship should be total".

Semantic constraints compare the student's solution to the ideal one. These constraints are usually more complex than syntactic constraints. For example. constraint 67 deals with composite multivalued attributes. Since such attributes can also be modelled as weak entities, the constraint has to compare a composite multivalued attribute in the ideal solution to a similar one or a weak entity in the student's solution. This constraint illustrates the ability of the system to deal with alternative correct student solutions that are different from the ideal solution specified by a human expert. KERMIT knows about equivalent ways of solving problems, and it is this feature of the knowledge base that gives KERMIT considerable flexibility.

KERMIT maintains two kinds of student models: short-term and long-term ones. Short-term models are generated by matching student solutions to constraints and the ideal solutions. The student modeller iterates through each constraint, checking whether the current problem state satisfies its relevance condition. If that is the case, the satisfaction component of the constraint is also verified against the current problem state. Violating the satisfaction condition of a relevant constraint signals an error. The pedagogical module uses the short-term student model to generate feedback to the student. On the other hand, the long-term student model is implemented as an overlay model. It keeps a record of each constraint's history: how often the constraint was relevant, and how often it was satisfied or violated. The pedagogical module uses these data to select new problems.

3.1. Interface

Students interact with KERMIT via its user interface (Figure 2) to view problems, construct ER diagrams, and view feedback. The top window displays the text of the current problem. The middle window is the ER modelling workspace where students create ER diagrams. The workspace was developed by integrating *Microsoft Visio* [15] with KERMIT. Feedback is presented in the textual form in the lowest window, and also verbally, through the animated pedagogical agent.

KERMIT's interface reduces the burden on the student's memory by showing the text of the problem, and also by showing the available constructs. The student can easily remind her/himself of the elements of the problem and the concepts of the ER model. Furthermore, this interface reinforces ER modelling by requiring the student to highlight the appropriate part of the problem text whenever a new construct is added to the ER diagram. The highlighted words are coloured depending on the type of object. When the student highlights a phrase as an entity name, the highlighted text turns bold and blue. Similarly the highlighted text turns green for relationships and pink for attributes. The feature is advantageous from a pedagogical point of view, as the student must follow the problem text closely. Many of the errors in students' solutions occur because they have not comprehensively read and understood the problem. These mistakes would be minimised in KERMIT, as students are required to focus their attention on the problem text every time they add a new object.

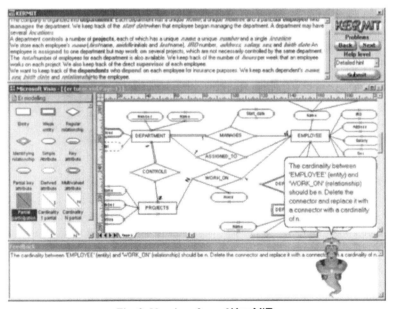

Fig. 2. User interface of KERMIT

Besides being useful from the pedagogical point of view, highlighting is also useful from the point of view of the student modeller for evaluating solutions. There is no standard that is enforced in naming entities, relationships or attributes, and the student has the freedom to use any synonym or similar word/phrase as the name of a particular object. Since the names of the objects in the student solution (SS) may not match the names of construct in the ideal solution (IS), the task of finding a correspondence between the constructs of the SS and IS is difficult. This problem is avoided in KERMIT by forcing the student to highlight the word or phrase that is modelled by each object in the ER diagram.

3.2. Pedagogical Module

The pedagogical module is the driving engine of the whole system. Its main tasks are to generate appropriate feedback messages for the student and to select new practice problems. KERMIT individualises both these actions to each student based on their student model.

There are are six levels of feedback, according to the amount of detail: *correct*, *error flag*, *hint*, *detailed hint*, *all errors* and *solution*. The first level of feedback *(correct)* simply indicates whether the submitted solution is correct or not. The *error flag* indicates the type of construct (e.g. entity, relationship, etc.) that contains the error. *Hint* and *detailed hint* offer a feedback message generated from the first violated constraint. *Hint* is a general message such as "There are attributes that do not belong to any entity or relationship". On the other hand, *detailed hint* provides a more specific message such as "*The 'Address' attribute does not belong to any entity or relationship*", where the details of the erroneous object are given. A list of hints on all violated constraints is displayed at the *all errors* level. The ER schema of the complete solution is displayed at the final level (*solution* level).

When the student gets a new problem, the feedback level is set to *correct*. The level of feedback is incremented with each submission until it reaches the *detailed hint* level. The system also gives the student the freedom to manually select the level of feedback, thus providing a better feeling of control.

When selecting a new problem, the student model is examined to find the constraints that have been violated most often. We have chosen this simple problem selection strategy in order to ensure that students get the most practice on the constructs with which they experience difficulties.

4. Evaluation

We performed an evaluation of KERMIT at the University of Canterbury, Christchurch in August 2001. This section presents the procedure and the results.

4.1. Procedure

The study involved sixty-two volunteers from students enrolled in the Introduction to Databases course. The students had learnt ER modelling concepts during two weeks of lectures and had some practice during two weeks of tutorials prior to the study.

This study involved a comparison of a group of students learning ER modelling by using the fully functional KERMIT against a control group who used a cut-down version of the system, referred to as ER-Tutor. The interfaces of both systems were similar, but ER-Tutor did not provide any feedback except for the complete solution. That way, both groups of students worked in the lab, but the ER-Tutor group had the feedback that is comparable to a classroom condition. The participants were randomly allocated to the control or the experimental group. Initially each student sat a pre-test and then interacted with the system in a single, two-hour session. The participants worked individually, solving problems at their own pace. There were 6 problems in total, presented to the two groups in the same order. All the important events such as logging in, submitting a solution and requesting help were recorded in a log specific to each student. Finally, the participants were given a post-test and a questionnaire.

A pre- and post-test were used to evaluate the students' knowledge before and after the session. To minimise any prior learning effects, we designed two tests (A and B) of approximately the same complexity. They contained two questions: a multiple choice question to choose the ER schema that correctly depicted the given scenario and a question that involved designing a small ER schema. In order to reduce any bias, the first half of each group was given test A as the pre-test and the remainder were given B as the pre-test. The students who had test A as their pre-test were given test B as their post-test and vice versa.

The questionnaire contained a total of fourteen questions. Initially students were questioned on previous experience in ER modelling and in using CASE tools. Most questions asked the participants to rank their perception on various issues on a Likert scale with five responses ranging from *very good* (5) to *very poor* (1), and included the amount they learnt about ER modelling by interacting with the system and the enjoyment experienced. The students were also allowed to give free-form responses.

4.2. Objective Analysis

Table 1 presents a few statistics about the study. The experimental group students spent more time interacting with the system than the control group. Although the difference is not significant, it is encouraging to note that students were more willing to interact KERMIT. The average times for completing a problem for both groups were very similar. These findings suggest that even though the students using KERMIT were forced to indicate the semantic meaning of each construct by highlighting a word in the problem text, their performance was not degraded.

We also analysed the logs to see how students acquired constraints, using the same approach as in [13]. We identified each problem-state in which a constraint was relevant. Each constraint relevance occasion was rank ordered from 1 up. For each occasion, we recorded whether a relevant constraint was satisfied or violated. We calculated, for each participant, the probability of violating each individual constraint on the first occasion of application, the second occasion and so on. The probabilities were averaged across all the constraints in order to obtain an estimation of the probability of violating a given constraint C on a given occasion. The probabilities

Table 1. Mean system interaction details

	KERMIT		ER-Tutor	
	Mean	s. d.	mean	s. d.
Time spent on problem solving (min.)	66:39	21:22	57:58	34:38
Time spent per completed problem (min.)	23:36	6:55	23:46	21:40
No. of attempted problems	4.36	1.45	4.10	2.55
No. of completed problems	1.75	1.14	1.97	1.20

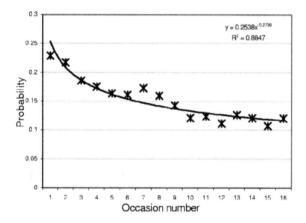

Fig. 3. Probability of violating a constraint as a function of the occasion when that constraint was relevant

were then averaged across all participants and plotted as a function of the number of occasions when C was relevant, as shown in Figure 3. To reduce individual bias, only the occasions in which at least two thirds of the total population of participants had a relevant constraint were used. The data points show a regular decrease. The power curve displays a close fit with an R^2 fit of 0.88. The probability of 0.23 for violating a constraint at its first occasion of application has decreased to 0.12 at its sixteenth occasion of application displaying a 53% decrease in the probability. The results of the mastery of constraints further strengthen the claim that the students learn ER modelling by interacting with KERMIT.

4.3.   Questionnaire Analysis

Table 2 displays a summary of the responses. The students in both groups required approximately the same time to learn the interface. Since KERMIT's interface is more complicated, we expected that students who used KERMIT would require longer to learn its interface. The difference in mean responses on the amount learnt is not significant. Both groups rated their enjoyment of the system on a similar scale.

The control group students rated the interface easier to use in comparison to the students who used KERMIT. The difference is statistically significant (t = 1.78, p < 0.01). This result was expected since KERMIT's interface is more complex than ER-Tutor's.

The difference for the ratings of the usefulness of feedback is statistically significant (t = 3.45, p < 0.01). These results are analogous with our expectations due to the difference in the information content presented as feedback from each system. Students who used KERMIT also had a better perception of the system as a whole. This was shown in their responses to whether they would recommend the system to others, where approximately 84% of the experimental group students indicated that they would, while the percentage of the control group students who had the same opinion was lower, approximately 68%.

Table 2. Means for the user questionnaire, pre- and post-test

	KERMIT		ER-Tutor	
	mean	s. d.	mean	s. d.
Time to learn interface (min.)	11.50	11.68	11.94	14.81
Amount learnt	3.19	0.65	3.06	0.89
Enjoyment	3.45	0.93	3.42	1.06
Ease of using interface	3.19	0.91	3.65	1.08
Usefulness of feedback	3.42	1.09	2.45	1.12
Pre-test	16.16	1.82	16.58	2.86
Post-test	17.77	1.45	16.48	3.08
Gain score	1.65	1.72	-0.10	2.76

4.4. Pre- and Post-test Performance

Table 2 also contains the results the students achieved in the pre- and post-tests. The difference in pre-test scores is insignificant, confirming that the two groups are comparable. The experimental group scored significantly higher on the post-test (t = 4.91, p < 0.01). Conversely, the difference in pre- and post-test of the group who used ER-Tutor is statistically insignificant. The difference in gain scores of the two groups is statistically significant (t = 3.07, p < 0.01). We can conclude from these results that students who used KERMIT learnt more than students who used the control system.

The effect size and power for the experiment were also calculated. Effect size is a standard method of comparing the results of one pedagogical experiment to another. The common method to calculate the effect size in the ITS community is to subtract the control group's mean gains score from the experimental group's mean gain score and divide by the standard deviation of the gain scores of the control group [2]. This gives the effect size of 0.63 for our experiment, which is comparable with the effect size of 0.63 in [1] and 0.66 in [11], where the session lengths were also 2 hours.

Another way to calculate the effect size is the ω^2 value [4]. For our experiment, ω^2 is 0.12, which is a relatively large effect size. We also calculated the power, measured as the fraction of experiments that would produce significant results for the same design, the same number of participants and the same effect size. Chin [4] recommends that researchers should strive for a power of 0.8. The power of this experiment was calculated as 0.75 at significance 0.05, which is an excellent result.

5. Conclusions

This paper presented KERMIT, an ITS for ER modelling. KERMIT's effectiveness in teaching ER modelling was shown in a classroom experiment. The participants who used the full version of KERMIT showed significantly better results in both the subjective and objective analysis in comparison to the students who practiced ER modelling with a conventional drawing tool.

The student modelling technique used in KERMIT (CBM) has previously been used to represent domain and student knowledge in SQL-Tutor [11,13] and in CAPIT [10]. In both cases, the analysis of students' behaviour while interacting with these systems proved the sound psychological foundations of CBM and the appropriateness of constraints as the basic units of knowledge. The research presented in this paper demonstrated that CBM can also be used to effectively represent knowledge in domains with open-ended tasks such as database modelling. This result further strengthens the credibility of CBM.

There are a number of future avenues that can be explored to further improve KERMIT. The current system only presents general hint messages on the errors in the student's solution. The feedback of the system could be enhanced to provide support for deep learning. We have recently started a new project, which will enhance KERMIT to support self-explanation.

Acknowledgements. The work presented here was supported by the University of Canterbury research grant U6430. We thank Ken Koedinger for advising on the evaluation study.

References

1. Albacete, P.L., VanLehn, K. The Conceptual Helper: an Intelligent Tutoring System for Teaching Fundamenatal Physics Concepts. In: Gauthier, G., Frasson, C. and VanLehn, K. (eds.). Proc. ITS'2000, Springer-Verlag Berlin (2000) 564-573
2. Bloom, B. S. The 2-sigma problem: The search for methods of group instruction as effective as one-to-one tutoring. Educational Researcher, 13 (1984) 4-16
3. Chen, P. P. The Entity Relationship Model - Toward a Unified View of Data. ACM Transactions Database Systems, 1 (1976) 9-36
4. Chin, D. N. Empirical Evaluation of User Models and User-adapted Systems. User Modeling and User Adapted Interaction, 11, (2001) 181-194
5. Constantino-Gonzalez, M., Suthers, D. A Coached Collaborative Learning Environment for Entity-Relationship Modeling. In: Gauthier, G., Frasson, C. and VanLehn, K. (eds.). Proc. ITS'2000, Montreal (2000) 324-333

6. Constantino-Gonzalez, M., Suthers, D., Icaza., J. Designing and Evaluating a Collaboration Coach: Knowledge and Reasoning. In: Moore, J. D., Redfield, C. L. and Johnson, W. L. (eds.). Proc. AIED 01, San Antonio, Texas, IOS Press (2001) 176-187

7. Elmasri, R., Navathe, S. B. Fundamentals of Database Systems. Addison Wesley (1994)

8. Hall, L., Gordon, A. Synergy on the Net: Integrating the Web and Intelligent Learning Environments. Proc. of WWW-based Tutoring Workshop at ITS'2000 (2000) 25-29

9. Hall, L., Gordon, A. (1998) A Virtual Learning Environment for Entity Relationship Modelling. SIGCSE bulletin, 30 (1998) 345-353.

10. Mayo, M., Mitrovic, A. Optimising ITS Behaviour with Bayesian Networks and Decision Theory. Int. Journal on Artificial Intelligence in Education, 12 (2001) 124-153.

11. Mitrovic, A., Martin, B., Mayo, M. Using Evaluation to Shape ITS Design: Results and Experiences with SQL-Tutor. UMUAI, 12 (2002) (in press)

12. Mitrovic, A., Mayo, M., Suraweera, P., Martin, B. Constraint-based Tutors: a Success Story. In: Monostori, L., Vancza, J. and Ali, M. (eds.). Proc. IEA/AIE-2001, Budapest, Springer-Verlag Berlin (2001) 931-940

13. Mitrovic, A., Ohlsson, S. Evaluation of a Constraint-based Tutor for a Database Language. Int. Journal on Artificial Intelligence in Education, 10 (1999) 238-256

14. Ohlsson, S. Constraint-based Student Modelling. In: Greer, J.E., McCalla, G (eds) Proc. of Student Modelling: the Key to Individualized Knowledge-based Instruction, Springer-Verlag Berlin (1994) 167-189

15. Visio, http://www.microsoft.com/office/visio/

Automatic Problem Generation in Constraint-Based Tutors

Brent Martin and Antonija Mitrovic

Intelligent Computer Tutoring Group
Department of Computer Science, University of Canterbury
Private Bag 4800, Christchurch, New Zealand
{bim20,tanja}@cosc.canterbury.ac.nz

Abstract. Constraint-Based Modelling (CBM) is a student modelling technique that is rapidly maturing. We have implemented several tutors using CBM and demonstrated its suitability to open-ended domains in particular. A problem with open-ended and complex domain models is their large size, necessitating a comprehensive problem set in order to provide sufficient exercises for extended learning sessions. We have addressed this issue by developing an algorithm that automatically generates new problems directly from the domain knowledge base. We present the algorithm and compare students' performance with generated problems to those using a teacher-authored problem set, and show the performance of the generated problem set to be superior.

1 Introduction

Constraint-Based Modelling (CBM) [8] is an effective approach that simplifies the building of domain and student models. We have used CBM to develop SQL-Tutor [5], an ITS for teaching the SQL database language. SQL-Tutor tailors instructional sessions in three ways: by presenting feedback when students submit their answers, by controlling problem difficulty, and by providing scaffolding information. Students have shown significant gains in learning after as little as two hours of exposure to this system [6].

SQL-Tutor contains a list of questions, from which one is selected that best fits the student's current knowledge state. In extended sessions with the tutor, the system may run out of suitable problems. We have overcome this by developing a problem generator, which uses the domain model to build new problems that fit the student model. We have implemented this extension to CBM and used it to generate a larger problem set for SQL-Tutor, which has also allowed us to use a problem selection algorithm that is tied more closely to the student model.

In this paper we describe the current implementation of SQL-Tutor. We then briefly introduce CBM and present our extension, which generates new problems. We then present the results of a six-week analysis of the new problem set. Finally, we summarise our work to date and indicate further areas we are investigating.

S.A. Cerri, G. Gouardères, and F. Paraguaçu (Eds.): ITS 2002, LNCS 2363, pp. 388–398, 2002.
© Springer-Verlag Berlin Heidelberg 2002

2   SQL-Tutor

SQL-Tutor [5] teaches the SQL database query language to second and third year students at the University of Canterbury, using Constraint-Based Modelling (CBM). This approach models the domain as a set of state constraints, of the form:

If   *<relevance condition> is true for the student's solution,*
THEN   <satisfaction condition> must also be true

The relevance condition of each constraint is used to test whether the student's solution is in a pedagogically significant state. If so, the satisfaction condition is checked. If it succeeds, no action is taken; if it fails, the student has made a mistake and appropriate feedback is given. CBM has advantages over other approaches such as model tracing [1] in that the model need not be complete and correct in order to function. Further, it is well suited to domains where the number of alternative solutions is large or the domain is open-ended.

Ohlsson does not impose any restrictions upon how constraints are encoded, and/or implemented. In SQL-Tutor we initially represented each constraint by a LISP fragment, supported by domain-specific LISP functions. In later versions we have used a pattern-matching algorithm designed for this purpose [4], for example:

```
(147
"You have used some names in the WHERE clause that are not from
this database."
 (match SS WHERE (?* (^name ?n) ?*))
 (or   (test SS (^valid-table (?n ?t))
       (test SS (^attribute-p (?n ?a ?t))))
"WHERE")
```

The syntax of the MATCH function is (`MATCH <solution name> <clause>` `(pattern list)`) where `<solution name>` is either SS (student solution) or IS (ideal solution) and `<clause>` is the name of the SQL clause to which the pattern applies (e.g. "SELECT"). The pattern list is a set of terms, which match to individual elements in the solution being tested. Each term may be a wildcard, variable, literal or list of literals. The latter denotes that the input element must be a member of the list. Subsequent tests of the value of a variable may be carried out using the TEST function, which is a special form of MATCH that accepts a single pattern term and one or more variables.

This language makes all of the logic for determining whether or not the constraint is satisfied transparent to the system, since it consists only of pattern matching and logical combination. Repeated functions such as "`^valid-table`" in the above example are simply macros, which are themselves defined in the same language. We have used this property to develop a problem solver that can generate correct solutions from student attempts by extracting the valid match fragments from each satisfied constraint and the *invalid* fragments from violated constraints. It then corrects the invalid fragments by comparing them to matched fragments of the ideal solution, and then combines them. If the student input is blank this algorithm reduces to a problem solver.

Unlike repair theory [9], we make no claim that this algorithm is modelling human behaviour. However, it has the advantage that a failed constraint means that the construct involved is *definitely wrong*: we do not need to try to infer where the error lies, so our algorithm does not suffer from computational explosion. For further details on this algorithm and the constraint language, see [4].

3   Generating New Problems

In the SQL-Tutor the next problem is chosen based on difficulty, plus the concept the student is currently having the most trouble with. The constraint set is first searched for the constraint that is being violated most often. Then the system identifies the set of problems for which this constraint is relevant. Finally, it choses the problem from this set that best matches the student's current proficiency level. However, there is no guarantee that an untried problem exists that matches the current student model: there may be no problems for the target constraint, or the only problems available may be of unsuitable difficulty. Further, since the constraint set is large (over 500 constraints), a large number of problems are needed merely to cover the domain. Ideally there should be many problems per constraint, in various combinations. In SQL-Tutor there is an average of three problems per constraint and only around half of the constraint set is covered. A consequence of this is that the number of new constraints (concepts) being presented to the student tapers off as the system runs out of problems. Figure 1 illustrates this. For a six-week open evaluation we found that the number of new constraints presented to the student is linear with the number of problems tackled ($R^2 = 0.83$), until around 40 problems have been solved. At this point the system runs out of suitable problems, and the number of new constraints presented drops to nearly zero.

The obvious way to address this limitation is to add more problems. However, this is not an easy task. There are over 500 constraints, and it is difficult to invent problems that are guaranteed to cover all constraints in sufficient combinations that

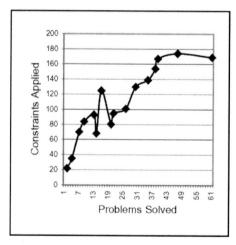

Fig. 1. New Constraints Applied

there are enough problems at a large spread of difficulty levels. To overcome this we have developed an algorithm that generates new problems from the constraint set. It uses the constraint-based problem solver described in section 2 to create novel SQL statements, using an individual constraint (or, possibly, a set of compatible constraints) as a starting point, and "growing" an SQL statement for which this constraint is relevant. This new SQL statement forms the ideal solution for a new problem. The human author need only convert the ideal solution into a natural language problem statement, ready for presentation to the student.

3.1   Building a New Ideal Solution

To build a new ideal solution we capitalise on the fact that the only reasoning that takes place within a constraint is pattern matching. Each pattern in the relevance condition of a constraint corresponds to a fragment of the solution that must be present for this constraint to be relevant. To create a new ideal solution that is relevant to a particular constraint, we begin by inserting the fragments from this constraint into our (currently blank) ideal solution. Since the pattern matches may contain variables, these must be instantiated. In SQL-Tutor, these variables may correspond to database table or attribute names, literals, relational operators etc. In some cases the value will be constrained by tests in the constraint, which resolve to a set of allowed values. For example, a variable representing a relational operator must contain a member of the set (>, <, <=, >=, =, <> or !=), so the algorithm may immediately instantiate the variable to a random element of this set. In other cases (e.g. literal comparisons, such as "role = 'Professor Dumbledore'") there is nothing to limit the value of one or more terms. However, such variables cannot be simply assigned a random value. For example, if the subject of the database being queried is movies, the condition "Title = 'Star Wars'" would be sensible, but "Title = 'sekfgdvfv'" would not. To overcome this problem we introduced a small set of further *instantiation* constraints, which restricts the value of such literals. The instantiation constraints also ensure that semantic consistency is maintained. For example, the instantiation constraint that checks for a valid literal in a comparison is:

```
(I8

    "Ensures that literal string comparisons in WHERE are with
     valid strings"

    (match SS WHERE
        (?* (^attribute-of (?n ?a ?t)) "=" (^sql-stringp ?s) ?*))

    (test SS (^valid-string (?s ?a ?t)))

    "WHERE"
)
```

where "Valid-string" is a macro that enumerates all the valid combinations of attribute names and literal strings. At this stage our new potential ideal solution consists of a set of disjoint fragments, which may or may not be valid SQL.

The constraint set in SQL-TUTOR (and in CBM domain models in general) consists of semantic constraints, which test that the student solution is answering the set problem and syntactic constraints, which simply test that the syntax of the solution is valid. We use this latter set as the input into the constraint-based problem-solver, which corrects any syntactic errors in the ideal solution we have generated so far, leaving a valid SQL query. The result when the problem solver has completed its task is a valid, novel SQL statement, for which the constraint from which it began is relevant. We have thus created a new ideal solution.

3.2   Authoring the New Problem Set

There are two ways we may use the problem generator to develop new exercises: by generating problems on the fly to fit the student model, or by authoring a problem set in advance. While the former gives the greatest flexibility in problem selection (for example, it would allow a problem to be created that fitted the student's n most problematic constraints), it requires that the system automatically generate the natural language problem text from the ideal solution. This is not an impossible task; however, the problem generation algorithm and the natural language translator would need to be guaranteed robust, otherwise the student may be presented with unintelligible or unsolvable problems. We have therefore adopted the latter approach, and used the algorithm to generate a problem set in advance. This does not preclude the development of a natural language converter; we are designing such a module, again using constraints and the constraint-based problem solver to perform this function.

For the purpose of this study, we used the problem generation algorithm to create a single problem per constraint, giving around 800 potential ideal solutions. We then chose the best of these, and converted them into natural language problem statements. On completion, we had a new problem set of 200 problems, which took only three hours of human effort to build, compared with many days for the human-authored set of 82 problems. Further, when we plotted the number of new constraints applied per problem (the same as the analysis of the control group in Figure 1), the cut-off rose from 40 problems to 60, indicating that the new problem set increased the length of time that a student could fruitfully engage with the system.

4   Evaluation

The motivation for Problem Generation was to reduce the effort involved in building tutoring systems by automating one of the more time-consuming functions; writing the problem set. Three criteria must be met to achieve this goal: the algorithm must work (i.e. it must generate new problems); it must require (substantially) less human involvement than traditional problem authoring; and the problems produced must be shown to facilitate learning to at least the same degree as human-authored problems. The first two were confirmed during the building of the evaluation system: the algorithm successfully generated problems, and the time taken to author the problem set was much less than would have been required for human authoring alone.

Additionally, if the method works, it should be possible to generate large problem sets, which will have the benefit of greater choice when trying to fit a problem to the user's current student model. We might therefore expect that given a suitable problem selection strategy, a system using the generated problem set would lead to faster learning than the current human-authored set, because we are better able to fit the problem to the student.

SQL-TUTOR was modified for this purpose and evaluated for a six-week period. The subjects were stage two university students studying a databases paper. At the end of the study the students were required to sit a lab test about SQL as part of their assessment, so they were motivated to use the system if they considered it might improve their performance. The students were broken into three groups. The first used the current version of SQL-TUTOR, i.e. with human-authored problems. The second group used a version with problems generated using the algorithm described. The third group used a version containing other research (student model visualisation) that was not relevant to this study. Before using the system, each student sat a pre-test to determine their existing knowledge and skill in writing SQL queries. They were then free to use the system as little or as often as they liked over a six week period. Each student was randomly assigned a "mode", which determined which version of the system they would use. At the conclusion of the evaluation they sat a post-test.

When the study commenced, 88 students had signed up and performed the pre-test, giving sample sizes of around 30 per group. During the evaluation this further increased as new students requested access to the system. At the conclusion of the study some students who signed up had not used the system to any significant degree. The final groups used for analysis numbered 24 (control) and 26 (experimental) students each. The length of time each student used the system varied greatly from not using it at all to working for several hours, with an average of two-and-a-half hours. Consequently, the number of problems solved also varied widely from zero to 98, with an average of 25.

There are several ways we can measure the performance of the system. First, we can measure the means of the pre-test and post-test, to determine whether or not the systems had differing effects on test performance. Note, however, that with such an open evaluation as this, it is dangerous to assume that differences are due to the system, since use of the system may represent only a portion of the effort the student spent learning SQL. Nevertheless, it is important to analyse the *pre-test* scores to determine whether the study groups are comparable samples of the population. This was found to be the case.

Second, we can plot the reduction in error rates as the student practices on each constraint. Each student's performance when measured this way should lead to a so-called 'Power law' [2,7], which is typical when the underlying objects being measured (in this case a constraint) represents a concept being learned. The steepness of this curve at the start is a rough indication of the speed with which the student, on average, is learning new constraints. Since each constraint represents a specific concept in the domain, this is an indication of how quickly the student is learning the domain. We can then compare this learning rate between the two groups.

Finally, we can look at how difficult the students found the problems. This is necessary to ensure that the newly generated problems did not negatively impact problem difficulty (either by being too easy or too hard). There are several ways we can do this. First, we can measure how many attempts the student took on average to solve a problem and compare the means for the control and test groups. Second, students were permitted to abort the current problem and could cite one of three reasons: it was too easy, it was too hard or they wanted to try a problem of a different

Table 1. Aborted Problems

Group	Aborted (%)	Too hard (%)	Too easy (%)	Diff Type (%)	Responded (%)
Control	26	24	42	34	84
Experiment	26	22	42	35	62

type. If the proportion of problems aborted rises, or the ratio of "too hard" to "too easy" problems is further from 1:1 than the control group, we might conclude that problem difficulty has been adversely affected.

In this study, we measured all of the above. We used the software package SPSS to compare means and estimate power and effect size, and Microsoft Excel to fit power curves. We now present the results.

4.1   Problem Difficulty

We measured problem difficulty both subjectively and objectively. We obtained subjective results by logging when students aborted a problem and recording their reason. If the problems were (overall) of a suitable difficulty, we would expect the ratio of claims of "too hard" to "too easy" to be approximately 1:1. Any significant move away from this ratio would indicate we have adversely affected problem difficulty. Further, the percentage of problems aborted should not rise significantly. Table 1 lists the results. "Aborted" indicates the proportion of all problems attempted that were aborted. "Too hard", "Too easy" and "Diff type" give the proportion of *aborted* problems for which the reason given was the problem was too hard, too easy, or the student wanted a problem of a different type, respectively. "Responded" indicates the proportion of aborted problems for which the student gave a reason.

These results suggest that for both groups the problems set are more often too easy than too hard. The percentage of problems aborted in each group was exactly the same, at around 26% of all problems. The ratio of "too easy" to "too hard" for the two groups is nearly identical, as is the proportion of problems aborted because the student wanted a problem of a different type. It therefore appears that the generated problems have had no effect on difficulty as perceived by the students.

Next, we measured the number of attempts taken to solve each problem. This gives an objective indication of how hard students found the problems. Table 2 lists the results (standard deviations are in parentheses). "Solved/student" indicates the average number of problems completed correctly. "Total time" is the average time spent at the system. This figure records the time that the user was actively using the system, from when they first logged in to when they last submitted an attempt. Thus, it excludes idle time where the user has forgotten to log out. "Attempts per problem" is the number of all submitted attempts (including those for problems the student abandoned), divided by the number of problems actually solved. "Time/Problem" similarly records the total time spent on the system divided by the number of problems solved. There was no significant difference in the objective measurement of problem difficulty: students took approximately the same amount of time and number of attempts in both groups. The number of problems solved and average total time

Table 2. Attempts per problem and time spent

Group	Solved/ Student	Tot. Time (hrs)	Attempts/ problem	Time/ Problem (min)	Pre-test mean
Control	23	2:37	3.96 (1.9)	6:14 (3.6)	4.82 (1.5)
Experiment	26	2:31	3.45 (1.2)	5:50 (3.2)	5.06 (1.5)
T-test			NO	NO	NO
Significant?			(p=0.31)	(p=0.71)	(p=0.48)

spent on the system was also almost the same for the two groups, suggesting that neither system was particularly favoured by students.

4.2   Learning Speed

We observed the learning rate for each group by plotting the proportion of constraints that are violated for the nth problem for which this constraint is relevant. This value is obtained by determining for each constraint whether it is correctly or incorrectly applied to the nth problem for which it is relevant. A constraint is correctly applied if it is relevant at any time during solving of this problem, and is *always* satisfied for the duration of this problem. Constraints that are relevant but are violated one or more times during solving of this problem are labelled erroneous. The value plotted is the proportion of all constraints relevant to the nth problem that are erroneous.

If the unit being measured (constraints in this case) is a valid abstraction of what is being learned, we expect to see a "power curve". We fitted a power curve to each plot, giving an equation for the curve where the initial learning rate is determined by the slope of the curve at n=1. Note that as the curve progresses learning behaviour becomes swamped by random erroneous behaviour such as slips, so the plot stops trending along the power curve and levels out at the level of random mistakes. This is exacerbated by the fact that the number of constraints being considered reduces as n increases, because many constraints are only relevant to a small number of problems. We therefore use only the initial part of the curve to calculate the learning rate. Figure 2 shows such plots, where each line is the learning curve for the entire group on average, i.e. the proportion of constraints that are relevant to the first problem that are incorrectly applied *by any student in the group*. The cut-off was chosen at n=5, which is the point at which the power curve fit for both groups is maximal.

Both plots exhibit a very good fit to a power curve. The differing slopes of the curves suggest a difference in learning rates between the Problem Generation group and the control group. To determine whether this difference is significant, we plotted curves for each individual student, and used this to determine the initial learning rate of each student. This increases the effect of errors even further, so we determined empirically the best cut-off point for each group, which was found to be n=4. We calculated the learning rate at n=1 for each student, and calculated the mean and significance. Table 3 summarises the results (standard deviations in parentheses).

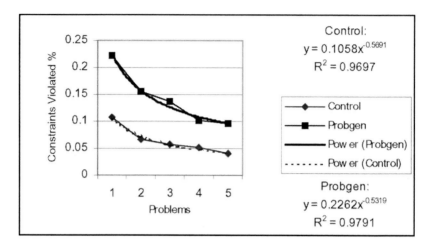

Fig. 2. Learning Performance

Table 3. Initial learning rates

Group	Slope	Fit (R^2)
Control	0.07 (0.04)	0.63 (0.29)
Problem Generation	0.16 (0.12)	0.68 (0.30)
T-test significant?	YES (p=0.01)	NO (p=0.61)

These results show that the slope at n=1, or initial learning rate, is almost twice as high for the experimental group. The difference is statistically significant at α=0.05 (p=0.01). A further test of the results is effect size and power. Using omega squared for effect size [3], we are striving for a power (repeatability) of 0.8, i.e. an 80% likelihood of reproducing this result using the same experimental conditions, and an effect size of around 0.15 (large). Using this method we obtained an effect size of 0.21, with a power of 0.794 at α=0.05, which is a very respectable result.

5   Conclusions

This paper identified the problem of producing enough exercises to tutor students in complex domains. We presented our solution for constraint-based tutors: an algorithm for generating problems directly from the domain model. We described this algorithm, and presented the results of a six-week evaluation using SQL-Tutor, where we aimed to show that the generated problems support learning at least as well as human generated exercises.

The results of the evaluation were extremely encouraging. It appears that the generated problem set *improved* student's learning speed by a factor of more than two. The exact cause of this improvement has not been identified; it may be purely because of the increased size of the problem set, or it may be because the problems represented better combinations of constraints. However, either of these is a positive outcome, since increasing the size of the problem set is likely to lead to greater combinations of constraints being represented, and we have shown that it is much easier to author large problem sets using the problem generation algorithm.

The problem generation algorithm does not come without cost. In order for the constraint-based problem solver to work satisfactorily, the constraint set must be sufficiently complete and correct; otherwise the generated solutions (including new ideal ones) may be incorrect. This imposes a greater burden upon the author of the constraint set. However, even this has a positive side: the better the constraint set, the more powerful it will be at diagnosis of student problems. We believe the extra effort is justified, considering the benefits observed.

6   Further Work

We are currently building an authoring system for constraint-based tutors that will incorporate all the various enhancements to CBM that we have developed, including the problem generation algorithm described. We have also begun designing constraints that will convert an SQL ideal solution into the natural language problem statement. If successful, we will incorporate problem statement generation into the authoring tool also.

When authoring the problem set for the study described, we weeded out many problems that were low quality. This arose mainly because of deficiencies in the instantiation constraints. We are looking more closely at this area, to try to identify the required properties of this constraint set, and to determine how it can be more easily deduced.

Acknowledgement. This research was supported by the University of Canterbury grant U6430.

References

1. Anderson, J. R., Corbett, A. T. and Koedinger, K. R. (1995). Cognitive Tutors: Lessons Learned. *Journal of the Learning Sciences* 4(2), pp. 167-207.
2. Anderson, J. R. and Lebiere, C. (1998). The atomic components of thought. MahWah, NJ, Lawrence Erlbaum Associates.
3. Chin, D. N. (2001). Empirical Evaluation of User Models and User-Adapted Systems. *User-Modeling and User Adapted Interaction* 11, pp. 181-194.
4. Martin, B. and Mitrovic, A. (2000). Tailoring Feedback by Correcting Student Answers. In Gauthier, G., Frasson, C. and VanLehn, K. (Eds.), *Proceedings of the Fifth International Conference on Intelligent Tutoring Systems*, Montreal, Springer, pp. 383-392.
5. Mitrovic, A. (1998). Experiences in Implementing Constraint-Based Modeling in SQL-Tutor. In Goettl, B. P., Halff, H. M., Redfield, C. L. and Shute, V. J. (Eds.), *Proceedings of the Fourth International Conference on Intelligent Tutoring Systems*, San Antonio, Texas, Springer, pp. 414-423.
6. Mitrovic, A. and Ohlsson, S. (1999). Evaluation of a Constraint-Based Tutor for a Database Language. *International Journal of Artificial Intelligence in Education* 10, pp. 238-256.

7. Newell, A. and Rosenbloom, P. S. (1981). Mechanisms of skill acquisition and the law of practice. In *Cognitive skills and their acquisition*. Anderson, J. R. (Ed.), Hillsdale, NJ, Lawrence Erlbaum Associates, pp. 1-56.
8. Ohlsson, S. (1991). Constraint-Based Student Modeling. In Greer, J. and McCalla, G. (Eds.), *Proceedings of the NATO Advanced Research Workshop on Student Modelling*, Ste. Adele, Quebec, Canada, Springer-Verlag, pp. 167-189.
9. VanLehn, K. (1983). On the Representation of Procedures in Repair Theory. In *The Development of Mathematical Thinking*. Ginsburg, H. P. (Ed.), New York, Academic Press, pp. 201-252.

Collaborative Ontological Engineering of Instructional Design Knowledge for an ITS Authoring Environment

Jacqueline Bourdeau[1] and Riichiro Mizoguchi[2]

[1] Télé-université, 4750 Henri-Julien, Montréal (Québec) H2T 3E4 Canada,
bourdeau@licef.teluq.uquebec.ca
[2] ISIR, Osaka University, 8-1 Mihogaoka, Ibaraki, Osaka, 567-0047, Japan,
miz@ei.sanken.osaka-u.ac.jp

Abstract. Intelligence in an ITS authoring system could rely on content-based engineering of instructional design (ID) knowledge, i.e. based on principles such as conceptualization, standardization and theory-awareness. An ontology-based architecture with appropriate ontologies has been proposed for a theory-aware ITS authoring system. Ontological engineering (OE) as a collaborative process jointly conducted by an OE expert and an ID expert is presented as a step on a roadmap towards a theory-aware ITS authoring system.

1 Introduction

What is (at) the core of Artificial Intelligence and Education (AIED) systems? This has been a question for as long as the field of AIED has come of age, and various answers have been suggested such as curriculum planning [1,2], student modeling [3,4], teaching expertise [5,6], and dialogue modeling [7,8,9], among others. Also suggested was the idea of intelligence implemented all over the periphery of an ITS rather than centralized at a core [10], as is for instance the case of adaptive hypermedia [11].

In this paper, the claim is that declarative knowledge about instruction could be the beating heart of an ITS, where shared intelligence among the designer/author and the authoring environment is the dynamic component for the interactive construction of instructional scenarios and learning environments. The goal of the work presented below is to explore the basic layer needed toward the architecture of an OE based authoring system, as described in [12]. The starting point and the main ideas are therefore shortly reminded in the next section.

2 Some Problems in ITS and in Instructional Technology Research

ITS research on knowledge representation so far has concentrated mainly on procedural knowledge, as opposed to declarative; cognitive modeling is often conducted from a naturalistic point of view. Authoring of ITS can be said fragmental [13]. ITSs have also been a research focus for years in Instructional Technology (IT),

S.A. Cerri, G. Gouardères, and F. Paraguaçu (Eds.): ITS 2002, LNCS 2363, pp. 399–409, 2002.

a field close to AIED, with the modeling of instructional design knowledge in authoring environments [14,15,16], or in an instructional design workbench [17].

An analysis of the existing in terms of components shows that few environments combine authoring tools and knowledge representation of instructional theories and principles, and that none of them possesses desired functionalities of an intelligent authoring system such as *Retrieve appropriate theories for selecting instructional methods* or *Provide principles for structuring a learning environment.*

Declarative knowledge is mainly absent in those systems, as is the maintenance of its integrity. OE has the potential to solve these problems by proposing a declarative knowledge modeling approach [18,19,20]; as a result, the semantic-based knowledge systematization could provide a gateway to learning objects and their management [21]. Instructional Design theories provide the principled knowledge to make high level design decisions such as instructional strategies [22], or to orient the lower level decisions such as learning material. However, tackling the systematization of instructional knowledge is not without major challenges; the two next sections will describe some of these challenges.

3   Collaborative Ontological Engineering of Instructional Design Knowledge: Challenges of Such an Enterprise

The ontological engineering process was conducted collaboratively by an OE expert and an ID expert. Among the many challenges of this enterprise are the following questions:

- Should a unification or an integration of theories be a goal, given that theories have competitive or complementary views?
- Should a unification or an integration of theoretical and practical knowledge be a goal, given that such a view is far from available and even questionable?
- By which criteria should we consider theoretical knowledge? Experimental evidence versus hypothetical or speculative? classical versus emerging?
- How can a common terminology be found and become acceptable by sometimes divergent theoreticians and practitioners?
- How to distinguish Learning Theories from Instructional Theories from Instructional Design Theories, when the many classifications available show serious variations and strong overlaps?
- How to specify these theories when, again, the many classifications of these show serious variations and strong overlaps?
- How to respect the integrity of each theory vs to integrate theories as questioned by Mayer [23] or Wasson [1]?
- How to link theoretical to practical knowledge?
- How to distinguish between domain and task ontologies and to link both in the case of an ontology-based ITS authoring system?
- What kind of attributes can be given to ***things*** when these things are theories? Cognitivist/constructivist? Validated/emergent?

A very particular question was raised: what should be the status of instructional design knowledge, domain or task knowledge? The following section describes the exploration that was conducted based on Gibbons' view of instructional technology as a design science.

4 Gibbons' Exploration into Instructional Technology Knowledge

The issue of considering ID knowledge as domain knowledge or task knowledge is whether to build it into the domain or into the task ontology; considering it as science means engineering the ID knowledge under domain knowledge. For this reason, the work of Gibbons on Instructional Technology (IT) as a design science was given special attention. What is Instructional Technology? The Association for Educational Communications and Technology (AECT) states: "Instructional Technology is the theory and practice of design, development, utilization, management and evaluation of processes and resources for learning." (www.aect.org). IT is composed of two main components: Instructional Design and Instructional Development [24]. Gibbons views IT as a design science in the sense of Simon [25], and attempts to relate theoretical knowledge to practical knowledge as done in the field of industrial design [26]. Classes of technological knowledge are proposed: 1) Fundamental Design Concepts (Operational Principle, Normal Configuration), 2) Criteria and Specifications, 3) Theoretical Tools, 4) Quantitative Data, 5) Practical Considerations, 6) Design Instrumentalities. As an example, a 'normal configuration' is defined as 'the general shape and arrangement that are commonly agreed to best embody the operational principle. Should these classes apply to IT Instructional design's operational principle could be: *to build an instructional system that sustains and fosters the learning process, ensures the quality and the effectiveness of learning.* This view has the potential to provide a framework for specifying IT knowledge, and stimulates reflection about the actual status of IT knowledge. For example, ID principles are defined as follows by Merrill [27]: a) a principle is a relationship that is always true under appropriate conditions, b) fundamental principles for instructional design do exist, c) these design principles apply regardless of the instructional program or practices involved, d) violating them results in a decrement in learning and performance. Given this definition, ID principles could be considered as 'Operational principles' in the sense of Gibbons.

Further considerations relate to the basic principles of knowledge systematization as they apply to the systematization of theoretical knowledge, and of multiple theories for the same field.

5 Knowledge Systematization of Theoretical Knowledge

Knowledge systematization has been done for human consumption to date. The results have mainly been described in natural language in the form of a book or a paper. It might be no problem if humans learn them. But, it becomes a problem when we try to make computers understand and use the knowledge. Knowledge systematization for computer-consumption from engineering point of view should enable a seamless flow of knowledge from theoretical world to practical world.

Our systematization project is done not for the sake of theory but for using the theory. By this, we mean that theories should be interpreted from an engineering point of view. Engineering is heavily based on the requirements of practice. For example, a head of a company might want to train some specific competencies/skills such as creative thinking, reasoning in an abstract space, negotiation in sales activities, planning, presentation, etc. of employees who have various background and experiences from novice to expert. Because of the variety of learning goals (competencies and skills) and of the heterogeneity of learners, a variety of theories can help the learning process. For example, although situatedness has been claimed to be one of the most critical factors in successful learning, it is not always considered that way in training practice. Human Resource Development divisions have identified that a skill which is too much specialized for a specific situation or domain to be applied to many situations is not what they need. Instead, what they need are skills which prove to be effective in many situations, that is, competencies. Needless to say, they never want too abstract knowledge which is hard to apply to real world situations, but at the same time, they also dislike inflexible skills which apply only in a specific situation. Another example is social interaction. Some learning theorists claim that social interaction is the essence of learning process; however, for a company which wants to train their employees' reasoning capability in an abstract space or their motor skills, social interaction may seem of little importance.

In short, contrary to the claim of some learning theorists that "this is the only learning theory which explains the learning process", the fact that a variety of learning theories exist may be viewed in a positive way. There exists a variety of requirements for effective learning, and each of them needs a most suitable theory and needs to be interpreted in the terms used in the application domain. Having a collection of the existing theories in an authoring system also allows to respond to the preferences of the instructional designers/authors and of their clients. Moreover, it might prove to be a stimulus to a reflective process on the side of the designers/authors as they consider the potential and relevance of each theory and the compatibility among them, eventually resulting in an improved level of quality. For these reasons, useful characterization of each theory is what we need from an engineering point of view.

When the enterprise is knowledge systematization, the necessary characteristics that systematized knowledge is expected to have are the following: 1) Concepts found in all the knowledge are clearly defined, 2) Concepts are organized in an *is-a* structure, 3) Dependencies and necessary relations among concepts are explicitly captured, 4) Each viewpoint used for structuring knowledge, if any, is made explicit, 5) Ready for multiple access, 6) Consistency is maintained. The above clearly shows that OE does contribute to the systematization of knowledge. Furthermore, when the user of the systematized knowledge is an engineer or a designer, which is our case, the set of viewpoints has to include practical points of view. One of our research goals is to make theories available for engineers and for designers/authors of ITSs.

6   Ontological Engineering, a Deconstructionist Approach

For an instructional scientist, OE starts with the deconstruction of the existing body of knowledge, both theoretical and practical. Although a risky enterprise, it is worth the journey. Needless to say, this restructuring process should not be considered a substitute to theory building. A simplified description of the OE process for Level 1 is: 1) Extract most essential concepts and most essential links among them; 2) Define them by their meaning, their attributes, and the semantic constraints on them. Ontological categories for a process are generally: actor (subject, thing which does actions), behaviour (verb, action, phenomena), object (thing being processed by actor), goal (state to be achieved), situation (context in which an action is done) and attributes (characteristics; of all of the above).

The first assumption is that "everything is concrete", and that concrete is defined as dimensioned by time and space.

The second assumption is that we have two kinds of worlds: 1) Concrete worlds (learning, instruction, instructional design) that we describe based upon the best possible approximation of what is existing, 2) Abstract worlds (learning, instruction, instructional design) where we reflect existing theories with the best possible fidelity. These are called Worlds of theories.

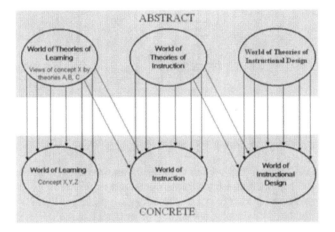

Fig. 1. Abstract and concrete worlds and how they relate to each other.

The third assumption is that we have two ontologies: 1) Domain ontology consists of the worlds of learning, instruction, instructional design, and of the worlds of learning theories, instructional theories, instructional design theories, 2) Task ontology consists of the context of use (by end-user and/or by intelligent system), *i.e.* the task of designing/authoring (ID task) or the sub-task of authoring (developing).

The fourth assumption is that theories are "things" in the world of theories: 1) Theories of learning, of instruction, of instructional design, 2) Theories of knowledge (epistemologies) on which theories of learning rely, 3) The worlds of theories is part of the Domain Ontology.

Definitions of the theoretical knowledge considered are: 1) A theory of learning is a conceptual system to describe, explain, predict and study *natural phenomena involved* in the learning process, 2) A theory of instruction is a conceptual system to describe, explain, predict and study *artificial activities for supporting, organizing, fostering, facilitating, accelerating or evaluating* the learning process, 3) A theory of instructional design is a conceptual system to describe, explain, predict and study the *design of artificial activities for supporting, organizing, fostering, facilitating, accelerating or evaluating* the learning process. Figure 1 illustrates a view of how the three worlds of theories relate to the three concrete worlds.

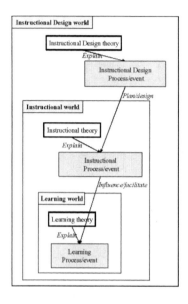

Fig. 2. A view of the three nested worlds.

One of the difficulties that we had in building ontologies of these theories is how to differentiate the relations and constraints contained in an ontology from those in the target theory, since an ontology itself is a theory of existence by definition and hence contains relations and/or constraints among objects just like a target theory is a set of relations/constraints among objects in the target world. We resolved this issue by giving each theory a primary identity with full relations/constraints it needs. Considering the fact that a theory tries to explain its target world we came up with a framework of our ontology building enterprise as shown in Fig. 2. It shows a nested structure of Learning, Instruction, and Instructional Design worlds. Each of the three kinds of theories explains processes/events which happen in each world. One of the major differences among the three kinds of processes/events is that while the lower two are real world pro-cesses/events, the other is a planning or design process. A theory needs to refer to objects existing in the target world when it tries to say something about them, which suggests that a theory may have its own set of objects, since any object in a theory is obtained according to the theory-specific articulation of the target world. In fact, a learning theory uses its own way of describing the learning process from its particular view. Each theory has its own viewpoint from which it views the target world. Although these distinctions are not perfect but questionable, they seem reasonable enough to serve the purpose of this work.

A tentative portrait of an ontology of instructional design was then sketched, following the steps recommended by the OE methodology for Level 1: a structured collection of terms, articulation of the world of interest, elicitation of concepts and of the *is-a* hierarchy among them.

7   Portraiting Domain and Task Ontologies of Instructional Design

A preliminary portrait of ID knowledge provides the main terms to be considered and how they can be structured. Three worlds compose the domain ontology, and two worlds the task ontologies. A structured collection of theories of learning and instruction is provided by Kearsley as an hypermedia base [28]. A view of learning theories from an ID perspective is found in Ertmer and Newby [29]. How Learning Theories view Learning is inspired from Mayer [23].

For the world of learning, the main concepts could be: learning activity, assignment, reading, interacting, problem-solving, learning phase, learning difficulties/remediation. For the world of theories of learning, the main concepts could be: theory of learning, epistemological ground, taxonomy, learning, motivation, attention, comprehension, memory, cognition, meta-cognition, learning phase, learning difficulties/remediation.

For the world of instruction, the main concepts could be: instruction, learning, instructional strategies, teaching, tutoring, assessment of learning. For the world of theories of instruction, the main concepts could be: theory of instruction, theory of learning, epistemological ground, taxonomy, learning, instructional strategies, teaching, tutoring, assessment of learning.

For the world of instructional design, the main concepts could be: instructional design, instruction, learning, instructional scenario, learning environment, selection of methods, selection of media, selection of assessment methods. For the world of theories of instructional design, the main concepts could be: theory of instructional design, theory of instruction, theory of learning, epistemological ground, taxonomy, learning, selection of methods, selection of media, selection of assessment methods.

As a conclusion to this preliminary portrait of knowledge relevant to the OE of ID knowledge, it is obviously too early to say whether these distinctions will reveal valuable; it is anticipated that a series of iterations may be needed before a satisfactory collection of terms is found.

8   Building These Ontologies into the Ontology Editor

The building of these ontologies into the Ontology Editor* fulfills the Level 1 of OE, and exposes the links and the hierarchy to constraint checking. Essentially, the building process consists, besides consolidating the terms and the hierarchy, in the specification of *Is-a* and *Part-of* relationships for each term. Generate and test is the preferred method, until a reasonable structure is obtained, and until all the constraints are fully respected. Another ontological category to be considered is *role*, as it proved to be a quite useful one in our case:

a) Instructional designer is a role (agent of design), with, as sub-roles, analyst of learning contents, of learners' characteristics, of learning context; designer of scenarios, of learning environments; developer of learning environments; collaborator with other designers, etc.

b) Instructor is a role (agent of instruction), with, as sub-roles, information presenter; discussion moderator; asking questions/answering questions; asking for/giving explanation; solving problems; collaborate; assess learning; game master; organizing lab experiment/field experiment; organize simulation/role play, etc.

c) Learner is a role (agent of learning), with, as sub-roles, asking/answering questions; asking for/giving explanation; solve problems; play simulation games; make assignments; pass examinations; self-manage learning; self-assess learning, etc.

An extract of the building within the Ontology Editor is shown in Fig. 3.

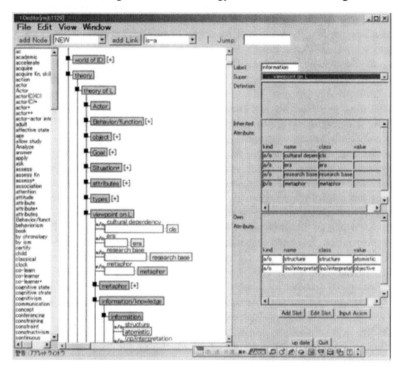

Fig. 3. Extract of the ontology built within the Ontology Editor

9   Further Work

The work towards a Level 1 of the ontology needs to be completed, in that the collection of terms must be stabilized, the hierarchy also needs to be stabilized, the relations need to be completed and refined, the definitions need to be completed, the semantic constraints need to be fully checked. A series of iterations is expected to be necessary to obtain a satisfactory Level 1.

Further steps on our roadmap include:

1) *Produce two detailed examples.* Based on the assumption that "everything is concrete", and that "concrete" means 'dimensioned by time and space", we plan to illustrate this idea with two concrete examples, specified within the Ontology Editor: Learner-Instructor interaction (what is it made of? Specify components and roles), Scenario building (what is it made of? Scenarize the desired functionalities).

2) *Elaborate functionalities of an ontology-based ITS authoring system.* The functionalities of such a system can be: Intelligent theory retriever, Intelligent navigator based on theories, Advisor to form an appropriate collaborative learning group, etc. Steps towards the identification of these functionalities are: 1) imagine what users can do with an ontology-aware authoring environment, 2) specify new functionalities, 3) build a scenario-based demo of functionalities, 4) test mockup and validate with users.

A long term perspective for this work is to provide the next generation of authoring systems with a scientific basis for semantic standards of learning objects and their management.

10 Concluding Remarks

We have presented a work in progress in AIED research that aims at -ontology-awareness for future ITS authoring systems. Collaborative ontological engineering of ID knowledge has been described, followed by the first results on a road map towards an ontology-aware authoring system.

The implications of "ontology-awareness" are meaningful, not only for AIED research into system building but also for knowledge sharing between humans and computers. OE enables humans to share theories with computers, and stimulates the quest for a consensus among humans. If an ontology represents a shared conceptualization in a community, OE has the potential to contribute to the building of such a conceptualization.

Discussions about the hierarchical nature of ontologies can help find general concepts by going up the hierarchy. The *is-a* and *part-of* hierarchies help humans in finding the essential differences between them. The first results described above represent a possible shared conceptualization. It may be far from complete, but it should provide a good start to come up with a richer agreement.

*The Ontology Editor was developed at Mizlab, Osaka University
(http://www.ei.sanken.osaka-u.ac.jp/oe/oe.html).

Acknowledgements. This work was supported by ISIR, Osaka University, where the first author spent a three month invited stay, Sept-Dec. 2001.

References

[1]   Wasson, B. (1996). Instructional Planning and Contemporary Theories of Learning, In P. Brna, A. Paiva & J. Self (Eds.). *Proc. of the Eur. Conf. on AIED*, 23-30, Lisbon: Colibri.

[2]   Nkambou, R. Gauthier, R., and Frasson, C. (1996). CREAM-tools: An authoring environment for curriculum and course building in an ITS. *Proc. of the 3d Int'l Conf. on CAL & Inst'l Sc. & Eng*, NY: Springer-Verlag.

[3]   Kay, J. (2000). *Accretion Representation for Scrutable Student Modelling*, Proc. ITS'2000, 514-523.

[4]   McCalla G., Vassileva, J., Greer, J. and Bull, S. (2000*). Active Learner Modeling*, Proc. ITS'2000, 53-62.

[5]   Goodyear, P. (1991). *Teaching Knowledge and Intelligent Tutoring*. Norwood, NJ: Ablex.

[6]   Granbastien, M. (1999). *Teaching Expertise is at the Core of ITS Research*, IJAIED, 10, 335-349.

[7]   Baker, M. (2000). *The roles of models in AIED research: a prospective view*. IJAIED, 11 (2), 122-143.

[8]   Katz, S., O'Donnell, G. and Kay, H. (2000). *An approach to analyzing the role and structure of reflective dialogue*, IJAIED, 11, 320-343.

[9]   Lajoie, S.P., Faremo, S. and Wiseman, J. (2001). *Identifying human tutoring strategies for effective instruction in internal medicine*. IJAIED, Special Issue on Modelling Teaching.

[10] Andriessen, J. and Sandberg, J. (1999). Where *is education heading and how about AI?* IJAIED,10, 130-150.

[11] Brusilovsky, P. (2000). *Course Sequencing for Static Courses? Applying ITS Techniques in Large-Scale Web-based Education*, Proc. ITS'2000, 625-634.

[12] Mizoguchi, R. and Bourdeau, J. (2000). Using Ontological Engineering to Overcome Common AI-ED Problems. IJAIED, Special Issue on AIED 2010, vol.11, 107-121. http://cbl.leeds.ac.uk/ijaied/

[13] Murray, T. (1999). *Authoring intelligent tutoring systems: an analysis of the state of the art*, IJAIED,10, 98-129.

[14] Merrill, D. (1993). An integrated model for automating instructional design and delivery, in Spector, M., Polson, P. and Muraida, D., eds.. *Automating Instructional Design: Concepts and Issues*, Engl. Cliffs, NJ: Educational Technology.

[15] Spector, M., Polson, P. and Muraida, D., eds., (1993). *Automating Instructional Design: Concepts and Issues*, Engl. Cliffs, NJ: Educational Technology.

[16] Tennyson, R. and Barron, A., Eds. (1995) *Automating Instructional Design: Computer-Based Development and Delivery Tools*. Springer, NATO ASI Series, Series F: Computer and Systems Sciences, vol. 140.

[17] Paquette, G. (2001). Telelearning Systems Engineering –Towards a New ISD Model, *Jl of Structural Learning and Intelligent Systems*, 14 (4), 319-154.

[18] Mizoguchi, R. and Sinitsa, K. (1996) *Architectures and Methods for Designing Cost-Effective and Reusable ITSs*, Proc. ITS'96, Montreal, pp. 1-21.

[19] Ikeda, M., Seta, K., and Mizoguchi, R. (1997) *Task Ontology Makes It Easier To Use AuthoringTools*. *Proc. of IJCAI-97*, Nagoya, Japan, 342-347.

[20] Chen, W. Hayashi, Y., Kin, L. Ikeda, M. and Mizoguchi, R. (1998) *Ontological Issues in an Intelligent Authoring Tool*, in Chan T-W., Collins A. & Lin J. (Eds.), *Proc. of ICCE'98*, vol. 1, 41-50.

[21] Wiley, D. (2001). *Instructional Use of Learning Objects*. Bloomington, Indiana: The Agency for Instructional Technology.

[22] Jones, M. (1988). *Instructional Systems Need Instructional Theory: Comments on a Truism*. Paper presented at the NATO Research Workshop "New Directions in Education Technology", Cranfield, England, November 10-13. (Tech. report, ARIES Lab., U. of Saskatchewan).

[23] Mayer, R. (1997). Learners as information processors. *Educational Psychology Journal*, 31 (3/4), 151-161.

[24] Seels B. and Richey R. (2001). *Instructional Technology: The Definition and Domains of the Field*. Washington, DC: AECT.

[25] Simon, H. (1969). *The Sciences of the Artificial*. Cambridge, MA: MIT Press.

[26] Gibbons, A. (2000). *The Practice of Instructional Technology*. Presented at the 2000 AECT conference, 48p.

[27] Merrill, D. (1994). *Instructional Design Theories*. Engl. Cliffs, NJ: Ed. Tech. Publications.

[28] Kearsley, G. *Explorations in Learning & Instruction: The Theory Into Practice Database*. http://tip.psychology.org/

[29] Ertmer, P. A., Newby, T. J. (1993). Behaviorism, cognitivism, constructivism: Comparing critical features from an instructional design perspective. *Performance Improvement Quarterly*, 6 (4), 50-70.

TeLoDe: Towards Creating an Intelligent Computer Algebra System

Iraklis Paraskakis

Department of Computer Science
CITY LIBERAL STUDIES
Affiliated Institute of the University of Sheffield
Tsimiski 13, 54 624 Thessaloniki, GREECE

Abstract. *TeLoDe* (Teaching Linear Ordinary Differential Equations) is an Intelligent Tutoring System (ITS), teaching how to solve Linear Second Order Ordinary Differential Equations with Constant Coefficients. *TeLoDe* augments *Maple*, a Computer Algebra System (CAS) by incorporating a teaching strategy module and declarative knowledge. *TeLoDe*'s teaching module is informed by *SIMTA* (Styles implemented by Methods Tactics and Actions). In *SIMTA* the contemporary concept of *teaching strategy* is rethought and viewed at two fundamental levels: *organisational level* and *operational level*. The *organisational level* deals with the *structure* of the teaching strategy whereas the *operational level* deals with the *manifestation* of that structure. A triple *generic* structure, *method*, *tactic*(s), *action(s)* represents the organisational level. The *teaching style* in *TeLoDe* is the *expository style* drawing from Ausubel's theory of meaningful reception learning. The expository style, utilising the declarative knowledge, provides the students with an environment where they are encouraged to actively construct their knowledge.

1   Introduction

Computer Algebra Systems (CAS), such as Maple are extremely powerful mathematical engines. Their strength is on solving symbolic problems i.e., CAS could be seen as powerful symbolic calculators. However, CAS cannot explain the steps or the logic involved in attaining the solution to a problem. This is CAS's Achilles' heel when it comes to consider them for use in education. This should not be interpreted that CAS systems cannot be used for educational purposes, but rather that their use in education has not reached their full and true potential.

As argued in [13], augmenting a CAS, by adding a teaching module and declarative knowledge, is a way of overcoming the inherent problems described above. TeLoDe, a prototype, is an augmentation of Maple. TeLoDe is an ITS prototype, based on Maple, and teaches how to solve a linear differential equation. The teaching module of TeLoDe is been informed by the SIMTA framework and, for demonstration purposes, the declarative knowledge of linear second order ordinary differential equation with constant coefficients has been developed.

S.A. Cerri, G. Gouardères, and F. Paraguaçu (Eds.): ITS 2002, LNCS 2363, pp. 410–420, 2002.
© Springer-Verlag Berlin Heidelberg 2002

TeLoDe's approach in teaching how to solve the aforementioned equations is based on the fact that the answer to the problem, the solution that is, is given by Maple. Consequently, TeLoDe's teaching focuses on issues like, understanding the nature, the existence and the 'look' of the solution. This way the student is placed on the advantageous position of being able 'check' Maple's answer to the specific problem. The problem solving techniques used in TeLoDe encourages the student to make hypotheses, conjectures and deductions through the extensive use of background knowledge where analogous cases, to their problem, are presented. Moreover, the techniques used are 'recycled', i.e., they have been used in solving other type of equations, which are very familiar to the student since these equations are present in the background knowledge of the student. This enables the student to see a pattern in one's approach in solving mathematical problems. TeLoDe's teaching is based on the use of the expository style. The expository style is based on Ausubel's theory of meaningful reception learning [3].

The expository style has been forged and implemented following the principles of the SIMTA framework. SIMTA institutes a novel thinking on the topic of teaching strategies, regarding their organisation and operation in the paradigm of multiple teaching strategies[1] and is the result of interdisciplinary research. SIMTA advocates that all teaching strategies operate in the paradigm of multiple teaching strategies and could be viewed at two fundamental levels: the *operational* and the *organisational* level. The *organisational level* deals with the structure of the teaching strategy whereas the *operational level* deals with the manifestation of that structure.

The rest of this paper is organised as follows. Section 2 presents an account of Computer Algebra Systems, their current use in tertiary education in the UK and what is meant by augmentation. Section 3 presents an overall description of the SIMTA framework and the expository style. Section 4 presents an account of TeLoDe

2   Computer Algebra Systems: The Present and Future

Computer Algebra Systems enable the exact solution of problems in symbolic form. This contrasts with the numerical analysis approach used in conventional computer languages such as FORTRAN or BASIC, where a numerical approximation is obtained. CASs are interactive and allow the user to define an expression, apply an operation and manipulate the output. Standard operations include algebraic simplification, calculus, (i.e., integration, differentiation, power series etc.), algebra, systems of equations, differential equations as well as the use of the system as arbitrary-precision desk calculators [9].

Maple [4], [5] is the product of Waterloo University in Canada. Maple is case sensitive. All Maple commands must be issued in lower case. This can be very

---

[1] The term "paradigm of multiple teaching strategies" indicates a collection of teaching strategies where each teaching strategy is able to offer an alternative view on the *same* problem i.e., they facilitate the accomplishment of the same goal. Alternative teaching strategies for the accomplishment of *different* goals cannot be considered to operate in the paradigm of multiple teaching strategies.

annoying because the system, for example, does not understand the complex notation **i** for imaginary numbers in lower case, requiring it to be in upper case only. For example to solve a quadratic equation the syntax is as follows:

$$solve(x^2 +2*x+1, x);$$

which returns

$$-1, -1$$

To integrate an expression the syntax is

$$int(x^2,x);$$

which returns

$$\frac{1}{3}x^3$$

To solve the inequality $x^2 + 3x + 2 \geq 2$ the syntax is as follows:

$$solve(x^2 + 3x + 2 \geq 2, x);$$

which returns

$$x \leq -3 \text{ and } x \geq 0$$

Maple is even capable to even capable to detect a case where an expression is discontinuous and thus it is not possible to evaluate a definite integral. Consider the example $\int_0^5 \frac{1}{1-x}dx$. Maple just returns the expression unevaluated whereas Mathematica, another CAS, does not check for singularities and merely substitutes the upper and lower values in the indefinite integral. This gives the result -ln(-4), which is simply wrong! Derive, another CAS, returns a value in the Complex domain which may be taken as an indication that something is 'wrong'. The fact that CAS make mistakes is central to our proposal for augmentation.

Contemporary use of CAS in tertiary education has concentrated on exploiting the plotting and animation facilities that CAS provide. Consequently, the powerful mathematical solving engine is used an ancillary fashion, in such a way to offer ways where the students can derive solutions to problems, derive the rules for differentiation and so on (for example see [14]). Three other projects that follow basic the same approach on the use of CAS in education are TRANSMATH, TMP and MathWise.

TRANSMATH is a project run by University of Leeds, [6], is based on Mathematica although Mathematica is seen as playing secondary role. Mathematica assists the teaching process by allowing animation, different plotting and enabling the user to see the effect of varying parameters. For example, TRANSMATH, using the Toolbook as front-end, leads the student step by step in finding the integral of a fraction, by pointing to long division of polynomials and guiding the student through to find the quotient and so forth [6]. The topics covered by TRANSMATH are:

- Introduction to Differentiation
- Indefinite Integration
- Ordinary Differential Equations

- Techniques of Differentiation
- Definite Integration

By contrast, in the TMP project at Imperial College [10], Mathematica plays a different role. Here the students are actively encouraged to "play" with Mathematica, that is, to learn to use the commands of Mathematica (At the University of North London a course entitled Computer Algebra exists which teaches students about Maple, its commands and how to use the package). This difference does not affect the overall role of CAS but rather the interaction between the student and Mathematica; the difference can be summarised as *learn to program Mathematica* as opposed to *learn to program the keypad* [12].

MathWise is another computer based learning package covering quite a range of topics from complex numbers to calculus [8]. MathWise is a product of the UK Mathematics Courseware Consortium, a project in the Teaching and Learning Technology Programme. It produces computer based learning modules for mathematics, particularly for science and engineering students. A number of universities collaborate in this project. Again Mathematica is the CAS upon which these modules are based. The aim in MathWise is the same as that at Imperial College and Leeds, to provide a tool to help in the teaching of the modules.

2.1   The Case for Augmenting CASs

As the projects cited above indicate, CASs are well established in the teaching of mathematics but have limitations. The teaching of mathematics topics is much the same it was before CASs, although they provide the ability to plot graphs, animate, and so on.

I would like to propose an alternative use of CASs in education, based on the unquestionable benefit of CASs' powerful solving engines. If the attainment of the solution of a problem could be entrusted to a CAS, then procedures such as transposition of a matrix, or how the quotient rule and the product rule in differentiation operate, or how the general solution of a differential equation is achieved, could be examined and assessed. The assessment of these procedures will consider the following two options:

1. Is it safe to entrust the whole process to a CAS?
2. How can the process be revised so that
   2a. the process is seen as a result of conceptual knowledge
   2b. there is a logical sequence between the steps in the process.

As a result more attention could be concentrated on the conceptual side of the topic and thus provide the student with a richer picture. This will allow rethinking of what is taught and how it is taught. At the same time the purpose of CASs is also rethought, since the role that they are now asked to play is more central than that defined in the projects mentioned previously.

To encompass this modification, CASs are required to "know" about the topics that they are required to cover in their procedural aspects. The knowledge currently possessed by CAS is only procedural. Moreover, since the procedural knowledge of CAS is in the form of a black-box [7], a glass-box would provide us with the option to follow the process of attaining a solution. The glass-box whilst utilising the functionality and power of a CAS at the same time will provide an interface where solutions to mathematical problems are done in human like manner. This augmentation of a CAS amounts to its transformation from an inherently non-pedagogical package to one offering pedagogical opportunities. Incorporating these considerations involves two tasks. First, CAS knowledge must be enriched by creating a glass-box for its procedural knowledge and by associating these procedures with declarative knowledge. Second, teaching strategies have to be built into the CAS.

3   Rationale and Architecture of the SIMTA Framework

The rationale of SIMTA is to develop a theoretical framework that can inform the structure of a teaching strategy module in an ITS. Through SIMTA, a new view regarding the concept of teaching strategy operating in a multiple teaching strategies paradigm is put forward. This view is underpinned by the following three premises:

- The *development/grouping* of teaching strategies operating in the multiple teaching strategies paradigm is *congruent* to a *common set of beliefs*[2]
- the current concept of a teaching strategy is uncoupled and revisited with the notion that a teaching strategy can be viewed at two levels, the *operational level* and the *organisational level*
- the *role* of a teaching strategy operating in the paradigm of multiple teaching strategies is to offer *alternative* representations of the *same* topic.

SIMTA is a two dimensional framework which is organised in a hierarchical fashion and supports the three factors, subject matter, student and tutor. SIMTA consists of four elements: *style*, *methods*, *tactics* and *actions*. Central to the organisation of SIMTA are the beliefs that

- a teaching strategy is 'freed' from the elements that are responsible for 'driving' the teaching strategy
- and that developing/grouping of teaching strategies operating in the paradigm of multiple teaching strategies is congruent to a common set of beliefs, which is responsible for 'driving' the teaching strategies.

A *teaching strategy* in SIMTA is defined in terms of a triple generic structure, namely *methods*, *tactics* and *actions* and operates under a *style*. The *style* encapsulates the common set of beliefs. The generic structure of a teaching strategy satisfies the premises

---

[2] The term *common set of beliefs* is equivalent to what [11] refers to as the assumed concepts, values and principles within educators' discourses, policies and practices. Such concepts, values and principles could represent one's beliefs regarding how learning is best achieved, what is education etc.

- that a teaching strategy must offer *alternative* representations of the *same* task at hand
- a teaching strategy is *repaired* before it is changed.

Consequently, a *teaching strategy* is concerned with the structure of the subject matter and the interaction of that structure with the student. The *method* is a mechanism for structuring the subject matter, the *tactic* is a mechanism for controlling the interaction between the tutor and the student, whereas the actions are low level mechanisms facilitating the interaction.

A *method* is the primary element of a teaching strategy in SIMTA and in fact acts as an identifier for the teaching strategy. The methods represent all possible ways of structuring a subject matter. Examples of methods are analogy, examples, generalisations, specialisations and investigations. Consequently, given a specific task a number of methods can be identified for that task and thus offer a number of *alternative* structures supporting the task at hand.

The *tactic* is a mechanism for facilitating the interaction of *a* method with the learner. Tactics represent generic dialogue structures and their spectrum ranges from *implicit* to *explicit* dialogue structures. Thus, a given method uses a number of tactics to facilitate interaction with the learner in more than one way, i.e., implicitly, explicitly or anything in between. Consequently, for a given task and a given method, a number of *alternative* interactions for *that* method with the learner are possible.

The *action* is a low level mechanism facilitating the tactic and is necessary for a computer tutor. Examples of an action are: display a statement, display a question, display a statement followed by a question, pick an example, etc.

From the above description it is shown that a teaching strategy as defined in SIMTA, adheres to the principle of offering alternative representations for a given task at two levels:

- the method level
- and the tactic level.

Alternatives at the level of tactic are considered to be *variations* of essentially the same teaching strategy, since the method is the primary element characterising the teaching strategy. However, alternatives at the method level are considered to be *different* teaching strategies because the methods that characterise the teaching strategies represent different structures, i.e., a change from the method of analogy to that of example. Figure 1 shows how two styles S1 and S2 are defined in the SIMTA framework.

As depicted in figure 1, under S_1 (*style* 1) the *methods* m_1 and m_3 are selected. In turn the *methods* m_1 and m_3 under S_1 use *tactics* t_1, t_2, t_3 and t_1 and t_3 respectively. Under the style S_1 the *tactic* t_1 uses actions a_1, a_2, and a_3 tactic t_2 uses a_2 and a_3 whereas t_3 uses a_2, a_3 and a_8. Again as depicted in figure 1, under S_2 (style 2) the methods m_1 and m_3 are selected. This time the methods m_1 and m_3 use different tactics to facilitate interaction of these methods and that reflects the fact that methods m_1 and m_3 operate under S_2 (style 2). The choice of actions is also different and these are a_4 and a_5 for t_2, a_6 and a_7 for t_4 and a_8 for t_5.

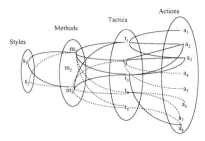

Fig. 1. Representation of multiple teaching strategies in a style (S1 is represented by the whole line whereas S2 is represented by the dashed line)

Therefore, one can see how these different combinations of methods and tactics, at both levels, result in a number of teaching strategies. However, given a specific task there is more than one manifestation both at the method level and at the tactic level. That is, there is more than one analogy or example and more than one implicit or explicit tactic. Thus, the question is how one selects between these different analogies or examples and the implicit or explicit tactics. The answer to this question is that selection depends on the *style*. The style ensures that only the congruent manifestations between these different methods and their tactics are grouped together.

4   An Overview of Ausubel's Theory of Learning and the Definition of the Expository Style

The expository style draws from Ausubel's theory of meaningful reception learning [1], [2], [3]. In reception meaningful learning the student is considered to be an active learner constructing their own knowledge. In the Ausubelian theory this is what is termed as a meaningful learning set that the student must possess. The teacher facilitates the learning by following a number of steps. First of all the lesson is organised in what is termed in Ausubel theory in Logically meaningful manner and then Potentially meaningful. In the first instance the topic to be taught is analysed to identify all links to other concepts/topics in an epistemological manner. These links are then filtered through the existing cognitive structure of a particular student, thus resulting in what is termed as potentially meaningful. Now the facilitation of the communication between the student and the teacher occurs either by progressive differentiation or integrative reconciliation. In the former case a more inclusive concept is first presented followed by more specific ones, thus differentiation whereas in the latter case the specific concepts are first shown followed by the more general and inclusive concepts. Moreover, Ausubel specifies that when a statement or question is made it has to be structured in a very specific and precise ways, or that the principal content must be in final form, as is termed in the Ausubelian theory.

To define the expository style, in accordance with the style definition, its type of learning and principles have to be defined. Therefore, the type of learning is *reception learning* and its principles are:

●Principal content/final form,

●Existing cognitive structure,

●Integrative reconciliation,

●Meaningful learning (potentially and logically meaningful),

● Progressive differentiation,

● Assimilation (subordinate, superordinate, combinatorial learning)

These principles will provide directions in manifesting the generic structure of methods, tactics and actions in such a way that when TeLoDe is activated under the expository style the teaching strategies will reflect the Ausubelian roots of the expository style (for a more detailed account of the expository style see [13]).

The above principles do not however, provide directions for the sequence of the strategies. Given that Ausubel's theory is developed in the paradigm of constructivism the strategies will move from implicit to explicit. In an implicit strategy, the tutor will provide the least possible information to the learner, whereas in an explicit strategy, the learner is given all the information. It has to stressed that in both cases, the statements will be couched in accordance with the principles of the expository style. Also, a strategy will only change its method when all its tactics have been exhausted. Likewise the methods will move from analogy to investigation to examples and finally to concept definition. This move is done on the contemplation that the analogy method is the most implicit method in TeLoDe followed by the investigation method, then the examples one and finally the concept definition method, considered to be the most explicit method.

5   Interacting with TeLoDe

TeLoDe is an augmentation of Maple by the inclusion of declarative knowledge, the expository style and a simple student model.

For the tutoring system to be activated the teaching style has to be selected and problem has to be given. Given the problem, the appropriate procedures and their sub-procedures are generated as well as the methods, tactics and actions that conform to the principles of the style are also been selected. Methods, tactics and actions that do not satisfy the principles of the chosen style are rejected.

If a procedure is strictly procedural, that is there is no declarative knowledge involved, then the student will be expected to carry out the work utilising Maples mathematical tools. Should a procedure be associated with declarative knowledge, then, in accordance with the principles of the expository style, the program will create a *meaningful structure*, that is a knowledge base constructed in order to facilitate the expository style. This is achieved by examining which methods can be sustained by the knowledge base utilising the principles of logically meaningful and potentially meaningful to the individual student. It has to be noted that at least the method of concept definition is always found to be valid.

Now the system is ready to interact with the student, who, in accordance with the expository style, must manifest a meaningful learning set. To demonstrate this interaction we will cite an annotated excerpt from the actual running of the program:

```
>main( prob, expl+4, exp, tact_lis, actions);
```

Prob indicates the problem, in our case linear second order ordinary differential equation with constant coefficients, *expl+4*, *expl* are the parameters that are set by the style and assist in the selection of the tactics that comply with the expository style, *tact_lis* represents all the tactics that are available to the system and *actions* all the actions available.

The system is now active and the first procedure with no associated declarative knowledge is displayed as follows:

```
   a) What is the type of the form of the solution in the
case of first order linear differential equation with
constant coefficients?
> The type of form of solution in the case of first order
linear differential equation with constant coefficients
is that of a function.
b) What is the type of the form of the solution in the
case of second order linear differential equation with
constant coefficients?
>( no answer)
c) The type of form of solution in the case of first
order linear differential equation with constant
coefficients is that of a function. What is the type of
form of solution in the case of linear second order
ordinary differential equation with constant
coefficients?
>( no answer)
d) What does the type of the form of the solution in the
case of linear second order linear differential equation
with constant coefficients depend on?
>( no answer)
         .
.( after above problem is resolved it comes back to
original problem)
         .
e) The type of form of solution in the case of second
order linear differential equation with constant
coefficients depends on the type of form of the unknown.
What does the type of form of the unknown in the case of
second order linear differential equation with constant
coefficients depend on?
>( no answer)
f) Here is an example of a second order linear
differential equation with constant coefficients
```

$$\frac{d^2 y(x)}{dx^2} + 2 \, \frac{dy(x)}{dx} + y(x) = 0$$

```
What is the type of form of solution in the case of
second order linear differential equation with constant
coefficients?
> The type of form of solution in the case of second
```

`order linear differential equation with constant`
`coefficients is that of a function.`

Upon initiation of the system, the methods of analogy, investigation, examples and definition become available. As analogy is the first method to be executed in accordance with the principles of utilising existing cognitive structure, reception learning, student being most active, the system asks the same problem but for a background concept (step a). The student replies correctly and the system moves to ask the question for the core concept (step b). As the student is not able to reply, the system makes an implicit correlation between background and core concepts (step c). As the student fails to realise that and the system has no more explicit tactics under analogy, it moves to the next available method, that of investigation (step c). In this case relationships in the core concept are examined and the student is being asked to state such relationships (step d). As the student does not reply to that, the system will try to revive such a relationship into student's memory by utilising background concepts for which the relationship holds and the student according to the student model knows. Once this has been resolved, the system comes back to the original problem and continues the method of investigation until all of its tactics are exhausted (step e). In this case the system moves to the next available method, that of examples and asks the student again (step f). As the student replies correctly the system moves on, but if the answer was wrong the system would have searched for an example from the background before continuing with the next method from the core knowledge.

6   Conclusions

In this paper we have presented TeLoDe an ITS prototype teaching how to solve linear second order ordinary differential equations with constant coefficients. TeLoDe shows that it is possible to build an Intelligent Computer Algebra System that fully exploit the capabilities of powerful mathematical solving engines such as Maple.

SIMTA has been central to the development of TeLoDe and brings a fresh approach to a rather difficult problem of computers in education. SIMTA signals a new impetus in our understanding of what is, what makes up and how a teaching strategy operates. Being able to unpack ,what was considered to be monolithic, the concept of teaching strategies, and define two new entities is a promising step forward as far as educational technology is concerned.

It this awareness that allows a novel and innovative explanation of the concept of teaching strategy and consequently of *multiple teaching strategies* as far as the organisation, operation and interaction, between the constituent teaching strategies, is concerned.

Informing TeLoDe's teaching strategy module by SIMTA, puts forward a new beginning for CASs. CAS's new role could be to undertake the procedural aspect of mathematics, which is an important one. Consequently, the human tutor could focus on the conceptual aspect of mathematics knowing that the students are trained on the procedural aspect by an ITS, whose objective is to train the students or reusing their background knowledge, forming conjectures and deductions and more important to be able to 'check' for the correctness of the results produced by the CAS.

As a result TeLoDe could mark a new beginning on the symbiosis between technology and human teachers. In this relationship, not only each one acts in a complementary way to the other but the co-operation is required for an educational goal to be achieved.

References

1. Ausubel, D. P. Educational Psychology: A cognitive view 2nd edition, 1978
2. Ausubel, D. P., Readings in school learning. New York: Holt, Rinehart and Winston, Inc., 1969.
3. Ausubel D. P, The psychology of meaningful verbal learning, Grune & Stratton. Inc., 1968.
4. Char W. B., Geddes O. K., Gonnet H. G., Monagan B. M., Watt M. S., *Maple: First Leaves, A Tutorial Introduction to Maple*, 2nd Edition, Waterloo Maple Publishing, 1988
5. Char W. B., Geddes O. K., Gonnet H. G., Monagan B. M., Watt M. S., *Maple Reference Manual*, 5th Edition, Waterloo Maple Publishing, 1990a
6. Cheng. S. Y., Kelly A. D., Maunder S. B., TRANSMATH- From Conception to Delivery, *Proceedings of International Conference in Hypermedia*, Sheffield, July 3-5 1995
7. du Boulay B., O'Shea T., Monk J., The Glass box inside the Black box: Presenting Computing Concepts to Novices, *International Journal of Man-Machine Studies*, Vol. 14, 1981
8. Harding R. D., Lay S., Moule H., Co-operative cross-platform development, *Association for Learning Technology Journal, (ALT-J)*, Vol. 4, No. 1, 1996
9. Hodgkinson E. D., *Algebraic Computing in Education*, Dept. of Applied Mathematics and Theoretical Physics, University of Liverpool, (Also presented at the Conference: Mathematics and Statistics Curricula in Higher Education for the 1990's), 1987
10. Kent P., Ramsden P., Wood J., *Multimedia for Teaching and Learning*, Times Higher Education Supplement pp. x-xi (London), 13 May 1994
11. Maurice St. H., A guide to commonplaces: on the use of loci in educator's discourse, Journal of Curriculum Studies, Vol. 23 No:1, 41-53, 1991
12. Noss R., Final report of the Transitional Mathematics project/TRANSMATH evaluation, on WWW at ULR: http://othello.ma.ic.ac.uk/articles/Evaluation Report, 1995
13. Paraskakis I., Rethinking Teaching Strategies: A Framework and Demonstration through Augmenting Maple, Unpublished PhD Thesis, The Open University, UK, 2000.
14. Watkins A., *A guide to using DERIVE*, Department of Mathematics and Statistics, Polytechnic of South West, Plymouth, 1990

An Intelligent Teaching Assistant System for Logic

Leanna Lesta and Kalina Yacef

School of Information Technologies, University of Sydney, Australia
kalina@it.usyd.edu.au

Abstract. This paper presents the Logic-ITA, an Intelligent Teaching Assistant system for the teaching/learning of propositional logic. Intelligent Teaching Assistant Systems are dedicated both to learners and teachers. The system embeds three tools: the Logic Tutor, the LT-Configurator and the LT-Analyser. The Logic Tutor is an intelligent tutoring system destined to the students. The other two tools are dedicated to the teacher. The LT-Configurator manages teaching configuration settings and material. The LT-Analyser is for monitoring the class' progress and collect data.

1   Introduction

Traditionally, Intelligent Tutoring Systems (ITS) are dedicated to learners. They help them learn at their own pace, following a curriculum tailored to their individual needs and receiving individualised feedback.

Intelligent Teaching Assistant Systems (ITAS) are dedicated both to learners and teachers [11]. They help learners as a traditional ITS would and they also assist the teacher in his/her tasks. The Logic-ITA is an example of Intelligent Teaching Assistant System for the domain of propositional logic. It was built with the aim of alleviating the problem of large numbers of students in classes, by adding an 'intelligent intermediary' between the teacher and the students.

It embeds an autonomous ITS for practicing formal proofs in logic, called the Logic Tutor [1]. In addition, the Logic-ITA also has two additional components dedicated to the teachers: the LT-Configurator and the LT-Analyser. Students can practice at their own pace, receive hints and appropriate feedback on their mistakes, and be provided with exercises adapted to their level. Teachers receive feedback from the system about the students' progress. All the interactions and exercises results are collected and stored in a database. Teachers and tutors can query this database to identify learning stages, common problems at a class level as well as a group or individual level.

The Logic-ITA has been integrated in our Languages and Logic course since 2001. This paper highlights the characteristics of the Logic-ITA. The following section presents the general architecture of the tool. Then sections 3 to 5 describe in turn the Logic Tutor, the LT-Configurator and the LT-Analyser. Section 6 describes a scenario of use. We then present the evaluation results and the conclusion.

S.A. Cerri, G. Gouardères, and F. Paraguaçu (Eds.): ITS 2002, LNCS 2363, pp. 421–431, 2002.

2   Architecture of the Logic-ITA

The Logic-ITA contains three tools: the Logic Tutor, the LT-Configurator, and the LT-Analyser. The Logic Tutor is for the students, whilst the other two tools are for the teacher. The general architecture is outlined below.

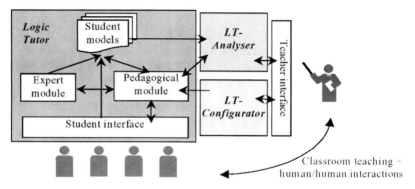

Fig. 1. General architecture of the Logic-ITA

The left hand part, the Logic Tutor, is an Intelligent Tutoring System dedicated to students. Several educational systems exist in the literature for this domain [4,9] with various styles of interface for representing the formal proofs. The novelty of the Logic-ITA resides in the added components on the right. We will present the three modules in turn in the next three sections.

3   The Logic Tutor

The Logic Tutor is an Intelligent Tutoring System that allows students to practice formal proofs, whilst providing them with context-sensitive feedback and tailored exercises. A multimedia presentation of the Logic Tutor can be found at [1].

Formal proofs are a way to prove a logic argument right. In logic, an argument is composed of a list (possibly empty) of premises and a conclusion. Premises and conclusion are well-formed formulas of propositional logic. The argument is said to be valid if the conclusion can be logically derived from the premises, by using laws of equivalence or rules of inference (both referred to as *rules* in the rest of the paper). A simple example is:

Premise 1: $(A \rightarrow (B \wedge C))$ Premise 2: A   Conclusion: B
This argument is valid, because we can first derive $(B \wedge C)$ from the 2 premises using a rule called *Modus Ponens*. Then we can derive B using the *Simplification* rule on the previous line.
In a formal proof, that could be represented as follows:

Premises Used	Line	Formula	Justification	Ref.Lines
	0	$(A \rightarrow (B \wedge C))$	Premise	
	1	A	Premise	
0,1	2	$(B \wedge C)$	Modus Ponens	0,1
0,1	3	B	Simplification	2

It should be noted that there are often many ways to prove an argument valid. What really matters is that the reasoning must be sound, i.e. that each line is validly derived and justified. In addition, a student's solution may contain "useless" steps, i.e. lines that are valid but that can be omitted because the conclusion does not rely on them. Although a solution with useless lines is less efficient, the result is nevertheless correct and students should be allowed to enter them. As a consequence, the Logic Tutor does not check a student's answer by just matching each step with one single stored solution (or a set of solutions) such as in plan-recognition techniques. It assesses the validity of each step on the fly.

Let us present briefly the main components of the Logic Tutor, by referring to Fig. 1.

The system creates and maintains a *Student Model* for each individual user. The student model is a mix of buggy and overlay models. It records all the attempted exercises along with the mistakes, and stores the student's level, performance in each exercise, results for each rule used and general student information. The student can at any time browse through this data. In the web-based version, he/she will be able to compare his/her level and results with those of the class. We believe that allowing students to scrutinise their student model enhances their learning [5,6] and this feature is also aligned with the requirement of user access to their own information [7].

The *Expert Module* contains the expertise of the system in propositional logic. It is able to check the correctness of students' answers dynamically as well as producing proper feedback when errors occur. Each line entered by the student is assessed, following a principle of cascading mistakes.

- First it checks that all the fields in the answer are filled with the right type of data.
- Then the syntax of the formula is checked. In case of mistake, the parser provides good error messages.
- Then the real cascade in the derivation begins.
  - The lower level represents general mistakes like incorrect reference line number and invalid application of the rule. For example the expert module may detect that the rule chosen by the student can be applied, but using lines other than those provided by the user. Or the expert module may detect that that rule cannot be applied but that another rule could be applied with the lines provided by the user. These are the hints that the system will provide to the user.
  - The higher level of mistakes deals with more specific mistakes, and uses a database of common mistakes. They also provide hints.

The *Pedagogical Module* is the main module of the system. It contains the high-level rules for sequencing the exercise training objectives, using the student model data. It updates the student model, and then suggests exercises for the student to solve. However, it allows the student to select other exercises or even to create a new one, thus leaving him/her in control of the learning. This is similar to the mechanism used in ELM-ART [3].

The pedagogical module is also based on the hypothesis that immediate feedback and hints facilitate the learning process [2, 8]. In case of a mistake detected by the expert module, the feedback provided is of good quality. It explains the mistake detected, re-explains the correct usage of the rule (contextualised with the current formulae), and provides hints when they are available.

Lastly the pedagogical module also contains HTML tutorial pages that can be consulted at any time during the solving of an exercise.

Overall the Logic Tutor offers students to practice at their own pace. Each step is thoroughly checked (a tedious task for the human teacher, partly because solutions are not unique) and the feedback provided is enlightening.

4   The LT-Configurator

The LT-Configurator is a super version of the Logic Tutor. It is intended for use by the teacher and manages all the teaching configuration settings and material.

4.1   Curriculum Sequencing Authoring Tool

The curriculum sequencing in the Logic Tutor is semi-dynamic, like in some other ITSs such as [10]. Through the LT-Configurator, the teacher defines students' learning levels and sketches the high-level sequencing of the progression through the levels. The finer grain of training objectives is decided on the fly with the data stored in the student model.

For learning to occur, students need to be challenged without being overwhelmed. A student starts at level 1. He/she will practice on various exercises for that level until it is sufficiently mastered. Then he/she is promoted to the next level up, and so on. The LT-Configurator allows the teacher to define exactly what "various" exercises and "sufficiently mastered" mean for the system. In particular for this domain, the important parameters are the type of rules used, the length of the exercise, the number of exercises and the performance result.

The teacher goes through the three following steps to set up the curriculum: the Groups, Levels and Progress configurations.

Groups Configuration. A Group is a collection of mutually exclusive sets of rules that are used to classify the exercises. The teacher can group the rules in meaningful sets. For example, it is generally a good idea to start with exercises using simple and familiar rules. These rules can be grouped in one. But a Group may contain several sets. As illustrated on Fig. 2, the teacher may define that, here, *Group 3*, will contain rules of either *Set 1* or *Set 2*. This means that an exercise using only rules of *Set1* will belong to *Group* 3, as would an exercise using only rules of *Set2*. But an exercise using rules of both *Set 1* and *Set 2* will not belong to this group. At any time, sets and groups can be modified.

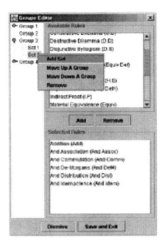

Fig. 2. A screen of Group configuration

When determining what level a particular exercise belongs to, the Logic Tutor examines the justifications used in the exercise's solution (provided by the teacher) and checks whether all these justifications are contained in one of the sets of this particular group. If so, the Logic Tutor associates the exercise with this group, otherwise the exercise moves on to be tested against the definition of the next group. This means that all exercises that would be suitable for the first group will not qualify for the second group and so on. So, for example, the last group will only be associated with the most difficult exercises that could not be associated with any lower group.

Levels Configuration. In the Logic Tutor, each exercise is assigned a *Level*. The level of an exercise is meant to reflect its relative difficulty and the degree of competence the user of the Logic Tutor should have before being posed the exercise. The Levels Configuration tool allows the teacher to define the number of levels and their properties, in terms of the following attributes:

- The maximum number of lines a solution to the exercise should have. The larger the number of lines, the more *thinking ahead* is necessary therefore the more difficult the exercise is.
- The maximum number of different rules used in solving the exercise. The larger it is, the more *different ways of reasoning* are involved hence the more difficult the exercise is.
- The Group the rules belong to. The group sets *a limit to the type of rules* that are necessary to solve the exercise by giving lower and upper boundaries.

Each student is also assigned a current level and is assigned exercises corresponding to the same level. Student levels are updated according to the progress configuration settings.

Progress Configuration. The Progress Configuration Editor allows the teacher to control how the system determines the student's level of competence. This level of competence is then used to determine which exercises the system will suggest next. As shown in Fig. 3, the left panel of the Progress Configuration tool contains a list of the available Levels (as set in the Levels Configuration, minus the first level, which is by default where they start). The right panel shows two tabs, "Parameters" and "Rules".

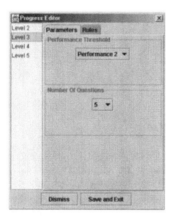 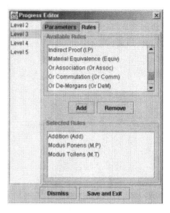

Fig. 3. Two screens in the Progress Editor

The *Parameters* tab allows the teacher to configure how the system determines when a student should be promoted to the next level. The lower menu, "Number Of Exercises", specifies a number n, such that the system will look at the last n exercises that the student has attempted in determining whether to promote them. The upper menu, "Performance Threshold" specifies how well the student must have performed (at least) in the last n exercises. The table below explains the meaning of Performance Threshold Levels.

Table 1. Performance Threshold Levels

Performance	Description
1	Found solution, no useless steps and no mistakes.
2	Found solution, no mistakes made but one or more useless steps.
3	Found solution, some mistakes made.
4	Did not find solution, no mistakes made.
5	Did not find solution, some mistakes made.

The *Rules* tab allows the teacher to specify a set of rules that the student must have used correctly in the last n exercises in order to be promoted.

So for example in Fig. 3, we can see that Level 3 is reached when the student has completed 5 or more exercises with a performance of 2 or better, i.e. 1, and that the *Addition, Modus Ponens* and *Modus Tollens* rules must have been used correctly in these exercises.

4.2   Management of Exercises

The teacher can create, add, and modify exercises, as well as adding comments and hints to them. He/she may choose to make partial solutions visible to the students. Exercises are then added to the exercise database for each level that has been defined. An exercise generator can also be used to generate exercises.

Exercise Databases. Exercises are sorted per level and stored in a database for that level. They are also indexed with the rules they involve. When they are saved, the levels of the selected questions are automatically calculated, based on the levels configuration.

The database contents for each level can be viewed, modified and deleted.

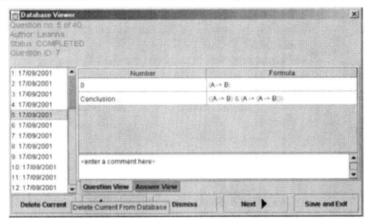

Fig. 4. Viewing database contents of a level (here the *Question View*)

The Logic Tutor suggests exercises that suit the student's needs by using the student model and the progress configuration parameters set by the teacher in the LT-Configurator. The Logic Tutor first delimits a set of exercises matching the level, the number of steps and the potential rules. This set contains only exercises not yet attempted by the student. Each of these exercises is given a weighting, equal to the average weight of the rules in the exercise. The rules are given weights according to the student model data. The weight of a rule is determined by the ratio of correct to incorrect uses of that rule by the particular student. The formula used to calculate this is as follows:

$$\text{Rule weighting} = 0 - (\text{TUC} - \text{TUI})$$

(TUC is equal to the number of times the rule has been used correctly and TUI is equal to the number of times the rule has been used incorrectly)

Where a rule has never been used, it is arbitrarily assigned a weight of 3. This means that the Logic Tutor will try to select exercises which require the unused rule in preference to exercises which require rules which the user has not used incorrectly a significant number of times. (A "significant number of times" here means incorrectly using the rule at least 3 more times than the number of correct usages of that rule.) However, if a rule has been used incorrectly a significant number of times, then the Logic Tutor will give preference to questions containing that rule over questions that contain an unused rule. The exercise obtaining the higher average weight will be selected for the student.

For example, if a student is at level 2 and has made repeated mistakes with, say, the *Modus Tollens* and *Addition* rules, an exercise using these two rules is more likely to be selected next.

Exercise Generation Tool. Exercises are entered by the teacher (or by the student) from his/her own material. However, the Logic Tutor needs a large database of exercises to ensure that students do not repeat exercises, and that exercises appropriate to their levels and needs are selected from the database. The Logic Tutor contains an exercise generation tool. Very basic in its interface, it generates a series of exercises based on the following criteria set by the teacher: (1) a list of premises, (2) a series of weights for the rules (the higher the weight, the more chances they are used in the derivation) and (3) the number of derivation steps (the greater the length is, the more difficult the exercise is).

The Exercise Generation tool starts from the list of premises, and applies rules selected according to their weight, following a forward chaining algorithm. It then stops at the number of steps defined by the teacher, and the formula reached then becomes the conclusion of the exercise, while the intermediary steps become a solution.

5   The LT-Analyser

The teacher can monitor the class's results, levels and problems through the *LT-Analyser*. These results are stored in a database and displayed graphically according to the criteria entered by the teacher. For example, the teacher may look at the performance results of the class on a particular exercise, or on all exercises involving a particular rule, or the distribution of levels among a given group of students, and so on.

Information taken from all the student models is stored in a database, updated daily as well as on request. As shown on Fig. 5, the LT-Analyser is composed of this database, in Microsoft Access, connected to Microsoft Excel. The teacher can then use the features of Microsoft Excel to query the database, visualise graphics and so on.

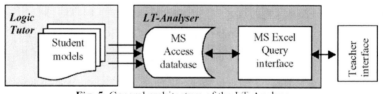

Fig. 5. General architecture of the LT-Analyser

Some examples of SQL queries that the teacher can make are:
- find rules causing the most mistakes (see Fig. 6a)
- find the most common mistakes, and how many times they were made

- find the exercises producing the most mistakes
- find types of errors per level of exercise.
- find the average performance for a particular exercise
- find the students who are stuck at a level
- find the students who make the same mistake more than 10 times.
- show the number of mistakes made per rule and per tutorial group (see Fig. 6b).

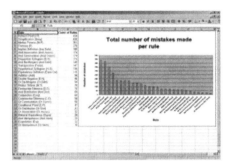 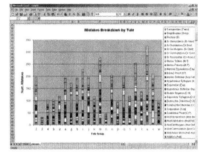

Fig. 6a and b. Samples of displays, one showing the breakdown of mistake per rule and the other showing the number of mistakes made, broken down per rule and per problem-solving sessions (called tutorials or tutes in Australia).

All the connecting parts have been set up, so the teacher, if he/she wants to, needs only deal with Excel as updates are automatically made.

6   Using the Logic-ITA: An Example Scenario

As we stated, the aim of the Logic-ITA is to both help the students and the teacher(s). Let us see how this can be achieved in a typical scenario example.

➢   The teacher sets up the system. In the LT-Configurator, the teacher defines groups, levels, and progress parameters. He/she supplies the database with exercises, possibly making use of the Exercise Generator. For some exercises, the teacher enters some hints such as "Look into using Modus Ponens rule", or restrictions such as "Try to solve it without using Commutation" or simply gives instructions such as "Solve this problem using Indirect Proof." For some other exercises, the teacher decides to provide a partial solution.

➢   Students use the Logic Tutor. We here enter the cycle of traditional use of an ITS. Students use it at their own pace, receive tailored feedback for the mistakes they make, have the choice of choosing a random exercise adapted to their level or selecting a particular one, or creating their own. At any time, they can view their student model contents, browse through their history of exercises... They all start off at level 1, with simple exercises suitable for that level. Then they progress through the curriculum.

➢   After asking students to do exercises X and Y, the teacher wants to check the results through the LT-Analyser. He/she queries the database to find out the common mistakes made and the rules that caused the most problems.

Simplification and Conditional Proofs were causing the most problems and the common mistakes were "The use of Simplication without Commutation" and "Wrong premises". He/she decides to re-explain the correct usage of these rules and insist on the common mistakes to avoid.

➢ The teacher looks at the progression rate in individual results. Two students appear to have recurrent problems and are stuck at the same level. The teacher obtains their student ID and approaches them individually for remedial action.

➢ The teacher consults the trend of results to see whether, in general, he/she is teaching at a reasonable pace for the class. It appears that students are doing very well. The pace can be increased.

7   Evaluation

We used an initial version of the Logic-ITA in 2001 with 442 enrolled students. We used the Unix version of the Logic-ITA during the semester and released the platform-free Logic Tutor (the ITS only) during the study week before the exam. We now have a web-based version ready for use in 2002.

We compared the results of the 2001 class, who used the Logic-ITA, with those of the 2000 class, who did not use the tool. We obtained encouraging results. As shown below, students obtained higher marks in 2001.

Table 2. Marks averages (and standard deviations). Students who did not sit the exam or did not hand in their homework are not counted, resulting in 379 marks for 2001 and 431 marks for 2000 at the final exam

	Weekly homework (3 marks)	Exam question (7 marks)
2000	1.86 (0.94)	3.31 (1.66)
2001	2.27 (0.94)	4.27 (2.73)

In addition, we conducted a survey on a voluntary basis with students and tutors. The feedback from the students was positive apart from the fact that students would have liked the freedom of using the tool from various locations. The web-based version should respond to those needs. Tutors appreciated the significant reduction in marking time as well as the expertise provided by the tool.

Tested at the class level, the LT-Analyser was found very helpful. It helped the teacher to re-direct the content of the lectures, address the common misconceptions and focus the revision lectures. In 2002 we plan to use it at a problem solving session level (tutorial group) and individual level (for students who agree to this).

8   Conclusion

In addition to helping students practice, the Logic-ITA helps the teachers by accomplishing the following tasks:

-     It replaces a large part of their expertise during one-to-one exercise sessions. The Logic Tutor is an autonomous ITS able to check students' answers, provide context-sensitive feedback and propose exercises adapted to the student's level and difficulties.

- The marking time is significantly reduced. Formal proofs are very tedious for a human to check, because there are many paths a student can take. Having each line expertly checked by the system means that teachers only have to look at the system's diagnosis.

- It displays the students' progress and difficulties in a concise or detailed way. The teacher can pinpoint individual problems as well as identify general trends. The content of the lectures can be adjusted to the class' current state of learning. Teachers can address common students' problems and can also identify in the mass the students who need special attention.

The last point means that, whilst the Logic Tutor is an adaptive system on its own, the Logic-ITA provides an additional level of adaptation to the student(s), which occurs at the teacher level. The Logic-ITA illustrates the concept of Intelligent Teaching Assistance. Whilst this still remains to be proven, we do not see major obstacles to apply this concept to another field where an Intelligent Tutoring System exists or can be built.

References

1. Abraham, D., Crawford, L., Lesta, L., Merceron, A., Yacef, K. (2001). The Logic Tutor: A multimedia presentation, Interactive Multimedia Electronic Journal of Computer-Enhanced Learning, October 2001 issue (http://imej.wfu.edu/articles/2001/2/03/index.asp).
2. Anderson, J.R., Corbett, A.T., Koedinger, K.R. & Pelletier, R. (1995). Cognitive tutors: lessons learned. The Journal of the Learning Sciences, 4(2), pp 167-207.
3. Brusilovsky, P., Schwarz, E., and Weber, G. (1996). ELM-ART: An intelligent tutoring system on World Wide Web. In C. Frasson, G. Gauthier, & A.Lesgold (Eds.), Third International Conference on Intelligent Tutoring Systems, ITS-96 (Lecture Notes in Computer Science, Vol. 1086), Berlin: Springer Verlag, pp. 261-269.
4. Croy, M.J. (1989) CAI and Empirical Explorations of Deductive Proof Construction. In The Computers and Philosophy Newsletter, Vol 4 , 111-127.
5. Kay, J. (2000). Invited keynote: Stereotypes, student models and scrutability. In Gauthier, G, Frasson, C & VanLehn, K (Eds): 5th International Conference on Intelligent Tutoring Systems, 19-30.
6. Kay, J. (2001). Learner control . International Journal on User Modeling and User-Adapted Interaction, 11 (1/2):111-127, Kluwer Academic Publishers.
7. Kobsa, A. (2001). Tailoring Privacy to Users' Needs (Invited Keynote). In M. Bauer, P. J. Gmytrasiewicz and J. Vassileva, eds.: User Modeling 2001: 8th International Conference. Berlin-Heidelberg: Springer Verlag, 303-313.
8. Mark, M.A. & Greer, J.E. (1995). The VCR tutor: Effective Instruction for device operation. The Journal of the Learning Sciences, 4(2), 209-246.
9. Scheines, R. & Sieg W. (1994). Computer Environments for Proof Construction. Interactive Learning Environments, 4 (2), 159-169.
10. Wiggins, G & Trewin, S. (2000). A System for Concerned Teaching of Musical Aural Skills. In Proceedings of the 5th International Conference on Intelligent Tutoring Systems, Gauthier, G., Frasson, C & VanLehn, K (Eds), pp 494-503.
11. Yacef, K (2002). Intelligent Teaching Assistant Systems. University of Sydney Technical Report 533.

The Design and Implementation of a Graphical Communication Medium for Interactive Open Learner Modelling

Vania Dimitrova, Paul Brna, and John Self

Computer Based Learning Unit, Leeds University, Leeds LS2 9JT, UK
{vania, paul, jas}@comp.leeds.ac.uk

Abstract. Our work explores an interactive open learner modelling (IOLM) approach where a learner is provided with the means to inspect and discuss the learner model. This paper presents the design and implementation of a communication medium for IOLM. We justify an approach of inspecting and discussing the learner model in a graphical manner using conceptual graphs. Based on an empirical study we draw design recommendations, taken into account in the implementation of the communication medium in STyLE-OLM - an IOLM system in a terminological domain. The potential and improvements of the medium are discussed on the basis of study with STyLE-OLM.

1   Introduction

A crucial issue in building intelligent tutoring systems capable of adapting to the needs of individual learners is maintaining computational models that represent the learners' preferences, needs and cognitive capacity [15]. Recently novel architectures that involve learners in diagnosis have been explored [2, 11, 13, 14, 19]. In line with these methods, we have investigated an approach, called interactive open learner modelling (IOLM), where learners are provided with the means to inspect and discuss the content of the models the systems build of them. Differently from the other overt diagnostic approaches, IOLM conceives diagnosis as an *ongoing dialogue* involving both a computer system and a learner that play symmetrical (to a certain extent) roles and construct together the learner model (LM). We argue that an IOLM system should involve the learner in a constructive interaction to reveal aspects of the learner's cognitive state. It should also provide suitable means for the learner to monitor the elicited LM, which may trigger new discussions that further alter the LM.

Our main goal has been to formalise the IOLM process in order to support the development of computer diagnosers that have the potential to elicit a more adequate picture of the student's knowledge and promote reflective thought [9]. Four aspects are vital in the design of an IOLM system [6]: defining suitable algorithms to extract the necessary domain knowledge for dialogue planning and diagnosis; managing diagnostic dialogue [7]; maintaining a jointly constructed LM [8]; and providing a communication medium for externalising and discussing the LM.

The purpose of this paper is to justify and present a graphical approach for designing and implementing a communication medium for IOLM. The role of such a medium is twofold: on the one hand it provides a means for rendering aspects of a learner's cognition, on the other hand, it enables both the learner and the computer to express their dialogue utterances.

S.A. Cerri, G. Gouardères, and F. Paraguaçu (Eds.): ITS 2002, LNCS 2363, pp. 432–441, 2002.
© Springer-Verlag Berlin Heidelberg 2002

The design of a communication medium for IOLM depends on the structure of the domain to be learned and the aspects of the LM which are open for inspection and negotiation. We have developed a framework for IOLM where domain knowledge algorithms are exemplified with Conceptual Graphs (CG) [17] and the LM is built as an extended overlay upon the domain knowledge [6]. Part of the LM that contains the learner's domain beliefs, which are represented with CGs, is externalised and discussed with the learner[1]. Accordingly, we have exploited a communication medium for IOLM that utilises graphically rendered CGs.

Next in the paper we will justify the use of a graphical communication medium for IOLM (section 2) and will present the design (section 3) and the implementation (section 4) of the medium used in STyLE-OLM - a demonstrator of IOLM in a terminological domain. The potential and improvements of the medium will be discussed on the basis of an evaluative study of STyLE-OLM (section 5).

2   Graphical Communication Medium for IOLM

The term medium is used here in accord with multimedia human-computer interactions as the physical 'carrier' to express and communicate information [3].

2.1   Externalising the Learner Model

A medium where a LM is open for a learner's inspection should meet certain criteria.

Understandability. Learners should be provided with a representation of the LM that they can easily understand. Studies reported in [14] and [19] suggest that learners tend to understand graphically rendered LMs. Well constructed diagrams aid processibility as they provide spatial clarity [12] and limited abstraction [18].

Effective Inspection. An effective representation must provoke inferential processes that may in turn provide for meta-cognition. Being less abstract than text, diagrams help people to confront their problem comprehension [4]. It is also expected that constructing external representations may promote self-explanation [4].

Reducing the Cognitive Load. LM inspection is in its nature a demanding cognitive task and LM representations that reduce the cognitive load are favourable. Well-constructed diagrams mirror the structure of what they represent and alleviate the inferential load [16]. Graphical representations that are capable of representing the information in a problem are processed quickly by the human visual system [4].

2.2   Discussing the Learner Model

The task of discussing a learner's beliefs imposes additional requirements to the design of a communication medium for IOLM.

Expressiveness. Both the system and the learner should be able to express their dialogue utterances when discussing the LM. Natural language is highly expressive and provides rich communicative means. It has been pointed out that the expressive

---

[1] We also include the LM reasoning rules that may lead to erroneous and incomplete beliefs [6].

capacity of semantic networks is comparable to linguistic modalities [18]. Moreover, if a particular graphical system has similar logical power as a sentential system, the graphical representation may be preferable because of its clarity [18].

Effective Communication. The communication medium has to enable participants to understand expressions constructed by the other party. Natural language may hinder diagnosis due to the complexity of determining learners' conceptual errors from vague, ambiguous, and ungrammatical learner utterances. Less abstract diagrammatic languages [18] might overcome this problem when appropriate dialogue control assistance is provided, for example the propositional content may be rendered with diagrams and the illocutions expressed with sentence openers [1].

Symmetry. Similarly to collaborative student modelling [2], IOLM is a collaborative process where the student and the system jointly maintain the content of the LM and have a common aim to create a more accurate LM. Symmetry is a vital feature in collaborative interactions [5], which implies that a common interaction language that provides both participants with equal expressive power in constructing their dialogue utterances and allows sharing dialogue maintenance roles is needed.

To sum up, flexibly structured communications that combine graphically rendered domain content with sentence openers that express illocutionary force are fruitful for LM inspection and discussion. Semantic networks, a diagrammatic representation with formally defined syntax and semantics and high logical expressiveness, can be used for the domain content. CGs are semantic networks with constraints on their nodes and links, which aids tractability. However, to the best of our knowledge, there is no empirical evidence that people can understand and construct propositions expressed with CGs. We, therefore, conducted a small study to investigate these aspects and inform the design of a communication medium for IOLM based on CGs.

3   The Design of a Graphical Communication Medium for IOLM

The communication medium in IOLM systems implements the interface with the learner. Initial evaluation of interface features at a design-specification stage before investing time and resources for implementation is feasible [10].

We conducted a small study aimed to reveal potential problems of communication based on CGs by examining whether people can *read, construct, manipulate,* and *communicate* with CGs. A conceptual graph is a kind of semantic network which comprises two types of nodes - concepts (represented with rectangles) and conceptual relations (represented with ellipses) - connected by directed arcs [17]. Figure 1 shows a CG constructed by a participant in the study to represent a given sentence.

Participants. The participants were twenty four secondary school students (sixteen-eighteen years old) with no prior knowledge of semantic networks and CGs. The experiment was conducted anonymously during a Computing lesson in a school environment. The participants were an appropriate target group for the terminological domain we had chosen to demonstrate our IOLM framework (see section 4).

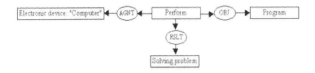

Fig. 1. A CG drawn by a learner to represent the sentence 'A computer is an electronic device which performs a number of instructions (program) on a set of data in order to solve a particular problem'. AGNT(agent), OBJ(object), RSLT(result).

Procedure and materials. Prior to the experiment, all participants were presented with a brief outline of its objectives in regard to a possible design of a computer-based communication medium. The study had three phases:

- *Training*, about half an hour, where an experimenter introduced the learners to the main CG notations. Each participant was given an *introductory text* with containing a CG overview and a *help text* with basic conceptual relations extracted from [17]. The students used both texts during the whole study.

- *Test*, half an hour, where the participnts worked individually using pen-and-paper on a set of questions related to the objectives of the study as follows: *reading* - identifying relations presented in a CG and extracting propositions rendered with CG; *building* - understanding the lexical and syntactic structure of the representation, extracting a semantic structure of a sentence and formalising it in terms of concepts and conceptual relations organised in CGs; *manipulating* - deriving semantic notations from structural changes as well as modifying the structure to present new semantic relations; *communicating* - understanding and constructing questions with CGs.

- Post-experiment *discussion*, approximately 10 minutes, where participants provided some commentaries and suggestions.

The materials included Computing facts familiar to the participants. All CGs were presented in a graphical form and textual sentences were provided when appropriate.

Results and Design Recommendations. The participants' answers to the test questions were classified in four groups - complete correct answer, incomplete correct answer (generally such answers were correct but did not cover all expected aspects), no answer, wrong answer, see Table 1.

Table 1. Summary of the students' responses to the four tasks examined in the study.

	Complete correct answers	Incomplete correct answers	No answer is given	Wrong answers
Reading CGs	54%	23%	15%	8%
Building CGs	13%	25%	33%	29%
Manipulating CGs	50%	10%	19%	21%
Communicating with CGs	79%	8%	13%	0%

The results of the study confirmed a design choice to use CGs in a medium for IOLM. The students understood information presented with CGs and, to a certain degree, expressed their knowledge by using CGs. Relationships between concepts were easily extracted and questions rendered with CGs were understood. CGs were relatively easily changed to represent the necessary meanings by adding new concepts/relations. Some students commented that the graphical representation helped them distinguish the domain concepts and relationships between them.

Whilst students could relatively easily understand CGs, they found it slightly more difficult to manipulate them correctly and found it quite difficult to construct new graphs. We outline below observed difficulties and draw design recommendations.

Problem. Learners may confuse conceptual relations. Some basic relations, e.g. ATTR (attribute) and CHAR (characteristic), are hardly distinguishable.

Recommendations. Using abbreviated relation names should be avoided. Patterns of often confusing relations may be collected (see section 5) and used in hints when a learner is believed to have mixed similar relations. The least possible number of basic, i.e. low level, relations [17] is recommended. High level relations which encode domain specific connections (e.g., in a Computing domain such a relation may be DEVELOPED) are less likely to cause ambiguity and should be preferred.

Problem. People tend to confuse link directions in CGs.

Recommendations. A textual equivalent supplied for each constructed graph may help learners identify wrongly directed arrows. Users should be provided with suitable means to correct their CGs.

Problem. Students may fail to build a new CG (from scratch) to express a textual sentence, while modifying existing graphs appears a relatively easy task.

Recommendations. In general, a graph modification should chiefly be encouraged in order to reduce the difficulty of constructing a conceptual graph. Ways to help the users build CGs should be provided, for instance, allowing the learners to inspect previously drawn graphs as well as allowing them to select and manipulate any of these graphs in order to utilise their graph constructions.

Problem. For some participants in our study it was difficult to distinguish the main concepts and the relations between them in the textual representation.

Recommendations. In order to avoid possible problems with constructing or altering conceptual graphs due to users' incapacity to elicit domain concepts and relations, a computer system may provide the learner with a clear indication of the CG 'vocabulary', e.g. all concepts and conceptual relations used in the particular application may be listed in an appropriate way.

The design recommendations have been taken into account in implementing the graphical communication medium in STyLE-OLM, outlined next.

4   The Communication Medium in STyLE-OLM

We will illustrate the implementation of a graphical communication medium for IOLM based on STyLE-OLM. STyLE-OLM is the Open Learner Modelling component in STyLE (Scientific Terminology Learning Environment) developed in the EU funded Larflast[2] project. STyLE-OLM is an environment for IOLM where learners can inspect and discuss aspects of their conceptual knowledge and influence

---

[2] The project involved partners from Bulgaria, UK, France, Romania, and Ukraine. See http://www-it.fmi.uni-sofia.bg/larflast/ for more details.

the content of the LM. STyLE-OLM is described in detail elsewhere [6, 9], the focus here is on the interface of the system presented with examples in a Finance domain.

STyLE-OLM provides a multimodal communication environment that combines graphics (graphically rendered CGs), text, and some interface widgets such as menus and buttons. In this environment, learners can inspect and discuss their knowledge about domain terms. There are two modes:

- **DISCUSS** where learners can discuss aspects of their domain knowledge and influence the content of the learner model (Figure 2);

- **BROWSE** where learners can inspect the current state of their LM (Figure 3).

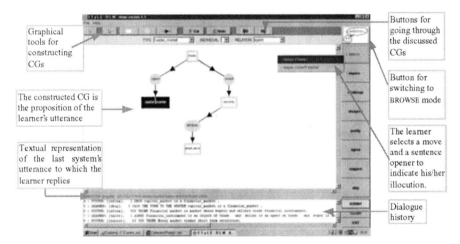

Fig. 2. STyLE-OLM in DISCUSS mode. A learner's reply to a system's question.

A picture at the top right of the window presents the current system mode. The learner switches between the modes by pressing the button with this picture.

In DISCUSS mode, users compose their dialogue utterances by defining a *propositional content* (represented with a CG) and an *illocutionary force* (represented in a dialogue move). Graphical tools (at the top) facilitate CG manipulation and construction. The learner is provided with suitable means to *add, delete* and *change* graphical objects. The dialogue moves are indicated with sentence openers.

The learners submit their utterances by pressing the *Submit* button at the bottom right of the screen. The system then generates a textual form of the utterance and asks the learners for confirmation. The learners can either return to the graphical window to make some changes or confirm their utterance in which case a system turn follows.

Both the student and the system contribute to the discussion in the same way - by selecting or creating a graph component and a dialogue move. The system's proposition appears in the drawing area as a conceptual graph and the illocutionary force is shown in the bottom of the drawing window, see Figure 2.

A text window at the bottom shows a generated transcript of the dialogue. The learner can go through the dialogue history either in its textual form or by using the arrows in the graphical tools at the top. He/she can alter any of the previously discussed graphs to construct the proposition of their utterance.

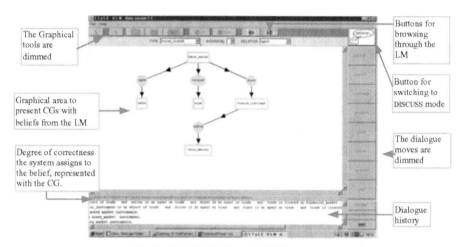

Fig. 3. STyLE-OLM in BROWSE mode.

In BROWSE mode, a user is allowed to inspect the jointly constructed LM elicited from the discussion. As Figure 3 shows, the layout in this mode is akin to the DISCUSS mode but the graphical widgets are disallowed. The bottom line of the graphical area shows the level of correctness that the system assigns to the beliefs in the LM. The arrows on the top allow browsing backwards and forwards through these beliefs.

5   STyLE-OLM Used with Learners

An experiment with seven subjects, postgraduate students at the authors' department, was conducted to examine the behaviour of STyLE-OLM and to analyse advantages of IOLM [9]. We discuss here only the use of the communication medium focussing on pitfalls and potential improvements, see [6] for full details of the study. Each learner attended an individual session, prior to which he/she was given an introductory text with Finance terms to study for a while and then asked questions about these terms. The learners' performance was assessed and initial LMs obtained (by hand). During half an hour training, which included instruction and guided walkthrough interaction with STyLE-OLM, learners got acquainted with the interface.

In a session with STyLE-OLM, the learners were asked to help the system obtain a better picture of their domain conceptualisations, which would facilitate adaptability in pedagogical situations like generating explanations, providing feedback, and selecting instructional materials. The learners were encouraged to discuss their domain knowledge, inspect their LMs and influence the content of these models. Each interaction lasted about half an hour and was terminated by the users. All sessions were monitored by the experimenter. Learners were given a questionnaire at the end of the sessions and some of them were interviewed to clarify unexplained aspects.

5.1   Outcomes

The communication medium was adequate for discussing and inspecting the LM. The participants did not experience major problems with constructing and understanding dialogue moves as well as examining LM beliefs in the LM.

Understanding Propositions Rendered in a Graphical Manner. At the beginning of each session, the learners mainly read the text shown in the bottom of the graphical window. After a while they became more confident with the graphics and in most cases examined both the CGs and the textual equivalents generated by the system. Although many learners found it useful to have both text and graphics to represent domain facts, it was often the case that the text was confusing (STyLE-OLM uses a simple template mechanism to generate sentences from CGs). Most learners commended the graphics when seeking to understand domain facts both in the system dialogue moves and the learner model. They found such representations helpful for articulating the main concepts and relations between them.

A major problem with the LM inspection concerned navigation. Learners usually switched to a BROWSE mode to search for information about the last stated fact, in order to see how their statements changed the LM or how the system assessed the correctness of these statements. Finding a particular graph in the LM often required considerable browsing through the LM. It seems beneficial to re-organise the beliefs in the externalised LM so that recently discussed ones appear first and provide search facilities so that beliefs related to a particular concept can be selected.

Constructing Propositions with Conceptual Graphs. Learners' opinions about the expressive power provided in STyLE-OLM to construct dialogue utterances varied. Some learners found the interface "a little idiosyncratic and non-standard" which "takes a lot of getting used to". Problems here refer mainly to changing graphical objects, selecting propositions, invalidating the last action, and spending much effort on finding terms. Although these issues do not demote the overall approach, they indicate the need to improve the user-friendly interface features.

Some learners experienced problems with justifications: to justify they needed to construct a new CG and select a sentence opener 'BECAUSE' - the statement being justified could potentially be lost and the argument obscured. For example, if after a system's challenge 'Why do you think that G', the learner justifies with 'It is true because G_1' (where G and G_1 express propositions represented with CGs). The learner's utterance does not have an explicit link to the statement he justifies and may obscure the understanding of the argument, for example, when reading the dialogue history. To address this problem, the CG language employed needs to incorporate contexts [17]. Contexts may bring more complexity for the graphical language. Further investigation is needed in order to utilise them in a communication medium.

The limited number of relations provided was the major obstacle for learners when constructing CG statements. There are two types of relations in STyLE-OLM - basic relations, such as 'agent', 'characteristic', etc. in line with [17] and domain oriented relations, such as 'operate_with', 'provide', 'trades_with', etc., identified by a Finance expert. The learners searched mostly for links of the second type and complained about missing relations (but rarely identified which ones). They seemed disappointed to be trapped in a language environment where very few verbs were provided. A proper expansion of the list of domain relations is required. The study also enabled us to identify sets of confusing basic relations, such as {actor, agent};

{patient, object, recipient, instrument}; {characteristic, attribute}; {operate_with, trade_with}; {support, provide}; {isa (in the meaning of part_of), contain}.

The participants in the study did not agree regarding their choice of graphics or text. The study is too limited to discuss this issue deeply, and further exploration is needed. In this line, [4] provides possible directions highlighting the difference between situations in which a presented external representation is interpreted and situations in which participants construct external representation (both types of situations need examination in respect to LM inspection and discussion).

6   Conclusions and Future Work

This paper presents the design and implementation of a communication medium for IOLM. Such a medium provides a means for learners to inspect and discuss the models the system builds of them. Based on relevant research, we have justified an approach of inspecting and discussing the LM in a graphical manner using conceptual graphs. We have presented an empirical study that examined whether people can read, build, manipulate and communicate with conceptual graphs. The study has informed the design of a communication medium for IOLM. Recommendations drawn from the study have been taken into account in the implementation of the communication medium in the STyLE-OLM system - an IOLM demonstrator in a terminological domain. We have presented the implementation of the communication medium in STyLE-OLM and have discussed its potential and possible improvements on the basis of an evaluative study of STyLE-OLM.

The paper illustrates a favourable application of a methodology found in Human-Computer Interaction research to the design of a communication medium in learning environments. The medium has been designed based on theoretical justification and empirical investigation, it has then been implemented and validated in a study with genuine learners, which has highlighted further improvements.

The work presented here is a step in a promising way forward to building learning environments that provide learners with control over the system's behaviour. It also demonstrates the development of an effective communication medium that reduces communication problems, facilitates reasoning about a learner's behaviour, and promotes meta-cognitive processes. Such a medium can be utilised in a wide spectrum of intelligent tutoring systems that enable learners to inspect and communicate knowledge to the system (e.g. interactive tutoring systems, learning companions) or to other learners (e.g. peer diagnosis, collaborative problem solving).

References

1.   Baker, M., & Lund, K. (1997). Promoting reflective interactions in a computer-supported collaborative learning environment. *Journal of Computer Assisted Learning*, 13, 175-193.
2.   Bull, S., Brna, P., & Pain, H. (1995). Extending the scope of student models. *User Modeling and User-Adapted Interaction*, 5(1), 45-65.
3.   Bunt, H. (1998). Issues on multi-modal human-computer interaction. In H. Bunt, R-J Beum & T. Borghuis (Eds.), *Multimodal Human-Computer Interaction: Systems, techniques, and experiments* (pp. 1-12). Berlin: Springer-Verlag.

4. Cox, R. (1999). Representation construction, externalised cognition and individual differences. *Learning and Instruction*, 9, 343-363.
5. Dillenbourg, P. (1999). Introduction: what do we mean by "collaborative learning". In P. Dillenbourg (Ed.), *Collaborative learning: cognitive and computational approaches* (pp. 1-19) Amsterdam: Pergamon.
6. Dimitrova, V. (2001). Interactive open learner modelling. PhD Thesis. Computer Based Learning Unit, Leeds University.
7. Dimitrova, V., Self, J.A. & Brna, P. (1999). The interactive maintenance of open learner models.In S.Lajoie & M.Vivet (eds.),*Artificial intelligence in education.* IOS Press, 405-412.
8. Dimitrova, V., Self, J.A. & Brna, P. (2000). Maintaining a jointly constructed student model. In S.Cerri & D.Dochev (eds.), *AI: Methodology, Systems and Applications*, Springer, 221-231.
9. Dimitrova, V., Self, J.A. & Brna, P. (2001). Applying interactive open learner models to learning technical terminology. In *Proceedings of UM2001*. Springer.
10. Johnson, P. (1992). *Human-Computer Interaction: Psychology, task analysis and software engineering*, London: McGraw-Hill Book Company.
11. Kay, J. (1995). The UM toolkit for cooperative user modelling. *User Modeling and User-Adapted Interaction*, 4, 149-196.
12. Larkin, J. H., & Simon, H. A. (1987). Why a diagram is (sometimes) worth ten thousand words. In J. Glasgow, H. Narayahan & B. Chandrasekaram (Eds.), *Diagrammatic reasoning - cognitive and computational perspectives* (pp. 69-109). California: AAAI Press/The MIT Press.
13. McCalla, G., Vassileva, J., Greer, J., & Bull, S. (2000). Active learner modelling. In G. Gauthier, C. Frasson & K. VanLehn (Eds.), *Intelligent tutoring systems* (pp. 53-62). Berlin Heidelberg: Springer-Verlag.
14. Morales, R., Pain, H., & Conlon, T. (2000). Understandable learner models for a sensorimotor control task. In G. Gauthier, C. Frasson & K. VanLehn (Eds), *Intelligent Tutoring Systems* (pp. 222-231). Springer, LNCS.
15. Self, J. A. (1999). The defining characteristics of intelligent tutoring systems research: ITSs care, precisely. *International Journal of Artificial Intelligence in Education*, 10, 350-364.
16. Shimojima, A. (1999). The graphics-linguistic distinction. *Artificial Intelligence Review*, 13, 313-335.
17. Sowa, J. (1984). *Conceptual structures: Information processing in mind and machine.* MA: Addison-Wesley.
18. Stenning, K., & Inder, R. (1995). Applying semantic concepts to analyzing media and modalities. In J. Glasgow, H. Narayahan & B. Chandrasekaram (Eds.), *Diagrammatic reasoning - Cognitive and computational perspectives* (pp. 303-338). California: AAAI Press/The MIT Press.
19. Zapata-Rivera, J-D., & Greer, J. (2000). Inspecting and visualising distributed Bayesian student models. In G. Gauthier, C. Frasson & K. VanLehn (Eds), *Proceedings of the 5th International conference on Intelligent Tutoring Systems* (pp. 544-553). Springer, LNCS.

Exploring Various Guidance Mechanisms to Support Interaction with Inspectable Learner Models

Diego Zapata-Rivera and Jim E. Greer

ARIES Laboratory, Department of Computer Science,
University of Saskatchewan, Saskatoon, Canada
Diego.Zapata@usask.ca

Abstract. Open or inspectable learner models have been used to support reflection, knowledge awareness, learner model accuracy, and negotiated assessment. Current systems employ many different mechanisms to present and to support human interaction with the learner model. This paper explores the interactions between learners and inspectable learner models using various guidance mechanisms (i.e. following a protocol, interacting with human peers and artificial guiding agents, interacting with the teacher, and exploring the model as part of a group). We report on a study carried out with fifth grade students who interacted with different configurations of inspectable learner modelling environments.

1 Introduction

Learner models should not be considered only as hidden components used to support instructional planning within ITSs. Researchers in the area of learner modelling have been exploring the potential of externalising the model to students and teachers [7]. Open or inspectable learner models have been used to support reflection, knowledge awareness, learner model accuracy, and negotiated assessment [1,2,4,5,6,8]. Recent findings show that learners are able to report their problem solving knowledge more accurately by interacting actively with their learner models. In a participative learning modelling approach, changes in learners' behaviour indicated evidence of learner's reflection and knowledge awareness [5]. Dimitrova et al. [2] explored interactive open learner modelling (IOLM) in which the learner's knowledge is challenged in order to encourage a negotiated diagnostic process. In this approach, negotiated assessment is enhanced by allowing the computer to choose among various diagnostic strategies in order to guide a constructive dialogue process with the learner. Dimitrova et al. reported that the quality of the model improved and there was evidence of reflective learning among participants.

Each of the current systems employs different mechanisms to present and to support human interaction with the learner model. But can we expect learners to learn and reflect on their knowledge by letting them browse freely through the model? Should we detect potential conflicts between the learner's and the system's view of the model and point them out to the student for further interaction? Could we just design a simple

S.A. Cerri, G. Gouardères, and F. Paraguaçu (Eds.): ITS 2002, LNCS 2363, pp. 442–452, 2002.

general protocol that learners can follow during their interaction with the model? Is there a benefit of having artificial guiding agents directing the learner's interaction with the model? How does the interaction with the model change when the teacher is involved in the process? In order to answer some of these questions, we have developed ViSMod [8], a visualization and inspection tool for Bayesian learner models, and ConceptLab [9], a knowledge construction and navigation system that employs conceptual maps as a representation of the learner. Using ViSMod and ConceptLab as our main learner modelling platforms, we have been exploring the effects of applying a learner modelling representation (i.e. Bayesian learner model and conceptual map) with various levels of guidance and support in the way learners interact with inspectable learner models.

In this paper, we describe ViSMod and ConceptLab, and present the study design and results of an experiment carried out with fifth grade students from a public elementary school who interacted with different configurations of inspectable learner modelling environments.

2   Inspectable Learner Modelling Tools

Our research on inspectable learner models has led us to experiment with inspectable Bayesian learner models and using conceptual maps as a representation of the student. Previous work on visualization and inspection of Bayesian student models - ViSMod [8] showed that students and teachers can successfully visualize a learner model as a graph using different visualization techniques, such as: colour, size, proximity of nodes (closeness), link thickness, and animation.

Using ViSMod it is possible to inspect the model of a single student, compare several students by comparing their models, navigate throughout the model changing focus according to students' and teachers' interests, and use several sources of evidence to animate the evolution of a new model. By allowing inspection of student models and the creation of what-if scenarios, ViSMod aims to support students' reflection, knowledge awareness, and refining of student models.

Considering the student as a part of a learning community in which situational factors play an important role in the learning process, we have developed a knowledge construction and navigation system called ConceptLab [9]. ConceptLab allows collaborative construction of XML-based conceptual maps. ConceptLab provides the possibility to link different kinds of resources to specific nodes. Students can create their own knowledge structure using a set of predefined concepts (common vocabulary given by the teacher) and use their own map to access class resources. These resources are suggested either by the teacher (initial links) or by classmates during the creation of their maps (collaborative browsing). As it is done with some constructivist tools, ConceptLab considers the object resulting from the student's work as his/her representation. In addition to allowing students to interact with their own map, ConceptLab makes it possible to overlay an initial Bayesian learner model on top of the model constructed by the student. Students can see the system's opinion about their knowledge and they can express their own opinion while interacting with the model. Information to initialise the underlying Bayesian learner model within ConceptLab can be obtained by using existing evidence about the student's knowledge (i.e. pre-assessment quiz). Figure 1 shows a screenshot of ConceptLab depicting a fragment of the model of a learner studying the biology cell.

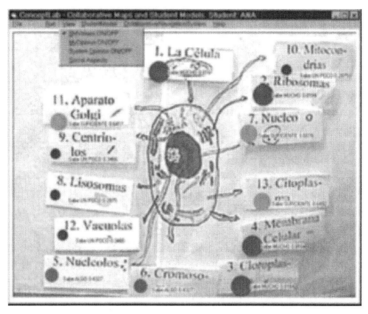

Fig. 1. ConceptLab. A learner model as an overlay on the conceptual structure created by the student. Spheres' size and colour are used to represent the student's knowledge on a particular concept.

3   Study Design

A study focussed on how students interact with different forms of learner models using different guidance mechanisms was conducted at the Joaquín Aristizabal School, a Colombian public elementary school. Participants were one hundred and ten fifth-grade students between the ages of ten and thirteen, as well as six teachers. The topic domain was the biology cell, learners were told about learner models, ViSMod, and ConceptLab. The learner model was first initialised for each student using the results of a pre-assessment quiz taken by all students. Students worked individually, in groups, in dyads with a human peer, in dyads with an artificial peer, or in dyads with the teacher.

While using ViSMod students were able to interact with a pre-defined Bayesian network that reflected the system's estimate of their knowledge. Students could change their own level of knowledge on any concept but were required to explain the changes. Prior to using ConceptLab, students were asked to create a conceptual map of a cell using paper, markers, and labels. They were prompted with some of the main concepts but were free to include some extra ones. Once they had created the paper-based model, a digital image of their concept map was imported into ConceptLab and connected to their Bayesian learner model. This allowed students to interact with the model which included information about the system's and the student's view of the learner model.

Teachers acted as facilitators letting students organise their work and decide the best way to create and/or interact with the model. In addition, teachers became active participants during a debriefing session focussed on negotiated assessment. A team of observers took note of students' and teachers' interaction with the learner-modelling environment. Both students and teachers answered a final questionnaire that covered general and specific questions about the learning activity, general suggestions, and their interaction with learner models using ViSMod or ConceptLab and the corresponding guidance tools.

Table 1. Inspectable student modelling scenarios

Scenarios	Participants	Learning Activity	Replications
Scenario 1	*Single Student*	*The student interacts freely with his/her model.*	*10*
Scenario 2	*Single Student*	*The student follows a protocol (solving a guiding questionnaire) while interacts with his/her model.*	*15*
Scenario 3a	*Single student with artificial guiding agent 'AGA'*	*Artificial peer points out interesting aspects of the model. It detects discrepancies between the system and the learners' view of the model, and points them out to the student.*	*11*
Scenario 3b	*Dyad of students human peers 'HP'*	*The student interacts with his/her model and explains it to his/her human peer who questions him about the model.*	*9*
Scenario 4	*Student, teacher*	*The student negotiates the final state of the model with the teacher.*	*6*
Scenario 5	*Group of five students*	*Groups of students interact with a group learner model and/or individual learner models. Different degrees of guidance are also tested in this scenario.*	*10*

Table 1 summarises the kinds of scenarios students and teachers walked through. Five general scenarios were defined in order to test a full range of possible environments based on inspectable learner models. Each scenario offers different characteristics such as different activities, different roles for student(s) and/or the teacher, different learner modelling tools, and different guidance mechanisms. The 110 students were each assigned to a scenario. Each scenario was replicated a number of times in the study (the last column in the table indicates the number of replications of this scenario were performed). After an initial group training session and pre-assessment quiz, the students worked within their assigned scenario for one session of one and a half hours. The experiment lasted for one week while all students were run through their assigned scenario.

In addition to ViSMod and/or ConceptLab, which were used in all of the scenarios, students in scenario 3a had the opportunity to interact with "Don Pacho" or "Doña Rita", two artificial guiding agents (AGA) designed to guide students during their interaction with their learner models. "Don Pacho" and "Doña Rita" represent two familiar characters for Colombian children. "Don Pacho" is a mature and gentle countryman who inspires respect and seems knowledgeable in many areas. "Doña Rita" is a young and kind schoolteacher who tries to help and guide students in a positive and gentle manner. Both agents can exhibit basic emotions, such as: happiness, sadness, anger, surprise and disgust through verbal and facial expressions based on Ekmans' basic emotions [3].

Changes in agents' emotional behaviour are triggered by the learner's level of knowledge on a particular concept, differences between the learners' opinion and the system's opinion on the learner's knowledge, and the interactions among the learner, the model, and/or the agent. In order to motivate students' interaction with the model, agents questioned students about their model (i.e. which concepts do you know better than the computer thinks you know them? do you agree with the model? do you want to change something?). The agents also directed the student to potential conflicting concepts (i.e. concepts in which the learner's and the system's opinion about the learner's knowledge differed significantly). Finally, the agents asked the learner for an explanation in cases where the learner had changed the level of knowledge, but he/she did not provide any justification. Figures 2 shows "Don Pacho" interacting with a student.

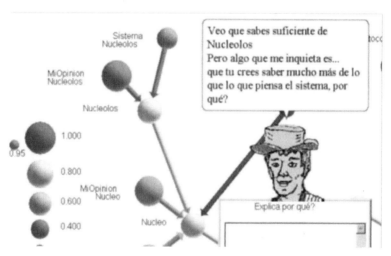

Fig. 2. *Don Pacho* asking the student to explain the difference between his/her assessment and the system's one on the concept *nucleolos*. A fragment of a Bayesian learner model of the biology cell is shown using ViSMod. It is possible to see how the learner's opinion and the system's opinion influence each node. In this example, size and colour are used to show marginal probability values representing the student's knowledge on a particular concept (e.g. 0.95 represents the student's opinion about his/her knowledge on *nucleolos*)

4   Results

Among the guidance mechanisms explored in this study to help students interact with their models are: following a fixed protocol (i.e. solving a guiding questionnaire that included general and specific questions about the model –scenario 2), interacting with a human peer (i.e. explaining the model to a peer – scenario 3b), interacting with an artificial guiding agent (Don Pacho or Doña Rita – scenario 3a), interacting with the teacher (i.e. as part of a negotiated assessment session – scenario 4), and exploring the model as a group (scenario 5).

We present results on the number and the type of changes made to the learner model by students, in the learners' browsing behaviour, and general observations made by the observers and the learners on the use of different learning modelling tools.

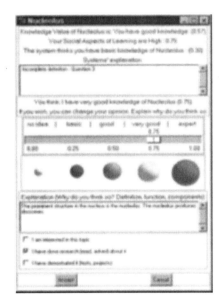

Fig. 3. Graphical interface used by students to change their knowledge on a particular concept (i.e. *nucleolus*). This figure was translated from the original in Spanish.

4.1   Changing the Learner Model

In order to interact with the model, similar graphical interfaces were available in both VisMod and ConceptLab. Figure 3 depicts one of the graphical interfaces students used to interact with the model. The upper frame shows the system's opinion (knowledge level and explanation) about the student's current knowledge on a particular concept. Students could change their opinion about their knowledge on a particular concept (middle and lower frame) by changing their level of knowledge, by providing information about the concept (i.e. its definition, function, and location), and by checking on any the self-assessment options that appear at the bottom of the window. This information remains available for students and teachers to explore. ITSs attached to these models can easily interpret information about students' knowledge levels and self–assessment options. At this moment, explanations are not interpreted to be used by an external ITS system.

4.1.1 Changing the Level of Knowledge

The number of times students increased their level of knowledge on their models seem indirectly proportional to the sophistication of guidance mechanisms offered (see figure 4). Although, scenarios 1, 2 and 5 seem to be similar regarding changes in level of knowledge, a closer look shows that students working in groups (S5) and students following a protocol (S2) revisited a particular group of concepts (see figure 5) and adjusted their knowledge gradually (i.e. by changing level of knowledge, concept domain explanations, and self assessment options). Students interacting freely with the model (S1) increased the level of knowledge of a large number of concepts. In fact, students in S1 made more changes to the model than students in any other scenario. It showed that students in S1 exhibited an unrestrained exploratory behaviour.

It is also possible to see that students preferred to increase their level of knowledge rather than to decrease it. Indeed, the only scenario in which increasing and decreasing the level of knowledge are balanced is S4. It seems that during a negotiated assessment session, the frequency in which the teacher and the student decided to increase and/or decrease the level of knowledge was similar. An interesting observation is that decreasing of level of knowledge was often presented at the end of the session. It appears that students, knowing that the teacher or a peer could explore their models in the future, decided to decrease their level of knowledge for some of the concepts just before ending the session. Changes in level of knowledge counted for a 35% of the total of changes made to the model.

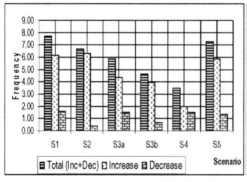
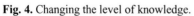
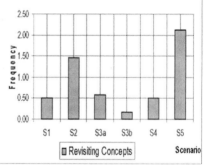

Fig. 4. Changing the level of knowledge.   **Fig. 5.** Revisiting concepts of the model

4.1.2 Explaining the Concepts and Self-Assessment

Figure 6 shows that the number of explanations added to the model was high for S1, S2 and S5, medium for S3a and S4, and low for S3b. It was noticed that while students explained their models verbally to their human peers (S3b), they were not concerned about registering their explanations into the model. On the other hand, students interacting with Don Pacho or Doña Rita (S3a) registered more explanations. Changes in domain concept explanations counted for a 31.4% of the total changes made to the model. Regarding the quality of explanations added to the model, it was found that more complete and detailed explanations were obtained in S4 followed by S3a, S5, and S2. Students in S1 gave a high number of short and incomplete explanations.

Students did use the self-assessment options to justify their level of knowledge on a particular concept. Changes on self –assessment options counted for a 33.6% of the total of changes made to the model. As it is shown in figure 7, students chose reading, doing research and asking ('I have read/done research'), and solving assignment and tests ('I have shown proof') as the main self-assessment options in most of the scenarios. In addition, it was found that in few occasions students used the domain content text box (middle frame in figure 3) to explain the reasons for decreasing their level of knowledge. Thus, it is necessary to offer a more ample range of self-assessment options to the student.

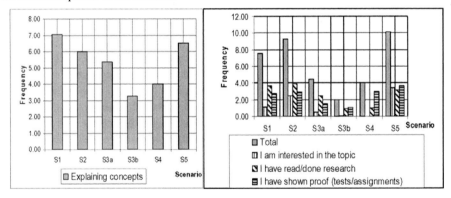

Fig. 6. Explaining the concepts of the model.   **Fig. 7.** Self-assessment.

4.2 Browsing Behaviour

As we expected, students' browsing behaviour became more structured when more sophisticated guidance mechanisms were available. Students in S4 traversed the model following structured paths from subtopics to topics. It appears the teacher influenced this order while negotiating with the student. Interestingly, students in S3b also explained their model to their peers in an organised manner. Initially, students in S3a visited several concepts without an apparent order, but since the guiding agent at some points of the session pointed particular nodes to the student, students followed the agent's directions and visited potentially conflicting nodes. Students working in groups (S5) also tried to maintain a hierarchical navigational order. Finally, students in S1 traversed the model in various ways without an apparent order.

4.3   General Observations

- *Using ViSMod vs. ConceptLab.* Although students in *ConceptLab* enjoyed the initial activity of creating their own conceptual map, once the model was in the computer, students did interact more with their learner models in *VisMod* than in *ConceptLab*. It seems that *VisMod* offered an interesting exploratory environment for students to interact by changing their knowledge and visualizing how their model got updated through the use of animation. Regarding the quality of explanations gathered and the effects of different guidance mechanisms, the response was similar in both systems.

- *Did we obtain a better learner model?* In order to analyse the quality of the final learner model we follow the criteria defined by Dimitrova et al. [2]. That is, (1) a better new learner model removes inconsistencies from the previous model, (2) represents a wider scope of learners' beliefs, (3) provides more explanations for learners' errors, (4) includes more valid information about the learner's knowledge, and (5) minimises the number of invalid assertions about the learner's knowledge. It is clear that our learner modelling tools help students to easily locate and remove inconsistencies from their models. Although, students working in S3a and S4 were guided by an artificial agent and the teacher respectively, which let them to find inconsistencies faster that the others, students in all of the scenarios adjusted their models to a degree they felt appropriate. This observation adds another criterion in deciding whether the model is better or not, namely '*learner satisfaction*'. Participants in our study found both tools useful in giving them a chance to express their opinions about their knowledge and the important role students appreciated the role the tools had on their final assessment. Regarding criterion 2, final learner models covered information about the student in a wider range of concepts in all of the scenarios. Regarding criteria 3, 4, and 5, students added explanations, changed the level of knowledge and provided self-assessment information in similar proportions. Thus, students explained their knowledge or lack of it, included valid information, and reduced invalid beliefs about their knowledge. Although the number and quality of students' contributions to the learner model varies from scenario to scenario, in general final learner models were considered to be better than the initial ones.

- *Did students learn while interacting with their learner models?* Although we did not run a post-assessment quiz, the final state of the model gives us an initial overview of the continuous assessment process that is generated with the interaction of the student with his/her learner model. By looking at this interaction and especially by focusing on the number and quality of the explanations provided by students and the self-assessment information obtained, we establish that there are clear indicators of students' engagement, motivation, and knowledge reflection.

- *Were artificial guiding agents effective?* Artificial guiding agents *Don Pacho* and *Doña Rita* attracted the attention and curiosity of students. Although agents had a positive effect in guiding students to particular concepts without forcing them, we believed that their role could be further enhanced by letting the agent offer interesting paths and external learning resources. In addition, the role of artificial guiding agents will become more important when interacting with big learner models and partial learner models from different domain areas.

- *Exploring learner group models.* Some students felt uncomfortable and had problems trying to convince the rest of the group to change their knowledge level on a particular concept. Some groups even changed their leader several times in an attempt to create a more stable situation in which everyone could contribute. This observation suggests that students prefer to reflect upon their own knowledge profile as opposed to a single group model. It also suggests that special support is needed to help groups to inspect and reflect upon a group model. More information about this finding can be found in [9].

- *Social aspects of learning.* Although our Bayesian learner models contained information about students' social aspects of learning (i.e. helpfulness, eagerness, and assertiveness), which was provided to teachers, students were not allowed to interact with this information. Further analysis of the effects of letting students interact with this kind of information remains as an open area to be explored.

5   Conclusions

A general message to take away is that exploring inspectable learning models using different guidance mechanisms result in a variety of effects on both the student and the learner model. It is important to take into account the goals of the learning session and the need of having an accurate learner model in order to decide which kind of support is more appropriate for a particular situation. Students in our study added important information to the learner model making it more accurate and reliable. Using ViSMod or ConceptLab in conjunction with different guidance mechanisms it is possible to support students' reflection, knowledge awareness, and refining of learner models.

In this paper, we have presented initial results on inspecting learner models using different guidance tools. Further exploration in this area will lead us to improve the design and to determine potential benefits of inspectable learner modelling environments.

Acknowledgements. We would like to acknowledge -COLCIENCIAS- Colombia and the Natural Science and Engineering Research Council of Canada for financial support. We would like to extend our thanks to teachers, observers, and students at the Joaquin Aristizabal public elementary school in Colombia for their participation in our studies.

References

1. Bull, S., & Shurville, S. (1999). Cooperative Writer Modelling: Facilitating Reader-Based Writing with Scrawl. Proceedings of the workshop 'Open, Interactive, and other Overt Approaches to Learner Modelling' at AIED'99. Le Mans, France, pp. 1-8.

2. Dimitrova, V., Self, J., & Brna, P. (2001). Applying Interactive Open Learner Models to Learning Technical Terminology. Proceedings of the 8th UM 2001, Springer, pp. 148-157.
3. Ekman, P. (1999) Basic emotions. In T. Dalgleish and T. Power (Eds.) The Handbook of Cognition and Emotion. Pp. 45-60. Sussex, U.K.: John Wiley & Sons, Ltd.
4. Kay, J. (1999). A Scrutable User Modelling Shell for User-Adapted Interaction. Ph.D. Thesis, Basser Department of Computer Science, University of Sydney, Sydney, Australia.
5. Morales, R., Pain, H., & Conlon, T. (2001). Effects of Inspecting Learner Models on Learners' Abilities. Proceedings of AIED'01. IOS Press, pp. 434-445.
6. Paiva, A., Self. J. & Hartley, R. (1995). Externalising learner models. Proceedings of World Conference on Artificial Intelligence in Education, Washington DC, pp. 509-516.
7. Self, J. (1988) Bypassing the intractable problem of student modelling. In Gauthier, G., and Frasson, C., (eds.), Proceedings of Intelligent Tutoring Systems ITS'88, 18-24.
8. Zapata-Rivera, J.D. & Greer, J. (2000) Inspecting and Visualizing Distributed Bayesian Student Models. Proceedings of the 5th International Conference on Intelligent Tutoring Systems, ITS 2000. Springer. 544-553.
9. Zapata-Rivera, J.D., & Greer, J. (2002). Construction and Inspection of Learner Models. In Proceedings of Computer Support For Collaborative Learning CSCL 2002, pp. 495-497.

Supporting Learning by Opening the Student Model

Danita Hartley and Antonija Mitrovic

Intelligent Computer Tutoring Group
Department of Computer Science, University of Canterbury
Private Bag 4800, Christchurch, New Zealand
Danita.Hartley@alliedtelesyn.co.nz, tanja@cosc.canterbury.ac.nz

Abstract. Intelligent tutoring systems (ITSs) provide individualised instruction by maintaining models of their students. Traditionally, these models have been hidden from the student. However, recent work in the area has suggested educational benefits in exposing the student model. This approach, known as open student modelling, allows the student to inspect their model thereby facilitating reflection, which is known to enhance the learning process. To date, few evaluations have been conducted to determine the effects that open student models have on learning. This is the focus of our work. In particular, we are interested in whether even a simple open model can have a positive effect on learning. We have exposed the student model in e-KERMIT, and performed an evaluation study. Subjective results from the study are encouraging, although a more extensive study is needed to draw reliable conclusions.

1. Introduction

Developing models of students' knowledge has been one of the central research topics in the area of ITS. Until recently, the learners have not been aware of the existence of student models. This situation has begun to change in the previous decade. Several projects focused on the effects of opening the student model on students' learning. The efforts range from simply visualizing the model, to actively involving the student in the modeling process through negotiation or collaborative construction of the model. The intention is to engage the student in thinking about his/her own knowledge, thus involving the student at the meta-cognitive level. The student model is not just a source of knowledge about the student of value to the system, but becomes an important learning resource on its own. Students who engage on the meta-cognitive level achieve significantly better results than students who do not [19].

In this paper we present our experiences in opening the student model of KERMIT [18], an ITS for database design. A high-level overview of the student model (SM) is always visible, but the student can explore the model in detail. The paper is structured as follows. Section 2 presents related work. KERMIT is briefly introduced in section 3, and its extension (e-KERMIT) is presented next. We performed an experiment described in Section 5, and the results of data analyses are given in the following sections. The conclusions are given in the final section.

S.A. Cerri, G. Gouardères, and F. Paraguaçu (Eds.): ITS 2002, LNCS 2363, pp. 453–462, 2002.
© Springer-Verlag Berlin Heidelberg 2002

2. Related Work

The representations used to visualize the student model range from simple skillometers to very complex ones. Skillometers allow for an easy to understand, high-level overview of the student model, and are used in ELM-ART [2] and cognitive tutors [1]. Some systems additionally allow the student to challenge and negotiate the content of the model. This process is referred to as open interactive [9], collaborative [6], cooperative [11] or participative [15] student modelling. Such approaches use more complex representations based on conceptual graphs [9], Bayesian networks [20], tree structures [11], tables [3, 4] and Prolog clauses [17].

TAGUS [17] is a learner modelling system that allows external agents (the student or an educational system) to inspect and modify the SM. The model is represented as a set of Prolog clauses, which makes communication with the student quite complex. The student can insert new information into the SM, and also can update, delete or revise it. Belief revision techniques are used to maintain the model.

The **um** toolkit [11] is a shell for building and inspecting student models. The student and the system maintain their private models, but can also share some information. The SM contains learner's preferences, attributes and beliefs. The student may inspect the model, ask for justifications of system's beliefs and modify them. The toolkit has been used to demonstrate a system that teaches students to use a text editor. 30% of students involved in a study inspected their student models, but more than half of the students did not show significant interest in the model.

Collaborative modelling allows the student to develop his/her model jointly with the system and maintain dialogues about its content. Mr. Collins [4, 5] teaches the use of pronouns in Portuguese, using a small knowledge base of 12 rules only. The student model consists of system's beliefs induced from the observed behaviour, and the student's beliefs, which are explicitly specified by the student. For each rule, the system maintains statistics of how the student has used it, and the student also specifies his/her confidence that he/she knows the rule. If the student's belief is the same or within one level of the system's belief, the student model is treated as correct. However, if the two beliefs vary significantly, the system asks the student to revisit his/her confidence, and presents recent attempts at the rule with justification of its own belief. The student may disagree with the system, and may need to answer additional questions in order to justify his/her confidence. The evaluation study shows that students are willing to inspect their SM and challenge it. However, the study involved only 9 participants, and the results are therefore not irrefutable.

[15] describes a learning system in which the student is to control a pole on a cart in a simulated environment. The student can inspect and modify the SM, and has to articulate the strategies used when working in the environment. The study revealed positive effects of the open SM on reflection. However, although the students showed improved awareness, their performance on a transfer task was poor.

StyLE-OLM [9] is an open learner modelling component of a system for teaching technical terminology in a foreign language. The student model is represented as a conceptual graph. Both the student and the system can question the SM, introduce or withdraw prepositions and justify claims. The system uses the belief modal logic and complex inference mechanism to produce a representation on which both sides agree. A limited study (with seven participants) revealed that more able students are better in reflecting on their knowledge. ViSMod [20] is a similar system that allows the student to create his/her model in terms of a Bayesian network.

Finally, several research projects focus on peer diagnosis as a way to involve students in reflection. PeerSM [6], PairSM [7], PhelpS [10] and ConceptLab [21] provide collaborative environments where groups of students discuss the content of SM. PeerISM [8] is an extension of this idea, where an artificial peer monitors the modelling process and advises on conflicting points. I-Help [12] is another system based on peer help, but learner models are distributed over various resources. Every learner in I-Help has his/her own agent, the goal of which is to contact suitable peers and negotiate with their agents about help that is needed. Thus, every agent needs to model his/her own students, but also other students in the system.

The above projects differ in the content of the student model, representation chosen for visualization, the type of interactions (inspection or negotiation) and the mechanism for dealing with conflicts. The area is still just emerging, and proper ways of evaluating developed systems is yet to be identified.

3. KERMIT – A Database Design Tutor

KERMIT (Knowledge-based Entity Relationship Modelling Intelligent Tutor) is an ITS aimed at the university-level students learning conceptual database design. The

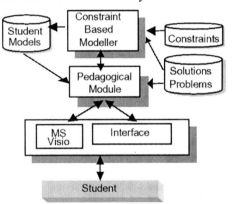

Fig. 1. The architecture of KERMIT

architecture of the system is illustrated in Figure 1. For a detailed discussion of the system, see [18]; here we present some of its basic features. KERMIT is a problem-solving environment in which 00students can practice database design using the Entity Relationship (ER) data model. The system consists of an interface, a pedagogical module, which determines the timing and content of pedagogical actions, and a constraint-based modeller, which analyses student answers and generates student models.

KERMIT contains a set of problems and ideal solutions, but has no problem solver. In order to check the correctness of the student's solution, KERMIT compares it to the correct solution, using domain knowledge represented in the form of more than 90 constraints. It uses Constraint-Based Modeling [16] to model knowledge of its students. The constraints cover both syntactic and semantic knowledge. An example of a syntactic constraint is ``An entity cannot be directly connected to another entity''. Semantic constraints relate the student's solution to the system's ideal solution, testing whether the student has modelled all requirements. There are constraints that check for equivalent, but not identical ways of modelling parts of a database in the student's and ideal solution. One of such constraints deals with multi-valued attributes of entities, which may alternatively be modelled as weak entities.

The interface is composed of three windows tiled vertically (see Figure 2). The top window displays the current problem and provides controls for stepping between problems, submitting a solution and selecting feedback level. The middle window is the main working area. In this window the student draws ER diagrams using the toolbar on the left side of the window. Feedback is presented in the lowest window in the textual form, as well as through an animated pedagogical agent.

4. e-KERMIT

As stated previously, our goal is to determine whether an open SM has an effect on student's learning. The systems presented in [9] and [21] are not full educational systems; in both cases only one isolated component has been developed. Conceptual graphs and Bayesian networks are used to represent domain knowledge, and also to represent the SM. Although such a decision is logical in these two cases, this is not possible in all situations. In the case of KERMIT, the knowledge base consists of a large number of constraints that are not related to each other. The constraints may be quite complex, and it is therefore not possible to visualize the SM in the same form as the underlying domain knowledge. Another difficulty comes from the size of the knowledge base, which is much bigger then in the mentioned systems. Therefore, we have decided to use a different representation. The open SM in e-KERMIT is a summary of the real SM, illustrated in a form of a hierarchy. The constraints are grouped according to the pedagogically important domain categories, while the individual constraints appear only as leaves in the hierarchy.

Following that, we modified KERMIT's interface to include the open SM, as shown in Figure 2. The only difference from the original interface is that the feedback window (the lowest part of the interface) is now divided into two parts. The left part of the window includes a summary of the student's progress, the number of problems the student has completed, the option of requesting the detailed view of their progress (the *Show Me More* button), and access to a tutorial on understanding the main progress view (the *Help* button). Summary statistics are shown because the main progress view is too large to display with the main interface. The summary of the SM provides constant feedback on progress and acts as an aid to remind and motivate students to further inspect their models. Figure 3 depicts the window that shows the hierarchical view of a student's progress, with some of the categories expanded. The window is split into two frames. The top frame displays the hierarchical taxonomy of ER knowledge, with progress statistics for each category. For example, consider the *Attribute Identification* category in Figure 3. The fraction to the right of the progress bar shows the student's score (33%) out of the percentage of material for attribute identification covered so far (44%). Besides summarizing the student's knowledge, the open model also presents a high level view of the domain, which supports student's understanding of the domain structure. By inspecting their models, students reflect on their knowledge, reconsider their beliefs about the domain concepts.

The lower frame provides a textbox that describes the currently selected category. This is an aid to provide an explanation for any part of the taxonomy that the student may have problems interpreting. In addition, the first time a student accesses their progress they are given a short tutorial on how to interpret what they see. The tutorial is made available at any time by clicking the *Help* button in the summary progress view in the main interface. The aim of the tutorial is to facilitate a quick understanding by giving students an introduction to how their progress is represented, and what the percentages convey.

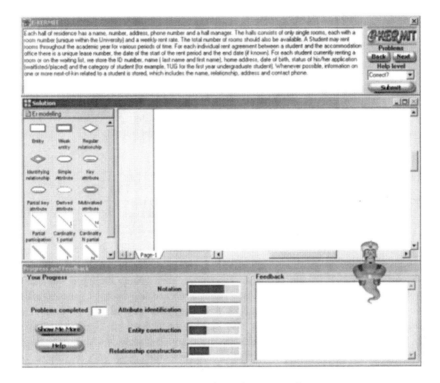

Fig. 2. The interface of e-KERMIT

5. The Experiment

An evaluation study was carried out with students enrolled in an introductory database course at the University of Canterbury. The experiment was run during the normal lab hours over the duration of one week. The evaluation focused on whether students learn more with an open SM, whether they inspect the models and feel that the open SM contributed to their learning. We were also interested in any differences between more and less able students with respect to the above.

The students were assigned to one of two groups: A control group interacted with the original KERMIT system, and the experimental group interacted with e-KERMIT. The groups were assigned to different rooms to prevent students from being exposed to both systems. Each student participated in a single session of up to 110 minutes.

Data collection consisted of four stages: pre-testing, system interaction, post-testing and subjective system assessment. Since participation was voluntary and laboratory attendance varies, it was hard to control group sizes. The pre/post tests consisted of three questions each, of similar difficulty. To minimise any effect resulting from variation in test difficulty, the tests were rotated between successive sessions.

6. Pre- and Post-tests

The results of the pre/post tests are shown in Table 1. The maximum mark was 22 in both tests. Students on average performed equally well on the pre-test, providing evidence that both groups were of comparable abilities. In both groups, the post-test mean was significantly higher than the corresponding pre-test mean (t=2.542, p=0.015 and t=4.905, p=0.000 respectively) revealing that students did improve their performance as the result of system interaction

Table 1. Pre- and post-test scores

Group	No. of students	Pre-test mean (SD)	Post-test mean (SD)
Control	26	16.12 (1.82)	17.77 (1.45)
Experimental	40	16.23 (2.59)	17.13 (2.37)

Within each group students were divided into more and less able subgroups based on their performance in the pre-test. The more able group included students who scored above the mean in the pre-test. Table 2 shows the average gains (difference between the post- and pre-test marks) and standard deviations. A 2x2 two-way randomised ANOVA revealed that the system used had no significant effect on student gain. The mean gains between the more and less able students in both groups were found to be significantly different (F(1,62)=45.881, p=0.001), but there was no significant interaction between the student ability and the system used. Further analysis revealed that only the less able students in both groups achieved a significant improvement (t=6.468, p=0.000 and t=3.534, p<0.005 respectively). Hence, system interaction appears to be more beneficial to the less able students.

Table 2. The results on the pre- and post-tests for the more and less able students

Group	Students	Pre-test	Post-test	Gain
Control – less able	15	14.80 (1.01)	17.13 (1.25)	2.33 (1.40)
Control – more able	11	17.91 (0.83)	18.64 (1.29)	0.73 (1.74)
Exper. – less able	22	14.41 (1.89)	16.14 (2.36)	1.73 (2.29)
Exper. – more able	18	18.44 (1.20)	18.33 (1.78)	-0.11 (1.75)

7. Log Analysis

The average interaction times of the two groups were not significantly different, as well as the total number of problems attempted/completed. However, students in the experimental group abandoned more problems (t=2.637, p=0.01). The mean time per solved problem was the same, but the time per uncompleted problem is significantly higher for the experimental group (t=1.817, p<0.1). It is tempting to suggest that students in the e-KERMIT group were willing to spend more time attempting to solve the problems than those in the control group, but a more extensive evaluation is needed to make this claim. Table 3 shows these results.

The students, on average, accessed their full progress model 1.36 times. This is possibly an underestimate of the real mean, because students may have opened the progress window only once and kept it open in the background. The tutorial was accessed on average 0.53 times in addition to the first time when progress was assessed. Comparison of the more and less able students revealed no significant difference between the mean number of times the SM and tutorial were accessed. There is no real correlation between the number of times students accessed their progress and their gain on the post-test for both the more able and less able students (r=0.344 and r=-0.146 respectively). 51.2% of the experimental group students accessed the main progress window. 66.7% of the more able students opened the main progress window, while only 45.5% of the less able ones did the same.

Table 3. Statistics from the logs

	Control group	Experimental group
Interaction time (mins)	66.65 (21.35)	67.65 (27.4)
Time/uncompleted problem	16.50 (13.31)	20.55 (14.47)
Time/solved problem	13.48 (7.23)	13.97 (7.68)
Attempted problems	4.36 (1.40)	3.89 (2.57)
Abandoned problems	2.61 (1.40)	1.78 (1.25)
Solved problems	1.75 (1.14)	2.11 (1.39)

8. Subjective Analysis

The questionnaire first asked how much ER modelling experience the students had previously had. Valid responses were *only lectures*, *lectures plus some work* and *extensive*. No students in either group said they had had extensive experience; however a surprising number of students (62.5%) in the experimental group answered with lectures plus work, while only 20% of the students in the control group answered with this response. Despite the suggested difference in experience between the two groups, results from the pre-tests revealed that the groups were of equal competence.

The time taken to learn the interface was asked next. Possible responses were *less than 5 minutes*, *10 minutes*, *30 minutes* and *most of the session*. The mean times were 11.3 minutes and 14 minutes for the control and experimental respectively. The Mann-Whitney U test revealed this difference is statistically significant (z=0.920, p=0.048) which is understandable, because the interface of e-KERMIT is more complicated as it includes visualisation of the student model. Students were also asked to estimate how much they learnt and how much they enjoyed learning with the system, on a scale from 1 (lowest) and 5 (highest). There were no significant differences for the means for the amount learnt (3.2 and 3.1) and for enjoyment (3.4 and 3.6) for the experimental and the control group.

Students in the control group were asked whether they would like to have access to an open SM. Of the 31 students who completed the questionnaire, 1 student said no, 10 were unsure and 20 said yes, thus favouring an open student model approach.

Experimental group students were asked questions about the open SM. 27 students said they examined the summary panel in the main interface, 2 mostly viewed the progress window and 8 used both views equally[1]. 9 students said they had difficulty in understanding their model, 18 had no problems and 9 said the model was understandable after explanation. Students were also asked whether they found the progress views useful, whether they examined their progress to identify weaknesses in their ER knowledge, and whether they felt that the opportunity to examine their progress assisted their learning. The responses to these questions are summarized in Table 4. 68.97% of the students who examined their progress found the open SM to be useful. The progress model was used to help identify weaknesses in ER knowledge by majority of these students, thus supporting reflective activity.

Table 4. Responses to questions about the open student model (OSM)

Question	Yes	No	Do not know	N/A
OSM useful?	45%	7.5%	12.5%	22.5%
OSM used to identify weaknesses?	47.5%	40%	0%	0%
OSM assisted learning?	67.5%	5%	22.5%	0%

9. Conclusions and Further Work

Open student modelling is claimed to enhance learning because it promotes reflective activity in the student [5, 9, 19]. However, evaluation of the effects of open SM is currently lacking. This research has focused on how even a simple open SM can affect learning. For this purpose we enhanced an ITS for database design, to present an overview of the student's progress. The resulting system visualises the SM as a hierarchy of categories, which conveys the structure of the domain.

An evaluation study was conducted to compare students' learning with KERMIT and e-KERMIT. The study focused on how the open SM in e-KERMIT affected learning, whether students would inspect their models, and students' subjective opinion of their model. The subjective results from this study are quite encouraging. The majority of students who examined their model found it to be a useful tool to aid in learning. Although the study failed to demonstrate any statistically significant improvements in post-test scores, students who used e-KERMIT performed at least as well as those who used KERMIT. Given that students were using the systems for only one hour, of which fourteen minutes was used to learn the interface, any benefits of an open SM were not expected to have a significant effect on student performance.

Students were not told explicitly to explore the SM, yet around half of them did inspect it. Responses from the questionnaire indicate that students reflected on their progress and domain weaknesses to some extent, although the majority of students said that they consulted mostly the progress summary in the main interface.

---

[1] Not all students have answered all the questions.

This study supports other findings [13, 19] that system interaction benefits the less able students more than the more able ones. We found that although the performance of the more able students in both groups did not improve after system interaction, the amount that these students thought they learnt, on average, was 3.1, which was the same for the less able group, who, in fact, had improved.

This work is a first step in evaluating the effects of a simple open SM on learning. To estimate the real effects, it is necessary to perform a longer study, allowing the SM to become more sophisticated and giving students more time to learn about the domain. We plan to conduct such a study in 2002.

References

1. Aleven, V., Koedinger, K. Limitations of Student Control: Do Students Know When They Need Help? In: G. Gauthier, C. Frasson and K. VanLehn (eds): Proc. ITS'2000, Springer-Verlag (2000) 292-303
2. Brusilovsky, P., Schwarz, E., Weber, G. ELM-ART: an Intelligent Tutoring System on World Wide Web. Proc. ITS'96 (1996) 261-269
3. Bull, S. See Yourself Write: a Simple Student Model to Make Students Think. In: A. Jameson, C. Paris and C. Tasso (eds): Proc. UM'97, Springer (1997) 315-326
4. Bull, S., Pain, H. Did I say what I think I said, and do you agree with me? Inspecting and Questioning the Student Model. In: J. Greer (ed), Proc. AIED'95 (1995) 501-508
5. Bull, S., Brna, P. & Pain, H. Extending the Scope of the Student Model. User Modeling and User Adapted Interaction, 5(1) (1995) 45-65
6. Bull, S., Brna, P. What does Susan Know that Paul Doesn't? (and vice versa): Contributing to each other's student model. In: B. du Boulay, R. Mizoguchi (eds), Proc. AIED 97, IOS Press, Amsterdam (1997) 568-570
7. Bull, S., Smith, M. A pair of student models to encourage collaboration. In: A. Jameson, C. Paris & C. Tasso (eds) Proc. 6th Int. Conf. on User Modeling, Springer (1997) 339-341
8. Bull, S., Brna, P. Enhancing peer interaction in the Solar system. In: P. Brna, M. Baker & K. Stenning (eds) Roles of communicative interaction in learning to model in Mathematics and Science: Proc. C-LEMMAS, Ajaccio, Corsica (1999)
9. Dimitrova, V., Self, J., Brna, P. Applying Interactive Open Learner Models to Learning Technical Terminology. In: M. Bauer, P. J. Gmytrasiewics, J. Vassileva (eds.) Proc. UM 2001, Springer (2001) 148-157
10. Greer, J., McCalla, G., Collins, J., Kumar, V., Meagher, P., Vassileva, J. Supporting Peer Help and Collaboration in Distributed Workplace Environments, IJAIED, 9, (1998) 159-177.
11. Kay, J. The UM toolkit for Cooperative Student Modeling. User Modeling and User-Adapted Interaction, 4 (1995) 149-196
12. McCalla, G., Vassileva, J., Greer, J., Bull, S. Active Learner Modelling. In: G. Gauthier, C. Frasson, K. VanLehn (eds), Proc. ITS'2000, Springer (2000) 53-62
13. Mitrovic, A. Investigating students' self-assessment skills. In: M. Bauer, P.J. Gmytrasiewicz and J. Vassileva (eds) Proc. UM-2001, Springer (2001) 247-250
14. Mitrovic, A., Ohlsson, S.: Evaluation of a Constraint-based Tutor for a Database Language. Int. J. on Artificial Intelligence in Education, 10(3-4), (1999) 238-256
15. Morales, R., Pain, H., Conlon, T. Effects of Inspecting Learner Models on Learners' Abilities. In: J. D. Moore, C. L. Redfield, W. L. Johnson (eds) Proc. AIED 2001 (2001) 434-445
16. Ohlsson, S.: Constraint-based student modeling. In: Greer, J.E., McCalla, G (eds): Student modeling: the key to individualized knowledge-based instruction, (1994) 167-189.

17. Paiva, A., Self, J. TAGUS – a User and Learner Modelling Workbench. User Modeling and User-Adapted Interaction, 4 (1995) 197-226
18. Suraweera, P., Mitrovic, A. Designing an Intelligent Tutoring System for Database Modelling. In: M.J. Smith, G. Salvendy (eds) (2001) 745-749
19. White, B.Y., Shimoda, T. A, Frederiksen, J.R. Enabling Students to Construct Theories of Collaborative Inquiry and Reflective Learning: Computer Support for Metacognitive Development. Int. Journal on AI in Education, 10 (1999) 151-182
20. Zapata-Rivera, J.D., Greer, J.E. Inspecting and Visualizing Distributed Bayesian Student Models. In: G. Gauthier, C. Frasson, K. VanLehn (eds), ITS'2000, Springer (2000) 544-553
21. Zapata-Rivera, J-D. Supporting Negotiated Assessment Using Open Student Models. In: M. Bauer, P. J. Gmytrasiewicz, J. Vassileva (eds) UM 2001, Springer (2001) 295-297.

Reasoning about Systems of Physics Equations

Chun Wai Liew[1] and Donald E. Smith[2]

[1] Department of Computer Science, Lafayette College, Easton PA 18042
liew@cs.lafayette.edu
[2] Department of Computer Science, Rutgers University, New Brunswick NJ 08855
dsmith@cs.rutgers.edu

Abstract. Many problems in introductory Physics require the student to enter a system of algebraic equations as the answer. Tutoring systems must be able to *understand* the student's submission before they can generate useful feedback. This paper presents an approach that accepts from the student a system of equations describing the physics of the problem and checks to see if it is correct. When it is not, the student's equation set is analyzed vis-a-vis one or more correct sets of equations, known physics concepts, and algebraic transformations. During this analysis credit-blame assignment is performed to identify one of several types of errors including 1) algebraic errors, 2) one or more omitted physics concepts, 3) incorrect instances of a required physics concept, and 4) use of an inappropriate physics concept. Experimental data collected from an introductory physics class is summarized and discussed vis-a-vis other methods. Results indicate that the techniques applied are effective at localizing most errors but that more work is needed to distinguish between algebraic and conceptual errors.

1 Introduction

One of the keys to being a good tutor is the ability to identify and localize the error in a student's answer and then generate useful focused feedback. Effective feedback enables students to correct their mistakes or conceptual errors without the tutor explicitly giving them the answer. An Intelligent Tutoring System (ITS) must not only determine if an answer is correct or incorrect but when incorrect it must localize and characterize the incorrect or missing part(s) of the answer. The degree to which an ITS can (1) localize an error in the answer, (2) identify the conceptual errors that contributed to the mistake and (3) analyze the problem context to generate feedback, greatly impacts on the effectiveness of the system.

Many problems in introductory Physics require the student to enter a set of algebraic equations as the answer. Tutoring systems must be able to *understand* the student's submission before they can generate useful feedback. This paper presents an approach that accepts from the student a system of equations describing the physics of the problem and checks to see if it is correct. When it is not, the student's equation set is analyzed vis-a-vis one or more correct sets of equations, known physics concepts, and algebraic transformations. The ability

S.A. Cerri, G. Gouardères, and F. Paraguaçu (Eds.): ITS 2002, LNCS 2363, pp. 463–472, 2002.

to apply algebraic transformations to the system of equations results in there being many equivalent forms of the answer that a tutoring system must be able to recognize and analyze. Most credit-blame assignment algorithms would map the student's equation to an equation in a solution set; however, it is computationally infeasible to either generate or store all the equivalent answers in this context. We have developed an algorithm that uses algebraic transformations to change the equations in the answer set into a form that is similar and suitable for comparison to the student's answer. The mapped equations are then compared and the similarities and differences are used to identify the errors that have been made.

2   Separating Physics from Algebra: An Example Problem

One of the many challenges to employing ITS techniques in a quantitative domain such as physics is the role played by algebra. It is required to solve such problem but at the same time enables misused concepts to masquerade as algebraic mistake. The resulting ambiguity (i.e., is the mistake algebraic or is the student confused about how to apply the physics concepts) presents a significant challenge to tutoring systems. In a perfect world the student would provide an *untransformed* set of equations that describe the physics of the problem and then proceed to algebraically solve them. In the real world, inputs provided by students are somewhere in between the desired *untransformed* equations and the final solution. The difficulty in generating effective feedback is exarcebated when algebra and physics are interwoven. To compound the problem, giving inappropriate feedback may often lead to a correct answer and even reinforce *bad habits* a student may have acquired.

To date all approaches to this problem, and there are few of them, compare the student's set of equations to a correct set of equations. The assumption is that the differences are sufficient to generate the appropriate feedback. As we will show in this paper it is difficult to (1) ensure that the appropriate equations are compared and (2) classify the error when the differences are identified. In the context of this paper, we are ignoring the issues of dimensional correctness of the equations. An earlier paper [1] describes our work in this area.

This section outlines the issues involved in ensuring that an equation in the student's set is appropriately and correctly mapped to an equation in the answer set. The discussion is illustrated with an example problem based on pulleys. A simple mechanism that is introduced early in the Physics curriculum is an Atwoods machine, a massless pulley with two masses, m_1 and m_2 hanging at either end as is shown in Figure 1. A common problem based on the Atwoods machine is to ask the student for the equation(s) that would determine the acceleration of the mass m_1, assuming that m_1 and m_2 are not equal.

A set of equations that would solve the problem is shown below. Equations 1, 2 and 3 deal with Force while Equation 4 is concerned with Acceleration.

$$T_1 - m_1 * g = m_1 * a_1 \qquad (1)$$

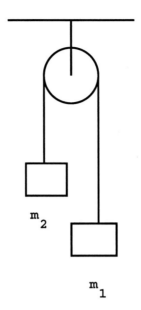

Fig. 1. Atwoods Machine

$$T_2 - m_2 * g = m_2 * a_2 \tag{2}$$
$$T_1 = T_2 \tag{3}$$
$$a_1 = -a_2 \tag{4}$$

This set of equations leads to the following solution

$$a_1 = (m_1 - m_2) * g/(m_1 + m_2) \tag{5}$$

An example of a set of equations that is different but also correct is:

$$T - m_1 * g = -m_1 * a \tag{6}$$
$$T - m_2 * g = m_2 * a \tag{7}$$

A student could enter any of the sets of equations (1 -4, 5 or 6-7 and they should be considered correct. These equations highlight some of the issues that an ITS has to deal with when it analyses a set of equations and attempts to identify the equations. The issues arise from the many equivalent syntactic forms of the equations. An ITS must be able to recognize and identify these equivalent forms of the equations. The recognition problems frequently cause an ITS to compare two equations that are not comparable. This results in the system generating feedback that is erroneous and therefore confusing to the student.

In comparing the student's equations with the answer set, an ITS must determine the mapping of the variables and subsequently equations from one set to the other. This process is complicated by several issues:

1. *variable renaming:* The student and the instructor may use different variable names to represent the same quantities. There is no restriction on the names of variables or choice of subscripts even though there are many standard variable names but there are also many commonly used variations, e.g., F, $Fnet$, F_1 usually represent a Force.

2. *simple aliasing of one variable:* Frequently, variables that have the same magnitude, coefficients and dimensions are aliased for one another. For example, the variables T_1 and T_2 in equations 1, 2 and 3 are equivalent to one another. In equations 6 and 7, there is only a single variable T_1 that is used to represent both, i.e., T_1 is an alias for T_2. When variables are aliased, then the number of equations in the set is also reduced.

3. *mapping of coefficients for a pair of variables:* Aliasing of variables also occurs when the coefficients are not the same. An example equation is:

$$a_1 = -a_2$$

In this case, the variables are not directly equivalent because they have different coefficients (sign and possibly magnitude).

4. *elimination of a class of "equivalent" variables:* There are many ways to specify the algebraic solution to a problem. These may involve using a greater or lesser number of variables and thereby a greater or lesser number of equations. Sometimes variables that are in an equivalent set are completely eliminated and in the process the corresponding equations that specify the equivalences are removed. For example, one very different but correct solution to the example problem is:

$$m_1 * g - m_1 * a = m_2 * g + m_2 * a$$

In this case, there is no variable representing the tension of the rope (commonly T, T_1, T_2). Instead that variable has been eliminated from the set and a corresponding equation has been eliminated.

5. *choice of coordinate axes:* For every vector, e.g., Force or Acceleration, there is a choice of coordinate axes. In the example problem, everything is aligned vertically but there is still the choice of whether the acceleration is positive in the up or down direction.

$$T_1 - m_1 * g = -m_1 * a_1 \tag{8}$$
$$T_1 - m_2 * g = -m_2 * a_2 \tag{9}$$
$$a_1 = -a_2 \tag{10}$$

The first set of equations (Equations 8-10) is consistent with a choice of a_1 being positive in the same direction downwards and opposed to T_1. The second set of equations below (Equations 11-13 is consistent with a_1 being positive in the upwards direction. An ITS should be able to detect and recognize the choice of axes, and thus the correctness of both sets of equations.

$$T_1 - m_1 * g = m_1 * a_1 \tag{11}$$
$$T_1 - m_2 * g = m_2 * a_2 \tag{12}$$
$$a_1 = -a_2 \tag{13}$$

All the above issues must be dealt with if a system is to make sense of the student's submitted answer, even with the help of a set of correct answers. The above issues arise from the use of algebraic shortcuts by the student, a use that cannot be and should not be discouraged. Unfortunately, their use obfuscates errors and makes it much harder for an ITS to identify errors and differentiate between conceptual and algebraic errors.

3   Related Work

Most Physics tutoring systems do not support the use of equations for input. Most of the systems either ask for numeric input or use multiple choice questions [2,3,4]. In an earlier version of the system[5], we described a technique for performing credit-blame assignment on single equations. This technique is unable to deal with the issues and complexities that arise when the answer is a set of equations instead of a single equation.

It is fairly easy to determine if an equation is correct if all the variables have been defined. One simple way is to substitute various values for the variables and evaluate the equation. This is the approach taken in many existing systems. It is much harder to determine what is wrong about an equation once it has been labeled incorrect. One simple approach (used in an early version of the ANDES system [6]) is to generate all possible correct equations and find the closest match to the student's submission. This turns out to be computationally infeasible as the space of possible equations is very large. The current ANDES system [7] instead generates a much smaller set of equations. This set represents the most common choices of coordinate axes (issue 5). The system uses an algebraic solver to determine the correctness of a student's equation. If the equation is incorrect, the system uses a set of mal-rules [8] to perturb its set of equations to find a closest match to the student's equation and thus generate feedback based on the mal-rule selected. This obviously can lead to cases where completely erroneous and confusing feedback is generated. Note that the system still has to deal with issues such as variable aliasing(Issue 2), mapping of coefficients (Issue 3), variable elimination (Issue 4) and choice of coordinate axes (Issue 5), when trying to map a student's answer to one that it has generated. This approach also requires a great deal of effort to create a knowledge base that has sufficient Physics knowledge to generate the required solutions and the choices. ANDES also takes the approach of verifying each equation as it is entered by the student. This gives the student immediate feedback as information is entered. The system can take this approach because all the variables have been defined *a priori*. The main concern for ANDES is to map the student's equation to a member of the set that is presently in the system.

4   Approach

The first step towards "understanding" a student's submission is to classify each equation as either (1) correct, (2) almost correct and (3) incorrect. The approach described in this paper compares the student's submission to a single solution set to classify each equation. Correctness preserving algebraic transformations are used to change one set of equations (e.g., the system's) into a form that is equivalent to the other (e.g., the student's), so that individual equations may be compared. Only a single set of equations is used unlike the multiple sets that are used in the ANDES system. The technique can determine the differences between an incorrect and a correct equation but has some difficulties in differentiating between algebraic and conceptual errors.

There are two types of algebraic transformations used in our system. The first is used to transform equations into a canonical sum of products form. The second type is used to transform the set by reducing the number of variables and hence the number of equations. These two types of transformations are used to transform the student's set of equations so that each equation can be heuristically mapped to an equation from the answer. Errors are identified by comparing each equation in the student's set with the corresponding equation from the solution set. Variables are not defined *a priori* but their dimensions are inferred by the system based on their name (e.g., a_n typically stands for Acceleration). Currently the student is required to enter all the equations before the system starts the analysis.

4.1   Algebraic Transformations

The two types of correctness preserving transformations are used to:

1. *transform equations to canonical form:* These transformations are rules for rewriting equations and transforming these equations into a canonical sum of products form. An example of these rules is one that multiplies each term by the divisor of a term. The primary effect of this rule is to remove all denominators. The canonical form is then used to *validate dimensions.* The dimensions of each variable and constant in the equations is inferred, thereby determining the dimensions of the equation. This can be done using a constraint based algorithm that is described in detail in [1].

2. *rewrite set equations to eliminate variables:*
   This type of transformation eliminates variables and thereby equations from the set. In a prior step, the dimensions of each variable is determined. The variables used in the student's set are then heuristically mapped to variables in the answer set. Any variables that are unmapped are then eliminated from the set using the transformations. The transformations are used for:
   - *the elimination of equivalent variables:* Equations in the form $v_1 = k * v_2$ are removed by substituting $k * v_2$ everywhere the variable v_1 occurs.
   - *the elimination of a class of variables:* The previous transformation eliminated variables that could be substituted for with an equivalent variable. There are times when a class of variables is not present in one or other set of equations. Usually, this happens when one set uses intermediate variables and the other does not. This transformation uses gaussian elimination to remove the variables from the set of equations.

4.2   Mapping Variables and Equations

Transformations are used to convert a set of equations so that it has the same number and type of variables as the set that it is being compared to. The variables from one set must then be mapped to the variables of the other set. The algorithm looks for a one-to-one match between the variables in the two sets of equations and handles simple aliasing of names. The heuristic technique uses knowledge of well-known variables (m usually represents Mass) and common use of subscripts to find a mapping.

Once all variables have been mapped, the algorithm maps equations in the student's submission to equations in the answer set. The algorithm only maps equations that have the same dimensions. The heuristic used determines how good a match is based on the terms in the equation, i.e., whether a term is present or absent in the equation that is being compared to. There is a pre-set limit on the maximum number of differences allowed. If the number of differences exceeds the limit, the equation is marked as unmapped, i.e., there was no corresponding equation in the answer set of equations.

4.3   Identifying Errors and Generating Feedback

Each of the student's equations is compared with the corresponding equation from the answer set to determine the differences between the student's equation and the correct equation. Some of the detectable differences are listed below:

- switch in sign, e.g., use of a $+$ instead of a $-$.
- missing or additional term: e.g., use of $m_1 * g + m_1 * a$ instead of $m_1 * g$.
- missing or additional trigonometric factor: e.g., use of $m_1 * g * sin\theta$ instead of $m_1 * g$.
- incorrect coefficient: e.g., use of a_2 instead of $-2 * a_2$.
- incorrect factor, e.g., use of m_2 in place of m_1.

All of these differences do not change the dimensions of the encompassing equation. Any mistakes that would change the dimensions of the equation would result in the equation being mapped to another equation. Trigonometric factors are dimensionless functions so their absence or presence does not change the dimension of the term or equation.

The switch in signs is a special case in that every other error can be identified and localized by examining only the equation in which it occurs. A switch in signs could be an error but could also represent a choice of an alternative set of coordinate axes. This can only be determined by verifying that the sign switch is consistently applied to all equations.

The final step is to generate feedback based on the critique of the equations. This is not the only place where feedback is generated. Feedback is generated immediately if any of the equations are found to be dimensionally incorrect or if the set of equations is incomplete, i.e., there are an insufficient number of equations.

The feedback that can be generated is based on the differences that are detected. This results in suggestions to consider (1) whether certain quantities are acting in concert or in opposition (incorrect signs), (2) the impact of a body on other bodies (missing or additional terms) and (3) that a body is acting (or not) at an angle with respect to another body (missing or additional trigonometric factors).

If there are unmapped equations in the student's answer, then there is a corresponding equation in the instructor's answer. The system will generate feedback suggesting that the unmapped equation does not lead to the solution and suggest considering the interactions between certain bodies in terms of Physics concepts, e.g., Force or Momentum. Earlier work in this area is described in [5]

4.4   Limitations

The errors that students make generally fall into one of the following categories:

- algebraic errors: This is detected as an incorrect equation.
- missing Physics concept error: This is detected as an missing equation.
- incorrect application of concept error: This is detected as an incorrect equation.

Problems arise when the system is unable to determine the type of error from the difference between the correct answer and the student's submission. This is caused by the use of algebraic transformations that are correctness preserving but have no corresponding Physics concept. For example, if a student chooses to (1) not use the intermediate variable T to represent tension in the rope and (2) to use a to represent acceleration, she would end up with the equation:

$$a = (m_1 - m_2) * g/(m_1 + m_2) \tag{14}$$

The use of algebraic transformations to reduce the set of equations, in this case to one equation, poses many problems to the ITS when a mistake is made. For example, if the student switches the $-$ sign for $a_1 = -a_2$, the equation above, Equation 14, is reduced to:

$$a = g \tag{15}$$

With the original set of equations (Equations 1-4), there are five places where such an algebraic error could have been made. On the other hand, the student could have made a conceptual error and not realized that the two blocks are moving in opposite directions and therefore generated the equation $a_1 = a_2$. If the student uses algebraic transformations and enters a reduced set of equations, the technique is unable to differentiate between these sources of errors. This is an example of where the student's use of algebraic transformations makes it hard for an ITS to generate useful feedback. The technique can localize and identify the difference between the student's answer and the correct answer but that is insufficient. The system needs to be able to identify the source of the difference, i.e., the error that was made.

The degree to which the student uses algebraic simplifications greatly impacts the ability of the algorithm to identify the source of an error. If the student made the above error and submitted either two or three equations, the algorithm would only have to disambiguate between an algebraic error and a conceptual error. In that case, the algorithm would assume that a conceptual error had been made and generate the appropriate feedback.

A more advanced mechanism would (1) enumerate the causes of the algebraic error, (2) identify the ones that are more likely to occur, (3) identify ways to disambiguate between the likely errors and then (3) prompt the user for information to disambiguate. For the above example, the system might prompt the user with "What is the relationship (equation) between the acceleration of the block of mass m_1 (a_1) and the acceleration of the block of mass m_2 (a_2)?". We are currently exploring this avenue of research.

5   Experimental Evaluation and Discussion

In the spring of 2001, we collected roughly 175 answers to two Physics problems from 88 different students. The two problems were (1) the Atwoods problem described in this paper and (2) a problem involving a moving pulley. The students were enrolled in an introductory Physics course for engineers and science majors.

Analysis showed that dimension errors occurred in roughly fifteen percent of the answers. These errors were detected by the algorithm and described in [1]. With the rest of the equations, the algorithm correctly maps variables in ninety percent of the equations. However, it only correctly maps seventy percent of the equations. Much of the difficulty lies in disambiguating between an equation is slightly incorrect and should be mapped from an equation that is fundamentally wrong and should not be mapped.

The ability to provide good and useful feedback is very dependent upon how well the algorithm maps the equations. There are three main categories of answers that the algorithm failed on. The first is where the student's choice of coordinate axes is not the same as the one in the answer. This is an area where the ANDES algorithm currently performs better. The second category is composed of answers where the algorithm incorrectly mapped the equations. If an equation has been correctly mapped, the algorithm performs well in determining what is incorrect about an equation. The algorithm can then correctly identify the errors and generate the appropriate feedback. Finally, there are answers where the equations were correctly mapped and the differences were identified but the algorithm could not determine the cause of the error. This was a small set because the students had been explicitly instructed to write down all the applicable equations and **not** to perform algebraic simplification. Even so, approximately twenty percent of the students used some algebraic simplifications and submitted reduced sets of equations.

6 Conclusion

Reasoning about sets of algebraic Physics equations is a difficult task that is further complicated when students use algebraic transformations to *simplify* their answer. This paper has described an approach for performing credit-blame assignment on a set of algebraic Physics equations submitted by a student. The technique is based on analysis and comparison of the student's answer (a set of equations) with a correct answer (another set of equations). The technique uses algebraic transformations to identify and map variables and equations from the student's set to the answer set. Mapped equations are compared and the differences are used to identify errors and generate feedback. The algorithm can detect and identify several types of errors including algebraic errors, omitted Physics concepts and incorrect applications of concepts. The technique has been evaluated on answers collected from students in an introductory Physics course at a small college. The results show that the algorithm successfully analyzes most of the submitted answers and generates the appropriate feedback.

References

1. Liew, C., Smith, D.: Checking for dimensional correctness in physics equations. In: To appear in Fourteenth International Florida AI Research SocietyConference. (2002)
2. Novak, G.M., Patterson, E.T.: Just-in-time teaching: Active learner pedagogy with www. In: Proceedings of IASTED International Conference on Computers and Advanced Technology in Education. (1998)
3. Hubler, A.W., Assad, A.M.: Cyberprof: An intelligent human-computer interface for asynchronous wide area training and teaching. In: Proceedings of Fourth International World Wide Web Conference. (1995)
4. Novak, G.M.: World wide web technology as a new teaching and learning environment. International Journal of Modern Physics **8, No. 1** (1997) 19–39
5. Liew, C., Shapiro, J.A., Smith, D.: What is wrong with this equation? error detection and feedback with physics equations. In: Proceedings of Thirteenth International Florida AI Research SocietyConference. (2000)
6. Gertner, A.S.: Providing feedback to equation entries in an intelligent tutoring system for physics. In: Proceedings of the 4th International Conference on Intelligent Tutoring Systems. (1998)
7. Shelby, R., Schulze, K., Treacy, D., Wintersgill, M., VanLehn, K., Weinstein, A.: An assessment of the andes tutor. In: Proceedings of the Physics Education Research Conference. (2001)
8. Cohen, P., Feigenbaum, E., eds. In: The handbook of artificial intelligence. Volume 2. William Kaufmann, Inc., Los Altos, CA (1982) 317–318

Principle Hierarchy Based Intelligent Tutoring System for Common Cockpit Helicopter Training

Robert A. Richards

Stottler Henke Associates, Inc. (SHAI)
1660 So. Amphlett Blvd., Suite 350
San Mateo, CA 94402, U.S.A.
Richards@shai.com, www.shai.com

Abstract. SHAI is developing a comprehensive Operator Machine Interface Assistant (OMIA) system. The system will assist operators learn the new common-cockpit MH-60R and MH-60S helicopters in an increasingly broad variety of mission tasks and analyses, using the wide assortment of sensor, navigation, and computational resources available. We are employing a principle hierarchy based intelligent tutoring system, to teach the Common Cockpit machine interface during simulated mission execution. The Intelligent tutoring system utilizes a SHAI developed ITS authoring environment that has been developed and enhanced for various other ITS projects. This paper describes the OMIA system, emphasizing the authoring tool's ability to develop visually the principle hierarchy and the evaluation finite state machines necessary to evaluate the student. In addition the decision tree enhancement to the authoring tool developed as part of this OMIA project, is described.

1 Introduction

The US Navy is introducing two new helicopters, the MH-60S and MH-60R (See Fig. 1.). Both of these helicopters utilize the *Common Cockpit* design. The Common Cockpit includes all the flight and mission instrumentation in both of the helicopters and enables both the pilot and co-pilot to share workload through dual flight and mission instrumentation, see Fig. 2. SHAI is building a training tool called the Operator Machine Interface Assistant (OMIA) that includes an intelligent tutoring system (ITS) to teach [1] the common cockpit. OMIA is currently in use by the US Navy and is being expanded to teach more of the overall domain.

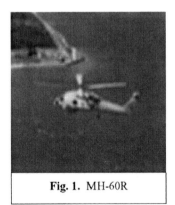

Fig. 1. MH-60R

OMIA utilizes a principle hierarchy based approach to the intelligent tutoring that interfaces to a scenario-based free-play simulation [2]. Much of the intelligent tutoring system aspects of the overall OMIA training system have been developed utilizing an ITS authoring tool (ITSAT) developed by SHAI. In addition, OMIA has

S.A. Cerri, G. Gouardères, and F. Paraguaçu (Eds.): ITS 2002, LNCS 2363, pp. 473–483, 2002.

required capabilities beyond the scope of the previous version of ITSAT and has thus enhanced ITSAT in a general manner to meet OMIA's needs.

Fig. 2. Common Cockpit

2   OMIA Training System

Two major components of the OMIA System are the ITS, and the scenario-based free-play simulator. The simulator allows the student to learn via free-play scenarios with a graphical user interface that closely matches that of the common cockpit mission displays. As shown in Fig. 3 the simulator communicates with the ITS, (via an external system interface) to update the student model, and to provide the student with remediations.

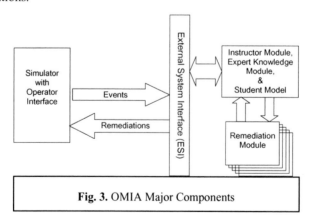

Fig. 3. OMIA Major Components

2.1   Simulator

The simulator provides an engaging interface between the student and the ITS. A

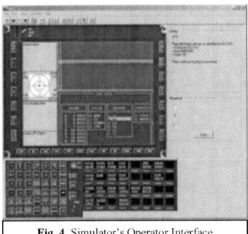

Fig. 4. Simulator's Operator Interface

student interacts with the simulator through a computer re-creation of the controls onboard the MH-60R/S, see Fig. 4. In addition to being an interface, this component also simulates the environment surrounding the helicopters using *scenarios*. Scenarios are authored using a visual editing tool, and determine the elements of the simulation. For example, sonar returns from pinging depend not only upon the settings chosen by the operator, but also on the environment and target submarine settings in the scenario file. Other entities, such as an enemy submarine or a friendly ship, can have agendas of their own. For instance, a submarine can be assigned the behavior "flee on detection." Even the fleeing behavior itself is customizable, as are all behaviors.

Of course, an operator might add objects such as sonobuoys to the simulation in real time. The flip side is that destroyed/sunk objects would be removed from the simulation as well. The ability to act upon the simulation and have it respond gives the students freedom to do the right thing, or to make mistakes. Either way, the system then has a better model of the student than before, and can use this to improve his learning experience. A graphical scenario generator [3] allows an instructor/author to create complex scenarios that include any number of intelligent agent entities (e.g., ships, submarines, and aircraft).

2.2   ITS Design

The OMIA ITS consists of the following major modules:
–   student model,
–   instructor,
–   expert knowledge, and
–   remediation.

This paper concentrates on the principle hierarchy and the tools used to manipulate the principle hierarchy. More information regarding other aspects of OMIA may be found in [4].

The Expert Knowledge Module utilizes a *principle hierarchy* representation, i.e., a collection of individual principles, arranged in a hierarchy. The principles are relatively low-level pieces of testable information. Each principle may also contain material that should be presented to the student as remediations. A very small sample of the principle hierarchy is shown below.
•   Acoustic

    ○   Active Sonar
- Dipping Sonar
  - Unintegrated for fast targets
  - Waveform selection
  - Configure before ping
  - Ping after configure
  -

The lower levels of the hierarchy are composed of specific principles which include the operational knowledge necessary to determine the appropriate action for a crewman to take in a particular set of circumstances. As events unfold, various principles come into play suggesting the appropriate conclusions and reactions resulting from new data and circumstances. The principle hierarchy, and associated knowledge about proper application of principles to scenarios, provides a facility for detecting at any time in a mission

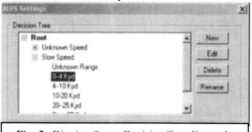

Fig. 5. Dipping Sonar Decision Tree Example

a correct action (e.g., evasive maneuvers) and/or determining a correct conclusion (e.g., target submarine is deeper than expected).

An example of an individual principle is "Use the unintegrated setting on the dipping sonar for fast moving targets." In this case, comparing a student's actions to the expert's is straightforward. A slightly more complicated principle is "Correct waveform selection for the dipping sonar." For this principle, the sonar settings suggested by the expert vary depending upon the environment and the expected target. A *decision tree* is used to represent the domain expert knowledge for principles such as this.

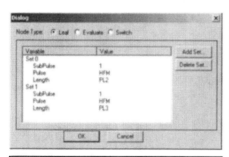

Fig. 6. Dipping Sonar Decision Tree Example Settings

Decision trees are graphically constructed tree diagrams where at each node a question is asked. The next node is chosen based on the answer to the current question. By traversing through this tree, one eventually arrives at the correct decision. A partial decision tree for determining dipping sonar settings based on submarine presumed speed and distance is shown in Fig. 5 and Fig. 6. In Fig.5 the highlighted *0 – 4 Kyd* is a leaf of the tree for a slow moving target at a range of 0 to 4 kiloyards. For this leaf the proper settings are shown in Fig. 6.

In this situation, there are two dipping sonar configurations that are appropriate.

3   Using the Intelligent Tutoring System Authoring Tool (ITSAT)

There are six categories of knowledge in the OMIA ITS system. These are;
–   The principle hierarchy.
–   The simulation scenarios, to be used as examples and exercises.
–   Descriptions (multi-media) which explain each principle.
–   Knowledge used to asses the correctness of student actions.
–   Knowledge used to assess a student's mastery of a principle given the history
         of his performance in relation to that principle.
–   Pedagogical knowledge.

SHAI has developed tools to assist in the development of all of these categories of knowledge. The SHAI developed ITS Authoring Tool (ITSAT) allows ITS authors to organize course principles, articulate teaching methods, specify courseware, and develop a case base of scenarios for students along with a specification of how the student's actions will be evaluated and their mastery of the required knowledge assessed. This paper demonstrates primarily the visual ITSAT environment with regards to the principle hierarchy and the finite state machines that contain the knowledge used to asses the correctness of student actions, i.e., they evaluate the student's knowledge of the principles.

3.1   Principle Hierarchy Editor

ITSAT's principal hierarchy screen is shown in Fig. 7. The *Hierarchy* tab has been developed and evolved during the course of many SHAI ITS projects [5] to provide

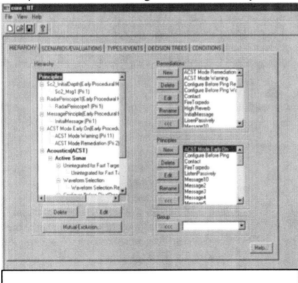

information about the principle hierarchy and the constituent principles and remediations as well as to provide a visual method of creating, manipulating and destroying principles and remediations. Each principle can be associated with multiple elements from the remediation section.

The left **Hierarchy** region shows the principle hierarchy and is used to organize the principles into the hierarchy itself. The bold entries in the

Fig. 7. ITSAT – Main Screen Showing Hierarchy Tab

hierarchy are groups, e.g., "Acoustics(ACST)". These groups represent areas of knowledge that encompass one or more principles. Under the groups are the principles, and under each principle are the principle's remediations. Objects in the hierarchy may be edited via a double click or the Edit button, while the Delete button removes items from the hierarchy.

Similarly, the **Remediations** region and the **Principles** region provide buttons to easily create, delete, edit, and rename items; as well as add items to the hierarchy (via the <<< key). The **Group** region provides the mechanism to create and add new groups to the principle hierarchy.

For example, there is a visual layer for creating or editing remediations, as shown in Fig. 8. In the remediation dialog, the *remediation type* indicates the type of this remediation file. This information determines how the file will be presented to the student. Types include, multimedia (i.e., video), text, picture, and default. In the case of *default* OMIA will ask Windows to open and display the file. One can test the remediation via the *Play* button; this will show how the remediation is presented to the student.

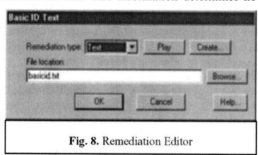

Fig. 8. Remediation Editor

3.2   Instructor, Student Model, and Remediation Modules

It is the job of the instructor module to determine when a student has failed a principle or conversely when a principle has been successfully applied. If for example the expert module indicates that a student should search for short range targets before long range targets, but the student does the opposite, he has failed this principle. The instructor module would then annotate the student's *student model,* and inform the remediation module, which may provide immediate feedback to the student (remediation) if appropriate.

The OMIA ITS contains *evaluation finite state machines* (EFSM) that describe what principles are active in a given situation, and evaluate a student's performance during the execution of a scenario. That is, it is the evaluation machines that are watching the actions of the student and determining which principles are being performed correctly or incorrectly. A scenario can have any number of evaluation machines that are evaluated simultaneously. ITSAT provides a visual tool for constructing, managing and editing the EFSMs.

A graphical representation of an EFSM is shown in Fig. 9. After a student performs an action, for example pinging the dipper, a different EFSM might check the student's waveform selection against that of the expert

Fig. 9. Evaluation Finite State Machine Editor

waveform selection. If the settings are correct, the student's percentage correct on waveform selection would increase. If wrong, his percentage on this principle would decrease and the remediation attached to this principle might be displayed.

EFSMs consist of states and transitions. Each state has a set of transitions; each transition has a destination state. During evaluation, the EFSM is considered to be in one of its states, called the "current state." From this current state, the EFSM evaluates each of the state's outgoing transitions. If one of these transitions "becomes true", it is taken to its destination state. This state then becomes the "current state" of the EFSM. Additionally, the student passes any of the transition's passing principles, and/or fails any of the transition's failing principles. This structure creates a set of directional paths that are used to determine how well the student reacted to events in the scenario.

3.3   Evaluation Finite State Machine (EFSM) Editor

ITSAT includes an evaluation machine editor. In the main window of the editor one can graphically create and connect states and transitions using the mouse. The text box below this window displays hints for editing the EFSM. The basic operations include:

- To create a state: Move the mouse over a blank portion of the window, and then right click. A box representing the state will appear.
- To create a transition: First select a state to be the source state. Then move the mouse over the state that will be the destination state for the new transition. Finally, right click. A transition will be created going from the source state to the destination state. The transition object itself is represented graphically as an oval.
- To select a state or transition: Move the mouse over the state or transition and click.
- To edit a state or transition: Move the mouse over the state or transition and double click.
- To delete a state or transition: Select a state or transition, and then press the delete key.

The descriptions button brings up the description editor for the evaluation machine that can be used to provide documentation.

As an example, in the EFSM shown in Fig. 9, the initial state, *ACST Mode*, is the top-most rectangle. When the action, *Key_DIP_CNFG* is taken, a transition is made to the *DIP_CNFG Menu* state. From this state, the machine can either transition on the dipper being configured (SetsValue) or on the key which closes the menu without changing any settings (Key_DIP_CNFG).

A major portion of the information content for an EFSM is contained within the transitions. Transitions can be activated based on either an *event* or a *condition*, or both. For example, a transition might be triggered on the event *OpenScenario* with a condition of *Scenario name equals Scenario*

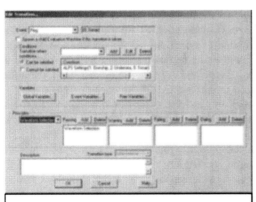

Fig. 10. Evaluation Transition Editor

Bravo. ITSAT provides a GUI to work with the transitions and is further described below.

3.3.1   Evaluation Transition Editor

The evaluation transition editor is shown in Fig. 10. Each transition has a list of conditions. In general, when these conditions are satisfied, the transition "becomes true" and is taken by the evaluation machine. A simple or complex set of factors can determine whether a transition is taken or not.

The event on which to match for the transition is set in the *Event* field. If an event is specified, this transition will only be taken if the event occurs AND all the conditions are met. If "None" is specified, the transition is taken any time the conditions are met. To the right of this field are the bindings of the event parameters. These event variables become bound to the particular event that occurred, and can be used as parameters to the transition's conditions.

If the *Spawn a child Evaluation Machine if this transaction is taken* box is checked, then the evaluation machine will remain in its current state and spawn a copy of itself when the transition would normally be taken. The spawned evaluation machine will begin evaluating at the transition's terminal state. This technique is useful for creating evaluation machines that need to evaluate a situation that can happen multiple times simultaneously.

The **Conditions** region displays all the current conditions for this transition. The drop-down list contains all possible conditions that can be added. If the "Can be satisfied" radio button is selected, then the transition will only be taken if all the conditions can be satisfied. If the "Cannot be satisfied" radio button is selected, then the transition will be taken only if all the conditions cannot be satisfied. Buttons are provided to; *Add* the selected condition to the current list of conditions, giving it default parameters; *Edit* the parameters of the condition via a Condition Editor; and *Delete* the condition from this transition. OMIA has enhanced the previous version of ITSAT to include the capability to have decision trees as one of the conditions. See below for more information on decision trees.

The **Variables** region allows editing of the different types of variables in a transition. These variables can then be used as parameters to the transition's conditions. Variables have a type, which indicates what type of object they can refer to, types include *Global, Event* and *Free*. Global variables are global in the sense that they are shared between the states and the transitions of the evaluation machine. Changes to the value of a global variable made in one transition will be seen by all transitions in that evaluation machine. Event and free variables are local variables. That means that they are only available in the context of the current transition. Free variables are declared as part of a transition, and the system will assign them to any object that causes the conditions to be satisfied. Event variables are parameters that are tied to an event. ITSAT includes variable editors for all types of variables.

The **Principles** region allows for adding/removing passing/failing principles for this transition. When a transition is taken, the student is credited with passing all the "passing" principles indicated, and is considered to have failed all the "failing" principles. To attach a principle to the transition, simply select it in the drop-down list. Then, choose to add it to one of four categories: passing, warning, failing, and dialog. When the transition fires, an action will be performed based on the category of the attached principle(s). For *passing* principles, a success will simply be noted in the principle hierarchy. *Warning* principles indicate that if the principle has a warning associated with it, then this warning should be displayed to the user. In the OMIA system, this is known as an enhancement and shows up on the multi-function display. A warning of *TryCOM1 PL4* is shown in Fig. 11. If a *failing* principle is attached it is noted that the principle was failed in the principle hierarchy.

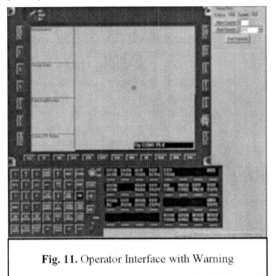

Fig. 11. Operator Interface with Warning

The *transaction type* field specifies what kind of transition this is. This provides feedback in the evaluation summary as to whether this transition is purely informational, whether it means some event occurred, or whether the student performed some action that caused this transition to be taken. In any case, this field is only applicable for transitions in which no principles are passed or failed, and it has no impact on the evaluation.

The *description* field annotates the transition with comments that may be displayed to the student after they're evaluated, i.e., in an ex postfacto summary report. The *comment* field is used to describe the transition in plain English, e.g., to provide explanation to other authors.

3.4   Decision Tree Editor

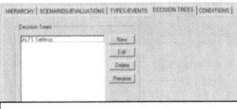

Fig. 12. Decision Tree Tab

OMIA's major contribution to the ITSAT tool is the addition of decision trees. A decision tree (DT) provides a powerful new type of event transition condition. The complex environment in which the MH-60S and MH-60R helicopters operate requires judgments that must take into account many variables. In addition, there are situations where multiple answers are correct. For multiple answer situations EFSMs could be constructed to handle them, but handling them in the context of the DT proved much cleaner.

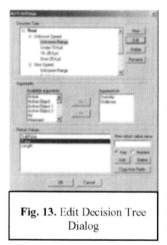

Fig. 13. Edit Decision Tree Dialog

The OMIA development could have built the DT capability outside the context of ITSAT, however, it was determined early that the power of DTs is formidable and should be included as a key component of ITSAT. The Decision Tree Editor follows the look and feel of the rest of ITSAT. The *Decision Tree* tab in ITSAT, as shown in Fig. 12, provides the basic mechanisms for creating *New* decision trees, as well as the ability to E*dit, Delete* and *Rename* decision trees.

The dialog accessed via the *Edit* button, see Fig. 13, begins to reveal the power of the decision tree editor. All DTs have a **Root** node, from the **Root** node one may add (*New*) nodes, as well as *Edit, Delete,* and *Rename* nodes. This dialog also allows for the selection of arguments available to the nodes and the return values.

There are a series of dialogs that allows for the creation of nodes, nodes can be one of three types, Leaf, Evaluate, or switch. An example of a complete leaf node is shown in Fig. 14.. This is the Leaf node for the Unknown Speed, Unknown Range branch of the decision tree shown in Fig. 13.

The decision tree editor addition to the ITSAT tool has proven valuable to the OMIA ITS development, both in the development of decision trees and in the maintenance and understanding of them.

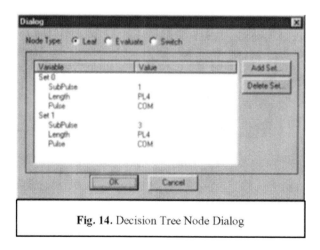

Fig. 14. Decision Tree Node Dialog

4 Conclusion

The complexity and number of the sensors under control of the crew on the MH-60S and MH-60R helicopters pose a difficult training task for the Navy. To meet this challenge SHAI is developing a comprehensive Operator Machine Interface Assistant system that employs a principle hierarchy based intelligent tutoring system. SHAI has exploited its own rapid development intelligent tutoring system authoring tool to construct the principal hierarchy, the evaluation finite state machines, decision trees and other portions of the ITS. The intelligent tutoring system authoring tool's capabilities have continued to expand as more and more SHAI ITS projects have found the tool valuable and then enhanced the tool to add any new capability required be particular ITS projects. The enhancements have been added under the same general framework so that added power and flexibility have come with only a small increase in user complexity. OMIA is no exception, the decision tree capability has been added during OMIA's development process. OMIA, benefiting from the power of ITSAT, has proven its value to the US Navy, as it is currently in use to train MH-60S crew as further development continues.

References

1. Bloom, B. S., (1984). The 2 sigma problem: The search for methods of group instruction as effective as one-to-one tutoring. Educational Researcher, 13(6): 4-16.
2. Bransford, J. D., Brown, A. L., & Cocking, R. R. (Eds.) (1999). How People Learn: Brain, Mind, Experience, and School. Washington D. C.: National Academy Press.
3. Stottler, R. H., & Vinkavich, M. (2000). Tactical action officer intelligent tutoring system (TAO ITS). I/ITSEC 2000 Proceedings.
4. Ludwig, Jeremy L. & Henry Jackson (2001). A Common Cockpit Training System. I/ITSEC 2001 Proceedings.
5. Stottler, R. H., Fu, D., Ramachandran, S. & Vinkavich, M. (2001). Applying a Generic Intelligent Tutoring System (ITS) Authoring Tool to Specific Military Domains. I/ITSEC 20001 Proceedings.

ASIMIL: Overview of a Distance Learning Flight-Training System

Michel Aka and Claude Frasson

Département d'informatique et de recherche opérationnelle
Université de Montréal
C.P. 6128, Succ. Centre-Ville
Montréal, Québec Canada H3C 3J7
{akakoasm, frasson}@iro.umontreal.ca

Abstract. This paper describes the implementation of a distance learning flight-training system. We described the various methods used during the implementation of the software (Virtual reality and Case Based Reasoning). ASIMIL proposes a client/server architecture that enables the user to have automated real-time assistance in addition to normal error detection.

1   Introduction

Recent years have led to the emergence of new Training approaches. The fast growth of computer technology and global network communications has made distance learning a reality. In general, Training takes form in two ways: Theory and practice.

Flight training is the main objective of the ASIMIL (Aero user-friendly SIMulation-based distance Learning) project. ASIMIL aims at developing a tool that will train and sharpen the skills of pilots in the Aeronautical domain. By the combining Virtual Reality (VR) and Case Based Reasoning (CBR) we hope to enhance the traditional training processes.

In "Functional requirements of a simulator prototype in Virtual Reality" [1], we defined the following requirements, covering most of ASIMIL's aspects:

The Control Requirements of the flight simulator describe the Physical aspects that have to be reproduced in the virtual environment. Control requirements also define what the learner can control during the flight.

- The Display requirements of the flight simulator describe the visual manifestation of instruments and the outside world. They also emphasize the importance quality and fluidity of the simulation.
- The Basic architecture requirements are defined in order to lead the implementation of the application. This application is required to work over TCP/IP (Transfer control protocol / Internet Protocol).

To meet these requirements we decided to implement a client/server application. Students (also called learners) practice by completing exercises that run on the client side of the application. Teachers (also known as instructors or experts) can monitor the learners' activities on the server side of the application. The exercises consist of

S.A. Cerri, G. Gouardères, and F. Paraguaçu (Eds.): ITS 2002, LNCS 2363, pp. 484–495, 2002.
© Springer-Verlag Berlin Heidelberg 2002

accomplishing multiple tasks in a three-dimensional (3D) simulation. Rules have to be respected and conditions have to be met in order to complete the exercises.

During the execution of an exercise, students may commit errors by not respecting the predefined sequence. In real life, when such a situation occurs, the human flight instructor is able to detect the error. But most importantly, he is able to determine the cause of this error in order to optimize the learner's knowledge acquisition. This is a very important factor in the learning process because the student is practicing and can be corrected at the same time; taking advantage of the instructor's experience. ASIMIL tries to mimic the presence of the human instroctor.

Several key elements influenced our choices of implementation:

- The proper identification of errors.
- The abundance of changeable parameters in each situation.
- The need to have adequate explanations and help corresponding to each situation.

The Virtual Aeronautical Instructor (VAI) is one of the main modules in ASIMIL. It identifies and reacts to all errors committed during the execution of the exercise. VAI's implementation is based upon Case Based Reasoning (CBR) technology. As an Artificial Intelligence (AI) technique, CBR enables us to solve problems by correctly identifying them and associating them to their corresponding solutions. VAI is not only used to understand mistakes but also to prevent them. A human Instructor is able, in some cases, to anticipate a failure or identify a situation that leads to an eminent error. VAI acquires its anticipation technique by monitoring the advices given by human instructors.

Through out this paper we will familiarize ourselves with VR and CBR. We will then focus on the implementation technique used to achieve the goals of this project.

2   VR and CBR: A Brief Description

2.1   Virtual Reality

Virtual Reality is a discipline that enables human beings to interface with multi-dimensional environments created by computer data [2]. By the alteration of senses (vision, sound and touch), Virtual Reality mimics a real environment or creates a new one that superimposes itself on to the real world. The user of a VR application is said to be immerged in a computer generated world [15].

2.2   Case Based Reasoning

Case Base Reasoning is a problem-solving paradigm [3][12]. Unlike other major AI approaches, CBR is able to utilize specific knowledge of previously experienced problems/situations (cases). It can generate a solution for a new problem by relying on similar past cases, and every time CBR solves a case or fails to do so, it memorizes it. As it encounters more and more new cases, CBR is able to gain experience. It is said to be revolutionary technique because it mimics the way humans learn by using past experience [4][14].

The seeds of case based reasoning can be found in the AI works of Roger Schank on Dynamic Memory [5].

Case memory is the structure where all cases of the CBR system are stored. There are two classes of Case Memory:

- Dynamic memory model: Here cases are organized in a hierarchical structure. Cases sharing similar properties are under the same general structure [6].
- Category and exemplar model: As an alternative way to organize memory, Ray Bareiss and Bruce Porter [7][8], proposed the Category and Exemplar model. The Category and Exemplar model has a network-oriented (figure 1) architecture. In this architecture features are linked to Exemplars and Categories. Exemplars represent sets of cases sharing common features. In the graph representing the Case Memory, these features are linked (directly or indirectly) to the Exemplar.

The way that CBR achieves problem solving can be divided into 4 main steps (figure 2):

- Case Retrieval: This is the process that identifies the best matching case (or cases) in the Case Memory in order to pair up the initial problem.
- Case Reuse: When the best-matching case for the initial problem has been found, we determine how that case's solution can be reused to fit the current situation.
- Case Revision: When Case Reuse generates a bad solution for a given problem, the CBR system has the opportunity to learn from its mistake. That method is called Case Revision.
- Case Retrain: After determining the new case's solution, a new index entry is created for the case if needed and the new case's structure is created. It is then added to Case Memory.

3   Architecture and Implementation of ASIMIL

3.1   General Architecture

On the top most level of architecture ASIMIL is a client/server application that operates over TCP/IP-compatible networks.

The role of the server side of the application is to regroups all activities that are in relation to the instructor. These activities consist of supervision, management, follow up and providing online Help. These functionalities are derived from the fact that the server is tied to the instructor's roll. The server can only manage a certain amount of connections (students/clients). This limitation is mostly imposed by network speed capacity and computational capabilities. The CBR engine is also implemented on the server side of the application.

The client (figure 3) side of the application provides the student with the tools necessary for him to learn and practice his piloting skills.

Also integrated in the client GUI a TTS agent reads out the all-incoming messages from server. This enables the learner to have knowledge of the instructor's words without taking his eyes off the cockpit.

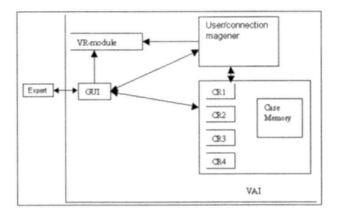

Fig. 1. Server Architecture

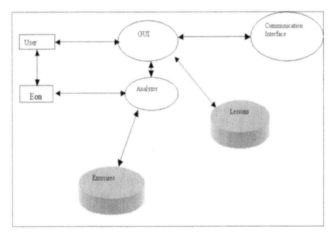

Fig. 2. Client-side architecture

3.2   Implementation

3.2.1   VR Module's Conception

In ASIMIL the VR module creates the 3D virtual environment inside which the learner will carry out his exercises.

This virtual environment is created in 2 steps:

- The modeling of all the objects to be present in the simulation. Modeling is done with the help of 3D Studio Max (Software that enables the user to create virtual environments).
- The integration of the various objects into a scene where every object has its own property. This work was realized thanks to Eon Studio (Software that enables the user to define interactivity and virtual objects' behavior) [13].

The simulation itself is completely independent from the rest of the software. It can be run as a normal flight simulator, where one would fly the plane without any precise objective.

In ASIMIL, the simulation communicates with VAI by sending and receiving messages. These messages are related to: The aircraft's position, the aircraft's orientation, the aircraft's speed, the aircraft's vertical speed, the flap's positions, the state of the Brakes, the state of the Gears, throttle, wind force, wind direction and visibility.

The Flight Dynamic Model (FDM) is the set of calculations and rules that regulates the aircraft's behavior in the virtual environment (Simulation). The earlier versions of the FDM were not adequate because they tried to simulate the aircraft's behavior instead of trying to make the plane move accordingly to the rules that make up its environment. In other words we simulated the laws of physics in the virtual environment including the forces that have an impact on the plane: Gravity, lift, drag and thrust.

In the current model in order for the plane to fly it has to overcome the force of gravity. Hence his lift has to be greater than that of the force that gravity permanently applied on it [11].

The computation required in ASIMIL's flight dynamic model happens in a cyclic manner. The forces are first computed to helps us determine the aircraft's ground speed and vertical speed. At the end of each cycle the new aircraft position is calculated. The cycle then repeats itself.

There are two types of simulations used in ASIMIL. They can be qualified as passive and active simulations.

When the learner starts an exercise and flies an aircraft in the virtual environment he uses the active simulation. The active simulation is able to capture the learner's input and modify
the simulation accordingly.

Remote viewing is the process through which the expert can follow the student's actions inside a virtual environment. The remote viewing takes place on the server side of the application and is made possible through the use of a simulation that is called passive. The passive simulation is only used on the server side of the application. Once the expert activates the remote viewing, the passive simulation is loaded. The passive simulation is very similar to the active simulation except it cannot be flown; instead it receives its input over the network from the client side of ASIMIL.

3.2.2   Analyzer Module

An exercise (Lift-off, Landing, Taxi, Straight level flight...) is a simulation that has to follow a predefined sequence in order for it to be carried out properly. A sequence is said to be an arrangement of items according to a specific set of rules, for example items arranged alphabetically, numerically, or chronologically [9].

In ASIMIL, a sequence is an arranged set of states that defines the precise chronological order that the learner's aircraft has to follow. In the following section we will take a look at the implementation of exercises, error detection, and post exercise assistance.

3.2.2.1   Definition of Current State and Concept

We define a state as a set of parameters that describe the simulation at a precise moment in time. The parameters can be divided into three categories:

- Aircraft's coordinates parameters
    - Aircraft's latitude and longitude
    - Aircraft's altitude
    - Aircraft's heading, pitch and roll
- Control panel's parameters
    - Aircraft's speed
    - Aircraft's vertical speed
    - Flaps' position
    - Breaks' state
    - Gears' state
    - Throttle
- Environmental parameters
    - Wind's direction
    - Wind's speed
    - Visibility

If St_i is the state of the simulation at time i we can say that:

$$St_i=([P_i],[CP_i],[ENV_i]) \ . \tag{1}$$

Where $[P_i]$, $[CR_i]$ and $[ENV_i]$ are respectively the set of values that represent the aircraft's coordinates, control panel parameters and environmental parameters at time i. These parameters are either Booleans or numerical values. When a parameter is a numerical value, it is represented by an interval. This form of representation (allowed interval of the parameter) is only used in the sequence and not used to describe the current state of the simulation. It is useful because it helps us generalize a sequence's state (a step) as an amalgam of acceptable states.

We call transition the transformation which, when applied to a state, leads us to the following state. Given a current state St_i, we can obtain St_{i+1} by applying the required T_i transformation at time i on St_i:

$$T_i(([P_i],[CP_i],[ENV_i]))=([P_{i+1}],[CP_{i+1}],[ENV_{i+1}]) \ . \tag{2}$$

$$T_i(St_i)=St_{i+1} \ .$$

By analogy the exercise sequence is also the series of transformations required to go from the initial state to the final state. Each transformation corresponds to the set of user inputs that will transform a given state into the next.

A concept is the notion that is associated to a step of the sequence. Each step of the sequence is characterized by a combination of concepts. The only step of the sequence that is not associated with a concept is the last step (St-n in the figure 4). Most of the time, there is only one concept associated to a step of the sequence. This is because usually one notion is enough to describe the transition that takes place

(Example: Brakes removal or 45 degrees right turn). But occasionally a sequence's transition may require more than one concept in its definition.

The expert's decision is another reason that would explain the fact that a step is associated to more than one concept. During the exercise's conception, the expert may feel that the presence of a given step St_i is useless in that course. Therefore the expert might remove the step St_i and associates its set of concepts $\{C-i\}$ to St_{i-1}'s. St_{i-1} will then be associated to $\{C-(i-1)\} \cup \{C-i\}$.

We just saw how concepts are paired up with exercise sequence steps, we will now see how concepts are linked to lessons.

3.2.2.2   Concepts

Concepts are both linked to exercises and lessons in two databases (Concepts-Lessons and Concepts-Exercises). Notions relative to a specific concept can be present in more than one lesson.

We could directly link steps of the exercise's sequence to their corresponding lessons without the intermediate of concepts. We chose to use concepts because it helps us better categorize these relations for the expert, especially during exercise creation. It must be pointed out that the sequence-steps/concepts/lessons architecture is completely transparent to the learner. The learner is only conscious of the mistake he did and is given the correct lessons at the end of the exercise.

3.2.2.3   Error Detection and Lessons Designation
Error detection
In ASIMIL, error detection is the process through which the analyzer is able to detect the user's mistake during the execution of the exercise.

We previously saw that the steps in the sequence correspond to the different states that the simulation has to follow. We also saw that steps of the sequence can represent a set of acceptable states. Now we will see how the sequence is checked.

Let $St_{current}$ be the current state of the simulation. $St_{current}$ does not need to have intervals to describe its numerical values because the precise values are obtained from the simulation.

An error occurs when the current state of the simulation does not correspond to the current state described in the sequence. In other words, there is an error when the sequence is not respected.

The algorithm used to detect an error at a given state is show in below.

Let $P_n(St_x)$ be the function that returns the nth parameter of step x. $P_n(St_x)$ can be an interval if it is a numerical value.

Let C be the set of broken concepts

The error detection () algorithm goes as follow:

```
START ----

          While n <= number of parameters of St_i do :
```

If $P_n(St_i)$ is a Boolean

    If $P_n(St_{current})$ is equal to $P_n(St_i)$ continue

       Else add the associated concept to the list of broken

concepts : $C = C \cup \{C - i\}$

    Else ($P_n(St_i)$ is a set of numerical value

    If $P_n(St_{current}) \in P_n(St_i)$ continue

       Else add the associated concept to the list of broken

concepts : $C = C \cup \{C - i\}$

    Get the next parameter: $n = n + 1$

Return C

END ----

During the error detection phase, the analyzer compares all the parameters of the current state with the parameters of the step of the sequence. If all the parameters match, nothing is done and we just move on to the next step. On the other hand, if two different parameters are found, the concepts associated to the current step of the sequence are noted. These concepts will find their use in the lesson designation phase.

Lesson Designation
In this phase, the analyzer will determine all the lessons that the user must study according to the errors that he made during the exercise. Before the analyzer can define the list of lessons to be revised it must first get the list of all the concepts corresponding to the user's mistake.

Let $Det(St_i, St_{current})$ the function that accomplishes error detection given a state St_i and a current simulation state $St_{current}$. That function returns the set of concepts (broken concepts) that are associated to St_i. $Det(St_i, St_{current}) = \{C - i\}$.

Let BC be the set of broken concepts at the end of an exercise.

$$BC = \bigcup_{i=o}^{i=f} Det(St_i, St_{current(i)}) = \bigcup_{i=0}^{i=f} \{C - i\} \ . \tag{3}$$

where f is the number of step in the exercise sequence and $St_{current(i)}$ is the current state of the simulation when the analyzer is at the ith step.

Once we have all the broken concepts all the lessons that are linked to these concepts are added to a list. The list is forwarded the GUI (Graphical User Interface) in order for them to be directly accessible by the user.

3.2.3   The Virtual Aeronautical Instructor

The Virtual Aeronautical Instructor is responsible for analyzing and explaining errors committed by the user. VAI can also anticipate user-mistakes and provide the student with assistance that might prevent an exercise-threatening situation. When VAI anticipates an error it informs the expert (if any is present) by using color codes applied on the user's name. These colors indicate the importance of the mistake. VAI comes as an addition to the Analyzer module which main roll is to correct and not assist.

A VAI case represents the state of the user's simulation at a given moment in time. Every case is associated with a paragraph that provides explanation and/or assistance.

The client side of ASIMIL periodically sends simulation update messages to the server. When these informations are received VAI uses it to make a target case (a case to be searched inside Case Memory). It then utilizes its CBR engine to retrieve eventual error-anticipations. An error-anticipation is possible only if the expert had made a previous anticipation in a similar situation.

When the user commits an error, the state of the simulation is sent to the server along with the set of concepts that had been broken. Again VAI builds a target case and searches the Case Memory for an error corresponding to the situation, if none exists it generates a new solution.

In case of delay, the client side of the application still provides the student with the response from VAI. However in case of major delay the response is simply disregarded. Non-the less the learner can carry on with his exercise since the analyzer module can determine what concepts were fouled.

3.2.3.1   VAI's Case Memory

A VAI case represents the state of the simulation at a given moment in time. VAI is able to detect and anticipate errors by comparing the current context of the simulation with similar contexts that led to errors present in the Case Memory. Every case is associated to the text that will be used to provide explanation to the learner. VAI's case Memory is the collection of all cases that are known to VAI. It is made of initial cases and the cases gained by experience. This Case Memory is organized in a Dynamic memory model pattern that has a hierarchical structure.

There are fourteen levels that constitute the hierarchy. The Case Memory has a maximum length of 14 branches. Each level uses a specific parameter for indexing (altitude, speed, heading, concepts…).

Let I_x represent the interval of possible integer values that the xth parameter.

$$I_x = \bigcup_{i=1}^{i=n} I_{ix}$$ where I_{ix} is the ith section of the interval I_x. It corresponds to the

i^{th} branch of a node.

Let $P_x(C)$ be the value of the xth parameter of the case C. During insertion and retrieval, in order to know the branch of the tree under which C is indexed, we look for the interval where:

$$P_x(C) \in I_{ix}.$$

At the xth level of the case memory, C can be found under the sub-tree referenced by the ith branch.

The interval division method was favored here because we were concerned about the size of case memory. If we had used the integer values of each parameter for indexing, we would have had a case memory structure too large to be implementable.

Table 1. Example of indexing using Interval repartition of the pitch

Pitch values	Index
<-20	0
[-20, -15[	1
[-15, -10[	2
[-10, -5[	3
[-5, 0[	4
...	...

VAI's treatment of new cases (target cases) is made in a cyclic manner. VAI's cycle is derived from the CBR cycle described by Aamodt and E. Plaza [3]. Through this cycle VAI is able to achieve situation identification, provide assistance to the user and gain experience. In order to find the appropriate phrases that will help the user, VAI has to retrieve the cases that resemble the most the target case. This is known as case retrieval.

3.2.3.2   Case Retrieval in VAI
Case Retrieval's roll lies on the ability to find a set of cases that are similar or equal to the target case. Case retrieval can be divided in sub steps known as: Feature identification, search and select.

Feature identification: Prior to performing a search in the case memory, in the case of a user-committed error, the information relative to user's simulation are used to create a target case. Once our target case is complete we can begin looking for it in the Case Memory.

Search and select: The objective of this step is to find the set of cases that resemble the most the target case. When the target case is in the Case Memory, we simply follow the index entries that correspond to its parameters to find it. When the target case is not in the Case Memory, all the cases in a precise subsection of Case Memory are compared to the target case. The comparison is done by a function that assesses the similarity between the target case and the cases in memory. The similarity is computed by calculating the difference of the cases parameters along with their respective weights. The case with the best similarity assessment is selected. Unfortunately, some times two or more cases happen to have very analogous similarity assessments; In this case they are all selected.

3.2.3.3   *Case Reuse in VAI*

Case reuse is the step where the explanation that will be given to the user is generated. Depending on the Case Retrieval's results Case Reuse will either copy or merge some cases' solutions to generate the target case's solution.

If the target case was already in memory then there is no need to apply Case Reuse. When Case Retrieval returns only one case, the solution is copied.
When the Case Memory returns more that one case then the solutions are concatenated and separated by "or". The target case is also marked as "not certified".

3.2.3.4   *Case Revision in VAI*

This step of VAI's cycle does not necessarily take place in real time. All the cases that are marked as "not certified" have to be reviewed by the expert. If the explanation and help do not correspond to the situation then the expert corrects the case. Cases that have recurrent complaints from user feedback are also marked as "not certified". This step helps VAI to better its error analyzing capabilities.

3.2.3.5   *Case Retain in VAI*

Once a new solution has been generated for the target case VAI can add it to its case memory. The target case is added according to the indexing method that makes up the Case Memory.

4   Conclusion

As a client/server software, ASIMIL is a tool that integrates Virtual Reality, Artificial Intelligence and distance learning. We have seen that assistance is brought to the user in real time and after each exercise when needed. The assistance provided in ASIMIL is mostly an automated process but it can also be given directly by the instructor thanks to the possibility of remotely viewing the learner's actions.

Future developments of ASIMIL consider the addition of user profile and improvements in the indexing method used by VAI. These improvements will also help in the automatic determination of the lessons that are to be taught to a user.

References

1. Francesca De Crescenzio: Functional requirements of a simulator prototype in Virtual Reality 4-9, in Proceedings for ASIMIL (2001).

2. Francesca De Crescenzio, Gouarderes G., Lefebvre P., Frasson C.: State of the art on Virtual Reality, in Proceedings for ASIMIL (2000).
3. Agnar Aamodt , Enric Plaza: Case Based Reasoning: Functional Issues, Methodological Variations, and System Approaches, in AI Communications 7-(1):39-59 (1994).
4. Anderson J. R.: The Architecture of cognition, Harvard University press, Cambridge (1983).
5. Schank R.: Dynamic memory; a theory of reminding a learning in computers and people. Cambridge University Press (1982).
6. Kolodner J.: Maintaining organization in dynamic long-term memory, in Cognitive Science Vol. 7 243-280 (1983).
7. Bareiss R.: Exemplar-Bases Knowledge Acquisition: A Unified Approach to Concept Representation, Classification and Learning. San Diego: Academic Press (1989).
8. Porter B., Bareiss R. and Holte R.: Concept learning and heuristic classification in weak theory domain. In Artificial Intelligence, vol. 45, no. 1-2, September 1990, pp229-263 (1990).
9. URL: http://www.its.bldrdoc.gov/fs-1037/dir-032/_4774.htm (1996).
10. Cognitive Systems: ReMind: Developer's Reference Manual, 220-230 Commercial St., Boston, MA 02109 (1992).
11. Shawn Blaszak,, Aaron Goldshall, George Suarez: http://library.thinkquest.org/2819/forces.htm (1996).
12. Jaczynski Michel: Etudes du Raisonnement par cas: recherche de cas similaire en utilisant des ensemble flous , Rapport de Stage de 3eme annee, DEA Informatique Universite de Nice (1993).
13. Eon Reality: Eon Reality Inc. http://www.eonreality.com/ (2002).
14. E. L. Rissland, J. Kolodner and D. Waltz: Case based reasoning. Morgan Kaufman editor, DARPA 89: CBR workshop 1-13 (1989).
15. URL : http://www.isi.edu/isd/VET/vet.html

Cognitive Modelling Approach to Diagnose Over-Simplification in Simulation-Based Training

Andreas Lüdtke, Claus Möbus, and Heinz-Jürgen Thole

University of Oldenburg, Department of Computer Science, Germany,
{luedtke, moebus, thole}@informatik.uni-oldenburg.de,
http://lls.informatik.uni-oldenburg.de

Abstract. Simulation-based training has become a standard in operational knowledge training for supervisory control in safety-critical environments. But traditional simulators do not support mental model formation of automated systems though these systems are a dominant part in modern control systems. Recently various "intelligent components" for this support have been suggested. But these approaches neglect the dynamic character of mental models. They focus on building a normative model at the beginning of the training but do not consider how it evolves due to knowledge acquisition processes. In this paper we present a model-based approach to diagnose success-driven learning in simulator training and to predict dangerous over-simplifications. Our research focuses on pilot training for automated cockpits.

1 Introduction

New developments in computer technology made high fidelity simulators with a very close resemblance to reality possible. Simulator training allows students to develop operational skills without harming their own life, that of others or real world equipment. But simulation-based learning has to be accompanied by good support and feedback on the learners' behaviour [7]. Recently several researchers emphasized the need for intelligent technologies that diagnose the student's performance and are able to assist the learner [1,8] and to adapt simulated scenarios accordingly [18]. As Connolly et al. [1] state it, "the focus of development efforts should be on incorporating intelligent technologies into these simulators rather than emphasizing the relative fidelity of the systems" (p. 535). In modern highly automated cockpits the need for "intelligent components" that support the construction of adequate mental models of the automatic systems has been pointed out [10,15]. Most tasks have been automated and the pilot's role can be understood as supervisory control [17]. He has to program the automatic systems, to observe their behaviour and to intervene when an error occurs. This role imposes increased demand on the mental capabilities. A crucial question is whether pilots can cope with them and are able to build an adequate mental model of the systems behaviour at the beginning of the training and will maintain it when gaining

S.A. Cerri, G. Gouardères, and F. Paraguaçu (Eds.): ITS 2002, LNCS 2363, pp. 496–506, 2002.

experience. Humans develop routine, which makes their performance faster. But on the other hand routine may also lead to over-simplifications (OS) [4] that appear to work well in normal situations but lead to error in exceptional cases. This may result in catastrophic human errors as a number of accidents show. Thus it is not enough to support mental model formation at the beginning of the training. Moreover we have to take into account knowledge acquisition processes that take part when the pilot applies his normative model. In this paper an approach based on a two-layered pilot model is presented. The first layer is a normative mental model of auto pilot (AP) behaviour and the second a success-driven knowledge acquisition process with access to the first layer. We intent to connect it to a flight simulator in order to diagnose OS based on the performance trace of the pilot student. In Ohlsson's categorisation [14] our pilot model is a simulation model, because it is able to construct the student's problem solving path step by step. Other approaches to pilot modeling (e.g. MIDAS [2], Javaux's and Oliver's approach [6]) differ from our model because they do not consider knowledge acquisition processes.

The cognitive approach relies on the empirically proofed ISP-DL (Impasse-Success-Problem Solving-Driven Learning) theory of knowledge acquisition [11, 13]. In our working group this psychological theory guided the development of IPSEs (Intelligent Problem Solving Environments) in various domains, for instance functional programming in the ABSYNT project. We have adapted the framework according to pilot domain requirements and used it to formalise normative operational rules for an AP system. The contents of the rules have been extracted from type rating documents and interviews. According to the ISP-DL theory experienced pilots will need less planning than novices, because they act according to stored and well-tried but still dynamically changing schemata [12]. Schemata are constructed through success-driven learning, optimised for routine situations but lacking specific features for exceptional situations. Thus they may be used to model OS.

After an introduction we present a brief explanation of a typical pilot error. The main part of this paper contains the detailed description of the modeling framework followed by an empirical case study.

2   Explanation of an Exemplary Pilot Error

An empirical study in a full-motion Piper Cheyenne flight simulator was conducted at Lufthansa Flight Training in order to identify and explain systematic pilot errors concerning the AP operation. The following error of subject A (fig. 1) happened in a step-climb manoeuvre and according to flight instructors could happen to almost every pilot:

After start the aircraft was cleared from air traffic control for 4000 ft. The pilot dialled this altitude in the 'Alerter' and selected it by pressing the ALTS-Button, which causes the AP to go into 'Altitude Select' mode. Then he pressed the ETRIM-Button to increase vertical speed (VS). Suggested VS for a climb is 2000 ft/min but it has to be adjusted to keep the indicated airspeed (IAS) above the 160 knts limit - increased VS causes IAS to decrease. The adjustment should be delegated to the AP by activating the IAS mode via the IAS-Button. Subject A waited for IAS to reach 160 knts in order to activate IAS mode in the correct moment. Approximately 300 ft before the selected altitude (Lead Point) the AP automatically transitions to 'Capture' mode and decreases VS so that the aircraft smoothly levels off. When finally 160 knts were reached and subject A pressed the IAS-Button the automatic transition to 'Capture' mode had already occured. Surprisingly for the pilot the aircraft did not level off at 4000 ft but continued to climb. Stabilising IAS is not allowed in 'Capture' mode. The problem was that transition to 'Capture' mode occurred exceptionally early and was not noticed, because the pilot had not expected it.

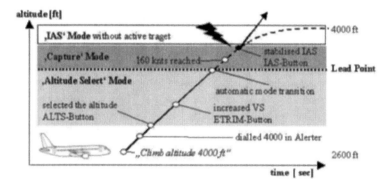

Fig. 1. Trajectory of the exemplary pilot error

To explain this error we constructed and analysed a formal model of the AP mode logic considering the relevant modes. Our analysis was guided by the work of Degani [3] and Leveson et al. [9]. Both suggested structural design features that may be a source for human error. We found a number of instantiations of these in the AP mode logic. For instance "inconsistent behaviour" in connection with the IAS-Button (fig. 2): When it is pressed in 'Altitude Select' mode, IAS mode becomes active, and the selected altitude is kept as an active target. But when pressed in 'Capture' mode though again IAS mode becomes active the selected altitude is no longer an active target - the manoeuvre is cancelled.

From the psychological perspective the "branching error" concept of Reason [16] applies to our scenario, because the initial sequence for both cases (160 knts reached in 'Altitude Select' or in 'Capture' mode) is the same (fig. 2). Then the pilot gets to a "critical decision point" before pressing the IAS-Button. He has to look carefully for the automatic mode transition. Formal interviews revealed that principally pilots know about that decision point, which leads to the assumption that initially both paths are represented in the mental model. But during training pressing the IAS-Button becomes a habit (bold arrows in fig. 2) because most times the transition occurs late enough. In accordance to the "branching error" concept we fade out alternative actions in our present pilot model based merely on the frequency of their successful application in the past.

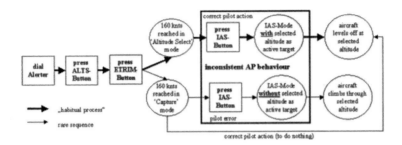

Fig. 2. Inconsistent AP behaviour after IAS-Button

3   Modelling Framework

To build the pilot model we take advantage of the goals-means-relation (GMR) modeling framework that was originally used in the ABSYNT project [11,12] to simulate knowledge acquisition processes. ABSYNT is a functional visual programming language, indeed a tree representation of pure LISP. Using a problem-solving monitor (PSM) a learner acquires basic functional programming concepts while working on programming tasks. The learner starts with basic pieces of knowledge acquired in theoretical lessons. If he succeeds in solving a familiar task, the knowledge he used is optimised by eliminating planning steps. Next time when working on a similar problem he will perform faster because of a shorter problem-solving path. In ABSYNT this process of success-driven learning is modelled by composition of simple GMR rules, which yields schemata and moreover whole solution cases. In the pilot context GMRs are used to represent the pilot's knowledge about how to operate the AP - the operational rules. Rule composition serves to model the development of "habitual processes" and OS in this context. In order to use the ABSYNT modeling framework in this way the two domains have been compared carefully in detail. The text that follows provides a summary of this comparison and a brief description of the knowledge representation for the pilot domain.

The main difference is that the pilot acts in a dynamic environment whereas the ABSYNT domain is static. The state of the aircraft constantly changes caused not only by the pilot but also by external influences. The modelling framework has to take this into account. First the various problem-solving activities have been compared. The ISP-DL theory states that the problem-solving process can be decomposed into phases very alike to the Rubicon Theory [5]:

- In the deliberation phase the problem solver decides to strive for the goal to solve a chosen or given task. Task goals in ABSYNT are specifyed by a predicative requirement that has to be fulfilled by a program yet to be created. In the pilot domain task goals are predicatively specifyed by flight parameters (e.g. altitude) to be achieved by a manoeuvre yet to be performed.
- In the planning phase the problem solver elaborates goals into implementable sub goals. In ABSYNT the result is a plan containing a set of language primitives the learner intends to arrange in the PSM. These actions only depend on goals and previously executed actions. Because of the dynamic environment the pilot must constantly check the current situation. He derives a plan containing a set of intended checks on the displays and movements of control instruments(CI).
- In the execution phase plans are executed. ABSYNT actions refer to mouse movements to arrange graphical icons in the PSM. In the pilot domain there are move-actions refering to movements of CI (e.g. pressing buttons) and check-actions refering to checks on displays to get information about the AP and the aircraft.
- In the evaluation phase the result of the actions is evaluated according to the task goal. In ABSYNT only the final program is evaluated, not those actions that have been "undone". In the pilot domain every single action is interpreted instantly by the AP and influences the goal achievement. Most times incorrect pilot actions can be alleviated by counteractions, but this increases pilots' workload and extends the manoeuvre time. So, the whole action trace has to be evaluated and not only the final result.

Next we present the comparison with regard to knowledge representation:

Concept	General Description	Characteristics in ABSYNT	Characteristics in the pilot domain
Goals	are derived and detailed during planning	represented by predicates describing a goal with associated sub goals	the predicates additionally describe instruments to be checked
Means	set of operator and leaf nodes	operator nodes represent programming language primitives; leaf nodes stand for parameters and constants	operator nodes represent move- and check-actions; leaf nodes represent state expressions that should be true after execution
GMR	associates a goal with a means	associates programming goals with LISP primitives	associates manoeuvre goals with pilot actions (checks and moves)

GMR rules	GMR is implemented in a set of rules in a Horn clause format. The GMR on the left hand side (Head) of a rule holds, if all GMRs on the right (Body) are true. There are four types of rules: task rules, goal elaboration rules, operator rules, and leaf rules		
Task rules	convert a task goal into a planning goal and impose constraints for the means	the task is to construct a program that fulfills the task goal	the task is to combine actions in an adequate chronological order and dependency that fulfills the task goal
Goal elaboration rules	differentiate a goal but the implementation is postponed	reification of goals made goal elaboration "executable" in the PSM	reification of goals is not desirable because of workload considerations
Operator rules	describe how goals can be achieved by operator nodes	describe the implementation of programming goals	describe the realisation of manoeuvre goals and constrain the execution of move-actions on the result of check-actions
Leaf rules	special type of primitive operator rules	describe the implementation of parameters and constants by leaf nodes	describe the result of pilot actions by pilot leaf nodes

The main differences in knowledge representation are the list of instruments I contained in the goal representation and the semantics of operators. First, we have chosen to extend the representation of goals, because the instruments pilots have to look for always depends on the present goal respectively manoeuvre. For example in a 'free climb' (without selected altitude) there is no 'Capture' mode, thus there is no need to look for it before pressing the IAS-button. By comparing I with the instruments considered in the associated check-actions sources for OS can be identified. Second, the semantics of operators differs in the control flow. In the pilot domain move-actions are only executed if preceding check-actions deliver that necessary preconditions are fulfilled. If not the move-actions are canceled. In ABSYNT there is no such dependency.

Finally we adapt the learning component. In ABSYNT rule composition was used to model changes in the learner's knowledge after he has successfully solved similar tasks (success-driven learning). Rules are composed if they have been used in succession few times and if certain constraints are fulfilled (see performance hypotheses below). Technically this is done according to the cut rule:

$$\frac{F \longleftarrow P \mathrel{\&} C, \qquad P' \longleftarrow A}{(F \longleftarrow A \mathrel{\&} C)\ \sigma} \qquad \begin{array}{l}\text{P, P', F must be atoms (here: predicates)}\\ \text{A and C can be conjunctions of atoms}\end{array}$$

The two clauses above the line resolve to the clause below the line by merging them and thereby eliminating P and P'. P and P' must have at least one identical instantiation. σ stands for the most general unifier and is applied to the whole resolvent. As an example we consider the following two GMR rules written here as Horn clauses:

```
gmr(check_act_ias(instr(speed-ind,mode-annunciation,ias-button)),Act)) ←
    gmr(check1_ias(instr(speed-ind)), Check1)) &
    gmr(check2_ias(instr(mode-annunciation)), Check2)) &
    gmr(act_ias(instr(ias-button)),Act)).

gmr(check2_ias(instr(mode-annunciation)), unequal(value(MA),capture)) ←
    value(MA), MA ≠ capture.
```

The second GMR in the body of the first rule and the head of the second one can be unified if $\sigma =$[Check2 / unequal(value(MA),capture)]. Applying the cut rule yields the composite:

```
gmr(check_act_ias(instr(speed-ind,mode-annunciation,ias-button)),Act)) ←
    gmr(check1_ias(instr(speed-ind)), Check)) &
    (value(MA), MA ≠ capture) & gmr(act_ias(instr(ias-button)),Act)).
```

By composing rules "habitual processes" are modelled, but there is a major difference in rule composition between ABSYNT and the pilot domain. In AB-SYNT composition always generates correct rules. Whereas in the pilot domain we constructed the rules in way so that composition can lead to the elimination of check-actions. In the example the check for the capture phase is replaced by the assumption that this phase is not active. This technique serves to model OS. In ABSYNT four hypotheses about performance differences between novices and experts were derived, where gaining expertise means continuously building more condensed schemata until whole solution cases emerge. At present we apply two of these hypotheses to show empirical indications for rule composition:

Time hypothesis. The selection and execution of each rule takes time, so a pilot using composites should be faster than someone using simple rules.

No-interleaving hypothesis. Actions contained in the same means are processed without interruption by other means. Thus actions in different means should not interleave. This enables to predict a partial order on action steps in different GMR rules. For actions in composites this is not possible.

In the pilot domain these hypotheses serve to diagnose based on the performance trace what rules have been composed and over-simplified.

4   Applicability of Rule Composition – An Empirical Case Study

During the case study 4 flight students have been taped on video. Subject A was filmed in 7 missions (7 * 1.5h). The results of a protocol analysis for subject A in step-climb and step-descent manoeuvres are described. Each manoeuvre protocol resulted from a transcription of a video sequence that was stopped and transcribed every 2 seconds. Manoeuvre time varied from 1 to 4 min.

First we investigated the time hypothesis. We analysed the time the subject needed for the first three manoeuvre actions: Dialling in the altitude, selecting it, and pressing the ETRIM-Button the first time (fig. 3 up to manoeuvre 10). The ETRIM-Button has to be pressed a few times until the desired VS is reached, but this time span heavily depends on environmental factors like wind and air pressure. Thus we considered only the initial stroke. When the times for manoeuvre 3, 4, 8, and 10 are considered as outliers we can draw a line connecting the remaining values. We interpret that the required time gets constantly shorter. The outliers can be explained by tasks that had to be performed in parallel to the climb or descent and by the initial VS before the manoeuvre. E.g. before the fourth manoeuvre VS was already 1500 ft/min, so there was no need to adjust it immediately and he could activate climb power (a parallel task) first.

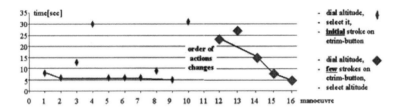

Fig. 3. Performance times for manoeuvres 1 to 11 and 12 to 16

One weak explanation for the faster performance is that the subject gets used to the location of the buttons. But according to our explanation the subject eliminates sub goals and thus needs less planning time. We model this speeding up by rule composition, which is plausible because the manoeuvres could be executed using the same set of rules.

Next we investigated the no-interleaving hypothesis. We assume that at the beginning of the training pilots have one simple rule for every single action, because there are individual constraints for each action. Thus according to the no-interleaving hypothesis for example altitude selection and decreasing VS should not interleave. But in the twelfth manoeuvre subject A starts to interleave exactly these two actions: He hits the ETRIM-Button a few times, then selects the altitude and continues with the ETRIM-Button until the prescribed VS is reached. This interleaving could be observed in all following manoeuvres. According to our model this interleaving is only possible if the subject has built a composite containing the actions for altitude selection and VS adjustment in the same means. He is no longer using the simple rules.

With this new rule set we investigated the time hypothesis again starting from the twelfth manoeuvre. We considered the same three actions as before, but this time in another order. We had to incorporate not only the initial stroke on the ETRIM-Button but all strokes he made before selecting altitude. This time span still leaves out the fine tuning of VS which heavily depends on environmental factors. As can be seen in fig. 3 (from manoeuvre 12 to 16) the time decreases with only one outlier. Because again all manoeuvres could be executed using the same set of rules (including the composite) and according to the time hypothesis our explanation is that further planning steps have been eliminated. In the 16th manoeuvre the subject commits the error described in section 2. This is the first time that the transition to 'Capture'-mode occurs before the 160 knts limit (the desired value for IAS stabilisation) is reached. The active mode is not noticed by the pilot and he stabilises IAS, which causes the plane to overshoot the cleared altitude. Thus we suppose that the necessary check has been eliminated during the rule composition and the resulting composite is over-simplified and applied under inappropriate conditions.

5   Conclusion and Further Work

We described a typical pilot error that was observed regularly in an empirical study we conducted at Lufthansa Flight Training during simulation-based pilot training. Based on theoretical work on system structure and human factors we found a hypothetical explanation of this error. The GMR modelling framework was adapted to the pilot context and serves the purpose of modelling a success-driven knowledge acquisition process by rule composition. This process leads to optimised knowledge ignoring necessary checks on display instruments, which can be understood as OS. Based on empirical data we have shown first indications for the applicability of our cognitive modeling approach. The model predictions will be used to improve learning environments for pilots. We envision integrating it with a flight simulator in order to diagnose OS of pilot students based on their performance trace. Identified OS shall be indicated to the flight instructor, how has to decide what to do. In further work the pilots' attentiveness to crucial automatic mode transitions of the AP has to be analysed thoroughly. Because in the empirical case study we observed, that the described error does not occur in situations with a high level of attentiveness. After the model is fully implemented and attentiveness is integrated it shall be evaluated as a whole.

Acknowledgements. We would like to thank the flight instructors and students at the Lufthansa Flight Training, especially the flight instructors Walter Dodel, Manfred Klapper and Christoph Ferenz. Many thanks also to Chief Flight

Instructor and Head of Training Harald Neumann who made the empirical study possible.

References

1. Conolly, C. A, 1Lt Johnson, J., MSgt Lexa, C.: AVATAR: An Intelligent Air Traffic Control Simulator and Trainer. In In B.P. Goettl et al. (eds.), Proceedings of the Fourth International Conference, ITS '98. Berlin [u.a.] : Springer (1998).
2. Corker, K.M.: Cognitive Models and Control: Human and System Dynamics in Advanced Airspace Operations. In N.B. Sarter, R. Amalberti (eds.), Cognitive Engineering in the Aviation Domain. Mahwah, NJ : Lawrence Erlbaum Ass. (2000).
3. Degani, A.: Modeling Human-Machine Systems: On Modes, Error, and Patterns of Interaction. Ph.D. Thesis. Georgia Institute of Technology (1996).
4. Feltovich, P.J., Spiro, R.J., Coulson, R.: The nature of conceptual understanding in biomedicine: The deep structure of complex ideas and the development of misconceptions. In D. Evans, V. Patel (eds.), Cognitive science in medicine: Biomedical modelling. Cambridge, MA : MIT Press (1989).
5. Gollwitzer, P.M.: Action phases and mind sets. In E.T. Higgins, R.M. Sorrentino (eds.), Handbook of motivation and cognition: Foundations of social behaviour, Vol 2. New York : Guilford Press (1990) 53-92.
6. Javuax, D., Olivier, E.: Assessing and understanding pilots' knowledge of mode transitions on the A340-200/300. In Proceedings of the International Conference on Human-Computer Interaction in Aeronautics, HCI-Aero'00 (2000).
7. de Jong, T.: Learning and Instruction with Computer Simulations. In Education & Computing, 6, (1991) 217-229.
8. Khan, T.M., Paul, S.J., Brown, K.E., Leitch, R.R.: Model-Based Explanations in Simulation-Based Training. In B.P. Goettl et al. (eds.), Proceedings of the Fourth International Conference, ITS '98. Berlin [u.a.] : Springer (1998).
9. Leveson, N.G., Pinnell, L.D., Sandys, S.D., Koga, S., Reese, J.D.: Analysing Software Specifications for Mode Confusion Potential. In C.W. Johnson (eds.), Proceedings of the Workshop on Human Error and System Development, Technical Report GAAG-TR-97-2. Glasgow Accident Analysis Group (1997).
10. Mitchell, C.M.: Horizons in Pilot Training: Desktop Tutoring Systems. In N.B. Sarter and R. Amalberti (Eds.), Cognitive Engineering in the Aviation Domain. Mahwah, NJ: Lawrence Erlbaum Associates (2000).
11. Möbus,C., Schröder, O., Thole,H.-J.: Diagnosing and Evaluating the Acquisition Process of Programming Schemata. In J.E. GREER, G. McCALLA (eds.), Student Modelling: The Key to Individualized Instruction. Berlin: Springer (1994).
12. Möbus,C., Schröder, O., Thole,H.-J.: Online Modelling the Novice-Expert Shift in Programming Skills on a Rule-Schema-Case Partial Order, in F. Schmalhofer, K.F. Wender, H. Böcker (eds.), Cognition and Computer Programming, Ablex Series in Computational Sciences, Norwood, N.J.: Ablex (1995).
13. Möbus,C., Thole,H.-J., Schröder, O.: Interactive Support of Planning in a Functional, Visual Programming Language. In P. Brna et al. (eds.), Proceedings AI-ED '93, World Conference on Artificial Intelligence and Education (1993) 362-369.
14. Ohlsson, S.: Some principles of intelligent tutoring. In Instructional Science 14. Amsterdam: Elsevier Science Publishers B.V (1986) 293-326.
15. Paries, J., Amalberti, R.: Aviation Safety Paradigms and Training Implications. In N.B. Sarter, R. Amalberti (eds.), Cognitive Engineering in the Aviation Domain. Mahwah, NJ: Lawrence Erlbaum Associates (2000).

16. Reason, J.: Action not as planned. In G. Underwood, R. Stevens (eds.), Aspects of Consciousness. London: Academic Press (1979).
17. Sheridan, T.B.: Supervisory Control. In Handbook of Human Factors and Ergonomics. New York [u.a.] : Wiley (1997).
18. Zhang, D. M., Alem, L.: Using Case-Based Reasoning for Exercise Design in Simulation-Based Training. In C. Frasson, G. Gauthier, A. Lesgold (eds.), Proceedings of the Third International Conference, ITS'96. Berlin [u.a.] : Springer (1996).

SIMPA: A Training Platform in Work Station Including Computing Tutors

Laurent Duquesnoy[1,2], Jean-Luc Berger[1], Patrick Prévôt[2], and
Françoise Sandoz-Guermond[2]

[1] Cellule multimédia – THALES ELECTRON DEVICES / Unité Tubes Intensificateurs
d'image et de Visualisation,
Z.I. Centr'alp, 38430 Moirans, France
{laurent.duquesnoy, jean-luc berger}@thales-electrondevices.com
[2] Laboratoire Interaction Collaborative, Téléformation, Téléactivités (ICTT), Bâtiment Léonard
de Vinci,
21 avenue Jean Capelle, 69621 Villeurbanne Cedex, France
{prevot, sandoz}@gprhp.insa-lyon.fr

Abstract. The know-how transmission becomes an essential condition of high
technology companies continuity. In response, we propose a multimedia training platform in operators work station, called SIMPA. It was developed within
the framework of a "Six Sigma" step, with a permanent concern of customers
satisfaction (learners, formative persons in workshops, and managers). Its foundation is to leave a large place in the autonomous activity of the learner, by in-
suring him a permanent pedagogical accompaniment, thanks to two computing
tutors (the professor and the companion); this answers the need of reduction in
time of human tutoring. SIMPA integrates all the tools of follow-up necessary
for the trainer to practise an indispensable debriefing at the end of each training
session. We experimented SIMPA in situation at TED / TIV[1;] the results are
convincing, as well in credibility of our computing tutors as in diversification of
pedagogical courses.

1   Introduction

As many high technology companies, the Moirans site of Thales Electron Devices
(TED/TIV[1]) is confronted today with the major stake of transmission of knowledge,
condition for the company continuity. Four main reasons explain that:
- from 1998 the setting up of **work organization in autonomous teams,** characterized by training needs for the versatility in the workshops,
- a context of **reduction in working time**, with the setting up of a 35-hour
  working week,
- the **population pyramid evolution**, with the emergence of a young population mixing with an ageing one,
- the **temporary workers training,** more and more called for punctual work
  growth; it must be fast and effective.

---

[1]   Thales Electron Devices, unité Tubes Intensificateurs d'image et de Visualisation (Image
Tube and Display).

S.A. Cerri, G. Gouardères, and F. Paraguaçu (Eds.): ITS 2002, LNCS 2363, pp. 507–520, 2002.
© Springer-Verlag Berlin Heidelberg 2002

In the operator's training domain on the Moirans site, we already provided a methodological response to these needs, through the contents structuring, the personalization of the pedagogical courses, and practises/theory alternation in the organization of our training activities [1]. With regard to the training evaluation, we developed a SEAMI[2]: System of Learner's Multimedia and Interactive Evaluation; its design benefited from recommendations resulting from a Principal Components Analysis made from a double experimentation from tool [2]. It appeared during these experiments the SEAMI could exceed its role of skill revealing corroborated; it is also a training tool in power, according to the model of pedagogy by the action. However, it preserved large gaps:

- its teaching structure was too rigid: single method of the illustrated textual QCM of videos;
- it wasn't possible to use it in self-tuition: no assistance or succeeded mediation;
- it didn't contain documentary space other only the 4 videos proposed;
- it didn't offer coherence with a personalized teaching course (pedagogical contract, formalized goals).

This article presents the step of design and the result of a model improved of SEAMI adapted to training; we called it **SIMPA**[3]: **Mediatized and Personalizable Interactive Support for Training.** Theoretical supportings and the practical application of our integrated computerized mediation model will be described on the simplified idea of the Intelligent Agents. We will copy our talk on the course of the project led according to the "Six Sigma" method that guided us in this step.

2   The "Six Sigma" Step

The development of SIMPA was treated from start to finish through a "Six Sigma"[4] project. This method relates to the development and the optimization of industrial process. It is a true methodology of implementation in project, that establishes the link between quality philosophy (to make well, first blow, for the customer), tools quality and statistical analyses. Focused on the measure, its permanent concern is the satisfaction of the customer need, taking into account all its requirements in the product or process specifications [3]. The successive stages of a project "Six Sigma" consisting in developing a new product are the followings:

- **"Define"**: Need description; definition of the goals, the perimeter and the schedule of the project. *R0 review;*
- **"Measure"**: Transcribe the voice of the customer in term of critical needs; hierarchisation and establishment of specifications for these needs; define means to measure them. *R1 review;*
- **"Analyse"**: Total design of the product; estimate of its capability. *R2 review;*

---

2 Système d'Evaluation de l'Apprenant Multimédia et Interactif.
3 Support Interactif Médiatisé et Personnalisable pour l'Apprentissage.
4 The term "sigma" indicates a statistical measuring unit which is the reflection of the capability of a process. Ideally, a capability of 6 sigma ensures a level of conformity of 99.99966 %.

- **"Design"**: Realization of the tasks of detailed design; Analyze of failure risks; Test plan in situation. *R3 review;*
- **"Verify"**: Check the robustness of the product; Plan of product transfer; lessons to be learnt from the project. *R4 review.*

All these stages give rise to reviews of validation (in the presence of the customers for the reviews R0, R2 and R4) for which a list of supplies is awaited. In our case, in the light of the gaps of SEAMI, the stage "Define" consisted in identifying the needs for a new multimedia training product. Let us detail our work according to stages of the "Six Sigma" steps.

3   Taking the Customers Needs into Account (Stage "Measure")

The project started on these 2 experienced needs:

- need for training supports on the work place with strong pedagogical contents intended to people in the field,
- need for competencies measuring instruments and traceability for training actions to manage the grids of versatility (card summarizing personal skills available in each workshop), within the framework of the system of Quality assurance ISO 9001.

3.1   Transcribe the Customer's Voice

We have 3 types of customers: the learners, trainers and managers, who are the pilots and the decision makers of our training activities. To identify their needs, the method requires to select and question a panel of them (we chose 10 interlocutors for each type of customer) and to gather and order their specific needs. So, we build for each type of customer a QFD matrix (Quality Function Deployment), also called **"House of Quality"**, in which it is obligatory to define a feature for each critical need of the customer [4]. The features are classified in Pareto (classification by decreasing values; see fig. 1) according to their respective load, calculated by multiplying their total importance by an estimated index of realization difficulty (between 1 and 5). Thus, the exploitation of QFD matrix structures the design step by giving a table of functioning on the command of the operations. From our total analysis of the needs a dominating feature F1 results, which constitutes the base of SIMPA: the **computerized functions of mediation** (weight of 1005 for a total weight of 4170 per 21 features).

Thanks to the R1 review, one identifies on the one hand the difficulties of realization. In our case, we have to take account of 2 incompatible aspects (*a priori*):

- developing functions of mediation integrated by means of computer while guaranteeing a support structure independent of the content,
- diversifying the suggested teaching activities modes while authorizing a use of the product in autonomy by the learners.

On the other hand, we detect early in the phase of design the essential points of the customers future satisfaction, and thus the success of the project. That results naturally in the installation of customers satisfaction indicators, elaborated at the end of the stage.

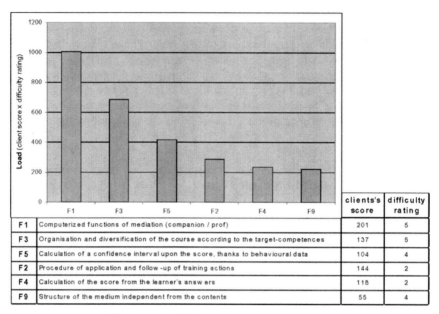

		clients's score	difficulty rating
F1	Computerized functions of mediation (companion / prof)	201	5
F3	Organisation and diversification of the course according to the target-competences	137	5
F5	Calculation of a confidence interval upon the score, thanks to behavioural data	104	4
F2	Procedure of application and follow -up of training actions	144	2
F4	Calculation of the score from the learner's answers	118	2
F9	Structure of the medium independent from the contents	55	4

Fig. 1. Pareto of the six priority features (on 21)

3.2 Customers Satisfaction

Three mainlines of customers satisfaction appear:
- response to specific needs: we propose to each customer a questionnaire out of its 5 main needs;
- efficiency of the result: we organize an assessment meeting convened by automatic follow-up after a few weeks of practical application in the field; it results in a concerted skills validation by an evaluation between all the actors of the training session;
- reduction in working time of the trainer: we check his total time of presence does not exceed 50% of the duration of the training.

4   Theoretical Bases of SIMPA (Stage "Analyse")

This stage gives rise to define the major choices which will guide the design of the product.

4.1 A Model of Framed Autonomy

One of the stakes of SIMPA is to reduce the attendance time of the trainers (their workload as a technical support being very strong) by adopting the **briefing–debriefing** tutorial model [5] described on fig. 2. Concretely the trainer leaves the training room after having presented the objectives and the day course; he carries out on his return an assessment adapted for each learner according to his traced activity during the autonomy phase. In our case the first session of training is devoted to discovering interface: it is **the run-up** [2].

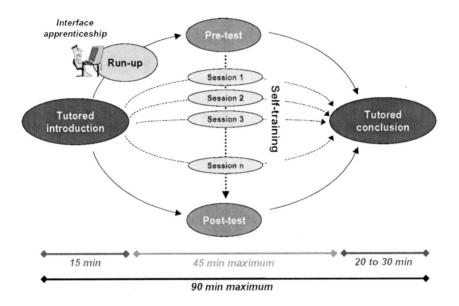

Fig. 2. The briefing–debriefing model

4.2   Structure of SIMPA

The heart of an application as SIMPA is composed of the **route book**, that is personal for each learner. His pedagogical contract is there drawn up (pedagogical objectives, course, possible specifications on the scores to obtain, methods of practical application, procedures of evaluation). This book grows rich by the follow-up of each training activity. From the route book, the learner navigate for each target-skill in the books dedicated to the **three types of knowledge** (theoretical and contextual knowledge, know-how in conformity, and be able to react in the event of risks) [1]. Lastly a book is dedicated to all the **documentary resources** in textual or multimedia form; these resources are worked out by the technical expert of the field in dialogue with the pedagogue. Fig. 3 shows the general architecture of the platform and its functioning.

4.3   Learning by Doing

We favour the autonomous activity of the learner; his course for each target-skill consists of a coherent series of exercises, called **teaching activities.** There is a balance to respect in the activities difficulty: if the difficulty is too weak, the learner answers by simple common sense without calling upon the documentary resources and thus without apprehending automatically the key concepts of the training. Conversely if the difficulty is too high the learner will be constantly in failure situation, and a feeling of discouragement will appear quickly. If one adds to these dangers the possible confusion of the learner within the environment from training or his possible incomprehension of the activities instructions, one admits without hesitation the need for **establishing a mediation in the absence of the human tutor.**

4.4   Mediation Criteria

To implement our feature F1, we proposed to exploit works of professor Reuven Feuerstein and his practice of the Instrumental Enrichment Program [6]. He defines cognitive functions (for example: "the need for precision in the data-gathering", "the need to plan one's control") to activate by the mediator during a training session. Our starting assumption is these cognitive functions are available for our learners, but little or badly invested because of the new situation or other parameters dependent on the environment or on the person's intentions. The goal of the mediation of the computing tutor is to request these cognitive functions so the suggested task can be accomplished successfully. One distinguishes 3 phases from the learner's mental activity [7] during the teaching activities which are proposed to him:
- **"I inform"**: the learner takes note of the environment, the nature and the facts of the case posed,
- **"I elaborate"**: the learner brings into play his cognitive mechanisms to solve the difficulty; this phase does not result inevitably in an observable behavioural activity,
- **"I act"**: the learner declares his answer.

We wish to take as a starting point the **mediation criteria** [8], classified below according to 3 types of intervention to adapt them on computer:
- **Spotting interventions:**
  - on the pedagogical objectives,
  - on the significance of the training,
  - on the course and the used means.
- **Regulation interventions:**
  - impulsiveness control,
  - mediation of the concentration,
  - mediation of the implication,
  - mediation of planning (to split up the difficulty).
- **Recognition interventions:**
  - mediation of the competence feeling,
  - mediation of the search of innovation and complexity,
  - positive management of the errors.

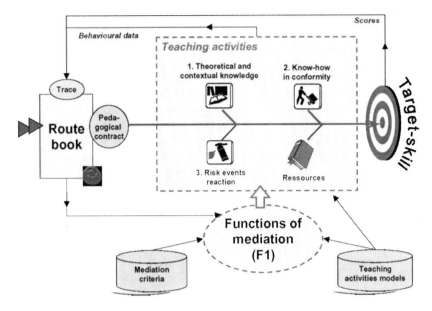

Fig. 3. General architecture of SIMPA

5   Detailed Design of SIMPA (Stage "Design")

5.1   A Library of Teaching Activities

SIMPA modules are designed around a fixed structure of decomposition of knowledge on which the pedagogue comes to graft, in dialogue with the technical expert a collection of adapted teaching activities. They are extracted from **a library of models,** until now composed of the following types:
- drag-and-drop labels (texts, photographs, videos or sounds), with 2 possible ways:
    - sequential (to respect a command of operations),
    - category index (all kinds of classifications in several categories),
- answer directly a Multiple Choice Questionnaire (MCQ),
- answer a MCQ launched by a keyword taped on keyboard,
- complete a phrase with holes,
- reconstruct a puzzle,
- complete a crossword grid,
- recognize active zones on an image,
- connect in pairs,
- validate or invalidate an assertion,
- extract the good elements from a given list.

This evolutionary list gives us a broad creation and field of application. Specific parameters, useful for the mediation mechanism, are dependant on each activity.

5.2 Actors of the Mediation

To mitigate the absence of human tutor during the training session, we developed 2 computing tutors: the professor and the companion. This binomial has a double function: on the one hand to instigate the interventions of the characters (who will intervene ? at which moments ?) by sparing possibilities of dialogue between them, and on the other hand to reveal fully **the duality of the ideal mediator:** at the same time to put oneself in the learner's place, and to guide him in his reflexion and his training course. As follows:

- **the professor** is based on the traditional guides developed in environments of interactive training or in the educational CD-Roms: he gives the instructions of each activity; as he knows the solutions, he expresses his joy in response of good answers of the learner;

- **the companion** is the regulator of the learner's behaviour: he is inspired by the pedagogical model of the "learning companion" [9]. He doesn't have the response to the exercises but his resources book is accessible permanently. Curiously, he doesn't fail to ask to the professor the utility of each new screen (pedagogical objectives).

These tutors share the mediation interventions. Because they don't manage any pedagogical adaptive strategy, we can't call them pedagogical agents as Claude Frasson defines them: reactive, instructable, adaptive and cognitive [10]. In fact, a pedagogical agent can be defined by three characteristics [11, 12]:

- adaptation: the agent is able to build a model of the learner;
- autonomy: the agent makes decisions on the basis of his knowledge;
- mobility: the agent can widen his space of search (on Internet for example), to dialogue with other agents to seek missing information.

Without developing complete "intelligent agents" [13], we gave to the tutors the following features, to approach a life-like behaviour [14]:

- **a permanent attention with the actions of the learner:** the eyes of the tutors follow the mouse movements, they bring pieces of advice and information about screen areas or the teaching activity in progress,

- **a diversity of the facial expressions:** the tutors are motionless (each one in a corner in bottom of the screen) but have a panel of about thirty different emotions. The animated elements are the eyes, the lashes, the eyebrows, the mouth and one hand. For the moment, they are not expressed directly by the word but by bubbles with the screen,

- **an interactivity with the results of the learner:** correction of the activities, evolution in the interventions of mediation given, automatic guidance control towards other screens of the course or documentary resources if the resolution of the current activity requires it (example on fig. 4).

In fact we counted on the **"persona" effect** described by James C. Lester and his team [15]: just the presence of a tutor animated in an environment of interactive training stimulates not only the intrinsic motivation of the learner but also their process of individual reflexion. Our goal is less to design an intelligent agent which adapts gradually to the learner's behaviour, than use the human adaptability confronted with a mediatized environment, since the conditions of interaction and credibility of the computing interlocutors are sufficient.

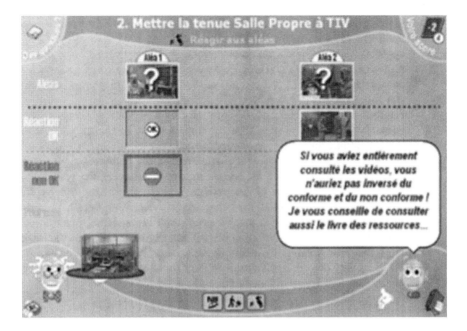

Fig. 4. Regulation intervention by the companion

5.3   The Mediation Mechanism

Without calling upon the techniques of the Artificial Intelligence (IA), we wanted to give to the computing tutors a credible talent for repartee. Thanks to the cyclic character of our training courses (a training action is divided into several target-skills, each one being a collection of teaching activities), we manage a limited number of teaching situations. So we built a mediation mechanism starting from a basic learner's behaviour, added by the processing of particular cases, as a function of the distance of the awaited behaviour. We identified these particular cases by a double series of tests on a panel of 25 learners in the company.

Concretely SIMPA modules are equipped with computer sensors which progressively generate **a training newspaper** with the activity of the learner (trace). One finds there the chronological order of his operations, devoted time, errors made as well as the obtained scores. This history is exploited by the tutors in order to clarify their interventions. One distinguishes the **thorough** (by the tutors) **and drawn** (by the learner) **interventions**. In the first case, the tutor interposes in the action by delivering his message on the screen; we reserve this type of intervention to defined cases: repetitions of the same mistakes, continuation of mistakes during the same activity. In the second case, the means to draw the attention of the learner are graduated from the most subtle (a wink of the tutor) to the most attractive (the tutor types with the pane). The tutor means his intention to intervene by a symbol representing the type of message which he wants to give. The drawing disappears since it is not any more topicality or when it is replaced by another message.

Except the spotting, these interventions are independent of the training contents. They are built according to the mediation criteria:

- **spotting:** at each arrival on a new screen, on request of the companion, the professor presents the teaching objectives. If the same page comprises several activities, he also gives a message of transition to present the activity that follows;
- **regulation:** interventions come from the tutors: if nothing occurs in an abnormally long time, in case of bad comprehension of the activities instructions (continuation of illogical actions), etc;
- **recognition:** with each click of the learner on the button *"I have finished"* (invariable means given to the learner to give his answer), the system generate an **internal bar code of the pedagogical situation**: well-ordered information upon the context and the behaviour (see details on fig. 5). The professor gives in case of good answer **a graduated recognition,** function of the difficulty of the exercise and number of tests to find the answer. On the contrary, the error is explicitly meant to the learner (in drag-and-drop for example, the badly placed labels return to their initial position), and the companion advises him according to the bar code.

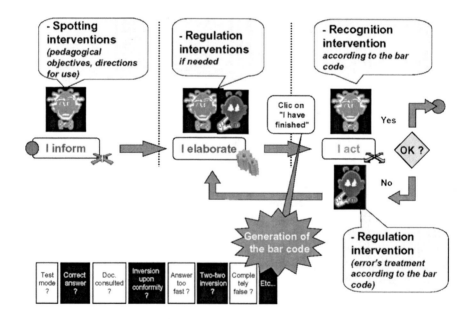

Fig. 5. Mediation mechanism in SIMPA

5.4 A Multi-users Platform

SIMPA modules were designed for triple use:
- **learning mode:** it's the greatest mode in term of mediation; the 2 tutors are present to accompany the learner, and the documentary resources are permanently accessible. Each activity suggested must be concluded so that one can declare complete the training course,
- **test mode:** the same activities are proposed, but the learner doesn't have any feedback on his actions: he has only one try to answer without knowing the accuracy of his answers. Only the professor is present (there is indeed no positive management of the errors to carry out) to manage navigation,
- **solution mode:** it is accessible at the end of the learning mode; all the activities are corrected, and the learner can freely come to re-examine the solutions of each screen, if it's results necessary during his later activity. This document constitutes a reference frame placed permanently at the disposal on the corporate network. There is no mediation for this using mode.

The platform recognizes two types of users: the learner and the trainer. The latter disposes of useful functions to control the learning session during his absence: management report of each target-skill, **uncertainty intervals on allotted scores** [1], **questions on computing post-it.** Let's also note that the trainer is the only one who is able to modify the pedagogical contract in the route book; in practice he draws up this contract in the presence of the learner.

6 Experiments and Estimate of the Mediation (Stage "Verify")

6.1 Experimental Device

We developed a SIMPA prototype on target-skills *"Slip on the clean room overalls" and "Communicate in the clean room"* within the framework of clean concept[5] training. It was tested according to the following experimental protocol: 25 people of the company, of all ages, sectors and expertise levels used this module 2 times, with an interval of 20 days. The purpose was to have a return of use on our mechanism of mediation: how the people react with the presence of the professor and the companion ? Do they have a credible and effective "behaviour" ? We thus proposed to our volunteers **an evaluation grid of the computing tutors.** In addition to the computer sensors which kept the trace of the actions, a human observer followed each test integrally, without intervening in the action, in order to identify the situations where the mediation proved to be insufficient.

6.2 Results Obtained

It appears that the companion is below the average for the first experiment (note obtained: 1.6 out of 4); his role was not marked enough, in particular with regard to the

---

[5] The clean concept indicates the whole means implemented to protect our products sensitive to the particulate contamination, and in particular the behavioural work rules in clean room.

assistance which he should have brought thanks to his resources book. On the other hand, as the first experiment the professor obtained a note of 3.1 out of 4. His actions on the instructions of the activities suggested and on guidance within SIMPA were the most noticed and appreciated. In fact his role was dominating because of the intuitive character of the good answers to the activities suggested. The clean concept is often a matter of good sense and the scores were high from the first experiment (5.3 out of 7). There were few errors and thus few opportunities given to the companion to appear. The test would have been more instructive on tougher target-skills, but our industrial constraints pushed us to choose the clean concept as experimentation subject.

We carried out some adjustments between the two experiments:

- **on mediation:** possible intervention of the companion during an activity elaboration (before the learner's click on "I have finished"), solution of blocking situations met with the first experiment (reconstitution of the puzzle, clarification of activities instructions, etc), more shunting toward the companion's resources book;
- **on navigation:** erase of inopportune mouse clicks during animations, more ergonomic presentation of the dialog box with the learner, access facilitation to professor's spotting messages.

After the second experiment, the companion reaches 2.5 out of 4 and the professor preserves his popularity with 3.3 out of 4. The general appreciation of SIMPA passes from 2.6 out of 4 for the first experiment to 3.3 for the second. The principal roles of our tutors are identified as follows by the learners:

Professor: - guidance during the course (21.5%),
            - activities Instructions (19.4%),
            - location in the course (16.1%).
Companion: - invitation to use documentation (38.3%),
            - invitation to consult the professor (25.5%),
            - relevant errors management (21.3%).

These results validate our choice of a bicephalous mediation; the comments collected in margin of the investigation near the volunteers indicate their total satisfaction toward this environment of interactive training.

6.3   Deployment of SIMPA at TED/TIV

The two target-skills used for our test were supplemented by five others to form today a complete training module on behavioural rules in clean room. One of the announced advantages of SIMPA was **the platform reproducibility** on a new training subject **in a very reduced time** (advanced industrial times: 15 days). We tested and validated this feature by carrying out within the requested times an entirely new one-hour training module on the critical points of a manufactoring process which inherits of course all the mediation functions of SIMPA.

The last asset of SIMPA is related to its computer architecture: each module has its own contents but its "brain" is shared. All the mechanisms of decision concerning the tutors are gathered in a single application on the corporate network. The improvement process is not only continuous but also **with retroactive effect;** this contributes to the facility of deployment of SIMPA at TED/TIV.

7   Conclusion and Prospects

The first results as well experimental as in situation of real use show us that the principal objectives of our "Six Sigma" project in designing new training supports SIMPA are achieved. The conditions of interaction and credibility of our computing tutors are satisfactory and guaranteed whatever the training contents. Our industrial constraints require less the system efficiency on a given subject than its good reproducibility for future needs in operator's training. The first training sessions carried out attest of a half-reduced time of human tutoring, and of a good satisfaction of the learners upon their computing tutors.

In term of pedagogy, the modular structure of the courses and the broad choice of teaching activities ensure the trainer a freedom and a great quality in the courses design. The objective is today for us to widen the equipment of SIMPA, at the same time in activities models and mediation capacity.

References

1. Duquesnoy, L., Berger, J.L., Prévôt, P., Sandoz-Guermond, F.: Méthode de conception et de suivi d'actions de formation multimédia en milieu industriel. Proceedings of the World Conference on Technologies de l'Information et de la Communication dans les Enseignements d'ingénieurs et dans l'industrie (TICE), Troyes (2000) 305-313
2. Duquesnoy, L., Berger, J.L., Prévôt, P., Sandoz-Guermond, F.: L'Analyse en Composantes Principales au service de la conception et la mise en oeuvre d'un support de formation multimédia. Proceedings of the Conference NîmesTIC, Nîmes (2001) 103-108
3. Pillet, M., Duret, D.: Qualité en production: de l'ISO 9000 à Six Sigma. Editions d'organisation (2001)
4. Breyfogle III, F.W.: Implementing Six Sigma – Smarter solutions using statistical methods. Whiley Interscience Publication (1999) 240-255
5. Prévôt, P., Akkouche, I.: Les Nouvelles Technologies Educatives et leurs usages. In: Connaissances et savoir-faire en entreprise: intégration et capitalisation. Editions Hermès (1997) 343-380
6. Feuerstein, R., Rand, Y.: Don't accept me as I am: Helping retarded performers excel. SkyLight Professional Development (revised edition) (1997)
7. Cardinet, A.: Pratiquer la médiation en pédagogie. Editions Dunod (1995)
8. Martin, J., Paravy, G. (Dir.): Pédagogies de la médiation – Autour du PEI. Editions Chronique Sociale (1990) 117-166
9. Abou-Jaoude, S.C., Frasson, C.: An Agent for Selecting Learning Strategy. Proceedings of the World Conference on Nouvelles Technologies de la Communication et de la Formation (NTICF), Rouen (1998) 353-358
10. Frasson, C., Mengelle, T., Aïmeur, E.: Using Pedagogical Agents in a Multi-strategic Intelligent Tutoring System. Workshop on Pedagogical agents in AI-ED World Conference on Artificial Intelligence and Education, Japan (1997)
    URL: http://www.iro.umontreal.ca/~frasson/FrassonPub/Acteurs-final.doc
11. Alberganti, M.: A l'école des robots ? L'informatique, l'école et vos enfants. Editions Calmann-Lévy (2000) 22-92
12. Johnson, W.L., Rickel, J.W., Lester, J.C.: Animated Pedagogical Agents: Face-to-Face Interaction in Interactive Learning Environments. In: The International Journal of Artificial Intelligence in Education 11 (2000) 47-78
    URL : http://www.csc.ncsu.edu/eos/users/l/lester/www/Public/apa-ijaied-2000.pdf

13. Bruillard, E.: Les machines à enseigner. Editions Hermès (1997) 177-222
14. Moreno, R., Mayer, R.E., Lester, J.C.: Life-Like Pedagogical Agents in Constructivist Multimedia Environments: Cognitive Consequences of their Interaction. Proceedings of the World Conference on Educational Multimedia, Hypermedia, and Telecommunications (ED-MEDIA), Montreal (2000) 741-746
15. Lester, J.C., Converse, S.A., Kahler, S.E., Barlow, S.T., Stone, B.A., Bhoga, R.S.: The Persona Effect: Affective Impact of Animated Pedagogical Agents. Proceedings of Conference on Computer-Human Interaction (CHI), Atlanta (1997)
URL: http://www.acm.org/sigs/sigchi/chi97/proceedings/paper/jl.htm.

Computer Aided Evaluation of Trainee Skills on a Simulator Network

Michelle Joab[1], Odette Auzende[2], Michel Futtersack[3],
Brigitte Bonnet[4], and Patrice Le Leydour[4]

[1]LIRMM & ERES, Université Montpellier II, 161 rue ADA, 34000 Montpellier, France
Michelle.Joab@lirmm.fr
[2]LIP6-POLE IA, Université Paris 6, cc 169, 8 rue du Capitaine Scott, 75015 Paris, France
Odette.Auzende@lip6.fr
[3]CRIP5, Université Paris 5, 10 avenue Pierre Larousse, 92245 Malakoff, France
Michel.Futtersack@math-info.univ-paris5.fr
[4]Thalès Training & Simulation - 1, rue du Général de Gaulle, Z.I. Les Beaux Soleils Osny
BP 226 - 95523 Cergy Pontoise cedex - France
{brigitte.bonnet, patrice.leleydour}@thales-tts.com

Abstract. The aim of the PPTS project (Pedagogical Platoon Training System) is to design and implement an evaluation environment for strategic and tactical skills, coupled to a network of full-scale simulators of the LECLERC tank. The three-level architecture adopted here is modelled on the levels of expertise, technical, tactic and strategic. The technical level is carried out by reactive agents, *the monitors*. They point out the important events of the exercise. The evaluation of tactical skills is carried out by cognitive agents, *the analysts*, which use the facts generated by the monitors to evaluate the tactical skills. The software architecture at analyst level provides a flexible solution to the problem of time in the evaluation of the exercise, whether the transitions between phases are sudden or gradual, whether the exercise is slow or rapid. We will complete this study with the strategic level.

1 Introduction

For many years, crew simulators have been used in civilian and military contexts for training purposes, including putting the trainees into extreme situations, such as military deployment in a war context. In the industrial context, many simulation-based training systems incorporate intelligent tutoring systems in order to improve the functionalities for the user (instructor or trainee) [1], [2].

If the simulators are put into a network, a group of trainees can be trained collectively [3]. However, this poses monitoring problems for the instructors, who have simultaneously to take into account the behaviour of each individual unit and the behaviour of the group as a whole. The aim of the automatic evaluation of the trainees discussed in this paper is to minimise the instructors' workload.

The PPTS project (Pedagogical Platoon Training System) is a joint project between the LIP6 and Thales Training & Simulation. It involves the design and the implementation of an evaluation environment for strategic and tactical skills within

S.A. Cerri, G. Gouardères, and F. Paraguaçu (Eds.): ITS 2002, LNCS 2363, pp. 521–530, 2002.

the framework of a LECLERC platoon simulator. This environment has to be an add-on to the existing instructor operating station.

A LECLERC platoon consists of four LECLERC tanks. The crew of a tank is made up of a tank commander, a pilot and a gunner. One of the tank commanders is also the platoon leader. To train a platoon, four LECLERC tank simulators are networked, communicate using the DIS (Distributed Interactive Simulation) standard and exchange data on an Ethernet network in the form of PDUs (Protocol Data Units). Four instructors are in charge of the four simulators; the instructor in charge of the platoon leader's simulator carries out the tasks of the chief instructor and more particularly observes the tactical behaviour of the platoon.

The simulation environment provides in real time each instructor with a 2D map of the terrain, of the current positions of all involved entities (manned simulators and virtual friendly and enemy entities which are controlled autonomously) and firings.

The instructors are continuously in demand; in addition, during certain phases of the exercise, such as combat, they cannot simultaneously make use of all the available sources of information. Since their cognitive workload is particularly high, some events may go unnoticed. Moreover, various elements which they consider important are not directly accessible at the instructor operating station in its current version: thus using the 2D map, the result of a firing is made visible only if it is successful (therefore if the enemy is destroyed) but the tank that has fired is not clearly identified.

The instructors therefore express their expectations in terms of enhancements and improvements to the existing instructor operating station. What they would like is an analysis tool to enable them not to miss a significant event, to highlight the relevant events for the evaluation of trainees, to help them to analyse the behaviour of each crew and of the platoon as a whole and to help them to justify their remarks during the debriefing session.

Section 2 introduces the problem of the evaluation of skills in a training session on a simulator and presents related work. Section 3 describes the three levels of skills under consideration (technical, tactical and strategic) which are reflected in the architecture of PPTS (section 4). Section 5 presents the current software development of the evaluator that implements the evaluation process at the technical level. Section 6 introduces the modelling of tactical skills currently being developed; section 7 provides the results and future work.

2   The Problem and State of the Art

We began our study of the evaluation of strategic and tactical skills of LECLERC tank crews by collecting existing expertise in the domain. We had documents which explained the "military doctrine" on this matter, we also observed how typical exercises performed on simulators were done and discussed this with instructors.

This initial study led to the following findings. The theoretical knowledge described in the documents is made up of principles the trainees have to respect. The application of these principles, however, leaves much room for personal interpretation and initiative. Though the fundamental criterion is the success of the mission, the means to do so may differ significantly from one platoon to another. Consequently, it is difficult to specify tactical skills in full. In addition it appears that errors come from an incorrect implementation of tactical know-how rather than from their ignorance. Errors often come from an incorrect perception or analysis of the situation. One of the problems we face is the difficulty to define the expertise of the evaluation of skills.

In a similar domain, Marsella and Johnson [4] use the situation assessment and the decision making capabilities of the synthetic entities to assess the trainee's performance. We use the data contained in PDUs to build the evaluation because this is the only significant information on how the exercise was done to be found on the network. Difficulties may be of a technical nature: large amounts of strongly noisy data are handled. Moreover the conceptual gap between the information provided and the strategic and tactical levels of the evaluation is considerable. This includes the characteristics (instantaneous position, speed, orientation, etc.) of each actor in the simulation, manned simulators or virtual entities, the occurrence of certain events (departure and results of firings). In addition, this data is incomplete, for example, the target of a firing is not always known. To build the evaluation, the nature of usable data therefore raises conceptual and technical difficulties because the situation cannot be characterised directly. The problem is that the analysis of this situation is the basis on which the decision which we aim to evaluate is made.

AETS (Advanced Embedded Training System) has been developed for tactical team training [5, 6]. It focuses on the Air Defense Team in a ship's Combat Information Centre. AETS processes high level actions (HLAs) from a large amount of data: all keystroke sequences, all trainee speech communications and all trainee eye movements. AETS builds an automated performance assessment and a cognitive diagnosis in succession.

Time is one of the important problems in the evaluation of an exercise. Instantaneous analysis is not sufficient because tactical and strategic choices can only be observed during a certain lapse of time. Only the occurrence of certain events (e.g. a firing) involves instantaneous analysis. Moreover the choice of a fixed temporal unit to delimit the analysis process is not relevant because the exercise alternates rapid phases and slow phases. The characteristic states of a situation are seldom reached in one go.

Loriette, Nigro and Jarkass [7] propose a two-level knowledge based architecture for the recognition of vehicle-driver manœuvres. The first level associates to time t (or to a time interval) one or more characteristic states in process, such as waiting to overtake, beginning to overtake or finishing overtaking. The second level concerns the recognition and validation of manœuvres, starting from a sequence of characteristic states detected by the first level and with a given duration. This two-level modelling can recognize and process characteristic situations but is insufficient to process the technical, tactical and strategic levels in our field of study.

The collective dimension of the instruction is one of the major aspects of our problem. The four manned simulators interact in a virtual world where they have to work in co-ordination to achieve a successful mission. How can co-ordination errors be distinguished from problems due to perception? Moreover, in the case of a collective co-ordination error, how can some of the responsibility be allocated to a particular crew?

Today this problem is often handled through multi-agent modelling of the team. Miller, Yin, Volz, Ioerger and Yen use a multi-agent architecture to design an intelligent collective training system (ITTS) [8]. These agents represent either virtual members of the team or a coach. The coaching agent supervises and interprets the activities of the members of the team and the way they interact. It has knowledge about the task, the structure of the team, the decision-making process and the mental state of the other members of the team. It uses the team model in order to detect individual errors. In [9], agents play the role of human instructor or team member in a virtual world. In the latter case, the virtual instructor interacts directly with the trainees to show what should be done whereas in [8] the coaching agent does not appear in the simulation.

3   The Three Levels of Evaluation

Managing a platoon is both an individual and a collective task. Several roles can be distinguished: the pilot, the gunner, the tank commander and the platoon leader. The success of a mission depends on the quality of the decisions taken by the platoon leader, on the correct understanding of the corresponding orders by the tank commanders and on the correct implementation of these orders by the pilot and the gunner.

The skills required for the management of a tank are of two kinds: technical and tactical. Technical skills are procedural know-how leading to elementary reflex actions. They may be individual or collective: "fire at a mobile target while moving" is an individual technical skill of the gunner while "move, observe and fire" is a collective technical skill of the crew. Simulators were often considered as perfect tools for an intensive "drill and practice" in order to acquire such technical skills.

Tactical skills allow the true resolution of a problem and require analytical and synthetic abilities. The problem for the platoon leader comes in the form of a very general objective "To hold the BROUTTAIS cross-roads while waiting to be joined by your unit" and of the description of a context (nature and potential movement of the enemy, nature of the terrain, weather conditions, logistic support).

In a training course an initial series of exercises is devoted to learning and practising technical tasks. Since the task to be achieved is very procedural, the work of the instructor is merely to check that the standard procedure is applied properly, or that the desired state has been reached.

The ambitious aim of PPTS is to help the instructors in the evaluation of the behaviour of a platoon in a tactical exercise because this evaluation is much more complex than the evaluation of technical skills.

As many tutoring systems, we adopt a knowledge-based approach to support the evaluation component. The expertise collected showed that the instructors consider three fundamental platoon attitudes in a tactical exercise: knowing how to protect oneself (protection), knowing how to move and knowing how to react facing the enemy (aggressive behaviour). The evaluation of these attitudes relies on the evaluation of skills at a lower level i.e. technical.

The overall evaluation of the mission is not restricted to observing whether or not the general objective has been achieved; it is completed by a set of remarks on how the exercise progressed, which is given to the trainees during the debriefing session. These remarks concern the quality of the protection, movement and aggressive behaviour and highlight their connection with the success or the failure of the mission.

The evaluation of a platoon is therefore a process relying on three levels of abstraction. The most concrete level is the evaluation of technical skills. These skills are independent and are expressed in terms of performance which can be observed by the instructor. The intermediate level is the evaluation of tactical skills, which depend on the effective implementation of a set of technical skills with respect to the current context and objective. The third level of the evaluation, which we call strategic, is the overall evaluation of the mission.

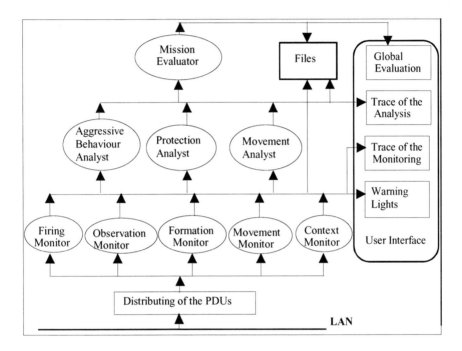

Fig. 1. PPTS Architecture.

4   PPTS Architecture

The information PPTS uses is very different from that used by the instructors. The input data of PPTS is the information that passes through the DIS network, encapsulated in PDUs. However this information does not have any teaching dimension; it is sent to ensure the overall consistency of the distributed simulation. Thanks to the PDUs each simulator has instantaneous knowledge of the other simulators, but this knowledge is limited to the aspects of some interest to it: their position, their speed, fires delivered, etc.

PPTS therefore has incomplete knowledge. The initial data is processed on three levels, according to the evaluation approach of the instructors. The general architecture of PPTS (Figure 1) follows these three levels of evaluation.

The **monitors** constitute the first level of the evaluation, that of the technical skills. The monitors are reactive agents (they operate practically in real time). When an interesting state is detected, the monitor immediately points it out to the instructor through the human-computer interface. At the same time, the monitor generates a set of facts in a working memory accessible to the analysts. A monitor does not make an explicit assessment, its role is only to recognize a behaviour, which will then be evaluated by the analysts.

The firing monitor identifies which tank fired and the type of ammunitions used and specifies the result of the firing: a target was reached, a target was just missed or the firing was lost. It indicates "doubles" (two tanks fired at the same target) and "redoublings" (the same tank fired twice at the same target).

The observation monitor examines the coverage of the observation (each tank is responsible for the observation in a sector) and the convergence of the observation.

The formation monitor recognizes the current formation of the platoon (line formation, diamond, battle, etc).

The movement monitor calculates permanently the respective distances between the tanks of the platoon and reacts if these are too small or too large. In addition, it is responsible for computing the speed of the platoon.

The context monitor detects the position and the level of threat of the enemy. It is responsible in particular for information about intervisibility: it indicates who should see who, because even if an object is visible in the observation sector of a tank, that does not mean that the gunner or the tank commander has seen this object.

The *analysts* use the facts generated by the monitors to evaluate tactical skills. There are three types of analyst: the protection analyst, the aggressive behaviour analyst and the movement analyst. Unlike the monitors, which are reactive agents, the analysts are cognitive agents in that they use the working memory to reason on phenomena with a certain duration and are able to make revisable assumptions. The modelling of the analysts is described in section 6. Their implementation is in progress. Their conclusions will be presented to the instructor and will be expressed at the same time in the form of facts memorised in a second working memory accessible to the mission Evaluator.

It will only intervene after the end of the exercise to evaluate the mission on an overall basis and to generate a document to be used by the instructors during the debriefing, or by the trainees away from the training session. The *mission evaluator* will exploit the facts generated by the analysts describing the development of the protection, aggressive behaviour and movement throughout the mission. This cognitive agent has not been yet modelled in the current state of the project.

The PPTS architecture is clearly bottom-up. Each level processes data resulting from the lower level. At the opposite, the PuppetMaster architecture [4] is top-down. The Situation Spaces correspond mostly to the PPTS tactical level, more precisely to the significant phases (see section 6). Our study of the expertise domain shows that every transition between phases is plausible so every analyst must have the capability to process independently.

5 Implementation of the Monitoring Level

The ALARME software implements the monitors which are instances of new C++ classes. As soon as the PDUs arrive, each monitor computes position, alignment and distance; detects in real time the events concerning it and sends information concerning these events to the user interface.

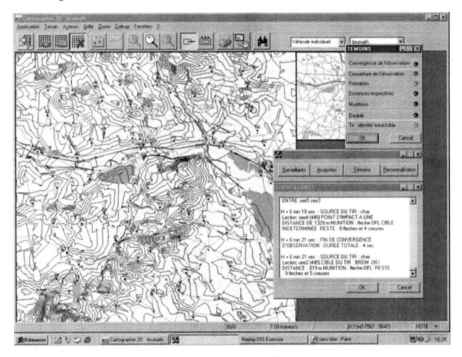

Fig. 2. The ALARME software.

When ALARME is launched, a menu bar proposes the display of various windows: the monitor log window, the analyst log window, the warning light window and the customising window (see Figure 2).

The monitors activate the warning lights corresponding to the events and display messages detailing these events. The customising window enables the instructors at all times to parameterise certain useful values for the warnings lights, for the analysis and also the overall comprehension of the exercise: the instructors can choose which warnings lights should be shown, can change the value thresholds for the activation of certain warnings, can allocate to each simulator a role within the platoon (platoon leader, assistant, subordinate), etc. This customised data is sent immediately to the monitors which modify their processing accordingly. Thus, if the platoon passes from a hilly area to a flat area, the tanks can occupy more ground and the threshold setting off an alarm for respective distances between tanks has to be increased.

Each monitor activates the corresponding warning lights. The context monitor detects in real time the events concerning the enemies (movement, visibility, etc.) which will be useful for the analysis but it is the only one not to send any information to the warning light and monitor windows.

6 Modelling the Analysis Expertise

Figure 1 shows the three levels of the PPTS architecture, which reproduce the hierarchical structuring of the domain knowledge: the technical, tactical and strategic levels. The monitors strictly speaking do not introduce an evaluation; their role is to highlight the significant events of the exercise. They provide the determining elements of the situation which make it possible for the analysts to evaluate the tactical progress of the exercise.

The analysts result from the expert knowledge of the instructors, from documents and from observation of actual exercises. The three identified analysts and the theoretical principles of the domain overlap. In addition, the rules which make explicit the evaluation of each of these tactical aspects refine the principles in order to obtain operational rules. Thus, to each analyst is associated a knowledge base and the monitors which supply it.

The **aggressive behaviour analyst** checks the offensive behaviour of the platoon, its reaction vis-a-vis the enemy, the level of engagement of LECLERC tanks in combat, the quality of the firings. The Firing and Context monitors supply this analyst, which reasons from the firings and from the level of the enemy threat.

The **protection analyst** evaluates the defensive behaviour of the platoon according to the context of the mission. For example, if the platoon is in the observation phase of an allied unit and if the enemy attacks this unit, the platoon has to react as if it were attacked directly. The firing, context, movement and observation monitors supply this analyst, which reasons from the firings, from the level of the enemy threat, from the platoon's movements and the observation coverage.

The **movement analyst** observes the platoon's movements and evaluates the adopted formations. The context, movement, and formation monitors supply this analyst, which reasons from the enemy presence, from the platoon's movements and the adopted formations.

From the analysis of the current context, the exercise is divided into phases. Certain phases are mutually exclusive, combat and speed, for example. On the other hand, other phases may coexist; for example, active monitoring is compatible with speed if it is a question of rapidly reaching a position to defend its ally.

The rules of the analysts were determined and differ according to the phases.

In the active monitoring phase, for example, the following protection rule is that if the enemy fires on an ally the platoon protects, at least one of the platoon's LECLERC tanks has to counterattack very quickly.

In the protection phase, for example, the following protection rule is that if the enemy threatens at least one of the LECLERC tanks when moving, the support tank has to fire within a very short lapse of time. This period is fixed according to the level of the enemy threat.

These protection rules are clarified by rules which evaluate the positive or negative behaviour of the platoon. When theses rules are candidates, they have a period of validity beyond which they are either triggered or become obsolete.

We have therefore organised the evaluation knowledge base into packages of rules associated with the various phases for each kind of analyst (aggressive behaviour, protection and movement). In addition, a rule package determines the type of current phase. The instructors of the domain have carried out an initial validation of the knowledge base.

Figure 3 describes an example of the activation mechanism of the evaluation rule packages. The main process MP "determine phase" monitors the processes involved in executing the rule packages of the analysts. The example above may be illustrated by the following case: a speed phase (P0) is detected at time t. At time t + 50, the platoon goes through a safety phase (P1). This excludes a speed phase so P0 is deactivated. P1 finishes when the platoon stops because it has become obsolete. We then go into the active monitoring phase (P2) when the platoon is able to protect an ally. To move into a better supporting position, the platoon passes into the speed phase (P3) without leaving the active monitoring phase.

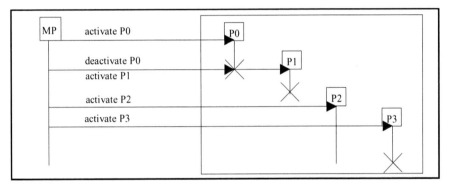

Fig. 3. Activating the rule packages of the analysts.

The main process MP detects the phases on the basis of certain indications. In the absence of these indications, it is not possible to detect the phase shifts and since certain phases complete themselves, certain moments of the exercise may not be characterised. On the other hand, when the situations are unstable, the phase shifts are likely to be detected inappropriately. The major problem lies in the fact that the main process MP is not always able to detect the transitions between phases. The following mechanism makes it possible to manage the transitions between the various phases of the exercise. When a phase is detected and confirmed during a sufficient lapse of time, the main process is able to end all the processes corresponding to incompatible phases. On the other hand, when the transitions are unstable or when the phases are compatible, the main process lets the processes proceed in parallel and triggers an arbitration process. This mechanism will be implemented in the next few months.

7   Conclusion and Future Work

We have designed an evaluator of skills coupled to a network of full-scale simulators. Using the three-level architecture adopted here, modelled on the three levels of expertise, technical, tactic and strategic levels, it is possible to build our system incrementally.

The domain expertise which enabled us to build the knowledge base of our evaluator reflects the principles expressed in the documents and the analysis of the exercises during actual training. This expertise mainly represents the skills of the platoon commander and especially makes it possible to evaluate the platoon taken collectively as a whole. Few rules exist to identify the expected skills of a given part of the platoon. Additional work will be done to refine the existing rules in order to evaluate the contributions of each tank to the collective performance of the platoon.

The technical level of the monitors provides an effective solution for the monitoring of the exercise. Indeed, the events detected by the warning lights provide the instructors with a first level of help, by giving them a relevant trace of the important events of the exercise which could also be used during the debriefing. This initial implementation has been validated by the instructors.

The software architecture at the analyst level provides a flexible solution to the problem of time in the evaluation of the exercise, whether the transitions between phases are sudden or gradual, whether the exercise is slow or rapid. Thus expiry periods for the rules, parallel activation of several packages of rules, the triggering of an arbitration process and the mutual exclusion of certain phases can be handled. To show that our architecture is general, we will validate it on other simulation domains.

References

1. Gecsei, J. and C. Frasson. SAFARI: an environment for creating tutoring systems in industrial training. in ED-MEDIA 94. AACE, Charlottesville, VA, USA; 1994; xiv+783 pp. 1994.(pp. 15-20).
2. Richard, L. and G. Gouardères. An Agent-operated Simulation-based Training System. in AI & ED 99: IOS Press.(pp. 343-351).
3. Ramesh, R. and D.H. Andrews, Distributed Mission training. Com. of the ACM, 1999. 42(9): p. 65-67.
4. Marsella, S.C. and W.L. Johnson. An instructor's assistant for team training in dynamic multi agent virtual worlds. in ITS '98. Springer.(pp. 464-73).
5. Zachary, W., et al. An advanced embedded training system (AETS) for tactical team training. in ITS '98. Springer.(pp. 544-53).
6. Zachary, W., et al., The advanced embedded training system (AETS): An Intelligent Embedded Tutoring System for tactical team training. International Journal of Artificial Intelligence in Education, 1999. 10(3-4): p. 257-277.
7. Loriette, S., J.-M. Nigro, and I. Jarkass. Rule-Based Approaches for the Recognition of Driving Maneuvers. in AISTA'2000: IOS Press.(pp. 141-146).
8. Miller, M.S., et al. Training teams with Collaborative Agents. in Intelligent Tutoring Systems, ITS 2000, Springer.(pp. 63-72).
9. Rickel, J. and W.L. Johnson. Virtual Humans for Team Training in Virtual Reality. in AI&ED99: IOS Press.(pp. 578-585).

Qualitative Assessment on Aeronautical Training with Cognitive Agents

Anton Minko[1], Guy Gouardères[2], and Orest Popov[3]

[1]Interactive STAR, Village d'entreprise 13, ZI de la Rivière, 33850
Léognan, France, anton.minko@star-ima.com
[2]Equipe ISIHM - LIUPPA - IUT de Bayonne, 64100
Bayonne, France, Guy.Gouarderes@iutbay.univ-pau.fr
[3]Faculty of Computer Science & Information Systems, Technical University of Szczecin,
Zolnierska Street 49, 71-210 Szczecin, Poland, popov@wi.ps.pl

Abstract. The present paper discusses the results of application of multi-agent technologies to the diagnostic of errors (and underlying cognitive gaps) in aeronautic training. Cognitive psychology issues related to errors constitute the base for ITS modelling. The model of reasoning based on qualitative simulation is proposed as the base for pedagogical evaluation of the trainee. As a result, simulation-based ITS using «learning-by-doing errors» approach is presented, where multi-agent architecture is used for threefold errors diagnosis: ergonomy, knowledge, psychology. The results of this research have found their applications in ASIMIL project.

Keywords. Simulation-based training, multi-agent systems, qualitative simulation, error diagnostic, aeronautics

1. Introduction

This paper describes how it is possible to improve aeronautical training with using «intelligent» simulators instead of traditional ones. Our work is situated in the field of intelligent tutoring systems for aeronautics (both pilots and mechanics). Today, training is performed mainly on complex simulators (like FBS or FFS[1], which represent the cockpit at scale 1:1). These simulators allow to reach a very high realism level and a good quality of training. However, there are several serious problems, in particular:

- the cost of this kind of tools remains very high and inaccessible for large public,
- the used approach (one trainer - one trainee) doesn't allow to increase the number of trained staff facing the constantly growing demand in aeronautical sector.

We propose a solution using a complete training environment, including:

- desktop simulator tightly combined with multi-agent ITS that performs anytime assessment by tracking the trainee in real-time. The main purpose of multi-agent

---

[1] FBS – Fixed-Based Simulator, FFS – Full Flight Simulator

S.A. Cerri, G. Gouardères, and F. Paraguaçu (Eds.): ITS 2002, LNCS 2363, pp. 531–541, 2002.
© Springer-Verlag Berlin Heidelberg 2002

-   architecture is rigorous error handling, which tends to approach human reasoning thanks to qualitative evaluation of errors committed by trainee
-   implementation, of such important learning concepts as Cognitive Task Analysis and Qualitative Assessment. The first one gives the base for procedural design, while the second one makes the learning more flexible for the trainee in real-time.

The compromise we are looking for and discussing in this paper consists in a way to mix the qualitative assessment with, first, a closely appraisal (due to real-time assessment required by users) and, second, an extreme rigour in evaluating trainee's mastery (in order to guarantee the secure quality of training). Precedent papers [GOU 2000], [POP 2001] already traced the outlines of future training system via using a Multi-Agent System (MAS) for qualifying trainee's errors. The work described in current paper, gives details of different error types, which can be qualified by MAS, as well as mechanism allowing to perform such qualification.

1.1. «Good Quality of Training» – What Does It Mean?

Indeed, it is necessary to precise what we imply under the good quality of training. Indeed, three different types of actors are to be taken into account, each of them having its own criteria of evaluation:

-   for aeronautical companies – before all, these are reliability and security guarantee offered by training with using concrete tools; this criteria is followed by another crucial factor, which is the cost of training;
-   for instructors –particular attention to the flexibility and customisation
-   for trainees – this is the easy-to-use aspect, and the credibility of the tool, i.e. the functional immersion (a thing to avoid absolutely is the situation where the tool transforms to the game).

1.2. Aeronautical Training Today and Tomorrow – Users Expectations

According to users, the general situation has been drawn as follows:

-   state-of-the-art educational software is not good enough – many programs use the same contents since early 90s while aircraft documentation is updated daily
-   lack of integration theory – practice: the courseware is purely theoretical («electronic manual») or purely practical (free-play simulator)
-   no personalization of learning path.

Among the expectations towards the new products we can notice the following ones:

-   high interest to turns today towards distance training over the Internet
-   interactivity (degree of freedom) becomes a more important factor
-   compliance with aeronautical standards (JAR, AICC) as guarantee of security.

ASIMIL tends to create simulation-based tool, which can be used by the trainee autonomously, over the Internet, with possibility to contact the trainer online. Via using intelligent agents, trainees see the courseware adapting to them (basing on diagnostics made about the trainee), and not the opposite.

In next sections we will present successively the place of multi-agent ITS in the model of training, the proposed classification of errors in three groups depending on supposed causes (ergonomy, knowledge, or psychology), and then we will describe the qualitative model used for evaluation of errors. Multi-agent architecture as well as an example about ITS functioning are presented in order to illustrate the solution chosen for the design and implementation.

2.   Training Process Modelling

The general problematic raised in the paper – how to get the quality of computer-mediated training comparable with the classic training? What do we need to add to simulators in order to get new quality of training? We found the answer in using ITS (intelligent tutoring systems) that modify the classic scheme of training, like it is shown on fig. 1:

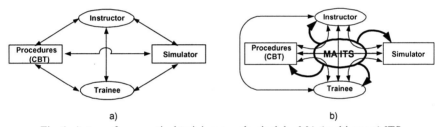

a)   b)

Fig. 1. Actors of aeronautical training: a – classical, b –MA (multi-agent) ITS

The role of instructor is paramount in training (Fig.1, a), because the instructor is the person who plans training session and chooses the appropriate pedagogical strategies in order to ensure the best quality of training. The main task of tutoring process automation consists in decreasing the instructor's charge, reached via decreasing his usual routine actions. Furthermore, the ITS is obliged to interact with all components of classical training loop (Fig.1, b) [POP 2001].

The logical analysis of the process of training using ITS allows to represent this process in the form of 3-level hierarchical structure: (Fig. 2) [GOU 2000].

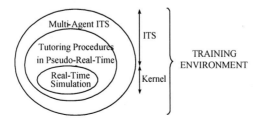

Fig. 2. The concept of training using intelligent tutoring system

The first level (or simulation kernel) is computer model of the aircraft (in our case this is the piloted aircraft as well as its systems). This kernel of simulation runs in real-time mode.

The second level is the level of procedures. This level is in charge of comparing the actions performed by the trainee, with the nominal actions prescribed by procedures. The level of procedures is a reactive one (only binary evaluation correct/incorrect).

The third level is that of intelligent training system (ITS). At this level the complete evaluation of trainee's actions is done (ITS accomplishes not only binary "correct/incorrect" estimation, but also performs the diagnostic of errors).

All three levels are inter-related: ITS uses the information about the simulator and procedures, and is able to control the simulator. The procedures level is also using the information on actions performed by the trainee, in order to reflect properly the current situation in the dynamic follow-up window.

Multi-agent architecture drives the third level of ITS, using agents of different types:
- reactive, which are bound to the kernel of simulator (they act according to « stimulus-reaction » principle)
- planned, which correct errors in the procedures, basing on a set of decision rules
- cognitive, which diagnose possible cognitive gaps (see below). The term "cognitive agent" is used in the sense of [FER 1999], i.e. "an agent is said to be cognitive if it can give a meaning to what it perceives, and one represents that understanding of the world as a mental or cognitive state", referring to the well-known Belief, Desire or Intentions.

3. From Error to Cognitive Gap

In aeronautical training, the error can not be viewed as simple deviation from the prescribed task. This definition is too restrictive. The designer's task consists in defining a number of alternative ways to reach a goal, in order to cover different solutions the trainee is likely to adopt. If we consider an error as a deviation from the standard, how to define exactly that standard? Three referentials could be planned [JAM 1996]: (a) referential of the prescribed task: the error is defined as non-respect of the procedure or non-application of paper manual's recommendations, (b) referential of operators in the same profession: the referential represents the set of tasks executed by an operator-type in the same profession, (c) referential of the operator himself: the individual activity of the operator is taken into account.

From the point of view of human-machine interaction, the definition of Reason [REA 1990] gives the view on the error as an intention of the operator. However, the operator's intention is unknown during the phase of interface design. The best suggestion designers can have is the task analysis. This analysis includes, in most of cases, a series of procedures corresponding to objectives prescribed to the operator. Implicitly, the intentions and the objectives of the operator are supposed to be identical. But, they are not necessarily the same.

In this relation, we need a system which doesn't simply analyse the errors from the point of view of lacking knowledge, but performs a complete diagnostic of an operator, detecting other disturbing factors susceptible to prevent the good procedure progress (hesitation, motivation lack, excessive concentration). So, we call Cognitive Gaps the omissions and/or deviations from the standard, which are introduced in the user's reasoning at a precise moment (time index) by one of these disturbing factors.

In [GOU 2000], we already established a primitive gaps typology ("tunnel", dropping and motivation gaps). The analysis of works performed by Rasmussen [RAS 1986], Norman [NOR 1991], Reason [REA 1990], maked us to extend that typology, distinguishing three different types of errors (or, more exactly, cognitive gaps):

- errors due to insufficient knowledge – this type of errors represents the primary hypothesis about the issue of an incorrect answer/action
- errors due to bad ergonomy of the ITS – these errors can be detected after the observations of trainee's interactions with common elements of ITS; if trainee doesn't master the tool because of interface issues, he/she loses motivation to learn and will not get good results in the end of training course
- errors related to psycho-physiological factors of human operator (i.e. human factor) – this type of errors is the most difficult to detect (such phenomena as lack of attention, discouragement, excessive concentration («tunnel effect»)); it needs more complex analysis of the whole training session from the beginning. These psycho-physiological discrepancies are analysed by the system in order to determine the level of trainee's self-confidence [AIM 2000].

All the three erroneous behaviours are characterised by the following symptoms:

- erroneous actions and/or
- excessive time delays while performing actions and/or
- chaotic overview of the cockpit (as if the person was looking for something lost).

Let us see to the following results observed in real planes (see table 1), assuming that approximate values of time needed for different operations is: signal detection – ~0.1 sec, visual image recognition – ~0.4 sec, decision making – max 3-4 sec, motion reaction – max 0.5 sec. It is easy to see that time of reaction should be comprised between 2 and 6 seconds.

Table 1. Approximate percentage of piloting errors. Distribution on 100 samples

Task	Description of faults	Quantity
Signal detection	Instrument value was not taken	4
	Calculus was made from another instrument	13
	Using of failing instrument	9
Signal recognition	Wrong calculus of values because of difficulty of reading (bad legibility)	14
	Wrong calculus of values because of instrument's complexity	18
	Wrong interpretation of instrument's scale	6
Signal identification	Wrong logical interpretation of instrument's values	17
Evaluation of situation	Wrong evaluation of the complete set of received signals	5
Choice of right method/action	Wrong actions (reactions) on signal	14

Signal detection task (26%) belongs to the group of psychology errors (bad trainee's concentration), signal recognition task (38%) is interpreted as ergonomic errors (ergonomy not adapted), and the rest of symptoms (36%) shows knowledge-related errors (trainee is not able to interpret received signals).

4. Error Modelling. Qualitative Simulation

In order to allow the ITSs to exit from the framework of classic symbolic inferences and to allow them to approach human efficiency, we need to have the means of representation of imprecise, qualitatitve knowledge as well as mechanisms of inferences on this knowledge. Non-deterministic control is very characteristic for training applications. This control is unavoidable because knowledge is acquired in a fragmentary fashion, and it is impossible to define a chain of logic reasoning a priori.

In this relation, two important factors are to be taken in consideration:

- strong dependence on the context (the same erroneous behaviour pattern can mean different errors in two different contexts)
- incomplete input information during the error diagnosis (*a priori*, it is impossible to gather and to take into account all sources of information used by the trainee during his activity on the simulator).

The first constraint was resolved via using additional small knowledge bases/plug-ins (which may be different for each procedure). For example, turn procedures are more restrictive in terms of aircraft stability than cruise flight procedures. ITS knowledge base already contains general rules related to cruise flight, while turn procedures overload their more restrictive parameters (taken in those plug-ins), what allows ITS to qualify trainee's performances in the right context.

In order to solve second constraint, we performed an analysis of several methods and techniques of the artificial intelligence, which use incomplete and/or qualitative knowledge in the engine of inference of ITS – Bayesian belief networks [GAN 2000], fuzzy logic, non-monotonic logic [WOO 1998], or qualitative simulation [KUI 1994].

We have chosen the qualitative simulation technique. This approach is based on the observation, according to which the human perceives and reacts in different situations in a very performant fashion, not by solving algebraic equations, but by reasoning on mental models of a qualitative nature. A qualitative model is represented as a network of influences between the parameters of the modelled system (in terms of positive, negative, or null influences between different parameters).

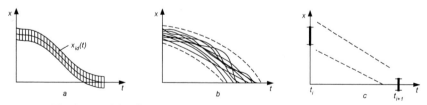

Fig. 3. Transition from numerical equation curve to qualitative curve

Fig. 3 (example taken from the evaluation of flight trajectory [KRA 1995]) illustrates transformation beginning from purely analytical evaluation (a); passing by two polynomial curves (b), where one needs to know only the type of equation (polynomial, sinusoidal etc.); finishing with classic qualitative linear form (c), which determines only the limits for hall of correct behaviour, represented by straight lines. This is an example of evaluation (see Table 2).

Table 2. Rating of trainee's actions (rating from 2 – the worst, to 5 – the best

	yaw	pitch	roll	yaw	pitch	roll	yaw	pitch	roll	yaw	pitch	roll
Value, °	0	15	0	1	0	5	2	0	0	0	5	90
Rating		5			5			5			1	
Value, °	0	15	5	1	0	10	2	0	5	0	5	60
Rating		5			5			5			3	
Value, °	0	15	10	1	0	15	2	0	10	0	15	60
Rating		4			5			5			2	
Value, °	0	15	15	1	5	0	2	0	15	0	15	45
Rating		4			5			5			5	
Value, °	0	10	15	1	5	5	2	5	5	0	20	45
Rating		5			5			5			3	
Value, °	0	5	15	1	5	10	2	10	15	0	20	60
Rating		4			5			5			3	
Value, °	0	5	10	1	5	15	2	10	90	0	20	90
Rating		5			5			1			2	
Value, °	0	0	10	1	10	5	2	15	30	0	0	45
Rating		5			4			4			4	
Value, °	0	0	15	1	15	15	2	15	45	0	0	30
Rating		5			3			3			5	

For example, during orientation in the air, the pilot operates with three angles - roll, pitch and yaw (supposing that other parameters are constant). For example, the roll at 15° allows the pilot to control the plane with more freedom, than the roll at 45°. Such tables of allow the designers of MA ITS to give a high level of intelligence to agents; this intelligence being close, to the reasoning performed by instructors.

5. Multi-agent System Representation

5.1. General Presentation of MA ITS[2]

Multi-agent technologies are widely used in the domain of ITS [FRA 1996], [GOU 2000], [RIC 1999]. Aeronautical training has five characteristics, which make it particularly well-suited for agents application: it is modular, decentralised, changeable, ill-structured, and complex.

5.2. ASITS Architecture and Its Application to ASIMIL

Three main components of an ITS (student, knowledge and pedagogical model) have been formerly built in the form of intelligent agent architecture as in Actors architecture [FRA 1996]. This architecture is presented on the fig. 4.

---

[2] Multi-Agent Intelligent Tutoring System

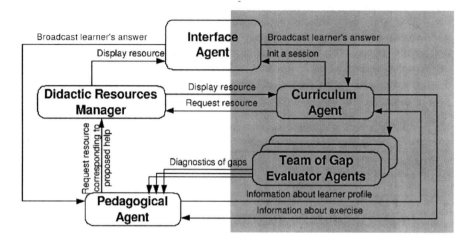

Fig. 4. ASIMIL architecture based on ASITS

Different agents of this architecture are:
-   Interface agent communicates between MAS and other components of system (simulator, virtual reality, procedures)
-   Curriculum agent tracks the evolution of the trainee in interaction with the training system and builds progressively the history of events
-   Team of Gap Evaluator Agents perform the diagnostic of trainee's errors following following axes: ergonomy-, knowledge-, or psychology-related gaps
-   Pedagogical - contains the pedagogical expertise and helps trainee after mistakes
-   Didactic resources manager searches for pedagogical resource (help etc.) to show.

5.3. Complex Gap Evaluation Strategies

In the real plane, or in CMOS-like simulator [GOU 2000], the instructor can verify knowledge by introducing a troubleshooting procedure. If the error appears, it is analysed later during the debriefing.

Tracking by agents in CMOS is demonstrated in [GOU 2000]. Today, presence of multiple agents – gap evaluators gives a possibility to diagnose multiple kinds of errors. Gap detector agent launches evaluations after the deviation is detected. Then gap is quantified, evaluated and forwarded to the pedagogical agent to be exploited (signalled to the trainee or stocked for reuse in debriefing phase).

5.4. Example of Agents Functioning

Fig. 5 shows two screens: simulator and Procedures (agents are not present on the interface – they manifest their activity by showing messages to the user). The procedure presented is entitled "Before take-off" preparation (actions that should be performed just before the plane begins the take-off). The user has to accomplish series of actions on the simulator, and procedures follow-up component will check, one after one, the accuracy of actions being performed by the learner. If the action performed by the learner doesn't correspond to the action required, red cross is fired.

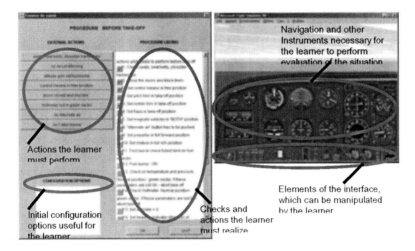

Fig. 5. Procedures follow-up system and the simulator (on the example of Microsoft Flight Simulator)

The diagnostic of errors (correct/incorrect action) being performed by Procedures, agents serve to detect and to diagnose cognitive gaps. This diagnosis is based on the analysis of trainee's interactions with the simulator, especially on the delays in reactions and of the number of useless actions (mouse clicks on the simulator window). For example, the fact of simply clicking three times on the simulator interface means that the trainee is not very familiar with it; another example – delay of more than 6 seconds while performing an action means that the trainee hesitates.

6. Current State of the Project

Design and implementation of a multi-agent system are being done using JADE platform. JADE (Java Agent DEvelopment framework) is a software framework for agent-based applications in compliance with the FIPA (http://www.fipa.org) specifications. The goal is to simplify the development while ensuring standard compliance through a comprehensive set of system services and agents. JADE can then be considered as an agent middle-ware that implements an agent platform and a development framework. It deals with all those aspects that are not peculiar of the agents internals and that are independent of the applications, such as message transport, encoding and parsing, or agent life-cycle.

According to project schedule, the evaluation is starting now. The more complete results will be available for May, 2002. The evaluation is twofold regarding agents functionality:

-   research validation using virtual users (virtual trainee) assisted by agents
-   users validation involving aeronautics professionals, instructors and IMA (Institut de Maintenance Aéronautique at Bordeaux, France) students.

7. Conclusions and Perspectives

In aeronautics, the complexity of aeroplane's cabin as well as number and layout of its instruments make the task of computer-assisted training (and, in particular, distance learning) very difficult. In state-of-the-art systems, the evaluation and certification are exclusively based on the instructor that follows the trainee step-by-step, relying on incomplete tracking and inferring prohibitive costs of current face-to-face training.

An important scientific problem of causal level, mainly issued from hardly observable parameters (but detectable on human-machine interface), was approached by the way of studying cognitive characteristics (difficulty, type of cognitive gap associated to the task), tracking environment variables (simulator state, learner profile) and evaluating by different agents the measure, or flexibility degree, of several stages of training.

Such characteristics as real-time follow-up by the instructor of trainee's cognitive discrepancies, making distinction among simulator-, procedures-, and cognitive tasks-related errors committed by the trainee, were objective of our research. The mastery of these variables via appropriate qualitative simulation as well as establishment of errors' hierarchy represent together the key advancement in relation to the precedent work [GOU 2000]. Now, the extension of errors' evaluation represents an unavoidable phase in the process of certification and accreditation of training courses, which will be likely to use ASIMIL software environment.

To meet this challenge, ASIMIL is developing a complete architecture, including the simulator equipped with virtual reality tools, a comprehensive multi-agent system, and online assistance feature.

Via experimentation and analysis of its current limits, this prototype allows to define future ways of investigation and type of research goals to assign to our works, which the next to come are: distance diagnostic, parallel management of several trainees working on the same simulator, detection and expression of emotions by ITS, etc.

Acknowledgements. This research was supported by ASIMIL project. ASIMIL (Aero user friendly SIMulation based dIstance Learning) project is a shared-cost RTD Project financed in 5th Framework, International Society Technologies Programme (IST-1999-11286), managed by Information Society DG of the European Commission. The project regroups 11 partners from 6 countries. Main objective of ASIMIL consists in exploring new approaches in aeronautical training, including distance learning, simulation, intelligent agents and virtual reality technologies.

We gratefully acknowledge the contribution of Alexander Tretyakov from IMA (ASIMIL partner) for qualitative evaluation experiments and the table used in this paper.

References

[AIM 2000] Aïmeur E., Frasson C. «Reference Model For Evaluating Intelligent Tutoring Systems» - TICE'2000, October 18-20 2000, Troyes – France.

[FER 1999] J. Ferber. Multi-Agent System: An Introduction to Distributed Artificial Intelligence. Harlow: Addison Wesley Longman, 1999

[FRA 1996] C. Frasson, T. Mengelle, E. Aïmeur, G. Gouardères. «An actor-based architecture for intelligent tutoring systems», Intl Conference on ITS, Montréal, 1996.

[GAN 2000] Ganeshan R., Johnson W.L., Shaw E., and Wood B.P. «Tutoring Diagnostic Problem Solving», In Proceedings of the Fifth Int'l Conf. on Intelligent Tutoring Systems, 2000.

[GOU 2000] G. Gouardères, A. Minko, L. Richard. «Co-operative Agents to Track Learner's Cognitive Gap», ITS-2000 – International Conference on Intelligent Tutoring Systems, Montréal, June 2000.

[JAM 1996] F. Jambon. «Formal modelling of task interruptions». Conference Human Factors in Computing Systems (CHI'96), Canada. ACM Press, 1996, pp. 45-46.

[KRA 1995] Krassovski A.A. «Basics of theory of simulators in aviation». Moscow, Machinostroenie, 1995, 304p. (in Russian)

[KUI 1994] B. Kuipers. «Qualitative Reasoning: Modelling and Simulation with Incomplete Knowledge». The MIT press, Cambridge, Massachusets, London, 1994

[NOR 1991] Norman K.L., «The psychology of menu selection: designing cognitive control at the human/computer interface», 1991.

[POP 2001] Popov O., Lalanne R., Gouardères G., Minko A., Tretyakov A. «The Structure of Multi-Agent Learning System and its Application in Aeronautical Training». Proc. of the 10th International Symposium SMC'01, Poland, 2001.

[RAS 1986] Rasmussen J. «Information processing and human-machine interaction: an approach to cognitive engineering», North-Holland, 1986.

[REA 1990] Reason J. «Human error». Cambridge University Press. Cambridge,1990.

[RIC 1999] Richard L. "Un système Multi-agents pour la modélisation d'Environnements Interactifs d'Apprentissage avec Ordinateur basés sur la simulation. Application à la formation de personnel de maintenance aéronautique", Thèse de doctorat de l'Université Toulouse III, 1999.

[WOO 1998] Wooldridge M, Parsons S. «Intention reconsideration reconsidered». Agent Theories, Architectures, and Languages – 5th International Workshop, ATAL'98, Paris, France, July 4-7, 1998 – pp.63-80.

Collaborative Discourse Theory as a Foundation for Tutorial Dialogue

Jeff Rickel[1], Neal Lesh[2], Charles Rich[2], Candace L. Sidner[2], and and Abigail Gertner[3]

[1] USC Information Sciences Institute, 4676 Admiralty Way, Marina del Rey, CA, 90292
rickel@isi.edu, http://www.isi.edu/isd/rickel
[2] Mitsubishi Electric Research Laboratories, 201 Broadway, Cambridge, MA, 02139
lesh,rich,sidner@merl.com, http://www.merl.com/projects/collagen
[3] MITRE Corporation, 202 Burlington Road, Bedford, MA, 01730
gertner@mitre.org, http://www.mitre.org/resources/centers/it/g068

Abstract. Research on intelligent tutoring systems has not leveraged general models of collaborative discourse, even though tutoring is inherently collaborative. Similarly, research on collaborative discourse theory has rarely addressed tutorial issues, even though teaching and learning are important components of collaboration. We help bridge the gap between these two related research threads by presenting a tutorial agent, called Paco, that we built using a domain-independent collaboration manager, called Collagen. Our primary contribution is to show how a variety of tutorial behaviors can be expressed as rules for generating candidate discourse acts in the framework of collaborative discourse theory.

1   Introduction

Our research objective is to develop computer tutors that collaborate with students on tasks in simulated environments. Towards this end, we seek to integrate two separate but related research threads: intelligent tutoring systems (ITS) and collaborative dialogue systems (CDS). Research on ITS [20] focuses on computer tutors that adapt to individual students based on the target knowledge the student is expected to learn and the presumed state of the student's current knowledge. Research on CDS (e.g., [8,11]), with an equally long history, focuses on computational models of human dialogue for collaborative tasks.

Effective instructional dialogue is best understood as a mixed-initiative interaction between tutor and student, in which the student works to solve problems while the tutor monitors the student's progress, providing feedback and hints when needed. Good human tutors aim to maintain progress in problem solving while supporting the student's sense of control and self-confidence, a balancing act that requires a high degree of interactivity and collaboration. Thus, it is natural to expect that a model of collaborative dialogue would provide a solid framework on which to build a conversational ITS. Furthermore, the flexibility of such a framework in supporting a wide range of collaborative interactions allows for the implementation of a variety of pedagogical strategies.

Unfortunately, there has been a surprising lack of cross-fertilization between these two research areas. Work on tutorial dialogue for intelligent tutoring systems (e.g., [4, 12,21]) has not leveraged general models of collaborative dialogue. Similarly, research

S.A. Cerri, G. Gouardères, and F. Paraguaçu (Eds.): ITS 2002, LNCS 2363, pp. 542–551, 2002.

on collaborative dialogues has focused on modeling conversations between peers or between an expert and novice, but has rarely addressed tutorial issues.

To help integrate ITS and CDS, we developed a tutorial agent in Collagen [15,16], a middleware system based on a long line of research on collaborative discourse [8, 7,6,11]. Collagen maintains a model of the discourse state shared by the user (e.g., student) and the computer agent (e.g., tutor). Agents constructed using Collagen use the discourse state to generate an agenda of candidate *discourse acts*, including both utterances and domain actions, and then choose one to utter or perform. Our domain-independent tutorial agent, Paco (Pedagogical Agent for Collagen), has already been used in several independent research projects [1,3,19].

Paco teaches students procedural tasks in simulated environments, building on ideas from earlier tutoring systems. While Paco engages in slightly more sophisticated con-versations than previous such tutors, our primary contribution is to show how various tutorial behaviors can be expressed as rules for generating candidate discourse acts in Collagen. Translating tutorial behaviors into the framework of CDS is a first step towards building tutoring agents that can leverage advances in collaborative discourse theory. A secondary goal of this work is to assess Collagen's value for building tutorial agents, both in terms of the theory it reflects and the software architecture it supports.

2   Pedagogical Approach

Paco supports simulation-based training, in which students learn tasks by performing them in a simulation of the real work environment. Paco repeatedly chooses a scenario, i.e., a task to perform starting from a particular simulation state, and then works through it with the student. Ideally, students should learn to flexibly apply well-defined procedures in a variety of situations.

Figure 1 shows an example dialogue from one implemented application of Paco that illustrates some of the key features we support. Paco is teaching the student how to operate the gas turbine engines that propel naval ships. Paco has previously taught the student how to engage an engine. Now, Paco is teaching the same procedure under slightly more complex conditions: (1) a high vibration alarm has occurred on the gas turbine generator, shutting down the generator, so the student will have to reset the alarm before starting the generator; and (2) a second engine is already running, so the student will have to stop it before starting the desired engine. The remainder of the paper will use this example dialogue to illustrate aspects of our design.

Our pedagogical approach is based on the apprenticeship model of learning [2]. To implement this approach, Paco uses a student model to dynamically interleave demon-stration and coached practice, using the approach introduced by Rickel [17]. As the student and Paco progress through a task, Collagen repeatedly identifies the set of valid next steps. Paco consults the student model to see whether the student has sufficient knowledge to choose one of them. (Any action that appears in the set of valid next steps is considered correct if performed by the student). If so, it expects the student to take the next step, and provides assistance only if the student requests it or makes a mistake. If not, Paco intervenes and teaches the student what to do next (e.g., lines 8-12 and 18-35). Thus, as Paco and the student work through tasks, initiative passes back and

(1) **Paco** sets the state of the simulator.

(2) **Paco** "I've reset the simulation so that we can try engaging an engine under slightly different conditions."

(3) **Paco** "Let's engage engine one."

(4) **Student** "Ok."

(5) **Paco** "You take it from here."

(6) **Student** "Let's start the generator."

(7) **Paco** "Good."

(8) **Paco** (Pointing) "Now, notice that the alarm light is on."

(9) **Paco** "Before starting a generator, always make sure that the alarm light is off so that you'll know when a new alarm appears."

(10) **Paco** (Pointing) "Press the alarm reset button on the generator in order to extinguish the alarm."

(11) **Student** presses the alarm reset button on the generator.

(12) **Paco** "Good."

(13) **Student** "Ok."

(14) **Paco** "You take it from here."

(15) **Student** presses the on button on the generator.

(16) **Paco** "Great."

(17) **Paco** "We succeeded in starting the generator."

(18) **Paco** (Pointing) "Now, notice that engine two is running."

(19) **Paco** "Before starting an engine, always make sure that the other engine is stopped."

(20) **Paco** "Let's stop engine two."

(21) **Paco** (Pointing) "First, press the disengage button on engine two in order to disengage the clutch."

(22) **Student** presses the disengage button on engine two.

(23) **Paco** "Right."

(24) **Paco** "The next step of stopping engine two is to close the fuel valves on engine two."

(25) **Student** "Ok."

(26) **Paco** "You take it from here."

(27) **Student** closes fuel valve one on engine two.

(28) **Paco** "Good."

(29) **Student** closes fuel valve two on engine two.

(30) **Paco** "Good job."

(31) **Paco** (Pointing) "The next step is to press the off button on engine two."

(32) **Student** presses the off button on engine two.

(33) **Paco** "Great."

(34) **Paco** (Pointing) "The indicator light tells us that engine two is stopped."

(35) **Paco** "So, we succeeded in stopping engine two."

(36) **Student** "Ok."

(37) **Paco** "You take it from here."

(38) **Student** opens fuel valve one on engine one.

(39) **Paco** "Good."

(40) **Student** opens the bleed valve on engine one.

(41) **Paco** "That was a correct action, but I wasn't expecting you to do it now."

(42) **Paco** "Let's go back to opening the fuel valves on engine one."

(43) **Student** opens fuel valve two on engine one.

(44) **Paco** "Great."

(45) **Student** presses the engage button on engine one.

(46) **Paco** "Whoops, you can't do that yet."

(47) **Student** "What next?"

(48) **Paco** (Pointing) "Press the on button on engine one."

(49) **Student** presses the on button on engine one.

(50) **Paco** "Good."

(51) **Student** "I think I should set the throttle speed."

(52) **Paco** "Right."

(53) **Student** "What should the speed be?"

(54) **Paco** "The speed should be stop."

(55) **Student** sets the throttle speed to stop.

(56) **Paco** "Good."

(57) **Student** presses the engage button on engine one.

(58) **Paco** "Good job."

(59) **Paco** "We succeeded in engaging engine one."

Fig. 1. An example dialogue in which Paco teaches steps in the current task (e.g., lines 21, 31), teaches that subtasks are finished (e.g., lines 17, 35), provides help when requested (e.g., line 48), passes initiative to the student when she should know what to do next (e.g., lines 5, 14, 26), provides positive feedback (e.g., lines 7, 16, 23), diagnoses and critiques incorrect actions (e.g., line 46), explains why steps needs to be done (e.g., line 9), discusses postconditions for actions (e.g., line 34), and keeps the student focused on the current subtask (e.g., line 42).

forth between them based on the student's prior experience. Whenever Paco decides that the initiative should shift, it lets the student know through verbal comments (e.g., "You take it from here").

Paco is fundamentally a tutor for supporting coached practice, but there are certain strategic pedagogical decisions within this approach that are flexible and easily changed. For example, while it is capable of demonstrating actions on the simulation, in Figure 1 Paco does not demonstrate any of the steps but rather prompts the student to perform them. Whether or not to demonstrate is a strategic decision that can be made based on properties of the domain and the student population. The contribution of this work is not to argue for or against particular instructional strategies, but rather to show that such decisions can easily be implemented in a collaborative dialogue system using straightforward discourse generation rules.

Paco represents the procedures it will teach using Collagen's declarative language for domain-specific procedural knowledge. This knowledge serves as a model of how domain tasks should be performed. Each task is associated with one or more *recipes* (i.e., procedures for performing the task). Each recipe consists of several elements drawn from a relatively standard plan representation. First, it includes a set of steps, each of which is either a primitive action (e.g., press a button) or a composite action (i.e., a subtask). Composite actions give tasks a hierarchical structure. Second, there may be ordering constraints among the steps that define a partial order over them. Third, a task and its steps can have parameters, and a recipe can specify constraints (bindings) among the parameters of a task and its steps. Finally, steps can have preconditions (to allow Collagen to determine whether a step can be performed in the current state) and postconditions (to determine whether the effects of a step have been achieved).

3   Collagen as a Foundation for Teaching Procedural Tasks

Collagen's main value for building tutoring systems is that it provides a general model of collaborative dialogue based on well-established principles from computational linguistics. The model includes two main parts: (1) a representation of discourse state and (2) a discourse interpretation algorithm that uses plan recognition to update the discourse state given the actions and utterances of the user and agent. Previous tutoring systems for procedural tasks do not include dialogue managers with this level of generality.

Based on the work of Grosz and Sidner [7], Collagen partitions the discourse state into three interrelated components: the linguistic structure, the attentional state, and the intentional structure. The linguistic structure groups the dialogue history into a hierarchy of discourse *segments*. Each segment is a contiguous sequence of actions and utterances that contribute to some *purpose* (e.g., performing a subtask). For example, lines 8 through 14 in Figure 1 represent a segment whose purpose is to reset the alarm, and this segment is part of a larger segment (lines 6 through 17) whose purpose is to start the generator. The segmentation scheme does not restrict the nature of the dialogue; Collagen allows segments with an unknown purpose, it allows dialogue about a single purpose to be split into multiple segments when it is interrupted by unrelated dialogue, and a single utterance can even include clauses belonging to different segments.

The attentional state represents what the user and agent are talking about or working on at a given moment. Tutors must track the attentional state in order to interpret the student's actions and utterances (i.e., guide plan recognition [10]), tailor suggestions, choose actions and utterances that serve as natural progressions of the dialogue (or properly mark unexpected shifts with cue phrases [7]), and recognize unnatural focus shifts by the student that may suggest misconceptions. Representing and tracking attentional state is simple for tutors that retain tight control over a fixed topic progression, but it becomes more complex in mixed-initiative dialogues where the student and tutor have more freedom to initiate topics for discussion and choose the execution order for tasks and subtasks.

Following Grosz and Sidner [7], Collagen represents the attentional state as a stack of discourse purposes called the focus stack. When a new discourse segment is begun, its purpose is pushed onto the stack. When a discourse segment is completed or discontinued, its purpose is popped off the stack. The stack mechanism allows Collagen to handle interruptions and digressions. Additionally, the attentional state maintained by Collagen includes an extension to the original model of Grosz and Sidner to capture which participant holds the conversational initiative. This allows Paco to decide when to explicitly pass the initiative to the student (e.g., "You take it from here.").

While the linguistic structure and attentional state closely reflect the actual temporal order of actions and utterances in the dialogue, the intentional structure represents the decisions that have been made as a result of those actions and utterances, independent of their order. As with attentional state, such information is most needed in mixed-initiative tutoring systems that do not impose a strict ordering on decisions. Collagen represents the intentional structure as *plan trees*, which are a partial implementation of SharedPlans [6]. Nodes in the tree represent mutually agreed upon intentions (e.g., to perform a task), and the tree structure represents the subgoal relationships among these intentions. Plan trees also record other types of decisions, such as whether a recipe has been chosen for a task, whether any of its parameters have been determined, and who is responsible for performing the task (e.g., student, agent, or both).

The heart of Collagen is the discourse interpretation algorithm, which specifies how to update the discourse state given a new action or utterance by either the user or agent. Its objective is to determine how the current act contributes to the collaboration. For example, the act could contribute to the current discourse segment's purpose (DSP) by directly achieving it (e.g., pressing a button when that action is the current DSP), proposing how it can be achieved (i.e., suggesting a recipe), proposing or performing a step in its recipe, or proposing a value for one of its unspecified parameters. If it does not contribute to the current DSP, Collagen must determine whether it is a shift in focus or an interruption. Collagen extends Lochbaum's discourse interpretation algorithm [11] with plan recognition, which can recognize when an act contributes to a DSP through one or more implicit acts [10,9].

Collagen performs "near-miss" plan recognition if it cannot find a correct interpretation of an act. It systematically searches for extensions to the plan tree that would explain the current act if some constraint were relaxed. For example, it can recognize acts that would violate an ordering constraint, unnecessarily repeat a step that was already performed, or perform a step that should be skipped because its effects are already satisfied.

Thus, near-miss plan recognition attempts to find plausible interpretations of student errors, providing a domain-independent capability for student diagnosis. Additionally, a domain author can define new types of errors or add explicit buggy recipes.

Figure 2 shows how Paco fits into the general Collagen architecture. The three software components in this architecture are the simulator, Collagen, and the agent (e.g., Paco). Paco and Collagen can be used in a new domain given only the appropriate domain task knowledge and an interface to the simulator. Collagen makes very few assumptions about the simulator. Primarily, it assumes that the user and agent can both perform domain actions (e.g., open a fuel valve) and can observe the actions taken by each other. Collagen makes no assumptions about the simulator's user interface. The simulator can, however, optionally specify a screen location for domain actions, which allows the agent to use a pointing hand to draw the user's attention to an object or indicate that the agent is performing an action.

Collagen represents utterances using an artificial discourse language derived from earlier work by Sidner [18]. The language is intended to include the types of utterances that people use when collaborating on tasks. Currently, Collagen's language includes utterance types for agreeing ("yes" and "OK") and disagreeing ("no"), proposing a task or action (e.g., "Let's start the generator"), indicating when a task has been accomplished (e.g., "We succeeded in stopping engine two"), abandoning a task, asking about or proposing the value of a parameter to a task or action (e.g., "What should the speed be?"), asking or proposing how a task should be accomplished, and asking what should be done next ("What next?"). Current work is extending Collagen's language to include additional elements from Sidner's language, especially to support negotiation about task decisions.

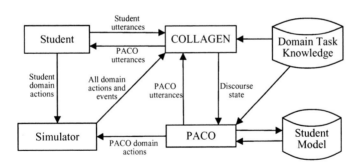

Fig. 2. Paco's Architecture

Since Collagen operates on statements in the artificial discourse language, it does not rely on any particular method of gathering input utterances or generating output utterances. Collagen provides a menu-driven user window that allows the user to construct utterances in English. We also use commercial speech recognition software and grammar rules as a shortcut to the menu-driven interface. To generate output utterances, Collagen uses a combination of domain-independent and (optional) domain-specific text templates. It displays the output strings in a window and speaks them using commercial speech synthesis software.

4   Tutorial Behaviors as Collaborative Discourse Acts

Table 1 summarizes our progress in mapping tutorial behaviors into a CDS framework. Due to space restrictions, it only describes a representative subset of Paco's current behaviors. The first column is a ranked list of tutorial act types. The second column describes procedures that generate zero or more instances of each act type from the current discourse state and student model. When it is Paco's turn, it constructs a prioritized agenda by evaluating the procedures for each act type, and then selects the highest ranked act in this agenda. The third column shows the semantics of each act type in Sidner's [18] artificial discourse language, which determines how the act will be interpreted by Collagen's discourse interpretation algorithm. Several of the act types have subcases, shown in the fourth column, which share the same basic semantics, but differ in how they are rendered into English (fifth column).

Paco uses several elements of the discourse state to generate its discourse acts, including the focus stack, the initiative, and plan trees. The focus stack is used, for example, to avoid teaching a step before its purpose is in focus. The focus stack also indicates when the student has interrupted the current task prematurely, which causes Paco to generate a candidate discourse act which would end the current interruption. In addition to the shared focus maintained by Collagen, Paco also maintains a *private focus* because it prefers to finish teaching an action before moving on. If the student starts working on another part of the task (thus popping the current focus from the shared focus stack) while there are still valid steps within Paco's private focus (e.g., line 40 in Figure 1), Paco will add a Correct Focus action (e.g., line 42) to the agenda, although Paco might choose to execute a higher-ranked element on the agenda first (e.g., line 41).

The conditions for generating discourse acts are easy to compute given the data structures maintained by Collagen. For example, several acts operate on the *valid next actions*, which refers to steps that can be executed next based on precondition and ordering constraints.Collagen computes this information during discourse interpretation. Additionally, Collagen's near-miss recognition computes the conditions needed to generate the various subcases of Negative Feedback (e.g., line 46). Finally, when the student asks for help (e.g., line 47) this pushes a discourse purpose of helping the student onto the stack which remains there until the agent provides the help (e.g., line 48).

Using the generic capabilities of Collagen to record information about a user, Paco maintains a simple overlay model [5] that records, for each step in a recipe, whether the student has been exposed to it. In Table 1, the condition "the student knows step ω" means that the student has been taught this step before. The condition "student knows step ω needs to be done" means the student has been taught all the steps that connect ω to the root of the current plan. Finally, Paco's student model also records which actions the student has been told that she has completed (e.g., line 17). The condition "the student knows when ω is complete" means that the tutor has told the student when ω was complete at least once before.

Paco's domain knowledge can include recipes that achieve the subgoal of explaining why a task step should be performed. Typically, these recipes are composed of one or more utterances of text written by a domain expert, but, in principle, explanation recipes can contain any type of primitive or abstract actions. Collagen's facilities for executing recipes in a collaborative setting are used to complete the explanation started by an

Table 1. Tutorial discourse acts

Act type	Add instance to agenda for...	Semantics	Subcases (if any)	Example gloss
Positive feedback (rank 1)	the user's most recent action α if it was, or it proposed, a valid next action and has not yet received feedback	$accept(should(\alpha))$	α finished subtask	Great job.
			α wasn't proposed by tutor	Nice.
			α caused unnecessary focus shift	That was a correct action, but I wasn't expecting you to do it now.
			α finished top-level goal	We're done with this scenario.
			none of above	Good.
Negative feedback (rank 1)	the user's most recent action α if it was, or it proposed, an invalid next action and has not yet received feedback	$reject(should(\alpha))$	α was already done	Whoops, you already did that.
			α's purpose was already achieved	Whoops, you didn't need to do that.
			α has an unsatisfied precondition	Whoops, you can't do that yet.
			executing α violates an ordering constraint	Whoops, it's too soon to do that.
End interruption (rank 2)	each step ω that is an interruption on the focus stack	$propose(\neg should(\omega))$	ω has known purpose	Let's stop closing the fuel valves.
			ω has unknown purpose	That is not relevant to our current task.
Teach complete (rank 3)	each non-primitive ω in the current plan such that ω is complete and the student does not know when ω is complete	$propose(achieved(\omega))$		We succeeded in closing the fuel valves.
Correct Focus (rank 4)	step ω if it is the tutor's private focus but not the action on top of the focus stack	$propose(should(\omega))$		Let's return to opening the fuel valves.
Give initiative (rank 5)	any valid next plan step ω that the student knows needs to be done, if the tutor has initiative and the student has not requested help	$propose(initiative = user)$	tutor has just proposed ω	Go ahead.
			tutor has not just proposed ω	You take it from here.
Explain Why (rank 6)	every plan step ω that is teachable (see Teach Step) and is currently unexplained and has an explanation recipe	first step of explanation recipe		Before starting an engine, always make sure that the other engine is stopped.
Teach step (rank 7)	every valid next plan step ω that the student does not know and whose parent is in focus	$propose(should(\omega))$	ω is primitive	Now, you should press the on button.
			ω is non-primitive	The next step of engaging the engine is to open the fuel valves.
Remind step (rank 8)	every valid next plan step ω that the student knows and whose parent is in focus	$propose(should(\omega))$		You need to press the on button.
Propose new scenario (rank 8)	purpose ω, if the current plan is complete, where ω is the next task to work on	$propose(should(\omega))$		Let's try another scenario. Let's engage engine one.
Shift Focus (rank 8)	every plan step ω that is not currently on top of the focus stack and the student knows has to be done and has a child c that is a valid next plan step and c is not known by the student	$propose(should(\omega))$		Let's open the fuel valves.

Explain Why action. This general approach could be used to support other types of multi-turn tutorial strategies as well [1].

The conditions for generating discourse acts represent necessary, but not sufficient, conditions for Paco to perform the act. An advantage of making explicit all necessary conditions for a discourse act is to make it easier to extend Paco with new discourse acts or extend other agents with the ability to perform Paco's tutorial actions [14]. Paco chooses which act to perform based on the rankings of the discourse acts, given in the first column of Table 1. For example, Paco prefers to give initiative when the student knows what to do next rather than teach or remind her what to do next. We hypothesize that different rankings or other methods for choosing an act from the agenda will produce different tutoring styles.

5   Evaluation

We assessed our progress on Paco through a formative evaluation with seven users. They had no prior experience with Paco or research in user interfaces, AI, or dialogue systems. Users received a single page of instructions, and then Paco instructed them on a sequence of seven tasks in the Gas Turbine Engine simulator, with a variety of initial conditions. The target task was to start engine one from an initial condition in which engine two is running. Paco first taught four subtasks of this target task, then taught the target task, and then had the users repeat this task twice more. Users completed the tasks in 20 to 30 minutes. Next, they filled out a survey and discussed their opinions with an interviewer.[1] To test Paco's effectiveness, five of the users were asked to teach the target task back to the interviewer.

The results suggest that Paco is a reasonable tutor. Most users commented positively on Paco's overall teaching skills, explanations, feedback, clarity of communication, and ability to understand what the user was doing. One user wanted the ability to ask "why" questions, three users wanted more rationales for actions (although two users praised Paco for providing rationales), and two users commented that Paco should not praise actions that the user should know well. After their session with Paco, users felt somewhat or very confident in their ability to perform the task. Of the users who taught the task back to the interviewer, three made no errors, one made a few minor errors but completed the task, and one forgot to turn off engine two so failed to complete the task.

6   Conclusion

By mapping tutorial acts into the framework of collaborative discourse theory, Paco provides a foundation for cross-fertilization between these two research areas. As our next step, we plan to broaden the types of tutorial acts we consider to include those used in recent analyses of human tutorial dialogues [13]. We are especially interested in the relationship of hinting and prompting to collaborative discourse theory.

References

1. B. Cheikes and A. Gertner. Teaching to plan and planning to teach in an embedded training system. In *Proceedings of the Tenth International Conference on Artificial Intelligence in Education*, pages 398–409. IOS Press, 2001.
2. A. Collins, J. S. Brown, and S. E. Newman. Cognitive apprenticeship: Teaching the crafts of reading, writing, and mathematics. In L. Resnick, editor, *Knowing, Learning, and Instruction: Essays in Honor of Robert Glaser*. Lawrence Erlbaum Associates, 1989.

---

[1] We thank Clifton Forlines for running and helping to design the evaluation.

3. J. Eisenstein and C. Rich. Agents and GUIs from task models. In *Proceedings of the Sixth International Conference on Intelligent User Interfaces*, pages 47–54, 2002. ACM Press.

4. R. K. Freedman. *Interaction of Discourse Planning, Instructional Planning and Dialogue Management in an Interactive Tutoring System*. PhD thesis, Northwestern University, 1996.

5. I. P. Goldstein. Overlays: A theory of modelling for computer-aided instruction. Artificial Intelligence Laboratory Memo 495, MIT, Cambridge, MA, 1977.

6. B. J. Grosz and S. Kraus. Collaborative plans for complex group action. *Artificial Intelligence*, 86(2):269–357, 1996.

7. B. J. Grosz and C. L. Sidner. Attention, intentions, and the structure of discourse. *Computational Linguistics*, 12(3):175–204, 1986.

8. B. J. Grosz [Deutsch]. The structure of task oriented dialogs. In *Proceedings of the IEEE Symposium on Speech Recognition*, Pittsburgh, PA, April 1974. Carnegie-Mellon University. Also available as Stanford Research Institute Technical Note 90, Menlo Park, CA.

9. N. Lesh, C. Rich, and C. Sidner. Collaborating with focused and unfocused users under imperfect communication. In *Proc. 9th Int. Conf. on User Modelling*, pages 64–73, 2001.

10. N. Lesh, C. Rich, and C. L. Sidner. Using plan recognition in human-computer collaboration. In *Proc. 7th Int. Conf. on User Modeling*, pages 23–32, 1999.

11. K. E. Lochbaum. A collaborative planning model of intentional structure. *Computational Linguistics*, 24(4):525–572, 1998.

12. N. K. Person, A. C. Graesser, R. J. Kreuz, V. Pomeroy, and the Tutoring Research Group. Simulating human tutor dialog moves in autotutor. *International Journal of Artificial Intelligence in Education*, 12:23–39, 2001.

13. R. Pilkington, editor. *Special Issue on Analysing Educational Dialogue Interaction*, volume 11 of *International Journal of Artificial Intelligence in Education*, 2000.

14. C. Rich, N. Lesh, and J. Rickel. A plug-in architecture for generating collaborative agent responses. In *Proceedings of the First International Joint Conference on Autonomous Agents and Multi-Agent Systems*, New York, 2002. ACM Press. Forthcoming.

15. C. Rich and C. L. Sidner. COLLAGEN: A collaboration manager for software interface agents. *User Modeling and User-Adapted Interaction*, 8(3-4):315–350, 1998.

16. C. Rich, C. L. Sidner, and N. Lesh. Collagen: Applying collaborative discourse theory to human-computer collaboration. *AI Magazine*, 22(4):15–25, 2001.

17. J. Rickel. An intelligent tutoring framework for task-oriented domains. In *Proceedings of the International Conference on Intelligent Tutoring Systems*, pages 109–115, Montréal, Canada, June 1988. Université de Montréal.

18. C. L. Sidner. An artificial discourse language for collaborative negotiation. In *Proceedings of the Twelfth National Conference on Artificial Intelligence (AAAI-94)*, pages 814–819, Menlo Park, CA, 1994. AAAI Press.

19. C. L. Sidner and M. Dzikovska. Hosting activities: Experience with and future directions for a robot agent host. In *Proceedings of the Sixth International Conference on Intelligent User Interfaces*, pages 143–150, New York, 2002. ACM Press.

20. E. Wenger. *Artificial Intelligence and Tutoring Systems*. Morgan Kaufmann, 1987.

21. B. P. Woolf. *Context-Dependent Planning in a Machine Tutor*. PhD thesis, Department of Computer and Information Science, University of Massachusetts at Amherst, 1984.

A Hybrid Language Understanding Approach for Robust Selection of Tutoring Goals

Carolyn P. Rosé, Dumisizwe Bhembe, Antonio Roque, Stephanie Siler,
Ramesh Srivastava, and Kurt VanLehn

LRDC, University of Pittsburgh
Pittsburgh, PA 15260 USA
rosecp@pitt.edu

Abstract. In this paper we explore the problem of selecting appropriate Knowledge Construction Dialogues (KCDs) for the purpose of encouraging students to include important points in their qualitative physics explanations that are missing. We describe a hybrid symbolic/statistical approach developed in the context of the WHY2 conceptual physics tutor (Vanlehn et al., 2002). Our preliminary results demonstrate that our hybrid approach outperforms both the symbolic approach and the statistical approach by themselves.

1 Introduction

Recent studies of human tutoring suggest that a productive activity for teaching is to have students explain physical systems qualitatively (Chi et al, 1981). The goal of the WHY2 project (Vanlehn et al., 2002) is to coach students as they explain physics systems in natural language in response to short essay questions such as, "Suppose you are running in a straight line at constant speed. You throw a pumpkin straight up. Where will it land? Explain." The WHY2 system has at its disposal a library of knowledge construction dialogues (KCDs), i.e., interactive directed lines of reasoning, each of which is designed either to elicit a specific idea (i.e., an elicitation KCD) or to remediate a specific misconception (i.e., a remediation KCD).

In order to do an effective job at selecting appropriate KCDs in response to student essays, the system must first analyze the student's essay to assess which key points are missing from the student's argument and which misconceptions the student may have based on what the student said. Thus, in this paper we explore a hybrid symbolic/statistical approach for robustly diagnosing student essay answers to qualitative physics questions in the context of the WHY2 conceptual physics tutor. In order to build an effective system, it is important both to give students the KCDs that they do need, and to avoid giving them extraneous KCDs that they do not need. Our preliminary results reported in this paper demonstrate that in both respects our hybrid approach outperforms both the symbolic approach and the statistical approach by themselves.

S.A. Cerri, G. Gouardères, and F. Paraguaçu (Eds.): ITS 2002, LNCS 2363, pp. 552–561, 2002.

2   The Role of KCDs in Why2

When students interact with WHY2, they are first presented with an essay question. After reading the essay question, the student types in an initial essay. The system then analyzes the student's essay in order to detect the presence of misconceptions and required concepts, which are determined when each of WHY2's problems are designed. The system then uses KCDs both for coaching students to insert missing required concepts (elicitation KCDs) and to remove the expression of misconceptions (remediation KCDs).

1-Tutor Let's say a car is moving along a straight road with a constant velocity, Vc. Let's say the car moves along the x-axis. An airplane ascends on take-off with a velocity Va, at an angle, theta, to the x-axis. Say the car and airplane have the same (constant) velocity in the x-direction, or $Vc_x = Va_x$.

For any given time interval, what is the relationship between the displacement of the car and the displacement of the airplane along the x-axis?

2-Student not sure

3-Tutor The displacement of a body in a given direction and over a given time interval is equal to what quantity multiplied by that time interval?

4-Student speed

5-Tutor The displacement of a body over a given time interval is equal to its average velocity divided by that time interval.

If something moves at a constant velocity of magnitude Vc, what is the magnitude of its average velocity across any time interval?

6-Student Vc

7-Tutor Super. Thus, since the car and airplane move at the same constant velocity in the x-direction, what is the relationship between their average velocities in the x-direction over any interval of time?

8-Student same

9-Tutor Correct. So if the average velocity in the x-direction is the same for the car and airplane for any given time interval, what is the relationship between the displacements of the car and airplane in the x-direction?

10-Student same

11-Tutor Okay. In general, if two bodies have the same constant velocity along a given direction, for any time point, their displacements along that direction will be the same.

Fig. 1. This figure contains an example remediation KCD for teaching the connection between velocity and displacement.

The ultimate goal of WHY2 is to coach students through the process of constructing explanations that are complete and do not contain any misconceptions. Knowledge construction dialogues (KCDs) are the main instructional tools used by WHY2 for coaching students. KCDs are interactive directed lines of reasoning that each teach a specific concept. Through these KCDs, students are lead step by step by a sequence of questions designed to guide them into discovering conceptual knowledge as independently as possible. They have a very simple underlying dialogue management mechanism, specifically a finite state push down automaton. And they make use of very simple shallow semantic parsing grammars to analyze student input, classifying it into one of a small number of pre-defined answer classes. KCDs have already been demonstrated to be effective for increasing students' conceptual knowledge of physics (Rosé et al., 2001).

To illustrate the revision cycle that WHY2 engages students in, take as an example the case where the student has the misconception that two objects with the same velocity and initial position may have different displacements from their points of origin. This can be remediated by engaging them in a dialogue about the relationship between velocity and displacement, as in Figure 1. Typical of KCDs, this KCD begins by introducing a scenario to make the underlying physics concept easy for students to relate to. The tutor's turn ends with a question. In Turn 2, the student indicates that he does not know the answer. Turns 3-10 form a subdialogue meant to respond to the lack of knowledge communicated by the student's Turn 2. In general, remediation subdialogues are provided to students each time the student fails to give a correct answer to a tutor's question. Thus, with main lines of reasoning having embedded remediation subdialogues, which in turn may have other embedded remediation subdialogues, KCDs follow a hierarchical structure. This hierarchical structure allows KCDs to tailor their instruction to the specific needs of the student. After the student completes the remediation KCD by demonstrating a correct understanding of the underlying physics principle, the student is then asked to correct the essay where the misconception was expressed.

1-Tutor If two objects have the same horizontal velocity, and if they start out in the same position, then what will be the relationship between the horizontal displacement of the two objects from the point of release?

2-Student same

3-Tutor Good. So if the horizontal velocity of the pumpkin is the same as the horizontal velocity of the runner, then what is the relationship between their respective displacements from the point of release?

4-Student they will equal each other

Fig. 2. This Figure contains an example Elicitation KCD about the connection between velocity and displacement.

If the system determines that a required concept is absent from a student's essay, the system engages the student in an elicitation KCD in order to encourage the student to articulate that concept. An example elicitation KCD is found in Figure 2. In this case the system is attempting to encourage the student to include a statement about the displacements of two objects being equal because

Recall:	NumberCorrectlyIdentified / CorrectPoints
Precision:	NumberCorrectlyIdentified / NumberIdentified
IncorrectPoints	TotalNumberPoints - CorrectPoints
IncorrectlyIdentified	NumberIdentified - NumberCorrectlyIdentified
False alarm rate:	IncorrectlyIdentified / IncorrectPoints
EssayQuality:	CorrectPoints / TotalNumberPoints
NumberCorrectlyIdentified:	Recall * CorrectPoints
NumberIdentified:	NumberCorrectlyIdentified / Precision
TotalKcdsGiven:	TotalNumberPoints - NumberIdentified
KcdsNeeded:	TotalNumberPoints - CorrectPoints
CorrectButNotIdentified:	CorrectPoints - NumberCorrectlyIdentified
KcdsCorrectlyGiven:	TotalKcdsGiven - CorrectButNotIdentified
KCD recall:	KcdsCorrectlyGiven / KcdsNeeded
KCD precision:	KcdsCorrectlyGiven / TotalKcdsGiven
KCDsNotNeeded	TotalNumberPoints - KcdsNeeded
KCDsIncorrectlyGiven	TotalKcdsGiven - KcdsCorrectlyGiven
KCD false alarm rate:	KCDsIncorrectlyGiven / KCDsNotNeeded

Fig. 3. This Figure summarizes our model for predicting KCD precision, recall, and false alarm rate from analysis precision, recall, and false alarm rate.

their respective velocities are equal. Elicitation KCDs are typically shorter than remediation KCDs. The idea behind them is that the student may already know the idea that they are meant to elicit and just has neglected to mention it in the essay. So they are short and ask questions meant to prompt the student to articulate the desired concept. If the student does not in fact know the desired concept, then the student will not be able to answer the questions correctly. In this way elicitation KCDs can be used as a tool for identifying student misconceptions and missing knowledge. In the case of discovering such a lack, the system will engage the student in a remediation KCD to remediate the student's incorrect answer. Once the student has demonstrated the ability to articulate the desired concept, the elicitation KCD is complete, and the system asks the student to insert that required point in the essay.

Essay Quality	KCD Precision	KCD Recall
0.10-0.30	0.98	0.98
0.40-0.70	0.86	0.86
0.80-1.00	0.23	0.23

Fig. 4. This Table illustrates how KCD precision and recall vary with essay quality, keeping 0.90 analysis precision and 0.90 analysis recall.

Essay Quality	KCD Precision	KCD Recall
0.10-0.30	0.94	0.97
0.40-0.70	0.72	0.86
0.80-1.00	0.13	0.22

Fig. 5. KCD precision and recall with 0.88 analysis Precision, 0.75 analysis Recall, and .08 analysis False Alarm Rate. Note that this is the result we get with our best combined approach to essay analysis described below in the Results section.

3   Selecting Appropriate KCDs

In order to build an effective system, it is important both to give students the KCDs that they do need, and to avoid giving them extraneous KCDs that they do not need. Neglecting to give a student a KCD that is needed means losing an opportunity to teach that student something that student needs to know. Giving a KCD that a student does not need means wasting a student's time, possibly distracting that student from what that student really needs to learn, and likely annoying or even confusing that student. Thus, we would like to build a system with a high KCD recall and low KCD false alarm rate, where we define KCD recall as the percentage of KCDs that a student needs that the system gives. And KCD false alarm rate as the percentage of KCDs that the student does not need that the system gives.

Nevertheless, analyzing student essays is a computational linguistics problem, and performance on this task is most naturally measured in terms of analysis precision, recall, and false alarm rate over a corpus of student essays. Analysis precision is the percentage of required points and misconceptions identified in the student essays that were actually present in those essays. Note that this is undefined in the case that no required points are identified. Related to this notion is analysis false alarm rate, which is the percentage of required points not present in the essay that were incorrectly identified by the system. Analysis recall is the percentage of misconceptions and required points present in student essays that were actually identified by the system. Note that this is undefined whenever there are no required points present in a student essay. Naturally, a system that is good at accurately identifying required points and misconceptions in student essays will also be good at selecting appropriate KCDs to engage students in. However, the relationship between analysis precision, recall, and false alarm rate and KCD precision, recall, and false alarm rate varies widely depending upon the quality of student essays. Thus, in order to make valid predictions about student experience with the system based on experiments over corpora of previously collected student essays, we built a mathematical model to compute KCD precision, recall, and false alarm rate from analysis precision, recall, and false alarm rate as it varies with different essay qualities. The model is summarized in Figure 3. From this model it is possible to predict how well we need to do at analyzing student essays in order to do a good job at selecting appropriate KCDs. It also makes it possible to make informed decisions about which out of a set of alternative language understanding approaches is most suitable based on their relative levels of analysis precision, recall, and false alarm rate.

We define Recall for analysis as the number of required points that WHY2 correctly identifies as present in a student essay (NumberCorrectlyIdentified) divided by the total number of required points actually present in the essay (CorrectPoints). Precision is NumberCorrectlyIdentified divided by the total number of required points that WHY2 identified, correctly or incorrectly (NumberIdentified). The number of points not correctly encoded in an essay (IncorrectPoints) is computed by subtracting CorrectPoints from TotalNumberPoints. To compute the false alarm rate, then, simply substract NumberCorrectlyIdentified from NumberIdentified and divide the resulting number by IncorrectPoints. EssayQuality is CorrectPoints divided by the total number of required points (TotalNumberPoints).

In order to project KCD precision, recall, and false alarm rate for different essay qualities, we need to transform these equations in order to compute values for NumberCorrectlyIdentified and NumberIdentified as they vary with essay quality. Thus, from the Recall equation we derive the equation that Number-CorrectlyIdentified is Recall multiplied by CorrectPoints. And from the Precision equation we derive the equation that NumberIdentified equals NumberCorrectlyIdentified divided by Precision. WHY2 gives an elicitation KCD for every required point not identified in the student essay. Thus, the total number of elicitation KCDs given correctly or incorrectly (TotalKcdsGiven) is TotalNumberPoints minus NumberIdentified. However, the number of KCDs that the student actually needs (KcdsNeeded) is TotalNumberPoints minus CorrectPoints. In order to determine how many KCDs were correctly given (KcdsCorrectlyGiven), we first need to know how many required points the student included in the essay that were not identified by WHY2 (CorrectButNotIdentified). If we know CorrectPoints and NumberCorrectlyIdentified, we can get CorrectButNotIdentified by subtracting NumberCorrectlyIdentified from CorrectPoints. Then, KcdsCorrectlyGiven will be TotalKcdsGiven - CorrectButNotIdentified, since a KCD will be incorrectly given if the student expressed the corresponding point but WHY2 missed it. Now we have enough information to compute KCD precision and recall. KCD recall is the percentage of KCDs that were given that the student needed, thus, KcdsCorrectlyGiven divided KcdsNeeded. And KCD precision is the percentage of KCDs given that were actually needed, thus, KcdsCorrectlyGiven divided by TotalKcdsGiven. To compute KCD false alarm rate, you must first determine the number of KCDs not needed (KCDsNotNeeded). You can compute this by subtracting KcdsNeeded from TotalNumberPoints. You also need to know how many KCDs were incorrectly given (KCDsIncorrectlyGiven). You can compute this by subtracting KcdsCorrectlyGiven from TotalKcdsGiven. Note that this is equivalent to CorrectButNotIdentified. Thus, KCD false alarm rate is KCDsIncorrectlyGiven divided by KCDsNotNeeded. Note that the projection of analysis precision and recall onto KCD precision and recall works out most accurately if we treat the undefined cases for analysis precision and recall discussed above as 1.0.

From this mathematical model we determined that as essay quality increases, it becomes much more difficult to do a good job at selecting appropriate KCDs for students. In fact, selecting appropriate KCDs for students with essay qualities of 0.80 or higher may well be completely out of our reach. In particular, even if analysis precision and recall are at 0.90, KCD precision, recall, and false alarm rate become unsatisfyingly low once essay quality is 0.70 or higher. See Figure 4. Thus, helping excellent students improve their ability to construct high quality conceptual physics explanations may require an entirely different approach. From this model we have also determined, not too surprisingly, that performance can remain reasonable even if analysis recall is low. A low analysis precision means students will not get KCDs that are needed. On the other hand, a low recall means that students will get KCDs that they do not need. In Figure 5 we see that if analysis recall is low but precision remains near the 0.90 level, KCD recall remains high. Although this phenomenon seems counter-intuitive at first glance, it makes sense when one considers that if precision remains the same but recall is decreased, then the total number of points identified will be smaller, thus the total number of KCDs given will be higher. When essay quality is low and many KCDs are needed, the likelihood is that increasing the number of KCDs given will increase the number of KCDs correctly given. Nevertheless, KCD precision seriously suffers for higher quality essays. By the time essay quality is at 0.40, a quarter of the KCDs given will be inappropriate, and over half of the KCDs given for essays of quality 0.70 or more will be inappropriate.

4   Combining Deep and Shallow Approaches to Language Understanding

Many successful tutoring systems that accept natural language input employ shallow approaches to language understanding. For example, CIRCSIM-TUTOR (Glass, 1999) and Andes-Atlas (Rosé et al, 2001) parse student answers using shallow semantic grammars to identify key concepts embedded therein. The AUTO-TUTOR (Wiemer-Hastings et al, 1998) system uses Latent Semantic Analysis (LSA) to process lengthy student answers. "Bag of Words" approaches such as LSA (Landauer et al., 1998) HAL (Burgess et al., 1998), and Rainbow (McCallum, 1996), have enjoyed a great deal of success in a wide range of applications. Recently a number of dialogue based tutoring systems have begun to employ more linguistically sophisticated techniques for analyzing student language input, namely the Geometry tutor (Aleven et al., 2001), BEETLE (Core et al., 2001), and WHY2 (Vanlehn et al., 2002). Each approach has its own unique strengths and weaknesses. "Bag of Words" approaches require relatively little development time, are totally impervious to ungrammatical input, and tend to perform well because much can be inferred about student knowledge just from the words they use. On the other hand, symbolic, knowledge based approaches require a great deal of development time and tend to be more brittle than superficial "Bag of Words" types of approaches, although robustness techniques can increase their level of imperviousness (Rosé 2000). To their credit, linguistic knowledge based approaches are more precise and capture nuances that "Bag of Words" approaches miss. For example, they capture key aspects of meaning that are communicated structurally through scope and subordination and do not ignore common, but nevertheless crucial, function words such as 'not'.

Recent work suggests that symbolic and "Bag of Words" approaches can be productively combined. For example, syntactic information can be used to modify the LSA space of a verb in order to make LSA sensitive to different word senses (Kintsch, 2002). Along similar lines, syntactic information can be used, as in Structured Latent Semantic Analysis (SLSA), to improve the results obtained by LSA over single sentences (Wiemer-Hastings and Zipitria, 2001).

A detailed description of our approach to language understanding is beyond the scope of this paper, but can be found in (Vanlehn et al., 2002). In brief, we use the CARMEL core understanding component (Rosé, 2000) for symbolic sentence level language understanding. It takes natural language as input and produces a set of first order logical forms to pass on to the discourse language understanding (DLU) module (Jordan et al., 2002). We use Rainbow (McCallum, 1996), a naive Bayes classifier, for an alternative "Bag of Words" sentence level language understanding approach. It assigns sentences to classes that are associated with sets of logical forms in the same representation language as CARMEL produces. Thus, output from either source is appropriate input for the DLU module. However, the classification approach has the drawback that it embodies the underlying simplifying assumption that students always express required points in a single sentence, which is not always the case. After sentence level processing, the DLU module combines the sentence level information by making abductive inferences about how the pieces of information fit together using Tacitus-Lite+ (Jordan et al., 2002). The resulting proof trees are then used as the basis for determining which required points are missing from student essays, when optional points are not mentioned or inferable from what is mentioned, and which misconceptions may be present. For our combined approach, we use a decision tree trained with the ID3 decision tree learning algorithm (Mitchel, 1997) to combine Rainbow's prediction with syntactic information in order to formulate a hypothesis about the classification of each sentence. we extract syntactic features for each sentence from the representation constructed by the parser. These features encode functional relationships between syntactic heads (e.g., (subj-throw man)), tense information (e.g., (tense-throw past)), and information about passivization and negation (e.g., (negation-throw +) or (passive-throw -)). We also extract word features that indicate the presence or absence of a root form of a word from the sentence. ID3 uses these features to construct a decision tree for identifying the correct classification of novel sentences.

5   Results

We conducted a series of experiments to evaluate our statistical, symbolic, and combined approach. We used as our test set a corpus of 33 essays collected during web-based tutoring sessions that were not used as development data. The web based tutoring sessions during which we collected this corpus involved university students and a human tutor where students were answering the question "Suppose you are running in a straight line at constant speed. You throw a pumpkin straight up. Where will it land? Explain." We divided these essays into a total of 130 sentence segments. For 77% of the data, three difference coders hand-classified each segment as having one or none of the 6 points required to solve the essay problem. We computed a pairwise Kappa coefficient to measure the agreement between coders, which was always greater than .75. We then selected one coder to complete the coding of the remainder of the data. We used that coder's data as a gold standard to use for measuring the performance of our alternative approaches. We computed average per essay performance over 25 trials of randomly selecting essays covering 10% of the corpus, training the decision tree using ID3 on the rest, and then testing the selected essays.

Since WHY2's domain specific knowledge sources are early in their development, we expected the symbolic only approach to perform poorly, and it did. It got an analysis precision of 17%, recall of 19%, and false alarm rate of 33%. Averaged over the essays in our test set, this translates in to a KCD precision of 64%, recall of 78%, and false alarm rate of 81%. The statistical only approach performed better overall with an anlysis precision of 75%, recall of 73%, and false alarm rate of 15%. This translates into an average KCD precision of 88%, recall of 90%, and false alarm rate of 27%. The combined approach performed best of all with an analysis precision of 88%, recall of 75%, and false alarm rate of 8%. Notice that the combined approach performs as well as or better than both the statistical and the symbolic approach on analysis precision, recall, and false alarm rate as well as KCD selection precision, recall, and false alarm rate. The most striking aspects of the results are that it achieves a 95% KCD recall, a full 5% increase over the statistical approach, which cutting the statistical approach's analysis false alarm rate in half. The results for this combined approach are displayed in Figure 5.

6   Conclusions and Current Directions

In this paper we have discussed the problem of selecting appropriate Knowledge Construction Dialogues (KCDs) for the purpose of encouraging students to include important points in their qualitative physics explanations that are missing. We have presented a model for projecting analysis precision, recall, and false alarm rate into KCD selection precision, recall, and false alarm rate. We used this model to inform the design of a heuristic for combining predictions from a symbolic and a statistical approach to essay analysis. We have demonstrated that our combined approach outperforms both the symbolic and the statistical approach alone in terms of both KCD selection precision, recall, and false alarm rate.

Acknowledgments. The authors would like to thank the rest of the Natural Language Tutoring group for their collaboration.

This research is supported by the Office of Naval Research, Cognitive and Neural Sciences Division MURI Grant N00014-00-1-0600 and NSF Grant 9720359 to CIRCLE, a center for research on intelligent tutoring.

References

1. V. Aleven, O. Popescu, and K. Koedinger. 2001. Pedagogical content knowledge in a tutorial dialogue system to support self-explanation. In *Papers of the AIED-2001 Workshop on Tutorial Dialogue Systems.*
2. C. Burgess, K. Livesay, and K. Lund. 1998. Explorations in context space: Words, sentences, discourse. *Discourse Processes*, 25(2):211–257.
3. M. Chi, N. de Leeuw, M. Chiu, and C. LaVancher. 1981. Eliciting self-exsplanations improves understanding. *Cognitive Science*, 18(3).
4. M. G. Core, J. D. Moore, and C. Zinn. 2001. Initiative management for tutorial dialogue. In *Proceedings of the NAACL Workshop Adaption in Dialogue Systems.*
5. M. S. Glass. 1999. *Broadening Input Understanding in an Intelligent Tutoring System.* Ph.D. thesis, Illinois Institute of Technology.
6. Pamela W. Jordan, Maxim Makatchev, Michael Ringenberg, and Kurt VanLehn. 2002. Engineering the Tacitus-lite weighted abductive inference engine for use in the Why-Atlas qualitative physics tutoring system. submitted.
7. W. Kintsch. 2002. Predication. to appear in the Cognitive Science Journal.
8. T. K. Landauer, P. W. Foltz, and D. Laham. 1998. Introduction to latent semantic analysis. To Appear in *Discourse Processes.*
9. Andrew Kachites McCallum. 1996. Bow: A toolkit for statistical language modeling, text retrieval, classification and clustering. http://www.cs.cmu.edu/ mccallum/bow.
10. Mitchel, T. 1997. Machine Learning. McGraw Hill.
11. C. P. Rosé, P. Jordan, M. Ringenberg, S. Siler, K. VanLehn, and A. Weinstein. 2001. Interactive conceptual tutoring in atlas-andes. In *Proceedings of Artificial Intelligence in Education.*
12. C. P. Rosé. 2000. A framework for robust sentence level interpretation. In *Proceedings of the First Meeting of the North American Chapter of the Association for Computational Lingusitics.*
13. K. VanLehn, P. Jordan, C. P. Rosé, and The Natural Language Tutoring Group. 2002. The architecture of why2-atlas: a coach for qualitative physics essay writing. In *Proceedings of the Intelligent Tutoring Conference.*
14. P. Wiemer-Hastings and I. Zipitria. 2001. Rules for syntax, vectors for semantics. In *Proceedings of the Twenty-third Annual Conference of the Cognitive Science Society.*
15. P. Wiemer-Hastings, A. Graesser, D. Harter, and the Tutoring Research Group. 1998. The foundations and architecture of autotutor. In B. Goettl, H. Halff, C. Redfield, and V. Shute, editors, *Intelligent Tutoring Systems: 4th International Conference (ITS '98)*, pages 334–343. Springer Verlag.

Beyond the Short Answer Question with Research Methods Tutor

Kalliopi-Irini Malatesta[1], Peter Wiemer-Hastings[*2], and Judy Robertson[1]

[1] Division of Informatics, University of Edinburgh, 2 Buccleuch Place
Edinburgh, EH8 9LW, Scotland
{kalliopm, judyr}@cogsci.ed.ac.uk

[2] School of Computer Science, Telecommunications, and Information Systems
DePaul University, 243 S. Wabash, Chicago IL 60604
peterwh@cti.depaul.edu

Abstract. Research Methods Tutor is a new intelligent tutoring system created by porting the existing implementation of the AutoTutor system to a new domain, Research Methods in Behavioural Sciences, which allows more interactive dialogues. The procedure of porting allowed for an evaluation of the domain independence of the AutoTutor framework and for the identification of domain related requirements. Specific recommendations for the development of other dialogue-based tutors were derived from our experience.

1 Motivations for a New Tutor

Recent advances in Intelligent Tutoring System technology focus on developing dialogue-based tutors, which act as conversational partners in learning. AutoTutor [5, 7], one of the prevalent systems in this field, claims to simulate naturalistic tutoring sessions in the domain of computer literacy. An innovative characteristic of AutoTutor is the use of a talking head as the primary interface with the user. The system is also claimed to be domain independent and to be capable of supporting deep reasoning in the tutorial dialogue.

One goal of the current project is to test these claims. Another motivation was the fact that the *domain* of AutoTutor, computer literacy, provides limited potential for activating deep reasoning mechanisms. By porting the tutor to a new domain, which requires in-depth qualitative reasoning, we can address issues of domain independence and framework usability in a concrete manner.

The new tutor, based on the AutoTutor framework, is built on the domain of Research Methods in Behavioural Sciences and thus was named Research Methods Tutor (RMT).

In this paper, we describe the issues that arose during the porting process. In particular, we will focus on the usability and extensibility claims of the AutoTutor

---

[*] This work was completed in Edinburgh University.

S.A. Cerri, G. Gouardères, and F. Paraguaçu (Eds.): ITS 2002, LNCS 2363, pp. 562–573, 2002.

system. Based on the results, concrete suggestions are made on feasible modifications of the framework.

1.1 AutoTutor

AutoTutor aims to collaborate with the student as human tutors do: by co-constructing the knowledge taught through a dialogue on a one-to-one basis.

The tutor presents questions and problems from a predefined curriculum script, attempts to comprehend learner contributions that are entered by keyboard, formulates dialogue moves that are sensitive to the learner's contributions (such as short feedback, pumps, prompts, elaborations, corrections, and hints), and delivers the dialogue moves with a talking head [5]. The talking head was intended to provide a more natural modality for the tutor-student dialogue. It also allows the tutor to give graded feedback, supporting the pedagogical and politeness goals of the system.

AutoTutor has seven modules: a curriculum script, language extraction, speech act classification, latent semantic analysis, topic selection, dialogue move generator, and a talking head. We will not describe all of these modules in detail. Nevertheless, sufficient information will be delivered in the relevant sections, in order to comprehensibly describe the development of the new tutor.

1.2 Main Research Goals

Our main goal was to explore more complex types of dialogue by porting the existing framework of AutoTutor to the new domain of Research Methods. Our secondary goal was to evaluate various aspects of the AutoTutor model. The main research questions addressed were:

How portable is the current software implementation? Does the system allow deep reasoning mechanisms to be activated in the tutorial dialogue of the new domain? Are the dialogue management and the knowledge representation adopted in the framework sufficient to cope with the requirements of a teaching domain that is richer in causal relationships? How does the absence of a user model affect the system's performance in the new conditions?

It should be noted that this evaluation is performed on a qualitative level and is only concerned with identifying system weaknesses and putting forward feasible suggestions for improvement. The teaching effectiveness of the tutor is not raised as an issue and thus will not be addressed throughout this article.

2 Research Methods Domain

As pointed out earlier, the depth of AutoTutor's conversations is limited by its subject. Computer Literacy attempts only to familiarise students with the basic concepts of computers, and does not get into any deep issues. Thus, many of AutoTutor's questions have a short-answer feel. A more complicated domain would set the grounds for testing if indeed the system can support deeper reasoning in the discourse. Instead of merely accessing simple facts, which are associated with the question, the students should have to make inferences, which lead them to discover or construct a conceptual link in their understanding of the topic.

Deep reasoning in RMT, is the process of a multi-turn dialogue between the tutor and the student. It is constituted of several steps. Firstly a principal concept of the domain is introduced through a fleshed out example. Then the role of the concept and its interaction with other secondary concepts is elicited through the dialogue. The tutor guides the discussion so as to help the student realise and articulate correctly the meaning of the concept and its interaction with other secondary concepts. Issues of causality that link different concepts are of particular interest in this process. As opposed to the computer literacy implementation, the RMT domain supplies a set of concepts that can be analysed beyond their definitional attributes, through worked examples.

At the current stage of this attempt only a subdomain of Research methods was chosen as teaching material, that of the fundamental concepts of True Experimental Design in Behavioural Research Methods. A possible future full-scale implementation of the tutor would aim to teach these concepts to first year college students in psychology or cognitive science, through a tutorial dialogue on specific experimental design examples. Prior preliminary knowledge of the domain by the students is assumed.

2.1 Learning from Examples

Examples are regarded as important components of learning and instruction. In the case of one-to-one tutoring it has been reported that most questions asked by tutors were embedded in a particular example [4]. Sweller [8] has suggested that worked examples have cognitive benefits over active problem solving. Active problem solving often leads to dead-ends, or lengthy, error ridden solution paths. Providing students with worked examples reduces the student's cognitive load by eliminating futile problem-solving efforts.

Others claim that examples are most beneficial when they are rich in context and anchored in real-world situations. These anchored examples include challenging material, are motivational in nature, and ultimately facilitate transfer to new problems [6, chapt. 1].

Based on this research it is apparent that grounding tutoring dialogues in examples is particularly important in one-to-one tutoring and thus in the design of Intelligent Tutoring Systems that aim to simulate naturalistic tutorial dialogues.

Motivated by the finding that most examples in naturalistic one-to-one tutoring dialogues originate from textbooks [6] and having already decided on a research methods related domain, a specific topic selection from the Cozby [1] textbook was decided.

The topic selection was influenced by existing studies of human-to-human tutoring in research methods conducted by Person [6]. The Tutoring Research Corpus of the Institute of Intelligent Systems at the University of Memphis was collected from upper-division college students who were enrolled in a course on research methods in psychology.

After a detailed study of the topics covered in the transcripts, and keeping in mind the remarks made regarding the value of grounding one-to-one instruction to examples, the topic selection for the new domain was derived from the eighth chapter of the Cozby textbook on Experimental Design. Using the transcripts of the related examples, in conjunction with the actual text from the chosen textbook, four example-based topics were selected as teaching material for the new domain.

2.2 Porting Procedure

After choosing the new domain, the porting procedure consisted of three steps, the collection of a sufficient corpus in order to train the language-understanding component, the development of a curriculum script based on the topic selection previously discussed and the creation of a lexicon of the concepts and terms to be introduced in the tutorial dialogue.

LSA and Corpus

Latent semantic analysis (LSA) is a major component of the mechanism that evaluates the quality of student contributions in the tutorial dialogue. In a study by Wiemer-Hastings et al. [9] LSA's evaluations of college students' answers to deep reasoning questions are found to be equivalent to the evaluations provided by intermediate experts of computer literacy, but not as high as more accomplished experts in computer science. LSA is capable of dealing with different classes of student ability (good, vague, erroneous, versus mute students) and in tracking the quality of contributions in the tutorial dialogue.

LSA is a corpus-based mechanism that represents texts as vectors in a high-dimensional space. Two texts can be compared by calculating the cosine between the vectors that represent them. The training of LSA starts with a corpus separated into units, which are called documents or texts. For the AutoTutor corpus, the curriculum script was used, with each item as a separate text for training purposes. The corpus also included a large amount of additional information from textbooks and articles about computer literacy. Each paragraph of this additional information constituted a text. The paragraph is said to be in general, a good level of granularity for LSA analysis because a paragraph tends to hold a well-developed, coherent idea.

In the first stage of processing a student's response, a speech act classifier assigns the student's input into one of five speech act categories: Assertion, WH-question, YES/NO question, Directive, and Short Response. Only the student's Assertions are sent to LSA for evaluation. The other types of speech acts are processed using simpler pattern-matching procedures.

LSA computes the similarity between any two bags of words. In AutoTutor one bag of words is the current Assertion given by a student. The other bag of words is the content of one of the curriculum script items associated with a particular topic, i.e., a model good answer or bad answer [5]. AutoTutor calculates a general goodness and badness rating by comparing the student contribution with the set of good and bad answers in the curriculum script for the current topic. More importantly, it compares the student response to the particular good answers that cover the aspects of the ideal answer.

In a study of LSA's ability to match the evaluations of human raters, it was concluded that the LSA space of AutoTutor exhibits the performance of an intermediate expert, but not an accomplished expert [9]. This was noted as satisfactory, since AutoTutor aims to simulate a human tutor that does not have specific training in tutoring within that domain.

In the development of the Research Methods Tutor, the same values for training LSA (dimension and threshold) were adopted. The documents originated from seven text books on research methods and from articles and tutorials published on the Internet. As explained earlier, the domain for the new tutor was restricted from General Research Methods in Behavioural Sciences, to the subset of True Experimental Design. Thus only the relevant chapters form each book were scanned. This choice was supported by Wiemer-Hastings et al. [9] finding that more text from the specific tutoring domain is better for LSA. Unfortunately this also made the collection of the corpus a very time-consuming and tedious procedure since only one or two chapters in each textbook were deemed relevant to the desired domain.

Corpus Size

The size of the training corpus for LSA is one important parameter of AutoTutor's language analysis mechanism. The corpus collected for the computer literacy domain was 2.3 MB of documents. A series of tests were performed on the amount of corpus and the balance between specific and general text [9]. As expected, LSA's performance with the entire corpus was best, both in terms of the maximum correlation with the human raters and in terms of the width of the threshold value range in which it performs well. One surprising result was that there was a negligible difference between a corpus consisting of 1/3 of the original items, and one which contained 2/3 of the original corpus. It was observed that there is not a linear relation between the amount of text and the performance of LSA. Another surprising finding was the relatively high performance of the corpus without any of the supplemental items, that is, with the curriculum script items alone.

The fact that there is very little difference in the performance of LSA between the 1/3 and 2/3 of the corpus, is a finding that will be used as a supportive argument for the corpus size collected for the Research Methods Tutor. The size of the corpus that was finally obtained on true experimental design is 750Kb. This renders it close to a third of the AutoTutor corpus. Since the whole procedure was extremely time consuming and the performance of the system was not expected to improve in the case the corpus size was doubled, that size was accepted as optimal for the purpose of this fist attempt in implementing RMT.

Development of Curriculum Script

The curriculum script is the module that organises the topics and the content of the tutorial dialogue. In the case of RMT, since the overall goal of this project was to demonstrate the feasibility of this approach instead of creating a full version of the tutor, only four topics in Experimental Design were developed. AutoTutor provides three levels of difficulty (easy, medium, difficult). In RMT the curriculum script included only the easy level since its short-term goal was to test the overall behaviour of the framework in the new domain.

The topics have a Graphic Display + Question + Answer format. The dialogue is initialised by the presentation of the example of an experimental design which the tutor and student are going to collaboratively work on improving. An image accompanies each subtopic of the topic covered in order to clarify the conceptual relationships that are being discussed. To make this clearer we will take a closer look at the curriculum script developed for one of the examples.

Initially the student is presented with the hypothesis that "Crowding impairs cognitive performance" and a preliminary experimental design on testing it. A multi-turn dialogue will follow, aiming in putting across the fundamental concepts of the topic taught. An image depicting the current experimental design is used to facilitate understanding (Figure 1).

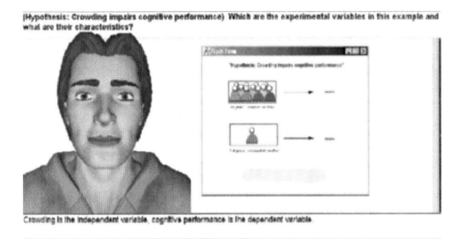

Fig. 1. RMT

Particular attention was given to constructing dialogue moves that promote deeper reasoning within the limits of the available dialogue moves. As opposed to the fact-based dialogues in the computer literacy domain, the new domain is taught through case-based dialogues. The formulation of the questions was done by adopting the dialogue structure of the tutoring transcripts available, to the form of hints, prompts, elaborations and splices. A major restriction in this approach was the fact that word order is not taken into account from the language understanding component. So, the design of the questions had to be done in such a way that word order was not of significance. This proved quite limiting since deep reasoning is achieved only through the discussion of causal relations were the direction of causality, and thus the word order in the phrase, does matter.

Lexicon

A set of definitions of the concepts introduced in the curriculum script and of other relevant terms that might arise in the tutorial dialogue, was derived from the textbook at hand and from the other sources used for the corpus collected.

3   Lessons Learnt and Problems Identified with AutoTutor

This section describes some problems encountered during the porting of AutoTutor to the Research Methods domain. These problems include: the knowledge representation approach, the ignorance of word order from the language understanding component and the dialogue planning mechanism. Further problems were encountered with the interface and tutoring dialogues during a small-scale evaluation session with AutoTutor. These are discussed in more detail below, as they are important obstacles in the way of developing a full version of RMT (pilot study section).

A primary limitation of the system, which is unavoidably reflected in all its modules, is the knowledge representation approach. The use of LSA shows satisfactory effects in "understanding" student contributions. Nevertheless, the fact that this understanding is local and limited in the sense that no more information can be extracted from LSA apart from a similarity metric to pre-stored information is problematic. While concepts and causal relationships have no means of being represented it is difficult to track the process of the tutorial dialogue in the new domain. The need of distinguishing between user input which was correct by chance and a user contribution that emerged from true understanding of the topic taught cannot be covered in the existing implementation.

During the porting process it became apparent that the ignorance of word order in a domain that supports deeper reasoning is severely restrictive. In the case of computer literacy it is unlikely that a student, with some preliminary knowledge of the subject, could contribute a phrase of incorrect word order i.e. "the computer is in RAM". Thus the fact that the tutor would consider the phrase correct is not as problematic. Unfortunately, in a discussion on experimental design a phrase like "the dependent variable has an effect on the independent variable" is incorrect. Although the system will have the correct phrase pre-stored, i.e. "the independent variable has an effect on the independent variable" in the case that the inverted order phrase above is typed it will fail to recognise the misconception and moreover will positively acknowledge an erroneous input.

The set of curriculum scripts provides a rich set of responses from which AutoTutor can choose, based on the evaluation of the student's contribution and on the dialogue selection rules. In other words the variety of responses is not dynamic since it is a set of canned text utterances. A discussion on experimental design can lead to various dialogue scenarios that are impossible to document in the curriculum script statically and under the restrictions imposed from the AutoTutor framework on the number of hints and prompts each subtopic is allowed to contain. Thus, because the information is pumped from a knowledge base and the utterances and explanations emerge from canned text, its performance is limited by the resources of its library.

AutoTutor's student modelling techniques are deliberately limited. Studies of human-human tutoring have shown that human tutors have relatively shallow understanding of their students' states of mind [6]. Thus, it was assumed that it is sufficient to keep a log of the tutorial dialogue and calculate the learner's ability based on the learner's assertions in all of the previous learner turns in the dialogue.

A major disadvantage of the absence of student modelling is that the tutor has no student profile stored and hence each time the student commences a new tutorial session she is considered as complete novice because there is no record of what he has been taught so far.

During the procedure of porting, unexpected difficulties were encountered due to the authoring of the curriculum script in a cumbersome token format. This is an issue that has already been identified by the Tutoring Research Group and is soon to be dealt with, with a creation of an authoring toolkit.

3.1 Pilot Study

A pilot study was designed in order to collect feedback on the actual characteristics of AutoTutor from the user's perspective. What concerned us was to investigate the claims made regarding the systems performance in terms of:

- quality of interface design
- dialogue management
- student model
- deep reasoning

Eight subjects were recruited in this study, amongst which four were PhD students in various disciplines (psychology, interface design, agent interfaces, cognitive science) and four were MSc students in cognitive science. Their feedback proved valuable both from an expert's and a user's perspective. It should be noted that these are not the normal target users for the AutoTutor system, that is, first and second year undergrads.

The subjects were asked to interact with the tutor for about 15 to 20 minutes, until they successfully covered three topics of the Hardware macro-topic and one topic of the Internet macro-topic. Then they were asked to fill in a questionnaire that inquired their overall opinion about the tutor and specific information regarding the aspects of interest listed above.

The overall impression of the tutor was recorded mostly as ''not very good'' (one subject found it good, six found it not very good and one found it as bad). This is a finding that justifies our interest in further investigating the tutor's actual performance.

Interface

Although literature on AutoTutor speculates that the agent interface is more effective than a conventional text-to-text application, there is no empirical data to back this intuitive claim. In an evaluation performed on the interface of the system by Link et al. [3], the factors that influence the perception of feedback delivered by an agent are investigated. The evaluation was derived by user ratings on how positive or negative the agent's feedback seems to be to users, in conditions where the speech parameters and facial expressions of the talking head were manipulated. Their results support the claim that verbal and nonverbal cues are additive. Specifically, participants relied on both linguistic expressions and the mouth curve.

There are several weaknesses in this evaluation approach that are worth mentioning. Firstly, only a small number of features of each of the two modalities was tested. The values of these features were chosen arbitrarily. Moreover the assumption that the agent should be designed to mimic a human tutor in his facial expressions and gestures is not supported by empirical evidence. In an analysis by Dehn [2] on the impact of animated interface agents it is made clear that such an assumption has yet to be validated.

In the same study, a systematic review of empirical evidence on agent interfaces is conducted. The conclusions report that although an agent character is largely perceived to be more entertaining, other dimensions, such as utility, likeability and comfortability are moderated by the kind of animation used and the domain in which the interaction is set. It is clearly stated that present studies do not suffice to enable us to make clear predictions as to what type of animations employed in what type of domain will result in positive attitudes towards the system. Another important point of this study is that all attempts on evaluation so far in this field, concerned limited short-term interactions with the systems. It is unknown if longer exposure to an animated agent might sustain or reduce the positive effect of entertainment ratings. It is interesting to see how these conclusions are verified from the feedback collected in the pilot study.

On the interface related questions, the feedback collected was mostly negative. The prevalent complaint in all users' suggestions was the poor quality of the agent's voice articulation. "Having to listen so hard made me lose parts of the information", reported one of the users. This feature had immediate impact in the focus of attention of the user. Users were distracted from the actual content of the tutorial dialogue, by the extra effort they had to use to understand the tutor's utterances. The log files of the tutoring session reveal that on average ten requests for repetition where made in sessions of approximately fifteen minutes duration. This is a high rate of repetition, considering that native English speakers where preferred as subjects, so that there would be no confounding effects by their level of mastery in English. Users were asked if they would prefer an agent interface over a conventional graphical user interface and the feedback collected shows that it is not obvious to the users that indeed an agent interface is better than a conventional one. This finding is consistent to the arguments put forward earlier on in this section.

The pilot study showed that the users found it difficult to interpret the agent's feedback. Most of them reported that they could not figure out if the agent was pleased with their contribution or if he thought it was incorrect. This increased the levels of their unease in the interaction with the system, since they had no knowledge of the progress of the tutorial. This dissatisfaction can be clearly observed both in the remarks the users put down at designated free comments area of the questionnaire. It was also pointed out that the prosody of the speech was unnatural, making it difficult to distinguish when the tutor was actually posing a question.

A novice user in computer literacy stated "I wasn't sure if answers were sarcastic, does "right" mean "you know nothing"? It made me feel, Oh my god I'm completely stupid!". This point is particularly important since we would expect the tutor to have a more positive and motivational impact on novices in the domain taught.

It is interesting to report some observations made of the users interacting with the system. The users took the agents' reactions seriously and were pleased when his feedback was evidently positive. One of the users said "I'd rather do this than read a book". They often made gestures back at him. According to Dehn [2] the extent to which the users perceive the agent as believable has immediate influence on their expectations from him. They often felt frustrated when correct contributions where dismissed with an ambiguous feedback gesture or even a negative one.

Dialogue Management

We aim to investigate the quality of the dialogue in terms of:

- coherence,
- clarity of the tutor's questions,
- interactivity,
- impression that the tutor understood the contributions.

Users rated the coherence of the dialogue as "intermediate". A problem identified was that many questions were too open-ended, resulting to a sense of confusion from the user's side.

Users were puzzled by some of the tutor's questions, especially the prompts, where it was not clear to them what the tutor was expecting.

Moreover the dialogue is structured in such a way that student initiative is very limited.[1] This leads to one-sided dialogues, in the sense that the tutor maintains the control of the tutorial flow and thus the student is not free to demonstrate her knowledge about the topic at hand. The student is restricted to answering questions and has no possibility of posing her own, apart from mere definition inquiries.

Regarding the limited sharing of control over the tutoring process, the users often felt frustrated towards the tutor because they felt there was no actual interaction. They felt limited to the tutor's instruction plan. Additional users' comments indicate that the session was not perceived to be interactive and that more user initiative was expected in order to conduct a truly collaborative dialogue.

Users reacted positively to the tutor's capability for answering to WH-questions. A problem observed in this functionality is that if the student poses a WH-question while the tutor is expecting an answer to an already given question, then the tutor jumps to answering the WH-question forgetting the previous question at hand. This is a weakness that is apparent in the whole of the dialogue management. As the tutor formulates a question, he expects the next student response to answer to that specific question. If the student types in a contribution long before the tutor finishes posing the question the tutor will still believe that the student input was a response to his question, unless it was a WH-question.

Student Model

It has been stated earlier that AutoTutor's approach to student modelling is deliberately very limited. This choice has serious implications in the flow of the tutorial dialogue. The tutor is often repetitive because he has no idea of the knowledge of the student. In the pilot study it was observed very often that the student knew the correct answer to a question, but LSA did not manage to match the correct answer with its pre-stored data. This caused the users to become frustrated by the tutor's repetitiveness.

The absence of a user model also has serious implications on the usability of the system. The tutor stores no profile of the user. This makes it pointless for someone to

---

[1] As student initiative we mean any student contribution to the dialogue that is not an answer to a question asked by the tutor.

attempt to use the system more than once because he will be forced to go through the same topics covered in his initial session with the tutor.

Deep Reasoning

The AutoTutor literature postulates that the tutor supports deep reasoning in the tutorial dialogue. This claim is difficult to investigate since the domain taught and the instruction approach adopted do not provide the ground for deep reasoning dialogue patterns. The domain of computer literacy does not permit reasoning mechanisms to be fully activated since it constrains the dialogue on a descriptive and definition oriented level. Concepts taught are mostly entities such as hardware components and there are no causal relationships between them that could trigger in-depth conversations.

4   Conclusions and Further Research

Our primary goal during this study was to investigate the feasibility of creating a new tutor based on the current AutoTutor system. It has become apparent that the domain of Research Methods increases the requirements from the system and that the current implementation does not suffice. The issues raised regarding the approaches of interface design, knowledge representation and dialogue management lead us to the conclusion that the current AutoTutor framework must be extended in order to support a new tutor such as RMT.

4.1   Feasible Suggestions for Improvement

The relationship between knowledge representation, language understanding and user modelling is evidently intricate. The current implementation has proved to be rather constraining. The addition of syntactic information in the language understanding component is deemed necessary for overcoming the word order problem and thus supporting deep reasoning in more demanding domains such as Research Methods. This will be a focus of our future research. Moreover, the dialogue planning approach should be reconsidered, aiming to provide functionalities that allow more student initiative and promote better understanding of the tutor's requests. More student initiative would help alleviate the tutor's repetition incidents since the user will be able to intervene in the tutorial dialogue and skip the delivered information that is already known. This will render the overall dialogue more interactive.

Dialogue planning should also be reconsidered. The current implementation imposes restrictions on the number of hints and prompts that can be associated with each good answer. The development of hint and prompt generators could help surpass the inflexibility of canned text and allow for a dialogue that is more tailored to the students needs.

Regarding the interface design, it is clear that further research is required into the effectiveness of interface agents. A short-term solution for dealing with the agent's poor articulation would be to accompany all utterances with the equivalent text bubbles. The effectiveness of a talking head over a talking head with speech bubbles and a conventional text-to-text interface has to be empirically tested in order to properly support the choices adopted by the system.

Overall the procedure of porting proved to be productive, since it shed light to issues that can only be identified through a hands-on investigation of the AutoTutor software implementation. The conclusions drawn aspire to provide useful guidelines for researchers in the field. Further research on the areas discussed will allow RMT to advance the state of the art in dialogue-based tutoring.

References

1. Cozby, P. C. (2001) Methods in Behavioural Research. *Mayfield Publishing Company, 7ᵗʰ edition.*
2. Dehn, D. M. (2000) The impact of animated interface agents: a review of empirical research.*Human-Computer Studies, 52, 1-22.*
3. Link, K. E. & Kreuz, R. J. & Graesser, A. C. and the Tutoring Research Group (2001) Factors that influence the perception of feedback delivered by a pedagogical agent. *International Journal of Speech Technology, 4, 145-153.*
4. Graesser, A. C. (1993) Questioning mechanisms during tutoring, conversation, and human-computer interaction. Memphis State University, Memphis, TN. ERIC Document Reproduction Service No. TM 020 505.
5. Graesser, A. C. & Wiemer-Hastings, K. & Wiemer-Hastings, P. & Kreuz, R. & the Tutoring Research Group (1999). AutoTutor: A simulation of a human tutor. *Journal of Cognitive Systems Research* , 1, 35-51.
6. Person, N. (1994) An analysis of the examples that tutors generate during naturalistic one-to-one tutoring sessions. *PhD thesis.* University of Memphis.
7. Person, N.K., Graesser, A.C., Kreuz, R.J., Pomeroy, V., & TRG (2001). Simulating human tutor dialog moves in AutoTutor. International Journal of Artificial Intelligence in Education , 12, 23-39.
8. Sweller, J. (1988) Cognitive load during problem solving: Effects on learning. *Cognitive Science,* 12, 257-285.
9. Wiemer-Hastings, P. & Wiemer-Hastings, K. & Graesser, A. C. (1999) Improving an intelligent tutor's comprehension of students with Latent Semantic Analysis. *In AI in Education,* 545-542. Les Mans, France.

A 3-Tier Planning Architecture for Managing Tutorial Dialogue*

Claus Zinn, Johanna D. Moore, and Mark G. Core

Division of Informatics, University of Edinburgh
2 Buccleuch Place, Edinburgh EH8 9LW, UK
[zinn|jmoore|markc]@cogsci.ed.ac.uk

Abstract. Managing tutorial dialogue is an intrinsically complex task that is only partially covered by current models of dialogue processing. After an analysis of such models identifying their strengths and weaknesses, we propose a flexible, modular, and thus re-usable computational framework, centered around a 3-tier dialogue planning architecture.

1 Motivation

Managing dialogue is an intrinsically complex task. Lewin *et al.* [1] note that dialogue management includes *turn-taking management*: who can speak next, when, and for how long; *topic management*: what can be spoken about next; *utterance understanding*: understanding the content of an utterance in the context of previous dialogue; *intention understanding*: understanding the point or aim behind an utterance in the context of previous dialogue; *context maintenance*: maintaining a dialogue context; *intention generation*: generating a system objective given a current dialogue context; and *utterance generation*: generating a suitable form to express an intention in the current dialogue context.

Now, how does dialogue management instantiate to the genre of tutorial dialogue? The work of Chi *et al.* [2] and our own analysis of a corpus of human tutorial dialogue indicate that a tutorial dialogue manager must (1) understand student utterances well enough to respond appropriately; (2) not ignore student confusion; (3) encourage the student to recognise and correct their own errors; (4) abandon questions that are no longer relevant; (5) handle multiple student actions in one turn; and (6) deal with student-initiated topic changes.

Whereas (1) stresses the need for a reasonably well performing input understanding engine, the latter tasks require the tutorial agent to monitor the execution of its dialogue strategies. In the case of failure, the agent needs to adapt its plan to the new situation: inserting a plan for a sub-dialogue to handle student confusion or a misconception (2+3), deleting parts of a dialogue plan because their effects are now irrelevant or already achieved (4+5), or reorganising sub-plans to handle topic changes (6). Consequently, there is no need for tutorial dialogue managers to generate elaborate discourse plans much in advance.

---

* The research presented in this paper is supported by Grant #N00014-91-J-1694 from the Office of Naval Research, Cognitive and Neural Sciences Division.

S.A. Cerri, G. Gouardères, and F. Paraguaçu (Eds.): ITS 2002, LNCS 2363, pp. 574–584, 2002.

Given the dynamics of tutorial dialogue — the large number of potential student actions at any point and the limited ability of the tutor to predict them — it is a more viable approach to enter a tutorial conversation with a sketchy high-level dialogue plan. As the dialogue progresses, the dialogue manager then refines the high-level plan into low-level dialogue activities by considering the incrementally constructed dialogue context. The dialogue manager therefore interleaves high-level tutorial planning with on-the-fly situation-adaptive plan refinement and execution.

2   The State-of-the-Art in Tutorial Dialogue Management

2.1   Models of Dialogue Processing

We review three industrial-strength models of dialogue processing, namely, *finite state machines* (FSMs), *form-filling*, and *dialogue components*, as well as an interesting cross-breed of FSMs and planning.

The FSM approach to dialogue management is characterised by defining a finite state automaton that contains all plausible dialogues. Necessarily, the dialogues are system-driven, turn-taking as well as system feedback are hardwired, and there is only a limited and well-defined amount of information available in each state of the network. A typical industrial dialogue system in the area of banking has 1500 states (personal communication, Arturo Trujillo, Vocalis plc).

Form-filling is a less rigid approach to dialogue management. Instead of anticipating and encoding all plausible dialogues, the dialogue engineer specifies the information the dialogue system must obtain from the user as a set of *forms* composed of *slots*. The structural complexity of possible dialogues is limited only by the form design and the intelligence of the form interpretation and filling algorithm. This algorithm may be able to fill more than one slot at a time, maintain several active forms simultaneously, and switch among them. In contrast to a FSM-based dialogue system, the user of a form-filling dialogue system can therefore supply more information than the system requested, or start a task before the system has offered to perform it. Form-filling systems are thus capable of performing *question accommodation* or *task accommodation*, respectively.

Dialogue components provide a modular add-on to dialogue engineering. In this paradigm, a dialogue, such as a bill payment dialogue, is divided into sub-dialogues, say, one to obtain a customer name and one to obtain his/her credit card number. Such sub-dialogues are specified in an object-oriented language, which allows the capture of common features. Atomic dialogues or *components* (*e.g.,* date) can be combined into complex dialogues called tasks (*e.g.,* bill payment=date+amount+bill-type), and tasks can be combined into *applications* (*e.g.,* banking=balance+bill payment+money transfer).

Although such dialogue components bring modularity to the form-filling approach, the problems of choosing among multiple refinements of a task, identifying which task the user is currently trying to perform, and detecting user-initiated switches among or abandonment of tasks, remain difficult and open.

Also, as in the other two approaches, no global dialogue history is maintained. This makes it hard if not impossible to properly handle meta-dialogues and other linguistic phenomena (*e.g.*, anaphora, ellipses) as well as to generate natural and effective feedback.

A major advantage of the three approaches is the robustness of their language understanding capabilities. Each approach has strong expectations about user input based on the state of the system. In the FSM approach, the nodes of the network can be attached to special grammars and language models; in the form-filling approach, one can associate actions with slot-filling events, for example, controlling the activation and combination of scoped grammars; in the dialogue components approach, grammars and language models may be associated with both atomic and complex components.

In each of the three approaches, all plausible dialogues (FSMs) or their content (form filling, dialogue components) have to be specified in advance. None of the approaches involve a deliberative component that can generate dialogue plans to achieve underlying goals, albeit dialogue components can be seen as instantiated plans. A deliberative component also proves useful in cases where the execution of the first planned dialogue strategy fails and re-planning is needed.

Dialogue management in the AUTOROUTE system combines deliberative planning with FSMs in a two tier approach [3]. The bottom tier consists of *dialogue games*, which are *generic* FSMs. Dialogue games encode typical adjacency pairs (*e.g.*, a question is followed by an answer which may be followed by a confirmation and an acknowledgement) that do not specify the content of the dialogue moves they contain. In the top-tier, a deliberative agent treats the I/O behaviour of a dialogue game as a primitive action. Given a goal, it generates a plan that has instantiated dialogue games as its primitive steps (*e.g.*, to pay a bill, obtain the date, amount, and bill-type; to obtain a date, play a question/answer game). Thus far, the AUTOROUTE approach has only been applied to the genre of information-seeking dialogues. Its planning architecture has not been fully exploited, and its re-planning capabilities allow only trivial cases of question and task accommodation. Moreover, turn taking is hardwired into the FSMs, which makes it hard to cope with situations where the user grabs the turn.

2.2   Previous Work in Tutorial Dialogue Systems

Existing tutorial dialogue systems perform dialogue management in an *ad hoc* manner. They adopt none of the aforementioned models of dialogue processing in their pure form; mainly, because none of the models explain how to generate effective tutorial feedback. We review the dialogue management in the tutoring systems AUTOTUTOR (domain: computer literacy) [4], ATLAS-ANDES (Newtonian mechanics) [5], and CIRCSIM/APE (circulatory system) [6] as well as in the EDGE explanation system (electrical devices) [7].

AUTOTUTOR's dialogue management can be regarded as an adaption of the form-filling approach to tutorial dialogue; to solve the feedback generation problem, it adds feedback moves to slots. AUTOTUTOR's dialogue management relies on a *curriculum script*, a sequence of *topic formats*, each of which contains a *main focal question*, and an *ideal complete answer*. The ideal complete answer consists of several sub-answers, called *aspects*. Each aspect includes: a list of anticipated bad answers corresponding to misconceptions and bugs that need correction; lists of prompts and hints that can be used to get the learner to contribute more information; and elaboration and summary moves that can be used to provide the learner with additional or summarising information. All of the moves are hard coded in English.

Using latent semantic analysis, AUTOTUTOR evaluates the student's answer to the main focal question against all the aspects of its ideal complete answer, and the anticipated bad answers. AUTOTUTOR gives immediate feedback based on the student's answer, and then executes dialogue moves that get the learner to contribute information until all answer aspects are sufficiently covered. The category and content of tutor dialogue moves are computed by a set of 20 fuzzy production rules and an algorithm that selects the next answer aspect to focus on.

While AUTOTUTOR's dialogue management performs well in the descriptive domain of computer literacy, it is unclear how well this approach will work in problem-solving domains such as algebra or circuit trouble-shooting. In these domains student answers will often require the tutor to engage the student in a multi-turn scaffolding or remediation sub-dialogue. Curriculum scripts are not nested and do not allow the representation of multi-turn dialogues.

The dialogue manager of **ATLAS-ANDES** teaches Newtonian mechanics and thus must address AUTOTUTOR's aforementioned limitations. It uses a combination of *knowledge construction dialogues (KCDs)*, which are recursive FSMs, and a generative planner [8]. The grammar of a KCD bears many similarities to an AUTOTUTOR curriculum script. A student answer to a tutor question can be divided into correct and incorrect sub-answers with associated tutorial remediations. Unlike AUTOTUTOR, this feedback may extend over multiple turns through the use of recursive KCDs.

While AUTOTUTOR requires a pre-defined and hand-crafted curriculum script, the ATLAS-ANDES approach allows on-the-fly generation of nested KCDs, using the APE discourse planner. The ATLAS-ANDES architecture is therefore similar to the 2-tier AUTOROUTE architecture: its KCDs are dialogue games that are more complex but domain-specific. The simple generic question-answer pair is replaced by a recursive automaton that can deal with a specific question and many anticipated possible correct and incorrect sub-answers. A compiler then maps KCDs into plan operators, which are used by APE to combine KCDs into larger recursive FSMs. Moreover, the developers of ATLAS-ANDES propose a solution to the rigidity that is typically associated with FSM-based systems. The reactive component of APE can skip around in the recursive KCD, for example, it can pop sub-networks that ATLAS-ANDES believes contain intentions that were already dealt with in prior dialogue.

In contrast, dialogue management in **EDGE** and **CIRCSIM/APE** is purely plan-based. EDGE provides two types of (STRIPS-like) operators: *discourse* and *content* operators. Discourse operators model Sinclair & Coulthard's four levels of discourse, namely, *transaction, exchange, move*, and *act* [9]. Content operators specify how to explain something. For example, "to describe a device: explain its function, its structure, and its behaviour". EDGE's content operators are quite general; their bodies contain abstract domain references that interface with a knowledge representation module. EDGE incrementally builds and executes plans. Before each tutor turn, the deliberative planner expands the current unfinished step with either a complex sub-plan or an elementary plan step. Elementary plan steps are then executed using simple template driven generation. Thus, planning is delayed as much as possible so that the most current student model can be consulted.

CIRCSIM/APE also incrementally constructs and executes plans, and uses simple template driven generation for realising elementary plan steps. However, a major drawback of CIRCSIM/APE (for others, see [10]) is that it embeds control in operators, unlike traditional planners, where control is separated from action descriptions. This makes writing operators difficult and puts an additional burden on the planner.

Conclusion. Although previous and ongoing work in tutorial dialogue systems has striven to support unconstrained natural language input and multi-turn tutorial strategies, there remain limitations that must be overcome: teaching strategies, encoded as curriculum scripts, KCDs, or plan operators, are domain-specific; the purely plan-based systems embed control in plan operators or, necessarily, conflate planning with student modelling and maintenance of the dialogue context; and all current tutorial dialogue systems except EDGE mix high-level tutorial planning with low-level communication management. These limitations can make systems difficult to maintain, extend, or reuse.

There is great benefit to be gained from integrating dialogue theories and dialogue system technology that have been developed in the computational linguistics and spoken dialogue systems communities with the wealth of knowledge about student learning and tutoring strategies that has been built up in the ITS community. It is therefore worth considering dialogue systems not designed for tutoring [3,11,12,13,14,15]. These systems do not allow for conversational moves extending over multiple turns and the resulting need to abandon, suspend, or modify these moves. However, these systems aim for dialogue strategies that are independent of dialogue context management and communication management concerns. These strategies contain no domain knowledge; they query domain reasoners to fill in necessary details. Furthermore, in systems explicitly performing dialogue planning, control is never embedded in plan operators. Our goal is to combine these beneficial features (modularity and re-usability) with the flexibility and educational value of tutorial systems with reactive planners.

3 A 3-Tier Architecture for Managing Tutorial Dialogue

We present a generic and modular architecture for the management of tutorial dialogue. It allows the effective combination of pedagogical strategies, domain knowledge, and dialogue management strategies, clearly separating the knowledge sources involved. Our overall architecture is depicted in Fig. 1. There are

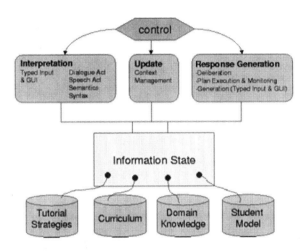

Fig. 1. A Modular Dialogue System Architecture.

three major modules, *interpretation*, *update*, and *response generation*. Each of the modules can access the *information state (IS)*, which captures the overall dialogue context and interfaces with external knowledge sources (*e.g.*, student model, domain reasoner, curriculum). In particular, the IS will need to contain a dialogue history that records all prior dialogue moves, and the *common ground*, the set of propositions that both dialogue partners have agreed upon in prior discourse. The IS also contains a list of salient objects to facilitate the treatment of linguistic phenomena such as anaphora. Moreover, the IS maintains any pending discourse obligations and provides access to the tutorial dialogue plan. This allows the system to deduce the issues that it needs to, or intends to address in future dialogue continuations.

In the remainder of this section, we describe only briefly the interpretation and update modules. We then focus on the response generation module that is based upon a 3-tier planning architecture, which we regard as enabling technology for managing tutorial dialogue.[1]

---

[1] An example that explains how we can simulate human-human tutorial dialogues in the 3-tier architecture is available from the authors upon request.

The interpretation module allows the student to interact with the system via text and graphical means. It then identifies the meaning and intention behind a student utterance. This includes its syntactic analysis, the construction of its propositional content, the recognition of its speech act, and the recognition of the intent behind the utterance (*i.e.*, the dialogue act). The latter is complemented by an evaluation of the student's answer or action for correctness).

The update module maintains the context. It is clearly separated from the response generation module. *Update rules* encode conversational expertise and define how to update the current context given a new dialogue act. Two example update rules are given below:

```
do DiagQuery:
    precond:     latest move is of type DIAG_QUERY
    effects:     add latest move to CDU
                 add obligation for hearer to address move to CDU
doAssert:
    precond:     latest move is of type assert
                 asserted content addresses a previous DIAG_QUERY or INFO_REQ, say Q1
    effects:     add latest move to CDU
                 remove speaker's obligation to address Q1
                 add hearer's obligation to address assertion
                 add that speaker is committed to propositional content of assertion
                 add that if hearer accepts assertion, then add assertion to common ground
```

The *update rule engine* fires the rule *doDiagQuery* if the latest dialogue move is a diagnostic query. As a consequence, such a move would be entered as part of the current discourse unit (CDU), and an obligation for the hearer to address this move would be created. The rule *doAssert* fires if the latest move is an assertion and if its asserted content addresses a previous diagnostic query or information request. If this is the case, then the latest move is added to the CDU, the speaker's obligation to address the question is deleted, the hearer is now obliged to address the assertion, and the propositional content of the assertion is a candidate for entering the common ground.

The response generation module computes appropriate tutorial moves and synthesises tutorial feedback as text or other modalities using a 3-tier planning architecture. Fig. 2 depicts its three levels: a *deliberative planner* that projects the future, anticipates and solves problems (top layer); a *plan execution and monitoring* system that performs adaptive on-the-fly refinement (middle layer); and an *action system* that performs primitive actions (bottom layer).

Top-tier: Deliberative Planning. The deliberation component synthesises plans from action descriptions at the highest possible level of abstraction. This abstraction not only minimises wasted effort, but also allows the middle layer to perform a maximum of situation-adaptive plan refinement. High-level planning results in a structured sequence of tasks that are passed to the *task agenda* of the middle layer; for each task, there is a reactive action package (see below) that achieves it, if successfully executed.

The deliberator is explicitly activated in two cases: when the tutor agent enters a tutorial dialogue, and during the dialogue when the middle layer fails to

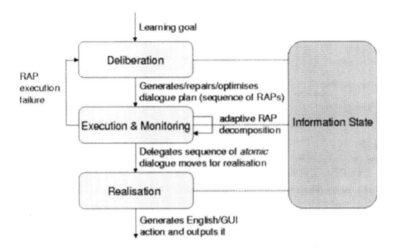

Fig. 2. A 3-tier Dialogue Planning Architecture

perform plan execution and therefore asks the top layer to perform a plan repair. However, the deliberative component has also a permanent background activity. It regularly inspects the agenda of the middle layer for two reasons: verifying whether pending discourse obligations (as recorded in the IS) are covered by the contents of the agenda, and searching to anticipate problems or to optimise the agenda's content. In both cases, the top layer can add or delete items from the task agenda as well as reorganise or aggregate them. The top and middle layer therefore need to synchronise their access to the agenda.

Middle-tier: Context-Driven Plan Refinement. Reactive Action Packages [16] are the basic blocks of a situation-driven plan refinement system. A Reactive Action Package (RAP) groups together and describes all ways to carry out a specific task in different situations. Fig. 3 displays (a simplified version of) the RAP *instruct_step*. It has three possible situation-specific ways of getting the student to perform a step in a procedure. Method M1 is applicable in any context. It spawns two sub-tasks, namely, the primitive task of generating a sequence of elementary dialogue moves, and the complex task of supplying feedback to the student's moves.

The RAP interpreter executes the contents of the agenda as follows. First, it selects the next task from the agenda. Then, it checks the selected task against the information state to see whether its effects have already been achieved. If this is the case, the task is deleted. Otherwise the interpreter identifies the RAP that can achieve the task. The methods of the identified RAP are checked, and the most appropriate of them is selected. If the chosen method is a primitive action, then it is delegated to the bottom layer for execution; if the method is a network of subtasks, then each subtask is put on the agenda, and a new interpretation cycle starts.

RAP: *instruct_step(?step)*
precond: nil
effects: instructed_step(?step)

method: M1
  context: nil
  tasks:
    t1: sequence assert(next_step(?step))
              direct(do(?step))
    t2: supply_feedback(did(?step))

method: M2
  context: didactic_mode(level(2))
          get_howto(?step, ?howto)
  tasks:
    t1: sequence assert(next_step(?step))
              assert(howto(?step, ?howto))
              check_student_understanding(ok)
    t2: direct(do(?step))
    t3: supply_feedback(did(?step))

method: M3
  contextsocratic_mode(level(2))
        get_effects(?step, ?effects)
  tasks:
    t1: sequence assert(next_desired_effects(?effects))
             diag_query(which_action_achieves(?effects))
    t2: supply_feedback(answered(which_action_achieves(?effects)))
    t3: direct(do(?step))
    t4: supply_feedback(did(?step))

Fig. 3. A RAP for Instructing a Step of a Procedure.

The execution of a RAP can fail for three reasons: its preconditions are not met, none of its methods are applicable, or the execution of one of its primitive methods fails. The RAP interpreter can cope with some failures, *e.g.*, it can try another applicable method. In the other cases, it has to call the top layer to cope with the failure.

Bottom-Tier: Action Execution. The bottom-tier is responsible for the execution of primitive dialogue actions. It gets a sequence of elementary speech acts and micro-plans the generation of multi-modal feedback (natural language utterances and GUI actions). The bottom-tier is supported by a sentence and media planner, both of which have access to the full dialogue context. In particular, these components consult the list of salient objects and the contents of the previous and current discourse unit to generate natural feedback that makes use of elliptical constructions and anaphoric expressions. Action execution fails if the micro-planner fails.

Turn-Taking Management. The tutoring agent releases the turn after it asks a question or requests that the student perform an action. In all other cases, the RAP interpreter "cycles" until a question or action request is generated. If the student takes the initiative and grabs the turn, then this dialogue act will be recorded in the IS, generating an obligation for the tutor to address the last student utterance. The top-layer then deliberates over the new situation and may change the contents of the agenda accordingly. Similarly, if the student fails to react within a time limit, then the interpretation module generates an appropriate dialogue act, which the update engine processes, generating an obligation for the tutor to address the student's silence. The deliberative planner can then decide to either give the student more time, or to take the turn to supply help.

4   BEE Tutorial Learning Environment — BEETLE

We have built BEETLE, a prototype implementation of our computational framework for managing tutorial dialogue that serves to both validate and propagate our ideas. It is primarily based on two technologies, the TRINDIKIT dialogue system shell [17] and the Open Agent Architecture (OAA) [18]. In line with our goal to provide a flexible, modular, and thus reusable architecture, domain reasoning is performed by a single agent. The BEER agent encodes BEETLE's knowledge about basic electricity and electronics. It has a rich LOOM representation of BEE concepts, can perform basic inferences in this domain, and has explicit representations of domain plans. BEETLE's deliberative planner, LONGBOW [19], creates instantiated dialogue plans from its general dialogue strategies by accessing the relevant domain knowledge represented in BEER.

At the time of writing, our 3-tier planning architecture is only partially implemented. The next major step is to replace LONGBOW and our hand-built plan execution and refinement layer with a state-of-the-art planning environment. We are currently investigating the use of the Open Planning Architecture (O-Plan) [20] and its successor I-Plan.

References

1. Lewin, I., Rupp, C.J., Hieronymus, J., Milward, D., Larsson, S., Berman, A.: Siridus system architecure and interface report. Tech. report, Siridis D6.1 (2000)
2. Chi, M.T.H., Siler, S.A., Jeong, H., Yamauchi, T., Hausmann, R.G.: Learning from human tutoring. Cognitive Science **25** (2001) 471–533
3. Lewin, I.: Autoroute dialogue demonstrator. Technical Report CRC-073, SRI Cambridge (1998)
4. Graesser, A.C., Wiemer-Hastings, K., Wiemer-Hastings, P., Kreuz, R.: AutoTutor: A simulation of a human tutor. Cognitive Systems Research **1** (1999) 35–51
5. Schulze, K.G., Shelby, R.N., Treacy, D., Wintersgill, M.C., VanLehn, K., Gertner, A.: Andes: A coached learning environment for classical newtonian physics. The Journal of Electronic Publishing **6** (2000)
6. Khuwaja, R.A., Evens, M.W., Michael, J.A., Rovick, A.A.: Architecture of CIRCSIM-tutor (v.3). In: Proceedings of the 7th Annual IEEE Computer-Based Medical Systems Symposium, IEEE Computer Society Press (1994) 158–163
7. Cawsey, A.: Explanatory dialogues. Interacting with Computers **1** (1989) 69–92
8. Jordan, P.W., Rosé, C., VanLehn, K.: Tools for authoring tutorial dialogue knowledge. In Moore, J.D., Redfield, C.L., Johnson, W.L., eds.: 10th International Conference on Artificial Intelligence in Education, IOS Press (2001) 222–233
9. Sinclair, J.M., Coulthard, R.M.: Towards an Analysis of Discourse: The English used by teachers and pupils. Oxford University Press (1975)
10. Freedman, R.: An approach to increasing programming efficiency in plan-based dialogue systems. In Moore, J.D., Redfield, C.L., Johnson, W.L., eds.: 10th International Conference on Artificial Intelligence in Education, IOS Press (2001)
11. Allen, J., Byron, D., Dzikovska, M., Ferguson, G., Galescu, L., Stent, A.: An architecture for a generic dialogue shell. Natural Language Engineering **6** (2000)
12. Pieraccini, R., Levin, E., Eckert, W.: AMICA: The AT&T mixed initiative conversational architecture. In: Proceedings of the 5th European Conference on Speech Communication and Technology (Eurospeech-97). (1997)

13. Larsson, S., Ljungloef, P., Cooper, R., Engdahl, E., Ericsson, S.: GoDiS - an accommodating dialogue system. In: Proceedings of ANLP/NAACL-2000 Workshop on Conversational Systems. (2000)

14. Rudnicky, A., Xu, W.: An agenda-based dialog management architecture for spoken language systems. In: Intl. Workshop on Automatic Speech Recognition and Understanding. (1999)

15. Chu-Carroll, J.: Form-based reasoning for mixed-initiative dialogue management in information-query systems. In: Proceedings of the 7th European Conference on Speech Communication and Technology (Eurospeech-99). (1999) 1519–1522

16. Firby, R.J.: Adaptive Execution in Complex Dynamic Domains. PhD thesis, Yale University (1989) Technical Report YALEU/CSD/RR#672.

17. Larsson, S., Traum, D.: Information state and dialogue management in the TRINDI dialogue move engine toolkit. Natural Language Engineering **6** (2000) 323–340

18. Martin, D.L., Cheyer, A.J., Moran, D.B.: The open agent architecture: A framework for building distributed software systems. Applied Artificial Intelligence: An International Journal **13** (1999) 91–128

19. Young, R.M., Pollack, M.E., Moore, J.D.: Decomposition and causality in partial order planning. In: Proceedings of the Second International Conference on Artificial Intelligence and Planning Systems, Morgan Kaufman (1994) 188–193

20. Currie, K., Tate, A.: O-Plan: the open planning architecture. Artificial Intelligence **52** (1991) 49–86

Teaching Case-Based Argumentation Concepts Using Dialectic Arguments vs. Didactic Explanations[*]

Kevin D. Ashley, Ravi Desai, and John M. Levine

Learning Research and Development Center

University of Pittsburgh
Pittsburgh, Pennsylvania, USA 15260
ashley@pitt.edu

Abstract. We compared two automated approaches to teaching *distinguishing*, a fundamental skill of case-based reasoning that involves assessing the relevant differences among cases in a context-sensitive way. The approaches are implemented in two versions of CATO, an ITS designed to teach law students basic skills of case-based legal argument. The original version of CATO employed a didactic explanatory dialogue. The newer version, CATO-Dial, teaches the same skill with a simulated dialectic argument in a courtroom setting. Our hypothesis was that students would learn better by engaging in the simulated argument than by receiving interactive explanation. We showed that students in the dialectic argument simulation group performed significantly better on certain sections of the post-test aimed at assessing transfer of their skills of distinguishing.

1 Introduction

In dialectical domains such as law, applied ethics, policy analysis, and business, where arguments by analogy are routinely employed in professional education and practice, the skill of distinguishing cases is fundamental. In law, practitioners regularly make arguments by drawing analogies between a target problem and past precedents. The argument asserts that the target should be decided in the same way as a cited source case by virtue of their relevant similarities. These are factual patterns the cases share that form the basis of legal reasons for deciding them in the same way.

Distinguishing is a way of responding to such arguments. A *distinction* is a factual difference underlying a legal reason to decide the target problem differently from the cited case. Not all differences are distinctions, only those that give rise to legal reasons for treating the cases differently. Such a difference may be a factual strength of a side (i.e., a party, either plaintiff, the one who commences suit, or the defendant) in the target problem not shared in the source case, or a factual weakness in the source case not shared in the target. For the cases used in our experiment, in which a student

---

[*] This material is based upon work supported by the National Science Foundation under Grant No. 9720359. We thank Professor Kevin Deasy, University of Pittsburgh School of Law, for his many contributions to this work.

S.A. Cerri, G. Gouardères, and F. Paraguaçu (Eds.): ITS 2002, LNCS 2363, pp. 585–595, 2002.

plays the role of the defendant's attorney, a distinction is defined as a pattern of facts that strengthens defendant's legal argument in the problem not found in the cited-case, or a fact pattern that weakens defendant's side in the cited-case not found in the problem. The legal reasons triggered by these factual strengths and weaknesses are based in legal policies and values in statutes, constitutions, and precedents [5].

One who distinguishes successfully must be sensitive to the argument context in which a source case has been used. The role a difference plays in an argument -- its underlying (here legal) significance depends on the other combinations of facts in the particular target problem and cited source case under comparison.

In observing student arguments, instructors note that students often evidence only shallow knowledge of the concept of a distinction. They may be able to find differences between cases but do not necessarily understand that only some differences are distinctions. Students may tend to ignore which side a difference favors, or they may view the significance of a difference independently of the other facts in the problem and cited-case. Because of their shallow knowledge, students may even make arguments which hurt, rather than help, their side's position.

Like other argument skills, the skill of distinguishing is ideally "picked up" by students through trial-and-error practice. In law school, students learn argumentation skills by engaging in classroom dialectical exchanges with a professor and other students and by participating in mock courtroom arguments in moot court competitions and legal writing classes. Students, however, are often reluctant to expose themselves in class by making arguments, and, in any event, could benefit from additional instruction outside the classroom. In an effort to meet this need, Aleven and Ashley [1, 2] developed the CATO program (i.e., Case Argument TutOrial), an Intelligent Tutoring System designed to teach beginning law students basic skills of making arguments with cases, including how to distinguish cases.

How can a tutoring system best teach students to learn to distinguish well? One approach, *didactic explanation*, involves presenting good and bad examples of distinguishing. The bad examples illustrate the various kinds of shallow knowledge, and the system explains why the examples are instances of unsuccessful argument. This is how CATO teaches distinguishing.

Alternatively, a *dialectic argument* approach might attempt to teach students distinguishing by engaging them in arguments and giving them an opportunity to learn the skill through a process of trial-and-error. From a technological viewpoint, this is a more difficult kind of pedagogical interaction to engineer. Before we undertook the effort to develop a large-scale didactic argument system, we wanted to see whether it was likely to make a difference in how well students learned. We therefore developed a variation of CATO, called CATO-Dial, which employs dialectic argument to teach distinguishing.

Our hypothesis was that students would learn the skill of distinguishing better by engaging in simulated argument than in interactive explanation. We speculated that role-playing and arguing would present information to students in a more relevant context and motivate them to process information more thoroughly. This would expose students' superficial knowledge and help them develop deeper knowledge concerning how a difference relates to underlying reasons, to the role it plays in the argument context, and to interactions with other facts in the problem and cited-case. We conducted an experiment to test our hypothesis that CATO-Dial can give students this kind of experience and benefit.

CATO-Dial's tutoring methodology is to engage students in argument dialogues that focus on case comparison. Traditionally, law school professors engage students in Socratic dialogues about cases that students read in their casebooks. While a number of Intelligent Tutoring Systems have been developed to teach legal subject matter [7, 13], few have focused on teaching legal argumentation skills or reasoning with cases. Legal argument is not as determinate a form of problem-solving as, say, physics or geometry. Legal problems rarely have provably correct answers; instead, there may be reasonable arguments on both sides of the dispute based on analogies to competing cases [3, 11]. The legal domain is also highly focused on texts, requiring any tutoring system to finesse the need for complex natural language processing.

Some early tutoring systems used argumentation to teach subject matter. For example, SCHOLAR [6] taught geography with a kind of Socratic dialogue. Collins and Stevens [9] concluded after systematic study that the best human tutors used a Socratic style. Their WHY system taught students about the causes of rainfall using an inquiry teaching method and Socratic dialogue. A subsequent tutoring system [15] incorporated the inquiry teaching method into an ITS shell and geography tutor. Using another argumentation dialogue strategy, playing devil's advocate, the OLIA ITS [10] defends the weaker position as it engages students in an argument / counter-argument dialogue. More recently, research suggests that students tutored manually with Socratic dialogues learned targeted physics concepts (i.e., rules) better than those taught with more didactic dialogues [12]. In the latter, the human tutor provided more explanation before asking questions but asked fewer open-ended questions.

2 Didactic Explanation vs. Dialectic Argument

A variety of tutoring systems have incorporated case-based reasoning to tell relevant stories, provide worked-out examples, adapt as students solve new problems, generate new problems, model students' knowledge, and provide advice to teachers. CATO, however, is one of the few that teaches a process of case-based reasoning, literally comparing and contrasting problems to past cases in order to draw and justify inferences about the problems [1, pp. 197-8].

CATO's instructional environment comprises a web-accessible Casebook and Workbook and a set of specialized computerized tools, accessible through an X-server connection to CATO running on a Unix workstation. The Casebook presents excerpts from important legal case opinions in trade secret law. Each is followed by a small set of argumentation and discussion questions, much as in an ordinary legal casebook. The Workbook guides students in using the CATO tools to analyze and respond to the argumentation and discussion questions.

In using CATO, students work with textual case summaries and abstract representations of cases in terms of *factors*. Each factor represents a stereotypical collection of facts, which tends normally to strengthen or weaken a conclusion that a side should win a particular kind of legal claim [3]. A Factor Hierarchy represents reasons why a factor makes a difference to the legal claim. Experiments show that CATO is an effective teacher [1, 2].

CATO helps students analyze target problems and compare them to past cases. It teaches novices to identify factors in a target, test hypotheses about their significance against cases in its database, and make legal arguments about how to decide the target problems citing cases. Novice users encounter target cases based on real litigated cases, such as the *Space Aero* case.[1] Users identify conflicting factors in the problem, which give rise to conflicting reasons about how to decide the problem. CATO then teaches them how to make legal arguments to resolve such conflicts.

CATO's Argument Maker tool provides a tutorial on distinguishing. In its original form, the tutorial engages students in an interactive exercise employing didactic explanation. Given a problem situation and case cited by a side in the dispute, students are invited to select from a menu the differences on which to focus in responding to the case by distinguishing. The program then explains whether that selection is a good or bad choice. If a bad choice, the program explains why and illustrates the rebuttal argument one might expect from the other side.

To enable CATO to employ dialectic argument in teaching distinguishing, we developed CATO-Dial, a modification of the program that engages novice users in courtroom-style arguments about target problems like the *Space Aero* case (or any other pair of relevant cases in its database) [4].

Here is an example students encountered with CATO-Dial's version of the tutorial on distinguishing, based on the *Space Aero* case. Students have identified conflicting factors in the *Space Aero* problem and have begun to consider the conflicting legal reasons about how to decide the problem associated with these factors. The Case Analyzer presents the two cases in a tabular form for comparing their factors. As shown in Figure 1, *Space Aero* has five factors, three of which favor the plaintiff (p) and two of which favor the defendant (d). The *Kubik* case, won by plaintiff (p), shares two of these factors, the relevant similarities (marked with "="). The relevant differences (i.e., distinctions) are the four unshared factors marked with "*". These favor deciding *Space Aero* for the defendant (i.e., differently from *Kubik*). Note that F1 and F19 strengthen the defendant in *Space Aero* and are not found in *Kubik*, whereas F7 and F21 strengthen the plaintiff's position in *Kubik* and are not found in *Space Aero*. F8 and F16 are also unshared factors, but they are *not* distinctions because they favor deciding *Space Aero* for plaintiff (i.e., the same as in *Kubik*). F8 favors plaintiff in *Space Aero*. Plaintiff won in *Kubik* despite F16.

CATO-Dial places the student in the role of an advocate, Perry Mason, Esq.,[2] who has to argue a case in court. As shown in Figure 2, the student may put arguments in the mouth of Perry Mason by selecting argument moves and values from a menu. CATO-Dial responds on behalf of the Judge, who mediates the proceedings, Hamilton Burger, Perry's opposing counsel, and Della Street, Perry's savvy assistant, who offers helpful hints. In the dialogue, Mr. Burger's responses (such as step 7 in Figure 2), generated by CATO-Dial, take advantage of any weaknesses in Mr. Mason's argument, based on the students' menu selections. The Judge's reaction is meant to

---

[1] In the *Space Aero* case, plaintiff Darling manufactured oxygen hoses for Navy aircraft and was the only company capable of their manufacture. Darling had committed over $250,000 in research for hose manufacture. Four long-time employees on Darling's hose-building team left to form Space Aero. Within one month Space Aero was able to manufacture hoses identical to Darling's. None of the defendants had any formal employment contract with Darling: each could be fired or leave at any time. Plaintiff's former supplier provided financial backing to Space Aero and conspired with the individual defendants to terminate their employment with Darling. Darling had disclosed the secret information to this supplier in prior dealings. Darling appeared to have taken minimal security measures.

[2] Based on E. S. Gardner's famous Perry Mason. See http://www.ozemail.com.au/~jsimko/.

underscore the student's mistake, and Della's hints, also generated by CATO-Dial, provide instruction on how to rectify them. CATO-Dial can engage in dialogues like this for any pair of relevant cases in its database.

CATO-Dial's dialectic argument contrasts with the didactic explanation of the original CATO. In the latter, the student is not engaged in as direct a manner. Instead, the student is presented with an argument that a hypothetical opponent could make. The footnote shows an excerpt from CATO's didactic explanation of why a student's distinction is incorrect.[3] Just as in step 5 of Figure 2, the student has chosen to distinguish the *Space Aero* case from the *Kubik* case using factors F8 and F16. The argument that CATO uses to show the inadequacy of the student's initial selection of distinctions is the same in both versions; the difference lies in the manner in which it is presented to the students and the way in which students are engaged in the task.

Space Aero	Kubik (p)
* F1 Disclosure-In-Negotiations (d)	* F7 Brought-Tools (p)
F8 Competitive-Advantage (p)	= F15 Unique-Product (p)
= F15 Unique-Product (p)	F16 Info-Reverse-Engineerable (d)
= F18 Identical-Products (p)	= F18 Identical-Products (p)
* F19 No-Security-Measures (d)	* F21 Knew-Info-Confidential (p)

Fig. 1. Case Comparison in Terms of Factors

COURT IS NOW IN SESSION
1. Judge: You may proceed, Mr. Burger.
2. Mr. Burger for Plaintiff: Your Honor, where plaintiff was the only manufacturer making the product [F15] and defendant's product was identical to plaintiff's [F18], plaintiff should win a claim of trade secrets misappropriation, as in Kubik, Inc. v. Hull, 56 Mich.App. 335, 224 N.W.2d 80 (1974).
3. Judge (to Defendant's counsel): Any response Mr. Mason?
4. Della Street (Whispering in Perry's ear): How are you going to respond on behalf of the defendant? ... Burger's analogy to the *Kubik* case is not very strong. Perry, you should distinguish the *Kubik* case, from the *Space Aero* problem. In the top part of this window, click on the factors that are the relevant distinguishing factors of the *Space Aero* problem and the *Kubik* case. If by mistake you clicked on the wrong factor, you can "turn off" that factor by clicking on it again. Finally, click on "Continue".

---

[3] Here is CATO's didactic explanation of why a student's selection of factor F8 as a distinction is incorrect. It makes a similar point re F16:

CATO: Suppose defendant made the following argument: "*Kubik, Inc. v. Hull.* is distinguishable, because in *Space Aero*, defendant's access to plaintiff's product information saved it time or expense [F8]. This was not so in *Kubik*." Would this really help defendant? When you have answered this question for yourself, please click on "Continue".

CATO: Plaintiff could respond to defendant's argument, as follows: "Your Honor, as defendant's counsel correctly pointed out, in the current problem, defendant's access to plaintiff's product information saved it time or expense [F8]. *Kubik*, which was won by plaintiff, does not have this strength on plaintiff's part but is otherwise similar to the problem at hand. Where this additional strength is present, a decision in favor of plaintiff is warranted even more strongly than it was in *Kubik*." In short, even though factor F8 is a difference, defendant cannot use it to distinguish *Kubik*. Defendant needs to focus on other differences, namely, on those differences that make *Space Aero* look stronger for defendant than *Kubik*.

5. <STUDENT: Distinguish *Kubik* [F8] [F16] (Continue)> **Mr. Mason for Defendant:** Kubik, Inc. v. Hull is distinguishable, because in *Space Aero*, defendant's access to plaintiff's product information saved it time or expense [F8] and plaintiff's product information could be learned by reverse-engineering [F16]. This was not so in *Kubik*.

6. Judge (to Plaintiff's counsel): Mr. Burger?

7. Mr. Burger for Plaintiff: Your Honor, as Mr. Mason concedes, in the current problem, defendant's access to plaintiff's product information saved it time or expense [F8]. *Kubik*, which was won by plaintiff, does not have this strength on plaintiff's part but is otherwise similar to the problem at hand. Where this additional strength is present, a decision in favor of plaintiff is warranted even more strongly than it was in *Kubik*. Your Honor, as defendant's counsel pointed out, in Kubik, plaintiff won in spite of the fact that plaintiff's product information could be learned by reverse-engineering [F16]. The current problem does not have this weakness on plaintiff's part and is otherwise similar to Kubik. If plaintiff won in Kubik, then a fortiori plaintiff should prevail in the current problem.

8. Judge (to Defendant's counsel): I am sorry Mr. Mason but at this time I am afraid I have to agree with Mr. Burger. Can you strengthen your argument?

9. <STUDENT: Help! (Continue)>

10. Della Street: Perry, here is a hint that may help you. Continue to select factors that can be used to distinguish the case. Even though factor F8 is a difference, defendant cannot use it to distinguish *Kubik*. .... Even though factor F16 is a difference, defendant cannot use it to distinguish *Kubik*. Defendant needs to focus on other differences, namely, on those differences that make *Space Aero* look stronger for defendant than *Kubik*. Continue to select factors that can be used to distinguish the case.... Then click on "Continue".

11. <STUDENT: Distinguish *Kubik* [F1][F19] [F7] [F21] (Continue)> **Mr. Mason for Defendant:** Kubik, Inc. v. Hull is distinguishable, because in *Kubik*, defendant knew that plaintiff's information was confidential [F21] and plaintiff's former employee brought product development information to defendant [F7]. This was not so in *Space Aero*. Also, in *Space Aero*, plaintiff did not adopt any security measures [F19] and plaintiff disclosed its product information in negotiations with defendant [F1]. This was not so in *Kubik*. These factors are reasons that *Space Aero* is stronger for defendant than is *Kubik*, and therefore, that *Kubik* should not be followed.

12. Judge (to Plaintiff's counsel): Mr. Burger?

13. Mr. Burger for Plaintiff: Your Honor, We concede that the defendant's argument can be used to distinguish the case.

14. Della Street: You're so brilliant Perry!

Fig. 2. Sample Dialectic Argument in CATO-Dial

3   Description of Experiment

We compared the impact of teaching distinguishing to senior undergraduates using the two versions of CATO. The students (20 males and 25 females) had all been accepted into law schools and were receiving preparatory instruction through a Summer Institute of the Council on Legal Education Opportunities (CLEO). The students were randomly assigned to two groups. The experimental group used the dialectic argument version of CATO-Dial and initially numbered 22 students. The control group worked with the didactic explanation version of CATO and initially numbered 23 students. After taking a pretest, each group worked in a series of eight two-hour sessions over a span of about one month from June 5 through July 11, 2000. For each session a student was paired with a different partner from the same group.

The pre-test comprised three questions which tested student's case-based argumentation skills. For Questions 1 and 2, students read a problem situation and three short cases. Students were asked to make and respond to arguments about the problem given the cases. Question 3 asked them to define the concepts of a relevant similarity and relevant difference.

During the first six instructional sessions, students in the experimental and control groups were treated identically. These sessions were designed to introduce students to making arguments with cases and to CATO or CATO-Dial, both of which behaved identically for these initial sessions. In Sessions 1 to 4, both groups of students familiarized themselves with the factor based representation system and the CATO environment. In Sessions 5 and 6 all students learned how to use the programs' Argument Maker tools to select cases to cite.

The control group and experimental group were treated differently in Sessions 7 and 8. These two sessions focused on teaching students how to distinguish cases. Students were expected to complete eight pair-wise case comparisons involving distinguishing. The eight pairs of cases were the same in both groups. The only difference was the manner in which CATO and CATO-Dial taught the lesson. The experimental group worked with CATO-Dial's courtroom dialogues like that in Figure 2. The control group worked with the original CATO didactic explanations.

After the students completed all eight sessions of classroom instruction with CATO or CATO-Dial, they took a post-test comprised of three argument questions (Questions 1, 2, and 3) and three transfer questions (Questions 4, 5, and 6). Questions 1, 2, and 3 were worded identically to the pre-test questions but Questions 1 and 2 involved a different problem and cases. The three transfer questions tested the following transfer skills: Question 4 required students to take on a new role – instead of making arguments they critiqued an argument. Question 5 tested students' recall of a particular problem situation they had encountered in the instruction. This problem had been used extensively in the teaching sessions as a basis of the argumentation lessons. Students were asked to make and respond to an argument about the problem, which they had to recall from memory, by analogizing it to and distinguishing it from a new case presented with the question. Question 6 required students to apply the skills they had learned with CATO or CATO-Dial to a new domain that they were unlikely to have encountered before: the copyright law doctrine of Fair Use.

A law professor and director of the summer CLEO program graded all but one of the pre-test and post-test questions. The grader was provided a one-page summary of grading criteria and instructed to assign a gestalt grade (between 1 and 10) to each question. He was blind as to the identity of the test writers, but did know which were pre-tests and which were post-tests. The exception was Question 5, the recall question, for which we developed an objective grading scheme. Students were awarded a maximum of ten possible points on the basis of how many of the factors in the problem they referred to in their argument. They received 1 point for citing a factor shared by the problem and case, 2 points for citing a factor in the problem not shared with the case, and 3 points for citing a factor in the problem that could be used to distinguish the case. In grading the recall question, the grader, an undergraduate research assistant, was blind as to which group the students were in.

4 Analysis

Post-test data were available for only 22 of the 45 students, 15 in the experimental group and seven in the control group. Of the 23 students whose data were not available, seven were from the experimental group and 16 were from the control group. Three students dropped out of the CLEO program and our study before Session 7. Five students did not show up for the post-test. Two students completed only the first question of the post-test. Thirteen students were dropped because they had not completed enough work in Sessions 7 and 8, the only sessions involving differential treatment of the experimental and control groups. In determining whether a student had or had not completed enough work in Sessions 7 and 8, the following criterion was adopted. If a student completed one or more of the eight pair-wise case comparisons presented in Sessions 7 and 8 using the relevant dialogue feature of CATO, he or she was retained. By relevant dialogue feature of CATO, we mean the didactic explanation mini-dialogue in the case of the control group and the dialectical argument in the case of the experimental group. In order to complete a pair-wise comparison, a student had to find all the relevant differences between the two cases. Whether a student completed a pair-wise comparison was assessed by examining the command log files of CATO or CATO-Dial for Sessions 7 and 8. Since students worked in pairs, if the log file failed to show completion of the pair-wise comparison, neither student in the pair received credit for that comparison. Conversely, if the log file showed completion, both students received credit.

Pre-test scores were analyzed for the 22 students, who provided both pre-test and post-test data. For each student, responses to the three pre-test questions were summed, and the mean response of students in the experimental group was compared to that of students in the control group, using a two-tailed t-test. Results showed no statistically significant difference between the two groups. Since the students were paired with different partners across sessions, we used the individual student rather than the pair as the unit of analysis for both pre-test and post-test analyses.

Post-test scores were also analyzed for the 22 students who provided both pre-test and post-test data. For each student, responses to the three argument questions (i.e., Questions 1, 2, and 3) were summed, as were responses to the three transfer questions (i.e., Questions 4, 5, and 6) (see Figure 3.) A two-tailed t-test indicated no significant difference in the mean post-test scores of the experimental and control groups with respect to the argument questions. For the transfer questions, however, the mean post-test score of the experimental group was significantly higher than that of the control group (t (6.8) =2.63, p < .05, effect size of 1.30).[4]

5 Discussion and Conclusion

The data confirmed in an interesting way our hypothesis that students would learn the skill of distinguishing better by engaging in simulated dialectical argument than in interactive didactic explanation. Whereas dialectic argument was not more effective

---

[4] Degrees of freedom for this test were reduced from 20 because Levene's test for equality of variances indicated that the variances of scores in the two groups were not equal.

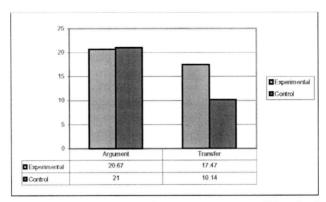

Fig. 3. Comparison of Mean Post-Test Scores on Argument and Transfer Questions

than didactic explanation in teaching distinguishing skills, it was significantly more effective in helping students transfer the skills they learned to new tasks and an unfamiliar legal domain. Dialectical argument may have induced students to construct a schema for making and responding to arguments, resulting in deeper knowledge and thus better performance on transfer skills.

Apart from the transfer difference, there was some other evidence that the experimental students had a deeper understanding of the importance that context plays in the task of finding distinctions. In addition to assigning numerical scores to answers, the grader evaluated the answers in terms of four grading criteria, each involving a simple binary positive-or-negative scale. Two suggestive, though nonsignificant, differences emerged, both of which favored the experimental group. Students in the experimental group were more often rated positively on the criteria "Avoids making opponent's argument" and "Avoids errors regarding which side strengths favor". These results support the conclusion that the experimental manipulation helped students to learn better when a difference is a distinction.

It is intriguing that a fairly superficial transformation from CATO to CATO-Dial in the presentation of the lesson on distinguishing had such dramatic benefits. After all, both programs presented the same basic information. The critical difference, we believe, is that CATO-Dial's dialectical argument simulation provided that information in a more useful way. The dialectical argument offers several potential benefits, any or all of which may explain the observed difference in transfer scores.

Students may have found the increased level of involvement in the courtroom simulation motivating and conducive to paying attention and learning. The courtroom role-playing context adds an element of competition to the task: the students may feel they are trying to defeat CATO-Dial. This context also adds a sense of fun to the task.

In addition, students may have found it is easier to understand the program's responses in CATO-Dial than in CATO. In the latter, the program is in the somewhat awkward position of explaining by example why a student's response is good or bad. The dialectical argument simulation, by contrast, provides a more natural context for illustrating the effect in an ongoing dialogue regarding a student's choices.

Role-playing in a courtroom argument, with that role's cognitive and emotional expectations, may also be important. For one thing, courtroom simulation explicitly prompts the student. An interactive style of human tutoring, in which tutors prompted students, supported learning even when tutors did not provide explanations and feedback [8]. For another thing, dialectical argument may induce a student to feel worse about making a mistake than does didactic explanation. If so, students are more likely to pay attention and to care about learning in the former context. Role-playing may also induce students to compare the cases more carefully and thus help transfer. In a recent investigation involving business school education, students who compared cases in a study phase were three times more likely to transfer the implicit principle of the cases to a new application than were those who simply read the cases for the purposes of advice-giving [14].

It is worth noting that students in the experimental group reported finding the dialogues somewhat (though not significantly) more helpful than did those in the control group. When asked, "When CATO did provide instructional feedback, how helpful was it?", students who used CATO-Dial rated it as more helpful than did students who used the original CATO ($\underline{M}$s = 6.76 and 5.56 out of 10, respectively.) This finding is consistent with the fact that many more students provided complete data in the CATO-Dial group than in the CATO group.

Law professors aim to teach research and argumentation skills that students can transfer to new legal domains and tasks. They know that law students are likely to practice in different areas of law than the ones students studied in law school, and that over the course of a student's legal practice, the laws are likely to change.

Consequently, the results of this study suggest that the CATO-Dial approach is potentially quite valuable. Our subsequent work will focus on converting as much of the CATO curriculum as possible to a dialectical format.

References

1. Aleven, V. (1997) *Teaching Case-Based Argumentation Through a Model and Examples*, Ph.D. Dis., U. Pittsburgh, unnumbered Tech. Rep. LRDC/ISP.
2. Aleven, V. and Ashley, K.D. (1997) "Teaching Case-Based Argumentation Through a Model and Examples". *Proc. 8th World Conf. AI in Ed. Soc.* 87-94. IOS Press: Amsterdam.
3. Ashley, K.D., (1990). *Modeling Legal Argument: Reasoning with Cases and Hypotheticals*. The MIT Press / Bradford Books, Cambridge, MA.
4. Ashley, K. D. (2000) "Designing Electronic Casebooks That Talk Back: The CATO Program". In *Jurimetrics* Vol. 40, No. 3, pp. 275-319.
5. Ashley, K.D. (2002) "An AI Model of Case-Based Legal Argument from a Jurisprudential Viewpoint." In *Journal of Artificial Intelligence and Law*. Kluwer: Dordrecht, Neth.
6. Carbonell, J.R. (1970). AI in CAI: An Artificial Intelligence Approach to Computer Aided Instruction. *IEEE Transactions on Man Machine Systems* 11(4) 190-202.
7. Centinia, F., T. Routen, A. Hartmann, and C. Hegarty (1995) "STATUTOR: Too Intelligent By Half?" In *Legal Knowledge Based Systems JURIX '95*. 121-132. Lelystad: Koninklijke.
8. Chi, Michelene T.H., S. Silver, H. Jeong, T. Yamauchi, and R. Hausmann (2001) "Learning From Human Tutoring" in *Cognitive Science*, Vol. 25, pp. 471-533.
9. Collins, A. and Stevens, A. L. (1982). "Goals and Strategies of inquiry Teachers". In *Advances In Instructional Psychology*, R Glaser (ed.) pp. 65-119. Hillsdale, NJ: Erlbaum.

10. Retalis, S., H. Pain and M. Haggith. (1996) "Arguing with the Devil; Teaching in Controversial Domains". *Int. Tutoring Sys., 3d Intl Conf., ITS-96.* 659-667. Berlin: Springer.
11. Rissland, E.L. (1990) "Artificial Intelligence and Law: Stepping Stones to a Model of Legal Reasoning". *Yale Law Journal* 99. 1957-1981. June 1990. Number 8.
12. Rose C. P., J. D. Moore, K. VanLehn, D. Allbritton. (2001) "A Comparative Evaluation of Socratic versus Didactic Tutoring", 2001 LRDC Tech Report LRDC-BEE-1.
13. Span, G. (1993) "LITES, an Intelligent Tutoring System for Legal Problem-Solving in the Domain of Dutch Civil Law". In *Proc. 4th Intl Conf. AI and Law*, 76-81. New York: ACM.
14. Thompson, L., Gentner, D. and Loewenstein, J. (2000) "Avoiding Missed Opportunities in Managerial Life." in *Org. Behavior and Human Decision Proc.*, 82, No. 1. May. pp. 60-75.
15. Wong, L., C. Quek, and C. Looi. (1997) "PADI-2: An Inquiry-based Geography Tutor". In *AI in Education*, Proc. AI-ED 97 World Conf. 47-54. Amsterdam: IOS Press.

An Intelligent Tutoring System Incorporating a Model of an Experienced Human Tutor

Neil T. Heffernan and Kenneth R. Koedinger

School of Computer Science
Carnegie Mellon University
Pittsburgh, PA 15213
(neil@cs.cmu.edu), (koedinger@cmu.edu)

Abstract. Symbolization is the ability to translate a real world situation into the language of algebra. We believe that symbolization is the single most important skill students learn in high school algebra. We present research on what makes this skill difficult and report the discovery of a "hidden" skill in symbolization. Contrary to past research that has emphasized that symbolization is difficult due to both comprehension difficulties and the abstract nature of variables, we found that symbolization is difficult because it is the articulation in the "foreign" language of "algebra". We also present *Ms. Lindquist*, an Intelligent Tutoring System (ITS) designed to carry on a tutorial dialog about symbolization. Ms. Lindquist has a separate tutorial model encoding pedagogical content knowledge in the form of different tutorial strategies, which were partially developed by observing an experienced human tutor. We discuss aspects of this human tutor's method that can be modeled well by Ms. Lindquist. Finally, we present an early formative showing that students can learn from the dialogs Ms. Lindquist is able to engage student in. Ms. Lindquist has tutored over 600 students at www.AlgebraTutor.org.

1 Introduction

The mission of the Center for Interdisciplinary Research on Constructive Learning Environments (CIRCLE) is 1) to study human tutoring and 2) to build and test a new generation of tutoring systems that encourage students to construct the target knowledge instead of telling it to them (VanLehn et al., 1998). CAI (Computer Aided Instruction) systems were 1st generation tutors. They presented a page of text or graphics and depending upon the student's answer, put up a different page. Model-tracing ITSs are 2nd generation tutoring systems that allow the tutor to follow the line of reasoning of the student. ITS have had notable success (Koedinger et al., 1997) despite the fact that human tutoring can look very different (Moore, 1996). One way they are different is that there is a better sense of a dialog in human tutoring and maybe this is important. After analyzing over 100 hours of untrained tutors in naturalistic tutoring sessions, Graesser et al. (in press) believe "there is something about interactive discourse that is responsible for learning gains."

The members of CIRCLE are working on 3rd generation tutoring systems that are meant to engage in a dialog with students, using multiple strategies, to allow students to construct their own knowledge of the domain. We have built a new ITS, called *Ms. Lindquist*, which not only is able to model-trace the student's actions, but

S.A. Cerri, G. Gouardères, and F. Paraguaçu (Eds.): ITS 2002, LNCS 2363, pp. 596–608, 2002.

can be more human-like in carrying on a running conversation, complete with probing questions, positive and negative feedback, follow-up questions in embedded sub-dialogs, and requests for explanation as to why something is correct. In order to build Ms. Lindquist we have expanded the model-tracing paradigm so that Ms. Lindquist not only has a model of the student, but also has a model of tutorial reasoning (e.g., Clancey, 1982). Based on observation of an experienced tutor and cognitive research, this tutorial model has multiple tutorial strategies at its disposal.

The task domain we are working on is symbolization, which is the task of writing an algebraic expression given a real-world problem context, often presented in the form of a word problem. Symbolization is important because if students cannot translate problems into algebra, they will not be able to apply algebra to solve real world problems. This domain makes it easy to avoid some difficult natural language issues because we can ask students to write algebraic expressions and those expressions are easy for the computer to "understand". We take advantage of this property of the domain to avoid any serious natural language processing; we also use pull-down menus to allow students to construct explanations. Instead, we focus our energies on modeling tutorial reasoning, which includes capturing the *pedagogical content knowledge (Shulman, 1986)* of an experienced human tutor. A tutor's "pedagogical content knowledge" is the knowledge that he or she has about how to teach a specific skill. A good tutor is not just one who knows the domain, nor is it simply one who knows general tutoring rules. A good tutor is one who also has content specific strategies that can help a student overcome common difficulties. We have set out to observe and model some of these strategies for our specific domain of symbolization. Lets look at one example of a content-specific pedagogical strategy for symbolization. The following was collected and transcribed from a one hour long one-on-one tutoring session between an experienced human tutor and an eighth grade student working on the "bike-trip" problem, which we use as one of several running examples.

240. Student: [reads problem[1]] Cathy took a "m" mile bike ride. She rode at a speed of "s" miles per hour. She stopped for a "b" hour break. Write an expression for how long the trip took.
241. S: uhm [Writes "s/m+b" but should be "m/s+b"]
242. Tutor: How do you calculate the amount of time it takes you? If you're, if you're, if you're riding at, let's make it simple. If you are riding at 20 miles per hour, OK, and you go 100 miles, how many hours did that take you?
243. S: Um 5
244. T: 5. And how did you get that 5? How did you use the numbers 100 and …
245. S: 100 miles divided by miles per hour
246. T: So you took the miles and divided it by the [garbled, but possibly "speed"]
247. S: Miles divided by s plus b equals time [Writes m/s+b]
248. T: Right.

The tutor in the above dialog appears to have done two things to scaffold this problem. First, the tutor focused on the problem of calculating the time actually on the bikes by decomposing what had been a problem with two operators into a problem that had only one operator. Presumably, this is because the student indicated he

---

[1] Throughout this paper, text in square brackets are comments, and S and T stand for "student" and "tutor" respectfully.

understood that the goal quantity was found by adding for the amount of the break ("b") to the time actually on the bikes.

The second scaffolding move the tutor did was to change the problem question from a symbolization question to a presumably simpler *compute question* by asking the student to calculate the speed using 100 and 20 rather than "m" and "s". Then in line 244 the tutor asked for the *articulation step* of "How did you get that 5?" Finally, the student is prompted for the *generalization step* of writing the expression using variables.

Our experienced tutor often invited the student to use concrete numbers. We call this strategy the *concrete articulation strategy (Gluck, 1999, Koedinger & Anderson, 1998[2])*. McArthur et al., (1990) also observed that human tutors often used what he called *curriculum scripts* and *micro-plans*, which often involved a series of questions designed to remediate particular difficulties. We use VanLehn's term for these scripts, *"knowledge construction dialogs"*, which emphasizes the fact that that we are trying to build a tutor that encourages students to build their own knowledge by less often *telling* them a hint and more often *asking* them a question.

The impediments to building a third generation tutor are not just technical. We think that if you want to build a good ITS for a domain you need to:

- Study what makes that domain difficult, including discovering any hidden skills, as well as determining what types of errors students make.
- Construct a theory of how students solve these problems. (We instantiated that theory in a cognitive model.)
- Observe experienced human tutors to find out what pedagogical content knowledge they have and then build a tutorial model that, with the help of the theory of domain skills, can capture and reproduce some of that knowledge.

The first step is reported elsewhere (Heffernan & Koedinger, 1997 & 1998), so we next explore the second and thrid steps.

2   Cognitive Student Model

Our student model is similar to traditional student models. We use the Turtle (Anderson & Pelletier, 1991) production system, which is a simplification of the ACT (Anderson, 1993) Theory of Cognition. A production system is a group of if-then rules operating on a set of what are called *working memory elements*. We use these rules to model the cognitive steps a student could use to solve a problem. Our student model has 68 production rules. Our production system can solve a problem by being given a set of working memory elements that encode the problem at a high level.

We model the common errors that students make with a set of "buggy" productions. From our data, we compiled a list of student errors and analyzed what were the common errors. We found that the following list of errors was able to account of over 75% of the errors that students made. We illustrate the errors in the context of the "two-jobs" problem, which has a correct answer of "5g+7(30-g)".

---

[2] Called the *inductive support* strategy in this prior work.

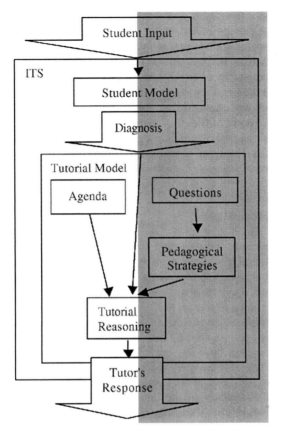

Fig. 1. Ms. Lindquist's Architecture

1) Wrong operator (e.g., "5g-7(30-g)")
2) Wrong order of arguments (e.g., "5g+7(g-30)")
3) Missing parentheses (e.g., "5g+7*30-g")
4) Confusing quantities (e.g., "7g+5(30-g)")
5) Missing a component (e.g., "5g+7g" or "g+7(30-g)" or "5g+30-g")
6) Omission: correct for a subgoal. (e.g., "7(30-g)" or "5g")
7) Combinations of errors (e.g., "5g+7*g-30" has the wrong order for "g-30" and is missing parenthesis)

These "buggy" productions are used to allow us to make sense of a student's input even if she has made several incorrect steps. We do not want a computer system that cannot understand a student if she gives an answer that has parts that are completely correct and parts that are wrong. We want the system to be able to understand as much as possible of what a student says and be able to give positive feedback even when the overall answer to a question might be incorrect.

Traditional model-tracing tutors have a bug message attached to each buggy production that generates a message through the use of a template. We do not do that.

We feel such an architecture confuses student reasoning with tutorial reasoning. We instead have the student model report its full diagnosis (which is represented with a set of working memory elements) to the tutor model that will then decide what to do.

If the student makes several errors, traditional model-tracing tutors are sometimes in a quandary as to what to do. Some ITSs do not deal with multiple bugs and instead rely on breaking down the problem into finer steps. A problem with this approach is that one cannot break down a skill like symbolization easily without decreasing the overall difficulty. Another solution is to ask the student what the subgoals should be and then tutor them on the subgoals individually (Corbett & Anderson, 1995.) However, a problem remains about what the ITS should do if the student makes more than one distinct error in a given input. This is addressed below.

3   The Tutorial Model

As mentioned already, we collected and transcribed one hour of experienced human tutoring. We wanted to observe what experienced tutoring in this domain looked like. The tutor worked as a full time math tutor for over a year before teaching middle school math for 5 years. She was given a list of symbolization problems and told her goal was get the student to learn how to solve such problems.

After transcribing the dialog, we have been able to extract some regularity in the tutorial strategies employed. One caveat: our tutorial model is informed by this observation of human tutoring, but it does not model any one individual or make claims to being the most effective model.

Now we will look at the components of the tutorial model shown in Figure 1. A fundamental distinction in the intelligent tutoring system (ITS) is between the student model, which does the diagnosing, and the tutorial models, which chooses the pedagogical plan that best responds to that particular diagnosis. It is composed of a tutorial agenda component as well as tutorial questions that can be used alone, or in combination, to generate a tutorial strategy. The system currently has 4 tutorial strategies. Through empirical study, we plan to learn which strategies are most effective. The tutorial model is implemented with 77 productions. This approach is similar to Freedman's (2000). We now describe how Ms. Lindquist decides what student difficulties to focus upon in the tutorial dialog.

Dealing with the diagnosis: The Focusing Heuristic
Ms. Lindquist uses a heuristic to decide what to focus the conversation on. This heuristic applies in cases when the student model's diagnosis indicates that the student had some correct elements and some incorrect elements. For instance, we considered giving the following positive feedback on an answer like that in line 242: "Your answer of 's/m+b' has some correct elements; it is true that you need to add the time of the break to the time on the bikes to find the total trip time." This feedback was meant to confirm the "+b" portion of the answer. After looking at what our human tutor did, we decided not to give positive feedback unless the student has two operands correct and the correct operator. We give an example of this in the context of the "two-jobs" problem:

T: [problem with answer of 5g+7*(30-g)]
S: 5g+7*g
T: No, but, 5*g does represent the amount Debbie earned bagging groceries. Let me ask you a simpler question. Can you tell me how much she made delivering newspapers?

If the student has made more than one error, the tutor decides to come up with a strategy to deal with each error. The errors are considered in the order they would be encountered in a post-order traversal of the parse tree of the correct answer (i.e., visited "bottom-up.") Therefore, the tutor might add multiple questions to the tutorial agenda depending upon the tutorial strategy selected for each error.

If a student says something the student model doesn't understand (e.g., "5/30-5*7/g" when the answer is "5g+7(30-g)") we will still want a robust ITS to be able to pick a reasonable strategy for a response. This is important because many times the tutor (humans or computers) will not be able to make sense of the student's input. Graesser et al. (in press) report in their study of human tutors that they "found that the human tutors and learners have a remarkably incomplete understanding of each other's knowledge base and that many of each other's contributions are not deeply understood... Most tutors have only an approximate assessment of the quality of student contributions." We want our ITS to be able to operate under these same difficult conditions and still be robust enough to say something reasonable.

Tutorial Agenda
Ms. Lindquist has a data structure we called the agenda, which stores the ideas she wants to talk about next. This agenda ordinarily operates like a push down stack, but we give an example of when the stack order is violated below in the section on the Concrete Articulation Strategy.

Tutorial Questions
The tutorial model can ask the following kinds of tutorial questions illustrated with an example of how the question can be phrased:
1) Q_symb : Symbolize a given quantity ("Write an expression for the distance Anne has rowed?")
2) Q_compute: Find a numerical answer ("Compute the distance Anne has rowed?")
3) Q_explain: Write a symbolization for a given arithmetic quantity. This is the articulation step. ("How did you get the 120?")
4) Q_generalize: Uses the results of a Q_explain question ("Good, Now write your answer of 800-40*3 using the variables given in the problem (i.e., put in 'm')")
5) Q_represents_what: Translate from algebra to English ("In English, what does 40m represent?" (e.g., "the distance rowed so far"))
6) Q_explain_verbal: Explain in English how a quantity could be computed from other quantities. (We have two forms: The reflective form is "Explain how you got 40*m" and the problem solving form is "Explain how you would find the distance rowed?")
7) Q_decomp: Symbolize a one-operator answer, using a variable introduced to stand for a sub-quantity. ("Use A to represent the 40m for the distance rowed. Write an expression for the distance left towards the dock that uses A.")

8) Q_substitute: Perform an algebraic substitution ("Correct, that the distance left is given by 800-A. Now, substitute "40m" in place of A, to get a symbolization for the distance left.")

Notice that questions 1, 3, 4, and 8 all ask for a quantity to symbolize. Their main difference lies in when those questions are used, and how the tutor responds to the student's attempt. Questions 5 and 6 ask the student to answer in English rather than algebra. To avoid natural language the student is prompted to use pull down menus to complete this sentence "The distance rowed is equal to <u>noun phrase</u> <u>operator</u> <u>noun phrase</u>." The noun phrase menu contains a list of the quantity names for that problem. The operator menu contains "added to", "subtracted from", "multiplied by" and "divided by."

Below we will see how these questions can be combined into strategies.

Tutorial Strategies

We will now look at three different tutorial strategies that Ms Lindquist uses; "Concrete Articulation", "Introduced Variable", and finally "Explain in English First" (There is a fourth strategy that we don't have space to illustrate. This strategy is that if a students makes an error the tutor tells the student the answer and then asks the student questions to see if the student understands the answer.) The first strategy we will look at is *Concrete Articulation* strategy.

Concrete Articulation Strategy

The concrete articulation strategy usually uses three questions of type Q_compute, Q_explain and Q_generalize. Here is an example of the dialog generated by Ms. Lindquist which we believe parallels the experienced human tutor closely.

T1: [Doing the "bike-trip" problem] Please write an expression for the total time the trip took. [Q_symb]

S1: s/m+b

T2: No. Let me ask you an easier question. Please compute the time actually on bikes if the speed was 20 miles per hour, and the distance ridden was 100 miles? [Q_compute]

S2: 5

T3: Correct. What math did you do to get that five? [Q_explain]

S3: 100/20

T4: Correct. Now write your answer of 100/20 using the variables given in the problem (i.e., put in 'm' and 's')? [Q_generalize]

S4: b+m/s

T5: Correct.

We will walk through what Ms. Lindquist did here. First, the student model diagnosed S1 ("s/m+b") as having the quantity "s/m" with reversed arguments (bug type #2.) The diagnosis also said that the student understood that the total trip time was the time of the break ("b") plus the time actually on the bikes. This diagnosis was passed to the tutorial model that could have selected among competing strategies. In this case, the tutorial model decided to conduct a *concrete articulation* knowledge construction dialog. Therefore, the tutor model generated questions for the *compute*, *explain/articulation* and *generalization* steps. The tutor put these three questions on the agenda.

At S2, the student answers the compute question correctly, and the tutor decides to continue with its plan. It has to be sensitive to what the student typed. If the student typed 100/20 instead of 5, then both the compute and explain questions would be removed from the agenda and the tutor would skip to the generalize step. An example of this sort of flexibility is demonstrated in T5. T4 was a question to articulate the time actually on bikes. The tutor was hoping the student would type "m/s" but instead the student answered "b+m/s." Only a pedantic tutor would not accept that answer as it indicates an understanding that subsumes the understanding required for the sub-goal. This is where the tutorial agenda behaves differently than a stack because Ms. Lindquist pops both of the questions off the agenda.

To show an example of how the previous situation could have come out differently, we now look at the following dialog:

T1: Hello. [Doing the "bike-trip" problem] Please write an expression for the total time the trip took. [Q_symb]

S1: help!

T2: Let me ask you an easier question. Please compute the time actually on bikes if instead the speed was 20 miles per hour, the time of the break was 2 hours, and the distance ridden was 100 miles? [Q_compute]

S2: 7

T3: Correct. What math did you do to get that 7? [Q_explain 7]

S3: 2+5

T4: Okay, but how did you get the 5? [Q_explain 5]

S4: 100/20

T5: Correct. Now, lets try this again, what math did you do to get the 7? [Q_explain 7]

S5: 2+100/20

T6:Correct. Now write your answer of '2+100/20' using the variables given in the problem (i.e., put in 'm', 'b' and 's')? [Q_generalize]

S6: b+m/s

T7: Correct.

This example is interesting in the way Ms. Lindquist responds at T4. The system has bug rules to apply to questions other than symbolization questions. In this case, the student model reported that the student's answer of "2+5" is a partially complete articulation but that the student didn't spell out where the "5" came from. So, the tutorial model is able to "dig-down" into the student's reasoning with an embedded sub-dialog. This involved adding the additional question of explaining how the student got the "5".

Introduced Variable Strategy

A second example of a tutorial strategy is what we call the *Introduced Variable* strategy, which was alluded to above when we looked at the student who answered the "two-jobs" problem with "A=5*g, B=30-g, C=7*B and D=A+C". Below we present an real example of Ms. Lindquist tutoring an ninth grader with this strategy. This strategy uses both Q_decomp and Q_substitute questions. Question Q_decomp sets the stage for this strategy, and is used to break down the originally composed problem into separate decomposed one-operator problems (as shown below in T2 and T3), introducing new variables when appropriate (as in T3.) The real meat of this strategy is shown at line 4, where the tutor introduces the variable "A" to stand for a sub-quantity. Question Q_substitute is used to scaffold the substitution step as shown in T5.

> T1: Hello. Jane is "j" years old. Peg is "p" years old. Mary is Peg's age minus Tom's age. Tom is 3 years younger than Jane. Peg is "x" years older that Mark. Write an expression for Mary's age. [Q_symb]
>
> S1: (p-3)-(3-j)+(p+x) [correct answer is "p-(j-3)"]
>
> T2: Hmm. No. Let me ask you and easier question. Use j and 3 to calculate Tom's age. [Q_decomp]
>
> S2: 3-j
>
> T3: Hmm. No. Try again please. What is Tom's age? Hint: pick one of these: j-3, 3-j, j+3, j*3, j/3, or 3/j. [This is a rephrasing as explained in the hint section below]
>
> S3: j-3
>
> T4: Correct. Calculate Mary's age. Use A instead of j-3 for Tom's age. [Q_decomp]
>
> S4: p-a
>
> T5: Correct. You are correct that p-A is Mary's age. Now, can you state this in terms of the numbers given in the problem. [Q_substitute]
>
> S5: p-(j-3)
>
> T6: Correct.

We note that this strategy is not one inspired by looking at human tutors but by our cognitive analysis that informed us that a crucial difficulty occurs when a student has to treat an expression (i.e., "j-3") like a number, so this strategy breaks that hard step into two steps (i.e., T4 and T5).

"Explain in English" Strategy

Mathematical communication is increasingly seen as a goal for students, and in particular translating between an algebraic representation, an English verbal representation, and a concrete representation of numerical instances (Schoenfeld et al., 1992, Koedinger & Nathan) Other researchers are also interested in wanting an ITS to elicit explanations from students (e.g., Conati et al., 1997.) We noticed in the dialog we collected from an experienced human tutor that she would often ask the student to explain how to compute a quantity in English and afterward, ask the student to say it in symbols (Heffernan, 2001). Therefore, we have implemented similar questions in the form of Q_represents_what and Q_explain_verbal as shown below:

> T1: Hello. [Doing the "bike-trip" problem] Please write an expression for the total time the trip took. [Q_symb]
>
> S1: m/s
>
> T2: What does "m/s" represent (e.g., the speed on the bike?)[Q_represents_what]
>
> S2: the total time of the trip
>
> T3: No, "m/s" represents the actual time on the bikes. Can you explain how you would find the total time of the trip using the time on the bikes? [Q_explain_verbal]
>
> S3: The total time of the trip is equal to [1st menu] "the amount of time for the break" [2nd menu] "plus" [3rd menu] "the actual time on the bikes". [Composed using three pull down menus.]
>
> T4: Good, now say what the total trip time is in symbols [Q_symb]
>
> S4: b+m/s
>
> T5: Correct

This strategy is based on the hypothesis that students will learn more if they are asked to explain in English how to compute a quantity.

Hints
Giving the students a hint is the simplest tutorial strategy we have and is a common way that a traditional model-tracing tutor gives help. Each question has a *hint chain*, which is simply a list of rephrasings of the question. The rephrasings get progressively more explicit, possibly, telling the student exactly what to do[3].

4   Early Evaluation

We have performed a early analysis of Ms. Lindquist, by comparing her to a traditional computer-aided instruction (CAI) control condition that simply told students the answer (if they got the problem wrong). This study answers the question of whether the dialogs Ms. Lindquist has with students lead to increased student learning, but ignores the question of whether it is worth the additional time. That is because we controlled for the number of problems, and not the amount of time. Students in the condition that received Ms. Lindquist were expected to take more time.

Procedure
The procedure and the results are more fully explicated in Heffernan's dissertation (2001). In summary, 20 high school students participated in the lab study. They were given pretests and posttests on symbolization. They were blocked into groups according to their pretests. Students preceded though the curriculum consisting of 68 problems. Students in the experimental condition received a partially random combination of the different strategies Ms. Lindquist is capable of.

Results
The students in the control condition, as expected, took half the amount of time, since they did not engage in dialogs with Ms. Lindquist. Students that engaged in a dialog with Ms. Lindquist, as opposed to those in the control condition, appeared to have benefited from engaging in those dialogs. We performed a ANOVA that showed only a marginally statically significant effect $(F(1,37)=2.6,p=.12)$ but with a respectable effect size of .7 standard deviations.

Discussion
Now that we have established that this dialogs appear to lead to better learning, our next experiment will control for "time on task" in order to determine if the additional time required to have a dialog is worth it.

The following example from this experiment nicely illustrates some of the aspects of Ms. Lindquist, including embedded dialogs (starting on lines 4 and 10), as

---

[3] The question of how explicit to make the "bottom-out", or last hint (i.e., "Do you tell the student the answer?"), is not a question that we, or this architecture, makes a commitment about. Some of our hint chains end with multiple-choice questions while others tell the student exactly what to type.

well as the embedded feedback shown at the beginning of line 8. The number of seconds it takes the student to respond is in square brackets.

1) Problem: Jane is "j" years old. Peg is "p" years old. Mary is Peg's age minus Tom's age. Tom is 3 years younger than Jane. Peg is "x" years older than Mark. Write an expression for Mary's age
2) Tutor: Hello. Please write an expression for Mary's age.
3) Student [143]: **Student hit the help button** *[should be p-(j-3)]*
4) Tutor: Let me try to give you some help. We will come back to Mary's age. Let me try to break this down for you. Please compute Mary's age if Jane's age was "20" years, and "Peg's age" was "40" years?
5) Student: [169]: **23** *[correct]*
6) Tutor: Correct. Using only 40, 20, and 3 write an expression for Mary's age.
7) Student [126]: **(20-3)-40** *[should be 40-(20-3)]*
8) Tutor: No. Your answer of "(20-3)-40" equals "-23", but you wanted to write an expression that equaled "23". Using only 40, 20, and 3 write an expression for Mary's age. Hint: Use 40 for Peg's age and 20-3 for Tom's age.
9) Student [47]: **(40-20)+3** *[should be 40-(20-3)]*
10) Tutor: Hmm. No.   Let me ask you a different question. Using only 20, and 3 write an expression for Tom's age.
11) Student [15]: **20-3** *[correct]*
12) Tutor: Correct. Now, lets try this question again: Using only 40, 20, and 3 write an expression for Mary's age. Hint: Use 40 for Peg's age and 20-3 for Tom's age.
13) Student [138]: **40-(20-3)** *[correct]*
14) Tutor: Correct. Now, say that again but this time use the variables from the problem.
15) Student [25]: **p-(j-3)** *[correct]*
16) Tutor: Correct

Notice that this example shows a student how could compute an instance (line 5), but had trouble articulating how to write the complete expression (lines 7, and 9), which is consistent with what our cognitive analysis predicted about the relatively difficulty of these tasks. Also consistent is the fact that using a variable, per se, does not appear to have been difficult (line 15). This students performance is consistent with our theory that *articulation*, and not comprehension of word problems or variables per se is what makes symbolizing difficult for students.

5 Conclusion

McArthur et al. criticized Anderson's et al. (1985) model-tracing ITS and model-tracing in general "because each incorrect rule is paired with a particular tutorial action (typically a stored message), every student who takes a given step gets the same message, regardless of how many times the same error has been made or how many other error have been made. ... Anderson's tutor is tactical, driven by local student errors (p. 200)" and goes on to argue for the need for a more strategic tutor. Ms. Lindquist meets that criticism. Ms. Lindquist's model of tutorial reasoning is both strategic (i.e., has multi-step plans) and tactical (i.e., reasons to produce output at the single question level.) She also intelligently handles multiple errors and reasons about the order in which to deal with them and then constructs a plan to deal with each of them. Ms. Lindquist is a modest step on the path to making a more dynamic tutor.

We have released Ms. Lindquist onto the web at www.AlgebraTutor.org, and have had over 600 students who have been tutored by Ms. Lindquist, the results of which are now in preparation. In addition she has won various industry awards from teacher related web sites such as *USAToday Education* and the National Council of Teachers of Mathematics. Ms. Lindquist is a system that combines the student modeling of traditional model-tracing tutors with a model of tutorial dialog based on an experienced human tutor. Early analysis reveals Ms. Lindquist can be effective, but more analysis is needed to determine where the biggest "bang for the buck" is to be found.

Acknowledgements. This research was supported by NSF grant number 9720359 to CIRCLE and the Spencer Foundation.

References

Anderson, J. R. (1993). *Rules of the Mind*. Hillsdale, NJ: Erlbaum.

Anderson, J. R., Boyle, D. F., & Reiser, B. J. (1985). Intelligent tutoring systems. *Science*, 228, 456-462.

Anderson, J. R., Corbett, A. T., Koedinger, K. R., & Pelletier, R. (1995) Cognitive tutors: lessons learned. *The Journal of the Learning Sciences*, 4 (2), 167-207.

Anderson, J. R. & Pelletier, R. (1991) A developmental system for model-tracing tutors. In Lawrence Birnbaum (Eds.) *The International Conference on the Learning Sciences*. Association for the Advancement of Computing in Education. Charlottesville, Virginia (pp. 1-8).

Clancey, W. J., (1982) Tutoring rules for guiding a case method dialog. In D. Sleeman & J. S. Brown (Eds.) *Intelligent Tutoring Systems* London: Academic Press. (pp. 201-226.)

Corbett, A. T., and Anderson, J. R., (1995) Knowledge decomposition and subgoal reification in the ACT programming tutor. in *Proceedings of Artificial Intelligence in Education* (pp. 469-476)

Conati, C., Larkin, J. and VanLehn, K. (1997) A computer framework to support self-explanation. In : du Bolay, B. and Mizoguchi, R.(Eds.) Proceedings of AI-ED 97 World Conference on Artificial Intelligence in Education. Vol.39, pp. 279-276, Amsterdam: IO Press.

Freedman, R. (2000) Using a reactive planner as the basis for a dialogue agent. In *Proceedings of the Thirteenth Florida Artificial Intelligence Research Symposium* (FLAIRS '00), Orlando.

Gluck, K. (1999). Eye movements and algebra tutoring. Doctoral dissertation. Psychology Department, Carnegie Melon University.

Graesser, A.C., Wiemer-Hastings, P., Wiemer-Hastings, K., Harter, D., Person, N., & the TRG (in press). Using latent semantic analysis to evaluate the contributions of students in AutoTutor. Interactive Learning Environments.

Heffernan, N. T. (2001). *Intelligent Tutoring Systems have Forgotten the Tutor: Adding a Cognitive Model of an Experienced Human Tutor*. Dissertation. Carnegie Mellon University, Computer Science Department. http://gs260.sp.cs.cmu.edu/diss

Heffernan, N. T., & Koedinger, K. R.(1997) The composition effect in symbolizing: the role of symbol production versus text comprehension. *Proceeding of the Nineteenth Annual Conference of the Cognitive Science Society* 307-312. Hillsdale, NJ: Erlbaum.

Heffernan, N. T., & Koedinger, K. R. (1998) A developmental model for algebra symbolization: The results of a difficulty factors assessment. In Proceedings of the Twentieth Annual Conference of the Cognitive Science Society, (pp. 484-489). Hillsdale, NJ: Erlbaum.

Koedinger, K. R., Anderson, J.R., Hadley, W.H., & Mark, M. A. (1997). Intelligent tutoring goes to school in the big city. *International Journal of Artificial Intelligence in Education, 8*, 30-43.

Koedinger, K. R., & Anderson, J. R. (1998). Illustrating principled design: The early evolution of a cognitive tutor for algebra symbolization. In *Interactive Learning Environments, 5*, 161-180.

Koedinger, K. R. & Nathan, M. J. (submitted to). The real story behind story problems: Effects of representations on quantitative reasoning. Submitted to *Cognitive Psychology*.

McArthur, D., Stasz, C., & Zmuidzinas, M. (1990) Tutoring techniques in algebra. *Cognition and Instruction*. 7 (pp. 197-244.)

Moore, J. D. (1996) Discourse generation for instructional applications: Making computer-based tutors more like humans. *Journal of Artificial Intelligence in Education*, 7(2), 118-124

Schoenfeld, A., Gamoran, M., Kessel, C., Leonard, M., Or-Bach, R., & Arcavi, A. (1992) Toward a comprehensive model of human tutoring in complex subject matter domains. *Journal of Mathematical Behavior*, 11, 293-319

Shulman, L. (1986). Those who understand: Knowledge growth in teaching. *Educational Researcher, 15*, 4-14.

VanLehn, K, Anderson, J., Ashley, K., Chi. M., Corbett, A., Koedinger, K., Lesgold, A., Levin, L., Moore, M., and Pollack, M., NSF Grant 9720359. *CIRCLE: Center for Interdisciplinary Research on Constructive Learning Environments*. NSF Learning and Intelligent Systems Center. January, 1998 to January, 2003.

An Instructional Assistant Agent for Distributed Collaborative Learning

Weiqin Chen and Barbara Wasson

InterMedia and Department of Information Science, P.O. Box 7800,
N-5020 Bergen, Norway
{weiqin.chen, barbara.wasson}@ifi.uib.no

Abstract. This paper presents an instructional assistant agent for FLE2 -- a distributed collaborative learning environment. We discuss the role of the instructional assistant agent and how it supports both the instructor and students in a distributed collaborative knowledge building process. We emphasize the supplementary role of the instructional assistant agent, which, on one hand, observes the distributed collaborative learning process and computes statistics for viewing, and on the other hand, detects possible problems and presents them to the instructor so that the instructor, if desired, gives feedback to the students so that they themselves can regulate the collaboration.

1 Introduction

In the context of distributed collaborative learning, the instructor's role is different from traditional instructor-centered environments, they are coordinators/facilitators, guides, and co-learners. They monitor the collaboration activities within a group, detect problems and intervene in the collaboration to give advice and learn alongside students at the same time.

The instructor's role in distributed collaborative learning depends heavily upon observation of the interaction. An intensive collaboration, however, which includes a relatively large number of messages or interactions, makes it difficult to follow. It is always time and effort consuming to analyze the collaboration, detect problems and give useful advice to regulate the collaboration. This problem has been intensively investigated. For example, IDLC [9] developed an Expert System Coordinator, GRACILE [1] implements two types of intelligent agents, mediator agents and domain agents. EPSILON [12] developed a facilitation agent to provide pedagogical support to students learning collaboratively on-line. Most of these efforts, however, have been placed on designing intelligent modules that replace the instructor's role in the collaboration. In order to obtain this goal, students are restricted to using "semi-structured" interfaces such as menu-driven or sentence-openers to collaborate that restrain the interaction channels and slow the communication process. Furthermore, the advice generated by these intelligent systems is based on its own understanding of the collaboration process, which has a high possibility of misinterpretation or misunder-

S.A. Cerri, G. Gouardères, and F. Paraguaçu (Eds.): ITS 2002, LNCS 2363, pp. 609–618, 2002.

standing. As a result, the advice might sometimes be inappropriate and confuse the students.

While closely related to these and other CSCL research efforts, our research has taken a somewhat different approach in that we have aimed at developing an instructional assistant agent, which, instead of taking the place of instructors, acts as a supplement to them. The instructional assistant, on one hand, observes the distributed collaborative learning process and computes statistics for viewing, and on the other hand, detects possible problems and presents them to the instructor so that the instructor, if desired, can give feedback to the students so that they themselves can regulate the collaboration. By providing advice and learning from feedback, the agent gradually improves its performance and builds up a trust relationship, until a point is reached where the agent is allowed to perform actions without the confirmation from the instructor. Within the DoCTA-NSS project (http://www.ifi.uib.no/docta) we are developing an instructional assistant for FLE2-distributed collaborative learning environment developed by Media Lab, Univ. of Helsinki in Finland.

Nwana [8] classified agent according to three ideal and primary attributes which agents should exhibit: autonomy, learning, and cooperation. Using the three characteristics, Nwana derived four types of agents in their agent typology: collaborative agents, collaborative learning agents, interface agents and smart agents. Although our instructional assistant agent has the ability to learn and to act autonomously, its ability to communicate with users is rather simple. In this sense, the instructional assistant agent falls into the interface agent category.

This paper is organized as follows. Section 2 briefly describes the FLE2 environment and the model of progressive inquiry. Section 3 discusses the role of the instructional assistant agent in FLE2. Its implementation and integration with FLE2 are discussed in section 4. Section 5 presents some related work, and our conclusion and suggestions for further consideration are given in section 6.

2   FLE2

FLE2[7] is a web-based groupware for computer supported collaborative learning (CSCL). It is designed to support collaborative process of progressive inquiry learning. According to Muukkonen et al. [7], the basic idea of progressive inquiry is that students gain deeper understanding by engaging in a research-like process where they generate their own problem, make hypotheses and search out explanatory scientific information collaboratively with others.

As a starting point, the instructor has to set up the context and the goal for a study project in order for the students to understand why the topic is worthwhile investigating. Then the instructor or the students present their research problems that define the directions where the inquiry goes. As the inquiry proceeds, more refined questions will be posted. Focusing on the research problems, the students construct their working theories, hypotheses, and interpretations based on their background knowledge and their research. Then the students assess strengths and weaknesses of different explanations and identify contradictions and gaps of knowledge. To refine the explanation, fill in the knowledge gaps and provide deeper explanation, the students have to do research and acquire new information on the related topics, which may result in new working theories. In so doing, the students move step by step toward answering the initial question.

To support collaborative progress inquiry process, FLE2 provides several modules, such as WebTop, Knowledge Building module, Chat module and Administration module. The Knowledge Building module is considered to be the scaffolding module for progressive inquiry, where the students post their messages to the common work-space according to predefined categories. The categories they can use are Problem, Working Theory, Deepening Knowledge, Comment, Meta-comment, and Summary. These categories are defined to reflect the different phases in the progressive inquiry process. The WebTop module is a supporting module where instructors and students can store and share resources such as documents and links. More details on FLE2 can be found in [7].

3   Role of Instructional Assistant Agent in FLE2

3.1   Role of Instructor in FLE2

In the context of CSCL, the instructor's role is different from traditional instructor-centered environments. Roehler and Cantlon [10] classified the instructor's role in distributive learning environments into five categories: offering explanations, inviting student participation, verifying and clarifying student understandings, modeling of desired behaviors and inviting students to contribute clues. In the collaboration process, apart from the subject-related problems which need instructor's help, there are also problems relating to the collaboration itself, such as "free-rider" where one student just leaves the task to others, "sucker effect" where a more active or able student was taken for a fee ride by other students in the group, and "status sensitivity effect" where high ability or active students takes charge and thus has an increasing impact on the group [11]. If these problems are not solved properly, the collaboration learning cannot obtain effective outcome.

In the collaborative learning process in FLE2, instructors can contribute to the progressive inquiry process in the following aspects: to setup a context, to enhance the discussion by presenting problems or working theories, to encourage students to join the knowledge building session by sending student emails with links to relevant and interesting notes in the knowledge building, and to upload learning materials and inform students and let them visit the new material.

Giving feedback on collaboration depends heavily upon the observation of the interaction. An intensive collaboration, however, which includes a relatively large number of messages in the Knowledge Building process, makes it difficult to follow. Although the messages are organized around a set of principles, it takes time and effort to analyze the collaboration, detect problems and give useful advice to regulate the collaboration. In order to lessen this problem, an instructional assistant agent is designed and developed that would observe the collaboration process, process the information collected and provide the instructor and the students with overview and advice on the collaboration process. In so doing, we hope to free the instructor from following every single activity in the collaboration process so that they can concentrate on the more important issues.

3.2   Role of Instructional Assistant Agent

3.2.1 As an Observer

As an observer, the instructional assistant agent looks over the shoulders of students and gathers information on the collaboration process and stores it in a database. Most web-based applications have a server side log that is mainly a comprehensive event report to help the administrator in troubleshooting. In a collaborative learning environment the information in most server logs is often insufficient and unreadable to help the instructor in regulating the learning process.

In the knowledge building process of FLE2, the main activity of the students is to post messages according to categories. Therefore, the information collected and stored by the agent includes the properties of the messages posted by the students. It includes:

- Category: to which category a message is posted?
- Student-Post: who post the message?
- Time-Stamp: when is the message posted?
- Msg-Correspond: to which message does the message correspond?
- Depth: at which depth of the thread is the message?

Additionally, the agent monitors the activities of the instructor and students in virtual WebTop so that it can get the updates and send notifications to other participants.

By querying the database, the instructional assistant agent is able to provide statistical information on the collaboration process. For example, how many notes have been posted in each category? How many notes have a certain students posted? How often does a certain student post messages? How many notes have each student posted in a certain category? How many notes have a certain student posted corresponding to a certain message?

The agent presents the statistical information in charts so that the instructor can follow the collaboration easily and detect problems quickly. Fig.1 shows an example of instructor's interface.

3.2.2 As an Advisor

As an advisor, the instructional assistant agent detects possible problems and provides advice to the students and instructors based on the information it obtained on the collaboration process. It gives advice by sending email or presenting advice when they log on. By looking into the collected information, the agent is able to detect possible problems such as someone is left out of the discussion or someone who is more active than others and steering the group. Thus the advice which the agent provides to the instructor aim at regulating the discussion. The agent can also detect updates in the collaboration by looking into the collected information. Therefore, the advice to the students aims at encouraging knowledge sharing and awareness.

In FLE2, the instructor is able to upload learning material, which s/he thinks is important for the students to read. When a piece of new material is uploaded by the instructor, the agent will automatically send email to the students to inform them of the new upload and advise them to visit the new material.

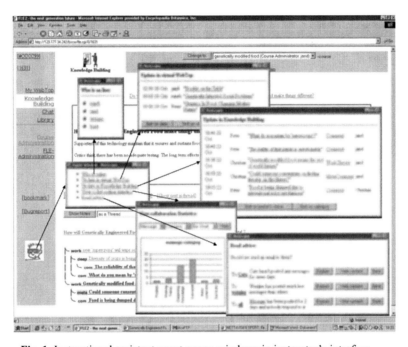

Fig. 1. Instructional assistant agent popup windows in instructor's interface

Figure 1 shows an example of the instructor interface. When the instructor selects the agent button, a pop-up window appears. The window contains links to "Who is online", "Update in virtual WebTop" and "Update in Knowledge Building", "View collaboration statistics" and "Read advice".

The "Who is online" takes the instructor to a window showing all the online group members. The instructor can send email or start a chat with them. The "Update in virtual WebTop" takes the instructor to a window showing all the updates since his/her last logon on the virtual WebTop of the group members with links to virtual WebTop of the members. By clicking the link, the instructor can go directly to the newly uploaded materials. The update list can be sorted on timestamp or poster's name. The "Update in Knowledge Building" has similar features with the "Update in virtual WebTop". It brings out all the newly posted messages on the knowledge building since the instructor's last logon. Each entry in the list includes link to the message and its properties, such as timestamp, category, name of the student who posted it and the link to its corresponding message. The "View collaboration statistics" link takes the instructor to a window where s/he can see a chart view of the statistical information of the collaboration. S/he can choose what to view (message-category or message-student, etc) and how s/he would like the information to be presented (pie chart, bar chat or line chart). By viewing the charts, the instructor can get a feeling of what has happened in the collaboration process and may detect possible problems quickly. The "Read advice" link takes the instructor to a list of advice generated by the agent. For each advice, the instructor can query the agent for an explanation on the advice provided. The agent then presents the related knowledge in the knowledge based. The advice mostly suggests the instructor to send an email to a specific student. If the instructor decides to follow the agent's advice, s/he can choose to send email by her/himself or delegate the agent to send an email. The agent records the instructor's actions on each piece of its advice and induces new rules based on the feedbacks.

The student interface has also an agent button which pops up a window containing links to "Who is online", "Update in virtual WebTop" and "Update in Knowledge Building". These links have same functions with those in the instructor's interface.

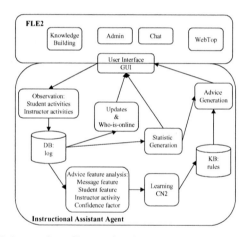

Fig. 2. Integration of instructional assistant agent and FLE2

4 Integration of Instructional Assistant Agent with FLE2

4.1 Architecture

Figure 2 shows the integration of the instructor assistant agent with the FLE2 server. The agent receives students and the instructor activities through the web server and the application servers in FLE2 and stores them in a database. The activities are mainly logon/off, updates on the virtual WebTop module, messages posted in the Knowledge Building tool and the chat log. Each of the activities has timestamp and other properties. For example, a message posted in the Knowledge Building tool should also include message content, post person, category, and corresponding message.

The instructional assistant agent itself is also an application server which is responsible for providing statistical information of the collaboration process, sending emails, providing advice and showing who is currently online. On the client side, there is a button, which by clicking, the instructor and students can go to an interface where they can get information from the instructor assistant agent.

The Statistic Generation module goes through the database, computes statistics on the collaboration process and presents them to the instructor and students in the form of tables or charts. These statistics are also used by the Advice Generation module, which produces advice by querying the database, using the statistics created by the Statistic Generation module, and reasoning on the knowledge base, which contains the instructor's expertise on how to regulate the collaborative knowledge building.

4.2 Implementation Details

4.2.1 Database and Knowledge Base

To add, access, and process data in the DB, we choose to use MySQL (http://www.mysql.com/), one of the most popular open-sourced SQL database management systems.

The expertise is represented in the form of production rules in the KB. In the beginning, the instructor can put some general rules in the KB. Based on these rules the agent generates its advice. Over time the agent learns from the instructor's feedback on the advice and induces more specific rules. When used for reasoning by the agent, specific rules have a higher priority than general rules. Externally, the rules are represented in RuleML (http://www.dfki.uni-kl.de/ruleml/). RuleML is an XML-based rule markup language. It allows rule storage, interchange and retrieval through WWW. Here is a simple rule example in RuleXL format:

"Send a msgNotification to a student (confidence factor is 1.0) if a message is marked as "new" to him/her". This rule corresponds to the message template No.3 in Section 4.2.3.

```
<imp>
  <_head>
    <atom>
      <_opr><rel>send</rel></_opr>
      <var>studentName</var>
      <var>msgID</var>
      <ind>msgNotification</ind>
      <ind>1.0</ind>
    </atom>
  </_head>
  <_body>
    <atom>
      <_opr><rel>new</rel></_opr>
      <var>msgID</var>
      <var>studentName</var>
    </atom>
```

```
    </_body>
</imp>
```

4.2.2 Learning

The learning algorithm we choose is CN2 [3]. It can induce new production rules periodically instead of doing it each time new feedback is provided. We believe that this feature fits asynchronous environments where real time update is not so crucial as compared to synchronous environments.

The input of the CN2 algorithm is the features of advice and the instructor's activities to the advice. The features of advice include:

- Message feature: category, student-post, timestamp, etc
- Student feature: last-logout, last-message-post, etc
- Confidence factor: how confident the agent is on the advice

The instructor's activities include send (delegate agent to send the advice to students), explain (ask agent to explain how it generates the advice) and view the content of the message to be sent to students.

Each advice presented to the instructor becomes one training example for the CN2 algorithm in the form of feature set: {msg_feature, student_feature, instructor_activity, confidence}.

Going through the training examples, CN2 creates a new set of rules and writes it out to KB in the form of RuleML. Afterward these new rules will be used in generating advice.

4.2.3 Email Template

The advice generated by the instructional assistant agent are based on pre-defined templates which mostly suggests the instructor send an email to a specific student. Some example email templates follow:

1. Hi [StudentName],

   Lately you have posted less messages than others, you may need to participate more.

   [InstructorName]

2. Hi [StudentName],

   [AnotherStudentName] has posted a message [LinkToMessage] corresponding to the message [MessageTitle] you posted. Would you like to read it?

   [InstructorName]

3. Hi [StudentName],

   [AnotherStudentName] has posted a message [link to the message], which is quite interesting but hasn't been paid much attention. I think you should read it.

   [InstructorName]

5 Related Work

Concerning agents in facilitating CSCL, three related works are worthy noting.

Constantino-Conzalez and Suthers [4] report their research on coaching collaboration in a synchronous distance learning environment with minimal reliance on the restricted communication devices such as sentence openers. They evaluate the potential contribution of tracking student participation and comparing students' individual and group solutions. The coach has the ability to recognize relevant learning opportunities and to provide advice that encourages students to take these opportunities. They identified several advice types such as discussion, participation, and feedback from which the coach can choose. The experiment results showed that reasonable collaboration advice could be generated without the need for expert solutions or discourse understanding. Our research is partially inspired by their work and aims at testing the role of agents in an asynchronous environment.

Dillenbourg [6] claims that the instructor retains a role in the success of collaborative learning. He further defines the "facilitator" role of an instructor as not to provide the right answer or to say which group member is right, but to perform a minimal pedagogical intervention (e. g. provide some hint) in order to redirect the group work in a productive direction or to monitor which members are left out of the interaction. He identified three main categories of agents in CSCL environment [5]: sub-agents, co-agents and super-agents. The instructional assistant agent presented in this paper fits in the super-agents category.

6   Conclusion and Future Plans

This paper presented our on-going project-an instructional assistant agent supporting the instructor and students in distributed collaborative learning. A prototype of the instructional assistant agent has been developed and is being tested. A formative evaluation of the prototype will be undertaken at a teacher workshop in Bergen at the end of April 2002. At this point we focus on functionality and users interface issues. A more thorough evaluation with focus on the performance of the agent will be carried out in conjunction with a large field trial in the DoCTA-NSS project in the fall of 2002. In this scenario, students in two grade 10 classes, one in Bergen and one in Oslo, collaborate on gene technology through FLE2. For the performance of the agent, the experimental research will focus on:

- Instructor reaction and judgments
- Student reactions   The role of domain knowledge
- The way of visualizing the statistics (e.g., is it easy for the instructor to interpret the information?)

Through the experiment we hope to learn if and how the interventions of the agent will assist the instructor and students in improving the task performance, the engagement and awareness in distributed collaborative learning environments. With the lessons learned, we hope to move one step further toward a plug-in agent which would be able to fit in any distributed collaborative learning environments.

Acknowledgments. This project is a part of DoCTA-NSS, a project funded by the ITU (IT in Education) programme of KUF (Norwegian Ministry of Church Affairs, Education, and Research). The authors would like to acknowledge J. Dolonen, R. Baggetun and S. Dragsnes who provided invaluable advice on the draft. The authors would also like to thank the anonymous reviewers for their constructive comments.

References

1. Ayala, G., Yano, Y.: Intelligent agents to support the effective collaboration in a CSCL environment. In: Carlso, P., Makedon, F. (eds.): Proc. of Ed-Telecom'96. Charlottevill, VA:AACE (1996) 19-24.
2. Baggetun, R., Dolonen, J., Dragsnes, S.: Designing Pedagogical Agent for Collaborative Telelearning Scenarios. In: Bjørnestad, S., Moe, R., Mørch, A., Opdahl, A. (eds.): Proc. of IRIS24. Ulvik, Norway (2001).
3. Clark, P., Niblett, T.: The CN2 Induction Algorithm. Machine Learning Journal. 4(1989) 261-283.
4. Constantino-Gonzalez, M., Suthers, D.: Coaching Collaboration by Comparing Solutions and Tracking Participation. In: Dillenbourg, P., Eurelings, A., Hakkarainen, K. (eds.): Proc. of ECSCL'2001. Maastriicht, the Netherlands (2001) 173-180.
5. Dillenbourg, P., Traum, D. Jermann, P., Schneider, D., Buiu, C.: The design of MOO agents: Implications from an empirical CSCW study. In: du Boulay, B., Mizoguchi, R. (eds.): Proc. of AIED'97. Amsterdam, IOS Press (1997) 15-22.
6. Dillenbourg, P.: What do you mean by collaborative learning? In: Dillenbourg, P. (eds.): Collaborative learning: cognitive and computational approaches. Amsterdam: Pergamon (1999) 1-19.
7. Muukkonen, H., Hakkarainen, K., Lakkala, M.: Collaborative technology for facilitating progressive inquiry: Future learning environment tools. In: Hoadley, C., Roschelle, J. (eds.): Proc. of CSCL'99. Standord University (1999) 406-415.
8. Nwana, H.: "Software agents: An overview". Knowledge Engineering Review. 3(1996) 1-40.
9. Okamoto, T., Inaba, A., Hasaba, Y.: The intelligent learning support system on the distributed cooperative environment. In: Greer, J. (eds.): Proc. of AIED'95. Charlottesville:AACE (1995) 210-218.
10. Roehler, L., Cantlon, D.: Scaffolding: a powerful tool in social constructivist classrooms. In: Hogan, K., Pressley, M. (eds.): Scaffolding Student Learning: Instructional Approaches and Issues. Cambridge, MA: Brookline Books (1997).
11. Salomon, G.: What does the design of effective CSCL require and how do we study its effects? SIGCUE Outlook, special Issue on CSCL, 3(1992) 62-68.
12. Soller, A., Cho, K-S, Lesgold A.: Adaptive Support for Collaborative Learning on the Internet. In: Peylo, C. (eds.): Proc. of the International Workshop on Adaptive and Intelligent Web-based Educational Systems held in ITS 2000. (2000).

Conflicts in Group Planning: Results from the Experimental Study of MArCo

Patricia Azevedo Tedesco*

Centro de Informática - UFPE. Av. Prof. Luiz Freire, s/n. Cidade Universitária,
Recife-PE. CEP: 50740-540, Brazil
pcart@cin.ufpe.br

Abstract. The emphasis on building co-operative/collaborative environments has brought out the matter of group interactions, together with the issue of conflicts. If well employed, conflicts can trigger cognitive changesa. In this paper, we present the results obtained in the experimental studies carried out to evaluate our framework for *detecting* and *mediating Meta-Cognitive* conflicts. The theoretical framework developed enables a computational system to analyse the ongoing interaction, to detect and to mediate conflicts. MArCo, our prototype, shows how our conceptual framework has been put to use. The results obtained in the experimental studies lead us to think that the approach is an interesting one, and should be developed further.

1 Introduction

People spend most of their daily lives as part of various groups. In doing so, they receive feedback, discuss different ideas, and get support for their endeavours. It is also the case that we spend a lot of time and effort in making decisions. This is a complex process, entailing various other subtasks: considering all different alternatives, weighing their pros and cons, and choosing the alternative that better satisfies our set of well thought out criteria. This can be quite overwhelming. Thus, research has shown (e.g. [1]) that when making decisions, groups tend to be more effective whereas individuals tend to be more efficient.

In this light, we set out to investigate how to provide support for consensual decision making (i.e. to collaboration). Research shows that conflicts are an inherent part of good quality consensual decisions – they help bring out different insights, ground points of view, and explore different alternatives [2]. A side effect of conflicts (when well employed) is the occurrence of *reflection* and *articulation*.

Thus, we have explored the idea that it is possible to build an artificial mediator that is able to detect and mediate conflicts, suggesting courses of action that might lead to more refined solutions[1]. For the detection, a model of *Meta-Cognitive* conflicts is needed. For the mediation, the system needs to know about the changes occurring in the group's plan, group and individual characteristics and the history of

---

* This work was done during the author's PhD at the CBLU - University of Leeds, and was sponsored by CAPES-Brazil.

[1] By more refined we mean solutions that bear indications that *reflection* and *articulation* have occurred.

S.A. Cerri, G. Gouardères, and F. Paraguaçu (Eds.): ITS 2002, LNCS 2363, pp. 619–629, 2002.

the interaction. The two main components of our framework are our computational models of *Meta-Cognitive Conflicts* and of *Strategic Changes*, described in [3,4].

This paper is organised as follows: next section presents an overview of MArCo, along with an example of its usage; we then discuss the experimental studies and their results. Lastly we present our conclusions and ideas for further work.

2   MArCo

MArCo stands for *Artificial Conflict Mediator*. It consists of a Java-based distributed interface that communicates with a Sicstus Prolog Server. The interface allows geographically separated group members to build plans. The Server enables MArCo to reason over the interaction. MarCo´s architecture is shown in Figure 1.

Participants contribute to the discussion via the dialogue and/or graph tools available. Once a user finishes her/his utterance, the contribution is then sent to the *Dialogue Record* (located at the interface) and to the *Dialogue Processor*.

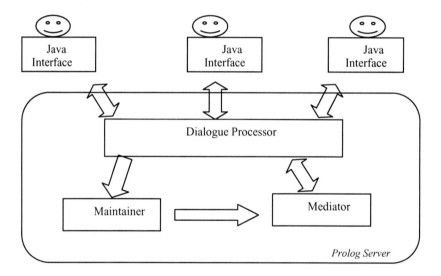

Fig. 1. MArCo's main Components and the flow of information

The *Dialogue Processor* is responsible for three main tasks.

1. ***Receiving users' utterances and mapping them into the BGI attitudes that describe their strategies.*** In order to model the agents' cognition when planning together we have adopted a Beliefs-Goals-Intentions model[2]. These attitudes can be inferred from the agents' dialogue. *Beliefs*, *Goals* and *Intentions* are directly related to the components of our plans, as follows:

---

[2] A BGI model can be seen as an especialisation of a BDI, since Goals can be understood as consistent desires, which we are commited to bring to happen.

- ***Intentions:*** represent actions the agents are committed to carrying out;
- ***Goals:*** represent the state of affairs the agents want to bring about;
- ***Beliefs:*** represent one of the following (depends on the context and contents of the utterance): (1) Constraints to our problems – *contextual beliefs;* (2) The ordering of and the justifications to our intentions– *domain beliefs;* (3) The agents' thoughts about the planning task – the *reflectors.*

2. Storing and manipulating the state transition automata that represent the DGs
3. Holding the text templates used by the *Mediator* to intervene in the discussion.

Once utterances are mapped, the *Maintainer* updates the Individual and Group Models (IMs and GM). IMs are updated whenever a member makes a contribution. Every time we have an agreement by the majority, the *Maintainer* updates the GM. Whenever the group finishes a DG, the system updates member's social roles[3].

MArCo's *Mediator* is responsible for both (1) detecting conflicts; and (2) deciding how to intervene, provoking *reflection* and *articulation*. The *Mediator* draws information from the GM and IMs, the dialogue history, the models of conflicts and strategic changes and of the task. Whenever the *Mediator* finds a disagreement about a focus it adds that fact to its knowledge base. Consider the excerpt shown below.

```
1.A.I Propose we do.before(a,(b,c) ).
2.B.I disagree, I think we should do.before(a,c ).
```

Here the *Mediator* signals an intention disagreement and asserts the following fact: *Disagreement([A,B], before(a,c), [a,b,c], int)*. Not all disagreements/conflicts are as explicit as this. If, further down the dialogue above, the *Mediator* notices *A* and *B* disagreeing about their intentions about *[a, b, c]*, or about a focus that contains part of it (e.g. *[a, b, d]*), it assumes that *A* and B were still arguing about their intentions regarding *a* and *b* and signals an intention conflict.

We should now discuss the language used in MArCo. When composing formulas, participants use the operators described in a prefix form. For example, the expression *after(a, b)* means that activity *a* is done after activity *b*. The operator *implies* can denote a causal link. For example, *implies(a, done(b))* means that *a* depends *b*. In some situations activities may be grouped together, as is the case in *before((a, b),c)*, meaning that *a*, followed immediately by *b*, is done before *c*. We provide natural language interpretations of the more complex expressions in the examples later on.

Let us now present an actual example. Suppose that we are dealing with *A* and *B*. Their individual models are IA and IB, and the group model is GM. In the beginning, the available dialogue moves are *inquire*, *statement*, *propose*, and *suggest*, corresponding to the initial moves of the four available DG's. *A* and *B* start their dialogue by trying to decide when Christmas sales start. The dialogue presented for this example was a translation of natural language dialogue obtained during the preliminary experiment described in [9]. The dialogues presented next section were actual ones, observed during the experimental study of MArCo.

```
1.Inquire(A,starts(xmas_sales, *)).
2.Statement(B, starts(xmas_sales, december).
```

---

[3] The social roles used are described in [8].

When *A* submits utterance 1 to MArCo, it is sent to the *Dialogue Processor,* who adds it to the *Dialogue History.* When utterance 2 is received, the *Dialogue Interpreter* sends the following message to the *Maintainer.*

beldom(B,starts(xmas_sales,december),[xmas_sales,december]).(*)

The *Maintainer* then checks if there is any domain belief in IB that is inconsistent with (*). A message is sent to the *Inference Mechanism,* that cannot make any further inferences (*). At this point, the dialogue moves available are: *challenge, prompt, clarify* and *critique.* Below we present the remainder of the current dialogue game:

```
3.Challenge(A, starts(xmas_sales,november)).
4.Critique(B,agree).
```

Upon receiving 3, the *Dialogue Interpreter* maps it onto two new domain beliefs:
beldom(A, not(starts(xmas_sales, december)), [xmas_sales,december]).
beldom(A,starts(xmas_sales,november)[xmas_sales,november]).

After that, a message is sent to the *Maintainer,* so that IA can be updated. Since IA is empty, there is no need to revise its belief set. Thus both *(a)* and *(b)* are added to IA. In the sequel, information is passed onto the *Mediator,* who, by analysing the pattern of the dialogue detects a belief disagreement, and asserts:

Disagreement([B,A], starts(xmas_sales,november), [xmas_sales,november], beldom)

On utterance 4, *B* agrees with *A*. Her critique is mapped onto:

Beldom(B, starts(xmas_sales, november), [xmas_sales, november]).(**)

The *Maintainer* then adds it to IB. After that the *Consistency Checker* finds that IB is now inconsistent, because of the presence of both (*) and (**). It then revises IB with respect to (**). Once this is done, it calls the *Inference Mechanism.*

At the end of the DG, the *Maintainer* updates the GM. Since both contributed equally to the discussion, MArCo registers them as *outspoken.*

Next, *A* and *B* discuss the duration of their project. After determining their problem context, the pair goes on to discuss how to organise the remaining activities, as shown in the excerpt below. There, the roles played by *A* and *B* did not change, with *A* being the *leader* and *B* playing the *follower.* There were no conflicts or mediator interventions. In order to exemplify the inferences performed by the *Inference Mechanism,* let us look at utterance 14. The *Inference Mechanism* starts by adding *before(production, distribution)* to the set of intentions in IA. It then tries to find any logical implications of the new sentence being added. Next it adds to IA: *Beldom(A, before(production,distribution), [production,distribution]),   Goal(A, ϕ)   where before(production,distribution)* $\mapsto \phi$ [4]

---

[4] By *before(production,distribution)* $\mapsto \phi$ we mean that the goal ϕ can be derived from the contents.

Once IA is consistent, the *Inference Mechanism* updates *A's* strategy.

```
Yes. I mean, the distribution and the... These two distribution things, they can only be done if the whole thing is
produced, actually.
14.Propose(A, before(production,distribution)).
Yeah.
15.Critique(B, agree).
I mean, probably together with advertising, this (distribution) can go in parallel, but this is definitely something you
can't do without having produced the whole thing.
16.Propose(A, parallel(distribution,advertising)).
Yes. So you mean that this will be done by the last week of October?
17.Critique(B, agree).
Yes. Last two weeks of October, because on the first of November they must start to sell it.
18.Propose(A, ends((1,k), first_november)).
Ah, Yes. I was confused by the 17 weeks.
19.Critique(B, agree).
And advertising campaign watch-for and hard-sell go in parallel.
20.Propose(B, parallel(m,n)).
Yes.
21.Critique(A, agree).
So, you can actually do the hard-sell campaign only if things are already in the shop. Is that true?
22.Inquire(B,(1,n)).
Yeah. You can do this is parallel, anyway.
23.Statement(A, parallel(1,n)).
Yes.
24.Critique(B, agree).
It is like you do the hard-sell campaign for two weeks and then the things are in the shops, so people can buy them.
25.Propose(A, before(n,1)).
Yeah.
26.Critique(B,agree).
Production run is the precedent activity, 8 weeks, can't be done in parallel with distribution?
27.Inquire(B,(j,k)).
I mean, this (production run) has to run before the distribution.
28.Statement(A, before(j,k)).
Hum Hum.
29.Critique(B, agree).
Ok. And in front of this production run we need one week training of labour, I think, because they can't do it.
30.Propose(A, before(i,j)).
Training of labour yes, before production run.
31.Critique(B,agree).
```

In the excerpt below contributions 36 to 40 show an explicit conflict. After the conflict, we see reflection, when user *B* declares that they needed to complete activity *b* in order to be able to do activity *d*. Figure 2 shows the state of the interaction at the point of disagreement (just after utterance 39) and the mediator's intervention.

```
I think that retooling can be done in parallel with training of labour.
32.propose(B,parallel(h,i)).
But this means that people will be trained with the old machines somehow. Is that true?
33.prompt(A).
I would say that retooling just... ah, because here they manufacture the moulds and they will fix the moulds and set the
machines. This can't be done in parallel, because let's say the work force has to be trained with them, so it can't be done
in parallel.
34.statement(B, implies(before(h,i), done(d))).
Yes. Ok, so...
35.critique(A,agree).
(dialogue proceeds here, adding more activities to the strategy, and drawing the graph)
Yes, manufacture of moulds. This has to be before the retooling and takes two weeks.
36.propose(B, before(d,h)).
Yes.
37.critique(A,agree).
Manufacture of moulds before the retooling and maybe before (A) the trial manufacture.
38.propose(A, before(d,f)).
Yes, but it is impossible.
39.counterpropose(B, and(before(b,d), before(d,f))).
Yes, it is possible.
40.critique(A,disagree).
Yes, it is impossible because you have detailed design of toy and moulds. How can you manufacture them without the
design?
```

When the *Mediator* intervenes after utterance 40, it tries to provoke *reflection* and *articulation* by first reminding the pair that they had not yet discussed the goals of their strategy and asking them to elaborate on their points of view.

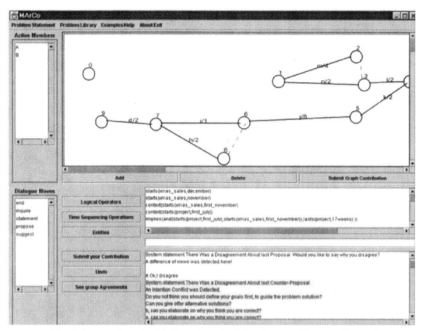

Fig. 2. Screenshot of MArCo, when the intention conflict was detected

3   The Experimental Study of MArCo

Our study of MArCo consisted of two *formative* evaluations. Firstly, we wanted to see whether the interface's functionalities allowed people to build their plans. Secondly, our goal was to investigate whether people's awareness of conflicts influenced the quality of their solutions. Moreover, we wanted to see if the mediator helped users to reflect on and articulate their ideas.

When the prototype was ready, we asked some colleagues to help us try its interface out. We were looking at issues of graph manipulation (is it possible to manipulate the graph with the tools provided?), of text formulas usage (Is the need to use a formal language too big a complication?), and of dialogue games (are we missing dialogue moves?). By observing users working with the interface, we found that the overall functionality of MArCo seemed fine.

During the second stage of the experimental study we observed seven pairs of users interacting through MArCo. Each user worked on a different machine. Out of fourteen participants, twelve were postgraduates, at Leeds University. The remaining two were Spanish language teachers. All participants had computer skills. Out of the twelve postgraduates, six were CBLU's PhD students, two were MEds, two were computing MScs, and the other two were Geography PhD students.

Five pairs used the prototype with the mediator turned on, and two used it without. Participants' interactions were recorded in a log file, to be later analysed. During the interactions we recorded interesting comments and questions. After participants finished their task they were interviewed.

3.1 The Results

We found evidence of all the conflicts predicted in our computational model. For the sake of space, we will only show the example in Figure 3. We refer the interested reader to [9], where we discuss all the instances of conflicts found in full detail.

```
1.A2.I think that.after(d,e).
    Activity d should come after e.
2.B2.I disagree,I think. and(implies(done(b),(d, e)),parallel(d,_e)).
    Activities d and e depend on the results of activity b, and should be done in parallel.
3.System.statement.A difference of views was detected here!
(Further down, the participants come back to the positioning of d and e)
4.B2.I Propose we do.parallel(e,(b,d)).
    Activity e should be done in parallel with b and d. Activity d is done after b.
5.A2.Could you explain why.
6.B2.I think that.implies(done(b),e).
    Activity e depends on the results of b.
7.A2.Ok,I.disagree.
8.System.statement.There Was a Disagreement About last Statement, would you like to
elaborate more on why you disagree?
A Belief Conflict was Detected.
Do you not think you should define your goals first, to guide the problem solution?
A2, can you explain why we should adopt your solution?
B2, can you explain why we should adopt your solution?
```

Fig. 3. An example of a Belief Conflict detected by MarCo

We found several evidences of strategic operations, mainly *revisions* and *additions*. No contractions were found, since participants were asked to put all the activities in the graph representation. Nevertheless, two of the pairs asked the observer if they could leave activities out of the graph. Figure 4 shows a *strategic concatenation*.

```
1.A4.I Propose we do. and((after(j,h),after(n,m)), (after(k,j), after(l, k))).
    Let's do activities j after h, n after m, k after j, and l after k.
2.B4.Ok,I.agree.
```

Fig. 4. Example of a Strategic Concatenation

After investigating whether the events we predicted occurred, we wanted to find out whether or not conflicts trigger changes, and if by detecting and mediating them, we can see indications of *reflection* and *articulation*. Thus, we analysed reflective activities within the context of conflicts, and their occurrence after the mediator's intervention. Our hypothesis was that a fair percentage of reflective activities happened after a *Mediator's* intervention. Whatever the cause, it gives us grounds to argue that the mediator helps to promote *reflection*. Some dialogue studies (e.g., [10]) show that better interactions for learning involve *clarify*, *challenge* and *justify* moves. Such moves indicate *reflection*. In MArCo, reflective activities are indicated by:

- **The user changing his/her mind.** We assume that changes are due to reflection.
- **The user elaborating on what was on his/her (or the group) model.** This can be done by making causal links between pieces of information or by introducing new lines of reasoning about the topic of the conversation.

- ***The user going back to what was previously discussed***. This indicates that s/he has found out that things were not clear, and wants to ground his/her point of view.
- ***The user challenging an utterance, or inquiring about its causes***. When asking for justifications, participants might either have other ideas in mind, or not have been able to work out the reasons for what has been said.

Let us now examine some reflective activities found in the study. The excerpt presented in Figure 5 happened during a disagreement between users A4 and B4. It represents an instance of reflection where users are trying to convince each other by elaborating on the causal links between the activities in question. In utterance 2, A4 states that he thinks we need to have done c to be able to do e. B4 then states that if they want to spend only 4 weeks with e, they need to do it in parallel with c.

```
1.B4.I Propose we do.parallel(c,e ).
2.A4.I think that.implies(c,e).
3.B4.I think that.implies(lasts(e,4),parallel(c,e)).
For e to take four weeks, c needs to be done in parallel with e.
```

Fig. 5. Reflective Activity during a Disagreement

Figure 6 shows another example of how the *Mediator* uses conflicts to try to provoke *reflection*. Utterances (1) and (2) present a disagreement about the ordering of d (following-up a previous discussion) and the *Mediator's* intervention. After the intervention, we can see B7 explaining that d needed b to be completed.

```
1.A7.I Propose we do.after(d,c).
2.B7.I disagree, I think we should do.after(d,b).
3.System.statement.There Was a Disagreement About last Proposal. Would you like to
say why you disagree?
An Intention Conflict was Detected.
Do you not think you should define your goals first, to guide the problem solution?
B7, can you elaborate on why you think you are correct?
A7, can you elaborate on why you think you are correct?
A difference of views was detected here!
4.B7.I think that.implies(d,done(b)).
        In order to do d, we need b to have been done.
5.A7.Ok,I.agree.
```

Fig. 6. Example of a Reflective Activity during a Conflict

3.2 Summary of the Findings

There are other pieces of evidence similar to the ones above in the experiment's log files. Considering all pairs, we found nine *Belief Conflicts*, five *Ordering Conflicts* and twelve *Intention Conflicts*. Most belief conflicts were found in pairs 2 and 3, and were mostly caused by members arguing about justifications for their attitudes. It is also true that reflective utterances (*clarifications*, *prompts*, *inquires*, and *justifications*), as well as other reflective activities appear more in the cases where conflicts were detected, as we thought.

In total, we have found fifty-eight reflective utterances. Twenty happened outside the context of a conflict. There were thirty-eight (65.5%) reflective utterances in the context of conflicts and/or disagreements (corresponding to individuals grounding their points of view and challenging their partners' positions). This corroborates our ideas that conflicts are a good opportunity to facilitate *reflection* and *articulation*.

Many of the reflective activities in the context appear after a conflict or disagreement was pointed out, indicating that the mediator's intervention was adequate. In the mediated pairs, there were thirty-three reflective utterances in a conflict/disagreement context. Out of these, twenty-one utterances happened after a conflict was detected. Table 2 shows the comparison between reflective activities during a conflict/disagreement and the ones happening after a conflict was detected.

Pairs 2 and 3 engaged into conflicts more often. The main difference between them was that pair 2 found that the mediator's interventions were sometimes too long. Pair 3, took their time to consider the mediator's interventions. Pair 4 had a fairly short interaction. With pair 6, there was quite a definite role division between the two participants. Thus, they did not have many conflicts or disagreements.

Table 2. Reflective Activities found during and after conflicts in the Mediated Pairs

Pair Number	Reflective Activities in the Context of Conflict/Disagreements	Reflective Activities After Conflict/Disagreements
Pair 2	11	5 (45%)
Pair 3	11	11 (100%)
Pair 4	3	1 (33%)
Pair 6	1	1 (100%)
Pair 7	7	3 (43%)

For comparison purposes, let us also discuss the results of the non-mediated pairs. In the dialogue of pair 1, who did not have the mediator turned on, we only found one intention and one belief disagreements, as well as one intention conflict (this was because one of the participants was much more experienced than the other). With this pair, only four reflective activities were detected. Three of these occurred within the context of their disagreements. Most correspond to clarification moves prompted by the less experienced participant. The explanations from the expert are quite short - and not questioned by the novice. Pair 5, also not mediated, had seven reflective activities, two of which happened in the context of their conflicts/disagreements. Both of these two reflective activities were by members trying to put their point across.

During the debriefing sessions, several issues arose. All participants said that they were aware of the conflicts, and were trying to articulate their views. They remarked that their awareness was due to the nature of the domain and to the dialogue game structure. They said that this might change in more complex domains, which makes the idea of the artificial mediator even more interesting. Participants remarked that mediator's interventions were adequate, and did help them think. They said that although they thought the interventions were sometimes too long, the pause in the interaction gave them time to stop and reflect. All the pairs liked the idea of working with it. One participant remarked that the mediator helped her plan her next moves better. When asked what they would do to improve the mediator, users suggested that: (1) the mediator should be clearer when pointing out group agreements; (2) use stronger statements; (3) point out the usefulness of the group agreements button more often; (4) including tools that helped planning and be as informed as possible.

The general assessment of the approach was quite positive, with participants comfortably working with an artificial mediator. Participants' experiences indicate that the approach is useful, and with improvements, it can certainly be used in different domains. The suggestions received have been recorded and are being considered for extensions of the prototype.

4   Conclusions and Further Work

This paper presented MArCo, our prototype, together with the results obtained from its evaluation. In order to implement the prototype, we have built computational models of conflicts and of the strategic changes they bring about. We have also analysed the interaction, group and individual models.

The approach implemented in MArCo contributes not only to Computer Science, but also to AIED. Artificial mediators can be seen as yet another way to support electronic meetings. The use of dialogue games helps people to be aware of the rationale for their decisions, and thus reach better informed solutions. These two issues also represent contributions to Computer Supported Co-operative Work.

There are many possible extensions to the work presented here. In fact, the author is working on two projects funded by CNPq that aim at investigating the following: (1) Group characteristics that can be used to support *Focus Groups* and *e-training* systems, and how we can enable intelligent agents to negotiate such a model. This investigation is currently being carried out as part of the AMADeUs Project. Here, Individual and Group Agents negotiate group formation and monitoring; (2) Interaction mechanisms that are more natural - and how we can give the mediator other clues as to how it can intervene more effectively; (3) Extending the mediator in MArCo, so that it can not only include other functionalities, but also be more effective in other domains; and (4) Including other agents that interact with the user and that can play different roles in the discussion (expert, devil's advocate).

References

[1]   Johnson, D.W., and Johnson, F. P., (1997). *Joining Together: Group Theory and Group Skills"*, Allyn and Bacon.
[2]   Hartley, P. (1997). Group Communication, Routledge
[3]   Tedesco, P. and Self, J. A. (2000a). "Using Meta-Cognitive Conflicts to Support Group Problem-Solving". In Gauthier, G., Frasson, C., and VanLehn, K. (eds.) *Proceedings of the 5th ITS'2000*, Lecture Notes in Computer Science, 1839, Springer Verlag, 232-241.
[4]   Tedesco, P. and Self, J.A. (2000b). "MArCo: using Using Meta-Cognitive Conflicts to Provoke Strategic Changes". In Sichman, J. and Monard, M.C. (eds.) *Proceedings of the IBERAMIA-SBIA 2000*, Lecture Notes in AI 1952, Springer Verlag, 186-195
[5]   Levin, J. A., and Moore, J. A., (1977). "Dialogue-Games: Metacommunication structures for Natural Language Interaction". *Cognitive Science*, 395-420
[6]   Pilkington, R. M., (1999). *Analysing Educational Discourse: the DISCOUNT Scheme*. Technical Report 99/2, Computer Based Learning Unit, The University of Leeds

[7]   Cohen, P. R., and Levesque, H. J., (1990). "Intention is Choice with Commitment", *Artificial Intelligence,* 42, 213-261

[8]   Tedesco, P. (2001b) "Using Using Group Models to support Group Planning Interactions in MArCo, Proceedings of the XII SBIE, pp. 202-210

[9]   Tedesco, P. (2001a) *Mediating Meta-Cognitive Conflicts in Group Planning Situations.* Unpublished Doctoral Dissertation, CBLU, The University of Leeds.

[10] de Vicente, A., Bower, A. and Pain, H. (1999). "Initial Impressions on using the DISCOUNT scheme". In Pilkington, R., McKendree, J., Pain, H., and Brna, P. (eds.) *Proceedings of the Workshop on Analysing Educational Dialogue Interaction.* Workshop at the AIED'99, Le Mans, France, 87-94

An Approach to Automatic Analysis of Learners' Social Behavior During Computer-Mediated Synchronous Conversations

Sébastien George[1,2] and Pascal Leroux[1]

[1] Laboratoire d'Informatique de l'Université du Maine (LIUM)
Avenue René Laënnec - 72085 Le Mans Cedex 9 - France
{george, leroux}@lium.univ-lemans.fr
[2] LICEF research center - Tele-university of Quebec
4750 avenue Henri-Julien, Montreal, Qc. H2T 3E4 – Canada
sgeorge@licef.teluq.uquebec.ca

Abstract. Studies have shown that when learners are working in groups, even when these groups are working remotely, they adopt a certain social behavior. It would seem particularly interesting to be able to determine these types of behavior automatically using a computer. Indeed, such information can be useful for the tutor working with the learners, for the learners themselves as well as for a computer system which aims to help these same learners. This paper presents an approach for automatic analysis of learners' social behavior during synchronous conversations. This approach is based on the specification and design of a textual conversation tool semi-structured by communicative acts and a computer agent to analyze the conversations automatically.

1   Introduction

The general context of our work concerns computer environments for distance learning and more especially environments designed to favor collective learning. Our work is based on a pedagogical approach that involves learners in collective activities, thus inciting them to share their knowledge in order to promote a social construction of knowledge. Our research field is therefore that of Computer-Supported Collaborative Learning [1]. In this field, the computer takes on various roles. Firstly, it allows remote learners to take part in a collective activity. Secondly, by means of specially adapted tools, it should favor collective work and exchanges between learners. Finally, it can also be used to analyze this collective activity in order to help the learners and give useful information to the tutors working with them. Here, our interest lies mainly in the computer analysis of these collective activities.

It is well known that social behavior appears within groups of people (moderator, independent, …) including virtual groups [2]. In an educational context, it is interesting to try to determine these social behavior profiles automatically within learner groups as these can be useful for the tutor, for the computer system and for the learners themselves. For the tutor in charge of a group, information concerning these profiles can offer a better understanding of social relationships within the group,

S.A. Cerri, G. Gouardères, and F. Paraguaçu (Eds.): ITS 2002, LNCS 2363, pp. 630–640, 2002.

thereby allowing him/her to give better guidance to the learners while the collective activity is taking place, and even use these profiles as an aid in creating future learner groups [3]. As for computer systems, automatic analysis leading to the definition of behavioral profiles would help to provide pointers for those trying to develop personalized advice and assistance for the learners. For the learners themselves, the fact of giving them information on their profiles would provide insight into their own behavior – a « mirror » effect [4] – and also provide insight into their work process.

The multiple benefits of automatic analysis of social behavior in a distance collective learning context have been listed above, the question is now how to achieve this automatic analysis. This paper therefore aims to present our work in this field, which is based mainly on the design, development and evaluation of a tool for computer-mediated synchronous conversations. In section three our proposition for automatically determining social behavior profiles is discussed, and in section four evaluation and first results are presented, but before this, section two lays out the theoretical bases resulting from Pléty's works on which we build our analysis of the social behavior of learners working in groups.

2   Basis for the Analysis of Learners' Social Behavior

Robert Pléty, researcher at the ethology of communications laboratory at the university of Lumière-Lyon 2 in France, has done a lot of work on the behavior of learners working in groups; namely he has analyzed the interactions of schoolchildren working in groups of four to solve algebraic problems [5]. To do this he started with a microanalysis of the verbal and gestural exchanges within the group, which led him to determine the behavioral patterns of the children. As regards learners working in groups, Pléty states that an organization is set up quickly and spontaneously, and that each of the partners can find his/her own place according to his/her personal knowledge and skills [5]. Pléty identified four typical behavioral profiles: the moderator, the valuator, the seeker and the independent. The characteristics of these four behavioral profiles are shown in Table 1.

Table 1. Behavioral profiles of learners working in groups (synthesis based on Pléty's work).

Profile	Volume of intervention	Type of intervention	Communicative gestures	Responses which follow
Moderator	High	Question or suggestion	Important (look and movements)	Positive responses
Valuator	Quite high	Reaction, answer and appraisal	Regulatory (eye movements)	Little responses
Seeker	Quite low	Very doubtful (questions)	Long inquiring looks	Questions well accepted
Independent	Low	Few suggestions or appraisal	Few eye movements	Intervention unanswered

According to this study, the four profiles can be found in almost all the groups analyzed (16 in all). The seeker and the independent take up their positions according to the relationship that develops between the moderator and the valuator. Thus, the learners define their roles within the group in such a way as to regulate for the best the exchanges and relationships between them [5].

We then wondered whether these same characteristics could be found in groups of learners working remotely through networks. Pléty partly answers this question when he says that the same aspects of connectedness, cohesion and leadership are found in networked learner groups as in ordinary groups [6]. Defining behavioral patterns for learners working in groups remotely would thus seem meaningful. This automatic analysis of social behavior could then be used to offer advice or provide personalized tools for the learners. For instance, a learner assuming the role of moderator could be given moderating tools dynamically. Thus we put forward the hypothesis that the behavioral patterns proposed by Pléty can be found in groups of learners working collectively at a distance. It is then a question of transposing Pléty's work into a context of computer-mediated conversation.

3   Proposition for the Automatic Determination of Social Behavior Patterns

3.1   Analysis of Conversation and Communicative Acts

Our work is mainly concerned with synchronous computer-mediated conversations in text form. This means of communication is well suited to today's network bandwidth and, moreover, it offers greater possibilities for automatic analysis of content.

A conversation can be seen as a series of conversation turns [7], that is to say a series of exchanges made up of speakers interventions, themselves composed of speech acts [8, 9] one of which is a directive act. When trying to analyze a conversation automatically, it is important to try to spot these directive communicative acts. One of the techniques used to analyze conversations consists in providing a semi-structured interface asking the user for a communicative act before he/she has freely typed the content of the message (hence the term semi-structured).

Even if there are drawbacks to using a semi-structured interface, such as lack of flexibility or additional constraints and discipline for the user [10], this technique can be considered useful in a learning context for the following reasons:

- the fact of having to type a message requires the user to think about what he wants to say and thus has an educational value [11, 12];
- a semi-structured interface encourages users to focus more on the task [13];
- the use of openers makes possible the automatic discussion analysis systems [14].

It would therefore seem appropriate to use communicative acts as a basis for structuring a conversation tool so that, on the one hand, semi-structured interfaces are well-suited to an educational context and, on the other hand, the social behavior profiles can be analyzed automatically. We are aware of the criticisms on this subject and aim to provide solutions, namely with regard to the following points:

- the structuring of the environment should itself encourage the use of the right communicative acts [15];
- too many acts make the interface difficult to use [16];
- the tool must allow the thread of the conversations to be made explicit [15].

3.2   Choice of Communicative Acts

The acts that we aim to integrate into a semi-structured conversation tool can be divided into five categories. Three of these categories can be found for example in the works of [17], namely: initiative acts, reactive acts and appraising acts. To these three basic categories we have added a further two. The first is the one we have called "greeting", and which can be found in the works of Clark and Schaefer [18]. The second category concerns auto-reactive acts. No reference has been found to this category in other works, and yet we feel it is essential to be able to react to one's own interventions. Although it is true that this category could be assimilated with reactive acts, we prefer to make a clear distinction between the speaker's reactive interventions to one of his/her own interventions, and his/her reactions to interventions made by others. Table 2 shows the acts identified for the five categories.

Table 2. The communicative acts suggested for a semi-structured conversation tool

Categories	Communicative acts
Greeting	Greeting
Initiative	Suggesting
	Asking
	Affirming
Reactive	Answering
	Querying
Appraising	Approving
	Disapproving
Auto-reactive	Clarifying
	Correcting

In order to make the work of selecting the communicative acts easier, we have tried to define a relatively limited number of acts which are semantically distinct and have distinguished ten in all. Compared to other classification systems for communicative acts, it must be said that the distinctions we make are less fine. However our main aim is to have a set of acts that are easy to use and yet sufficient for the analysis we intend to use them for: to determine behavioral profiles. It must be said that Table 2 is a result of bringing users into contact with our conversation tool.

Moreover, during a conversation, communicative acts are part of a sequence and we feel that the idea of adjacency pairs proposed in the works of Clark and Shaefer [18] is particularly appropriate here. According to these authors an adjacency pair is composed of two ordered utterances produced by two speakers, the form and content of the second utterance being dependant on the first. The idea of adjacent pairs is used here with a double objective in mind: making it easier to structure the conversations and helping to limit the inappropriate selections of communicative acts. The Fig 1. shows the adjacency pairs we have selected. The left-hand point represents the starting point of a new discussion, thus a user can begin a discussion with a greeting act or by an initiative act. To take another example, starting with a suggestion, a user can "query" this suggestion or appraise it. Each time a user intervenes, he/she can react to his/her own intervention by clarifying or correcting what has just been said. It can also be noted that the flowchart has no final point. This is intended to allow debates to develop. This aspect is important in a learning context to encourage learners to go into their ideas in depth.

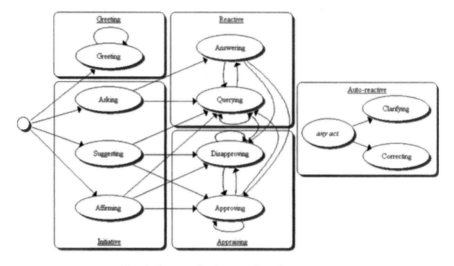

Fig. 1. Communicative acts flowchart

3.3   Conversation Trees

There are a great deal of synchronous written communications tools (chat tools) on the market today. However, these tools are poorly adapted for sustained conversations. They operate on the basis of stacking up messages from users in a temporal way. We feel this operating system can be criticized on several counts. The stacking of messages one behind another according to the order in which they arrived poses problems in the context of a synchronous conversation. Indeed, the time taken to type the texts does not allow an immediate answer to a message. As a result, these time-lags cause overlapping of the interventions which makes it difficult to follow the conversation. Two messages can be close together at the interface whereas they are not necessarily connected, and, inversely, two messages which are related may be separated by other messages. The consequence of this major drawback is that the conversation is difficult to have, and to follow [19].

In order to compensate for the problem of overlapping, we suggest equipping the conversation tool with a tree representation of the messages. The principle is to connect each message with the one it answers or reacts to. New discussion topics start at the beginning of the tree, the others are attached to existing messages. The advantage is that this way of representing the discussion takes into account both the threads of discussion and the topics. Further research has been done into the tree representation of synchronous conversations. Since our tool was created, we have however come across another similar work of research. Indeed, an interface prototype called Threaded Chat has recently been developed in Microsoft©'s research laboratories [20]. An experimental study of this tool has shown it to be promising, and that it helps in decision making. However, in this tool each message is only displayed on one line, which means that the user has to scroll it horizontally to be able to read it all. The tool presented in part 4.1 does not suffer from this ergonomic problem as messages are displayed on several lines when necessary.

3.4   Calculating Behavioral Profiles

From the aforementioned specifications concerning the design of a conversation tool, an automatic analysis system can be designed to identify the four typical behavior profiles identified by Pléty. We present here the formulae used by the computer agent we designed to calculate the behavioral profiles. These heuristic formulae are based on the indications given in Pléty's works and were refined during evaluations. The first formula calculates the participation coefficient of a given participant, p, by dividing the number of messages sent by this participant by the average number of messages[1] sent by the participants as a whole. This gives the following formula:

$$ParticipationCoeff(p) = \frac{NumberOfMessages(p)}{AverageMessages} \times 50$$

If the number of messages sent by a participant is equal to the average, then the participation coefficient for that participant is 50. A coefficient which is close to 0 indicates little participation, whereas a coefficient which is close to 100 indicates a high level of participation in the conversation[2].

Four different formulae make it possible to calculate the coefficients corresponding to the four profiles: moderating, valuating, seeking and independence coefficients. For example, the moderating coefficient for participant p is calculated as follows:

$$ModeratingCoeff(p) = \frac{NumberOfInitiativeMessages(p)}{TotalNumberOfMessages(p)} \times \frac{TotalNumberOfActs}{NumberOfInitiativeActs} \times 50$$

In this formula, *NumberOfInitiativeMessages(p)* corresponds to the number of initiative (suggesting, affirming, asking) messages sent by the participant, and *TotalNumberOfMessages(p)* indicates the total number of messages sent by this participant. The ratio between these two terms is multiplied by the ratio between the total number of communicative acts (10) and the possible number of initiative acts (3). Whenever this coefficient is close to 0, it shows that the participant is not a moderator, whereas a coefficient close to 100 indicates the behavior of a moderator. The other coefficients are all calculated in a similar way to this one.

Thereafter, the behavioral profiles are calculated by weighting the quantitative participation coefficient with one of the more qualitative coefficients described above. A weighting coefficient[3] is applied in order to obtain values that are both relevant and representative. Thus, the formula to calculate the moderator profile of a participant is:

---

[1] This average takes into account the presence of a participant so as to avoid miscalculation if a participant arrives during a meeting.

[2] In all our calculations, any coefficient of more than 100 will be rounded down to 100.

[3] Weighting coefficients were fixed after prior evaluations that had been carried out.

$$ModeratorProfile(p) = \frac{ParticipationCoeff(p) + 2 \times ModeratingCoeff(p)}{3}$$

In this case the 2/3 weighting gives more importance to the moderating coefficient. It should be noted that all profiles are calculated throughout a conversation and change in time. Part 4.2 presents a tool designed to observe the evolution of these profiles.

4   Evaluating a Computer-Mediated Conversation Tool

From the proposal presented above we developed a computer-mediated conversation tool and an automatic analysis system which we then incorporated into an environment developed to support distant project-based learning. This environment, which is called SPLACH[4], comprises all the tools necessary for collective project-based activities (synchronous and asynchronous conversation tools, application sharing tool, scheduling tool, a tool to write reports) [21, 22]. The interest in incorporating all these tools into the same environment lies, on the one hand, in making the system easier to use for the learners, and, on the other hand, allowing the collective activities to be analyzed by the system to give the users advice. Analysis of synchronous conversations is part of this environment.

4.1   The Synchronous Conversation Tool Developed

Fig.2 shows a screen dump of the learner interface of the SPLACH environment during a synchronous meeting. In the top left-hand part, learners taking part in a meeting can share a document in order to work on it together. During a meeting the synchronous conversation tool is at the bottom of the screen. In order to encourage the feeling of awareness between the participants at a meeting, their photos are shown on the right-hand side of the screen. Moreover, "smiley" buttons allow each participant to indicate his/her mood (☺ ☺ ☹) which is displayed next to their photo, thereby enabling them to indicate their feelings without typing any text.

As has been explained in part 3.3, interventions are displayed as on a tree in the conversation tool. Each intervention begins with an icon which symbolizes the communicative act chosen by the user. To intervene, the user clicks either on an existing message or at the end of the conversation on the line "click here to start a new discussion". In either case a menu appears showing the list of possible acts (according to the sequences defined in part 3.2). Furthermore, users are informed when someone is typing a message. Thus, an icon in the bottom left-hand corner of the sender's photo indicates that a message is being typed, also stating which kind of message, in other words the communicative act chosen. For example, in figure 2, the question mark in the bottom left-hand corner of Benoît's photo indicates that he is typing a "querying" message. This information allows the users to expect to receive a

---

[4] SPLACH is the French acronym for "Support d'une pédagogie de Projet pour L'Apprentissage Collectif Humain" which can be translated as "Support Project-Based Learning for Collective Human Learning".

Fig. 2. The SPLACH environment interface during a meeting

message without worrying about the time-lag in answering inherent to textual conversation tools (feedback on user activity).

4.2   Evaluation at the Tele-University of Quebec

Evaluation of the SPLACH environment was carried out in a distance education context at the Tele-university of Quebec. Six students studying programming at a distance formed two teams for about six weeks. The overall objective was to collectively write a computer program, each student being responsible for certain functions of the program. These teams were followed by one of the Tele-university tutors, also using the SPLACH environment. In all there were over 70 hours of connections to the server, of which about fifteen were synchronous conversation. The synchronous conversation tool was much appreciated by the students who were not bothered by the fact of having to choose a communicative act, even though they could not always find any immediate use in doing this. A manual analysis of the use of communicative acts shows that the students very often used it adequately (only between 10 and 15% of the acts selected did not correspond to the content of the message). Choosing acts from a dropdown menu seems appropriate. The evaluation showed that the behavioral profiles calculated corresponded to what was happening in the conversations. The formulae written for the calculations therefore seemed relevant to the context we used them in.

Figure 3 shows a tool designed to visualize the evolution of these profiles during a conversation. For the moment this tool has been designed with a view to experimental observation, but the tutor could be given it to help him follow the learners' progress, or the learners themselves could use it to gain insight into their own behavior.

Each graph corresponds to a particular type of profile and the curves show how the profiles of the users at the meeting evolve in time (X axis). Thus the "moderator" graph in figure 3 indicates that the user called Luc was the main moderator during this meeting, whereas Michel was the least. It can, however, be noted that Michel was the main "seeker", and that none of the participants were really "independent".

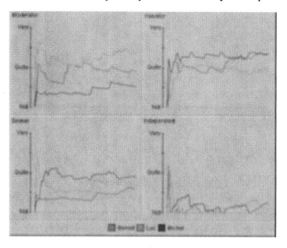

Fig. 3. The tool to visualize behavioral profiles

5   Conclusions and Futures Directions

This paper describes an approach to automatically determine the behavioral profiles of learners during synchronous computer-mediated conversations. The first results obtained from an evaluation would seem to confirm our hypothesis that the behavioral profiles set out by Pléty can be found in groups of learners working remotely. The computer specifications of the conversation tool which is semi-structured with communicative acts allow these profiles to be calculated by the system.

We are aware that the calculations could be refined by taking into account other variables and by carrying out more specific experiments. Thus, we do not take the reactions to the interventions into consideration for the calculations (the intervention of a moderator, for instance, also typically leads to reactions from others). For the moment we prefer to have relatively uncomplicated calculations which involve few parameters. Nevertheless, in our incremental design method, we are bearing in mind the idea of taking reactions to the interventions into consideration in order to refine the calculations. A further research direction to follow-up our work involves a deeper study of the tool to visualize behavioral profiles, and in a wider sense the instrumentation of the tutor working with learners in a collective learning context.

Acknowledgements. The work presented in this paper has been done during the PhD work of the first author at the computer science laboratory of Le Mans University (LIUM) in France. The first author is currently doing post-doctorate work in the LICEF research center at the Tele-University of Quebec in Montreal. The authors would like to thank the France/Quebec cooperation commission for their support. The authors also wish to express their gratitude to the students of the Tele-university of Quebec and to Jacques Rivard for enabling them to carry out the evaluations in real-life situations.

References

1. Bannon, L. J., Issues in Computer-Supported Collaborative Learning, C. O'Malley, (Ed.), NATO Advanced Workshop on CSCL, Maratea, Italy (1989).
2. Rheingold, H., Les communautés virtuelles. (Addison-Wesley France, Paris, 1993).
3. Dillenbourg, P., Baker, M. J., Blaye, A., C.O'Malley, The evolution of research on collaborative learning, Learning in Humans and Machines: Towards an Interdisciplinary Learning Science , 189- 211 (1996).
4. Jermann, P., Soller, A., Muehlenbrock, M., From mirroring to guiding: A review of state of the art technology for supporting collaborative learning, European Conference on Computer-Supported Collaborative Learning (Euro-CSCL 2001), Maastricht, Netherlands (2001), pp. 324-331.
5. Pléty, R., L'apprentissage coopérant, Ethologie et psychologie des communications (ARCI Presse Universitaire, Lyon, 1996).
6. Pléty, R., Comment apprendre et se former en groupe (Retz, 1998).
7. Sacks, H., Schegloff , E. A., Jefferson, G., A Simplest Systematics for the Organization of Turn-Taking for Conversation, Language 50, 696-735 (1974).
8. Austin, J. L., How to do Things with Words (Oxford, 1962).
9. Searle, J. R., Speech acts: an essay in the philosophy of language (Cambridge University Press, 1969).
10. Suchman, L. A., in Computer-Supported Cooperative Work . (Kluwer Academic Publishers, 1994), vol. 2, pp. 177-190.
11. Winograd, T., A Language/Action Perspective on the Design of Cooperative Work, Human-Computer Interaction 3, 3-30 (1987).
12. Flores, F., Graves, M., Hartfield, B., Winograd, T., Computer Systems and the Design of Organizational Interaction, ACM Trans. on Office Information Systems 6, 153-172 (1988).
13. Baker, M. J., Lund, K., Promoting reflective interactions in a computer-supported collaborative learning environment, Journal of Computer Assisted Learning 13, 175-193 (1997).
14. McManus, M. M., Aiken, R. M., Using an Intelligent Tutor to Facilitate Collaborative Learning, Innovating Adult Learning with Innovative Technologies. Elsevier Science B.V. , 49-64 (1995).
15. Robertson, J., Good, J., Pain, H., BetterBlether: The Design and Evaluation of a Discussion Tool for Education, International Journal of Artificial Intelligence in Education 9, 219-236 (1998).
16. Soller, A., Linton, F., Goodman, B., Lesgold, A., Toward Intelligent Analysis and Support of Collaborative Learning Interaction, S. P. Lajoie, M. Vivet, (Eds.), Ninth International Conference on Artificial Intelligence in Education, Le Mans (IOS Press, 1999), pp. 75-82.
17. Bilange, É., Modélisation du dialogue oral finalisé personne-machine par une approche structurelle, Informatique, Thèse de Doctorat, Université de Rennes I (1991).
18. Clark, H. H., Schaefer, E. F., Contributing to Discourse, Cognitive Science 13, 259-294 (1989).

19. Herring, S., Interactional Coherence in CMC, Journal of Computer-Mediated Communication 4, http://www.ascusc.org/jcmc/vol4/issue4/ (1999).
20. Smith, M., Cadiz, J. J., Burkhalter, B., Conversation Trees and Threaded Chats, Proceedings of the 2000 ACM Conference on Computer Supported Cooperative Work, Philadelphia, Pennsylvania, USA (2000), pp. 97-105.
21. George, S., Leroux, P., Project-Based Learning as a Basis for a CSCL Environment: An Example in Educational Robotics, European Conference on Computer-Supported Collaborative Learning (Euro-CSCL 2001), Maastricht, Netherlands (2001), pp. 269-276.
22. George, S., Apprentissage collectif à distance. SPLACH : un environnement informatique support d'une pédagogie de projet, PhD in computer science, Université du Maine (2001).

Going Beyond the Problem Given: How Human Tutors Use Post-practice Discussions to Support Transfer

Sandra Katz[1] and David Allbritton[2]

[1] Learning Research and Development Center, University of Pittsburgh
Pittsburgh, PA 15260 USA
katz+@pitt.edu
[2] Department of Psychology, DePaul University, 2219 N. Kenmore Ave.
Chicago, IL 60614 USA
dallbrit@depaul.edu

Abstract. Recent studies reveal that human tutoring sessions do not always end when the student has solved a problem. Instead, tutors and students frequently use a post-practice discussion to bring new topics to the table or to continue problem-solving discussions. One of the main roles of post-practice dialogues is to support transfer—that is, the student's ability to apply concepts and adapt familiar solution strategies to unfamiliar problems. Several developers of intelligent tutoring systems have implemented post-practice modules, with similar aims. However, in contrast to the integrated instructional planning that human tutors apparently perform, automated planning of reflective activities is typically done independently of instructional planning during problem solving. We present a framework for describing reflective plans that are distributed between problem solving and debrief and evidence that reflective discussions support transfer in elementary mechanics.

1 Introduction

In recent studies of one-on-one tutoring, we observed that students and tutors frequently continue their discussion of a practice problem after the student has solved it (e.g., [1]). The primary goals of post-practice discussions appear to be to deepen students' conceptual knowledge, to develop problem schemas—i.e., strategies for solving particular types of problems—and, as a result of both processes, to enhance transfer—the ability to apply concepts and adapt familiar solution strategies to unfamiliar problems. Prior research has shown that instruction to enhance conceptual understanding and schema acquisition supports transfer (e.g., [2, 3]).

Several developers of intelligent tutoring systems (ITSs) have incorporated post-practice reflective modules into their system, with similar aims (e.g., [4]). Unfortunately, there is little research to guide the development of automated modules for reflection. Three main questions need to be addressed:

1. What roles do post-practice discussions perform in human one-on-one tutoring?

S.A. Cerri, G. Gouardères, and F. Paraguaçu (Eds.): ITS 2002, LNCS 2363, pp. 641–650, 2002.
© Springer-Verlag Berlin Heidelberg 2002

2. How are these roles carried out? For example, what is the relationship between reflective dialogues during and after problem solving? What goals are achieved during each phase and what tactics do tutors use to achieve these goals?
3. Do post-practice dialogues enhance learning? Is it even worthwhile to implement post-practice reflection in intelligent tutoring systems?

In previous research, Katz and colleagues [1] investigated the instructional roles of post-practice discussions in avionics and their effectiveness in eliminating misconceptions. Avionics experts debriefed novice technicians on their solutions to problems in the Sherlock ITS (e.g., [4]). The researchers observed that misconceptions were more likely to be eliminated if discussions about them were distributed between problem solving and debrief instead of taking place during problem solving alone. This study therefore corroborated previous research which showed that learning is supported by reflective activities such as conducting team debriefs—when coupled with pre-briefs [5]—and prompting students to respond to „reflection questions" following worked examples [6].

In the study reported on in this paper, we investigated the instructional roles of post-practice discussions in elementary mechanics, their relationships to problem-solving dialogues, and the effectiveness of particular aspects of these discussions. Towards these ends, we analyzed dialogues between physics tutors and students, as students solved problems in the Andes ITS (e.g., [7]). One motivation for this study was to see if the findings from [1] were corroborated in a different domain. In addition, we used pre-test to post-test gain scores to provide a more rigorous measure of the effectiveness of post-practice dialogues.

As we will demonstrate, our analyses of the post-practice dialogues in mechanics corroborated the findings in [1] in several respects. First, these dialogues performed instructional roles similar to those identified in avionics. Second, like the avionics tutors, the physics tutors adapted the post-practice discussions to the needs of individual learners [8]. Third, the reflective dialogues supported near transfer, as measured by pre-test to post-test gain scores on problems similar to those that students solved in Andes. Finally, these discussions were often intricately connected to discussions that took place during problem solving.

The latter finding is especially important for automated planning of reflective dialogues. It suggests that reflective planning modules should specify which instructional goals to address when—during problem solving versus during a post-practice discussion—and how to achieve these goals. However, to our knowledge, no intelligent tutoring systems attempt to generate integrated plans for reflection. To address this problem, we analyzed a sub-corpus of the post-practice dialogues in basic mechanics—in particular, those that extended problem-solving discussions. We then developed a framework for specifying distributed strategies for reflection that can guide the design of automated reflective planners.

2   Methods

2.1 Procedures and Corpus

Fifteen student volunteers taking an introductory physics course at the University of Pittsburgh were randomly assigned to one of seven human tutors, also paid volunteers. Tutors had prior experience teaching physics in a classroom or one-on-one tutoring setting; some had done both.

Students first took a pre-test to measure their background knowledge in physics. They then worked on 24 problems in Andes during 3-5 sessions, which each lasted approximately 2-4 hours. The tutor and student sat in separate rooms and interacted via teletype. Andes' automated coaching was suppressed so that all of the help that students received came from the live tutors. The system automatically logged students' actions and conversations with their tutor. To highlight the roles of post-practice dialogues and their potential impact on student-tutor interaction during problem solving, we presented the problems in one of two formats, „debrief" and „no debrief." At the start of each problem, the experimenter told participants whether they would be allowed to discuss the problem further after the student solved it. Students worked on twelve problems in each of these within-subject conditions.

After the last problem, students took a post-test which was identical to the pre-test. The tests consisted of 13 qualitative questions from a standard test of elementary mechanics called the Force Concept Inventory and 37 quantitative problems.

The corpus consists of 315 transcripts, 160 from „debrief" problems, 155 from „no debrief" problems. (Due to time constraints and other factors, four students did not complete the 24-problem set.) The post-practice discussions varied from a single comment to nearly 100 dialogue turns. We marked the start of these discussions at the point where the tutor confirmed that the student's answer was correct. We then segmented the post-practice dialogues into sub-dialogues, one sub-dialogue per topic. The sub-dialogue is our unit of analysis. For simplicity, we refer to sub-dialogues as 'post-practice dialogues.' The corpus consists of 164 coded post-practice dialogues. The corpus and experimental procedures are described in more detail in [8].

To simplify the exposition, the dialogue examples presented below deal with one central principle in mechanics, Newton's Second Law (NSL). This principle basically states that an object accelerates when there is an unbalanced or „net" force acting on the object. Furthermore, the net force is equal to the object's mass times its acceleration ($F\_net = m * a$). Conversely, the forces acting on a stationary object are balanced (the sum of the forces acting on it equals zero).

2.2 Dialogue Analysis

The post-practice dialogues were coded to address the following questions:

1. What relationships hold between problem-solving dialogues and post-practice dialogues, with respect to the roles and novelty of the subject matter addressed?

2. Do particular aspects of post-practice dialogues correlate with learning (as measured by pre-test to post-test gain scores), specifically:

- *Dialogue initiator*—the frequency of tutor-initiated and student-initiated dialogues in a student's corpus
- *Instructional role*—the frequency of dialogues in a student's corpus that abstracted concepts, problem-solving strategies, and tactics (Table 1)
- *Information status*—the frequency of dialogues in a student's corpus that restated discussions that took place during problem solving, extended problem-solving discussions, or brought new topics to the table

Table 1. Instructional roles of post-practice dialogues that potentially support transfer

Conceptual generalization: help the student understand concepts associated with the current problem and how these concepts apply to various physical situations.
Conceptual specialization: clarify the distinction between related concepts—e.g., the difference between instantaneous, average, and constant acceleration.
Correct knowledge gap: explain a concept or state a piece of declarative knowledge that the student apparently lacks; often done to resolve a misconception.
Correct misconception: correct a piece of faulty knowledge or a flawed mental model
Strategic generalization: help the student: (1) understand that the strategy used in the current problem applies to a whole class of problems—e.g., all conservation of energy problems, (2) recognize that a particular schema applies to the task at hand, or (3) adapt a schema to physical situations that differ in particular ways.
Alternative strategies: teach different strategies for solving the same problem or for achieving a particular solution step, or help the student understand why one strategy is preferable or equivalent to another.
Problem-solving tactics: teach „tricks of the trade" for solving quantitative problems, such as breaking complex problems into more manageable sub-goals, reading the problem statement carefully, and expressing relations symbolically before instantiating variables.

Instructional Role and Information Status. In [8], we describe the complete taxonomy of reflective dialogue roles that were identified in the elementary mechanics corpus and used to code it. Table 1 summarizes the roles that potentially support transfer. Any given post-practice dialogue can have more than one role, as we illustrate presently.

Sometimes post-practice discussions extend discussions that took place during problem solving. This is very much the case with the lesson excerpted in Table 2. During problem solving, the tutor focuses on strengthening the student's understanding of Newton's Second Law (turns 1-8) and on helping him to apply the corresponding formula ($F\_net = m * a$) to the current problem (turns 8-20), which involves a stationary object. The post-practice dialogue contains three segments that perform the following roles: (1) reinforce the student's ability to apply NSL to a static situation (turns 1-2), (2) help the student see that NSL also applies to a dynamic situation—*strategic generalization* (turns 3-8) and (3) reinforce the student's concept of NSL—*conceptual generalization* (turns 9-12).

Table 2. Example of a post-practice dialogue that elaborates on a problem-solving dialogue. S = student; T = tutor. Ellipses represent deleted text. Comments are in italics. Spelling errors have been corrected

Andes Problem Statement	
A rock climber of mass 55 kg slips while scaling a vertical face. Fortunately, her caribiner holds and she is left hanging at the bottom of her safety line. Find the tension in the safety line.	
Problem-solving Dialogue	**Post-practice Dialogue**
1. **S:** first I will need the tension formula! I think it is T = F * a	1. **T:** Now…what if I switched the problem around a bit and now I told you that this guy is going to rappel down the cliff and the maximum tension in the rope is 450 N; if he hangs there, will the rope break?
2. **T:** whoa! Where are you coming up with these equations?… What the heck does that formula mean?	
3. **S:** I can't remember the rest of it.	2. **S:** yes
4. **T:** Ok, first of all…what does Newton's 2nd law say?…	3. **T:** ok. So he is now going to move down the rope. Knowing all that, that the maximum tension in the rope is 400, how could you find the minimum acceleration he would need to not break the rope?…
5. **S:** The force the person is being pulled down with is m * a so the rope is pulling up on him the same amount, but not negative	
6. **T:** why does it say that? I hope you understand that this is not an action reaction pair.	4. **S:** set T = 400
7. **S:** I didn't think so—just that the tension of the rope is holding the person steady.	5. **T:** well I want you to write out the equations in the lines and show me. Start with Newton's Second Law.
8. **T:** Newton's equation…says what—that the sum of the NET force = m * a. NET also means unbalanced. What is the net force in this case? How many forces act on this guy?	*The student works on the problem in the Andes equation boxes.*
	6. **S:** he has to go at least with an a = - 2.53 m/s/s
9. **S:** 0	7. **T:** ok well, I will assume you did the calculation right…But does this make sense to you?
10. **T:** 0 forces act on him?	
11. **S:** no, the net force is 0. There are two forces.	8. **S:** yes
12. **T:** good; what are they?	9. **T:** there are two very important things his law says and they have just been illustrated in this problem. The first is that an unbalanced force produces an acceleration. Another way to think of this problem is that you have to account for 139 N.
13. **S:** the tension of the rope and gravity	
14. **T:** well, his weight right?…in this case w = m * g. So we have 2 forces—tension up, weight down equal to zero, right?	
15. **S:** right	10. **S:** right
16. **T:** it should like this: T – m * g = 0. So now what is the tension equal to?	11. **T:** that 139 is the unbalanced force and this is what produces the acceleration. Also it says that the acceleration always points in the same direction as the unbalanced force is acting. Right?
17. **S:** the guy's weight	
18. **T:** which is what? Calculate it.	
19. **S:** 593 N (*N = Newtons*)	12. **S:** yes
20. **T:** yeah	

At other times post-practice dialogues raise topics that were not discussed during problem solving, as in the dialogue on the same topic excerpted in Table 3, from a different tutor and student. In contrast with the multi-functional dialogue in Table 2, the post-practice dialogue in Table 3 deals only with „going beyond" the student's understanding (turn 13), by applying NSL to a dynamic situation. Perhaps this tutor saw no need to reinforce the student's ability to apply NSL to a static situation because the student just did this effortlessly. The contrast between these two dialogues demonstrates the adaptive nature of post-practice discussions [8].

Table 3. Example of a post-practice discussion that "goes beyond" the currrent problem. There was no coaching during problem solving. S = student; T = tutor. Ellipses represent deleted text. Comments are in italics. Spelling errors have been corrected

---

1. **T:** Okay—now consider what would happen if the climber were slipping down at an acceleration of say, a. Would tension be the same?
2. **S:** No
3. **T:** ...If a is positive down, is T large or smaller?...what would the tension be then? No calculations. Suppose you cut the rope, what's a?
4. **S:** Whatever a is, it accelerates without opposition
5. **T:** so what is its value?
6. **S:** in this case gravity
7. **T:** uh – gravity is a force—give me a number
8. **S:** 9.8 m/s
9. **T:** right that's acceleration *due to gravity*--not gravity
10. **S:** okay
11. **T:** so what is the tension if the a is almost g...if the rope is cut?
12. **S:** 0
13. **T:** exactly...the solution is fine -- I'm going beyond....
14. **S:** I follow now; if the person is still moving, the tension can still be calculated using the person's mass and the downward acceleration.
15. **T:** true – give me a quick equation...

Taken together, the dialogues in Tables 2 and 3 represent the two main types of information status categories in our coding scheme: „new" and „old." These categories are further subdivided into the four descriptors shown in Table 4.

Table 4. Information status categories

„Old" Dialogues:

Elaboration: Elaborated dialogues add information to a problem-solving discussion.

Restatement: Restated dialogues have a precursor during problem solving. However, they do not add information; they merely summarize or restate what came before.

„New" Dialogues:

New/domain-based: These dialogues are unrelated to any discussion that took place during problem solving. The subject matter focuses on the domain (e.g., physics).

New/general: These dialogues are also unrelated to any discussion that took place during problem solving but their content is not domain-based. Instead, they deal with assessing performance, motivating the student, bolstering confidence, session management, etc.

---

3   Results and Discussion

3.1   Evidence That Post-practice Dialogues Support Learning

Two people coded the dialogue features described in the preceding section. Fifteen transcripts were selected at random to test for inter-rater reliability. Thirteen transcripts contained a debrief session and the coders' judgments of whether a debrief occurred were in perfect agreement (100%). The coders agreed on both the number of sub-dialogues and the sub-dialogue boundary locations for 12 of the 13 debrief transcripts (92%). Agreement rates were 92% for initiator (kappa = .83), 85% for information status (kappa = .78), and 94% for instructional role (kappa = .77).

We measured learning in terms of *overall gain score* from the pre-test to post-test, *qualitative gain score*—with respect to the 13 qualitative questions—and *quantitative gain score*—with respect to the 37 quantitative questions. Two raters scored the tests. Agreement was 92.6% (kappa = .84).

We searched for correlations between these three measures of learning and the following features of the post-practice dialogues that each student participated in: (1) the total number of post-practice dialogues, (2) the number of dialogues that carried out the abstraction functions described in Table 1, (3) the number of abstraction dialogues that were student-initiated and tutor-initiated, and (4) the number of dialogues tagged with each of the information status categories described in Table 4, plus the aggregated categories „new" and „old." Five factors correlated significantly ($p < .05$) with both overall gain score and quantitative gain score (we list the correlation statistics for overall gain score followed by the same for quantitative gain score): the total number of debrief dialogues that a student and his tutor engaged in (r = .39; r = .37); the number of dialogues that elaborated upon problem-solving dialogues (r = .59; r = .59); the number of „Old" (elaborated and restated) dialogues (r = .52; r = .48); the number of abstraction dialogues (r = .55; r = .52); and the number of abstraction dialogues that were initiated by the tutor (r = .56; r = .49). None of the examined factors correlated significantly with qualitative gain score, although there was a trend for tutor-initiated abstraction dialogues (r = .34, $p < .10$).

These results suggest that post-practice dialogues correlate with learning—in particular, near transfer—especially when they abstract the concepts and strategies associated with the current problem, elaborate or restate problem-solving discussions, and are initiated by the tutor. As a more rigorous test of the effectiveness of post-practice reflection, we conducted a follow-up study in which forty-six students solved problems in Andes in one of three conditions: with automated reflection questions after problem solving—similar to those that the human tutors in the current study asked students—and discussion with a human tutor; with the same reflection questions followed by canned feedback (without a human tutor), or with no reflection questions. Students learned more with the reflection questions than without, but the canned feedback and human tutored conditions did not differ significantly [8]. Taken together, these two studies corroborate prior research on the effectiveness of post-practice discussions (e.g., [1, 5, 6]), and support the practice of incorporating reflective modules within ITS's.

3.2   A Framework for Specifying Distributed Plans for Reflection

Most reflective dialogues in the mechanics corpus elaborated upon problem-solving dialogues. If we consider only dialogues that dealt with domain material, 78 (48%) were distributed across problem solving and debrief („old"), while 43 (26%) were coded as *new—domain*. The high frequency of distributed post-practice dialogues, coupled with the finding that elaborated dialogues—and „old" dialogues in general—correlated with learning, prompted us to examine the sub-corpus of tutor-initiated distributed dialogues more closely, in order to develop a framework for specifying distributed plans for reflection that can be implemented in ITS's.

Like any dialogue plan, reflective dialogue plans have three essential elements: a *goal* and its *sub-goals*, *tactics* for achieving these goals, and *content* to fill the speech acts that implement selected tactics. However, automated generation of integrated plans for reflection like those that human tutors produce would require some special considerations, such as how instructional goals should be distributed between problem solving and post-practice reflection. We propose the following framework for specifying reflective plans and illustrate it with reference to Tables 2 and 5:

- **Overall Goal**: Goal specification involves two main elements:
  1. *Goal Descriptor:* the type of goal, according to theories of intention in discourse (e.g., [9])—e.g., *enabling* understanding or the ability to perform an action; *convincing* the hearer to carry out an action; *motivating* the hearer, etc.
  2. *Object:* the knowledge piece that the tutor wants the student to understand or be motivated to learn; the action she is trying to convince the student to take, etc.
- **Manner:** How should the goal be achieved? There are three considerations:
  1. *Staging:* Which goals should be achieved during problem solving, which during the post-practice discussion? In the example (Tables 2 and 5), the tutor focuses on applying NSL to a static situation during problem solving and on applying NSL to a dynamic situation during the post-practice discussion. However, the tutor needs to enhance the student's understanding of NSL before she can help him to apply it. She distributes this subgoal between problem solving (Table 2, turns 1-8) and the post-practice dialogue (Table 2, turns 9-12).
  2. *Scope of intervention:* To what extent should a goal or sub-goal be achieved, whatever stage it occurs in? For example, what particular knowledge pieces should be addressed in an explanation or interactive dialogue? In the example, the problem-solving dialogue partially addresses the concept of NSL. The tutor distinguishes NSL from the principle of action-reaction pairs (Table 2, turns 4-8), and formally states NSL (Table 2, turn 8). The post-practice dialogue adds to this explanation, reifying the main relation expressed in the equation and stating the relationship between the net force and direction (Table 2, turn 11).
  3. *Tactics:* What tutoring tactics—e.g., hints, Socratic-style dialogues or „directed lines of reasoning" [10], didactic explanations—should be used to achieve each goal and sub-goal? Tutors frequently combine tactics. For example, the tutor in Table 2 shifts from an interactive approach (turns 2-7) to a didactic approach (turn 8) when the former does not seem to be working.

- **Content:** What subject matter should be included in the speech acts that implement tutoring tactics?

Table 5. A distributed plan for achieving the main goal of the dialogue shown in Table 2. S = student; & = and; | = or

Overall Goal:	
Descriptor: enable-understanding	
Object: how to apply Newton's Second Law	
Problem-solving Plan	**Post-practice Reflection Plan**
Goal Descriptor: enable-understanding	**Goal Descriptor:** enable-understanding
Object: apply NSL to static situation	**Object:** apply NSL to dynamic situation
Constraints: (S understands Newton's Second Law & S is familiar with formal representation of NSL & S has difficulty applying NSL to static situation)	**Constraints:** (S understands Newton's Second Law & S is familiar with formal representation of NSL & S can apply NSL to static situation)
Tactics: (didactic | directed line of reasoning)	**Tactics:** (didactic | directed line of reasoning | What-if scenario)

As in other types of discourse planning, constraints govern the selection of goals in reflective dialogue planning. Constraints form the „left-hand" (conditional) side of planning rules. As shown in Table 5, the problem-solving goal of enabling the student to apply NSL to a stationary object can not be executed unless the student has a basic understanding of what NSL means and how to represent it formally. When a cognitive prerequisite specified in a planning rule is not met, a repair dialogue addressing that rule should be posted to the planning agenda (e.g., Table 2, turns 2-8). Conversely, some constraints block execution of a reflective dialogue goal. For example, if a student does not have difficulty with applying NSL to a static situation, then no instruction on this skill should take place during problem solving (Table 5), for a static problem. This was the case with the student in Table 3.

Constraints also govern the selection of tutoring tactics, the distribution of instruction between problem solving and post-practice reflection (*staging*), and the extent to which a distributed goal is addressed in each stage (*scope of intervention*). In addition to accounting for cognitive constraints, reflective dialogue planners should account for affective constraints (e.g., the student's level of frustration) and logistical constraints (e.g., the amount of time remaining in the student's session). For example, the tutor in Table 2 seemed to consider the student's frustration level when she shifted from interactive to didactic tactics. Achieving this level of sophistication in automated planners presents a challenge, especially for student modeling and natural-language processing technology.

4   Conclusions and Future Work

This study supports prior research on the effectiveness of post-practice dialogues (e.g., [1, 5, 6]), and hence supports the practice of incorporating reflective modules in ITS's.

Perhaps the most important implication of this research is that the planning of post-practice discussions should not take place independently of instructional planning during problem solving. Human tutors apparently generate integrated, distributed plans. In order to develop rules for automated reflective planners, further research on human tutoring is needed to identify the types of constraints that govern the selection, distribution and execution of instructional goals. Our research will continue in this direction, with the aim of providing precise guidance for the design of automated reflective dialogues that can do what human tutors do—take students beyond their current level of understanding and problem-solving ability.

Acknowledgements. This research was supported by grants from the Spencer Foundation (grant number 199900054) and the Office of Naval Research, Cognitive Science Division (grant number N00014-97-1-0848). The data presented and views expressed are not necessarily endorsed by these agencies. We thank James Carlino, Beth Nicholson, and Annalia Palumbo for their assistance.

References

1. Katz, S., O'Donnell, G., & Kay, H. (2000). An approach to analyzing the role and structure of reflective dialogue. *International Journal of Artificial Intelligence and Education*, 11, 320-343.
2. Kieras, D.E., & Bovair, S. (1984). The role of a mental model in learning to operate a device. *Cognitive Science*, 8, 255-273.
3. Marshall, S. P. (1995). *Schemas in Problem Solving*. New York, NY: Cambridge University Press.
4. Katz, S., Lesgold, A., Hughes, E., Peters, D., Eggan, G., Gordin, M., Greenberg., L. (1998). Sherlock 2: An intelligent tutoring system built upon the *LRDC Tutor Framework*. In C. P. Bloom and R. B. Loftin (Eds.), *Facilitating the Development and Use of Interactive Learning Environments* (pp. 227-258). New Jersey: Lawrence Erlbaum Associates.
5. Smith-Jentsch, K. A., Zeisig, R. L., Acton, B., & McPherson, J. A. (1998). Team dimensional training: A strategy for guided team self-correction. In J. A. Cannon-Bowers & E. Salas (Eds.), *Making decisions under stress: Implications for individual and team training* (pp. 271-297). Washington, DC: APA.
6. Lee, A. Y., & Hutchison, L. (1998). Improving learning from examples through reflection. *Journal of Experimental Psychology: Applied, 4(3)*, 187-210.
7. Gertner, A. & VanLehn, K. (2000). Andes: A Coached Problem Solving Environment for Physics. In G. Gauthier, C. Frasson, and K. VanLehn (Eds.), *Proceedings of the 5th International Conference, ITS 2000* [133-142], Montreal, Canada.
8. Katz, S., & Allbritton, D. (submitted). Adaptive tutoring that takes place after a problem has been solved.
9. Mann, W., & Thompson, S. (1988). Rhetorical structure theory: Towards a functional theory of text organization. *TEXT, 8(3),* 243-281.
10. Hume, G. D., Michael, J., Rovick, A., & Evens, M. (1996). Hinting as a tactic in one-on-one tutoring. *Journal of the Learning Sciences, 5(1)*, pp. 23-47.

Conception of a Language Learning Environment Based on the Communicative and Actional Approaches

Johan Michel and Jérôme Lehuen

LIUM, Université du Maine, Avenue Olivier Messiaen, 72085 Le Mans Cedex 9, France
{Johan.Michel, Jerome.Lehuen}@lium.univ-lemans.fr

Abstract. This paper's aim is to give a conceptual framework about the conception of a Computer Assisted Language Learning environment based on the communicative and actional approaches. In this environment, the learner is implicated in a task that he/she has to complete by interacting with a partner using his/her language competencies. Given a task, different ways exist to accomplish it and the different competencies of the learner can then be solicited with different types of interaction. Works accomplished in human computer dialogue give models to manage this interaction.

1   Introduction

Some language learning methods emphasize communication as the main source of acquisition of language skills. Some also focus on the importance of performing tasks existing in the real world and so, on the immersion of language students in a world where they can act via language. These two approaches of language learning are the communicative one and the "actional" one. We believe they can both be useful to design a Computer Assisted Language Learning (CALL) environment. Our environment is designed for foreigners wanting to learn French language.

The communicative approach views language learning happening through communication between people. The focus is on communicative competencies more than on grammar rules and vocabulary. Related works exist and so we can mention the FLUENT system developed by Florence Reeder and Henry Hamburger [7] and [12], the works by Patrick Boylan and Alessandro Micarelli [2], and in a broader view, the work by Hiroaki Ogata and al [11].

The "actional" approach considers the learner, the language user, as a social actor involved in actions in his/her life. Actions are performed in domains, considered as life sectors. In a particular domain, some language activities take place in order to perform tasks. Tasks are problems to solve and goals to reach. Those language activities are receiving and producing texts, texts are dialogue sequences occurring in this particular domain and inducing language activities during the accomplishment of the task. The learner has got general competencies (skills, abilities and aptitudes), including communicative competencies. Those communicative competencies permit the learner to imagine strategies to complete tasks. The strategies use results in text production from the language user, and the evolution of the task produces texts from peers that the learner can perceive and understand. This approach is described in [4].

S.A. Cerri, G. Gouardères, and F. Paraguaçu (Eds.): ITS 2002, LNCS 2363, pp. 651–660, 2002.

Our view is influenced by both of those approaches. They are not conflicting and we can determine a common space shared by those approaches. The learner is involved in a task (the actional approach) for which communication with a partner is requested (the communicative approach). It's designed here with an environment that enables the learner to immerse in a virtual world where the learner can act by using natural language and also by manipulation of tools to accomplish tasks. He/she does it with a virtual agent, the latter being his/her partner in the interaction. The task is a pretext to install a dialogue between the learner and the companion. Goal-oriented interaction and dialogue are the key concepts of the "actional" and communicative approach. Works accomplished in Human Computer Dialogue (HCD) give a slot of reusable techniques and models in order to manage and structure the dialogue and the interaction [9]. A lot of work has already been done in tutorial dialogues in education [1] but we believe HCD could be used in a different way, not only as a tutorial one but also to provide a discussing companion to the learner implicated in an activity. Around this activity, an environment has to be created to permit the learner to get clues and explanations about the activity he/she performs. This environment could be seen as a pedagogical environment, including the virtual world where the interaction takes place. This environment includes another virtual agent that we call a tutor.

This paper illustrates our approach and is divided into three parts. The first one describes the environment in regard to the activities. The second one explains how the system can manage the interaction. The third one links the activity and the interaction problems.

2   Environment and Activities

This section describes first the environment and the activities possible in such an environment.

2.1   Environment

This description doesn't include considerations about the pedagogical dimension (and then considerations about the interface that should be imagined to support it) but it only deals with the world where the learner is implicated in an activity with a partner. The user is facing an interface representing a virtual world currently implemented as a classic 2D graphic environment. This virtual world can be described in terms of actors, accessories and a set. One actor is implicated in an activity (a problem situation) with the learner: this is the virtual partner. The accessories are tools and objects useful for the activity. The set is meant to be as close as possible to the authentic context where the activity occurs. Some objects can be included directly into the set but can't be used in any ways by the learner or the virtual partner.

The learner and the virtual partner can act within this world. Two ways of acting in the world exist, there are verbal actions and non-verbal actions. The user dialogues with his/her partner via a dialog panel and can manipulate directly objects and tools on the interface to complete the requested tasks. The virtual partner is also designed to act on the objects of the world and to dialogue with the learner.

The non verbal actions that the learner can perform on the interface are the following: pointing out an object or a place (click / double-click on the object / place), moving an object (drag and drop the object), putting two objects in relation (drag and drop the object on an other).

With these specifications, activities, being the accomplishment of tasks, can take place. For example, if the world is a kitchen, the virtual partner would be a kitchen boy, the accessories would be common kitchen tools and ingredients, and the task could be the preparation of a meal with some interactive specifications depending on learning objectives. We can represent the model of this environment on Figure 1.

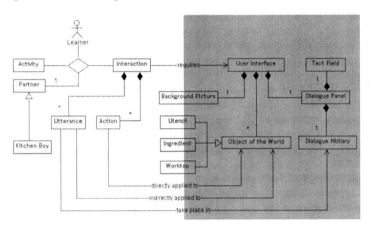

Fig. 1. The environment in the cooking domain example (UML diagram)

2.2   Activities

The activities constitute an essential point of our approach. An activity is a situation in which the knowledge is embedded in the interaction between the learner and the environment. Our definition of a pedagogical activity is close to the task approach (as a general didactic framework) as seen by the didactic engineering in a language class [5], the latter including both "actional" and communicative dimensions. In this section, first, we present the points we have retained for our issue. Afterwards, we describe a model that defines an activity when using an interactive learning environment. Then, we mention the actors implicated in this activity and their different roles. Then, the global structure of the activity is presented.

2.2.1 The Task Approach
The didactic task approach is characterized by six points [5]:

1. The tasks request language use and are organized around a problem situation.
2. The tasks accomplishment implicates the use of different means.
3. The problem situation creates a context in which each linguistic form gets its meaning.

4. The proposed task anticipates and actualizes procedures of use equivalent to those used outside of the class.
5. The tasks are structured in different linked stages, determined by the product to develop and by pedagogical criteria.
6. The contents and results are relatively open.

Our approach includes the three first characteristics. The first is represented by the fact that the learner is directly implicated in an activity (depending on the problem situation) and that language use is requested. The second deals with the different means of help and evaluation given to the learner. The third is about the contents of the interaction, those contents being organized around the problem situation, we will detail them later when describing the interactive possibilities. The fourth deals with how the accomplished task can change the way the learner uses language, including its use in everyday life. This is the goal of such an environment by providing problem situations close to everyday life. We assume it is possible to manage to reach such goals. The fifth one seems unrealistic in a CALL environment, we can not really control the learner use in a long term perspective and know about his/her real skills and capacities, but we can give him/her a picture of what he/she can do at a given time in a given situation and the help to permit him/her to gain his/her missing competencies. The sixth could be divided following the two mentioned concepts: in a CALL environment, it seems difficult to have really open contents, but results mostly depend on the learner's attitudes.

The learner is in fact implicated into two different levels of activity, defining two levels of interaction at the same time for the learner, one we could call pedagogical interaction including the other one linked to the completing of the task.

2.2.2   A Model to Define an Activity in an Interactive Learning Environment

This model comes from researches performed around the concept of interaction in learning environments [4] [6]. Those environments were dedicated to mathematics learning but their conclusions are interesting in our study. One activity (they are called interaction situation in the references) is defined by five characteristics:

1. The "learning objectives" (skills or competencies the learner should gain).
2. The "problem situation" the learner has to solve.
3. The "data" (problem state), the "tools" (domain tools, help) given to the student to solve the problem;
4. The learner's possible reactions.
5. The system's reactions

We can take this model and adapt it to design precisely our situation: (1) the learning objectives define the skills and competencies that can be tested and are meant to be acquired in the interaction; (2) the problem situation is a task accomplishment; (3) the "data" are defined by the way the task has been completed (the activity state); (4) the learner's reactions would be changed here into the learner's actions, those actions being possible verbal or non-verbal acts. Those actions have to be included in the context they occur, to get their meanings; (5) the system's reactions at this level of interaction are constituted by the tutor's interventions. To precise this idea, at the second level of interaction, during the problem situation solving, the system's reactions are constituted by the partner's interventions.

2.2.3 The Virtual Agents

To create a social context into the environment, we have chosen the idea of having companions to participate in the interaction. Some interesting works have already been done in this research field [8] and we have decided to have two virtual agents to interact with the learner. One is a partner, the other, a tutor. The learner interacts with those two characters:

- The partner is the character implicated in the problem situation with the learner. The problem situation is organized in a way that the learner and this partner must communicate to manage to succeed in the problem solving. Its role is to make the learner dialogue and act. The organization of the dialogue is detailed in section 3.

- The tutor is meant to present the task to complete, to help the learner if he/she is stuck during the interaction with the partner. Its role is also to present the results at the end of the activity to point out to the learner what was done correctly and what was not done correctly.

2.2.4 The Activity's Global Structure

The pedagogical activity takes place through three stages:

1. The problem situation is presented to the learner by the tutor.
2. The learner is implicated in a task (the problem situation) to complete with a partner. The tutor can give him/her clues or help during the interaction.
3. The learner receives results of the evaluation made with the interaction marks. This evaluation is given by the tutor.

The two levels of interaction appear clearly here: one happening all along the pedagogical activity, the other one only during the second stage when the user is interacting also with the partner in the problem situation. The problem situation is a pretext to install an interaction between the learner and the partner. The problem situation is defined by an applicative task and the competencies involved in the interaction. This dialogue induces that the learner uses his/her communicative competencies to manage to complete the task, i.e. resolving the problem situation. The nature of the task influences the nature of the interaction and thereby, the nature of the dialogue exchanges. The nature of the exchanges, delimited by the task nature, can also be influenced by the partner interventions and then engage some competencies of the learner. Those competencies can then be evaluated, but this article does not deal nor with natural language processing problems nor with the evaluation of the learner's interventions. Figure 2 presents the activity global structure.

The next section deals with the organization of the interaction between the learner and the system when implicated in the second stage.

3   Interaction Managing Model

The key concept in such a kind of environment is interaction. We need to identify the elements needed to design the model of interaction between the user and the system

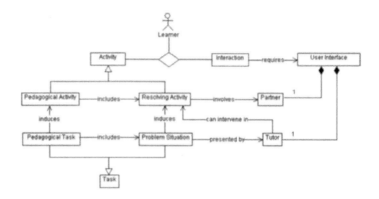

Fig. 2. Task, activity, partner and tutor (UML diagram)

(via the partner) during an activity. From the system, we must have a representation of the context in which the interaction happens, and a set of possible attitudes and reactions towards the learner's acts. With these considerations, we can attempt to build a model to manage the interaction.

3.1   Context

To understand the learner's acts on the interface, the context is essential. Two dimensions define the context in which the interaction occurs: the state of the world and the state of the activity. The state of the world is defined by the state of the objects (position, physical characteristics, etc.). The state of the activity is defined by how far and how the task has been accomplished. To be able to represent the state of the activity, we need a model of the task to complete.

To design the task precisely, we can use the Task-Method paradigm [13]. This model permits to break the task down in different sub-tasks by the ways of different methods. Two types of methods exist: the decomposition methods which break down tasks into sub-tasks (and recursively) and the operational methods which constitute the leaves of the task-tree by determining the procedure to be carried out. Inside this kind of representation, we must also have a correct relation between verbal and non-verbal acts. One verbal act could be replaced by a non-verbal act by the learner or the virtual partner in the interaction and conversely.

With such a representation, we can observe the activity issued from the task (the accomplished sub-tasks, the operations still to perform to reach the task or sub-tasks' goals). This permits to see the actual state of the activity (where we are in the task completing) and the near future of the task (where the activity seems to tend). This makes it possible to see if the user is acting correctly or if he/she is diverging from the given task. The world and the activity states are strongly linked because the task may implicate special positions or actions for some specified tools.

3.2   System Reactions Inside the Interaction

The system is requested to be able to react to the learner's acts. The representations of those reactions towards the learner are done through the attitudes and interventions of the two virtual agents. The context, described in the previous section, gives a framework in which the learner's acts can be interpreted. If the learner is acting correctly without any mistakes, the virtual partner keeps on going in the activity.

But the learner can also perform acts that the system (represented by the virtual partner) might not understand. Different kinds of misunderstandings or non-expected phenomena are possible. There can be linguistic problems in an utterance of the learner. There can be unexpected acts from the learner with some objects or tools in the world in the task context. There can also be inconstancies between what the learner means in the dialogue with the virtual partner and the acts he/she performs in the world. In these cases, some sub-dialogues not linked directly to the task accomplishment are initiated by the virtual partner to permit understanding. If bigger problems appear, the tutor intervention could be requested.

3.3   Interaction Managing Model

We can now define our model to manage the interaction from the system's point of view. The latter is based on the concept of Minimal Unit of Interaction (MUI) [9]. The MUIs are structures containing a set of information related to an act (utterance or action) of the system (via the virtual partner) and to an act (utterance or action) of the learner. This enables the system to delimit a significant unit of interaction, which then permits the choice of the system reaction. The MUI structure is shown in Figure 3.

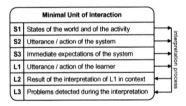

Fig. 3. Model of a Minimal Unit of Interaction

Each MUI is initialized with the three first fields [S1, S2, S3] which define the system's (the partner) utterance/action and its context. The three following fields [L1, L2, L3] are filled after the learner produced an utterance/action coded in L1. The field L2 is the result of the interpretation and L3 gives the problems detected during the interpretation. If any problem occurs, it's then possible to construct a reaction of the system to induce a correction or a reformulation from the learner. These representations of one step of the dialogue (one exchange) can be included in a broader model to manage the interaction.

The interaction managing model is oriented with two different axes: the managing axis (representing time and activity progress) and the incidental axis (representing the solving of linguistic or interactional problems). This approach is inspired by some

HCD works [10]. If there's no problem during the interaction, the managing diagram is implemented: the interaction is happening along the activity axis. But if there's a problem, like the misunderstandings evoked in section 3.2, the incidental diagram is implemented (1). We get there a sub-dialog including several MUIs (2). When this sub-dialog is closed (3), the interrupted interaction can be resumed (4). We can see it on Figure 4. The particularity of these diagrams is to be recursive. This is why the model is able to produce complex hierarchic structures as in Figure 5. This structure contains seven MUIs, three managing diagrams and three incidental diagrams.

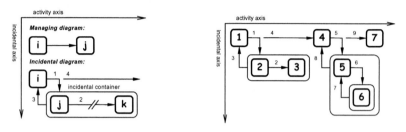

Fig. 4. Managing & incidental diagrams   **Fig. 5.** Example of a hierarchic structure

4   Activities and Interaction

In this section, we illustrate the approach with examples coming from an applicative task and a world we have imagined: the kitchen world and the preparation of a course. This also presents to the learner a cultural dimension which is cooking, one of the main cultural elements in France.

The second stage is organized around a problem situation. The problem situation is defined by an applicative task and the competencies involved during the interaction. So the interaction in the applicative task between the learner and his/her partner can be organized in different activity types depending on the problem situation to be created. The problem situation definition includes different competencies. Some communicative competencies can be identified: comprehension and expression. They define what we call interaction types.

In the comprehension type, the interaction is composed of actions from the learner and utterances from the partner. Conversely in the expression type, the interaction is composed of learner utterances and actions from the partner. With those interaction types, we can define activity types.

From an applicative task, we can imagine the ways to solve it and using the interactive types, we can represent the problem situations that induce the activity types. The activities are designed with two major elements: an interaction type and a stake for the learner in the interaction. The stake permits to define the role of interaction leader in the activity, this role being shared by the learner and the partner. Those activity types can be defined by three characteristics:

– What kind of interaction type occurs in the activity?
– Who's leading the interaction, is it the learner or the virtual partner?
– What's the objective for the learner in this kind of interaction?

With those characteristics, the tutor can present the activities to the learner before he/she gets implicated.

4.1 Two Activity Types to Engage Comprehension

In the first activity type, the leader is the learner. The purpose is to foster the learner's understanding. The latter performs actions on the environment, once given a description of the problem situation solving. The partner's reacts by describing and commenting the actions. In the kitchen context, the learner can prepare a course. The kitchen boy describes and comments what the learner is doing.

In the second activity type, the leader is the partner. The purpose is to test the learner's understanding of the partner's instructions. In the kitchen context, the kitchen boy dictates the recipe to the learner. The learner tries to execute it. The learner's actions permit an evaluation of his/her comprehension.

4.2 Two Activity Types to Engage Expression

In the third activity type, the leader is the learner. The purpose is to make the learner express himself/herself concerning a request of the partner in an activity. The request is supposed to be understandable by the learner; the goal is to see what the user produces from the request. In the kitchen context, the kitchen boy asks the learner to dictate him the recipe to the kitchen boy, and the kitchen boy tries to execute it.

In the fourth activity type, the leader is the partner. The purpose is to make the learner express himself/herself by analyzing and describing the partner's actions. The learner describes what the partner is doing. In the kitchen context, the kitchen boy prepares a course and asks the learner to describe his/her actions.

Other activities can be imagined but it's too early to present them. They could implicate more dialogue interaction between the learner and his/her partner. Other applicative tasks can give facilities to create other activity types.

5 Conclusion

In this paper, we present a work in progress concerning the conception of a Computer Assisted Language Learning (CALL) environment based on considerations coming from the communicative and "actional" approaches. These considerations bring us to focus more on the interactional aspects of the language than on its grammatical aspects. The objective is to improve the learner's linguistic and communicative competencies by engaging him/her in activities which require interactions with a partner. This is a major constraint to design the activities. In this context, we also need a model of interaction which can manage communication problems. So we bring up a model giving a structured representation of the interaction based on works about Human-Computer Dialogue.

At the moment, a "Wizard of Oz" experimentation allows us to validate our approach and we have developed a prototype of the environment including two simple activities. The dialogue model has been implemented in several systems and has been validated.

References

1. Aleven, V.: Tutorial Dialogue Systems. In: proceedings of Workshop at AI-ED'2001 10th International Conference on Artificial Intelligence in Education, San Antonio, USA (2001)
2. Boylan, P., Micarelli, A.:Learning languages as "culture" with CALL. Calvi, L., Geerts, W. (eds.), CALL, Culture and the language curriculum, London, Springer (1998) 60–72
3. Council of Europe: Common European framework for languages. CUP (2001)
4. Delozanne, E.: Explications en EIAO, études à partir d'ELISE, un logiciel pour entraîner à une méthode de calcul de primitives. Thèse de l'Université du Maine (1992)
5. Dolz, J., Scheunwly, B., Thévenaz, T., Wirthner, M.: Les tâches et leurs entours en classe de français. Colloque DFLM (2001)
6. Dubourg, X.: Modélisation de l'interaction en EIAO, une approche évènementielle pour la réalisation du système REPERES. Thèse de l'Université de Caen (1995)
7. Hamburger, H.: Foreign language immersion: Science, practice, and a System. In: JAIED Special Issue on Language Learning, Vol. 5(4) (1994) 429–453
8. Hietala, P., Niemirepo, T.: The competence of learning companion agents. In: International Journal of Artificial Intelligence, n°8 (1998) 178–192
9. Lehuen, J.: A Dialogue-Based Architecture for Computer Aided Language Learning. In: Papers from the AAAI Fall Symposium on Building Dialogue Systems for Tutorial Applications, Cape-Cod, USA (2000) 20–27
10. Luzzati, D.: A Dynamic Dialogue Model for Human-Machine Communication. In: The Structure of Multimodal Dialogue II, Taylor, Néel & Bouwhuis (eds.), Benjamins, Amsterdam (2000) 207–221
11. Ogata, H., Liu, Y., Ochi, Y., Yano, Y.: Agent-Mediated Language-Learning Environment based on Communicative Gaps, Gauthier, Frasson, Van Lehn (eds.), ITS'2000, Montréal (2000) 454–463
12. Reeder, F.: Could you repeat the question? In: Papers from the AAAI Fall Symposium on Building Dialogue Systems for Tutorial Applications, Cape-Cod, USA (2000) 144–147
13. Trichet, F., Tchounikine, P.: DSTM: a framework to operationalize and refine a Problem-Solving Method modeled in terms of Tasks and Methods. In: International Journal of Experts Systems and Methods, 16 (1999) 105–120

Deriving Acquisition Principles from Tutoring Principles

Jihie Kim and Yolanda Gil

Information Sciences Institute, University of Southern California
4676 Admiralty Way, Marina del Rey, CA 90292, U.S.A.
{jihie, gil}@isi.edu

Abstract. This paper describes our analysis of the literature on tutorial dialogues and presents a compilation of useful principles that students and teachers typically follow in making tutoring interactions successful. The compilation is done in the context of making use of those principles in building knowledge acquisition interfaces since acquisition interfaces can be seen as students acquiring knowledge from the user. We plan to use these ideas in our future work to develop more proactive and effective acquisition interfaces.

1 Introduction

Transferring knowledge from humans to computers has proven to be an extremely challenging task. Over the last two decades, an array of approaches to interactive knowledge acquisition have been proposed. Some tools accept rules and check them against other existing rules [13,22]. Some tools acquire knowledge suitable for specific tasks and problem solving strategies [29]. Other tools focus on detecting errors in the knowledge specified by the user [21,23,31]. Some systems use a variety of elicitation techniques to acquire descriptive knowledge [18,35] often in semi-formal forms. There are some isolated reports of users with no formal background in computer science that are now able to use acquisition tools to build sizeable knowledge bases [24,14,10]. However, the majority of the burden of the acquisition task still remains with the user. Users have to decide what, how, and when to teach the system. Current acquisition tools do not take the kind of initiative and collaborative attitude that one would expect of a good student, mostly reacting to the user's actions instead of being proactive learners.

We set off to investigate how the dynamics of tutor-student interactions could be used to make acquisition tools better students to further support users in their role of tutors of computers. Given the success in deploying educational systems in schools and their reported effectiveness in raising student grades [26], we expected the tutoring literature to have useful principles that we could exploit. Another strength of tutoring work is that it is typically motivated by extensive analysis of human tutorial dialogues [17], which the knowledge acquisition literature lacks.

This paper describes our analysis of the literature on tutorial dialogues and presents a compilation of useful principles that students and teachers follow in

S.A. Cerri, G. Gouardères, and F. Paraguaçu (Eds.): ITS 2002, LNCS 2363, pp. 661–670, 2002.
© Springer-Verlag Berlin Heidelberg 2002

making tutoring interactions successful and that could be useful in the context of interactive acquisition tools. We plan to use these ideas in our future work to develop more proactive acquisition interfaces.

The paper begins with a discussion of the similarities and differences between instructional systems (educational software and human tutoring) and interactive acquisition tools. We then present fourteen learning principles that we believe can be immediately incorporated into our current tools. Finally, we describe how acquisition interfaces can interact with users using these principles.

2   Tutorial Dialogues in Instructional Systems and in Interactive Knowledge Acquisition

In instructional systems (both educational software and intelligent tutoring systems), the tutor's role is to help the user (student) achieve some degree of proficiency in a certain topic (the lesson). In interactive acquisition interfaces, these roles are reversed. Acquisition tools can be seen as students learning new knowledge from the user (teacher) and they should be able to use some of the strategies that good learners pursue during a tutoring dialogue. Ideally, it should also be able to supplement the user's skills as a teacher by helping the user pursue effective tutoring techniques. This would help the user teach the material better and faster to the system, as well as delegate some of the tutor functions over to the system.

In essence, we are trying to investigate what it takes to create a good student, while most ITS work has focused on creating good teachers. We believe that the work in educational systems and acquisition systems share a lot of issues and they may be able to contribute to each other in many ways. In fact there has been work that bridges these two communities. For example, there have been recent interests in acquiring knowledge for intelligent tutoring systems [34]. We think that technology built by the knowledge acquisition community will be useful for building tools to help users develop the knowledge and models used in ITS.

There are some issues that interactive acquisition interfaces will not face. Human students in need of tutoring often have a lack of motivation that the instructional system has to address [28]. Instructional systems need to use special tactics to promote deep learning, such as giving incremental hints instead of showing the student the correct answers. Finally, our student will not be subject to the cognitive limitations of a typical human student, and can exploit memory and computational skills that would be exceptional (if not infrequent) for human students.

3   Principles in Teaching and Learning

We have been investigating various tutoring principles[1] used by human tutors and educational software [16,41,17]. Although human tutors provide more flexi-

---

[1] In the tutoring literature these are often referred to as tutoring strategies. We prefer to refer to them as tutoring principles, since we found that they can be implemented

ble support, the tutoring principles supported by educational software are often inspired by human tutors [33] and we derive learning principles from both. Table 1 shows a summary of the principles that we found useful. The rest of this section describes these principles and discusses how they could be adopted in acquisition systems. More details on how current acquisition techniques are related to these principles are described in [20].

Instructional systems contain other components such as student models and domain models, but here we are focusing on tutoring principles and leave user modeling as future work.

Table 1. Some Tutoring and Learning Principles

Teaching/Learning principle	Tutoring literature
Introduce lesson topics and goals	Atlas-Andes, Meno-Tutor, Human tutorial dialog human learning
Use topics of the lesson as a guide	BE&E, UMFE
Subsumption to existing cognitive structure	human learning, WHY, Atlas-Andes
Immediate feedback	SOPHIE, Auto-Tutor, LISP tutor Human tutorial dialog, human learning
Generate educated guesses	Human tutorial dialog, QUADRATIC, PACT
Keep on track	GUIDON, SCHOLAR, TRAIN-Tutor
Indicate lack of understanding	Human tutorial dialog, WHY
Detect and fix "buggy" knowledge	SCHOLAR, Meno-Tutor, WHY, Buggy, CIRCSIM human learning
Learn deep models	PACT, Atlas-Andes
Learn domain language	Atlas-Andes, Meno-Tutor
Keep track of correct answers	Atlas-Andes
Prioritize learning tasks	WHY
Limit the nesting of the lesson to a handful	Atlas
Summarize what was learned	EXCHECK, TRAIN-Tutor, Meno-Tutor
Assess learned knowledge	WEST, Human tutorial dialog

References: Atlas [40], Atlas-Andes[37], BE&E [12], Buggy [6], CIRCSIM-tutor [44], EXCHECK [30], GUIDON [9], Human tutorial dialog [17], human learning [33,19,27, 3,11,15], LISP Tutor [2], Meno-Tutor [43], PACT [1], QUADRATIC [36], SCHOLAR [8], SOPHIE [5], TRAIN-Tutor [42], UMFE [38], WEST [7], WHY [39].

– **Introduce lesson topics and goals.**

In the beginning of the lesson, tutors often outline the topics to be learned during the session and try to assess the student's prior knowledge on these topics. For example, the advance organizer approach [3] lets the student see the big picture of what is to be learned and provides what the tutor's argument will be in order to bridge the gap between what the student may already know and what the student should learn. In educational systems, such as Meno-Tutor [43], as the tutor introduces general topics it asks exploratory questions in order to assess the student's prior knowledge. In fact,

---

as goals, strategies, or plans during the dialogue, or simply be taken into account in the design of the interaction.

there are similar findings in teacher-student dialogs. Teachers often let students express how good or bad they are at given topic [17].

Adopting the above tutoring principle, acquisition tools should start their dialogue by asking for the topic of the current lesson and establish assumed prior knowledge. The topic of the lesson could be given as a set of terms to be defined, or a set of test problems that the system should be able to solve at the end of the lesson. Once the user specifies the topic, the system may assist the user to assess the current knowledge base in terms of the topic and bring up possibly relevant background knowledge. Missing prior knowledge can prompt a sub-dialogue for a background lesson.

– **Use topics of the lesson as a guide.**
In planning tutorial dialogues, instructional systems check what is being learned against the topics of the lesson [12] and try to avoid unfocused dialogue and digressions. In the process of learning, the terms brought up during the lesson are connected to the concepts learned [38].

As in instructional systems, acquisition tools can use the topics of the lesson in checking how much progress the user made in building the knowledge base and in relating the terms introduced in the session to those topics.

– **Subsumption to existing cognitive structure.**
The subsumption theory by Ausubel [3] emphasizes that learning new material involves relating it to relevant ideas in the existing cognitive structure. The integration of new material with previous information can be done by analogies, generalizations and checking consistency. Through analogy, novel situations and problems can be understood in terms of familiar ones [19]. Effective human tutors ask for similarities and differences for similar cases [11]. In educational systems such as Atlas-Andes [37], the system points out differences between similar objects (e.g., speed vs. velocity) in terms of what they are and how they are calculated. Human tutors help students generalize when there are several similar cases [11]. For example, they suggest or point out the need to formulate a rule for similar cases by asking how the values of certain factors are related to the values of the dependent variables. Educational systems, such as Atlas [40], encourage students to abstract plans from the details to see the basic approach behind problem solving. Finally, cognitive dissonance theory [15] points out that people tend to seek consistency among their cognitions (i.e., beliefs, opinions). When there is an inconsistency (dissonance), something must change to eliminate the dissonance.

Acquisition systems should follow this principle and assist users to: 1) learn new concepts from analogous concepts that already exist, 2) generalize definitions if similar things exist (and there could be plausible generalizations), and 3) make all new definitions consistent with existing knowledge.

– **Immediate feedback.**
Many educational systems provide immediate feedback on the quality of student's responses [5,2]. The studies of feedback in a variety of instructional

context find that immediate feedback is much more effective than feedback received after a delay [27]. Similarly, in the tutorial dialog study by Fox [17], tutors show immediate recognition of every step the student makes and their silence tends to presage the student's confusion. It is reported that in providing feedback, human tutors are more flexible than educational software, using high bandwidth communication to guide the students [33].

Based on this principle, we can make acquisition tools more actively involved in providing and obtaining feedback. For example, in addition to reporting how newly entered knowledge was understood and what errors were found, tools can ask for feedback on how results or answers being generated match the user's expectation.

- **Generate educated guesses.**
  Some educational systems invite guesses on questions either in the process of letting the student discover the answers [36] or in the process of assessing the student's knowledge[1]. Likewise, in the studies of human tutoring, student often display their understanding by finishing the tutor's utterance and the tutor finds out what students understood by inviting their guesses (utterance completion strategy) [17].

  We can extend the existing capabilities of acquisition tools to provide educated guesses on how to fix problems based on their context. For example if there are salient features such as an action that can fix two errors at the same time, maybe it should be suggested as a most promising next step. If the guesses were wrong, it may be an indication of further missing knowledge and the system can show its surprise to the user and ask for further help.

- **Keep on track.**
  If the student gives an incorrect answer, the tutor must immediately get the student back on track [8]. Some systems also detect change of directions [42] or check if the questions are irrelevant to the case at hand [9].

  Novice users of interactive acquisition interfaces often have difficulty in understanding if they are on the right track and if they are making progress [24]. We believe that acquisition interfaces should keep track of information regarding the progress made throughout the session and the tasks that remain to be addressed in the dialogue.

- **Indicate lack of understanding.**
  Studies in human tutoring show cases where students themselves indicate lack of understanding of introduced terms [17], but tutors also point out the specific aspects that need to be understood by the student.[11].

  Some acquisition tools indicate to the user what is missing in the knowledge base [24] and users often use it to decide what to do next. Diagnosis questions should be useful to detect misunderstandings and missing knowledge.

- **Detect and fix "buggy" knowledge.**
  Many educational systems have a tutoring goal of diagnosing the student's "bugs" [43,39,6] and question answering is often used in checking student's

knowledge. However, simply telling that an error has occurred is much less useful than reminding the student of the current goal or pointing out a feature of the error [32]. If there are insufficient or unnecessary factors in a student's answers, experienced tutors pick counter examples to highlight the problem [11]. In the process of checking, when the tutor does not understand the answer, sometimes the student is asked to rephrase the answer [8].

Most acquisition systems have a way of detecting errors and gaps in the knowledge base. However, as in the case of educational systems, instead of simply telling the errors found it is more useful to show the explanation of how and where the errors were found.

- **Learn deep models.**
The tutor and the student should focus on deep conceptual models and explanations rather than superficial ones [40]. Students should not only be expected to give the right answer but to do so for the right reasons. For example, when the student's answer is right, educational systems ask how the correct answer is generated [1,40]. In some cases, to be able to ensure that the student understood the explanation educational systems use a set of check questions [37]. Studies of human tutoring show that students themselves occasionally try to check the reasoning behind the answers provided [17].

Current acquisition tools do not have a good basis to evaluate or pursue depth in their knowledge base, though this is a long recognized shortcoming. One thing acquisition tools can do is to provide a way of enforcing users to check how the answers were generated and see if the system provides the right answer for the right reasons.

- **Learn domain language.**
Another interesting aspect of a lesson is learning to describe the new knowledge in terms that are appropriate in the domain at hand. Educators want to ensure that the students learn to talk science as a part of understanding of the science [40]. Teaching is more difficult when the student organizes and talks about knowledge in a different way than the tutor does [43].

Acquiring domain language has not been a focus of knowledge base development in general. If an acquisition tool has a notion of checking the terms the users bring up in the process of entering knowledge, they can be highlighted to draw the user's attention.

- **Keep track of correct answers.**
Instructional systems keep track of the questions that the student is able to answer correctly as well as those answered incorrectly, which drives further interactions with the student. Some systems try more specific or simpler version of questions to keep better track of progress. [37].

Some acquisition tools keep track of whether some set of test cases are answered correctly. However, they can be more actively used in guiding the acquisition dialog in terms of helping the user understand the current status of the knowledge base. For example, the acquisition tool can volunteer its own assessment of the kinds of questions that can be answered.

- **Prioritize learning tasks.**
  To handle multiple tasks and sub-tasks to be done, educational systems use priority rules. For example, systems can focus on errors before omissions and shorter fixes before longer fixes, prior steps before later steps, etc [11].

  Similarly, some acquisition systems use a priority scheme to organize errors based on their type and the amount of help the system can provide.

- **Limit the nesting of the lesson.**
  It appears that it is useful to limit the nesting of lessons to a handful [40], which seems it would help our acquisition tools keep track of what is going on as much as it helps a human student.

- **Summarize back to teacher what was learned.**
  Many educational systems summarize the highlights at the end of the lesson [43,30]. For example, EXCHECK prints out review of the proof for the student to give a clear picture of what has been done [30]. In some systems, when the tutor has given several hints, a summary may be given to ensure that the student has correct information just in case the student gave right answer by following hints without understanding the procedures [42].

  Acquisition tools do not actively provide a summary unless the user explicitly queries the knowledge base. Providing a summary of what has been learned in terms of the purpose of the lesson will be very useful for the user.

- **Assess learned knowledge.**
  In their dialogs with human tutors, students often indicate how well they understand the topic as well as what has been learned [17]. Also some educational systems have a way of isolating the weaknesses in the student's knowledge and propose further lessons on those areas [7].

  Only some acquisition tools perform this kind of assessment. We believe that volunteering the assessment of how well the system understands certain topics will be very useful for the users.

4 Using Principles in Knowledge Acquisition

Based on our observations of teaching and learning principles described in the previous section, we are developing a system called SLICK². The principles are used to steer the dialog with the user, and result in a more goal-oriented behavior that makes the system a more proactive learner.

We have designed SLICK as a front-end dialogue tool that can be layered over the functionality of existing acquisition interfaces. We are exploring the use of SLICK with SHAKEN [10], a tool that allows end users to specify process models in terms of their substeps and the objects involved, uses graphical input,

---

² Skills for Learning to Interactively Capture Knowledge

and allows users to test the process model by asking questions and running a simulation. We are also using SLICK as a front-end dialogue tool for EXPECT [4], a tool that allows users to specify problem solving in terms of methods and submethods, uses a structured editor for input, and allows users to pose both parameterized and instantiated problems for testing. In each case, the general learning principles described in this paper are operationalized by taking into account the features of the specific acquisition interface, in terms of the kinds of target knowledge they capture, the input modality offered to the user, and the testing and error checking strategies used. For example, the topic of the lesson in SHAKEN is a top-level process description and a set of objects that are involved in that process, while in EXPECT the topic of the lesson is given by a set of top-level problem solving goals. SLICK analyzes whether new terms introduced by the user relate to the topic of the lesson, checking this in SHAKEN by querying their appearance in the current expanded process description details and in EXPECT by checking their use in problem solving trees. We are also investigating how to include in SLICK useful dialogue management and user interaction techniques, as well as self-awareness capabilities that would enable it to assess the system's competence and confidence on the lesson topics as the dialogue with the user progresses.

5   Conclusion and Future Work

We have presented an analysis of instructional systems in terms of tutoring and learning principles and described how they could be useful in the context of interactive acquisition tools. We believe that they will play a central role in making acquisition tools proactive learners. We have started to incorporate these principles in our work and we are planning to perform user studies to collect feedback on the effectiveness of this addition.

Acknowledgments. This research was funded by the DARPA Rapid Knowledge Formation (RKF) program with award number N66001-00-C-8018. We would like to thank Ken Forbus, Lewis Johnson, Jeff Rickel, Paul Rosenbloom, David Traum, and Jim Blythe on their insightful comments on earlier drafts.

References

1. Aleven, V. & Koedinger, K. (2000). The need for tutorial dialog to support self-explanation. In *Proceedings of the AAAI Fall Symposium on Building Dialogue Systems for Tutorial Applications*.
2. Anderson, J. R., Conrad, F. G., & Corbett, A. T. (1989). Skill acquisition and the lisp tutor. *Cognitive Science*, 13:467–506.
3. Ausubel, D. (1968). *Educational psychology: A cognitive approach*. New York, Holt, Rinehart and Winston.
4. Blythe, J.; Kim, J.; Ramachandran, S.; and Gil, Y. (2001). An integrated environment for knowledge acquisition. In *Proceedings of the IUI-2001*.

5. Brown, J. S., Burton, R., & de Kleer, J. (1982). Pedagogical natural language and knowledge engineering techniques in SOPHIE I, II, III. In Derek, S. & Brown, J. S., (Eds.), *Intelligent Tutoring Systems*. New York, Academic Press.

6. Brown, J. S. & Burton, R. R. (1978). Diagnostic models for procedural bugs in basic mathematical skills. *Cognitive Science*, 2:155–191.

7. Burton, R. & Brown, J. (1979). An investigation of computer coaching for informal learning activities. *International Journal of Man-Machine Studies*, 11:5–24.

8. Carbonell, J. R. (1970). AI in CAI: An artificial intelligence approach to computer-assisted instruction. *IEEE Transactions on Man-Machine Systems*, 11(4):190–202.

9. Clancey, W., (Ed.) (1987). *Knowledge-Based Tutoring:The GUIDON Program*. MIT press.

10. Clark, P., Thompson, J., Barker, K., Porter, B., Chaudhri, V., Rodriguez, A., Thomere, J., Mishra, S., Gil, Y., Hayes, P., & Reichherzer, T. (2001). Knowledge entry as the graphical assembly of components. In *Proceedings of K-CAP-2001*.

11. Collins, A. & Stevens, A. L. (1982). Goals and strategies of inquiry teachers. *Advances in Instructional Psychology*, 2:65–119.

12. Core, M. G., Moore, J. D., & Zinn, C. (2000). Supporting constructive learning with a feedback planner. In *Proceedings of the AAAI Fall Symposium on Building Dialogue Systems for Tutorial Applications*.

13. Davis, R. (1979). Interactive transfer of expertise: Acquisition of new inference rules. *Artificial Intelligence*, 12:121–157.

14. Eriksson, H., Shahar, Y., Tu, S. W., Puerta, A. R., & Musen, M. (1995). Task modeling with reusable problem-solving methods. *Artificial Intelligence*, 79:293–326.

15. Festinger, L. (1957). *A Theory of Cognitive Dissonance*. Stanford University Press.

16. Forbus, K. & Feltovich, P., (Eds.) (2001). *Smart Machines in Education*. AAAI press.

17. Fox, B. (1993). *The Human Tutorial Dialog Project*. Lawrence Erlbaum.

18. Gaines, B. R. & Shaw, M. (1993). Knowledge acquisition tools based on personal construct psychology. *The Knowledge Engineering Review*, 8(1):49–85.

19. Gentner, D., Holyoak, K. J., & Kokinov, B. N., (Eds.) (2001). *The analogical mind: Perspectives from cognitive science*. MIT press.

20. Gil, Y. & Kim, J. (2002). Interactive knowledge acquisition tools: A tutoring perspective. http://www.isi.edu/expect/papers/Interactive-KA-Tools-gil-kim-02.pdf (internal project report).

21. Gil, Y. & Melz, E. (1996). Explicit representations of problem-solving strategies to support knowledge acquisition. In *Proceedings of the Thirteenth National Conference on Artificial Intelligence*.

22. Ginsberg, A., Weiss, S., & Politakis, P. (1985). SEEK2: A generalized approach to automatic knowledge base refinement. In *Proceedings of IJCAI-85*.

23. Kim, J. & Gil, Y. (1999). Deriving expectations to guide knowledge base creation. In *Proceedings of the Sixteenth National Conference on Artificial Intelligence*, pp. 235–241.

24. Kim, J. & Gil, Y. (2000). Acquiring problem-solving knowledge from end users: Putting interdependency models to the test. In *Proceedings of the Seventeenth National Conference on Artificial Intelligence*.

25. Kim, J. & Gil, Y. (2002). Proactive learning for interactive knowledge capture. http://www.isi.edu/expect/papers/KA-Dialog-Kim-Gil-02.pdf (internal project report).

26. Koedinger, K., Anderson, J., Hadley, W., & Mark, M. (1997). Intelligent tutoring goes to school in the big city. *International Journal of Artificial Intelligence in Education*, 8:30–43.
27. Kulik, J. & Kulik, C. (1988). Timing of feedback and verbal learning. *Review of Educational Research*, 58:79–97.
28. Lepper, M., Woolverton, M., Mumme, D., & Gurtner, J. (1993). Motivational techniques of expert human tutors: Lesson for the design of computer-based tutors. In Lajoie, S. & Derry, S., (Eds.), *Computers as Cognitive Tools*, pp. 75–105. Hillsdale.
29. Marcus, S. & McDermott, J. (1989). SALT: A knowledge acquisition language for propose-and-revise systems. *Artificial Intelligence*, 39(1):1–37.
30. McDonald, J. (1981). The EXCHECK CAI system. In Suppes, P., (Ed.), *University-level Computer-assisted Instruction at Stanford: 1968-1980*. Stanford.
31. McGuinness, D. L., Fikes, R., Rice, J., & Wilde, S. (2000). An environment for merging and testing large ontologies. In *Proceedings of KR-2000*.
32. McKendree, J. (1990). Effective feedback content for tutoring complex skills. *Human Computer Interactions*, 5:381–413.
33. Merrill, D. C., Reiser, B. J., Ranney, M., & Trafton, J. G. (1992). Effective tutoring techniques: A comparison of human tutors and intelligent tutoring systems. *The Journal of the Learning Sciences*, 2:277–305.
34. Murray, T. (1999). Authoring intelligent tutoring systems: An analysis of the state of the art. *International Journal of Artificial Intelligence in Education*, 10:98–129.
35. Novak, J., (Ed.) (1998). *Learning, Creating, and Using Knowledge: Concept Maps as Facilitative Tools in Schools and Corporations*. Lawrence Erlbaum.
36. O'Shea, T. (1979). A self-improving Quadratic tutor. *International Journal of Man-Machine Studies*, 11:97–124.
37. Rose, C. P., Jordan, P., Ringenberg, M., Siler, S., VanLehn, K., & Weinstein, A. (2001). Interactive conceptual tutoring in Atlas-Andes. In *Proceedings of AI in Education*.
38. Sleeman, D. H. (1984). Inferring student models for intelligent computer-aided instruction. In Michalski, R. S., Carbonell, J. G., & Mitchell, T. M., (Eds.), *Machine Learning: An Artificial Intelligence Approach*, pp. 483–510. Springer.
39. Stevens, A. & Collins, A. (1977). The goal structure of a Socratic tutor. In *Proceedings of the National ACM Conference*.
40. VanLehn, K., Freedman, R., Pamela, J., Murray, C., Osan, R., Ringenberg, M., Rose, C., Schulze, K., Shelby, R., Treacy, D., Weinstein, A., & Wintersgill, M. (2000). Fading and deepening: The next steps for Andes and other model-tracing tutors. In *Proceedings of ITS-2000*.
41. Wenger, E., (Ed.) (1987). *Artificial Intelligence and Tutoring Systems*. Morgan Kaufmann.
42. Woolf, B. & Allen, J. (2000). Spoken language tutorial dialogue. In *Proceedings of the AAAI Fall Symposium on Building Dialogue Systems for Tutorial Applications*.
43. Woolf, B. P. & McDonald, D. D. (1984). Building a computer tutor: Design issues. *IEEE Computer*, 17(9):61–73.
44. Zhou, Y., Freedman, R., Michael, M. G. J., Rovick, A., & Evens, M. (1999). What should the tutor do when the student cannot answer a question? In *Proceedings of FLAIRS-99*.

Collaborative Discovery Learning of Model Design

Crescencio Bravo[1], Miguel A. Redondo[1], Manuel Ortega[1], and M. Felisa Verdejo[2]

[1]Dpto. de Informática. Universidad de Castilla - La Mancha.
Paseo de la Universidad, 4. 13061 Ciudad Real (Spain)
{cbravo,mredondo,mortega}@inf-cr.uclm.es
[2]Dpto. de Lenguajes y Sistemas Informáticos. Universidad Nacional de Educación a
Distancia. Ciudad Universitaria, s/n. 28040 Madrid (Spain)
felisa@lsi.uned.es

Abstract. Design and simulation environments are tools offering contrasted benefits for discovery learning in multiple domains. However, when these domains are complex the problems that the students have to solve during their learning justify the necessity to carry out the design activity itself in groups. From the perspective of modelling and simulation in collaboration, we present DomoSim-TPC, a system supporting collaborative learning in Domotics[1]. The system provides shared workspaces integrating tools for domain problem solving with generic but customized tools to support collaborative decisions and discussions. The potential of this synthesis to support learning tasks in modelling is described. We outline the mechanisms offered by the system and discuss our solution compared to other relevant systems.

1 Introduction

Computer simulation tools allows nowadays the modelling and simulation of complex problems in very diverse fields such as Engineering, Experimental Sciences, Economy, Statistics, or Sociology. Scientific discovery learning is an approach which considers the learner as an active agent in the knowledge acquisition process. In discovery environments learners are engaged in constructivist activities, and they acquire knowledge through a process of subjective construction starting from the experience rather than through the discovery of an ontological reality [6]. In 1997 a committee of scientific advisers handed the President of the United States of America a list of the most promising constructivist applications and simulations were on top of the list [18]; this gives an idea of the importance of this discipline.

When we face domains requiring modelling and simulation techniques, collaboration is usually necessary [9], this is the case to solve complex design problems. According to Guzdial et al [8], collaboration in problem solving activities provides not only an appropriate performance but also promotes reflection, a mechanism enhancing learning processes. Thus, using this approach: (1) groups of students can solve more interesting and more complex problems than individual students and (2) the students that work in groups need to communicate, make

---

[1] Domotics: It is the technical discipline that studies housing automation. It is also called intelligent building design.

S.A. Cerri, G. Gouardères, and F. Paraguaçu (Eds.): ITS 2002, LNCS 2363, pp. 671–680, 2002.
© Springer-Verlag Berlin Heidelberg 2002

arguments and give opinions to other members of the group, encouraging the kind of reflection that leads to learning.

We have built an environment for collaborative learning of model design that uses simulation. Using this environment the students, organized in groups, can solve problems selected from a collection. We consider design as a discipline that requires the construction of some scenario under a variety of constraints. This scenario is the model that the students will be able to test on a simulation tool. They will obtain a solution to a proposed problem in a refinement process involving guided discussion. The environment itself allows the teachers to manage the problem collection, the definition of activities, the monitoring of the learning process, the tutoring of students and the analysis of the activities.

The domain in which we have materialized our theoretical positions is Domotics. This discipline is taught as a subject in Secondary Education (Technical Training) and in Technical University Colleges of Industrial Engineering in Spain, and it covers the subject of house automation or intelligent buildings design. We have developed a modelling tool including (1) a set of operators relative to different management areas (activators, receivers and systems that have to be placed on the layout of a house), (2) a set of parameters and (3) some relations between the operators [5].

This paper describes our collaborative simulation environment. In section 2 we will refer to simulation applications in which groups of people take part and some systems that make use of simulation in collaboration situations. Then, we will define in detail our environment and the principles under which it has been developed. Finally, some conclusions will be drawn and future work will be outlined.

2   Collaboration and Simulation

CSCL (Computer-Supported Collaborative Learning) is a paradigm that focuses on the social dimension of learning processes and promotes the use of the technology as a tool mediating [11] and facilitating co-constructive activities. It seems interesting to apply CSCL with simulation scenarios. We call this symbiosis Computer-Supported Collaborative Simulation (CSCS).

First of all, let us mention some kinds of simulations that can be confused with this new term or that have similarities with it. **Interactive simulation** is a reproduction of reality, which stimulates the scientific curiosity and research practice. In **distributed simulation** different simulators act as elements of a distributed simulation at a greater scale [12]. A very similar simulation type to the one we propose is **participative simulation**, in which the participants are agents in a simulation such as players in a wide range of computer-supported games [19].

A number of systems exploring the idea of collaborative simulation have been implemented. Following the participative approach we can mention SESAM (Software Engineering by Simulation of Animated Models) [17], created at the University of Stuttgart. It has been developed to study the concepts of Software Engineering and how to apply these concepts to practical situations. The system supports the simulation of the development cycle of a software project, representing software products, documents of diverse types, fictitious participants (clients, project members, etc.) and the evolution of the project in the time line based on a model. A model builder and a player (student) collaboratively analyse the phenomenon of

Software Engineering by means of the construction, validation and refinement of a software project model.

ERCIS is a system of participative and distributed simulation based on DIS (Distributed-Interactive Simulation). DIS is a training system for military applications. It can be used to create a Group-Distance Exercise (GDE), in which participants are distributed in different locations. ERCIS [3] is a system of GDE that supports the teaching in the handling of the RBS-70 missile unit. ERCIS has two main components: the team simulators and the simulation server. The simulation server controls a microworld of the group's environment, including simulation of aircrafts, the exercise scenario and some geographical information. ERCIS has an important pedagogic value. The GDE systems can automate the registration and evaluation of execution statistics. It is also possible to record the sessions and to reproduce them in order to improve the effectiveness in post-action revisions.

Other systems do not follow any of the aforementioned approaches, but they allow some kind of collaboration among the users. Two examples are SIMPLE and LESP.

VacSim [14] is a simulation system designed to learn the basic principles of vacuum-pump technology for semiconductors manufacturing, and it is framed in an environment of engineering learning based on simulation called SIMPLE (Simulated Processes in a Learning Environment). It is based on learning traces, which seem specially interesting in simulations, for example in manufacturing and chemical processes where the sequence and time of the actions can have a dramatic effect in the simulated world. The collaboration is reflected by facilitating the communication between the teacher and the student and among students by sharing execution traces of the simulation.

The LESP[2] environment (Learning Environment for Simulation of Particulate Models of Matter) allows the study of matter as a set of particles. It is based on the combination of multiple representations (macroscopic phenomena in form of particle models, combined with text, animation and videotape) with constructive activities (the learners being creators of theoretical models of particles). LESP combines the easiness of use of a visual learning environment with a complex physical simulation and a modelling program. Its e-mail module allows sending and receiving messages about the built models, enabling the attachment of LESP simulation files; this allows the student-student and teacher-student discussion about the models.

3 Collaborative Simulation for the Learning of Design

We have built a Computer-Supported Collaborative Simulation (CSCS) environ-ment, called DomoSim-TPC, for learning domotic design. It is based on the CSCL principles, developing ideas of Problem-Based Learning [2] and Learning by Design [10]. Its characteristics are described next.

3.1 Description of the Learning Situation

With the use of DomoSim-TPC, teaching Domotics in Secondary Education and University involves also a modification of the educational protocol. First, the teacher

---

[2] http://www.uni-essen.de/chemiedidaktik/LESP/bestellen.html, visited in Jan. 2002.

carries out a presentation of basic theoretical contents. Next, students are organized in small groups whom the teacher assigns the resolution of design problems selected from an available library of problems. The problems have a characterization and include specific didactic objectives according to the criterion of the teachers. The students use DomoSim-TPC to design the models that, they consider, satisfy the requirements of the proposed problem. During this process the learners discuss and justify the design decisions that they have taken, building a common knowledge base. In addition, they can carry out a simulation of the model to test its behaviour in extreme situations and this way to check the fulfilments of the expected requirements. Students work in collaboration and at distance, taking advantage of the enriching aspect provided by the different visions that the students from different colleges have. Finally, teachers and students discuss and reach conclusions about the experience.

3.2 Modular Architecture: Workspaces

The system has three different workspaces with diverse tools. Teachers use the first one, and students use the second one. The third one is a workspace for student-student and teacher-student coordination. In the student's workspace there are two important tools for collaborative problem-solving: (1) the **Planning of Model Design**, that facilitates that the student builds a plan -a set of abstract design actions- by means of an intermediate representation language [15], and (2) the **Model Design and Simulation**, that allows them to refine the previous plan to build a model solution and to test the model by simulation [4]. In the following we focus on the Model Design and Simulation Tool.

3.3 Activities and Problems

The aim students have to achieve is the design of a model solving a particular problem. A problem is described by a formulation, some restrictions, requirements, and the house or building plan to "domotize".

Students are organized in groups and the teacher proposes the realization of problem solving activities to these groups. There is a collection of generic problems, created by experts in the domain and teachers by means of authoring tools. The collection is organized in three complexity levels: high, medium and low. This parameter together with a configurable help level allows the system to offer scaffolding [16] in the learning process. Thus, students will gradually solve problems starting with the ones with smaller complexity to reinforce the intrinsic structure of the problem resolution process. In this way knowledge is built by means of a leverage process of re-elaboration and integration. For difficult problems less detailed help is provided while for easy problems greater help is offered because problems are solved from small to big complexity and when students face a difficult problem they have already solved ones which are easier. Thus, help fades along the learning process.

3.4 Coordination and Communication Tools

In the Coordination space there is a variety of tools allowing the communication and the coordination among the participants: Chat, Recent News Board, Electronic Mail and Session Agenda. During the *model design and simulation* stage two extra synchronous tools can also be used: the Guided Chat and the Decision Making Tool.

Collaborative interactions for problem solving include two interdependent cognitive tasks: solving the problem (model design) and collaborating. Besides task-oriented action, collaboration requires communication to exchange information relative to the domain, to coordinate actions and to reach agreements. Collaborative interactions involve explanation, reflection, verification, discussion, argumentation, etc. For this reason we have decided to include a chat linked to the design tools. This chat is defined as *guided* because it does not allow the introduction of free text. Students have to select from a pre-set of goal-oriented communicative acts. This solution offers two advantages, on one hand students clearly express in a form understandable for everybody their personal perspective, on the other the system provides a structure for the conversation. This approach has been explored in a number of proposals such as the one in Baker & Lund [1].

The Decision-Making Tool proposes a question to the group to reach a decision about some topic. There are three kinds of questions: those that have an affirmative or negative answer, those that have a *real value* as an answer and those that have an alternative between a set of possible answers. When all the students have responded to the question, or there is a configurable timeout, the pooling result is shown in a new window.

3.5 Design and Simulation of the Problem Solution

The Model Design and Simulation Tool accessible from the student's workspace is used to build a solution to a domotic problem. To carry out this process the students of the work group must follow a collaboration protocol [13], used in order to coordinate the phases in a problem solving session. A protocol is described as a state-transition diagram in which each node of the diagram represents a state in the protocol. Each state represents a workspace in which to perform a kind of task. The protocol we propose (fig. 1) presents three nodes matching three different workspaces named "subspaces".

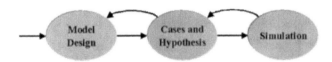

Fig. 1. State diagram of the collaboration protocol.

The first subspace to be accessed when an activity is selected is the Design subspace. Here, students carry out the sub-task of designing a model. When they consider they have solved this phase, they can move to the Simulation Cases and Hypothesis subspace, in which they outline hypothesis and check whether these are verified and they can also propose new test-cases and select another in the case library to run a simulation. Once a case has been chosen, the group can move to the Simulation subspace (fig. 2) to check and evaluate the quality of their solution by observing the behaviour of their model.

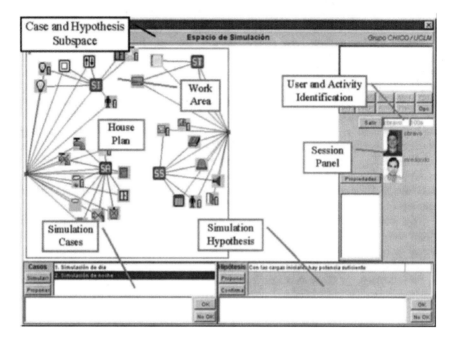

Fig. 2. Simulation case selection and hypothesis verification.

Figure 2 shows the different areas of the window corresponding to the Case and Hypothesis subspace:

- Work area: It is a shared electronic whiteboard where the designed model is displayed; it contains the house plan and the operators. In figure 2 we can see a single room (a lounge) with four subsystems.
- House plan: It is the representation of the plan on which the problem is defined.
- The user and activity identification area.
- Session Panel: It contains the list of participants in the work session.
- Selection and proposal of simulation cases: In this area simulation cases related to the problem and the new ones proposed by the students are shown.
- Outlining and verification of simulation hypothesis: Hypothesis are essential to deeply understand the mechanisms that govern the simulation. The hypothesis are expressed as sentences in natural language. In this area the incorporated hypothesis of the problem and the ones proposed by the students are displayed.

To materialize both the processes of proposition and selection of cases and the proposition and verification of hypothesis we have taken into account the Language/Action Perspective [20]. Communicative acts are carried by *Propose (Proponer)*, *OK*, *NO OK*, *Simulate (Simular)* and *Confirm (Confirma)* buttons that represent speech acts. Once the group have reached consensus about a certain case to simulate, the users can access the Simulation subspace. The Case and Hypothesis panels disappear and the Environment and Guided Chat panels (fig. 3) became visible so that the simulation can start.

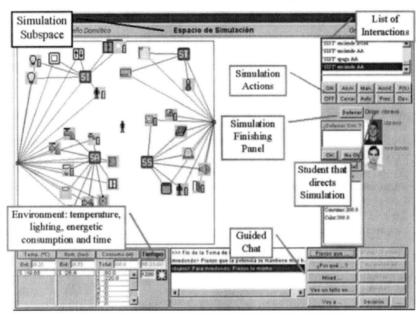

Fig. 3. Collaborative session of simulation in real time.

The system provides for different roles. The student who has proposed the case to simulate leads the participation and other students observe and communicate. The leader student can alter the automatic behaviour of the model, that is to say, of the automatized house, switching operators on or off, opening or closing doors, causing accidents, etc. To do this, he/she will select an object and will press a button to perform a simulation action (see fig. 3). The teacher role can control the simulation session by stopping it temporarily, for example, to propose a question, to promote a reflection, etc. The interactions carried out by the system and the interactions performed by the student are displayed on the whiteboard in a graphic way and in the list of interactions in a textual way (see fig. 3). This way students will check if the model behaviour is the one expected. The students can talk and collaborate by means of the communication and coordination tools. When the simulation finishes the Case and Hypothesis subspace is accessible again.

From the Case and Hypothesis subspace the group can return to the Design subspace to make changes in the model, motivated by the observation and experimentation carried out in the simulation phase, so that a problem is solved in successive refinements combining design and simulation.

3.6 Collaborative Support

The previous subspaces integrate different mechanisms that support the design and simulation process in collaboration:

- Mechanisms of direct manipulation: Students design and simulate the model by means of elementary actions of direct manipulation. The outstanding feature of this paradigm is the acceleration of learning, facilitating the intuitive and effective use of the systems and reducing and preventing errors. The metaphor of the collaborative electronic whiteboard based on the object-action model is used. This model provides a structure to increase the user's control. There are tele-pointing capabilities too, that allow users to show ideas by pointing, crossing out, etc.
- Support for communication and coordination: When the students go designing and simulating the solution they can make use of the Guided Chat and the Making-Decision Tool to exchange information, to coordinate actions and to reach agreements.
- Awareness techniques: To facilitate the collaboration in real time a great importance has been given to awareness. Awareness is the perception and knowledge of the interaction that other people make in a shared workspace [7]. This is reflected in the following aspects: (1) the students can see the mouse pointers of the rest of group members all the time, each one with each participant's representative colour; (2) each student's state is maintained and represented (editing, parameterisation, selecting, linking, designing, drawing and communicating); (3) the interactions made by other students, besides being visualized on screen in real time, are reflected in the message area like a history of the design session (it is also possible to activate an alert sound). All this allows users to know what other students are doing, what intentions they have, etc.

In table 1 the different mechanisms that are offered in the three subspaces for the execution of the corresponding tasks are summarised and compared.

The design and simulation tasks are carried out by means of direct manipulation following the electronic whiteboard metaphor and the object-action model. The objects are the domain operators (activators, sensors, systems and links) and the actions that are applied on them are insertion, selection, deletion, movement, link between operators and parameterisation. During the realization of both tasks the student can use communication and coordination tools to facilitate collaboration among the participants. Taking awareness into account, the following functionalities are offered: teledata (shared data model), a list of the interactions performed and the participants' name and photo; in the Design subspace, telepointers and each participant's state (that indicates what he/she is doing: edit, select, communicate, etc.) are also shown. The Case and Hypothesis subspace is used for a more specific task and there are not communication and coordination tools. It is also based on the object-action model but in this case the student does not work with a whiteboard and icons but with forms, which represent objects, and buttons, which represent actions.

Table 1. Collaboration Support Mechanisms to the collaboration in the different subspaces.

Subspace	Collaboration Support Mechanisms		
	Direct Manipulation	**Communication and Coordination**	**Awareness**
Design	Electronic Whiteboard Object-Action Model Objects: domain operators Actions: edition, parameterisation and link	Guided Chat Decision-Making Tool	Teledata Telepointers Interaction List Session Panel: photo, name and state
Cases and Hypothesis	Object-Action Model Objects: cases and hypothesis Actions: propose, ok, not ok	---	Teledata Interaction List Session Panel: photo and name
Simulation	Electronic Whiteboard Object-Action Model Objects: Domain operators Actions: on/off, open/close, manual/automatic ...	Guided Chat Decision-Making Tool	Teledata Interaction List Session Panel: photo and name

4 Conclusions and Future Work

In this paper we have presented a synchronous collaborative environment for complex domain learning based on modelling and simulation. The system offers different shared workspaces to the users according to their role (student and teacher). The main workspace, in which problem solving activities are carried out, is structured through a collaborative protocol identifying three subspaces: model design, outlining of cases and hypothesis, and model simulation. These subspaces integrate tools for the domain problem solving with generic but customized tools to support collaborative decisions and discussions. The tools use different mechanisms for the realization of the tasks: direct manipulation based on the object-action model, communication and coordination support, and awareness techniques to facilitate real time collaboration.

We have applied our research to the Domotics domain. The environment has been evaluated by experts in this domain and by teachers, and it has been tested in real situations of experimentation in Technical Training Schools. This way, its practical utility and the validity of the proposals of this work have been demonstrated. This is the formative evaluation.

Our oncoming goal is to perform the summative evaluation, i.e., to obtain quantitative and qualitative data from the experiences in order to draw conclusions about this approach and to extend our positions to other domains in which the design and simulation are justified.

References

1. Baker, M.J. & Lund, K.: Flexibly structuring the interaction in a CSCL environment. Brna, P., Paiva, A. & Self, J.A. (Eds.) Proceedings of the European Conference on Artificial Intelligence in Education. Lisbon: Editicoes Colibri (1996)
2. Barrows, H.S. & Tamblyn, R.: Problem-based learning: An approach to medical education. New York: Springer (1980)

3. Berglund, E. & Eriksson, H.: Distributed Interactive Simulation for Group-Distance Exercises on the Web (1999) (http://www.scs.org/oldConferences/wmc98/websim/wbms/d21/Ws.html).
4. Bravo, C., Bravo, J., Ortega, M. & Redondo, M.A.: A Simulation Distributed Cooperative Environment for the Domotic Design. Proceedings of 4th International Workshop on Computer Supported Cooperative Work in Design. Compiégne (Francia) (1999)
5. Bravo, J.: Planificación del diseño en entornos de simulación para el aprendizaje a distancia. Tesis Doctoral. Universidad Nacional de Educación a Distancia. Madrid (1999)
6. von Glasersfeld, E.: Radical constructivism and Piaget's concept of knowledge. F.B. Murray (Ed.) The impact of Piagetian theory. Baltimore: University Park Press (1979) 109-122
7. Gutwin, C. & Greenberg, S.: Workspace Awareness. Position paper for the ACO CHI'97 Workshop on Awareness in Collaborative Systems, organized by Susan E. McDaniel & Tom Brinck, Atlanta, Georgia, March 22-27 (1997)
8. Guzdial, M., Kolodner, J., Hmelo, C., Narayanan, H., Carlson, D., Rappin, N., Hübscher, R., Turns, J. & Newstetter, W.: Computer Support for Learning through Complex Problem Solving. Communications of the ACM, april, vol. 39, no. 4 (1996)
9. Kafai, Y.B. & Ching, C.C.: Talking Science Through Design: Children's Science Discourse Within Software Design Activities. A. Bruckman, M. Guzdial, J. Kolodner & A. Ram (Eds.), Proceedings of ICLS'98. Atlanta, Georgia (1998) 160-166
10. Kolodner, J.L.: Educational Implications of Analogy: A View from Case-Based Reasoning. American Psychologist, vol. 52, no. 1 (1997) 57-66
11. Koschmann, T. (Ed.): CSCL: Theory and practice of an emerging paradigm. Lawrence Erlbaum Associates (1996)
12. Loper, M. & Seidensticker, S.: The DIS Vision: A map onto the future of distributed simulation. Orlando, Florida: Institute for Simulation and Training (1994)
13. Miao, Y. & Haake, J.M.: Supporting Concurrent Design by Integrating Information Sharing and Activity Synchronization. Proceedings of the 5th ISPE International Conference on Concurrent Engineering Research and Applications (CE98). Tokyo, Japan (1998) 165-174
14. Plaisant, C., Rose, A., Rubloff, G., Salter, R. & Shneiderman, B.: The design of history mechanisms and their use in collaborative educational simulations. Proceedings of CSCL'99 (1999)
15. Redondo, M.A., Bravo, C., Ortega, M. & Verdejo, M.F.: PlanEdit: An adaptive tool for design learning by problem solving. Proceedings of AH'2002. Málaga (Spain) (2002)
16. Rosson, M.B. & Carroll, J.M.: Scaffolded Examples for Learning Object-Oriented Design. Communications of ACM, abril, vol. 39, núm. 4 (1996)
17. Schneider, K. & Nakakoji, K.: Collaborative Learning as Interplay between Simulation Model Builder and Player. Proceedings of CSCL'95 (1995)
18. Shaw: President's Committee of Advisors on Science and Technology, Report to the President on the Use of Technology to Strengthen K-12 Education in the United States. Panel on Educational Technology (1997)
19. Stevens, V.: Participatory simulations: Building collaborative understanding through inmmersive dynamic modeling. Massachusetts Institute of Technology (1998) (http://www.media.mit.edu/~vanessa/part-sims/thesis.html)
20. Winograd, T.: A Language/Action Perspective on the Design of Cooperative Work. Greif, E. (Ed.) CSCW: A Book of Readings. Morgan-Kaufmann (1988)

A General Platform for Inquiry Learning

Beverly Park Woolf [1], John Reid [2], Neil Stillings [2], Merle Bruno [2],
Dan Murray [3], Paula Reese [1], Alan Peterfreund [4], and Kenneth Rath [1]

[1] University of Massachusetts
Bev@cs.umass.edu
413 549 6036
Fax: 413 545 1249
http://ccbit.cs.umass.edu/ckc/index.html
[2] Hampshire College
[3] University of Rhode Island,
[4] Peterfreund Associates

Abstract. This research explores the use of software to move higher education towards more active student learning including inquiry, problem-based and cooperative learning. Active students ask their own questions, engage in hypothesis generation, make and test predictions about theories, are involved in reasoning and address their own misunderstandings. These activities place heavy demands on the faculty and are rarely allowed in large classrooms. The challenge is to support this type of inquiry learning without also adding and excessive burden to faculty time.

We have built and evaluated software that supports inquiry learning in classrooms. The software supports students to reason about a phenomenon, make mistakes and monitor their own scientific processes. Intelligent tutoring and a discovery approach guide students' inquiry in problem-cases. The software provides some of the efficiency needed to make inquiry-oriented instruction more widely available and enhance problem-solving activities during classtime.

We are expanding this model for inquiry-based learning across three domains, several institutions and teaching style. Student performance will be measured, providing empirical evidence for the portability of inquiry-oriented instruction for college-level classrooms. We will evaluate the comparative results concerning the differential effects of these interventions in each environment.

1   What Is Inquiry Learning and Why Is It Difficult?

One great educational challenge is to keep students engaged in authentic and active work. For example, science students should explore actual scientific problems and history students should explore source documents, including tax records and police records, to identify causes and effects of historical events. Using the inquiry method, students learn about theories and how theories are derived. They are active in knowledge construction, learn what questions to ask, how to make predictions about theories and how theories and rules can be tested. Inquiry learning provides a well-described approach to constructivist learning. Performing less authentic "hands-on" activities does not guarantee that students see the work as relevant [Wenk, 2000].

Teachers in a typical classroom ask 95% of the questions, mostly requiring short answers [Graesser & Person, 1994; Hmlo-Silver, '02]. The student's apparent task is to absorb and understand explicit concepts and to exhibit this understanding in largely

S.A. Cerri, G. Gouardères, and F. Paraguaçu (Eds.): ITS 2002, LNCS 2363, pp. 681–697, 2002.

factual and definition-based multiple choice examinations. Additionally, large introductory courses are often taught in lectures attended by several hundred students in which an instructor often presents information carefully organized into digestible packages. Problem-solving and student-centered activities are difficult for the faculty member to organize. Yet, it is a mistake to suppose the mere acquisition of facts may be useful in the future [Dewey 1938]. Rather, the understanding of the structure of a discipline, and not only learning facts, will have the greatest impact on students [Bruner, 1963].

Arranging inquiry learning is labor intensive, typically requiring one trained facilitator for each group of students, especially for small (5-6 students) group in secondary and graduate mentoring. This is not always practical. Though inquiry-oriented and problem-solving instruction has proven effective in dedicated small-college settings such as Hampshire College [Stillings et al., 1999], moving it to large post-secondary classrooms is often thought to be too labor intensive. Based on prior NSF research,[1] using faculty interviews and structured classroom observations, we found that compared to more traditional instruction, inquiry-oriented instructors devoted significantly more time to activities designed for the acquisition of inquiry skills and that these practices led to greater changes in students' inquiry skills and epistemologies. Inquiry teachers often select appropriate cases and counter-examples and encourage students to generate their own hypotheses, make predictions, reveal their misconceptions and test their ideas [Hmelo-Silver.'02]. Such inquiry, specifically case-based learning, is frequently used in medical schools, where actual patient cases are presented for diagnosis.

Inquiry learning mirrors the method scientists use to solve problems. Authentic scientific reasoning is *not* based primarily on the ability to take good notes and demonstrate the understanding of a body of information. The need for people to develop inquiry reasoning is more pressing than ever, because citizenship in a high-technology world requires scientific reasoning and disciplined thinking. Broad agreement exists that students must understand how scientists think [AAAS, 1993; NRC, 1996; AAHE 1997]. Reports stress the importance of creating environments in which students are engaged in long-term investigations and cognitive problem solving. Students need to solve messy problems without nearby authoritative help in the form of an answer sheet held by the instructor.

Excellent undergraduate projects have encouraged students to work in teams, ask their own questions, refine hypotheses so they can be answered through analyzing evidence, and develop and implement ways to gather such evidence in the laboratory or library [D'Avanzo & McNeal, 1997]. Yet, research suggests [Derry, 2000] that facilitating classes structured this way is difficult for novice faculty, who may not know how and when to intervene appropriately. One goal of faculty intervention is to help students understand what they do not know.

Unfortunately, most computer-assisted teaching systems are also structured toward traditional delivery of concepts, facts and findings: they direct students to a single correct answer and often push education further away from inquiry-oriented instruction. Discipline-specific CD's often serve as an encyclopedic review. Many

---

[1] NSF KDI REC 9729363 Inquiry Based Science Education: Cognitive Measures and System Support. Stillings, PI. This research program on inquiry-oriented instruction based at Hampshire College included comparative investigation of ongoing, sustainable educational settings that involve varying degrees of inquiry-oriented reform.

intelligent tutoring systems (ITS) fall into this same teacher-centered paradigm, in which the teacher (computer) directs the learning, asks the questions and evaluates the answers. Existing technology often encourages student preparation prior to class or allows in-class activities to focus on problem solving while still maintaining adequate content coverage, e.g., ClassTalk or a web-based student homework systems [Wenk et al., 1997; Dufresne et al., 1996]. Lecture-less workshop classes are dedicated to in-laboratory solution of computer-based problems [Laws, 2000; Beichner, 2000]. Often in problem-based learning (PBL) or case studies lectures, the instructor determines what questions are asked. However, there is little empirical evidence concerning the success or portability of such inquiry-oriented models for the traditional college-level classroom.

Roschell ['02] notes that early paradigms in educational technology focused on the relationship of student to computer (with the computer controlling the students (e.g., CAI) vs. the student controlling the computer (e.g., logo). Lately the paradigm has moved more towards the role of representational issues, including model-based intervention or co-operative learning discourse among teachers and students.

The research described falls into this latter paradigm. The computer places the student in the center as the main focus of activity, a student's problem-solving behavior is the objective (goal) and model tracing is the tool. Inquiry learning software moves the role of the computer to that of inquiry-based teacher, where the teacher acts as guide and coach.

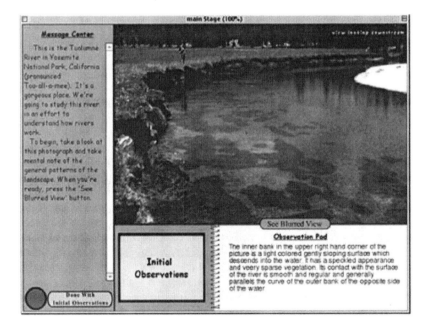

Fig. 1. View of a bend in the Tuolumne River, Yosemite National Park with Observation Pad beneath for students to enter detailed observations.

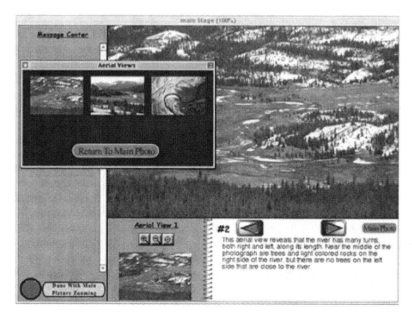

Fig. 2. The student "moves" around the site and views the landscape from many vantage points by choosing related views, both close-up and aerial photographs.

2 Software to Support Basic Inquiry Infrastructure

Researchers at the University of Massachusetts have focused on developing a universal (portable) infrastructure to support certain types of inquiry learning. The software guides students through exploration of ill-structured problem spaces, with the goal to help students become critical self-directed learners, who are cognizant of the limits of their own knowledge [Hmlo-Silver, 2002]. The goal is *not* to teaching specific content in the module. We developed structured tools, which are generic and reusable, to support students in construction of their own knowledge and assessment of their inquiry reasoning ability, diagnostic strategy, and problem solving strategy.

We have shown that our software can support students' observations and interpretations of a specific phenomenon. Additionally, it supports: (1) small student groups interacting, increasing active thinking across the class; (2) individual interaction with software promoting richer and more broadly based interaction among the students in discussion; (3) recording of students' observations and reasoning to be commented on by the instructor; (4) hypothesis testing and revision by making quantitative data about the field sites available to the student; and (5) cautious teacher adoption of inquiry teaching methods.

This basic inquiry framework has been successfully applied in geology classes to study the Toulumne River, Figures 1 -2. It was developed as part of an NSF award,[2] a research program on inquiry methods that also focused on developing software to support inquiry in linguistics, geology and forest ecology. The research enabled us to characterize scientific inquiry interactions between students and instructors in the classroom and to support hypothesis generation, experimental data collection and analysis and model building. In the Toulumne module, students type in observations about photographs, make hypotheses and use data to confirm or refute their hypotheses. The module is based on an expedition approach using 35mm slides or field trips in introductory classes at Hampshire College, taught by John Reid. The software has been evaluated in three institutions in Massachusetts and Rhode Island.

The software gently moves students through five inquiry phases, Table 1. In *Phase 1*, the student is asked to study a photograph of an environmental phenomenon (Figures 1-2) and to consider interesting features. In *Phase 2,* the student is asked to compile as complete a list of observational facts as possible, couching them in language that is rich in detail (see Observation Pad, bottom of Figures 1-2). The student can select from a gallery of photographs and zoom in at will on all of them (Figure 2). As the student types in observations, each one is linked with markers to spots on the zoomed in photograph. The module automatically recalls comments made by the student for use in the final report. In *Phase 3*, the student types in one or more hypotheses, identifies causes for the observed phenomenon and predicts data that will either support or refute the hypotheses. In *Phase 4*, the student gathers data about the phenomenon to test the hypothesis. In the Toulumne module, the student can study databases on water velocity, river depth or grain size. Before doing each field measurement, the student predicts the graphical representation of the variable, Figure 3, as though he or she were standing in the river at each measurement location with, for example, a flow meter or a depth probe. The student manipulates a slider bar graph to indicate hypothesized data points. In *Phase 5* an organized sequential review of all student observations, hypotheses, data and explanations are presented, Figure 4. The student can re-order the text for better organization of the final report, edit individual observations or hypotheses, and revisit any point of the inquiry process to reassess the data or modify the hypothesis. Once satisfied with the synthesized work, the report is printed out or sent electronically to the teacher for evaluation.

Students have used this software (see evaluation, Section 5) and have worked in teams to ask their own questions, placing fewer demands on the faculty. The software 1) ensures that *students remain* active. Students are writing observations and justifying the need for additional data to support conjectures, e.g. flow, depth, and grain data in geology. Using the infrastructure, students can stop to read source material, ask questions, gather evidence, critique a hypothesis and judiciously find support for their hypotheses; 2) improve students' *inquiry-based strategies.* Learners benefit when the inquiry cycle (captured by the five phases) and their thinking are made visible; they recognize when to ask for input and learn how to find a solution to an impasse; 3) provides *social support for learning.* Making observations with the

---

[2] NSF KDI REC 9729363 Inquiry Based Science Education: Cognitive Measures and System Support, Stillings, P.I.,.

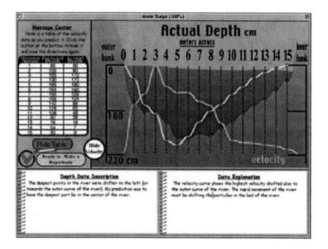

Fig. 3. The student manipulates bar graph sliders to enter hypothesized data.

software exists within a social context, i.e., students work in groups, across computers or several on one computer to suggest new observations or propose new ideas; 4) helps students gain *enhanced conceptual understanding*. Processes, such as the origins of rivers (discussed above) or medical diagnosis (discussed below), have always been difficult to convey via text or traditional lecture, yet conceptual understanding of the process is key to understanding; 5) *encourages autonomous learning*. The software requires students to use their intuitions to connect existing ideas to new ideas. Software provides less support as students take responsibility for their own learning, questioning, reflection and investigation.

3 Inquiry into Three Domains

One fundamental innovation of this research is to support inquiry skills in a variety of classes and institutions and to demonstrate that intelligent inquiry modules are transferable to distinct student populations and scalable to different sized schools.[3] Then students in varying classes will be encouraged to question processes, make mistakes and to monitor their own scientific processes. The next version of the software will port the inquiry model described above into three disciplines (civil engineering, biology and geology), in a variety of post-secondary institutions (a community college, small liberal arts college and both a medium and large university) and within a variety of teaching styles (traditional large lecture-based, small case-based classes), see Table 2.

[3] This work is supported by the Department of Education, Fund for the Improvement of Post Secondary Education, Comprehensive Program, #P116B010483.

Fig. 4. During the last phase, the module offers an organized sequential review of observations and hypotheses. The student can edit and re-order their observations for better organization of their final report.

The biology module, listed in Table 2, explores case studies for introductory Human Anatomy courses and explore the scientific basis of medicine through authentic medical cases, a case-based method of instruction adapted from materials used at Harvard Medical School [Waterman, 1995; Waterman, Matlin, and D'Amore, 1993; Matlin, 1992; Hafler, 1991]. In the existing introductory biology class at Hampshire College, pioneered by Merle Bruno and Chris Jarvis, students work in teams to diagnose medical cases presented through descriptions of patient histories, physical exams and laboratory findings. They study how diseases are transmitted, physiological effects of disease, and the immune response to disease-causing microorganisms. The biology module will enhance students' abilities to be self sufficient and critical learners. Specifically, students will identify key elements of the medical problem, determine the essential information needed, seek out and find that information, clearly and concisely discuss findings with peers and work together to synthesize experimental approaches to a solution. Students will be given medical test results and subsequent symptoms or responses to treatments only when appropriate.

The inquiry modules in civil engineering examine issues in bridge failure and water-quality. They will be used in the freshman and junior civil and environmental engineering courses, which are traditional lecture-style classes. Field trips are prohibitive for engineering classes due to the large size classes. "Virtual field trips" such as we are building, will more effectively and dynamically introduce students to environmental engineering and water resources issues, will effectively integrate the trip with concepts introduced in lecture, and will provide measurement style trips pertinent to environmental engineering. Incorporating the modules at several points within the curriculum will ensure that students not only form a strong foundation of the basic principles of environmental engineering, but that they also learn to actively build upon that foundation.

Table 1. Using the inquiry infrastructure in various domains, classes and teaching styles.

Discipline	Activity	Original Teaching Style	Institution
Civil Engineering	Water Quality Hydrology	Traditional lecture-based classes	University of Massachusetts
Human Biology	Medical-diagnosis	Small case-based classes	Hampshire College (Merle Bruno)
Geology 1	Toulomne River Field Trip	Large traditional lecture-based classes	University of Massachusetts
	Toulomne River Field Trip	Small problem Based classes	Greenfield Community College
Geology 2	Evolution of New England	Small inquiry-based classes	Hampshire College
Geology 3	Glaciers and Ice Fields	Medium sized traditional lecture-based classes	University of Rhode Island
Geology 4	Neotechtonics	Medium sized traditional lecture-based classes	Skidmore College

The three disciplines represent three distinct populations of students with distinct learning styles, i.e., engineers tend to be more analytic; biology students tend to be headed towards a career in the life sciences; and geology students often represent a cross section of liberal arts majors and non-scientists. We will evaluate whether inquiry software supports students in all these disciplines to formulate questions and generate competing hypotheses and explore data related to their questions. We will test whether students can initiate experiments, search source documents to collect appropriate data, analyze data, make judgments about their findings, revise their initial question and hypotheses, and reflect upon their experiences and their inquiry process [White and Frederiksen, 1998].

4   Structured Tools to Support Top Level Inquiry Skills

In building the inquiry software, we developed tools that engage students in a fundamental dialectic process. We wanted students to be involved in reasoning, to address their own misunderstandings and to focus on inquiry or critical thinking. Tools have been designed for each of the five inquiry phases identified above in Table 1. These tools gently support students to 1) critically reflect on a situation and thoroughly observe phenomenon; 2) synthesize observations into a coherent set of interpretations and predictions; 3) ask for data to confirm the hypothesis and 4) learn to assess and trust the validity of their own hypotheses independent of a mentor's input. The generalized software platform will enable faculty to position graphics and data for inquiry learning.

Table 2. Explicit roles assumed by students as part of the problem solving team.

Student Role	Tasks
Recorder	Compiles a computer list of all team member contributions, such as: What do we know? What do we need to know?
Facilitator	Ensures that everyone in the group gets a chance to speak and that everyone does contribute.
Skeptic	Helps keep the group "honest" asking: How do we know that? Could there be any other explanations?
Task Manager	Keeps the group "on task." Asks: Have we listed everything we know? What hypotheses (or diagnoses) are we considering? What do we need to do next?
Accuracy Coach	Asks: Where did you get that information? Did everyone understand that explanation?

Phase 1. Orientation of Student to the Environment

During the *Orientation* phase, students are presented with a biology, geology or engineering situation and guided to carefully observe it and synthesize their observations into a coherent set of interpretations and predictions. Students form teams during this phase with each student assuming an explicit role, see Table 4. A student who claims to be unable to handle a specific role will be encouraged to take on that role. Table 3 identifies some of the comments/questions presented by the tutor during this phase. *Fuzzy View* presents the initial photograph in an unfocused view to encourage students to provide very general, high level comments about the contour of the river or phenomenon.

Table 3. Questions and Comments made by the Tutor during Phase 1.

Phase 1. Orientation	Tools
What do you observe about this (river, patient, bridge)? Is there anything notable or unusual about (it, her)?	*Fuzzy View*
Several views of this site are available. You may enlarge this picture or move to other views.	*Photo Gallery* *Zoom-in Tool*

Phase 2. Make Observations to Identify Factors and Features

During the *Observations* phase, students organize their discussions around three questions, see Figure 5: What do we know? What do we think we know (begin to think about hypotheses)? What more do we need to know? Each typed message is placed in a column marked "Facts," "Ideas," "Learning Issues," or "Action Plan." The software automatically recalls comments made by the student for use in the final report. The answers given by students in response to: "What more do we need to know?" fall into two categories: topics that students can look up in resources in the software; and topics that require more information about the phenomenon, event or patient. Separating questions into these lists helps students understand the difference between observations and interpretations.

During the observation phase in a classroom, a faculty member might use a variety of student-active teaching strategies in a variety of disciplines and classroom situations [How Change Happens, 2000]. The software mimics some of these strategies. For instance it ensures that teams assign themselves learning tasks (without being able to judge the quality of those tasks). Also it does not supply data (in Phase 4) until students have thoroughly pursued material they can look up or work out themselves. So the medical module assesses whether a student has asked enough questions during Phase 2 and proposed sufficient hypotheses during the Phase 3 to *merit* seeing additional findings about the patient. In other words, the student must probe the problem for him or herself.

Cycle of Case Inquiry

Teams receive and read "page one"
What do we know?
What do we think we know?
What more do we need to know?
Teams assign themselves learning tasks
Students assume individual homework
assignments
Students report findings to teams.
Repeat cycle until case is solved.

Fig. 5. The cycle of case-based activities required to solve inquiry problems.

Determining "sufficiency" of student observations or hypotheses is still a research issue. Obviously the system might count the number of observations, but numerous observations that are inane would be counted as better than a few that are insightful. Currently, the Toulomne Module records the location of the student's observation on each photograph to determine whether relevant portions of the phenomenon have been missed. The student is then asked to comment about selected locations. We also have had some success searching key words in student observations; however issues of spelling and syntax confound this measure. We determine "sufficiency' of hypotheses through the Structured Hypothesis Tool, see Phase 3, below.

Intelligent inquiry modules will guide students towards additional observations, questions or experiments as needed. The nature of the module's feedback is the very essence of where inquiry environments gain their power. The software will effectively have "prompt cards" to use during each phase [Hmelo-Silver, 2002]. The prompt facility will ask for clarification of terms written down in the fact column and ask, "what does that term mean?" If the student can not clarify or define ideas, these become learning issues.

During Phase 1, each student took on an explicit role and was made responsible for certain tasks, Table 4. At the next meeting, students share the results of their homework assignments and construct new sets of lists. This process is repeated until the questions asked could be answered only by learning more about the situation (bridge, patient or phenomenon). Students are then given "Page Two" (e.g., the engineers report, the Emergency Room findings, the velocity measurements) and continue the process. Table 4 indicates some of the activities supported and tools in Phase 2.

Table 4. Questions and Comments made by the Tutor during Phase 2.

Phase 2. Observations	Tools
Teams receive and read "page one" Students record: "What do we know?"	*Observation Pad (Figures 1-2)*
Students record: What do we need to know? Students record: What must we learn?	*Identify focus of Attention*

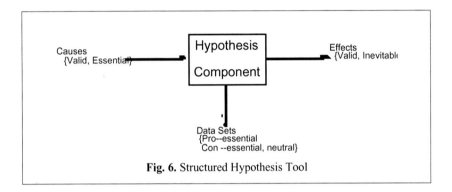

Fig. 6. Structured Hypothesis Tool

Phase 3. Propose Hypotheses, Make a Prediction or Plan an Experiment

In the *hypotheses* phase, students suggest hypotheses and ask for data. Clearly open-ended student input can not be parsed, as good natural language analysis does not yet exist. Clearly, the more the tutor can understand about the student's hypothesis, the more specific it can be in its feedback. Given the state of the art, this means the more constrained the software model has to be to understand the student's input. There is a trade-off between allowing the student the freedom to generate their own hypothesis (as opposed to a pre-programmed one) and thus engage in a less-constrained mode of thinking and having pre-programmed computer feedback based on the pre-programmed data/hypothesis sets that challenge and evaluates students responses.

Fig. 7. Possible causes of a bridge failure

Here the software goal is to push the student for an explanation or definition of their hypothesis. The software asks the student to explain the hypotheses and define the words used. Students first type in causes for the observed phenomena in the Open

Hypothesis Pad, similar to Figure 2. Subsequently, students are asked to use the Structured Hypothesis Tool, Figure 6, which has an external component to assist a student in writing down solution factors. This tool makes hypothesis explicit and helps students recognize whether data supports or refutes their hypothesis. The Structured Hypothesis Tool provides nodes and arcs to help student delineate causes and effects of hypotheses. In the case of a failed bridge, a series of possible causes are presented in separate nodes, Figure 7, and students move causes and effect nodes and arrows to generate a flow chart describing their hypothesis, Figure 8. Resources available in this phase are described in Table 5.

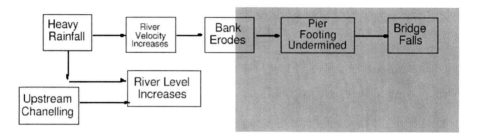

Fig. 8. A structured hypothesis constructed by the student.

Table 5. Activities supported during Phase 3.

Phase 3. Hypothesis Formation	Tools
Students provide multiple open hypotheses Students construct individual delineated hypotheses	*Hypotheses Pad* *Structured Hypothesis Tool* *(Figure 6)*

Phase 4. Gather, Measure and Analyze Data

In the *design and data collection* phase, students request data to confirm or refute their hypotheses. Here the goal is to push the student to express causes of the phenomenon. Placing their knowledge in public view helps them see the limits of their understanding. They also evaluate the hypotheses and focuses on the inquiry, examining the fit between hypothesis and accumulating evidence. Hopefully, students learns to assess and trust the validity of their hypotheses independent of a mentor's input, during this phase. For example, manipulated slider bar within a graph enables students to indicate hypothesized data points of the velocity and depth of the Toulomne River, Figure 3. Before doing each measurement, the student is asked to predict the value of the variables.

During this phase, the student is asked to consider the cost of requesting data as students must learn not to immediately ask for expensive or invasive studies (e.g., empty the river to diagnose a bridge failure) before more reasonable examinations (e.g. examine newspaper weather reports) are attempted. Students are encouraged to determine for themselves whether the data supports or refutes their hypothesis.

The tutor will assess what the student does not comprehend, based on previous sites visited or data requested and will direct the student to an earlier inquiry phase, possibly requiring a return to the hypothesis generation stage if data gathered does not support the hypothesis. Intelligent feedback is based on analysis of an individual's history of observations, data gathering and any deficiencies or lack of complete exploration. Resources available in this phase are shown in Table 6. Sticky notes allow students to record facts, data, and possible causes and effects of hypothesis that students want to return to.

Table 6. Questions and Comments made by the Tutor in Phase 4.

Phase 4. Gather, Measure and Analyze Data	Tools
Cost of Data	*Slider bars(Figure 3)*
Student reorders data, labels page	*Sticky notes*
Tutor checks consistency of data	*Prompts student*
Tutor asks general questions: "What do you want to do now?"	*Identify focus of attention*

Phase 5. Write Conclusion and Final Report

In the *report* phase, students print out a report of their input at every phase. The report is sent electronically to the teacher for evaluation. The goal here is to summarize all causes and hypotheses and to establish a common ground, which helps students synthesize the data and move the group along in the process (Hmlo-Silver 2002).

A graphical sequential review of all observations, hypotheses, data and explanations is presented to the student, Figure 4. This review can be edited and re-ordered for better organization. The *final case review* contains hypotheses, diagnoses and recommendations and is written as though the team is a consulting expert reporting back to the client, e.g., health care provider, state engineers. The student writes the report within the context of the software, but are free to use a text processor and copy the report into the *Final Case Review Tool*. The written report must be well documented, based on the findings (e.g., in the medical case on symptoms, history, and physical findings) and the research done by the team. Students must indicate: What tests were done? Which differential diagnoses/hypothesis did these tests either support or eliminate? How did these tests support or eliminate the diagnoses/hypothesis considered?

The software will also support a variety of writing assignments, some related directly to the case and others designed to teach students to find and read analytically, primary research articles, see Table 7. Software will support the *case log* which contains information and reflections of the problem solving processes, including notes on team members' report, notes from text or library work, sudden (or deliberate) insights about other routes to follow, other information to look up, and brainstorming lists of other ways of thinking about the case. Table 8 indicates some of the activities supported and tools in Phase 5.

Table 7. Homework assignments provide practice in finding and reading primary research articles and in developing background for the case groups.

Software Writing Assignments

- Case Logs
- Interim case reports
- Final report for each case
- Statistical Problems
- Experimental design analyses
- Article summaries and revisions
- Final paper

Table 8. Questions and Comments made by the Tutor during Phase 5.

Phase 5. Final report	Tools
Is this your final conclusion?	
(If wrong hypothesis) Have you thought about …?	*Final Case Review Tool (Figure 4)*
(If right hypothesis but wrong data) Did your data support your hypothesis?	

5   Evaluation of Learning

Several classroom tests of the Tuolumne River module showed that the software can support inquiry learning. The first evaluation took place at Hampshire College, small private liberal arts college in which inquiry learning is central to every class. The test demonstrated that software use resulted in participation from a greater proportion of the students and generated more and richer hypotheses than did inquiry-style lectures using inquiry-based lectures with the same photographs. Student entries into the software notebooks confirmed the involvement of the entire class and the post-class discussion confirmed the students' active involvement in pursuing hypotheses. These results provide preliminary support for the hypothesis that software can enhance an already-successful technique of inquiry instruction. There was a high level of engagement on most students' parts and the involvement of all students, especially the quiet and retiring ones, had more depth, and produced a product that can be adequately assessed by the instructor. This is particularly helpful to women students who are commonly less assertive in putting forth their ideas in the inquiry-based classroom setting. Students with no prior knowledge of river processes provided sophisticated interpretations indicating that the discovery we seek is possible with a wide range of students.

The second evaluation was in a large university with engineering majors. The students were generally positive about the software, stating that the module was thought provoking and helpful for learning how to think about observations and data as they relate to the formation of hypotheses regarding a natural system. The students thought the time and energy spent on this module was valuable. Among the most positive features they listed:

- Prediction of the graphs (velocity and depth).
- Hypothesizing and drawing conclusions after seeing the various graphs.
- Making of our own graphs using our own hypothesis and then getting to see how they compared to the real thing.
- Getting the user to think and analyze, data take observations, and relate the information to form a hypothesis.
- It caused you to think and come up with an interesting hypothesis.
- I learned the reason for the formation of a river. I can apply what I learned to the formation of other water lands.
- Quality of graphics and the quality of the photos of the river.

Among the weakest features of the software they listed:

- A little more explanation after productions would have been nice.
- Conclusions or a way to see if you were right.
- There should be a section at the end to summarize the information that you have learned. Maybe, a section at the end to re-write and formulate a new hypothesis.

6   Future Work

We are addressing the student comments as well as other software limitations. For example
The data collection phase will be augmented to provide flexibility for a teacher to add new data. Authoring tools are being built to ensure instructor extensibility and facilitate moving the framework to new disciplines. The reporting phase will be enhanced to supply the student with sufficient editing capabilities.

Once the software is deployed in three domains, we will evaluate results concerning the differential effects of interventions in each environment. We will identify feasible teaching and learning activities that produce inquiry-related cognitive change in student learning. Evaluation across three domains will also test whether technology provides the efficiency needed to make inquiry-oriented instruction widely available. Student performance across institutions and learning styles will be measured. The intelligent inquiry platform should affect the content and pacing of first year courses. Certainly, students will progress at different rates through the material and individual students spend more time on the importance and application of concepts as opposed to just learning facts and procedures.

Acknowledgement. We gratefully acknowledge support for this work from by the Department of Education, Fund for the Improvement of Post Secondary Education, Comprehensive Program, #P116B010483 and the National Science Foundation, KDI

REC 9729363 Inquiry Based Science Education: Cognitive Measures and System Support. Stillings, PI. Any opinions, findings and conclusions or recommendations expressed in this material are those of the authors and do not necessarily reflect the views of the granting agencies.

References

Advisory Committee to the NSF Directorate for Education & Human resources (1996). Shaping the Future: New Expectations for Undergraduate Education in Science, Mathematics, Engineering, and Technology. NSF 96-139. Arlington, Va. NSF.

American Association for the Advancement of Science (AAAS): Project 2061 (1993). Benchmarks for Science Literacy. New York: Oxford.

Bruner, J. S. (1963). The Process of education. Cambridge MA: Harvard University Press.

Bruno, M and Karas, C (2000) The Case of the Older Shoulder. A medical case study used in Human Biology class, Natural Science 121 Hampshire College. http://demeter.hampshire.edu/%7Ecjarvis/NS121/index.html

Bruno, M. S. and S. Karas, 2000. The Case of the Older Shoulder: a resource for case-based teaching. http://demeter.hampshire.edu/~mbruno/ns121

Bruno, M.S. and C.D. Jarvis. 2001. It's Fun, But is it Science? Goals and Strategies in a Problem-Based Learning Course. The Journal of Mathematics and Science: Collaborative Explorations.

Beichner, R. (2000) SCALE_UP Dissemination and Replication, FIPSE Grant # P116B000659.

D'Avanzo, C and McNeal,(1997) A. Inquiry teaching in two freshman level course: Sam e core principles but different approaches. In D'Avanzo, C and McNeal,(eds.) Student-active science: Models of innovation in college science teaching,. Philadelphia, PA: Saunders Press.

D'Avanzo, C and McNeal,(1997) A. Inquiry teaching in two freshman level course: Sam e core principles but different approaches. In D'Avanzo, C and McNeal,(eds.) Student-active science: Models of innovation in college science teaching,. Philadelphia, PA: Saunders Press.

D'Avanzo, C., & McNeal, A. P. (1997). Research for all students: Structuring investigation into first-year courses. In A. P. McNeal & C. D'Avanzo (Eds.), Student-active science - Models of innovation in college science teaching. Philadelphia, PA: Saunders College Publishing (pp. 279-300).

Derry, S.J., Seymour, J., Steinkuehler, C., & Lee, J., (2001) From ambitiiious vision to partially satisfying reality: an evolving socio-technical design supporting community and collaborative learning in teacher education. American Education Research Association Journal, 31, 104-137, Seattle, WA.

Dewey, J. (1938). Experience and education. New York: Macmillan Publishing Company.

Dufresne, R., Gerace, W., Leonard, W., Mestere, J., Wenk, L, (1996) Classtalk: A Classroom Communication system for active learning, Jounral of Computing in Higher education, Spring 1996, Vol. 7 (2), 3-47.1996

Graesser, A.C., & person, N. (1994). Question asking during tutoring. Annual Meeting of the American Education Research Association

Hafler, Janet (1992) The Role of the Tutor and Learning Agenda in Problem-Based Tutorials, in: Tutoring Excellence: Faculty Development for the New Pathway, 1(2):4,5, Harvard Medical School Office for Educational Development.

Hmelo-Silver, (2002) C. Collaborative Ways of Knowing: Issues in Facilitation, Proceedings of the Conference on Computer Support for Collaborative Learning, Gerry Stahl, Ed., 2002, Boulder Colorado.

How Change Happens, 2000

Laws, P., (2000) Workshop Science: Implementation of a Project-Centered Curriculum for Non-Scientists, FIPSE Grant # P116B000927.

Matlin, Karl S. (1992) *Cell Biology by the Case Method*, Department of Pathology, Harvard Medical School.

National Research Council (NRC) (1996). National Science Education Standards. Washington, D.C.: National Academy Press.

NCTM (Nation al, Council, of Teachers of Mathematics) (1991) Professional; standard oft teaching mathematics. Reston, VA.

NRC (National Research Council) 1996 National Science 4eEducation standards. Washington, D.C., National Academy Press.

Roschelle, J. & Pea, R.,(2002) A Walk on the WILD side: How wireless Handhelds May Change CSCL, *Proceedings of the Conference on Computer Support for Collaborative Learning,* Gerry Stahl, Ed., 2002, Boulder Colorado.

Stillings, N. A., Ramirez, M. A., & Wenk, L. (1999a). Assessing critical thinking in a student-active science curriculum. Presented at NARST meeting, Boston, MA March 28-31, 1999. Waterman, Margaret A. (1995) *Introduction to Case Writing for the Life Sciences*, presented to the Coalition for Education in the Life Sciences, Madison, WI.

Stillings, N. A., Ramirez, M. A., & Wenk, L. (1999b). Assessing critical thinking in a student-active science curriculum. Presented at the annual meeting of the National Association for Research in Science Teaching, Boston, MA March 28-31, 1999.

Stillings, N. A., Ramirez, M. A., & Wenk, L. (2000).Teaching and learning the nature of science in inquiry-oriented college science courses. Presented at the 2000 AERA meeting, New Orleans, LA, April 24-28, 2000.

Waterman, Margaret A. (1995) *Introduction to Case Writing for the Life Sciences*, presented to the Coalition for Education in the Life Sciences, Madison, WI.

Waterman, Margaret A., Karl S. Matlin, Patricia A. D'Amore (1993) *Using Cases for Teaching and Learning in the Life Sciences: An Example from Cell Biology*, presented to Coalition for Education in the Life Sciences, Woods Hole, MA.

Waterman, Margaret A., Karl S. Matlin, Patricia A. D'Amore (1993) *Using Cases for Teaching and Learning in the Life Sciences: An Example from Cell Biology*, presented to Coalition for Education in the Life Sciences, Woods Hole, MA.

Wenk, L. (1999). Developmental measures as evaluation tools for inquiry science programs. Presented at the 1999 NARST Annual Meeting, Boston, MA March 28-31, 1999.

Wenk, L. (2000). Improving science learning: Inquiry-based and traditional first-year college science curricula. Doctoral dissertation, School of Education, University of Massachusetts, Amherst.

Wenk, L., Dufresne, R., Gerace, W., Leonard, W., Mestere, J., (2000) Technology-assisted active learning in large lectures., Chapter 24. (2000)

White and Frederiksen, 1998

Assessing Effective Exploration in Open Learning Environments Using Bayesian Networks

Andrea Bunt and Cristina Conati

Department of Computer Science, University of British Columbia
201-2366 Main Mall, Vancouver, B.C, V6T 1Z4
bunt@cs.ubc.ca, conati@cs.ubc.ca

Abstract. Open learning environments provide a large amount of freedom and control, which can be beneficial for students who are able to explore the environment effectively, but can also be problematic for those who are not. To address this problem, we have designed a student model that allows an open learning environment to provide the students with tailored feedback on the effectiveness of their exploration. The model, which uses Bayesian Networks, was created by an iterative design and evaluation process. The successive evaluations were used to improve the model and to provide initial support for its accuracy and usefulness.

1 Introduction

Open learning environments are computer-based educational systems that place less emphasis on supporting learning through explicit instruction and more on providing the learner with the opportunity to explore the instructional domain freely, acquiring knowledge of relevant concepts and skills in the process [4][7]. In theory, this type of active learning should enable students to acquire a deeper, more structured understanding of concepts in the domain [7]. Also, owing to the unguided nature of the interaction, the hope is that, in addition to skills in the target instructional domain, the learner can practice and acquire meta-cognitive skills associated with effective exploration [4].

Empirical evaluations, however, have shown that a student's ability to benefit from interacting with open learning environments depends on a number of student-specific features, including activity level [4][7], whether or not the student already possesses the meta-cognitive skills necessary to learn from exploration [7] and general academic achievement [6]. Students who are inactive or lack the necessary cognitive skills often fail to initiate enough meaningful experiments; they can have difficulty interpreting and generalizing the results of the experiments that they do initiate [7][8], thus incurring sub-optimal learning.

The above findings indicate that the effectiveness of open learning environments could be improved by providing real-time support for the exploration process, tailored to each student's individual needs. Such support should be provided only when necessary, to avoid interfering with the unrestricted nature of

S.A. Cerri, G. Gouardères, and F. Paraguaçu (Eds.): ITS 2002, LNCS 2363, pp. 698–707, 2002.
© Springer-Verlag Berlin Heidelberg 2002

this learning activity. Therefore, having a student model that can detect when a student is not benefitting from the exploration process is crucial. In this paper, we describe such a model. Our model relies on Bayesian Networks to assess the effectiveness of the student's exploration process and was built using an iterative design and evaluation process. Two successive user evaluations were conducted to define the structure of the model and to validate our approach. The model has been implemented in the Adaptive Coach for Exploration (ACE) [2]. Using the Student Model's assessment, ACE provides tailored hints to guide and improve the students' exploration of mathematical functions.

Modelling students' exploration presents unique challenges, for two main reasons. First, in more structured educational activities, such as problem solving and question answering, there is usually a definition of correct behaviour, which allows this behaviour to be represented and recognized in a formal model. In contrast, in open learning environments there is no clear understanding of what constitutes successful exploration in general. Second, it is hard to obtain reliable information on the student's exploratory behaviour. The amount and quality of information available to a user model to perform its assessment is referred to as the bandwidth issue [9]. The less explicit information on the user's relevant traits or behaviours the model is able to obtain, the higher the uncertainty in the modelling process. The bandwidth problem is especially difficult for student modelling in open learning environments. Both exploratory behaviour and related meta-cognitive skills necessary for effective learning are not easily observable unless the environment's interface forces students to make them explicit. However, forcing students to articulate their exploration steps clashes with the unrestricted nature of open learning environments. Thus, a model for exploratory behaviour is bound to deal with low bandwidth information, which introduces a high level of uncertainty into the modelling task.

Because of these challenges, there has been little work on how to monitor and assess student behaviour in open learning environments. ALI's student model [3] indicates whether or not the student has encountered the important concepts in the target environment and understood them through experimentation. This model, however, deals with quite high bandwidth information obtained directly by both engaging students in tutorial dialogs and requiring them to take quizzes. Other systems tackle a restricted version of the problem of modelling exploration. A student model that can assess a student's ability to either confirm or reject hypotheses is described in [10]. Smithtown [7] tracks when a student violates rules of good experimentation, such as manipulating more than one variable at a time. Neither model, however, addresses the issue that some students are inactive in open learning environments and can have difficulty initiating a set of experiments that effectively covers the exploration space.

The rest of the paper describes how we tackle the challenges of modelling exploratory behaviour in ACE's student model. We formalize effective exploration behaviour by designing the student model iteratively using the results of an evaluation with human subjects. We address the uncertainty owing to the low bandwidth problem using Bayesian Networks.

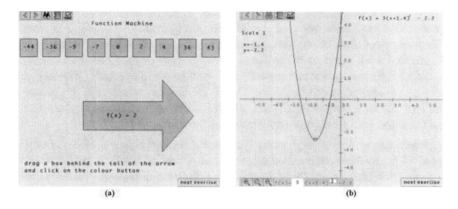

Fig. 1. The Machine Unit (a) and the Plot Unit (b).

2   The ACE Open Learning Environment

ACE [2] is an intelligent open learning environment for the domain of mathematical functions. ACE's activities are divided into units and exercises. Units are collections of exercises whose material is presented with a common theme and mode of interaction. Exercises within the units differ in function type and equation. Currently, ACE supports only different types of polynomial functions.

Figure 1 shows the main interaction window for two of ACE's units: the *Machine Unit* and the *Plot Unit*. ACE also has a third unit, the *Arrow Unit*, not displayed for lack of space. We have also omitted the help pages and the feedback panel, which normally appear to the right of and below the main window, respectively. The *Machine Unit* (fig. 1(a)) and the *Arrow Unit* allow the student to explore the relationship between an input and the output of a given function. In the Machine Unit, the exploration consists of dragging any number of inputs displayed at the top of the screen to the tail of the function "machine" (the large arrow shown in fig. 1(a)), which then computes the corresponding output. The Arrow Unit allows the student to match a number of inputs with the correct outputs and is the only activity within ACE that has a clear definition of correct and incorrect behaviour. In the *Plot Unit* (fig. 1(b)), the student can explore the relationship between the graph of a function and its equation, as well as graph properties, such as slopes and intercepts. The student can manipulate a graph either by dragging it around the screen (using the mouse) or by editing the equation box.

3   The Student Model

The Student Model aims to generate an assessment of the student's exploration of the ACE environment that the system can use to support the student's exploration. As the description of the ACE interface in section 2 shows, the student's

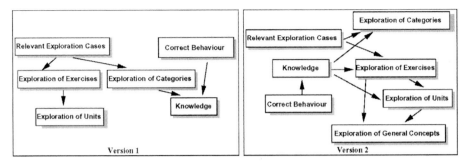

Fig. 2. A High-Level Description of the First and Second Versions of the Student Model

actions within the available activities have low bandwidth because, although they are easy to track, they provide limited information about the student's reasoning. The Student Model uses Bayesian Networks to model and manage the resulting uncertainty[5].

One of the main challenges in using Bayesian Networks is to define the network's structure to accurately represent the probabilistic dependencies among the variables of interest. In our model, this problem is exacerbated by the difficulty of defining correct exploratory behaviour (see sec. 2). Our approach was to use an iterative design process, which we describe in this section. We first built a version of the Student Model using our intuition of what constitutes effective exploration in ACE and evaluated the model in a formal study. We then used the study results to redesign the model and conducted an evaluation of the changes. By building and evaluating two versions of the model, we were able to gain valuable insight into (i) what factors contribute to effective exploration of the ACE environment and (ii) how to formalize these factors in the Student Model. Because of space limitations we are not able to describe all the details of this iterative process. Further information can be found in [1] and [2].

3.1 Version 1 of ACE's Student Model

Figure 2 (Version 1) shows a high-level description of the types of nodes in the first version of the model's Bayesian Network and the influences among them. There are two classes of nodes: exploration nodes and knowledge nodes. To assess exploration, the model uses the student's coverage of the *relevant exploration cases*. Relevant exploration cases represent the salient function-related concepts that should be explored in each exercise to gain a thorough understanding of the target material. Exploratory behaviour is modelled at different levels of granularity, including the exploration of individual exercises ("Exploration of Exercises" in fig. 2), of groups of related exercises ("Exploration of Units" in fig. 2) and of exploration cases that appear across multiple exercises ("Exploration of Categories" in fig. 2). The set of relevant exploration cases for a particular exercise depends on both the unit the exercise belongs to and the type of function presented in the exercise. For example, in the Plot Unit, if the student is exploring a constant function, she should experiment with positioning the graph at both positive and negative intercepts, while a linear function would also require experimenting with different slopes. Exploration cases in the Machine and Arrow units involve different categories of inputs, such as small positive numbers and large negative numbers. All exploration nodes are binary variables where a True value represents the probability that the student has effectively explored the corresponding item (i.e., an exploration case, exercise, unit or category). Knowledge nodes ("Knowledge" in fig. 2) represent the knowledge of function related concepts. These nodes are updated using a combination of student actions that indicate exploration and any explicit evidence of their knowledge ("Correct Behaviour" in fig. 2). In this version of ACE, explicit evidence of knowledge is available only in the Arrow Unit. A True value for a knowledge node means that the student understands the related material. The Conditional Probability Tables (CPTs) in the Bayesian Network were constructed using our best estimates of the corresponding probabilistic dependencies, which were tested and refined through the evaluation described later.

Figure 3 shows a more detailed portion of the network representing the exploration of two exercises in the Machine Unit (nodes "e_1" and "e_2"). The exploration case nodes for each exercise (nodes "$e_i Case_i$" in fig. 3) influence both their corresponding exercise node and the exploration category that they belong to. For example, "$e_1 Case_1$" is a relevant exploration case in exercise "e_1" and is an instance of the exploration category consisting of small positive inputs ("exploredSmallPosInputs" in fig. 3).

Direct evidence of the students' exploration is introduced into the network through the relevant exploration case nodes. The value of a relevant exploration case node is changed to True when the student performs interface actions that the system considers to be an indication of the student having explored that case. Each unit in ACE has a different interpretation of what this entails. For example, in the Machine Unit, a case is considered explored when the student drags an input to the "machine" that is an instance of that case. For instance, in figure 3, the node "$e_1 Case_1$" would be set to true when the student drags a small positive input. In the Plot Unit, a case is considered explored when the student either drags and drops the graph to a position belonging to a particular case (e.g., drags the line to a location where it has a positive y-intercept) or edits the function equation to change the graph in a meaningful way (e.g., changes the equation so that the slope of the graph is negative).

The Student Model's assessment is used by ACE's coaching component [2] to support the student's exploration in two ways. The first is through tailored hints, which the student can obtain on demand. The Coach determines the focus of a hint (i.e., what aspect of the current exercise should explored further) by searching the Bayesian Network for a relevant exploration concept node that has a low probability. The second kind of support is provided when a student tries to move on to a new exercise. When this happens, the Coach examines the probability that the student has effectively explored the current exercise. If that

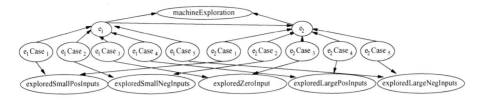

Fig. 3. A Portion of the Network Related to Exercise Exploration in the Machine Unit

probability is too low, the Coach generates a warning to explore the exercise better and to ask for a hint if needed.

The first version of ACE's Student Model was evaluated in a formal study described in [2]. Subjects in the study were first-year university students who had not taken a university math course. Two of the statistically significant results from the study provided initial support for the Student Model's accuracy and usefulness:

1. The more exercises the students effectively explored according to the Student Model, the more they improved on the post-test.
2. The more hints the students asked ACE for, the more they improved on the post-tests. Since the concepts targeted by the hints are based on the Student Model's assessment, this is an indication that the model can enable the Coach to provide relevant feedback that helps guide the students' exploration.

Analyzing students' behaviour during the study also uncovered two main problems with the model's assessment. First, a category of exploration assessment was missing from the model. Second, the model under-estimated the exploratory behaviour of knowledgeable students. In the next section, we describe these inadequacies and the new version of the model that we built to address them.

3.2   Version 2

Figure 2 (Version 2) shows the high-level structure of the second version of the Student Model. The differences between this model and the previous version are the addition of "General Exploration Concepts" nodes and the dependencies between the knowledge nodes and exploration nodes. We now describe both of these changes.

General Exploration Concepts.   The study uncovered that some students thoroughly explored many exercises but consistently exhibited poor exploration of exercises that targeted the same general concepts (e.g., exercises with constant functions). The Coach could determine that the student had exhibited poor exploratory behaviour in a couple of exercises. However, since the first version of the model maintained an assessment of cross-exercise exploration only through categories of relevant exploration cases (see fig. 2 (Version 1)), the

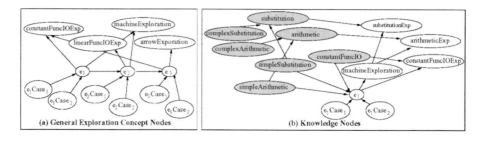

Fig. 4. Example Portions of the Bayesian Network in the Second Version of the Model Showing (a) the General Exploration Concepts and (b) the Knowledge Nodes

Coach had no way of knowing that both exercises targeted the same general concept. We addressed this Student Model inadequacy by adding a new type of node to the network, which represents the exploration of general concepts ("Exploration of General Concepts" in fig. 2 (Version 2)). These nodes allow the model to maintain an assessment of how effectively students are exploring concepts that appear in multiple exercises or units, but that do not correspond to any of the relevant exploration cases within the exercises. Figure 4(a) illustrates how these general exploration concepts appear in the network, which in this example involve the exploration of input/output in constant and linear functions ("constantFuncIOExp" and "linearFuncIOExp" in fig. 4(a)).

Knowledge Nodes. The study also revealed that several highly-knowledgeable students (identified via a pre-test) rightfully ignored unnecessary warnings from the Coach to explore an exercise further, and chose not to explore concepts they already understood. The model's inadequacy in these situations was that its exploration assessment was based solely on how active students were during the interaction, captured by the relevant exploration case nodes. The model did not take students' knowledge into account in deciding if and how much they actually needed to explore to improve their understanding.

We modified the second version of the Student Model to incorporate information on the student's knowledge into the model's assessment of effective exploration. Thus, in the new model, low exploration activity on certain concepts is only a sign of poor exploration if the student does not already know those concepts. Student knowledge is incorporated into the assessment by having each exploration node influenced by a set of related knowledge nodes.

The semantics of both knowledge nodes and exploration nodes also changed in the new model. In the previous version, knowledge nodes represented general knowledge of material assessed through both exploratory behaviour and explicitly correct behaviour, when demonstrated (e.g., in the Arrow Unit). In the new model, knowledge nodes represent only knowledge related to non-exploratory activities and receive evidence only from the students' explicitly correct behaviour (including pre-test results, when available). Similarly, while in the previous version probabilities for exploration nodes were simply a quantitative measure of

Table 1. Results from the Evaluation of the Second Version of the Student Model

	Version 1	Version 2
# Subjects	14	5
# Unnecessary warnings	62	2
Total # warnings	163	42
% of warnings that were unnecessary	38%	5%
# Premature passes	6	5
Total # exercises to be assessed	154	55
% of premature passes	4%	9%

the student's coverage of the relevant exploration cases, they now represent the likelihood that the student has explored the related concepts sufficiently to understand them. This assessment depends on both the student's exploratory actions and knowledge of the related topic.

Figure 4(b) illustrates an example of the relationship between knowledge nodes and exploration nodes. Exercise 1 involves knowledge of simple substitution, simple arithmetic and the input/output of constant functions. Therefore, the corresponding exercise node "e_1" depends on knowledge nodes for those concepts (the shaded nodes "simpleSubstitution", "simpleArithmetic" and "constantFuncIO" in fig. 4(b)), as well as the relevant exploration cases (e.g., "e_1Case_1" in fig. 4(b)). The CPT for each exploration node is designed so that if the student has high knowledge of the related concepts, the probability that the student needs to explore more thoroughly is low. When there is a low probability that the student knows the corresponding concepts, the probability that the student needs to explore more thoroughly is based on the adequacy of the student's coverage of the relevant exploration cases.

4 Evaluation

After revising ACE's Student Model in light of the observations made during the first evaluation, we ran a second study to determine the effectiveness of the changes. In particular, before going to a fuller scale evaluation we wanted to verify that the changes in the model actually improve the way ACE issues warnings. As discussed in section 3.1, the Coach issues a warning to explore further when a student tries to leave an exercise before the Student Model assesses that the exercise was explored effectively. Ideally, the assessment of this Student Model compared with that of the previous version should result in the Coach intervening less frequently with the high ability students, while still supporting the students who are experiencing difficulty with the exploration process. In addition, the model should be able to detect situations in which students are systematically failing to explore general concepts, such as the input/output of specific function types.

A total of five subjects participated in the study. As in the previous study, the subjects were first-year university students who had not taken a university math course. Subjects participated in one session that lasted at most 80 minutes and consisted of a pre-test, a session with ACE and a post-test. The pre-test and post-test consisted of 39 questions, divided equally into questions on i) function output recognition and generation, ii) graph and equation property recognition and iii) graph-equation correspondence. One researcher observed each session and ACE was instrumented to produce log files of the students' interface actions. The pre-test scores were used to set the values of the knowledge nodes in the model before the students started using ACE.

To verify that the new model reduced unnecessary interruptions for more knowledgeable students, without becoming too lenient with less knowledgeable ones, the logs from both the old and new study were analyzed by hand for two event counts: the number of unnecessary warnings that ACE generated and the number of premature transitions to new exercises that ACE allowed. Unnecessary warnings were considered to occur when the Coach generated a warning to explore an exercise further, despite it being clear from the pre-test that the student already understood the concepts associated with that exercise. A premature pass occurred when the Student Model determined that the student had effectively explored the exercise, but the student did not appear to understand the associated concepts on the post-test.

Table 1 shows the results of the analysis. As desired, the new Student Model resulted in a substantial reduction in the percentage of warnings that were deemed to be unnecessary (from 38% with the old model to 5% with the new model). The number of premature passes did rise slightly (from 4% to 9%). This indicates that the model, at times, overestimates the students' exploratory behaviour. Instances of the Student Model over-estimating exploratory behaviour were also observed in the first evaluation. Although knowledge is now taken into account together with the students' actions to assess effective exploration, the model still has no way to assess whether or not the students actually use this knowledge to reason about the outcome of their exploratory actions. We plan to address this problem in future versions of the model.

Unfortunately, we could not evaluate accuracy of the second change (the addition of general exploration concept nodes) since, unlike in the first study, none of the subjects poorly explored any of the more general concepts.

5   Conclusions and Future Work

There is mounting evidence that students need support in open learning environments (e.g., [7]). This support cannot be provided in a tailored and timely manner without knowing when and why a student is having difficulty exploring. This paper has presented the details of a Student Model that assesses the effectiveness of a student's exploration in ACE, an open learning environment for mathematical functions.

We built two versions of the Student Model. Results from the evaluation of the initial version provided confirmation of the model's accuracy and usefulness, but also uncovered some problems. The second version considerably improved the model's performance since knowledgeable students received fewer unnecessary interventions, and yet ACE continued to support students who were experiencing difficulty with the exploration process. These results support our belief that having a Student Model assess the effectiveness of a student's exploratory behaviour can help provide the tailored support that many students need to learn from open learning environments.

Future work on the ACE Student Model will be to continue improving the model's assessment of effective exploration. Our studies showed that while it is important for students to perform the right set of exploratory actions, these actions alone are not always sufficient to learn the targeted material. The students need to proactively reason about their actions. Thus, we plan to include in our model additional factors that would permit a more accurate assessment of the student's exploration. These factors include the student's tendency to self-explain, whether or not the student is attending to results of her exploration, and the time spent on each relevant exploration case.

References

1. A. Bunt. On creating a student model to assess effective exploratory behaviour in an open learning environment. Master's thesis, University of British Columbia, 2001.

2. A. Bunt, C. Conati, M. Huggett, and K. Muldner. On improving the effectiveness of open learning environments through tailored support for exploration. In J.D. Moore, C.L. Redfield, and W.L. Johnson, editors, *AIED 2001*, pages 365–376, San Antonio, TX, 2001.

3. A. D'Souza, J. Rickel, B. Herreros, and W.L. Johnson. An automated lab instructor for simulated science experiments. In J.D. Moore, C.L. Redfield, and W.L. Johnson, editors, *AIED 2001*, pages 65–75, San Antonio, TX, 2001.

4. M. Njoo and T. de Jong. Exploratory learning with a computer simulation for control theory: Learning processes and instructional support. *Journal of Research in Science Teaching*, 30(8):821–844, 1993.

5. J. Pearl. *Probabilistic Reasoning in Intelligent Systems*. Morgan Kaufmann, Los Altos, CA, 1988.

6. B.J. Reiser, W.A. Copen, M. Ranney, A. Hamid, and D.Y. Kimberg. Cognitive and motivational consequences of tutoring and discovery learning. Technical report, The Institute for the Learning Sciences, 1994.

7. V.J Shute and R Glaser. A large-scale evaluation of an intelligent discovery world: Smithtown. *Interactive Learning Environments*, 1:55–77, 1990.

8. W.R. van Joolingen and T. de Jong. Supporting hypothesis generation by learners exploring an interactive computer simulation. *Instructional Science*, 20, 1991.

9. K. VanLehn. Student modeling. In M. C. Polson and J. J. Richardson, editors, *Foundations of Intelligent Tutoring Systems*, pages 55–78. Erlbaum, Hillsdale, NJ, 1988.

10. K. Veermans, T. de Jong, and W.R. van Joolingen. Promoting self-directed learning in simulation-based discovery learning environments through intelligent support. *Interactive Learning Environments*, 8(3):229–255, 2000.

Hierarchical Representation and Evaluation of the Student in an Intelligent Tutoring System

Joséphine M.P. Tchétagni and Roger Nkambou

Université du Québec à Montréal
tchetagni.josephine@uqam.ca nkambou.roger@uqam.ca

Abstract. In this paper, we present an approach to hierarchical knowledge representation for the student's evaluation in propositional logic. The *hierarchical evaluation* consists in assessing the student's state of knowledge at several levels of granularity. The relevance of the method is justified by the need for a precise and flexible diagnosis of the learner's skills in a given domain. For that purpose, we shall model the propagation of the evaluation from a specific level of knowledge content to more general levels, using Bayesian inferences and neural networks classifications.

1 Introduction

"Intelligence" in an intelligent tutoring system (ITS) is ensured with tools which enable efficient management of the available information. One of the keys is the system capability to provide the learner with a personalized, adaptive but effective teaching. Thus, to adopt a suitable strategy, these teaching features require the system to be aware of the cognitive and behavioural skills associated to a particular student, to diagnose the student's errors or misconceptions, and to adjust the system beliefs about his current state of knowledge. This paper proposes a hierarchical representation of the student's model in an ITS (McCalla et al. [5]). We aim at showing that this approach can provide an efficient support for a global evaluation and a precise diagnosis. Our objective here is to validate this assertion by defining and justifying this idea, using propositional logic as the matter to be learned. In what follows, section 1 reviews student modeling methods, section 2 explains our approach and we show why it is relevant in section 3. Section 4 gives an outline of our future works concerning the validation aspects.

2 The Student Model: Related Works

The aim of the student's model (SM) should be to guide the tutor in taking the teaching decisions that are best adapted to a learner. However, a comprehensive student modeling is a difficult task, as these decisions must take into account several factors: the learner's current knowledge and behavioural characteristics, the goals of the training session, etc. These parameters are not easily assessable

S.A. Cerri, G. Gouardères, and F. Paraguaçu (Eds.): ITS 2002, LNCS 2363, pp. 708–717, 2002.
© Springer-Verlag Berlin Heidelberg 2002

from a man-machine interaction, thus various possibilities may be available when designing the SM. In the SM, the first question to be answered is *what* is to be represented. Here two philosophies of knowledge representation exist: *state models* where the student's knowledge is represented at given stages of the learning process and *procedural models* (Anderson et al. [1]) where the process through which the student solves problems is represented. State models are adapted in learning concepts while procedural models are more appropriate in acquiring skills. Overlay models (Carr and Goldstein [2]) and buggy models (Fung [4]) are knowledge representation approaches that determine *how* to express the student's knowledge. In overlay models, the student's knowledge is considered as a subset of the domain knowledge which should be incremented. However, buggy models further enable the modeling of faulty information in system knowledge. A more recent approach consists in representing knowledge as a set of contextual constraints that the student behaviour or responses should comply with (Mitrovic et al [6]). When implementing these concepts, Bayesian graphs (Conati et al.[3]) provide an intuitive approach to diagnosis, our main concern in this paper. They make it possible to represent in specific contexts, the dependencies between different elements of knowledge in term of posterior probabilities.

3   Our Approach

Our aim here is not to propose a new domain knowledge representation approach, but rather, to *position the learner's state of knowledge* with respect to a knowledge element, that intervenes in a given domain. Assuming that a knowledge base already exists in the system, we have developed from this base, a hierarchical structure including the items of interest for a given training session, in order to view the student knowledge with respect to this hierarchy, by mimicking it.

3.1   Hierarchizing the Learning Content

When converting domain knowledge into a hierarchical representation, five levels of granularity can be identified, namely the domain (level 1), the subjects (level 2), the sub-subjects (level 3), the concepts (level 4) and the exercises (level 5) through which the student acquires concepts. Level 4 comprises *primitive or basic concepts* and *generic or composite concepts*. For instance, concepts such as *logical conjunction, logical disjunction* and *logical negation* are primitives while the *logical implication* is generic. In fact, a composite concept is a knowledge unit the definition (intuitive or formal) of which is based on a combination of several basic concepts. In this hierarchy, the nodes in each level refer to a knowledge unit. For example, Figure 1. shows at level 1 the domain of *mathematics*, at level 2, the subjects of *logics* and *integral calculus*, at level 3 the sub-subjects of *propositional logic, predicate calculus, fuzzy logic*, at level 4 the concepts of logical *OR, AND, NOT* and at level 5, there are some exercises linked to these concepts. Indeed, the links represent the decomposition of a given knowledge unit into more specific ones (*hierarchical or external links*), but they can also model the dependencies between elements of a single granularity (*internal links*). For example at the sub-subject level, the forward link between *fuzzy logic* and *propositional logic* models the fact that the latter is a pre-requisite to learn the former, while the forward links between *propositional logic* the logical concepts *OR, AND, NOT* model the decomposition of the sub-subject into concepts. Furthermore, the primitive concepts will be connected to basic exercises, while the generic ones will be connected to more elaborate exercises, which are characterized by a synthesis of the basic knowledge acquired by solving related basic exercises. It is therefore necessary to express the pre-requisite relations even at this bottom level. For example, problems concerning *implication* or *conjunctive normal form* (CNF) should be considered only after the solving of problems involving basic logical operators.

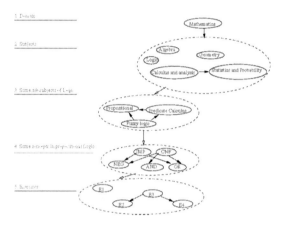

Fig. 1. A hierarchical domain knowledge view

Table 1. A hierarchical model for domain knowledge representation

Level	Designation	Information	
1	Labels	Mathematics	
2	Labels	Logic	
3	Labels	Proposition	Predicate
	Meta-K[1]	*Probability*(Masters Predicate Level_2)/(Masters Boole Level_2) = 0.5	
4	Labels	Primitive(OR)|Primitive(NEG)|Generic(IMP)| Generic(FNC)	
	Meta-K	*Probability*(Masters IMP Level_1) / (Masters (OR, NEG) Level_1)= 0.8	
		Probability (Masters EQU Level_1) / (Masters IMP Level_1) = 0.8	
5	Labels	Depend on the knowledge representation used	
	Meta-K	(Do Exercises (Generic)) → (Do Exercises (Primitive))	

3.2   Domain Knowledge Representation in the Hierarchy

As we noticed earlier, the representation of domain knowledge in this hierarchy does not relate to its real contents. Thus, we have used labels to designate the elements in each level and posterior probabilities to express their dependencies. In Table 1, level 4, the representation for concepts linked to the sub-subject of *propositional logic* is shown. But level 5 deals with the exercises to be solved by the learner, thus the representation paradigm to be used depends on the nature of the knowledge involved (procedural, analytical or declarative).

Table 2. Student model on the basis of the domain knowledge hierarchy

Level	Designation	Information
1	Mastery	(Mathematics, LEVEL)
2	Mastery	(Logic, LEVEL)
3	Mastery	$Probability$(Propositional, LEVEL)⎾$Probability$(Predicates, LEVEL)
4	Mastery	$Probability$(OR, LEVEL)⎾$Probability$(NEG, LEVEL)⎾$Probability$(IMP, LEVEL)
5	Trace	Depend on a predefined format

3.3   Modeling the Student in the Knowledge Hierarchy

The framework we are proposing here concerns the student's performance in solving problems. As stated earlier, the SM will mimic the hierarchical representation, thus at each level and for each label there will be indicators expressing the student's *LEVEL* of mastery with respect to the corresponding contents (Table 2). Student assessment at the fifth level will directly use data from a trace of the training session. At higher levels, it will be carried on inferences based on performance values from the lower levels. These inference rules indicate the level of mastery to be assigned for a concept, sub-subject or subject, when the levels of mastery in related finer granularities are given. Here, we have used posterior probabilities relations to model those dependencies (as in Table 1).

3.4   Assessing the Student State of Knowledge

Since the student's evaluation is based on inferences, this process should begin at the fifth level. We do not intend to perform a pre-test prior the launching of a training session for the SM initialisation; we will rather collect information related to problem solving in a training session. Thereafter, cognitive and/or behavioural skills to be considered in the evaluation process have to be defined. The skills are sometime slightly linked to the nature of the problem. For example in natural sciences (medicine, biology, etc.), memory and attention are important, while in pure sciences (mathematics, physics), abstraction capability (cognition) and concentration may be needed. Hereon, we shall only consider criteria related to the student's knowledge and his assessment will be simply based on his performance during the exercises solving activities. To this end, a statistical approach, which only takes into account the student's final solution, may be adopted. In this case, we have considered the proportion of solved exercises over the total number of tried exercises. A more refined approach allows the follow up and the assessment of the student on the basis of the number of correct steps performed in the solving process. A last approach will consist in taking into account the coherence of the student reasoning. Here, the question is: *what is the relevance of step (i+1), considering steps $\{i, i\text{-}1, i\text{-}1, \ldots 1\}$*? A paradox appears when a student adopts a perfectly coherent, but completely incorrect path right from the first step of the problem solving process.

Information not directly linked to the knowledge content may also help in the student's assessment and may further favour its accuracy. Hence, criteria such as the time spent in solving the associated exercises, the number of steps in solving exercises (compared to the maximum or average number of steps fixed by a domain expert), the numbers of variables used, the time spent in solving similar problems presented successively and the number of tutor's interventions, are parameters which may be involved in assessing the student.

Once these criteria are chosen, one should infer the student's level or class of mastery (from levels 1, 2 and 3 as defined earlier) for the concept related to the exercises considered. For each class, conditions of membership are defined in different ways. They may be deterministically stated by listing some features that the student's performance should have; for example { *(NUMBER of EXERCISES SOLVED = HIGH, TIME FOR SOLVING = MEDIUM)*} $\rightarrow S \in level\_2$. Alternatively, more flexible conditions define a bound on the probability that a student will master a concept. For example, these conditions may be expressed as *If probability/{S masters LOGICAL AND }] >* 0.8 *thenS* $\in$ *level_1 performance class*. A clear and precise definition of these conditions will require domain expert advice and empirical data sets of former students. The next challenge is to determine how to obtain these values for a particular student. Neural network computation provides a classification of students when membership conditions are deterministic while statistical techniques provide an estimate of the probability that the learner masters.

Indeed, a multi-layer artificial neural network trained with a back-propagation algorithm classifies a student on the basis of the values of the criteria listed above, for his particular data. In Figure 2, the network will have m inputs where m is the number of criteria chosen among the ones stated above. In this illustration example, m=3 and the inputs to the network are the criteria *"NUMBER OF SOLVED EXERCISES"*, *"AVERAGE TIME to solve EXERCISES"* and *"NUMBER OF TUTOR INTERVENTIONS"*. The output layer contains three units, each corresponding to a performance level. Note that the network is in fact a 2-stage network since it first assigns the student's parameters to one of the classes *HIGH, LOW* or *MEDIUM*, before the final classification on the basis of the class of those parameters.

Statistical calculations on the other hand evolve with the frequence at which a parameter is observed or not. For example, if the evaluation criterion is the *"NUMBER OF SOLVED EXERCISES"*, a learner's level of knowledge with re-

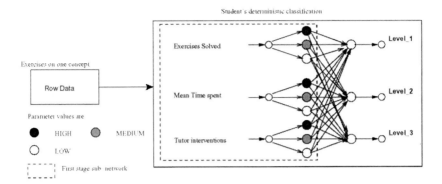

Fig. 2. A neural network architecture for student assignment to a performance class

spect to a concept I may be estimated by taking the frequence p_i of exercises that he successfully solved. Now, the question is to determine how these inferences can be carried on, from the level of exercises to the top level of subjects when the conditions of membership to a performance class are bounds on the probability of mastering a concept, a sub-subject or a subject.

3.5   Updating the Learner Model Using Bayesian Reasoning

Diagnosing the student's level of mastery for a sub-subject is carried out from the aggregation based on his level of mastery for the concepts related to this sub-subject. The same process will happen by aggregating performance values from sub-subjects to subjects and so on. Furthermore, as stated above, inferences may be performed from a knowledge unit to another one in the same level, allowing the tutor or an adaptive agent of the student's model to deduce the student's level concerning a knowledge not yet learned and to eventually optimize the learning process by skipping some basic exercises. The architecture proposed in this paper may be seen as a Bayesian network, since the diagnosis of the learner knowledge at each level in the model is built from *a priori* information related to his state of knowledge at the level below (Figure 3).

Therefore, one should first set posterior probabilities for each knowledge unit in the architecture from the level of the domain to the levels below. This may be achieved by using a neural network classifier similar to the one in Figure 2. In fact, as Ruck et al. [8] showed, a multi-layer perceptron trained with any algorithm minimizing the mean square error between an output unit and the target output approximates the posterior distribution of classes corresponding to that output, *given* the actual network input. In this case, the network output may be interpreted as the probability of mastering the concept, given a *prior knowledge* of former results on subjects (and composite concepts if necessary) related to that concept. To better understand how, lets examine the case where we are looking for an estimate of *Probability[(Mastery of < Basic Concept >) = Level_1/(Mastery of < Composite concept >) = Level_j]* (for example *Prob-*

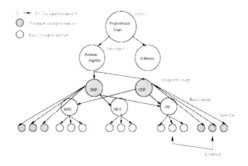

Fig. 3. The student model as a Bayesian network

ability[(Mastery of OR) = Level_1)/(Mastery of IMP) = Level_1)]). We argue that the input patterns to the neural network should be those that were used to evaluate *Probability[(Mastery of < Composite concept >)].* Those input patterns consist of some features of exercises *directly* linked to the parent composite concept, for example, the number of times that the basic concept intervenes in the solved exercises. Furthermore, since sub-subjects and subjects are not directly linked to exercises in the architecture, posterior probabilities of the form *Probability[(Mastery of <Concept>)=Level_i/(Mastery of <Sub-subject>)=Level_j],* *Probability[(Mastery of <Sub-subject>)=Level_i/(Mastery of <Subject>) = Level_j]* cannot be derived from exercises resolution data. We think that those values should rather be established on the basis of an expert judgment for the following reason: from the granularity of concepts and above, the learning matter is more and more dense while our main goal was in fact to avoid defining exercises covering a whole sub-subject or subject.

Once the Bayesian network is set with prior and posterior probabilities, a particular student assessment can take place based on evidence from his exercises solving activities: once an exercise is solved, this evidence is propagated throughout the network in the bottom-up direction. In this architecture, there are restrictions on the way evidence propagates throughout the network. This is due to the fact that two child nodes may influence their (same) parent, without influencing each other: they are not *d-connected.* This is especially true for primitive concepts node, which should not be related, since they refer to a minimal content to be learned.

3.6   Nodes Interactions and Evidence Propagation

Now, our goal is to illustrate two restrictions on the propagations throughout the network. For this demonstration example, the SM probabilities are initialized with arbitrary values. Since inferences will be triggered each time an exercise is solved, "concept nodes" are considered as *observation nodes* via the resolution of one associated exercise. Nodes at the upper levels are considered as *target nodes* since assessment will apply with respect to a sub-subject or a subject.

Exercises linked to a generic concept comprise some elements of basic concepts, but those linked to a basic concept require only knowledge related to it. Therefore, evidence from a generic concept will influence *backward* its ancestors and *forward* all the corresponding children nodes. Nonetheless, evidence from a basic concept will *only* propagate backward to its ancestors. This is intuitive since for example solving a generic exercise is likely to improve the knowledge of *all* the basic concepts which appear in that exercise, but solving an exercise associated to a primitive concept only improve the knowledge of a parent generic concept.

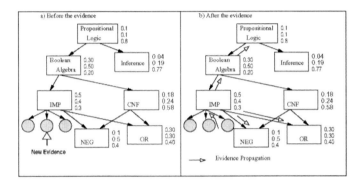

Fig. 4. Network Initial state and evidence propagation at the node *IMPLICATION*

An exercise related to the "*IMPLICATION*" node has been solved in figure 6.a) and arrows in figure 6.b) show the resulting propagation. Beliefs concerning its chidren, "*OR*" and "*NOT*" have changed through the forward propagation of $\pi(OR)$ and $\pi(NOT)$ messages, while the beliefs about its ancestors have changed through the backward propagation of $\lambda(BOOLEAN\,ALGEBRA)$ and $\lambda(PROPOSITION\,ALLOGIC)$ messages. Furthermore, the update in the node "*BOOLEAN ALGEBRA*" does not propagate back to the node "CNF" since any change in the knowledge of "*BOOLEAN ALGEBRA*" due to "*IMPLICATION*" should not influence the knowledge of the CNF concept, unless it is explicitly specified by linking the "*IMPLICATION*" node to the "*CNF*" node. Figure 7.b) shows the propagation resulting after the solving of an exercises related to "*NEG*". Beliefs about "*IMPLICATION*" changed, as well as beliefs about the other ancestors of "*NEG*". But there is no change on the belief about the "*OR*" node albeit the fact that it has a parent node in common with "*NEG*" node. This means that basic concepts with the same parent node should not be *d-connected*. This could be achieved using an *OR-GATE* between basic concepts and their parent node.

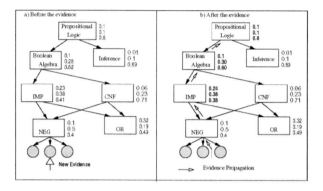

Fig. 5. Network Initial state and evidence propagation at the node *"OR"*

4   Relevance of the Approach

In a learning context, it is useful to partition the domain knowledge in order to ease the evaluation process. The student's assessment can be simplified by designing his knowledge state at various levels of granularity. The hierarchical presentation of learner's knowledge can be justified from the fact that the domain knowledge generally covers several subjects, and learning will involve a part of the whole. Furthermore, for long-term training purposes, it is necessary *to assess the student's state of knowledge with respect to several elements of the domain matter*, in case these elements influence learning content in later training stages. In the example of learning of the sub-subject of *propositional logic*, while examining what happens when the student's evaluation is made in a global way, we notice how difficult it is to take into account the student's preliminary state of knowledge. For instance, if the *conjunction* and *disjunction* concepts have already been learned, there is no mean through which the corresponding exercises can be ignored in the session planning process. Thus, the hierarchical approach to the learner's model simplifies the evaluation process since the learning content at each level of granularity can be considered independently. Furthermore, it makes training more flexible because, if one wishes to learn a subject or a particular concept, the appropriate structure is already available. The students state of knowledge on the whole learning domain can be easily stated in terms of his state of knowledge vis-à-vis the different parts of this domain. Finally, in case of incoherence or misconception about a knowledge item which was assumed to be well mastered, it is easier to track back the evaluation process.

5   Conclusion

The main contribution of this work is the proposition of an approach that takes advantage on the fact that the student's assessment in finer grain knowledge content is more tractable. Thus, the learner's performance is effectively evaluated with respect to more specific knowledge units while his state of knowledge for coarser grained knowledge content is inferred using a Bayesian network. Future works will focus on the validation process where our main concern will be the implementation of the student solving process representation and the estimation of posterior probabilities, using the CyberSciences ITS (Nkambou and Laporte [7]) as our testbed.

References

1. R. Anderson, J. and R. Pelletier. A development system for model-tracing. *Journal of Artificial Intelligence in Education*, 4(4):397–413, 1992.
2. B. Carr and I. Goldstein. *Overlays: a Theory of Modeling for CAI*. AI Memo 406, MIT, 1977.
3. C. Conati, A. Gertner, K. VanLehn, and M. Druzdzel. On-line student modeling for coached problem solving using bayesian networks. In A. Jameson, C. Paris, and C. Tasso, editors, *User Modelling: Proceedings of the Sixth International Conference, UM97*, pages 231–242, Vienna, July 1997. Springer Verlag.
4. P. Fung. Do-it-yourself student modelling. *Computer Education*, 20(1):81–87, 1993.
5. I. McCalla, G. and E. Greer, J. *Granularity-Based Reasoning and Belief Revision in Student Models in Student Models: The Key to Individualized Edu cational Systems, J. Greer and G. McCalla (eds.)*. New York: Springer Verlag, 1994.
6. A. Mitrovic, M. Mayo, P. Suraweera, and B. Martin. Constraint-based tutors: a success story. In Laszlo Monostori, József Váncza, and Moonis Ali, editors, *IEA/AIE*, volume 2070 of *Lecture Notes in Computer Science*, pages 931–940. Springer, 2001.
7. R. Nkambou and Y. Laporte. Cooperating agents in a virtual laboratory for supporting learning in engineering and science. In V. N. Alexandrov, Jack Dongarra, Benjoe A. Juliano, René S. Renner, and Chih Jeng Kenneth Tan, editors, *International Conference on Computational Science*, volume 2074 of *Lecture Notes in Computer Science*, pages 366–376. Springer, 2001.
8. W. Ruck, D., K. Rogers, S., M. Kabrisky, E. Oxley, M., and W. Suter, B. The multilayer perceptron as an approximation to a bayes optimal discriminant function. *IEEE Transactions on Neural Networks*, 1:296–298, 1990.

CLARISSE: A Machine Learning Tool to Initialize Student Models

Esma Aïmeur[1], Gilles Brassard[1], Hugo Dufort[2], and Sébastien Gambs[1]

[1] Université de Montréal, Département IRO
C.P. 6128, Succursale Centre-Ville, Montréal (Québec), H3C 3J7 CANADA
{aimeur,brassard,gambsseb}@iro.umontreal.ca
[2] Netvention Inc., 33 Prince Street, Suite 307
Montreal (Québec), H3C 2M7 CANADA
hdufort@netvention.com

Abstract. The initialization of the student model in an intelligent tutoring system is a crucial issue. It is not realistic to assume that each new student has the same prior knowledge concerning the topic being taught, be it nothing or some "standard" prior knowledge. We introduce CLARISSE, which is a novel categorization method. We illustrate this tool with the identification of categories among students for QUANTI, an intelligent tutoring system for the teaching of quantum information processing. In order to classify a new learner, CLARISSE generates an adaptive pre-test that can identify with high accuracy the learner's category after very few questions.

1 Introduction

In Intelligent Tutoring Systems (ITSs), the *student model* assesses the current state of a student's knowledge and makes inferences about the gaps in his skills. Students want to be active and challenged to reason about the material they are taught. They also need sophisticated feedback, customized curriculum, help and adapted guidance.

To do so, we need to categorize student profiles in order to bring together people who share similar prior knowledge. This makes it possible to focus more quickly on the needs of students. This categorization is important for several reasons. The tutor will be able to select the topics to be taught in a more appropriate manner. Moreover, if a student wishes to exchange his ideas on a given topic with fellow students, it is much easier if they share prior knowledge and common interests.

The initialization of the student model is one of the most important problems that faces ITSs. This initialization could be long-term or short-term [9]. The quality of tutoring depends highly on the relevance of the information acquired during the initialization process. Pre-tests are often used to initialize the student model and it is very convenient when these pre-tests are built per categories.

Quantum mechanics explains the behaviour of elementary particles. Quantum information is very different from its everyday classical counterpart: it cannot be

S.A. Cerri, G. Gouardères, and F. Paraguaçu (Eds.): ITS 2002, LNCS 2363, pp. 718–728, 2002.

measured reliably and it is disturbed by observation, but it can exist in a superposition of classical states. *Quantum Information Processing* (QIP) is the new and exciting field that studies the implication of quantum mechanics for information processing purposes [8]. This is the realm of futuristic concepts such as quantum cryptography, quantum computing, quantum teleportation and the computation of distributed tasks with vastly reduced communication cost. Some of these ideas are still theoretical, but others have been implemented in the laboratory. In the past few years, QIP has grown tremendously in worldwide interest and activity, especially since Peter Shor's momentous discovery that quantum computers—if only they could be built—would defeat most cryptographic schemes currently in use over the Internet to protect the transmission of sensitive information such as credit card numbers [18], leaving unconditionally secure quantum cryptography as a leading alternative [5].

In this paper, we introduce CLARISSE: a novel tool for initializing the student model. We illustrate the working of CLARISSE in the context of QUANTI [1,2], which is an ITS currently under development for the teaching of quantum information processing. The automatic teaching of QIP is important because this revolutionary new field is still cruelly lacking experts despite all the attention it attracts. More to the point of this paper, however, our main interest in QIP stems from the challenge of categorizing student profiles because of its inherent multidisciplinarity that draws on computer science, mathematics, physics and chemistry.

2 The Curriculum and the Student Model

2.1 The Curriculum

The curriculum is based upon the knowledge base of our Intelligent Tutoring System QUANTI (currently under development), for which a novel web-based elicitation algorithm was developed to help experts during the knowledge acquisition phase [1,2]. The knowledge representation used is a form of semantic network, a graph where nodes (called *entities*) are pieces of knowledge and edges represent *relations* between these nodes.

The network of *concepts* forms the highest level of the knowledge base. Each concept in turn can be broken up into a semantic network. In this network, the concept itself plays the role of *root* in the data structure. The network is made of three different kinds of nodes: components, characteristics and examples. A *component* represents one of the pieces of knowledge that forms the concept. A *characteristic* is generally linked to either a component, in which case it expresses one of its features, or to another characteristic. An *example* serves to illustrate a component.

2.2 The Student Model

The student model is composed of three sub-models: the cognitive model, the affective model and the inferential model.

The *cognitive model* is in charge of representing the learner's knowledge of the domain—what he knows and what he does not know, and to which extent. This part is implemented using an *overlay* model that derives its structure directly from the structure of the curriculum. As the curriculum, the overlay model is made of semantic networks, each being the reflection of their counterparts in the curriculum. Recall that each node is a piece of knowledge. Our goal is to know the level of understanding of the learner. A percentage is associated with each node that represents the level of understanding: 0% means that the user knows nothing (or that we have assumed that he knows nothing) about this particular piece of knowledge, 100% means that he has totally mastered the subject. The main focus of this paper is on how to initialize these values for a new learner.

The *affective model* records the affective profile and the emotional state of the learner. This is an important part in any ITS, but we do not discuss it further because it is peripheral to the issues considered in this paper. The *inferential model* draws inferences about the student from the data available in the cognitive and affective models. In turn, these inferences themselves modify and update these two models.

2.3 Initialization of the Cognitive Model

To initialize the cognitive model, the simplest solution would be to assume that a new learner knows nothing about the domain before starting his first lesson: the level of understanding for each node is set to zero. However, new students are not necessarily unfamiliar with the domain taught by the ITS. Therefore, a better approach is to evaluate the learner with a questionnaire called *pre-test*, which is given before the start of the first session.

For an evaluation to be as accurate as possible, the ideal solution would require to ask at least one question for each node. This is done with an *exhaustive* pre-test. In practice, this method is often too demanding for the student. The number of questions asked of the student during the pre-test could be very high and the student, who is eager to start the course, may feel desperate.

In an *intelligent* pre-test, the questions are focused on the more important nodes. Once these values are measured, the mechanisms of the inferential model are activated in order to propagate these values inside the network. This allows us to reduce the number of questions, but there is a tradeoff between the number of questions in the pre-test and the accuracy of the model. With an intelligent pre-test, the system has to use inferences for the nodes for which it has not asked a question directly to the learner. This reduces the information reliability. The *adaptive* pre-test [3,16], which chooses the next question by taking into account the answers to previous questions, is an example of an intelligent pre-test.

Categorization is another way of avoiding to bury the student under a ton of questions. Each student has unique characteristics and behaviour. However, it is often possible to observe patterns among students and to group students with similar features within *categories*, sometimes called *stereotypes* [14]. Once the categories are discovered, the only task left when a new learner arrives is to be able to determine to which category he belongs. The number of questions required for determining the category of a student is generally much smaller than for an intelligent pre-test. To each category, there corresponds a different initialization of the values of the nodes. This is the approach taken here.

3   Categorization Method

3.1   State of the Art

Categorization is a form of unsupervised learning. We know that we want to find something but we do not know exactly what it should look like. The categories are not known *a priori*: they are revealed by the categorization process. Categorization can be defined as the task of finding structure within data.

Two families of categorization methods exist. The earlier one, which contains the *mathematical and statistical approaches*, does not provide any explanation as to why we end up with these categories or the relations between the items. We concentrate on the second family: the *symbolic and conceptual approaches* [4,7,17]. They try not only to regroup items that are close but also to find how the attributes of the items are similar or different between each other. This makes it possible to provide explanations for the categories thus created. Rules are issued in order to separate items into different groups. Rules can be used recursively for the separation of items. For example, once a rule has been used for splitting a partition of items into two categories, it is possible to choose another rule for the creation of smaller categories within one of these main categories. Among the methods proposed thus far, we note UNIMEM [15], CobWeb [10] and WITT [13].

3.2   CLARISSE

To successfully initialize student models, we use a categorization method. Mathematical clustering by itself is not satisfactory because we want to find categories in an initial set of students, and rules that can be used to categorize new students. For this purpose, we developed a categorization method called CLARISSE, which stands for CLusters And Rules ISSuEd. It works by recursively splitting an initial set of items and building a binary tree that is then used to identify categories.

CLARISSE can be used to process any type of entries; we call each entry an *item*. Items are made of *descriptors*, which are single-valued attributes. The value of each descriptor must be defined, and all items must be comparable in terms of descriptors. Each descriptor has a range of acceptable values, or *domain*. In the usual application of CLARISSE to Intelligent Tutoring Systems, items are *students*, descriptors are *questions* (from a questionnaire), and domains are *question types*.

In CLARISSE, each item can be represented by a point in an N-dimensional space where N is the number of descriptors. If each descriptor has K possible values, then there are $2^K 2^N$ ways of splitting the descriptor space at each step of the method. (This formula must be adapted if the number of possible values is not the same for each descriptor.) CLARISSE reduces the search space to the most promising combinations of descriptors and values.

Great care must be taken when defining domains. In particular, the *semantic distance* between possible values should be defined very precisely. A domain can be defined as a finite range of integer or real values, or as a discrete space of labelled attributes, in which case a matrix of semantic distances must be supplied.

To drive the categorization process, CLARISSE relies on a measure of *category utility* (CU) [12]. This measure tells us how much a category is well defined. According to [6], two factors must be taken into account when calculating the CU: given any item that belongs to some category, the *dissimilarity* indicates how much this item can be differentiated from any item that belongs to another category, whereas the *internal coherence* indicates how much this item is similar to all the other items in the same category. The role of the internal coherence is to prevent the creation of "junkyard" categories that contain orphaned items.

CLARISSE derives the internal coherence of a category from a measure of the entropy in the descriptors. In order to reduce this entropy, items can be *swapped* between categories, but there is a price associated to this action: our measure of internal coherence *and* our measure of dissimilarity might suffer from it. Since it is recursive and it can use backtracking, CLARISSE can try various ways of partitioning clusters, which yield slightly different results that are sorted by category utility.

Here is a sketch of how CLARISSE works.

- Start with an initial set M containing n items.
- To execute a mathematical clustering, we need to select two prototypes (or seeds) among the n items in M. We choose S_1 and S_2 as the farthest items in the descriptor space. This is one of many possible strategies. This operation takes time in $O(n^2)$.
- Apply mathematical clustering (aggregation) to S_1 and S_2 by use of either the centroid method, the farthest neighbour method, or the nearest neighbour method, to obtain clusters C_1 and C_2. The complexity of these methods ranges from $O(n^2)$ to $O(n^3)$, and affects the properties of clusters in ways that we shall not discuss here. See [13].
- Choose a descriptor D_0 whose values can be partitioned in a way that maximizes the dissimilarity between C_1 and C_2. Once such a descriptor is found, try to find additional descriptors D_i that can be used with D_0 to refine our partition of the descriptor space, without critically reducing the quality of C_1 and C_2. The conjunction $\{D_0 \wedge ... \wedge D_i\}$ of such descriptors is called a *rule*, which we note R.
- If some items in C_1 and C_2 are cut from their parent cluster by the application of R, then try to swap these items between C_1 and C_2. As we said above, there is a price associated with this swapping: it is the loss of internal coherence in the receiving cluster. This price, which we call *item displacement cost*, must be counterbalanced by the gain in overall partition quality. We weigh this price using an internal parameter, which we call *belonging weight*.

- After trying all the rules that look promising, keep the best candidate. Swap items between C_1 and C_2. The candidate rules (that were not used) are kept in a set, and are available in case we choose to backtrack and try another path.
- Recursively apply these steps on C_1 and C_2. If some category contains only one item, or all of its items are indistinguishable, that category is final.

In Fig. 1, two mathematical clusters (represented by dashed ovals) were built around seeds S_0 and S_1. CLARISSE found a rule on Y: *all items with $Y < 5$ are in category C_1 and all items with $Y \geq 5$ are in category C_0.* Three *fringe items* (represented by white circles) were swapped in the process. The resulting categories are both coherent and explainable.

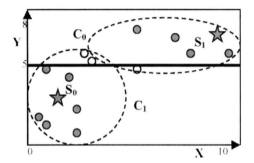

Fig. 1. Example of a partition in the R×R plane

4 The Experiment: Methodology and Analysis of the Results

To identify student categories in quantum information processing, we used a sample of the target public as training set. We built a questionnaire containing 30 multiple-choice questions covering themes ranging from classical logic and matrices to advanced quantum information processing topics. Answers were rated using three values: good (10 points), bad (3 points), very bad (0 points). These ratings correspond to the descriptor space distances used in the clustering algorithm. Each question is used as a descriptor in the clustering process, and thus in our case CLARISSE is working in a 30-dimensional descriptor space.

Students, teachers and researchers (in physics and in computer science) were asked to participate on a voluntary basis through a web-based questionnaire using HTML pages and JavaScript. Over a one-week period, we received 31 answers from Australia, Canada, France, Israel, Japan, the Netherlands and the United States. Results were passed through a validation program, and formatted as an input file to CLARISSE.

Of course, we are aware that this initial experiment can be seen at best as a way to sharpen our tools. Indeed, the complete classification of students in a field as rich as quantum information processing would require a far greater number of questions as well as data from at least as many participants as there are questions. It would be unrealistic to base the student model of an Intelligent Tutoring System entirely on so little data. Nevertheless, the results obtained by CLARISSE were used to validate the approach in a convincing way, pending a more thorough experiment.

Using its built-in heuristics for inducing variations in its parameters, CLARISSE found only one stable cluster tree, which involved seven clusters. The resulting solution leads us to challenge two well-established beliefs, but care must be exercised given that our current experiment was not conducted on a sufficiently large scale.

Myth #1: *Categories must represent the students' technical background.*

No strong correlation was found between a student's technical background and his results. Profiling students by merely asking them about their technical background, the courses they have taken during the previous year, or their current activities, is not precise enough for an ITS to be efficient. Tutoring is about fulfilling the student's pedagogical needs, and these needs can vary greatly among students with the same technical or pedagogical background.

Myth #2: *Categories must represent partitions in the distribution of scores.*

We found only a weak correlation between scores and categories: the weakest students were grouped in two well-defined categories, but the remaining students were so tightly grouped that any *ad hoc* method would fail to detect subgroups. For example, if we examine the questionnaires whose scores fall in the 80%-90% range, we find that even though the standard deviation is small, different people have made different mistakes. Some of these errors are repeated across a significantly large group of questionnaires; by observing this trend, the presence of categories is revealed.

It turns out that raw results, as used in traditional tutoring, are not giving much information when we try to categorize students. Most teachers have time constraints that prevent them from looking for patterns in their pupils' results. Machine learning tools, such as CLARISSE, can greatly enhance the thoroughness of their analysis.

4.1 The Cluster Definition File

Using analysis of the coherence variation through the cluster tree, CLARISSE partitioned it into 7 categories that showed high coherence. Each category is identified by:

- A value of internal coherence. Generally, a high coherence shows a high density of the category's descriptor space.
- Its list of members from the original set.
- An ordered list of rules that oppose this category to all other categories that were found. These rules form a hierarchical rule system, which can be used to quickly classify a new student.
- A list of the most significant descriptors. These descriptors are used to initialize the student model in an ITS, whenever a student falls into this category.

4.2 Classifying New Students

The main purpose of this process is to classify new students who wish to follow a course in quantum information processing. We define inclusion/exclusion rules for each cluster, which helps us build a hierarchical rule system. For example, there could be an *inclusion* rule for some category that would state that any student who gave a very bad answer to some specific question is included in that category, or an *exclusion* rule that excludes any student who gave the good answer to that same question. It turns out that only 6 of the 30 questions in the original questionnaire are used in these rules. These questions were marked as highly significant by CLARISSE, since they were used to discriminate between emerging categories.

Fig. 2 shows this rule system. Categories are ordered from those that contain highest-ranking scores to those that contain lowest-ranking scores. Failing to validate a capability sends you lower in the decision tree. For each category, a description of the typical members is given. To classify a new student in one of the seven categories, it suffices to ask him questions on at most three concepts with the adaptive pre-test that derives from Fig. 2. Once classified, the student receives the category's standard profile (a set of descriptors) and thus we can initialize his student model in our ITS.

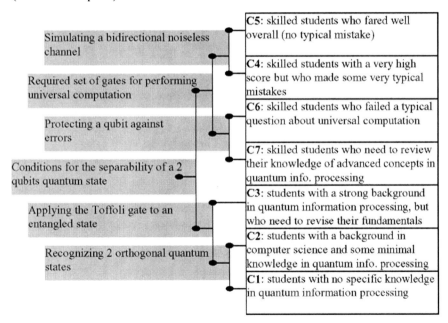

Fig. 2. Decision tree used to classify new students

Because we received four filled questionnaires *after* compiling these results, we decided to validate our method by using the six significant descriptors to classify the new participants. Table 1 shows an evaluation of our results. In two cases, we had a perfect match between the participant's descriptors and the category's descriptors, while in the other two, we had a lower level of success. With a success rate of 61.5%, 26.6%

(8/30) of the third participant's nodes in QUANTI would have been initialized incorrectly. This is much better than no initialization at all, and wrong values will eventually be corrected by the inferential agent. The fourth participant has a better fit, with an 88.2% success rate.

Table 1. New students are categorized and their student model is initialized

Student	Category	Number of descriptors in the category definition	Number of descriptors that matched the participant's answers	Success rate
A	C7 - skilled	15	15	100%
B	C5 - highly skilled	16	16	100%
C	C2 - basic knowledge	13	8	61.5%
D	C6 - skilled	17	15	88.2%

Student C in Table 1 somehow falls between categories 1 and 2, and would have been best classified in category 1. When encountering such a case, CLARISSE should be asked to integrate this *hard to classify* student in its training set. Thus it is important to enrich the categories with new students from the population whenever possible, for instance by adding some students on the training set on a regular basis, or by asking a few students to pass the pre-test now and then.

Now that seven categories have clearly been identified, the initial values of the student model have to be computed for each of these categories. Once this phase is completed, the only task left is to use the decision tree in order to recognize to which category each new student belongs. The decision tree plays the role of a small adaptive pre-test whose goal is to classify a student in one of the seven categories. The battery of questions asked of a student is not fixed: the next question asked may depend on the answers to the previous questions.

Each question in the questionnaire is linked to one or several nodes in the cognitive model. This allows us to initialize the student's level of understanding for those nodes. If more than one question point to a node, a weighted average is calculated to set the level of understanding for that node. Once this phase is completed, the inferential model is used to propagate values inside the cognitive model. Once all the initial values for a particular category have been processed, they are stored. When a new learner is detected to belong to that category, his student model is initialized accordingly.

5   Conclusions

Nowadays, a significant amount of research focuses on the enhancement of learning effectiveness of web-based educational systems, which increases the likelihood that distance learners might benefit from this technology-based approach to education.

The main purpose of a student model is to provide the tutor with the information necessary to select a suitable instructional action. The initialization of the student model is one of the most important problems that faces Intelligent Tutoring Systems. It can be complex and difficult, especially when students come from different areas and do not share the same prior knowledge.

In this paper, we introduced CLARISSE, an efficient machine learning tool to categorize student models. The application of CLARISSE to quantum information processing identified seven well-defined categories of students, each having a different set of values for the cognitive model. The process allowed us to challenge two well-established myths. CLARISSE also provided an adaptive pre-test that can classify a student in one of these categories with at most three questions. This is much fewer than would have been required by an exhaustive pre-test, or even compared to the 30 questions in the original questionnaire used in the experimentation.

In earlier work [11], CLARISSE had been tested on various other clustering problems, yielding promising results. We used it to build an identification key for mushrooms, to categorize 120 countries using social development indicators, and to categorize students for various other ITSs such as a spreadsheet tutor and a racquetball tutor.

References

1. Aïmeur, E., Blanchard, E., Brassard, G., Fusade, B. and Gambs, S., "Designing a Multidisciplinary Curriculum for Quantum Information Processing", *Proceedings of Artificial Intelligence in Education: AI-ED'01*, pp. 524–526, 2001.

2. Aïmeur, E., Blanchard, E., Brassard, G. and Gambs, S., "QUANTI: A Multidisciplinary Knowledge-Based System for Quantum Information Processing", *Proceedings of International Conference on Computer Aided Learning in Engineering Education: CALIE'01*, pp. 51–57, 2001.

3. Arroyo, I., Conejo, R., Guzmand, E. and Woolf, B.P., "An Adaptive Web-based Component for Cognitive Ability Estimation", *Proceedings of Artificial Intelligence in Education: AI-ED'01*, pp. 456–466, 2001.

4. Bauer, M., Gmytrasiewicz, P. and Pohl, W., Workshop "Machine Learning for User Modeling", *Proceedings of the Seventh International Conference on User Modeling*, 1999.

5. Bennett, C.H., Brassard, G. and Ekert, A.K., "Quantum Cryptography", *Scientific American*, pp. 164–171, October 1992.

6. Biswas, G., Weinberg, J. and Fisher, D., "ITERATE: A Conceptual Clustering Algorithm that Produces Cohesive Clusters", 1995, available on the Internet at URL: http://cswww.vuse.vanderbilt.edu/~biswas/Papers/kdd/iterate-oilabs.html .

7. Bloedorn, E., Mani, I. and MacMillan, T.R., "Machine Learning of User Profiles: Representational Issues", *Proceedings of the National Conference on Artificial Intelligence*, pp. 433–438, 1997.

8. Chuang, I.L. and Nielsen, M.A., *Quantum Computation and Quantum Information*, Cambridge University Press, 2000.

9. De Koning, K., and Bredeweg, B., "Exploiting Model-Based Reasoning in Educational Systems", in *Smart Machines in Education,* K.D. Forbus and P.J. Feltovich (Eds), pp. 299–330, 2001.

10. Fisher, D., "Knowledge Acquisition via Incremental Conceptual Clustering", *Machine Learning* **2**, pp. 139–172, 1987.

11. Dufort, H., *Évaluation et adaptation automatique de cours dans un système tutoriel intelligent*, Masters thesis under the direction of Esma Aïmeur, Université de Montréal, 1999.

12. Gluck, M.A. and Corter, J.E., "Information, Uncertainty, and the Utility of Categories", *Proceedings of the Seventh Annual Conference of the Cognitive Science Society*, Hillsdale: Lawrence Erlbaum Associates, pp. 283–287, 1985.

13. Hanson S.J., "Conceptual Clustering and Categorisation: Bridging the Gap between Induction and Causal Models", *Machine Learning: An Artificial Intelligence Approach* **3**, 1990.

14. Kay, J., "Stereotypes, Students Models and Scrutability", *Proceedings of Intelligent Tutoring Systems: ITS 2000*, pp. 19–30, 2000.

15. Lebowitz, M., "Experiments with Incremental Concept Formation: UNIMEM", *Machine Learning* **2**, pp. 103–138, 1987.

16. Millàn, E., Pérez-de-la-Cruz, J.L. and Svàzer, E., "Adaptive Bayesian Networks for Multilevel Student Modelling", *Proceedings of Intelligent Tutoring Systems: ITS 2000,* pp. 534–543, 2000.

17. Raskutti, B. and Beitz, A., "Acquiring User Preferences for Information Filtering in Interactive Multi-Media Services", *Proceedings of PRICAI*, pp. 47–58, 1996.

18. Shor, P.W., "Polynomial-Time Algorithms for Prime Factorization and Discrete Logarithms on a Quantum Computer", *SIAM Journal on Computing* **26**, pp. 1484–1509, 1997.

Incorporating Learning Characteristics into an Intelligent Tutor

Declan Kelly [1] and Brendan Tangney [2]

[1] National College of Ireland, Dublin, Ireland
dkelly@ncirl.ie
[2] University of Dublin, Trinity College, Ireland
tangney@tcd.ie

Abstract. This paper introduces, EDUCE, an ITS that utilises individual learning characteristics to generate presentations in diverse and sensitive ways. In EDUCE, the pedagogical framework classifies the educational content and the learner characteristics in the student model along two dimensions: Gardner's Multiple Intelligences and Bloom's learning goals. The two dimensions represent the philosophical underpinning in the design of instructional strategies and for understanding the student behaviour. It is through the provision of a variety of instructional strategies, that EDUCE aims to motivate and engage the learner. This paper describes the principles, architecture, design and implementation of EDUCE. It shows how educational theory may underpin the design of an ITS and how a pedagogical component that accommodates learning characteristics may be incorporated into an ITS. It also shows how to develop a mechanism by which the learner can choose between alternative instructional approaches.

1 Introduction

An Intelligent Tutoring System tries to model a student's knowledge, style and preferences in order to help navigate them through the learning process in an individualised manner that meets their needs. It provides appropriate help, suggest the next step in the learning cycle and presents material in a way that matches their preferences. There is however some debate on the benefit of such systems, with some proponents claiming significant improvements in learning [28] but other studies being more critical [23]. One way forward may not be in asking questions about the application of new technologies in terms of media such as text, video, or sound but in asking about the way students learn via the new technology [5]. In particular customized learning offers considerable potential [18] in that it should allow learners to take the initiative and choose from a diversity of instructional methods, e.g. problem-based learning, project-based learning, simulations, tutorials, and team-based learning [2]. This approach has implications for the role of the instructional designer where there will be less involvement in direct instructional decision making and more concentration on the mechanisms by means of which decisions are made. It follows that the only viable way to make decisions about instructional strategies is to do so

S.A. Cerri, G. Gouardères, and F. Paraguaçu (Eds.): ITS 2002, LNCS 2363, pp. 729–738, 2002.

dynamically using a system that is constantly observing the student and is capable of continuously updating information about the student's progress, attitude, expectations [27].

This research introduces, EDUCE, an ITS that uses a rich and sophisticated pedagogical model that allows for the delivery of material in diverse and student sensitive ways. It recognises the need to select a pedagogical model that caters for student's with individual learning characteristics. It stands in contrast to most current ITS, and self-instructional material, that implicitly, or explicitly, adopts a specific pedagogical model of instruction and expects the student to conform to it [22]. EDUCE offers a domain independent pedagogical framework that allows for the delivery of material in a variety of ways.

The word „educe" originates from the Latin „educere" meaning to „lead out, bring out or develop from latent or potential existence". The motivation behind EDUCE, is that intelligence is not a fixed static entity, but something that resides inside a person, and can be enhanced significantly through education and awareness. The belief is that matching the instructional methods with the learning characteristics of the student can help this process. Through the provision of a variety of instructional strategies, EDUCE aims to motivate and engage the learner in spontaneous, creative and ingenious ways in order to draw out the latent knowledge.

EDUCE classifies the educational content and the learner characteristics in the student model along two dimensions. Gardner's multiple intelligences concept [10], [11], [12], provides one dimension in which the student characteristics are described. The multiple intelligence concept defines intelligence as the capacity to solve problems or fashion products that are of value and states that there are eight different ways to demonstrate this intelligence. Learning goals provide the other dimension and are defined at three levels – the memorization of facts, the understanding of concepts and ability to solve problems.

EDUCE provides a learning environment in which students can choose material according to their needs and preferences. Material is presented to students along with opportunities to select alternative instructional strategies. EDUCE dynamically records all actions the student makes, and updates the students profile accordingly. It uses this information, when making decisions, to present the learner with suitable educational material. At the end of each topic, a summary report gives the learner the opportunity to view how they interacted with the system and thus learn something about their own learning style. Currently, science is the subject area for which content is being developed. EDUCE is currently at the prototype stage and is being evaluated to measure student satisfaction, motivation and learning effectiveness.

This paper emphasises two points. Firstly, students learn in different ways and modelling learning characteristics enhances the quality of ITS design. Secondly, an ITS can incorporate mechanisms, independent of the subject domain, that allow the student to avail of customised learning and choose between instructional approaches. The following sections illustrate these points by describing the principles, architecture, design and implementation of the student model, pedagogical model, domain model and presentation module in EDUCE.

2   Related Work

Research on learning styles has shown that students learn differently, that they process and represent knowledge in different ways, that performance is related to how students learn, that some students learn more effectively when taught with preferred methods and that is possible to diagnose learning style and make prescriptions [21], [7]. It has been shown that the approaches used by learners are dynamic and open to adaptation according to the particular context of learning. The research also provides a wealth of insight into individual differences and orientations to learning that can be translated into instructional design. Different studies report that when the learner's individual learning style is taken into account, the quality of the learning material is enhanced [17], [20]. However, observing and defining learning characteristics is difficult and traditionally questionnaires and psychometric tests are used to assess and diagnose learning characteristics [14], [19].

Several system adapting to the individual's learning characteristic have been developed [4], [6]. However it is not clear which aspects of learning characteristics are worth modelling, how the modelling can take place and what can be done differently for users with different learning styles [3]. In attempts to build a model of student's learning characteristics, feedback from the student is obtained using questionnaires, navigation paths, answers to questions, directly requesting feedback, allowing the user to update their own student model and to make specific adaptations such as sorting links or viewing stretch text.

Machine learning techniques offer one solution in the quest to build a model of learning characteristics [24], [25]. Typically these systems contain a variety of instructional types such as explanations or example and fragments of different media types representing the same content, with the tutoring system choosing the most suitable for the learner. Another approach is to compare the students performance in tests to that of other students, and to match students with instructors who can work successfully with that type of student [13]. Other systems try to model learning characteristics such as logical, arithmetic and diagrammatic ability [16].

EDUCE builds on existing research by modelling the learner's psychological characteristics through the multiple intelligence concept and through the identification of learning goals.

3   Student Model

The student model in EDUCE is inspired by the Multiple Intelligence concept. The psychological profile and the learning characteristics of the student are defined along two dimensions, the student's intelligence and learning goal. In the student model, a two dimensional array of variables, corresponding to each combination of intelligence and learning goal, stores the weighting factor that indicates the students preferred learning characteristics. Other information also stored in the student model includes the navigation history, the time spent on each learning unit, the answers given to questions and the different sections covered.

There is no universally accepted definition of intelligence. The classical viewpoint is that intelligence could be measured by giving tests with right and wrong answers, and characterising the ability that underlies intelligence with a unitary trait, for example the IQ test score [26]. An alternative view is the multiple intelligence concept. Rather than seek to understand the content or elements of intelligence, the objective is to understand what people do when they are engaged in intelligent behaviour. What is important is the way in which people combine knowledge, strategies, and metacognitive process to solve problems important to them. Intelligence is seen not as fixed static entity, but something that can be enhanced and amplified significantly through education and training.

Gardner identifies eight intelligences involved in solving problems, in producing material such as compositions, music or poetry and other educational activities. The intelligences include the logical/mathematical, linguistic/verbal, visual/spatial, bodily/kinesthetic, musical/rhythmic, interpersonal, intrapersonal and naturalist. Logical/mathematical intelligence consists of the ability to detect patterns, reason deductively and think logically. Linguistic/verbal intelligence involves having a mastery of the language and includes the ability to manipulate language to express oneself. Spatial intelligence is the ability to manipulate and create mental images in order to solve problems. Musical intelligence encompasses the capability to recognise and compose musical pitches, tones and rhythms. Bodily-Kinesthetic intelligence is the ability to learn by doing and using mental abilities to co-ordinate bodily movements. The interpersonal intelligence is the ability to work and communicate with other people. The intrapersonal intelligence involves knowledge of the internal aspects of the self such as knowledge of feelings and thinking processes. Naturalist intelligence involves the ability to comprehend, discern and appreciate the world of nature.

Gardner states that everybody possesses the different types of intelligences to different degrees and that they operate together in an orchestrated way. The theory suggests that even though different intelligences do tend to be stronger in some people, everybody has the capacity to activate all the intelligences and in different situations, different intelligences or a combination of intelligences may be used.

Educational goals and learning outcomes is the other dimension in the student's learning profile. The learning goal may be to learn facts, rules or action sequences, to learn concepts and principles, or to learn how to solve problems [8]. Alternatively the learning goals may be classified at levels ranging from knowledge, comprehension, application, analysis, and synthesis to evaluation [1]. The student's goals, either implicitly or explicitly stated, has a strong influence on how the student uses the system, and in EDUCE educational material is provided to meet this need. EDUCE defines learning goals at three levels – the memorization of facts, the understanding of concepts and ability to solve problems.

4   Pedagogical Model

The pedagogical model in EDUCE uses the intelligence and the learning goal of the student to influence the instructional strategy used in presenting the material. Instructional strategies are defined as patterns of practice that recur in the delivery of content. The choice of strategy will depend on the specific intelligence being explored and the learning goal. To access each of the intelligences, there is a set of practical techniques, methods, tools, media and instructional strategies. For example, to emphasis the logical and mathematical mind, strategies such as the use of abstract symbols and formulas, calculations, deciphering codes, forcing relationships, graphic and cognitive organisers, logic and pattern games, number sequences and patterns, outlining, problem solving and syllogisms may be employed [15]. Table 1 gives an example of how different intelligences are accessed when learning about scientific experiments.

Table 1. A sample of the different instructional strategies that can be used for the different intelligences when learning about experiments

Intelligence	Instructional Plan
Linguistic/Verbal	Record the steps in the experiment
Logical/Mathematical	Identify the pattern of a successful experiment
Visual/Spatial	Draw pictures of the experiments
Bodily/Kinesthetic	Carry out the experiment
Musical/Rhythmic	Listen to the sounds in the experiment
Interpersonal	Discuss with another student the results
Intrapersonal	Conduct reflections on the experiment
Naturalist	Use nature examples in explaining the experiment

Learning goals also influence the instructional strategy to use. For example, if the goal is to teach facts and rules, direct instruction that explicitly presents, clarifies and explains is useful. If the goal is to teach concepts, patterns and abstractions, indirect instruction that involves the expression of learner ideas and a process of inquiry and analysis may be appropriate. When the goal is to teach problem solving, self-directed instruction that places much of the responsibility on the learner along with an emphasis on synthesis, evaluation and metacognition would be suitable.

The task of choosing the correct instructional material involves deciding which material closely matches the model of the student. The classification task may be expressed as *ChooseInstructionalStrategy: I* $\rightarrow$ *R* where *ChooseInstructionalStrategy* is the function to learn, *I* is the range of possible instructional material, and *R* denotes the set of real numbers. *ChooseInstructionalStrategy* is an evaluation function that assigns a numerical score to each possible piece of instructional material. Each piece of instructional material is characterised by the same features as the student model: intelligence and learning goal. The instructional material that scores the highest numerical score will be chosen as the most appropriate to present. Currently this function is implemented by first identifying the intelligence/learning goal combination with the highest value in the student model. The piece of material giving the highest score for that intelligence/learning goal combination is selected. The student's response to the instructional strategy chosen is used to update the student model. Feedback comes from recording the pages visited and the options selected. A count is kept of how often a student uses a particular intelligence. The count is incremented every time a page that explores this intelligence is viewed. The scores for each intelligence/learning goal combination are normalized to give a comparative score of the preferred learning style. As the record of student behaviour increases, the quality of the decisions made improves, keeping the student engaged and motivated with material compatible with the learning characteristics.

5   Domain Model

The domain model is structured in two hierarchical levels of abstraction, concepts and learning units. Concepts represent the sections, and subsections into which the knowledge base is divided. Each section consists of learning units that contain the content for that particular concept. Learning units may contain different media types such as text, image, video, audio and animation. Different content for the same concept is provided for students with different intelligences and learning goals.

In the teaching of a concept, key instructional events identify the process in which learners acquire and transfer new information and skills [9]. These key instructional events may be summarised into four specific stages, structuring, modelling, coaching, and fading [2].   Structuring is the process of getting learners ready to learn by selecting, organizing and previewing the content to be presented. During the structuring phase, the instructor captures the attention of the learners and focuses it on the outcome of the lesson. Modelling is a teaching activity that involves demonstrating to learners what they need to do (in the form of action sequences), to say (in the form of facts and concepts) or to think (in the form of problem solving or learning-to learn strategies). Coaching is that stage of the instructional process during which learners convert memories into actions as a result of the modelling process. Effective coaching gives opportunities for practice, guiding it by prompting, questioning and providing motivation. Fading is the event that most directly achieves transfer of learning. The practice of fading involves the removal of external supports such as prompts or reinforcers, and the provision of independent transfer.

Subject experts, in the field of science, provide the educational material for EDUCE. Concepts and the relationships between them are first identified in the material.   Multiple learning units for each concept and instructional event are subsequently developed for use with each intelligence and learning goal. Material is consequently organised for the key instructional events of structuring, modelling, coaching and fading. The organization of the domain knowledge allows the student to choose alternative presentations of the same content when moving from one concept to another, from one instructional event to the next and even within the same instructional event.

6   Presentation Module

EDUCE uses learning characteristics, inferred from the interaction of the student with the system, to adapt the presentation of the content and the teaching strategies. Adaptive decisions are made based on the choices the learner makes as they navigate the system. The choice of presentation and instructional strategy is dynamic and is dependent on the current action the student is making and on previous actions.

There is two distinct forms of adaptation technology in EDUCE, adaptive presentation at the content level and adaptive navigation support at the link level. Adaptive presentation includes text, multimedia and modality adaptation. Adaptive navigation support includes direct guidance and link annotation. In EDUCE, adaptive presentation is implemented using stretch text, page variants and fragment variants. Stretch text enables the user to view extended information on the same page by activating a hotword. The extended part of the page may subsequently be collapsed back to the hotword to reduce the amount of information on screen. Page variants store different presentations of same content. On presenting a page, the system selects the page using the information in the learner model. EDUCE also allows learners to view alternative pages by following links. However the same choices are not presented to all students. Different learners will have different choices presented depending on their learning characteristics. Alternative fragment variants store the variety of choices the student may make.

Adaptive navigation support takes place by suggesting to the learner a page of instructional content that will match their learning characteristics. Direct local guidance takes place by suggesting the most relevant link from the current page. The learner can let the system decide what the next best page is by selecting the default next page. Link annotation takes place by augmenting links with visual cues. Links that may be useful to the learner are highlighted. Adaptive guidance also takes place at the end each of lesson unit. As the student moves onto the next concept, the chance is given to express satisfaction or dissatisfaction with the delivery of instructional. The student has a choice, to continue with the same instructional style, to try something different but similar, or to try a random instructional style.

All actions of the user are collected and used to evaluate their satisfaction with the method of instructional delivery. If the learner does not select alternative instructional strategies during the delivery of a concept, the current model of the student is assumed correct and reinforced. If the student selects alternative presentations to what was originally given, the student model is updated accordingly. In Fig. 1, a screen shot is given of part of a lesson unit. Here, social studies is being studied using the logical/mathematical intelligence. The student is being introduced to inductive thinking patterns using an attribute web. Verbal/linguistic intelligence is also being encouraged by asking the student to write on the web. The student may progress through the lesson by selecting the next button. The content of the page will be automatically generated based on the knowledge in the student model. However, if the student prefers another mode of instruction, they may select alternative instructional strategies. The student is given the option to work in a group, which if selected may suggest, that the student is more comfortable using interpersonal intelligence. The option is also given to view pictures in helping find the characteristics of the school. If the option is selected, it may suggest the student prefers the visual/spatial approach.

7   Implementation

EDUCE is a web based ITS and is being implemented using Java and XML technology. In EDUCE, the domain knowledge base holds the educational content in XML format. An XML file for each section of material stores the learning unit content. The student knowledge base stores individualised student models in tables within a database. The pedagogical manager is implemented in Java. It is responsible for retrieving information from the student model and making decisions about which instructional strategy to use. The presentation manager receives input from the pedagogical manager and manages the presentation of information through the use of

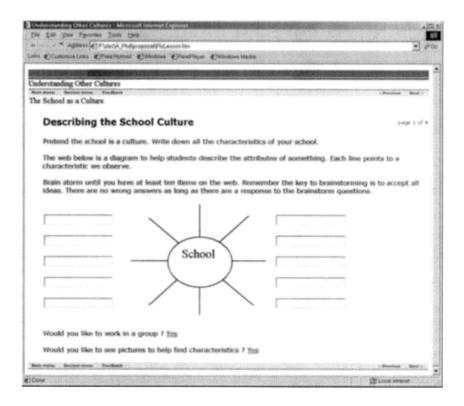

Fig. 1. A Typical page in EDUCE.

XSLT stylesheets. The action monitor observes, monitors and handles all feedback from the student in the form of links activated, buttons pressed and text entered. The student manager, implemented in Java, analyses feedback from student and updates the student model.

8   Conclusions and Future Work

In this paper, we presented EDUCE, an ITS that identifies individual learning characteristics and generates presentations in diverse and sensitive ways to match these characteristics. The motivation behind EDUCE is that students can be best engaged by matching instructional strategies with learning characteristics. The paper emphasised that ITS design should concentrate on the mechanisms that allows learners to choose between instructional approaches. The paper also shows that this can best done by identifying and using learning characteristics.

In EDUCE, we showed how a domain independent pedagogical framework could classify the student and educational content in two dimensions, intelligence and learning goal. We argued that students learn differently and by modelling learning characteristics, the quality of the ITS design is enhanced. Moreover we illustrated in

EDUCE, how to including a pedagogical component, that identifies learning characteristics, making the system becomes more flexible and adaptable to individual learner needs. The architecture, design and implementation of EDUCE was described in detail. Currently, EDUCE is at the prototype stage, with content being developed and being evaluated with students to measure satisfaction, motivation and learning effectiveness. Future work will involve extensive empirical studies to evaluate how can students with different learning characteristics be supported.

Presently, EDUCE makes pedagogical decisions using explicit rules to identify suitable instructional material. It may indeed be possible to explicitly model how different categories of student preferred different models of presentation. However this is time consuming and makes the assumption we know what the correct learning theory is. It also makes the assumption, that we can articulate the rules for updating the student model and for making pedagogical decisions. Machine learning algorithms can help, as they are particularly useful in poorly understood domains where humans might not have the knowledge to develop effective algorithms and in domains where the system must dynamically adapt to changing conditions. The identification of learning characteristics is a domain in which machine-learning algorithms may be useful as teaching students in an effective manner, is an ongoing area of research, and students are different and learn in a different ways. Future work involves the identification and implementation of a machine-learning agent that can be used in the identification of leaning characteristics.

References

1. Bloom, B. Engelhart, M., Hill, W., Furst, E., & Krathwohl, D. (1956): Taxonomy of educational objectives. The classification of educational goals. Handbook I: Cognitive domain. Longman Green.
2. Borich, G., Tombari, M. (1997): Educational Pscyhology: A contemporary Approach. Longman 1997.
3. Brusilovsky, P. (2001): Adpative Hypermedia. User Modeling and User-Adapted Instruction, Volume 11, Nos 1-2. Kluwer Academic Publishers.
4. Carver, C., Howard, R., & Lavelle, E. (1996): Enhancing student learning by incorporating learning styles into adaptive hypermedia. 1996 ED-MEDIA Conference on Educational Multimedia and Hypermedia. Boston, MA.
5. Clark, R. E. (1983): Reconsidering research on learning from media. Review of Educational Research, 53(4).
6. Danielson, R. (1997): Learning Styles, media preferences, and adaptive education. In: Proceedings of the workshop "Adaptive Systems and User Modeling on the World Wide Web", Sixth International Conference on User Modeling, UM97.
7. Dunn & Dunn (1978): Teaching Students through their individual learning styles: A practical approach.Prentice Hall, Reston Publishing.
8. Gagné, R. M. (1985). Conditions of Learning. New York: Holt.
9. Gagné, R. M., Briggs, L. & Wagner, W., (1992). Principles of instructional design. Harcourt, Brace.
10. Gardner H. (1983) Frames of Mind: The theory of multiple intelligences. New York. Basic Books.
11. Gardner H. (1993): Multiple Intelligences: The theory in practice. New York. Basic Books.

12. Gardner H. (2000): Intelligence Reframed: Multiple Intelligences for the 21st Century. Basic Books
13. Gilbert, J. E. & Han, C. Y. (1999): Arthur: Adapting Instruction to Accommodate Learning Style. In: Proceedings of WebNet'99, World Conference of the WWW and Internet, Honolulu, HI.
14. Honey, P. and Mumford, A. (1986, 1992): The Manual of Learning Styles. Peter Honey, Maidenhead.
15. Lazaer, D. (1999): Eight Ways of Teaching: The Artistry of Teaching with Multiple Intelligences, SkyLight.
16. Milne, S. (1997): Adapting to Learner Attributes, experiments using an adaptive tutoring system. Educational Pschology Vol 17 Nos 1 and 2, 1997
17. Rasmussen, K. L. (1998): Hypermedia and learning styles: Can performance be influenced? Journal of Multimedia and Hypermedia, 7(4).
18. Reigeluth, C.M. (1996): A new paradigm of ISD? Educational Technology, 36(3).
19. Riding, R. J. (1991): Cognitive Styles Analysis, Learning and Training Technology, Birmingham.
20. Riding, R., & Grimley, M. (1999): Cognitive style and learning from multimedia materials in 11-year children. British Journal of Educational Technology, 30(1).
21. Riding, R. & Rayner. S, (1997): Cognitive Styles and learning strategies. David Fulton Publishers.
22. Rowntree, D. (1992): Exploring open and distance learning materials. London: Kogan page
23. Russell, T. L. (1998): The "no significant difference" phenomenon. North Carolina State University, Raleigh.
24. Specht, M. and Oppermann, R. (1998): ACE: Adaptive CourseWare Environment, New Review of HyperMedia & MultiMedia 4,
25. Stern, M & Woolf. B. (2000): Adaptive Content in an Online lecture system. In: Proceedings of the First Adpative Hypermedia Conference, AH2000.
26. Terman (1925): Mental and physical traits of a thousand gifted children. Genetic studies of genius: Vol 1. Standford CA. Standord University.
27. Winn, W. (1989): Toward a rational and theoretical basis for educational technology. Educational Technology Research & Development, 37(1).
28. Woolf, B., Regian, W. (2000): Knowledge-based training systems and the engineering of Instruction. Handbook of Training and Retraining.

Simultaneous Evaluation of Multiple Topics in SIETTE

Eduardo Guzmán and Ricardo Conejo

Departamento de Lenguajes y Ciencias de la Computación.
E. T. S. I. Informática. Universidad de Málaga. Apdo. 4114, 29080 Málaga. SPAIN
{guzman, conejo}@lcc.uma.es

Abstract. SIETTE is an efficient web-based implementation of a *Computer Adaptive Test*. The inference machine used is based on *Item Response Theory*. New enhances in the evaluation mechanisms, question selection and finalization criteria have been introduced. New evaluation mechanism allows giving structured knowledge estimation about all topics evaluated in a test. Question selection criteria are able to automatically select a balanced number of items from all topics, so teachers do not need to accomplish this task manually. This paper shows that SIETTE can successfully be integrated into web-based Intelligent Tutoring Systems with structured curriculum, in order to make initial estimations of the student's knowledge level, or even to update the student's model after his exposition to instructional components.

1 Introduction

One of the most important features of an Intelligent Tutoring System (ITS) in comparison to Computer Aided Learning Systems is that ITS adapts to each particular student giving a personalized training [1]. Generally, in web-based ITSs, students can access different instructional components. There students learn different topics, but the ITS does not have any information about how it is accomplished. Therefore, this kind of systems needs some diagnosis module to accomplish a tracking about the examinee's ability. The role of assessment in an ITS is, consequently, the measurement of the state of the knowledge at each time.

Traditionally, ITS have domain knowledge model about the subject being taught, and an instructional planner. The instructional planner decides the best next step in the instructional process. The knowledge model may be composed by a set of nodes that represent the estimated knowledge about each topic of the subject. As a consequence, when a new student begins a course in an ITS, some mechanism is required to have an initial estimation of the student's ability. A first solution could be the realization of a pre-test of each topic involved in the subject. This solution will be acceptable if the number of different topics is small. Otherwise the realization of a test session for each topic can be a very hard and boring task.

SIETTE is a web-based tool to assist teachers and instructors in the evaluation process. Tests offered by this tool are *Computer Adaptive Tests* (CATs) [2], where the evaluation process, the item selection criterion, and the tests finalization criterion are based on a psychometric theory called *Item Response Theory* (IRT) [3].

S.A. Cerri, G. Gouardères, and F. Paraguaçu (Eds.): ITS 2002, LNCS 2363, pp. 739–748, 2002.

In this paper, some improvements to the former evaluation mechanisms of SIETTE [4] are presented. The new version of SIETTE is now able to give a structured estimation of the proficiency in each topic after a test session. This estimation mechanism is even able to use multidimensional questions, that is, questions whose resolution depends on the student's knowledge about more than one topic. All these features make the student model of SIETTE more detailed, and as a result, enhance its use as an evaluation module inside web-based ITSs for curriculum-structured domains.

The structure of the paper is as follows: first, a brief introduction to CATs is presented. In section 3, the main components of SIETTE and how the adaptation operates are summarized. Following, the hierarchical structure of the knowledge base of SIETTE is explained. Then the new enhances added to the evaluation mechanism, are introduced, mainly focusing on the *unidimensional* evaluation. Next, an example of a test session is proposed. The paper finishes with some conclusions.

2   Computer Adaptive Tests

A CAT can be defined as a test administered by a computer where the presentation of each item and the decision to finish the test are dynamically adopted based on the student's answers. In more precise terms, a CAT is an iterative algorithm that starts with an initial estimation of the examinee's proficiency level and has the following steps: (1) All the questions in the knowledge base (that have not been administered yet) are examined to determine which is the best item to ask next according to the current estimation of the examinee's knowledge level. (2) The question is asked, and the examinee responds. (3) According to the answer, a new estimation of the proficiency level is computed. (4) Steps 1 to 3 are repeated until the stopping criterion defined is met. This procedure is illustrated in Fig. 1.

The selection and finalization criteria are based upon a Bayesian procedure that can be controlled with parameters that define the required accuracy. The number of questions is not fixed, and each examinee usually takes different sequences of questions, and even different questions.

The main advantage of adaptive testing is that it reduces the number of questions needed to estimate the knowledge level of the student, and that estimation's accuracy is much higher than the estimation achieved by randomly picking the same number of questions [5].

3   The SIETTE System

SIETTE is structured in two parts: (1) a set of author's editors, which allow the teachers to include and modify questions (called *items*), and to hierarchically structure all these *items* in a set of different topics (this structure is called *curriculum*). All these *items pools* are stored in a knowledge base. (2) A virtual classroom where students can take tests about different domains. These tests are generated according to teachers' specifications and are adaptive.

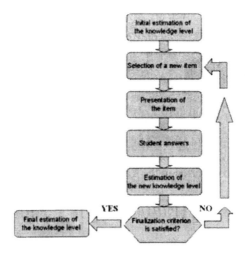

Fig. 1. Flow diagram of an adaptive test. (Adapted from [11])

The system can be used in two different ways: as an independent evaluation tool or as a component of the diagnostic module of an ITS with a curriculum structured knowledge base [6].

While the student is taking the test, the system creates and updates a student model, which mainly stores his knowledge distribution at each stage of the evaluation process. Until this moment, SIETTE has been presented as a system able to measure only one variable called knowledge level (*latent trait* in IRT). This knowledge level is an aggregated value that measures the understanding and know-how of a student in certain subject.

3.1 The Adaptation Mechanism in SIETTE

In IRT, each item i in a test is assigned an *Item Characteristic Curve* (ICC) which is a function, $f : (-\infty, +\infty) \rightarrow [0,1]$, representing the probability of a correct answer to that item, given a certain student's knowledge level θ. Let us represent this probability by the expression: $P(U_i=1| \theta)$ or just P_i. Logically, the probability of failing the question is $P(U_i=0| \theta) = 1-P(U_i=1| \theta)$, or simply Q_i. It is usually assumed that ICCs belong to a family of functions that depend on one, two or three parameters. These functions are based on the normal or the logistic distribution function. SIETTE uses the three-parameter logistic model [7], where the ICC is described by:

$$P_i = P(U_i = 1|\theta) = c_i + (1-c_i)\frac{1}{1+e^{-1.7a_i(\theta-b_i)}} \tag{1}$$

c_i is the guessing factor, b_i is the difficulty of the question and a_i is the discrimination factor. The guessing factor is the probability that a student with no knowledge at all answers the question correctly. The difficulty represents the knowledge level in which the student has equal probability to answer or fail the question, besides the guessing factor. The discrimination factor is proportional to the slope of the curve.

The value of θ is estimated using the response to each item of the test. It is done by a Bayesian method [8], where the probability distribution of the student's knowledge level is calculated, by the Bayes' rule.

A discrete implementation of IRT is used in SIETTE. The latent trait θ can only take K discrete values (from 0 to $K-1$). The ICCs are represented by a vector of K components, whose values are initially calculated from the discretizacion of formula (1), but they are dynamically updated by the on-line learning module [5].

If the test is composed by n items, given the ICCs, the *a posteriori* estimated knowledge level can be inferred in the following way:

$$\overline{P(\theta|u)} = \left\| \prod_{i=1}^{n} \overline{P_i(\theta)}^{u_i} (\overline{1 - P_i(\theta)})^{(1-u_i)} \overline{P(\theta)} \right\| \tag{2}$$

A distribution of the probability of θ is obtained applying Bayes' rule n times. So, SIETTE does a Bayesian classification of the examinee in one of the K classes of knowledge levels according to his answers to the n items proposed.

3.2 Hierarchical Structure of the Curriculum

The items pool is stored into a knowledge base. One for each of the subjects or domains to be evaluated. Each knowledge base is formed by three types of objects:

- *Topics:* They are hierarchically structured forming the *curriculum*. SIETTE can operate with an undefined number of levels in this hierarchy. Each final node of the *curriculum* corresponds to an unique concept or a set of indiscernible concepts in the evaluation sense. Intermediate nodes of the hierarchy represent aggregations of the subtopics of the lower hierarchy according to an inclusion relation. The model of the student associates a knowledge level to each of these (intermediate or terminal) topics. The curriculum structure is defined by the teacher. Independence between nodes of the curriculum that are not directly related is assumed.
- *Items:* They must be explicitly associated to one or more terminal or intermediate topics. This association indicates that the knowledge about a set of topics is required to correctly answer the item. The relation between the knowledge of this topic and the item response is given by an ICC.

In the old version of SIETTE, items only were able to evaluate only one topic. Therefore, each item had one associated *unidimensional* ICC. In the new version, two additional relations can be found between topics and items:

First, items can be associated to more than one topic. For these kind of items, the ICC is *multidimensional* and represents the probability to correctly answer to an item in terms of the combination of the knowledge levels of the required topics. An important constraint that will reduce the complexity of he problems is that an item will be only associated to several topics if these topics are sons of the same topic, i.e., these topics are siblings. In section 4.2 the evaluation mechanism for these items is briefly described.

Second, each item is also associated with all the ancestors in the *curriculum* hierarchy. That is, an item defined to evaluate the topic T_{abc} it can be also used to evaluate the topic T_{ab}, the topic T_a, ; or even the whole subject, where T_{abc} is a subtopic of T_{ab}, etc. This implies having $p+1$ characteristic curves, where p is the depth of the topic to which the topic initially belongs. Let us suppose that each curve is *unidimensional*. These curves represent the probability of correctly answer the item, given the knowledge level of each node respectively. Section 4.1, shows how the evaluation is accomplished in this case.

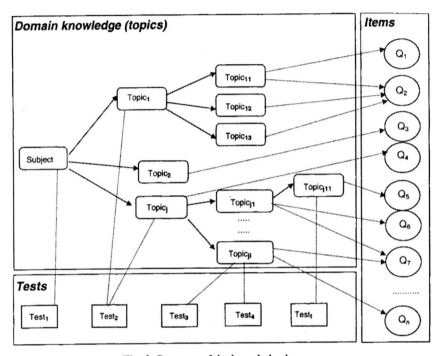

Fig. 2. Structure of the knowledge base

Tests: A test represents an evaluation session. Its main objective is to obtain an estimation of the examinee's knowledge level about one or more topics of the *curriculum*. Therefore, tests are defined in terms of the topic or topics being evaluated. Items which correspond to a test, are those required to accomplish the assessment. There is not a direct relationship between tests and items. This relationship is established through topics. Moreover, in SIETTE, a test can only be associated to sibling topics in the hierarchy.

Two evaluation modes for a test can be prefixed: *aggregated*, if only the evaluation of this node of the *curriculum* is required; or *complete*, if an exhaustive evaluation of all nodes of the sub-tree whose root is the topic, is required.

4 Evaluating Multiple Topics in SIETTE

In the former version of SIETTE, if a test involved items from several topics, the final knowledge level obtained was a global estimation for all these topics. Also teachers had to explicitly indicate the percentage of items from each topic that appear in a test session.

For an independent evaluation for each topic, a different test for each topic was required. The use of SIETTE as an evaluation module in an ITS requires a more detailed evaluation information. Therefore some extensions of IRT are needed, since classical approach of CAT using IRT as an inference machine are only valid for an aggregated estimation.

4.1 Unidimensional Evaluation

The evaluation process is carried out in parallel for each node of the hierarchy, taking the root node topic as the starting point. In this case, the student model is formed by the probability distributions of the knowledge level in each topic assessed. Formally, if a test is composed by the items $Q_p,...,Q_n$ where $(u_p,...,u_n)$ is the vector of responses to these items, the estimation of the knowledge level of the topic k will be obtained from the distribution $P(\theta_k \mu_p,...,u_q)$ which is proportional, like in formula (2), to:

$$\forall k \quad P(\theta_k) \times \prod_{i=p}^{q} P_i(\theta_k)^{u_i} (1 - P_i(\theta_k))^{(1-u_i)} \tag{3}$$

where $(u_p,...,u_q)$ is the subset of responses to the items associated to topic k or to some of its descendants; $P_i(\theta)$ represents the ICC of the item i, given the knowledge level about the topic k; and $P(\theta)$ is the *a priori* density function or initial estimation of the student knowledge level about the topic k.

For instance, to evaluate the knowledge level of the topic j (T_j), see Fig. 2, all items associated to its descendants can be used. For instance, item Q_5 associated with topic T_{jll}. As a result, the knowledge in topics T_{jll}, T_{jl} and T_j can be simultaneously updated using the characteristic curves associated to item Q_5 for each one of these topics. In the same way, if item Q_n is posed to the student, the knowledge about the topic T_{jl} will be updated. The estimation process of the knowledge level about the topic T_j will be modified too according to the new evidence.

This way of evaluation establishes a particular dependency between the values of knowledge levels of certain topics regarding other topics. Hence, if all items were associated to terminal nodes in the *curriculum*, the process would imply the evaluation of them and the inference of the value of the ascending nodes by the aggregation of their direct descendants. The inverse process is not possible.

Concerning the adaptive mechanism, there are several alternatives. One alternative is to calculate the influence of the possible application of an item in all the student's knowledge level vectors for all the nodes of the hierarchy, and to establish a criterion of minimum average of the expectations of the *a posteriori* variances. In this case, the system will select an item about the topic whose knowledge estimation is the poorest.

As a result, the responsibility of balanced selection of items of each topic is left to the inference machine.

4.2 Multidimensional Evaluation

Sometimes, the answer to an item depends on the knowledge of more than one concept (topics in SIETTE). As a result, multidimensional models should be used to evaluate them. In SIETTE, the calculus of the *a posteriori* probability, in this case, is relatively simple. ICCs are transformed into *s* dimensional matrices of *k* components. Clearly, the size of these curves is exponential in terms of the number of topics, but from a practical point of view, the problem is tractable for values of k' that can be processed in a reasonable response time. The mechanism used to evaluate multidimentional items will be described in future works.

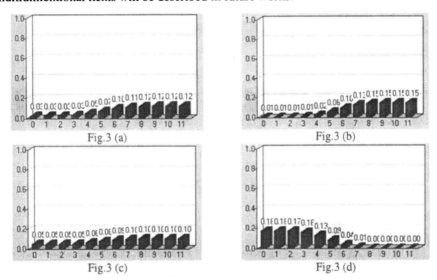

Fig. 3. Knowledge distribution for each topic after posing five items

5 An Example

In this example, the behaviour of a simulated examinee is going to be analysed. A test session accomplished by the examinee is represented. Let us consider a test of the subject of *Introduction to Compilers* [9]. It is formed by four topics: *(a) Introduction, (b) Lexical Analysis, (c) Syntactic Analysis,* and *(d) Semantic Analysis.* It has been configured with a number of items for each session between 10 and 20. The knowledge is classified into twelve categories (from 0 to 11). All student models begin with constant knowledge distributions for all topics, equal to 0.083. ICCs of all items are unidimensional with difficulty 5 and discrimination factor 0.7.

The goal of this analysis is to show the enhances in the adaptive mechanism of item selection. These enhances make the system able by itself to automatically choose the most adequate items in order to infer the examinee's knowledge level in each topic. In an item pool where all items have the same difficulty, the adaptation is done according to the topic, not to the item difficulty.

The expected behaviour of the system is that it should pose more items from those topics where the examinee's ability is more uncertainty. That is, if examinee succeeds or fails in the main part of items, the system will be soon able to estimate a knowledge level. In contrast, if he sometimes succeeds but occasionally fails, the estimation process is more difficult, and therefore requires a higher number of items.

Let us suppose that the examinee has good knowledge of topics *(a)* and *(b)*, no knowledge about topic *(d)* and intermediate knowledge about topic *(c)*. He will always answer correctly to items of topics *(a)* and *(b)*, and incorrectly to items of topic *(b)*. For items of topic *(c)*, he will answer to one correctly, incorrectly to the next item, and so on.

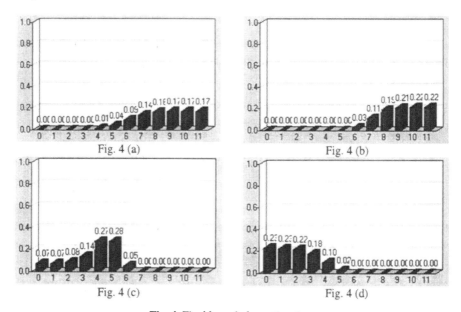

Fig. 4. Final knowledge estimation

In a first stage, the system should make an initial estimation of the ability in all topics. In Fig. 3 probability distributions curves of the examinee's knowledge after posing five items are shown. All distributions except the one for topic *(c)* (Fig. 3 (c)) begin to have a certain slope, which indicate that examinee has a well defined level in these topics. On the other hand, the curve for the topic *(c)* is not so inclined because the examinee has given right answers to some items and wrong answers to other items. The test has not reach at a conclusion about his knowledge level in this topic. The estimation of the knowledge is more difficult in this case. Let us take into account that all items have a difficulty equal to 5. Reasonably, examinee should be classified into the knowledge level 5, because his knowledge is intermediate, but he is failing half of items, which makes the estimation process more complex.

Now the expected behaviour of the system is that to pose more items for topic *(c)* than for the other topics, since the estimation is more difficult. The curves for the other topics will have each time a smaller variance, i.e., its dispersion will be smaller and the estimation more accurate.

The test finished because the maximum number of items has been reached and not because the adaptive finalization criterion (Fig. 4). For this reason, although curves show low variance, any of the levels have a probability significantly greater than the former level.

Table 1 shows the final percentage of items posed to the examinee. The maximum corresponds to topic *(c)* which makes sense because the behaviour of the student was not consistent, so the knowledge level of the topic has been more difficult to estimate. In spite of that fact, table 1 shows that the percentage of items posed from each topic is balanced. Obviously, the knowledge of those topics in which the examinee has always succeeded or failed has been quickly estimated.

Table 1. Statistics of the first examinee's test session

Topic	Correctly answered items	Incorrectly answered items	Total number of items	Estimated knowledge level	Percentage of total items
(a)	3	0	3	11	15%
(b)	6	0	6	11	30%
(c)	5	4	9	5	45%
(d)	0	2	2	0	10%

6 Conclusions

An improved adaptive mechanism based on IRT has been presented. SIETTE provides tests where student's knowledge level can be estimated according to the topics, subtopics and concepts in the hierarchically-structured curriculum. These features make this system useful as a diagnostic tool in a web-based ITS. On the other hand, Web based ITSs generally use instructional components which do not give feedback about the influence of tutorial component in the student's learning process. In this case, SIETTE can be integrated in such tutorial components to compensate their lack of feedback mechanisms. By means of a test of all topics covered by the instructional component, the ITS can obtain information about how this instruction has modified the student's proficiency.

In previous versions of SIETTE, teachers were enforced to set the percentage of items to be presented to examinees. This was done to guarantee that items of all topics were presented and that the number of items of each topic was balanced. Thanks to the modifications introduced, the adaptive mechanism of item selection is able to automatically select the most adequate percentage of items of each topic. This is an implicit consequence of the searching for a better estimation of the knowledge in each topic.

The multidimensionality introduced in the curriculum makes for a more realistic assignment of items to topics. Often teachers are enforced to assign an item to a certain topic, when it could be also assigned to other topic. In these cases, the assignment to only one topic despises relevant information for the estimation of knowledge about other topics. The use of multidimensional items has also some influences in the finalization of the test, since these items are useful to estimate knowledge in several topics, and as a result, a lower number of items is required to finish the test.

On the other hand, the main problem of the integration of SIETTE in an web-based ITS is that the ITS and SIETTE must have a common structured *curriculum*, or at least, a correspondence may be established between the student model used in the tutoring system and the *curriculum* settled in SIETTE. Moreover the values returned by SIETTE are coarse data that has been obtained from the observations. ITSs might have mechanisms to indirectly infer the values of knowledge in certain topics from knowledge estimation in other topics. For instance, if a student has demonstrated a high knowledge level in a topic, a low knowledge level in another topic, which is one of its prerequisites, will be very unlikely. SIETTE does not manage this kind of relations between topics. These inferences must be accomplished by the ITS. There are systems [10] that manage more complex models, but it implies a very high computational cost.

The system can be tested at http://www.lcc.uma.es/SIETTE

References

[1]   Self, J. (1990) Theoretical foundation for Intelligent Tutoring Systems. AAAI/AI-ED 1990; 45.
[2]   Wainer H. (1990). *Computerized adaptive testing: a primer.* Hillsdale, NJ: Lawrence Erlbaum Associates.
[3]   Lord, F. M. (1980). *Applications of item response theory to practical testing problems.* Hillsdale, NJ: Lawrence Erlbaum Associates.
[4]   Ríos A., Millán E., Trella M., Pérez-de-la-Cruz J., Conejo R. (1999). *Internet Based Evaluation System*, In: *Artificial Intelligence in Education AIED'99*, Le Mans (1999) 387-394.
[5]   Conejo, R., Millán, E., Pérez-de-la-Cruz, J., Trella, M., (2000). An empirical approach to on-line learning in SIETTE. In *Proceedings of ITS'2000*, Montreal. Springer-Verlag. 57-60.
[6]   Trella, M., Conejo, R. (2000). ITS Web based Architecture for Hierarchical Declarative Domains, in: *Young Researchers Track Proceedings, ITS'2000*, Montreal 57-60.
[7]   Birnbaum, A. (1968). *Some latent trait models and their use in inferring an examinee's mental ability.* In Lord, F. M. & Novick, M.R. (ed.) *Statistical theories of mental test scores.* Reading, MA: Addison-Wesley.
[8]   Owen, R. J. (1975). A Bayesian sequential procedures for quantal response in the context of adaptive mental testing. *Journal of the American Statistical Association 70*, 351-356.
[9]   Aho, A.V., Sethi, R., Ullman, J.D. (1987). Compilers: principles, techniques and tools.
[10]   Millán, E., Pérez-de-la-Cruz, J. L., Suárez, E. (2000). An Adaptive Bayesian Network for Multilevel Student Modeling. In *Proceedings of ITS'2000.* 534-543.
[11]   Olea J.,Ponsoda, V.: Tests adaptativos informatizados. In Muñiz, J.(ed) *Psicometría.* 1996. Madrid: Universitas.

Toward Measuring and Maintaining the Zone of Proximal Development in Adaptive Instructional Systems

Tom Murray[1] and Ivon Arroyo[2]

[1] Cognitive Science, Hampshire College, Amherst, MA 01002
[2] Computer Science, University of Massachusetts, Amherst, MA 01003
tmurray@hampshire.edu, ivon@cs.umass.edu

Abstract. Intelligent tutoring Systems (ITSs) adapt content and activities with the goals of being both effective and efficient instructional environments. They have goals for students to be challenged and guided in an optimal way-- without being too overwhelmed with difficult material or too bored with easy or repetitive material. We propose a particular definition of the zone of proximal development (ZPD) as a general way to describe what all ITSs try to do, and we propose a foundational analysis of instructional adaptivity, student modeling, and system evaluation in terms of the ZPD. We give an operational definition of the ZPD and give an example of its use, and summarize how instructional methods such as scaffolding can be used to maintain ZPD-learning. We also explain how our definition of the ZPD can lead to a more complete model for efficient and effective instruction than common mastery learning criteria.

1 Introduction

Many exposés in educational technology build upon educational constructs such as scaffolding, apprenticeship learning, and the zone of proximal development (ZPD), that can be traced back to Vygotsky. These concepts are rarely clearly defined or operationalized [1]. The field of intelligent tutoring systems (ITS) is based on building models and it behooves us to try to specify our principles in a computational form. Our goal in this paper is to give a specific and concrete model showing one possible implementation of the concepts of zone of proximal development and scaffolding. We propose that the model is general, not in reflecting a general version of the diverse interpretations of Vygotskian constructs, but in its applicability to ITS design issues.

The most complete treatment of ZPD in the ITS community to date has been by Luckin and du Boulay in the context of the Ecolab ITS [2] [3]. They use the phrase Zone of Available Assistance (ZAA) to refer to the amount of instructional resources (hints, problem sets, etc.) available to a student in a particular learning scenario, and Zone of Proximal Adjustment (ZPA) to refer to the subset of these resources that are best suited for a learner in a particular situation. ZPD, ZAA, and ZPA are not defined in any measurable or operational way; they are rough concepts used to describe the pedagogical approach used in designing Ecolab, and it is not clear what aspects are generalizable to other applications of ZPD-based ITSs (or Vygotskian Instructional

S.A. Cerri, G. Gouardères, and F. Paraguaçu (Eds.): ITS 2002, LNCS 2363, pp. 749–758, 2002.
© Springer-Verlag Berlin Heidelberg 2002

Systems, VIS, as Luckin calls them). The knowledge representation schemes used in Ecolab are intricate, innovative, and appropriate for the application. The domain model uses two linked topic networks, one for taxonomical knowledge and one for rules. Learning activities and progressive levels of hints are generated based on the current topic focus and student model values. The student model value for each topic is interpreted as how close the learner is to being able to solve the activity without help (this frames the construct in Vygotskian terms, but is not significantly different from the more standard interpretation of an overlay student model value as topic "mastery level"). The elementary data used to infer the student state comes from 1) the degree of hinting needed to complete activities, and 2) the level of difficulty of the activities. The value for a topic comes from considering student success with the topic's associated activities, in combination with the student model values of its prerequisite topics (using a Bayesian Belief Net). In the end, though the system has a sound design and evaluations suggest it is effective, it is unclear in general what the ZPD is or how it should be measured, and much of the methodology is ad-hoc or 'best guess'. In this paper we give an analysis of the construct of ZPD for use in ITSs and try to operationalize its definition so that it can generally applied. Our analysis is in an early stage and we do not elaborate on implementation-specific ad-hoc details, because, though ad-hoc heuristics are necessary in all ITS design, describing one set of them would not contribute to a general theory. The operational aspects of ZPD in Ecolab are problem difficulty and hint difficulty, in the context of determining topic mastery level for instructional effectiveness. We extend this theory by operationalizing efficiency as well as effectiveness, and operationalizing notions of both upper and low levels of the ZPD. Our exposition centers around the idea of adapting instruction to keep students within a "zone" where they are neither too frustrated nor too bored. We propose a particular method for measuring this zone and we elaborate on the variety of means available to an ITS for trying to keep students in this zone if it is inferred that they have slipped out of it (by using different types of scaffolding for instance).

We could say that the primary goals of all instruction is for learning to be both efficient and effective. I.E. we want the learner to learn as much as possible in as little time as possible. The primary method ITS's use to attain these goals is to adapt instruction to the needs of the learner and to the pedagogical properties of the content. To be both efficient and effective we want to provide just the right number and content of expository interactions (content and feedback) and interrogative interactions (exercises or activities). Vygotsky describes the zone of proximal development as "the distance between the actual development level as determined by independent problem solving and the level of potential development as determined through problem solving under adult guidance or collaboration of more capable peers" [4, pg 86]. The ZPD is commonly used to articulate apprenticeship learning approaches [4]. In the prototypical description of learning in the ZPD the learner is involved in a task that is realistic in terms of its complexity and context, and is apprenticing with an expert mentor. Instruction progresses from simply observing the expert perform the task to taking on increasingly difficult components of the task (individually and in combination) until the apprentice can do the entire task without assistance. The assistance is called "scaffolding" and the removal of assistance is called "fading." Such a scenario of learning in the ZPD has implications for the design of learning environments and educational activities, but has limited implications for adaptive instruction. The description reminds us that authentic tasks involve the use of multiple concepts and skills in a concerted way, and that learners must be engaged ("situated") in an integrated task context to learn the sub-skills in their proper context and relationships. It articulates a zone within which tasks are too difficult to accomplish without assistance, but which can be accomplished with some help. However, it does not give much guidance on how to determine that zone, what and when to scaffold, and when and what to fade. Our goal in this paper is to give a concise operational definition of the ZPD, and to discuss how to maintain learning in the ZPD.

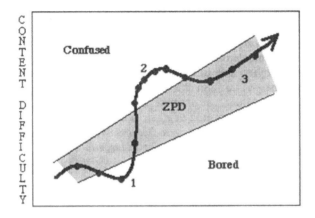

Fig. 1. ZPD Illustration

Our sense of the term ZPD is compatible with how it is used in many contexts. We want to give assistance in order to keep the learner at their leading edge– challenging but not overwhelming them. The ZPD can be characterized from both cognitive and affective perspectives. From the cognitive perspective we say that material should not be too difficult or easy. From the affective perspective we say that the learner should avoid the extremes of being bored and being confused and frustrated. (But *some* cognitive dissonance is usually necessary). Both boredom and confusion can lead to distraction, frustration, and lack of motivation. Of course the optimal conditions differ for each learner and differ for the same learner in different contexts.

Figure 1 illustrates our meaning of the ZPD. It shows a "state space" (or "phase plane") diagram illustrating a student's trajectory through time in the space of tutorial content difficulty versus the student's evolving skill level. The dots on the trajectory indicate either unit time or lesson topics, and are included to illustrate that progression along the trajectory is not necessarily linear with trajectory length. For example, the dots are bunched up in some placed and spread out in others. In practice, each tutor (human or machine) has limited resources and possibilities of assisting the student, so the "effective ZPD" is defined by the difficulty of tasks possible if the student is given the *available* help (Luckin & du Boulay's ZAA). We are only concerned with the effective ZPD for a particular learning environment. This zone will also differ according to each student's tolerance for boredom and confusion. The ZPD is neither a property of the learning environment nor of the student; it is a property of the interaction between the two. We say that the student or learning is "in the ZPD" when the student demonstrates efficient and effective learning. The delineation of the exact zone that is the goal for instruction (shaded area in the figure) is defined by the instructional strategy, and is not a property of the student per-se. This is similar to saying that the criterion for mastery learning is defined by the instructional strategy. We can not directly control the cognitive properties of the student, so it is the *tutor* that must adapt to keep the student in the ZPD.

Though this concept of ZPD makes intuitive sense and provides an attractive metaphor for designing instruction and analyzing learning, it is not operationalized. What is this zone and how do we determine 1) if the student is in it or 2) how to adapt instruction to keep the learner in it? It might seem that the goal of measuring when a student is in the ZPD is intractable and impossible to operationalize. But a human tutor has a workable estimate of when the student is in the zone. Alos, students have a great deal of flexibility and tolerance for non-optimal instruction, so we can reasonably aim to just put them in the "ball park." We can tell when a student is clearly *not* in the ZPD at the two extremes. If a learner indicates that they are bored or if they consecutively answer many similar problems correctly, we can infer that they are in the bored-zone. If a learner is unable to solve a problem using the available means of assistance (i.e. have reached a non-constructive impasse) then we can infer that they are in the confused-zone.

2   Mastery vs. ZPD Learning

Before describing our operational definition of the ZPD we need to articulate a simple but general framework for adaptive instruction upon which to base our discussion. At a course level we can say that all instruction is comprised of three elements: sequencing content, providing opportunities for practice, and giving feedback. Intelligent tutors can adapt at all three levels. For most of our discussion we will make the simplifying assumption that all content is organized into "topics" and topic "difficulty levels." Difficulty levels are used to describe the different levels of performance or understanding within a topic. We need to include difficulty levels so that we can define a problem "equivalency set" (or simply "problem set") as a set of problems, activities, interactions, etc. associated with a particular topic and difficulty level. We assume that a "mastery learning" instructional method is used. That is, the learner is repeatedly given problems (and feedback) for the same learning goal until they demonstrate its mastery in some way. The repetition of this material does not need to be sequential, i.e. the tutor can put the learning goal on hold and treat different topics, but it does not forget the goal to come back and treat the unmastered topic. Note that the number of "tries" (problem solution attempts) is the same as the number of hints plus one (a "hint" can be a simple as "wrong, try again"), which is equivalent to the number of mistakes made on a problem attempt.

Our assumption that mastery learning is used can be almost universally applicable to ITSs if we define mastery learning broadly. Mastery does not imply perfection, but satisfactory performance. Learners can do better than the "mastery" level for a content unit, but the instructional goal of the system is for the student to achieve mastery on a content unit (or units) before moving on. To *not* use mastery learning implies skipping a content unit when it is not mastered. However, missing prerequisites will eventually have to be dealt with when they are needed. Thus for

ITSs the goal of effectiveness is met. But mastery learning does not address efficiency. It only assumes that there is *enough* instructional material, practice opportunities, and help (feedback and scaffolding) available to the learner for them to eventually master each learning goal. The mastery criterion does not measure or detect whether a student achieves mastery in an inefficient way, for example through a slow and tedious process or through an inconsistent and frustrating one. Incorporating the ZPD into systems goes "beyond mastery" in a sense, by introducing the goal of efficiency along with effectiveness (mastery). We can say that ITSs have two goals: content mastery (primarily effectiveness) and keeping the student in the ZPD (primarily efficiency). Of course these goals are not independent. If the student is confused or bored this inefficient learning will usually lead to loss of effectiveness.

Next we make the point that, in the ZPD paradigm, it is not desirable to have a student get all of the answers correct. If a student consistently gets the first 3 problems correct on every topic, and then moves on to the next topic, the student is probably not being challenged enough. So the best case is for the student to fail at some items and to have multiple attempts at problems.

3   An Operational Definition of the ZPD

Wertsch [1] and others have attempted to give a clearer definition of the ZPD than is available from Vygotsky's sketches of the construct, but even more precise operational definitions are required for machine tutors. Hadgaard [5, p. 350] notes that the ZPD is "an analytic tool necessary to plan instruction and to explain its results". Our operational definitions of tutoring within the ZPD can be used for both system evaluation and for computer tutoring strategies, as we shall demonstrate in subsequent sections.

Mastery criterion. First we will operationalize mastery learning in a common fashion. The mastery learning criterion determines when the student can move on to the next content unit, while the ZPD measurement will determine whether the student learning was efficient for the previous (or current) problem set. It is not practical to infer mastery (or ZPD) based on one task. We will call P the minimum number of times a learner should be given a problem exercise on a particular topic. Here is an example problem sequence showing the number of hints given on problems in a problem set: (3, 1, 0, 0). The student needed 3 hints on the first problem, 1 hint on the second, and then got two correct without hints. There are several possible methods for defining mastery criterion for a problem set. We choose the criterion of getting M out of the previous N correct. This method has the property that problems done before the moving window of N problems do not affect the score (ancient errors are forgiven). It also tolerates guesses and slips as noted below. Further, we will allow N to be equivalent to P (the minimum number of problems allowed), because this streamlines the method and we can think of no good reason to complicate the scheme by making them different. Let us look at a number of possible sequences ("hint vectors") to illustrate this "M out of P" mastery criterion.

1. (3, 1, 0, 0). A prototypical sequence. The learner gets better and reaches mastery.
2. (0, 4, 3, 1, 0, 0). The first problem seems to have been a lucky guess.

3. (4, 4, 0, 0, 3, 0). The fifth problem seems to have been a "slip" or random error.
4. (2, 2, 2, 1, 1, 0, 0). Illustrates very gradual learning or improvement.
5. (4, 4, 0, 0). Illustrates sudden learning or improvement---an "aha" experience.

All of these sequences achieve mastery under the criterion of getting two correct out of the last three problems (in #3 the final 2 problems would not have been needed).

ZPD criterion. Our criterion for ZPD assumes that there is *some* mastery criterion in effect, but any reasonable criterion for mastery could be used in place of the "M out of P" method above and the following analysis of ZPD would still hold. Remember that our goal is to challenge the student just the right amount: not too much, not too little. Challenge level can be inferred from the number of failed attempts or hints needed to solve a problem. It does not make sense to measure whether the learner is in the zone for one problem. Being in the zone is determined for a problem *set* (or more generally for some sequence of problems). We want just the right number of hints in a problem set, which we will call "H." We do not want "less than or equal to H" (this contrasts with mastery criterion where we could accept M "or more" correct answers). As with mastery learning, there are alternative ways to implement this general idea. Compare problem sequences #4 and #5 above, showing gradual and "aha" learning. For these two sequences any criterion that counts the total hints in the *last N* attempts would give differential results for what we think are equivalent examples in ZPD terms. So our goal is to have the student get *exactly* H hints in the problem set, regardless of the number of problems seen. Or, to be more practical, we want the student to stay in the zone of getting H +/- DH (delta H) hints.

We say that the learner is in the bored zone and the problems are too easy if they need less than H-DH hints. We say that they are in the confused zone and the situation is too difficult if they need more than H+DH hints. The exact values for P and H will strongly depend on the content and pedagogical goals and style. These values may even differ for different topics or activity types in a tutorial. As we will note later, they may also be adapted based on the student model.

Let us give our operationalized definition of the ZPD a name: "Specific ZPD" or **SZPD** (like "specific heat" in material science). The SZPD has three parameters, **H**, the goal number of hints in each problem set, **DH**, the allowed variation in H to consider the situation within the ZPD, and **P**, the minimum number of problems the student is guaranteed to see (under normal circumstances). The SZPD is a property of the system's instructional strategy. The measurable learner property is **H***, the actual number of hints given in a problem set. We define **Z**, a measurement of how close the student's performance in a problem set is to the goal: $Z = H^* - H$. The area $Z > DH$ delineates the confused zone, and the area $Z < DH$ delineates the bored zone. It is left to the instructional designer to specify the default SZPD parameters for a particular system, and how the system will respond to the learner being in the bored or confused zones. Ultimately it is a matter of empirical testing to determine the values of H, DH, and P that correspond to the teaching and learning style desired.

Finally we will mention another method for determining whether the learner is in the ZPD---asking them. The system can provide buttons for indicating that the learner is confused or bored, or that the material is too difficult or easy. This information can be used instead of or in combination with the more analytic SZPD method in determining how the system reacts to non-ZPD learning.

4   An Example of Using the SZPD to Evaluate an ITS

In this section we describe how we are using the SZPD to evaluate a pool of data obtained from use of a mathematics ITS, Animalwatch [6, in press]. The analysis looks at a set of trials in which different hinting strategies were used. The goal is to determine which hinting (or "help") strategies are best suited for particular types of individual differences (such as gender and cognitive developmental level). The data analysis is not yet complete, and results will be published in a future paper. In this paper we simply use the study to illustrate use of the SZPD for system evaluation.

4.1   Animalwatch

Animalwatch is an Intelligent Tutoring System for basic arithmetic and fractions that offers word problems about endangered species. It takes the student through a series of word problems dynamically chosen from a large database of word problem templates, which are instantiated with appropriate operands, depending on the student's current proficiency. When the student enters an incorrect answer, Animalwatch provides help through progressive hints.

We are in the process of using our operational definition of the ZPD in the analysis of a pool of data obtained from the use of Animalwatch over several years. We have done some analysis of hint effectiveness before on this system and concluded that students behaved differently with different hint styles [7]. This time, we will integrate data from uses of Animalwatch over a period of 3 years (including 300 subjects). This is a post-hoc formative evaluation–the system was designed and the data was gathered prior to the formulation of our SZPD theory.

Our study focuses on how students with different cognitive abilities benefit from hints with different levels of abstraction ("concrete" and "formal" hints). The problem selection mechanism is the same for all versions of the ITS, only the hinting methods vary. We measured students' cognitive development level with a Piagetian cognitive development pre-test instrument. Students were randomly assigned to two different versions of Animalwatch: one providing concrete help, another providing formal numeric help.

4.2   Analysis of Animalwatch Data

We said before that the ZPD is a property of the interaction between the learner and learning environment. Thus, we expect similar students to have a different average number of hints (H*) for different hint methods (i.e. they take longer or shorter to reach mastery). In our analysis we assume a goal value for H and compare students' Z values (how far they are from H) for sequences of equivalent problems. A problem equivalency set in Animalwatch consists of problems for a particular topic (e.g. subtraction) and a specific difficulty (e.g. three-digit subtraction involving borrowing). Due to the problem and topic selection strategies (described in [9]) the problems in an equivalency set are not always seen sequentially (i.e. problems from other sets may be interspersed).

We have hypotheses about how Z values should change for students of similar cognitive ability who have been provided concrete or formal hints. Table 1 shows fictitious data that illustrates our hypothesis: that we expect low cognitive development student to perform better when given concrete help and high cognitive development students to do better with formal help. The table assumes a value of H=5 (for example, in the top left data cell Z=H*-H=7-5=2). We also expect high cognitive development students to have lower Z values than low cognitive development students, as we expect them to need fewer hints in order to reach mastery. Statistically significant findings in the data would enable us to create adaptive hinting strategies in future versions of the system, where we could change the hinting style based on cognitive development level.

Table 1. Fictional Z values for low and high cognitive development students vs. help type

	High cognitive development	Low cognitive development
Concrete help	(3,2,1,1,0,0) Z=2	(3,2,3,1,0,0) Z=4
Formal help	(3,1,1,0,0) Z=0	(3,3,2,1,2,1,0,0) Z=7

The example in Table 1 compares individual students, but statistical analysis requires aggregating over each of the four groups of students. Rather than use the hint sequence for a single student and problem set, we average the hints for all students in a group for a particular problem set. We compare student Z values by averaging the first problem seen by all students in a group, then the second problem, etc. So that the hint vectors in Table 1 becomes a sequence of the average number of hints received for the Nth problem in a problem set. For example if two students' hint vectors were (4,2,1,0,0) and (3,2,1,1,0) the vector for the average hints is (3.5, 2, 1, 0.5, 0) and the Z value for H=5 would be (7 - 5 =) 2. We plan to compare these "composite Z values" for the four groups indicated in Table 1, and across the various topic levels (problem equivalency sets) in the tutorial.

The Z value gives us an overall look at ZPD behavior aggregated over a problem set, but we may also want to investigate at a smaller grain size what is happening within the problem sets. For example, this would help us distinguish the "gradual" vs "sudden" learning behaviors in example hint vectors #4 and #5 above. To do this we will be producing and inspecting graphs that illustrate four hint vectors averaged over for each group in Table 1: A. is for High-Cdevel/Concrete, B. is Low-Cdeve/ Concrete, C. is High-Cdevel/Formal, and D. is Low-Cdevel/Formal. We intend to use such graphs to visually compare (and use the associated hint vectors to analytically compare) ZPD-learning among subject types and across problem sets.

5   The ZPD for Planning, Scaffolding, & Adaptation

In this section we look at the types of adaptations that an ITS can make when it is determined that the tutoring session has drifted outside of the ZPD.

Keeping the student in the ZPD involves maintaining an optimal degree of new material, and/or level of challenge. The term "scaffolding" is used to describe tutorial interventions or decisions serving this goal. It is not our goal to give a definition of scaffolding that most accurately reflects either Vygotsky's theories or modern theories of apprenticeship learning [8]. Rather, we make a reasonable appropriation of the term to refer to any instructional decision or method that has the goal of keeping the learner in the ZPD. The general methods commonly used include: adaptive content sequencing, providing cognitive tools, and hinting and related forms of feedback and help including partial problem solutions.

"Hints" are problem solving assistance that gives information or focuses attention in ways that improve the chances that the learner will be able to solve a problem. The major other form of help is problem decomposition scaffolding. In this method the problem is broken into components which are individually easier to solve. Some forms of scaffolding will assist with problem decomposition and other higher order skills to allow the learner to focus on domain specific schema formation, while other forms of scaffolding will assist the learner in domain-specific skills or answers so that they can practice the overall approach to the problem.

It is also possible to "scaffold" both known and unknown skills. The case of scaffolding unknown skills is clear. But the tutor can also automate a task the student already knows how to do or that is inconsequential to the current learning goals. For example, providing a graphing tool for students that already know how to create graphs, or where using and understanding graphs is important but learning how to construct them is not an important goal.

We have already mentioned the common method of providing progressive levels of hints. Different types of help differentially benefit learners with different characteristics. As mentioned above, this argues for providing not only different levels of hints but different types of hints and help.

6   Conclusion

In this paper we offer an analysis of the Vygotskian constructs of scaffolding and the zone of proximal development within the context of adaptive instructional system design and evaluation. We say that scaffolding is any instructional assistance, intervention, or planning that assists the learner in maintaining a learning experience that is within the ZPD. We define the ZPD as a zone of instructional interaction wherein the material given to the learner is neither too difficult nor too easy, or, to phrase it in affective terms, wherein the learner is neither too bored nor too confused, as they progressively master instructional objectives. In posing this definition we extend the traditional concerns of instructional systems (and extend the traditional interpretation of the ZPD) from one concerning only effectiveness to also explicitly include the goal of efficiency. We assume that in all individually paced instruction there is some mastery criterion, so that learning effectiveness is guaranteed for competed topics. When we add the goal that just the right amounts and types of information, practice tasks and help is given, we address efficiency as well as effectiveness.   We maintain that the primary goals of all adaptive instructional systems are effectiveness and efficiency.

The learner's state and progress can be determined by analysis of pretests, task performance, direct communication (as in "I'm confused") and other actions (such as tool use and navigation).   We focus here on task performance and measure ZPD learning by counting the number of problem attempts (or hints given) for a set of equivalent problems. We define the "specific ZPD" (SZPD) as having three parameters: H (the goal number of hints in a problem set), DH (the allowable deviation from this goal), and P (the minimum number of problems in a problem set, as determined by the mastery criterion). The SZPD parameters are properties of the instructional strategy.

The SZPD can be used for post-hoc analysis and formative evaluation of systems, or it can be used for in dynamic adaptation in tutoring strategy rules. To illustrate its use, we give an example of our in-progress use of the SZPD in a post-hoc evaluation of a mathematics tutor. The goal of the evaluation is to determine the relative effectiveness of different hinting styles vs. learner gender and cognitive development level.

Our proposal for an operational definition of the ZPD (the SZPD) is a specific and practical method for measuring ZPD-learning. In contrast, the question of how adapt or respond to non-ZPD learning (i.e. how to scaffold and fade) is an under-constrained problem with many degrees of freedom. We have described the purposes and characteristic of various forms of scaffolding as a step towards articulating and discovering the appropriate applicability conditions for these various forms.

References

[1] Wertsch, J. (1984). "The zone of proximal development: Some conceptual issues." In B. Rogoff, J. Wertsch (Eds.) *Children's Learning in the "Zone of Proximal Development"* pp. 7-18. San Francisco: Jossey-Bass Inc.

[2] Luckin, R; du Boulay, B. (1999a) Ecolab: the development and evaluation of a Vygotskian design framework. International Journal of Artificial Intelligence in Education. Volume 10. Number 2. pp. 198-220

[3] Luckin, R; du Boulay, B. (1999b). Capability, Potential, and Collaborative Assistance. *Proc. of User Modelling-99,* J. Kay (ed). Springer: NY, pp. 139-148.

[4] Vygotsky, L.S. (1978). *Mind in Society: The development of higher psychology processes.* Cambridge MA: Harvard University press.

[5] Hadegaard, M. (1991). The zone of proximal development as basis for instruction." In L. C. Moll (Ed) Vygotsky and education: instructional implications and applications of sociohistorical psychology. New York: Cambridge University Press, 1990. pp. 155-172.

[6] Beal, C. R., & Arroyo, I. (in press). The Animal Watch Project: Creating an intelligent computer math tutor. In S. Calvert, A. Jordan, & R. Cocking (Eds.) Children in the digital age. New York: Praeger.

[7] Arroyo, I.; Beck, J.; Woolf, B.; Beal, C.; Schultz, K. (2000) Macroadapting Animalwatch to gender and cognitive differences with respect to hint interactivity and symbolism. Proceedings of the Fifth International Conference on Intelligent Tutoring Systems. Montreal, Canada. June 2000. pp. 574-583.

[8] Collins, A., Brown, J.S., Newman, S. (1989). "Cognitive Apprenticeship: Teaching the Craft of Reading, Writing, and Mathematics. In (L.B. Resnick (Ed.) *Knowing, Learning, and Instruction.* Hillsdale, NJ: Erlbaum.

Getting to Know Me: Helping Learners Understand Their Own Learning Needs through Metacognitive Scaffolding

Rosemary Luckin and Louise Hammerton

Human Centred Technology, School of Cognitive & Computing Sciences University of Sussex, Brighton
BN1 9QH UK
rosel@cogs.susx.ac.uk, Tel:++44 1273 678647

Abstract. Software scaffolding has been successfully employed within educational technology to help bridge the recognition-production gap between what learners want to achieve and what they are able to effect themselves without assistance. Such work has however concentrated on scaffolding the learner at the domain level with less attention to the potential for providing explicit support at the Metacognitive level. Evidence from previous work has shown that less able and less knowledgeable learners are especially ineffective at selecting appropriately challenging tasks and seeking appropriate qualities and quantities of support and guidance [1, 2]. But how can we make learners more effective at reflecting on their own needs, at seeking appropriate challenges and appropriate support? We have used a participatory design approach to assist young learners in the design process so that they can, in turn, assist us as we develop Metacognitive scaffolding strategies. These strategies have been implemented in Ecolab II. Early results are encouraging and suggest that low ability children can too be scaffolded to greater success.

Keywords. Metacognition, Software Scaffolding, Vygotsky, Learner modelling.

1 Introduction and Background

The Zone of Proximal Development (ZPD) [3, 4] requires collaboration or assistance for a learner or group of learners from other more able partners. This need for collaborative assistance arises from the belief that the activities which form a part of the child's effective education must be just beyond the range of her independent ability. The more able partners, whether peers, teachers, or computers must provide appropriately challenging activities and the right quantity and quality of assistance. This is an appealing and persuasive idea that lies at the foundation of all applications of scaffolding [5] whether through technology or human interaction. The key factor at the heart of successful scaffolding is not only the ability of the more able learner/teacher to offer appropriate help, but also their ability to withdraw or fade the support they offer when the learner is ready. The implication of this for those playing

S.A. Cerri, G. Gouardères, and F. Paraguaçu (Eds.): ITS 2002, LNCS 2363, pp. 759–771, 2002.

the role of the more able partner is that they need to have a good model of how well the learner is doing in order to both provide and withdraw assistance appropriately. This is true both for human and software learning partners.

In order to explore the way in which software might offer adaptive scaffolding through the operationalisation of Vygotsky's Zone of Proximal Development within a learner model, we developed the Ecolab I software. This work built upon previous work on software scaffolding [6-10] and required the production of a Vygotskian software design framework. This framework was implemented within the Ecolab I software and concentrated on the design of domain level of scaffolding. The domain selected was that of ecology and the software we developed scaffolded the learner about feeding relationships, food chains and food webs. In doing this it largely ignored Metacognitive issues. In the evaluation study of the Ecolab I, children performed well and their knowledge of food web ecology grew. Learning gains were made when learners were encouraged to take on challenging tasks in combination with the appropriate level of collaborative support through the adaptive scaffolding techniques implemented in the software. However, only the most able children showed any awareness of their own learning needs [11], or any skill at selecting appropriately challenging activities and seeking suitable levels of assistance.

In developing Ecolab II, we have therefore turned our attention to the design of scaffolding at the Metacognitive level. In this paper we briefly introduce the original Ecolab I software, discuss the potential role of Metacognitive scaffolding and describe our participatory design work with children. The Ecolab II software is then described. We concentrate in particular on the Metacognitive scaffolding implemented and the accompanying learner modelling adjustments. Finally, we discuss our ongoing evaluation of the software and the nature of our future work.

2   The Original Ecolab I System

The original Ecolab I was an interactive learning environment that helped children learn about food webs and chains. It provided a flexible software environment in the form of a simulated ecology laboratory. The animals and plants which the child selected to put into this simulation could be viewed from different perspectives. For example, their energy levels could be seen in the form of a bar chart and the feeding relationships that exist between them could be seen as food chain or web diagrams. The simulation could be run in different modes and in increasingly complex phases. Any changes that occurred when the simulation was run could then be viewed through different perspectives. In addition to this simulation, there were adjustable activities that could be completed with assistance from the system. This assistance, or collaborative support, was available in several ways:

- First, there were five levels of graded help specific to the particular situation. These varied with regard to the quality of the help that they provided. The higher the level of help the greater the control taken by the system and the less scope there was for the child to fail [12].
- Second, in addition to offering the child specific hints to ensure the activity was completed successfully, the difficulty level of the activity itself could be

adjusted. This is referred to as *Activity Differentiation*. There were three differentiation levels.

In order to provide this collaborative support a learner model was maintained by the system. This consisted of an overlay of the system's curriculum knowledge representation graph (an adaptation of Goldstein's Genetic Graph, [13]). In the domain knowledge representation each node in the graph represented an element of the curriculum, something that the child needed to understand: a relationship or a level of terminology abstraction. In the overlay learner model there were 2 values, or *tags*, associated with each node. The first value: the *ability belief* tag was the system's 'belief' about the child's independent ability. The second value: the *collaborative support* tag was a quantitative representation of the amount of collaborative support that the system needed to provide for the child in order to ensure her success at that node. These tags allowed the modelling of the system's beliefs about which areas of the curriculum were outside the child's independent ability and the extent of the collaborative support required to bring each of these areas within her collaborative capability. This model enabled the system to draw inferences about a learner's potential from the system's beliefs about her capability. These inferences could then be used to make decisions about which area of the curriculum should be learnt next, at what level of difficulty and with how much initial system support.

In fact, in the original version of the Ecolab I [1] the sophistication of the learner model was varied in order to create three variations of the system: NIS, WIS and VIS. VIS implemented the learner model just described, whereas NIS and WIS were more rudimentary. NIS made no decisions for the child and simply recorded a visible map of the areas of the curriculum that the child had tried. WIS also recorded areas of the curriculum tried and, in addition, kept track of the level of help that the child had used. This information was used by the system to generate suggestions to be made to the child about what they should try next, and to apply a contingent strategy [7] to the selection of the next help level.

The evaluation of the Ecolab I highlighted the benefits that accrue when learners are challenged and intellectually extended. It also illustrated the difficulty that such young learners have in achieving such intellectual extension without explicit direction from the system. This direction does not necessarily have to mean system control. A suggestion, such as that offered by the WIS system variation, can often be enough. A system which can assist a learner to take more control for her own extension, which models a learner's developing collaborative skills as well as her developing understanding of the curriculum is the logical extension that we are exploring through Ecolab II.

3   The Role of Metacognitive Scaffolding

Metacognition can be broadly referred to as any knowledge or cognitive process that refers to, monitors, or controls any aspect of cognition. Flavell [14] distinguishes between Metacognitive knowledge and Metacognitive regulation. Metacognitive knowledge refers to information about one's cognitive processes and is subdivided further into knowledge of oneself, task and strategies. Metacognitive regulation incorporates a variety of executive functions and Metacognitive strategies such as planning, resource allocation, monitoring, checking, and error detection and correction. Successful students continually evaluate, plan and regulate their progress, which makes them aware of their own learning. When confronted with an effortful cognitive task it is those with greater Metacognitive abilities that tend to be more successful [15]. Our aim, in the development of Ecolab II, is the creation of an environment that provides Metacognitive support. Our focus is particular. We are concerned to help learners improve their help seeking and task selection skills, and through this their performance at the domain level.

In order to design a Metacognitive scaffolding framework we sought to increase our understanding of how we might support a learner's ability to challenge his or her own skill level and seek appropriate assistance. We did this by exploring children's perceptions of, and attitudes towards challenge and help. An adaptation of the 'Wizard of Oz' technique [16] was adopted to examine further the issues of help and challenge. The 'Wizard of Oz' technique is commonly used to simulate human computer interfaces. The „wizard's" existence is usually unknown to the user, but he or she is responsible for making decisions about how the system will respond to the user's actions. It is a useful technique for evaluating potential alternative interfaces or functionality without the need to fully implement these alternatives within the system under development. In the adaptation of this technique for our studies, children worked in pairs. One child adopted the role of the computer and the other adopted the role of a user of that computer. The child user knew that the wizard existed. In fact, both user and wizard worked on the same apparatus and could view each other's interactions continuously. Initially, the interfaces and functionality were not implemented in software. The interfaces were paper-based and the child taking the role of the computer provided the functionality by operating what was, in effect, a paper computer. In later studies we used a semi-functional prototype to stimulate discussion. These activities with learners have enabled us to gather detailed information about what children think will be helpful and why, both for themselves and for others (for more information see [17-19]). It is this information that we have used in the development of Ecolab II. It is important to note at this juncture that our learner centred design approach does aim to produce an optimally usable interface. However, while this should reduce (and hopefully eradicate) the need for help targeted at assisting users in their use of the system's features it is not our aim to reduce the need for help at the conceptual level of the domain. If a child is working in their ZPD then they should need help. It is our aim to scaffold them to select optimally useful help at that conceptual level i.e. with the domain of food chains and webs.

4   Ecolab II Architecture

The original version of the Ecolab I provided 'help' at the domain level i.e. at the level of individual actions such as when an animal moved or ate another animal or plant. This help was available when the learner was completing these specific actions and they made an error. As explained earlier, the VIS version of the original Ecolab I software aimed to act as an instructional partner for the child, providing collaborative assistance in terms of the adjustment of activities and the provision of help. The learner model at the heart of Ecolab I was used to decide what topic should be learnt next by the child and how much help the system should provide. The WIS version of the Ecolab I allowed the child greater autonomy to select the activity and help levels. The system merely suggested that the child should consider doing a task or selecting a particular level of help. Ecolab II is designed to combine aspects of the original VIS and WIS systems. Rather than just making a suggestion, it offers different qualities and quantities of prompt to try to get the child to consider what they should do next: be it selecting a task or how much help to ask for.

4.1 Help at the Meta Level

The Metacognitive learner model is implemented so that help is available at four points:

1. When the child is selecting what they are going to learn about.
2. When the child is deciding what level of challenge to choose.
3. When the child is in need of help at the domain level.
4. During interactions as a reminder to use the *progress* button.

In each of the first three of these cases three levels of help are available. For example, when a child needs help at the domain level the following help would be available:

Level 1 Don't forget that the Ecolab can help you
Level 2 Why not ask for some **more/less** help
Level 3 Try Level **X** help (e.g. Level 3 help)

This Meta level help is in addition to the domain level help available in the original Ecolab I. In addition to this the child is offered feedback on their progress through the curriculum via a *progress* button within the interface.

4.2 Meta Level Modelling

In Ecolab II there is a 2-layered model of the child. One layer is at the domain level and the other is at the Metacognitive level. In addition to the *ability belief tag* maintained in the original Ecolab I (and described in Section 2 above), Ecolab II also maintains a *Meta ability belief tag*. This value is used to measure how aware the child is of their own learning needs and represents the system's 'belief' about the child's Metacognitive ability, in the same way that the *ability belief tag* represents the system's 'belief' about the child's ability at the domain level. Both values are updated every time a new activity is selected or domain level help is used.

4.3 Alice and Ecolab II

The following scenario and figures clarify the nature of the learner experience with Ecolab II:

Alice who is 10 years old, has completed two activities using Ecolab II and decides to choose a new activity. She clicks on the 'New Activity' button and a dialog box appears suggesting she should click on the *progress* button. After clicking on the progress button Alice is given five options for progress information: Activity Success, Activity Progress, Challenge Progress, Action

Progress, Help Progress. She chooses Challenge Progress. A dialog box appears *'You have chosen activities at the lowest level of challenge, do you think you are challenging yourself enough?'* (Fig. 1.) Alice clicks on 'New Activity' again and this time a dialog box opens with ten different activity nodes to choose from (Fig. 2). As she has already interacted with Ecolab II, a model has been created by the system about what it believes her current domain and Metacognitive ability levels are. The previous two activities Alice has completed have been in 'Zone 1' and both been at 'Challenge Level 1' so the Ecolab II suggests *'Try moving into a new zone'*. Alice chooses activity node 'Food 2' in 'Zone 2'.

Fig. 1.

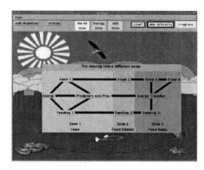

Fig. 2.

A dialog box appears with three choices of challenge and a suggestion *'Try choosing a more challenging activity'* (Fig. 3). Alice chooses 'Challenge Level 2' and is given the corresponding activity, which involves finding out about food chains and what happens to the organisms that make up a food chain. Alice already has several plants and animals added to the Ecolab II so she decides to use the 'Eat and Be Eaten By' action command to build a food chain. She creates a food chain with *'Tadpole eats Pondweed and is eaten by Heron'*. Unfortunately, 'Tadpoles' are not eaten by 'Herons' so a dialog box appears with four choices of help and a suggestion *'Don't forget that the Ecolab can help you'* (Fig. 4). Alice chooses 'Help Level 2' and is told *'Tadpoles are not eaten by Herons, don't forget you can click on different plants and animals to find out more about them'*. Alice clicks on the 'Tadpole' and finds out that it is eaten by 'Stickleback'. She continues working on the Ecolab building more food chains.

4.4   The Ecolab II Model of Alice

As Alice completes her activities and uses action commands in Ecolab II the system updates its internal model of both how much it 'believes' she understands feeding relationships and how much it 'believes' she understands her own learning needs. This information is used to adjust the help level the system suggests that she use (Learner focused Scaffolding, [20]), to alter the difficulty of the activity the system suggests that she select (Task focused Scaffolding, [20]), and to select the level of Metacognitive support she is given (Metacognitive Level Scaffolding).

Fig. 3.   **Fig. 4.**

5   Evaluation of Ecolab II

In order to explore the way in which children used the Meta level help and the appropriateness of our Meta level modelling techniques we conducted an evaluation study in a local primary school at the end of 2001. We measured children's learning with Ecolab II using the same paper pre-test and post-test as was used in the original Ecolab I evaluation study [11].

5.1 Participants

The children were all members of the same class and were between 9 and 11 years of age. There were 32 children, 16 boys and 16 girls. All the participants had already learnt about food chains and food webs with their teacher as part of their normal classroom activity in the half term prior to the study. Of the 32 children who started the study, only 26 completed all sessions between and including pre- and post-test. The six who did not complete these sessions had been absent during the evaluation period. The children participating in this study were not involved in the previous participatory design studies.

5.2 Procedure

Prior to using the software each child carried out the written pre-test. They were instructed to answer as many questions as they could. Children were given help with the reading of questions if they needed it. Before using the software the children were given a short questionnaire that asked questions about their computer usage. Ecolab II was then demonstrated to them explaining all its functionality. Once the demonstration had finished the children were given a software pre-test to complete using Ecolab II and five minutes 'free-play' to give them time to familiarise themselves with the software. After the 'free-play' session each child had 25 minutes to use the software. They were instructed to „explore the Ecolab, to see what they could find out" and were encouraged to undertake the activities available on the system. The same written and system-based tests were given to the children again once their 25-minute session was over. The written tests were completed in the children's classroom. The computer sessions were carried out in the school's multi-media suite with a maximum of 4 children at a time, with all children present always belonging to the same user group. The computer session time was very limited so plans are being made for a larger scale study with a different group of children in the early summer of 2002.

As part of the school's routine assessment procedure the children had all completed a Cognitive Ability Test (CAT). Using these scores and the results from the pre-test the children were allocated to one of three ability ranges: high, average and low. The children's class teacher was then asked to assess the three groups and confirm that the ability distributions were fair and that they reflected his own assessment of the children. The use of the ability measures ensured that both of the user groups contained the same range of abilities and allowed investigation of the performance of the different systems with children of different abilities.

6   Results

Both the original Ecolab I evaluation and the current study with Ecolab II looked at whether the different variations of the Ecolab I had been more or less effective in increasing the child's learning gain in terms of their knowledge of feeding relationships. The effects for the different ability groups were considered to assess each system and each system variation's efficacy across different abilities.

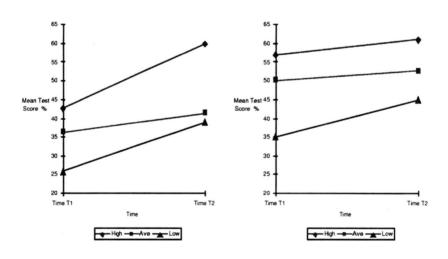

Fig. 5. Ecolab I (n=26)   **Fig. 6.** Ecolab II (n=26)

Figs 5 & 6 Ability by Time interaction

6.1 Overall Learning Gain in Ecolab I and Ecolab II

In the original Ecolab I system it was the more able learners who faired best overall as illustrated in Fig. 5. As mentioned earlier, it was only the brightest children who demonstrated a useful level of awareness about their own learning needs in the Ecolab I evaluation. The scores at pre test were higher in the Ecolab II study than the Ecolab I evaluation. This is not explained by the ability levels of the children in the class, which were similar for both studies, and is likely to be the effect of a shorter time period between the class teaching session on food chains and webs and the software evaluation study.

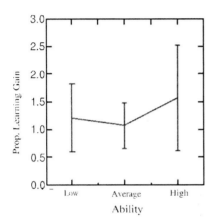
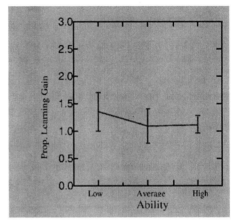

Fig. 7. Ecolab I (WIS)   **Fig. 8.** Ecolab II

Figs 7 & 8: Proportional learning gain and ability, means and 95% confidence intervals.

In Ecolab II the situation was rather different. Here it was the low ability children who made the largest learning gains (Fig 6). Figs 7 and 8 below illustrate the proportional learning gains made by the different ability groups using the WIS version of the Ecolab I (Fig 7) and the Ecolab II software (Fig 8).

An analysis of the variance (ANOVA) on the Ecolab II pre-test and post-test data, with one within subject variable (time), and one between subjects variable (ability: High, Average, Low) indicates that the difference between the ability groups is significant ($F(2,23) = 3.51$, $R^2=.24$, $p =.05$). A comparable analysis of the pre-test and post-test data for the WIS users of Ecolab I indicates that the difference between the ability groups was not significant ($F(2,7) = 2.38$, $R^2=.25$, $p =.167$), though was of a similar magnitude.

6.2 Interacting with Ecolab I and Ecolab II

Here we look at the children's interactions with the software. We have adopted the same approach in our analysis of Ecolab II as we used for Ecolab I. For each child who uses the software a summary record of their interactions is produced from the logs maintained during their sessions of system use. These are then analysed to explore:

- The character of the different interactions

- The nature of the collaborative support provided by the system for the child.

As with Ecolab I we found two characteristics that could clearly be seen as either present or largely absent within the interactions. These were referred to as:

- **Busyness**: considered to be a characteristic of interactions in which the children completed an average or above average number of actions of any type, such as adding an organism to their Ecolab world or making one organism eat another.

- **Exploration**: considered to be a characteristic of an interaction if the child had been involved in some sort of action that challenged her intellectually.

The relationship between these interaction characteristics, a child's ability and her learning gain provides useful evidence about what appears to constitute an effective interaction. Children who were willing to take on a challenge were thus categorised as *Explorers*.

Table 1. Comparison of interaction characteristics – non-exploring, exploring, and busy/exploring – for children with below and above average learning gain.

	Ecolab I			Ecolab II		
	Non-explorer	Explorer	Busy-explorer	Non-explorer	Explorer	Busy-explorer
Above average	2/13	11/13	9/13	2/11	9/11	7/11
Below average	8/13	5/13	2/13	9/15	6/15	2/15
odds ratio* (95% CI)	0.11 (0.02, 0.74)	8.80 (1.35,57.4)	12.4 (1.83, 83.8)	0.15 (0.02, 0.94)	6.75 (1.06, 42.8)	11.4 (1.65, 78.4)
* All of the odds ratios are significantly different from chance, which is 1, using a χ^2 test.						

Table 1 shows that the importance of taking on a challenge, or being an explorer, is consistent between Ecolab I and Ecolab II. However, in Ecolab II the exploring characteristic was present amongst all ability levels indicating a positive development from Ecolab I: within which only the more able children took on and benefited from a challenge. By contrast, in Ecolab II the low ability children did particularly well (Fig 8). There is also evidence to support the importance of the co-occurrence of Busyness and Exploration. Table 1 illustrates that the majority of children with above average learning gains displayed both busyness and exploration characteristics, whereas very few of the children with below average learning gain did. The odds ration analysis illustrates the consistency of these results between Ecolab 1 and Ecolab II. Children who display the exploring and busy characteristics are 11.4 times more likely to be amongst the learners achieving above average learning gains with Ecolab 2 and 12.4 times more likely with Ecolab I.

6.3 Collaboration between Learner and Ecolab I and Ecolab II

In the same way that the interaction characteristics of Busyness and Exploration were used to differentiate the types of interaction children engaged in, two characteristics were found to be the most useful for differentiating the nature of the collaboration that went on between system and learner, these were:

- Seeking **Lots** of help i.e. learners requested an above average number of instances of help

- Seeking a **Deep** level of help i.e. an above average level of help was sought.

In the Ecolab II evaluation, the collaborative features found to be significant to the success of an interaction were once again both the quantity and the quality of the help used by the learner. This can be seen in Table 2 below, in which a high percentage of the children with above average learning gains used a high level and an above average amount of system assistance.

Table 2. Help Characteristics of Children Using Ecolab II

	High Level of System Assistance Used	Above Average Amount of System Assistance Used
% Children with ABOVE average learning gains	73% of children	82% of children
% Children with BELOW average learning gain	47% of children	33% of children

There was a slight change in emphasis from Ecolab I, with quality of help rather than quantity of help appearing to have a marginally greater impact.

The combination of exploring a challenge and seeking help was once again a characteristic of many of the children who learned the most:

- 64% of the children who achieved above average learning gains displayed the Exploring interaction characteristic in combination with the use of above average quantities and qualities of system assistance

by contrast:

- 7% of the children who did not achieve above average learning gains displayed the Exploring interaction characteristic in combination with the use of above average quantities and qualities of system assistance.

7 Conclusion

We accept that the number of children involved in the evaluation, and their length of system usage was limited. Nevertheless, when children's interactions are considered in the light of their post-test performance and original ability group membership the findings are interesting. There are clearly some consistent factors that are shared by learners who achieve higher learning gains. These are a willingness to take on a challenging activity and to seek assistance in its completion. This is consistent with the concept and process of the ZPD and is true for both Ecolab I and Ecolab II. However, in the original Ecolab I system these characteristics were more commonly found in the more able, who in turn produced higher test score increases. The story is rather different in this respect with the Ecolab II system evaluation. Here it is the less able learners who perform particularly well. This is an interesting and encouraging finding. All too often software is more easily appropriated by more able children who will inevitably learn more than their less able peers. We are still analysing the data we have collected to explore which particular system features appear to be the most effective. Further empirical work, involving longer periods of system use and more tightly focused parameters are planned in pursuit of this greater understanding. We are also refining a pre and post test rationale for assessing children's metacognitive ability.

Acknowledgements. Many thanks to Benedict du Boulay, Daniel Wright and the its 2002 reviewers for their many helpful comments on earlier drafts of this paper, and to the children and teachers of Blacklands Primary School, Hastings, Uk.

References

1. Luckin, R. and B. du Boulay, *Ecolab: the Development and Evaluation of a Vygotskian Design Framework*. International Journal of Artificial Intelligence and Education, 1999. 10(2): p. 198-220.
2. Wood, H.A. and D. Wood, *Help seeking, learning and contingent tutoring*. Computers and Education, 1999. 33(2-3): p. 153-169.
3. Vygotsky, L.S., *Mind in society: the development of higher psychological processes*. 1978, Cambridge, MA: Harvard University press.
4. Vygotsky, L.S., *Thought and Language*. 1986, Cambridge, Mass: The MIT Press.
5. Wood, D.J., J.S. Bruner, and G. Ross, *The role of tutoring in problem solving*. Journal of Child Psychology and Psychiatry, 1976. 17(2): p. 89-100.
6. Soloway, E., et al., *Learning theory in practice: Case studies of learner-centred design*, in *CHI 96 Human Factors in Computing Systems: Common Ground*, M.J. Tauber, Editor. 1996, ACM press: Vancouver. p. 189-196.
7. Wood, D., et al., *EXPLAIN: Experiments in planning and instruction*. Society for the Study of Artificial Intelligence and Simulation of Behaviour Quarterly Newsletter, 1992. 81: p. 13-16.
8. Rosson, M.B. and J.M. Carroll, *Scaffolded examples for learning object-oriented design*. Communications of the ACM, 1996. 39(4): p. 46-47.

9. Bliss, J., Askew, M. & Macrae, S., *Effective teaching and learning: scaffolding revisited.* Oxford Review of Education, 1996. 22(1): p. 37-61.
10. Jackson, S.L., J. Krajcik, and E. Soloway, *The Design of Guided Learner-Adaptable Scaffolding in Interactive Learning Environments.* CHI 98 Human Factors in Computing Systems, 1998: p. 187-194.
11. Luckin, R., *'ECOLAB': Explorations in the Zone of Proximal Development.* 1998, School of Cognitive and Computing Sciences, University of Sussex.
12. Wood, D.J., Wood, H. A. & Middleton, D. J., *An experimental evaluation of four face-to-face teaching strategies.* International Journal of Behavioural Development, 1978. 1: p. 131-147.
13. Goldstein, P., *The genetic graph: a representation for the evolution of procedural knowledge*, in *Intelligent Tutoring Systems*, D. Sleeman and J.S. Brown, Editors. 1982, Academic Press: New York.
14. Flavell, J.H., *Metacognition and cognitive monitoring: A new area of cognitive-developmental inquiry.* American Psychologist, 1979. 34: p. 906-911.
15. Brown, A.L., *Metacognition, executive control, self-regulation, and other more mysterious mechanisms.*, in *Metacognition, motivation, and understanding*, F. E. Weinert and R.H. Kluwe, Editors. 1987, Lawrence Erlbaum Associates.: Hillsdale, New Jersey:. p. 65-116.
16. Dahlback, N., A. Jonasson, and L. Ahrenberg, *Wizard of Oz studies: Why and How?* Knowledge Based Systems, 1993. 6: p. 258-266.
17. Luckin, R. and L. Hammerton. *„OK, I'll have someone help me for a change" Talking to children about task difficulty and help seeking to inform software scaffolding design.* in *International Conference on Communication, Problem-solving and Learning.* 2001. University of Strathclyde, Scotland.
18. Hammerton, L. and R. Luckin, *You be the Computer and I'll be the Learner: Using the 'Wizard of Oz' Technique to Involve Children in the Software Design Process*, in *Proceedings of 10th International Conference on Artificial Intelligence in Education: AI-ED in the Wired and Wireless Future.*, J. Moore, W.L. Johnson, and C.L. Redfield, Editors. 2001, IOS Press: Amsterdam. p. 551-553.
19. Hammerton, L. and R. Luckin, *How to help? Investigating children's opinions on help: To inform the design of Metacognitive Software Scaffolding*, in *AIED2001 Workshop Proceedings: Help provision and help seeking in Interactive Learning Environments.*, R. Luckin, Editor. 2001, St Mary's University: San Antonio. p. 22-33.
20. Luckin, R., *Knowledge construction in the zone of collaboration: scaffolding the learner to productive interactivity*, in International Conference of the Learning Sciences, A. Bruckman, et al., Editors. 1998, AACE: Atlanta, Georgia. p. 188-194.

Using Production to Assess Learning: An ILE That Fosters Self-Regulated Learning

Philippe Dessus and Benoît Lemaire

Laboratoire des Sciences de l'Education
Université Pierre-Mendès-France
BP 47 – 38040 Grenoble Cedex 9, France
{Philippe.Dessus,Benoit.Lemaire}@upmf-grenoble.fr

Abstract. Current systems aiming at engaging students in Self-Regulated Learning processes are often prompt-based and domain-dependent. Such metacognitive prompts are either difficult to interpret for novices or ignored by experts. Although domain-dependence per se cannot be considered as a drawback, it is often due to a rigid structure which prevents from moving to another domain. We detail here *Apex*, a two-loop system which provides texts to be learned through summarization. In the first loop, called *Reading*, the student formulates a query and is provided with texts related to this query. Then the student judges whether each text presented could be summarized. In the second loop, called *Writing*, the student writes out a summary of the texts, then gets an assessment from the system. In order to automatically perform various comprehension-centered tasks (i.e., texts that match queries, assessment of summaries), our system uses LSA (Latent Semantic Analysis), a tool devised for the semantic comparison of texts.

1 Introduction

This paper is about Lesgold's "two fundamental laws of instruction" [1]: (1) "Not everyone who passes a test on a topic knows what appears to have been tested"; and (2) "Not everyone who fails a test on a topic lacks the knowledge that appears to have been tested". Referring to these two laws, it is worth studying the means to reduce the gap between student knowledge and its assessment by a system. Apex, the system we are developing, aims at decreasing this gap by comparing the texts judged to be learned by the student to their summary. The architecture of our system is composed of a main loop, divided into two components, one devoted to reading, the other one devoted to writing:

- *In the Reading component*, the student reads texts and, after each one, is asked a judgment of learning. The first text is selected according to a natural language query provided by the student. Other texts are successively selected by the system according to the student judgment of learning of the prior ones.
- *In the Writing component*, the student writes out a summary of what has been read. The system compares this summary to the texts the student has

S.A. Cerri, G. Gouardères, and F. Paraguaçu (Eds.): ITS 2002, LNCS 2363, pp. 772–781, 2002.

judged as being learned. The student is warned in case the self-assessment is not coherent with the assessment by the system. The summary is then revised as often as the student wishes.

In order to automatically perform these comprehension-centered tasks (i.e., texts that match queries, assessment of summaries), our system relies on LSA (Latent Semantic Analysis), a tool devised for the semantic comparison of texts that we will describe later. The features described above exist in the current research literature within two lines of research: ILE, for Interactive Learning Environments and SRL, for Self-Regulated Learning.

2   *Apex* = ILE + SRL

To date, systems called ILE are either *production-centered*, qualitatively assessing production to help students write texts [2,3] or solve problems [4]; or *comprehension-centered* [5,6], providing students with texts related to their comprehension of previously delivered texts. The main features of ILEs are the following [7]: (a) *students are autonomous*, the guidance of ILEs is less formal than traditional ITS, (b) *focus on non-domain knowledge*, ILEs are more domain-independent than traditional ITS, and they tend to foster students' metacognitive skills, (c) *vary teaching styles*, since knowledge transmission is not the core goal of ILEs, they adopt various teaching styles (i.e., dialogue, assessment, scaffolding, etc.), (d) *authentic learning*, situations presented in ILEs are more authentic, giving students opportunities to develop real-life skills (i.e., writing and revising summaries, self-assessment of understanding, etc.).

We combine this notion with another line of research: SRL, which relies on four assumptions [8] : (a) the learner is an active participant in the learning process, (b) learners can monitor, control and regulate some aspects of their own cognition, motivation and behavior, (c) there are some goals the learner can set in order to carry on with the learning process, (d) self-regulated activities are mediators between learners and performance (e.g., reading or writing).

Few research has been done to promote SRL within ITS. One of the reasons could be that "computer-assisted SRL" is an oxymoron: "self-regulated" means that the student is free to perform a given activity, while the very notion of tutoring means that the computer constraints the student activity.

A way to address this drawback is to integrate the SRL theory within an ILE rather than in an ITS. We will first describe some trends about SRL research, then we will present LSA. Finally, we will detail our system, *Apex 2.0*.

3   Self-Regulated Learning

3.1   Theoretical Framework

We adapted the model of Self-Regulated Learning, detailed in Butler and Winne [9]. These authors describe their model as follows (see Fig. 1): firstly, the student constructs a representation of the learning task through his or her prior knowledge (e.g., beliefs, knowledge on domain and strategy, motivational beliefs). This representation is used to set learning goals that are progressively attained by diverse tactics and strategies. Then these goals generate products, both internal (cognitive and emotional) and external (behavior, performance). This last phase is subject to two sorts of metacognitive processes: (a) it is first *monitored* by the student, who can reassess goals and change his or her strategies through internal feedback; (b) then, performance can be cognitively *controled* [10]. In other words, learning occurs when the teacher helps students to formulate and monitor their own goals instead of doing it in their place, from an expert point of view. We now describe systems devoted to assist this goal formulation in various academic activities, and therefore to foster SRL.

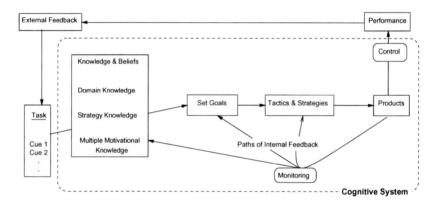

Fig. 1. A Model of Self-Regulated Learning (after [9,10])

3.2   Related Work on Computer-Aided SRL

One of the first SRL-centered computer programs was *Reading Partner* [6]. It delivers metacognitive questions during reading. *Reading Partner* includes neither a user model nor a domain model: the prompts delivered are linked to each text a priori. *Writing Partner* [3] is another system developed within the same framework: it delivers guidance during the writing process through diverse predefined metacognitive questions for assessing writing quality. Although these systems have been positively tested, some drawbacks remain: (a) there are few differences between control group and experimental group, although they are attributed to the non-solicited prompts group, (b) there is no adaptivity to the student. Second generation of SRL systems aims at integrating SRL management into ITS with such adaptivity. We now present systems in this line of research according to the main processes involved: reading, writing or learning.

Reading-Centered SRL-systems. *Listen* [5] is a reading tutor equipped with speech recognition that listens to students and helps them learn to read. Text read aloud sentence per sentence by students is analyzed by *Listen*, which in turn provides online feedback: speaking a word or several words, spelling aloud a word by phonemes or by syllables. Vocabulary help is available through Word-Net. *Listen* also allows students to read stories close to both their interest and their reading ability. Although this system is mainly devoted to reading, another module allows students to write stories.

Writing-centered SRL-systems. *Business Letter Tutor* [2] is a case-based system that helps secretaries to write business letters. First the system gets some characteristics of the letter to be written, then it delivers to the secretary the closest letter from its database. Each letter of the database is indexed with meta-tags and a neural network-based processing performs the matching.

Learning-centered SRL-systems. *Autotutor* [11] is a LSA-based ITS in the domain of computer literacy. One of the purposes of *Autotutor*, for which LSA is required, is to answer unrestricted student questions by matching them with domain content. Another functionality of *Autotutor*, named *"Selection of next good answer aspect"* (GAA) uses LSA to select the next dialogue content to cover, within a set of pre-computed GAA. This selection is computed according to three criteria: (a) the matching of the next GAA with the zone of proximal development (*Autotutor* selects the next GAA to cover which similarity with the previous one would be both *below* a specified threshold—too similar, i.e., already covered—and still *above* other less related aspects); (b) its coherence (i.e., semantically close) with the preceding GAA; (c) its resemblance with the uncovered content.

Comments. Most of the systems presented above are both prompt-based and domain-dependent. Firstly, they rely on a domain theory (i.e., composition process, misconceptions on a specific domain) to propose prompts that should influence students' metacognitive processes (i.e., "What more do you need to know in order to solve this problem?"). Zellermayer et al. [3] showed that such prompts require a low cognitive load only if they are unsolicited. Boekaerts [12] showed that direct teaching of such strategies did not systematically entail a long term use. We showed above that prompt delivering has some drawbacks: weak portability to another domain content, difficult prompt interpretation—prompts can either be problematic for novices or ignored by experts.

Secondly, current ITS are domain-dependent. They generally contain a predefined knowledge structure that is used to select content. This structure is required to formulate a lesson goal given the student profile. This structure also both mimics expert domain knowledge and constrains further implementations to other domain contents.

Our system aims at two goals: no delivering metacognitive prompts and being domain-independent. It also includes some features of the previous systems. Firstly, we decided to offer a minimal guidance to the student in order to promote autonomy: the student will be responsible to stop at any time the delivery of content material to enter the assessment part and vice versa. Secondly, in order to promote SRL processes, students are asked to judge their learning, just following the exposition to the content. Finally, our system both comprehension and production-centered, like *Listen*. In order to tightly link both processes, we rely on a unique formalism to represent the content material and the student production. Both are represented as texts. However, the semantics of texts needs to be represented since the system has to perform comparisons between student production and content. The "next text to be read" like in *Autotutor* or *Listen* is also selected according to a semantic representation. For these reasons, all texts are represented in the LSA formalism, a model which is now described.

4   Presentation of the System

4.1   LSA: A Knowledge Representation System for *Apex 2.0*

As we mentioned earlier, our system is based on two main loops. The first one selects texts to be read by the student, the second one assesses learning by comparing a text written by the student to the texts he or she has read. Both processes require a semantic matching between texts. Therefore, we relied on LSA, a tool which performs a semantic comparison between texts based on the statistical analysis of huge corpora [13,14]. Two words are considered semantically similar if they statistically occur in semantically similar paragraphs all over the corpus. Two paragraphs are said semantically similar if they contain semantically similar words. For instance, *weapon* and *gun* are semantically similar since they appear statistically in similar paragraphs (i.e., they occur with similar words like *shot*, *crime*, etc.). This mutual recursion is solved by a form of factorial analysis which assigns each word to a high-dimensional vector (about 300 dimensions).

Each word being represented by a vector, it is straightforward to assign each new set of words to a new vector, by simple sum of vectors. If we consider that each knowledge source can be represented by a set of words, we can say that LSA is a knowledge representation system. Of course, it is not efficient for reasoning on the representation, for instance drawing inferences, since the 300 values defining a vector do not have an intelligible meaning per se. Semantic networks or description logics are much more powerful formalisms for this purpose. However, LSA is more appropriate for comparing representations, which is not the case for symbolic formalisms. A semantic comparison of two sets of words, i.e., two vectors, is performed by simply computing the cosine of their angle. A semantic comparison is therefore a number between -1 (no similarity) and 1 (highest similarity). The number of dimensions plays an important role. If the number of dimensions is too small, too much information is lost. If it is too big, not enough dependencies are drawn between vectors. Dumais [15] showed that a size of 100 to 300 gives the best results in the domain of language. We will not present in detail the mathematical aspects of LSA which are detailed elsewhere [13].

We claim that LSA is an adequate tool for our purpose for several reasons. Firstly, Dumais [15] showed that LSA improves text retrieval performance up to 30%, compared with standard methods. Secondly, another line of research on LSA showed its capabilities to assess comprehension through text exposition [16]. Actually, these authors showed that LSA is as good as humans to assess the comprehension of students who have read a set of texts on a given topic and produced an essay about this topic [17]. Thirdly, a more recent line of research showed LSA's capabilities to model user within an ITS [11,18]. LSA can be used to find the most appropriate text to provide to a student, given the texts read. The idea, close to *Autotutor's* GAA, is to select a text which is neither too close nor too far from the student model.

4.2   Previous Versions of *Apex*

Our system is a follow-up of previous versions of *Apex* presented elsewhere [19]. We describe here the main functionalities of these versions in order to highlight what is new in *Apex 2.0*. *Apex* is a domain-independent ITS that can automatically assess the semantic content of student essays.

- *Apex 1.0* takes as input a student essay and returns an assessment based on a semantic comparison with the relevant parts of the course. For each relevant unit of the course, the system informs the student about the way the content is covered. For instance, the system could say "*You have covered very well the section about* X. *You have covered badly the section about* Y". Then the student is asked to work on the essay once more. Assessments at the paragraph level were delivered as well as a general grade. We compared this last measure with human grades and found a correlation of .59.
- *Apex 1.2* is a Web version of the system, written in PHP and MySQL. It can manage several students, several teachers and several courses. A student can pick up a course, select a topic, write an essay, get an assessment, revise the essay accordingly, etc. Teachers can add new courses and structure them.
- *Apex 1.5* analyses the student essay in order to split it into coherent parts. Instead of comparing the essay as a whole, each part is compared with the relevant parts of the course. Therefore, indications to the student are more precise. Consequently, the correlation with human grades raises to .62.

These systems assess student essays but they do not help students to improve their knowledge. The student would know which part of the course was not well understood but the student might not know what to do to fill this gap. In other words, these systems take care of the control but not of the learning. Therefore, our goal was to design a system that would do both. In addition, we thought that it would be important to take into account student comprehension. It is useful to know whether the student has learned something about the text that has been presented. This information could be used to select the next text.

4.3   An Overview of *Apex 2.0*

The Reading and Writing loops (Fig. 2) rely on three kinds of markers associated to each text: *provided, summarizable, deliverable*. This information is updated after each student action. Each marker indicates:

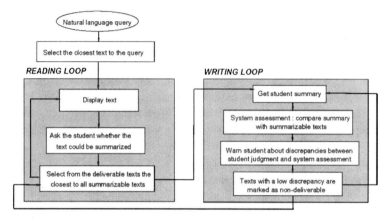

Fig. 2. Apex architecture

- whether the text has been already *provided* in the current Reading loop. This is to ensure that the system is not providing the same text twice in the same Reading loop. Initially, all texts are marked as not provided;
- whether the text has been judged to be *summarizable* or not. This information is asked after the student has read a text. It is used for comparison with the system assessment. We could have directly asked the student to indicate whether the text was learned or not but we think this would be too hard a question. We think it is better to get this information by means of a question related to the way the text could be summarized, especially because this is the task the student will perform in the Writing loop. Initially, all texts are marked as not summarizable;
- whether the text is *deliverable* or not. Texts that are both judged as summarizable by the student and positively assessed by the system are permanently marked as non-deliverable. They will no longer be provided to the student. A text is positively assessed if it is semantically close enough to the text written by the student. Initially, all texts are deliverable.

The Reading loop. The goal of the Reading loop is to provide the student with texts. Texts are selected according to an initial natural language query formulated by the student and to what the system knows about the student from the beginning of the session. We tested the system with a corpus in sociology of education (56 documents, 29,024 words). We also added a 137,598-words corpus in the same domain which was only used for improving the semantic comparison accuracy. All these texts were beforehand analyzed by LSA and represented as vectors in a 300-dimensions semantic space. Suppose a student composes the following query: *"I'd like to work on the school effects"*. *Apex 2.0* would find the closest text to this query and provide the student with this text. The student reads the text. Then the student is required to click on one of the two buttons: *"I think I could sum it up"* or *"I don't think I could"*. If the first choice is selected, the text is marked in the system as summarizable.

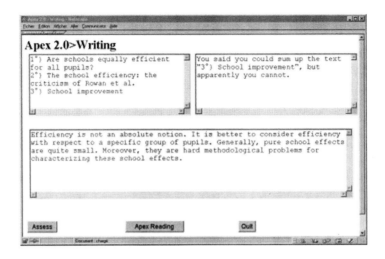

Fig. 3. Screendumps of *Apex 2.0* Writing module

The system then selects the next text which is, from all deliverable texts not already provided in the current Reading loop, the closest text to all summarizable texts. The idea is to select a text which content is mostly related to what the student is supposed to have learned. To do that, the system computes the average semantic proximity between each text and all summarizable texts. If no text has been marked as summarizable yet, it means that the system is not able to select the next text. Therefore, the student is asked to rephrase the initial query. After a while, the student can decide that enough texts have been provided. The student then enters the Writing loop.

The SRL process solicited here is concerned with cognitive monitoring. In confronting their reading goals to the texts proposed by the system, students can refine them. They can thus get a more precise view of the content to learn.

The Writing loop. The student writes out a text summarizing the content of all texts read during the Reading loop. Of course, only the texts judged as summarizable are supposed to be summarized. The system displays the title of all of them (upper left pane of Fig. 3). The goal of the Writing loop is to know whether the student is really able to summarize these texts. The way to do that is to compare two assessments: the first one, performed by the student after each text has been read (i.e., summarizable or not) and the second one performed by LSA (i.e., deliverable or not). This latter assessment is performed as follows: the student summary is computed by LSA and represented by a vector. This vector is then compared with all the texts the student has previously judged as summarizable. If the similarity is high enough (above a threshold arbitrarily set at .5), the text is marked as non deliverable. If the similarity is too low the text remains deliverable and the student is warned: "*You said you could summarize* *the text* X *but apparently you cannot*". This information can be used by students to revise their summary, in that case the Writing loop starts again. Otherwise, the student re-enters the Reading loop.

The SRL process dedicated to this loop is cognitive control. In writing a summary that is semantically compared with the source texts, the student can keep in mind the parts that are not summarized well. In turn, the summary can be reviewed to more adequately match with the source texts. This way the student is able to have a better grasp of the content delivered during this loop.

5   Further Work and Limits

We plan to test *Apex 2.0* in experimental conditions, in which subjects perform various learning goals (e.g., reading for learning, studying for an exam, completing a brief essay). We will measure some dependent variables such as: number of goal refinements, number of texts read, number of revisions of the text, etc. A next version of *Apex* will address some current limits: (a) the judgment of learning could be refined by allowing the student to highlight parts of texts considered as learned; (b) text deliverability could also be a priori defined by the teacher, in order to allow content selection by the teacher; (c) in order to help students who begin learning a content, teacher predefined queries would be proposed to them; (d) in order to scaffold the student activity it would be adequate to diminish progressively the help provided.

6   Discussion

Apex 2.0 can be distinguished from other SRL-based systems on two points: a unique formalism and no intrusive hints. Firstly, most ITS use separate knowledge bases to model respectively users, pedagogical moves, and content. Knowledge is formalized either by the teacher or the domain expert. Our system imposes neither a specific formalization nor a rigid model because all the necessary knowledge resides within a unique formalism. Secondly, current systems are prompt-based, i.e., systems usually provide metacognitive hints that are (or not) taken into account by users. Our system is rather an attempt to emphasize the gap between the content judged to be learned and the content actually learned. In that way students can try to reduce this gap either by writing better summaries or by judging more objectively their learning.

The question of transfer remains to be investigated. Adequate metacognitive prompts could lead to internalization by the user, who would be able to perform metacognitive skills *without* guidance. To date, this domain is seldom inquired, and we would test if abilities developed within *Apex 2.0* remain after its use.

Acknowledgements. We thank E. de Vries and B. Camou for their thoughtful comments on an earlier version of this paper, and P. Bressoux for providing the text of the course.

References

1. Lesgold, A.: Toward a theory of curriculum for use in designing intelligent tutoring systems. In Mandl, H., Lesgold, A., eds.: Learning Issues for Intelligent Tutoring Systems. Springer, Berlin (1988) 114–137
2. Boylan, P., Vergaro, C.: Metacognition in epistolary rhetoric: A case-based system for writing effective business letters in a foreign language. In Lajoie, S.P., Vivet, M., eds.: Artificial Intelligence in Education. IOS Press, Amsterdam (1999) 305–312
3. Zellermayer, M., Salomon, G., Globerson, T., Givon, H.: Enhancing writing-related metacognitions through a computerized writing partner. American Educational Research Journal **28** (1991) 373–391
4. Veermans, K., de Jong, T., van Joolingen, W.R.: Promoting self-directed learning in simulation-based discovery learning environments through intelligent support. Interactive Learning Environments **8** (2000) 229–255
5. Mostow, J., Aist, G.: Evaluating tutors that listen. In Forbus, K.D., Feltovich, P.J., eds.: Smart Machines in Education. AAAI, Menlo Park (2001) 169–234
6. Salomon, G., Globerson, T., Guterman, E.: The computer as a zone of proximal development: Internalizing reading-related metacognitions from a reading partner. Journal of Educational Psychology **81** (1989) 620–627
7. Self, J.: The role of student models in learning environments. Trans. of the Institute of Electronics, Information and Communication Engineers **E77-D** (1994) 3–8
8. Azevedo, R.: Using hypermedia to learn about complex systems: A self-regulation model. In: Help Workshop of the AI-ED 2001 Conference, San Antonio (2001)
9. Butler, D.L., Winne, P.H.: Feedback and self-regulated learning: A theoretical synthesis. Review of Educational Research **65** (1995) 245–281
10. Nelson, T.O.: Cognition versus metacognition. In Sternberg, R.J., ed.: The Nature of Cognition. MIT Press, Cambridge (1999) 625–644
11. Graesser, C., Person, N., Harter, D., the Tutoring Research Group: Teaching tactics and dialog in Autotutor. International Journal of Artificial Intelligence in Education **12** (in press)
12. Boekaerts, M.: Self-regulated learning : a new concept embraced by researchers, policy makers, educators, teachers, and students. Learning and Instruction **7** (1997) 161–186
13. Deerwester, S., Dumais, S., Furnas, G., Landauer, T., Harshman, R.: Indexing by Latent Semantic Analysis. Journal of the American Society for Information Science **41** (1990) 391–407
14. Landauer, T., Foltz, P., Laham, D.: An introduction to Latent Semantic Analysis. Discourse Processes **25** (1998) 259–284
15. Dumais, S.: Improving the retrieval of information from external sources. Behavior Research Methods, Instruments and Computers **23** (1991) 229–236
16. Wolfe, M., Schreiner, M., Rehder, B., Laham, D., Foltz, P., Kintsch, W., Landauer, T.: Learning from text: Matching readers and texts by Latent Semantic Analysis. Discourse Processes **25** (1998) 309–336
17. Kintsch, E., Steinhart, D., Stahl, G., Matthews, C., Lamb, R., the LSA Group: Developing summarization skills through the use of LSA-based feedback. Interactive Learning Environments **8** (2000) 87–109
18. Zampa, V., Lemaire, B.: Latent Semantic Analysis for user modeling. Journal of Intelligent Information Systems **18** (2002) 15–30
19. Lemaire, B., Dessus, P.: A system to assess the semantic content of student essays. Journal of Educational Computing Research **24** (2001) 305–320

The AMBRE ILE: How to Use Case-Based Reasoning to Teach Methods

Nathalie Guin-Duclosson, Stéphanie Jean-Daubias, and Sandra Nogry

Laboratoire d'Ingénierie des Systèmes d'Information
Université Claude Bernard - Lyon 1
Nautibus, 8 bd Niels Bohr, Campus de la Doua
69622 Villeurbanne Cedex
FRANCE
{nguin, sdaubias, snogry}@bat710.univ-lyon1.fr

Abstract. Designing an Interactive Learning Environment (ILE) requires work within a multi-disciplinary team [9]. In this paper, we describe the designing process of the ILE AMBRE, the purpose of which is to teach methods. We show how, based on didactic work, we chose to represent the expert knowledge to be taught to the learner through Artificial Intelligence techniques. We also describe how we adjusted the Case-Based Reasoning paradigm (CBR), derived from Artificial Intelligence, to teaching abstract knowledge based on problem classes. Last we describe a Cognitive Psychology experiment we conducted in order to test the appropriateness of the thus designed EIAH to the goals of the AMBRE project.

1 Introduction

This paper describes the multidisciplinary work conducted in the framework of the AMBRE project. The purpose of the project is to complete an Interactive Learning Environment (ILE) to teach methods. Derived from didactic studies, these methods are based on a classification of problems and solving tools.

In order to teach abstract knowledge, we suggest to use the Case-Based Reasoning paradigm (CBR). Our theory is that the use of cases already experienced by the learner to solve problems and the comparison between experienced cases and problems to be solved can help the learner acquire abstract knowledge (schemata, problem classes).

In the first part of this paper, we describe the knowledge that we would like the learner to acquire through the AMBRE ILE, and how we represent it within an Artificial Intelligence system. We then present how such expertise can be connected with CBR, and describe existing work regarding ILE using CBR. In a third section, we show the teaching process, which the AMBRE project is based on, as well as the first ILE prototype implemented. We finish with a description of an experiment intended to test the appropriateness of the prototype to the goals of the project, the results of the experimentation leading us to express recommendations for designing the AMBRE ILE.

S.A. Cerri, G. Gouardères, and F. Paraguaçu (Eds.): ITS 2002, LNCS 2363, pp. 782–791, 2002.
© Springer-Verlag Berlin Heidelberg 2002

2   How to Represent the Knowledge to Be Taught?

Didactic studies suggest teaching explicitly the methods, which, in a small domain, help to guide the problem solving process [14][15]. These methods are based on a classification of problems and of solving tools. They help select the solving technique that is best suited to a given problem.

As part of the AMBRE project, we consider relying on a problem solver to help the learning, particularly in order to provide the learner with explanations. The problem solver should therefore work according to the methods it wishes to have acquired, not according to the most general expert methods of the domain [4]. Thus, the solver should be designed and derived from the targeted knowledge.

In order to represent such knowledge, we use the SYRCLAD [7] solver architecture which enables to explicit in a declarative way a problem classification and the reformulation and solution knowledge associated with it. Thus it enables to model the knowledge to be observed in learners, not only the knowledge of an expert.

In a given domain, an expert (didactician, teacher...) defines a hierarchy of problem classes. In order to be able to use that hierarchy to classify a problem, an expert should define the reformulation knowledge that allows computing the values of discriminating attributes of the classification hierarchy. Some classes in the hierarchy, referred to as operational, are specific enough for each one to be associated with a solving technique suited for the problems in that class (according to the system).

Solving a problem then consists first of all in an operationalisation phase, where the system uses the reformulation knowledge and the domain problem classification graph to determine what class the problem is in and to build a new model of that problem (referred to as operational model). This model is mainly composed of the discriminating attributes of the hierarchy, but also of attributes which distinguish the problem from its class. This operational model no longer has surface features (i.e. problem elements irrelevant to the solution) of the descriptive model. The solving in itself then consists in applying the solving technique associated with the class of problem to the operational model, in order to get a solution to the posed problem.

The purpose of the AMBRE project is to design an ILE the purpose of which is to have the learner acquire a solving method based on a problem class hierarchy and on solving techniques associated with those classes. However, it does not always seem appropriate to present such a hierarchy to the learner explicitly. In some domains, the terms defining solving techniques and classes are not necessarily used institutionally and are unknown to the learners. Therefore we consider a process where the learner is more active, where he or she builds his own method, by representing a class of problem by a prototype problem. We believe that the case-based reasoning paradigm can help the learner acquire such a method.

3   Use Case–Based Reasoning

3.1   From SYRCLAD to CBR

Case-Based Reasoning can be described as a set of sequential steps (elaborate, retrieve, adapt, test/revise, store) that is often represented by a cycle [13]. We liken such a cycle (steps in bold type in Figure 1) to a solving method implemented with the SYRCLAD architecture (steps in italics type in Figure 1).

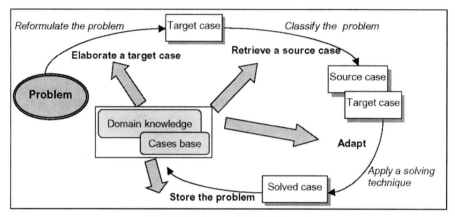

Fig. 1. SYRCLAD and the CBR cycle

The problem reformulation step can be seen as a target case elaboration step, even if that step is then advanced since it uses classification knowledge and reformulation knowledge. The problem classification can also be matched with a source case retrieval step, the retrieved source case then constituting the prototype case of the problem class that a SYRCLAD solver would have determined. Adapting the solving of that source case to the target case is then like applying the solving technique to the operational class represented by the prototype. In order to store the solved problem, one can consider that the SYRCLAD solver connects the new case with a problem class. The SYRCLAD solver does not use the revision step of usual CBR cycle, since the solving is always correct. In the AMBRE ILE, revision is included in each step of the cycle, as it is explained in part 4.

Our objective is to have acquired a solving method based on a problem class hierarchy by presenting examples of solved problems to the learner, and guiding the solution of new problems using case-based reasoning. We wish the « expert-student » knowledge after the learning can be modelled like in Figure 2: based on a cases base, the learner has built operational classes represented by a prototype problem, and these problem classes can be organised in a hierarchy.

3.2   CBR Uses in ILE

The CBR paradigm is a technique that has already been used in various parts of an ILE.

Modelling the learner's knowledge can be done using CBR [18], like the assessment of the leaner [10]. By comparing the learner's model with other learners' assessments (forming a cases base), CBR can also help select a learning strategy [5], or build a path in a hypertext [8].

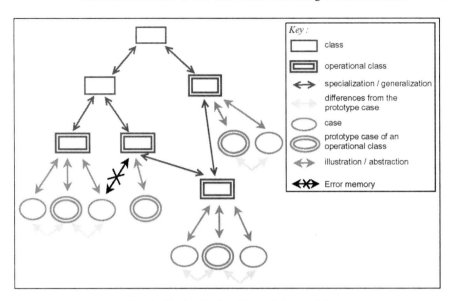

Fig. 2. "Expert-Student" knowledge model

The closest application of our theory is Case-Based Teaching [17]. Systems based on this learning strategy present a close case to the learner when the leaner is having difficulty solving a problem, or when facing a problem he or she never came across before (in a new domain or a new type). In these systems there are several levels of interactivity between the learner and the computer environment [19]. The learner can ask the system to find a similar example and explain how that case was solved; the system can also offer the entire solution to the learner's exercise like in CATO [1].

The Virtual Participant [12] is an example of case-based teaching. It is a virtual assistant intervening in virtual lectures to present cases to the learners. The cases base includes problems posed by persons taking part in the lecture, and solutions (offered by the same persons). This environment has been tried in a course where forum type lectures were given. From one year to the other, the participants experienced similar problems; thus the Virtual Participant helps meet their expectations more efficiently by offering similar cases experiences by previous year students.

4   The Learning Principle in AMBRE

In the case of the AMBRE project, the purpose was to have the learner acquire a solving method for problems in one domain. To do so, the first step is to present him, in an interactive manner, the solving of a few typical problems (serving as cases base initialisation). The learner is then assisted in solving new problems (usually in the same class as the submitted examples): the environment guides the learner's solving of the problem by following each step of the CBR cycle (see Figure 3). Elaboration, retrieval, adaptation and storage are done by the learner, but guided by the system.

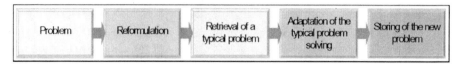

Fig. 3. The solving steps in AMBRE

4.1 Elaboration of the Target Case

The first step consists in reformulating the problem to be solved. The learner is asked to build a new formulation of the submitted problem, step by step. Actually this task consists in identifying the structural features of the problem to be solved (i.e. relevant features for the solution, as opposed to surface features), by finding attributes of the operational problem model. The system relies on the classification graph to guide the reformulation. It reviews the student's answers and explains possible mistakes in order to reach an agreement with the student on a correct reformulation. The reformulation (operational model) no longer has most of the initial problem's surface features, and becomes a reference for the remainder of the solving.

4.2 Retrieval of a Source Case

The second step of the solving consists in the learner comparing the problem to be solved with those he or she has already solved by identifying differences and similarities in each case. He or she should choose the prototype problem (source case) that seems the nearest to the problem to be solved, such nearness being based on reformulated problems, not on surface features. By choosing a prototype exercise, the learner implicitly identifies the class of problems associated with the problem to be solved. The system diagnoses the student's proposal and may suggest and justify a better choice, in order to reach an agreement with the student on the reference problem.

4.3 Adaptation of the Source Case Solution to the Target Case

In order to complete the solving, the learner should adapt the solution of the source case (the reference problem) to the target case (the problem to be solved). At this point, we are hopeful that little by little, the learner will relate a solving plan to the problem class. The system prepares such an adaptation by outlining differences and similarities between the source case and the target case. When both cases belong to the same operational class, adapting the solution of the prototype problem comes to applying the solving technique associated with its respective class to the values of the significant attributes of the problem to be solved (those that distinguish the problem from the class it is an instance of). The solving technique, known to the system, is not explicitly known to the learner. That is why the learner should rely on the source case solution and adapt it to the target case.

It can be considered that in a first phase, the system will show the learner how to carry out the adaptation step with an example, in order to introduce the interface tools helping to achieve the adaptation. When the learner puts forward an adaptation resulting in a solution proposal, the system diagnoses the proposal and may provide explanations on corrections to be made in order to reach a correct solution.

4.4 Storage of the Target Case

Once the problem is solved, the learner should add it to the cases base, i.e. insert it in the problems structure he or she has built. During that phase, the learner should identify, explicitly this time, the problem class associated with the problem to be solved. This task will often consists in relating the new case to a prototype problem, therefore in inserting it in a group of existing problems. A group of problems includes all problems in the same operational class. Obviously the learner should be given an opportunity to change the selection of the prototype problem representing a group. In addition, it may be advisable that the prototype problems all belong to the same family of problems (in the meaning of surface features), so as to better focus on structure differences.

It may occur that the new case does not belong to an existing group of problems, and the learner can then create a new group whose prototype problem is the problem he or she has just solved. It may also occur that one (or several) sub-groups of problem need to be created within a group, the sub-group being also represented by a prototype problem. The purpose is to represent an operational class, sub-class of another operational class; to the sub-class is related a more specific solving technique than the one related to the parent class.

Last, the learner should be given tools to help him, if he or she wishes, distinguish problem groups from one another, by building an initial hierarchy. To do so, it is advisable that he or she uses attributes of operational models, which he or she is familiar with through the problem reformulation step.

5 Prototype Evaluation

A prototype of the AMBRE ILE was made (see Figure 4 for the retrieval step) for the numbering problem domain (final scientific year level)[1]. The prototype reproduces the operation of the system with a limited number of problems, as the Artificial Intelligence modules of the systems have not been integrated yet. Indeed, for the AMBRE environment to provide the functions described in the above section, conventional ILE modules, i.e. the expert module, the learner's model, the diagnosis module, the educational module and the aid and explanation module should be completed and the SYRCLAD solver integrated.

Prior to developing the entire ILE, we wanted to assess the impact of the CBR paradigm on method learning by observing, at first, the behaviour of users with the prototype.

---

[1] The problem class hierarchy for this domain was determined as part of the "Combien?" work group, composed of Artificial Intelligence researchers and mathematic teachers [6].

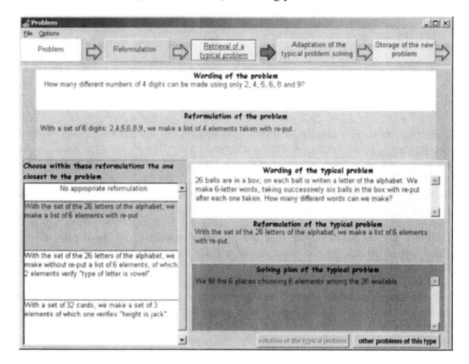

Fig. 4. The prototype retrieval step

As part of this preliminary evaluation, conducted according to cognitive psychology techniques, two hypotheses were tested:

- the use of CBR paradigm facilitates the induction of problems categories,
- the use of the CBR paradigm helps improve the learner's performance by problem solving.

Below, we describe the experiment conducted and the results obtained.

5.1 Experimentation

This first evaluation consists of a comparison study of the use of two prototypes; the first prototype guides the solving according to the ILE AMBRE principle, and therefore integrates the CBR paradigm. The second prototype offers, as a control condition, a simple solving of the same exercises in the same environment, but without any special guiding.

Before and after the training with the prototype (see Figure 5), the learners solve two paper-pencil tasks:

- a problem solving task helping to measure the learners' performance,
- a problem categorisation task (classification of ten exercises wordings based on solution similarity) providing indication of learners' classification.

The experiment was conducted with 64 students in their final scientific year, in the classroom in order to reproduce actual use conditions.

The tasks offered in pre-test and post-test were analysed and compared. For the categorisation task, the classifications given by the learners were subjected to a descriptive analysis using the Barthélemy and Guénoche taxonomy [2]. For the problem-solving task, the answers were processed using a variance analysis.

Prototype use traces were also analysed in order to observe software use conditions and determine most frequent errors.

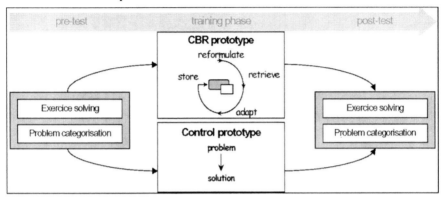

Fig. 5. Experimentation plan

5.2 Results and Discussion

First of all the results of this first experiment show that the prototype using the CBR paradigm facilitates problem classifying according to relevant features for the solving, but only with some learners. Then, during the post-test, there is no significant problem solving performance difference between both groups (those using the CBR prototype and those using the control prototype). In addition, use traces outline the difficulties experienced by the learners in finding the closest source exercise in the retrieval step; they often proceed by trial-error. Thus, even if the reformulation step helps explain structure features, it does not facilitate the use of such features in the retrieval step.

Therefore these results do not validate our hypotheses (problem category induction facilitation and improved problem solving performance). One could assume these disappointing results come from the difficulty experienced by some learners during the retrieval step (the way we presented this step on the interface should be improved). These results are also partly due to the lack of system flexibility, which does not allow the learner to circulate between the various process steps.

5.3 Advice for Designing the ILE

The results of the experiment underline the need to improve the ILE prototype before carrying on with the tests. The retrieval step seems the most important one to develop. There should be more incentives to compare the target problem and the typical problems. To do so, we should offer tools to the learner facilitating such comparison. We have already imagined the techniques which in the next version of the prototype, will help outline the similarities and differences between the problem to be solved and the case base derived problems. In addition, transition from one step to the other should be made possible so the learner may understand the impact of the choice of the typical problem on the remainder of the resolution (the adaptation step), and so he or she can relate the retrieval and storage step. One can assume that by offering greater freedom for movement between CBR steps, the learner's awareness of the relationship between such steps will be made easier. The integration of artificial intelligence modules in the prototype should add flexibility, particularly for this point.

6 Conclusions and Prospects

This paper described the AMBRE ILE project, which relies on the CBR solving cycle to have the learner acquire a problem solving method based on a classification of problems in the domain. For this study, we designed and implemented a prototype of the ILE using the CBR paradigm to facilitate method learning by guiding the student towards problem classification and solving tools. Thus we took into account, in addition to the CBR paradigm, cognitive psychology studies that demonstrate the importance of using examples when elaborating abstract knowledge [3]. In order to assess the impact of this paradigm on problem classification and solving tools, we set up an experiment comparing the prototype to a prototype without CBR.

Although the results of this first cognitive evaluation do not confirm our hypotheses, they give a better understanding of the learner's behaviour and views. This enables us to express recommendations that should make easier, in the AMBRE ILE, the learner's classification of problems and solving tools. The new prototype, integrating at least part of the artificial intelligence modules, and taking into account the recommendations expressed after the first experiment, should help us set up new experiments with a view to assessing the impact of the CBR on learning problem classes and on learning solving tool classes. A longitudinal study would also be useful to observe the learner's problem classification as time passes. Last, additional experiments on learning from examples will help provide a better understanding of how to induce some learning processes, and thereby help method teaching.

References

1. Aleven, V., Ashley, K.D.: Teaching Case-Based Argumentation through a Model and Examples - Empirical Evaluation of an Intelligent Learning Environment. Artificial Intelligence in Education (B. du Boulay and R. Mizoguchi Eds.), IOS Press (1997) 87-94
2. Barthélemy, J.P., Guénoche, A.: Trees and Proximity Representations. Wiley J., London (1991) 238
3. Cummins, D.: Role of Analogical Reasoning in the Induction of problem categories. Journal of Experimental Psychology: Learning, Memory, and Cognition, Vol. 5 (1992) 1103-1124
4. Delozanne, E.: Explications en EIAO: études à partir d'ÉLISE, un logiciel pour s'entraîner à une méthode de calcul de primitives. Phd, Université du Maine, Le Mans, France (1992)

5. Gilbert, J.E.: Case-Based Reasoning Applied to Instruction Method Selection for Intelligent Tutoring Systems. Workshop 5: Case-Based Reasoning in Intelligent Training Systems, ITS'2000, Montreal (2000) 11-15

6. Guin, N., Giroire H., Tisseau G.: Le classement de problèmes : une méthode de résolution de problèmes pour le module expert d'un EIAO. Application aux problèmes de dénombrement. In proceedings of "Quatrièmes journées EIAO de Cachan" (Guin, D., Nicaud, J.-F, Py, D. Eds.), Eyrolles, France (1995) 113-124

7. Guin-Duclosson, N.: SYRCLAD: une architecture de résolveurs de problèmes permettant d'expliciter des connaissances de classification, reformulation et résolution. Revue d'Intelligence Artificielle, vol 13-2, Paris : Hermès (1999) 225-282

8. Héraud, J.-M., Mille, A.: Pixed: vers le partage et la réutilisation d'expériences pour assister l'apprentissage. In Proceedings of international symposium TICE 2000, Troyes, France (2000) 237-244

9. Jean, S.: PÉPITE: un système d'assistance au diagnostic de compétences, Phd, Université du Maine, Le Mans, France (2000)

10. Khan, T.M.: Case-Based Evaluation for Student Modelling. Workshop 5: Case-Based Reasoning in Intelligent Training Systems, ITS'2000, Montreal (2000) 16-22

11. Kolodner, J.: Case Based Reasoning. San Mateo, CA: Morgan Kaufmann Publishers (1993)

12. Masterton, S.: The Virtual Participant: Lessons to be Learned from a Case-Based Tutor's Assistant. Computer Support for Collaborative Learning, Toronto (1997)

13. Mille, A.: Associer expertise et expérience pour assister les tâches de l'utilisateur, Habilitation à diriger des recherches, Université Claude Bernard, Lyon, France (1998)

14. Rogalski, M.: Enseigner des méthodes en mathématiques. Commission Inter-Irem Université, Enseigner autrement les mathématiques en Deug A première année, bulletin Inter-Irem (1990) 65-79

15. Rogalski, M.: Les concepts de l'EIAO sont-ils indépendants du domaine? L'exemple d'enseignement de méthodes en analyse. Recherches en Didactiques des Mathématiques, vol 14 n°1.2 (1994) 43-66

16. Sander, E.: L'analogie, du naïf au créatif. Paris, l'Harmattan (2000)

17. Schank, R., Edelson, D.: A Role for AI in Education: Using Technology to Reshape Education. Journal of Artificial Intelligence in Education vol 1.2 (1990) 3-20

18. Shiri, A., Aimeur, E., Frasson, C.: SARA: A Cased-Based Student Modelling System. Fourth European Workshop on Case-Based Reasoning, Lecture Notes in Artificial Intelligence, n° 1488, Dublin, Ireland (1998) 425-436

19. Tourigny, N., Capus, L.: Towards Making Intelligent Training Systems Using Examples more Flexible and Reusable by Exploiting Case-Based Reasoning. Workshop 5: Case-Based Reasoning in Intelligent Training Systems, ITS'2000, Montreal (2000) 23-28

Model-Based Reasoning for Domain Modeling in a Web-Based Intelligent Tutoring System to Help Students Learn to Debug C++ Programs

Amruth N. Kumar

Ramapo College of New Jersey
505 Ramapo Valley Road
Mahwah, NJ 07430-1680
amruth@ramapo.edu

Abstract. The benefits of using Model-Based Reasoning for domain modeling are several-fold. We analyze these benefits and illustrate them in the context of a Web-based Intelligent Tutoring System. The system is designed to teach students to analyze and debug C++ programs for semantic and run-time errors. We have evaluated one instance of the Model-Based tutor, which deals with debugging pointers in C++, in several sections of Computer Science II course. We will present the results of these evaluations, which confirm the learnability of Model-Based tutors.

1   Introduction

We are developing an Intelligent Tutoring System to help students learn the C++ programming language by analyzing and debugging C++ code segments. Among the six levels of abstraction of educational objectives proposed by Bloom [4], we target application (use methods in new situations, solve problems using knowledge) in our ITS, as opposed to program synthesis, which has been the focus of many earlier works (e.g., LISP Tutor [15], PROUST [10], BRIDGE [6], ELM-ART [7] and Assert [3]). Our work focuses on tutoring programming constructs rather than the entire programming enterprise. It focuses on semantic and run-time errors in C++ programs as opposed to syntax errors that a compiler would detect.

We have been using Model-Based Reasoning [8] to model the domain for our tutoring system. In Model-Based Reasoning, a model of the domain is first constructed, consisting of the structure and behavior of the domain. In our case, this would be a model of the C++ language, consisting of objects in the language and their mechanisms of interaction. This model is used to simulate the correct behavior of an artifact in the domain. In our case, the model is used to simulate the expected behavior of some particular C++ language construct, e.g., C++ pointers. The correct behavior is compared with the behavior predicted by the student for that artifact. The discrepancies between these two behaviors are used to hypothesize structural discrepancies in the (mental model of the student

S.A. Cerri, G. Gouardères, and F. Paraguaçu (Eds.): ITS 2002, LNCS 2363, pp. 792–801, 2002.
© Springer-Verlag Berlin Heidelberg 2002

for that) artifact. In our case, the behavioral discrepancies are used to generate feedback to tutor the student. Figure 1 illustrates the architecture of an Intelligent Tutoring System that uses Model-Based Reasoning for domain modeling (figure is adapted from [9]).

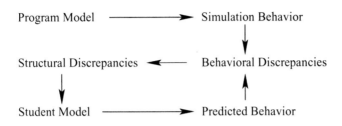

Fig. 1. Architecture of Model-Based Reasoning for Tutoring Program Debugging

Insofar as the domain model is complete, Model-based reasoning is comprehensive in its coverage of possible behavioral (and hence, structural) discrepancies. This is not necessarily true of Rule-Based systems (e.g., production rules used in ACT-R theory [2]), which cannot address behavioral discrepancies unless they have been explicitly encoded into the tutoring system. Similarly, Case-Based Reasoning systems are primarily constrained to the types of cases already entered into the knowledge base [16]

In the next section, we will discuss and analyze the benefits of using Model-Based Reasoning in our tutoring system. In Section 3, we will describe the currently implemented features of the tutoring system. In Section 4, we will present the results of evaluating the tutor in several sections of our Computer Science courses. Finally, we will discuss conclusions and future work in Section 5.

2   Model Based Reasoning for Domain Modeling in an Intelligent Tutoring System

There are several advantages to using Model-Based Reasoning for domain modeling in Intelligent Tutoring Systems.

Domain Model is the Expert Module: We need not include the answers to problems in the ITS. The model knows the correct answer, i.e., it is capable of solving each problem to obtain the correct answer. Therefore, the domain model doubles as the runnable expert module. Constraint-Based Modeling [14] does not require the inclusion of a runnable expert module either. However, it targets the knowledge that prescribes user's actions whereas Model-Based reasoning targets the knowledge that describes the domain's behavior. In this sense, the two could co-exist in an Intelligent Tutoring System. There have been more recent efforts to extend Constraint Based Modeling to include a runnable expert module [12].

Dynamic Generation of Problems: Limited problem set has been recently recognized as a potential drawback of encoding a finite number of problems into a tutor [12]. Using Model-Based Reasoning for domain modeling can easily address this drawback. Since domain models based on Model-Based Reasoning are capable of solving problems on their own without being told the correct solution, a tutor using such models need not be restricted to administering only the problems that have been encoded into it. When coupled with a scheme for generating problems, such a tutor can potentially administer an unlimited number of problems to the learner.

One scheme used in literature to dynamically generate problems is by using BNF-like grammar, e.g., [11]. In this scheme, problems are generated by randomly instantiating the grammar. Each rule of grammar can be carefully designed with specific pedagogical objectives in mind. We have used such a generative scheme with our Model-Based tutor to be able to generate an unlimited number of problems. (Please See Figure 2, where templates are BNF-like grammar rules).

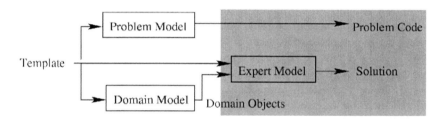

Fig. 2. Generative Architecture of a Model-Based Tutor

Randomizing a template to generate problems is acceptable in the domain of program analysis and debugging, since the context of the problem is fully captured in the templates. However, this is not necessarily true in all the domains, e.g., in the legal domain [13], the context is much richer and harder to capture in templates.

One criticism that may be leveled at the process of randomizing a template is that it could generate only trivial variations of a "typical problem." In the programming domain, this is not true. Randomizing can yield sufficiently interesting and non-trivial variations of a problem. E.g., consider the following snippet of correct C++ code:

```
{
        int *variablePointer;
        int count = 32;
        variablePointer = &count;
        cout << *variablePointer;
}
```

One random variation of the template from which this code was generated is:

```
{
     int *variablePointer;
     {
          int count = 32;
          variablePointer = &count;
     }
     cout << *variablePointer;
}
```

Whereas the original code was correct, the new code suffers a dangling pointer, a rather sophisticated semantic error in C++ programming.

There are several benefits to coupling a tutor with a problem generator:

- The tutor is capable of administering problems on a particular topic to a student as long as the student needs, or until the student has mastered the topic.
- In addition to tutoring, the tutor may also be safely used to test students. Using a tutor to test students has many advantages: since students are already familiar with the interface of the tutor from tutoring sessions, they feel comfortable taking a test in this environment, with all the concomitant advantages of online testing. Since the tutor randomly generates problems, tests are individualized, deterring plagiarism.

Model-Based Generation of Explanatory Feedback: Model-Based Reasoning facilitates the generation of explanation during simulation of the model. In other words, as the tutor executes the model of a C++ program, it can simultaneously generate explanations about the behavior of the program. We use this feature to generate feedback in two steps in our tutor:

- **Process Explanation:** Each line of code in the C++ program triggers an explanation of what it does.
- **State Explanation:** In addition, each object involved in a line of code explains why it is in an invalid state, if it is indeed in an invalid state.

State explanation segments are inserted into process explanation at appropriate points to produce a generic explanation. This generic explanation is postprocessed based on the student model to produce feedback at various levels of granularity:

- **Simulative Feedback:** The feedback includes a complete explanation of the behavior of the program. This feedback is used for novices, for the first few problems in a tutoring session, and in instructional (as opposed to problem-solving) mode.
- **Diagnostic Feedback:** The feedback includes only those lines of explanation that correspond to an error in the program. This feedback is used after the first few problems in a tutoring session, once the student starts making progress towards the educational objectives of the tutor;

- **Customized Feedback:** The feedback includes only those lines of explanation reported by the processes and objects flagged as being deficient in the student model.

To date, we have implemented simulative and diagnostic feedback in our tutor. The elegance of using Model-Based Reasoning for domain modeling is that the domain model naturally facilitates the generation of feedback, and no separate rules or constraints have to be encoded for this purpose.

One drawback of using Model-Based Reasoning for domain modeling is that building the domain model is an expensive task both in terms of time and expertise. However, once such a domain model is built, it will be able to handle any problem, and not just those previously encoded into the tutor. Unlike Rule-Based Reasoning or Case-Based Reasoning, Model-Based reasoning is not brittle. An implication of this is that the learner can enter his/her own problems into the tutor and test/learn from them, e.g., in Figure 2, we replace the template by problem(s) entered by the learner. Such a facility in a tutor would be very powerful in promoting learning. Table 1 summarizes some of the ways a Model-Based tutor could be used.

Table 1. Ways of Using a Model-Based Tutor

Problems Generated By	Problems Solved By	Type of Tutor Use
Tutoring System	Learner	Tutor or Test Learner
Learner	Tutoring System	Solve for Learner
Tutoring System	Tutoring System	Demonstrate to Learner

3   A Tutor for C++ Programming

We have been developing a tutor to help students learn C++ by analyzing and debugging C++ programs for semantic and run-time errors. We have used Model-based Reasoning for domain modeling in this tutor. Currently, the tutor knows about variables, scope, pointers, dynamic allocation and rudiments of function calls. We plan to develop several tutoring modules from this single domain model, addressing different aspects of C++ programming. One tutoring module that we have tested in several sections of Computer Science courses deals with pointers in C++. This module contains nearly 40 problem templates, and addresses dangling pointers and lost objects in C++.

Currently, the tutor provides four types of feedback:

- **None** - the tutor does not even indicate whether the learner's answer is correct. This is useful when the tutor is used for online testing in a class.

- **Demand** - the tutor provides feedback only on demand from the learner. The feedback provided may be minimal (states whether the learner's answer is correct or not), diagnostic (points out where the code has semantic errors) or simulative (explains the behavior of the code line by line).
- **Error-Flag** - The tutor signals the correctness of the learner's answer by immediately changing the color of the learner's answer, red for incorrect and green for correct. The learner may follow-up by asking for feedback.
- **Immediate** - When the learner enters an incorrect answer, the tutor guides the learner through three levels of hints: **abstract** (e.g., "Remember, you have a dangling pointer if a pointer is dereferenced before it is assigned"), **concrete** (e.g., "Is valuePointer referenced before it is assigned?") and **bottom-out** (e.g., "Well, valuePointer has been assigned before it is referenced. Therefore, it is not a dangling pointer.").

The interface of the tutor consists of a left panel for the program, and a right panel for the problem, answering options and feedback provided to the user. The user is led through a clockwise flow of action that is intuitive: from the program to the problem statement, answering options, grading button, feedback, and the button to generate the next problem.

4   Evaluation of the Tutor

We have evaluated the tutor on C++ pointers in several sections of Computer Science II course. In this section, we will discuss the results of these evaluations, addressing both cognitive and affective aspects of learning with the tutor.

4.1   Cognitive Learning with the Tutor

Tutor in Isolation: In Fall 2000, we tested the tutor in two sections (N=19 combined), by administering a pretest, followed by practice using the tutor, and a post-test. These were not controlled tests. The author was the instructor in both the sections. The pretest and post-test scores were out of 40. Table 2 lists the figures from the tests.

Table 2. Results of Testing the Tutor in Isolation

(N=19)	PreTest	PostTest	Effect Size
Average	12.21	26.74	2.16
Standard Deviation	6.70	8.73	

The Effect Size is calculated as (post-test score - pretest-score) / standard-deviation on the pre-test. An effect size of 2.16 sigma indicates that the tutor facilitated learning among the students. It compares favorably with the result that individual human tutors can bring students 2 sigma above normal classroom instruction [5].

Tutor Versus Printed Workbook: In Spring 2001, we again tested the tutor in two sections (N=33 combined), using the pretest-practice -posttest protocol. We conducted a controlled test - between the tests, the control group practiced with printed workbooks, whereas the test group practiced with the tutor. The author was not the instructor in the sections. The pretest and post-test scores were out of 40. Table 3 lists the figures from the tests.

Table 3. Results of Testing the Tutor Versus Printed Workbook for Practice

(N=33)	PreTest	PostTest	Effect Size
Users of Tutor for Practice			
Average	13.00	23.06	1.52
Standard Deviation	6.61	10.12	
Users of Workbook for Practice			
Average	15.24	24.71	1.33
Standard Deviation	7.10	10.54	

Practicing with the tutor appeared to be slightly better than practicing with the printed workbook, although the difference is not statistically significant.

Minimal Versus Simulative Demand Feedback in the Tutor: In Fall 2001, we conducted a controlled test of the tutor in one section (N=16). This time, we tested two versions of demand feedback for the tutor: minimal versus simulative. In minimal feedback, the tutor corrects the user's answer, but does not explain the correct answer. In simulative feedback, in addition, the tutor explains the correct answer. We used the same pretest-practice-posttest protocol as before, with fixed times for each step. Incorrect answers were penalized. The author was not the instructor in either class. The pretest and post-test scores were out of 80. Table 4 lists the figures from the two tests.

Table 4. Results of Testing the Tutor with Minimal Versus Simulative Feedback

(N=16)	PreTest	PostTest	Effect Size
Group Receiving Simulative Feedback			
Average	11.00	25.63	1.41
Standard Deviation	10.35	23.77	
Group Receiving Minimal Feedback			
Average	8.25	17.38	1.63
Standard Deviation	5.60	14.62	

The results seem to indicate that simulative demand feedback may not be any better than minimal feedback. Informal comments from the students seemed to suggest that simulative feedback is too verbose. All the same, it is encouraging to see that using the tutor did help the students improve their performance.

4.2   Affective Learning with the Tutor

Students filled out a feedback form after the controlled tests in Spring 2001, in which they provided feedback about the instrument they had used for practice between pretest and post-test (workbook for control group and tutor for test group, N=33). These feedback forms clearly indicate that the tutor facilitates affective learning. On a Likert scale of 1 (Strongly Agree) to 5 (Strongly Disagree), the average scores of the test group (students who used the tutor as the practice instrument) and control groups (students who used the printed workbook as the instrument of practice) on the questions of the feedback form are shown in Table 5.

Table 5. Affective Results of Testing the Tutor Versus Printed Workbook

Feedback Question "Instrument" is Tutor for Test Group "Instrument" is Workbook for Control Group	Test/ Tutor Users	Control/ Workbook Users
1. It was easy to (learn to) use this instrument	2.13	2.29
2. The problems posed by the instrument were clear	1.94	1.94
3. The instrument listed interesting problems	2.13	2.35
4. The problems were repetitive and boring	3.44	3.06
5. The instrument provided useful feedback	2.20	3.06
6. The instrument helped me learn the material	2.31	2.88
7. Using this instrument was time-consuming	3.88	3.12
8. The instrument should be made available to all students	1.56	2.65
9. If this instrument is made available, I will use it	1.93	2.65
10. I would like to see such instruments on other topics	1.44	2.59

Question 1 indicates that the tutor was easy to learn if we use the control group's score as the basis, since presumably, students do not need to "learn" how to use a printed workbook designed like a typical textbook. The problems in the printed workbook were themselves generated by the tutor, and the results for Question 2 validate this. Questions 3 and 4 seem to indicate a slight Hawthorne effect in that students using the online tutor felt the problems were more interesting and less repetitive and boring, although the types of problems were the same for both the tutor and the printed workbook. Question 5 clearly indicates the superiority of the tutor, which provided detailed problem-specific feedback whereas the printed workbook just listed the correct answer for each problem. Questions 6 and 7 indicate that the tutor facilitated better affective learning than the printed workbook, which is encouraging. Questions 7 through 10 clearly indicate the students' preference for the tutor over the traditional printed workbook.

5   Conclusions and Future Work

We plan to extend the Model-based domain model of the tutor to handle semantic and run-time errors associated with storage classes, arrays, structures, loops, nested selection statements, and their applications in C++. We plan to reify the tutor's interface by asking the user to not only choose the error in a program but also indicate the line of code where the user thinks the error has occurred. We also plan to continue to successively refine and evaluate the tutor in the future semesters.

Acknowledgements. Partial support for this work was provided by the National Science Foundation's Course, Curriculum and Laboratory Improvement Program under grant DUE-0088864.

The author would like to thank Ken Koedinger, Kurt VanLehn, Vincent Aleven and Noboru Matsuki for the opportunity to participate in the *2001 CIRCLE Summer School on Building Intelligent Tutoring Systems* held in Pittsburgh, PA.

References

1. Anderson, J.R., Farrell, R. and Sauers, R.: Learning to Program in LISP. Cognitive Science, 8 (1984) 87-130.
2. Anderson, J.R.: Production Systems and the ACT-R Theory. In Rules of the Mind. Hillsdale, NJ: Lawrence Erlbaum & Associates, Inc. (1993) 1-10.
3. P. Baffes and Mooney, R. J.: A Novel Application of Theory Refinement to Student Modeling. Proceedings of the Thirteenth National Conference on Artificial Intelligence, Portland, OR, August (1996) 403-408.
4. Bloom, B.S. and Krathwohl, D.R.: Taxonomy of Educational Objectives: The Classification of Educational Goals, by a committee of college and university examiners. Handbook I: Cognitive Domain, New York, Longmans, Green (1956).
5. Bloom, B.S.: The 2 Sigma Problem: The Search for Methods of Group Instruction as Effective as One-to-One Tutoring. Educational Researcher, Vol 13 (1984) 3-16.
6. Bonar, J. and Cunningham, R.: BRIDGE: Tutoring the programming process, in Intelligent tutoring systems: Lessons learned. J. Psotka, L. Massey, S. Mutter (Eds.), Lawrence Erlbaum Associates, Hillsdale, NJ (1988).
7. Brusilovsky, P., Schwarz, E. and Weber, G.: ELM-ART: An intelligent tutoring system on the World Wide Web. Proceedings of ITS 96 : Third International Conference on Intelligent Tutoring Systems, Montreal, Quebec, June (1996).
8. Davis, R.: Diagnostic Reasoning Based on Structure and Behavior. Artificial Intelligence, 24 (1984) 347-410.
9. deKleer, J. and Williams, B.C.: Diagnosing Multiple Faults. Artificial Intelligence, 32 (1987) 97-130.

10. Johnson, W.L.: Intention-based diagnosis of novice programming errors. Morgan Kaufman, Palo Alto CA (1986).
11. Koffman, E.B. and Perry, J.M.: A Model for Generative CAI and Concept Selection. International Journal of Man Machine Studies. 8 (1976) 397-410.
12. Martin, B. and Mitrovic, A.: Tailoring Feedback by Correcting Student Answers. Proceedings of Intelligent Tutoring Systems (ITS) 2000. G. Gauthier, C. Frasson and K. VanLehn (eds.). Springer (2000) 383-392.
13. Muntjewerff, A.J. and Breuker, J.A.: Evaluating PROSA, A System to Train Solving Legal Cases. Artificial Intelligence in Education: AI-ED in the Wired and Wireless Future. J.D. Moore, C.L. Redfield and W.L Johnson (ed.), IOS Press, Amsterdam (2001) 278-285.
14. Ohlsson, S.: Constraint-based Student Modeling. In J.E. Greer, G. McCalla (eds.) Student Modeling: The Key to Individualized Knowledge-Based Instruction (1994) 167-189.
15. Reiser, B., Anderson, J. and Farrell, R.: Dynamic student modeling in an intelligent tutor for LISP programming, in Proceedings of the Ninth International Joint Conference on Artificial Intelligence, A. Joshi (Ed.), Los Altos CA (1985).
16. Reyes, R.L. and Sison, R.: A Case-Based Reasoning Approach to an Internet Agent-Based Tutoring System. In: Moore, J.D. Redfield, C.L. and Johnson, W.L. (eds.): Artificial Intelligence in Education: AI-ED in the Wired and Wireless Future, IOS Press, Amsterdam (2001) 122-129.
17. Sack, W., Soloway, E. and Weingrad, P.: From PROUST to CHIRON: ITS Design as Iterative Engineering: Intermediate Results are Important! In J.H. Larkin and R.W. Chabay (Eds.), Computer-Assisted Instruction and Intelligent Tutoring Systems: Shared Goals and Complementary Approaches. Lawrence Erlbaum Associates, Hillsdale, NJ (1992) 239-274.

Using Computer Algebra Systems as Cognitive Tools

The ACTIVEMATH group: Jochen Büdenbender, Adrian Frischauf,
Georgi Goguadze, Erica Melis, Paul Libbrecht, and Carsten Ullrich

DFKI Saarbrücken, D-66123 Saarbrücken, Germany
activemath@activemath.org

Abstract. We describe how Computer Algebra Systems (CASs) can be
used as cognitive tools in a learning environment. In particular, we show
how a CAS is employed in ACTIVEMATH, how different types of CAS-
exercises are designed, and how feedback can be produced with the help
of the very same CAS. We report the results of a first preliminary formative evaluation of ACTIVEMATH' CAS-exercises in a university course
and some modifications of ACTIVEMATH caused by this evaluation.

1 Introduction

The ACTIVEMATH learning environment [9] presents a variety of (interactive)
learning materials to the student rather than exercises or examples only. The
course materials include motivations, concepts, elaborations, exploratory animations, worked-out examples, and exercises with feedback.

As its name suggests, ACTIVEMATH emphasizes the active role of the student
and leaves space for exploratory learning. This feature is greatly supported by the
integration of cognitive tools. Currently, ACTIVEMATH integrates the Computer
Algebra Systems (CASs) MAPLE and MUPAD and a proof planner as cognitive
tools. They provide the backbone for interactive problem solving that does not
need pre-defining few possible problem solutions, and for dynamically producing
local (problem solving) feedback to the user's actions. Furthermore, the user's
exercising performance is used to update ACTIVEMATH's long term user model.

The term *cognitive tool* was coined in [7] and generally denotes instruments
supporting cognitive processes by extending the limits of the human cognitive
capacities, e.g., the working memory. When applied to learning, such tools can
help, e.g., to remember, to practice, to hypothesize, to solve a problem. In particular, when learning is difficult because it is too complex or because several
things have to be done at the same time, these tools can help considerably. This
is well-known for simulation tools [6], dynamic geometry systems, etc.

In this paper, we mainly describe how specific interactive exercises with CASs
can be designed and report on their actual usage. To begin with, let's summarize
why the Computer Algebra Systems can support active learning of (mathematical) problem solving. They help the learner a) to *explore* a problem interactively
and *directly experience* the result of a calculation, even a complex one; b) to

S.A. Cerri, G. Gouardères, and F. Paraguaçu (Eds.): ITS 2002, LNCS 2363, pp. 802–810, 2002.

focus on a particular subtask or skill in solving a problem rather than paying all the attention to a detailed computation; c) to correct misconceptions and errors and support her by local *feedback*; d) to learn how to handle the cognitive tool for after-learning usage.

In the remainder of the article, we discuss some advantages and difficulties of integrating CASs into ITSs. Section 3 concretely looks at CAS-exercises in ACTIVEMATH. Section 4 contributes a preliminary formative evaluation and reports our experiences with ACTIVEMATH' CAS-exercises in real-life mathematics lessons attended by first-year university students.

2   Computer Algebra Systems

There exist quite a number of CASs that are used for professional and for educational purposes, e.g., MAPLE [1] or MUPAD [10]. These systems are stand-alone and have elaborate algorithms to perform even complicated computations. As stand-alone tools they have been used in some schools but as far as we know there is no learning environment integrating a CAS. Instead, existing ITS use their specific problem solving modules such as the physics problem solver in Andes [2].

However, the CAS facilities differ largely from those specifically designed problem solvers: on the one hand, a CAS computes only one solution path and does not compute the search space for a solution as, e.g., the physics problem solver does in Andes. A CAS does neither directly provide information evaluating the user's input apart from correct/incorrect and impossible inputs. On the other hand, a CAS is a very powerful stand-alone system that can solve complex and complicated problems. This makes it a cognitive tool that can help to solve even real-world problems in a school lesson's time.

For developers of ITSs and authors the use of an existing third-party CAS has the disadvantage that the CAS is a black-box system as opposed to a white-box system the developers would have implemented or can at least modify themselves. This makes enhancing the CAS with more functionalities rather difficult. In comparison, when the developers of a learning environment have also implemented the service system, they can easily adapt it to suit the pedagogical and technical needs of the ITS (which would also be possible if the system was available as open source).

In what follows we investigate the questions (1) what can be done with such black-boxes, (2) what is the advantage for an ITS that integrates a CAS, and vice versa (3) what is the advantage of not just taking the stand-alone CAS but rather integrating it into the larger learning environment? As for the third question, when a CAS is integrated into a context which presents conceptual content and examples, it is possible for the learner to see the big picture of the domain and to refer to or being referred to knowledge that is relevant for solving an exercise such as definitions, similar examples, or missing prerequisite knowledge. Moreover, such an environment offers user-adaptivity, a feature that stand-alone CASs are not designed to provide. For instance, ACTIVEMATH can restrict the available features of a CAS: a student who is learning mathematical integration should not use a CAS to solve his exercises completely, but using the CAS as a calculator for auxiliary calculation is acceptable.

3   CAS-Exercises in ACTIVEMATH

The philosophy of ACTIVEMATH suggests that the user controls her exercise activities herself and no single solution needs to be followed as long as a correct solution results at some point. Moreover, since handling the CAS can be one of the learning goals, the user's input is CAS commands.

Figure 1 shows a screen shot of a CAS-exercise session. With the start of an exercise, a console appears. It displays the text of the exercise again such that problem and later the solution can be seen in *one* window. In Figure 1 the text asks to prove an inequality. The learner performed three calculation steps which all were correct. However, her first attempt to finish the exercise was not successful, because the result can further be simplified to $0 \leq (a + b)^2$ which is *obviously* correct because of the square on the right side. After two more steps the learner successfully finished this exercise and received a positive feedback.

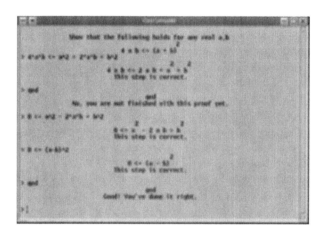

Fig. 1. An example CAS-session

The student can save the current dialog as a text. This allows to quickly resume a session and to inspect a solution later. Furthermore, the student can annotate CAS-exercises (as well as any other learning material) with public or private notes. ACTIVEMATH also offers a scratch pad facility, for auxiliary calculations. A CAS can be used to produce visualizations. ACTIVEMATH uses these to more adequately present mathematical concepts which have a dynamical aspect, e.g., the convergence of a sequence or the definition of the velocity of a body.

3.1   Integration Mechanism

We have developed a framework that allows an easy integration of existing mathematical systems within ACTIVEMATH. In this framework, the CAS is started on the server via a console applet on the client in the browser. A proxy handles the communication between the CAS (where the student's answers are evaluated), the console (to provide input/output), and ACTIVEMATH (e.g., to update the user model).

3.2   Exercise Types

ACTIVEMATH offers a variety of exercises in general. This includes multiple choice questions, proof planning exercises, CAS-exercises, and control questions. We experimented with two different types of CAS-exercises, single-step exercises, where only one input is required, and multi-step exercises, where each single step is evaluated and feedback is given. In addition to the usual check of correctness of a step, multi-step exercise results are evaluated with respect to the finality of the input (see Figure 1).

3.3   Local Feedback in CAS-Exercises

In ACTIVEMATH we distinguish between global and local feedback [8]. Global feedback may be given after reading, navigating, and, of course, exercising. In the case of exercising with a CAS, the result of the exercise session updates ACTIVEMATH's user model, e.g., if the student fails to solve an exercise for a certain concept, its mastery value is decreased. Subsequently, this can trigger suggestions for learning certain content, solving certain exercises, etc. As opposed to global feedback, local feedback is given during exercising and refers to the activities in the learner's problem solving attempts. This local feedback is what is commonly provided by most ITS [5].

   In this section we analyze how the CAS integrated into ACTIVEMATH can be employed for producing local feedback for CAS-exercises. The philosophy of ACTIVEMATH suggests the following: to allow for more than a single solution, to relieve the author from the burden of foreseeing and implementing every possible (in)correct solution step, and to exploit the capabilites of the CAS. The idea is to use the CAS to compute whether an input satisfies a *test condition* and to deliver feedback depending on the answer. We distinguish between five classes of test conditions:

   i test the equality of the input with respect to a predefined value. For example, if the user has to find the Euler indicator of a given number, his input will also be a number which is checked for equality against a solution either provided by the author or calculated by the CAS.
   ii check the validity of an expression in which the input is a subexpression. For example, if the correct input is supposed to be the inverse of a given permutation, then the product of these two should be equal to the identity

permutation. Any mathematically incorrect input does not satisfy the test condition and thus, results in a feedback stating that this product is not equal to the identity and hence, the input is incorrect. Such a feedback is meant to stimulate further learning by wondering how the feedback is related to the original task.

iii test the equivalence of the input with respect to a given expression. This leaves quite some freedom for the user's input because it is judged only modulo equivalence rather than equality. Here, an important case is the check for equivalence in a sequence of transformations/manipulations of formulas (e.g., equations) as shown in Figure 1. Only the correctness but not the progress towards a goal is judged.

iv test the equivalence of the solution set corresponding to the input and the solution set corresponding to a given formula. This method can be used if the exercise deals with (in)equations. Theoretically, this class is equal to class (iii). Practically however, this method helps to overcome the cases when the CAS is not able to check for equivalence directly.

v test whether the input is sufficiently simplified. For example the input `limit(x+2, x=2)` will not be accepted as the final solution of an exercise, even if it is correct. This term should be further simplified to 4, which will be accepted.

In the following we elaborate on how these classes of test conditions are used to provide several kinds of feedback. A common classification of feedback distinguishes between Knowledge of Result, Knowledge of Correct Result, Answer Until Correct, and Elaborated Feedback. The CAS-exercises in ACTIVEMATH cover them by the five types of local feedback explained in the following:

Help. Since the student inputs her calculation steps via the CAS input syntax, a Help function explains the appropriate CAS commands for this exercise. Help can be accessed by typing "help". This function can also be used to author hints for the student.

Input-Error. A common type of errors is incorrectly written input. These input errors may have different causes: (1) incorrectly typed commands or expressions (given the CAS language) which cannot be interpreted by the CAS or (2) a misconception of the intended input. The first, e.g., unbalanced brackets, could be avoided by a schematic input editor provided with the planned *intermediator* described in the section 'near future'. Errors caused by misconceptions occur, when the user's input is syntactically correct but does not represent the right kind of mathematical object. In this case, the CAS' calculation of the test condition fails. If the CAS can detect the failure, appropriate feedback can be provided.

Correct/Incorrect. If an exercise requires direct input of the solution, the CAS can check it and inform the learner immediately about the correctness of her input. If the answer is correct, the exercise session ends. Otherwise, the learner is invited to provide a new input. In exercises that require several calculation steps before the final solution, every step is evaluated and feedback about its correctness is given. The check for correctness depends on the mathematical objects which occur in the solution steps. We use the classes described in (i) -

(v). An example for (iii) is the exercise "Please enter the power set of $\{1,7\}$" where the learner's input is compared to the solution $\{\emptyset, \{1\}, \{7\}, \{1,7\}\}$

Elaboration-on-Error. In some exercises the feedback can be more elaborate than simply 'correct' or 'incorrect'. An exercise which needs a comparison of solution sets (iv) is the following: "Solve the inequation $1 \leq x \leq 4$, where x is a real number". The correctness of the student's input can be checked by comparing it with the correct solution which is $x \in [-2, -1] \cup [1, 2]$, e.g., with the following CAS code: `if bool(solve(new,x) = solve(solution,x)) then result:=1 end_if` where `new` contains the learner's input and `solution` is the correct solution. One option for an elaborate feedback is to point the learner to elements belonging to her solution set but not to the set of the correct solution and vice versa.

Show-Solution. Finally, an authored solution or one automatically computed by the CAS is yet another kind of feedback in CAS-exercises in ACTIVEMATH. If the author provides a pre-determined solution, the learner can access it by typing "solution" and then the exercise is considered finished immediately. This feature can be suppressed for pedagogical reasons.

4 Preliminary Empirical Evaluation

4.1 Experimental Design

The target population for ACTIVEMATH is university-level students with different skills and mastery-levels in mathematics. Hence, to evaluate if and how the current version of ACTIVEMATH influences the student's active problem solving and learning (including usability considerations), we were planning to run a real-life study with 100 first-year students in obligatory weekly sessions augmenting the lectures of an introductory calculus course at the university of Saarland. Disappointingly, due to the unforeseen last-minute choice of the lecturer and administrative difficulties, we were unable to carry out the study in a better coordination with the lecturer's material and homeworks and in *obligatory* sessions, i.e., with as many as 100 students and with the opportunity to test groups of students. That's real life... Still, at the moment we are more interested in an evaluation with a real-life setting than in a lab experiment with ideal but somewhat unrealistic conditions.

We had to resort to varying numbers of voluntary attendants with an average of six students for one semester and could not include a proper pre-test but had to rely on the student's last school grades in mathematics. Thus, we decided to observe the attending students, to record their questions and the human tutor's answers to gain an initial understanding of how and if CAS-exercises are usable and contribute to active learning. Moreover, we had to make use of the content of a full calculus course that is based on the rather traditional textbook [3] that was already encoded in ACTIVEMATH and to a number of additional interactive exercises.

As a result, we conducted a preliminary formative evaluation with the objective to successively improve ACTIVEMATH functionalities and design. The evaluation was conducted over one semester with first-year students of computer science. They attended the obligatory course *Mathematics for computer scientists* that covered calculus up to integration in one dimension. The course comprised four hours lecturing per week, homeworks, and weekly traditional obligatory exercises as well as our additional voluntary ACTIVEMATH session once a week.

At the beginning, 29 out of 150 students registered for the voluntary AC-TIVEMATH session which was our sole empirical source. Because of the optional nature of the ACTIVEMATH sessions the number of attendees dropped considerably during the semester. In interviews, the students explained that they were under time pressure and avoided any activity not directly contributing to the homeworks or to the announced examination.

The evaluation sessions took place in computer rooms, where every student had her own computer and each session was attended and supervised by a tutor who first briefly introduced the handling of ACTIVEMATH and later gave hints and answered their questions (all recorded).

Apart from the observations and the recording of questions and answers we used the methods questionnaires and interviews. Before the actual ACTIVEMATH sessions 29 students filled an on-line questionnaire and at the end a second questionnaire was filled by six students only and more interviews were conducted to compare with the student's initial attitudes and motivation.

4.2   Results

The first questionnaire showed a rather low average mathematics grade. The last mathematics school grades varied from 1 (very good) to 4 (sufficient), with an average of 2.75 (satisfying). All students frequently used a computer prior to the evaluation. Former use of learning software was restricted to vocabulary trainers in a few cases. The second questionnaire and interviews invariably showed that the student's motivation and attitudes towards mathematics and active learning increased.

Qualitative Observations. Our observations confirmed a strong increase of learning motivation. Students enjoyed using CAS-exercises, especially to explore new content. The feedback even led to little competitions among the students in which each student wanted to solve the exercises first.

These "competitions" can explain another unexpected observation: the more elaborate feedback was considered less important. The students were more interested in whether their solutions were correct or incorrect. We assume that the need for elaborate feedback will increase when the exercises become more difficulty and when no human feedback is available.

In fact, we noticed that the need for help by the human tutor gradually decreased. Initially, the students had problems using ACTIVEMATH, in particular, problems with the CAS-syntax. This was remedied by the implementation of the help facility.

Similarly, the navigation behavior of students changed during the semester. In the first sessions, the students traversed the curriculum in a book-like manner (going forward or backward page-wise). After they became more familiar with the system, they navigated more freely and took advantage of the overall content presentation of ACTIVEMATH. Then, they also used the dictionary, e.g., to search for additional exercises. Not surprisingly, students with good mastery felt more secure about the content and, hence, used the advanced features, e.g., inspected the user model to find out about their weaknesses, whereas weaker students were more focused on solving exercises and did not make so much use of additional features ACTIVEMATH offers for self-guided learning.

Technical Problems and Their Solution. We identified a number of technical problems in the realistic course setting, in particular, when many students attended a session.

Performance. The system's performance dramatically decreased when a large number of students simultaneously used ACTIVEMATH. Hitherto ACTIVEMATH was not developed with regard to efficiency, so that several standard optimization solutions, e.g., caching of content, were not yet implemented. As a first alleviation, we run the knowledge base now within the same process rather than as a resource-intensive independent process.

Presentation. The presentation of mathematical formulas in the console as well as in the ACTIVEMATH HTML pages is not at all perfect yet. This is due to the browser-based presentation. Therefore, we are investigating a SVG or MATHML presentation for the browser. The current CAS-console is implemented as a rather basic java applet that requires no additional software installation but can offer a limited user interface only. The next version of the CAS-console will require a newer java version with enhanced graphical capabilities. Several small presentation problems, e.g., an unnecessary amount of brackets in the formulas, were solved quickly. ACTIVEMATH' learning materials are not stored as predefined HTML pages, but encoded in an knowledge representation that separates content from presentation. This allows to adapt the presentation rather straightforward because only a single presentation rule has to be changed.

5   Conclusion and Near Future

We have integrated Computer Algebra Systems into the learning environment ACTIVEMATH and employed their computational power to support active and exploratory learning as well as evaluation and feedback for the student's problem solving actions.

Three of the most interesting technical novelties for ITSs in general – apart from the technical integration of CASs – might be the distinction between five classes of test conditions for user input in CAS, the dynamic generation of several types of local feedback in CAS-exercises with the help of the CAS, and the saving of the student's solution for later usage.

We conducted a preliminary formative study to evaluate the content and design of CAS-exercises and their surroundings in ActiveMath. The results were promising in terms of exploratory learning and increased motivation and also gave rise to some technical changes that made the interface more effective for students.

To address those questions that we were unable to investigate in the described preliminary evaluation, we are planning to conduct a more formal study with more students. In one of the next studies we not only plan to test the actual post-performance but also plan to investigate the question how the difficulty and complexity of exercises influences the student's use and benefit from ActiveMath.

As a first step towards an authoring tool, we will prepare templates for each class of test conditions to facilitate the creation of CAS exercises.

For the technical development, very soon the integration of CASs into ActiveMath will be augmented by an *intermediator*, a module that provides several useful functionalities among others abstract input syntax, abstract authoring language, user-adaptive help and feedback, and more sophisticated detection of syntax errors.

An extended version of this paper is available as a technical report [4].

References

1. B.W. Char, G.J. Fee, K.O. Geddes, G.H. Gonnet, and M.B. Monagan. A tutorial introduction to MAPLE. *Journal of Symbolic Computation*, 2(2):179–200, 1986.
2. C. Conati, A.S. Gertner, K. VanLehn, and M. Druzdzel. On-line student modeling for coached problem solving using baysian networks. In A. Jameson, C. Paris, and C. Tasso, editors, *User Modeling: Proc. of UM97*, pages 231–242, 1997.
3. B.I. Dahn and H. Wolters. *Analysis Individuell*. Springer-Verlag, 2000.
4. The ActiveMath group. Using computer algebra systems as cognitive tools. Technical Report RR-02-01, DFKI Saarbrücken, Saarbrücken, 2002.
5. B. Jacobs. Aufgaben stellen und Feedback geben. Technical report, Medienzentrum der Philosophischen Fakultät der Universität des Saarlandes, 2001.
6. W.R. Joolingen and T. Jong. Design and implementation of simulation-based discovery environments: the SMISLE solution. *Journal of Artificial Intelligence and Education*, 7:253–277, 1996.
7. S. Lajoie and S. Derry, editors. *Computers as Cognitive Tools*. Erlbaum, Hillsdale, NJ, 1993.
8. E. Melis and E. Andres. Evaluators and suggestion mechanisms for activemath. Technical report, DFKI, 2002.
9. E. Melis, E. Andres, G. Goguadze, P. Libbrecht, M. Pollet, and C. Ullrich. Activemath: System description. In J. D. Moore, C. Redfield, and W. L. Johnson, editors, *Artificial Intelligence in Education*, pages 580–582, 2001. IOS Press.
10. Andreas Sorgatz and Ralf Hillebrand. MuPAD. *Linux Magazin*, (12/95), 1995.

The Design of a 'Motivating' Intelligent Assessment System

Katerina Georgouli

Technological Educational Institute (T.E.I.) of Athens, Department of Informatics, Agiou Spiridona, 12210 Egaleo
kgeor@teiath.gr

Abstract. This paper intends to present the design of an intelligent assessment system, which attempts to assess the student in arithmetic word problem solving. During assessment, the system keeps track of the aptitudes, which the student shows, concerning the answers he/she gives to special types of problems and in the same time it observes aspects of the student's motivational state. More precisely, motivation aspects deal with a) the effort the student shows in solving the different types of problems and b) with the independency and the confidence that characterize his/her behaviour. The system tries to adapt itself according to the above information, in order to motivate the student, offering her the appropriate help and the possibility to follow an individualized way through the objective items of the assessment.

Keywords. Intelligent Tutoring Systems, Adaptive Assessment, Motivation, Problem Solving.

1. Introduction

Many attempts have been made in the field of Artificial Intelligence (AI) to implement acceptable by the schoolteacher systems [1,2]. The first and still foremost contribution of AI to education is the so-called intelligent tutoring system (ITS). In particular, ITSs are computer-based learning systems which attempt to adapt themselves to the needs of learners and are therefore the only such systems which attempt to 'care' about what the student knows, wants to do, is able or unable to understand, tries to avoid, etc [3]. For a tutoring program to be classified as 'intelligent', it must have 'human-like' tutoring capabilities, like being able to adjust the content and delivery of the lesson to the needs of the student by analysing responses and behaviour. This is usually done, by tracing the path of the student's understanding through the curriculum.

On the other hand, one of the main concerns in Education is to make the instruction an interesting and engaging experience for the student. In fact, very little research has been done in motivational aspects of instruction in ITSs, although many of them use multimedia facilities to motivate the student. The need for basic computational models of motivation and the use of the design-based approach of artificial intelligence to lay down such models is advocated by many of the

S.A. Cerri, G. Gouardères, and F. Paraguaçu (Eds.): ITS 2002, LNCS 2363, pp. 811–820, 2002.
© Springer-Verlag Berlin Heidelberg 2002

researchers in the area. There already exist a few useful models [5,6], characterized by their efforts to organize into some structure variables that have been shown empirically to affect student motivation, including some of the inner conceptions of the student. In the cognitive perspective, student motivation is defined in terms of the individual's commitment and persistence in choices of plans and actions. Keller [7] in his ARCS Model defines four components that influence the motivation of a learner: attention, relevance, confidence and satisfaction. The information needed for a motivation diagnosis is selected by questionnaires, verbal communication, self-report, expert systems and sentic modulation [8]. Lepper et al. [4] were between the first researchers who suggested that some additions should be made to a computer tutor in order to provide it with an ability to detect a student's motivational state. Computer diagnosis of motivation is usually done by adding specialized motivational components in the standard ITS architecture. Del Soldato et al. [9], more recently, has suggested some additions that should be made to a computer tutor in order to be able to detect a student motivational state. Particularly, she added two new modules to the traditional ITS architecture: a motivation modeller and a motivational planner. In this way, her system was able to detect the student's motivational state, concerning his effort and confidence, exploiting the pattern of standard reactions.

In this paper, we present the design of an intelligent assessment system able to adapt itself to the student's aptitudes and motivational state. The system concerns students who show remarkably low performance in a domain and who need to be faced in a special way. The design follows the prevailing expert system and student modelling approach and has in general the architecture of an ITS. In section 2, we consider the knowledge representation and in section 3, the architectural ideas, which permit the system to detect the student's aptitudes, to diagnose her motivational state and to react appropriately. In section 4, we focus on the student modelling aspects, which guide the adaptation of the system. In section 5, we present in brief the results of a preliminary evaluation of the prototype system that has been implemented according to the proposed design. The results we present here, concern mainly the accuracy of the provided by the system student profile and the reliability of those aspects of the student model that guide the adaptation of the system.

2. Knowledge Representation

In our system, the domain knowledge is split into small "chunks" of knowledge, called *Learning Units* (LU), which are linked to one another through semantic associations of the type, *is-part-of*. Learning units that represent the different types of problems of the domain are called *basic learning units (BLUs)* and are grouped, according to their common characteristics, to major groups called *Classes of Learning Units (CLU)*, which in their turn are grouped to major classes of CLUs, called *Major Classes of Units (MCLUs)*. This way, MCLUs, CLUs and BLUs establish a semantic network of learning units, defining the declarative domain knowledge of the system. The declarative domain knowledge is stored in the form of frames in the expert system.

Counters associated to specific slots of the LUs contain information about the student's performance to each LU. The values of these counters reflect the extent to which the system believes the student has mastered each LU. Another set of counters is about motivational aspects related to the LU. Motivational knowledge deals with the effort the student shows in finding the right answers in certain types of problems and the overall confidence and independency she shows during assessment. All the above-mentioned counters compose only a part of the student model. The rest of it concerns the student's aptitudes. This kind of knowledge deals with "meta-cognitive" skills and contains declarative knowledge about the student's observed through assessment individual characteristics. Some of these characteristics are efficiency in manipulating specific CLUs, ability in calculations and estimation of the expected result etc. The concepts used in this kind of knowledge are closer to the general terms that teachers often use to evaluate students.

Aptitudes and motivational knowledge is the only kind of declarative knowledge that is accessed by the system in order to decide whether to adapt itself or not to the student's individual characteristics. The above described object oriented knowledge representation permits the existence of components and procedures that can be used from different modules of the system.

Curriculum knowledge is about the conceptual network of the different BLUs the problems of which the student has to solve during the assessing process. Curriculum knowledge expresses: a) the sequencing in which the problems of each BLU might be presented through assessment and b) the transformations that are permitted to take place in this sequencing in order the student to be able to follow an individualized way through the conceptual network of the domain knowledge. The curriculum knowledge is stored in a dynamic list called *presentation scenario (PS)*. The PS consists of *Curriculum Units (CUs)*, each of which belongs to a different BLU. When the system adapts itself to the student the sequencing of the CUs is changed, forming this way a new PS. The PS in effect at the beginning of each assessing session is called *starting presentation scenario (SPS)* and the one in effect at each assessing moment is called *current presentation scenario (CPS)*. The system provides a default PS as SPS but also a new SPS might be designed through the authoring environment of the system.

Each CU is described through a set of attributes which characterize a) the placement of the CU in the PS, b) whether a CU is important and must be presented anyway to the student or it is not important and might be bypassed, c) whether the association between the CU and the next CU at the sequencing is 'loose' and can be *broken* when the system decides to bypass the CU or to move it into another place in the PS or whether it is 'strict' and must be never changed (prerequisite CU).

3. The Architecture of the System

Typically, an assessment system is an educational system that should be able to identify as quickly and as accurately as possible the gaps in the student's knowledge of the subject domain and to check the reasons for that. Computer-based assessment, in order to be able to adapt itself to the student individualities, like an expert human tutor does, should be mainly able a) to decide about how to present the assessing material and what to assess next, following the curriculum sequencing [10] and b) to take under consideration the motivational state of the student [11]. Curriculum sequencing is essentially a control path through the objective items of the assessment and is usually explicitly predicted when designing an assessment test. The design of our system, in order to overcome the rigidity of the curriculum's explicit design, supports an internal curriculum sequencing transformation mechanism, lying on the student' s aptitudes and her motivational state.

The architecture of the system has a tripartite model [3,12], which includes the standard ITS architecture as a subset (Figure 1).

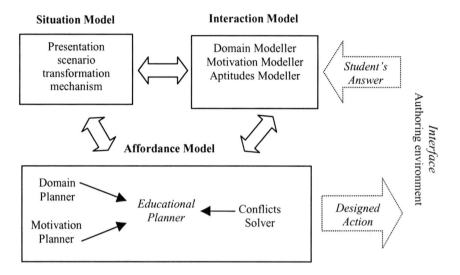

Fig. 1. The architecture of the intelligent assessment system

3.1. The Affordance Model

The Affordance Model is a part of the system, which contains pedagogical expertise about the assessing strategy in use in the form of productive rules. It is a multi-part component, composed of the domain planner, the motivation planner and the conflicts solver. These three components send proposals to the educational planner who takes the final educational decisions.

The domain planner detects the current state of the learner's knowledge, according to the domain student model, and proposes the appropriate next step, traversing the curriculum sequencing in a progressive manner in the direction of the existing ultimate goal. Its main characteristic is than it is more than a typical planner, taking also into consideration student's detected weaknesses and aptitudes.

The motivation planner takes into account the student's motivational state and decides: a) about whether to advance or not in the traversal of the PS and b) the appropriate help to offer in order to maintain the motivational student's state, as suggested by Lepper, Woolverton, Mumme, & Gurtner [4].

The educational planner is responsible to reconcile output from the two first planners, to call the conflicts solver to solve any existing conflict between the domain planner and the motivation planner advices and to decide about: a) to advance or not in the PS, b) when and what kind of help to provide and c) whether to change or not the sequencing in the PS. This latter responsibility is the one that permits the system to adapt itself according to the student model, offering the student the possibility to follow an individualized way through the conceptual network of the different BLUs.

3.2. The Situation Model

The Situation Model is responsible to maintain the CPS through the assessment process. A *presentation scenario transformation mechanism (PS-TM)* is included to it in order to retrieve the knowledge about the curriculum sequencing in a specific assessment moment and to carry out the needed transformations in it during adaptation. The PS-TM realizes the ordered by the educational planner transformations, when the importance of the CUs and the semantic associations between the different CUs permit it, redirecting the 'loose' semantic associations between the different CUs of the PS.

3.3. The Interaction Model

The Interaction Model uses three different modellers, which attempt a 'closed' student modelling based on the aptitude and motivational aspects of the student's behaviour.

Table 1. Example of domain modeller's behaviour

Student's performance	Diagnosis	Update of counters	Classification of given answer
She gave up		increase give-up counter	
Right intermediate problem steps	Correct result		Right («belief»100%)
	Wrong result	Increase give-up counter	Right («belief»80%)
Wrong intermediate problem steps	Correct result according to the wrong steps	Further diagnosis is needed	Almost wrong («belief» will be given after studying the aptitudes model)
	Correct result according to the right steps	Increase inattention counter	Almost right («belief» will be given after studying the aptitudes model)
	Wrong result	Further diagnosis is needed	Wrong («belief»100%)

The domain modeller uses the overlay student modelling technique comparing the student's answers with the ones the system already knows as correct. In order to decide about the correctness or not of a given answer, the modeller takes also under consideration the aptitude characteristics of the student, giving according to them a percentage of belief to its judgment. The modeller analyses the student's answers in order to build a model of what the student knows. The analysis is based on the diagnostic rules, in order to classify an answer as "right", "almost right", "almost wrong" or "wrong". The student's performance in the different LUs is measured as a function of the number of presented problems and the number of each type of responses given for them, accompanied by a certainty factor expressing the belief of the system to the above estimation (see Table 1 for an example). The approach the domain-based modelling mechanism adopts is very simplistic, but a more sophisticated one without affecting the basic architecture of the system can easily replace it. In fact, we already experiment with such an approach based on fuzzy neural networks with promising results.

The motivation modeller generates its part of student model observing the student's characteristic reactions, which specify her motivational state, e.g. the requirements for help, the giving ups, her persistence to give an answer, etc. The motivation modeller focuses on three motivational aspects, as proposed by del Soldato et al. [9], namely effort (or persistence), confidence and independence. Effort refers to how a task was achieved, confidence relies mostly on the student's beliefs on his efficiency to solve the problem, and independence relies on the perceived feeling of needing or not needing help in order to complete the solution steps. Effort is the only motivational aspect that is measured separately for each BLU and CLU in the system. Confidence, effort and independence are characterized as "low", "average" or "high", incremented or decremented in large or small steps during each interaction, according to the rules of the motivation modeller (see Table 2 for an example).

Table 2. Rules of effort[1] modelling

Performance	Steps	Help	Effort
Gave up	none		None
	few	no	Effort to low
		yes	Decrease of effort
	many	no	Increase of effort
		yes	Effort to average
Answered		no	Increase of effort
		yes	Effort to average
Out of time	few	no	Effort to average
		yes	Effort to low
	many	no	Effort to high
		yes	Increase of effort

In our design, additionally to the domain-based modeller and the motivation modeller, a third modeller is considered based on student's general aptitudes issues, the *aptitudes modeller*. The aptitudes modeller generates its student model studying the overall student performance and attempts to identify the student's strengths and weaknesses like preferences and specially good performance at specific CLUs, ability to manipulate problems with difficult semantic structure or big numbers, ability in calculations and in estimation of the expected result etc. In Table 3, aptitudes

---

[1] Effort is expressed as a function of the student's persistence to solve the presented problem even, if he has to ask for help.

modeller reconciles information about the student's performance, give-ups and the effort she shows and concludes about the student's preference to a specific CLU.

In next section, we will study more precisely the student modelling aspects, which guide the adaptation of the system.

Table 3. Rules of preference modeling

Performance	Effort	Give-ups	Preference
Very good	Average or high	None	Big
Good	Average or high	None	Big
		Few	Medium
	Low	None	Medium
		Many	Little
Quite good or bad	Average or high		Little
	Low		No preference at all

4. 'Motivating' Aspects of the System

Motivation is offered to the student in two different ways.

First, the motivation planner takes into account the student's motivational characteristics and advises the educational planner about whether: a) to offer help or not, in order to maintain the motivational student's state and b) to advance or not in the traversal of the CPS.

Table 4. Examples of decisions of the conflicts solver

Proposals of Domain modeller	Proposals of motivation planner	Decisions of Conflict solver
The student performs well. Present a more difficult type of problem	Present again the same type of problem in order to help the student become more confident	Present a new problem of the same type of problems
The student performs badly. Present a new problem of the same type of problems	Present again the same type of problems in order to help the student to become more confident	Present a new problem of the same type of problems giving the student hints to overcome her bad performance
Wrong answer to the problem. Give help based on the diagnosis of the mistake and present a more difficult type of problems	The student must become more confident, experiencing the feeling of success	Present a new problem of the same type of problems giving the student information about the mistake she did in the last problem
Wrong answer to the problem. Give help based on the diagnosis of the mistake	The student must become more independent	Present a motivating message instead of help.

For example, the motivation planner proposes to insist in presenting the same type of problems when the student has very low confidence and needs to be encouraged. Solving the same problem and succeeding to give a right solution will help the student to experience the feeling of success and become more confident. The planner, in order to help the student to improve her independence and persistence, proposes the refusal of a help request urging her to try harder. When there are conflicts between the proposals of the motivation planner and those of the domain planner, conflicts solver is asked to take the final decisions (see Table 4 for some examples).

Second, the educational planner decides whether to adapt or not the sequencing in the CPS to the student's aptitudes and motivational state. That is, the educational planner decides to re-sequence the CUs in the CPS when the student shows a big preference in problems belonging to a specific CLU and in the same time he has a very low overall performance and confidence, and needs to be encouraged. Then, all the CUs belonging to BLUs of this CLU are grouped and moved in the first places of the rest of the sequencing that has to be presented. For example, if there are types of problems (BLUs) that have as context (CLU) 'money' or 'volume' and the low-confident student performs much better in solving of problems of money than of volume, then from now and then all types of problems that have as context 'money' will always be presented before the equivalent types of problems having as context 'volume'.

5. Evaluation of the Prototype

A prototype assessment system has been implemented based on the design model presented in this paper. For the implementation, we used the GC Lisp V programming language, GoldWorksIII expert system environment (from GoldHill Inc.) and Visual Basic VI (from Microsoft). The system, called ASSA (Adaptive System of Student Assessment), assesses the ability of low-attaining pupils to solve simple word arithmetic problems of addition and subtraction and runs on Windows95/98 (from Microsoft).

Two experts in the design of educational software, three teachers of elementary school, five expert teachers in special education and a cognitive scientist have attempted a preliminary evaluation of the prototype system. The evaluation process used here is more akin to the evaluation of Expert Systems, involving the empirical testing of the knowledge base against the judgmental accuracy of experts and ground-truth measures of accuracy. The evaluators experimented with the system in the laboratory under the designers' supervision. Only three pupils have been used at this preliminary evaluation stage. In next paragraphs, we present the followed evaluation procedure and the evaluation results, which concern mainly the reliability of these aspects of the student model, which guide the adaptation of the system, the accuracy of the provided by the system student profiles, produced by different performance histories and the stability of the assessment results.

During evaluation, the adaptive characteristics of the system and the student modelling aspects, which guide the adaptation, were firstly explained in details to the expert evaluators. Next, the evaluators were urged to design a presentation scenario of their convenience and to use it as a SPS for all their subsequent experiments. Then, the subjects were asked to experiment with the assessing process in several sessions, producing different characteristic performances and motivation behaviours at each of them. For each experiment, the student profile was demonstrated to the experts, who had to comment about its accuracy. When the experiments were over the subjects were asked to remark about the efficiency of the motivational factors used in student modelling, the reliability of the measurements of student's individual characteristics (motivational and aptitudes) and the stability of the assessment results.

All evaluators approved the overall adaptive performance of the system and the reliability of the measurements during student modelling. Nevertheless, those experts, who studied the system from the cognitive point of view, reserved themselves to denote convinced about the ability of the system to perform a thorough assessment aiming at a detailed student model. They asked for a more detailed diagnosis of wrong answers and a more appropriate design of hints and provided help. The cognitive scientist expressed her doubts about the efficiency of the motivational factors used in student modelling and argued that knowledge about motivation diagnosis may be elicited based on theories of motivation, observations or 'common sense', but in order to test the validity of this knowledge a number of experiments must be devised.

Although the number of pupils was very small in order to draw accurate conclusions, the assessment results were proved to be stable, remaining always the same when they were produced by similar assessment histories and the produced student profiles have been characterized as accurate, according to the rules of the three distinct modellers and the motivational factors in use. Our intent is to proceed with an evaluation in real class conditions, using a satisfactory number of pupils in order to obtain more accurate results.

6. Conclusion/Future Work

This paper presents the design of an adaptive to the student's individualities and motivational state assessment system, based on expert system and student modelling techniques. The system is able to detect the current state of the student's achievement, her aptitude characteristics, her motivational state, and react with the purpose of adapting the curriculum sequencing to the student's individual strengths and motivational characteristics.

During assessment the system tackles the objectives to be assessed, in a systematic way according to their sequencing in the presentation scenario, which represents the assessment curriculum. The presentation scenario sequencing might be dynamically changed according to the educational rules and the aptitude and motivational characteristics of the student. At the end of each assessment session, the different kinds of knowledge, which derives from the firing of the rules, are formatted and provided to the teacher as the student's learning style profile. This kind of information is believed to be very useful to the teachers especially to those who have not enough time or experience to follow a similar assessment procedure.

The system has been validated by a number of experts with promising results. First results have shown that the system is able to adapt its assessing strategy to the student's cognitive strengths and to implement motivational tactics in a satisfactory level. Although the implementation of a domain-based student model was not of first priority in our work the need of a more efficient student modelling method emerged and the need of the enrichment of the pedagogical rules, concerning the provision of help was obvious too.

Resulting from the evaluation results, our future work will be to extend our research in the area of fuzzy neural networks for student modelling. This method has been proved to be efficient enough, offering successful student models. We intend to implement it in our prototype system and to study the differences between the new and the old version of ASSA in relation to the produced student profiles and the corresponding adaptive behaviors. Next move will be to adopt the most efficient of the two student modeling methods and design a new web-based assessment system in a more sophisticated domain.

References

1. Boulay, B. du, Luckin, R., and del Soldato, T.: The Plausibility Problem: Human Teaching Tactics in the 'Hands' of a Machine. International Conference on Artificial Intelligence in Education: Open Learning Environments: New Computational Technologies to Support Learning, Exploration and Collaboration, Le Mans, France, IOS Press (1999).
2. Koedinger, K., Anderson J.: Intelligent Tutoring Goes to School in the Big City". *International Journal of Artificial Intelligence in Education* 8 (1997) 30-43.
3. Self, J.: The defining characteristics of intelligent tutoring systems research: ITSs care, precisely. *International Journal of Artificial Intelligence in Education 10 (1999) 350-364.*
4. Lepper, M. R., Woolverton, M., Mumme, D., & Gurtner, J.: Motivational techniques of expert human tutors: Lessons for the design of computer-based tutors. Computers as cognitive tools. S. P. Lajoie, & S.J Derry, (eds), Hillsdate, NJ: Erlbaum Associates (1993) 75-105.
5. Aubé, M.: Towards Computational Models of Motivation: A much needed foundation for social sciences and education. *International Journal of Artificial Intelligence in Education*, 8(1) (1997) 43-75.
6. Viau, R.: La motivation en contexte scolaire, Saint-Laurent:ERPL(1994).
7. Keller, J. M.: Strategies for stimulating the motivation to learn. *Performance and Instruction Journal*, 26 (1987) 1-7.
8. de Vicente, A., & Pain, H.: Motivation Diagnosis in Intelligent Tutoring Systems. Proceedings of *ITS '98,* Springer-Verlag, (1998) 86-95.
9. del Soldato, T., & du Boulay, B.: "Implementation of Motivational Tactics in Tutoring System". *International Journal of Artificial Intelligence in Education* 6 (4) (1995). 337-wing378.
10. Gouli, E., Kornilakis, H., Papanikolaou, K., Grigoriadou, M.: Adaptive Assessment improving interaction in an Educational Hypermedia System. In: Avouris, N., Fakotakis, N. (eds): Advances in Human-Computer Interaction I. Proceeding of the Pan Hellenic Conference with International Participation in Human-Computer Interaction, (2001) 217-222.
11. Dowling, C., and Kaluscha, R.: Prerequisite Relationships for the Adaptive Assessment of Knowledge. Artificial Intelligence in Education. G. J. Charlottesville, V.A. Association for the Advancement of Computing in Education (AACE) (1995) 43-50.
12. Prentzas J., Hatzilygeroudis I. and Koutsojannis C.: A Web-Based ITS Controlled by an Expert System, Proceedings of the IEEE International Conference on Advanced Learning Technologies (ICALT 2001), Madison, Wisconsin, USA (2001) 239-40.

Human or Computer? AutoTutor in a Bystander Turing Test

Natalie Person[1], Arthur C. Graesser[2], & The Tutoring Research Group[2]

[1] Rhodes College, Department of Psychology, Memphis, TN 38112
person@rhodes.edu
[2] University of Memphis, Department of Psychology, Memphis, TN 38152-3230
a-graesser@memphis.edu

1 Introduction

Since the development of the first digital computer in the 1940s, the notion of computer intelligence has received considerable attention from computer scientists, philosophers, and psychologists. The question of whether it is possible to create a computer program that possesses human intelligence has spurred much debate. Turing (1950) argued that computers are not capable of thinking and provided several theological, psychological, and sociological arguments in support of his position. To determine a computer program's intelligence, Turing proposed several benchmark methods. One such method requires humans to decide whether they are interacting with an actual computer program or another human via computer mediation. According to Turing, a computer could be described as intelligent if it could deceive a human into believing that it was human. The two studies presented here were designed to determine whether AutoTutor could pass a variation of the Turing test, the Bystander Turing Test. The subsequent sections of this paper address the following: (1) the AutoTutor system, (2) the Bystander Turing Test, (3) the two empirical studies, and (4) the conclusions of the studies.

2 Description of AutoTutor

AutoTutor is a generic computer tutor architecture that can be used for a variety of content domains [3], [5], [10], [12]. The Tutoring Research Group (TRG) has recently developed two versions of AutoTutor, one for computer literacy and one for conceptual physics. The computer literacy AutoTutor is designed to help students learn basic computer literacy topics covered in an introductory course (e.g., hardware, operating systems, and the Internet). The conceptual physics AutoTutor is designed to help students learn Newtonian physics.

AutoTutor's architecture is comprised of six major modules: (1) an animated agent, (2) a curriculum script, (3) language analyzers, (4) latent semantic analysis (LSA), (5) a dialog move generator, and (6) a Dialog Advancer Network [7], [9], [11], [12], [13], [15], [16]. AutoTutor initiates the conversation with the learner by selecting a question or problem from the curriculum script for the learner to solve. Students learn about computer literacy or physics by engaging in a conversation with the animated

S.A. Cerri, G. Gouardères, and F. Paraguaçu (Eds.): ITS 2002, LNCS 2363, pp. 821–830, 2002.

agent. AutoTutor scaffolds the conversation with a series of dialog moves that are frequently used by effective human tutors [4], [8]. The dialog moves included in AutoTutor are Pump, Prompt, Hint, Assertion, Correction, Summary, and three kinds of Short Feedback (positive, negative, and neutral).

Although the selection of dialog moves is complex in AutoTutor, a summary of this process is as follows. After each typed student contribution, a series of language analyzers operate on the words in the student's contribution so that the contribution can be classified into one of five speech act categories: Assertion, WH-question, Yes/No question, Frozen Expression, or Prompt Completion. The quality of the Assertion classifications is determined by latent semantic analysis (LSA). LSA is also used to monitor several other parameters that are important in tutoring (e.g., topic coverage, student ability). The dialog move generator is controlled by a series of production rules that utilize the LSA parametric data. The dialog move generator selects one or a combination of pedagogically appropriate dialog moves from the curriculum script. These moves are conveyed to the student via the animated agent. The Dialog Advancer Network (DAN) manages the turn-taking and provides AutoTutor responses to all of the speech act categories.

3   The Bystander Turing Test

The original Turing test is based on the Imitation Game. In the Imitation Game, the participants are a man, a woman, and an interrogator. The interrogator is physically separated from the man and woman. The object of the game is for the interrogator to decipher which participant is male and which is female by evaluating their responses to questions posed by the interrogator. Turing proposed replacing one of the humans (i.e., the man or woman) with a computer. If the interrogator cannot discern whether the responses are generated by the computer or by the human, the computer program is said to pass the Turing Test. Specifically, the computer program is emulating human thought and intelligence if it can process human language, utilize knowledge it has been given before and receives during the interactive session, and use stored knowledge to engage in an intellectual conversation with the learner [14].

The Bystander Turing Test (BTT) is a variation of the original Turing Test. In the BTT, participants rate whether particular dialog moves in tutoring transcripts are generated by AutoTutor or by skilled human tutors. We converged on this variation of the original Turing Test for two reasons that are based on our observations of human tutors attempting to tutor students in computer-mediated environments. First, human tutors have tremendous difficulty responding in real-time to student input. Given that AutoTutor responds immediately to student contributions, noticeable time lags caused by human tutors' need to think would potentially influence an interrogator's decisions. Second, human tutors frequently make errors when typing their responses. Hence, AutoTutor's text-to-speech generator would mispronounce a considerable number of words, and unquestionably, affect an interrogator's judgments.

The conversations included in both BTT studies were constructed in the following way. Two hundred and eighty-two conversations were randomly selected from several thousand conversations that had taken place between college students and the computer literacy AutoTutor. In each of the 282 conversations, a particular AutoTutor dialog move was deleted along with all subsequent conversational turns. Six skilled human computer literacy tutors were asked to read each conversation and then fill in the blank lines with what they would say to that student at that juncture in the conversation.

After the human tutor responses (i.e. dialog moves) were collected, packets containing 36 conversations were assembled. Each packet contained 18 conversations in which all tutor dialog moves were generated by AutoTutor and 18 conversations in which the last dialog move in the conversation was generated by a human tutor. To the extent possible, the AutoTutor dialog move categories (e.g., Pump, Prompt, Assertion) were evenly distributed across the 18 authentic AutoTutor conversations. Participants in each study were asked to read the entire conversation and evaluate the last dialog move. The evaluation questions differed in the two studies and will be discussed in the next two sections.

3.1 Study 1

The participants were 64 students who were either enrolled in a computer literacy course or who had completed the course at the University of Memphis. The participants received extra credit in a course for their participation. All participants read and signed an informed consent form before the experiment began. Testing packets were then given to the participants which included 36 conversations, 18 of the conversations ended in an AutoTutor dialog move and 18 ended in a human tutor dialog move. After each conversation, participants rated the last tutor dialog move on a six-point scale, 1 indicating the dialog move was definitely generated by a human and 6 indicating the dialog move was definitely generated by a computer (see Table 1).   After providing ratings for all 36 conversations, participants were asked to describe any strategies they had developed for identifying which dialog moves were generated by the computer and which were generated by humans. The analysis of these open-ended responses will not be discussed in this paper.

3.2 Study 2

The participants were 24 undergraduates at Rhodes College, a small liberal arts college located in Memphis, Tennessee. The students participated in the study to fulfill research requirements for introductory psychology classes. The materials and procedure for Study 2 differed from Study 1 in the following ways. After reading each conversation, participants provided three six-point scale ratings for the last tutor dialog move in each conversation. The additional questions were added to assess the teaching effectiveness and conversational appropriateness of the dialog moves. The three rating questions used in Study 2 are provided in Table 1. After the participants completed all 36 dialog move ratings, they were asked to describe any strategies they had developed for identifying the speakers of the dialog moves. Lastly, participants were asked to complete a computer knowledge questionnaire. This questionnaire was included to determine whether computer knowledge is a moderating factor in participants' ability to discriminate human versus computer tutors.

Table 1. Dialog Move Assessment Questions Used in Study 1 and 2

(Used in Study 1 and 2)

1. The last tutor response/question is

1	2	3	4	5	6
Definitely Human	Probably Human	Not sure, but guess Human	Not sure, but guess Computer	Probably Computer	Definitely Computer

(Study 2 only)
2. In terms of conversational appropriateness, the last tutor response/question is (do not circle between the bars):

1	2	3	4	5	6
Definitely Inappropriate	Probably Inappropriate	Not sure, but guess Inappropriate	Not sure, but guess Appropriate	Probably Appropriate	Definitely Appropriate

(Study 2 only)
3. In terms of effective teaching, the last tutor turn response/question is

1	2	3	4	5	6
Definitely Ineffective	Probably ineffective	Not sure, but guess Ineffective	Not sure, but guess Effective	Probably Effective	Definitely Effective

4   Results and Discussion

A series of independent samples t-tests were performed to determine whether the human and computer means differed for the three six-point scale assessment questions used in Study 1 and 2. The means for the three questions are reported in Table 2. A series of one-way ANOVAs were performed to determine whether participants were relying on dialog move category information when providing ratings for the three assessment questions. Means and likelihood values from these analyses are reported in Tables 3, 4, and 5. The results from all of these analyses are reported and discussed below.

4.1   Who Said It? (Question 1)

Independent samples t-tests were performed to determine whether participants could distinguish AutoTutor versus human-generated dialog moves in Study 1 and Study 2. For the "Who said it?" question, mean ratings on the six-point scale for the last dialog move in each conversation were compared (see Table 2). Results from both studies indicated that participants could not discriminate between dialog moves generated by AutoTutor and those generated by humans, $t(142) = 1.45$, $p > .10$; $t(142) = .68$, $p > .10$; Study 1 and Study 2, respectively. Hence, AutoTutor passed the Bystander Turing Test when observations were collected at a fine-grained level (i.e., at the level of individual dialog moves, as opposed to interacting with AutoTutor versus a human for 30 minutes). Simply put, the college students could not tell whether the dialog move was generated by a computer or by a human computer literacy tutor. AutoTutor therefore does a fairly good job of simulating skilled human tutor dialog moves.

Table 2. Means and Standard Deviations for Assessment Questions in Study 1 and Study 2

	Study 1					
Question	Computer			Human		
	Mean	s.d.	n	Mean	s.d.	n
1. Who said it?	3.52	0.44	72	3.62	0.38	72

	Study 2					
Question	Computer			Human		
	Mean	s.d.	n	Mean	s.d.	n
1. Who said it?	3.72	0.91	72	3.82	0.76	72
2. Conversationally appropriate?	4.07	0.82	72	4.13	0.77	72
3. Effective teaching?	3.76	0.78	72	3.81	0.67	72

One alternative explanation of why the speaker discrimination was so low involves the dialog move categories. Perhaps the college students used the dialog move category information to diagnostically decide whether a computer or human produced the dialog move. College students may have been penalized in their predictions if they were poor guessers for some categories, but accurate guessers for others. We do know that the distribution of dialog moves of human tutors is radically different from the distribution of dialog moves in the AutoTutor sample. For example, human tutors tend to generate helpful Assertions whereas AutoTutor tries to get the learner to do the talking through Hints and Prompts.

Although sophisticated guessing could conceivably account for the poor discrimination in college students predicting computer versus human, a closer look at the data would reject this alternative explanation. We discovered that the likelihood that the college students believed a dialog move was generated by a computer was absolutely equivalent for all six dialog move categories included in Study 1 and all seven dialog move categories included in Study 2. The likelihood values were computed by considering the proportion of four, five, and six ratings on the "Who Said It?" question for each dialog move category (see Table 1). The means and likelihood values of the dialog move categories are reported in Table 3. One-way ANOVAs indicated that there were no significant differences among the dialog move categories. Thus, the college students did not show a bias among the different dialog move categories by rating particular categories as more likely to be generated by a computer.

Another potential explanation for low speaker discrimination is that the human tutors adopted the conversational style of AutoTutor. Although the human tutors were instructed to generate exactly what they would say to a student at a particular point in a tutoring conversation, the human tutors may have been inadvertently affected by the previous AutoTutor dialog moves. Thus, the human tutors may have generated succinct dialog moves that are inherent in AutoTutor's curriculum script.

Table 3. Means and Likelihood Values of Dialog Move Categories for the "Who Said It?" Question

		Study 1		
Dialog Move Category	Mean	s.d	Likelihood	n
Pump	3.47	0.43	0.50	24
Prompt	3.66	0.41	0.56	22
Prompt completion	3.55	0.48	0.50	26
Hint	3.68	0.36	0.55	20
Assertion	3.49	0.37	0.51	29
Correction	3.60	0.40	0.53	23
Total	3.57	0.41	0.52	144

		Study 2		
Dialog Move Category	Mean	s.d.	Likelihood	n
Pump	3.93	0.78	0.60	27
Prompt	3.72	0.93	0.59	27
Hint	4.06	0.93	0.64	21
Assertion	3.62	0.83	0.55	38
Correction	3.67	0.82	0.56	21
Summary	3.50	0.53	0.58	6
Feedback	3.94	0.01	0.72	3
Total	3.77	0.84	0.59	143

Study 1: One-way ANOVA for Means, $F(5,138) = 1.07$, $p > .10$; One-way ANOVA for Likelihood Values, $F(5,138) = 1.20$, $p > .30$

Study 2: One-way ANOVA for Means, $F(6, 136) = 0.94$, $p > .10$; One-way ANOVA for Likelihood Values, $F(6,136) = 0.50$, $p > .10$

(NOTE: The Prompt Completion Category was not included in the Study 2 analyses because there was only one occurrence.)

4.2 Conversationally Appropriate? (Question 2)

For the question designed to assess conversational appropriateness (Question 2), an independent-samples t-test yielded no mean differences between human and computer generated dialog moves, $t(142) = 0.44$, p > .50. That is, participants considered dialog moves generated by AutoTutor to be as conversationally appropriate as those generated by human tutors (AutoTutor mean = 4.07, Human mean = 4.13). The fact that the means did not differ and were closer to the more favorable extreme of the six-point scale is a promising indicator that AutoTutor is a competent conversational partner. As mentioned in the discussion of the "Who said it?" (Question 1) results, the human tutors may have adopted the conversational style of AutoTutor rather than generating the dialog moves they would have produced in an actual human-to-human tutoring session. Even if this was the case, the participants in Study 2 considered the dialog moves in both speaker conditions to be conversationally appropriate. Hence, even if AutoTutor does not emulate the style of human tutors in human-to-human sessions, AutoTutor does deliver dialog moves that were deemed acceptable and believable.

One of the fundamental design goals of AutoTutor is to create a system that helps students construct answers and explanations by delivering dialog moves that are pedagogically effective and conversationally appropriate. In order to determine whether particular dialog move categories were considered more conversational than others and to determine whether some dialog move categories were too computer-like, we compared the means and likelihood values of the dialog categories in two one-way ANOVAs. The means, likelihood values, and statistical results for the "Conversationally Appropriate?" question are reported in Table 4. Recall the means are the average six-point scale ratings on the "Conversationally Appropriate?" question (see Table 1), and the likelihood values are the proportions of four, five, and six ratings for each dialog move category. For example, 60% of the Pump moves received a four, five, or six rating irrespective of the speaker. The results from the one-way ANOVAs indicated no significant differences among the means or likelihood values for any of the dialog move categories. Thus, no dialog move category was considered more or less conversationally appropriate than any other, and all of the categories received high ratings approximately 70% of the time.

4.3   Effective Teaching? (Question 3)

The third assessment question addressed the pedagogical effectiveness of particular dialog moves. For the "Effective Teaching?" question, an independent-samples t-test indicated no mean differences between computer- and human-generated dialog moves, $t(142) = 0.30$, $p > .10$ (see Table 2). Therefore, participants were not using speaker characteristics when making holistic judgments about the pedagogical quality of the dialog moves.

Table 4. Study 2 Means and Likelihood Values of Dialog Move Categories for the "Conversationally Appropriate?" Question

Dialog Move Category	Mean	s.d.	Likelihood	n
Pump	3.97	0.86	0.66	27
Prompt	3.94	0.86	0.64	27
Hint	3.84	0.88	0.62	21
Assertion	4.20	0.68	0.71	38
Correction	4.26	0.72	0.74	21
Summary	4.61	0.39	0.89	6
Feedback	4.67	0.44	0.89	3
Total	4.09	0.79	0.69	143

Study 2: One-way ANOVA for Means, $F(6,136) = 1.65$, $p > .10$; One-way ANOVA for Likelihood Values, $F(6,136) = 1.52$, $p > .10$

In keeping with the dialog move category analyses performed for the other assessment questions, we wanted to discern whether the participants viewed some dialog move categories as more effective teaching strategies than others. Two one-way ANOVAs were performed to determine whether statistical differences occurred among the means and likelihood values for the dialog move categories. Both one-way ANOVAs indicated significant mean and likelihood value differences among the dialog move categories. LSD post-hoc tests were performed to determine the specific differences among the means and likelihood values. All means, likelihood values, and statistical results for the "Effective Teaching?" dialog move analysis are reported in Table 5.

In the "Effective Teaching?" means analysis, participants considered Assertions, Corrections, Summaries, and Feedback moves to be more effective teaching categories than Pumps, Prompts, and Hints, $p < .05$. The likelihood analysis produced a similar pattern of results; Assertions, Summaries, and Feedback moves had significantly greater proportions of high ratings (participants rated them a 4, 5, or 6) than Pumps, Prompts, Hints, and Corrections, $p < .05$. The differences between particular dialog move categories for the "Effective Teaching?" question should take few educational researchers or practitioners by surprise. Assertions, Summaries, and Corrections, are information delivery moves that have different pedagogical functions; however, these moves do not require students to actively elaborate their own knowledge. Thus, participants showed clear preferences for dialog moves that minimized the cognitive effort of the students and maximized the informational output of tutors.

Table 5. Study 2 Means and Likelihood Values of Dialog Move Categories for the "Effective Teaching?" Question

Dialog Move Category	Mean	s.d.	Likelihood	n
Pump	3.54^a	0.64	0.57^a	27
Prompt	3.53^a	0.78	0.51^a	27
Hint	3.52^a	0.90	0.55^a	21
Assertion	4.04^b	0.61	0.68^b	38
Correction	3.96^b	0.61	0.63^a	21
Summary	4.39^b	0.39	0.78^b	6
Feedback	4.33^b	0.17	0.89^b	3
Total	3.78	0.73	0.61	143

[a,b] Means and likelihood values that share a superscript do not statistically differ.
Study 2: One-way ANOVA for Means, $F(6,136) = 3.91$, $p < .001$; One-way ANOVA for Likelihood Values, $F(6,136) = 2.82$, $p < .05$

These results are consistent with many educators's beliefs that students prefer to be passive recipients of information that is spoon-fed to them rather than learners who actively engage in the learning process by generating explanations and asking questions. Participants did consider the Feedback dialog moves to be effective teaching strategies; however, this finding should be interpreted with caution given the few instances of Feedback moves ($n = 3$) in the Study 2 sample.

5 Conclusions

A number of conclusions can be drawn from the findings of these two bystander Turing studies. The participants in both studies were unable to discriminate dialog moves that were generated by humans from those generated by AutoTutor. Therefore, AutoTutor is, to some extent, achieving many of the design goals of AutoTutor's developers by simulating the dialog moves of effective human tutors and delivering them in conversationally appropriate ways. Future studies, however, should include conditions in which randomly generated dialog moves from human tutors and AutoTutor are inserted in the turn that participants evaluate. If participants can discriminate random moves from non-random ones but cannot discriminate human versus computer, then we will have more compelling evidence that AutoTutor's dialog move selections are on par with those of human tutors.

The dialog move category analyses indicated that participants did not associate particular dialog categories with the speaker categories nor did they consider any of the categories to be more conversationally appropriate than others. However, the participants did consider some dialog move categories to be more effective teaching strategies than others. This finding reflects participants' beliefs about what constitutes effective teaching strategies as well as their beliefs about how students learn. Unfortunately, these beliefs are not compatible with current research devoted to effective pedagogy. This incompatibility between student beliefs and tutors' pedagogical goals presents the same problems for developers of intelligent tutoring systems as those frequently encountered by teachers and human tutors. Effective teachers and tutors encourage students to take an active role in the learning process by structuring tasks and dialogs in ways that force students to engage in behaviors such as asking questions, recognizing misconceptions, generating explanations, and synthesizing information from multiple sources [1], [2], [4], [13]. Such student behaviors are not only rare without teacher intervention but frequently cause cognitive distress in students. ITS developers must therefore strive to design systems that preserve effective pedagogy without overly frustrating students.

Acknowledgements. This research was supported by grants from the National Science Foundation (SBR 9720314 and REC 0106965) and the Department of Defense Multidisciplinary University Research Initiative (MURI) administered by the Office of Naval Research under grant N00014-00-1-0600. Any opinions, findings, and conclusions or recommendations expressed in this material are those of the authors and do not necessarily reflect the views of ONR or NSF.

References

1. Chi, M.T.H.: Constructing self explanations and scaffolded explanations in tutoring. *Applied Cognitive Psycholog, 10* (1996) S33-S49

2. Chi, M.T.H., Bassok, M., Lewis, M. W., Reimann, P., & Glaser, R.: Self-explanations: How students study and use examples in learning to solve problems. *Cognitive Scienc, 13* (1989) 145-182

3. Graesser, A.C., Hu, X., Susarla, S., Harter, D., Person, N.K., Louwerse, M., Olde, B., & the Tutoring Research Group: AutoTutor: An Intelligent Tutor and Conversational Tutoring Scaffold. *Proceedings for the 10th International Conference of Artificial Intelligence in Education* San Antonio, TX (2001) 47-49

4. Graesser, A.C., Person, N.K., & Magliano, J.P.: Collaborative dialogue patterns in naturalistic one-to-one tutoring sessions. *Applied Cognitive Psychology 9* (1995) 1-28

5. Graesser, A.C., Person, N.K., Harter, D., & the Tutoring Research Group: Tactics in tutoring in AutoTutor. In the *ITS 2000 Proceedings of the Workshop on Modeling Human Teaching Tactics and Strategies* Montreal, Canada (2000) 49-57

6. Graesser, A.C., Wiemer-Hastings, K., Wiemer-Hastings, P., Kreuz, R., & TRG: AutoTutor: A simulation of a human tutor. *Journal of Cognitive Systems Research 1*(1999) 35-51

7. Graesser, A.C., Wiemer-Hastings, P., Wiemer-Hastings, K., Harter, D., Person, N., & the Tutoring Research Group: Using latent semantic analysis to evaluate the contributions of students in AutoTutor. *Interactive Learning Environments 8* (2000) 129-148

8. Person, N.K., & Graesser, A.C.: Evolution of discourse in cross-age tutoring. In A. M.O'Donnell and A. King (Eds.), *Cognitive perspectives on peer learning* Mahwah, NJ: Erlbaum (1999) 69-86

9. Person, N.K., Graesser, A.C., & the Tutoring Research Group: Designing AutoTutor to be an effective conversational partner. In the *Proceedings for the 4th International Conference of the Learning Sciences* Ann Arbor, MI (2000) 246-253

10. Person, N.K., Graesser, A.C., Bautista, L., Mathews, E.C., & the Tutoring Research Group: Evaluating Student Learning Gains in Two Versions of AutoTutor. In J.D. Moore, C.L. Redfield, & W.L. Johnson (Eds.) *Artificial intelligence in education: AI-ED in the wired and wireless future* Amsterdam, IOS Press (2001) 286-293

11. Person, N.K., Graesser, A.C., Harter, D., Mathews, E.C., & the Tutoring Research Group: Dialog move generation and conversation management in AutoTutor. *Proceedings of the AAAI Fall Symposium: Building Dialogue Systems for Tutorial Applications* Falmouth, MA: AAAI Press (2000) 45-51

12. Person, N.K., Graesser, A.C., Kreuz, R.J., Pomeroy, V., & the Tutoring Research Group: Simulating human tutor dialog moves in AutoTutor. *International Journal of Artificial Intelligence in Education 12* (2001b) 23-29

13. Person, N.K., Klettke, B., Link, K., Kreuz, R.J., & the Tutoring Research Group: The integration of affective responses into AutoTutor. *Proceedings of the International Workshop on Affect in Interactions* Siena, Italy (1999) 167-178

14. Turing, A.M.: Computing Machinery and Intelligence. In E.A. Feigenbaum & J. Feldman (Eds.) *Computers and thought.* New York: McGraw-Hill (1950)

15. Wiemer-Hastings, P., Graesser, A.C., Harter, D., and the Tutoring Research Group: The foundations and architecture of AutoTutor. *Proceedings of the 4th International Conference on Intelligent Tutoring Systems* Berlin, Germany: Springer-Verlag (1998) 334-343

16. Wiemer-Hastings, P., Wiemer-Hastings, K., and Graesser, A.: Improving an intelligent tutor's comprehension of students with Latent Semantic Analysis. *Artificial Intelligence in Education* Amsterdam: IOS Press (1999) 535-542

Representational Decisions When Learning Population Dynamics with an Instructional Simulation

Nicolas Van Labeke and Shaaron Ainsworth

ESRC Centre for Research in Development, Instruction & Training
School of Psychology, University of Nottingham,
University Park, Nottingham, NG7 2RD, UK.
{nvl,sea}@psychology.nottingham.ac.uk

Abstract. DEMIST is a multi-representational simulation environment that supports understanding of the representations and concepts of population dynamics. We report on a study with 18 subjects with little prior knowledge that explored if DEMIST could support their learning and asked what decisions learners would make about how to use the many representations that DEMIST provides. Analysis revealed that using DEMIST for one hour significantly improved learners' understanding of population dynamics though their knowledge of the relation between representations remained weak. It showed that learners used many of DEMIST's features. For example, they investigated the majority of the representational space, used dyna-linking to explore the relation between representations and had preferences for representations with different computational properties. It also revealed that decisions made by designers impacted upon what is intended to be a free discovery environment.

1   Introduction

Research with multi-representational tutoring systems and learning environments has revealed that learning with multiple external representations is a demanding process but one that if successfully mastered can lead to a deep understanding of the domain [e.g. 1,2]. DEMIST is a multi-representational simulation designed to explore when learning with MERs is effective. It implements the DeFT framework for learning with MERS and by evaluating how people learn with DEMIST, we also evaluate the underlying framework. This serves a dual function. By analyzing learners' behaviour we can understand more about the demands of complex information processing and by understanding these demands adaptive multi-representational learning environments can be created. To accomplish this, we intend to perform design experiments based on manipulating the parameters of the DeFT framework. However, before this can be achieved we have sought to discover if DEMIST is effective and how learners would respond to an environment which provides so much representational flexibility. To begin we therefore summarise the DeFT framework and how DEMIST embodies it before turning to the details of the study.

The DeFT Framework [3] provides an account of the different pedagogical functions that MERs can play, the design parameters that are unique to learning with MERs and the cognitive tasks that must be undertaken by a learner.

S.A. Cerri, G. Gouardères, and F. Paraguaçu (Eds.): ITS 2002, LNCS 2363, pp. 831–840, 2002.

There are three key functions of MERs: to complement, constrain and construct. MERs complement each other by supporting different complementary processes or containing complementary information. When two representations constrain each other, they do so because one supports interpretation of the other. Finally, MERs can support the construction of deeper understanding when learners abstract over representations to identify the shared invariant features of a domain. Each of these functions has a number of subclasses (see [4]). The cognitive tasks that a learner must perform to learn with MERs include understanding the properties of the representation and the relation between the representations and the domain. Additionally, learners may have to select or construct representations. The cognitive demand unique to MERs is to understand how to translate between two representations and there is much evidence that this is complicated. DeFT describes five key design dimensions that uniquely apply to multi-representational systems:

1. *Redundancy*: How information is distributed. This influences the complexity of a representation and the redundancy of information across the system;
2. *Form*: The computational properties of a representational system;
3. *Translation*: The degree of support provided for mapping between representations
4. *Sequence*: The order in which representations are presented;
5. *Number*: The number of (co-present) representations supported by the system.

DEMIST [3] allows systematic manipulations of these design parameters. It aims to support learners in the development of their knowledge of the concepts and representations important in understanding population dynamics. It provides a number of mathematical models, for example, the Lotka-Volterra model of predation which learners can explore. To investigate these models, users are presented with a potentially very large set of representations. Hence, DEMIST also aims to support learners" understanding of how domain general representations such as X-Time graphs are used in this domain, to introduce them to the specific representations of population dynamics (such as phaseplots and life tables) and to encourage their understanding of the relationship between these representations.

The study we report in this paper represents the first attempt to evaluate if DEMIST is effective. However, an equally important goal was to discover how learners would use a simulation-based learning environment which includes so many representations. We subscribe to the view that learning is best considered an active process where learners take responsibility for their own achievements, but were worried about whether DEMIST provides sufficient support to guide learners new to the domain. Therefore a key design goal was to keep track of users' behaviour with DEMIST. Furthermore, few simulation environments provide learners with quite so much choice about what representations to interact with and how many to work with simultaneously. Therefore we have little information about learners' representational preferences. Hence, this experiment explores decisions learners make when provided with many complex representations.

2   System Description

DEMIST (see figure 1) is built around the authoring of instructional scenarios. The basis for its design is a formal description of an instructional simulation that describes the task of authoring simulations with SIMQUEST [5,6]. Each scenario consists of a sequence of *Learning Units* that instantiate a particular mathematical model. The parameters of the mathematical model are combined as *experimental sets* that can be instantiated by various sets of initial conditions. This allows the learner to explore the same model under different experimental conditions.

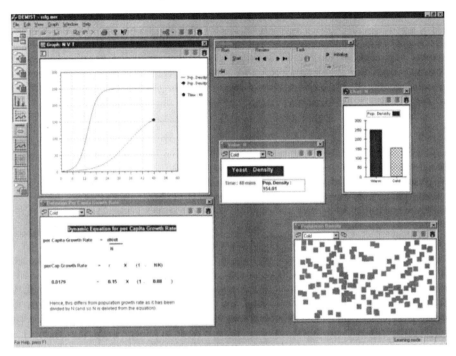

Fig. 1. DEMIST in learning mode.

Each of these Learning Units includes a set of representations such as table, XY-Graph, Histogram, Animations which display one or many of the variables and parameters extracted from the mathematical model. Representations can be automatically displayed or only shown when the learner requests them and the order in which they appear can be specified by an author or left under learner control. One of the features of DEMIST, unique to our knowledge among the simulation environments, is that the translation between representations can be varied. DEMIST currently allows three levels of translation: *independent* (actions on an ER are not reflected onto other ERs), *map relation* (selecting a value in one ER shows all the corresponding relationships in other ERs) and *dyna-linked* (modifying the information in one ER is reflected onto all the other relevant ERs). There are a small number of additional activities available to the learners. In particular, they can make *hypotheses* about the values of the model in the future or perform *actions*, which allows the learner to act on a value at the current stage of the simulation and change it. They can choose which representations they use to perform these activities and depending on the degree of translation could check the consequences of these actions on other representations (e.g. predict that the population density will have doubled in size in 10 years by adding a hypothesis to the relevant row of a table and see a point added to the graph corresponding to that prediction).

3   Method

The experiment used three of DEMIST's models of population dynamics, starting from the simplest: *Single-Species Unlimited Growth* (SSUG), *Single-Species Limited Growth* (SSLG) and *Two-Species Predation* (TSP). Each of these models consisted of three learning units, which focused on particular phenomena that is characteristic of that model (e.g. doubling time for exponential growth, carrying capacity for limited growth [7]). The learning units specified the representations to be included and any learning activities to be performed. To provide learners with a large relatively unconstrained space to explore, the following authoring decisions were made:

- *Information*: representations contain up to three dimensions of information. Pairs of representations could therefore have full, partial or no redundancy;
- *Form:* large representational system (between 8 to 10 ERs for each unit), which varied in their relevance and ease of interpretation;
- *Sequence:* learner choice of sequence of representations;
- *Number:* a maximum of five co-present representations. A small number of representations were selected to be displayed at the beginning of each unit;
- *Translation:* full dyna-linking allowing learners to reflect actions onto other ERs.

For the purposes of this study we were less interested in examining the informational properties of a representation. Hence, we categorised the representations according to a taxonomy of representation type which focused on the format and operators of the representations. For example, all tables were classified as one type of representation, tabular, whether they contained values of population density, growth rate or environmental resistance. Similarly all representations that could have been considered as animations were so grouped. The analysis of the type of representations provided in the experiment together with the number of representation of each type available by model can be seen in table 1.

Table 1. Categorization of ERS in DEMIST

	Description	SSUG	SSLG	TSP
X v Time Graph	Line graph of data across time	6	5	4
X v Time Graph (log)	Logarithmic scaled line graph	2		
XY Graph	Line graph that plots two dimensions of data where one is not time.	2	5	4
Chart	Two-dimensional bar chart	4	3	3
Pie Chart	Proportions of two or more values			3
Concrete Animation	Dynamic ER with a pictorial element	1	2	4
Table	Tabular representation	4	3	4
Dynamic Equation	Dynamic ER that contains explicit mathematical expressions	3	4	2
Terms	Dynamic ER with explanatory text and often a current value	2	1	
Value	A very simple representation that provides only a data label and value	3	3	3

3.1 Participants

18 participants were involved in the experiment. All were students or researchers at Nottingham, and their prior experience in mathematics and biology was recorded (students with degrees in biology or mathematics were excluded from the experiment). One of them crashed the software during the experiment, making the data unreliable for analysis. The results are based on the remaining 17 participants.

3.2 Pre- and Post-test

The pre-test and the post-test consisted of multiple-choice questions, 11 for the former, and 22 for the latter. The pre-test was developed to assess whether subjects had any relevant prior knowledge and was deliberately designed to include items that were most likely to be familiar. The post-test included more difficult items and repeated 10 of these pre-test questions. One key feature of the questionnaire design was the development of three types of question. The first focused on domain concepts (e.g. what will happen to the prey population if some predators are removed?), the second on interpreting specific representations (e.g. which of these four graphs of population density against time is characteristic of SSUL?) and the third on multi-representational understanding (e.g. finding the odd-one-out among four different representations of supposedly the same dataset). These questions were designed to assess if multi-representational simulations such as DEMIST can support learning about representations and the relation between representations as well as the more traditional conceptual issues.

3.3 Procedure

Participants were first given the un-timed pre-test and were then introduced to DEMIST and the main features of the interface explained. The experimenter remained present to clarify any questions that learners may have about the interface but did not provide direct guidance. Participants were warned they only had one hour to complete the three tasks and the experimenter occasionally reminded them about the time. However, generally participants had complete control over the amount of time and the nature of their interactions with DEMIST. After one hour, participants were stopped and immediately given the post-test. They completed the test in their own time and were then debriefed and paid for their participation.

4   Results

The learners had some prior knowledge of the domain. If they had been guessing, they would have been expected to get a total of 25% of the questions right as each question had one right answer and three distractors. As can be seen from table 2, the average pre-test score was 42.3% which is significantly above chance ($t = 4.3$, $df = 16$, $p < 0.001$).

Table 2. Pre-Test and Post-Test results.

	Overall		Concept		Single ER		MERs	
	Mean	St.Dev.	Mean	St.Dev.	Mean	St.Dev.	Mean	St.Dev.
Pre-Test (11 items)	42.3%	16%	41.2%	23%	52.9%	21%	11.8%	22%
Post-Test (22 items)	55.6%	15%	61.3%	27%	59.9%	10%	33.8%	26%

Closer analysis revealed whether or not questions of different types (i.e. conceptual, single ER, MERs) were answered differently. Conceptual and Single ER questions were answered above chance, however those relating to MERs were answered significantly below chance (t = 2.5, df= 16, p=.024). This pattern of results confirms our intuitions that these types of question were harder than the others.

The post-test consisted of 10 items from the pre-test and 12 more items. Again the performance of participants was significantly above chance at 55.6%, (t= 8.5, df = 16, p<.0001). Table 2 shows that overall there was a significant increase in the percentage of questions that subjects got right from pre-test to post-test (t = 3.1, df =16, p<0.008). As the post-test included more difficult items than the pre-test, we compared subjects' performance on those questions that were present on both the pre and post-test. Scores significantly improved on these questions from an average of 45.9% at pre-test to 62.3% at post-test (t = 4.9, df = 16, p <.0001). Finally, we looked at performance on post-test items by type of question. Performance on all questions was now significantly above chance accept for those questions which dealt specifically with MERs (t=1.4 df = 16, p=.188) which was now at chance.

There was only limited time available for this intervention and in future we would like to have longer sessions. So given these factors we are content to observe significant improvement in learning outcomes.

4.1 How Do Learners Use DEMIST?

The second goal of the study was to explore learners' representation use to discover whether they had strong preferences about the representations.

Number of Simultaneous Representations
Learners had the choice to work simultaneously with between one and five representations plus the controller. The majority of learners spent most of their time working with three representations (40.4% of total time) or four representations (31.7%). Working with one representation at a time was very unpopular and working with two only slightly more common. There is a relatively high standard deviation for the use of 5 co-present representations (mean 19.1%, St.Dev. 13.12%). No one chose to use the maximum number of five representations for more than half the session and some participants never used more than four representations.

Exploration of the Representational Space
We examined the total number of representations that the participants activated (using a time threshold of 10 seconds to avoid including Ers opened in error). Participants tended to explore as much as possible of the representational space, activating a total

of 73 representations on average out of the 80 available. However, this does imply that they used the representations equally. To examine which representations learners preferred we calculated the amount of time each type of representation was used. As not all representations were available in all learning units, we first calculated the maximum possible availability (see table 1). Secondly, we grouped all representations of the same type together even if they contained different information. This allowed us to express the use of each type of representation as a function of its availability. So, for example in table 3, the low value for the pie chart does not mean that it was available rarely, it shows that even when available, it was not selected.

Table 3. External Representations Usage.

	Mean	St.Dev.	No. of Reps	Translation	Hypothesis
X v Time Graph	73%	21%	9/15	532	151
Terms	70%	26%	3/3	2	0
Value	60%	12%	3/9	1	0
Chart	33%	19%	2/10	13	0
XY Graph	29%	24%	2/11	257	0
Concrete Animation	28%	21%	2/7	4	0
Table	28%	20%	2/11	178	4
Dynamic Equation	21%	19%	1/9	0	0
Pie Chart	9%	10%	0/3	0	0
X v Time Graph (log)	8%	12%	0/2	16	5

Key – The use of a representation expressed as a percentage of maximum potential usage, standard deviation, the number of representations of a given type opened automatically by the system as well as the total number of that type, and the number of translation and hypothesis requests over the expt.

The first analysis we performed on this data was to examine how influenced learners had been by the initial selection of representations for a unit. During piloting it had become evident that some learners were unhappy unless they were provided with an initial set of representations, hence for each unit we selected two or three representations to open automatically. However, learners were free to close those representations at any time. We found a striking correlation between our provision of representations and the ones that learners spent the most time working with ($r = 0.85$, $n = 10$, $p < 0.02$). For this reason, a large degree in the variance of percentage of use is not based on a learner's choice of representations, it is based on the system's choice. The ERs that learners selected for different amounts of time than that predicted simply by automatic selection include the XY graph which was used more than expected, and the table and concrete animation, which were used less.

Acting on Representations
Representations are used for both display and action, where actions are a request to translate information, predict a value at some future point or to modify current values. The trace logs provided information about which ER was associated with the

initiating action for translating and for stating hypotheses. The total number of these requests for the 17 participants can be seen in table 3. There is enormous variance in these values. The X v Time Graph was used for 98% of all hypotheses. For translation requests, again the X v Time Graph was the most common accounting for 58% of all requests, but the XY Graph (25%) and the Table (12%) were also used appreciably. These latter figures are particularly interesting as they do not reflect the percentage of time that learners chose to display the representations (see table 3). Translation requests from the XY graph are plausibly about trying to understand a new and difficult to interpret representation, whereas from the table perhaps its familiarity was being used by learners to help interpret other representations.

5   Discussion

This study provides useful information to begin work on design experiments on the DeFT parameters. They have confirmed that DEMIST can teach learners with little prior knowledge about the representations and concepts involved in population dynamics. This is encouraging as in normal use we would expect to allow learners to use DEMIST for substantially more than the one hour available for this study.

Analysis of the test material has shown that understanding the relation between representations may be the most difficult aspect of the domain. Learners performed worse on these items at pre-test and only got 34% of the MERs answers right at post-test. This confirms earlier studies which have shown that relational understanding is difficult for learners (e.g. [8,9]). How best to support translation between representations, is one of the aspects of DeFT that has been implemented in DEMIST. We can vary the level of automatic support between ERs in ways that we refer to as contingent translation. Learners new to the domain should be provided with fully dyna-linked MERs. This scaffolding will be reduced as their knowledge improves so that they take increasing responsibility for mapping information across ERs. The relatively poor performance on the MERs items in the study provides further evidence for the importance of empirical research in this area and highlights the need to develop test material that is sensitive to multi-representational understanding.

This study was also concerned with addressing how learners would behave if they were given the representational flexibility that DEMIST provides. We were interested in exploring what their representational preferences were and whether they would spontaneously choose to use features such as translation. A number of interesting details were revealed about learners' behaviour, some of which we had not expected.

Firstly, we were disconcerted to observe how much of learners' representational selection was based on an initial set of representations presented by the computer. Essentially, the vast majority of learners chose to work with these representations only exploring alternatives towards the end of a learning unit. This may well cause us to redesign the learning units. The decision to "pop up" pre-selected representations had been made after piloting. However, we viewed the system presentation of representations as gentle guidance about useful places to start and emphasised this during the introduction to the system. This does not seem to have been learners' interpretation. Of course, perhaps we chose the "best" representations for each unit and the learners simply agreed with this choice. This is possible as we based our selection of representations on the way that they were used in textbooks (e.g. Gotelli

1998). A future experiment could compare different ways of selecting initial ERs varying between none/random /"worst"/"best" to provide information about how much guidance a supposedly discovery environment like DEMIST ought to provide.

Other results that may have implications beyond DEMIST's domain include the number of co-present ERs that learners chose to use. There was a strong bias for three or four ERs. Learners rarely chose to focus on only one or two at a time. Some learners did seem happy to go to five, the maximum we allowed in this study but others limited their selection to three. Many simulation environments provide a fixed number of representations. We would argue that ideally this decision should be under learner control, but where not, limiting the number of co-present ERs to three or four seems to fit with most learners representational preferences.

We also examined learners' actions to see which ERs were used to request translations. Learners made quite a number of translation requests (an average of 59 per participant). The majority of these were from the X-Time graph but significant numbers were from the XY graph. This was surprisingly high given its low general percentage presence. We interpret this behaviour of one of attempting to use DEMIST's translation features to understand this complex representation by relating it to other more familiar representations. We had expected to see more learners selecting familiar representations and requesting translation from this known point. This was arguably what occurred with the table. However, representations such as "value" which we had included for this function were not used in this way. It provokes an interesting instructional question of whether learners should start from the familiar and interpret a new representation from its standpoint or start with the unfamiliar and complex and then see how it relates to the familiar. Finally, learners only stated hypotheses with X-Time graph. This is disappointing as one of the benefits of dyna-linking is that learners could construct hypotheses on different ERs and see how this was mapped to other ERs. For example, they could have added values to the table (which is an easy and precise operation) and then this value would be reflected onto other representations such as the XY graph. We need to find a way to emphasise this strategy as it is a more active way of understanding relations between representations than simply selecting common dimensions of information.

We had expected to observe a systematic relationship between representation usage and learning. There was no evidence for this. One reason for this may be the lack of variability between learners' ER use – e.g. sticking to system selection, examining but not really using all of the representation space, choosing three or four representations, etc. However, this result also highlights a flaw in relying solely on the traditional experimental method. For example, if learners chose to spend a large amount of time with an XY graph, we can't tell from the traces if the explanation is that they didn't understand the representation and were trying to interpret it or whether they were in fact fully conversant with it and recognised that it was a useful way to understand the domain. If we want to understand the process of learning with MERs we need to take a more fine-grained approach to data collection. A key next stage in the project will be to conduct a micro-genetic study (e.g. [10]) with one or two learners where we will take detailed protocols about their goals, strategies and decisions.

This study has revealed DEMIST to be a suitable environment to ask questions about how learners should best be supported when they learn with MERs. It is based on a rich domain which is best understood by reference to multiple linked representations. We have shown that students can begin to understand the domain in a short amount of time but that the more complex issues will require more time and strategic support. Hence, we will be following a two-pronged research agenda. Using detailed protocol analysis we hope to build a more complete picture of the process of learning in this domain which could ultimately form the basis of a computational model (e.g. [11]). Second, we can perform design experiments which systematically vary the DeFT parameters (e.g. amount of translation, number of co-present ERs). A combination of these two approaches should help uncover design principles for how best to support the complex information processing that MERs require.

References

[1]   Cox, R. and Brna, P. (1995). *Supporting the use of external representations in problem solving: the need for flexible learning environments*. International Journal of Artificial Intelligence in Education **6**(2/3): 239-302.

[2]   de Jong, T., Ainsworth, S., Dobson, M., van der Hulst, A., Levonen, J., Reimann, P., Sime, J., van Someren, M.W. and Spada, H. & Swaak, J. (1998). *Acquiring knowledge in science and math: the use of multiple representations in technology based learning environments*. Learning with Multiple Representations. M. W. van Someren *et al.* Oxford, Elsevier.

[3]   Van Labeke, N. and Ainsworth, S. (2001). *Applying the DeFT Framework to the Design of Multi-Representational Instructional Simulations*. AIED'2001 - 10th International Conference on Artificial Intelligence in Education, San Antonio, Texas, IOS Press.

[4]   Ainsworth, S. (1999). *The functions of multiple representations*. Computer & Education **33**(2/3): 131-152.

[5]   de Jong, T. and van Joolingen, W.R. (1998). *Scientific discovery learning with computer simulations of conceptual domains*. Review of Educational Research **68**: 179-202.

[6]   Kuyper, M., *Knowledge engineering for usability : Model-Mediated Interaction Design of Authoring Instructional Simulations*. Ph. D. Thesis. University of Amsterdam, (1998).

[7]   Gotelli, N.J. (1998). *A Primer of Ecology*. Sunderland, MA, Sinauer Associates.

[8]   Ainsworth, S., Bibby, P.A. and Wood, D.J. (2002). *Examining the effects of different multiple representational systems in learning primary mathematics*. Journal of the Learning Sciences **11**(1): 25-62.

[9]   Tabachneck, H.J.M., Leonardo, A.M. and Simon, H.A. (1994). *How does an expert use a graph? A model of visual & verbal inferencing in economics*. 16th Annual Conference of the Cognitive Science Society, Hillsdale, NJ: LEA.

[10]   Schoenfeld, A.H., Smith, J.P. and Arcavi, A. (1993). *Learning: the microgenetic analysis of one student's evolving understanding of a complex subject matter domain*. Advances in instructional psychology, volume 3. R. Glaser. Hillsdale, NJ, LEA. **3**: 55-175.

[11]   Tabachneck-Schijf, H.J.M., Leonardo, A.M. and Simon, H.A. (1997). *CaMeRa: A computational model of multiple representations*. Cognitive Science **21**(3): 305-350.

Integration of Automatic Tools for Displaying Interaction Data in Computer Environments for Distance Learning

Aloys Mbala, Christophe Reffay, and Thierry Chanier

Laboratoire d'Informatique de l'Université de Franche-Comté
16, route de Gray, 25030 Besançon Cedex
{mbala,reffay,chanier}@lifc.univ-fcomte.fr

Abstract. Our research concerns distance learning (DL). We are interested with distributed collaborative learning. In this approach, it is important to have indicators permitting the appreciation of durability and the evolution of groups involved. We think that actors responsible for the organisation and the working of groups (tutor for each group and coordinator of the DL session for all groups and its progress in general) can from the types of interactions and their amounts, get revealing elements permitting them to appreciate the state of a group and its evolution. From the analysis of interactions seen during a distance learning experimentation that we led, we show here that the disappearance of a group as we observed could be discerned practically in real time. It justifies for us, the necessity to set up in distance learning environments, agents capable of assisting the coordinator of the training and the tutors in their tasks.

1 Introduction

Current computer environments for distance learning don't have tools which assist learning groups nor support their cohesion. With reduced size groups, involved in a collaborative learning process, this limitation becomes a crucial problem. When one or two members of such groups abandon, the whole group may disappear.

Conversely, the existence in a group of some motivated and dynamic people creates an auspicious group dynamics to the effectiveness of collaborative learning. It is therefore important to be able to form groups or to reorganise them on the fly, in such a manner that every group gets a critical mass, sufficient to generate the beneficial effects expected in this type of pedagogy. In DL, roles of group support and observation often rely on two types of actors : the tutor responsible for his/her group and the coordinator, who has a view on every group and who is responsible of the progress of the whole training course.

We show in this paper that during the training period, one can foresee the evolution of the group from very simple indicators (frequency and number of interactions). It becomes possible to design tools to support group management for the coordinator and the tutor. We analyse interactions recorded during a DL experimentation, named *Simuligne*, and we put in perspective the evolution of interaction data and the behaviour of the groups as we observed. From these intra-group interaction data, it would have been possible to predict the progression of these groups.

S.A. Cerri, G. Gouardères, and F. Paraguaçu (Eds.): ITS 2002, LNCS 2363, pp. 841–850, 2002.

This leads us to the conclusion that DL platforms must be endowed with supplementary functionalities permitting to display in real time individual involvement and group behaviour. This new type of environment we call it SIGFAD, a French acronym of '*Soutien des Interactions dans des Groupes de Formation A Distance*'. We introduce a specification of the system, based on the MaSE methodology, a multiagent based approach. MaSE permits, from an initial set of requirements, to develop all steps going from prose specification to an implemented agent system.

2   Theoretical Foundations

The management of user groups in DL is fundamental. There exist many reasons for this. The positioning and integration of learners in the group help us to remedy various phenomena which are largely identified as parts of DL, notably : sociological isolation of the learner, loss of motivation. The group constitutes the immediate materialisation of the accompaniment of the learner (this is also valid for other actors, but since the learner is the main issue of every learning enterprise, we'll often restrict to its unique evocation).

Collaborative learning has a natural context in DL, precisely due to the fact that it supposes social interactions among users that create a sociological setting in a manner preventing isolation and maintaining motivation. Some authors used the expression '*distributed collaborative learning*' to refer to the implementation of collaborative learning in DL [11].

Many researchers highlight the fact that in computer-supported distance learning, it is difficult to evaluate the level of interaction and communication among individuals [13]. It is quite surprising, because all user's actions are recorded in log files. These data can be analysed and information about interaction and communication among individuals becomes available. In fact, if researchers made this remark, it simply means that they had no system to analyse log data and to display intra-group interactions. Developing such systems is our current concern.

In general, one can notice an evolution of research on collaborative learning from how individuals do function in a group to the group itself becoming the unit of analysis [8]. This evolution is supported by human and social theories like Activity Theory (AT) that take into consideration persons interacting with each other, with tools such as computers, symbolic or natural languages [1].

In the context of distributed collaborative learning, the group takes a singular importance. It is the role of tutor to bring and maintain cohesion in the group. The coordinator of the training period has a further more crucial role. He is the one in charge of good progression over the training course and is concerned with the upbringing of various groups. In fact, there should be a minimum quantity of interactions occurring in each group and for this reason, the coordinator may have to reorganise groups, close some or reinforce others. We need a critical mass (in terms of active persons) in every group that can generate sufficient intra-group interactions and productions. Many studies aim at designing systems for supporting group interactions [15], [21].

3 The Study

We designed and managed a DL experimentation of ten weeks. Its purpose was to collect data which would be analysed later and give a better understanding of which factors influenced the progression of a DL course. It concerned forty English-speaking learners split up in four small size basic groups A, G, L, N. We call them basic groups because there were other groups (i.e. the M one which gathered all users). The experimentation named *Simuligne* consisted in participating into a global simulation (frequently used by language teachers in intensive face-to-face classes); every basic group had to participate in a competition to designate the French virtual city which could welcome learners of an English university for their summer school. The challenges for every basic group were then to elaborate the candidature (entirely written in French) for the Open City competition. Every basic group had one tutor and a couple of native persons who served as peer companions for learners. Natives were students of Faculty of Letters of *Université de Franche-Comté* (Master in French as Foreign Language). A coordinator helped tutors planned the activities by discussing with them in a designated group restricted to tutors and natives. The group members didn't know themselves before and the whole course was entirely computer-mediated at a distance. Our course has been implemented on WebCT™.

The course was divided in three stages (not taking into account the preliminarily one where everyone introduced him/herself and discovered technical features of the environment). Each stage comprised several activities. Every interaction and communication data occurring during the course were recorded. Tutors and the coordinator had only access to the basic evaluation tools offered by the WebCT platform, which will be referred to as CEDIL (CEDIL stands for Computer Environment for DIstance Learning) in the follow-up.

Let us now give a conceptual description of a Simuligne activity (the reader interested in a more general view of CEDIL used during Simuligne will find it in [3]).

The activity theory (AT) proposed by Leontiev (quoted in [12]) is the most suitable one to explain the structure of a Simuligne activity because it takes into account the group as the basic unit of analysis and gives a central position to the concept of activity. Fjuk et al. [12] argues that AT gives conceptual accounts of work and development, and the role of artefacts (like the computer) within social contexts. Figure 1 presents a model of a Simuligne activity, adapted from the basic structure of activity of Engelström [9]. An activity has an object/goal and is part of a stage; it means that the course has a number of stages, each one composed of a number of activities. An activity is composed of tasks. A subject uses a tool to achieve a task. A subject can be a member of several groups, but he has a unique status in a given group. The usual concepts of 'division of labour' and 'rules' of AT are implemented in our model using status and tasks. We added the notion of time (not present in Engeström's activity) : an activity possesses an earliest date of beginning and a latest date of end. In other words a subject, with a given status in a group, uses tools (each one linked to a task) for achieving an object of an activity during a length of time.

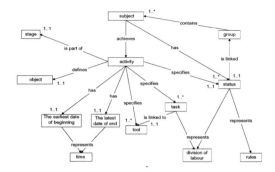

Fig. 1. Conceptual model of a Simuligne activity

The general diagram of CEDIL is shown in figure 2. Every user (login + password) is a member of a course (which we used as group) and have a permanent status in the group. CEDIL offers four user profiles: learner, administrator, designer and pedagogic assistant, giving different rights and tools to each of them. We had to implement each Simuligne status (learner, coordinator, tutor, native) as a CEDIL user profile. We had three status in a basic group: learner implemented as learner CEDIL profile, native also implemented as CEDIL learner profile, tutor implemented as CEDIL designer profile. The coordinator was implemented as CEDIL administrator profile but could also connect herself in every basic group as a silent learner in order to observe what happened in the group. We should also notice the absence of reference to the community (group) in CEDIL; we had to implement our Simuligne groups as CEDIL courses as palliative.

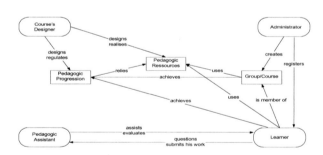

Fig. 2. The General Diagram of CEDIL

During Simuligne, which took place from the 30th of April to the 07th of July 2001, we observed a decrease of activities in the group L to the point that we had close it on May 30. The two remaining active learners were transferred to another group.

We present figures of interaction accumulated weekly in the first four weeks of Simuligne. Tables 1 and 2 respectively present the accrued percentages of the number of times a member accessed his/her group and the duration of his/her online connection. These data give an estimation of the level of activity of the group, because individual activity happened off-line (and are not measured here). From the first week, group L had a relatively low level of activity, especially in terms of connection time.

Table 1. Accrued percentages of number of entries in CEDIL groups. Week 1 is the first week of stage E1, actual beginning of the simulation, after the completion of the preliminary stage E0.

Basic groups	Week1	Week1+2	Week1+2+3	Week1+2+3+4
A	35,39%	31,21%	30,47%	29,73%
G	22,17%	27,34%	29,01%	30,15%
L	21,75%	20,95%	20,16%	19,44%
N	20,68%	20,50%	20,36%	20,68%
Total	100,00%	100,00%	100,00%	100,00%

Table 2. Accrued percentages of connection time per basic group

Basic groups	Week1	Week1+2	Week1+2+3	Week1+2+3+4
A	42,03%	34,99%	33,47%	32,31%
G	18,09%	23,16%	23,93%	25,55%
L	17,94%	17,54%	17,72%	17,27%
N	21,93%	24,31%	24,88%	24,87%
Total	100,00%	100,00%	100,00%	100,00%

Tables 3 and 4 respectively present the accrued percentages of number of intra-group read mails and intra-group posted mails. In CEDIL, groups are insulated in the sense that mails are only available within the group: a user can send/receive mails only to/from a member of his group. This means that the number of mails posted or read partly denotes the vitality of the group. Group L appears again as having a lower level of activity (particularly noticeable when looking at posted mail). On the contrary, group G progressively appears as the most active one whichever table one looks at.

Tables 5 and 6 present the accrued percentages of number of messages read and posted in the forums respectively. Due to the conception of Simuligne, this is probably the most significant indicator of the level of activities in a group. We should keep in mind that during the period covered by our study (30th April to 30th May), the forum was certainly the tool the most frequently used. Eight forums were opened in every basic group during the period covered by our study. It is not therefore surprising that the group L that died out on May 30 presents some extremely low forum-oriented interaction rates.

The data contained in the previous tables were extracted from the HTTP server log file. This file registers every user's action in a different line containing information like the IP address of the user, his CEDIL login name, the date and the type of action, the size of the file. These data are not directly available in the log files. We extracted

Table 3. Accrued percentages of number of intra-group read mails

Basic groups	Week1	Week1+2	Week1+2+3	Week1+2+3+4
A	29,15%	23,61%	21,81%	20,92%
G	13,70%	20,69%	25,65%	31,15%
L	19,24%	19,88%	18,84%	17,40%
N	37,90%	35,82%	33,70%	30,53%
Total	100,00%	100,00%	100,00%	100,00%

Table 4. Accrued percentages of number of intra-group posted mails

Basic groups	Week1	Week1+2	Week1+2+3	Week1+2+3+4
A	27,62%	24,09%	22,88%	22,24%
G	20,95%	25,41%	29,01%	35,12%
L	17,14%	15,51%	15,09%	14,05%
N	34,29%	34,98%	33,02%	28,60%
Total	100,00%	100,00%	100,00%	100,00%

Table 5. Accrued percentages of number of read messages in forums

Basic groups	Week1	Week1+2	Week1+2+3	Week1+2+3+4
A	50,65%	42,39%	40,27%	38,16%
G	25,26%	28,27%	26,62%	26,26%
L	12,66%	13,55%	13,69%	13,94%
N	11,43%	15,79%	19,43%	21,64%
Total	100,00%	100,00%	100,00%	100,00%

Table 6. Accrued percentages of number of posted messages in forums

Basic groups	Week1	Week1+2	Week1+2+3	Week1+2+3+4
A	57,75%	50,26%	49,46%	47,71%
G	19,01%	23,28%	20,43%	19,82%
L	8,45%	9,26%	9,32%	9,45%
N	14,79%	17,20%	20,79%	23,02%
Total	100,00%	100,00%	100,00%	100,00%

the data from raw information contained in log files, saved them in databases and built them from appropriate SQL queries. These manipulations are essential, and current statistical analysis tools of HTTP logs can not provide such interaction data.

Furthermore, one needs to go inside several CEDIL files in order to build group interaction data.

We present in the next table, the durations of connection to instruction pages from the beginning of the session to the 30th of May. The durations are not presented weekly as the other data but also reveal that group L paid few attention to instructions. The durations were calculated from data recorded in specific files of CEDIL.

Table 7. Connection times to instruction pages

	Number of access	Duration (hh mm ss)	Duration (in seconds)	Percentage
A	626	103h06m03s	371 163	32,26%
G	364	99h18m26s	357 506	31,08%
L	379	56h22m43s	202 963	17,64%
N	390	60h46m40s	218 800	19,02%
Total	1759		1150432	100,00%

Up till now, we can conclude that information collected in log files can provide, after judicious computer operations, interaction data to the users in such manner that they can know daily and even in real time the situation of the group and predict their evolution. For conciseness reasons, we presented in the previous tables weekly data aggregates, but this could be also done per day and even in smaller time units as an hour. We would want to highlight the fact that if some authors argue that "*in computer-supported distance learning classes, it is often difficult to know to what extent individuals are interacting and how much they communicate with other class members*" [13], it simply denotes the absence of requisite functionalities in DL platforms. The existing platforms need to be coupled to systems that collect interaction information in appropriate places, computerize them and display judicious data on the state and the durability of the groups.

4 SIGFAD, a Multiagent System to Assist Users Involved in DL

In section 3, we reported a computer-mediated DL experimentation. In this training course, we had four basic groups and one of them disappeared. In fact, we closed this group because we noted its very weak level of activity and because the minimum number of active persons expected to play a role in the simulation was not attained. The remaining two learners were "sent" to another group. We took this decision (closing the group and transferring learners) after examining the daily journal of the coordinator and the information collected from different log and tracking-actions and processed by simple programs. The kind of information displayed in the previous tables were not accessible and come from a post processing.

We argue that existing DL platforms must be provided with automatic tools that will make it possible for one to know the state of a group, the behaviour of users and predict in real time the evolution of the DL training course. The objective of showing different types of interaction data as done in the previous section is to demonstrate that judicious indicators can be built from data recorded in different files. Computer scientists are challenged to build these automatic indicators and to provide them to users in such a manner that offers a straightforward and immediate usage.

The agent paradigm is a good solution to this challenge. This paradigm is suitable to the metaphor of *personal and intelligent assistant* [16]. Good reviews of the concepts of agent and multiagent systems can be found in [2], [10], [19]. We used the notion of agent to specify a multiagent system, named SIGFAD, which purpose is to provide assistance to users in DL. This section presents the beginning of its specification.

When designing and specifying SIGFAD, we used Multiagent Systems Engineering (MaSE), a methodology for developing heterogeneous multiagent systems. MaSE uses a number of graphically based models to describe system goals, behaviours, agent types and agent communication interfaces. MaSE is also associated with a tool, agentTool, which supports the methodology. For a detailed review of MaSE and the associated agentTool environment, see [5], [6], [22].

The first task when designing agent and multiagent systems is to identify goals and sub-goals. In MaSE, this is made during the Capturing Goals step. This step consists of two sub-steps: identifying goals and structuring them in a Goal Hierarchy Diagram. The Goal Hierarchy Diagram of SIGFAD is shown in figure 3.

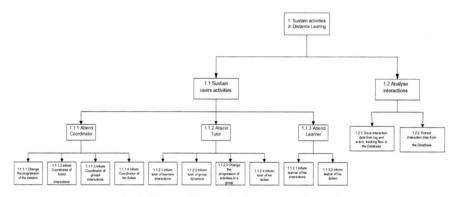

Fig. 3. The Goal Hierarchy Diagram of SIGFAD

At this state of our conception, the main objectives of SIGFAD concern the maintenance tasks of the groups. Even though in the previous sections we insisted on coordinator's and tutors' roles, it is obvious that learner's actions (actions of any group member in general) also influence the durability of the group. The goals of SIGFAD are then threefold, with regards to coordinator, tutors and learners. The coordinator deals with the adjustment of activities (suspend some activities, report others, lengthen or modify time limits). This is done by evaluating tutors activities and group performances. He must also appreciate his own participation to the environment. A tutor has to identify learners' failures in order to dispense weaker learners of certain tasks; he has to appreciate the state of his group, to predict its durability and also to display his own participation. Learners need to know their own participation and what activities have to be achieved in a given period. In SIGFAD a goal called 'analyse interactions' is defined. This goal consists of having access to tracking-actions pages of CEDIL and HTTP server log files, extracting interaction data and saving them in a database, analyse automatically interaction data and display indicators related to the progression and the state of individuals and learning groups.

5 Future Work and Conclusion

Beyond the data analysis presented here, it is necessary to note that the construction of judicious indicators requires to elaborate mathematical models which from the interaction data available, such as those shown in the previous section, will automatically compute variables reflecting the state and the progression of committed groups. We investigate at the moment the analysis social networks which can be usefully applied in DL to build parameters related to the cohesion of the group or the centrality of a given member of the group [18]. Up to now, we exhibited the objectives of SIGFAD. The next stage of our work will consist in specifying our system entirely by achieving all steps of MaSE. These steps include the description of system behaviours, agent types and agent communication interfaces.

The data analysis presented in this paper is certainly partial and we don't argue that agent systems based only on counting messages can support actors in DL. This analysis showed however that automatic tools for displaying users' participation miss in the existing DL platforms. These automatic tools don't exist actually and can't be replaced by current commercial analysis tools of web logs. In order to display on the fly this information, we need tools which will help appreciate the state of the groups, predict their evolution, reorganise them if necessary. These tools, if available, could also permit the appreciation of the quantity and the quality of intra-group interactions and therefore take judicious actions to encourage them. Based on the agent paradigm, we proposed these required functionalities as a multiagent system, named SIGFAD. We presented its Goal Hierarchy Diagram. It is the main output of the Capturing Goal, first step of MaSE, a methodology for designing heterogeneous multiagent systems.

Acknowledgment. Simuligne was born in a trans-disciplinary research project named ICOGAD, which partners are: the department of Language Learning at The Open University, UK, the Computer Science Laboratory of the Université de Franche-Comté, and the Psychology Laboratory of Université de Nancy 2, France. Special thanks to the French Minister of Research (MRT) and its cognitive science programme (Programme Cognitique 2000) which supports the ICOGAD project.

References

1. Baker, M.,. "The roles of models in Artificial Intelligence and Education research : a prospective view". *International Journal of Artificial Intelligence in Education*, 11. (2000) 122-143
2. Bradshaw, J. M. "An Introduction to Software Agents". In *Software Agents*. Ed. J.M. Bradshaw. Menlo Park, Calif. : AAAI Press (1997)

3. Chanier, T. "Créer des communautés d'apprentissage à distance". *Les dossiers de l'Ingénierie Educative, no 36 sur "Les communautés en ligne", octobre.* Centre National de Documentation Pédagogique(CNDP) : Montrouge (2001) 56-59.
4. Charlier, B., Daele, A., Cheffert, J-L., Peeters, R., Lusalusa, S. "Learning collaboratively in a virtual campus : teachers' experiences". ISATT 99. Dublin (1999)
5. Deloach, S., A. "Analysis and Design using MaSE and agentTool". *The 12th Midwest Artificial Intelligence and Cognitive Science Conference* (2001)
6. Deloach, S. A., Wood, M. F., Sparkman, C. H. "Multiagent Systems Engineering". *International Journal on Software Engineering and Knowledge Engineering. World Scientific Publishers. Vol. 11 n° 3* (2001) 231-258.
7. Dillenbourg, P. "What Do You Mean By "Collaborative Learning"". In P. Dillenbourg (Ed.) *Collaborative Learning : Cognitive and Computationnal Approaches.* Amsterdam : Pergamon/Elsevier Science (1999) 1-19.
8. Dillenbourg, P., Baker, M., Blaye, A., O'Malley, C. "The evolution of research on collaborative learning". In E. Spada & P. Reiman (Eds*) Learning in Humans and Machine: Towards an interdisciplinary learning science.* Oxford. Elsevier (1996) 189-211
9. Engelström, Y. *Learning by expanding. An activity-theoretical approach to developmental research.* Orienta-Konsultit Oy, Helsinki (1987)
10. Ferber, J., *Les systèmes multi-agents : vers une intelligence collective.* Intereditions (1997)
11. Fjük, A. *Computer Support for Distributed Collaborative Learning. Exploring a Complex Problem Area.* Dr. Scient. Thesis5. Department of Informatics. University of Oslo (1998)
12. Fjük, A., Nurminen, M. I., Smordal, O. "Taking Articulation Work Seriously – an Activity Theoretical Approach". *TUCS Technical Report N° 120.* 16 p. (1997)
13. Haythornthwaite, C. "Networks of Information Sharing among Computer-Supported Distance Learners". *Proceedings of the Third International Conference on Computer-Supported Collaborative Learning* (1999) 218-222.
14. Jermann, P., Soller, A., Muehlenbrock, M. "From Mirroring to Guiding : A Review of State of the Art Technology for Supporting Collaborative Learning". *Proceedings of the First European Conference on Computer-Supported Collaborative Learning* (2001)
15. Kusunoki, F., Sugimoto, M., Hashizume, H. "A System for Supporting Group Learning that Enhances Interactions". *Proceedings of the Third International Conference on Computer-Supported Collaborative Learning* (1999) 323-327.
16. Maes, P. "Agents that Reduce Work and Information Overload". In *Software Agents*, ed. J.M. Bradshaw. Menlo Park, Californie, AAAI Press (1997)
17. Nurmela, K., Lehtinen, E., Palonen, T. "Evaluating CSCL Log Files by Social Network Analysis". *Proceedings of the Third International Conference on Computer-Supported Collaborative Learning* (1999) 434-442.
18. Reffay, C., Chanier, T. "Social Network Analysis used for modelling collaboration in distance learning groups" (2002) This volume.
19. Weiss, G., Dillenbourg, P. "What is 'multi' in multi-agent learning". In P. Dillenbourg (Ed.) *Collaborative Learning : Cognitive and Computationnal Approaches.* Amsterdam : Pergamon/Elsevier Science (1999)
20. Wertsch, J.V.. "A socio-cultural approach to socially shared cognition". In Resnick, L., Levine, J., Teasley, S. (Eds). *Perspectives on Socially Shared Cognition.* Hyattsville, MD: American Psychological Association (1991) 85-100
21. Whatley, J., Staniford, G., Beer, M., Scown, P. "Intelligent Agents to Support Students Working in Group Online". *Journal of Interactive Learning Research.* vol. 10, N° 3/4. AACE, Charlottesville (1999)
22. Wood, M. F., Deloach, S. A. "An overview of the Multiagents Systems Engineering Methodology". *Proceedings of the First International Workshop on Agent-Oriented Software Engineering.* Ciancarini P., Wooldridge, M. (Eds). Lectures Notes in Computer Science, Vol. 1957. Springer Verlag. Berlin (2000)
23. Wooldridge, M. "Intelligent Agents". In G. Weiss (Ed). *Multiagent Systems*, The MIT Press. (1999)

Directing Development Effort with Simulated Students

Joseph E. Beck

Robotics Institute
Carnegie Mellon University
Pittsburgh, PA. U.S.A.
joseph.beck@cmu.edu

Abstract. Our goal is to find a methodology for directing development effort in an intelligent tutoring system (ITS). Given that ITS have several AI reasoning components, as well as content to present, evaluating them is a challenging task. Due to these difficulties, few evaluation studies to measure the impact of individual components have been performed. Our architecture evaluates the efficacy of each component of an ITS and considers the impact of a particular teaching goal when determining whether a particular component needs improving. For our AnimalWatch tutor, we found that for certain goals the tutor itself, rather than its reasoning components, needed improvement. We have found that it is necessary to know what the system's teaching goals are before deciding which component is the limiting factor on performance.

1 Introduction and Motivation

An intelligent tutoring system (ITS) is a complex piece of software. In addition to using a student model (SM) to interpret the student's actions and a pedagogical module to selecting teaching decisions, there is also the tutor itself. ITS designers must be concerned with how hints actually appear on the screen, the pedagogical principles used, what types of problems and feedback are available, etc.

It is not surprising that little work has been done at assessing which components of the system work and which do not. The work by Shute [6] at testing the efficacy of her tutor's pedagogical decisions is one of the rare examples of this type of evaluation. Given that this research showed the existing pedagogical module might not have been helpful, there is considerable potential gain from using this type of evaluation.

Unfortunately, there are two factors working against this approach. First, human evaluation studies are expensive. Even if subjects aren't paid, getting an ITS ready for "prime time," installing it in the lab to be tested, and diagnosing why it doesn't work on their computers costs a large amount of time. Second, there is the problem of combinatorics: studying whether the pedagogical module is helpful or not gives 2 experimental conditions. If one is interested in the SM's effectiveness that gives 4 conditions. If there are 3 different types of hints, and you are curious which one works best... Finding sufficient subjects for all of these conditions can be difficult.

This difficulty is unfortunate, as examining each component's impact not only tells us how well our past efforts worked, but it also informs us where we should direct our future efforts. If an evaluation shows that improving the SM would greatly enhance performance, it might not be sensible to spend effort on improving the ITS's hints.

S.A. Cerri, G. Gouardères, and F. Paraguaçu (Eds.): ITS 2002, LNCS 2363, pp. 851–860, 2002.

Therefore, our goal is to find a low-cost way to assess the performance of each component of an ITS. If we can determine which components are not performing as well as they should be, we will have a method for directing development efforts in an ITS. Our approach for this is to use simulations of actual students [7] We conduct this research in the context of the AnimalWatch [1] arithmetic tutor.

2 Prior Use of Simulated Students

VanLehn et al. [7] performed some of the first work with simulated students, or *simulees*. These simulees were constructed via a detailed cognitive task analysis of how students solve problems. This work emphasized constructing a runnable model of student behavior and using it to test systems. The testing was primarily to make sure the tutor's behavior was not overtly incorrect. For example, the simulees were able to detect that some words were used and only defined in later lessons. This idea of using such "fake" data for evaluating a tutoring system is appealing.

Other work in using simulated students for ITS design was done by Mertz [4]. This work constructed a learning agent based on the Soar architecture [5]. The problems and instructions were recoded so as to be understandable by the Soar agent, and then the simulated learner would attempt to solve the task. The Soar agent screened an intelligent tutor for weaknesses in its design. Since Soar learns from trial to trial, sub procedures that are useful will be reused in later exercises. This learning allows the tutor designer to consider ordering of exercises, or even how to best place the components for solving a particular exercise.

However, this process is time intensive: every piece of textual instruction and every problem situation within the tutor must be converted into a representation understandable by Soar. Furthermore, to determine if the ITS's lessons are well constructed, it is necessary to examine the production rules learned by the Soar-agent.

This technique uncovered several potential flaws in the tutor's design: missequenced problems, needless divergence from standards used in other problems, and inefficient problem solving procedures. This list of detected problems is interesting and impressive. Although expensive to construct, it is not clear that an automatic detection scheme that did not involve fine-grained cognitive modeling would be capable of doing this.

A drawback of such schemes is that they can be difficult to construct and require expert knowledge. Furthermore, if the same cognitive modeling approach is used to design and to test the system, there is a problem with circular reasoning.

3 Our Architecture

Although this paper explores using ADVISOR as an evaluation tool, ADVISOR's goal is to automate decision-making in an ITS. ADVISOR learns how students behave by observing a population of users and, with these data, generates a set of teaching strategies that optimize instruction. The teaching strategies adjust the tutor's behavior to try to meet a configurable teaching goal. Currently, teaching goals are specified on a per problem basis. So goals such as "learn the curriculum quickly" are not permitted. However, goals such as "Present problems so that the student makes one mistake per problem, limit the amount of help the tutor gives, and try not to have it take too much or too little time," *are* permitted. Of course, it is necessary to quantify exactly how important each restriction is, how much time is "too little," etc.

To build ADVISOR, we used a layered ML architecture. This design allowed each component to be considered and optimized independently of other aspects of the project. One layer of learning is concerned with describing student behavior in different contexts. The other layer determines how to map this description of the student's behavior onto a correct teaching action, see Fig. 1.

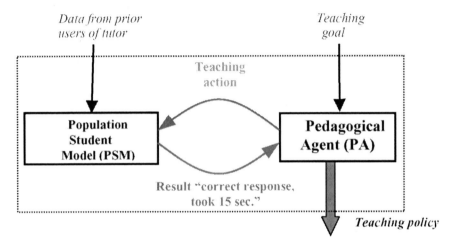

Fig. 1. ADVISOR architecture

3.1   The Population Student Model

The population student model (PSM) is responsible for predicting how the student will react in given situation. The PSM is constructed by data mining logs of previous users of the tutor. The current PSM used 10,000 interactions with students. Note that an "interaction" refers to the student submitting a response to the tutor, not to the number of actual users. In this case, 100 students used the tutor for 3 to 5 hours.

When we analyzed the interactions between students and the AnimalWatch tutor, we had 48 features to describe the current situation [2], and each interaction was cast in terms of those features. Given a feature vector to describe the current situation, and labeled training instances, it is straightforward to use a supervised machine learning technique to construct a model that maps the set of descriptive features to how the student will behave. Specifically, the PSM takes the set of features and predicts:

1.   How long the student will take to respond
2.   Whether the student's response will be correct

This PSM was constructed using linear regression [2]. However, the specific technique used is not important for this discussion.

Two important points are that the PSM makes different predictions for different students, and it is capable of acting as a simulee. Since the PSM makes its predictions based on features that describe (among other things) the student using the tutor, it will give different predictions for different students. So, although it is derived from data from a population, it is not a "stereotype" approach to student modeling. The PSM can take an arbitrary state and predict how the student will behave. For example, when queried about how the student will perform in state S, the PSM would compute:

1. Probability of correct response, and the time the student required.
2. Probability of an incorrect response, and the time the student required.

The two probabilities will sum up to 1.0, but the predicted times differ.

3.2   The Pedagogical Agent

The Pedagogical Agent's (PA) job is to interact with the PSM, and to use it to compute how it should teach to meet the specified teaching goal. By experimenting with the PSM, the PA is able to determine a policy (i.e. strategy) to meet the goal. The PA makes the same teaching decisions that the AnimalWatch tutor does:

- The topic on which the student will work (e.g. subtract whole numbers)
- The problem on which the student will work (e.g. 6-4 Vs. 1003-847)
- What feedback to provide to the student in event he makes a mistake

Since the PA examines the effects of teaching actions on this simulation of a student, it is not necessary to experiment with actual students to determine how to teach them. This architecture was tested in a classroom and found to work [3].

Finally, we have a simulation of an ITS, specifically the AnimalWatch mathematics tutor (ADVISOR is not specific to a particular ITS). This simulation determines which teaching actions are available to the PA at each point.

Although several simulations are required for ADVISOR, building each of them is not difficult. The hardest is a simulation of the student. We have chosen to build a simulation of the student (the PSM) that works at a coarse grain size by only predicting time and correctness of the student response. This coarseness limits the scope of the current ADVISOR architecture, but, by avoiding fine-grained details, model construction cost is lower and the simulation is more computationally tractable.

The original purpose of ADVISOR was to learn an optimal teaching policy. However, its component architecture and its ability to reason without using additional human subjects, make it ideal for examining the performance of each part of an ITS.

4   Goals

The goal of this research is to use the ADVISOR architecture to determine how to direct engineering effort on an ITS. This work is being done in the context of the AnimalWatch tutoring system, which is designed to teach arithmetic.

To evaluate ADVISOR, we examine how well it can perform in what we call the *target time* task. For this task, ADVISOR must get students through a problem in a specific amount of time. If ADVISOR takes the specified amount of time it receives a reward of 1.0, but is penalized linearly for taking a longer or shorter amount of time. For example, for a penalty of 0.025 per second and a goal of 45 seconds, if a student finished a problem in 38 seconds, ADVISOR would receive a reward of 1.0 - (45-38) * 0.025 = 0.825. ADVISOR's task is to get as large a reward as possible.

An important point to note is that the objective of a high target time is not to make the student's life difficult or to mislead him. Rather, it is a method for controlling problem difficulty. A teacher interested in basic skills practice (e.g. math fact retrieval) could set a goal of 5 seconds as a target time, a teacher interested in making students think about each problem could assign a goal of 45 seconds.

For a goal of 45 seconds, ADVISOR cannot give a very simple problem to the student since he would solve it very quickly (e.g. repeatedly presenting 1+1 would not achieve a high reward). With respect to feedback, if a student provides an incorrect response after 5 seconds, ADVISOR can provide non-specific help such as "try again." If a student enters an incorrect response after 40 seconds, the tutor will have to provide effective help in order to avoid being penalized. So ADVISOR's strategy will have to be dynamic based on how the student is progressing through the problem.

It is possible to argue that mistakes rather than time are a better measure of student performance. There is merit to this argument, but neither metric does a good job at telling the entire story. Observing sixth-graders using the AnimalWatch tutor shows several cases of a student getting a problem such as "6+7" and answering it immediately. Other students stop, put up six fingers, and then count with their fingers to reach the final total. Stating that both of these students made no mistakes glosses over tremendous differences in how challenged they were by this problem.

There is nothing specific about the ADVISOR architecture requiring it to optimize time. We have run experiments where ADVSOR had to minimize the amount of help students received, the number of mistakes they made, while also being heavily penalized for providing problems the students can solve without error. Of course, this goal is somewhat contradictory, and all facets cannot be simultaneously optimized, but ADVISOR did mange to find a solution that was somewhat surprising.

We tested ADVISOR with 120 different target times (from 1 second up to 120 seconds). For these tests we used a variety of simulated students. At the start of each simulation run a student was generated randomly according to the distribution of characteristics in the population we used to train the PSM (e.g. proficiency at certain topics, score on Piaget test of development). Fig. 2 shows performance on this task. For example, when given a target time goal of 36 seconds, ADVISOR received an average reward of 0.6 (averaged across 500 runs of the simulation). This set of simulation runs was done with the standard PSM, but a fairly weak PA. Performance starts out fairly low (0.45), for time goals of 25 seconds it reaches its maximum (0.80), and performance smoothly falls off from there.

One question is why doesn't ADVISOR achieve a performance of 1.0 for all time goals? If it has a simulation of the student to work with, a simulation of the tutor, and can look ahead to see longer term effects, what is holding it back? These restrictions are precisely the set of issues that are (or should be) considered when evaluating an ITS: the accuracy of the SM, the quality of the pedagogical model's decisions, and the quality of the actual tutorial interventions. Although hard to evaluate in the general case, considering the target time task and seeing performance graphically makes this clearer. What are the limiting factors of ADVISOR's performance?

1. *Weakness in the Pedagogical Agent.* The PA is not capable of reasoning perfectly with the information provided by the PSM. To search far enough ahead to consider all of the possibilities is not possible.

2. *Inaccuracy of the Population Student Model.* The PSM is not a perfect model of students. When the PA queries it to determine the effect of a teaching action, the PSM returns two possibilities, each with an associated probability. The first is the state resulting from an incorrect response; the second is the possibility the student will be correct. Since the PA is uncertain about the effects of its actions, this limits possible performance.

3. *Lack of flexibility of AnimalWatch tutor.* AnimalWatch has a broad, but limited, selection of hints and problem types. Perhaps in some situations, a certain kind of hint would be ideal but does not exist?

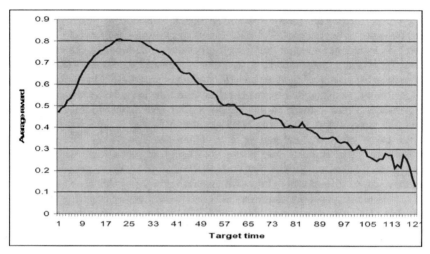

Fig. 2. ADVISOR's performance

All of these act to limit ADVISOR's performance. The questions we must ask is *when* are each of these the limiting factor, and *how much* can be gained by improving each component. We now construct a set of experiments to determine this.

5   Methodology and Experiments

To determine what constrains ADVISOR's performance, we vary the performance of the PA and PSM. Specifically, we attempt to construct an "optimal" version of each.

5.1   Optimizing the PA

A PA in an actual ITS must reason quickly. We set an upper limit of 0.25 seconds per decision as acceptable performance, since students are often impatient. With this limit, the PA cannot search as deeply to estimate the future repercussions of the PA's decision. We call a PA that can reason in less than 0.25 seconds per decision an "efficient" PA. Fig. 2 is from a PA of this type.

How well could a PA perform that had unlimited time to reason? Obviously, no ITS will ever have that much time, but removing the time constraint lets us explore the *maximum* impact of making the tutor's reasoning more efficient.We simulate this by allowing the PA to search many moves ahead and use either a heuristic function or rollouts to evaluate the leaf nodes. For use in an actual tutor, this does not give acceptable response times. Even in simulation runs, this is not practical.

Fig. 3 shows this performance. Efforts at improving the PA can move the curve representing efficient performance closer optimal performance. Possible ways to do this include making the search more efficient by using pruning techniques, or using machine learning to select actions. *However this is done, the maximum payoff for the design and engineering effort is the curve marked "Perfect PA."*

Note that for most time range, performance is still not close to 1.0. This indicates that there are other weaknesses in ADVISOR's reasoning.

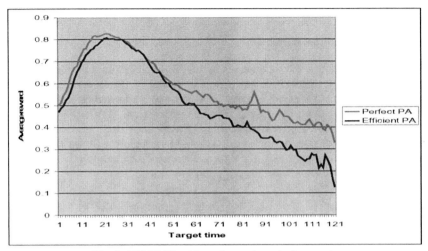

Fig. 3. ADVISOR with perfect pedagogical reasoning

5.2 Optimizing the PSM

How can we improve the performance of the optimal PA that is shown in Fig. 3? One method is to simulate how ADVISOR would perform given a perfect model of the student. Obviously, we don't have such a model. However, we can pretend we do by making the PSM's predictions deterministic. When the PA considers an action, it queries the PSM and receives two possible outcomes for whether the student will give the correct response or not. When the PA is done considering possible actions, and performs one of them, it informs the PSM of this fact. At this point, the PSM tells the PA which of the two outcomes actually occurs. Thus, the PA can plan ahead with some uncertainty, but is forced to accept an unlucky outcome.

We can simulate a "perfect" PSM by determining ahead of time which of the two events will occur. When the PA queries the PSM for possible outcomes, the PSM immediately decides which of the two will occur. It then sets the probability of that outcome to 1.0 and the probability of the other outcome to 0. This knowledge of how the student will behave allows the PA to plan perfectly.

Obviously this model is only perfect in the context of the simulation, so isn't applicable for a deployed tutor. However, it lets us examine the effect of having a perfect SM. Analyzing performance of a perfect SM gives us insight into the maximum gains we can get from improving student modeling through techniques such as eye tracking, finding a better set of features to provide to the PSM, etc.

Fig. 4 shows ADVISOR's performance with a perfect PSM. The top curve refers to a version of ADVISOR with an optimal PA and a perfect PSM. The bottom curve is the performance with an optimal PA with the standard PSM (the same as the top curve from Fig. 3). For time goals of less than 15 seconds there is little gain from improving the PSM. However, for time goals greater than 20 seconds there is a large difference in performance, so spending effort on the PSM makes sense *in this context*.

5.3   Impact of AnimalWatch

We have examined how the weaknesses in the PSM and PA limit performance. In the top curve of Fig. 4, ADVISOR has a perfect model of the student, and can search enough interactions ahead to achieve near-optimal performance with this model. Since this removes two of the three listed constraints on ADVISOR's performance, we must consider the fact that the AnimalWatch tutor itself is a constraint. Any remaining deficiencies in performance (i.e. anything below 1.0) are the fault of the tutor itself. For low target times, the tutor is the major constraint on performance. For high target times the tutor is not the main limiting factor.

6   Results

We have examined how weaknesses in the PSM (i.e. the student model in a typical ITS), the PA (i.e. the pedagogical module), and AnimalWatch (a proxy for a generic ITS) limit performance. What can we do with this knowledge?

Fig. 5 shows graphically the potential gains from improving each component of the system. The area between the bottom two curves represents the possible gains from improving the pedagogical agent. The area between the middle and top curves represents possible gain from improving the SM. The area above the top curve is how much can be gained by making the AnimalWatch tutor more flexible.

The first item to notice is that work at improving the system *must be in the context of a particular goal*. If the goal is to build a system where students practice basic math fact retrieval (e.g. a target time of 5 seconds per problem), spending effort at improving the system's ability to reason about the student and predict how he will act (i.e. the PSM or student model) is a waste of time. Similarly, improving the tutor's ability to select teaching actions (i.e. the PA or pedagogical module) is probably not productive. The best way to achieve gains is to broaden the scope of the AnimalWatch tutor; the lack of performance is not the fault of the AI. This fits with our observations of the tutor. AnimalWatch was designed to present students with somewhat lengthy word problems. For target times of 5 seconds, questions such as "What is 5-3?" would be more appropriate, and did not exist in our system.

For target times of 15 seconds or greater, there is a large gain for improving performance of the PSM. Thus, if researchers (or the teachers) are interested in having students solve problems of this type, continuing research on student modeling for this task is warranted. Target times must be around 60 seconds before finding methods to improve the tutor's pedagogical reasoning become profitable.

Thus, before tinkering with a system or performing research to improve it, it is necessary to determine the goals for the system. If the system will be presenting problems that require students to spend more than 60 seconds on the problem, there is not much point is finding ways to improve the PA. Although we have found the PSM might be hard to improve, there is a large potential gain for most target times.

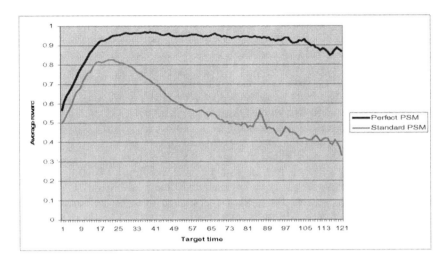

Fig. 4. ADVISOR with a perfect student model

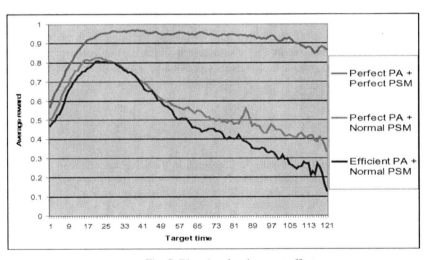

Fig. 5. Directing development effort

7 Conclusions and Future Work

Although ADVISOR was designed to learn how to teach students, we have had success at applying it to answering questions about how to direct development efforts.

By first enumerating constraints on performance, and then simulating their removal, it is possible to experimentally determine effects of improving various part of the tutor.

This technique permits designers to not conduct expensive ablation studies. Although such studies are known to be useful, the relative lack of them indicates a lack of eagerness to undertake an expensive (and possibly fruitless!) evaluation.

Therefore, by computationally modeling student performance and simulating a tutoring system, we can build systems whose teaching policies can be easily altered. This adaptability is a benefit to end users of the tutor. But we can also adjust the system's performance in the lab to direct future design work.

Two large outstanding issues are the grain-size of the PSM's reasoning and the PA's teaching goals. The PSM predicts student actions at a gross level, and does not attempt to reason at a cognitive level. This restricts the ADVISOR architecture to not being able to reason bout why a student might be confused.

Currently, teaching goals are on a per-problem basis. In principle, it is possible to construct a PA that reasons about the curriculum, but that would require many interactions with the PSM to predict that far into the future. This search is not computationally tractable or likely to be accurate. One possibility is to construct a higher level agent responsible for guiding the student through the curriculum, and have this agent interact with a different, more coarse-grained, PSM. Both of these are hard problems, but the ADVISOR architecture is not incapable of this scaling.

We have presented the results of using ADVISOR to perform an ablative evaluation of the AnimalWatch tutor. Prior research has shown the potential of simulating students. The results presented suggest that simulating other components of an ITS has considerable power for economically addressing a variety of issues.

Acknowledgements. This work has been funded from the National Science Foundation program HRD 9714757. Any opinions, findings, and conclusions or recommendations expressed in this material are those of the authors and do not necessarily reflect the views of the National Science Foundation. Beverly Woolf, Carole Beal, Ivon Arroyo, Rachel Wing, and David Marshall were instrumental in creating and evaluating AnimalWatch.

References

1. Arroyo, I.. Learning Algebra with the Computer. In *Workshop on "Learning Algebra with the Computer" at the Fifth International Conference on Intelligent Tutoring Systems*. 2000
2. Beck, J.E. and Woolf, B.P.. High-level Student Modeling with Machine Learning. In *Fifth International Conference on Intelligent Tutoring Systems*. p. 584-593. 2000
3. Beck, J.E., Woolf, B.P. and Beal, C.R.. ADVISOR: A machine learning architecture for intelligent tutor construction. In *Seventeenth National Conference on Artificial Intelligence*. p. 552-557. 2000
4. Mertz, J.S., Using a Simulated Student for Instructional Design. *Artificial Intelligence in Education*, 1997. **8**: p. 116-141.
5. Newell, A., *Unified Theories of Cognition*. 1990, Cambridge, Massachusetts: Harvard Universtiy Press.
6. Shute, V.. SMART Evaluation: Cognitive Diagnosis, Mastery Learning and Remediation. In *Artificial Intelligence in Education*. p. 123-130. 1995
7. VanLehn, K., Ohlsson, S. and Nason, R., Applications of Simulated Students: An Exploration. *Journal of Artificial Intelligence in Education*, 1994. **5**(2).

An Evaluation of Intelligent Learning Environment for Problem Posing

Akira Nakano, Tsukasa Hirashima, and Akira Takeuchi

Kyushu Institute of Technology
Department of Artificial Intelligence
680-4 Kawazu, Iizuka 820-8502, Japan `nakano@minnie.ai.kyutech.ac.jp`

Abstract. In this paper, we describe an Intelligent Learning Environment which realizes the learning by problem posing. In the learning by problem posing, a learner poses problems through the interface provided by the ILE. The ILE has a function to diagnose the problems posed by the learner. By using the results of the diagnosis, the ILE helps the learner to correct wrong problems, or leads her/him in the next step of problem posing. We have developed the ILE. In this paper, we also report an experimental evaluation in an elementary school. By using the result of the experiment, we examined (1) usability of the ILE and (2) effectiveness of the ILE. In the ILE, the interface was implemented in Java, and the diagnosis module was implemented in Prolog. The current environment deals with simple arithmetical word problems solved by an addition or a subtraction.

1 Introduction

Several researchers about problem posing of arithmetical word problems suggested that problem posing is important to learn arithmetic. For example there are task analysis of problem posing [1], [2], examination of learning effects of problem posing [3], and case studies in classroom [4], [5]. Besides, "the Curriculum and Evaluation Standards for School Mathematics (in USA,1989)", and "Professional Standards for Teaching mathematics (in USA,1991)" also indicated that it was important for learners to experience to pose problems. However, despite the importance of problem posing, it is not popular as a learning method in reality. In Learning by Problem Posing, in order to judge whether the problem is correct or not, a teacher has to examine each problem which learners posed. Therefore, it is difficult for teachers to use problem posing as a learning method.

Based on this consideration, we are developing an Intelligent Learning Environment which realizes the learning by problem posing. The domain of the ILE is arithmetical word problems solved by an addition or a subtraction. In the ILE, when a learner poses a problem, the ILE diagnoses the problem and helps her/him to correct the wrong problem, or leads her/him in the next step of problem posing [6]. We have already developed a prototype of the ILE and used it in the lecture of the class experimentally [7]. However, in the experiment because we could not keep enough computers to provide each student, two

S.A. Cerri, G. Gouardères, and F. Paraguaçu (Eds.): ITS 2002, LNCS 2363, pp. 861–872, 2002.

or three students used one ILE. Therefore although we confirmed that learners could pose problems on the ILE, we could not evaluate the ILE in detail.

In this paper, we report an evaluation of the ILE based on individual use by 4th grade elementary school students in class. In this experiment, we evaluate the ILE from the following two viewpoints, (1) whether the students can pose problems by using the ILE or not, and (2) whether the use of the ILE is effective to improve the student's ability of problem posing or not. We call the former viewpoint "usability" and the latter viewpoint "effectiveness". To evaluate the two points, we carried out pre-test, post-test, questionary for both students and teachers, and collected log data of problem posing in the ILE. So, in order to consider about the usability, at first, we analyzed if subjects used the ILE enough. We then checked if the subjects whose results in the pre-test were low could pose solvable problems in the ILE. Moreover, we put several questions to several teachers who observed this class of problem posing on the ILE.

We compared the results of the pre-test and the post-test in order to evaluate the effectiveness. If the result of the post-test is significantly higher than the result of the pre-test, we can judge the ILE is effective in problem posing, not only the quantity of posed problems but also the quality of them are important to evaluate the ability of problem posing. Because there is no standard method to evaluate the ability of problem posing, we also prepare a scoring method of posed problems in this paper.

2 ILE for Problem Posing

2.1 Solution-Based Problem Posing

To develop an ILE for learning by problem posing, categorization of problem posing is important. We have categorized problem posing in the following three types:(1) Problem-Based Problem Posing, (2) Story-Based Problem Posing, and (3) Solution-Based Problem Posing [7].

The ability to pose problems is necessary to solve problems of which solution are not known. However, the ability often cannot be acquired only to solve problems. Therefore, the practice to pose problems is a promising way to acquire the ability.In this paper, we deal with "Solution-Based Problem Posing". Solution-Based Problem Posing is the most popular type of problem posing, because it is effective to master the solution method directly [8], [9]. To deal with other types of problem posing on computer is our future work.

Solution-Based Problem Posing is an effective practice to learn arithmetic. In Solution-Based Problem Posing, first, a solution method is given beforehand, then, learners pose problems which can be solved by the solution method. We call the solution method "stated solution". The stated solution is defined by a learner, or given by a teacher or a system. Based on a stated solution, the learner has to pose problems which can be solved by the stated solution. Finally, the solution method of the problem posed by the learner has to be equal to the stated solution. We call the solution method of the posed problem "derived solution". That is, when the derived solution is equal to the stated solution or when the derived solution is judged the stated solution, the result of the problem posing is correct in Solution-Based Problem Posing. So, we think that Solution-Based Problem Posing is a learning method to learn relation between problem and solution.

2.2 Framework of ILE for Problem Posing

We developed an ILE for Solution-Based Problem Posing. We describe the ILE of problem posing based on the solutions in this section. The domain is arithmetical word problems which can be solved by an addition or a subtraction. Fig. 1 shows the framework of the ILE. In the ILE, when a learner poses a problem, the ILE diagnoses the problem in Problem Diagnosis Module. Moreover, by using result in Advice Generator, the ILE helps her/him to correct the wrong problem, or leads her/him in the next step of problem posing. The Problem Diagnosis Module and the Advice Generator and knowledge used in these modules are implemented by Prolog. Client and other module and information of Server are implemented by Java.

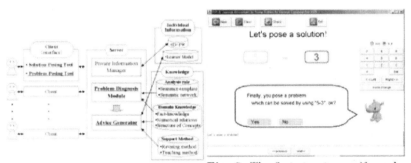

Fig. 1. The framework of the ILE.   **Fig. 2.** The first step to specify problem formula.

Next, we explain graphical user interface in the ILE. The interface of the ILE provides learners with two steps to promote problem posing. In first step, a learner specifies a stated solution before s/he poses a problem, e.g., "5-X=3". We call this solution method like "5-X=3" "problem formula". So, in Fig. 2, the learner specifies a stated problem formula "5-X=3". In second step, s/he poses problems which can be solved by the stated problem formula. In order that the ILE judges whether the result of the learner's problem posing is correct or not, the ILE checks whether the derived problem formula is equal to the stated problem formula or not. Fig. 3 is the interface to pose a problem. This interface is explained in more details. Currently, the ILE can deal with only Change-Problem [10]. In Change-Problem, the quantity in "the initial situation" is changed to the quantity in "the final situation" by the "change action". The Change-Problem usually consists of three sentences: the first sentence describes the initial situation, the second sentence describes the change action, and the

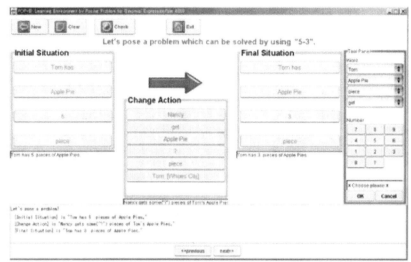

Fig. 3. The second step to pose problems.

third sentence describes the final situation. Therefore, we prepare a "problem template" that composed of three "single sentence templates". In Fig. 3, the problem template is shown in the left side panel. By filling in the blanks of three single sentence templates, the problem is completed. Moreover, in order to filling in the blanks of the templates, the ILE provide learners with several concepts in concept panel beforehand and ten-key. In Fig. 3, these are shown in the right side panel. In issue panel, the ILE provide learners with information generated based on the result of first step. In comment panel, the ILE provide learners with advice which is feedback about result of their operation in the interface and is generated in Advice Generator. Moreover, we explain the problem template in detail. The initial situation has the four information: "owner", "object", "number", and "unit". This means that "owner" has "object" and the number of "object" is "number", then, the unit of the number is "unit". The change action has the five information: "actor", "object", "number", "unit", and "action". The ILE deals with the type of action where object moves between the object's owner and other people, i.e., between two peoples. For example, the action where A receives B's object from B is dealt with. However, the ILE does not deal with the type of action where object moves among three people. For example, the action where A receives B's object from C is not dealt with. The final situation has the four information: "owner", "object", "number", and "unit". In learning by problem posing, the problem template and the sentence templates restrict the expression of problems. However, we think that using these templates don't lose the main effect of learning by problem posing, because, at learning by arithmetical word problem, we think that it is most important to consider relation between concepts and numerical relations.

3   Experimental Use of the ILE

A prototype of the ILE has been already developed. So two elementary school teachers permitted us to use the ILE in their arithmetic classes after they had used the ILE by themselves. Subjects were 55 students of elementary school in 4th grade. In this experiment, we could keep enough computers to provide each student. We evaluate the ILE from the following two viewpoints, (1)whether the students can pose problem by using the ILE or not, and (2) whether the use of the ILE is effective to improve the student's ability of problem posing or not. We call the former viewpoint "usability" and the latter viewpoint "effectiveness". The process of the experiment is as follows.

(p1): We took 20 minutes to teach how to pose Change-Problems with several examples.
(p2): In the pre-test, the subjects posed problems on paper in 10 minutes. We provided the subjects with problem formulas, and then, the subjects posed problems that can be solved by the problem formulas. In this pre-test, the following problems formulas were provided: "6+9=?", "12-5=?", "7+?=15", "11-?=4", "?+9=13" and "?-7=6".
(p3): The subjects posed problems with the ILE. 10 minutes were taken to explain the way to use the ILE, and 30 minutes were used to pose problems. Then, 4 teaching assistants were supporting how to use the ILE always.

(p4): As the post-test,the subjects posed problems on paper again in the same method of (p2).

(p5): We asked teachers and the subjects several questions.

Through the experiment, we gathered the following data: (d1) logs of problem posing on the ILE, (d2) scores of problem posing on paper before using the ILE and after using the ILE, (d3) answers that teachers and students filled questionnaires.
In this section, we explain the evaluation of the ILE based on these data.

3.1   Usability of the ILE

In lesson of problem posing on paper, it is difficult for a teacher to support each learner and it is difficult for the learner to write sentences on paper. Therefore, some students maybe fail to pose problems, because they are not good at write sentences. Therefore, the ILE provides learners with feedback to correct wrong problem and to lead them next problem posing. Moreover, the ILE provides learners with a tool to make sentences with combination between concepts. Therefore, learning by using the ILE is not practice to write sentences, but it is practice to make relations between concepts and numerical relation. From the results, we expected that the ILE would be usable for learners.

We evaluate the usability of the ILE from the following four viewpoints. At first, (1) we analyzed the number of posed problems with the ILE. Then, (2) we checked if the subjects whose results in the pre-test were low could pose solvable problems in the ILE. Next, (3) we put several questions to teachers who participated at this class of problem posing on the ILE. By using the questions their impressions for the lesson of problem posing with the ILE are examined. Finally, (4) we put several questions to subjects. By using the question, their impressions for the learning of problem posing with the ILE are examined.

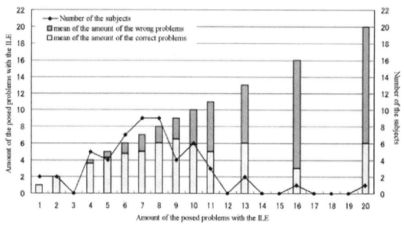

Fig. 4. The relation among amount of the posed problems with the ILE, a distribution of the subjects and the contents of the use of the ILE.

Fig. 4 shows two graphs at the same time. One graph is line graph which shows relation between amount of the posed problems with the ILE and number of the subjects. The other one is bar graph which shows relation between amount of the posed problems with the ILE and the contents of the posed problem with the ILE. At first, we explain each graph as follow. In the line graph of Fig. 4, the horizontal axis shows amount of the posed problems with the ILE, and the vertical axis shows number of subjects (the vertical axis is shown in the right side of Fig. 4). For example, when the value in the horizontal axis is 7, the value in the vertical axis is 9. It means that the number of the subjects who posed 7 problems with the ILE is 9. In the bar graph of Fig. 4, both the horizontal axis and the vertical axis shows amount of the posed problems with the ILE (the vertical axis is shown in the left side of Fig. 4). That is, the value in the horizontal axis is the same value in the vertical axis. There are two cases in the contents of the posed problems with the ILE; one is that a subject posed a problem which is judged correct by the ILE, the other is that the subject posed the problem which is judged wrong by the ILE. For that reason, we divided one bar into two colors. Therefore, at each bar in the graph, the length of the part which is dark color shows "mean of the amount of the posed wrong problems" (The "wrong problem" means that the posed problems is judged wrong by the ILE) and the length of the part which is light color shows "mean of the amount of the posed correct problems" (The "correct problem" means that the posed problems is judged correct by the ILE). For example, when the value in the horizontal axis is 7, the value in the vertical axis is 7, and then, in the bar, the length of the part which is dark color is 2 and the rest, i.e.; the part which is light color is 5. It means that the subjects who posed 7 problems with the ILE posed wrong problems and correct problems at the rate of 2 to 5. That is, their correct answer rate is 71%. By using both the line graph and the bar graph, for example, we can know at the same time that the number of the subjects who posed 7 problems with the ILE is 9 and their correct answer rate is 71%.

In the experiment, the mean of the amount of the problems posed by total subjects is 7.5. Forty-seven % subjects posed problems more than the mean of the amount of the problems posed by total subjects (i.e.; forty-seven % subjects posed more than 8 problems). We guess they posed problems actively with the ILE, although they posed many wrong problems (the correct answer rate of the subjects is 57%). Fifty-three % subjects posed problems less than 7.5 with the ILE. However, they did not pose so many wrong problems (the correct answer rate of the subjects is 79%). So, we guess that the subjects used the ILE carefully not to pose wrong problems. Four students posed less than two problems although the all problems were correct. Their log data of all operation of the ILE show that they did not operate the ILE at all in the second half of the class. So, we guess that the subjects did not use the ILE to pose problems.

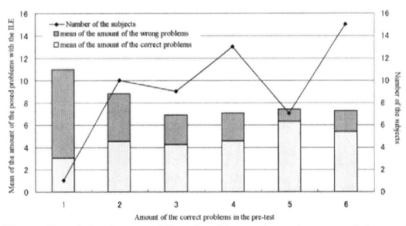

Fig. 5. The relation between ability of problem posing and amount of the posed problems with the ILE.

Next, we check if the subjects whose results in the pre-test were low could use the ILE and if the subjects could pose solvable problems in the ILE. Fig. 5 shows two graphs at the same time. One graph is line graph which shows relation between amount of the correct problems in the pre-test and number of the subjects. The other one is bar graph which shows relation between amount of the correct problems in the pre-test and amount of the posed problems with the ILE. At first, we explain each graph as follow.

In the line graph of Fig. 5, the horizontal axis shows amount of the correct problems in the pre-test, and the vertical axis shows number of the subjects (the vertical axis is shown in the right side of Fig. 5). For example, when the value in the horizontal axis is 3, the value in the vertical axis is 9. It means that the number of the subjects who posed 3 correct problems in the pre-test (in the pre-test, we judged correct problem when the posed problem can be solved).

In the bar graph of Fig.5, the horizontal axis shows amount of the correct problems in the pre-test, and the vertical axis shows mean of the amount of the posed problems with the ILE (the vertical axis is shown in the left side of Fig. 5). In the same way as the bar of Fig. 4, we divided one bar into two colors. Therefore, at each bar in the graph, the length of the part which is dark color shows "mean of the amount of the posed wrong problems" and the length of the part which is light color shows "mean of the amount of the posed correct problems". For example, when the value in the horizontal axis is 3, the value in the vertical axis is 6.9, and then, in the bar, the length of the part which is dark color is 2.7 and the rest, i.e.; the part which is light color is 4.2. It means that the subjects who posed 3 correct problems in the pre-test posed wrong problems and correct problems at the rate of 2.7 to 4.2. That is, their correct answer rate is 61%. By using both graphs, for example, we can know at the same time that the number of the subject who posed 3 correct problems in the pre-test is 9 and their correct answer rate is 61%.

By using Fig. 5, at first, we classify the subjects into several types based on the result of the pre-test. Subjects who could pose six correct problems or five correct problems in the pre-test are 22. We consider that they have the high level ability of problem posing. So, we call them "high level subjects". Subjects who could pose four correct problems or three correct problems in the pre-test are 22. We call them "middle level subjects". Subjects who could pose two correct problems or a correct problem in the pre-test are 11. We call them "low level subjects".

Next, we examine how each type subject used the ILE. The correct answer rate of the low level subjects is 48%, i.e., the worst in these level subjects. The correct answer rate of the high level subjects is 78%, i.e., the best in these level subjects. From this result, we consider that it reflects the difference of ability of problem posing. The mean of the amount of the correct problems with the ILE of the low level subjects is 4.4, i.e., the worst in these level subjects.

The mean of the amount of the correct problems with the ILE of the high level subjects is 5.7, i.e., the best in these level subjects. From this result, we consider that it reflects the difference of ability of problem posing, too. However, the low level subjects could pose several correct problems on the ILE. Therefore, we judge that the ILE was not hard for the low level subjects to use. Moreover, we consider that the result shows the function in order to correct wrong problem is a factor of the result. We consider that the reason in which the high and middle level subjects used the ILE carefully in order not to pose wrong problem.

Moreover, in order to judge whether amount of the use of the ILE is enough or not, we asked teachers and the subjects several questions. Table 1 shows the result in which we asked teachers who used the ILE and presented 4 questions. These are as follows: (t-1) Did you judge that subjects using the ILE were earnest at the class?, (t-2) Did you judge that the subjects can use the ILE smoothly?, (t-3) Were feedback of the ILE helpful for subjects when they posed wrong problems? and (t-4) Were feedback of the ILE helpful for subjects when they posed correct problems? And, in order to investigate usability, we asked user of the ILE (i.e., they are this subject). Table 2 shows the result in which we asked subjects 3 question. These are as follows: (s-1) Did you enjoy problem posing on the ILE?, (s-2) Were feedbackof the ILE helpful for you when you posed wrong problems? and (s-3) Were feedback of the ILE helpful for you when you posed correct problems?

Table 1. An evaluation of the teachers.

Question	Yes	No	So-so
(t-1)	6	0	1
(t-2)	7	0	0
(t-3)	6	0	1
(t-4)	5	0	2

Table 2. An evaluation of the 4th grade students.

Question	Yes	No	So-so
(s-1)	17	8	0
(s-2)	48	6	1
(s-3)	41	10	4

Subjects' behavior at class (t-1,t-2) and subjects' interest (s-1) and the function of the ILE (t-3, t-4, s-2, s-3) are evidence of the above our interpretation which is that the subjects posed enough correct problems on the ILE. In the result of the Table 1 and the Table 2, these are evaluated high. That is, we think that the teacher thought this class using the ILE succeeded as class of learning by problem posing and subjects are interested in this class.

In order to judge whether the ILE is learning material for learning by problem posing that elementary school students can use easily or not, we showed two Figures and two Tables and our interpretation of these data. In the result based on two Figures (Fig. 4 and Fig. 5), almost subjects, even the subjects who posed few problems, could pose correct problems with the ILE. Moreover, in the result of two Tables (Table 1 and Table 2), the teacher answered that the subjects could use the ILE and the function of the ILE was good, and the subjects answered that the class of the ILE was interesting. Therefore, in these results, we judge that the usability of the ILE is high.

3.2   Effectiveness of the ILE

In problem posing on the ILE, a learner has to find the proper combination among concepts and numerical relations. Because to find the proper combination is an important task of problem posing, the practice should be effective to improve problem posing ability.

Therefore, we evaluate the effectiveness of the ILE from the comparison of the scores of the pre-test and the post-test. First, the method to give a score to

each posed problem, and then the result of the comparison of the scores of the
pre-test and the post-test is explained.

Scoring Method of Posed Problems

Difficulty in problem formula. Problem formula has three types: (α) A
!^ B=X,(β) A !^ X=C,(γ) X !^ B=C (A, B, C are numerical values. X is
a variable). "A" is the number in the initial situation, "B" is the number
of the change action, and "C" is the number in the final situation. "X" is
the number that is derived by the solution. In the α type, the answer is in
the final situation. So this type of problem is the easiest one. In the β type,
the answer is in the change action. In the γ type, the answer is in the initial
situation. In learning by problem solving, generally, problems which can be
solved by α type equation are the problems of the easiest type in these three
types. And, problems which can be solved by γ type equation are the problems of the most difficult type. We think that there is the same difficulty of
arithmetically thinking in problem solving and problem posing. So, we use
the difference of formula type to score the posed problems.

Difficulty of operation. We think that each verb lets us remind each operation. For example, "give" usually reminds us of "subtraction", and "receive"
usually reminds us of "addition". This is the simplest pattern of the combination of a verb and an operation. For example, if we posed a problem by using
"give" simply, the problem is like this: "Tom has 5 pieces of apple pies. Tom
gives Nancy some pieces of his apple pies. Tom has 3 pieces of apple pies.
How many pies of apple pies does Tom give Nancy?" We call the operation
reminds by the verb "simple reminded operation".
Meanwhile, in the problem posing, not only the verb in the change action
but also the combination of other concepts in the change action should be
considered in order to decide the operation. So, all problems are classified in
two cases. One is that an operation of derived problem formula is the same
with the simple reminded operation. And then, the other is that an operation
of derived problem formula is different from the simple reminded operation.
We call this case "operation with the gap". The gap means that there is
difference between operation of derived problem formula and the simple reminded operation. For example, the case in which there is the gap is "Tom
has 5 pieces of apple pies. Nancy gives Tom some pieces of her apple pies.
Tom has 8 pieces of apple pies. How many pies of apple pies does Nancy give
Tom?" The operator of derived problem formula is "addition", but the simple
reminded operation of "give" is "subtraction". Therefore, this problem has
the gap. So, we judge that a problem which has the gap is more difficult than
a problem which does not has it.

Result of comparison between pre-test and post-test.

In evaluation of
the effectiveness of the ILE, we investigate whether the ability of problem posing
of all subjects is improved or not, by using the ILE.

We explained the method to evaluate each posed problem. The scoring method is as follows: if the problem type is the α type problem, the score of the problem is one. If the problem type is the β type problem, the score of the problem is two. If the problem type is the γ type problem, the score of the problem is three. Moreover, only if the problem has gap between an operation of derived problem formula and a simple reminded operation, the score of the problem is incremented one.

So, by using the scoring method of the posed problems, we can get each learner's scores of the pre-test and the post-test. We evaluate the effectiveness by using the difference of the scores between the pre-test and the post-test. In the pre-test and the post-test, the highest score is 18.

Table 3. A comparison between the pre-test and the post-test.

test	subjects	mean	standard deviation
pre-test	55	7.4	3.7
post-test	55	9.6	4.0

So, we tried t-test in order to investigate a change between the mean of scores of the pre-test and the post-test. Table 3 shows the relation of both tests. In the result, the difference of the change is significant. (Mean of the pre-test=7.4, Mean of the post-test=9.6; t-test, t(55)=2.00, p <.001). Therefore, we think that the ability of problem posing of the 4th grade subjects is improved by using the ILE.

4   Conclusions

We evaluated (1) the usability of the ILE and (2) the effectiveness of the ILE through the use of the ILE in the class of elementary school.

In the evaluation of the usability of the ILE, we presented that almost subjects, even subjects who posed few problems in pre-test, could pose correct problems with the ILE. Moreover, in order to judge whether amount of the use of the ILE is enough or not, we asked teachers and the subjects several questions. In the questions, the teacher answered that the subjects could use the ILE and the function of the ILE was good, and the subjects answered that the class of the ILE was interesting. Therefore, in the result, we judge that the ILE has enough usability for use in the class.

In the evaluation of the effectiveness of the ILE, at first, we proposed the scoring method of problem posing. And then, we reported the effectiveness of the ILE based on result of t-test about the difference of the change between mean of the scores of the pre-test and mean of the scores of the post-test. In the result, we judge the subjects who used the ILE improved in the ability of problem posing, i.e., the ILE also has enough effectiveness for learning of problem posing.

The problem posing in the ILE (problem posing based on stated problem formula) is one of Solution-Based Problem Posing. Of course, we think that it is necessary to develop other ILE based on other type of Solution-Based Problem

Posing. At present, an evaluated environment in the ILE is an environment to pose problems based on a stated problem formula. However, we are developing other environment to pose problems based on information which is specified only calculation procedure to solve the posed problem, e.g., the information is "5-3". Moreover, we will develop the other types of problem posing, i.e., Problem-Based Problem Posing and Story-Based Problem Posing. To realize the learning environment of the two types of problem posing is also our future work.

Acknowledgements. This research is supported in part by Grant-in-Aid for Scientific Research from the Ministry of Education, Culture, Sports, Science and Technology of Japan, the Telecommunications Advancement Foundation, and Artificial Intelligence Research Promotion Foundation.

References

1. Silver, E.A., Mamona, J., Posing Mathematical Problems: An Exploratory Study. *Journal of Research in Mathematics Education*, vol. 27, No. 3, pp 293–309, 1996.
2. Lyn D. English, Children's Problem Posing Within Formal and Informal Contexts. *Journal of Research in Mathematics Education*, vol. 29, No.1, pp 83–106, 1998.
3. Ellerton, N.F., Children's made up mathematics problems: A new perspective on talented mathematicians. *Educational Studies in Mathematics*, 17, pp 261–271,1986.
4. Silverman, F.L., Winograd, K., Strohauer, D., Student-generated story problems. *Arithmetic Teacher* 39, pp 6–12,1992.
5. Silver, E.A., Cai, J., An Analysis of Arithmetic Problem Posing by Middle School Students. *Journal of Research in Mathematics Education* vol. 27, No.5, pp 521–539, 1996.
6. Nakano, A., T. Hirashima, A. Takeuchi, "A Learning Environment for Problem posing in Simple Arithmetical Word Problem". *Proc. of ICCE2000* pp 91–98, 2000.
7. Nakano, A., T. Hirashima, A. Takeuchi, "An Intelligent Learning Environment for Problem Posing and Its Evaluation – In the case of Arithmetical Word Problems Solved by an Addition or a Subtraction" *Proc. of ICCE2001* pp 1242–1249, 2001.
8. Nakano, A., T. Hirashima, A. Takeuchi, "Problem-Making Practice to Master Solution-Methods in Intelligent Learning Environment". *Proc. of ICCE '99* pp 891–898, 1999.
9. Hirashima, T., A. Nakano, A. Takeuchi, "A Diagnosis Function of Arithmetical Word Problems for Learning by Problem Posing" *Proc. of PRICAI2000* pp 745–755, 2000.
10. Silver, E.A., "On mathematical problem posing. For the Learning of Mathematics". *For the Learning of Mathematics* 14 (1), pp 19–28,1994.

Using Edit Distance Algorithms to Compare Alternative Approaches to ITS Authoring

Shaaron Ainsworth, David Clarke, and Robert Gaizauskas

School of Psychology, University of Nottingham, Nottingham, NG7 2RD, UK
Department of Computer Science, University of Sheffield, Sheffield, UK
{sea,ddc}@psychology.nottingham.ac.uk;
robertg@dcs.sheffield.ac.uk

Abstract. One of the traditional goals of an Intelligent Tutoring System is to provide domain content for learners that is appropriate to their needs. A key component of this knowledge is the sequence in which instructional activities are performed and so unsurprisingly this is often a key task in ITS authoring. In order to understand this process better it is important to have accurate quantitative ways of classifying the difference between alternative sequences of ITS material. Edit distance algorithms provide a useful way of capturing this knowledge but suggest that weights need to be careful adjusted to capture important aspects of ITS sequences. The weighted algorithm is illustrated with examples from three studies using the REDEEM ITS authoring tool. This technique has allowed us to compare authors' sequences in a way that is robust, quantifiable and that provides insights into ITS authors' pedagogical principles.

1 Introduction

One key characteristic of Intelligent Tutoring Systems is that they can offer alternative sequences of domain material or exercises to learners that are adapted to each learner's specific requirements. It is also clear from research in human and machine learning that the rate or quality of what is learnt can depend upon the sequence in which material is presented (see Langley, 1995 for a review).

ITS authoring tools aim to make the production of ITSs more efficient and effective. Many of these ITS authoring tools focus on the way that alternative sequences of material could be generated by combining user expertise and ITS techniques (e.g. IDE, DOCENT, ISD Expert, see Murray, 1999). REDEEM, though classified by Murray as primarily concerned with tutoring strategies, requires users to spend significant amounts of time in making decisions about curriculum sequencing.

In this paper, we discuss ways of analysing alternative sequences of domain material generated by teachers using the REDEEM ITS authoring environment. We begin by briefly describing how authors create sequences of material in REDEEM and discuss why it is useful to have objective techniques for comparing these alternative sequences. We then consider techniques that could be used to analyse these sequences. Each technique is first illustrated with a simple example and then we describe how the method was used to analyse four teachers' use of the REDEEM

S.A. Cerri, G. Gouardères, and F. Paraguaçu (Eds.): ITS 2002, LNCS 2363, pp. 873–882, 2002.

authoring tools. The paper ends by considering whether this technique has generality beyond our particular domain.

REDEEM (Major, Ainsworth & Wood, 1997) allows authors with little technological knowledge to create simple ITSs. Unlike many ITS authoring tools, REDEEM does not support the construction of domain material. Instead authors import existing computer-based material and then use the REDEEM tools to overlay their teaching expertise. The REDEEM shell uses this knowledge, together with its own default teaching knowledge, to deliver courseware adaptively to meet the needs of different learners. The courseware for REDEEM consists of individual frames of material. The author is faced with five main tasks to 'REDEEM' it, which are "what to teach", "how to teach", "who to teach", "what each student will learn" and "how each student will learn". All of these aspects of authoring impact upon the resultant sequences of material. Authors describe student categories by grouping the students. These can either be fixed or can change according to students' performance during the teaching sessions. They describe teaching strategies by manipulating sliders of dimensions of teaching such as position and amount of testing, type of help, and number of responses per question. The dimensions that have the greatest impact on sequences are "general to specific" – which adjusts the weights in the array so that general or specific material is preferred and "student control" that describes the freedom students have to choose their own sequences through the material. These decisions are then combined so that each student category is associated with a teaching strategy and with appropriate sections of the domain material.

2 Why Are ITS Sequences Worth Analysing?

Each learner interacting with a REDEEM ITS receives a particular sequence of domain material, non-computer tasks and exercises/questions. These sequences are primarily but not completely determined by the decisions of the author. There are a number of reasons why we are interested in characterising these sequences, particularly the sequences of domain material, in a precise and quantitative way.

The first reason to examine the sequence of domain material (pages) in a REDEEM ITS is to compare it to the underlying CBT. Creating sequences with REDEEM is time consuming. Hence, we need to determine how much authors impose their own sequences. If they create sequences with a fixed structure that are similar to the original CBT, there is little reason to use REDEEM for this function. Using a sequence analysis technique will provide information to answer this question.

Secondly, we want to compare different authors' sequences for the same domain and groups of learners. If authors create similar sequences to each other, there is likely to be a perceived appropriate sequence for teaching this course (low inter-author differences). Alternatively, if authors create sequences that differ substantially, this suggests there is no canonical view of domain structure in the domain (high inter-author differences). Furthermore, the more constrained the authoring, and hence the less freedom for the ITSshell to compute sequences, the more the likely authors are to have seen a strong prerequisite structure in the domain. Examining these sequences allows us to compare authoring across different courses. In the short-term such comparisons could be used to suggest when it is appropriate to use tools such as REDEEM. In the long-term, this may be a useful way to acquire domain taxonomies.

Thirdly, each author is required to specify sequences for each student category. Some teachers may construct very similar sequences for all learners (low intra-author differences). Alternatively, teachers may provide highly differentiated structures by selecting very different sequences for alternative types of learners (high intra-author differences). Looking at inter and intra author differences provides a valuable way of capturing and analysing important aspects authors' of mental models of teaching.

Fourthly, some sequences maybe more effective than others. Many approaches to instructional design consider the sequence of concepts and procedures to be crucial (e.g. Gagne, 1984). Hence, we might expect that some REDEEM ITSs would be differentially effective. Learning outcome studies with REDEEM ITSs may be able to pinpoint more precisely why certain sequences are more effective than alternatives.

Finally, when using REDEEM in a discovery learning mode, where students have control over the sequences of materials and problems they access, the resultant sequences can be compared either against each other or against some canonical view of the course structure. Again, this may help in the difficult process of relating design decisions and learner experience to learning outcomes.

3 Techniques for Analysing REDEEM Sequences

There are many aspects of REDEEM ITSs that are susceptible to sequence analysis. The one we focus on in this paper is the sequence of pages (i.e. domain content). The technique that we have explored recently, and which provides the focus for this paper, is the use of a particular string similarity algorithm: edit or Levenshtein distance.

3.1 Levenshtein Distance

The basic idea underlying Levenshtein distance (LD) is that the difference between two strings (sequences) is the minimal number of edit operation that transforms one string into another where edit operations are defined as deletions (del), insertions (ins) or substitutions (sub). For example, assuming that each is equally weighted at 1, the edit distance between Biarritz and Briar is five. This technique is used in a variety of applications, for example, in spelling correction, plagiarism detection, DNA sequence analysis, and even bird song (e.g. Sankof, & Kruskal, 1983).

Table 1. Levenshtein Distances (LD) for Four Example Sequences and Original CBT

CBT	Author A	Author B	Author C	Author D
Triangles	Triangles	Triangles	Circles	Rectangles
Squares	Rectangles	Rectangles	Triangles	Vertices
Rectangles	Squares	Squares	Squares	Circles
Vertices	Vertices	Vertices	Rectangles	Quadrilaterals
Polygons	Polygons	Circles	Vertices	Squares
Circles	Quadrilaterals		Polygons	Polygons
Quadrilaterals	Circles		Quadrilaterals	Triangles
				Vertices
LD CBT v ITS	4	4	2	7

We used this technique to compare the courses generated by four authors working with REDEEM to an original course. This domain is primary shapes so we provide here a simplified example sequence of pages on basic shapes. Thus the input data looked something like those in Table 1.. As described above, authors have a number of ways they can perturb the sequence from the original CBT. They can change the order of pages (the actions of authors A and C), they can delete pages (author B) and they can chose to repeat pages (amongst the actions of author D). This analysis revealed that Author C had the closest sequence to the original CBT (only *circles* has moved), whereas author D has the largest distance as she has repeated *vertices* and changed the position of almost every page. There may be many ways to achieve the minimum transformation. For example, there are four possible alignments for String B with a LD of 4 (these alignments can be seen with triangles represented as "t", etc)

- del Sqs, sub Verts with Sqs, sub Polys with Verts, del Quad {tsrvpcq $\Rightarrow$ t-rsvc};
- sub Sqs with Rects, sub Rects with Sqs, del Polys, del Quad {tsrvpcq $\Rightarrow$ trsv-c};
- del Squares, insert Squares, del Polygons, del Quad { tsr-vpcq $\Rightarrow$ t-rsv-c };
- ins Rects, del Rects, del Polygons, del Quad {t-srvpcq $\Rightarrow$ trs-v-c-}

In fact, the data were substantially more complicated than this. The CBT consists of 71 unique pages which could be combined in multiple ways. Each teacher chose to create five student categories (Group A to Group E), which were rank ordered by the teachers (Ainsworth, et al 2000), and assigned them different material or teaching strategies. It should be noted that each REDEEM ITSs had been iteratively developed by each teacher until they were satisfied with the outcome. Thus, what we analyse here is a sequence of material that was generated by the tools/author partnership assuming that students do not get reclassified during their interaction with the REDEEM shell. It is best thought of as a teacher's view of the prototypical domain structure. These sequences were then compared to the original CBT.

Table 2. Analysis of Four Authors' Sequences

	Teacher 1				Teacher 2				Teacher 3				Teacher 4			
	Len	Del	Rep	LD	Len	Del	Rep	LD	Len	Del	Rep	LD	Len	Del	Rep	LD
Group A	39	32	0	65	54	20	7	69	36	35	0	66	58	24	11	70
Group B	46	25	0	65	54	20	7	69	44	28	1	59	62	20	11	68
Group C	82	3	14	76	73	5	7	69	43	29	1	65	76	10	15	72
Group D	82	3	14	76	66	12	3	59	66	6	1	66	88	1	18	83
Group E	44	27	1	67	66	12	3	59	43	29	1	65	84	5	18	82
Mean	58.6	18.2	5.8	69.8	62.6	13.8	5.4	65.0	46.4	25.4	0.8	64.2	73.6	12.0	14.6	75.0
St.Dev	21.5	14.1	7.5	5.7	8.4	6.3	2.2	5.5	11.4	11.2	0.4	2.9	13.2	9.8	3.5	7.0

Key - Len: Length of ITS sequences. Del: The number of pages deleted. Rep: The number of pages used more than once. LD: The LD between the CBT and the ITS.

It can be seen from Table 2 that the LDs for all ITSs were high. If all of pages in the CBT were included in the ITS in the same order, the LD would obviously be 0. In fact, the average LD was 68.5. The explanations for these values are threefold and differ depending on the teacher and the group. Firstly, there was a large number of deletions. For example, the ITSs created by the authors for Group A had between 35 and 24 pages deleted from the original CBT. Secondly, some authors are using pages more than once. This reached a maximum of 18 repetitions for Teacher 4 (groups D and E). This decision has the greatest impact on the LD scores. If length of course is correlated with LD, there is a significant positive correlation ($r = 0.88$, $df = 18$, $p < 0.01$). Thus, the longer the course the more it differed from the original sequence.

We were also interested in determining how far each ITS differed from a theoretical maximal misalignment. A REDEEM ITS that is shorter than the CBT of length N has a maximum LD from the original CBT of the length of the CBT (in this case a LD of 71), whereas one that is longer has a maximum LD from the original CBT of length of the REDEEM ITS. One indication of how the ITSs differed from the CBT can be seen by comparing how far each of the ITSs differed from this maximum score with total similarity scoring 0% and total disagreement 100%. Each of these LDs was compared to their maximum potential LD and on average the REDEEM ITSs scored 92.5% of this potential. Accordingly, this measure seems to reveal that the prototypical ITS sequences created by the teachers from the CBT bore little similarity to the sequence in the underlying CBT.

3.2 Weighted Levenshtein Distance

It can be seen from Table 2 that the LD values are all high with little variability. It is tempting to conclude that all the teachers produced similar sequences to each other, if not to the original CBT. However, this is not borne out by the data. A further problem with the application of this technique can be seen in the example data from Authors' A and B (Table 1.); i.e. that many sequences can result in the same LD. However, the most important objection to using LD to compare ITS structures is that it does not s capture important aspects of these data. If you consider the examples of Authors C and D above, *triangles* which occurs first in the CBT has been shifted by one position in the ITS to be addressed second for author C, but has been shifted six places to be taught 7th for author D. Intuitively, we would say that that Author D has altered the CBT more than Author C, yet the effects on the LD are equal. Similarly, the effects of deleting a page would seem in educational terms to be a more radical decision than simply moving it by one position. However, the former would produce a LD of 1 (one deletion) and the latter 2 (one insertion and one deletion or two substitutions).

Hence, it became apparent that the simple unweighted Levenshtein algorithm was not suitable for capturing important aspects of the way that the CBT had been perturbed to create the REDEEM sequences. Yet, the basic idea of analysing the distance between the sequences in terms of minimum number of transformation operations seemed useful. One feature of the LD not mention above is that the basic edit operations may be differentially weighted in computing the overall edit distance, i.e. there is no reason that sub, del and ins must each have a weight of one. We therefore modified the algorithm such that each operation had different weights according to intuitions about their relative significance in educational terms

- Deletion – a page in the CBT that is not in the ITS: $1 + (1/Length(Source))$
- Substitution – a page in the CBT that is not in the same position in the ITS: (absolute difference between position in ITS – position in CBT)/ Length(Source).
- Insertion – a page in the ITS that is not in the CBT: $1 + (1/Length(Source))$

These were chosen for the following reasons. Deletions represent a greater change than simply moving an item (hence the addition of the constant 1). Furthermore, deleting a page from a short course has a bigger impact than deleting a page from a longer course (hence 1/(length of source)). The reasoning is identical for an insertion. For substitutions, the more a page changes position, the greater the change regardless of the direction of change (hence the absolute differences between the positions, normalised by the dividing by the length of the source since the significance of a move of N position is relative to the overall length of the CBT). Of course, these are not the only possible weights one could use. We have created and analysed a number of different weights. But, this combination coincided with the intuitions of authors concerning how different their ITSs were to the CBT. This approach can be demonstrated by using the algorithm on the example strings given in Table 1.

Table 3. Weighted Levenshtein Distances Between CBT and Example Sequences

	Author A	Author B	Author C	Author D
Weighted LD	0.57	2.57	1.42	3.28

The weighted LDs (WLDs) are now absolutely and relatively different to the ones given in Table 3. The ITS with the lowest LD is now Author A's. This reflects the fact that she has no deletions and has swapped position of two pairs of pages shifting each by only $1/7^{th}$ of the course. This can be achieved by four substitutions of $1/7^{th}$. Author B had a larger WLD than LD because she has deleted pages from the CBT to create her ITS, as well as swapping *squares* for *rectangles* (two dels of $1+1/7^{th}$, 2 subs of $1/7^{th}$). Author C can achieve her sequence with 5 subs. Finally, Author D has moved all of the pages around by many places and *vertices* which is best modelled as an insertion of *vertices* (at a cost of $2/7^{th}$) and then six subs.

We claim that these WLDS provide a more sensible interpretation of the difference between the ITSs and the CBT than the original LDs. Important differences (amount that a page has been moved and whether it is no longer present) are now included, but the notion of minimum differences between the two strings has been preserved.

4   Analysing REDEEM Sequences with the Weighted LD Algorithm

We identified five reasons why it would be useful to quantify the differences between sequences generated by REDEEM. The final two reasons involve learner outcomes, but the first three address authoring issues. Hence, we use the WLD metric to answer these questions based on the authoring of the four teachers described above.

4.1   Comparing REDEEM Sequences to the Underlying Courseware

The ITSs created by the four primary educators from an original 71 page course on primary shapes were used for this comparison. The Weighted Levenshtein Distance algorithm compared their perturbation from the CBT to obtain these WLD measures.

This first thing to note for the WLDs is the differences in the relative as well as absolute values to the original LDs. There is no systematic relationship between the LDs and the WLDs (r=-0.16). The WLD is revealing aspects of the data that were not observed with the unweighted algorithm. Deleting pages has, by intent, an even greater impact on WLDS than on LDs. For example, the LD for Teacher 1's ITS for group A that had the second highest number of deletions was 65 (equal lowest LD), the WLD for the same sequence was 40.51 (second highest). There is a significant negative correlation between course length and WLD (r = 0. 63, df, = 18, p <0.01), i.e. those sequences with high WLDs tended to be those whose length was short.

Table 4. Weighted Analysis of Four Authors' Sequences

	Teacher 1				Teacher 2				Teacher 3				Teacher 4			
	Len	Del	Rep	WLD	Len	Del	Rep	WLD	Len	Del	Rep	WLD	Len	Del	Rep	WLD
Group A	39	32	0	40.51	54	20	7	29.72	36	35	0	45.3	58	24	11	38.51
Group B	46	25	0	26.46	54	20	7	29.72	44	28	1	45.3	62	20	11	36.03
Group C	82	3	14	26.46	73	5	7	22.6	43	29	1	39.29	76	10	15	29.64
Group D	82	3	14	35.02	66	12	3	27.59	66	6	1	21.38	88	1	18	40.92
Group E	44	27	1	40.97	66	12	3	27.59	43	29	1	39.29	84	5	18	27.31
Mean	58.6	18.2	5.8	33.84	62.6	13.8	5.4	27.44	46.4	25.4	0.8	38.11	73.6	12.0	14.6	34.48
St.Dev	21.5	14.1	7.5	7.17	8.4	6.3	2.2	2.91	11.4	11.2	0.4	9.82	13.2	9.8	3.5	5.811

Key - Len: Length of ITS sequences. Del: The number of pages deleted. Rep: The number of pages used more than once. LD: The LD between the CBT and the ITS.

The WLDs are relatively high, but it is difficult to quantify this. As with the original LD, the minimum possible WLD is still 0. However, the concept of theoretical maximum that was used with the LD is not a sensible way of determining the greatest perturbation with the WLD. To achieve this maximum WLD an educator would be required to make decisions that realistically have no likelihood of being made, i.e. to delete all but one of the pages from the CBT and then repeat that single page indefinitely. Therefore, to gain some understanding of the degree to which the authors had changed the course, we computed the maximum WLD given no deletions or substitutions. This is achieved by moving each page its maximum possible distance from the source to the target which in this case of 71 items gives a WLD of 35.49.

4.2 Comparing Author ITS Sequences to Each Other

Each author created five different ITSs for the purposes of this study and assigned them to different student categories. Hence, the ITS sequences can be compared to each other. Each row in Table 5 shows the WLDs between a pair of ITSs (e.g. Group A and Group B) for each teacher. The higher a teachers' average WLD score, the more the ITSs were differentiated to individual learners. Teacher 1 had the highest WLD score and standard deviation. Her ITS content was the most differentiated to particular learners' perceived needs. Teachers 2 and 4 by contrast had much lower mean WLDs suggesting they created ITSs with the most overlap. Teacher 2 created a "core" ITS sequence which she amended slightly for her upper and lower groups whereas Teacher 4 created different ITSs for each group but with no strong outliers.

This analysis shows how ITS authoring tools can compare approaches to teaching by providing information about how much a teacher tends to differentiate content for different learners. However, this is only one of the decisions that teachers make about how to adapt to different learners as they also adjust their teaching strategies. We have previously examined strategies created by these four authors using REDEEM (Ainsworth et al, 2000) so we were able to see if teachers who differentiate their teaching by content also differentiate by strategy. We found the same rank order if teachers approaches were ranked by either strategy or content (T1 > T3 > T4 > T2).

Table 5. Analysis of ITS sequences by Student Category and Teacher

ITSs		T1	T2	T3	T4
A	B	59.5	0.0	49.1	8.6
A	C	59.5	22.3	46.4	23.5
A	D	57.4	29.5	46.4	36.6
A	E	58.3	29.5	31.1	40.7
B	C	0.3	22.3	10.1	16.2
B	D	36.4	29.5	10.1	29.3
B	E	43.4	29.5	22.4	33.4
C	D	36.4	7.1	0.0	13.7
C	E	43.4	7.1	33.4	18.0
D	E	7.1	0.0	12.8	4.6
Mean		40.18	17.67	28.23	16.49
St. Dev		21.35	12.69	17.13	15.46

4.3 Comparing ITSs for Different Groups and Different Courses

We have also used the WLD to examine agreement about the needs of different learners. There may be some students where there is much higher agreement than others about the appropriate sequence of material. The authors created different ITSs for each five groups of learners (Table 6). Each sequences was then compared to the other ITSs for that student group (e.g. all 4 ITSs for group A were compared, a total of 6 comparisons). The more the authors agreed about how to teach a group of students, the lower the score should be. In fact, the average WLDs were distinctly high suggesting there is no consensual view of learner's content needs in this domain.

Table 6. Analysis of Mean Distance between Sequences by Student Category

	Group A	Group B	Group C	Group D	Group E
Mean WLD	49.65	47.05	43.36	52.69	46.33
St.Dev	12.52	12.77	11.55	7.03	11.66

Finally, we are interested in whether this measure can identify those domains that should benefit most from being REDEEMed. Topics may vary in the extent to which authors desire to construct their own sequences or in the extent to which they differ from each other. We used the WLD measure to compare authoring for two other domains we have been studying. The first, Communication and Information System

Protocols, is a multi-chapter course developed by the Royal Navy. Table 7 shows the results for four of these courses each authored by two Naval authors. We compare each REDEEM course to the CBT and then compare each author's ITS to each other.

Table 7. Weighted LD Analysis of Four Royal Naval Courses by Two Authors

	Author 1 & CBT	Author 2 & CBT	Author 1/Author 2
CISP1 (Ln 28)	4.16	3.35	1.25
CISP2 (Ln 37)	9.22	8.32	0.51
CISP3 (Ln 48)	9.67	8.88	1.37
CISP4 (Ln 52)	11.92	10.2	1.18
Mean	8.74	7.69	1.08
St.Dev	3.28	2.99	0.39

The second domain is Genetics for 14 to 16 yr olds. "Genetics 1" is a 48 page course and "Genetics 2" is 73 pages. Two different teachers have authored these courses for their pupils. We report the WLDs for each ITS created (five for Teacher 1, three for Teacher 2) compared to the CBT, but do not compare the teachers' authoring to each other as there is no equivalence across their different learner categories.

Table 8. Weighted LD Analysis of Secondary School Genetics

T 1 Groups	T1 & Gen1	T1 & Gen2	T2 Groups	T 2 & Gen 1	T2 & Gen2
5	26.6	41.7	D2	16.5	31.0
4	26.6	41.7	D6	10.9	27.1
3	25.7	41.7	T (top)	6.0	24.4
2	17.6	41.3			
1 (top)	17.6	35.5			
Mean	22.82	40.38		11.13	27.50
St.Dev	4.78	2.73		5.267	3.32

These analyses provide data about how different domains and the contexts in which they are used impact upon they way authors use REDEEM. There are lower WLDs for the Navy courses compared to the school courses with a striking overlap between the trainers' sequences. This confirms our views that these authors were using REDEEM to follow courses which were strongly constrained by pre-requisites (Ainsworth, Williams & Wood, 2001). This is also visible in the authoring of a single strategy for all learners. By contrast, the genetics courses reveals a different picture. Here the authors have relatively low intra-author WLD scores but larger and different CBT v REDEEM WLD scores. This corresponds to their goal of differentiating content to adapt to their pupils needs whilst working to (alternative) curriculum goals.

5 Summary

In this paper we have described a novel way of examining course authoring by using the Levenshtein Distance algorithm with weights that are specifically adapted to the issue of ITS sequences. We have created this measure to provide a quantitative expression of the difference between sequences generated by teachers' use of an ITS authoring tool which alters the way that learners are presented with material. Although it is not the only approach to comparing sequences, we have found it a useful way to identify when authors most diverged from the original courseware (CBT – ITS differences), from each other (inter-author differences) and across their class of learners (intra-author differences). Using this technique has begun to answer questions about conditions under which use of REDEEM is likely to prove most beneficial, has helped us identify domains for which there is more agreement about the appropriate sequences, and has provided quantitative ways of classifying approaches to teaching students and courses. Furthermore, it should be possible to use the WLD measures to drive multivariate methods such as multi-dimensional scaling where aspects of authoring and teaching style become apparent from the number, uniformity and universality of the dimensions that arise.

We have presented the WLD technique in the context of REDEEM, we hope that it is apparent that its potential application as a measure for quantifying differences in sequences of teaching material is much broader than REDEEM alone.

Acknowledgements. This research conducted at the ESRC Centre for Research in Development Instruction and Training and also supported by the Office of Naval Research under grant N00014-99-1-077. We would like to thank the teachers for being such informative authors. Shirley Grimshaw and Ben Williams were invaluable in collecting the data.

References

Ainsworth, S.E., Grimshaw, S.K. & Underwood, D.J. (1999) Teachers as designers: Using REDEEM to create ITSs for the classroom. Computers & Education, 33(2/3),171-188.

Ainsworth, S.E. Underwood, J.D. & Grimshaw, S.K. (2000) Using an ITS authoring tool to explore educators' use of instructional strategies. In G. Gauthier, C. Frasson & K. VanLehn (Eds.) Intelligent Tutoring Systems: 5th International Conference ITS 2000. pp 182-191.

Ainsworth, S.E., Williams, B.C & Wood, D.J. (2001) Using the REDEEM ITS authoring environment in naval training. In T. Okamoto, R. Hartley, Kinshuk, & J.P. Klus (Eds) IEEE International Conference on Advanced Learning Technologies, pp 189-192. Los Alamitos.

Gagne, R. (1985) The Conditions of Learning, 4th, Holt, Rinehart, and Winston,.

Langley, P. (1995) Order effects in incremental learning. In P. Reimann and H. Spada, (Eds), Learning in humans and machines. Pergamon: pp 154-165,.

Levenshtein V.I. (1966) Binary codes capable of correcting deletions, insertions and reversals. Cybernet. Control Theory. 10:707-710

Major, N., Ainsworth, S.E., & Wood, D.J. (1997) REDEEM: Exploiting Symbiosis Between Psychology and Authoring Environments, Int. Jour. of AI in Education 8(3/4), 317-340.

Murray, T. (1999). Authoring intelligent tutoring systems: An analysis of the state of the art. Int. Jour. of AI in Education 10, 98-129.

Sankof, D. & Kruskal, J.B. (1983). Time Warps, String Edits and Macromolecules. Addison-Wesley, Reading, Massachusetts.

Are ITSs Created with the REDEEM Authoring Tool More Effective than "Dumb" Couresware?

Shaaron Ainsworth and Shirley Grimshaw

School of Psychology, University of Nottingham, Nottingham, NG7 2RD, UK
{sea, skg)@psychology.nottingham.ac.uk

Abstract. The REDEEM authoring tool allows teachers to create simple ITSs from existing CBT by imposing their pedagogical preferences about how students should best be taught. In this study we compared learning outcomes of 86 14-16 yr old students who studied genetics with CBT and with ITSs constructed for them by their class teacher who had expert knowledge of both the topic and these students. We found that performance of the students improved from pre-test to post-test but learning outcomes were not influenced by type of learning environment. Detailed analysis of participants' performance suggested that REDEEM could enhance knowledge by directly questioning students but that features such as differentiation did not impact upon performance. We discuss possible interpretations for these results in the light of evaluation issues for ITS authoring tools.

1 Introduction

One of the primary goals of the research and development of Intelligent Tutoring System (ITS) Authoring Tools is to deliver the benefits that ITSs bring to learning in a cost and time effective manner. Research has shown that learners interacting with individualised computer tutors can generate impressive learning outcomes (*e.g.* Mark & Greer, 1995; Lesgold, Lajoie, Bunzo, & Eggan, 1992). To date, there have been few evaluations of the products of ITS authoring tools (ITSATs) to see if they deliver similar improvements in learners' knowledge and skills. So far, probably the only ITSATs that can claim large scale empirical evaluation are XAIDA (Hsieh., Halff, & Redfield, 1998).

One reason for the small number of evaluations of ITSATs relative to ITSs s is that determining the success of an ITSAT is more complicated given the need to evaluate the authors' as well as the learners' experiences (e.g. Murray, 1997). If the evaluation goal is not simply to determine whether an ITS is effective but also to identify what features lead to this success, then proving causal relations between aspects of the ITS design and positive learning gains is very complicated To be done successfully, large scale experiments are required. Furthermore, the effectiveness of any learning environment is influenced by its context of use (e.g. Wood, Underwood & Avis, 1999). For authoring tools, these methodological and philosophical issues are multiplied because any resulting ITS is a combination of the options for authoring offered to users, the authors' decisions, and the systems' interpretation and delivery of those decisions.

S.A. Cerri, G. Gouardères, and F. Paraguaçu (Eds.): ITS 2002, LNCS 2363, pp. 883–892, 2002.

In this paper, we report a substantial study of a teacher's use of REDEEM to develop ITSs for Genetics that were subsequently used by 80 children in her class. Consequently, we hoped to answer the question of whether the REDEEM, in the hands of an expert teacher, can deliver effective learning outcomes.

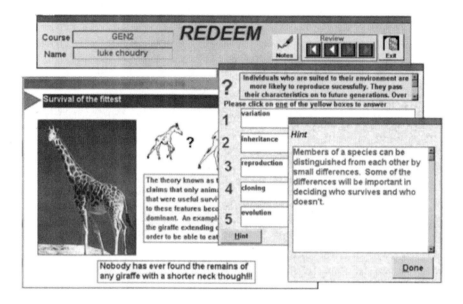

Fig. 1. REDEEM running Genetics 2

2   System Description

REDEEM (Major, Ainsworth & Wood, 1997) is designed to allow teachers and trainers with little technological knowledge to create simple ITSs. Unlike many ITS authoring tools, REDEEM does not support the construction of domain material. Instead authors import existing computer-based material as domain material and then use the REDEEM tools to overlay their teaching expertise. The REDEEM shell uses this knowledge, together with its own default teaching knowledge, to deliver the courseware adaptively to meet the needs of different learners.

The courseware for REDEEM consists of individual pages of material that can contain text, animations, simulations, exercises and multi-media. Having selected domain material, the author is faced with five main tasks to 'REDEEM' it. Essentially, authors provide a domain model by describing characteristics of the existing material which allows the ITS Shell to sequence and structure it. They supplement the material with additional questions and provide hints to their solution (see Figure 1). Then authors individualize a course to meet the requirements of their specific learners. They classify their students into categories (based upon any dimension that they choose) and then assign different content to these categories.

Different teaching strategies are created by manipulating dimensional sliders of eight components of instruction (e.g. student control, position and amount of question, amount of help, number of attempts at questions). They also assign questions of appropriate styles and difficulty to strategies. These strategies are then associated with student categories. Thus, there are essentially two stages to REDEEM authoring; in the first stage the domain material is enriched but it remains essentially non-adaptive CBT; in the second stage the CBT is individualized to the needs of learners by macro-adapting the teaching strategies and the content to student categories. These can dynamically adjust during a student's interaction with the system.

3   Current Experiment

Previous studies with REDEEM have focussed on the experience of authors in domains as diverse as "Shapes" in primary maths and "Communication and Information System Principles" with the Royal Navy (see Ainsworth, Grimshaw & Underwood, 1999; Ainsworth, Williams & Wood, 2001). They have shown that REDEEM is one of the most usable ITS authoring tools. It requires only 90 minutes to train authors. The majority of the tools are simple to use, especially those used for macro-adaptation. Authoring with REDEEM is time efficient. Authors have taken between 1 and 4 hours to develop an hour of instruction. So we have demonstrated that ITS production with REDEEM is relatively efficient but the key question of whether it is effective had not been addressed.

To answer this question, we recruited a secondary (high) school teacher and provided her with two previously developed ToolBook courses that teach the age 14-16 UK curriculum on the topic of Genetics. She was asked to author her ideal ITSs for the pupils that she taught. These pupils then took part in learning outcome studies. As REDEEM ITSs are based on existing courseware, we have an unusual and interesting possibility for comparing learning outcomes. Most comparisons compare ITSs to either individual human teaching, classroom teaching or to alternative versions of themselves. Ablation experiments where particular design features are removed and performance of the systems compared (e.g. Cohen, & Howe, 1988) are an increasingly common technique. Essentially, with REDEEM we can perform a massive but controlled ablation experiment where the learning outcomes from those students working with stand-alone courseware can be compared to learning outcomes with REDEEM ITSs. If learning outcomes are higher with REDEEM, then we can conclude that the REDEEM/Author partnership in the situation provided better support for learning than the non-intelligent courseware.

3.1   REDEEM ITSs and Courseware

The courseware used in this experiment was two ToolBook courses developed by another teacher prior to this study. The first, Gen1, was 48 pages long and covered the topics of inheritance, genes, variation and cell division. The second, Gen2 was longer at 72 pages and covered dna structure, evolution and reproduction. They consist of text and graphics declarative material with some multimedia, simple exercises and a glossary. Navigation is limited to "go next page" and a hotlink to glossary. A workbook was created to contain the same non-computer tasks as those by REDEEM and some blank pages to make notes.

The teacher's authoring with the REDEEM Tools created ITSs with the following characteristics. They had additional interactivity compared to the CBT. She created many questions and for the majority of these, also authored multiple levels of hints. She described pages where she wanted students to reflect, which prompts REDEEM to offer its notes tool. She developed a number of non-computer tasks (e.g. worksheets) which were authored to appear at appropriate times. She described the characteristics of the domain material to create the semantic network for the REDEEM Shell. She often chose to develop sections that addressed the same topics at varying levels of complexity. This was either done by creating a "core" section on a topic such as genetic engineering and then adding additional material for a "hard" section or by creating two distinct sections such as "easy" and "hard" fertilization.

She then chose how to adapt the ITSs to the perceived needs of different learners. She created five different categories of learners based on her judgements of their relative aptitude (A to E). Each category was assigned different material and teaching strategies (summarized in Table 1.). Some aspects of her strategy such as using no questions before material covered, when to assign non-computer based tasks and whether to teach material from general to specific were common to all strategies.

Table 1. Summary of ITSs Created for Five Categories of Learner

	Group A	Group B	Group C	Group D	Group E
Content Difficulty Amount	difficult 44 & 60 pages	quite difficult 44 & 50 pages	easier 32 & 44 pages	easier 30 & 44 pages	easier 30 & 44 pages
Questions Types Difficulty Amount	all types med. & hard 36 & 39 ?s all	all types med. & hard 36 & 39 ?s all	all types easy & med. 24 & 24 ?s no more than 1 per page	no matching easy & med. 23 & 24 ?s no more than 1 per page	no matching easy & med. 23 & 24 ?s no more than 1 per page
Strategy Autonomy Help Answers- deduced	choose sections selects ? type help on error multiple attempts at ?	choose sections selects ?s help on error multiple attempts at ?	no choice ? after section help on error multiple attempts at ?	no choice ? after section help on error & request 2 attempts at ?	no choice ? after page help on error & request 2 attempts at ?

3.2 Design and Participants

In order to reduce the effects of participant variance, a within subjects design was employed. All participants received one course under REDEEM and one as the courseware, i.e. half received REDEEM Gen1 and CBT Gen 2 and half CBT Gen 1 and REDEEM Gen2. 45 boys and 41 girls aged between 14 and 15 years old took part in the experiment. No attempt was made to have equal number assigned to different categories as this was an important part of the author's teaching strategy. Hence numbers in the five categories were 8 (A), 30 (B), 23 (C), 15 (D) and 10 (E).

3.3 Materials

Developing fair pre and post-test material is particularly complex given the differentiation by content and strategy that REDEEM provides. Furthermore, some of the material is directly questioned for (some) groups by REDEEM. Hence, performance on these items could be enhanced by simple memorisation rather than understanding. Rather than excluding the material, we chose to address this issue by creating three types of question:

- REDEEM questions – directly questioned by REDEEM;
- Surface Transformation questions – which addressed the same issue as a REDEEM question but transformed (e.g. questions about the inheritance of brown or blue eyes was mapped onto aliens with purple and pink eyes)
- Non REDEEM questions – the material to answer the question was presented to all students but not directly questioned.

In total, a 60 item multi-choice quiz was developed. It consisted of 30 questions on Gen1 and 30 on Gen2 each further subdivided into 10 REDEEM, 10 Surface Transformation (ST) and 10 Non-REDEEM (Non) questions.

3.4 Procedure

1. Pre-tests were given to the participants in their school classroom just prior to the intervention
2. Intervention: The pupils came to the University of Nottingham to study the Genetics material. Each session lasted between 30 and 90 minutes. The minimum number of sessions a pupil attended for was two and the maximum was five. Two computing labs were used each equipped with 32 PCs. There were up to three experimenters and two teachers on hand to deliver non-computer tasks, provide help with the interface to the software and provide classroom management.
3. Post-tests were given within two weeks of participants finishing the study.

4 Results

To examine the effects of the intervention, a [2 by 2 by 2] ANOVA was carried out on the pre-test and post-test data. The design of the analysis was 2(genetics 1, genetics 2) by 2(pre-test, post-test) with a between subjects factor of group (REDEEMgen1/CBTgen2, REDEEMgen2/CBTgen1). Twelve subjects were excluded for non completion of a test. Analysis revealed a significant main effect of time ($F_{1,72}$ = 74.52, MSE = 7.62, p < 0.0005), and a significant main effect of course ($F_{1,72}$ = 5.06, MSE = 8.25, p = 0.028) with subjects scoring higher on Genetics 2 than on Genetics 1. There were no significant interactions. Consequently, it would appear that subjects were slightly more familiar with the Genetics 2 material at the beginning of the study and that they all improved over time, but that there was no differential improvement associated with the course they had experienced through REDEEM rather than as CBT. Furthermore, the degree of the improvement whilst statistically significant was not impressive in educational terms.

Table 2. Pre and Post Test Scores by Course and Type of Intervention

	Genetics 1				Genetics 2			
	REDEEM (n = 40)		CBT (n = 34)		REDEEM (n = 34)		CBT (n = 40)	
Time of test	Mean	S D	Mean	S D	Mean	S D	Mean	S D
Pre-test/ 30	11.00	3.37	11.71	3.01	12.68	3.94	11.83	3.69
Post-test/ 30	14.38	4.83	14.18	3.75	15.47	4.63	14.30	3.69

Given the design of the test material, we could explore whether improvement on all three types of question was equal. We predicted that for the questions on the course they had experienced through REDEEM, they would perform significantly better on REDEEM and ST questions than on Non questions (Table 3). There should be no difference for CBT material as they were not asked any questions during that part of the intervention. If significant differences are present at post-test, this would suggest that the differences we are observing are related to the actual questions rather than to the way the material has been presented to the subjects. Two [2 by 3 by 2] ANOVAs were performed on the REDEEM and CBT data respectively, with two within-subjects factors, time and question type and one between-subjects factor, course.

Table 3. Question Types Scores by Course and Time (REDEEM Only)

	Genetics 1 (n = 41)				Genetics 2 (n = 34)			
	Pre-test		Post-test		Pre-test		Post-test	
Question type	Mean	S D	Mean	S D	Mean	S D	Mean	S D
REDEEM/10	3.66	1.61	5.24	1.95	4.21	2.06	5.62	2.31
ST/ 10	3.63	1.55	4.78	2.03	4.71	1.96	5.74	1.90
Non/ 10	3.63	1.73	4.32	1.71	3.76	1.23	4.12	1.79

For the REDEEM data, as before there was a significant main effect of time ($F_{1,73}$ = 42.75, MSE = 2.79, p < 0.001) and question type ($F_{2,146}$ = 10.89, MSE = 2.49, p < 0.001). There was a significant interaction between question type and course($F_{2,72}$ = 4.10, MSE = 2.78, p <0.02). Simple Main Effects showed that question type had a significant impact on genetics 2 ($F_{2,144}$= 12.40, p <0.001) but not on genetics 1 ($F_{2,144}$= 1.58). Furthermore, there was a significant interaction between time and question type ($F_{2,146}$ = 5.41, MSE = 1.67, p < 0.005). Simple Main Effects revealed that there were no significant differences between the question types at pre-test ($F_{2,288}$ = 1.28) but that there were at post-test ($F_{2,288}$ = 13.64, p <0.001). Post hoc comparisons showed that REDEEM and ST questions improvement significantly from pre to post-test (q= 7.54, p <0.001 & q= 5.67, p <0.001) whereas non-REDEEM questions did not (q = 2.70). Analysis of the CBT data showed a single significant effect, that of time ($F_{1,73}$ = 45.64, MSE = 1.72, p < 0.001). Thus, we can conclude that the difference between the question types that we observed with the REDEEM were a result of the nature of the intervention rather than an artefact of the questions asked.

One further interesting analysis of the pre-test and post-test data concerns the teacher's categorisation. We were interested to see this categorisation corresponded to learner's pre-test scores and whether there was any differential impact upon performance. Table 4 shows the scores for these categories based on their performance on the pre-tests. There was a significant correlation between participants scores on the pre-test and their category for both courses($r = 0.66$, $N = 85$, $p < 0.001$ and $r = 0.73$, $N = 86$, $p < 0.001$). This suggests that the teacher categorisation, which was blind to the pre-test score, had been accurate. However, there was no interaction between categories and time; all groups made similar progress from pre to post-test.

Table 4. Pre-test Scores by Category and Course

	Genetics 1		Genetics 2	
Cat	Mean	S D	Mean	S D
A (n=8)	15.13	1.71	18.5	2.22
B (n=30)	12.73	1.99	13.4	3.68
C (n=23)	9.96	2.87	10.57	4.14
D (n=15)	8.53	2.64	8.67	5.61
E (n = 9	8.44	2.06	8.22	1.73

The last analysis conducted examined if REDEEM impacted on the time that students were taking to learn the material.

Table 5. Times in Seconds per Course and Per Page by Category

		Genetics 1			Genetics 2		
Cat		Mean	No of pages	Time per page	Mean	No of pages	Time per page
A	RED.	9316	44	212	7862	60	131
	CBT	3180	29	110	3050	40	76
B	RED.	5126	44	114	5110	50	102
	CBT	2874	29	99	2581	40	65
C	RED.	4727	32	140	3348	44	76
	CBT	3039	29	104	3720	40	93
D	RED.	5329	30	170	3976	44	90
	CBT	3220	29	111	3333	40	83
E	RED.	4159	30	135	3257	44	74
	CBT	3190	29	110	1681	40	42

To calculate the amount of time the participants had spent learning we totaled the time they spent over each session from first to last mouse click. The total time per course was obviously influenced by the course length. Hence, we divided total time by the number of pages in the course to determine the mean amount of time in seconds per page. Analysis by [2 by 5 by 2] ANOVA showed a significant main effect of intervention ($F_{1,72} = 8.64$, $p < 0.005$) with page times longer for REDEEM than for CBT. There was a significant interaction between intervention and course ($F_{1,72} = 10.65$, $p < 0.002$) which confirms that REDEEM took longer to complete than CBT irrespective of course. We inspected this data to see if learners who spent longer on the course showed differential improvement. There was no systematic relationship between improved performance and time for the CBT groups ($r = 0.10$, and $r = 0.04$ for Gen1 and Gen2), but there was a weak relationship for the REDEEM groups ($r = 0.32$, $p < 0.02$) and ($r = 0.27$, $p < 0.07$) for Gen1 and Gen2. It seems that time per se is not an important determiner of learning outcomes, but that if students spend time on the activities provided by REDEEM then this may improve their understanding.

5 Discussion

The results of this study showed that whilst children in all conditions improved their knowledge of genetics, there was no differential impact of REDEEM on learning outcomes. There were slight indication of potential benefit in that questions on the post-test which had been asked by REDEE showed the greatest degree of improvement and that students who spent longer working with REDEEM learnt more. We were also happy that given the generally inappropriately low times spent with the learning environments, that REDEEM appeared to slow the students down. However, this is not the strong endorsement of REDEEM's benefit that we were looking for.

In order to understand these results, we face a very large credit assignment problem. The explanation of the lack of difference between REDEEM and CBT could rest with a number of different factors and, while we have our favourites, we first identify as many of them as possible.

The first plausible candidate is these REDEEM ITSs were no more effective at supporting learning than the underlying CBT. This could be either because the system's delivery of the author's decisions was not advantageous or that the authoring itself was not sensitive to learners' needs. Generally, we judged the authoring by the class teacher to be excellent. She had a detailed knowledge of the topic, which allowed her to create a very clear domain structure and to provide questions and exercises on issues which she knew were both important and likely to be difficult.. She also had a detailed knowledge of the students, which was evident in the way that her judgements of their knowledge of Genetics correlated so highly with their pre-test scores. It is true that some of her teaching strategy decisions were not the ones we personally would have made (e.g. limiting help on request and fixing fairly strict number of attempts at questions). However, this is just opinion as there is no independent evidence as to whose views of teaching were the most appropriate for these students. Hence, there is little support for the statement that the responsibility for the lack of difference lies with the decisions of the author. However, it could be that the REDEEM tools do not ask teachers the "right" questions about their pedagogies or that the REDEEM shell delivers them in a way that it is inappropriate. REDEEM may be just in insufficiently intelligent ITS.

A related explanation rests with the learner. The CBT and REDEEM both deliver the same (apart from differentiated content) material. Consequently, whilst it may be easier to learn this material when you are interacting with a system that asks you questions, provides hints to their solution, provides you with an on-line note tool, etc, it is of course still possible to learn without these facilities. Thus, another reason why there is little difference between the CBT and REDEEM is that learners' may be compensating for the lack of support by working harder.

The second type of explanation concerns the courseware. Unlike other ITS authoring tools, REDEEM relies on the pre-existing content. REDEEM's goal is to enhance the teaching of this content by providing additional interactivity and to differentiate this material and interactivity by providing alternative teaching strategies and content. If this underlying courseware is not of good quality then REDEEM may be unable to do much to enhance it. Furthermore, if the courseware is already rich in interactivity and allows for learners with different needs then perhaps REDEEM's feature are superfluous. This is not an explanation that appears likely in this case. The CBT had already been used in a school classroom and contains much clearly presented and relevant information. However, given its very limited interactivity (only a few simple exercises per course) and scope for different interpretations of the material, it might be expected that it could be enhanced by REDEEM's features.

The third type of explanation lies in the design of the study. It could be the case that the pre and post-tests were not sufficiently sensitive to learning outcomes However, there were no floor or ceiling effects and performance on the test is highly correlated with teacher's judgements. Secondly, for ethical reasons the teacher replicated limited aspects REDEEM's functionality with the CBT. For example, as we had access to the source of the CBT she asked us to construct a sequence through the CBT which matched her views of teaching. We were also able to easily delete and include material as she desired. Workbooks were provided for learners with exercises and notes pages and patrolling teachers acted as motivation for their completion. This is a quite realistic way to use the CBT as teachers are unlikely to teach with courseware that does not fit their teaching and curriculum needs but does provide a more rigorous test of REDEEM's additional features. Finally, because the school was unable to provide a computer room at the necessary times, the pupils were brought to the University of Nottingham for these lessons. This unfortunately led to the learning experience for pupils as being somewhat removed from their everyday schooling. It also meant that given the time constraints this imposed a single intervention session lasted up to 90 minutes. This was longer than desirable.

Finally, we need to acknowledge significant problems with participants' motivation. Many, though by no means all of the students, did not wish to learn about this topic. This was evident from the general time spent on reading material and interacting with exercises. REDEEM provides student history inspection tools and it was notable that many pupils were skipping through pages without reading them. The trace logs from the CBT if anything revealed an even worse picture. REDEEM may provide more features that support learning, but learners need to engage with the system if they are to benefit from those features. Hints are only helpful if you read them, exercises only beneficial if you complete them and on-line note tools only valuable if you write in them.

We see a number of avenues for future research that will attempt to address which of these explanations are correct. Firstly, we are examining the process measures of students' interaction with the CBT and, particularly with REDEEM, to identify if there are any systematic patterns between what learners were doing on the system and pre-test/post-test performance. For example, we can measure the number of attempts at questions, the amount of time reading hints and the number of time help was requested, the amount of note taking etc. Secondly, we are currently attempting to replicate this study in a way that removes some of these problems. We have identified a school with good existing computer facilities and are now running the learning environments in normal lessons. Accordingly, we hope that by sacrificing some control of conditions, we have gained a significant advantage in terms of realism with hopefully a concomitant impact upon learner motivation. Thirdly, we are also following the opposite approach. The teacher in this study (and others we have run) are very keen to use the differentiation features that REDEEM provides. From an experimental viewpoint is less than ideal as there are multiple differences between

REDEEM ITSs and the underlying CBT. Consequently, we have developed a number of smaller ITSs (teaching photography, Freud and digital computing) with much less differentiation of features and are running more controlled design experiments in the laboratory. This allows more systematic comparisons of the relative contribution to learning that various of REDEEM's functions can provide.

REDEEM provides features that aid its use in the classroom above and beyond that of CBT. It provides student history and modelling, swift customisation of content and strategy and a common interface to many different courses. Consequently, as long as it does not deliver *worse* learning outcomes there is good reason to use it. We hope that future evaluation will uncover the conditions when REDEEM is more effective than CBT. If this does not prove to be the case then research can take us in two opposite direction. Firstly, we could modify the REDEEM tools so that they deliver the features that aid classroom integration but don't attempt to improve pedagogy. This will significantly reduce the time required for authoring. Secondly, we can modify REDEEM so that has more sophistication and intelligence and will probably require longer authoring times. Both routes remain viable options to explore in the research and development of authoring tools that best support the teacher/learner/system triangle.

Acknowledgements. This research was supported by the ESRC at the ESRC Centre for Research in Development Instruction and Training. We would like to thank Wendy Crossland for her help in authoring and running the study.

References

Ainsworth, S.E., Grimshaw, S.K. & Underwood,.J.D. (1999) Teachers as designers: Using REDEEM to create ITSs for the classroom. *Computers and Education,* 33(2/3),171-188.

Ainsworth, S.E., Williams, B.C & Wood, D.J. (2001) Using the REDEEM ITS authoring environment in naval training. In T. Okamoto, R. Hartley, Kinshuk, & J.P. Klus (Eds) Proceedings of the IEEE International Conference on Advanced Learning Technologies, pp 189-192. IEEE Computer Society, Los Alamitos, CA.

Cohen, P., & Howe, A. (1988). How evaluation guides AI research. AI Magazine, 9 , 35-43.

Hsieh, P.Y., Halff, H.M. and Redfield, C.L. (1998). Four easy pieces: Development systems for knowledge-based generative instruction. *Int. Jour of AI in Ed*, 9, 1–45,

Lesgold, A., Lajoie, S., Bunzo, M. & Eggan, G. (1992). Sherlock: A coached practice environment for an electronics troubleshooting job. In J. Larkin & R. Chabay (Eds.), *Computer based learning and intelligent tutoring* (pp. 202-274). Hillsdale, NJ: LEA.

Major, N., Ainsworth, S.E., & Wood, D.J. (1997). REDEEM: Exploiting symbiosis between psychology and authoring environments, *Int. Jour of AI in Ed 8(*3/4), 317-340.

Mark, M.A. & Greer, J.E. (1995) The VCR tutor: Effective instruction for device operation. *Journal of the Learning Sciences*, 4(2), 209-246.

Murray, T. (1997). Expanding the knowledge acquisition bottleneck for intelligent tutoring systems. *Int. Jour of AI in Ed,,* 8(3-4), 222-232.

Murray, T. (1999). Authoring intelligent tutoring systems: An analysis of the state of the art. *Int. Jour of AI in Ed*, 10, 98-129.

Wood, D.J., Underwood, J.D.M. & Avis, P. (1999) Integrated Learning Systems in the Classroom. *Computers and Educati*on, 33(2/3), 91-108

StoryML: An XML Extension for Woven Stories

Petri Gerdt[1], Piet Kommers[2], Jarkko Suhonen[1], and Erkki Sutinen[1]

[1] Dept. of Computer Science, University of Joensuu, Finland
{pgerdt,suhonen,sutinen}@cs.joensuu.fi
[2] Dept. of Educational Technology, Univ. Twente, The Netherlands
P.A.M.Kommers@edte.utwente.nl

Abstract. StoryML is an XML-based representation of metadata elements connected to collaboratively written stories. The StoryML specification gives means to interpret and specify the core characteristics of stories. Hence, StoryML supports the functionality of information retrieval, filtering and adaptive representation of stories. These intelligence properties make collaboratively written stories a significant platform for truly activating, open learning environments.

1 Introduction

In this paper we elaborate the concept of *woven stories*, first presented in [3], into the direction of an intelligent learning environment. A woven story is the result of several authors' efforts in a shared writing space, where the authors may write story sections and link them together. A woven story is thus a hyperdocument or alternatively hyperspace, which consists of an arbitrary set of story sections and links between them. The woven stories idea differs from collaborative writing in that the participating authors may not have a common goal to write a document jointly. Instead, they explore their ideas and express their views, for example different authors might want to change the ending of a story by writing an alternative ending in a new story section. A woven story is visualized as a graph, where the story sections are represented by nodes and the relations between them by links. We have explored the concept of woven stories in a experimental Internet-based application labeled Woven Stories 2, or WS2 for short [2].

The opportunity to adapt the hyperspace, consisting of stories, according to the specific characteristics and needs of the users is interesting. This adaptation means for example that the stories would be represented to different users in different ways. Also it would be useful to the user of woven stories to retrieve subsets of collaboratively written stories. To achieve adaptation, filtering and retrieval in woven stories, we need a way to define an extension for collaboratively written stories.

We have developed a XML-based specification for woven stories which is referred to in this paper as *StoryML*. The StoryML specification specifies a data structure for capturing the characteristics of a woven story: the story sections, associations and the authors who have participated in the authoring effort. We present a description of the core element set of the StoryML in Section 3.

S.A. Cerri, G. Gouardères, and F. Paraguaçu (Eds.): ITS 2002, LNCS 2363, pp. 893–902, 2002.

One of the key concepts in the development of StoryML is metadata. With metadata elements one can store all the necessary information related to a specific domain. The core StoryML elements have been inspired by the Dublin Core metadata initiative [1]. Furthermore, StoryML draws elements from issues related to collaborative writing and collaborative concept mapping.

The woven stories concept supports open problem solving in a way that it does not force the user to act in a predefined manner. The intelligence of the woven stories empowered by StoryML comes with the adaptation of stories. This adaptation can be utilized for example during the learning process to illustrate individualized learning paths.

Traditionally, intelligent tutoring systems have supported the learner in his or her learning process to follow a more or less optimal root from a given starting point into the desired learning goal or objective. The tutoring system has tried to help the learner according to his or her preferences as given by the user model. In the scheme of woven stories, however, we emphasize the active role of the learner. The intelligence, or adaptivity, of a learning environment should be guaranteed by tools which help the learner to actively compose a meaningful environment for the learning process. To achieve this functionality an effective metadata scheme, in this case StoryML, is needed.

2   Woven Stories

Our view on systems realizing the woven stories idea is a family of web-based applications that allow users to compose their stories, and link appropriate story sections with pre-existing sections authored by someone else. As a co-authoring environment, woven stories support the user not only as his or her individual cognitive tool, but also as a shared platform to reflect ideas and thought processes of other users with related interests. Thus, a group of users can apply woven stories to tasks such as creative, open problem solving [2].

2.1   Uses of Woven Stories

The combination of the fact that human narrative thoughts may build upon existing recent expressions and at the same time benefit from alternative thought directions from the parallel co-authors is a potential source of progress in the coming future. The key issue is what mechanisms we develop as viable and fruitful ones for this intertwining process. In these efforts to make meaningful linking and reuse of knowledge sources on the web our woven stories project is not unique. A relevant discipline in this respect is the one initiated by research groups under the IEEE like the group in standard-upper-ontology [9]; its main goal is to find a solid basis for classifying and interrelating conceptual entities automatically. The lesson drawn from their work so far is that linguistic expressions can be utilized to convey the thinking process rather than to capture and represent the solid meaning underneath. This is the reason why woven stories do not attempt to rely on formalisms for the interlinking of narrative elements; it attempts to facilitate the human participants to anticipate to thought-provoking ideational junctions, without giving away one's own complete message.

The utilisation of woven stories is in its early days; a number of application domains have been identified so far:

1. The educational use is in composition and structural awareness in formulating thoughts and accepting lateral connotations and even conflicting perspectives.
2. Communication and mutual understanding in multicultural settings. Explaining technological and scientific constructs soon promotes a paternalistic and colonialist relation between teacher and audience. Woven stories allow us to anticipate to the mental process of successive integration and conceptual reconciliation; the new topic should become interwoven with familiar, preferably ideographic elements from the local culture, myths and episodic repertoire.
3. In the construction of new knowledge also the idea of a matrix of cross-fertilizing ideas seems much more fruitful than the mechanism of comparing conflicting ideas pair wise and deciding 'which is the true one' all the time.
4. The notion that concepts can better be understood in competing contexts is a well-received in rhetoric and theorem-proving: The attack by hybrid non-native seems to articulate the identity of a concept rather than threatening it. A good example is the ontology browser [7].
5. Finally, woven stories help us to redefine the most intrusive element we allowed in cognitive psychology, learning theory and theories about social representations: Concepts themselves. Based upon our pre-occupation with how to emulate human intelligence, we have adopted "object-oriented" ramifications about how to imagine "concepts". This is not a trivial entity as a factor "X" in order to reason about anonymous phenomena. As long as we confront students and designers with the name for a mental expression, we should have at least attempt to clarify its nature. It will be clear that in epistemic analyses we do not successfully characterize the phenomenological nature of concepts. Woven stories and concept mapping are the two more prominent methods to make students and designers aware of the perceptual and reflective nature of concepts.

2.2 The Dependency between Woven Stories and Concept Mapping

It is not so long ago that we started to think again about explicit representations of our thoughts. Cognitivism gave an impulse to accept the human mind as a world than can effectively be explored. Simon and Newell's work opened a new tradition of defining human problem solving as a rule-driven production process. The succeeding era of building expert systems showed exactly to what point this formalism works: Just before we ask ourselves how the human mind succeeds in controlling the direction and the span of the search.

It seems that both the procedural and the declarative representation are necessary. On top of that, the human problem solving capacity needs configurational awareness. This is exactly enabled by schematic representations. The types of knowledge can be classified along two dimensions: Episodic vs. semantic and declarative vs. procedural. It has become clearer lately how episodic memory plays a crucial role in the transition from declarative into procedural knowledge. Students with a good short-term memory capacity tend to rely less on episodic knowledge; these students seem to have the natural gift to transform new information into operational knowledge. The students with a weaker short-term memory need to reconstruct earlier given information via situational cues and via semantic elaborations like analogue reasoning; we call them students with a holistic style, as they need to recruit a large repertoire of prior knowledge before the factual date can be reconstructed.

The serialistic students proved to be much quicker learners. However in the mid and long term the serialists show a weaker integrated knowledge structure; the speed of memory prevents them from making connections with what they already know. After few years of study the holistic-style students show an easier and more flexible problem-solving style [5,6].

The study further showed that concept mapping fits best to the natural study style of the holists. It proved to be difficult to make serialistic students benefit from the concept mapping approach. The typical reason why holists benefited more from the concept map was that it releases the short-term memory load. The typical correlation between holistic style and the problems to perceive and report information in the original sequence seems to do with the lack of episodic encoding. Here we expect to find woven stories as a beneficial compensation for the problems holistic students have in chronologic reports. In summary: woven stories and concept mapping have the natural tendency to be mutually supportive. In global terms we may expect that the serialistic students will benefit more from concept mapping, while the holistic students get a typical compensation from the woven stories approach.

The clear distinction between stories and concept maps is the episodic nature of stories. A node in a concept map is often related only to its neighbouring concepts. One might say that a concept map represents only the local information of a particular concept. On the contrary stories typically represent episodes that consists of a several sub-sequent story sections connected by links. The analysis of episodes could be useful to make assumptions about the students' reasoning during the learning process. Moreover, information on different *episode patterns* could be stored by the StoryML specification, and actual story lines corresponding to a given pattern could be retrieved on demand. An example of episode patterns is a sequence A-B-A which represents a three step dialog, between students A and B.

3   Definition of StoryML

In a general sense, metadata can be called as a "data about data". The term "metadata" itself refers to background information about something[4]. Metadata can be associated to data which stores descriptive information of learning objects existing in a particular learning space. In many cases, metadata is dependent on the usage of the learning object. For example in the case of adaptive learning materials there can be metadata elements which store the data used in the adaptation or personalization process.

The reasons for creating and using metadata in general situations is to improve the possibilities of retrieval as well as to support control and management of the described resources. To make the creation process of metadata elements easier and to achieve interoperability between systems from diverse origins, several metadata standards have been developed. To describe the essential characteristics of a particular woven story we need a method to store the metadata for the attributes of such data entities. In the context of StoryML the metadata elements describe the characteristics and background information of stories.

StoryML draws elements from issues related to collaborative writing and collaborative concept mapping. One of the key ideas in woven stories and StoryML is the combination of collaboratively writing and linking a set of story sections. Collaboratively written text needs a special storing format, as any part of it may include contributions from many authors, and these must be separable in order to indicate different contributions. Collaborative linking of a set of story sections needs a visualization that shows clearly the structure of relations between them. In woven stories this is done by representing the collection of sections as a graph that is stored in the StoryML. The visual objects in the graph are linked to the story sections; in fact, the graph visualization represents the entire woven story. Furthermore the graph representation needs a special storing format to indicate contributing authors. The StoryML core element set is a stand-alone representation of a woven story at a given time. We present a summary of the core element set in Subsection 3.1.

3.1   The StoryML Core Element Set

The StoryML core element set is divided into five main categories represented by separate elements, which are summarized in Table 1.

Table 1. The main categories of the StoryML core element set.

Element	Description
General	General information about the woven story.
Content	The content (story sections) of the woven story written by an arbitrary number of authors.
Association	Contains the associations or links included in the woven story.
Visualization	Contains the representation of the woven story as a graph.
Author	Data about the authors who have contributed to the woven story.

The *General element* and its subelements store general information about a particular woven story, such as the name and intention of it. A woven story has a name that is used to refer to it as a whole. As a woven story can be used to serve different goals, an intention statement is included in the General element to let the authors decide and document a common goal. In addition to the intention the General element includes a description of the woven story which summarizes the content of the woven story in a free form. The description can for example be an invitation or an announcement to new writers, or simply an abstract of the content. The General element has a subelement, Creator, which stores information about the software tool used to implement the woven story. The General element includes a unique identifier, by which possible extensions are linked to the woven story.

The *Content element* stores the data of the set of story sections belonging to a woven story. The sections may include text, links and images and they may be written by an arbitrary number of authors. Thus the story sections are represented by a flexible structure which can be reformed to reflect the potentially complex authorship of a single section.

The *Association element* describes the associations between the collection of story sections in a woven story. These associations are restricted in the core element set of the StoryML to include only the links among the story sections and links to external content (not for example version history, which can be viewed as an association between versions too). Each of the associations may be described by a free form description.

The structure of a woven story is visualized by a graph. The *Visualization element* stores information that describes the visual representation that the authors have decided to use for their woven story. The Visualization element includes subelements for nodes and arcs, which together form the basis of the graph representation. The nodes represent separate story sections in the woven story, every one of the nodes representing a specific section. The only exception to this are external links, in which case a node represents external content located somewhere in the web. The arcs which connect nodes represent links (associations) between the story sections.

The *Author element* stores information about the authors who have participated in the writing of the woven story. This data includes personal data submitted by the authors themselves, such as their names, affiliations and interests. Two important information fragments stored within this element are the login name and color of each user. Both of these are required to indicate authorship in the woven story. The story sections may include a list of authors, who have participated in the writing of it, and their contributions in the actual text may be colored according to their allotted colors.

3.2   Data Management and StoryML

It is unrealistic to think that the user of the woven stories environment stores or even has to store all the necessary data to the StoryML elements. There are three different ways to collect the data in the environment. First, the data can be explicitly stored by the user or group of users. Secondly, the environment using StoryML can automatically or semi-automatically create some of the elements dynamically according to the content and relationships between story sections. Thirdly, data can be retrieved from the available user model. The elements that can be generated automatically by the application are, for example, the author of the node, the time of the contribution or the ID-number of the story node.

The user model of the authors can be used to get the data determining the visual appearance of a particular story node. In this way the system can adapt the representation of the story according to the specific preferences of the user. One of the most intuitive visual attributes would be the color of the nodes and arcs used to highlight a part of a woven story. The user model can be also dynamic, so that it can change according to the behavior of the user.

From the computational point of view, the methods of storing the metadata of a particular story section is quite easy to implement. The difficult part emerges when we are dealing with complex relations between the story nodes. Of course the students can add the relational information by themselves, but it is difficult to imagine that all the students can relate their ideas to the writings of other students or even to their own writings. Besides, it is basically impossible for an author to figure out complex relations between his own text and the contributions of the others.

A rich, ontologically sound relational information about the story nodes can help us to improve the functionality of a woven story environment. We can apply the relation information to make the environment adaptive to the needs of different users. Also the filtering of the woven story can be achieved using the relational information of the story.

A solution to the problem of creating relational or content dependent metadata elements is a content analysis of the story nodes. There are several heuristics to analyse the content of the text. For example the <!metaMarker> program is designed to provide an "information context" in the form of a rich set of metadata elements for a variety of time and resource intensive tasks [8]. <!metaMarker> has been originally developed to automatically organize customer service requests or incoming email streams according to their subject contents. It also automatically identifies such things as the emotional "tone" of the message and the intention or goal of the author of the message. The <!metaMarker> program uses Natural Language Processing (NLP) and Machine Learning (ML) for automatic metadata generation.

To adapt <!metaMarker> to extract metadata elements specific to educational material, the initial target elements from GEM and Dublin Core were categorized into three groups depending on how they will be extracted. Some elements such as "author" or "publisher" were directly extracted from the texts by applying educational material specific sublanguage grammar. Other elements such as "quality" or "relation", which are implicit in the texts, were derived through the discourse model analysis of the educational materials. This gives us an opportunity to apply such applications as <!metaMarker> also in the woven stories environment to create the relevant metadata elements of story nodes.

Of course there are still problems in the automatic text analysis. It is not entirely certain that we will get the needed information. Furthermore it is highly possible that in some cases we will get a false result from the automatic analyser. One solution to this is to make the creation of the metadata elements semi-automatic. In a semi-automated system a program can automatically create essential information or hints to the person responsible for creating the metadata of the text or in our case the metadata of a story section. The person can complement the automatic analysis according to the information received from the system. In this way we can combine the speed of automatic text processing with the opportunity of having a kind of backup check of the information received from the system.

In the context of the woven stories, the metadata creator can be the author of a story node, peer users in the system or the teacher/creator of the writing situation. In educational context the teacher could be able to add relative information of story nodes according to the information received from an automatic content analyser. This will help the student, because complex relations between story nodes are not trivial. An automatic system can help the teacher to help the student to relate his writing to other writings in many different ways.

4   Applications of the StoryML

The idea of woven stories is very useful in *distance education* settings. The students can use the system to collaboratively write stories or various types of documents. They can see the development of the story and the relations between different nodes in the story line. On the other hand the woven stories concept can be seen as a way to represent the learning process of the student or students. During the learning process of a particular subject there might be several interactions between different students or nodes in the story line. The learning process (path) can be analysed by examining various sections of the story.

An example of the educational use of woven stories is the case of a distributed learning task. Let us consider a situation where a group of students receive a learning goal that they must achieve collaboratively. In this situation the woven story application can support the students by presenting the individual efforts. Hence, the students can figure out if they have reached the given goal. For example, the parallel learning paths of the group members might be represented as alternative paths between two nodes A and B.

StoryML can be constructed to support the *analysis of the nature of discursion in stories*. For example during the assessment of collaborative work it would be useful to get information about students who have encouraged or opposed other students during the collaborative work. Those students who have been active and really contributing to the ongoing work could receive better marks for the assignment. This would give a teacher an opportunity to assess the students' participation and contribution to the learning activity processed by the woven stories system. In addition, the student could use the above information to self-evaluate his own contribution to the collaborative learning task. Maybe the information received from the application could help the student to make new discoveries of his own thinking.

The *time dimension* of stories is also important. It gives the students means to self-reflect their own or other students' paths during the learning process. In this way the students are able to make conclusion about the relations of story sections or the development of ideas.

The StoryML specification gives us *tools to define different relations between story sections*. The system can automatically or semi-automatically inform a student or a teacher about different factors in a particular woven story. For example a woven stories application using StoryML can notify the student about similar topics or the same kind of story sections in the hyperspace that are related directly to what he is writing or doing. On the other hand it might be useful to inform a student about totally different contents or opinions, so that the student might get some novel ideas from other students. Also, if the story nodes represent the learning process or path of particular student, the application could advice the student to take the next step in the learning path. For example, in the case where the student is stuck in his studies and he is making the same mistakes (circling in the learning space), the application could show him the right direction.

The StoryML specification supports the *implementation of adaptive functionality*. The user model maintained by an woven stories application makes it possible to present the hyperspace according to specific characteristics of the user. One example is to present the hyperspace differently to a heterogeneous population of users. Thus, an woven stories application can present different presentations of the same hyperspace by showing different types of story lines and relations according to several attributes present in the StoryML. The StoryML specification can act as a basis of the adaptation function.

The educational application of StoryML specification supports the means to adaptively offer particular learning materials to the learner. With the woven stories application the learner can choose from a repository of learning materials (e.g. from particular course or several courses) such objects that are relevant for his own learning goal or motivation. Hence, the StoryML specification gives us a tool to represent the individual *learning stories* of a particular learner. In this way the different learning styles and learning goals are represented in a form of various learning paths or stories with in the same learning space. The learner can for example browse through different kinds of learning paths and select the one that fits to his own learning style.

To develop this idea further, we can imagine that the learner makes his own contributions and associations during the learning process. With the woven stories application the learner can modify the existing learning materials (e.g. content and relationships) and hence enhance the repository with the modified, graph-structured representation of the contents. In this way the repository of learning material comes richer every time there is a novel way of understanding the knowledge and information presented through the learning material. Furthermore, the learning material becomes more adaptive and personalized.

5   Conclusion

The StoryML specification introduced in this paper serves as a starting point to the formalization that can be used to represent the hyperspace of woven stories in an educationally meaningful way. The continuing development of both the concept of woven stories and the metadata attached to a particular woven story is underway. The StoryML core set will develop further as we get more insight into the nature of the data stored in StoryML, and its actual utilization used by a student. Furthermore, we are enhancing our existing woven stories application, the WS2, to support the StoryML specification in order to exploit the possibilities offered by it. Knowledge and experience gathered during the development process of the application as well as feedback from its users will be essential in the further development of StoryML.

From the educational point of view the concept of woven stories empowered by StoryML supports flexible and adaptive ways of learning. This modification of woven stories supports the learner individually, not by forcing or guiding her to behave in a predefined way.

References

1. Dublin Core Metadata Initiative. Dublin Core metadata element set, version 1.1: reference description, 1999. Available at:
   http://dublincore.org/documents/1999/07/02/dces/
2. P. Gerdt, P. Kommers, C. Looi, E. Sutinen: Woven Stories as a Cognitive Tool. *Cognitive Technology 2001*, LNAI 2117, Springer-Verlag, 2001, 233 – 247.
3. Harviainen, T., Hassinen, M., Kommers, P., Sutinen, E.: Co-authoring Stories over the Internet. In *Advanced Research in Computers and Communications in Education* (Eds. Cumming, G., Okamoto, T., Gomez, L.), IOS Press, Amsterdam, 1999.
4. Heery, R.: Review of metadata formats. *Program*, 30(4):345-373, 1996.
5. Huai, H.; *Cognitive Style and Memory Capacity: Effects of Concept Mapping as a Learning Method*. Doctoral Thesis, University of Twente, 2000.
6. Huai, H., Kommers, P.: Concept Mapping as a Learning Strategy for Autonomous Students with a Serialistic Cognitive Style. In *International Journal of Continuing Engineering Education and Life-Long Learning*, 11 (1/2), 135 – 151, 2001.
7. The Ontology Browser. Internet WWW-site,
   url: http://ontology.teknowledge.com:8080/rsigma/SKB.jsp (December 12, 2001).
8. Paik, W. Automatic Generation of Eduactional Metadata Elements to Enable Digital Libraries. *Proceedings of the 9th Internaltional Conference on Computers in Education* (ICCE/SchoolNet2001), Seoul, Korea, November 12-15, 2001, 1406 – 1413.
9. Standard Upper Ontology (SUO) Working Group, IEEE P1600.1, Internet WWW-site, url: http://suo.ieee.org/, 2002 (January 31, 2002).

An Agent That Helps Children to Author Rhetorically-Structured Digital Puppet Presentations

Paola Rizzo[1], Erin Shaw[2], and W. Lewis Johnson[2]

[1] Department of Computer Science
University of Rome "La Sapienza"
Via Salaria 113, 00189 Rome, Italy
rizzo@dsi.uniroma1.it
http://www.dsi.uniroma1.it/~rizzo

[2] Center for Advanced Research in Technology for Education
Information Sciences Institute, University of Southern California
4676 Admiralty Way, Marina del Rey, CA 90292-6695 USA
{shaw,johnson}@isi.edu
http://www.isi.edu/~shaw/
http://www.isi.edu/isd/johnson.html

Abstract. This paper describes a pedagogical agent that helps children to learn to author structured presentations about explanations of concepts. Using a Rhetorical Structure Theory analysis of a source Web page, the agent performs pedagogical tasks to support the user's understanding of rhetorical relations, stimulates reflection about the relations between the structure of the original text and the structure of the presentations, and suggests ways to improve the user's performance. Upon completion of the authoring, the presentations are organized into coherent structures that can be performed by animated characters, or Digital Puppets, in a learning-by-teaching classroom context.

1 Introduction

When properly designed, multimedia presentations result in deeper learning, compared to equivalent textual presentations [1]. Likewise, authoring multimedia presentations forces students to organize their thoughts and clarifies their understanding of the subject material, encouraging the development of important procedural and metacognitive skills while achieving mastery of the subject matter.

To support both multimedia presentation and multimedia authoring, we are developing a system aimed at young children for authoring and generating Digital Puppet presentations. Digital Puppets (DPs), like animated pedagogical agents (APAs) [2], are animated characters that help learners understand a subject. Like APAs, DPs use text-to-speech software and a variety of nonverbal gestures to provide voiceover narration and personalized commentary, which have been shown to be particularly effective multimedia presentation methods [3]. Like APAs, we expect DPs to evoke a positive affective response in the viewer, referred to as the *persona effect*, which is produced even by lifelike characters that do not perform autonomous

S.A. Cerri, G. Gouardères, and F. Paraguaçu (Eds.): ITS 2002, LNCS 2363, pp. 903–912, 2002.
© Springer-Verlag Berlin Heidelberg 2002

pedagogical behaviors [4]. Unlike APAs, however, DPs are not necessarily intelligent or autonomous; hence, we call them puppets.

How can we assist students in structuring their knowledge and explanations about a subject, so as to create coherent and effective presentations? Agents such as Adele, STEVE, and Herman [5, 6, 7] are designed to generate explanations based upon knowledge structures that support explanation. But young children have relatively poor understanding of what counts as causation, evidence, etc. As a consequence, agent authoring tools such as Diligent [8] and VIVIDS [6] are too complex to be used by children. In contrast, off-the-shelf Web page and presentation building tools provide little structure, and no guidance as to how to think about the knowledge students must present.

As a basis for structuring knowledge and explanations we have adopted Rhetorical Structure Theory (RST) by Mann & Thompson [9]. According to the RST, a coherent natural language text is structured in terms of functional relations that hold between parts of it. The relations, such as elaboration, motivation, and evidence, represent different pragmatic goals within the authoring tool. The goals provide a high-level structure for presentation authoring.

We focus in this paper on a pedagogical agent that assists with presentation authoring by monitoring the user's performance, and by intervening to assist him. The tutor is embedded in the Digital Puppet System's authoring tool. Using an RST analysis of the source text, the agent performs pedagogical tasks to support the user's understanding of rhetorical relations, stimulates reflection about the relationships between the structure of the original text and the structure of the presentations, and suggests ways to improve the user's performance. Upon completion of the authoring, the authored paragraphs are organized into coherent structures that can be presented by DPs in a learning-by-teaching classroom context.

2   Related Work

The Digital Puppet system is, at its core, a tool for building knowledge representations, and is similar to systems like Belvedere [10] and ConvinceMe [11]. These hypothesis-oriented tools address high school and undergraduate level scientific inquiry into broad-based problems in a collaborative setting. In contrast, we present an RST-based tool for young children whose goal is to explain the relationships of local artifacts (paragraphs of text) in a learning-by-teaching context. Tools that address rhetorical issues, such as argument construction, e.g., SenseMaker [12], and explanation construction, e.g. Explanation Constructor [13], are fundamentally similar, though are not RST- or agent-based.

As far as we know, no computer-based learning environment is aimed at teaching students how to organize presentations of a target text according to rhetorical principles. Most Intelligent Language Tutoring Systems (ILTS) focus on vocabulary and grammar; some systems (e.g. [14]) help learners plan the essay by dividing it into functional units like introduction, body, and conclusion, but the text to be written is self-contained and does not constitute a presentation of some other text.

The Rhetorical Structure Theory is used in the area of natural language processing for both analyzing and generating texts in terms of rhetorical relations [15, 16]. Burstein et al. [17] use the RST to automatically summarize GMAT essays produced by students. Their work differs from ours in that the GMAT essay is a self-contained text, and the summary provided to the student does not outline the rhetorical structure of the essay nor of the summary. André et. al [18] use an RST-based planning system for controlling an agent that displays animated presentations of Web pages or multimedia material. Our system is focused on helping the user to author the text of a presentation, rather than on automatically building multimedia presentations, and the text authored by the children is organized into a coherent structure using templates, rather than by means of a planning algorithm. Other works on ITSs use natural language methods, such as performatives designed from speech acts, for producing coherent and effective dialogues between system and student [19]. Here, we use the RST to guide students through the process of building coherent presentations.

3   The Digital Puppet System

Digital Puppet presentations are authored in the Digital Puppet System (DPS), which was created for authoring a simplified version of Adele (Agent for Distance Education), a Web-based animated pedagogical agent technology [5]. Whereas Adele is designed to support simulation-based learning, DPS serves a complementary functions, to augment Web-based presentations. There are three types of users of the DPS: designer, author, and viewer. The designer annotates the text of a Web page using the RST relations; the author, a fourth grader, creates a puppet-enhanced presentation about a Web page; and the viewer, a classmate, teacher, or even the author herself, plays the resulting presentation. The DPS, which includes the pedagogical agent and RST annotation tool [20, 21], is illustrated in Figure 1.

Fig. 1. The DP system, including the pedagogical agent and RST annotation tool

The DPS consists of three main parts: (1) The designer's tools for annotating the text, (2) the authoring tool for creating the presentation, which this paper is focused on, and (3) the browser environment for playing the presentations. The pedagogical agent is embedded in the authoring tool, where it monitors and assists the author. The operation of the system can be summarized in the following steps:

Designer
1. A Web page on the topic of study is either selected or created by a teacher or instructional designer, and is input to an RST-based manual annotation tool.

2. The designer, by means of the tool, generates a paragraph-level RST analysis of the page and produces hierarchical markup tags that represent the tree of rhetorical relations, that are inserted into the Web page using XHTML.

Author

3. The RST-annotated Web page is read in and displayed by the DP authoring tool.

4. The RST agent interacts with the author, explaining the meaning of the RST relations, highlighting the structure of the page, and suggesting ways to structure the presentations.

5. The DP authoring tool is a Java application that enables the learner to further annotate the Web page for the purpose of adding introductory and explanatory presentation text. RST relation boxes are presented as a means of outlining, or structuring, the presentation. The authored text and associated interactive buttons are inserted into the page with Java Script.

Viewer

6. At anytime, the presentation-enhanced Web page can be displayed and tested in a Web browser. The authoring tool creates a display Web page with two frames. In one frame, it inserts a JavaScript function called the Puppet Control Engine, which controls the Digital Puppet's animated behavior and communicates with the client-based text-to-speech engine. In the other frame, it displays the annotated Web page that includes a synthesis of the authored text for each explanation. The tool then calls a browser to display the results.

7. The viewer activates the Digital Puppet presentation by clicking on the interactive buttons that have been placed before relevant paragraphs, i.e. annotated paragraphs of the Web page by the DPA tool. The puppet then presents the material to the viewer. In our initial version of the system, the interaction between the puppet and viewer is minimal; the puppet may ask questions but cannot respond.

The author's interface to the DPA tool is shown on the left in Figure 2. The Web page is displayed in the main window, to the left. The user writes an introduction to the page in the small window at the top-right. She then selects a paragraph from the original page and writes an explanation about it in a second small window (bottom-right). An annotation button is inserted before the main paragraph so that the authored text can be retrieved for editing, and ultimately, presentation. The authored text is linked to the original text by means of a cause relation that has been selected by the author from a list of possible rhetorical relations. The agent monitors the author's activities and makes suggestions as appropriate, or provides help on demand via the Help button. To activate the presentation, the author clicks on a button on the toolbar.

The viewer's interface to the Web browser and the Digital Puppet is shown on the right in Figure 2. The Web page is augmented with small buttons that, when pressed, activate the animated puppet to present explanations that were authored for a particular paragraph. The puppet uses a client-based text-to-speech synthesizer to narrate the presentation and an XML-based animation engine to perform the presentation. The teen persona of the Digital Puppet is designed as a character with whom younger students can easily identify, and as a role model.

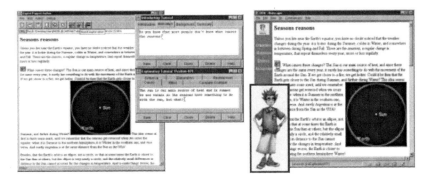

Fig. 2. DP authoring tool interface (left) and the puppet-enhanced Web page (right)

4 Organizing Presentations Using Rhetorical Structure Theory

According to the RST [9], a text can be analyzed in terms of a tree of relations, each of them holding between two non-overlapping text spans named nucleus and satellite respectively. The nucleus is more important for expressing the writer's intention, and is independent of the satellite. A relation specifies a set of constraints on nucleus and satellite, and a pragmatic effect that the writer intends to produce in the reader. For example, the "evidence" relation has as intended effect that the reader's belief in the nucleus is increased. The following text, taken from [9], p. 10, and regarding a federal income tax program, shows an instance of this relation; the first span is the nucleus, while the second span is a satellite providing evidence for the nucleus: "(1) The program as published for calendar year 1980 really works. (2) In only a few minutes, I entered all the figures from my 1980 tax return and got a result which agreed with my hand calculations to the penny."

Table 1. Rhetorical relations for the Introductory and the Explanatory Tutorials

Introductory Tutorial	Explanatory Tutorial
Introduction	Cause
Background	Result
Motivation	Evidence
	Compare/Contrast
	Elaboration
	Restatement

We have selected and partially modified a subset of the relations originally proposed in [9], and we have classified them according to their purpose: 1) structuring an *Introductory tutorial*, i.e. a text that introduces the Web page as a whole, and 2) structuring *Explanatory tutorials*, i.e. texts that are aimed at explaining specific portions of the Web page (see Table 1). For Introductory relations, the whole text of the Web page is considered a nucleus, for which three types of satellite information are to be provided by the author: the introduction, the background, that should increase the reader's ability to comprehend the nucleus, and the motivation, that should foster the reader's desire to read the original text. As for the Explanatory, the author is requested to identify some important spans within the original text, and to provide one or more satellites for each of them, choosing suitable relations. For example, the author might provide some evidence or restatement for several concepts mentioned in the original text.

The connection between the original text (i.e., the Web page) and the authored text is illustrated in Figure 3. Each piece of text written by the author corresponds to a relation. There is only one introductory presentation, comprising three pieces of text, one per relation. There may be several explanatory presentations, each comprising at least one piece of text about a unique paragraph.

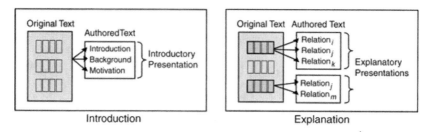

Fig. 3. Relations between the original text and the authored texts

5 Pedagogical Tasks and Knowledge of the Tutor

In order to realize RST-based presentations, especially the explanatory ones, the author should perform three tasks while interacting with the DPA tool: (1) understand the basic structure of the original text; (2) build sensible relations between the original text and the texts to be authored; (3) edit the texts of the presentations. The tutor helps the author perform these tasks by executing several types of behaviors, that can be classified according their "focus", i.e. the issue they concern, and to four pedagogical functions: *stimulating reflection, supporting comprehension, encouraging action,* and *improving performance* (see Table 2 for examples).

Tutor's Behaviors Focused on the Original Text
Thanks to an a priori RST analysis of the original text, the pedagogical agent is able to highlight, comment, and explain the following items in the original text:

1. The paragraph containing the basic nucleus, and the most significant satellite paragraphs. This information helps the author to choose which paragraphs to work on first, or can be used by the agent for giving feedback to the author about his choice of paragraphs to annotate.

2. The rhetorical relations holding between paragraphs. This helps the author understand the structure of the original text, provides him with examples of the relations he wishes to edit, and gives him guidelines about how to structure his own explanatory text.

Table 2. Examples of pedagogical behaviors of the agent

		FOCUS		
		Structure of original text	Preparation of authored text	Relation between original and authored text
F U N C T I O N S	**Stimulating reflection**	*What do you think is the most significant paragraph?*	*Do you think what you have is long enough?*	*Can you think of other relations you may write wrt this paragraph?*
	Supporting Comprehension	*Look, this paragraph is an example of an evidence*	*For writing some evidence, look at the following example...*	*When explaining a result, it is good to provide some evidence for it*
	Encouraging action	*Try to identify some evidence in the text. If you can't, I can help you.*	*Maybe you could write something more...*	*Why don't you try to elaborate on this comparison?*
	Improving performance	*What you have highlighted is not a generic elaboration, it is a comparison*	*I suggest that you try to rewrite the text in your own words*	*It would be good to elaborate on this evidence*

Tutor's Behaviors Focused on Relations between Original and Authored Texts

The RST is a descriptive rather than a prescriptive theory; hence, the tutor can only give some general suggestions about the relations to choose for linking the authored paragraphs to paragraphs in the original text, based on preferences shown in Table 3. The preferences are based on the idea that a relation instance in the original text should be linked to the most relevant and specific relation instances in the authored text.

Table 3. Preference-based rules for suggesting relations to author

If relation instance in original text is:	Then agent suggests user author:
Cause	Result, then Evidence, then Elaboration
Result	Cause, then Evidence, then Elaboration
Compare-contrast	Elaboration
Evidence	Compare-contrast, then Elaboration
Elaboration	Restatement
Restatement	[no specific suggestion]

Tutor's Behaviors Focused on the Authored Text

Two kinds of performance variables about the author can be continuously measured by the agent: *global* and *local*. Global variables refer to the relations and relation instances the author creates, regardless of the specific paragraphs they are attached to. Local variables refer to the relations and relation instances concerning specific paragraphs in the original Web page. The variables are listed in Table 4. In the names of the variables, the prefixes "o-" and "a-" stand for "original" and "authored" respectively. Some of the variables are computed on the basis of two constants:

total_rels, the number of all the relations the author can choose from (see Table 1); and *total_o-pars*, the number of paragraphs in the original text.

The agent can also keep track of other variables that refer to the actual actions performed by the user: *tool_actions*, concerning the author's use of the tool in general (for example, how often and about what topic help is requested), and *task_actions*, regarding the user's progress during the authoring task (for example, how often he edits, clears and deletes relations).

By means of these variables the agent can notice, for example, whether the author is (a) over/under-using some relations; (b) adequately explaining the original text or ignoring some parts of it; (c) plagiarizing the original text; (d) authoring text that is too long or short with respect to the original paragraph. The values of the variables are used for inferring the author's needs and for triggering agent's behaviors aimed at, for example, encouraging him to experiment with all the available relations, or better explaining to him the overlooked relations.

Table 4. Global and local variables for measuring the authoring task outcomes

Global Variables			Local Variables
About a-relations	**About a-instances**	**About o-paragraphs**	
total_a-rels: number of used relations	*total_a-insts*: number of all authored relation instances	*total_explained_o-pars*: number of annotated original paragraphs	*relative_a-rels*: number of a-relations authored for each o-paragraph
relative_a-rels: percentage of *total_a-rels* to *total_rels*	*a-inst_length*: length of each authored piece of text	*relative_explained_o-pars*: percentage *of* *total_explained_o-pars* to *total_o-pars*	*ao_length_distance*: difference between length of o-paragraph and length of the a-text
a-rel_insts: number of instances authored for a given relation			*ao_distance*: semantic distance between o-paragraph and a-paragraph

6   Evaluating the RST-Based Approach

The work presented in this paper is new and ongoing. During the 2001-2002 school year we are scheduled to perform field trials of the authoring tool at an Elementary School in Los Angeles Unified school district with English Language Learners (students whose first language is not English). Our evaluation plan calls for a preliminary study to evaluate the usability of the tool and understanding of the task, and a pilot study to assess its effectiveness. To evaluate how well an arbitrary ten-year-old might create an RST-structured presentation, we asked a fourth grader to prepare a sample presentation. His answers give us an indication of the challenges we will face in our future work, including how to parse awkward sentences, how to assist at both grammatical and semantic levels, and how to synthesize authored components:

Intro: "Hi my name is Dale Lin. I am Doing a report of seasons."
Motivate: "Say if your in the USA and you wanted to go some where cold you would go down to the southern hemisfear because it would be winter there"
Evidence: "The cause of seasons is that it is on one imaginary line called and axis. The earth rotates around the axis and form an angle of 23.4. the the ear start to tilt and a cause a certin amout of area."
Backgrnd: "The axis cause a tilt that mak the north or south hemisfear to receive more sun then the other."

The challenge is then to turn the authored results into a coherent presentation. We may be able to catch some of the grammatical errors before the components are synthesized, and the authoring tool enables the student test out a presentation before it is performed for the peer group. However, we expect for younger children, especially children whose first language is not English, that there will be awkwardness and that the awkwardness will be a catalyst for learning. The following is an example of one synthesis of the components above. Italicized text is the student's verbatim text:

Hi! My name is Oliver, and I will be speaking for *Dale* today. We are *doing a report of seasons*. It's good to know *what causes the seasons*. Why? *Say if your in the USA and you wanted to go some where cold you would go down to the southern hemisfear because it would be winter there.* What causes the seasons? *The cause of the seasons is that it is on one imaginary line called and axis. The earth rotates around the axis and form an angle of 23.4. The ear start to tilt and a cause a certin amout of area. The axis cause a tilt that mak the north or south hemisfear to receive more sun then the other.*

For the pilot study [22], as designed by Mayer, we will work with a class of fourth grade students. We will evaluate both learning performance and outcomes for both a puppet and control group, analyzing the performance based on learning process dimensions such as number of self-explanations, and inquiry episodes generated by students, to determine whether the Digital Puppet learners scored significantly higher on process measures of cognitive activity during learning. To study the learning outcomes, we will analyze the data from a battery of instruments in order to determine whether the Digital Puppet task improved student learning.

Acknowledgements. We would like to thank Kate LaBore for her support and insightful comments, Nancy Chang, for performing the student evaluation, Andrew Marshall, who created the first animation engine for Adele, Karyn Cordova, who is creating the new animation engine, Daniel Marcu and Edward Hovy for insightful discussions, and Stefano Levialdi and Marilena De Marsico for useful comments on a previous version of this paper. This work was supported by an internal R&D grant from the USC Information Sciences Institute, and by a scholarship from NATO and the Italian National Research Council awarded to Paola Rizzo during her visit to the USC.

References

1. Mayer R. E.: Multimedia Learning. Cambridge University Press, Cambridge, UK (2001)
2. Johnson, W.L., Rickel, J.W., Lester, J.C.: Animated Pedagogical Agents: Face-to-Face Interaction in Interactive Learning Environments. International Journal of Artificial Intelligence in Education 11 (2000) 47-78
3. Moreno, R. and Mayer, R. E.: Engaging students in active learning: The case for personalized multimedia messages. Journal of Educational Psychology, 92 (2000) 724-733
4. Lester, J. C., Converse, S. A., Kahler, S. E., Barlow, S. T., Stone, B. A., Bhogal, R. S.: The persona effect: Affective impact of animated pedagogical agents. In: Proceedings of CHI '97 (1997) 359-366
5. Shaw E., Johnson W. L., Ganeshan R.: Pedagogical agents on the Web. In: Proceedings of the Third International Conference on Autonomous Agents (1999) 283-290

6. Johnson, W.L., Rickel, J., Stiles, R., Munro, A.: Integrating Pedagogical Agents into Virtual Environments, Presence: Teleoperators and Virtual Environments 7(6) (1998) 523-546

7. Lester, J. C., Converse, S. A., Stone, B. A., Kahler, S. E., Barlow, S. T.: Animated pedagogical agents and problem-solving effectiveness: A large-scale empirical evaluation. In: Proceedings of the Eighth World Conference on Artificial Intelligence in Education. IOS Press, Amsterdam (1997) 23-30.

8. Angros, R., Johnson, W.L., Rickel, J.: Agents that Learn to Instruct. In: AAAI 1997 Fall Symposium Series: Intelligent Tutoring Systems Authoring Tools, Technical Report FS-97-01, AAAI Press, Menlo Park (CA) (1997)

9. Mann W. C. and Thompson S. A.: Rhetorical structure theory: A theory of text organization. Technical Report ISI/RS-87-190, Information Sciences Institute, University of Southern California, Marina del Rey, CA. (1987)

10. Suthers, D. D.: Representational Support for Collaborative Inquiry. In: Proceedings of the 32nd Hawai'i International Conference on the System Sciences (HICSS-32), Maui, Hawai'i (CD-ROM), Institute of Electrical and Electronics Engineers, Inc. (1999)

11. Schank, P, and Ranney, M.: Improved reasoning with Convince Me. In: Human Factors in Computing Systems CHI '95 Conference Companion, Association for Computing Machinery, New York, NY (1995) 276-277

12. Bell, P. Using argument representations to make thinking visible for individuals and groups. In: Proc. Computer Supported Collaborative Learning '97, University of Toronto (1997) 10-19

13. Sandoval, W. A., and Reiser, B. J.: Evolving explanations in high school biology, Paper presented at the Annual Meeting of the American Educational Research Assn., Chicago, IL (1997)

14. Rowley, K. and Crevoisier, M.: MAESTRO: Guiding students to skillful performance of the writing process. In: Proceedings of the Educational Multimedia and Hypermedia conference, Calgary, CA. (1997)

15. Marcu D.: The Rhetorical Parsing of Unrestricted Texts: A Surface-Based Approach. Computational Linguistics, 26 (3) (2000) 395-448

16. Hovy, E.H.: Automated Discourse Generation Using Discourse Structure Relations. Artificial Intelligence 63(1-2), Special Issue on Natural Language Processing (1993) 341-386.

17. Burstein, J. and Marcu D.: Towards Using Text Summarization for Essay-Based Feedback. In: La 7e Conference Annuelle sur Le Traitement Automatique des Langues Naturelles TALN'2000, Lausanne, Switzerland (2000)

18. André, E., Rist, T., Müller, J.: Integrating Reactive and Scripted Behaviors in a Life-Like Presentation Agent. In: Proc. of the Second Int'l. Conf. on Autonomous Agents (Agents '98), Association for Computing Machinery (1998) 261-268.

19.Penstein Rosé C. and Freedman R.: Building Dialog Systems for Tutorial Applications. In: AAAI Fall Symposium 2000, AAAI Press Technical Report FS-00-01, Menlo Park (CA) (2000)

20. Marcu D., Amorrortu B., Romera M.: Experiments in Constructing a Corpus of Discourse Trees. In: The ACL'99 Workshop on Standards and Tools for Discourse Tagging, Maryland (1999) (RST tool: http://www.isi.edu/licensed-sw/RSTTool/index.html)

21. O'Donnell, M.: RSTTool 2.4 – A Markup Tool for Rhetorical Structure Theory. In: Proceedings of the Int'l Natural Language Generation Conference (INLG'2000), Mitzpe Ramon, Israel (2000) 253-256

22. Johnson, W.L., Mayer, R., and Shaw, E.: K12 Agents: USC/ISI grant 12-1540-0002 (2001)

"You Cannot Use My Broom! I'm the Witch, You're the Prince": Collaboration in a Virtual Dramatic Game

Rui Prada[1], Ana Paiva[1], Isabel Machado[2], and Catarina Gouveia[3]

[1]INESC-ID and Instituto Superior Técnico - Rua Alves Redol, 9, 1000 Lisboa, Portugal.
+351 21 3100219
{Ana.Paiva,Rui.Prada}@inesc.pt

[2]CBL, University of Leeds, UK & INESC-ID and ISCTE - Rua Alves Redol, 9, 1000
Lisboa, Portugal. +351 21 3100312
Isabel.Machado@inesc.pt

[3]Faculdade de Ciências de Educação – University of Lisbon and INESC-ID Rua Alves
Redol, 9, 1000 Lisboa, Portugal. +351 21 3100312
Catarina.Gouveia@inesc.pt

Abstract. In this paper we discuss how collaboration issues are addressed in the context of *Teatrix*, a virtual environment aiming at providing the children with the means for collaboratively creating a story on a virtual stage. The children create stories using a set of pre-defined scenes and *dramatis personae* – characters that have specific roles in the play, which they control to a certain extent). Each child expects the story to evolve in reaction to her/his character's actions and the overall story emerges from the collaboration of different children. Based on this premise we conducted some evaluation experiences, in order to assess to what extent *Teatrix* promoted collaboration and what types of collaboration were particularly elicited by the application.

1 Introduction

Children as young as three engage in the art of make-believe, exploring the boundaries between reality and fantasy. The transition from the make-believe play of the preschooler to more structured theatricals is evident in children's efforts to set up little plays [9]. One of the most important aspects of drama is that it provides a collaborative type of activity where children engage in a play actively, with several senses. Aristotle refers to this as "enactment": which means to act rather to read [5]. However, due to its physical grounding, acting is often seen as an activity done independently from the creation of stories and the writing processes. In fact, creating stories is often regarded as an individual activity and collaboration plays little role in it.

Merging acting, reading and writing into a single collaborative virtual environment, and supporting it, was one of the main goals of the research here presented.

The product of such research is a virtual environment for story creation, *Teatrix*, which aims at giving effective support for young children (7-9 years old) to develop:

S.A. Cerri, G. Gouardères, and F. Paraguaçu (Eds.): ITS 2002, LNCS 2363, pp. 913–922, 2002.
© Springer-Verlag Berlin Heidelberg 2002

1. their notions of narrative, through the dramatization of several situations;
2. their ability to take a second and third person perspective across the experience of a wide range of situations.

This paper is organised as follows: first we describe some of our findings concerning collaboration in dramatic games. Then, we give a summary of *Teatrix*, describing how it provides support for collaborative story creation, and we present some results of the evaluations conducted with *Teatrix*. Finally, we discuss some pending issues and propose some future work.

2   Collaboration in Dramatic Games

Our research was grounded on a set of experiences run in the school "O Nosso Sonho". During the experiences we observed children of several ages performing fairy tales in two different settings: theatre and puppet scenarios. The school follows an educational approach where different types of activities are done in different rooms. Every day, each child has the possibility to choose his/her daily activities by choosing the room to go to. Drama is one of these activities and one of the most chosen ones (drama is done in the "*Dramatic Room*"). Children enjoy the dressing up, the make-up to become someone else, the acting, the singing, and even to be in the audience.

So, in order to better understand and influence the creation of a virtual theatre we collected 14 performances done in the "Dramatic Room" (each performance with young actors with ages between 4 to 8) and observed the interactions between children and with the teacher. This analysis was not trivial as interactions in a dramatic game may occur at different levels, in parallel and between different participants.

In the dramatic games, we were able to distinguish two types of interactions:

1. "*performance level interactions*": children interact through their characters by their actions and sentences, and;
2. "*co-ordination interactions*": children may provide signals to the others, give orders, make demands or simply inform the others about something. Further, children's actions are often dictated by their common goal, and co-ordination actions may appear, like for example, in the middle of one performance when one child not involved in that particular scene, steps out of the stage to find a "little basket" to give to the *Red Riding Hood*.

Being collaborative in nature, and as with many other collaborative activities (see [4] for an overview of collaborative learning), we can find that dramatic games are influenced by several different factors. In particular:

1. *The age of the children*: we found that 5 to 6 year old children did not manage to stay in character easily and needed a significant help from the teacher in order to "act". Differently, the 7 to 8 year old were much more at ease with their characters. This result may stress the importance that perspective taking plays in collaborative activities and the lack of ability not to center on their own perspective found in the younger groups.

2. *The group heterogeneity/homogeneity:* since the groups performing were quite large (from 4 children to 8) the influence of heterogeneity was not seen as very significant. However, we noticed that our groups with both genders tended to produce better plays than with only male actors (we didn't have the opportunity to have a female only play). Also, larger groups are more difficult to control, and thus the play tends to be weaker in terms of narrative result.

3. *Teacher intervention:* in our dramatic room the teachers play two essential roles: 1) the stage director, deciding where each child should go, and signal them to start or finish; 2) the narrator: it is often the teacher that sets up the story ("One day, a family that lived..."). Although both roles can be performed by children (in fact, some children do like to take a lead in coordinating the whole performance), these two activities are usually done by the teacher. We found that, if the teacher is not very active in the directives given to the young actors (in two of the performances the teacher had a minimal role in it), the play may turn into something completely different from what had been agreed upon. For example, we had a group performing *Hansel and Gretel* where half of the group decided they wanted to be wolves and attack the two children in the forest. Another group decided they just wanted to pretend that they were riding motorbikes. Also, interaction between the children, both at the *co-ordination* and at the *performance* level, becomes weaker and conflicts tend not to be solved.

4. *Story/Task:* the type/genre of the story to be performed may also influence the collaboration established, as some stories do foster interaction and coordination more than others. Since our experiments were all conducted with fairy tales (*Red Riding Hood, The Three Little Pigs, Hansel and Gretel,* and *Cinderella*) we did not achieve any results on the influence of the story in the collaboration of the children during the dramatic games.

5. *The audience:* we did performances both with and without an audience and the interactions between the actors were slightly different in each case. The audience introduces both a critic element in the performance and at the same time a disturbing one. We found that the performances without an audience lead to a much better control of the characters, but children were not as enthusiastic about it as with an audience. In our case, the audience was sometimes too disturbing, and often children from the audience would step in the stage interfering with the whole performance (note that the *Dramatic Room* is a classroom and not a theatre).

3 Overview of *Teatrix*

Based on the above findings and taking into account the dramatic games activity of the school we designed *Teatrix* as a game for story creation (see [6] [7]). Following a theatrical metaphor, the environment is divided in three modules strongly related with the theatrical performances.

The first module (*Backstage*) offers the children the possibility to prepare the scenes, props and characters for each story (in relation with what happens in the backstage of a theatre during the preparation of a play).

Fig. 1. *Teatrix*: Backstage Module.

The second module (*On Stage*) provides the children with the possibility to initiate one story, based on a previous preparation, and to start the acting (on stage performance). The performance is done in a collaborative 3D world. The story creation only evolves if the children work together to achieve a common goal: their story. From the story creation process a "*film*"-like object is created. This '*film*'-like object offers the children with a product, which they can analyze and even to reconstruct in future performances.

The third module (*The Audience*) is based on the artifact produced from the story creation process. In this module, children can be the audience of their own performances and have the opportunity to write about their work. With this module we wanted to provide the children with the means for watching and discussing what they've produced. By supporting the discussion of the story we aimed to promote a better understanding of the characters interactions, and to encourage the children to reflect on the emotional and intellectual parts of the story [3].

4 Collaboration in *Teatrix*

Teatrix runs in a networked classroom where each child (or group of children) uses a computer to access to the *Teatrix* environment. *Teatrix* was implemented using a distributed architecture, and since it is a cooperative environment several children can work on the same story simultaneously. *Teatrix* can support collaboration in two of the three modules of the environment: *Backstage* and *On Stage*. Although one can imagine the collaborative writing to be done in the *Audience* module, *Teatrix* does not support it at the moment.

Controlled Character

Available actions for the control

Item in *bag*

Fig. 2. *Teatrix*: On Stage Module.

In the *Backstage*

The most important activity children have to do collaboratively with the *Backstage* is to choose the actors and roles for the play. Children can choose the roles they play in the story, according to a taxonomy of roles proposed by Propp [8]. The roles are:

- *Villain* - the role of the villain is to disturb the peace of the happy family, to cause misfortune, damage or harm. The villain may be a dragon, a devil, a witch, a stepmother, or even a little boy or a girl.
- *Hero/Heroine* - Propp presents two types of heroes: the seekers, which go in search of a loved/needed element; and the victimized heroes, whom are themselves the victims of the villainy.
- *Magician* - has special functions in the story and can be represented in many forms. The magician provides the hero with a certain magic object needed to complete the quest, and usually tests him first with a simple task. Plays the role of *Donor* in Propp's definition.
- *Beloved one and Family* - Usually described in the initial situation, and it is often subject to harm by the villain. The family is many times the requester of the heroes' quest.
- *Helper* - Helps the hero on his/her quest. Gives relevant information, rescues him/her from a misfortune situation or directly help the hero, side by side, in the defeat of the villain.

Each role has a set of *functions* associated with, this set of *functions* characterises the character's behaviour and goals in the story, and the combination of the role with the actor originates the concept of a "*character*" (*dramatis personae* [7]) that the child will have to control. The interesting aspect of this is that children in *Teatrix* do not mind being witches and villains as much as in a "real dramatic game".

The mechanism for choosing the roles is simple: one child is the responsible for creating the settings and selecting the actors involved in the story. It is usually that child that then initiates the story performance in the 3D stage. To do that, s/he invites the others to select their own characters to control (and thus their role in the story). Once a character is chosen by one of the children, the others cannot choose it. Children see this part as a game and there is normally no negotiation involved. They just want to be involved in it.

In the Virtual Stage

In the virtual stage, as in a real stage, collaboration is necessary in order to attain the objective that is "the performed story". Children control their characters using actions from the set of possible actions associated with the character being controlled. The choice of the actions is done from a control window they can choose *walk*, *pick* an object (which the character will keep in the bag – see Fig. 2) or even *talk* to other characters. Amongst the possible actions to choose from, there are some that involve the *use* of an object (which they have to collect and keep). Using certain objects may implicate other characters and the result may be something happening to those characters. For example, a little boy may use a stick to hit and harm the witch. With the use of actions provided in the control window, the child can control the actions his/her character will perform, even if these are against the goals established by its role (a child controlling a villain may not want it to harm anyone).

Further, at the *performance* level, the interaction between the children is achieved from both the actions that involve other characters, but also though the *talk* action that allow children to make their characters communicate through speech with the others. These actions performed by the characters constitute the fundamental ingredients of the play and consequent movie. Thus, children collaborate with the others to make their "collaborative story" an entertaining story (to be watched in the audience module).

However, interactions may also occur with system-controlled characters, which are characters that exist in the story and that are not controlled by any child. Such characters have their behaviours and goals as a result of the role they play in the story (see [7] for more details on the system controlled agents).

5   Results

Teatrix is already installed in a Portuguese school "O Nosso Sonho" and we have been testing it since March 2000. Children work together in a distributed environment (see [6] and [7] for more details on the distribution mechanism and NIMIS environment) each one controlling his/her own character. Each child is using his/her own computer/working place (in the NIMIS classroom they have a LCD tablet embedded in the table which is used as the interface with pen based input). Also, as they are all in the same room, they can talk to each other in particular for coordinating their actions in the 3D worlds.

First Experiences with *Teatrix*

We did the first tests and evaluations of *Teatrix* during 2000 and at the beginning of 2001. From the first experiences we realized that the roles of the characters were well understood, as well as the whole creation metaphor. In general, children liked to play with it (they see it as another game they can play together).

However, the first evaluations also showed that:

1. children were a bit disappointed with the control they had over the characters since it did not provide them with the means to develop their character's performances or to fully express their creativity. The problem of controlling characters at different levels has already been addressed by [1] and recently by [10]. Similarly, and to overcome our particular problem, we designed another type of control (the "Hot Seating") that can be seen as a kind of mental control of the character. The "Hot Seating" tool is based on research by Dorothy Heathcote [2] on acting in classroom drama. The idea is that a child is seated on the "Hot Seating", and s/he is asked to freeze her/his character's actions. S/he should step out of the character's behaviour and justify why the character is acting in that way. S/he can also inspect the emotional state of the character and its goals, and change the behaviour accordingly (more details on the control of the characters and the "Hot Seating" can be found in [11]).

2. children did most of the coordinating type of interactions by talking (shouting!) to each other over the tables. For example, "I'm following your witch", or "you cannot use my broom". This fact justifies that in the future we will be working on the creation of a clear and explicit support for *co-ordination* level interactions.

Recent Experiences with *Teatrix*

More recently we have been developing a systematic work that has lasted for about three months with a group of six children (8-11 eleven years old), in the school *"O Nosso Sonho"*. This study was conducted in three phases:

Phase 1. We began our work by introducing *Teatrix* to the children, a few of them had already some experience from the past year but the majority of the group was at *beginner* level. First we let them try the system on their own (with little guidance from us). They worked in groups of two or three. Our goal was to allow children to explore the story creation process in *Teatrix* only with the experience they got from the stories they performed in the *Dramatic Room*.

Phase 2. After the first period of exploring, we have introduced *Teatrix* in a tutorial session. To promote a collaborative situation, we gave the group the responsibility to develop a specific task where they would build a story all together, to perform afterwards in *Teatrix*. All these sessions were observed and recorded in video format.

Phase 3. In the final phase, we created an initial setting (prepared in the *Backstage*). The story set up, named "witches, wizards and witchcrafts..." had two characters: Pedro (a boy) and Inês (a girl). The two characters played antagonist roles, so one was a *villain* and the other a *hero*. Each group of 3 children had to choose their character to control and the group had the flexibility to assign the roles of the two characters. To give extra motivation for this story an initial situation was presented to the group: *"The summer holidays ended and Pedro and Inês are coming back to the Dark Raven school for another school year. To decide who will be the leader of the year, every student has to go into the haunted forest and find the enchanted magical wand. Pedro starts to harass Inês by telling that he is the one that is going to win and he bets a jewellery bag with her. Throughout this journey, the teachers challenge the apprentices of wizards and witches, and in each moment there is a new quest...".*

The collaboration was analyzed by considering the interaction performed through the characters by their actions in the virtual world and by the direct interaction between children in the classroom. After the experiment we interviewed the children about what they had done, and how they had understood their role and the objective of the story creation process.

First, we asked the children for their opinion about *Teatrix*, in order to understand the representations that they had about the characters, roles, scenes and props. The results showed that children liked *Teatrix*, and they understood the characters' roles, the scenes, etc. While we were interviewing the children about what they liked most about this experiment with *Teatrix*, one child told us that he liked it when they found the villain in a scene and the villain moved towards his character and hit him with a stick. This and similar statements show that children realise the importance of interactions between characters for the story to evolve and also that the role of the characters changes the way the interaction flows. As expected, we identified two levels of collaboration between students using *Teatrix*: (1) *co-ordination* interactions and (2) *performance* level interactions as described below:

1. a) the children working in a group discuss their ideas and the decisions they made: what objects to pick and what to do with them. We observed that those children always had the need to discuss what to do with their mates. We were able to observe one particular moment, where children were very excited because they were almost reaching the magic wand, they knew it had to be in the current scene because they had looked everywhere else. They all wanted to direct the character and make him walk; they were standing up and shouting. One child took the control and started to ask everyone what they thought would be the best way of searching and reaching for the wand. Quite naturally, all children started talking to each other, listening and deciding according to all opinions.

1. b) the two groups worked together to build the story by sharing ideas, theories and experimenting through collaborative activities towards a common goal which they successfully achieved. Sometimes, besides controlling different characters, the decisions about one character were established between all children of both groups. They stood up and cross over the tables pointing up to the other monitor. They

seemed to understand the task as something to be performed by everyone. It was clear that making stories involved more than just playing with the characters in the virtual world. It involved the real context and the use of the computer and to go back and forward from the virtual world into a deep social involvement.

2. Concerning *performance* level, occurring in the virtual world, children constantly looked for the other character, exchanging objects, performing actions and trying to communicate with him. We could clearly identify the climax of the moment when they finally met the other character. They become so excited, standing up and couldn't stop looking at the monitor.

Children were highly motivated to work with *Teatrix,* and although the system had some problems during its use, children interpreted them as magical phenomena of the program itself. For example, two girls were walking with their character towards a door, trying to go to another scene, but (as the system crashed) they ended facing a "blue wall". Later, during the interview, they explained it was something that had happened to prevent them to go where they wanted, so to them it became part of the game, part of that story.

6 Conclusions

In this paper we show how a story creation environment can trigger and promote certain types of collaborative activities. We started by briefly describing *Teatrix* and the factors that influenced its design. Then we analysed the types of collaborative activities one can find in *Teatrix*. We believe that the work here presented allows us to understand to some extent how we can support the *co-ordination type of interactions* and *collaboration*, and more importantly if we do really need to support them through a virtual environment.

References

1. Blumberg, B. and Galyean T.: "Multi-level Control for Animated Autonomous Agents: Do the Right Thing...Oh, Not that" in Creating Personalities for Synthetic Actors, Ed. R. Trappl and P. Petta, Springer, 1997.
2. Bolton, G.: "Acting in classroom drama: a critical analysis", Pub. Stoke-on-Trent : Trentham, 1998.
3. Dautenhahn, K.: "Story-Telling in Virtual Environments". *Working Notes Intelligent Virtual Environments,* Workshop at the 13th biennial European Conference on Artificial Intelligence, Brighton, UK, 1998.
4. Dillenbourg, P., Baker M., Blaye A. & O'Malley, C.: "The Evolution of research on collaborative learning", in Spada E. & Reiman P. (eds) Learning in Humans and Machine: towards and interdisciplinary learning science, Oxford, Elsevier.
5. B. Laurel: *Computers as Theatre*, Addison-Wesley, 1993.

6. Machado, I., Prada, R. & Paiva A.: "Bringing Drama into a Virtual Stage", *in Collaborative Virtual Environments*, ACM Press, 2000.
7. Paiva, A., Prada R. & Machado, I. "Heroes, villains, magicians...: *Dramatis Personae* in a virtual story creation environment" In "Intelligent User Interfaces" ACM Press, 2001.
8. Propp V.: *Morphology of the Folktale*, University of Texas Press, 1968.
9. Singer D. & Singer J.: *The House of Make-Believe*, Harvard University Press, 1990.
10. Sengers, P.: "Semi-Autonomous Avatars" presentation and poster at the Autonomous Agents' 2000.
11. Paiva A. & Machado, I.: "The Child Behind the Character". In the Special Issue on " Socially Intelligent Agents - The Human in the Loop", of the Journal *IEEE Transactions on Systems, Man, and Cybernetics*, 31(5), 2001.

Feedback on Children's Stories via Multiple Interface Agents

Judy Robertson[1] and Peter Wiemer-Hastings[2]*

[1] University of Edinburgh
ICCS/Division of Informatics
2 Buccleuch Place
Edinburgh EH8 9LW Scotland
[2] DePaul University
School of Computer Science,
Telecommunications, and Information Systems
243 South Wabash Avenue
Chicago IL 60604 USA

Abstract. This paper describes StoryStation, an intelligent tutoring system designed to give ten to twelve year old children feedback on their creative writing. The feedback is presented via eight animated interface agents. Each agent gives a different sort of support to the writer including: a thesaurus, a dictionary, feedback on vocabulary and characterisation, help with spelling, help with plot structure, example stories to read and help with the interface itself. This paper focuses on the strategies for generating feedback to the children and discusses some issues in presenting this feedback through the interface agents.

1 Introduction

Writing stories is hard work. Many writers find it stressful; they might worry about whether an idea is any good, whether the story will interest the reader, whether their spelling is adequate or even whether their handwriting is legible. Children need a lot of encouragement, help, support and feedback during the writing process. After investing so much effort in writing a story, each pupil deserves to have it read and appreciated. Unfortunately, even the best teachers don't have time to give each pupil the support she needs.

A possible solution to the problem is to use an intelligent tutoring system to give the children help and feedback on their stories. A tutoring system can never be an appreciative, amused, scared or sympathetic audience but it can create more time for the teacher to be an appreciative reader. The tutoring system can give lower level suggestions and support to children while the teacher is engaged in high level discussions about stories with other pupils.

* This work was supported by grants from the James S. McDonald Foundation and from the EPSRC. The pilot study reported here was carried out in conjunction with Charlotte Moss. Thanks are also due to the pupils and staff of Sinclairtown Primary School and St Columba's Primary School, Fife, Scotland.

S.A. Cerri, G. Gouardères, and F. Paraguaçu (Eds.): ITS 2002, LNCS 2363, pp. 923–932, 2002.
© Springer-Verlag Berlin Heidelberg 2002

StoryStation is an intelligent tutoring system designed to provide support and feedback to children on a variety of writing skills, based on a prototype described in (Wiemer-Hastings and Graesser, 2000). The system is outlined in Section 3, and the mechanism for supplying feedback to the pupils is described in more detail in Section 4. Much of the feedback is acknowledgement and praise for good work; through recognition of the children's best efforts at mastering writing techniques, StoryStation encourages them to use the same skills in the future. StoryStation provides dictionary and thesaurus facilities, a bank of example stories written by other children, help with spelling, plot structure, and vocabulary usage and techniques for portraying story characters. Each of these features is presented to the user through an animated interface agent. Figure 1 shows the interface to StoryStation.

Fig. 1. The interface to StoryStation

Flower (1994) described how important it is for students to learn strategies to manage the multiple constraints involved in writing. She characterized writing as the "negotiated construction of meaning", and described a variety of voices that speak during the process of composition. Voices correspond to the different types of constraint that impinge upon the process. The term voice emphasises that the constraints are not innocent bystanders to the process. Instead, they are actively involved, pushing the writer in different directions. Thus, the writer must "negotiate" with these voices to achieve a solution which creates meaningful text, and (at least partially) satisfies the constraints. The biggest problem is that the pupil is not normally consciously aware of the voices. This project's goal is to help the writer convert these ethereal forces into concrete considerations that she is consciously aware of and then can reason about. Thus, in StoryStation, we have chosen to embody different aspects of writing as unique animated pedagogical agents.

Instead of an "all knowing" computer telling the pupil that something they have done is incorrect, several characters give their "opinions" on the pupil's composition. Different characters can also disagree with each other. Thus, pupils can learn about the constraints inherent in writing and the interactions between them, and build strategies for managing them.

StoryStation has been developed in a conjunction in close consultation with pupils and teacher at a local state funded primary school. We have used a child centred design strategy in which a team of eight children and two teachers have helped the researchers at all stages of the project. One of our collaborators is a retired teacher with forty years of teaching experience; her expertise and knowledge of the Scottish National Curriculum have been invaluable to the project. We have also worked with primary six and seven classes in three other schools while gathering story corpora and testing aspects of StoryStation, on subjects outside our design team. We have chosen to work in state funded schools with pupils of a range of ability levels and socio-economic backgrounds. The software is still under development, but as part of our development methodology we have conducted formative evaluation of some aspects of it. These studies are outlined in Section 5. In this paper we focus on some issues concerning the presentation of feedback to the pupils, and the strategies we have developed for this. We will empirically compare the effectiveness of these strategies in future work.

Agent interfaces may seem intuitively appealing, especially for children's software, but what effect do such interfaces have on their motivation and learning? As discussed in Section 2, there is currently no conclusive or consistent evidence that they are effective. We intend to explore these questions in future studies using StoryStation. The paper concludes with some lessons learned from the pilot work so far, with some implications for future research in this area.

2   Background

Several computer writing environments were developed in the late 1980s (Britton and Glynn, 1989; Sharples et al., 1988). The design of these environments was informed by research on the cognitive processes during the composition process (e.g. Flower and Hayes, 1980). Such writing environments provided appropriate representations of the composition at different stages of the process (e.g. planning, generating, revising) and the facility to switch between the representations in order to cater for different writing styles.

More recently, research into writing systems has refocused on providing emotional as well as cognitive support for writers. T'riffic Tales (Brna, Cooper and Razmerita, 2001) is a cartoon creation program designed for five year olds who are learning to write. Pupils can ask for help with their stories from an emotional pedagogical agent named Louisa. The design of Louisa was informed by research into empathic interactions between class teachers and their pupils. The designers take the view that a pedagogical agent should provide emotional support — care, concern continuity, and security — for learners as well as cognitive, domain related support. They propose a cycle of behaviours for such an agent which signals to the pupil that help is available, provides help in an engaging, interactive manner, and ensures thes pupil that further help is available if needed (Brna, Cooper and Rasmerita, 2001).

This model seems particularly appropriate in the writing domain. Bereiter and Scardamalia (1982) report empirical evidence on the effects of encouraging and prompting novice writers. It was found that children would write more on a subject if they were initially asked to write as much as possible and were prompted to continue at points when they claimed to have nothing more to write. These very simple interventions tripled writing output. The prompts were content-free motivational prompts such as "You're doing well. Can you write more?". Bakunas (1996) found that discourse-related prompts which suggested a structure for ideas were even more helpful than purely motivational prompts in the context of generating ideas for an essay. These empirical results suggest that interactions with animated agents which exhibit encouraging, empathic behaviours will be beneficial for writers.

The preceding discussion of appropriate design for pedagogical agents does not focus on the effectiveness of such agents in comparison to "traditional" graphical user interfaces. However, it cannot be assumed that animated pedagogical agents are more effective than GUIs in terms of either students' motivation or learning. Indeed, Dehn and van Mulken (2000) review empirical studies of the impact of animated agents on the user's experience with using the software, her behaviour while using it and her performance on the task with which the agent is intended to assist. The authors report that there are few empirical studies which address these issues, and that the results are inconclusive. They conclude that the literature to date "does not provide evidence to for a so-called persona effect, that is, a general advantage of an interface with an animated agent over one without an animated agent" (Dehn and van Mulken; 2000: p. 17). Furthermore, the methodological validity of some studies is questionable. For example, Lester et. al (1997) concluded that the presence of the animated agent in an intelligent tutoring system improved the learners' problem solving skills. Dehn and van Mulken point out that these conclusions are suspect because there was no control condition that provided the same advice without an animated agent.

Given the lack of evidence due to a small number of studies, some of which are confounded, Dehn and van Mulken call for further methodogically sound studies in this area. We intend to conduct such studies during the course of the StoryStation project.

3   StoryStation Overview

StoryStation is being developed using a child centred design methodology, adapted from (Druin, 1999; Scaife and Rogers, 1999). We have worked closely with a team of eight (ten to twelve year old) pupils in a state funded primary school during the design process. As part of this process, the pupils have evaluated other pieces of writing software, suggested ideas for the software features, designed and animated interface agents, and created icons for the interface (see Wiemer-Hastings and Robertson, 2001). We have also conducted larger scale requirements analysis with two classes, interviewed teachers, and started exploratory work into agent interactions through a Wizard of Oz pilot study (see Section 5).

The software is designed to be most effective when assisting children with a story re-telling task. This activity is used in classrooms as a way of focusing young writer's attentions on writing skills rather than the imaginative skills of creating a story plot. The writer's task is to recount a story he has heard or read before. As he does not have to devote cognitive resources to thinking of a storyline, he can spend more time writing descriptions of the scenes and characters. A story re-telling task is also easier to support in an intelligent tutoring system because there is more information available about what the user is trying to achieve. However, many StoryStation features can be used for any writing task, including factual writing assignments

StoryStation is a work in progress. At the time of writing the backend language processing features are complete, as are the student modelling and teaching rules. The interface is under development, and is not yet integrated with the backend. StoryStation can also be used in a batch mode to process stories from text files and generate feedback files in the absence of a user.

The features of StoryStation are as follows. Firstly, there are some simple facilities to assist the users as they create their stories, but which do not contain intelligent feedback. Interface help is provided in the form of documentation written by the pupils in the design team. There is also a library of example stories, collected from pupils in a variety of local primary schools after visits by storytellers. The purpose of this feature is to give children ideas for their own stories from reading and critiquing stories written by their peers. The same stories will be the basis of writing tasks using StoryStation. StoryStation also provides an interface to the dictionary and thesaurus features of WordNet (Miller et al, 1993) because the classes we have worked with regularly use such resources for writing exercises.

In addition to these simple features, there are some forms of support which require some natural language processing techniques. We describe these in the following paragraphs.

Pupils may have difficulty in writing coherent plots, even when re-telling stories with which they are familiar. Although they are capable of orally re-telling the plots, the difficulty of the writing task interferes with the re-telling, resulting in incoherent stories. Furthermore, certain writing techniques are best used in particular plot episodes. For example, lengthy character descriptions generally work better at the beginning of a story because descriptions would slow down the pace of exciting events. As another example, a writer might use shorter sentences to make an action sequence more exciting (Corbett, 2001). It is possible to supply help and suggestions on plot structure if the user is writing a known story. By setting the user a story re-writing task, a reasonable strategy for reducing cognitive overload, StoryStation can use an algorithm based on latent semantic analysis (Landauer and Dumais, 1997) to match the user's plot episodes with episodes in the model story. In this way, it can remind the pupil of plot episodes which she might have forgotten, help the pupil improve coherence by re-ordering episodes, and suggest appropriate techniques for improving particular episodes.

Spelling help was the most frequently requested feature during the requirements gathering exercise. In spite of a move towards the process approach to writing, where a drafting process encourages children to focus on spelling in the later stages of editing, many children are constantly worried by their spelling difficulties. During a recent Wizard of Oz pilot study we observed that lower ability pupils found constant help with spelling reassuring. StoryStation is integrated with Microsoft Word's spell checker. We have found this spell checker to be 80-85% reliable when checking children's stories. StoryStation also supplies spelling support in the form of personalised word banks of commonly misspelled words, specialist vocabulary, and language suitable for particular stories. These have been adapted from vocabulary notebooks which are used by the classes we have worked with for the same purpose.

The vocabulary and characterisation features of StoryStation adopt the strategy of praising the pupils for good use of particular techniques by highlighting "good words" in the pupil's story. "Good words" is a classroom shorthand for long words, unusual words, or words which are not within the pupil's everyday vocabulary. It can also highlight phrases where the pupil has described a character's appearance, personality or feelings, and good dialogue segments. In the classroom, praising a pupil for using a writing technique was until recently less common than reprimanding her for mistakes. However, the schools involved in the project have recently adopted a writing scheme which specifies that teachers should not correct a story in the absence of the author; instead she should highlight parts of the story she enjoyed. Later, in the presence of the author, she can discuss the mistakes and offer suggestions. This approach is considerably more motivating than traditional approaches to marking (see Dunsbee and Ford, 1980) and the class teacher reports that it is working well.

Storystation identifies "good words" by checking the familiarity of each story word in a corpus. The corpus is derived from the mean familiarity and age of acquisition data from the MRC Psycholinguistic database (Coltheart, 1981), and frequency statistics from the British National Corpus (BNC). It can also identify alliteration and minimal pairs (both examples of manipulating language for poetic effect) using the phonetic information in the MRC.

The feedback on characterisation techniques is based on a story characterisation scheme described in Robertson (2000). StoryStation checks the user's story for words which are associated with descriptions of characters' appearance, personalities, feelings and speech. Word lists for each of these categories were derived using WordNet. First of all, seed words for each category were collected from the Linguistic Inquiry and Word Count (LIWC) corpus (Pennebaker et al., 2001); stories which had been human-rated using the story analysis scheme (Robertson and Good, 2001); and the researcher's intuition. These word lists were then extended by searching for synonyms, hyponyms and hypernyms in WordNet. The word lists were hand filtered and refined on several story collections. The resulting software was then tested on a fresh corpus which had previously been human-rated using Robertson's story analysis scheme. Preliminary analysis indicates that inter-rater reliability is acceptable.

StoryStation's method of generating feedback is described in the next section.

4   Generating Feedback

StoryStation generates feedback for the pupils using its student models, curriculum models and some heuristics encapsulated in tutoring rules. It builds a student model for the current user's story with entries for spelling, word count, number of different words, mean BNC frequency, proportions of nouns, adverbs, adjectives and pronouns, counts of connective usage (such as "and", "because", "but"), and counts of characterisation techniques. The tutoring rules use this information to decide what feedback to give on each aspect of the story. Firstly, if the user has previously asked for feedback during the current session, the tutoring rules will compare the current student model to the previous model for the same session to see whether the pupil has improved the story by taking StoryStation's advice. Secondly, if the user has not asked for help on this story before, the tutoring rules will compare the current student model with the user's most recent student model from a previous session. Thirdly, if this is the user's first session with StoryStation, the tutoring rules compare the fields in the user's current student model to expected values from the curriculum models. The curriculum models contain the norms for each of the five Scottish National Curriculum levels. These were derived by using processing a corpus of 140 stories for each of the linguistic measures stored in the student model and finding the quintiles for each measure. The quintiles provide threshold values for each curriculum level. StoryStation keeps a record of the curriculum level which a child is working towards (this information is supplied by the teacher), and can therefore compare every field in the student model against the threshold value for the appropriate curriculum level.

Note that the third method of comparison is the least reliable because it assumes that the corpus of 140 stories are representative of the children's stories in general. StoryStation's performance will become more reliable over time because it will be able to use the user's previous performance as a benchmark.

The tutoring rules are used to generate overall and specific feedback. The overall feedback on the story gives the user general information about her progress in spelling, vocabulary and characterisation. For example, it could encourage the pupil by mentioning that her spelling has improved since last time, or suggest that she could make her story even better by using the thesaurus to find good vocabulary. These indications of progress will also be useful to the teacher.

StoryStation can also give specific feedback to the pupil at a word or phrase level. It can identify spelling mistakes, offer spelling suggestions, and highlight other features which require the user's attentions. It highlights "good words", and use of characterisation techniques in order to praise the child and encourage her to try using similar techniques in her next story. It can also highlight repetitive use of language, for example overuse of "and", and give general suggestions on how the user could improve this. A discussion of the success of the feedback strategies in pilot work is given in the next section.

5   Pilot Results and Implications for Future Work

As part of the design process, we have consulted with pupils and teachers throughout the project. Two informal pilot studies are of interest here - a Wizard of Oz study to explore children's reactions to feedback from animated agents, and a field study to discover how children respond to the StoryStation feedback.

The purpose of the Wizard of Oz study was to discover what pupils thought of the animated agents and whether they took their advice. In this case, the advice was actually typed in by a teacher or another pupil, but appeared to the user as if it came from the agents. Interviews with eight pupils indicated that the pupils mainly appreciated the agent's advice and enjoyed their support. When asked how the agents made them feel, one pupil mentioned: "It made me feel more confident. You know you're not making mistakes in words". Another said "It made me feel happy because it was helping me with my spelling. and the words I didn't know".

One pupil did not enjoy his experience with the agents and seemed upset by one of their comments. The "wizard" who supplied his advice was another pupil, and he bluntly stated that the story did not make sense. When asked about his experiences with the agents, the pupil said "[the advice] made me feel 'Oh, I must be rubbish at my writing then'". It appeared that the pupil had never considered whether it was wise to take the agent seriously or not; he had assumed that the agent had some authority and so was upset by its censure. This implies that careful phrasing of advice is required to avoid demoralising pupils.

A further field study was conducted to see how the children responded to feedback generated by StoryStation. This feedback came in the form of a printed page containing general comments and an annotated version of the pupil's first draft of a story. Twenty three pupils were given this form of feedback on their stories and were asked to redraft the stories after reading the advice.

The pupils did make the changes suggested in the feedback. They worked systematically through the annotated story and changed spelling mistakes and corrected overuse of the connective "and". They appeared to take less notice of the general advice at the start of the feedback and were slightly puzzled by the fact that the purpose of some of the highlighting was simply to praise them. However, once the researchers read out the highlighted praise, reinforcing that the pupils had done well, the pupils understood and were pleased. During interviews with two groups of five pupils, it seemed as though the more able, more articulate pupils appreciated the feedback more than the less able, shyer pupils. This is possibly because meta-level skills for understanding feedback and responding accordingly are less developed in less able writers.

Some pupils were confused by the colour coding of the comments, but others quickly learned that they only needed to make changes for red and orange highlights, saying "you can just ignore the rest". One boy who had difficulty with spelling pointed out that the colour coding was demoralising for him. He said "I know I'm not that good at spelling but I like to try to put in good words, but then my whole page gets coloured in yellow". He was discouraged that his best efforts lead to a lot of negative seeming feedback. This suggests that more spelling support is required during the writing process, and that the feedback strategy for poorer spellers should be modified.

The results of this pilot study suggest that pupils are not accustomed to receiving detailed specific praise on aspects of their writing. To gain the most from StoryStation, pupils may need some help in changing their expectations about story "corrections". They should be taught to respond to positive as well as negative feedback, and to value their own work.

It may also be the case that more able pupils are better equipped to respond appropriately to advice on their writing, and that less able writers need further support in interpreting and acting on advice. Future studies will explore whether ability is a factor in the effectiveness of advice presented by agents and a traditional graphical user interface.

6 Conclusions

StoryStation is a unique writing environment for children that provides significant support for a story-retelling task. By involving pupils and teachers in every stage of the design process, we have created a system that is well-tailored to the pupils' preferences and writing processes. StoryStation provides both positive and constructive negative feedback to the pupils. By associating the different types of feedback with different agents, we hope to help the pupils learn the metacognitive skills required to manage the different constraints on the writing process.

In future research, we will use StoryStation as a testbed for addressing a number of important questions regarding how best to support children's writing. In particular, we can examine the effects of animated pedagogical agents on learning and motivation. Preliminary results have already shown the feasibility of our approach, and suggested new research questions.

References

Bakunas, B. (1996). Promoting idea production by novice writers through the use of discourse-related prompts. Applied Psycholinguistics, 17, pages 385-400.

Bereiter, C. & Scardamalia, M. (1982). From Conversation to Composition: The Role of Instruction in A Developmental Process. In Glaser, R., Editor, Advances in Instructional Psychology Volume 2. Lawrence Erlbaum Associates.

Britton, B. and Glynn, S. (Eds) (1989). Computer Writing Environments: Theory, research and design. Lawrence Erlbaum Associates, New Jersey.

Coltheart, M. (1981). "The MRC Psycholinguistic Database" Quarterly Journal of Experimental Psychology, 33A, 497-505.

Corbett, P. (2001). Write your own chillers: create your own spine-tingling stories and terrifying tales. Belitha Press, London.

Dehn, D. and van Mulken, S. (2000). "The impact of animated inerface agents: a review of empirical research". International Journal of Human-Computer Studies 52 1-22.

Druin, A. (1999) "Cooperative Inquiry: Developing New Technologes for Children with Children". Proceedings of CHI '99. ACM Press.

Dunsbee, T. and Ford, T. (1980). Mark My Words: A study of teachers as correctors of children's writing. NATE, London.

Ellis, S. and Friel, G. (1998). 5-14 Teacher Support: Learning to Write, Writing to Learn: Imaginative Writing. Scottish Consultative Council on the Curriculum.

Flower, L. (1994) The construction of negotiated meaning: A social cognitive theory of writing. Southern Illinois University Press, Carbondale, EL, 1994.

Flower, L. and Hayes, J. (1980). The dynamics of composing: making plans and juggling constraints. In Gregg, L.W. and Steinberg, E. R., Editors, Cognitive Processes in Writing. Lawrence Erlbaum Associates.

Graves, D. (1983). Writing: Teachers & Children At Work. Heinemann Books.

Hietala, P. and Niemirepo, T. (1998). "The Competence of Learning Companion Agents" International Journal of Artificial Intelligence in Education (1998) 9, 178-192.

Landauer, T.K. and Dumais, S.T. (1997) "A solution to Plato's Problem: The latent semantic analysis theory of acquisition, induction, and representation of knowledge" Psychological Review 104:211-240.

Lester, J. Converse, S., Kahler, S, Barlow, S., Stone, B., Bhoga, R. (1997). "The Persona Effect: Affective Impact of Animated Pedagogical Agents" in Proceedings of CHI 97, Atlanta.

Miller, G. , Beckwith, R., Fellbaum, C., Gross, D. and Miller, K. (1993). Introduction to WordNet: An On-line Lexical Database. Onlline publication, available at ftp://ftp.cogsci.princeton.edu/pub/wordnet/5papers.pdf

Pennebaker, J.W., Francis, M.E., & Booth, R.J. (2001). Linguistic Inquiry and Word Count (LIWC): LIWC2001. Mahwah, NJ: Erlbaum Publishers.

Robertson, J. (2000). The effectiveness of a virtual role-play environment as a story preparation activity. PhD thesis, Edinburgh University. Available at www.cogsci.ed.ac.uk/~judyr .

Robertson, J. and Good, J. (submitted). "Using a Collaborative Virtual Role-Play Environment to Foster Characterisation in Stories". Submitted to Journal of Interactive Learning Research.

Scaife, M. and Rogers, Y. (1999). "Kids as Informants: Telling us what we didn't know or confirming what we knew already?" in Druin, A. (Ed). The Design of Children's Technology: How we Design, What we Design and Why. Morgan Kaufman.

Wiemer-Hastings, P. and Graesser, A. (2000). "Select-a-kibitzer: A computer tool that gives meaningful feedback on student compositions." Interactive Learning Environments, pp 149-169.

Wiemer-Hastings, P. and Robertson, J. (2001). "Story Station: Children's story writing software". Poster at AIED 2001.

Informing the Detection of the Students' Motivational State: An Empirical Study

Angel de Vicente and Helen Pain

Institute for Communicating and Collaborative Systems; Division of Informatics,
The University of Edinburgh
{angelv,helen}@dai.ed.ac.uk

Abstract. The ability to detect the students' motivational state during
an instructional interaction can bring many benefits to the performance
of an Intelligent Tutoring System (ITS). In this paper we present an
empirical study which provided us with a considerable amount of knowledge regarding motivation diagnosis. We show how this knowledge was
formalised in order to create a set of motivation diagnosis rules that can
be incorporated into a prototype tutoring system. We also briefly present
how these motivation diagnosis rules were evaluated in another study.

1 Introduction

Many tutoring systems attempt to motivate the student by using multimedia,
games, etc. This approach seems to be based on the idea that it is possible to
create instruction that is motivating *per se*. However, as Keller mentions in [6],
it is not always the case that if the instruction is of good quality motivation
will follow. There has been some previous work that has dealt explicitly with
motivation in ITSs (e.g.[4,5,9]), but these have dealt mainly with instructional
planning, and not so much with motivation diagnosis. We believe that there is
a pressing need for more research in this area [2], and we focus in this paper
on how to elicit and formalise knowledge to diagnose the student's motivational
state during an interaction with an instructional system.

The issue of how human teachers detect their students' motivation has been
virtually unexplored in AI and Education research. Introspection and observational studies could throw some light into this issue, but they may be of limited
usefulness for motivation diagnosis in ITSs. In a traditional instructional setting
or any other social interaction there is a vast amount of information available
through various communication channels, such as facial cues, posture, etc. [1],
and there has been some interesting research on incorporating some of these cues
in instructional systems (e.g. [10]). But many such cues that help us detect other
people's emotions (or motivation) are perceived unconsciously, which makes it
difficult to elicit emotion (or motivation) detection knowledge.

In order to limit the amount of sources of information available for knowledge elicitation, we designed a study in which a tutor is asked to infer a student's
motivational state. But in order to do so, the only information that is available

S.A. Cerri, G. Gouardères, and F. Paraguaçu (Eds.): ITS 2002, LNCS 2363, pp. 933–943, 2002.
© Springer-Verlag Berlin Heidelberg 2002

to her[1] is the pre-recorded screen interaction of a student with an instructional system. That is, the tutor is only able to see on a computer screen the interface of the instructional system which the student was manipulating. We expected that it would be easier for tutors to rationalise their motivation diagnosis knowledge in this setting than if they were presented, say, with video-recordings of tutoring interactions. At the same time, we believed that the knowledge inferred in this way would be easier to formalise in terms of information available to the instructional system (such as the duration of the interaction with the system, mouse movements, etc.).

2   Background on Recorded Interactions

As explained above, the participants of this study watched a number of recorded interactions of a student with a prototype ITS for learning Japanese numbers. This prototype ITS (MOODS) is a simple tutoring system with an added motivation self-report facility. This means that the student is able to report about his perceived motivational state during the interaction with MOODS. As a result of a previous study [3], we had a number of recorded interactions with the system, which were used as the basis for the study presented in this paper.

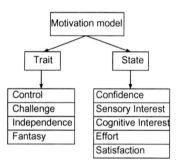

Fig. 1. Motivation model

The self-report facility available in MOODS is based on a motivation model which is presented in figure 1[2]. The model is based on the relevant literature (e.g. [6,7,8]) and it is composed of a number of motivational factors, which are divided in two classes: trait variables, or 'permanent' characteristics of the student; and state variables, or more 'transient' characteristics. Definitions for all these variables are given in table 1.

---

[1] In this paper there are two main characters: the participants of the study, and the students whose interactions with an instructional system were replayed. In order to facilitate readability we use female pronouns to refer to the study participant and male pronouns to refer to the students. This has no relation to their actual gender.

[2] A more detailed description can be found in [3].

Table 1. Definitions of motivation model variables

Variable	Definition
Control	Refers to the degree of control that the student likes having over the learning situation (i.e. does he like to select which exercises to do, in which order, etc. rather than let the instructor take these decisions?).
Challenge	Refers to the degree that the student enjoys having challenging situations during the instruction (i.e. does he like to try difficult exercises that represent a challenge for him?).
Independence	Refers to the degree that the student prefers to work independently, without asking others for help (i.e. does he prefer to work on his own, even if he finds some difficulties, and try to solve them by himself rather than asking for collaboration or help from others?).
Fantasy	Refers to the degree that the student appreciates environments that evoke mental images of physical or social situations not actually present (i.e. does he like the learning materials being embedded in an imaginary context?).
Confidence	Refers to the student's belief in being able to perform the task at hand correctly.
Sensory interest	Refers to the amount of curiosity aroused through the interface presentation (i.e. appeal of graphics, sounds, etc.).
Cognitive interest	Refers to curiosity aroused through the cognitive or epistemic characteristics of the task (i.e. regardless of the presentation issues, does the student find the task at hand cognitively appealing?).
Effort	Refers to the degree that the student is exerting himself in order to perform the learning activities.
Satisfaction	Refers to the overall feeling of goal accomplishment (i.e. does the student think that the instruction is satisfying and that it is getting him closer to his goals?).

The trait variables in our motivation model are: control, challenge, independence and fantasy. There seems to be agreement on the importance of control and challenge for student's motivation. Fantasy, although not often included in theories of motivation in Education, seems to be a factor that can play an important role in engaging the student (e.g. [8]). Independence, as defined in table 1, is related to challenge, but also to interpersonal motivations, such as: cooperation, competition and recognition [8].

The state variables represent transient characteristics of the student that relate to the material being learned. In figure 1 the state variables are presented in a more or less 'chronological' order. Thus, considerations of how confident he feels about succeeding in the task will likely take place before engaging in the task. This, together with the interest (both sensory and cognitive) that the lesson arouses in him, will influence the effort that he will put into the task. Satisfaction, as defined in table 1, represents the overall feeling of goal accomplishment, and will be influenced by all the variables above, plus by the outcomes of the task [6].

3   Materials

The participants of this study were asked to watch the recorded interactions of a student with MOODS, and they were asked to infer and comment on the motivational state of the student during the interaction. For this, we developed A_MOODS, which can be used to replay the actions of a previous student interaction with MOODS and to predict his motivational state. The A_MOODS interface can be seen in figure 2.

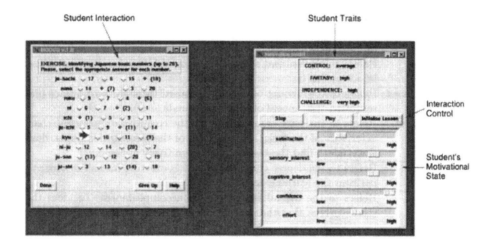

Fig. 2. A_MOODS interface.

The actions made by the student are replayed in the window to the left (with title MOODS v.1.0). To facilitate the viewing of the student interaction, an arrow (around the centre of the window in figure 2) indicates the mouse movements.

The window to the right (titled Motivation model) consists of three frames.

1. The top frame is a representation of the *student traits* of the motivation model (described in section 2). The values for these were obtained through a questionnaire during the self-report study described in [3].
2. The three buttons in the middle of the window control how the student interaction is replayed.
   - The replay of the student interaction starts when *Play* is pressed, and stops when *Stop* is pressed.
   - The button *Initialise Lesson* allows the user to 'rewind' the interaction to the beginning of the current lesson.

- The replay of the interaction is done in real time, except for the replay of the theory lessons. In this type of lesson there is very little student activity, and therefore the system simply shows a message regarding how long the student took to learn the lesson[3]. After this the interaction continues.
3. The bottom frame is a representation of the student's *motivational state*, as discussed in section 2 (The task of the participants for this study was to predict the likely values of these motivational variables as the instruction replay took place).

In order to let the participants update the student's motivational model, the interaction stops by default in any of the following three situations:

1. When the student presses any of the buttons (Done, Give Up, or Help), but before any feedback is given by the system.
2. After feedback is presented to the student.
3. When a new lesson is presented to the student.

In these cases a small message[4] is shown to remind the participant to update the motivational model. If the participant does want to update the motivational model or comment on any aspect of the instruction at any other time, she can stop the interaction by pressing the *Stop* button.

4   Methodology

For this study 10 post-graduate students with previous teaching and/or tutoring experience volunteered to participate. After reading the study instructions, the interaction with A_MOODS started. The interaction can be summarised as follows:

1. The participant was given information about the trait characteristics of a student.
2. Then she was shown a replay of the student's interaction with MOODS.
3. Throughout the interaction, and particularly at any stop points, the participant was encouraged to give verbal comments on the student's motivational state and the possible factors affecting it.
4. Whenever the interaction was paused the participant was asked to update the motivational state if she had enough information to make an inference. And she was asked to verbalise the reasoning behind her inferences.
5. When the student pressed any of the three buttons available (Done, Give up, or Help), the participant was also encouraged to comment on the type of feedback that she thought would be the most appropriate to give to the student at that moment.

Throughout the duration of the study, the participant's comments were recorded on an audio disc, and were later transcribed and analysed.

---

[3] A sample message of this type is: "The student used 147 seconds to study this lesson".

[4] "Please update the motivational model. Afterwards press 'Play' to continue."

5 Results

Before the study started, most of the participants commented on the perceived difficulty of the task. They expected not to be able to make any inferences based on the information provided. Contrary to their expectations, most of the participants made a considerable number of reasoned inferences about the student's affective state, and at the end of the study they commented that the task was actually not so difficult and that there was quite a lot of information available to them in order to perform these inferences.

On average, the time participants spent with the system was around 36 minutes. In this time, an average of 4 lessons were covered, and 8.5 inferences were made per participant. In total we collected 85 inferences. The excerpt below illustrates the type of comments that participants made during this study.

Interviewer:

And [...] why do you think he is satisfied at this point?

Participant:

Well, [...] he is hovering the mouse over the answers each time, he wasn't randomly moving the mouse, he is looking for the answer, [...] and that he didn't take a long time to answer the questions. To me that would suggest that the task is interesting enough to complete with some attention and to do it properly, if you like. [...] So, I would increase the satisfaction here, just for the fact that he did it with confidence.

Inferred rule from excerpt. Based on the excerpt above, we were able to elicit the rule presented in figure 3. Because the mouse movement through the interface is not random, the participant could infer that the student was paying attention to the task and because it was performed quickly, she inferred that he was confident. And given that:

1. He was interested in the task
2. He was confident
3. He performed the task well

the participant could infer that the student would be highly satisfied. The dashed arrow and the box in figure 3 represent another rule, but serve to illustrate that performing a task quickly can also mean lack of interest, but it is the combination of other evidence that can lead us to believe that, in this case, a quick performance was due to high confidence.

Elicited motivation diagnosis rules. By analysing all the recorded interviews with participants, we elicited 85 rules similar to that in figure 3. Given a rule, we consider its *inputs* the factors on which the inference of that rule is based. For example, *inputs* to the rule in figure 3 are *Mouse movements, Quickly performed,*

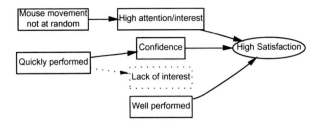

Fig. 3. Inference rule from excerpt.

Confidence, etc. The *output* of the rule is its conclusion: *High Satisfaction* in the case of figure 3.

In figure 4 we analyse the elicited rules according to their *input* categories. As we can see, the input factors more often mentioned by the participants were those related to students' performance. The main category in figure 4 is that of *Characteristics of performance*, which was mentioned in 41 out of the 85 provisional rules elicited. This category includes a number of characteristics which relate to the way a student performed during the interaction, such as the order in which he did the exercises, whether he gave up or not, etc.

The second most mentioned broad *input* category was that of *Teaching materials*, in which we include subcategories such as the *Difficulty of the teaching materials*, issues regarding the *History of the interaction*, etc. Although not mentioned as often as *Performance* or *Teaching materials* issues, it can be seen in figure 4 that the student's *Motivation model* and his *Motivational traits* were also considered on a number of occasions as input factors for some of the inference rules.

In figure 5 we can see which output categories were mentioned most often by the participants. Not surprisingly, since this was the main purpose of the study, most of the inference rules have as their *output* a category relating to student's *Motivational model*. But we can see that there were also a number of cases where the *output* of some of the rules was related to other categories. For example, there were some rules in which the participants reasoned about the student's knowledge on the subject, about the feedback that should be provided to the student, etc.[5]

Due to lack of space we cannot present here the complete set of rules inferred from this study, but by way of illustration we present in table 2 some of the rules related to the detection of the factor *Satisfaction*. Each rule has a reference code in the first column of the table (starting with the letters *IS* for the rules that

---

[5] It is interesting to note that some of the results of this study contrast with those of the self-report study mentioned earlier [3]. Thus, participants in this study made fewer inferences about student's effort than about his satisfaction. On the other hand, participants of the self-report study reported their effort on more occasions that their satisfaction. A similar situation arises with the factors *Cognitive interest* and *Sensory interest*.

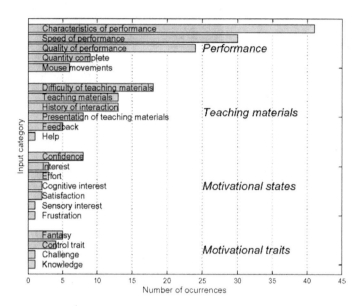

Fig. 4. Occurrences for each input category.

infer a high satisfaction value and starting with the letters *DS* for the rules that infer a low satisfaction value).

Each column represents an *input* factor, which are presented into the same broad categories as in figure 4. The different factors[6] given as input for the rules are:

- Performance
    - **Quality**. Correctness of the answers provided to the exercises.
    - **Speed**. Time spent in doing the instructional unit.
    - **Give up**. Whether the student chose to give up the lesson or not.
- Teaching Materials
    - **Difficulty**. Level of difficulty of the current exercise.
    - **pre(Diff)**. Level of difficulty of the previous exercise.
    - **Control**. Level of control available in the current lesson.
    - **Feedback**. Characteristics of the feedback provided (*Enc*: Encouragement).
- Motivation model
    - Value of the corresponding factor in student's motivational model.
- Motivation traits
    - Value of the corresponding factor in student's motivational traits model.

---

[6] The complete set of rules has a larger number of input factors, but they are not listed here as they were not mentioned for the sample rules given in table 2.

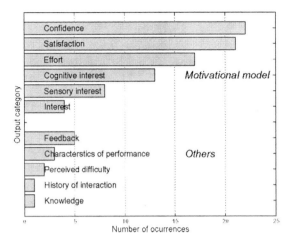

Fig. 5. Occurrences for each output category.

6   Discussion and Further Work

As mentioned earlier, participants in this study were initially quite convinced that the task would prove extremely difficult and that it would be virtually impossible for them to extract any useful information about student's motivational state without being able to see him. But despite the original doubts of most participants, we have seen that we were able to infer a large number of motivation diagnosis inference rules.

More importantly, by only showing them the student's interaction with the tutoring system, these rules are based on very concrete aspects of the interaction, such as mouse movements, quality of performance, etc., which can be easily detected in a tutoring system. On the other hand, we believe that if the participants had been able to see the student himself, many of the inferences about his motivational state would have been based on their gestures, posture, etc., which would prove much harder to detect in a regular tutoring system.

This study offered us some clues as to which aspects of the instruction seem to be the most relevant in order to detect students' motivational state, and it provided us with a promising amount of motivation diagnosis rules. But the validity of these rules remains to be analysed. Cross-participant comparison does not seem to be an appropriate way to validate the given set of rules, as the number of rules elicited is not large enough to provide a sufficient number of rules which can be applied under the same conditions. Also, comparison with the self-report study presented in [3] is not appropriate becausethere is no reason to believe that the self-report is necessarily accurate, as 'false' readings can be given under certain circumstances. For example, if the student is too engaged, he would probably forget to update the motivational model. Also, it is likely that

Table 2. Sample diagnosis rules

	Quality	Speed	Give up	pre(Difficulty)	Difficulty	Control	Feedback	Confidence	Effort	Cognitive interest	Control	Output
	Performance			*Teaching Materials*				*Motivation Model*				*Mot. Traits*
IS1	High							High	High			High
IS3	High				Enc							Inc
IS4	High				Enc				High			High
IS5									High			High
IS7	High	Fast	X >X									Inc
IS9					High					High		High
DS1	Low						Low	Low				Low
DS2	Avg		Yes									Low
DS4		V. Slow										Dec
DS7					V. Low					High		Dec

students will attempt to 'please' the tutoring system by providing artificially positive readings of their motivation [11].

Therefore, we evaluated these rules by performing another study in which participants were presented with an instructional interaction context and were asked to rate the rules that could be applied under those conditions. This study gave us a chance to find which rules from the current set are generally accepted as valid, and which ones are not. We will be reporting this study shortly.

In conclusion, we can say that the results of this study suggest that it is feasible to infer motivation diagnosis knowledge based only on the information provided by the computer interaction with a tutoring system. We have managed to gather a considerable number of motivation diagnosis rules, although the validity of these has to be proven yet, which we plan to do in a further study.

Acknowledgements. We thank Jeff Rickel, Kaśka Porayska-Pomsta, Thomas Segler, Ben Curry, Manolis Mavrikis and anonymous reviewers for useful comments on previous versions of this paper. This research was partially supported by grant PG 30660835, Ministerio de Educación y Cultura, Spain.

References

1. Flora Davis. *La Comunicación No Verbal*, volume 616 of *El Libro de Bolsillo*. Alianza Editorial, Madrid, Spain, 1976. Translated by Lita Mourglier from: "Inside Intuition - What we Knew About Non-Verbal Communication"; McGraw-Hill Book Company, New York.

2. Angel de Vicente and Helen Pain. Motivation diagnosis in intelligent tutoring systems. In Barry P. Goettl, Henry M. Halff, Carol L. Redfield, and Valerie J. Shute, editors, *Proceedings of the Fourth International Conference on ITS*, pages 86–95, Berlin, 1998. Springer.

3. Angel de Vicente and Helen Pain. Motivation self-report in ITS. In Susanne P. Lajoie and Martial Vivet, editors, *Proceedings of the Ninth World Conference on Artificial Intelligence in Education*, pages 648–650, Amsterdam, 1999. IOS Press.

4. Teresa del Soldato. *Motivation in Tutoring Systems*. PhD thesis, School of Cognitive and Computing Sciences, The University of Sussex, UK, 1994. Available as Technical Report CSRP 303.

5. Kim Issroff. *Investigating Computer-supported Collaborative Learning from an Affective Perspective*. PhD Thesis, Institute of Educational Technology, The Open University, 1996.

6. John M. Keller. Motivational design of instruction. In Charles M. Reigeluth, editor, *Instructional-design Theories and Models: an Overview of their Current Status*, pages 383–434. Lawrence Erlbaum Associates, Hillsdale, New Jersey, 1983.

7. Mark R. Lepper and Thomas W. Malone. Intrinsic motivation and instructional effectiveness in computer-based education. In Snow and Farr [12], chapter 11, pages 255–286.

8. Thomas W. Malone and Mark R. Lepper. Making learning fun: A taxonomy of intrinsic motivations for learning. In Snow and Farr [12], chapter 10, pages 223–253.

9. Yukihiro Matsubara and Mitsuo Nagamachi. Motivation system and human model for intelligent tutoring. In Claude Frasson, Gilles Gauthier, and Alan Lesgold, editors, *Proceedings of the Third International Conference on ITSs*, pages 139–147, Berlin, 1996. Springer-Verlag.

10. Nathalie Person, Bianca Klettke, Kristen Link, and Roger Kreuz. The integration of affective responses into AutoTutor. In *International Workshop on Affect in Interactions. Towards a New Generation of Interfaces (Annual Conference of the EC I3 Programme)*, October 1999.

11. Byron Reeves and Clifford Ivar Nass. *The Media Equation: How People Treat Computers, Television and New Media Like Real People and Places*. Centre for the Study of Language and Information, US, New York, 1998.

12. Richard E. Snow and Marshall J. Farr, editors. *Conative and Affective Process Analyses*, volume 3 of *Aptitude, Learning, and Instruction*. Lawrence Erlbaum Associates, Inc., Hillsdale, New Jersey, 1987.

Modeling Students' Emotions from Cognitive Appraisal in Educational Games

Cristina Conati and Xiaoming Zhou

Department of Computer Science, University of British Columbia, Vancouver, BC, Canada,
{conati, xzhou}@cs.ubc.ca

Abstract. We present a probabilistic model that assesses student emotional reaction during interaction with an educational game. Following a well-known cognitive theory of emotions (the OCC theory), the model predicts a student's emotional state by assessing the student's appraisal of her interaction with the game, in light of the student's goals and personality. We illustrate how the model relies on a Dynamic Decision Network that is based on both the OCC theory and observations from two user studies.

1 Introduction

Learner motivation is a key component for the success of any pedagogical activity. Electronic games for education are learning environments that try to increase the learner's motivation by embedding pedagogical activities in highly engaging, game-like interactions. However, several studies show that, while these educational games are usually successful in increasing student engagement, they often fail in triggering learning [7]. The studies indicate that this happens because many students play the games without actively reasoning about the underlying instructional domain, and thus fail to learn from the game activities.

To overcome this limitation of educational games, we are designing pedagogical agents that, as part of game playing, generate tailored interventions aimed at stimulating the student to learn better from the game. However, in order not to interfere with the high level of engagement that is a key asset of educational games, these agents need to take into account the players' affective states in addition to their cognitive states when deciding how to act.

Toward this end, we are devising a probabilistic model of student affect that our pedagogical agents can use, along with an assessment of student learning, to generate interventions that improve learning without compromising engagement. The model relies on a Dynamic Decision Network (DDN) [9] to probabilistically integrate information on both the possible causes of affective reaction and its observable effects (e.g., a change in the student's facial expression). Leveraging any evidence available on the student's emotional state is crucial, because in this modeling task the different sources of evidence are often ambiguous, and vary significantly with both the student and each particular interaction.

In this paper, we focus on the part of the model that reasons about the causes of student's affect by relying on the OCC cognitive theory of emotions, developed by

S.A. Cerri, G. Gouardères, and F. Paraguaçu (Eds.): ITS 2002, LNCS 2363, pp. 944–954, 2002.
© Springer-Verlag Berlin Heidelberg 2002

Orthony, Clore and Collins [8]. The OCC theory describes a person's emotions as the result of that person's appraisal of how the current situation fits with the person's goals and preferences. Our DDN models a student's appraisal mechanism during interaction with an educational game. It does so by representing how game events relate to the students' goals, as well as how these goals probabilistically depend on the students' traits and playing behavior.

Because affective user modeling is a rather new research area, only a few computational modes of user affect have been devised to date. A model that, like ours, is based on the OCC theory is discussed in [4]. This model is not probabilistic, and does not specify how to identify users' goals, traits and preferences. A model that uses fuzzy rules to assess anxiety in combat pilots is described in [5]. Because of the specificity of the modeling task, the model does not need to deal with the high level of uncertainty involved in modeling affect in less constraining interactions, like those generated by educational games. The affective model proposed in [1] relies on a probabilistic approach, but it uses only evidence on the effects of emotional arousal, not on its causes. For this reason, the model can assess only intensity and valence (i.e., whether the emotion is positive or negative) of the user's emotional states. [6] discusses how eyebrow movements and posture can provide partial evidence to infer a student's engagement while interacting with a computer-based tutor.

In the rest of the paper, we first present the educational game that we currently use as a test bed for our research. We then describe how our model was built by integrating the OCC cognitive theory of emotions with observations we collected in two user studies. We conclude with a discussion of future work.

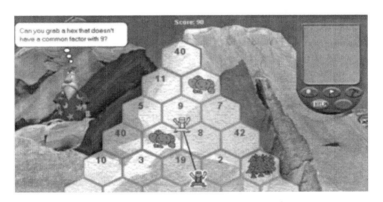

Fig. 1. Screenshot of the Prime Climb interface

2   The Prime Climb Educational Game

Prime Climb is a game designed by the EGEMS (Electronic Games for Education in Math and Science) group at the University of British Columbia to help students learn number factorization. In Prime Climb, two players must climb ice-faces divided in numbered sections (see Fig. 1). Each player can only move to sections with numbers that do not share any factors with that occupied by the other player. A player who makes a wrong move falls and the climbing team looses points. For instance, the player at the bottom in Figure 1 fell because she moved to section 42, which shares factor 3 with section 9, where the other player is. To help the students understand factorization, Prime Climb includes tools to inspect the factorization of the numbers on the mountain, accessible via the PDA at the top-right corner of Fig. 1.

Before climbing a mountain with a peer, each player must get certified by doing practice climbs with an instructor. This instructor is one of the intelligent agents that we are designing to improve the pedagogical effectiveness of Prime Climb. The function of this agent is to be the student's climbing partner during the practice climbs and provide hints (both unsolicited and on demand) that help the student to reason about number factorization, without compromising her level of engagement. These hints include (i) making the student think about the reasons for a fall, and (ii) giving specific advice on how to avoid or recover from a fall (see Fig. 1, on the left). The affective model that we describe in the rest of the paper is devised to assess student affect during the interaction with the climbing instructor. The model is used by the instructor (the *agent*, from now on) to decide when and how to provide help. We chose to model student affect during the practice climb phase of the game to test our approach on a simpler scenario before extending it to the more complex task of modeling student affect during the climbs with a peer.

3   A Dynamic Decision Network to Model Student Affect

Modeling student affect during the interaction with an educational game is a task frequently permeated with uncertainty. One cause for this uncertainty is that often the same situation can induce a variety of different emotional states in different students, depending upon student properties that are not always easily observable (e.g., goals, preferences, personality). A second cause of uncertainty is that the bodily expressions that are symptoms of emotional arousal (e.g., changes in facial expressions, increased heart rate) can be difficult to assess precisely and seldom support a one-to-one mapping with emotional states.

To handle the high level of uncertainty in this modeling task, we explicitly represent the probabilistic nature of the relations between student emotional states, their causes and effects using Dynamic Decision Networks (DDNs) [9]. DDNs are an extension of Bayesian networks [9] that can model, in addition to static random variables, (i) an agent's deliberate actions, represented as decision variables; (ii) the agent's preferences over the possible outcomes of the actions; and, (iii) the evolution of variables over time. The advantage of a model based on DDN is that it can leverage any evidence available on the variables related to emotional states to make predictions for any other variable in the model. For instance, we can assess both emotional states and personality traits from bodily expressions (i.e., the *effects* of the emotions), if a sufficient number of bodily expressions can be reliably observed (see *diagnostic assessment* in Figure 2). Or, the student's emotional state can be assessed using existing information on relevant student's traits and the current situation (i.e., the *causes* of emotions), even if there is little evidence on bodily expressions (see *predictive assessment* in Figure 2). Furthermore, DDNs provide algorithms that can compute, at any decision point, the agent action with the maximum expected utility, thus providing a decision theoretic basis for the agent behavior.

In this paper, we focus on the part of the model that performs predictive assessment (more details on the diagnostic part can be found in [2]). Figure 2 shows two time slices of the DDN that forms our model of student's affect. The nodes in Figure 2 represent classes of variables in the actual DDN. The part of the network above the nodes *Emotional States* represents the relations between possible causes and emotional

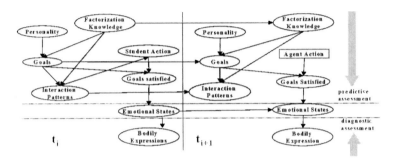

Fig. 2. Two time slices of the DDN to model student affect

states, as they are described in the OCC cognitive theory of emotions devised by Ortony, Clore and Collins [8]. In this theory, emotions arise from valenced (positive or negative) reactions to situations consisting of events, actors and objects. The valence of one's emotional reaction depends upon the desirability of the situation for oneself, which in turn is defined by one's goals and preferences. For instance, an event that matches one's goal can generate positive emotions such as *joy* for the event, *admiration* toward the actor that caused the event, or *pride* if the actor is oneself. Corresponding negative emotions for an event that interferes with one's goals are *distress*, *reproach* and *shame*.

To apply the OCC theory to the assessment of emotions in Prime Climb players, our DDN includes variables for goals that students may have when playing the game, summarized in Figure 2 by the nodes *Goals[1]*. The object of the student's appraisal is any event caused by either a student's game action (node *Student Action* in Figure 2, time slice t_i) or an agent's action. Agent actions are represented as decision variables in the model (e.g., the rectangular node *Agent Action* in Figure 2, slice t_{i+1}) indicating points in which the agent makes choices about if and how to intervene in the game[2]. The desirability of an event in relation of the student's goals is represented by the nodes class *Goals Satisfied*, which in turn influences the student's emotional state.

User's goals are a key element of the OCC model, but assessing these goals is not trivial, especially when asking the user directly is not an option, as is the case in educational games. Thus, our DDN also includes nodes that can help the model infer the student's goals from indirect evidence. What goals a student has can depend on both the student's *Personality* [3] and *Factorization Knowledge*, as represented by the

---

[1] We currently do not explicitly represent player preferences in our model.
[2] Due to space constraints, we omit the description of how the model is used to inform the agent's choice.

links connecting the corresponding nodes with the *Goals* node in Figure 2. Also, the student's goals can influence how a student plays the game, as this influence is represented in the DDN by the link between the nodes *Goals* and *Interaction Patterns* in Figure 2. In turn, interaction patterns can be inferred incrementally from specific features of the student's individual actions at each time slice. Thus, observations of both the relevant student's traits and game actions can provide the DDN with indirect evidence for assessing the student's goals.

In Figure 2, the links between nodes in different time slices indicate that the values of the corresponding variables evolve over time and that their value at time t_i influences the value at time t_{i+1}. These links model, for example, the fact that a student is more likely to feel a given emotion at time t_{i+1} if the student felt it at time t_i. A new time slice is added to the network when either the student or the agent performs an action. However, only two time slices are maintained at any give time, because the influence of previous time slices can be summarized as prior probabilities in the first of the two active slices (e.g., slice t_i in Figure 2). We now describe in more detail the nodes that allow predicting student emotions from situation appraisal.

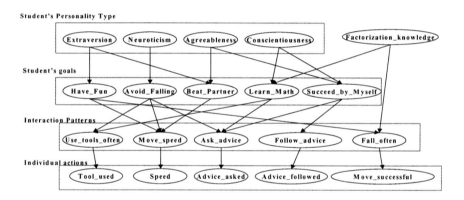

Fig. 3. Student traits, goals and moving patterns in one time-slice of the DDN

4   Nodes and Structure of the Appraisal Model

The elements of the appraisal model that do not derive directly from the OCC theory are the result of combining other relevant findings from psychology with our intuition and with observations of students playing Prime Climb. These observations were collected from two Wizard of Oz studies, involving 23 students who engaged in practice climbs with the climbing instructor agent. Students could ask the agent for help at any time by clicking on a help button available in the interface. An experimenter (Wizard) controlled the agent from a computer placed in a separate room, and provided help both unsolicited and on-demand.

Before playing with Prime Climb, students were given a pre-test to evaluate their knowledge of number factorization. Afterward, they filled out a questionnaire probing, among other things, what high level goals students had while playing the game. In both studies, an observer recorded students' behaviors. In the second study (involving 10 of the 23 students) we also collected log files of the interactions.

Student goals. Our model currently includes 5 high level goals that students playing Prime Climb may have. As shown in Figure 3, these goals include *Have Fun*, *Avoid Falling*, *Beat Partner*, *Learn Math* and *Succeed by Myself* (i.e., without the agent's help). The goals *Have Fun*, *Learn Math* and *Avoid Falling* are plausible goals that students may establish given the nature of the game. The goal *Succeed_by_Myself* was clearly shown by some students who not only avoided asking the agent for help, but also looked annoyed when the agent volunteered it. The goal *Beat Partner* is inconsistent with the nature of the game, as climbing the Prime Climb mountain is designed to be a collaborative effort. However, 8 out of the 23 subjects in the Wizard of Oz studies selected this goal in the post-questionnaire (see Table 1), and the goal is consistent with findings indicating that certain personality types tend to be competitive even during collaborative interactions. The goal nodes in the DDN are currently Boolean, where a T value represents the probability that a player has the corresponding goal.

Table 1. Number of students that selected each goal in the post-questionnaire

Have Fun	Avoid Falling	Beat Partner	Learn Math	Succeed By Myself
14	15	8	12	8

Student personality traits and math knowledge. Because personality is known to influence one's goals and behaviours [3], our model contains nodes and links representing student personality types and their relations to student goals in playing Prime Climb. Thus, when accurate priors are available for personality nodes, the DDN can use them as additional information to estimate the probability of goals, if goals cannot be directly established. Nodes and links for personality types have been chosen following the Five-Factor Model of personality [3]. In the Five-Factor Model, personality traits are structured as five domains - *neuroticism, extraversion, openness, agreeableness and conscientiousness*. As Figure 3 shows, our affective student model currently includes variables for only four of the five domains, because *openness* did not seem directly relevant to our task. The links modeling relationships between the four personality nodes and the student's goals are based on the definitions of the four domains in the Five-Factor Model. For example, an agreeable person is defined as "*fundamentally altruistic..... eager to help...and believes that others will be equally helpful in return*". By contrast, the disagreeable person is "*egocentric, sceptical of others' intentions, and competitive rather cooperative.*" Thus, in our model, the conditional probabilities for the *Beat-Partner* and *Succeed-by-Myself* goals reflect the fact that they are likely for a disagreeable person, and unlikely for an agreeable one. Personality nodes currently have two values, representing the extremes of the corresponding personality types.

In addition to personality, another student trait that may influence student goals is knowledge of number factorization. This trait is represented in our DDN by the variable *Factorization Knowledge* in Figure 3, and influences the goal *Learn_Math* because of our intuition that having high math knowledge can make a student less interested in learning math through the game. However, further studies in which we have information on the subjects' personality are needed to accurately specify the dependencies between domain knowledge, personality and goals.

Interaction patterns. Another source of information that can be used to infer students' goals is how they play the game. Our data indicate several dependencies between students' goals and their playing behavior. For instance, we found that (i) a student who wants to succeed by herself is unlikely to ask the agent for advice; (ii) a student who has the goal to learn math is more likely to access the Prime Climb tools to inspect number factorization; (iii) students that have the goals *Have_Fun* and *Beat_Partner* are more likely to move quickly, while students that want to avoid falling are more likely to move slowly. As Figure 3 shows, our model currently includes variables for five interaction patterns that our data indicate to be directly linked to students' goals: *Use_tools_often*, *Move_speed* (indicating how quickly the student moves from one number to another), *Ask_advice*, *Follows_advice*, *Fall_often*. One of these interaction patterns, *Fall_often*, is influenced by both the goal *Have_Fun* and by the student's factorization knowledge. This allows the system to model the fact that a few students kept falling because they found it amusing. Thus, the model considers frequent falls as an indication of either lack of factorization knowledge or the goal to have fun.

Student individual actions. Evidence for interaction patterns is collected directly from individual student interface actions, described by the nodes at the bottom of Figure 3. Every time the student performs an action, a new time slice is created in the dynamic network, and the relevant nodes describing the action and its outcome are set as evidence. The node *Tool_used* is set every time the student activates one of the tools available to inspect number factorization. The outcome of a student's move (i.e. whether the student fell or not), provides evidence for the node *Move_successful*, while the speed of a move provides evidence for the node *Speed*. *Advice_asked* is set to true every time the student asks the agent for advice, while the value of *Advice_followed* depends upon whether or not the student followed the agent's advice.

Some of the nodes describing student actions also provide evidence defining the situation used in the appraisal process (described later in this section). Two of these nodes are shown in Figure 4: *Move_successful*, described above, and *Ahead-of-partner*, which is also instantiated after a student move and indicates whether or not the student is ahead of her partner after the move. The values of these nodes influence how the DDN models the student's appraisal of her action's outcome.

Agent actions. Agent actions are represented as a decision node in the DDN, (e.g., node *agent action* in Figure 4). Like student actions, each agent action adds a new slice to the DDN. We currently summarize the agent's actions as three different values of the decision node: (1) *Hint* (an indirect suggestion to help the student overcome a climbing impasse); (2) *Move To* (explicitly telling the student where to move); (3) *Reflect* (asking the student to reason about the outcome of a move).

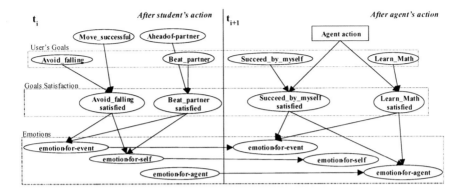

Fig. 4. Sample of the nodes involved in action appraisal and emotion assessment

Situation appraisal. The appraisal mechanism which dictates how the outcome of the student or agent actions relates to student goals is represented in our DDN by the links between goal nodes, action nodes and a new layer of nodes representing goal satisfaction (see Figure 4). For each goal node *g* in the DDN, a corresponding Boolean node *g_satisfied* describes whether goal *g* is satisfied after each agent or student action (Figure 4 shows a sample of the goal satisfaction nodes in the network). For example, if the student has the goal *Avoid_Falling* and makes a move at time t_i, the value of the node *Avoid_Falling_satisfied* in that time slice depends upon whether the move is successful. Similarly, if the student has the goal *Succeed_by_Myself*, the probability of the goal *Succeed_by_Myself_satisfied* decreases if the agent gives general advice about how to climb, and decreases even more if the agent explicitly tells the student where to move. The values of the goal satisfaction nodes are the direct cause of the student's emotional states, as we describe next.

Student emotional states. While the OCC theory specifies 22 emotion types, we currently represent in our DDN only the 6 that are more directly relevant to assessing student engagement during the Prime Climb practice climbs. Two of these emotions, *joy* and *distress*, are directed toward the event that is the object of student appraisal. Two other emotions, *pride* and *shame*, are directed toward the student herself and arise when the student caused the appraised event. The other two, *admiration* and *reproach*, are directed toward the agent, when the agent caused the event. The three pairs of emotions are represented in the network by three corresponding two-valued nodes (see Figure 4), *emotion_for_event*, *emotion_for_self* and *emotion_for_agent*, because we currently assume that the emotions in each pair are mutually excusive and that each interaction event simply changes the probability that the student can be in either of the two emotional states. Further empirical validations may lead us to move to a model in which each emotion is represented by a different variable. Currently, the model does not include a separate node for the student's emotion toward the climbing partner because in this phase of the game the climbing partner is the agent.

In each time slice, all the goal satisfaction nodes are linked to the *emotion_for_event* node, to represent the result of event appraisal. In addition, goal satisfaction nodes are linked to the *emotion_for_self* node if the time slice includes a student's actions (see Figure 4, slice t_i), or to the *emotion_for_agent* node if the time slice includes an agent's action (see Figure 4, slice t_{i+1}). Links between emotion nodes across time slices model the evolution of emotions over time. In particular, the conditional probabilities for an emotion node with no parent goal satisfaction node (e.g., *emotion-for-self* in Figure 4) model the fact that an emotion fades over time if no event revives it.

Keeping the distinction between the student's emotions toward self and toward the agent is important to help the agent decide how to act. For example, if the probability of *shame* is high the agent can decide to provide hints aimed at making the student feel better about her performance, while if the probability of *reproach* is high the agent needs to take actions that allow it to regain credibility.

5   Sample Assessment

To exemplify the workings of our model, we illustrate the assessment it generates during a simple simulated interaction. In this interaction, the student   (i) moves quickly, (ii) never falls and (iii) is often ahead of the partner. Four times during the interaction (marked by the asterisks on the bottom axis in Figure 5), the agent asks the student to reflect on the outcome of a move and the student ignores the advice.

Suppose that we don't have any knowledge of the student's personality. Since the student repeatedly ignores the agent's advice, the probability of the interaction pattern *Follow_advice* decreases, and that of the goal *Succeed_by_Myself* consequently increases (see Figure 5, bottom chart). The probability of the goals *Have_Fun* and *Beat_Partner* also increases, because both goals receive evidence from the fact that the student moves quickly (see Figure 3). The middle chart in Figure 5 shows the corresponding assessment of the student's emotional state. The probability of *reproach* increases slightly every time the agent intervenes, because the intervention interferes with the goal *Succeed_by_Myself*; then it   slowly decreases over the time slices when the agent lets the student be. Despite the four agent interventions, the goal *Succeed_by_myself* is satisfied in the majority of the time slices because the student always makes successful moves without following the agent's advice. The goal *Beat_Partner* is also likely to be satisfied, because the player stays mostly ahead of the partner. Thus, the probability of *pride* constantly increases, while the probability of *joy* increases in all but those slices corresponding to the agent's interventions.

Changes in the probabilities of goal nodes also propagate upward to influence the assessment of the student's personality. The probability of the personality type *Disagreeablenes* increases because it is supported by both goals *Succeed_by_Myself* and *Beat_Partner,* while the probability of the personality type *Extraversion* increases because of the support coming from the goal *Have_Fun* (see top chart in Figure 5).

As we mentioned at the beginning of the paper, the assessment of the affective model should be combined with an assessment of student learning to enable the agent to improve this learning   without   compromising student engagement. Consider, for instance, the example   described above. The affective model clearly indicates that the

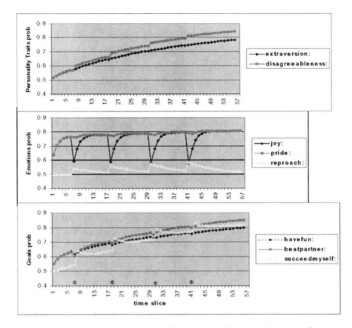

Fig. 5. Sample assessment of goals, emotions and personality

student feels reproach for the agent when it tries to make the student reason about her moves. This suggests that the agent should avoid intervening in the student's playing. However, the four agent's interventions in this example might be justified if the agent had some reason to believe that some of the student's successful moves were not due to a real understanding of the factorization of the numbers involved. The agent might also have decided that causing the student's reproach wouldn't seriously compromise her engagement, because the high probability of *joy* and *pride* indicates that overall the student is enjoying the game. Finally, recognizing that the student most likely has the goal of having fun, the agent might try to compensate for its pedagogical interventions by generating actions that have the sole purpose of amusing the student.

6   Conclusions and Future Work

We have presented a probabilistic model that relies on a Dynamic Decision Network to assess student emotions during the interaction with an educational game. The model was built by integrating the OCC cognitive theory of emotions with data gathered during two user studies. It assesses affect by predicting how student goals, personality and knowledge influence student appraisal of the interaction with the game.

Several are the directions for future work. First, we will refine the model by running additional studies with students for which we have a personality assessment. Third, we will integrate the affective model with a model of student learning, and define the utility functions that will guide the selection of agent actions in the DDN. Lastly, we will extend the model to assess student affect during the climb with a peer.

References

1. Ball, G. and J. Breese. Modeling the emotional state of computer users. in *Workshop on 'Attitude, Personality and Emotions in User-Adapted Interaction', UM '99*, 1999.
2. Conati, C. Probabilistic Assessment of User's Emotions During the Interaction with Educational Games. To appear in *Journal* of *Applied Artificial Intelligence*.
3. Costa, P.T. and R.R. McCrae, Four ways five factors are basic. *Personality and Individual Differences*. 1992. **13**(1) p. 653-665.
4. Elliott, C., J. Rickel, and J. Lester,. Lifelike Pedagogical Agents and Affective Computing: An Exploratory Synthesis. *Artificial Intelligence Today , Lecture Notes in Computer Science 1600*, M. Wooldridge and M. Veloso (eds.), 1999. Springer Verlag. 195-212.
5. Hudlicka, E. and D. McNeese. Assessment of User Affective and Belief States for Interface Adaptation: Application to an Air Force Pilot Task. *Journal of User Modeling and User-Adapted Interaction*, 2002. **12**(1): p. 1-47.
6. Kaapor, A., S. Mota, and R. Picard. Toward a learning companion that recognizes affect. in *AAAI Fall Symposium: 'motional and Intelligent II'*, 2001. AAAI Press.
7. Klawe, M. When Does The Use Of Computer Games And Other Interactive Multimedia Software Help Students Learn Mathematics? in *NCTM Standards 2000 Technology Conference*, 1998. Arlington, VA.
8. Orthony, A., G.L. Clore, and A. Collins. The cognitive structure of emotions, 1988. Cambridge University Press.
9. Russell, S. and P. Norvig. Artificial Intelligence: A Modern Approach, 1995. Morgan-Kaufman.

An Affective Module for an Intelligent Tutoring System

Barry Kort and Rob Reilly

Massachusetts Institute of Technology,
20 Ames Street, Cambridge, MA USA 02139
{bkort, reilly}@media.mit.edu

Abstract. There is a growing body of evidence that supports the claim that affect plays a critical role in decision-making and performance as it influences cognitive processes [1], [2], [3]. Despite this body of research the role and function of affect is not generally recognized by the disciplines that address the broad issues of understanding complex systems and complex behavior, especially in the presence of learning. The innovative models and theories that have been proposed to facilitate advancement in the field of human-computer interaction (HCI) tend to focus exclusively on cognitive factors. Consequently, the resulting systems are often unable to adapt to real-world situations in which affective factors play a significant role. We propose several new models for framing a dialogue leading to new insights and innovations that incorporate theories of affect into the design of (affect-sensitive) cognitive machines.

1 Introduction

The emerging discipline of Affective Computing has begun to address a variety of research, methodological, and technical issues pertaining to the integration of affect into HCI (e.g., machine recognition of affective states of the user, synthesis of affective states of cartoon avatars or embodied agents, applications incorporating social-emotional intelligence). In order for Affective Computing to become a discipline it should be supported by: a novel model that supports model-based reasoning, and, an innovative learning cycle model that integrates/accounts for and responds appropriately to affect.

2 Background

Intelligent Tutoring Systems (ITSs), which were introduced a decade ago, were envisioned as the next generation of Computer Assisted Instruction systems (CAI). "When first introduced...ITSs were announced and avowed as the future of education and training" [4]. Despite some initial successes [5], [6], [7], [8], [9], "ITSs have not yet seen general acceptance" [4]. And today the ITS community "is still talking about the

S.A. Cerri, G. Gouardères, and F. Paraguaçu (Eds.): ITS 2002, LNCS 2363, pp. 955–962, 2002.

promise of this technology while searching for the leverage that will encourage its widespread adoption and classroom use" [4].

Woolf [9] observes that typical ITSs consists of:

- •a **Domain Knowledge Module**, which contains the information that the tutor is teaching,
- an **Expert Module**, is more than a mere representation of the data, it is a model of how an expert human teacher would present the Domain Knowledge,
- a **Student Module**, which maintains information that is specific to each user and how far they have progressed,
- a **Tutor/Pedagogical Module**, which is responsible for deciding how and when the domain knowledge is presented; this module emulates the pedagogical approach of an expert teacher (e.g., when to present a new topic, which topic to present, when a review is needed),
- a **Diagnostic/Misconception Module**, which contains the rules used to identify misperceptions, gaps and misunderstandings on the part of the user,
- a **Communication Module**, which is the user interface (e.g., keyboard, mouse, sentic device, screen display/layout). This module answers the question: "How best to present the material to the learner?" and,
- Jerinic and Devedzic [4] have added an **Explanation Module**, which is "define[d as] the contents of explanations and justifications of the ITS's learning process, as well as the way they are generated" .

It's important to note that the typical ITS largely ignores a user's emotional (affective) state. There is no 'Affective Module' that would provide for emotional (affective) scaffolding based upon a learner's affective state. In a preliminary study Aist, et al.[10], found support for the contention that emotional (affective) scaffolding can improve the state-of-the-art, at least when provided by a human. It seems apparent that ITSs must learn how to recognize, interpret and react appropriately to a person's affective state. Clearly "there is an interplay between emotions and learning, but this interaction is far more complex than previous theories have articulated"[11].

3   Science and Story Making: Towards an Affective Module

To begin to conceive of an Affective Module for an ITS, let's start by examining the current real-world educational model. The current model, as shown in Figure 1, begins with 'data,' which is a collection of answers to questions that the learner has not yet seen fit to ask or needed to ask. Such data becomes 'information' when it answers a question that the learner cares to ask. For the most part, a teacher, who must somehow motivate the student to care enough to seek the answers found in the data, supplies these questions. Studying is like 'panning for gold' where the answers are the 'nuggets' buried in a ton of otherwise uninteresting gravel. Once we have our 'nuggets of information' how do we organize them into a 'body of knowledge'? We may think of 'information' as the pieces of an unassembled jigsaw puzzle, whereas 'knowledge' is the assembled jigsaw puzzle. That is, the question-answer pairs are organized into a coherent structure, in the logical and natural order in which new questions arise as soon as old ones are answered.

Fig. 1. Current Model: Primarily Supports Rule-based Learning

The assembled 'jigsaw puzzle of knowledge' reveals a previously hidden picture— a 'big picture,' if you will. Or to put it another way, the assembled 'jigsaw puzzle of knowledge' is a tapestry into which is woven many otherwise hidden and previously unrevealed stories.

Fig. 2. New Model: Supports Model-based Reasoning

The novel model shown below in Figure 2 goes beyond the current model shown in Figure 1. The focii of attention shifts to the construction of 'knowledge' and to the extraction of meaningful 'insights' from the 'big picture.' When 'knowledge' is coupled with a personal or cultural value system, 'wisdom' emerges. In other words, wisdom allows us to harness the power of knowledge for beneficial purposes.

'Wisdom' affords us the possibility of extracting the stories woven into the tapestry of knowledge. So from 'wisdom' we craft the bardic arts of story making and story telling. The ancients crafted myths and legends. These were the prototypical stories of their cultures, which were intended to impart 'wisdom.' A story is thus an anecdote drawn from the culture. A well-crafted anecdote or story has value both as an amusement and as a source of insight into the world from which it is drawn. And the plural of 'anecdote' is data—a collection of anecdotal stories or evidence. This observation closes the loop in Figure 2.

Figure 2 suggests a novel model that, on a fundamental level, supports an improved educational pedagogy. This will serve as a foundation for the next part of our model— how a learner's affective state should be incorporated into the overall model.

4 Models of Emotions and Learning

In an attempt to install/build/re-engineer the current state of educational pedagogy, educators should first look to expert teachers who are adept at recognizing the emotional state of learners, and, based upon their observations, take some action that scaffolds learning in a positive manner. But what do these expert teachers *see* and how do they decide upon a course of action? How do students who have strayed from *learning* return to a productive path, such as the one that Csikszentmihalyi [12] refers to as the "zone of flow"? This notion that a student's affective (emotional) state impacts learning and that appropriate intervention based upon that affective state would facilitate learning is the concept that we propose to explore.

To prove our point, note that skilled humans can assess emotional signals with varying degrees of precision. For example, researchers are beginning to make progress giving computers similar abilities to accurately recognize affective expressions [13], [14], facial expressions [15], [16], [17], [18], [19], [20], and gestural expression [21], [22]. Although computers only perform as well as people in highly restricted domains, we believe that:

- accurately identifying a learner's cognitive-emotive state is a critical observation that will enable (human or computer-based) 'mentors' to provide learners with an efficient and pleasurable learning experience, and,
- unobtrusive highly accurate technology will be developed to accurately assess actions in less restricted domains (see e.g., [23]).

Anxiety ↔ Confidence
Ennui ↔ Fascination
Frustration ↔ Euphoria
Dispirited ↔ Enthusiasm
Terror ↔ Excitement
Humiliated ↔ Proud

Fig. 3. Emotion sets possibly relevant to learning

Our own preliminary pilot studies with elementary school children suggest that a human observer can assess the affective emotional state of a student with reasonable reliability based on observation of facial expressions, gross body language, and the content and tone of speech. If the human observer is also acting in the role of coach or mentor, these assessments can be confirmed or refined by direct conversation (e.g. simply asking the student if she is confused or frustrated before offering to provide coaching or hints). Moreover, successful learning is frequently marked by an unmistakable elation, often jointly celebrated with "high fives." In some cases, the "Aha!" moment is so dramatic, it verges on the epiphanetic. One of the great joys for an educator is to bring a student to such a moment of triumph. But how can computers acquire this same level of proficiency as that of gifted coaches, mentors, and teachers?

Our first step is to offer a model of a learning cycle, which integrates affect. Figure 3 suggests six possible emotion axes that may arise in the course of learning. Figure 4 interweaves the emotion axes shown in Figure 3 with the cognitive dynamics of the learning process. In Figure 5, the positive valence (more pleasurable) emotions are on the right; the negative valence (more unpleasant) emotions are on the left. The vertical axis is what we call the Learning Axis, and symbolizes the construction of knowledge upward, and the discarding of misconceptions downward. Students ideally begin in Quadrant I or II: they might be curious or fascinated about a new topic of interest (Quadrant I) or they might be puzzled and motivated to reduce confusion (Quadrant II). In either case, they are in the top half of the space if their focus is on constructing or testing knowledge. Movement happens in this space as learning proceeds. For example, when solving a puzzle in *The Incredible Machine*, a student gets a bright idea how to implement a solution and then builds its simulation. If she runs the simulation and it fails, she sees that her idea has some part that doesn't work—that needs to be diagnosed and reconstructed. At this point the student may move down into the lower half of the diagram (Quadrant III) into the 'dark teatime of the soul' while discarding misconceptions and unproductive ideas. As she consolidates her knowledge—what works and what does not—with awareness of a sense of making progress, she advances to Quadrant IV. Getting another fresh idea propels the student back into the upper half of the space (Quadrant I). Thus, a typical learning experience involves a range of emotions, cycling the student around the four quadrant cognitive-emotive space as they learn.

If one visualizes a version of Figure 4 and 5 for each axis in Figure 3, then at any given instant, the student might be in multiple Quadrants with respect to different axes. They might be in Quadrant II with respect to feeling frustrated and simultaneously in Quadrant I with respect to interest level. It is important to recognize that a range of emotions occurs naturally in a real learning process, and it is not simply the case that the positive emotions are the good ones.

We do not foresee trying to keep the student in Quadrant I, but rather to help him see that the cyclic nature is natural in learning science, mathematics, engineering or technology (SMET), and that when he lands in the negative half, it is an inevitable part of the cycle. Our aim is to help students to keep orbiting the loop, teaching them to propel themselves, especially after a setback.

A third axis (not shown) can be envisioned as extending out of the plane of the page—the cumulative knowledge axis. If one visualizes the above dynamics of moving from Quadrant I to II to III to IV as an orbit, then, when this third dimension is

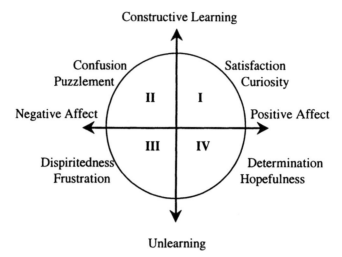

Fig. 4. Four Quadrant model-relating phases of learning to emotions in Figure 3

added, one obtains an excelsior spiral. In Quadrant I, anticipation and expectation are high, as the learner builds ideas and concepts and tries them out. Emotional mood decays over time either from boredom or from disappointment. In Quadrant II, the rate of construction of working knowledge diminishes, and negative emotions emerge as progress wanes. In Quadrant III, as the negative affect runs its course, the learner discards misconceptions and ideas that didn't pan out. In Quadrant IV, the learner recovers hopefulness and positive attitude as the knowledge set is now cleared of unworkable and unproductive concepts, and the cycle begins anew. In building a complete and correct mental model associated with a learning opportunity, the learner may experience multiple cycles until completion of the learning exercise. Note that the orbit doesn't close on itself, but gradually spirals around the cumulative knowledge axis.

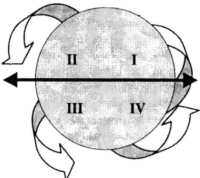

Fig. 5. Circular and helical flow of emotion in Four Quadrant model

We are in the process of performing empirical research on this model. We have conducted several pilot research projects, which appear to confirm the model.

5 Conclusion

Our models are inspired by theory often used to describe complex dynamic interactions in engineering systems. As such, they are not intended to explain how learning works, but rather to provide a framework for thinking and posing questions about the role of emotions in learning. As with any metaphor, the model has its limits. The model does not encompass all aspects of the complex interaction between emotions and learning, but begins to describe some of the key phenomena that needs to be considered in metacognition.

These models go beyond previous research studies not just in the range of emotions addressed, but also in an attempt to formalize an analytical model that describes the dynamics of a learner's emotional states, and does so in a language that supports metacognitive analysis.

Acknowledgement. This material is based upon work supported by the National Science Foundation under Grant No. 0087768. Any opinions, findings, or conclusions or recommendations expressed in this material are those of the author(s) and does not necessarily reflect the views of the National Science Foundation.

References

1. Damasio, A.R. (1994). <u>Descartes Error: Emotion, Reason and the Human Brain</u>, G.P. Putnam Sons: NY.
2. Goleman Daniel. (1995). <u>Emotional Intelligence</u>. Bantam Books: New York.
3. Picard, Rosalind W. (1997). <u>Affective Computing</u>. MIT Press: Cambridge, MA.
4. Jerinic, Lj. and Devedzic, V. (2000). A Friendly Intelligent Tutoring Environment – Teacher's Approach, ACM SIGCHI Bulletin Vol. 32, No. 1, January 2000, pp. 83-94.
5. Anderson, J. (1990) Analysis of Student Performance with the LISP Tutor. In Frederiksen, N., Glaser, R., Lesgold, A.M. and Shafto, M. (Eds.), <u>Diagnostic Monitoring of Skill and Knowledge Acquisition</u>, Hillsdale, NJ: Lawrence Erlbaum.
6. Bonar, T. (1988). Byte-sized Tutor. In J. J. Psotka, L. D. Massey and S. A. Mutter (Eds.) <u>Intelligent Tutoring Systems: Lesson Learned</u>, Lawrence Erlbaum Associates.
7. Russell, D, Moran, T.P., and Jordan, D.S. (1988). The instructional design environment. In J. J. Psotka, L. D. Massey and S. A. Mutter (Eds.) <u>Intelligent Tutoring Systems: Lesson Learned</u>, Lawrence Erlbaum Associates
8. Sleeman, D. (1987). PIXIE: A Shell for Developing Intelligent Tutoring Systems. <u>Artificial Intelligence in Education</u>, Vol. 1, 239-265.

9. Woolf, B. (1987). Theoretical Frontiers in Building a Machine Tutor. In Kearsley, G. P. (Ed.) Artificial Intelligence and Instruction-Application and Methods, Addison-Wesley, Reading, 229-267.

10. Aist, G., Kort, B., Reilly, R., Mostow, J., and Picard, R.W. (2002). Computer Tutor Plus Human Wizard: Adding Human-Provided Emotional Awareness to an Automated Reading Tutor that Listens, Poster session ITS 2002, France.

11. Kort, B., Reilly, R., and Picard, R.W. (2001). Theoretical Frontiers in Building a Machine Tutor. In Kearsley, G. P. (Ed.) Artificial Intelligence and Instruction-Application and Methods, Addison-Wesley, Reading, 229-267.

12. Csikszentmihalyi, M. (1990). Flow: The Psychology of Optimal Experience, Harper-Row: NY.

13. Picard, Rosalind W. (2000). Toward Computers that Recognize and Respond to User Emotions, IBM Systems Journal, Vol. 39 (3 and 4), p. 705.

14. Scheirer, J., Fernandez, R., Picard, R.W. (1999), Expression Glasses: A Wearable Device for Facial Expression Recognition, Proceedings of CHI, February 1999.

15. Bartlett, M., Hager J.C., Ekman, P., and Sejnowski, T. (1999). Measuring Facial Expression by Computer Image Analysis. Psychophysiology, vol. 36, pp. 253-263.

16. Cohn J, Kanade, T., Moriyama, T., Ambadar, Z., Xiao, J., Gao, J., and Imamura, H. (2001). A Comparative Study of Alternative FACS Coding Algorithms, Technical Reports, Robotics Institute, Carnegie Mellon University, November, 2001. Available at: http://www.ri.cmu.edu/pubs/pub_3853.html

17. Donato, G., Bartlett, M.S., Hager, J.C., Ekman, P., and Sejnowsk, T.. (1999). Classifying facial actions, IEEE T. Pattern Analy. and Mach. Intell., vol. 21, pp. 974--989, October 1999

18. DeSilva, L.C. Miyasato, T. Nakatsu, R. (1997). Facial emotion recognition using multimodal information, in Proc. IEEE Int. Conf. on Info., Comm. and Sig. Proc., (Singapore), pp. 397-401, Sept 1997

19. Ekman, P. (1997). Facial Action Coding System, Consulting Psychologists Press.

20. Essa I., Pentland, A. (1997). Coding, analysis, interpretation and recognition of facial expressions, IEEE Transactions on Pattern Analysis and Machine Intelligence, vol. 19, pp. 757--763, July 1997.

21. Chen, L.S., Huang, T.S., Miyasato, T., and Nakatsu, R. (1998). Multimodal Human Emotion/Expression Recognition. Proceedings of 3rd International Conference on Automated Face and Gesture Recognition, pp366-371.

22. Huang, T.S., Chen L.S, and Tao, H. (1998). Bimodal Emotion Recognition by Man and Machine. ATR Workshop on Virtual Communication Environments.

23. Kapoor, A., Mota, S. and Picard, R.W. (2001). Towards a Learning Companion that Recognizes Affect, Proceedings of AAAI 2001.

Perceived Characteristics and Pedagogical Efficacy of Animated Conversational Agents

Kristen N. Moreno, Bianca Klettke, Kiran Nibbaragandla, and Arthur C. Graesser

Department of Psychology, University of Memphis
Memphis, TN 38152
{kmoreno, bklettke, a-graesser}@memphis.edu,
kiran_bhai@hotmail.com
http://www.psyc.memphis.edu/faculty/moreno/
http://www.psyc.memphis.edu/students/klettke/klettke.htm
http://mnemosyne.csl.psyc.memphis.edu/home/graesser/

Abstract. We investigated college students' perceptions of a diverse sample of animated conversational agents. We also examined the pedagogical efficacy of those agents. We found that people perceive differences among the agents on several dimensions, such as likeability, and that the agents differ in pedagogical efficacy. However, none of the characteristics that we measured accounted for differences in pedagogical efficacy across the agents. We discuss implications for the field of agent studies with particular emphasis on the creation of pedagogically effective conversational agents and suggest directions for future research.

1 Introduction

In recent years, technology-based learning has assumed an increasingly larger role in education, as evidenced, for example, by the increasing availability of online degrees and distance learning courses. Intelligent tutoring systems are comparatively sophisticated examples of learning technology. Although the first computerized tutoring programs emerged many years ago, recent enhancements include the addition of animated conversational agents that play the role of tutors [23]. These pedagogical agents provide an anthropomorphic interface that potentially affects the tutor-student interaction. They can be programmed to speak, gesture, and emote in response to student contributions in a tutorial dialogue [5, 6, 14, 16, 17, 21, 25, 28]. The incorporation of human-like conversational features into such systems may facilitate the engagement of humans in the learning environment, and could potentially affect the pedagogical efficacy (i.e., the usefulness as a teaching device) of intelligent tutoring systems. However, the issue of whether pedagogical agents facilitate, inhibit, or do not affect the pedagogical efficacy of intelligent tutoring systems has yet to be settled definitively.

The number of intelligent information systems featuring animated conversational agents has dramatically increased in recent years. Some examples include STEVE, a virtual-reality tutor developed for naval training [12, 13, 26]; COSMO, a program that assists people learning to troubleshoot networking problems [16, 28]; Herman the Bug, which teaches children about botany by helping them to design plants that will

S.A. Cerri, G. Gouardères, and F. Paraguaçu (Eds.): ITS 2002, LNCS 2363, pp. 963–971, 2002.

survive in different environments [16]; AiA, a navigational aid for web-based information [1, 2]; and LANCA, a distance learning program featuring four networked agents that work in concert to provide optimal learning strategies depending on the individual learner's progress [7]. The Tutoring Research Group at the University of Memphis has developed two intelligent information systems that feature animated conversational agents. One system, HURA Advisor [8, 22], was designed to facilitate navigation and information retrieval about ethical concerns in the use of human participants in research. The other system, AutoTutor [9, 10], is an intelligent tutoring system designed to tutor college-level students in physics and computer literacy by engaging them in a multi-turn conversation in natural language.

As animated conversational agents become more prominent, it becomes increasingly important to understand the factors that affect the quality of interactions between conversational agents and humans. The information systems developed by the Tutoring Research Group feature an animated conversational agent intended to facilitate the interaction between humans and the information systems, so we have been keenly interested in the factors affecting such interactions. Indeed, much of our current research [e.g., 19] is explicitly aimed at discovering and understanding any characteristics that may affect the pedagogical efficacy of agents, with the ultimate goal of designing more effective, pleasant, and entertaining tutors and navigational guides. Such research is also underway in many of the other labs cited above.

Clippit, the paperclip agent that appears in various Microsoft Office applications, was perhaps one of the earliest widely available interactive agents. Although Clippit was designed to facilitate the use of Microsoft Office programs by offering an assortment of potentially helpful tips, many people preferred to use the programs without the assistance of the agent. Animated conversational agents may affect humans' experience of technology in many ways. They can potentially facilitate the interaction by serving as a navigational guide, helping the user decide what to do next. They can enhance the user's enjoyment of the program, as in the case of the "persona effect," or the finding that people prefer learning from programs that feature conversational agents over those that do not include agents [2, 4, 15]. Furthermore, the inclusion of animated agents in intelligent tutoring systems appears to enhance some types of learning. For example, the Tutoring Research Group has found that students who interacted with AutoTutor (which features a pedagogical agent) performed better on measures of learning outcomes than did students who passively read relevant textbook material or students who received no tutoring [9, 24]. The effect size for AutoTutor on learning gains was comparable to that of human tutors. Similarly, Moreno, Mayer, Spires, and Lester [20] found that middle school and postsecondary students performed better on transfer (but not retention) tests following a tutorial about botanical anatomy and physiology featuring a pedagogical agent [16], as compared to those who did not interact with a pedagogical agent during the learning exchange. Atkinson [3] also found evidence of enhanced performance on word problems following interactions with a pedagogical agent, as compared to conditions not featuring an agent. Thus, agents provide a potentially valuable addition to some technology-based environments, especially on certain learning tasks. Nevertheless, agents can also annoy or even discourage the user, thereby obstructing human-computer interactions (as may have been the case with Clippit). Furthermore, agents may not facilitate all types of learning [20]. It is therefore important to understand the factors that affect people's reactions to animated conversational agents.

The various animated conversational agents featured in currently available software programs present great variety in terms of characteristics that may affect their interactions with humans [14, 23]. Some agents resemble humans (e.g., AutoTutor, STEVE, ADELE [27]), whereas others are based on non-human organisms (e.g. Herman the Bug, Microsoft's Peedy agent) or even inanimate objects (e.g., Microsoft's Robby agent). Agents may vary in their gender, age, race, and other demographic variables. They can be programmed to simulate different personality traits, such as humor, supportiveness, or irritability. The agents that currently accompany many software programs can emulate a variety of characteristics that may affect interactions between humans and computers. One question of interest is whether people are sensitive to differences among agents. Do people perceive agents as differing on basic personality dimensions? Do such differences affect learning of the material? In the present research, we addressed this issue by examining college students' impressions of 9 different agents, as well as their impact on learning. Unlike previous empirical studies on this topic, which investigated only a single agent, we explored a diverse array of agents. A broad diversity of agents ensures a meaningful assessment of the correlations among agent features, learning, and impressions of users. Without this diversity, the methodological problem of restricted range of the stimulus materials results in insensitive assessments of the correlations.

The current research addressed two questions pertaining to the pedagogical efficacy of animated conversational agents. We first investigated whether the agents differed in pedagogical efficacy. That is, do people learn more effectively from some agents than from others? It may be that all pedagogical agents present information with equal efficacy. However, if people perceive differences among agents, then those differences could potentially affect learning.

We were also interested in determining the mechanisms through which any effects on learning might be mediated. That is, what characteristics of pedagogical agents may cause people to learn more (or less) effectively from them? To address this question, we examined the relationship between people's perceptions of each agent and that agent's pedagogical efficacy. For example, one factor that could potentially affect pedagogical efficacy is likeability. Perhaps people learn more effectively from a likeable agent than from an unlikeable one. Surprisingly, some research has indicated that likeability is unrelated to learning. However, as we have noted, many of the studies that have examined the relationship between liking and learning have used a narrow set of stimuli. Given the broad variability among existing conversational agents, we sought to include a wide and varied sample of agents in this research. Finally, we were interested in whether perceptions of comprehensibility affected learning. Quality of the voice would seem to be a critical determinant of pedagogical efficacy. People cannot learn from tutors whom they cannot comprehend [29]. We also examined the credibility of the agents, the quality of the presentation, and the synchronization of the facial animations and speech output in relation to learning.

2 Method

2.1 Participants and Design

Participants were 36 Introductory Psychology undergraduates (53% female) from the University of Memphis. They received course credit in exchange for their participation. The design of the study was within-subjects (i.e., each participant saw all 9 agents). The order in which each participant saw the agents was randomized.

2.2 Agents

There were 9 animated pedagogical agents. The Tutoring Research group created several of these agents (Anna, Bianca, Kiran, Marco, and Professor) using the Microsoft Agent software package [18]. The rest were pre-existing Microsoft Agent characters (Charlie, Genie, Gourdy, and Merlin). The agents differed only in appearance and voice. We used various male and female Microsoft Agent voices. Examples of agents created by the Tutoring Research Group appear in Figure 1. The agents were presented in XTrain [11], a program designed to integrate Microsoft Agent characters with text, pictures, HTML, Macromedia Flash, and Director files.

Fig. 1. Examples of agents used in the study

2.3 Procedure

Participants heard information about topics in 3 content areas: computer literacy, physics, and psychology. Three pedagogical agents presented the tutorial information for each topic area. Different agents presented each content area, for a total of 9 agents. Moreover, the assignment of agents to topic was counterbalanced across participants so that each agent spoke about each topic an equal number of times. The agents communicated the information by engaging in a three-way conversation among themselves (i.e., the participants did not converse with the agents). Each three-way tutorial interaction lasted approximately 7 minutes. We have included the physics dialogue in Excerpt 1 as an example:

Excerpt 1. Tutorial dialogue on physics

Agent 1. Well, should we move on to physics now? Here is a question: Suppose a man is running in a straight line at constant speed. He throws a pumpkin straight up. Where will it land? Explain.

Agent 2: Ok, I know that the pumpkin is in free fall once it has left the man's hand.

Agent 3: Also, neglecting air resistance there is only one force acting on the pumpkin once it has left the man's hand.

Agent 1: And remember: force, acceleration, and velocity are all vector quantities.

Agent 2: Right. Also, Newton's second law, net force equals mass times acceleration, is true for the components of those quantities taken in any direction.

Agent 3: However, there is no horizontal component of force on the pumpkin once it has left the man's hand, so the horizontal component of acceleration is zero.

Agent 1: So, that means that when a component of acceleration is zero, the corresponding component of velocity does not change.

Agent 2: Yes, but remember, the pumpkin and the man were traveling with the same horizontal velocity when the pumpkin left his hands.

Agent 3: Oh, I got it. The man had to exert a vertical force on the pumpkin to give it a velocity component in the vertical direction. This force ceased when the pumpkin left his hand.

Agent 1: Yeah, once in free fall the acceleration of the pumpkin is due to Earth's gravitational pull and is constant.

Agent 2: In this case, it means that the acceleration reduces the upward velocity of the pumpkin to zero and then to negative values as the pumpkin travels downward.

Agent 3: Ok, therefore, if the horizontal velocity of the man does not change, then it is the same as that of the pumpkin.

Agent 1: So, to sum up, when the height of the man's hands above the ground matches that of the pumpkin, they will be in the same place and the man can grasp the pumpkin.

Following each tutorial dialogue, the participant immediately rated the agents on several dimensions before continuing to the next topic. To ensure that participants knew which agent they were rating, a picture of the agent being rated was printed in upper left corner of each rating sheet. Participants rated each agent on the dimensions of likeability, comprehensibility, credibility, quality of presentation, and synchronization of speech and animation, using 6-point scales that distinguished positive from negative impressions. For example, the rating scale for likeability is 1 = disliked very much; 2 = somewhat disliked; 3 = not sure, but guess disliked; 4 = not sure, but guess liked; 5 = somewhat liked; and 6 = liked very much. Participants did not further explain their preferences.

After the participants had heard all 3 tutorial dialogues and had rated all 9 agents, they completed a cloze recall task as an index of learning. This task required participants to fill in particular phrases from the agents' conversations. The recall task was based on statements extracted from the agents' conversations. Some examples from the physics cloze recall measure of learning appear in Excerpt 2:

Excerpt 2. Example items from the learning index on physics

1. The pumpkin is in _____ once it has left the man's hand.
2. Neglecting _____, there is only one force acting on the pumpkin once it has left the man's hand.
3. Force, acceleration, and velocity are all _____.

Each recall test item was then scored for both accuracy (proportion of words recalled correctly) and source (which agent said it). This allowed us to examine whether learning differed across the agents.

3 Results

Participants rated all 9 agents on several scales. We assessed their perceptions of the agents' likeability, comprehensibility, credibility, presentation quality, and synchronization of voice and animation. Table 1 presents the means for these variables.

Table 1. Means and F scores for perceptions and learning by agent

Agent	Like-ability	Compre-hensibility	Credi-bility	Quality	Synchro-nization	Learning
Genie	4.72	4.83	3.58	4.75	3.81	.41
Marco	4.34	4.34	3.54	4.57	3.29	.36
Gourdy	4.11	4.58	3.25	4.28	3.58	.35
Anna	3.03	3.09	2.77	3.26	1.06	.33
Kiran	4.36	3.81	4.00	4.53	3.31	.31
Bianca	3.81	3.53	3.31	3.92	2.97	.28
Profes-sor	3.17	4.03	3.77	4.03	1.83	.27
Merlin	5.05	5.06	3.78	5.00	1.00	.26
Charlie	3.33	2.50	2.78	3.19	2.25	.25
F	10.96**	13.02**	5.99**	9.83**	15.97**	2.46*

Note. Higher values indicate more positive responses. All Fs have df = 1, 35. $* p < .05.$ $** p < .001$

One question of interest was whether participants perceived differences among the agents on these dimensions. To assess this question, we computed a repeated-measures analysis of variance (ANOVA) on each dimension. Indeed, as Table 1 indicates, these ANOVAs revealed significant differences among the agents on all dimensions. People perceived some agents to be more likeable, comprehensible, and credible than other agents. They also indicated differences in the quality of the presentations and the synchronization of voice and animation across the 9 agents. Thus, people do in fact perceive differences across agents on these dimensions.

Table 1 also presents the results for the learning index by agent. A repeated-measures ANOVA indicated that these recall scores also differed significantly across the 9 agents. This suggests that people do indeed learn more effectively, as indicated by performance on a cloze recall task, from some agents than from others. Thus, in answer to one of our questions of interest, we found that agents do indeed differ in their pedagogical efficacy.

Another objective was to investigate possible factors that could influence the pedagogical efficacy of agents. To examine this issue, we computed correlations between the scales measuring people's perceptions of the agents and scores on the learning index. If people perceive differences among the agents and the agents differ in pedagogical efficacy, then it stands to reason that perceived differences among the agents might account for observed differences in learning. As Table 2 indicates, all scales measuring participants' perceptions of the agents were significantly and positively correlated with each other. Interestingly, however, none of these factors correlated significantly with performance on the learning index. This suggests that, although the participants clearly learned better from some agents than from others, none of the assessed dimensions, including likeability and comprehensibility, could explain the observed differences in performance on the learning index.

Table 2. Correlation matrix for dependent variables

	Likeabi-lity	Compre-hensibility	Credibili-ty	Quality	Synchron-ization
Comp	.50**				
Credibility	.51**	.33**			
Quality	.54**	.59**	.49**		
Synch	.56**	.54**	.31**	.53**	
Learning	.03	.07	-.02	.04	.03

Note. Comp = Comprehensibility. Synch = Synchronization. **$p < .001$, in subject analyses

4   Discussion

We designed this study to assess perceptions and pedagogical efficacy of animated agents. We began by examining whether people perceive differences among various agents. Our results indicate that people do indeed perceive such differences. Ratings differed across agents on every dimension assessed in this study. Some agents were liked more than others, some were easier to comprehend, some were more credible, better synchronized, and better presenters. Indeed, that these dimensions were significantly and positively intercorrelated suggests that these five factors varied together. Generally, a positive reaction on one of the dimensions was associated with positive reactions on the other dimensions, and vice versa.

We also found that people learn more effectively from some agents than from others. That is, these agents differed in their pedagogical efficacy, as evidenced by significant differences across the agents on the learning index. This finding has important implications, both for the field of agent studies in general and for our research program in particular. Our ultimate goal is to create animated conversational agents for inclusion in intelligent tutoring systems (AutoTutor) and information systems (HURA Advisor). Thus, we are interested in maximizing the pedagogical efficacy of agents. We now know that agents do differ in pedagogical efficacy. Thus, it is important to continue research into the factors that affect the efficacy of pedagogical agents.

Our third (and perhaps most important) question of interest pertained to the specific characteristics that might explain the observed differences in the pedagogical efficacy of these agents. Unfortunately, our results were equivocal on this question. Although people indicated different perceptions across agents on all of the dimensions assessed in this study, none of these dimensions correlated significantly with performance on the learning index. As such, although it is clear that pedagogical agents differ in their effectiveness as tutors, the question of what characteristics of pedagogical agents facilitate (or inhibit) learning remains open. Of special interest is the lack of relationship between liking and learning. Following the Clippit debacle, much research has been directed at constructing likeable agents. But perhaps this research does not focus on the most crucial question. Our results suggest that, at least for the purposes of intelligent tutoring systems, it may be more sensible to focus on developing pedagogically effective agents, regardless of how well they are liked. Rather than asking what makes an agent likeable, perhaps we should ask what makes an agent a good teacher. Of course, liking could remain an important variable even in the absence of an impact on pedagogical efficacy. People may be more likely to begin or to continue using a tutoring system that features a likeable, entertaining, supportive agent. But the current results suggest that liking does not affect the pedagogical efficacy of animated conversational agents.

Acknowledgements. This research was supported by grants from the National Science Foundation (REC 0106965) and the Department of Defense Multidisciplinary University Research Initiative (MURI) administered by the Office of Naval Research under grant N00014-00-1-0600. Any opinions, findings, and conclusions or recommendations expressed in this material are those of the authors and do not necessarily reflect the views of ONR or NSF. The authors thank Blair Terry and Genna McCallie for assistance in coding the data.

References

1. André, E., Rist, T.: Controlling the behavior of animated presentation agents in the interface: Scripting versus instructing. AI Magazine 22(4) (2001) 53-66
2. André, E., Rist, T., Müller, J.: Integrating reactive and scripted behaviors in a life-like presentation agent. Proceedings of the Second International Conference on Autonomous Agents. Minneapolis-St. Paul, MN (1998) 261-268
3. Atkinson, R.K.: Optimizing learning from examples using animated pedagogical agents. Journal of Educational Psychology (in press)
4. Baylor, A.L.: Investigating multiple pedagogical perspectives through MIMIC (Multiple Intelligent Mentors Instructing Collaboratively). Proceedings of Artificial Intelligence in Education (AI-ED) International Conference. San Antonio, Texas (2001)
5. Cassell, J., Pelachaud, C., Badler, N., Steedman, M., Achorn, B., Becket, T., Douville, B., Prevost, S., Stone, M.: Animated conversation: Rule-based generation of facial expression, gesture and spoken intonation for multiple conversational agents. Computational Graphics 28 (1994) 413-420
6. Elliott, C., Rickel, J., Lester, J.: Lifelike pedagogical agents and affective computing: An exploratory synthesis. In M. Wooldridge and M. Veloso (eds.): Artificial Intelligence Today. Springer-Verlag, Berlin (1999) 195-212
7. Frasson, C., Martin, L., Gouardères, G., Aïmeur, E.: LANCA: A distance learning architecture based on networked cognitive agents. Intelligent Tutoring Systems (1998) 593-603
8. Graesser, A.C., Hu, X., Person, N.K.: Teaching with the help of talking heads. Proceedings of the IEEE International Conference on Advanced Learning Technologies. Los Alamitos, CA: IEEE Computer Society (2001) 460-461
9. Graesser, A.C., Person, N., Harter, D., Tutoring Research Group: Teaching tactics and dialog in AutoTutor. International Journal of Artificial Intelligence in Education (in press)
10. Graesser, A.C., VanLehn, K., Rosé, C.P., Jordan, P.W., Harter, D.: Intelligent tutoring systems with conversational dialogue. AI Magazine 22(4) (2001) 39-51
11. Hu, X.: Xtrain 1.0 [computer software]. The University of Memphis: Advanced Learning Technologies Laboratory (1998)

12. Johnson, W.L.: Pedagogical agent research at CARTE. AI Magazine 22(4) (2001) 85-94
13. Johnson, W.L., Rickel, J.: Steve: An animated pedagogical agent for procedural training in virtual environments. SIGART Bulletin 8 (1998) 16-21
14. Johnson, W.L., Rickel, J.W., Lester, J.C.: Animated pedagogical agents: Face-to-face interaction in interactive learning environments. International Journal of Artificial Intelligence in Education 11 (2000) 47-78
15. Lester, J.C., Converse, S.A., Kahler, S.E., Barlow, S.T., Stone, B.A., Bhoga R.S.: The persona effect: Affective impact of animated pedagogical agents. Proceedings of CHI '97. Atlanta, GA (1997) 359-366
16. Lester, J., Stone, B., Stelling, G.: Lifelike pedagogical agents for mixed-initiative problem solving in constructivist learning environments. User Modeling and User-Adapted Interaction 9(1-2) (1999) 1-44
17. Loyall, A.B., Bates, J.: Personality-rich believable agents that use language. Proceedings of the First International Conference on Autonomous Agents. Marina del Rey, CA, ACM (1997)
18. Microsoft: Microsoft Agent 2.0 [computer program]. Author (1998)
19. Moreno, K.N., Person, N.K., Adcock, A.B., Van Eck, R.N., Jackson, G.T., Marineau, J.C.: Do people stereotype animated agents? (2002) Manuscript under review
20. Moreno, R., Mayer, R.E., Spires, H.A., Lester, J.C.: The case for social agency in computer-based teaching: Do students learn more deeply when they interact with animated pedagogical agents? Cognition and Instruction 19 (2001) 177-213
21. Person, N.K., Craig, C., Price, P., Hu, X., Gholson, B., Graesser, A. C., Tutoring Research Group: Incorporating human-like conversational behaviors into AutoTutor. Agents 2000 Proceedings of the Workshop on Achieving Human-like Behavior in the Interactive Animated Agents. Barcelona, Catalonia, Spain (2000) 85-92
22. Person, N.K., Gholson, B., Craig, S., Hu, X., Stewart, C., Graesser, A.C.: HURA Advisor: A web-based intelligent agent who manages mixed initiative dialog to optimize information retrieval. Proceedings of the 2001 IEEE Conference on Communications. IEEE (2001)
23. Person, N.K., Graesser, A.C.: Pedagogical agents and tutors. In J.W. Guthrie (ed.): Encyclopedia of Education. New York: Macmillan (in press)
24. Person, N.K., Graesser, A.C., Kreuz, R.J., Pomeroy, V., Tutoring Research Group: Simulating human tutor dialog moves in AutoTutor. International Journal of Artificial Intelligence in Education 12 (2001) 23-29
25. Person, N.K., Klettke, B., Link, K., Kreuz, R.J., Tutoring Research Group: The integration of affective responses into AutoTutor. Proceedings of the International Workshop on Affect in Interactions. Siena, Italy (1999) 167-178
26. Rickel, J., Johnson, W.L.: Animated agents for procedural training in virtual reality: Perception, cognition, and motor control. Applied Artificial Intelligence 13 (1999) 343-382
27. Shaw, E., Johnson, W.L., Ganeshan, R.: Pedagogical agents on the web. Proceedings of the Third International Conference on Autonomous Agents (1999) 283-290
28. Towns, S.G., Callaway, C.B., Voerman, J.L., Lester, J.C.: Coherent gesture, locomotion, and speech in life-like pedagogical agents. IUI '98: International Conference on Intelligent User Interfaces. ACM Press (1998) 13-20
29. Whittaker, S.: Computer mediated communication: A review. In: Graesser, A., Gernsbacher, M.A., Goldman, S.R. (eds.): The Handbook of Discourse Processes. Mahwah, NJ: Erlbaum. (in press)

Learning about the Ethical Treatment of Human Subjects in Experiments on a Web Facility with a Conversational Agent and ITS Components

Arthur C. Graesser[1], Xiangen Hu[1], Natalie K. Person[2], Craig Stewart[3], Joe Toth[4],
G. Tanner Jackson[1], Suresh Susarla[1], and Matthew Ventura[1]

[1] University of Memphis, Department of Psychology, Memphis, TN 38152-3230
{a-graesser, xhu, gtjacksn, ssusarla} @memphis.edu
mventura45@hotmail.com
[2] Rhodes College, Department of Psychology, Memphis, TN 38112
person@rhodes.edu
[3] Carnegie Mellon University, Pittsburgh, PA 15213
craigste@andrew.cmu.edu
[4] Institute for Defense Analyses, Alexandria, VA 22311
jtoth@ida.org

Abstract. The Human Use Regulatory Affairs Advisor (HURAA) is a web-based help facility that provides training on the ethical use of human subjects in research, and that serves as an information retrieval system on ethical policies. The content for HURAA is derived from United States Federal agency documents and regulations. HURAA has a number of components that go beyond conventional page-turning or hypertext systems, including (1) an animated conversational agent that serves as a navigational guide for the web facility, (2) an enhanced multimedia introduction, (3) lessons with case-based and explanation-based reasoning, and (4) document retrieval through natural language queries or a *Point & Query* facility. The effectiveness of HURAA was tested on a small sample of participants (N = 18) who were assigned to either the full HURAA version or a conventional computer-based training version.

1 Introduction

The use of human participants in experiments needs to follow ethical principles that protect their safety and that provide benefits to the individuals and society. These principles are articulated in documents prepared by a number of United States Federal agencies, organizations, and governing bodies, such as the National Institutes of Health [18], the Department of Defense [4], [6], and particular branches of the US military. Most of these ethical principles have been adopted by other countries, and may end up having widespread acceptance throughout the world in the future.

All research projects must be reviewed and approved by the Institutional Review Boards (IRBs) affiliated with the organizations that sponsor the research. Violations of the ethical principles, directives, and approval process can potentially result in termination of all research projects in the organization until the problems are corrected. In fact, governing boards have recently shut down all research conducted

S.A. Cerri, G. Gouardères, and F. Paraguaçu (Eds.): ITS 2002, LNCS 2363, pp. 972–981, 2002.

at US universities and other institutions for several months, so the ethical conduct of research is a matter to be taken very seriously. Therefore, the Institute for Defense Analyses and the Office of Naval Research funded a project to build a web-based help/training facility for research ethics, in an effort to communicate and adhere to the ethical policies. The name of the web site is the Human Use Regulatory Affairs Advisor (HURAA), and is accessible at http://xhuoffice.psyc.memphis.edu/huraa.

There were a number of broader objectives that guided the design of HURAA. First, there needed to be a task analysis on the clients who would use the web facility. The users of the HURAA are high-ranking military officials under the US Secretary of Defense, who must approve research protocols involving human subjects in studies sponsored by the Department of Defense (DoD); these users focus on fundamental ethical issues, but not the nuts-and-bolts procedures of filling out forms and gaining approval from the IRB. Second, the layout and design of the web facility was to incorporate available guidelines in human factors, human-computer interaction, and the Advanced Distributed Learning (ADL) Initiative of DoD. Third, the architecture and the HURAA components needed to be conformant with the ADL standards for reusable instructional objects, as specified in the Sharable Content Objects Reference Model (SCORM, version 1.1 or 1.2) [21].

It is the fourth objective that is particularly relevant to the ITS community. HURAA was designed to optimize both learning and information retrieval. One of the objectives of the ADL mission is to promote the speed and quality of learning in web-based distance learning environments [7], [21]. Most eLearning facilities incorporate hypertext and hypermedia facilities, which meta-analyses have established are, on the average (with notable exceptions), equal to or better than learning by reading printed documents or listening to lectures in classrooms [16]. HURAA therefore incorporated hypertext/hypermedia. However, HURAA pushed the envelope one step further by incorporating some of the sophisticated pedagogical techniques that have been implemented in intelligent tutoring systems (ITS) during the last two decades. More specifically, HURAA incorporated pedagogical techniques that are case-based, explanation-based, and question-based. Most of these ITS capabilities are designed to promote deep learning, rather than mere shallow learning [1], [2], [3], [9], [10], [14], [22]. Some segments of HURAA have persuasive multimedia that are intended to hook the user to continue on the website in addition to facilitating learning [17]. These segments are pitched for learning at the shallow end of the continuum, but the intent is to optimize attention and motivation.

Regarding information retrieval, HURAA implements multiple methods of accessing information in a large space of documents. HURAA has hypertext and glossaries, the conventional methods of information retrieval. But HURAA goes further. It has a Point&Query facility [8], which provides answers to context-sensitive Frequently Asked Questions (FAQs). Users also can type in questions or descriptions in English; HURAA then responds by accessing relevant documents identified through the use of recently developed techniques in computational linguistics [13], including latent semantic analysis [15].

The interchange between HURAA and the user is managed by an animated conversational agent and by discourse mechanisms that are designed to facilitate the dialogue [9], [19]. Many users will be high-level decision-makers with very little time to visit the site (i.e., 30 minutes or less), so HURAA needed to be engineered to maximize its coverage of critical information in the minimum amount of time. This required some efficient dialog management techniques that are available in the fields of human-computer interaction and discourse processes. For example, the conversational agent briefly identifies the functions of major interface components the user clicks on, and offers recommendations on next steps when each web page is first accessed. This prevents the first-time user from spending undue time analyzing the functions of interface features and figuring out what they are supposed to do next. Navigational guidance is one of the important functions of the conversational agents that have been developed in recent years [12].

It is beyond the scope of this paper to describe the complete architecture and implementation of HURAA. Instead, we will focus on the modules that contributed to three benchmark tasks that were included in a performance evaluation that was conducted on 18 participants. The participants were university graduate students and upper-division undergraduates who were seeking approval of their own research projects from a local IRB. Therefore, they had a vested interest in understanding the ethics of human experimentation. The participants received introductory material on ethics and HURAA, completed lessons that involved case-based and explanation-based reasoning, and performed searches for answers to test questions. Half of the participants received the full HURAA version and half a Standard version with conventional page-turning and hypertext capabilities. The Standard version was designed to have information equivalence to the HURAA version so that any differences in performance could not be attributed to an imbalance of information available to the users.

2   Relevant Modules of the HURA Advisor

The seven major modules of HURAA are Introduction, Historical Overview, Lessons, Explore Issues, Explore Cases, Decision Making, and Query Documents. Links for these seven modules are always present on the web page, in the banner on the left of the screen display. This section describes the modules and HURAA facilities that are directly relevant to the performance evaluation.

2.1   Introduction

The Introduction Module is a multimedia movie that plays immediately after a new user has logged in. It is available for replay by returning users. The Introduction is intended to impress the user with the importance of protecting human subjects in research. It introduces the user to the basic concepts of the Common Rule [4], [18], the Belmont Report's coverage of beneficence, justice, and respect for persons, and the Seven Critical Issues that must be scrutinized when evaluating any case [5]: Social and scientific value, accepted scientific principles, fair subject selection, informed consent, minimizing risks and maximizing benefits, independent review, and respect for subjects. The Introduction also describes for the user "what" the site is, "who" should use the site, "why" the site is important, "how" the site works, and "when" the site should be used. It consists of a "voice-over" accompanied by images designed to illustrate the concepts being discussed. The Introduction was prepared by an accomplished expert in radio and web-based entertainment industries, after rounds of feedback from a panel of DoD personnel. The corresponding content in the Standard version is simply a sequence of pages with text, which are read by the learners at their own pace. The verbal content was identical in both versions.

2.2 Lessons

This module comprises five lessons that teach the user about the Seven Critical Issues identified [5] and how to apply them to particular cases that involve ethical abuses. This is a form of case-based reasoning. For example, one of the lessons presents the user with a description of a biomedical study. The user is then presented with the Seven Critical Issues and must decide, on a six-point scale, the extent to which there is a problem with each issue in that case. The user then receives feedback comparing his/her responses with those of a panel of experts from the DoD, along with a brief explanation. Discrepancies between the learner's decisions and the judgments of the experts are highlighted in some fashion (e.g., in italics or in red). In the full-blown HURAA (i.e., not the experimental version), cases are dynamically selected on the basis of the user's previous responses, to ensure full coverage of the Seven Critical Issues. That is, the selection of the next case (N) would tend to cover issues that were not problems in previous cases or were incorrectly identified by the learner in the previous cases. However, a fixed set of 5 cases was included in the experimental version of HURAA that was used in the evaluation.

Figure 1 shows a screen shot of one of the lessons that involved case-based and explanation-based reasoning. The animated conversational agent appears in the upper left on all screens in the web site, providing navigational guidance throughout the session. Below the agent is a banner of 7 main modules (Introduction, Historical Overview, etc.) and 7 secondary modules (Glossary, Archives & Links, etc.). The screen shot would appear after the learner had read about a particular case that was problematic with respect to some (but not all) of the critical issues. The case takes up a single screen and is (re)read at the learner's pace. After the case is read, each issue is rated by the user on a 6-point scale that segregates "Problem" from "No Problem" decisions. The issue is defined at the right of the rating box for each issue, as the issues are rated, on-by-one. After the learner rates all issues, HURAA provides feedback on the user's ratings. That is, an issue is flagged and highlighted if there is a discrepancy between the learner's judgment and the judgment of an expert in research ethics. An explanation of the discrepancy is also presented.

Signal detection analyses are performed on the learner's decisions as a measure of performance. These analyses measure how discriminating a learner is in detecting cases that do versus do not have problems with particular ethical issues. A decision is a hit (H) if both the learner and expert agree that an issue is potentially problematic for the particular case. A decision is a correct rejection (CR) if both agree that an issue is not potentially problematic for a case. A miss (M) occurs when the expert believes there is a potential problem, but the learner doesn't. A false alarm (FA) occurs when the learner believes there is a problem, but the expert believes there is no problem. The experts were 7 individuals in the DoD who had experience and training in research ethics. A d' score is also computed that assesses how well the learner can discriminate cases with versus with out problems. A *d'* score of 0 means the learner is not at all discriminating whereas the score increases to the extent that the user is progressively more discriminating (with an upper bound of about 4.0).

The Standard version simply had the learner read the cases and then read the experts' decisions and explanations about whether or not there is a problem with each of the seven issues. They also read definitions of each of the seven issues.

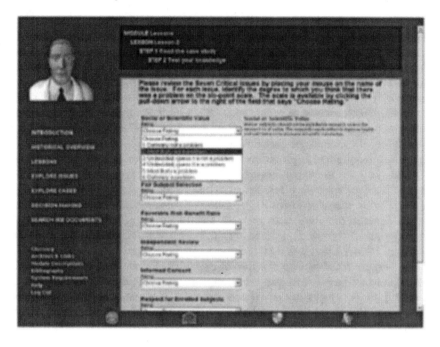

Fig. 1. Screen Shot of the HURAA Advisor

2.3 Query Documents

This module allows the user to ask a natural language question (or description) and then generates an answer by retrieving high matching excerpts from various documents and HURAA content. The user can select any or all of the following documents in the search: The IRB Guidebook, the DoD Directive, the Army regulations, the Navy regulations, the Air Force regulations, HURAA Issues (the seven critical Belmont issues), or HURAA cases. For each document that the user selects, the highest matching paragraph from the document space is selected by the computational linguistics software and is displayed in a window. Beneath this window, the headings for the next four results appear. If the top choice is not the one that the user needs, s/he can click on the headings to read those excerpts. The search engine that is used to identify the optimal matches is latent semantic analysis [11], [15]. Latent semantic analysis (LSA) has recently been proposed as a statistical representation of a large body of world knowledge. An LSA space can be created and tested for a very large corpus of documents in a short period of time (within a month). From the present standpoint, LSA has the potential for accessing paragraphs in the document space that are relevant to questions users ask.

The Standard version did not allow the learners to search for answers to questions through natural language queries. Instead, the learners had to search linearly through a large document space, through hypertext, or through a Glossary.

The participants were instructed to search the document space in order to find answers to 4 test questions. Performance was measured by retrieval time and the likelihood of retrieving the correct paragraph out of the large document space.

2.4 Animated Conversational Agent

This is a talking head with synthesized speech, facial expressions, and pointing gestures. The Agent tells the user what to do next when the user first encounters a web page. For example, when the user enters the Explore Issues Module, the Agent says, "Select the issue that you would like to explore." The talking head moves to direct the user's attention to some point on the display. For example, the talking head looks down when he says, "You may select one of the options below me." The talking head also tells the user what each primary and secondary module is supposed to do, after the user rests the mouse pointer over the module link for more than 2 seconds. The Agent is designed to project an authoritative persona and to help the user navigate through the interface more quickly. Many novice users are lost and don't know what to do next when they encounter a page. The Agent is designed to reduce this wasted time. The Standard version does not have the Agent as a navigational guide.

2.5 Point & Query

The interface displays a question mark (?) for some hot spots. When the user clicks on the question mark, a menu of questions appears. The user selects a question by clicking on it, and then the answer appears. Thus, the user can quickly ask a question with two clicks of a mouse. Users are also exposed to good, relevant questions because the designer of the P&Q handcrafts these Question-Answer items. P&Q can be viewed as a context-sensitive Frequently Asked Question (FAQ) facility [8]. The P&Q facility was available in the HURAA version but not the Standard version.

3 Evaluation of the Performance of the HURA Advisor

After the participants finished the Introduction, the lessons and the retrieval tasks described above, they were given a posttest. The posttest had two major components from the standpoint of the present paper. First, they were tested on their memory for the introductory material. Second, were given two additional cases and asked to decide which of the Seven Critical Issues were potentially problematic. These posttest data, plus the results of the search task, provided the outcome measures of performance.

3.1 Memory for Introductory Material

Memory was assessed in three tests: Free recall, cued recall, and the cloze task. The free recall presented a series of concepts that the participants were asked to define or describe. For example, they were asked "What are the three principles of the Belmont Report?" After finishing the free recall task, the cued recall test was administered. The cued recall test had more retrieval cues than the free recall test, e.g., Autonomy is one of the three principles of the Belmont Report. Describe Autonomy." The cloze procedure has the most retrieval cues. It takes verbatim segments of the introductory text and leaves out key words, which the participant fills in. For example, one of the segments is "Human subjects should not be included in research unless the research is of _____, either in improving health and well-being, or in increasing _____." There are progressively more retrieval cues for content to be retrieved as one goes from free recall to cued recall to the cloze task.

Memory was found to be better for the HURAA version than the Standard version. The proportion of free recall items correctly recalled was significantly higher in the HURAA version than the Standard version, with means of .65 and .50, respectively, $F(1, 16) = 6.75$, $p < .05$, $MS_{error} = .01$. The effect size of the advantage of HURAA over the Standard version was 1.25 standard deviation units. The cued recall and cloze task also showed higher means for HURAA than the Standard version but the means were not quite significant. The proportions of items recalled correctly in the cued recall test were .66 versus .57, with an effect size of .41. The proportions of words filled in correctly in the cloze task were .56 and .39, with an effect size of .89. We anticipate that these differences will be significant when more participants are run and there is more statistical power. Nevertheless, the free recall task showed an advantage of HURAA over the Standard version even with the low sample size. The multimedia effects of HURAA, which were designed to be captivating and persuasive, apparently did have a significant impact on memory for the introductory material. It should be noted that there was no significant difference in the time spent comprehending the Introduction in the two versions, with means of 4.6 and 3.1 minutes ($p > .10$), respectively; however, for technical reasons, a precise time could not be obtained for this timing measure.

3.2 Identification of Potentially Problematic Issues in Cases

The posttest assessed how discriminating the participants were in identifying potentially problematic issues on two cases. The cases were selected systematically so that 6 of the issues were problematic in one and only one of the two cases; one of the issues was problematic in both cases so it was not scored. Hit rates, false alarm rates, and d' scores were collected for each participant and analyzed. The results uncovered no statistical differences between the HURAA and Standard versions. The means were nearly the same for hit rates (.67 versus .61), false alarm rates (.33 and .33), and d' scores (.91 versus .65) in the HURAA and Standard versions, respectively. The effect size for d' scores was .35, with an advantage for HURAA, but the difference was not significant. It appears that there was no pedagogical advantage in having participants actively decide which issues were problematic and receive explanations about discrepancies with experts. It is just as effective to have the participants simply read the experts' decisions and explanations for each of the 7 issues. The amount of time spent completing this task did not significantly differ for the HURAA and Standard versions, with means of 20.9 versus 18.9 minutes, respectively ($p > .25$).

Our original prediction was that participants receiving the HURAA version would be more discriminating in identifying problems with particular cases. This prediction rested on the assumption that there would be benefits in having the users (a) actively decide and rate cases on potentially problematic issues and (b) receive explanatory feedback on all discrepancies between the ratings of participants and ethics experts. However, there apparently was no advantage in the process of active decision making and receiving selective feedback and explanations for discrepancies. It was just as good to simply deliver the ratings and explanations of the experts on all issues. Perhaps differences will emerge with a larger sample of subjects, with greater statistical power. The good news is that the means were in the predicted direction.

3.3 Retrieval of Answers to Questions

We measured the speed and accuracy of retrieving answers to the 4 questions given to the participants. For example, two of the test questions were "Find out what the specific limitations are on the uses of prisoners in research." and "Find out what a medical monitor is in human subjects research." The amount of time it took to find answers to the 4 questions did not significantly differ for the HURAA and Standard versions, with means of 22.3 versus 23.3 minutes, respectively. However, the accuracy was significantly higher for HURAA than the Standard version, with mean scores of .76 and .54, respectively, $F(1, 16) = 6.82$, $p < .05$, $MS_{error} = .03$, effect size = 1.22 standard deviation units. Therefore, the natural language queries produced a much higher accuracy than the conventional methods of searching documents for answers.

4 Final Comments

The results of our performance evaluation support the claim that most of the distinctive features of the HURA Advisor had advantages over the conventional page-turning or hypertext systems. This is good news for those who develop enhanced multimedia, natural language query systems, and intelligent tutoring systems in general. However, it is appropriate to hedge and acknowledge that a larger sample of participants needs to be run before we can defend these claims more strongly. The fact that HURAA was implemented on a web site suggests that it is feasible to implement some components of intelligent tutoring systems, with a high degree of tutor-learner interactivity, in web-based distant learning environments. In another project, we are currently running ITS systems with natural language, multi-turn, tutorial dialog on web sites [10]. The timing of the turn-by-turn tutorial dialog is fast enough to have normal conversations on the web. Sophisticated ITS systems will become more widespread to the extent that the software moves from the desktop to the Internet.

A.C. Graesser et al.

Acknowledgements. This research was directly supported by contracts from the Office of Naval Research (N61339-01-C1006) and the Institute for Defense Analyses (AK-2-1801), and was partially supported from grants by the National Science Foundation (REC 0106965) and the DoD Multidisciplinary University Research Initiative (MURI) administered by ONR under grant N00014-00-1-0600. Any opinions, findings, and conclusions or recommendations expressed in this material are those of the authors and do not necessarily reflect the views of ONR, IDA or NSF.

References

1. Aleven, V., Koedinger, K.R., & Cross, K.: Tutoring answer explanation fosters learning with understanding. In S.P. Lajoie and M. Vivet (Eds.), Artificial intelligence in education. Amsterdam: IOS Press (1999) 199-206
2. Anderson, J. R., Corbett, A. T., Koedinger, K. R., & Pelletier, R.: Cognitive tutors: Lessons learned. The Journal of the Learning Sciences 4 (1995) 167-207
3. Ashley, K.D.: Modeling legal argument: Reasoning with cases and hypotheticals. Cambridge, MA: MIT Press (1990)
4. 32 CFR 219: Protection of Human Subjects, Department of Defense (1991)
5. Emmanuel, E. J., Wendler, D., & Grady, C.: What makes clinical research ethical? Journal of the American Medical Association 283 (2000) 2701-2711
6. DoD Directive 3216.2: Protection of Human Subjects in DoD supported research, Department of Defense (1993)
7. Fletcher, J. D.: Technology, the Columbus effect, and the third revolution in learning. In M. Rabinowitz, F.C. Blumberg, & H. Everson (Eds.), The Impact of Media and Technology on Instruction. Mahwah, NJ: Lawrence Erlbaum Associates (in press)
8. Graesser, A. C., Langston, M. C., & Baggett, W. B.: Exploring information about concepts by asking questions. In G. V. Nakamura, R. M. Taraban, & D. Medin (Eds.), The psychology of learning and motivation: Vol. 29. Categorization by humans and machines. Orlando, FL: Academic Press (1993) 411-436
9. Graesser, A.C., Person, N., Harter, D., & TRG: Teaching tactics and dialog in AutoTutor. International Journal of Artificial Intelligence in Education (in press)
10. Graesser, A.C., VanLehn, K., Rose, C., Jordan, P., & Harter, D.: Intelligent tutoring systems with conversational dialogue. AI Magazine 22 (2001) 39-51
11. Graesser, A.C., Wiemer-Hastings, P., Wiemer-Hastings, K., Harter, D., Person, N., & TRG: Using latent semantic analysis to evaluate the contributions of students in AutoTutor. Interactive Learning Environments 8 (2000) 129-148
12. Johnson, W. L., & Rickel, J. W., & Lester, J.C.: Animated pedagogical agents: Face-to-face interaction in interactive learning environments. International Journal of Artificial Intelligence in Education 11 (2000) 47-78
13. Jurafsky, D., & Martin, J.H.: Speech and language processing: An introduction to natural language processing, computational linguistics, and speech recognition. Upper Saddle River, NJ: Prentice-Hall (2000)
14. Koedinger, K.R., Anderson, J.R., Hadley, W.H., & Mark, M.A.: Intelligent tutoring goes to school in the big city. International Journal of Artificial Intelligence in Education 8 (1997) 30-43
15. Landauer, T.K., Foltz, P.W., Laham, D.: An introduction to latent semantic analysis. Discourse Processes 25 (1998) 259-284
16. Liao, Y.C.: Effects of hypermedia on students' achievement: A meta-analysis. Journal of Educational Multimedia and Hypermedia 8 (1999) 255-277

17. Mayer, R.E.: Multimedia learning: Are we asking the right questions? Educational Psychologist 32 (1997) 1-19
18. NIH 45 CFR 46: National Institutes of Health Code of Federal Regulations, Protection of Human Subjects (1991)
19. Person, N.K., Graesser, A.C., Kreuz, R.J., Pomeroy, V., & TRG: Simulating human tutor dialog moves in AutoTutor. International Journal of Artificial Intelligence in Education 12 (2001) 23-29
20. Protection of Human Subjects in Department of Defense
21. Sharable Content Object Reference Model (SCORM), Version 1.1. www.adlnet.org.
22. VanLehn, K., Jones, R.M., & Chi, M.T.: A model of the self-explanation effect. The Journal of the Learning Sciences 2 (1992) 1-59

Design and Evaluation of a Navigation Agent with a Mixed Locus of Control

Judith Masthoff[1]

University of Brighton, UK
Judith.Masthoff@brighton.ac.uk

Abstract. The effectiveness of a Navigation Agent has been evaluated, which determines a path through course material tailored to the individual student. *Lesson selection* by the agent showed an advantage for students who were unable to monitor their own learning process. *Initiative* by the agent --where the agent also chooses the moment for selecting another lesson-- reduced the time needed to finish the task by stimulating the students to study the lessons in a balanced way. The experiment also provides evidence that a mixed locus of control is preferable to either the student or the agent exclusively taking the initiative and selecting lessons.

1 Introduction

Many interactive instruction systems are based on a large database of information (explanations, interactive exercises). A vital question is how to make that database accessible to students, in a way that optimally supports the individual student's learning process. There are three general approaches.

In the first approach, the students navigate through the database themselves, using, for instance, menu structures. Self-navigation can be supported in various ways. Firstly, the database can be visualized, for instance by cone trees visualizing hierarchical information [9], or "subway lines" visualizing cohesion [4]. Secondly (as described in [1]), links can be annotated with information about the history of a student's actions (for instance, "has read"), and the system's prediction regarding the suitability of a page given that history (for instance, "ready to be learned"). Annotation can occur in an interesting multitude of ways, such as by words, traffic light symbols, font size, font type, etc. Thirdly, the information space can be restricted to a set of 'appropriate' pages. In hypermedia this is done through link hiding [1]. In computer games (and some old computer-assisted instruction systems), the idea of levels is used: users can only reach the following level when they have performed sufficiently well on the lower level. However, despite all these support methods, navigation often remains a difficult task, particularly in the case of a large database.

In the second approach, 'guidance' is used: part of the system navigates for the user, selecting successive lessons and exercises. This is used in lecturing by a human teacher. The idea is that the teacher knows better what a good order is in which to

---

[1] The author is supported by Nuffield grant NAL/00258/G. The work has been carried out while working at Eindhoven University of Technology.

S.A. Cerri, G. Gouardères, and F. Paraguaçu (Eds.): ITS 2002, LNCS 2363, pp. 982–991, 2002.

learn the material, and reduces the cognitive load of the students by 'navigating' for them. In [6] a system is described in which anthropomorphic agents guide the user through a database using a narration metaphor. It has been one of the main research areas in Intelligent Tutoring Systems to produce systems that can do adaptive navigation (mostly called 'sequencing'). In adaptive hypermedia, a "Continue" link is often provided [1], clicking which results in the system selecting the next page.

In the third approach, a mixture of self-navigation and guidance is used. This is very commonly used in adaptive hypermedia systems, which tend to provide a combination of a "Continue" link and adaptive link annotation.

Orthogonal to this "who selects the next lesson" dimension, is the dimension of "who decides *when* to go to another lesson". This can be (1) always the student, (2) always the system, or (3) a combination of both. In self-navigation, it tends to be the student (though a system could say "Your lesson has finished. Please select another."). In most systems, guidance means that the system will select the next lesson when asked by the student. Whilst the system selects the lesson, the *initiative* for the navigation is still the task of the student. This in contrast to traditional lecturing, where the teacher tends to take the initiative. The system always taking the initiative might lead to the users feeling a lack of control [8]. Like [5], we advocate the third option, namely a *mixed locus of control* in which both the user and the system can navigate and who takes the initiative depends on the interaction, in particular on the student's performance. Such a mixed locus of control in the area of navigation is also described by [11]. Indirect evidence for the effectiveness of a mixed locus of control has been found by Swanson (as reported in [10]). Swanson found that total student control (as in discovery learning) was good for the most able students, but was particularly ineffective with low-ability students, who benefited most from contingent tutoring. Total teacher control (as in lectures) produced intermediate results.

This paper will briefly present a Navigation Agent, which can select an appropriate next lesson for the student, and can also take the initiative for navigation. It is not our intent, however, to present the perfect Navigation Agent. Rather, the focus is on a comparative evaluation of different approaches to navigation. As mentioned by [3], controlled evaluation of adaptive navigation support has been rather limited. Sometimes combinations of navigation support are evaluated at the same time, making it difficult to find results. For instance, [3] mentions that the Continue button was used in over 90% of times, which made it difficult for them to assess the effect of the adaptive annotations. Also, big variations in students' navigational behavior occur, which make it difficult to find statistically significant results [2]. We hope to show a way in which evaluation of adaptive navigation can be conducted with more success.

2 Design of the Navigation Agent

The Navigation Agent should determine a path through the course material at run time, taking the current estimation of the foreknowledge, goals, and capabilities of the student into account at any moment, as well a description of the course material. The estimations are changed on the basis of the interaction with the student, the lesson selection by the student, or explicitly by the student.

2.1 The Kind of Course Material the Agent Will Work with

The course material should consist of lessons which are described by attributes such as the foreknowledge needed to study the lesson, and the goals accomplished by studying the lesson. For more advanced behavior, the agent will also need other attributes, like the learning style of a lesson etc, but it is outside the scope of this paper to discuss this. Each lesson should contain exercises, and the student's performance on the exercises will be available to the agent.

2.2 Which Lesson to Select

2.2.1 Determination of a Sequence of Lessons

A sequence of lessons is determined such that if it is studied from beginning to end, the student has sufficient foreknowledge to study each subsequent lesson, and eventually all the student's goals are reached. Note that this is a simplification, as in fact the sequence may need to meet additional criteria, related to the predicted effort it will take to study each lesson and the learning style of the student [7]. A sequence that meets these criteria is determined by recursion. Departing from the goal of a student, lessons are searched with which that goal can be reached. The foreknowledge associated with these lessons should be achieved before they are studied, and the same procedure is used to obtain a sequence resulting in that foreknowledge.

There can be many situations in which the agent would need to construct a new sequence [7]. However, for the purpose of the experiment, the Agent's task has been simplified: by experimental design both its expectation of the students' goal and their foreknowledge are accurate. Also, no alternative paths are possible in the material.

2.2.2 Whether to Select a More Difficult or an Easier Lesson

When the Agent selects a lesson, it needs to decide whether to select a more difficult or an easier lesson. An easier lesson should be selected if the student is performing poorly in the current lesson and a more difficult lesson should be selected if the student performs well. When an easier or more difficult lesson is not available, the current lesson should be selected. There are several ways in which "poorly" and "well" can be defined, for instance by using the number of successive correct or incorrect responses. We consider the student's performance in a lesson to be "poor" if the last presented exercise of that lesson has been answered incorrectly, and less than 50% of the items of that lesson have been mastered. The student's performance in a lesson is considered to be "good" in all other cases.

The student's performance in the current lesson cannot be used:

- When the student was not in any lesson at the moment of navigation, for instance at the beginning of the course or when trying a so-called final test (see below). In that case a more difficult lesson will be selected.
- When the student was reading the instructions of a lesson and had not started practicing. There are three possible interpretations of the student choosing another lesson while reading the instructions: the lesson seemed uninteresting (not leading towards a goal), or it seemed too easy (understandable without practicing), or it seemed too difficult. In the first two cases, a more difficult lesson is needed. In the

last case, an easier lesson is needed. We hypothesized that it is more likely that it is one of the first two. So, we decided that a more difficult lesson would be selected always when the student was reading instructions for the first time. The experiment will explore whether this decision was correct.

2.2.3 Selection of the Next Lesson

Given the sequence and the decision on whether to select an easier or more difficult lesson, the selection of the next lesson is easy unless there is a mixed locus of control. When only the agent can select lessons, the next lesson should be the previous or next lesson from the sequence for an easier or more difficult lesson, respectively. For instance, if the sequence is 1-2-3-6-12, and the agent has last selected lesson 3, then the more difficult lesson will be 6, and the easier lesson 2.

However, in the case of a mixed locus of control, the student could also have selected lessons and, hence, the current lesson may not be part of the sequence, or an easier or more difficult lesson may require more than one step in the sequence. For instance, consider a sequence 1-2-3-6-12. When the student has selected 12 and next navigation towards an easier lesson is required, the selection of that easier lesson should depend on the past performance of the student on lessons 1, 2, 3, and 6. The same holds when the student has selected a lesson outside the sequence, like 7.

The last lesson selected by the agent could be used as the index in the sequence from which the previous or next one is chosen. However, if, for instance, the student had selected lesson 3 before and had performed well at it, it seems reasonable to use lesson 3 as the index in the sequence rather than, for instance, lesson 1. So, we decided to increase the index in the sequence to a lesson selected by the student whenever the student performed well on that lesson, "well" being defined as above.

2.3 When to Take the Initiative

The Navigation Agent should take the initiative to navigate whenever the student is performing very well or very poorly on the current lesson. There are several ways in which "very well" and "very poorly" can be defined, for instance by using the number of successive correct or incorrect responses, or by looking at asymptotic performance. We define the student's performance as "very good" if the student has answered the exercise last presented in that lesson correctly and at least 80% of the items in that lesson have been mastered. The student's performance in a particular lesson is considered to be "very poor" if the student has made more than three mistakes, the item last presented was answered incorrectly, and at most 20% of the items of that lesson have been mastered. As a consequence, the agent will only take the initiative to navigate when the student is doing exercises, and not when reading instructions. More sophisticated mechanisms might include the time spent on the instructions relative to the time spent on the exercise, and the number of times the instructions are consulted.

3 Evaluation of the Navigation Agent

The purposes of this experiment were as follows. In the first place, the advantage of an efficiently-functioning lesson selection mechanism should be determined. A simple, but regularly applied form of user navigation, namely a menu structure, was used as a baseline. The effect of combining user navigation and guidance should also be determined. We hypothesized that weaker students benefit more from lesson selection by the system. Note that we decided not to include adaptive link annotation, as this would have required more experimental conditions and hence more subjects.

In the second place, the acceptance by the students of automatic lesson selection should be determined. This acceptance may depend, among other things, on the correctness of the choice of an easier or more difficult lesson. We hypothesized that automatic lesson selection is more effective and acceptable when combined with the possibility of user navigation.

3.1 Method

3.1.1 Design and Procedure

Five conditions were used in a between-subjects design: a "Menu condition", a "Guidance condition", a "Mixed condition", a "TGuidance condition" and a "TMixed condition". In all conditions, the subjects were instructed to study "Square Dance" lessons in such a way that they would learn to perform the "Slide through" as quickly as possible. They could try to pass the "Slide through" test as often as and whenever they wanted. The experiment ended when the test was completed correctly. No feedback was given during the test.

Subjects could practice lessons for as long as they wanted. In the "Menu condition" and the "Guidance condition" they were instructed to press a "Quit lesson" button whenever they wanted to study another lesson. In the Menu condition, pressing this button resulted in the appearance of a menu screen, from which they could select a lesson. In the Guidance condition, pressing the button resulted in the automatic selection of a lesson according to the algorithm described above. In the Mixed condition, subjects could use both a menu and guidance. They were instructed to press a "Menu" button whenever they wanted to select a lesson through the menu, and to press a "Pick lesson" button whenever they wanted a lesson to be automatically selected for them.

In the TGuidance and TMixed conditions, the initiative for the selection of another lesson could be taken both by the Navigation Agent and the student. The agent used the criteria as described above to decide when guidance was needed. Subjects were informed that the system might take the initiative.

The times were recorded at which subjects decided to change lesson, selected a lesson, and selected the test. It was also recorded which lesson was selected by the subject or the agent, which exercise items were studied and whether the subject responded correctly to the exercise. Immediately after the experimental session, subjects had to fill out a questionnaire in which they could indicate any problems they had experienced during the course, how well they liked it, why they selected the lessons in that particular order (in the Menu and Mixed condition), how they liked the order selected for them (in the Guidance and Mixed condition), and when they used the menu and when the automatic selection (in the Mixed condition).

3.1.2 Subjects
Fifty-six subjects with university or higher vocational training participated in the experiment. The average age was 25. All subjects had computer experience, none had heard of Square Dance. Subjects were randomly assigned to an experimental condition: 14 to Menu, Guidance and Mixed, and 7 to TGuidance and TMixed.

3.1.3 Materials
Square Dance is performed by a group of eight dancers, moving according to the instructions given by a "caller". In the computer course, subjects had to move the dancers by 'remote control' in accordance to an audio call by the computer. The understandability of the interface and the material had been tested in pilot studies. This domain was chosen because the average Dutch person has never heard of it.

The course consisted of fourteen lessons. Each lesson comprised an instruction and an exercise part. The first two lessons explained basic terminology. In the third lesson, the remote control was explained and the basic movements of the dancers were practiced. In the other lessons, more advanced dance movements were presented. According to an experienced square dancer, the order of the lessons in the menu is good for a student who has to learn all the movements of the course. The sequence determined by the Agent consisted of Lesson 1, 2, 3, 6, and 12. The instructions of Lesson 12 indicated that Lesson 6 constituted prerequisite material.

3.2 Results

An overview of the results is given in Table 1. The total time was calculated from the moment the subjects started the course after reading the general instructions till the moment they started the last test. Lessons are called "superfluous" when other than lessons 1, 2, 3, 6, and 12. Figure 1 shows the average time spent on each lesson.

Table 1. Overview of results

	Menu	Guidance	TGuidance	Mixed	TMixed
Total time					
Mean	33'42"	27'12"	22'50"	27'24"	22'3"
Standard deviation	14'3"	9'11"	8'32"	12'23"	3'37"
Av. time superfluous	9'23"	0	0	4'17"	
Av. # student initiative	10.2	6.6	1.7	7.3	5.6
Pick lesson	-	6.6	1.7	3.3	3.9
Menu	10.2	-	-	4	1.7
Av. # agent initiative	-	-	4	-	3.3
Some examples paths (-selection by student, = selection by agent)	1-2-3-12-6-12 1-2-3-4-5-6-7-12 12-1-2-3-4-5-12-6-7-8-12	1=2=3=6=12		1=2=3-12-3=6=12 1=2=3=6-4=12-5-6=12	

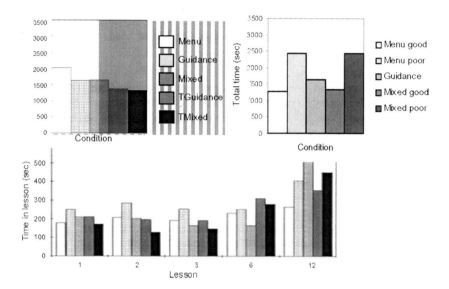

Fig. 1. Average total times (top), and times per relevant lesson (bottom) per condition.

In the Menu condition, a lot of subjects followed the lessons in the order of the menu till they decided to select the lesson on the Slide through (e.g., 1-2-3-4-5-6-7-12). Three subjects started with the lesson on the Slide through (12). In the Guidance and TGuidance conditions, all the subjects followed the same path (1-2-3-6-12).

In the TGuidance condition, the use of the Quit Lesson button always resulted in the selection of the current lesson. In the Mixed condition, three subjects always used the Menu button, three subjects always used the Pick lesson button, and eight subjects used both. When both were used, the Menu button was used frequently to select an easier lesson. In the TMixed condition, the Menu button was mostly used to return to an easier lesson, and the use of the Pick lesson button often resulted in the selection of the current lesson. Only one subject spent some time on superfluous lessons.

Table 2. Results of statistical analyses. Symbol - denotes not significant

Contrast	Total time	Time per lesson
Menu versus Guidance	-	Sign. lessons 5, 7, 8
Menu versus Mixed	-	Sign. lessons 5, 7, 8
Guidance versus Mixed	-	Sign. lessons 3, 4
Menu versus TGuidance and Tmixed[2]	$F(1,1)=7.17\ p<.017$	Sign. lessons 5, 7, 8
Guidance and Mixed vs. TGuidance and TMixed	-	-
TGuidance versus Tmixed	-	-
Poor versus Good navigators Menu and Mixed[2]	$F(1,1)=22.05 p<.0033$	
Poor navigators Menu and Mixed vs. Guidance[2]	$F(1,1)=11.31 p<.00033$	
Good navigators Menu and Mixed vs. Guidance	-	

---

[2] According to the Bonferroni principle, effects are significant with a familywise α–level of .05, .01, or .001, respectively, when $p<.017$, $p<.0033$, or $p<.00033$, respectively.

A MANOVA was performed on the total time and the time spent on each lesson, with the condition (Menu, Guidance, Mixed, TGuidance, TMixed) as a between-subjects factor. Six contrasts were performed. See Table 2 for the results.

A post-hoc analysis was performed in which the subjects of both Menu and Mixed were divided into two groups: one group with subjects who studied at least two superfluous lessons, and one with the remaining subjects. We will call the first group the poor navigators and the second group the good navigators. In Menu, nine subjects belonged to the poor navigators, and five to the good navigators. In Mixed, four subjects belonged to the poor navigators, and ten to the good. Figure 1 shows the results per subgroup. Three contrasts were performed, see Table 2 for the results.

3.3 Discussion

3.3.1 Effect of Who Selects the Next Lesson

Lesson selection by the system (Guidance and Mixed condition) has not led to a statistically significant decrease in the total time, even though, on average, six and a half minutes less were needed than in the Menu condition. The lack of a statistically significant effect is probably due to the large variance between subjects. This does not come as a surprise: from our literature review (see section 1) and past experiments [7], we expected a large variation of navigation behavior within a group of subjects, and we expected poor navigators to benefit more from guidance than weak navigators.

The results in Guidance are more homogeneous than in Menu and Mixed. The results suggest that, especially in Menu, the group of subjects can be divided into two groups: a slow and a fast group. An explanation may be that in Menu some subjects merely follow the sequence of the menu, while others are much better at deciding which lessons are relevant. The heterogeneous results in Mixed may be explained by some subjects being more reluctant to use guidance than others. These explanations are confirmed by the navigation paths, and by the time spent per lesson.

The significant effects of condition for the contrasts between the poor and good navigators, and the poor navigators and the Guidance condition indicate that the poor navigators need more time than the good navigators and the subjects in the Guidance condition. This implies an advantage of using guidance for students who are unable to monitor their own learning process. As nine of the fourteen subjects of the Menu condition are poor navigators, determining a good path through the course material seems a difficult task, therefore guidance seems necessary.

It can be argued that subjects had only limited information available for the navigation (for instance, no link annotation). On the other hand, the number of lessons was very limited, the foreknowledge relations between the lessons was limited, and the lessons needed to reach the goal were quite easy to find: Lesson 12 had the same name as the goal and mentioned the need for Lesson 6, and besides these two lessons only the first lessons were needed, which all had a name starting with "basic".

The student always selecting the lesson (Menu condition) has the disadvantage that a great deal of time was spent on superfluous lessons: on average one third of the total time in that condition. This is confirmed by the significant effect of condition on the fifth, seventh, and eighth lessons in the comparisons between Menu and both Guidance and Mixed. The system always selecting the lesson (Guidance) has the advantage that only relevant lessons are studied as a natural consequence of the lesson selection algorithm used. The Mixed condition has the advantage that less time is spent on superfluous lessons than in the Menu condition (5' less) and also less time is spent on the first lessons than in Guidance (3'30" less). Subjects may be more aware of the need to decide the moment of navigation for themselves, because they also have the possibility to select the lesson themselves, as in the Menu condition.

Many subjects in the Guidance condition complained that it seemed impossible to obtain an easier lesson. One subject used the "Quit lesson" button in the instruction part of the lessons, without doing any exercises, till she reached the twelfth lesson and did not manage to quit that lesson. It is clearly incorrect always to select a more difficult lesson when lesson selection is requested while the student is reading the instructions of a lesson for the first time. This example also shows an advantage of the Mixed condition: it allows the student to correct bad selections by the system.

3.3.2 Effect of Who Takes the Initiative

There is a tendency in favor of the agent taking initiative: on average TGuidance took 4'22'' less than Guidance (a decrease of 16%), and TMixed took 5'21'' less than Mixed (a decrease of 19%). This is supported by a significant effect of condition on the total time for the contrast between the Menu and the TGuidance and TMixed conditions, while the contrasts between Menu and Guidance and between Menu and Mixed were not significant. So, the initiative of the Navigation Agent seems to decrease the time needed to complete the task.

In TMixed, in contrast to Mixed, hardly any time was spent on superfluous lessons: only one subject spent some time on these. A possible explanation is that the agent frequently took the initiative for selecting another lesson and that the subjects agreed with that selection. This is confirmed by the fact that the agent took the initiative 3.3 times on average, and that the menu button was less often used than in Mixed.

On average, more time was spent on the sixth lesson in TGuidance and TMixed than in the Guidance and Mixed respectively: 5'9'' compared to 3'53'', and 4'40'' compared to 2'44''. There was no significant effect of condition on the time spent on this lesson for this contrast. However, it suggests that the cause of the difficulty which some of the subjects experienced with the twelfth lesson, especially in Mixed -- namely that they did not spend enough time on the sixth lesson-- has disappeared.

The results in the TMixed condition are more homogeneous than in the other conditions. The variance may have been reduced by a combination of two factors, namely a stimulation due to the initiative of the agent to spend enough time studying the relevant lessons (seemed lacking in Mixed) combined with a possibility to use the menu button for fast consultation of a specific easier lesson (lacking in both Guidance and TGuidance). This suggests that TMixed should be preferred to TGuidance.

4 Conclusions

An approach has been described in which initiative and lesson selection *by the Navigation agent* can be combined with initiative and lesson selection *by a student*. In a controlled experiment, the effectivity of both lesson selection and initiative by the agent was explored. Lesson selection by the agent proved to be advantageous for students who were unable to monitor their own learning process. Initiative by the agent reduced the time needed to finish the task by stimulating the subjects to spend enough time studying the relevant lessons. Both guidance initiated by the agent and a mix of user navigation and guidance lead to a reduction in learning time. A mixed locus of control reduces the variance between students, thus making the learning process more predictable.

There are several directions for further research. In the first place, research should be done on how quickly the Navigation Agent can discover deviations from the initially assumed foreknowledge and goals, and how fast it can adjust the difficulty of the path through the course material to the abilities of the individual student. In the second place, the lesson selection should be tested in more complex domains. In the third place, research should be done to further improve the *timing* of initiative, especially with respect to the initiative to return to an easier lesson. Finally, the effect of giving the student more information for self-navigation is worth investigating.

References

1. Brusilovsky, P. (2001) Adaptive hypermedia. User Modeling and User Adapted Interaction, Ten Year Anniversary Issue (Alfred Kobsa, ed.) 11 (1/2), 87-110
2. Brusilovsky, P. & Pesin, L. Adaptive navigation support in educational hypermedia: An evaluation of the ISIS-Tutor. Journal of Computing and Information Technology 6 (1), 1998, 27-38.
3. Eklund, J. & Brusilovsky, P. The value of adaptivity in hypermedia learning environments: A short review of empirical evidence. In: P. Brusilovsky and P. De Bra (eds.) Proceedings of Second Adaptive Hypertext and Hypermedia workshop, Computing Science Report No. 98/12, Eindhoven University of Technology, 1998, 13-19.
4. Espinosa, R. & Baggett, P.(1993). A design for accessing multimedia information using cohesion. In M. Brouwer-Janse and T. Harrington (Eds.), Human-machine communication for educational systems design. Berlin: Springer.
5. Gentner, D. Interfaces for learning: Motivation and the locus of control. In F.L. Engel, D.G. Bouwhuis, T. Bösser, & G. d'Ydewalle (Eds.), Cognitive modeling and interactive environments in language learning. Berlin: Springer, 1992.
6. Laurel, B., Oren, T., & Don, A. Issues in multimedia interface design: media integration and interface agents. Proceedings of the ACM CHI conference on human factors in computing systems, 1990, 133-139.
7. Masthoff, J. *An agent-based interactive instruction system.* PhD Thesis. Eindhoven University of Technology, 1997.
8. Norcio, A.F., & Stanley, Adaptive human-computer interfaces. *Naval Research Laboratory Report 9148, 1988.*
9. Robertson, G., Mackinlay, J., & Card, S. (1991). Cone trees: Animated 3d visualizations of hierarchical information. Proceedings of the ACM CHI '91 conference on human factors in computing systems, 189-194.
10. Snow, R.E., & Swanson, J. Instructional psychology. *Annual Review of Psychology, 43,* 1992, 583-626.
11. Takeuchi, A., & Otsuki, S. Intelligent tutoring system: Coordinating mixed initiative with strategic dialogue by soft scenario. Transactions of the IEICE, E73, 1990, 308-314.

Adding Human-Provided Emotional Scaffolding to an Automated Reading Tutor That Listens Increases Student Persistence

Gregory Aist[1], Barry Kort[2], Rob Reilly[2], Jack Mostow[3], and Rosalind Picard[2]

[1] With Project LISTEN 1996-2001; now Visiting Scientist, MIT Media Lab;
and Research Scientist, Research Institute for Advanced Computer Science, Mail Stop T27-A,
NASA Ames Research Center, Moffett Field CA 94035-1000 USA
GregoryAist@yahoo.com
[2] MIT Media Lab, Building E15, 77 Massachusetts Ave., Cambridge MA 02139 USA
http://affect.media.mit.edu/AC_research/lc/
[3] Project LISTEN, RI-NSH 4213, Carnegie Mellon University,
5000 Forbes Ave., Pittsburgh PA 15213
http://www.cs.cmu.edu/~listen

Everyone agrees emotions are important, and some have even built supportive language into their ITSs, such as praise. But what is the effect of such emotional scaffolding, and is it worth including in a system that is already providing cognitive scaffolding? This poster presents the first statistically reliable empirical evidence from a controlled study for the effect of human-provided emotional scaffolding on student persistence in an intelligent tutoring system. We conducted an experiment that added human-provided emotional scaffolding to an automated Reading Tutor that listens.

A human wizard sat in a room with a television connection to the room where the student was seated, and either observed the student (control condition) or provided emotional scaffolding (experimental) such as praise ("Very good") or encouragement ("You're doing fine"). Students were 2nd-5th graders, including boys and girls.

Each student participated in one session with emotional scaffolding, and in a second (control) session without emotional scaffolding. Each session was divided into several portions. After each portion of the session was completed, the Reading Tutor gave the student a choice: continue, or quit.

We measured persistence as the number of portions the student completed. Human-provided emotional scaffolding added to the automated Reading Tutor resulted in increased student persistence, compared to the Reading Tutor alone – at least for the boys. Boys persisted on average twice as long with emotional scaffolding as without; however, many of the girls were already at or near maximum persistence:

Boys: $N=7$, 6.1 ± 3.4 (expt.) vs. 2.7 ± 2.4 (control), $p=.007$ by paired T-test.

Girls: $N=7$, 11.0 ± 4.9 (expt.) vs. 10.0 ± 4.5 (control), $p=.582$ by paired T-test.

Increased persistence means increased time on task, which generally leads to improved learning. If these results for reading turn out to hold for other domains too, the implication for intelligent tutoring systems is that they should respond with not just cognitive support – but emotional scaffolding as well.

S.A. Cerri, G. Gouardères, and F. Paraguaçu (Eds.): ITS 2002, LNCS 2363, p. 992, 2002.

An Approach of Reinforcement Learning Use in Tutoring Systems

Abdellah Bennane

DINF-VUB, Vrijie Universiteit Brussel; 2, pleinlaan, B-1050 Brussels, Belgium
http://dinf.vub.ac.be ; abennane@vub.ac.be

Machine learning is a domain of artificial intelligence research, which develops a learning process theory and builds machines, which learn to construct or change new or old knowledge, in exploiting the information received from exterior. So, learning is perceived to be a key indicator of intelligence, and likewise a condition of artificially intelligent systems. One of the domains where the machine learning was applied is the design of intelligent tutors, especially in the construction and maintenance of the student model which is often elaborate in order to facilitate the teaching decision-making. The declared goal is to build an intelligent tutor, which does not need teaching strategy knowledge. The system that we propose requires only domain knowledge; an internal learning agent will generate the remainder. This system is composed of two components: a teaching environment and an internal learning system, henceforth **(ILS)**. The teaching environment contains knowledge base, evaluation unit, reward unit, and communication unit. **(a)** We believe that a teaching situation is the elementary component of content. The situation includes a static part, and a dynamic part, which corresponds at the same time to the learner activities and to the various control modes from these activities. The presence of a student model will supply the system with a memory that will summarize the exchanges generated between the environment and the student. We make no distinction between the student model and the **ILS**. **ILS** is composed of the following elements: a reward update unit that updates the learning system base after evaluation of the student action; a selection unit that allows selecting an action according to a policy (pedagogical strategy), a learning unit that allows the processing of policy by referring to the experience of the system itself. Therefore, initialization with a minimal teaching expertise is not required. The knowledge base fields of the **ILS** are: current situation; action; following situation; and reward. It is a quadruplet: (situation (x), action (a), next situation (y), reward (r)) which means that the action (a) carried out for the state (x) results in a new state (y) and a reward (r). Adopting this approach means that one can simplify the teaching module from the classical architecture of ITS.

We presented an approach that allows the construction of an objective teaching strategy by using the observable data from the interaction between the students and the teaching environment. Using reinforcement learning allows designing an agent, which exploits these data in order to produce a pedagogical policy. It may remove the pedagogical module from the classical architecture of the intelligent tutors. The advantages of this approach is that it allows the discovery of strategies adapted to the individualized learning, is transferable from one context to another, and may be less time and energy consuming.

S.A. Cerri, G. Gouardères, and F. Paraguaçu (Eds.): ITS 2002, LNCS 2363, p. 993, 2002.
© Springer-Verlag Berlin Heidelberg 2002

An MPEG-4 Authoring Tool Dedicated to Teachers

Dominique Deuff[1], Nicole Devoldère[1], Béatrice Foucault[1], Isabelle Chanclou[1], Delphine Mantsos[2], Cédric Gégout[3], and Michael Picaud[3]

[1] France Télécom R&D
Technopôle Anticipa - 2, avenue Pierre Marzin - 22307 LANNION cedex
tel : +33 2 96 05 03 11
dominique.deuff@francetelecom.com
[2] France Télécom (Paris)
[3] France Télécom R&D (Rennes)

This work deals with a multimedia authoring tool for teachers. This authoring tool is based on MPEG4 technology in order to allow creation of standard links between the multimedia elements (texts, images, videos, sounds, 3D or 2D synthetic objects).

We have attached on the MPEG4 core, peripheral "tool-modules" which basic functionalities are creation, management and edition of multimedia elements. For these modules we made a distinction between two categories of media. The modules for the first category are not designed to create media but to provide the functionalities for the media, such as the possibility of creating anchors, therefore of rendering the zones of the images responsive. The modules for the second category can create media, for instance, writing a text or designing a diagram.

To be teacher friendly, the authoring tool user interface has been built with ergonomics and simplicity in mind. The authoring tool does not have a menu-based interface like most existing software. In order to guide a novice teacher, the interface is based on a succession of frames. Thus for each action he has to do, the user interacts with one frame to go to the next frame.

The tool was designed to guide the teacher, but this latter remains an active participant in his choices. He selects media from a remote database and creates links between media to build and organise an educational content.

References

1. Information technology - coding of audio-visual objects; part1: systems, 1998. ISO/IECJTC1/SC29/WG11 N2501.
2. Cédric Gégout, Voula Zoi, Jonh Melas, Nicolas Mitrou, and Caccia Giusepe. An mpeg-4 framework for modern networked multimedia applications authoring. *International conference on Media Futures*, pages 133–135, 2001.

S.A. Cerri, G. Gouardères, and F. Paraguaçu (Eds.): ITS 2002, LNCS 2363, p. 994, 2002.

Resource Reuse and Broadband User Modelling in ie-TV

Benedict du Boulay and Rosemary Luckin

Human Centred Technology Research Group
School of Cognitive & Computing Sciences
University of Sussex, Brighton BN1 9QH UK
bend@cogs.susx.ac.uk rosel@cogs.susx.ac.uk

The convergence of communications and information technology within education, as well as more widely, means that concepts developed within ITS & AIED are now applicable to a wider range of wired, and more interestingly 'wireless', technologies. In [1] we outlined the educational rationale of a Broadband User Model (BbUM) that would support the individualisation of the interactions, both between the technology and a user and between collaborating users, for a system able to deliver a variety of resources in a range of media, including interactive TV. At the heart of any such system there needs to be a database of resources from which the user, the educational designer or the system itself, including the user model, can select. Some of these resources will be items that were developed for other purposes, such as self-contained TV programmes, books or simulation programs. Others will be resources developed with such a system in mind. In either case the use and reuse of these resources depends on careful tagging at a level of granularity that enables them to be used both in their entire original form as well as in parts. For example, imagine that a TV programme is being indexed and that it consists of a number of items, originally in a chronological sequence. The tagging might indicate that one item is analogous to another or generalises it. Labelling the items makes explicit some of the implicit pedagogic relationships that underpin the design of the original programme. This enables the possibility of recomposing the TV programme in some other sequence that reflects a different overall pedagogical structure to the original. Moreover, each item is also tagged in terms of its position in some domain scheme. A prototype system has been implemented that employed a database searchable in a variety of ways, including the keywords matched against video/TV captions and/or automatically transcribed speech. Metadata included such fields as ID, title, ownership, media type, format, and duration. Content categorisation included topic, target user group, and interactivity. Form categorisation included problem, concept, description, and explanation or example.

References

1. R. Luckin and B. du Boulay. Imbedding AIED in ie-TV through broadband user modelling (BbUM). In J. D. Moore, C. L. Redfield, and W. L. Johnson, editors, *Artificial Intelligence in Education: AI-ED in the Wired and Wireless Future*, pages 322–333. IOS Press, Amsterdam, 2001.

S.A. Cerri, G. Gouardères, and F. Paraguaçu (Eds.): ITS 2002, LNCS 2363, p. 995, 2002.
© Springer-Verlag Berlin Heidelberg 2002

Integrating Adaptive Emotional Agents in ITS

Jessica Faivre[1], Roger Nkambou[1], and Claude Frasson[2]

[1] University of Quebec in Montreal, Department of Computer Science
faivre.jessica@courrier.uqam.ca. roger.nkambou@uqam.ca
[2] University of Montreal
frasson@iro.umontreal.ca

A wealth of emotional models, with starkly differing views concerning the relation between cognition and emotion, generally show emotions like a mechanism facilitating human adaptation and social integration. Cognitive reflection can help us to guide and moderate our emotions and few differences in affective states may have a pronounced impact on cognitive processes. When people are in positive affective states, information processing is strongly influenced by heuristics, stereotypes, or scripts, whereas in negative affective states, they tend to be more conservative, linear, and sequential in their thinking process which is more easily affected by the implications of specific information provided in the situation. The main question is "how different affective states are linked to different styles of information processing?".

Emotion's management in ITS implies the design of emotional agents improving interaction in training systems and affective mechanisms who modify the way in which learning takes place later on. Providing consistent support (advice, confidence, encouragement) and expressions of interest by vocal expression of speech and body language, an animated actor could be able to induce, influence a particular mood state to the learner (emotional contagion) or at least a positive impression. Nevertheless, methodological problems arise with new pedagogical strategies of computer-based tutoring: "how detect and assess emotional states and their influences without interfere with the natural learning process?". The learner's mental processes are not directly observable and, to date, the most objective approach for assessing changes in a person's affective state, in an unobtrusive manner, is via assessing sentic modulation using mechanisms to sense posture, eye-gaze and facial expressions. However, it is very difficult to exactly know which attributes and values are relevant when differentiating between many emotional states, because in natural interaction, prototypic expressions of basic emotions occur relatively infrequently.

According to the relations between emotion, cognition and action in contextual learning and avoiding the recourse of external sensors, we work on an ITS model based on multiagent architecture in which two Adaptive Emotional Agents have been integrated. One is designed to elicit and to analyse the learner's emotional experiences by mean of his interactions with the system acting like a "behavioural planner" by adapting his own behavioural rules according to current the learner's "emotional actions", whereas the second manifests the tutor's emotional non-verbal expressions arising from plan generation and execution through body gestures, facial expressions in a 3D embodied agent. The Tutor Agent manages the learning session by making decisions on the contents, the

S.A. Cerri, G. Gouardères, and F. Paraguaçu (Eds.): ITS 2002, LNCS 2363, pp. 996–997, 2002.
© Springer-Verlag Berlin Heidelberg 2002

appropriated resources to present and the tutorial strategies to adopt. It has his own Emotional State based on the OCC Model and Cognitive State (strategies, plans, scenarios, pedagogical goals, knowledge) to analyse the student's actions and results comparatively to its own desires or beliefs.

The project is just in its early stages, experimental projects will be conceived and several points will be enriched. They concerns methodological problems of the reliability with the recognition of the learner's emotions by coding and classifying them in real-time application with significant degree of psychological colourability, then the determination of what kind of emotions could be considered pedagogically adequate or not in scenarios, and the interaction frequency necessary to maintain the student's attention, depending on context, cognitive and emotional styles.

Targeted Detection: Application to Error Detection in a Pedagogical System

Hélène Giroire[1], Françoise Le Calvez[2], Jacques Duma[3],
Gérard Tisseau[1], and Marie Urtasun[2]

[1] LIP6, Université Paris 6, `<firstName>.<surname>@lip6.fr`
[2] CRIP5, Université Paris 5,
`<firstName>.<surname>@math-info.univ-paris5.fr`
[3] Lycée technique Jacquard, Paris, `dumajd@club-internet.fr`

In a learning environment (tutorial system), the problem of the detection of students' errors is fundamental. When an error is detected, the tutorial system can choose the best time to provide information and explanations in order to help the student make progress. The mechanism of error detection must be able to draw from knowledge about the studied domain and to adapt itself to various pedagogical strategies. In an interactive system, the problem of the detection of students' errors arises in an incremental manner, at each input of information.

The learning environment that we are building [1], the software "Combien?" (How many? in French) is a pedagogical system to help students learn combinatorics using mathematical language. In this system, the student builds via an interface a solution of the exercise whose internal representation is a tree-like structure.

Furthermore, we have designed a targeted detection mechanism [2] which makes it possible to identify a pattern associated with a condition binding some of the variables in a conceptual tree structure.

This mechanism can be used for the incremental detection of errors in the building of a tree-like structure. The concept of target (new input element to be analysed) allows us to take into account the interactive aspect. In order to detect and explain the errors, the system needs specific knowledge. This knowledge is grouped in a data structure named error schema. Two important components of each error schema are a tree-like pattern with distinguished variables and a condition of error binding these variables.

In the Combien? software, we implemented error detection using the targeted detection method. For each class of problem, we defined an error schema data base. In the school year 2001-2002, this Combien? software was used for combinatorics teaching at secondary school (final year). Some students used the software before their combinatorics course, and the others after the course. In both cases, the students (in groups of three) solved the exercises without the teacher's help. The contextual aids of the system were sufficient in themselves.

References

[1] Tisseau G., Giroire H., Le Calvez F., Urtasun M., and Duma J., *Design principles for a system to teach problem solving by modelling.* Lecture Notes in Computer Science N° 1839, ITS'2000, pp. 393-402, Springer-Verlag, Montréal, 2000.
[2] Giroire H., Le Calvez F., Duma J., Tisseau G., Urtasun M., *Un mécanisme de détection incrémentale d'erreurs et son application à un logiciel pédagogique* RFIA 2002, pp. 1063-1072, Université d'Angers, Janvier 2002.

S.A. Cerri, G. Gouardères, and F. Paraguaçu (Eds.): ITS 2002, LNCS 2363, p. 998, 2002.
© Springer-Verlag Berlin Heidelberg 2002

The Design of ENCAL, a Learning Environment Utilising Multiple Linked Representations

Andrew G. Harrop

Computer-Based Learning Unit University of Leeds LS2 9JT England
A.G.Harrop@cbl.leeds.ac.uk,
http://www.cbl.leeds.ac.uk/~andrewh

With the increasing sophistication of society's intellectual tools has come increasing difficulty in teaching the use of those tools. This research focuses on one such tool, the elementary calculator. Simple as this device looks, it has been found that most pupils of the age when they learn its use in school need help when using calculators, especially if they are using them with problems involving more than one operation... [1].

To use a calculator, a real-world problem must be restated in symbolic form. The requisite cognitive process requires the mapping of mental models to representations. The computer-based learning environment ENCAL (Entities, Notation, CALculator) can be viewed as an embedded cognitive model of the solution process, centered on three Multiple, Equivalent, Linked, Representations (MELRs) — iconic (real - world, concrete), datatree (intermediate representation of dataflow) and calculator (abstract arithmetic).

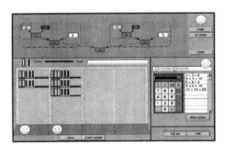

Fig. 1. The ENCAL environment — Bottom left panel, iconic representation of problem; top panel, datatree; bottom right, calculator representation.

A pilot evaluation of ENCAL showed that all three representations were necessary for user understanding of problems compared to say two representations. The datatree appeared to provide pupils with a good cognitive model of the situation by offering an intermediate link between the concrete and the abstract extremes, thus helping users to understand more clearly evaluation procedures.

References

1. Wiebe, J. H.: Calculator memory and multistep problems, Arithmetic Teacher, **37** 1 (1989) 48–49.

S.A. Cerri, G. Gouardères, and F. Paraguaçu (Eds.): ITS 2002, LNCS 2363, p. 999, 2002.
© Springer-Verlag Berlin Heidelberg 2002

Supporting Interaction Analysis for Collaborative Learning

Akiko Inaba, Ryoji Ohkubo, Mitsuru Ikeda, Riichiro Mizoguchi, and Jun'ichi Toyoda

I.S.I.R., Osaka University, 8-1 Mihogaoka, Ibaraki, Osaka, 567-0047 Japan
inaba@ai.sanken.osaka-u.ac.jp

Many of software designers of CSCL environment have been suffering from complex and subtle educational requirements offered by clients. One of major causes of the problem they face is the lack of shared understanding of collaborative learning. We do not know what design rationale of CSCL environment is and even do not have common vocabulary to describe what the collaborative learning is. In this research, we are aiming at supporting such complex instructional design (ID) process of CSCL environment. To fulfill the aim we have been constructing an ontology to represent CSCL session[1,2]. The ontology will work as both vocabulary to describe the session and design patterns referred to during the instructional design process. To represent learning scenarios using the ontology will facilitate users' shared understandings and reuse the scenarios. It is useful to store and provide effective learning scenarios as design patterns. As the first step to fulfill our aim, we adopt learning theories as foundation to analyze, design, and develop the learning sessions. The design patterns inspired by the theories provide design rationale for CSCL design.

Currently, laying the ontology and CSCL models formulated in terms of the ontology as basis, we have been conducting a project aiming at developing various kinds of ID support systems for CSCL. In this poster, we introduce the 'Theory-based Interaction Analysis (TIA)' support system. We can observe various kinds of interaction among members of a learning group during collaborative learning session. The key to understanding CSCL lies in understanding the rich interaction between individuals. However, it is difficult for even human users to analyze them in order to clarify what types of collaboration have occurred in the session and what educational benefits have been expected for the members through the session. So, we propose an *interaction analysis support system* that helps users to abstract essence of interaction from raw protocol data, and to understand what types of collaboration have been occurred in the session, and then infers educational benefits expected to be gained by the members through the interaction process. We describe what interaction analysis is and why the interaction analysis is difficult for educational practitioners and CSCL designers, and propose an interaction analysis support system to reduce the difficulties, and interaction patterns that are core part of the system. The interaction patterns represent typical interaction processes, which are abstracted, desired interaction process inspired by learning theories. The system compares learners' interaction process with the typical interaction patterns to infer whether the process is effective for the learners or not.

S.A. Cerri, G. Gouardères, and F. Paraguaçu (Eds.): ITS 2002, LNCS 2363, pp. 1000–1001, 2002.

At this stage, we rely on learning theories to construct interaction patterns and pick up utterance-labels for abstracting raw protocol data. For future work, we will

extend the system to embed a module that users can store new interaction patterns to the system. By this extension, the user uses their best practice as typical collaborative learning patterns. Moreover, we will construct a collaborative learning support system in which learners select utterance-labels or use sentence-openers, and the system identifies the state of collaborative learning and advises the learners on their learning process.

References

[1] Inaba, A., Supnithi, T., Ikeda, M., Mizoguchi, R., & Toyoda, J. 'How Can We Form Effective Collaborative Learning Groups?' Proc. of ITS2000, 282-291 (2000)
[2] Inaba, A., Tamura, T., Ohkubo, R., Ikeda, M., Mizoguchi, R., & Toyoda, J. 'Design and Analysis of Learners' Interaction based on Collaborative Learning Ontology' Proc. of Euro-CSCL2001, 308-315 (2001)

A Support Environment for Novice Web Searchers

Anna Lloyd

University of Sussex, Brighton BN1 9QH, UK
annall@cogs.susx.ac.uk

This study is part of an ongoing investigation into the feasibility of a software support environment for novice Web searchers, which aims to alleviate some of the frequently-encountered problems of frustration, disorientation, delay, confusion, and failure to find what is sought [1].

Previous work, e.g. [2], characterise the process of searching, with suggestions for user interface design; but it may also be useful to educate the user in effective search techniques and to foster their metacognitive awareness [3] of the search process, including planning, monitoring and reflecting; and it may also be useful to provide context-sensitive help that adapts to the user's level of expertise.

A 'low-tech' prototype of the support environment, consisting of coloured cards, is illustrated on the poster (see [4] for the advantages of low-tech prototyping). It was thought that the card system would be easier for novices than an html prototype. There were three types of colour-coded card, for 'sign-posting', 'activity', and 'information', and they were connected by simulated hypertext links in which relevant text on one card was highlighted, indicating to the participant that they should turn over and read another card which had a matching title. The experimenter was nearby to give extra help if it was needed.

Eleven paid participants, self-defined as 'novice web searchers', aged 13 to 39, were allowed 30 minutes to search the Web for information about anything that interested them, and the cards were on the table next to the computer. The sessions were recorded on video and the participants completed a questionnaire.

The video recordings and questionnaire responses revealed (a) useful information about the layout, sequence, and design of the software prototype to be developed; and (b) a number of situations in which the role of the experimenter could be replaced by an adaptive software component. The participants generally had favourable impressions of the prototype and its ability to teach them about Web searching, which is encouraging for future work.

References

1. anonymous: Are We There Yet, Dad? Cartoon on a Greetings Card, December 2001
2. Shneiderman, B., et al: Clarifying Search - A User-Interface Framework for Text Searches. D-Lib Magazine (1997) January
3. Forrest-Pressley, D.L., et al (eds): Metacognition, Cognition, and Human Performance. Academic Press (1985)
4. Preece, J., et al: Human-Computer Interaction. Addison-Wesley (1994)

S.A. Cerri, G. Gouardères, and F. Paraguaçu (Eds.): ITS 2002, LNCS 2363, p. 1002, 2002.
© Springer-Verlag Berlin Heidelberg 2002

Towards More Affective Tutoring Systems

Manolis Mavrikis[1] and John Lee[2]

[1] Department of Mathematics and Statistics,
[2] Division of Informatics; Cognitive Science
The University of Edinburgh, EH9 3JZ, Scotland, UK
manolis@maths.ed.ac.uk J.Lee@ed.ac.uk

During the last few years education has been experiencing significant change thanks to the rapid advancement of IT. On the other hand, it seems that little attention has been paid on some aspects of conventional teaching. Recently though, research in the help-seeking process (such as 'contingent instruction' [3]) together with the increased interest in issues relating to the affective aspects of tutoring systems in a large number of publications shows, once more, the importance of these issues.

Our previous work [2] targeted Dynamic Geometry Environments (DGEs) (such as Cabri), which were already successfully integrated into classroom. This integration though has risen new issues and limitations one of which is the difficulties students phase when working in an asynchronous way. By conducting a detailed experiment we were able to see that students manifested their emotional state, apart from facial and vocal expressions, by their mouse activity. Frustrated, confused and bored student exhibit a different mouse activity than usual while trying actions on the objects, toolbars and menus.

Based on the above we designed a Dynamic Authoring aNd Tutoring Environment ($DANTE$), which, by a feedback mechanism, monitors students' help solicitation process, their goal achievement as well as their mouse activity (toolbar, menus clicks, object manipulation), and provides a type of contingent and affective feedback that helps students interpret their actions into a meaningful way and consequently prevent the abandonment of the task.

The same mechanism is currently applied on $WàLLî\int$, a Web-based Assistant for Learning in a Locally Integrated System. By employing a prototype of the system (http:///www.maths.ed.ac.uk/~manolis/wallis) we collect data and analyse further students' mouse activity and the way they solicit help. Observations during their interaction with the system will be instrumental in eliciting rules for emotional detection (similar to [1]) which can be utilised by the system, in order to 'sense' students affective state.

References

1. de Vicente, A. and Pain, H. (2002). Informing the detection of students motivational state: an empirical study. To appear in the same issue.
2. Mavrikis, M (2001). Towards more Intelligent and Educational Dynamic Geometry Environments, MSc Thesis, The University of Edinburgh, Division of Informatics
3. Wood, H. (1999), Help seeking, learning and contingent tutoring In Computers & Education **33**(2-3):153-169.

S.A. Cerri, G. Gouardères, and F. Paraguaçu (Eds.): ITS 2002, LNCS 2363, p. 1003, 2002.

Mobile Lessons Using Geo-referenced Data in e-Learning

Claude Moulin[1], Sylvain Giroux[2], Antonio Pintus[1], and Raffaella Sanna[1]

[1] CRS4, VI Strada OVEST , Z.I. Macchiareddu , C.P. 94, 09010, Uta (CA) – Italy
{moulin, pintux, raffa}@crs4.it
[2] Dept. of mathematics and computer science, University of Sherbrooke, Canada
sylvain.giroux@dmi.usherb.ca

MOBILE LESSON: We coined the term "mobile lesson" for courses held outside of a classroom. During these courses, all actors are mobile. Themes tackled in such lessons are as varied as geophysics and mineralogy in geography, monuments in history, trees and ecosystems in biology, or distance measuring in physics and geometry, dialects in linguistics... Mobile lessons are not a new teaching technology or strategy, but new mobile devices may render it more efficient and more attractive. We believe that going on the field, looking for information and above all observing actual phenomenon, therefore acting in a more personal and autonomous way, are really helping students to build their knowledge.

SOFTWARE: The software we built addressed both the edition of a mobile lesson content and the management of the students on the field. The implementation rely on e-mate, a framework for mobile personalized geo-referenced services. If necessary, e-mate generates a user interface on the fly for a device (PCs, PDAs, etc.). The implementation was done in Java and questions were specified in XML.

EXPERIMENTS: Teachers of a high school in Sardinia (Italy) developed a mobile lesson for the archaeological site of Nora. This site is interesting from an historical point of view because it contains both Punic and Roman ruins. First teachers prepared the lesson. They went to Nora with a GPS system and point out the coordinates of significant locations we called "hot spot". Then students were taught on the Roman civilization in the classroom. Next, the class moved to Nora. Teams of two or three students were equipped with a laptop connected to a GPS. Students were free to go wherever they wanted on the site. They had to discover the hotspots previously identified by the teachers. Labels like "the roman theatre" give the name of the hot spot. But just finding the theatre was not enough, because this place represent a squared area whose side is more than forty meters long. The students had to find the "exact" position picked up by the teacher, near the theatre. Why the teacher chose this point was a question they had to answer. If they met difficulties to find the right place, then explanations, help and hints were supplied gradually. Thus, students had to move and ask to the software if they were at the right place or not[1]. If it was the case, other questions in relation with their position were asked. These may be general questions about the place but often they were questions about what the students can see at the very moment from that precise position. A score was associated for the discovery of locations and for right answers to questions for motivating the students a bit more.

---

[1] Tests made on the precision of GPS, lead us to accept a position as right if it was at most at eight to ten meters of the chosen point. This precision was satisfying.

S.A. Cerri, G. Gouardères, and F. Paraguaçu (Eds.): ITS 2002, LNCS 2363, p. 1004, 2002.
© Springer-Verlag Berlin Heidelberg 2002

Shared Scientific Argumentation for Lab Work in Physics: An Application of Ethnomethodology in the Conception Process

Nadège Neau and Alain Derycke

Laboratoire TRIGONE, Bât B6, Cité scientifique,
59655 Villeneuve d'Ascq, France
{Nadege.Neau, Alain.Derycke}@univ-lille1.fr
http://noce.univ-lille1.fr

In order to perform science apprenticeship in University, we would like to produce a tool supporting scientific argumentation for experiments in Physics labwork. We present here the conception approach, using ethnomethodology paradigm. Our objective is to define guidelines for the conception of software supporting scientific argumentation. Our approach is context centred and user centred. It means that our goal is to define an analyze of labwork like it is in real situation, the failings, the requirement, in order to design a tool which could support student's thought. This analyze is based on ethnomethodology paradigm. So, our work can be devised in two parts: firstly teacher's point of view, secondly student's point of view.

In a first time, we interviewed several teachers about labwork. They explained their work, labwork sessions conception, the execution of the work, the evaluation of the students work. With these interviews, we defined a protocol which describes pedagogical labwork objectives from the teacher point of view. The protocol will be used for the conception of the use context of the future tool (which is about to be designed).

In a second time, we used ethnographic techniques of observation. We video recorded students during their activity in labwork. Image and sound can give very important information about the interaction between students working together (often by two). Our point of view is focalised on the two students, not each one separately. We are looking for all type of failings, in order to describe which elements of information should be included in a future tool supporting interaction and particularly argumentation. We will be able to define guidelines to support interaction in the context of labwork.

This new conception approach in CSCL is focalised on the interaction of students in order to produce a tool, which could support scientific argumentation. We think that an analyze based on the use context is necessary to define a usable tool better than a general approach which could be applied in different contexts but wouldn't be able to be really efficient in the specific case of the labwork.

S.A. Cerri, G. Gouardères, and F. Paraguaçu (Eds.): ITS 2002, LNCS 2363, p. 1005, 2002.
© Springer-Verlag Berlin Heidelberg 2002

Student's Setup to Access a WEDS

Marilyne Rosselle, Pierre Gillois, Josette Morinet, and François Kohler

SPIEAO, Faculté de Médecine, UHP-Nancy I, 54505 Vandœuvre cedex, France
ml.rosselle@ifrance.com, {gillois,kohler}@spieao.u-nancy.fr and
morinet@uhp-nancy.fr

This research[1] is part of the French-speaking Virtual Medical University (UMVF[2]) project. French educational medicine system is shifting from local evaluation to national evaluation. Therefore that could allow students to share pedagogical resources, and to access inter-university courses from any place. Moreover, the medicine-educational-process does not only take place at the university but also in the hospital, at home or in an office. At home, students need to adjust their computing environment in order to receive and view the educational resources supplied by the UMVF-WEDS (Web-Based Education Delivery Systems). In the setup-stage, he may need some help, according to his computing qualification level. Therefore we provide him with a setup-program.

Services concerning the management of students' computing environment installation and its testing have been enlightened : set-up services and test services; those services are not supplied by any well-known WEDS. In hospitals, education implies to consider the connection between the university network and the hospital network. That raises some additional problems, especially when students have to consult confidential clinical cases. Other services will also be required because of the specific medicine context (e.g. emptying caches before quitting public computers in universities) and because of the possible home uses (e.g. calculating connection costs and download times).

Therefore, we first extend the student's profile, considering his computing qualification level and his localization (place and type of computing environment). Second, we list several categories of documents that the computing environment should restore in order to allow the use of the resources available on the WEDS. Third, from these categories, it has been possible to define the required types of software and hardware. Fourth, all this information has been recorded in a reference-frame. Fifth, all requirements have been clearly specified in UML in order to be implemented. Seventh, new categories of users, that should be includes in WEDS design have been draw up : setup-users, testers and reference-frame's managers. And eighth, we acutely insist on the need of a sample-lesson (provided by the WEDS) to prove whether the computing environment is able to work correctly or not, before the student use it for studying.

The use of exchange protocol for medical image and information like DICOM or HL7 should also be considered. This research domain is still raising issues which could become valuable supports to improve WEDS in the years to come.

---

[1] Full version available at URL: http://www.spieao.uhp-nancy.fr/umvf/
[2] http://www.umvf.prd.fr/

S.A. Cerri, G. Gouardères, and F. Paraguaçu (Eds.): ITS 2002, LNCS 2363, p. 1006, 2002.
© Springer-Verlag Berlin Heidelberg 2002

Learner Evaluation in Web-Based Learning Environments

M. Rubens, P. Trigano, and D. Lenne

UMR CNRS 6599 HEUDIASYC - Université de Technologie de Compiègne BP 20529
60206 COMPIEGNE Cedex – France
Tel : (33) 44 23 45 02   Fax : (33) 44 23 45 02
{rubens,philippe.trigano,dominique.lenne}@hds.utc.fr

The main goals of evaluation are to provide to a human tutor the level of each learner, to give the learner the mean to be aware of what is understood, and finally to allow the system to adapt itself to the learner's level of understanding. Since we are working with Web-based Learning Environment a part of our work is to improve *questionnaires with multiple choices (QMC)*.

We use dynamic *QMC* that can ask new questions depending on the answers of the learner. To create this kind of questionnaire we chose the "curriculum" representation of the course. We chunk the course into *knowledge units (KU)* and we organize them hierarchically. Each *KU* contains information about the part of the course it belongs to, the list of *prerequisite KUs*, and the list of *accessible KUs*. For a k1 knowledge unit, the *prerequisite KUs* are the knowledge that can facilitate the comprehension of k1; and so the *accessible knowledge* are the KUs that should be easily learnt due to the comprehension of k1.

The knowledge units are organise into a graph which is used to manage the questions of the *QMC*. All the questions of the *QMC* are predefined with their propositions. Each answer of the learner is analysed and if the answer is wrong, the system will run over the graph of knowledge to ask new questions about the *prerequisite knowledge*. This procedure will continue until there is a good answer or if there is no more *prerequisite knowledge*.

In future work, we will concentrate our research on the evaluation of a group of learners in the case of collaborative works. Our idea is to evaluate the individual productions of each learner and then to regroup all these individual evaluations to make a global evaluation. To make it we are thinking of using a *Multi-Agents System (MAS)*. In this *MAS* we will use two different sorts of agents.

The first one is the *Cognitive Agent (CA)*. This agent retrieves all the individual evaluation, and then makes statistic manipulations to give a global evaluation of the work. We are also interested in the global evaluation of the group, considered as a whole entity. Another agent could be useful for such an evaluation. The second sort of agent of our system is the *Personal Agent (PA)*. A *PA* is locally associated to a student to assist, to help and to evaluate him It is also in charge of all the communications (with the *CA* and the other PAs (and so the learners)). Finally we plan to use the global evaluation to precise the learner evaluation, looking for typical mistakes or critical comportments.

Our work concerns the cognitive evaluation of the learner. At present this evaluation is dedicated to the individual learner but it will be extended to a group evaluation by using our Multi-Agents System.

S.A. Cerri, G. Gouardères, and F. Paraguaçu (Eds.): ITS 2002, LNCS 2363, p. 1007, 2002.
© Springer-Verlag Berlin Heidelberg 2002

A Constructivist Knowledge Base Architecture for Adaptive Intelligent Tutoring Systems

Ashraf Saad and A.R.M. Zaghloul

Georgia Institute of Technology, Electrical and Computer Engineering, GTREP/ECE,
Savannah, GA 31405, USA

In order to support human learning, knowledge representation in intelligent tutoring systems must support: a constructivist approach to knowledge formation, dynamic additions and deletions of knowledge, the ability to reuse knowledge in multiple contexts, the ability to represent abstractions, and the ability to represent expertise. In order to support these requirements, we propose a network architecture that is fundamentally different from both neural and semantic networks [1]. It is comprised of two fundamental elements: nodes and links. A node represents a fundamental knowledge building block, or *knowledge quantum*, or a certain abstraction that is fundamentally derived to represent a collection of knowledge quanta. Nodes can belong to one of possible abstraction layers. Links relate nodes within a given layer or in different layers. A fundamental principle underlying our network architecture is that of local connectionism: each node is only aware of its rules of interactions with possible neighboring nodes, whether these nodes lie within the same layer or in other layers. The creation of inter-layer and intra-layer links leading to the formation of the knowledge base must be achieved using learning algorithms that lend themselves to a local connectionism approach, such as spreading activation [2]. Once knowledge is rooted on such a fundamental premise, we believe that it can be readily applied to multiple learning and disciplinary contexts. Fundamental issues that are being addressed by our research include those pertinent to fundamental knowledge representation, knowledge abstraction as well as the nature and development of expertise. We hope that our work will shed a light on the learning mechanisms employed by human beings that will lead to the development of intelligent tutoring systems that can emulate and support such learning processes.

References

1. Saad, A. and Zaghloul, A.R.M.: An Evolutional Network Architecture for Developmental Knowledge Bases, proceedings of the Second International Conference on Development and Learning, MIT, Cambridge, MA, USA, June 12-15, 2002, (2002) in press
2. Saad, A.: A Multi-Agent Spreading Activation Network Model for Online Learning Objects, Multi Agent-Based Learning Environments workshop proceedings, 10th International Conference on Artificial Intelligence in Education, San Antonio, TX, May 19, 2001, (2001) pp. 55-59

S.A. Cerri, G. Gouardères, and F. Paraguaçu (Eds.): ITS 2002, LNCS 2363, p. 1008, 2002.
© Springer-Verlag Berlin Heidelberg 2002

Qualitative Models of Interactions between Two Populations

Paulo Salles[1], Bert Bredeweg[2], Symone Araujo[1], and Walter Neto[1]

[1]Universidade de Brasilia, Instituto de Ciências Biológicas, Campus Darcy Ribeiro,
70.910-900 Brasilia - DF, Brasil
psalles @unb.br
[2]University of Amsterdam, Department of Social Science Informatics; Roetersstraat 15,
1018 WB Amsterdam, The Netherlands
bert@swi.psy.uva.nl

Negative and positive interactions between populations such as competition, predator-prey and symbiosis, under the influence of environmental factors, have been pointed out as the main organising forces of communities. Due to explicit representation of knowledge and of causal relations, qualitative simulations can be useful for students to have insights on structure and behaviour of interacting populations. Our work is based on a library of model fragments representing basic population processes (such as natality and mortality), so that it is possible to derive complex community behaviour from 'first principles' [1]. Six types of interactions were modelled: neutralism (0,0), amensalism (0,–), commensalism (0,+), predator-prey (+,–), symbiosis (+,+) and competition (–,–). The symbols {–, +, 0} represent, respectively, negative, positive or no effects from the other species. We define a 'basic interaction model', in which population1 produces some effect (*effect1on2*) that affects natality (*born2*) and mortality (*dead2*) of population2, while this one has an effect (*effect2on1*) which influences *born1* and *dead1*. These influences may be positive or negative, according to the interaction type. For instance, in the predator-prey model *effect1on2* has a positive influence on *dead2* (increases mortality of prey) and *effect2on1* has a negative influence on *dead1* (decreases mortality of predator). Simulations with these models show typical behaviour of each interaction type, such as coexistence and competitive exclusion. The simulation models are organised according to educational learning routes, following the general scheme discussed in [2]. Moving along these routes means progressing along dimensions such as *Order*, *Structural Change*, *Generalization*, *Specialization*, *Analogy* and *Inverse*. For example, amensalism is *analogous* to commensalism because one population is not affected by the other one. Ongoing work includes using interaction models in order to represent more complex community behaviour and testing learning routes in the classroom.

References

1. Salles, P., Bredeweg, B.: Building Qualitative Models in Ecology. In Ironi, L. (ed.): Proceedings of the 11th International Workshop on Qualitative Reasoning. Instituto di Analisi Numerica C.N.R. Pubblicazioni n° 1036, Pavia, Italy (1997).
2. Salles, P., Bredeweg, B.: Constructing Progressive Learning Routes Through Qualitative Simulation Models in Ecology. In Biswas, G. (ed.) Proceedings of the 15th International Workshop on Qualitative Reasoning. Saint Mary's University, San Antonio, TX (2001).

S.A. Cerri, G. Gouardères, and F. Paraguaçu (Eds.): ITS 2002, LNCS 2363, p. 1009, 2002.
© Springer-Verlag Berlin Heidelberg 2002

An Adaptive Distance Learning Architecture

Hassina Seridi-Bouchelaghem and Mokhtar Sellami

Badji Mokhtar Annaba University, Laboratoire de Recherche Informatique (LRI).
BP12 Sidi Amar, Annaba, 23000 Algeria.
H_seridi@yahoo.com, sellami@univ-annaba.net

This paper presents the core architecture of an adaptive distance learning environment which combine the recent knowledge representation methods and intelligent distance learning environment. It describes the services that are involved in the production and generation of adaptive course to learners according to their profiles.

We define a methodology based on the notion of "point of view" which is aimed in the reutilization and capitalizing of knowledge in order to improve and help the course authors in their activities. These points of views are the different perception which an observer can be having in terms of his position in the space.

In our system, we are preoccupied from the didactical components reutilization and the dynamical construction of the course which is adapted to the learner characteristics; having account the different author's point of views. Our system offers the following services : an individualized course is delivered to the learners according to their profiles, their progress, their learning style and their teaching style, allow the authors to exchange points of views, incite the authors to follow a constructional methodology, the system should not allow them to gather the didactical items in order to construct their courses. It should rather allow them to identify the notions which are introduced in the courses. It is a matter of distinguishing shape and contents by using XML and RDF. It allow the reutilization by creating a didactical components library and improve the adaptability in so far as the same material may be introduced according to the learner's pedagogical wills by using XML (DTD, XSL).

All the advantages of the system derive from the integration of technologies such as the XML paradigm, Servlets and distributed databases.

The distance learning and continuous vocational school take an increasing importance. Collaborative environment sustained by computer have received a growing interest by researchers. New models are necessary to put into a effect such environment including human companionship. We will take into consideration the collaborating and cooperating work in our next work.

S.A. Cerri, G. Gouardères, and F. Paraguaçu (Eds.): ITS 2002, LNCS 2363, p. 1010, 2002.
© Springer-Verlag Berlin Heidelberg 2002

Modelisation and Automation of Reasoning in Geometry. The ARGOS System: A Learning Companion for High-School Pupils

J.P. Spagnol

Université Paris 5: Crip5 équipe SBC 45 Rue des Saints-Pères
75270 PARIS CEDEX 06
spaj@math-info.univ-paris5.fr

ARGOS is a Knowledge-based system for automated theorem proving (ATP) which can automatically solve geometry problems at high-school level. An expert, or the user, gives to ARGOS at the same time declarative knowledge and the way to explain it in a proof and the system automatically builds different kinds of rules implementing different ways of using knowledge: classical ways as forward and backward chaining but also dynamically creating new objects or launching conjectures in mathematical problem solving. For each exercise solved, the system builds a proof that is written in the way a mathematics teacher would write it and adapted to the user's level. The system also tries to meta-explain its research mechanisms indicating its dynamic creations and conjecture calls in the written proof.

Before initiating a demonstration the user may set the system's parameters. He/she may also ask for a proof of a certain school level, prioritise knowledge or forbid certain domains, emphasize certain rules and ban others, and set a deadline for the research. The system also has several explanatory levels. Several facts, visible on the figure, are not explained by a teacher. They must be deduced by ARGOS and it can explain these depending on the user's parameterisation. In ATP it is difficult to implement efficient research strategies and heuristics to select and dynamically create new objects adapted to the exercise. The ARGOS system often solves a problem by its learned deduction and creation strategies. If not it can consider the problem from the different points of view linked to the conjectures calls. These may have been proved or not, but the consequent creations, guided by the goal, can help the demonstrator to progress. If it finds a solution the system introduces into the written proof the dynamically created objects and the conjecture calls used to solve the problem. So the written proof gives a solution and tries to meta-explain to the reader the ideas and heuristics which led to the proof. The system is at present experimented with eighth-grade pupils. They successively give to the system every new knowledge introduced by their teacher. They also have to write the manner they would explain it in a concrete deduction step. So they can test their redactionnal template by giving problems to ARGOS. The system sends back an answer, in the pupil's explanation way, for every proposed conjecture about any teacher's exercise. Considering the robustness of the ARGOS system we can imagine a pupil putting any sort of conjecture to the system. The pupil can test any idea coming from the observation of the figure. So he/she can gradually build a proof for the exercise following his/her own ideas and not forced by the software. For details, see http://perso.club-internet.fr/jps0123/.

S.A. Cerri, G. Gouardères, and F. Paraguaçu (Eds.): ITS 2002, LNCS 2363, p. 1011, 2002.
© Springer-Verlag Berlin Heidelberg 2002

Adequate Decision Support Systems Must Also Be Good Learning Environments

Joshua Underwood and Rosemary Luckin

School of Cognitive & Computing Sciences, University of Sussex, BN1 9QH, UK
{joshuau, rosel}@cogs.susx.ac.uk

Decision support must provide adequate explanation; to do this decision support systems (DSSs) must also support learning. Users who want to understand the reasoning behind DSS output are expressing a desire to learn. During evaluations of our DSS, comments referring to its potential for use as a learning aid have been common. While DSSs may be useful in training if accompanied by sufficient learner motivation, access to experts, etc, they are not generally designed to actively support learning. Our evaluations lead us to the conclusion that ITS components and the application of established educational theory are necessary elements in the design of acceptable DSSs. Here, we describe our existing DSS and how it can be extended and reconfigured to provide adequate learning support.

Our prototype DSS[1] for brain tumor diagnosis supplements imaging data with information from magnetic resonance spectra. As few radiologists have the expertise necessary to read spectra we use Pattern Recognition (PR) techniques to automate interpretation. We provide explanation by supporting human case-based and statistical reasoning through: 1) Comparison of new cases with similar cases of known pathology and disease typical spectra. 2) A classification overview plot of the training database, generated by the PR techniques. In this plot the new case is highlighted, close cases are spectrally similar and cases of the same pathology form clusters. Users can select cases in the overview and inspect and compare them. In evaluations, expressions of users' learning needs have been particularly evident and have led to the inclusion of reference materials, expert comments, and note-taking facilities. The need to motivate radiologists to use MRS data has also been highlighted.

While the existing DSS enables a self-motivated learner to engage in situated, exploratory and independent learning, the addition of teaching strategies and a student model will allow: 1) An active scaffolded and individualized exploitation of the overview for case-based teaching, via presentation of prototypical and exemplar cases. 2) Motivation through selective presentation of challenging cases. 3) Active guidance on the use of integrated web-based resources for collaborative learning and knowledge sharing. Our poster illustrates these claims in three scenarios.

The building blocks for the integrated learning/decision support system envisaged here exist in the current DSS. However, much work remains to be done at the level of cognitive analysis and application of appropriate learning theory.

---

[1] For details see http://www.cogs.susx.ac.uk/users/joshuau/interpret/index.html

S.A. Cerri, G. Gouardères, and F. Paraguaçu (Eds.): ITS 2002, LNCS 2363, p. 1012, 2002.
© Springer-Verlag Berlin Heidelberg 2002

Author Index

Lecture Notes in Computer Science

For information about Vols. 1–2270
please contact your bookseller or Springer-Verlag

Vol. 2307: C. Zhang, S. Zhang, Association Rule Mining. XII, 238 pages. 2002. (Subseries LNAI).

Vol. 2308: I.P. Vlahavas, C.D. Spyropoulos (Eds.), Methods and Applications of Artificial Intelligence. Proceedings, 2002. XIV, 514 pages. 2002. (Subseries LNAI).

Vol. 2309: A. Armando (Ed.), Frontiers of Combining Systems. Proceedings, 2002. VIII, 255 pages. 2002. (Subseries LNAI).

Vol. 2310: P. Collet, C. Fonlupt, J.-K. Hao, E. Lutton, M. Schoenauer (Eds.), Artificial Evolution. Proceedings, 2001. XI, 375 pages. 2002.

Vol. 2311: D. Bustard, W. Liu, R. Sterritt (Eds.), Soft-Ware 2002: Computing in an Imperfect World. Proceedings, 2002. XI, 359 pages. 2002.

Vol. 2312: T. Arts, M. Mohnen (Eds.), Implementation of Functional Languages. Proceedings, 2001. VII, 187 pages. 2002.

Vol. 2313: C.A. Coello Coello, A. de Albornoz, L.E. Sucar, O.Cairó Battistutti (Eds.), MICAI 2002: Advances in Artificial Intelligence. Proceedings, 2002. XIII, 548 pages. 2002. (Subseries LNAI).

Vol. 2314: S.-K. Chang, Z. Chen, S.-Y. Lee (Eds.), Recent Advances in Visual Information Systems. Proceedings, 2002. XI, 323 pages. 2002.

Vol. 2315: F. Arhab, C. Talcott (Eds.), Coordination Models and Languages. Proceedings, 2002. XI, 406 pages. 2002.

Vol. 2316: J. Domingo-Ferrer (Ed.), Inference Control in Statistical Databases. VIII, 231 pages. 2002.

Vol. 2317: M. Hegarty, B. Meyer, N. Hari Narayanan (Eds.), Diagrammatic Representation and Inference. Proceedings, 2002. XIV, 362 pages. 2002. (Subseries LNAI).

Vol. 2318: D. Bošnački, S. Leue (Eds.), Model Checking Software. Proceedings, 2002. X, 259 pages. 2002.

Vol. 2319: C. Gacek (Ed.), Software Reuse: Methods, Techniques, and Tools. Proceedings, 2002. XI, 353 pages. 2002.

Vol.2320: T. Sander (Ed.), Security and Privacy in Digital Rights Management. Proceedings, 2001. X, 245 pages. 2002.

Vol. 2322: V. Mařík, O. Štěpánková, H. Krautwurmová, M. Luck (Eds.), Multi-Agent Systems and Applications II. Proceedings, 2001. XII, 377 pages. 2002. (Subseries LNAI).

Vol. 2323: À. Frohner (Ed.), Object-Oriented Technology. Proceedings, 2001. IX, 225 pages. 2002.

Vol. 2324: T. Field, P.G. Harrison, J. Bradley, U. Harder (Eds.), Computer Performance Evaluation. Proceedings, 2002. XI, 349 pages. 2002.

Vol 2326: D. Grigoras, A. Nicolau, B. Toursel, B. Folliot (Eds.), Advanced Environments, Tools, and Applications for Cluster Computing. Proceedings, 2001. XIII, 321 pages. 2002.

Vol. 2327: H.P. Zima, K. Joe, M. Sato, Y. Seo, M. Shimasaki (Eds.), High Performance Computing. Proceedings, 2002. XV, 564 pages. 2002.

Vol. 2329: P.M.A. Sloot, C.J.K. Tan, J.J. Dongarra, A.G. Hoekstra (Eds.), Computational Science – ICCS 2002. Proceedings, Part I. XLI, 1095 pages. 2002.

Vol. 2330: P.M.A. Sloot, C.J.K. Tan, J.J. Dongarra, A.G. Hoekstra (Eds.), Computational Science – ICCS 2002. Proceedings, Part II. XLI, 1115 pages. 2002.

Vol. 2331: P.M.A. Sloot, C.J.K. Tan, J.J. Dongarra, A.G. Hoekstra (Eds.), Computational Science – ICCS 2002. Proceedings, Part III. XLI, 1227 pages. 2002.

Vol. 2332: L. Knudsen (Ed.), Advances in Cryptology – EUROCRYPT 2002. Proceedings, 2002. XII, 547 pages. 2002.

Vol. 2334: G. Carle, M. Zitterbart (Eds.), Protocols for High Speed Networks. Proceedings, 2002. X, 267 pages. 2002.

Vol. 2335: M. Butler, L. Petre, K. Sere (Eds.), Integrated Formal Methods. Proceedings, 2002. X, 401 pages. 2002.

Vol. 2336: M.-S. Chen, P.S. Yu, B. Liu (Eds.), Advances in Knowledge Discovery and Data Mining. Proceedings, 2002. XIII, 568 pages. 2002. (Subseries LNAI).

Vol. 2337: W.J. Cook, A.S. Schulz (Eds.), Integer Programming and Combinatorial Optimization. Proceedings, 2002. XI, 487 pages. 2002.

Vol. 2338: R. Cohen, B. Spencer (Eds.), Advances in Artificial Intelligence. Proceedings. 2002. X, 197 pages. 2002. (Subseries LNAI).

Vol. 2342: I. Horrocks, J. Hendler (Eds.), The Semantic Web – ISCW 2002. Proceedings, 2002. XVI, 476 pages. 2002.

Vol. 2345: E. Gregori, M. Conti, A.T. Campbell, G. Omidyar, M. Zukerman (Eds.), NETWORKING 2002. Proceedings, 2002. XXVI, 1256 pages. 2002.

Vol. 2347: P. De Bra, P. Brusilovsky, R. Conejo (Eds.), Adaptive Hypermedia and Adaptive Web-Based Systems. Proceedings, 2002. XV, 615 pages. 2002.

Vol. 2348: A. Banks Pidduck, J. Mylopoulos, C.C. Woo, M. Tamer Ozsu (Eds.), Advanced Information Systems Engineering. Proceedings, 2002. XIV, 799 pages. 2002.

Vol. 2349: J. Kontio, R. Conradi (Eds.), Software Quality – ECSQ 2002. Proceedings, 2002. XIV, 363 pages. 2002.

Vol. 2350: A. Heyden, G. Sparr, M. Nielsen, P. Johansen (Eds.), Computer Vision – ECCV 2002. Proceedings, Part I. XXVIII, 817 pages. 2002.

Vol. 2351: A. Heyden, G. Sparr, M. Nielsen, P. Johansen (Eds.), Computer Vision – ECCV 2002. Proceedings, Part II. XXVIII, 903 pages. 2002.

Vol. 2352: A. Heyden, G. Sparr, M. Nielsen, P. Johansen (Eds.), Computer Vision – ECCV 2002. Proceedings, Part III. XXVIII, 919 pages. 2002.

Vol. 2353: A. Heyden, G. Sparr, M. Nielsen, P. Johansen (Eds.), Computer Vision – ECCV 2002. Proceedings, Part IV. XXVIII, 841 pages. 2002.

Vol. 2359: M. Tistarelli, J. Bigun, A.K. Jain (Eds.), Biometric Authentication. Proceedings, 2002. XII, 373 pages. 2002.

Vol. 2363: S.A. Cerri, G. Gouardères, F. Paraguaçu (Eds.), Intelligent Tutoring Systems. Proceedings, 2002. XXVIII, 1016 pages. 2002.

CPSIA information can be obtained at www.ICGtesting.com
Printed in the USA
LVOW031547041211

257765LV00002B/33/P